AMERICAN DEMOCRATIC SOCIALISM

BOOKS BY GARY DORRIEN

Logic and Consciousness

The Democratic Socialist Vision

Reconstructing the Common Good

The Neoconservative Mind: Politics, Culture, and the War of Ideology

Soul in Society: The Making and Renewal of Social Christianity

The Word as True Myth: Interpreting Modern Theology

The Remaking of Evangelical Theology

The Barthian Revolt in Modern Theology

*The Making of American Liberal Theology:
Imagining Progressive Religion, 1805–1900*

*The Making of American Liberal Theology:
Idealism, Realism and Modernity, 1900–1950*

Imperial Designs: Neoconservatism and the New Pax Americana

*The Making of American Liberal Theology:
Crisis, Irony, and Postmodernity, 1950–2005*

Social Ethics in the Making: Interpreting an American Tradition

Economy, Difference, Empire: Social Ethics for Social Justice

The Obama Question: A Progressive Perspective

Kantian Reason and Hegelian Spirit: The Idealistic Logic of Modern Theology

The New Abolition: W. E. B. Du Bois and the Black Social Gospel

*Breaking White Supremacy: Martin Luther King Jr.
and the Black Social Gospel*

*Social Democracy in the Making: Political and
Religious Roots of European Socialism*

In a Post-Hegelian Spirit: Philosophical Theology as Idealistic Discontent

American Democratic Socialism: History, Politics, Religion, and Theory

AMERICAN DEMOCRATIC SOCIALISM

History, Politics, Religion, and Theory

Gary Dorrien

Yale

UNIVERSITY

PRESS

New Haven and London

Yale University Press books may be purchased in quantity for educational, business, or promotional use. For information, please e-mail sales.press@yale.edu (U.S. office) or sales@yaleup.co.uk (U.K. office).

Set in PostScript Electra type by IDS Infotech, Ltd.
Printed in the United States of America.

Library of Congress Control Number: 2020943020
ISBN 978-0-300-25376-4 (hardcover : alk. paper)

A catalogue record for this book is available from the British Library.
This paper meets the requirements of ANSI/NISO Z39.48-1992 (Permanence of Paper).

10 9 8 7 6 5 4 3 2 1

For Maxine Phillips, Norm Faramelli, and Dan Frankot,
treasured friends in the struggle

Contents

PREFACE

The convention that democratic socialism is hopelessly un-American has become unsettled. In Europe, Social Democracy has created mixed-economy welfare states that extend the rights of political democracy to the social and economic realms. The government pays for everyone's healthcare, solidarity wage policies restrain economic inequality, and higher education is free. These achievements have been difficult to imagine in the United States, until recently. If democratic socialism is about providing universal healthcare, rectifying economic inequality, abolishing structures of cultural denigration and exclusion, and building a peaceable and ecological society, it sounds pretty good to the generation of U.S. Americans that grew up under neoliberal globalization and does not remember the Cold War.

This book is an interpretation of the history, politics, and theory of U.S. American democratic socialism. It tells a story about intertwined secular democratic socialist and religious socialist traditions, and to readers for whom socialism is a secular subject the intertwining may feel like two books in one. I shall argue that Christian socialism has been far more important in American democratic socialism than previous books on this subject convey. Repairing the deficit matters in its own right and brings into view the African Americans and women who came to socialism through the doors of religious movements, especially the social gospel. The project of making democratic socialism American has long involved religious, black freedom, and feminist movements lacking much history in Continental traditions of democratic socialism.

My forty years of scholarship and social justice activism lie behind this book as a whole and occasionally register directly in the last three chapters. One side of my work is social ethical and political, focusing on ethical and political theory, economic democracy, racial justice, feminism, ecology, militarism and empire, and postcolonial criticism. The other side is philosophical and theological, focusing on Kant, Hegel, post-Kantian idealism, philosophy of religion, metaphysics, philosophical and theological ethics, and modern theology. To me these lines of intellectual inquiry are complementary, partly because both sides of my work draw upon Christian socialist and secular democratic socialist wellsprings.

I gravitated as a college student to the secular democratic socialism of Karl Polanyi and Michael Harrington and the Christian socialism of Walter Rauschenbusch and Martin Luther King Jr. I have been deeply involved ever since in social justice activism and scholarship within and outside democratic socialist organizations. In theory there was a question to answer when this book moved into the early 1970s and drove to the present day: Should I hide behind a mask of putative objectivity? In truth I did not seriously consider the mask. This book occasionally marks my personal involvement in subjects under discussion without rehashing the arguments I made at the time. These personal nuggets are in the text to keep it real, not to win an argument.

This book went into production at Yale University Press in February 2020, just as Bernie Sanders seized the lead in the Democratic nomination for president and just before Covid-19 officially reached pandemic status. It felt precarious on both counts to meet the publishing deadline, but I took consolation that there would be room for editing tweaks before the book went to press. I assumed that Sanders would fall short sooner or later; meanwhile we New Yorkers fixed anxiously on Italy.

The world changed with stunning, sweeping, devastating brutality. Italy was ravaged, and in New York City we wondered fearfully: Will we be devoured like Italy? Soon New York was worse than Italy. Covid-19 overwhelmed New York City hospitals and piled up bodies in makeshift morgues. It surged north, south, and west across the nation, worse than any other nation, exposing that the mighty United States of America was less prepared than any comparable society to handle the onslaught. The federal government did the minimum while President Donald Trump sprayed his news conferences with a firehose of lies and self-congratulation. State governors shut down their economies to flatten the curve of infection and save hospitals from crashing. Black and brown Americans in densely populated neighborhoods suffered the worst, as usual, while healthcare workers struggled heroically to save as many lives as possible. Americans as a whole got a taste of what it is like to live in a state of hypervigilance. Feelings of anxiety, fear, and vulnerability that many black Americans experience as normal life became, for a while, the daily bread of nearly all Americans. In April alone the U.S. economy lost twenty-one million jobs, a doubly disastrous figure for a nation that ties healthcare coverage to a job. The following month some states began to reopen their economies before 98 percent of the U.S. population had been tested even once.

Back in February, Sanders had surged in the Democratic race while former vice president Joe Biden stumbled through the early primaries with a wan message about restoring political normalcy. Five major candidates clogged the moderate lane, all warning that the socialist Sanders was too left wing to defeat Trump. Massachusetts senator Elizabeth Warren tried to find a lane between the five moderates and Sanders and failed. The field consolidated with breathtaking speed, narrowing to Biden versus Sanders, just as contagion fear swept the nation.

In May I got a chance to tweak the edited manuscript. Stay-at-home orders were beginning to expire across the nation. The scale of economic damage caused by the contagion had begun to register. Biden pondered in his basement whether he dared to move left, as Franklin Roosevelt did in 1933.

Then came an explosion in Minneapolis, Minnesota, that ripped across the nation and much of the world. George Floyd, an African American man, was killed by a Minneapolis police officer who pressed his knee on Floyd's neck while staring with icy nonchalance at onlookers. Cities erupted in rage and trauma, reacting to the stark cruelty of the murder and the fact that three other police officers did nothing to stop it. Floyd was the latest black American to be brutalized to death by white police as though his life did not matter. His murder was yet another reminder that there is no vaccine for antiblack racism or any kind of racism.

Every major U.S. American city is a tinderbox of racial grievance and despair, trapped in America's distinctly vicious legacy of anti-black racism: 246 years of chattel slavery, 100 years of segregation and disenfranchisement, and 50 years of weaponizing racism to gain political power. For decades, American socialists rarely gave top priority to the struggle against racism. Yet the U.S. American socialist tradition is also distinctly complex and accomplished concerning racial justice, counting the foremost leaders of the civil rights movement among its proponents. Today the same injustices that created socialist and black freedom movements in the first place are very much with us, driving and compounding other crises of recent origin. My next-to-last opportunity to tweak this Preface occurred just after Biden named U.S. Senator Kamala Harris as his running mate. This historic announcement was justly hailed on the liberal-left and marked by earnest resolutions to pull Biden and Harris to the left. As a highly accomplished woman of color, with a multicultural background, from the Wall

Street wing of the Democratic Party, Harris is a symbol of the challenges that the entire American liberal-left faces in addressing the intersections of race, gender, sexuality, class, and the eco-crisis. Electoral politics is merely one of the venues for this struggle, but always necessary to it, as the history of American democratic socialism demonstrates. The November 2020 election put Biden and Harris in the White House, where they confront a Republican Party that has lurched completely into right-wing nationalism and a progressive wing of the Democratic Party that has had it with neoliberal inequality.

This is the second book I have written since my late friend James Cone was lost to us. For thirteen years he read every book I wrote while it was still a work in progress. I missed him when I wrote *In a Post-Hegelian Spirit* (2020), but that book is philosophical and would have irritated him, evoking a question he often asked me: "How can you go on about Hegel? People are dying!" I had trouble letting go of the present book because my best reader and critic had no hand in it. This may explain how I overcame my customary shyness about asking friends, outside readers, and students to spot my howlers and wayward arguments. My heartfelt thanks go to Fynn Adomeit, Daniel Beers, Byron Belitsos, Amy Carr, Heath Carter, Tess Gallagher Clancy, Stephen Crouch, Jacob Dorn, Robert Ellsberg, Jacob Gonzalez, Hannah Griggs, Richard Healey, Obery Hendricks Jr., Jason Hicks, Ban Htang, Maurice Isserman, Catherine Keller, Geoffrey Kurtz, Michael Lerner, Davis Logan, Kelly Maeshiro, Felipe Maia, Cynthia Moe-Lobeda, Maxine Phillips, Elijah Prewitt-Davis, Joerg Rieger, Matthew Sitman, Aaron Stauffer, Daniel Steinmetz-Jenkins, Ian Storey, Kevin Wall, and Lawrence Wittner.

For the rights of access to materials in archived collections I am grateful to Butler Library and Burke Library, Columbia University, New York, New York; the Socialist Party of America Papers, William R. Perkins Library of Duke University, Durham, North Carolina; the Reinhold Niebuhr Papers, Library of Congress, Washington, DC; the Rauschenbusch Family Collection, American Baptist Historical Society–Samuel B. Colgate Memorial Library, formerly at Colgate–Rochester Seminary, Rochester, New York, now at Mercer University, Atlanta, Georgia; the Washington Gladden Papers, Ohio Historical Society, Columbus, Ohio; the W. E. B. Du Bois Library, University of Massachusetts, Amherst, Massachusetts; the Henry Demarest Lloyd Collection, Wisconsin State Historical Society, Madison, Wisconsin; the Oswald Garrison Villard Papers, Houghton Library, Harvard University, Cambridge, Massachusetts; the Norman Thomas Papers, New York Public Library; and the Democratic Socialists of America Collection, Tamiment Library, New York University, New York, New York.

I am deeply grateful for the fourth time to my superb editor and friend at Yale University Press, Jennifer Banks, and to her second-to-none team: production editor Susan Laity, copyeditor Lawrence Kenney, and assistant editor Abbie Storch. Thanks as well to my proofreader, Fred Kameny.

There are many ways to interpret the history of U.S. American democratic socialism. Mine is an intellectual history approach framed in a contextual fashion that focuses on the chief democratic socialist organizations in U.S. American history and that makes a case for the importance of religious socialists to the subject. The book contains a great deal of social history, but it is not a social history, let alone a social history of the broadest possible conception of the subject. With few exceptions, the figures I feature belonged to the main organization of their time that advocated democratic socialism and took for granted that doing so is a prerequisite of democratic socialist seriousness.

The words "America" and "American" naturally recur constantly in this book, reflecting historic ordinary usage and the fact that only the United States put "America" in its name. However, I repeatedly sprinkle the term "U.S. American" into the text to register that citizens of the United States do not own the terms "America" and "American." I have a simple rule about italicized emphases within quotations: NEVER add or subtract one. Every cited italicized emphasis comes from the original quote. One might reasonably expect that after writing many books on these subjects I would have figured out when, and when not, to capitalize socialist, communist, social democrat, romantic, and the like, but I am prone to dwell on the murky in-between cases that editorial rules oversimplify, and then become confused by the exceptions. Special thanks to Susan and Lawrence for saving me from this proclivity. As always, I am grateful to my longtime indexer Diana Witt, who compiles only superb indexes.

Abbreviations and Acronyms

AAA	Agricultural Adjustment Act
AAS	American Anti-Slavery Society
ABM	Anti-Ballistic Missile
ACA	Affordable Care Act
ACLU	American Civil Liberties Union
ACTWU	Amalgamated Clothing and Textile Workers Union
ACWA	Amalgamated Clothing Workers of America
ADA	Americans for Democratic Action
AEA	American Economic Association
AFDC	Aid to Families with Dependent Children
AFL	American Federation of Labor
AFL-CIO	American Federation of Labor–Committee for Industrial Organization
AFSCME	American Federation of State, County and Municipal Employees
AFT	American Federation of Teachers
ALP	American Labor Party
ARU	American Railway Union
ASU	American Student Union
ATWU	Amalgamated Textile Workers of America
BLF	Brotherhood of Locomotive Firemen
BSCP	Brotherhood of Sleeping Car Porters
CALCAV	Clergy and Laity Concerned About Vietnam
CCF	Cooperative Commonwealth Federation
CDC	Centers for Disease Control and Prevention

CDM	Coalition for a Democratic Majority
CIO	Committee for Industrial Organization
CIO	Congress of Industrial Organizations
CISPES	Committee in Solidarity with the People of El Salvador
CORE	Congress of Racial Equality
CPLA	Conference for Progressive Labor Action
CPPA	Conference for Progressive Political Action
CSF	Christian Socialist Fellowship
CSU	Christian Social Union
DDP	German Democratic Party
DGB	Trade Union Confederation
DSA	Democratic Socialists of America
DSOC	Democratic Socialist Organizing Committee
EJA	Economic Justice Agenda
ERAP	Economic Research and Action Project
FOR	Fellowship of Reconciliation
FSC	Fellowship of Socialist Christians
GMA	General Managers Association
HUAC	House Special Committee to Investigate Un-American Activities
ILGWU	International Ladies' Garment Workers' Union
ILP	Independent Labour Party
ISL	Independent Socialist League
ISR	*International Socialist Review*
ISS	Intercollegiate Socialist Society
IWW	Industrial Workers of the World
KAOWC	Keep America out of War Congress
KPD	Communist Party of Germany
LID	League for Industrial Democracy
MFDP	Mississippi Freedom Democratic Party
MIA	Montgomery Improvement Association
NAACP	National Association for the Advancement of Colored People
NAM	New American Movement
NDP	New Democratic Party
NEC	National Executive Committee
NIRA	National Industrial Recovery Act
NPL	Non-Partisan League
NRA	National Recovery Administration
PCA	Progressive Citizens of America
PL	Progressive Labor

PNAC	Project for the New American Century
PS	Socialist Party [France]
PSM	People for Self-Management
PWWC	Post War World Council
RYM	Revolutionary Youth Movement
SANE	Committee for a Sane Nuclear Policy
SCLC	Southern Christian Leadership Conference
SDA	Students for Democratic Action
SDF	Social Democratic Federation
SDS	Students for a Democratic Society
SFIO	French Section of the Workers' International [France]
SI	Socialist International
SLF	Seattle Liberation Front
SLID	Student League for Industrial Democracy
SLP	Socialist Labor Party
SNCC	Student Nonviolent Coordinating Committee
SP	Socialist Party
SPD	Social Democratic Party [Germany]
SPL	Socialist Propaganda League
SRU	Social Reform Union
STFU	Southern Tenant Farmers' Union
SWP	Socialist Workers Party
SYL	Socialist Youth League
TPP	Trans-Pacific Partnership
UAW	United Auto Workers
UDA	Union for Democratic Action
UE	United Electrical Workers
UMWA	United Mineworkers of America
UNIA	Universal Negro Improvement Association
URL	Union Reform League
USPD	Independent Social Democrats [Latvia]
WCTU	Woman's Christian Temperance Union
WCU	Working Class Union
WFM	Western Federation of Miners
WHO	World Health Organization
WNC	Woman's National Committee
WRL	War Resisters League
WSA	Worker–Student Alliance
YPSL	Young People's Socialist League
YSL	Young Socialist League

AMERICAN DEMOCRATIC SOCIALISM

RADICAL DEMOCRACY, JEWISH UNIVERSALISM, AND SOCIAL DEMOCRACY

Americans have long debated two contrasting visions of what kind of country they want to have. Both are ideal types linked to mainstream forms of conservative and progressive politics. The first is the vision of a society that provides unrestricted liberty to acquire wealth, lifts the right to property above the right to self-government, and limits the federal government to national defense and protecting the interests of elites. The logic of this ideal is right-libertarian or right-nationalist, legitimizing the dominance of the wealthy, the aggressive, and the corporations in the name of individual freedom. The second is the vision of a realized democracy in which the people control the government and economy, self-government is superior to property, and no group dominates any other. The logic of this ideal is democratic socialist or left-progressive, extending the rights of political democracy into the social and economic spheres.

Right-libertarianism is powerful in American life despite being impossible, setting freedom against democratic equality. Democratic socialism is supposedly so un-American that it must be called by other names. But it has a rich history in the United States, even by its right name. Democratic socialists founded the industrial unions and many trade unions, pulled the Progressive movement to the left, played leading roles in founding the National Association for the Advancement of Colored People (NAACP), founded the first black trade union, proposed every plank of what became the New Deal, and led the civil rights movement of the 1950s and 1960s. Today democratic socialist activism is surging as a protest that global capitalism works only for a minority and is driving the planet to eco-apocalypse.

This book interprets the entire history of U.S. American democratic socialism, beginning with radical democrats of the early American Republic and ending with proposals for a Green New Deal and a new labor party. Four arguments frame the narrative as a whole and inform the specific arguments of each chapter: (1) The entire American democratic socialist tradition has sought to Americanize democratic socialism by speaking the language of individual liberty, trying to build a coalition party of the democratic left, and grappling with American racism, cultural diversity, Exceptionalist mythology, and activist religion. (2) Religious socialism has been more important in American democratic socialism than scholarship about it conveys. (3) The best traditions of socialism are like the original socialist movement in being predominantly cooperative and decentralized. Nationalization is only one form of socialization and usually not the best one. The best American traditions of democratic socialism have emphasized bottom-up economic democracy instead of centralized government interventions from above. (4) The convention that democratic socialism is too idealistic to be a realistic alternative must be challenged. There damned well better be an alternative to severe inequality and destroying the planet. Sociologist Max Weber famously contended that no ethic of ideal ends belongs in politics, where only a realistic ethic of responsibility is appropriate. All American democratic socialist leaders have struggled with themselves, their organizations, their opponents, and their circumstances over what might be possible.

The first three chapters of this story track the first American socialist organizations to the end of the Socialist Party's golden era. This book describes America's first great socialist leader, Eugene Debs, as a thoroughly American lover of working-class people who adopted a magical idea of socialist deliverance. It shows that women and African Americans came to democratic socialism mostly through Christian socialism, as did the first great hope of radical industrial unionism, the Knights of Labor. It lingers over the founding of the Socialist Party in 1901 and the wondrous stew of radical democrats, neo-abolitionists, Marxists, social gospel Christians, Populists, feminists, trade unionists, industrial unionists, Single Taxers, social democrats, anarcho-syndicalists, and Fabians that joined it. It argues that the early party was remarkably successful at politics, despite its labor problem, and had little trouble speaking American, despite its Marxian cast. It contends that the craft unionism of the American Federation of Labor (AFL) fatally truncated the labor movement and the kind of socialism that was possible in the United States, thwarting the Socialists from scaling up and from creating a labor party. It commends the Socialists who bravely opposed World War I and bore the persecution of the U.S. government only to be devastated by the meteor of world Communism. Afterward they tried to build a farmer-labor-socialist-progressive party but were defeated by obstacles new and old.

The Debsian heyday ended in shattered despair, yielding the dismal run-up to Norman Thomas Socialism, as it was called—the central subject of chapter

4. Norman Thomas Socialism was a three-sided struggle to renew the democratic socialist idea, hold off the Communist Party, and get a farmer-labor-socialist-progressive party off the ground. Thomas was eloquent, personable, astute, courageous, and not cut out to be a party leader. He symbolized the shift of the Socialist Party from being primarily working class to being primarily a vehicle of middle-class idealism. The New York garment unions were the financial rock of the party until 1937, when Thomas and the left wing drove them out. Afterward there was no financial rock.

Every chapter of this book mixes narrative and theory, blends the renowned and the wrongly forgotten, and takes seriously the maxim of Debs that there is no such thing as an unorganized socialist. Socialist movement organizations are featured in every chapter except chapter 7 and are always in view without exception. Debs realized there were plenty of individual socialists out there who never joined anything. He empathized with the nonjoiners, being a romantic American individualist who couldn't bear the wrangling of political conventions. Yet he rightly told his vast audiences that socialism is inherently social and organizational; the only kind worth talking about binds together with others in solidarity and struggle. This book is movement-oriented in the fashion of its subject and in accord with my customary contextual approach to intellectual history.

Chapters 4 and 5 describe the forty-year period in which Thomas stood at the center of American democratic socialism, befriended black Socialist unionist A. Philip Randolph, and grappled with Communism, the New Deal, united front politics, World War II, and the Cold War. In the 1920s Socialists touted that Thomas was a Presbyterian minister and Princeton graduate, not a threatening Bolshevik. In the 1930s they watched Franklin Roosevelt carry out 90 percent of their platform and disastrously carped against him. They could have touted the Socialists on Roosevelt's team who helped to implement the New Deal, but that would have undercut the tack the party took. The Socialists played leading roles in organizing the Congress of Industrial Organizations (CIO) unions and led the dominant CIO union, the United Auto Workers. Their united-front activism mostly backfired, and the party dwindled, surpassed even by a Communist Party that was shrewd enough to support Roosevelt. Thomas and the Socialists allowed into the party a band of Trotskyites who sabotaged the party and stole its youth section. Another exodus ensued when Thomas and the Socialists held out too long against World War II. Afterward Thomas adamantly opposed Soviet domination of Eastern Europe and pro-Soviet American leftism, supporting the purge of Communists from CIO unions. In 1958 he balked at admitting a group of former Trotskyites into the party, fearing they would take it over, which they promptly did.

These were the Shachtmanites, disciples of Max Shachtman, a former associate of Bolshevik hero Leon Trotsky. The Shachtmanites were brainy, cunning, scholastic, aggressively parasitic, fiercely ideological, consumed with the
right kind of anti-Communism, which they called anti-Stalinism, and at every
historical turn, strange. They were still Leninists when they broke from Trotsky
in 1939 and were more Leninist than they claimed when they morphed in the
mid-1950s toward democratic socialism. Michael Harrington was their youthful
star. Brilliant, energetic, and charming, he befriended black Socialist-pacifist
organizer Bayard Rustin and brought Shachtmanites into the civil rights movement. Rustin joined the Shachtmanites, Harrington and Rustin helped the
Shachtmanites take over the party, and Harrington was anointed the successor
to Debs and Thomas. He didn't deserve the title during the early years that he
heard it in speaker introductions. Harrington deserved it only after he broke
from the Shachtmanites in 1972 and broke up the Socialist Party.

The idea that democratic socialism should be radical is contested in every
generation by socialists who are radical about hardly anything. From the beginning the Socialist Party had a wing of stodgy social democrats who prized their
perches in the AFL. Most were German state socialists based in Milwaukee or
Chicago or Jewish garment unionists based in New York. Many became top
party officials dubbed the Old Guard. Debs fought them fiercely, especially
during the party's first dozen years, targeting the AFL leaders. The Old Guard
was never just one thing, and it evolved through the eras of Debs, Thomas, and
Harrington. Max Hayes, bitterly derided by Debs as an Old Guard sellout, tried
valiantly to rally the Socialist wing of the AFL. James Oneal, a Debs ally of the
early party, became an Old Guard stalwart in the 1930s without changing his
politics, except for one thing—the tragedy of Soviet Communism. The Old
Guard of the 1950s helped the Shachtmanites overtake the Socialist Party, with
dripping irony, as these groups had previously despised each other. In every
generation the Old Guard—whoever it was deemed to be—was accused of having inordinate self-regard and betraying socialism. Thomas treated the Old
Guard generously up to the point that he drove most of it out of the party. It was
always tempting for left-Socialists to claim the Old Guard held them back. If
only they could be rid of the grumpy conservatives! But the Socialists did not
fail solely because they had an Old Guard.

The Marxian ideology that American Socialists more or less borrowed from
German Social Democracy disparaged reform causes as second-order and
pedestrian and reform parties as balefully bourgeois. Their attitude showed
when they worked in reform movements and tried to create a labor party.
Thomas dispelled much of the socialism-only ethos that the party inherited

from its Marxian past but acquiring new habits came hard. Many Socialists within and outside the Old Guard held racial biases that blinkered how they practiced socialism. The party took a decent position on racial justice and did little about it, falling far short of the Communist Party, even though Randolph was a prominent national figure and closely allied with Thomas. Randolph, Rustin, Harrington, James Farmer, Ella Baker, Norman Hill, and former Communists Stanley Levison and Jack O'Dell changed this picture, helping Martin Luther King Jr. unite the established civil rights movement based in New York City with the new, youthful, church-based movement of the South. Randolph and Thomas, followed by King and Harrington, are central figures in my interpretation of U.S. American socialism. All were dedicated to keeping secret that King's social gospel was democratic socialist.

The Shachtmanites had a vision of a realigned Democratic Party that put trade unions at the center, supported the civil rights movement, drove out the party's Dixiecrat flank, and welcomed Shachtmanites as union and party leaders. They were done with the warhorse doctrine that Socialists should never ally with bourgeois parties except as a strategy to build a new labor party. The Democratic Party, they claimed, was becoming a labor party in disguise. Shortly after the Shachtmanites swung the Socialist Party behind this strategy, a group of ambitious college students based in Ann Arbor, Michigan, proclaimed that a New Left was needed. The leaders of Students for a Democratic Society (SDS) lumped together all the competing groups and ideologies of what they derisively called the Old Left. Thomas got a pass, as did Harrington at first, but SDS said it took no interest in Old Left faction fights over Marxian ideology, Communism, union organizing, and the working class. Anti-Stalinist social democrats were surely better than pro-Soviet Communists, but only by degree. To SDS, the Old Leftists sounded too much alike, not fathoming what it was like to be a college student in 1962.

My telling of the SDS story and its influence on American socialism emphasizes the early affinities between SDS and the Student Nonviolent Coordinating Committee (SNCC), the emergence of Black Power and radical feminism in the later SDS and SNCC, and the howling alienation the New Left never outgrew. Chapter 6 recounts that the New Left was born in a fractious relationship with the Socialist Party while depending on funding from trade unions in the party. The so-called Old Left, being cast as old and bygone, denied that privileged college students who never learned their Marxism had anything to teach them. The socialist drama of the early 1960s pitted hardened survivors of the 1930s against gently raised youth of the 1950s. It built to a spectacular crash as SDS and SNCC self-imploded, leaving the Old Left socialists to say, I told you so. The black New Left struggled with the role models it inherited from the 1950s while the white New Left was too alienated to find any; social critic C. Wright Mills came the closest to being a half exception. Both wings of the New Left wrongly spurned the hard-won wisdom of the Old Left about Communist vanguardism and dictatorship, while giving birth to liberation movements that enriched how socialists conceived of social justice and battled for it. Harrington blew his chance to be a bridge figure between the Old Left and New Left— until the 1970s.

Chapter 6 revolves around Harrington, King, and the socialist organizations that Harrington cofounded in 1973 and 1982. I will argue that the 1970s was a lost decade in American politics marked chiefly by confusion and banality. It was a period of absorbing the turbulent legacy of the 1960s, the genocidal horror of the Cambodian revolution, and the daunting transformation of the world economy. The economic boom of the post–World War II era ran out, yielding a structural economic shift and its miserable combination of stagnation and inflation. Stagflation defied Keynesian correction, confounding the social democratic left, which called the new situation post-Fordism. The bitter ideological divides in the Socialist Party blew it apart in 1973, ending the party of Debs and Thomas. The Shachtmanites bridled at the anti–Vietnam War movement, Black Power, and radical feminism, founding a new organization called Social Democrats USA. Harrington led a faction of progressive social democrats into a new organization called the Democratic Socialist Organizing Committee (DSOC), building a vehicle for Old Left social democrats, select veterans of the New Left, and youthful newcomers from George McGovern's Democratic presidential campaign. Meanwhile Harrington argued that the rightward trajectory of the Shachtmanites represented something too important not to name. He called it neoconservatism, a tag that stuck. The Shachtmanites and Cold War liberals he named went on to become the most consequential intellectual-political movement of their time, winning high positions in three Republican administrations and mocking Harrington for befriending feminists and anti-anti-Communists.

The idea of DSOC was to create a multi-tendency organization uniting the generations of the progressive democratic left. DSOC was more Old Left than New Left, wearing its anti-Communism proudly. Yet DSOC achieved the Communist Party dream of the Popular Front periods of 1935–39 and 1941–45, creating a united front organization, this time without Stalinism. DSOC won the battle against the neoconservatives for influence in the Democratic Party only to get blown away by the next great turn in American politics. Harrington and DSOC sought to ride into power in 1980 when their ally Edward Kennedy challenged Jimmy Carter for the Democratic nomination. Kennedy failed to unseat Carter, and the neocons rode into power to run the foreign policy and education departments of Ronald Reagan. DSOC was too deflated by defeat and disdainful of Carter to rally for him against Reagan. Many blamed the hapless and unlucky Carter for the alarming triumph of the Reagan right, but Harrington stressed that Reagan became powerful by offering clear, bad, popular answers to complex structural problems. The left needed new answers calibrated to the new realities of global capitalism.

The democratic socialist left confusedly debated the fiscal crisis of the state and two academic cottage industries called market socialism and analytical Marxism. DSOC merged in 1982 with a New Left organization, the New American Movement, to form Democratic Socialists of America (DSA). There was no mistaking the symbolism of DSA. Both of the merging organizations sought to heal the leftover rift between the Old Left and New Left. By 1982 the leftists who knew what they believed belonged to an ascending cultural left that privileged race, gender, and sexuality, building on the social movements of the sixties. Meanwhile a long-departed Italian Communist leader, Antonio Gramsci, won a tremendous vogue for contending that the left wrongly cedes the entire cultural realm to the right.

Gramsci died in a Fascist prison cell in 1937. He argued that capitalism exercises hegemony over the lives of people where they live, in schools, civic organizations, religious communities, newspapers, media, and political parties. Hegemony is the cultural process by which a ruling class makes its domination appear natural. Gramsci contended that if the left had any serious intention of winning power, it had to contest the right on the cultural level. This argument swept much of the Socialist left in the 1980s, giving Marxists a sort-of-Marxian basis for appropriating the cultural leftism of identity politics, difference feminism, and other forms of cultural recognition.

The idea that socialism is compatible with liberal democracy and the related idea that socialism is compatible with capitalist markets have long histories in cooperative, ethical, and religious traditions of socialism. Both ideas, however, were anathema to orthodox Marxists. The storied debate over revisionism in German Social Democracy was principally about the role of democracy in socialism, giving rise to a self-conscious name, democratic socialism. But even the Social Democratic founders of democratic socialism did not claim that socialism is compatible with capitalist markets. Market socialism is the idea that there must be a way to combine socialist planning and cooperation with capitalist markets. This idea, though implicit in democratic socialism, is much harder to justify on Marxian grounds than the idea that socialism is inherently democratic. Harrington's theoretical work revolved around these two sets of problems.

He argued that good socialism is radically democratic, and it deals constructively with capitalist markets. On democracy he cast Marx as a radical democrat much like himself. On market socialism Harrington argued that capitalist markets should work within socialist plans, until he shifted in the 1980s to an emphasis on social democratic plans within capitalist markets, while fudging the difference.

Harrington was a market socialist in both phases of his later career, but the coming of neoliberal globalization chastened him. He cheered when his friend François Mitterrand became the president of France and instituted an ambitious socialist program. Then Mitterrand made a bitter retreat in the face of overpowering economic forces, and Harrington pulled back. The fate of Mitterrand's government marked everything that Harrington said about market socialism in his last years.

In some usages market socialism is synonymous with economic democracy, and in others it is not. Today this discussion is a global enterprise that draws on the foundational theories of Polish neo-Marxists Oskar Lange and Włodzimierz Brus. My analysis focuses on American political economists and social theorists Fred Block, Robert Dahl, David Ellerman, John Roemer, Leland Stauber, and Thomas E. Weisskopf in dialogue with British theorists Saul Estrin and David Miller. Roemer was also a major player in analytical Marxism, along with political economists and theorists G. A. Cohen, Jon Elster, and Eric Olin Wright. Here the Marxian focus on structural conflict was refashioned through rational-choice game theory to explain the crisis of the welfare state. Rational-choice Marxists describe welfare state capitalism as a structural conflict among capitalists, state managers, and workers in which each group rationally maximizes its material interests. Like market socialists, analytical Marxists renewed socialist theory with an intellectual project that remains a significant endeavor.

But these were not the discussions that drove the left in the 1980s and 1990s. This book shifts gears in chapter 7 because cultural left academics took over the left and changed the subject. The democratic left cratered everywhere except the academy, where it surged with controversial new forms of theory and activism—difference feminism, queer theory, critical race theory, and identity politics. Many social democrats charged that cultural leftism betrayed the socialist commitment to economic redistribution. Sociologist Todd Gitlin, literary critic Irving Howe, and philosopher Richard Rorty protested that the new discourses of cultural difference and even vanilla multiculturalism ruined the left by reducing it to identity politics. Some democratic socialists, notably social philosophers Nancy Fraser and Cornel West, fused socialist theory and cultural left criticism, while political theorists Joseph Schwartz and Michael Walzer tried to temper the social democratic critique of cultural leftism. But the left fought bitterly over Marxist retentions and cultural recognition, especially out-side DSA. Chapter 7 keeps DSA in view but on the margin, where it struggled through the 1990s and early twenty-first century merely to hang on. My analysis of cultural leftism features the work of West, gender theorist Judith Butler, fem-inist theorist bell hooks, Jewish theologian Michael Lerner, and social philoso-pher Iris Marion Young. It builds to an extensive analysis of Fraser's theory of redistribution, recognition, and participation as interlinked scales of justice, leading to Fraser's contention that a third wave of feminism has emerged among feminists demanding alternatives to the authority of the modern nation-state.

Today the next socialist left is being forged by third-wave feminists, liberation-ists of color, unionists, and youthful opponents of neoliberal inequality, many of whom came of age politically in the Bernie Sanders Democratic primary campaigns of 2016 and 2020. I shall argue that Sanders renewed American dem-ocratic socialism by running the two greatest campaigns ever waged by an American socialist and that he is better described as a social democrat than as a democratic socialist. His description of democratic socialism closely resembles how European Social Democratic parties have described it for the past century, as an advanced welfare state politics of economic rights. Sanders supports a ver-sion of codetermination in which workers control up to 45 percent of board seats and 20 percent of shares. Similar planks in European platforms have long marked the boundary between modern social democracy and outright demo-cratic socialism. Sanders emphatically rejects centralized government owner-ship and does not discuss forms of social ownership that differ from it. The fact that he shares this habit with many European Social Democrats does not mean that he or they are right that socialism no longer has anything to do with worker ownership, public ownership, or mixed models of them. In one crucial respect Sanders is much more radical than the adjusted European Social Democracy of the past half century. European Social Democrats stopped talking about social ownership and the class struggle at the same time, but Sanders has dramatically revived the language of the class struggle.

Occupy Wall Street, in 2011, was a harbinger that people are fed up and a breaking point had been reached. Forty years of letting Wall Street and the big corporations do whatever they want yielded belated protests against flat wages, extreme inequality, and the rule of neoliberal capitalism. Sanders railed through-out the neoliberal era against inequality and exclusion. Then he spoke to the surge against it. Many youthful types who cut their political teeth in his cam-paign are struggling to build a different left from the one they inherited, creating social justice networks within and outside the orbit of the Democratic Party. Some are swelling the socialist wing of the Democratic Party in the fashion of

U.S. congressional stars Alexandria Ocasio-Cortez and Rashida Harbi Tlaib. Some are reviving the dream of a left coalition party, and others are reviving an older dream of a labor-socialist party that marginalizes middle-class progressives.

IMAGINING DEMOCRATIC SOCIALISM

The original idea of socialism goes back to Charles Fourier in France and Robert Owen in England in the 1820s. Fourier argued that social disorder is caused chiefly by poverty, a condition he suffered firsthand. Owen founded cooperative communities after achieving spectacular success as an up-from-poverty manufacturer. Both sought to achieve the unrealized demands of the French Revolution, which never reached the working class. Instead of pitting workers against one another, a cooperative mode of production and exchange would allow them to work for one another. Socialism was about organizing society as a cooperative community. The traditions of socialism flowing from Fourier and Owen conceived of it as worker ownership at the firm or guild level. Some French and British socialists wanted the state to finance producer cooperatives, and others were vehemently opposed, but all were averse to state socialism—an oxymoronic pairing to them. Karl Marx, a German revolutionary exiled in England, shared this aversion to state socialism, but Marx was vague and utopian about the communist solution, which shielded him from acknowledging that his commitment to collective ownership had a state collectivist upshot. The British Fabians cast aside all such pretensions, straightforwardly identifying socialism with centralized government collectivism. Thus the two most consequential traditions of socialism promoted state socialism while denying it (Marxism) or welcoming it with bureaucratic enthusiasm (Fabianism).

Marx and Frederick Engels contended in *The Communist Manifesto* (1848) that capitalism is inherently self-destructive and would soon be swept away by a proletarian revolution. In the 1860s Ferdinand Lassalle and Wilhelm Liebknecht founded Germany's first two Social Democratic parties, while Marx waged stormy battles with Russian anarchist Mikhail Bakunin in the First International, which destroyed it. Soon there were many kinds of socialism featuring variable approaches to the state, political democracy, the labor movement, and socialization. "Social Democracy" originated as the name for socialist parties that worked to achieve socialism through political struggle and running for office. They claimed that being revolutionary and running for office went together, which sparked contentions over what it meant to be revolutionary or democratic. The task of distilling the principles of "orthodox Marxism" fell to German socialist leader Karl Kautsky, who combined the revolutionary vision of *The*

Communist Manifesto, the political program of the German Social Democratic Party (SPD), and a philosophy of economic determinism he called dialectical materialism. In 1889, six years after Marx died, Socialists founded the Second International, this time excluding anarchists while making room for various schools of semi-Marxian and non-Marxian socialism. British ethical radical William Morris was a prominent semi-Marxian, while British Fabians Sidney Webb and George Bernard Shaw founded the Fabian movement on the idea that modern society was gradually evolving into democratic state collectivism.

Orthodox Marxism was not as dialectical as Kautsky claimed, and it reduced every social problem to class conflict between workers and capitalists. Both things diminished the socialist vision by harnessing the most powerful critique of capitalism—Marxism—ever devised. There is no core that unites the many schools of socialism except the original idea of organizing society as a coopera-tive community. The Fourier and Owen traditions carried well beyond their European origins, inspiring American radical democrats and progressives to dream of a society based on cooperative ethical values. Some founders of the U.S. Republican Party were homegrown radical democrats who identified with Fourier, and others were German '48ers who fled Germany after the failed rev-olution of 1848. Many of the '48ers knew Marx personally, and both camps linked slavery to capitalism, as Marx did; to them it could not be that European socialism was hopelessly un-American. If America was to become a decent soci-ety that broke the nexus of slavery and economic domination, it had to extin-guish America's original sin and prevent capital from dominating labor.

"Democratic socialism" bears the fateful history of Continental socialism in its self-conscious utterance. Nineteenth-century British socialists did not call themselves democratic socialists, even though most of them were, because democracy was not controversial in British socialism and few British socialists were Marxist. Democracy was controversial and divisive in Continental Marxism. Marxists agreed with democratic socialists that capitalism is antagonistic toward democracy and socialism is intrinsically democratic, but Marxists contended that existing democracy was a bourgeois fraud. Real democracy would emerge only from a proletarian revolution that abolished the class system and its division of labor. For a socialist to lionize democracy as the best road to socialism was ridiculous. Socialism was the road to democracy, not the other way around. Democracy would come by making the state irrelevant, as Marxists believed, or by smashing the state, as anarchists believed.

Kautsky-style Marxism subordinated democracy to a Marxian vision of revo-lutionary deliverance. Running for office and accepting democratic norms were acceptable only as tactical means to achieve the revolutionary end. Democratic socialists named themselves self-consciously in reaction, refusing to subordinate democracy and liberal rights to a catastrophe vision of deliverance or the demands of a left-wing dictatorship. They said socialists had to be democratic and liberal on their way to achieving socialism, and not merely on tactical grounds. SPD leader Eduard Bernstein rocked the SPD in 1898 by saying it forcefully. To put it negatively, "dictatorship of the proletariat" was a repugnant Marxian phrase conveying that socialists sought to disenfranchise the bourgeoisie—an odious nonstarter. Bernstein's classic case for democratic socialism was tagged as a revisionist betrayal of Marxism, which linked forevermore the terms "democratic socialist" and "revisionist." But "revisionism" names a perennial necessity in every intellectual tradition—the willingness to revise a stale orthodoxy. The Social Democrats who founded the Second International believed that socialist revolutions were inevitable wherever capitalism arose and puzzled that no socialist revolution had occurred anywhere. Not only were they wrong about socialist revolutions occurring in all industrialized societies. It didn't happen in any until Russia became a belated, disputed, and troubling exception.

Self-named "democratic socialism" thus began in Continental Europe as the principled democratic wing within Social Democracy. Democratic socialism was part of Social Democracy, its revisionist flank. Social Democracy was a name for the broad socialist movement, and democratic socialism named the flank of social democrats that insisted on the liberal democratic road to socialism. But Social Democracy began to acquire a different meaning after World War I, when socialists won electoral power and shed much of their Marxism. Their prolonged struggle against Russian Soviet Communism was formative and defining, as was their swing away from collective ownership after World War II. Social Democracy came to signify what democratic socialists actually did when they ran for office and gained power. They did not achieve democratic socialism, a vision of radical economic democracy. They added socialist programs to the existing system, building advanced welfare states undergirded by mixed economies. Social Democracy became synonymous with the egalitarian reformist policies of the modern welfare state.

In *Social Democracy in the Making: Political and Religious Roots of European Socialism* (2019), I analyzed the European history of the logic by which the gap between the ideals and the politics of democratic socialism triggered revisionist movements. In Germany the revisionist watersheds were the Bernstein drama of 1898–99 and the Bad Godesberg Program of 1959 that committed the SPD to Bernstein's pluralistic ethical socialism. In Sweden a similar watershed occurred in 1928 under Per Albin Hansson, who built the model European Social Democratic party, a powerhouse of Bernstein socialism. In 1951 the Frankfurt

Declaration of the refounded Socialist International formally took the Bernstein option of emphasizing democratic socialist values and deemphasizing nationalization and the class struggle. In Britain the Labour Party revised its Fabian orthodoxy in 1955, espousing pluralistic economic democracy under party leader Hugh Gaitskell and politician-theorist C. A. R. Crosland.[1]

Each of these revisionist episodes was a creative response to a stagnant orthodoxy *and* a blow to socialist confidence. By the end of World War II the divergence between democratic socialism and social democracy was something quite definite, not merely a rhetorical convention, albeit with room for exceptions at both ends. Democratic socialists held out for some form of public or worker ownership, at least to some degree, and social democrats backed off from socializing enterprises, at least most of the time. This difference marks what should be called democratic socialism from social democracy—a significant distinction, even as fluidity and exceptions are possible on both sides. Crosland played the leading role in breaking the customary identification of socialism with nationalization, which yielded generations of social democrats who claimed that socialism is about economic rights, not social ownership. But even Crosland took for granted that democratic socialists need to fight for as much economic democracy as they can get, creatively fashioning new forms of social ownership. What came instead was a social democratic tradition that settled for establishing economic rights through the welfare state.

I do not press this distinction to disparage the past half century of social democracy. I shall argue that social democracy at its best continues to struggle for creative forms of economic democracy and thus reduces the gap between democratic socialism and social democracy. But democratic socialism is not merely a catchall expression for the politics of achieving an advanced welfare state. Today every Social Democratic and workers' party is struggling to rethink its mission in the face of economic globalization and reactionary movements based on racism and xenophobia. In Germany the SPD has capitulated to neoliberal capitalism and become habituated to its junior-partner alliance with the Conservative Party, albeit with codetermined enterprises. In Sweden the Social Democratic Party has disavowed its historic attempt to democratize major enterprises, the Meidner Plan, which folded in 1992 after a ten-year run. Every European Social Democratic party is battling to save its social insurance programs while fighting off a rising tide of hostility toward immigrants. Meanwhile Sanders-style purported radicalism fixes on demands that European Social Democrats achieved a half century ago. Germany, Sweden, Denmark, Norway, and even struggling Britain invest in the common good in ways that vastly surpass the United States.

U.S. American democratic socialists fell behind their European counterparts after starting better than most of them. The United States had vibrant radical democratic traditions before and after Europeans invented socialism. American radical democrats began to call themselves socialists in the 1850s after German immigrants created the first American socialist organizations. German American social democrats were the heart of the Socialist Labor Party, founded in 1877 along with a smattering of native-born anarchists and Marxists. Christian socialism sprawled across the nation in the 1880s and 1890s, often taking a Populist form. Populists railed against banks and monopoly trusts, calling for free silver—the coinage of silver dollars at a fixed weight ratio of 16-to-1 against dollar coins made of gold. They launched powerful organizations and parties of their own, seeped into the Democratic Party, and often graduated to socialism. Very soon after the Socialist Party was founded in 1901 it rivaled the cultural diversity of the entire Second International. German trade unionists anchored the strongest Socialist organization, in Milwaukee, where social democracy was a culture, not merely a cause. Jewish garment workers from Russia and Russian Poland anchored a storied Socialist movement in New York, espousing a universalistic creed in Yiddish. Chicago Socialists ran the national office of the Socialist Party and major publishing outlets. Rebellious tenant farmers in Oklahoma, red populists in Texas, syndicalist miners in Colorado and California, and populist Socialists across the Midwest and West supported a vast network of Socialist periodicals, summer camps, and state parties.

For thirty-eight years collectively between 1910 and 1960 Milwaukee was run by three Socialist mayors—Emil Seidel, Daniel Hoan, and Frank Zeidler—all of whom burnished its reputation as one of America's best governed cities. They didn't mind that the press called them sewer socialists because they built superb public works projects that were models for the nation. The leading Socialist periodical, *Appeal to Reason*, was published in Kansas and topped 900,000 subscribers in its heyday. *The National Rip-Saw*, morphing out of *Appeal to Reason* and reaching a similar audience of farmers, Populists, Christian socialists, and rebels, boasted 160,000 subscribers. *The Jewish Daily Forward*, written in Yiddish, was the Bible of New York Jewish socialism, averaging 150,000 subscribers for decades. Scores of Socialist weeklies had upward of 30,000 subscribers between 1900 and 1920, showing that socialism had no trouble speaking American. One of them, the *Texas Rebel*, fairly raged to its 28,000 readers that if you really believe in government of the people, by the people, and for the people you have to be a socialist; in fact, you are one.

AMERICAN SOCIALIST HISTORIOGRAPHY

Most scholarship on American socialism contends that its significant tradition was the Communist one and the Socialist Party never had a chance of becoming significant. Two classic books published in 1952 dominated this field for a generation, summarizing opposite traditions of assessment that yielded a similar verdict. Political scientist Ira Kipnis, in *The American Socialist Movement*, argued that the Socialist Party was doomed from the beginning by its accommodating social democratic reformism. Kipnis said the right wing of the party led by Milwaukee journalist-politician Victor Berger was consumed with winning elections, and the mainstream of the party led by New York journalist-politician Morris Hillquit was only slightly less opportunistic. The party debated immediate demands and true Marxism at its founding but adopted the wrong answer. It got a chance to correct its course in 1905, when the Industrial Workers of the World (IWW) was founded, but Debs did not stick with the IWW, and most of the party loathed the anarcho-syndicalism and violence of the IWW. The party lost its last chance of becoming important when it censured its left flank of IWW members in 1912 and expelled IWW leader Bill Haywood from the executive committee the following year. Kipnis contributed mightily to the legend that the IWW Wobblies were the real thing and the flanks led by Hillquit and Berger were sellouts. The real thing was anarchist in hating government and syndicalist in contending that worker syndicates should run the country. True leftism versus opportunism explained the failure of the Socialist Party, culminating in the Haywood drama. Had Kipnis peeked ahead to World War I he would have had to explain how it was that Hillquit and Berger stoutly opposed the war while nearly all the party's intellectuals—some of them true-believing left-wingers—capitulated to it.[2]

Sociologist Daniel Bell, in *Marxian Socialism in the United States*, agreed from an opposite standpoint that the party was hopelessly futile from the beginning, contending that every Socialist leader espoused a utopian vision of social transformation that made the party alien to American society and marginal in it. According to Bell, AFL leader Samuel Gompers was the wise hero who figured out how to make social democratic gains in capitalist America, whereas Debs, Hillquit, and Berger clung to an un-American fantasy. Subsequently the Socialist Party crawled onward at the national level only because it had a compelling figurehead, Thomas. Just as Kipnis looked down on his subject from the superior vantage point of pro-Communist radicalism, Bell looked down as a Cold War liberal, having recently outgrown his youthful attachment to Norman Thomas Socialism. The Socialists, Bell said, were ideologues in a pluralistic and technocratic society that eventually put an end to ideology itself.[3]

These rival books cast a long shadow over scholarship on the American left. The fact that they drove to the same conclusion about the futility of American democratic socialism solidified this verdict as a convention. Cold War liberalism, combining anti-Communist containment and the domestic reforms of the New Deal, dominated the scholarship and politics of the 1950s and early 1960s. To render the legacy of American democratic socialism less negatively, one had to take the Kipnis and Bell outcome for granted while alleviating the story of their harshness. Two political historians, Howard Quint and David Shannon, took this approach in the mid-1950s, winsomely playing up that a remarkable array of Americans identified with the Socialist Party over the decades. Quint, in *The Forging of American Socialism* (1953), and Shannon, in *The Socialist Party of America* (1955), suggested that American democratic socialism could not have been such a hopeless idea if it attracted so many prairie Populists, Jewish garment workers, Protestant clerics, old-American patricians, and sewer socialists. Quint covered the period between 1865 and 1901 and Shannon from 1901 to 1950. They got the main thing right without grasping the defining sociological weakness of the party. The Socialist Party was a social movement bound by an ideology and a very weak organizational structure. It was never an organized political party that overcame its factional disputes, and its ideological separatism thwarted the labor party option back when it was a real option. Quint and Shannon eschewed interpretation to the point of failing to explain what went wrong for American democratic socialists; presumably, what went wrong was self-evident.[4]

Many scholars specialized in the ostensibly more important subject, American Communism. In 1957 political historian Theodore Draper, a former correspondent in the 1930s for the Communist *Daily Worker*, wrote a pioneering, detailed, astute, and devastating insider history, *Roots of American Communism.* Draper argued that the Communist Party surpassed the Socialist Party because it slavishly carried out every shift, reversal, alliance, and conspiracy ordered by its masters in Moscow. This was a story of orders transmitted by Kremlin bosses to their compliant servants in New York. Whatever laudable things American Communists did—defending the poor, supporting black Americans, helping to found the CIO, trying to create a Farmer–Labor party—were incidental by comparison. Communists, whenever so ordered, were willing to reverse direction, sabotage unions and coalitions, and lie about anything, especially their own politics. Draper portrayed American Communism as more evil than stupid. Socialism was deeply alien to American society, exactly as Bell said, and the only kind that succeeded in America was totalitarian, never mind that Communist and pro-Communist dupes shielded themselves from realizing what sort of outfit they defended. Many scholars amplified Draper's picture of America's homegrown

Communist menace, notably Shannon, Irving Howe, Lewis Coser, Nathan Glazer, and Harry Overstreet. Nearly always they came from Socialist, pro-Communist, or Communist backgrounds themselves, citing former Communists who became professional anti-Communists. Jay Lovestone and Benjamin Gitlow, upon falling from the top of the American Communist hierarchy, were pioneers of the former-Communist anti-Communist genre; later there were many others, notably James Burnham, Max Eastman, and Whittaker Chambers.[5]

Scholarship on U.S. American Communism shifted dramatically when scholars applied the social history approach to it, focusing on Communists who never got a directive from Moscow. Maurice Isserman wrote the breakthrough social history *Which Side Were You On?* (1982), reinterpreting the role of American Communism in the Popular Front campaigns of the thirties and forties. Isserman contended that Communists fled the party in the late 1950s because the Cold War abolished any prospect of a new Popular Front, not because they were disillusioned by Soviet rule at the Draper level. A gusher of social histories ensued, usually focusing on black Communists and the CIO unions, where Communists controlled or exercised dominant influence in 15 internationals numbering approximately 1.4 million members. Ronald Schatz, Mark Naison, Bruce Nelson, Robin D. G. Kelley, and Michael Goldfield were pioneers of the social history genre. Kelley's *Hammer and Hoe: Alabama Communists during the Great Depression* (1990) made a seminal contribution, detailing the struggles of Alabama Communists against the racist police state of Alabama in the 1930s and 1940s. Kelley stressed that Alabama Communists came from the working class, had little or no connection to Euro-American traditions of radical politics, and consisted mostly of religious black wage earners and sharecroppers, housewives, and renegade liberals. Reflecting on the chasm between black Alabama Communists and the party bosses in New York, Kelley noted aptly that if black Alabamans had waited "patiently for orders from Moscow, they might still be waiting today."[6]

American democratic socialism exploded under the Communist eruption of 1919, fought American Communism at the Draper level for decades, and fell behind the Communists in the 1930s in racial justice activism and organizing CIO unions. The New Left revisionism that famously disputed Cold War liberalism in the 1960s and yielded the social histories of the 1980s extended to how the early Socialist Party should be understood. Political historian James Weinstein was the leading New Left revisionist about the Socialist Party. In *The Decline of Socialism in America* (1967) he contended that Kipnis and Bell were too prejudiced against their subject to get it right. Kipnis said the sellout leaders who opposed Haywood sealed the party's fate; Bell said Woodrow Wilson's liberalism sealed the party's fate, making socialism irrelevant in American life; Weinstein showed that Socialist activism increased after the anarcho-syndicalists bolted and Wilson entered the White House, contrary to Kipnis and Bell. Moreover, *none* of the party's left-wing leaders (Debs, Ella Reeve Bloor, Louis Boudin, Emil Herman, Kate O'Hare, Charles Ruthenberg, and Rose Pastor Stokes) or its leading left-wing intellectuals (Frank Bohn, Jack London, J. G. Phelps-Stokes, and William English Walling) dropped their Socialist politics.[7]

I take the latter point from Weinstein while stressing that American socialism never acquired anywhere near the labor movement base of the British Labour Party and the Continental Social Democratic parties. The early Socialist Party was too extraordinary for its own good, combining so many ethnic groups, regional cultures, and social movements that Debs and Hillquit saw no need to ally with anybody except on Socialist terms, while Debs and Haywood castigated the entire AFL as a corrupt sellout. Even after the party lost the Haywood anarcho-syndicalists, it remained a thriving political force that improved its record on racial justice, supported the rights of women, and welcomed a surge of immigrants. The party's early factionalism gave way to a more coherent democratic socialism, to the extent that such a thing was possible in a ramshackle federalist structure, and Debs forged a genuine friendship and political bond with Hillquit. The Socialist Party outperformed all its European counterparts in the electoral arena up to 1918 *despite* its small size and union base. The vicious government persecution of the party for its antiwar stand might have been enough to cripple it irreparably; as it was, the Communist eruption tore apart the entire Socialist world. The American Communist Party arose at the expense of the Socialist Party it devastated.

Most historical scholarship on American democratic socialism underplays the importance of racism and black Socialists, feminism and feminist Socialists, and religious socialism and thus misses as well how these subjects relate to each other. I am grateful to scholars who have addressed one or more of these issues. Sally Miller and Mary Jo Buhle wrote pioneering works on women in the Socialist Party, filling a crucial gap; Jack Ross extended Weinstein's basic story line about the Socialist Party and added an appreciative twist about the Old Guard; Heath W. Carter superbly detailed the working-class roots of the social gospel in Chicago, highlighting Catholic unionists; Philip S. Foner was the first scholar to give George W. Woodbey and other black socialists their due. The socialist contention that all forms of oppression are secondary to the class struggle naturally yielded accounts of white male Socialists saying so. But Christian socialism was not a latecomer in the United States, it spread across the entire nation, and it did not take a back seat to nonreligious socialism.[8]

Most of the women who came into the socialist movement came through social gospel socialism. The United States was like Britain in producing vital Christian socialist traditions that spoke to broader middle-class audiences than the Socialist parties, demanded to be included in Socialist politics, built significant organizations, and outlasted the Marxist traditions. Kipnis dismissed the Christian socialists in three quick strokes, noting that George Herron was briefly famous, something called the Christian Socialist Fellowship existed, and all Christian socialists, being religious, were of course opportunists. On occasion Kipnis cited a Christian Socialist cleric saying something moralizing about public morality. Christian socialism itself he dispatched with a single sentence: "Since the Christian Socialists based their analysis on the brotherhood of man rather than on the class struggle, they aligned themselves with the opportunist rather than the revolutionary wing of the party." The party's many Christian socialist leaders and authors, whoever they were, could not have mattered, since they were religious.[9]

Bell similarly pushed aside the Christian Socialists, without employing "opportunist" as a broad-brush epithet. He devoted a footnote to the Christian Commonwealth colony at Commonwealth, Georgia, noted that Edward Bellamy's Fabian nationalist utopia *Looking Backward* (1888) won most of its fame through Christian socialist clergy, and observed that a cleric named George Herron was "one of the leading figures of the party." That was it. Even a bit of following up on Herron would have vastly enriched Bell's picture of American socialism, but he wasn't interested. It could not be that these people mattered. The struggles for racial justice and feminism had no role in Bell's story, so the Christian socialist roles in both didn't matter either. Bell's very insistence that socialism is always religious—that is, eschatological—exempted him, he thought, from paying attention to any actual religious socialists, whether or not they were indebted to Marx.[10]

Herron was a lecture circuit spellbinder and Congregational cleric who befriended Debs, showed Debs how to translate ethical idealism and populism into sermon-style socialist evangelism, and electrified the social gospel movement by calling America to repent of its capitalist, racist, sexist, and imperialist sins. W. D. P. Bliss was a tireless organizer and Episcopal cleric who tried to unite the reform movements and failed to persuade the Socialist Party that uniting the reform movements was its mission. Woodbey was a brilliant black Baptist cleric who spoke for the Socialist Party and the IWW, was beaten and jailed for doing so, and tried to improve how the party and the Wobblies talked about racial justice. W. E. B. Du Bois had one foot in the black church, joined Socialists Mary White Ovington and William English Walling in willing the NAACP into existence, and provided intellectual leadership for black social gospel radicals. Walter Rauschenbusch, the leading social gospel socialist of his time, never quite joined the Socialist Party because its atheist ethos repelled him. Kate O'Hare was a brilliant prairie Socialist writer and speaker who reflected the racism of her milieu and attracted a following exceeded only by Debs. Vida Scudder was a prolific organizer, writer, Episcopal laywoman, feminist, and lesbian who worked with Bliss and tried to drag Rauschenbusch into the Socialist Party.

These apostles of Christian socialism absorbed more Marxist theory than they usually found it prudent to cite. Bliss and Herron were like Debs in coming to socialism through the Populist movement and its outraged moral sensibility. Bliss, Herron, Scudder, and Rauschenbusch struggled with the paradoxes of their ethical Christian idealism for socialist activism, but, like Debs, they believed the class struggle and the limits of middle-class American moral idealism compelled them to be socialists. They said so eloquently a generation before Reinhold Niebuhr became famous for saying it. Marxian social democracy and Populism were the two main highways into American socialism. Christian socialism was the third, and much of the Populist movement *was* Christian socialist. Chapters 2 and 3 contend that Christian socialism played a greater role than scholars of American socialism have said; afterward the point comes through without requiring any special mention.

INVENTING AMERICAN DEMOCRATIC SOCIALISM

Early U.S. American socialism was both homegrown and imported. Thomas Paine, a leading propagandist of the American Revolution, was an apostle of the radical democratic insistence that citizens have a right to information and a right to act on what they know. He clashed with other American Founders over believing in it more than they did, giving birth to an American tradition contending that liberal rights apply to all citizens and are achieved through democracy. America's first labor party, the Workingmen's Party of New York, was also the world's first labor party. Founded in 1829 by Robert Owen socialists— machinist Thomas Skidmore, mechanic-journalist George Henry Evans, and Owen's son Robert Dale Owen—it quarreled, split, and folded in two years, propelling Skidmore and Evans into the agrarian movement for free land, albeit as rivals. Evans became America's leading proponent of the view that achieving public control of land is the key to creating a good society. *Webster's Dictionary*, in 1848, registered this identification of socialism with free land, defining socialism as "a social state in which there is a community of property among all the citizens; a new term for AGRARIANISM."[11]

Agrarians clashed with each other over party politics, as did abolitionists for similar reasons; meanwhile the two movements intertwined. William Lloyd Garrison founded the New England Anti-Slavery Society in 1832 and the American Anti-Slavery Society (AAS) in 1833. He opposed any involvement in politics or government because the U.S. Constitution was a proslavery document, and, to him, abolitionism was a moral crusade. Subsequently he acquired a similar commitment to feminism. Abolitionist leaders Henry Stanton and Gerrit Smith opposed Garrison on politics and feminism, bolting the AAS in 1840 to form the Liberty Party. They contended that moral crusading alone would not abolish slavery; the movement had to get political. One newspaper, the *New York Tribune,* and its legendary editor, Horace Greeley, pressed the political argument brilliantly but with abolitionist-agrarian-feminist-socialist politics. Greeley founded the *Tribune* in 1841 and stocked it with radical democrats Charles Dana, Margaret Fuller, George Ripley, and Fourier's first American disciple, Albert Brisbane. They campaigned for abolition, free land, women's rights, and communal socialism, urging the Whig Party to oppose slavery and the monopoly of land.[12]

Greeley lost the abolitionist argument in the Whig Party but created a journalistic powerhouse peaking at a circulation of 200,000 in its weekly national edition. One of his most avid readers was Abraham Lincoln, and from 1852 to 1862 Greeley's chief writer on Europe was Karl Marx. The closest thing to a steady job that Marx ever held was writing for the *Tribune.* He hated having to grub for a living by writing mere journalism that editors presumptuously edited but did it anyway. He wrote 350 bylined articles, his alter ego Engels wrote 125, and many more passed as anonymous editorials. Marx wrote dispatches on China, British politics, British imperialism in India, American slavery, Continental European counterrevolutions, and economics. He said it mattered very much to see the world through a Marxist lens, something very different from standard progressive commentary. The structure of economic ownership determines the character of an entire society, and socialism is the collective ownership of the means of production—a sufficient condition for fulfilling the essential aspirations of human beings.[13]

From this perspective the *Tribune* trafficked mostly in bourgeois newspaper twaddle, even from its socialist writers. Some American socialists graduated to Marxism upon reading Marx, and others stuck with non-Marxian forms of ethical or religious socialism. Marx policed what counted as a socialist argument, contending that socialism had to be proletarian-revolutionary or was otherwise worthless. Pre-Marxian critiques of capitalism missed what matters, the extraction of surplus value that exploits workers and steals the fruit of their labor.

Labor cannot be emancipated through reforms or emancipated only for white workers. Parliamentary democracy is not the road to a classless society. Questions concerning racial and gender oppression are subordinate to the labor question. Marx had a steely realism about politics, even in *The Communist Manifesto*. He was usually willing to deal with labor and socialist movements as he found them, contending that proletarians had to make whatever alliances with liberals and democrats it took to advance the revolution. But he heaped ferocious invective on pretty much everyone who disagreed with him. He sundered the First International by clashing with anarchists. He blasted German Social Democrats in 1875 for uniting on the basis of Ferdinand Lassalle's democratic state socialism, conveniently overlooking that the other German Social Democratic party in the merger was mostly radical democratic too, not Marxist. He sneered at American Socialist women and radical democrats who said the labor question is also a women's question. He repudiated England's only Marxist party, H. M. Hyndman's Social Democratic Federation (SDF). To Marx it was pointless for socialists to unite on the basis of radical democratic causes instead of Marxism.[14]

Greeley's circle had a few European socialist exiles before Europe erupted in republican revolutions in 1848. Then Marx and Engels issued *The Communist Manifesto*, the revolutions failed, and a gusher of German socialists fled to the United States. Some played major roles in founding the Republican Party and served as military commanders in the Union Army. Gustav Koerner was the pioneer German socialist connection to Lincoln. He fled political persecution in Germany in 1833; landed briefly in St. Louis, Missouri, where American slavery abhorred him; settled near Belleville, Illinois, and befriended Mary Todd while studying for the bar in Lexington, Kentucky. Koerner befriended Todd's future husband, Lincoln, on the way to a distinguished career in Illinois law and Democratic politics, serving on the state Supreme Court and as lieutenant governor. He commiserated with Lincoln when Lincoln dropped out of politics in 1849, introducing him to German socialist '48ers who landed in Illinois, Wisconsin, and Missouri. Koerner was a player in the Midwest stirrings for a party opposing any further expansion of slavery, which led to the national founding of the Republican Party in 1856.

One '48er, Herman Kriege, was a former leader of the League of the Just, a European Christian Communist group that morphed in 1847 into the Communist League and commissioned Marx and Engels to write the *Manifesto*. Kriege converted to the cause of free land after he landed in the United States and read Evans, which got him promptly expelled by Marx from the Communist League. Another '48er, Wilhelm Weitling, was the League of the Just's most prominent writer and speaker before he fled to the United States. In Germany he called himself a socialist Luther; in the United States he swiftly ditched revolutionary socialism in favor of an Owen idea, a labor exchange bank. Weitling reasoned that in America the merchant capitalist was the source of monopoly, so common ownership of property was pointless. America needed to socialize the process of exchange, combining a central bank with producer cooperatives. Other '48ers included Friedrich Karl Franz Hecker, Carl Schurz, Fritz Anneke, August Willich, Hermann Korff, Friedrich von Beust, and Joseph Weydemeyer. Some influenced Lincoln's decision to reenter politics in 1854, when the first Republican gatherings were held in Wisconsin and Michigan.[15]

Hecker was a prominent 1848 agitator, fled to Illinois in September 1848, cofounded the Illinois Republican Party in 1856, campaigned against Know-Nothing Americanism, served as a brigade commander in the Union Army, and opposed Lincoln when he took a conciliatory approach to the defeated Confederacy. Schurz immigrated in 1852, settled in Wisconsin, linked slavery to capitalism, organized German American support for Lincoln, commanded troops as a general at Bull Run, Chancellorsville, Gettysburg, and Chattanooga, and served as a U.S. senator from Missouri. Willich outflanked Marx to the left in the Communist League, enlisted Engels as his assistant, fled to Cincinnati in 1849, ran the socialist Republican newspaper *Republikaner*, and served as a brigadier general in the war. Weydemeyer began as a Prussian military officer, opted for revolutionary journalism, befriended Marx and Engels, migrated to New York in 1851, and served as a lieutenant colonel in the war.[16]

These figures were colorful additions to a fiery abolitionist stew of radical liberals, radical democrats, humanists, Christian evangelicals, socialists, feminists, disaffected Whigs, and formerly enslaved neo-abolitionists. Explicitly Marxian networks existed in the 1850s only in German working-class sections of northern cities. Weitling's attempt to found a national convention of German socialists flopped, as did Weydemeyer's attempts to spread Marxism in New York. But radical democratic, neo-abolitionist, free land American socialism flourished, converting many of the German '48ers. Unitarian abolitionist cleric Theodore Parker spoke for many radicals by floridly describing America as a virgin impregnated by a freedom-seeking people and married to humankind. In 1850 he described the democratic ideal as a government of all the people, by all the people, and for all the people. Lincoln's Gettysburg Address of 1863 immortalized this ideal. Many abolitionists absorbed a socialist worldview while fighting to abolish slavery and establish Radical Republicanism in American politics. After the war they contended that "socialism" was the best name for the radical democratic ideal of Parker and Lincoln.[17]

Lincoln's strong egalitarianism could be harnessed as readily to the capitalist exaltation of free labor as to socialism. His ideal was a society of small producers that used American opportunity to rise in society through their merit. But the socialists caught Lincoln's socialist inflection whenever he linked physical slavery to economic domination, believing he was almost one of them. In 1858 Lincoln said that politics is an eternal struggle between the principles of the common right of humanity and the divine right of kings. What matters is to enlist wholly for the right principle and against the wrong one. Democrats charged that Republican opposition to the spread of slavery was moralistic, making Republicans unfit for politics. Lincoln played the political game, steering clear of abolitionism while making moral arguments about the rights of humanity. In 1859 he told the Wisconsin State Agricultural Society that labor is not only superior to capital but greatly so. This theme became a staple of his 1860 campaign for the presidency, exhorting workers not to surrender their economic or political power.[18]

Lincoln treasured his alliance with Greeley and sought to live up to it. The Homestead Act of 1862 was a light version of Greeley's call to give land to the landless; Greeley pressed Lincoln for two years to issue the Emancipation Proclamation; and Lincoln selected Greeley's managing editor, Dana, as assistant secretary of war. Dana was the connection for the Marxists, non-Marxian social democrats, and communal socialists who won military commissions in the Union Army. A generation later, after socialists had been airbrushed out of the story of Lincoln and the Republican Party or refashioned as liberals, their successors overcompensated in correcting the record. Black socialist cleric George W. Slater Jr. claimed that Lincoln was a flat-out socialist, upping the ante only slightly on a customary socialist boast.[19]

The socialist appeal to the spirit of Lincoln was much like the argument that Christian socialists made when they claimed that socialism and religion go together. American socialists, like all Christian socialists, had to cope with the fact that socialist rhetoric about abolishing capitalism evoked fears of class war and proletarian smashing. Christian socialism, wherever it took root, sought to mitigate this threat. Marxists, radical democrats, anarchists, and trade unionists charged that churches obviously sided with the capitalist class and did not care about the poor and afflicted. The founding Christian socialists countered that a different kind of Christianity was possible and that antireligious socialism is not saving. Socialism had to be Christianized before destructive forms of it shredded the churches, universities, and government, and it had to be disciplined by liberal democratic values. Otherwise it betrayed its defining radical democratic impulse—that socialism *is* democracy applied to the economic realm.

England had deep traditions of cooperative, Christian, and ethical socialism, which enabled Christian socialists to play major roles in socialist movements and the British Labour Party. Continental Europe was very different, nearly always pitting Social Democratic parties and state churches against each other, which prevented Christian socialists from breaking through or even from existing. In the United States, Christian socialists were uniquely advantaged and disadvantaged. America's Puritan evangelical heritage was an advantage, teaching that Christianity has a social mission to build a good society and the state a sacred duty to protect liberty. The lack of a national state church was an advantage, allowing room for activist social religion. Homegrown Christian feminism linked to the temperance movement was another advantage, one which led to religious socialist feminists who did not accept Marx's authority on the woman question. The abolitionist factor—something shared with the British tradition—was very important. Many of the founding British and American Christian socialists conceived Christian socialism as the next phase of the abolitionist struggle. They were socialists because they were neo-abolitionists; on both sides they shucked off the taunt that they were moralistic. Herron, Woodbey, Du Bois, Ovington, and Albion Tourgée epitomized this two-sided claim. But America had a distinctly capitalist ethos and a Constitution that canonized proslavery eighteenth-century liberalism—to the befuddlement of immigrant socialists.[20]

The First International—the International Workingmen's Association—was born in London in 1864, belatedly giving Marx something to join. The United States got its first national union in 1866 with the founding of the National Labor Union, which advocated an eight-hour workday, financial reform, and political activism. It expired after three years, not lasting long enough to be accepted into the International. Many leaders of the populist Greenback Party, founded in 1873, came from the National Labor Union; meanwhile the only chartered American sections of the International were the German Workingmen's societies. In 1857 Friedrich Sorge, a German '48er and music teacher, founded the Communist Club in New York. The following year it merged with a Lassallean Workingmen's society; in 1869 it morphed into a group called New Democracy; and in 1871 the group disbanded and reorganized as Sections Nine and Twelve of the International. Section Nine consisted of the German and Irish founders of American trade unionism led by Sorge, Cigar Makers Union founder Adolph Strasser, United Brotherhood of Carpenters founder Peter McGuire, and Strasser's protégé Samuel Gompers. Section Twelve consisted of New England abolitionists, radical democrats, and feminists led by two radical feminist sisters, Victoria Woodhull and Tennessee Claflin.[21]

Woodhull overcame a turbulent early life in Ohio to become a renowned feminist advocate of divorce and the right to free love. She made a fortune as a magnetic healer and spiritualist, befriending Cornelius Vanderbilt, and in 1870 Vanderbilt helped Woodhull and her sister establish the first brokerage firm on Wall Street run by women. The firm was hugely successful, heightening Woodhull's already controversial reputation as a spiritualist, con artist, radical feminist, provocateur, wily operator, and defender of sex work. Later in 1870 she and her younger sister founded a newspaper, *Woodhull and Claflin's Weekly*, to promote their causes and Woodhull's campaign for the presidency of the United States.

Woodhull contended that the Fourteenth and Fifteenth Amendments established the right to vote for all citizens, including women. She joined the First International and brought many of her readers into it, which threatened the German American Socialists. Everything about her offended them, including her air of Yankee superiority. Gompers later put it vividly: "Section Twelve of the American group was dominated by a brilliant group of faddists, reformers, and sensation-loving spirits. They were not working people and treated their relationship to the labor movement as a means to a 'career.' They did not realize that labor issues were tied up with the lives of men, women, and children—issues not to be risked lightly. Those pseudo-Communists played with the labor movement. This experience burned itself into my memory so that I never forgot the principle in after years."[22]

Marx had a very similar feeling about the U.S. American feminist socialists. These people were not the real thing and could not be trusted. In 1872 Woodhull's group of self-described intellectuals held a convention of their own, and Sorge convened a separate group. Both groups sent delegates to the 1872 convention of the First International at The Hague, where Marx declared that Sorge's group was legitimate and Woodhull's was not. Marx was embroiled in the last phase of his battle to prevent Bakunin from taking over the International, so he transferred the office of the International from London to New York—far from him and Bakunin.

This dubious honor, for Sorge, meant that his fractious group got to preside over the death of the International. Woodhull ran for president in 1872 as the candidate of the Equal Rights Party, advocating women's suffrage and equal rights. Her running mate was black abolitionist leader Frederick Douglass, but she was arrested just before the election for obscenity, charged with slandering famous liberal Protestant cleric Henry Ward Beecher over his alleged adulterous affair with Elizabeth Tilton, the wife of Beecher's longtime ally. Whatever votes Woodhull received were not recorded. Four years later American socialism got its formal founding with the liquidation of the International. Sorge reorganized Section One as a new political party, the Workingmen's Party of America. Its core was a group of Lassallean social democrats that split off from the International in 1874 in solidarity with the first of Germany's two Social Democratic parties, the General German Workers' Association—the democratic state socialist party founded by Lassalle in 1863. Germany's two Social Democratic parties united at Gotha in 1875, buoying the hopes of American social democrats. Socialism was ascending, despite the sorry sundering of the First International.

THE SOCIALIST LABOR PARTY, THE KNIGHTS OF LABOR, THE SINGLE TAX, AND THE AFL

Sorge, Strasser, McGuire, Typographical Union founder Albert Parsons, and journalist J. P. McConnell, Marx's onetime secretary in London, were the founders of the new Workingmen's Party. They united too late to run a presidential candidate in 1876, throwing their support to the Greenback Party demanding the circulation of fiat money from the government. In 1877 the socialists held their first national convention and took a new name, Socialist Labor Party (SLP). Ideologically the party had three factions, and culturally it split two ways between the American-born and the recently arrived, but the party was overwhelmingly German and German speaking. There was a small faction of anarchists, a large faction espousing the parliamentary state socialism of Lassalle, and a trade union faction that called itself Marxist.

The Lassalle group was dominated by recent immigrants and identified with Lassalle's former party in Germany. It took pride that the German Social Democratic unity platform of 1875 was basically the Lassalle program of democratic state socialism and political activism—just as Marx angrily contended in *Critique of the Gotha Program*. The union faction of SLP founders had longer backgrounds in the United States and conceived Marx as a revolutionary unionist who spurned political activism. The SLP grew impressively, claiming ten thousand members by 1879, despite battling constantly over which faction was redder than the other. In 1878 the Greenback Party elected fourteen members to Congress and some SLP leaders pressed for an electoral alliance with the Greenback populists. The success of the Greenback movement was too great to brush aside. In 1880 the SLP and the Greenback Party joined forces at the national level, while the SLP attracted members of the Knights of Labor—an upstart union founded by a Christian communal socialist.[23]

The Knights of Labor launched something that was not to be—a national union with a communal socialist agenda and no exclusions based on race, gender, or trade skill. Uriah Stephens, a Philadelphia tailor who studied for the Baptist ministry, founded it in 1869, calling it the Noble and Holy Order of Knights of Labor. In the beginning it was a fraternal society of tailors replete with Mason-like secrecy and religious rituals. Stephens organized the Knights as a voluntary association of producers open to all workers wanting to create a cooperative society. He wanted no parasitic nonproducers in the Knights, so he barred bankers, land speculators, lawyers, liquor dealers, and gamblers from joining. He argued that Gilded Age capitalism was hopelessly corrupt and predatory, America needed a worker organization dedicated to creating a good society, and fraternal-like secrecy was the only way to protect members from being persecuted or killed. The Knights outgrew their fraternal beginning while Stephens urged the Greenbacks and Labor socialists to consolidate. He bonded his organization to Greenback–Labor, forging a coalition of populists, Labor socialists, and cooperative religious unionists. Stephens ran for Congress in 1878 as a Greenback–Labor candidate, the same year the Knights officially opened their membership to African Americans and women.

But the Knights chafed at the secrecy policy, Bible rituals, and Stephens's anti-Catholic Protestantism. In 1879 the organization voted to go public, and Stephens resigned in protest. The Knights argued about it for three years before going public in 1882. Their new leader was Terence Powderly, a Catholic Republican former machinist and current mayor of Scranton, Pennsylvania. Under Powderly the Knights grew spectacularly, becoming the nation's first industrial union and its first successful nationwide union, period. In 1880 it had twenty-eight thousand members; in 1884 it had one hundred thousand members, surging with Catholic recruits; by 1886 it had eight hundred thousand members. Along the way it dropped its Noble and Holy Order moniker, shed its aversion to strikes, supported various third-party movements, and campaigned for five reforms: an eight-hour workday, equal pay for equal work, a graduated income tax, producer cooperatives, and abolition of child labor and convict labor. The Knights boasted racially integrated local assemblies in the North and tolerated segregated assemblies in the South. Their secrecy and radicalism were anathema to many Catholic hierarchs, but two cardinals, James Gibbons and John Ireland, stoutly defended them.[24]

In 1883 the Knights added a sixth policy cause, Henry George's Single Tax, which taxed the entire increment in the value of land. George was an autodidactic Christian deist born in 1837 in Philadelphia. He dropped out of school at fourteen, traveled widely, worked his way up as a journalist in California, loathed the railroad monopolies, and ruminated on a depressing phenomenon: wherever capitalism spread it generated new wealth and excessive misery. Specifically, wherever American capitalism spread, speculators grabbed the land, prices soared, economic activity contracted, wages and prices dropped, and desperate majority populations struggled not to starve. In 1869 George had a Damascus Road moment while walking the streets of New York, overwhelmed by the city's extreme inequality. He vowed to devote the rest of his life to reforming the system. Ten years later, in *Progress and Poverty*, he argued that landownership is the root of all social evil. As long as land values increase, those who work the land are forced to pay more for the right to work.[25]

George was against monopoly, not capitalism. Steeped in Adam Smith–David Ricardo classical economics, he said it was legitimate to derive earnings from the application of labor or capital but not to extract wealth as rent. Rent unjustly charges producers for the right to produce. It is a toll levied by monopoly, expropriating wealth for something—mere possession—that performs no useful function. Since God created the land for everyone, and society creates the increment in the value of land, the increment should go to society. Sufficiently taxing the land—a Single Tax appropriating the entire unearned increment in the value of land—is the key to creating a just society. Confiscating land, George said, is unnecessary; all that is needed is to confiscate rent.

Progress and Poverty electrified an enormous reading public as soon as it was published in the United States (1879) and England (1880). Within a few years it had sold seven million copies in ten languages, an astounding achievement for a bulky tome on economics. Nearly every Socialist, Christian socialist, and Progressive platform of the 1880s and early 1890s in the United States and Britain endorsed George's Single Tax or the outright socialization of land. George grew accustomed to being lionized by socialists who chided him for going halfway. His simplicity and vaguely Christian basis were crucial to his impact. He stressed that the Single Tax changed everything without making heroic demands on the political system. It did not require sweeping transformations of human consciousness or society or rest on a theory of class war or stigmatize capitalists who actually produced something. To succeed, it only needed to win a few elections. On his sensational lecture tours George called himself an apostle of the kingdom of God, declaring that the Single Tax would unleash new creative powers of the human spirit. If rent were abolished, the sterile waste of centuries of parasitic landlords would be wiped away, and the barren places "would ere long be dappled with the shade of trees and musical with the song of birds."[26]

Marx grieved in his last years that George single-handedly distracted socialists from what matters: surplus value and the self-destruction of capitalism. He told Sorge that George was a throwback to the radical disciples of Ricardo who revised Ricardo's theory of rent shortly after his death. They, too, wanted rent to be paid to the state as a substitute for taxes. A long line of French socialists came

next, pining to socialize land; now George was famous for recycling their backward fantasies. Marx shook his head at squishy land socialists: "They leave *wage
labor* and therefore *capitalist production* in existence and try to bamboozle
themselves or the world into believing that if ground rent were transformed into
a state tax *all the evils* of capitalist production would disappear of themselves."
When so-called socialists called for land socialization, he said, they actually
reestablished capitalist domination "afresh on an even wider basis than its present one." At least George was honest about trying to save capitalism. Yet Marx
caught the historic importance of the George phenomenon: "On the other
hand, George's book, like the sensation it has made with you, is significant
because it is a first, if unsuccessful, attempt at emancipation from the orthodox
political economy."[27]

The Greenback–Labor alliance was short-lived, unable to ride out an economic upturn. Greenback presidential candidate James Weaver, an Iowa
Greenback member of Congress, won only three hundred thousand votes in
1880. The SLP membership plummeted to fifteen hundred, and party leaders
lost their tolerance for coalition politics. They disliked English-speaking politics
and were no longer willing to pretend otherwise. After the election the SLP
broke apart. The revolutionary wing followed Parsons into the anarchist
International Working People's Association, the so-called Black International of
Bakunin. By 1885 its American section had seven thousand members and was
centered in Chicago. Many others followed Strasser and McGuire into a new
union founded in 1881, the Federation of Organized Trades and Labor Unions
of the United States and Canada, headed by Strasser's cigar industry protégé,
Samuel Gompers. The Federation founders advocated a hard-nosed, practical,
socialist unionism based on the skilled trades, which they called Marxism.
America needed the real thing, they said, not the romanticism of the Knights,
the anarchist fanaticism that wrecked the First International, or the feckless
political activism that wrecked the SLP.

The Knights had a moment of glory, winning strikes against Jay Gould's
Union Pacific Railroad in 1884 and the Wabash Railroad in 1885. A flood of new
members poured into the Knights from the autonomous Railroad Brotherhoods.
In March 1886 the Knights struck against Gould's Union Pacific and Missouri
Pacific Railroads, tying up five thousand miles of track. More than two hundred
thousand workers struck in Arkansas, Illinois, Kansas, Missouri, and Texas. But
the Brotherhood of Locomotive Engineers and Trainmen refused to honor the
strike, state militias in Missouri and Texas intervened against the strikers, and
the strike unraveled. The failure of the Southwest railroad strike devastated the
Knights, setting off the chain reaction that created the AFL in 1886.[28]

The first May Day—May 1, 1886—dramatically symbolized that the United States was not an exception to the class struggle. In 1884 the Federation unionists passed a resolution declaring that if the eight-hour workday were not enacted by May 1, 1886, a one-day general strike would commence. Powderly ordered the Knights not to strike, believing the Federation overplayed its hand. On the first May Day many Knights spurned Powderly's plea against the general strike, joining the Black International anarchists and Federation unions in demonstrations. Massive parades of striking workers marched in Chicago, New York, Detroit, Cincinnati, Baltimore, Milwaukee, Boston, St. Louis, and Pittsburgh. Two days later Chicago police officers killed four protesters at a strike against the International Harvester plant; the following day someone threw a bomb into a crowd at a protest at Haymarket Square, killing one police officer and wounding others. Parsons and six other anarchists were convicted of conspiracy to throw the bomb, despite a weak case against them, and Parsons and three others were hanged for it. In October the Supreme Court ruled that states could not regulate interstate commerce passing through their borders, annulling the legal power of states over numerous trusts, railroads, and holding companies. In November the SLP backed George's spectacular United Labor Party campaign for mayor of New York City, which bested Republican candidate Theodore Roosevelt but lost to Tammany machine Democrat Abram S. Hewitt. In December the Federation unionists merged with defecting Knight craft unions to form a powerful new union federation, the AFL.[29]

A new generation of socialist and Christian socialist leaders emerged from the first May Day, the Haymarket tragedy, the George campaign, and the founding of the AFL, just as the AFL founders began to say that bread-and-butter unionism was much better than socialism. Daniel De Leon, the father of American revolutionary unionism, was the first of the newcomers to become a major player in American socialism.

He came to the SLP from an unlikely background. Born to a wealthy family of Sephardic Jews in Curaçao, Dutch West Indies, where his father was a surgeon in the Royal Netherlands Army and a colonial official, De Leon studied at the University of Leiden without graduating. He moved to New York in 1874, taught Greek and Latin at a prep school in Westchester, earned a law degree at Columbia University, practiced law in Texas for four years, returned to New York in 1882, and decided he would rather be an academic. He won a prize lectureship at Columbia by lecturing about European imperialism in Latin America, beginning his first three-year term of lectures in 1883 and his second in 1886.

What went wrong is disputed. De Leon said he was fired from Columbia for supporting George's mayoral campaign. Columbia said his subject was too marginal to justify a position for him on the faculty. Columbia is more believable, as historians routinely judge that De Leon was a "pathological liar" prone to highly "peculiar fictions," especially about himself, though of course Columbia was wrong about imperialism. De Leon joined the Knights in 1888 and the SLP in 1890, just as the SLP bitterly split over its recent flirtation with George progressives. The smaller SLP faction disavowed political action, and the larger faction vowed to run pure socialist candidates. Engels, writing to Sorge, said American socialism would be better off if every German in the SLP disappeared. The smaller faction split off to form its own SLP in Cincinnati, defiantly keeping the name, and De Leon joined the old SLP in New York just as it hit bottom.[30]

De Leon's brilliance and his status as a *Gelehrte* (professor) dazzled his new German American SLP comrades. He quickly overwhelmed them with his cunning, controlling, dogmatic personality, his flair for sectarian invective, and his talent for theory. De Leon took over the party and its English language paper, contending that one part of Marxist theory remained to be developed—how to take power. De Leon and Lenin regarded De Leon as the American Lenin, though De Leon said that in America Socialists had to gain power through the ballot—"the weapon of civilization"—not through the methods of Marxist (or, later, Leninist) class war. Outright class war applies only to lower civilizations. De Leon argued that trade union Marxism is hopelessly flawed because its leaders inevitably become functionaries in the capitalist system, as happened in the AFL. The road to power is to wage the political and economic revolution *simultaneously*, because winning either struggle without the other is self-defeating and corrupting. The SLP needed to be a revolutionary party that captured the unions as its first order of business.[31]

De Leon began with the Knights because it was more vulnerable than the AFL. He infiltrated the Knights' New York assembly and persuaded the western assemblies to join him in ousting Powderly, but the new grand master reneged on his bargain with De Leon, so De Leon countered by founding the Socialist Trades and Labor Alliance. Now the SLP was creating a dual union—the worst of all crimes to Gompers—while boring into the AFL. De Leon tried to enter through the front door, but Gompers won a convention vote in 1890 blocking the SLP. That set off three years of bitter fighting about it. Gompers wailed that his "union wrecking" foes in the SLP were led by "a professor without a professorship, a shyster lawyer without a brief, and a statistician who furnished figures to the republican, democratic, and socialist parties." De Leon was the professor, Morris Hillquit the lawyer, and Machinist union secretary Thomas J. Morgan the statistician.[32]

Socialists nearly captured the AFL in 1893 and 1894, barely losing a policy vote in 1894 calling for the socialization of all means of production and distribution. They took their revenge by ejecting Gompers from the presidency, replacing him with miner John McBride. But the coalition of Socialists and Populists unraveled, and Gompers climbed back into office the following year. De Leon was very good at causing a ruckus and at arguing that Marx would have agreed with him. The Socialists had able leaders who dreamed of winning the AFL to socialism. Cleveland printer Max Hayes and cigar maker unionist J. Mahlon Barnes were ringleaders of this cause through the golden era of the Socialist Party. Dual unionism, however, was the Achilles heal of De Leon's strategy. Every SLP leader wanted the AFL to become socialist, but nearly half the party opposed De Leon's devotion to manipulation, indoctrination, and dual union subversion. Always he took his defeats badly, purging whoever didn't go along with him. To him, all reform movements were stupid, feminism was the worst, feminist men were unbearable, revolutionary unionism was the only true socialism, and American socialists needed to defer to him. In 1899 the SLP brawled and split over whether it wanted to be as sectarian as De Leon. The schism was a bitter affair yielding two fistfights and a court case. The losing side of the court battle was based in the Jewish textile unions and led by Hillquit.

Morris Hillquit was born Moshe Hillkowitz in 1869 in Riga, Latvia, a German cultural outpost on the western frontier of the Russian Empire. Politically, Riga was part of Russia; culturally and linguistically, it was German; from both sides it treated native Letts as conquered nobodies devoid of history or standing. Hillkowitz spoke German at home and in his early schooling but later studied at a Russian Gymnasium where he absorbed the lore of Holy Russia. He thus grew up bilingual, German without being German, and Russian without setting foot in Russia. Until 1884 his family owned a factory. Jewish merchants were crippled in 1861 when Tsar Alexander II abolished serfdom; twenty years later a bomb-throwing anarchist killed the slight-reforming Tsar Alexander II, and Russian Jews suffered for it. The anti-Jewish pogroms of 1881 and 1882 drove half a million Jews out of Russia and Poland, while Alexander III conducted a brutal policy of Russification in the provinces.

Hillquit fled to New York in 1886 with his mother and three siblings, joining his father and older brother, who had left two years earlier. The family barely survived the harsh conditions of Manhattan's Lower East Side. Hillquit toiled in a shirt-making sweatshop while struggling to learn English, helping his family pay for its two-room tenement. He bonded with fellow socialist immigrants with an intellectual bent, readily deciding he was a social democrat, not an anarchist. Anarchists declaimed and emoted about blowing up factories and smashing the government. Most of Hillquit's neighborhood anarchists were German followers of firebrand Johann Most, though Hillquit knew about Russian anarchism. He was immune to it, preferring the practical idealism of Marxian social democracy, later reflecting that socialism was never "a religious dogma to me. I accepted its philosophy as convincing on the whole, without insisting on every article of the Marxian creed for myself or my comrades."[33]

He joined the SLP in 1887 on his eighteenth birthday. Hillquit admired its German leaders, finding them far superior to the 10 percent of the party that was American-born. In New York the SLP had two Jewish sections—Section 8 was small and spoke Yiddish, Section 17 larger and spoke Russian. Both groups sought to emulate the United German Trades, a powerful union of German-speaking immigrants aligned with the SLP. United German Trades began as a press union and grew into a federation with clout. Some immigrants tried to survive by peddling; most found work in the garment industry; others subsisted as bakers, cigar makers, house painters, or factory workers. Middlemen contractors working for the manufacturers mercilessly exploited the workers, especially Jews, who had almost no history of union organizing.

The few attempts to start Jewish unions were stillborn. Language was a barrier to SLP organizing because only one of the SLP Jews, Abraham Cahan, was fluent in Yiddish. Cahan was a twenty-seven-year-old Russian exile who grew up in Belarus, dropped religion for socialism as a teenager, identified with the revolutionaries who killed Alexander II, fled Russia in 1882, and joined the SLP in 1887. His great passion was to create a reading public of Jewish socialists. He goaded Hillquit and others to learn Yiddish, which was hard for Russian speakers. Hillquit and his SLP Jewish comrades soon realized that building a Jewish labor movement from the bottom up would take decades, struggling for years at the one-to-one level. They reversed the normal organizing process by building from the top down, founding the United Hebrew Trades federation in 1888.

Two representatives of the Yiddish section and two of the Russian section launched the organization at the SLP headquarters on East Fourth Street. Hillquit was the junior partner on the Russian side, deferring to a revolutionary stalwart, Leo Bandes, who had served time in Russian prisons. They started with a threefold mission—coordinate Jewish union organizing, organize new unions, and convert Jewish workers to socialism. At the time there were only two Jewish unions—typesetters and Yiddish theater singers. United Hebrew Trades started with the typesetters and singers, won a few battles, and branched out to the garment industry, which became the bedrock of American Jewish socialism. It also organized bakers, retail clerks, bookbinders, musicians, and soda workers.

Cahan had a dream to create a Socialist paper for Yiddish speakers. He and Hillquit shook down German unions for the seed money that created *Arbeiter Zeitung* (Workers' News) in 1890. It ran four pages, belonged to the SLP, and was an instant success, reaching immigrants who thrilled at reading about their lives in their language. Cahan wrote snappy human-interest stories, and Hillquit wrote earnest articles about Social Democracy. They clashed over Yiddish because Hillquit said Yiddish was a corrupt and illiterate German dialect beneath his dignity, and Cahan said Hillquit wrote stuffy German in Hebrew characters.

Cahan's Jewishness was simultaneously defining and irrelevant to him. He later explained: "We regarded ourselves as human beings, not as Jews. There was only one remedy to the world's ills, and that was socialism." In 1897 he founded *The Jewish Daily Forward (Forverts)*, named after a legendary Social Democratic paper in Berlin. It was deeply Jewish while denying that its socialism had a Jewish character. Cahan showed Yiddish readers that socialism didn't have to screech dogmatically in stale jargon. The *Forward* was a family paper, addressing the anxieties and confusions of an immigrant people in a new land. A wildly popular advice column, "Bintel Brief" (a bundle of letters), dispensed homely counsel about dealing with Gentiles, American customs, employers, immigration officials, and husbands who drank. Cahan presented socialism as a replacement for the authority of the rabbi, in the idiom of the synagogue. The *Forward* grew into a national treasure, assimilating Yiddish-speakers into American life and informing them about the struggles of the international working class. Its identification with secular, socialist, Yiddish culture intensified with the arrival of the Bundists—Russian and Polish Russian socialists who fled after the 1905 Russian Revolution. Cahan steered constantly between critics who said the paper was too socialist and not socialist enough. The *Forward* launched celebrated Yiddish writers Sholem Aleichem, Isaac Bashevis Singer, and Sholem Asch and exerted a powerful influence in Jewish unions.[34]

Hillquit and Cahan came up together, though Cahan was somewhat trapped by his success. On two occasions he stepped away from the *Forward* to establish his career as an English-writing journalist and novelist but staying away proved impossible for him. The paper was his creation and legacy. Hillquit was complex, reflective, and highly assimilated, modeling himself after Kautsky. Modulated Social Democratic Marxism was his mainstay, in a self-consciously American vein. In the 1890s he earned a law degree from New York University and seethed under De Leon's dictatorial and conspiratorial severity, later recalling, "He excelled any person I ever knew in unscrupulousness of attack, inventiveness of intrigue, and picturesqueness of invective." By 1899 Hillquit's minority faction of the SLP was done with De Leon, breaking with him in combustive fashion. The following year the Hillquit group held a convention in Rochester, New York, proposing to ally with the Social Democratic Party of America, a new party of populist socialists led by Eugene Debs.[35]

Debs began as a Brotherhood of Locomotive Firemen secretary in 1875, absorbing its fraternal ethos. He drifted to the populist left, converted to industrial unionism in 1893, and founded the American Railway Union (ARU). Craft unionism split the workers in a given enterprise into separate crafts defined by specific functions. Industrial unionism organized all the workers in an enterprise into one union. The AFL had a few industrial unions, but it was overwhelmingly a bastion of conservative, insular, racist, sexist craft unionism, which eventually drove Debs out of the Firemen and away from the AFL. His conversion to industrial unionism shocked the railroad Brotherhoods, as he seemed to be a model craft unionist.

The ARU arose and fell spectacularly, crushed by the government in 1894. Debs moved further left and almost won the Populist presidential nomination in 1896 but decided at the last moment he didn't want it. Had Democratic candidate William Jennings Bryan won the presidency in 1896 Debs might not have become a Socialist. As it was, he announced his conversion in 1897, which promptly made him America's leading socialist, before Debs knew what kind of socialist he wanted to be. He created a new party in 1897, Social Democracy of America, which had a schism that created the Social Democratic Party of America in 1898, which wasn't the answer either. Shortly after he found the answer, Debs had trouble remembering his tangled path to it. On the lecture circuit he told a romantic-radical version of his story that misled historians David Karsner, McAlister Coleman, and Nathan Fine. The historians who got him right — Ray Ginger and Nick Salvatore — grasped that Debs adopted a simplistic socialist creed partly because it took him so long to come to it.[36]

FOUNDING THE SOCIALIST PARTY

To create the Socialist Party of America, the parties led by Debs and Hillquit had to overcome their immense distrust of each other and get through the national election of 1900. They could not have succeeded lacking the personal authority Debs and Hillquit brought to the merger. Debs was eloquent, radical, courageous, very emotional, charismatic, sentimental, and inimitable, with a large and needy ego, enthralling teeming crowds year after year. He was a Paine-tradition deist who mixed easily with Marxist atheists and yet won the devotion of over three hundred social gospel clerics, who joined the party. He absorbed the antinomian strain of radical Protestantism that fired America's native radicalism from Puritan heretic Anne Hutchinson to abolitionist leader William Lloyd Garrison to feminist icon Susan B. Anthony. Debs was thoroughly Midwestern American, exuding unpretentious sincerity and enthusing that America's ideals were liberty and equality, in contrast to Europe's. He insisted that Thomas Jefferson and Abraham Lincoln would have been Socialists had they lived to see what became of the Democratic and Republican Parties. His socialism was based on the class struggle but steeped in his devotion to personal liberty, virtue, and the power of the ballot. It was also rigidly binary, chaining his party to a simplistic socialism versus capitalism choice that blinkered his legacy on racial justice, feminism, reform movements in general, trade unions, and making socialism relevant to U.S. American politics. In particular, his either/or denigrated and thwarted the Socialists who tried to expand the Socialist flank of the AFL.

Debs insisted that socialism was the only answer to every social problem. Any compromise with capitalist-anything was corrupt. Unions that didn't promote revolutionary socialism were corrupt, never mind that trade unions are inherently conservative institutions, offering security and stability through collective bargaining. Debs believed his socialism-only fundamentalism was Marxist, though he took barely a pass at Marxology. Hillquit applied Marxian orthodoxy to America with a pragmatic temper, constantly steering his party between antipolitical syndicalism and mushy reformism. Victor Berger, the leader of the Milwaukee social democrats, regarded himself as the American Bernstein, espousing a revisionist Marxism that insisted on its Marxist basis. Marxian social democracy was simultaneously conservative, radical-utopian, and obfuscating in its European and American contexts. It did not oppose reform causes but spurned the radical democrats, feminists, ethical socialists, and unionists who made immediate demands for universal individual rights, woman suffrage, union rights, nationalized banks, universal education, social insurance, and free land, always on the ground that reform movements for these causes delayed the revolution. The Socialist Party clashed over whether it should make any such demands or regard farmers as workers. But when Socialists ran for office they nearly always emphasized their reform demands, not socialism—which galled Debs.

Feminism proved to be harder to subordinate than other reform demands. Woman suffrage grew into a powerful national movement in the early twentieth century, and nearly all the party's feminist leaders came straight from it. Most of them had backgrounds in Christian temperance and suffrage activism, where women ran the organizations and the meetings. In the Socialist movement they had to deal with men who said that women's issues were low priority compared even to workplace reforms or nationalized banks. The party's first female leaders, while accepting that woman suffrage was a bourgeois reform issue, sometimes noted that feminist criticism cut deeper. In fact, there was a Marx–Engels basis for saying so.

Marx and Engels were deeply influenced by the matrilineal theory of the origins of human society propounded by American anthropologist Lewis H. Morgan. Morgan descended from a prominent Connecticut Yankee family and began his pioneering research on the Iroquois Confederacy in the early 1840s. He made his living as a lawyer in Rochester, New York, went on to study numerous Native American tribes, and got into politics, serving in the 1860s as a Republican New York State Assemblyman and Senator. His early work *Land of the Iroquois* (1851) compared systems of kinship. His landmark book, *Systems of Consanguinity and Affinity of the Human Family* (1871), put the study of kinship at the center of modern anthropology, contending for the unity of humankind. His capstone work, *Ancient Society* (1877), heightened his claims about the centrality of family and property relations to social evolution, delineating three stages of human development: "savagery," "barbarism," and "civilization."

The first stage was defined by the use of fire and bow, the second by the development of agriculture and domestication of animals, and the third by the development of alphabets and writing. Marx and Engels seized on Morgan's picture of stateless "primitive" societies founded on communal property and female givers of life, which they ranked with Darwin's theory of natural selection and Marx's theory of surplus value. Marx labored on a book based on *Ancient Society* but never finished it. Engels rewrote and completed Marx's book in 1884, the year after Marx died. It was titled *The Origin of the Family, Private Property, and the State*, and it had canonical status in Marxism.[37]

Engels contended that female inequality was rooted in the system of private property, which turned males into patriarchs anxious to secure the descent of their property to their male heirs. The first division of labor was between men and women, assigning childrearing to women. The first class opposition set husbands against their wives, and the first class oppression was the oppression of females by males. Engels explained that three basically different forms of marriage evolved through human history, corresponding to the three stages of human development charted by Morgan. "Savagery" practiced group marriage, "barbarism" instituted pairing marriage, and "civilization" instituted monogamy, "supplemented by adultery and prostitution." Polygamy and male dominion over female slaves were innovations within higher forms of barbarism, wedged between pairing marriage and monogamy. For women, Engels stressed, this was not a progress story. Women had sexual freedom under group marriage that they lost under barbarism, while men got more freedom and power at each stage. Monogamous marriage was an economic institution designed to safeguard a family's property, usually providing exemptions for men via prostitution and adultery. In the modern age, he said, there were two kinds of it—Catholic and Protestant. Catholic parents found suitable wives for their bourgeois sons, while Protestant bourgeois sons were allowed to find their own wives within their own class, more or less freely. Engels surmised that Catholicism abolished divorce because the church realized it had no cure for adultery. Protestantism marked an advance by allowing marriage to be based, at least to a certain degree, on love. But in both cases every marriage was a marriage of convenience determined by the class position of the participants.[38]

Engels did not claim that communism would abolish monogamous marriage or its families. Under communism, he reasoned, marriage would be based on love. Individual men and women would come together to form families out of mutual attraction. The bourgeois ideal of romantic monogamous marriage would be achieved for the first time in history: "Far from disappearing, it will only begin to be completely realized." Once the means of production were turned into social property, wage labor would disappear, along with the proletariat, coerced marriage slavery, and prostitution. "Monogamy, instead of declining, finally becomes a reality—for the men as well." Engels was sweeping and vague about what that meant. He said private housekeeping would become a social industry and the "care and education of the children" would become a public matter. The fact that he threw "care" together so casually with universal education set off much contention about whatever he surely did not mean. Socialism, on Marxist terms, was less advanced than communism, but Engels did not claim that even communism abolished the original division of labor. Perhaps "care" belonged to a distinct category? Perhaps the socialist aim in this area reassigned child-rearing to society? Or perhaps men needed to change?[39]

The male leaders of the Socialist Party were not interested in changing. They supported suffrage feminism as an electoral demand, accepted female members, and stuck to their proletarian-labor focus. They lauded the women who broke through as Socialist leaders, stressing that women played no such roles in the Republican and Democratic parties, while taking for granted that female Socialists needed to focus on socialism, not women's issues. Eight women served as elected delegates at the founding convention in 1901. May Wood Simons was the crucial one, having come to the party through the SLP and her marriage to Algie M. Simons. He was a research assistant to social gospel economist Richard Ely at the University of Wisconsin, worked in the mid-1890s for the University of Chicago Settlement, joined the SLP, and became editor of the Chicago SLP paper *Worker's Call*. She attended Northwestern University, taught school briefly, worked at the Chicago Settlement, and joined the SLP while struggling to figure out what socialism meant for women. Her SLP pamphlet of 1899, *Woman and the Social Problem*, was her answer. It was pure Engels-Marxism, emphasizing that the working poor did not benefit from bourgeois marriage.

Simons said capitalism exploited women and men similarly in workplaces and imposed distinct hardships on women in the home and family. Young industrial workers couldn't afford to marry and support families, which caused an explosion of "illegal sexual relations." They lived in tiny, crowded, depressing homes resembling the sweatshops in which they toiled for starvation wages. Only socialism, she contended, would emancipate industrial workers from the misery of poverty, vice, promiscuity, illegitimacy, and desperation: "It is to socialism alone that the home life must look for its rescue and purification." Social institutions could do the cooking, sewing, laundry, and cleaning, freeing women to do what they wanted, which might occasionally include cooking, sewing, and the rest. In her early socialist career Simons did not believe that women should have an organization of their own in the party. In 1908 the party created one, against its own ideology, because most of its female leaders were protégées of feminist socialist Christian Prohibition icon Frances Willard, who taught them that women need to have their own organizations.[40]

Simons was the party's first female lecture performer, speaking at Chautauqua camps through the Midwest. Soon there were two others who soared beyond her as public figures, Lena Morrow Lewis and Kate Richards O'Hare. Lewis lit up camps and street corners across the country, and O'Hare was a sensational speaker who demanded the largest convention halls available. In 1907 the Congress of the Second International at Stuttgart, Germany, encouraged member parties to make special efforts to recruit women. American socialist author John Spargo responded by proposing a national committee exclusively for women, which was debated at the 1908 convention. Female delegates divided sharply over this proposal; some wanted nothing to do with special treatment of any kind, but the Willard veterans carried the day, helped by Simons, who declared that she had changed her position. Socialists needed to recognize that women had it worse than men under capitalism. If the party wanted female members, it had to create a special place for them. This argument won a Woman's National Committee headed by Simons—which was more than the Socialists ever did for black members.[41]

Debs ran for the American presidency five times as the Socialist candidate, while refusing its debates over socialist ideology and strategy. He opposed World

War I after nearly the entire intelligentsia of the party bailed out, accepting the prison cell that European Socialists and American Socialist intellectuals averted over the same choice. He spearheaded a powerful, heterogeneous, popular, growing, but never big enough party that never won the labor movement following that European socialists won readily. The golden era ran out when America intervened in the war, the government viciously persecuted the Socialists, and Communism shredded the Socialists. Belatedly the Socialists tried to build a broad coalition democratic left party. The United States would have much more social democracy today had they succeeded.

Their best opportunity to do it occurred before the Socialist Party existed, when Debs refused the Populist nomination and deflated the Populist movement. The Old Guard talked about it seriously in 1909, when the British Labour Party was new and unproven. Hillquit and others talked about it again in 1919, when Labour made a great leap forward and American socialism imploded. The entire party took a pass at it in 1924, when Socialists cosponsored Robert La Follette's presidential campaign on a Farmer-Labor-Socialist-Progressive fusion ticket, a one-off episode for the AFL. The Socialists talked about it constantly in the 1930s and 1940s, when FDR stole their platform and the question of allying with Communists constantly plagued the debate. By the time Socialists settled for caucus status in the Democratic Party they lacked anywhere else to go. Their shrewd attempt to realign the Democratic Party paid huge dividends for the nation but not for them. The issues they left on the table by failing to build a coalition party of the left are very much with us.

2

SOCIAL GOSPEL SOCIALISM, THE LABOR MOVEMENT, AND THE SOCIALIST PARTY

The founders of the Socialist Party believed they could transform capitalism into economic democracy by winning elections and supporting radical unionism. Some lobbied for immediate demands and others condemned immediate demands as opportunism, but in the early going all supported political activism. For a while, which was later called the golden age, they were remarkably successful, building by far the strongest left organization in the United States. Starting with 10,000 members in 1901, by 1912 the party boasted 118,000 members, 300 periodicals, and 1,200 elected public officials. It had strong leadership bases in Chicago, New York, and Milwaukee and a vast following of lumberjacks, miners, clerics, tenant farmers, and railroad workers in the western states. Ideologically, the Socialist Party had a right flank of pro-AFL Social Democrats led by Victor Berger, a centrist flank of assimilated Marxists led by Morris Hillquit, a left flank of anti-AFL populists led by Eugene Debs, and an ultraleft flank led by Bill Haywood that eventually opted for anarcho-syndicalism. But the first three groups were not sharply defined until the Wobblies forced the ideological issue. The deepest divide in the party was always cultural. And party officials in Chicago were puzzled that the party had so many Christian clerics.

The profusion of these clerics and of suffrage activists confounded Socialist officials who equated socialism with atheism and did not fathom the social gospel. The white social gospel, founded by Congregationalists, Episcopalians, and Baptists in the 1880s, was a response to the charge that churches did not care about exploited workers. The black social gospel, founded by Methodists, Baptists, and Episcopalians, also in the 1880s, was an attempt to create a new abolitionism. Christian socialists on both sides of the color line tried to fuse the two wellsprings of the social gospel, wanting the Socialist Party to be a vehicle of ethical neo-abolitionist socialism, which did not happen.

Washington Gladden, a Congregational pastor, and Richard Ely, an Episcopalian political economist, founded the original social gospel organizations on a Progressive platform, differently fudging whether they were socialists. George Herron, George W. Woodbey, W. D. P. Bliss, Vida Scudder, George Slater, Reverdy Ransom, and Walter Rauschenbusch did not fudge, challenging middle-class Americans to overcome their fear of socialism. This difference distinguished the reformist mainstream of the social gospel from its socialist left wing, but mis-leadingly. Nearly every social gospel leader supported producer cooperatives and public ownership of natural monopolies, and the explicitly socialist wing rejected the later Ely's identification of socialism with state socialism. In a broad sense of the term, nearly all social gospel leaders were socialists, although some said it was important to deny it.

GLADDEN, ELY, AND THE COMING OF DEBS

Gladden and Ely came from humble backgrounds that stuck with them long after they became national figures. Gladden grew up poor, rural, and semi-orphaned in upstate New York. He was five years old when his father died in 1841; soon after, Gladden was dispatched to his uncle's meager farm. Fortunately, his uncle was a book reader. Ely's background was equally modest, though he acquired an aristocratic temperament and a desire for academic respectability that put him in the conservative wing of the social gospel. The early social gospel owed its structural dimension mostly to Ely's expertise in political econom-ics. Gladden and Ely were prolific and industrious advocates of liberal rights, democracy, intellectual freedom, and almost everything else about modernity. They simply refused to believe that modern progress, in the economic sphere, culminated with capitalism; there had to be a stage beyond capitalism.

As a youth Gladden switched from Presbyterianism to Congregationalism because the local Congregationalists were abolitionists. His autodidactic drive carried him to Williams College in Williamstown, Massachusetts, where he graduated in 1860. Later that year Gladden began his first Congregational pas-torate in Brooklyn, New York, where he lasted a few months. Brooklyn terrified him; the city felt like a buzzing, impersonal monster, and his congregation was debt-ridden and factional. Then the Civil War broke out. Overwhelmed by the city, the moment, and his shortcomings, Gladden collapsed emotionally. He moved to the quiet climes of Morrisania, New York, where he found healing and converted to liberal theology, reading American theologian Horace

Bushnell. Bushnell convinced him not to accept any doctrine that offended his sense of what is good or true. Gladden preached an early version of social gospel liberalism in New York and New England and went on to journalism at a progressive Congregational newspaper, the *Independent*. In both contexts he acquired social ideas, contending that Christianity had to become relevant to a changing social order. Gladden did not conceive of liberal theology and social Christianity as different things; to him they were complementary sides of one thing. This conviction persuaded many readers to equate the two ideas, fusing liberal theology and the social gospel.[1]

Gladden took his bearings from the golden rule: All are commanded to love their neighbors as themselves, so employers and employees should practice cooperation, disagreements should be negotiated in a spirit of other-regarding fellowship, and society should be organized to serve human welfare rather than profits. Gladden preached that God is the Spirit of love divine that dwells in every human heart and unites the human race as a divine society. The virtues of other-regarding cooperation are practicable only for individuals and small groups; thus the early Gladden was against corporations *and* big unions. All individuals combine traits of egotism and altruism, he reasoned, and both are essential to a good society. There is such a thing as self-regarding virtue, for a society with no competitive vigor would have no dynamism. The problem was that commercial society rested on competitive vigor alone. Gladden was slow to see that this was a structural problem, not merely a moral one, but he was among the first to say that it mattered.

Ely was born in 1854 and grew up on a farm near Fredonia, New York. His father was a self-taught engineer, impoverished farmer, and devout Presbyterian with a severely gloomy temperament. Calvinist predestination contributed mightily to the gloom, which drove Ely into the Episcopal Church during his college days at Columbia University. He later explained that Anglican humanism "offered a fuller and richer life." As a youth Ely devoured his father's library, enrolled at Dartmouth College, won a scholarship to Columbia in 1872, and graduated in 1876, winning a fellowship to study abroad. Ely started at the University of Halle, where he learned about the German historical school of economics led by Karl Knies, Adolf Wagner, and Gustav von Schmoller. He transferred to Heidelberg to study under Knies, embracing his teacher's view that economics is a historical discipline, not a natural science.[2]

Ely earned his doctorate at Heidelberg in 1879 and began his teaching career two years later at Johns Hopkins University in Baltimore, Maryland. At first it was a temporary position. American economists revered laissez-faire doctrine, Ely's approach was heresy, and he had to prove that students would take his classes. He clashed with faculty colleagues, especially the obstreperous Simon Newcomb, who couldn't bear Ely's pushy progressivism. Many colleagues disliked Ely's preoccupation with reform politics, an unseemly fixation for an academic. Ely proved them right, and wrong, by writing a flurry of books and attracting students. These were the signature works of the early social gospel and socialist movements, and all were on political economics. His first book, in 1883, introduced American readers to French and German socialism, opining that Christian socialism offered a better basis for socialism than its professorial versions. His second book, in 1884, contended that all economic systems are shaped by cultural and political contingencies, exactly as the German historical school said. Economics is not a science about an economic state of nature, it should not espouse unchangeable concepts, and a good society safeguards the common good by managing economic outcomes. His third book, in 1885, said that America was developing a socialist tradition that had a constructive role to play in reform politics.[3]

The riskiest and most novel of his early books was the next one, *The Labor Movement in America* (1886). American newspapers condemned unions as coarse, violent, selfish, gangster-prone, and un-American. Ely pushed back, contending that fear and prejudice prevailed in this area, plus the self-interests of newspaper owners. He surveyed the varieties of union organizing and argued that unions are mostly good for democracy. Unions were civilizing vehicles because they helped many Americans feel included in American society: "Today the labor organizations of America are playing a role in the history of civilization, the importance of which can scarcely be overestimated; for they are among the foremost of our educational agencies, ranking next to our churches and public schools in their influence upon the culture of the masses." Ely praised the Knights of Labor in particular, advising Americans not to believe what newspapers said about it. He later recalled that he felt compelled to address "this spectacular crisis of the eighties," which represented "an unprecedented, unparalleled opportunity for the church."[4]

Ely and Gladden were diligent organizers, like the British Christian socialists they admired. In 1885 they teamed with economists John Bates Clark and Henry C. Adams to found the American Economic Association, which Ely served for seven years as founding secretary and later as president. The same year, Ely and Gladden teamed with social gospel minister Josiah Strong to launch an activist ecumenical vehicle convening huge summer gatherings, the Inter-denominational Congress. In 1890 Ely, Gladden, and Lyman Abbott launched a summer program on social Christianity at the Chautauqua Society in upstate New York that later morphed into the American Institute of Christian

Sociology, led by Ely. Ely's summer lecturing at Chautauqua boosted his renown. In 1891 he and Bliss founded an American branch of the Christian Social Union (CSU), a British Anglican organization led by upcoming luminaries Scott Holland and Charles Gore. To Ely and Bliss, English Anglican socialism was the gold standard, especially the CSU. Ely and Gladden organized with a sense of urgency, imploring that Gilded Age capitalism was a crisis for American Christianity. Social Darwinism justified selfishness, it bonded readily with economic orthodoxy, it justified cruel policies by appealing to academic dogmas, and its growing popularity in American culture was morally toxic for American society. Every social gospel organization issued this warning, while Ely and Gladden struggled to say exactly where Darwinian science veered into something toxic.[5]

Herbert Spencer was the theorist of Social Darwinism and by far the preeminent intellectual of the late nineteenth century. An English Victorian polymath, Spencer coined the phrases "Social Darwinism" and "survival of the fittest," fitting these concepts into a vast mechanistic system. One could not be a philosopher, natural scientist, or social scientist in the late nineteenth century without mastering Spencer's fusion of Darwinian natural selection, Lamarckian development, Malthusian population theory, early thermodynamics, laissez-faire economics, and libertarian politics. Darwin taught that human beings consist of one species ranging in groups he called races from the savage to the civilized. The advanced groups, he said, were sure to exterminate and replace the "savage races" throughout the world, which would widen the gap between human beings and apes, though Darwin painted this picture in summary fashion and moved on, not wishing to elaborate. Spencer elaborated extravagantly. He featured Darwinian natural selection and won Darwin's endorsement of the phrase "survival of the fittest" but denied that natural selection was the main mechanism for generating biological diversity. Spencer contended that every individual's biological development (ontogeny) recapitulates the entire evolutionary development (phylogeny) of its species. The environment acts directly on organisms, yielding new races, and the survival of a race depends on its interaction with its environment. If there is a one-to-one correspondence between phylogeny and ontogeny, such that ontogeny repeats forms of the ancestors, the characteristics of less developed races must exist within the more advanced races.[6]

Life is a continuous process of development from incoherent homogeneity (protozoa) to coherent heterogeneity. Races are real and hierarchically ordered, with traits that can be measured. Any political intervention that impedes this natural process is harmful. All state-supported poor laws, education, sanitary supervision, and other measures that impede natural weeding out are repugnant. So are imperial ventures that waste resources and produce bloated, centralized governments. Spencer's word on these topics settled the issue for many in the Gilded Age. German Social Darwinist Ernst Haeckel, the foremost biologist of the late nineteenth century, summarized the upshot of this ideology, opining that the hierarchical ordering of the races was obvious, intelligence was obviously the key distinguishing factor, Africans were obviously at the bottom of the human order, and any government policy that helped the unfit to survive was odious. Haeckel claimed that whites had an unbroken history of superiority. In fact, the Caucasian "Mediterranean man" was the only species (excepting the "Mongolian") to have arisen above nature to the status of civilization: "The Caucasian, or Mediterranean man *(Homo Mediterraneus)*, has from time immemorial been placed at the head of all the races of men, as the most highly developed and perfect."[7]

The founders of the social gospel were informed, intimidated, attracted, and appalled by Spencer's system. They shared this situation with upcoming U.S. American philosophers William James, Josiah Royce, and Borden Parker Bowne and the founders of U.S. American sociology, notably Lester Ward, Charles Cooley, and Albion W. Small, and young W. E. B. Du Bois, whose early writings on race were steeped in neo-Lamarckian Social Darwinism. The founders of the social gospel pored over Spencer's works for instruction and errors, by necessity. All of them took much of his system to be an authoritative scientific description of how the world works. All played leading roles in persuading the churches that Darwinian biology had to be taken seriously and was compatible with Christianity. All rejected or played down some aspect of Spencer's system, but they had to reckon with Spencer's immense authority. Moreover, an optimistic, vaguely religious version of Social Darwinism with a strong progress motif was popular in American culture. America was said to be thriving because it was so competitive, bustling, capitalist, and short on government intervention. American society was evolving in a good direction, so Darwinism was not to be feared.[8]

In the academy a harsher version of Social Darwinism also gained influence. Yale sociologist William Graham Sumner taught Spencer's *Study of Sociology* without the happy progress motif. Sumner had a dismal view of where social evolution was headed, and he played up the antitheistic aspects of Social Darwinism, offending religious leaders. In the 1860s he studied biblical criticism at Göttingen, which ended his plan to become an Episcopal priest. Branching into social and historical studies, in 1870 he read Spencer's essays — later collected as *The Study of Sociology* — which converted him to Social

Darwinism. Two years later Sumner joined the Yale faculty to teach political and social science. An eccentric figure, riveting in the classroom, he gave cheeky, opinionated lectures that propagandized for Social Darwinism in the name of "the science of society," a phrase he preferred to sociology. Sumner refused to teach women, railed against government, and exhorted his well-born male students to resist all schemes to lift up the poor and weak. His aggressive teaching sparked a public controversy over the boundaries of the new social science. Religious leaders deplored Sumner's bias against Christian ethics; he replied that he studied society just as he studied nature, scientifically. Sociology would not get anywhere as a science if it had to defer to religious objections.[9]

Was Social Darwinism a doctrine? Sumner tried to head off a debate on this question by contending that what mattered was the scientific understanding of society, not any doctrine. Upholding a doctrine, even one as sound as Social Darwinism, was not the point. Thus he preferred not to speak of sociology, which sounded like a bundle of ideas or doctrines. What mattered was the disinterested, scientific pursuit of truth. On the other hand, he said, "Social Darwinism" was a very good name for the truth disclosed by science. Spencer's vast systemic description of a brutal struggle for survival corresponded exactly to the real world of nature and history, which made a mockery of ethical humanism. Social evolution is about the competition of life for the limited resources of nature. Culture is the cultivation of physical and psychosocial traits that advance the struggle for life.

Sumner derided moralists who pleaded for the weak and the poor. He vehemently denied that government exists "in some especial sense, for the sake of the classes so designated, and that the same classes (whoever they are) have some especial claim on the interest and attention of the economist and social philosopher." Some moralists even said that a society's moral health should be gauged by how it treats its most vulnerable members. That was ridiculous, Sumner said. It is perverse to suppose that the "training of men is the only branch of human effort in which the labor and care should be spent, not on the best specimens but on the poorest." Sumner allowed that there is such a thing as progress in civilization. He was not a reactionary who wanted to turn back the clock on male suffrage or education for the masses. But progress is slow and slight, it always has a negative side, and it is easily wrecked by sentimentality toward the poor: "Under our so-called progress evil only alters its forms, and we must esteem it a grand advance if we can believe that, on the whole, and over a wide view of human affairs, good has gained a hair's breadth over evil in a century."[10]

Sumner's blend of laissez-faire economics and Darwinian natural selection made a strong bid to set American sociology against religious and humanistic ethics. Social Darwinism promised to remedy the ostensible weakness of laissez-faire orthodoxy—its dependence on deduction, trafficking in fixed concepts deduced from supposed traits in human nature. Social gospel academics created a new field of study, social ethics, partly to fend off the challenge of Social Darwinism. Francis Greenwood Peabody, at Harvard, and Graham Taylor, at Chicago Theological Seminary, were the key founders. To Gladden and Ely, as to Peabody and Taylor, it did not matter that Sumner lacked Spencer's commanding intellectual prestige since no one rivaled Spencer. Ely absorbed Spencer more deeply than did Gladden, Peabody, and Taylor because they were rock-bottom moralists, and Social Darwinism was a nonstarter for Christian morality. Moreover, Gladden believed that cooperation played a larger role in the struggle for survival than every Social Darwinist said.[11]

But the social gospel founders did not know how to draw the line between Darwinian biology and its application to other areas. They took help where they could get it. Gladden and Ely leaned on Darwin's leading American popularizer, John Fiske, to wring a spiritual worldview out of Darwinian theory. Fiske argued that Darwinism is compatible with a religious sensibility and even the existence of God. Gladden and Ely cheered the nation's first sociology department at the University of Chicago, where social gospel progressives Small, Shailer Mathews, and Taylor said that sociology should be sociohistorical, not biologically reductionist, and society should be shaped by progressive reforms, not erratic Darwinian weeding out. For most social gospel founders, the moral issue cut the deepest. Social Darwinism was an overreach because it denigrated the gospel command to see Christ in the poor and vulnerable. Ely was less sturdy than other founders in this area, his paternalism was stronger than his justice convictions, and he became a superpatriot during World War I. The later Ely odiously supported immigration policies favoring white Nordics, very much in line with the trade unionists and Protestant gentility he sought to unite. In the early going, however, Ely's training in German historicism was a bulwark for American socialism. It steeled him against laissez-faire orthodoxy and Spencer's antistatism, undergirding the signature social gospel arguments for unions, state taxation policies, public ownership of utilities, and industrial reforms.[12]

Ely put it generically upon founding the American Economic Association (AEA). Economists E. J. James and Simon Patten wanted the organization to call for government regulation of the economy. Ely, aiming for a bigger outfit, said it was enough to say that laissez-faire orthodoxy is wrong as politics and morality. The AEA believed in economic evolution and relativity, leaving room for various views about how far government intervention should go. Ely laid down four principles: (1) the positive work of the state is an indispensable condition of human progress; (2) political economics must avoid doctrinal dogmatism; (3) the clash between labor and capital must be mediated by the church, state, and academy; (4) progressive economic development and progressive legislation go together. Nearly fifty founders convened in Saratoga, New York, to affirm these principles, where Ely stressed number 3: "We who have resolved to form an American Economic Association hope to do something toward the developing of a system of social ethics. We wish to accomplish certain practical results in the social and financial world, and believing that our work lies in the direction of practical Christianity, we appeal to the church, the chief of the social forces in this country, to help us, to support us, and to make our work a complete success, which it can by no possibility be without her assistance." The AEA founders included clerics Gladden, Lyman Abbott, Leighton Williams, Amory Bradford, Newman Smyth, R. Heber Newton, and J. H. Rylance. They responded creatively to an upsurge of craft, industrial, and federated trade unionisms represented, respectively, by the Railroad Brotherhoods, the Knights of Labor, and the Federation of Trades and Labor Unions.[13]

Eugene Victor Debs became a Socialist by moving from craft fraternalism to craft unionism to industrial unionism. He was born in 1855 in Terre Haute, Indiana, and gently raised by French immigrant parents who named him after two French authors, Eugène Sue and Victor Hugo. Debs's father, Daniel, grew up in textile business prosperity in Colmar, Alsace, and married a Catholic employee of the family business. He was disinherited for marrying her, fleeing to the United States in bitter reaction and poverty. Debs's parents ran a grocery store in Terre Haute and taught their four children that anyone could succeed in America by working hard and being virtuous. Debs grew up feeling deeply bonded to his nurturing parents, Terre Haute, and the Midwest in general, and never lost the feeling.

The later Debs, regaling crowds with the story of his life, romanticized the frontier democracy and small-town values of Terre Haute, lamenting that industrial capitalism devoured both. He seemed to forget that the pioneers were ambitious capitalists and that his early unionism was far from radical or even unionist. As a youth Debs absorbed his father's love of French republican authors, prizing Hugo especially. Yet he dropped out of school at the age of fourteen, later explaining that his struggling family needed him to work. In fact, his parents subsisted well enough and begged him to stay in school. Debs couldn't wait to join the world of grown-up workers. He began as a locomotive paint-scraper, moved up to railroad fireman, lost his job in the depression of 1874, worked as a grocery business accounting clerk, and witnessed the founding of the Brotherhood of Locomotive Firemen (BLF) in 1875. Then he joined the Terre Haute lodge of the BLF and was elected secretary, with no clue that union work would be radicalizing for him.[14]

The BLF was a benevolent fraternity providing insurance and death benefits for members. Firemen needed affordable life insurance because accidents were common on the railroads, and firemen didn't make enough money to buy private insurance. If they were injured or killed they had to rely on charity. The only solution was to organize a cooperative insurance fraternity of the workers themselves. Debs plunged wholeheartedly into this work. By day he worked as a wholesale grocery accounting clerk; at night he wrote scores of letters to BLF lodges across the country, inquiring about accidents and benefit claims. Debs was compliant and service-minded, reliably supporting Brotherhood officials. He scaled the ranks of the BLF by winning over its leaders and workers, exuding the BLF motto of "Benevolence, Sobriety and Industry." He was plain and earnest in the fashion that midwesterners loved, but more so, radiating an intense sincerity. In 1877, addressing the BLF convention in Indianapolis, Debs decried an ongoing strike against the Baltimore-Ohio and Pennsylvania Railroads, imploring that strikes are always destructive. The following year he was appointed associate editor of the *Locomotive Firemen's Magazine*, and two years later he was promoted to grand secretary and treasurer of the BLF and editor of the magazine.

Debs trained in autodidactic fashion for these posts, poring over Voltaire's *Philosophical Dictionary*, Appleton's *Encyclopedia*, and Horace Greeley's *New York Tribune*. He practiced speechmaking in front of a mirror, memorizing snatches of Thomas Jefferson, Thomas Paine, and Patrick Henry. He founded a literary club that brought famous speakers to Terre Haute, welcoming freethinking orator Robert Ingersoll and abolitionist icon Wendell Phillips. Debs revered both of them, especially Phillips for moving on to the labor movement after the abolitionist struggle was won. Feminist leader Susan B. Anthony got a rockier reception than Ingersoll and Phillips; Debs shocked Terre Haute by inviting her in the first place and then praising her. In 1885 he was elected to the Indiana state legislature as a Democrat and married a very bourgeois German woman, Katherine Metzel of Pittsburgh. Debs began to change shortly after he married her, in step with a radicalizing labor movement, which stranded Kate Debs emotionally.

He traveled constantly for the BLF and was influenced by Firemen who supported the Knights. For Debs the labor movement was thousands of brothers; for Kate Debs it was a faceless mass of rough people to whom she could not relate. She compensated by building a large, ornate house in a wealthy section of Terre Haute filled with gables and a blue-tile fireplace in every room. Debs and Kate were considerate to each other and supportive of each other; for many years she transcribed his speeches and letters longhand. But he was gone most of the time, and both regretted that they were far from being soulmates. In 1885 the BLF convention sprouted a left flank that seethed about overlong hours, yellow-dog contracts prohibiting employees from joining a union, and BLF leaders that submitted. It demanded a vote on the no-strike provision in the BLF constitution and abolished it. The convention proceeded to depose every BLF officer except Debs and Frank Sargent, ordering Debs to convey a message to the upcoming Brotherhood of Locomotive Engineers convention—the BLF was now a labor organization, wanting labor solidarity with the Engineers.

The union version of the BLF was still a mostly conservative enterprise, culturally and politically. Debs held together a strange concoction of conservatives that barely tolerated unionism and a left flank that wanted a fighting democratic union. He succeeded resoundingly, becoming legendary in the union for his personal, one-by-one, self-sacrificing devotion to the workers. He asked workers what they needed, slept in the upper berth, took the smallest portion when food was scarce, never complained about travel accommodations, treated waitresses respectfully, and emptied his pockets to workers in need. On one occasion a fireman needed a watch to win a promotion; Debs promptly gave the man his own. He spent some social capital by editorializing for an eight-hour workday, which brought the BLF into an alliance, on this issue, with the Federation of Organized Trades and Labor Unions. Thus began the friendly phase of his relationship with Federation leader Samuel Gompers.

Gompers was a Jewish immigrant from London who came to New York at the age of thirteen, already working in his family's meager cigar business. Since his father belonged to the British Cigarmakers' Society, Gompers grew up learning about trade unions and a bit of socialist theory. At the age of fourteen he joined the Cigar Makers Local Union No. 15. Gompers learned German and Marxism through his German shop mates, acquiring a mentor, Karl Laurell, formerly a secretary of the First International. The German protégés of Ferdinand Lassalle outnumbered the German Marxists in New York, but Laurell taught Gompers that Lassalle-style Social Democracy wrongly fixed on political activism. The real road to socialism was through the trade unions. Gompers scaled the ranks of the Cigar Makers Union, making president in 1875. In 1881 he and Adolph Strasser founded the Federation of Trades and Labor Unions at a convention in Pittsburgh; Gompers wanted to call it the Federation of Organized Trade Unions. The difference was crucial for what became the AFL in 1886, which merged the original federation with craft workers defecting from the Knights. Gompers had an iron will and a rigid creed:

organize workers, control shop conditions, build a financial foundation, charge high fees to finance insurance benefits, allow no union to strike without the consent of the Federation, and concentrate on the skilled and craft workers. His devotion to the last principle eventually yielded another creedal rule that defined the AFL: Adhere to business principles.

The early Gompers was a socialist who believed he was America's best Marxist, and the early AFL welcomed the African Americans who had recently poured into the Knights. But the craft unions that constituted the early Federation and then the AFL were brazenly racist, and Gompers-style trade unionism had a business logic that gradually erased his socialist convictions. These two things folded together in the early 1890s to create a very white, male, business union federation that fought off AFL socialists who tried to turn the AFL socialist. In the 1880s Gompers shed his socialism without dropping its crude economic determinism. His creed owed much of its efficacy to being very simple. Economic power, he said, "is the basis upon which may be developed power in other fields. It is the foundation of organized society."[15]

Gompers took for granted that the state always reflects the power of the dominant economic groups. The state intervenes only to protect the domination of big business. Therefore, constructive unionism spurns politics and tries to avoid conflicts with the state. Gompers said labor had to combine to fight capital because workers belong to a distinct class, but the goal of trade unionism is not to create a socialist society. He accepted industrial society and its hierarchical class structure, contending that the purpose of a union is to improve the position of workers within a capitalist society. Trade unions exist to win higher wages and better working conditions for trade workers, not to help workers transcend their status as workers. As late as 1894, after four years of fighting off bitter challenges from Socialists for control of the AFL, Gompers still claimed to believe that unions transformed "the ethics of industry, society, and the state." But by then he was a hardened champion of constructive unionism. Socialism and industrial unionism, he said, are emotional, reckless, and destructive, and political activism of any kind is needlessly divisive and dangerous. Gompers boasted that he corrected the mistake of the SLP Lassalleans who repeated the mistake of the German Lassalleans. He was still a better Marxist than they were, never mind that he was no longer a socialist and was adamantly opposed to a labor party. Constructive unionism federated the craft unions and compelled the competing political parties to curry union favor, just as Marx, supposedly, would have advised.[16]

Debs chafed from the beginning at privileged class unionism, but he worked for a railroad Brotherhood that was more provincial and racist than the AFL.

The BLF and all other railroad Brotherhoods barred black members, spurned Catholics and immigrants, and had to be dragged into alliances with other unions. The Engineers were the best-organized railroad Brotherhood and the one most opposed to allying with other unions. Debs treated everyone respectfully, urging Firemen to relinquish their prejudices against blacks, immigrants, and joining the AFL. He also refused to scold. He was one of them, accepting Jim Crow in its Midwest version. He went out of his way to befriend Gompers, respecting that Gompers built a powerful federation and at least knew what he believed. Gompers regarded Debs as an exceptionally genial and hardworking type—the person best suited to lure the Firemen into the AFL.

Debs had stronger feelings, pro and con, about the Knights. He admired the noble motto of the Knights—An injury to one is the concern of all—and their emphasis on local producer control. But he believed the Knights lurched too far into prostrike romanticism, and their lack of a strong centralized organization was a fatal flaw. The Knights soared spectacularly in 1884 and 1885 but crashed just as swiftly. In 1885 Knights leader Terence Powderly prematurely ordered striking packinghouse workers in Chicago to return to work. The strike was broken, and the Knights perished in Chicago. The following year the Knights struck dramatically against the Gould railway in the Southwest, the Brotherhood of Locomotive Engineers and Trainmen opposed the strike, state militias intervened, and the Knights were crushed. The anti–trade union majority of the Knights angrily ordered Knights to withdraw from the craft unions, and many responded by joining the AFL.

Debs puzzled and stewed over these events, trying to decide what he believed while managing lower-stakes factionalism in the BLF. He loved the universal solidarity ethic of the Knights but believed they lost their way. He defended the Knights most of the time but advised Firemen not to join them and was appalled by the Haymarket anarchists; the later Debs, upon turning radical, had to revise how he felt and talked about the Haymarket martyrs. Debs felt pressured by the first May Day and chastened by the surge of Knights into the AFL. In 1888 he muddled through a failed BLF strike against the Burlington Railroad, chagrined that he spent most of it talking out of both sides of his mouth. The following January he endorsed the Knights unequivocally for the first time, regretting that it took so long. If labor did not unite and fight, he declared, all would be lost. Labor had to fight to save American civilization, not only itself. This was partly a warning to himself, well after pro-Knights Christian socialists dished out stronger fare to their audiences.

Debs straddled constantly between BLF believers in harmonious service and militants demanding strikes and rank-and-file control. Some protested that he was better at inculcating hero worship than at uniting the union with persuasive arguments. Debs heard this complaint for the rest of his career, not always responding appropriately, as he needed to be admired. In 1890 he tried to unite the Firemen, Switchmen, Brakemen, Engineers, Railway Conductors, and Railway Telegraphers in a national federation. Debs made a two-sided argument for a strong federation: Each Brotherhood had to be autonomous *and* the federation needed a hierarchical corporate structure stocked with labor specialists like him. Militants protested that this proposal handsomely benefited well-paid union officials like Debs, contradicting his democratic politics. Debs won over the militants without capitulating to their demands, but his assiduous efforts to unite the Railroad Brotherhoods failed. The Engineers tried to sabotage the Switchmen, the Engineers were expelled, the Conductors and Telegraphers withdrew in solidarity with the Engineers, and by 1892 only the Firemen and Switchmen were still trying to federate. Debs concluded sadly that the path to uniting the railroad workers was not through the Railroad Brotherhoods.[17]

The rise of the unions forced white churches to take the social gospel seriously. Ely's book on the labor movement won a large readership and respectful reviews, plus a backlash at Johns Hopkins to get rid of Ely. Newcomb declared in the *Nation* that no one holding Ely's views about unions deserved to teach at any American university. Ely's supporters countered that his books were fair-minded, peaceable, and constructive. His next books came even faster, with two books in 1888 on taxes and social problems and two in 1889 on political economy and social Christianity. *An Introduction to Political Economy* (1889) lauded Spencer for mapping the agenda of sociology with distinguished ambition and ripped Spencer for his crude speculations, ideological dogmatism, and "blindness to the facts of life." Ely said Lester Ward's *Dynamic Sociology* was much better, grounding a new field in a sociohistorical perspective. Good sociology and political economics needed each other, and both gave ballast to social gospel theology and Progressive politics. In *Social Aspects of Christianity* (1889) Ely published his stump speeches, conveying the mood of an ascending movement. It was a best-selling landmark; for twenty years the book was assigned to every young minister participating in a Conference of the Methodist Episcopal Church. Ely said the gospel divided into theology and sociology and united in the love commandment of Christ to love each other. It was fine for theologians to rattle on about God's loving nature, but good theology dared to change society, translating the second commandment into sociology.[18]

Ely taught social gospel theologians to say that religion and science work together as the progressive unfolding of truth. He never doubted that ideas govern the world, because the divine indwells all things. Good theology is guided by the same truths discovered by social science, and the best versions of both eschew dogmatism. Thus social Christianity did not baptize ideologies or pet theories. It was harmonious, rational, scientific, ethical, and averse to fighting. Church and state, rightly ordered, were harmonious, as were religion and science, and even labor and capital. Ely treasured Anglican socialist Frederick Denison Maurice for theologizing about the divine unity of the world. Theologies pitting faith against reason, or the church against the state, betrayed God's sacramental presence in all things. Reason and the state are sacred vehicles of the divine Logos pervading the world and are no less sacred than faith and the church. Social Christianity, to Ely, was comprehensively idealistic, calling for church, state, family, academy, and industry to work together to advance human progress. Socialism was helpful as an aid to this work and not as a creed.[19]

Ely disliked the stock exchange but did not condemn it unreservedly. He supported the nationalization of railways and other natural monopolies but not the nationalization of everything productive. He asked readers to send money to the AEA, "a real legitimate Christian institution" advancing a simple aim: "To find out the underlying principles of industrial society, and to diffuse information among the working classes and all classes." Ely tried to hold the AEA to this description, but orthodox economists poured into it, and he tired of defending his chair at Johns Hopkins. He could be abrasive, which soured his reputation at Johns Hopkins. He dismissed the marginal utility school of Carl Menger and William S. Jevons, which denied that value should be calculated from the cost of production or labor embodied in the product. Ely dismissed even Alfred Marshall's second-generation revision, which explained the discrepancy in the value of goods and services by referring to their secondary utility. Value is a function of utility derived from the cumulative desires of consumers and determined at the margin, depending on the relationship between desires and supply. To Ely, every attempt to refine the idea of a natural free market was pointless, whether or not Marshall was a socialist, as he sometimes averred. Ely stuck to his core convictions that economic systems evolve into new forms through adaptation and regulation, and capitalism must be steered in the right direction. America needed a third way between state socialist authoritarianism and laissez-faire anarchy, and the church had a role to play in achieving it. But the church, he said, preferred to traffic in "platitudes and vague generalities," so it had to be pushed.[20]

Ely prized his reputation as a fair-minded analyst of the labor and capital problem. His books touted his academic expertise and the fact that his German teachers helped to build the first welfare state. He said the best economists selectively appropriated socialist ideas and were usually German because Germany had the best universities. He was averse to radical rhetoric about the class struggle or anything else. Ely was a social gospel Fabian, contending that society was evolving toward a cooperative commonwealth. Then in 1889 he pulled back from socialist gradualism, claiming that the best social gospel fixed on specific reforms and was not socialist. Occasionally, in front of the right crowd, he said he was still a Christian socialist, as long as he got to define it. Edward Bellamy, a Christian socialist journalist from Chicopee, Massachusetts, published a best-selling utopian fantasy in 1888, *Looking Backward.* Young Bostonian Julian West awakes in 2000 to an America of nationalized banks and essential industries, communal kitchens, and dreamy, idyllic, peaceable harmony. The book electrified a huge audience of middle-class book clubs and spawned a Fabian-like movement calling itself Nationalism and led by Protestant ministers. Ely told a Boston crowd of Bellamy nationalists in 1890 that religion and nationalism were both important, and he rejoiced that some Christian socialists were both: "Christian Socialism—if you will take it in my conservative sense—is what I think we need; that is religion coupled with Nationalism."[21]

But much of the Christian socialism that emerged in the 1880s did not share Ely's elitist, managerial, Fabian sensibility. He did not like the romantic radicalism of Herron or the solidarity radicalism of Bliss, and he had second thoughts about government socialism. Ely worried that movements for state socialism tend to be totalizing, not knowing when to stop. State socialists suppressed private production, assigning the role of production to the government. They were against private capitalists, not capital, proposing to abolish capitalists as a class by making every member of the community a capitalist, nationalizing capital. When socialists said that labor creates all wealth, they did not deny that land and capital are factors of production. They meant that land and capital are passive factors in production and that owners should not benefit from any wealth creation in which they do not personally play an active role. Ely said he still believed in cooperative socialist reforms that left room for local self-determination and close-at-hand adjustments, but radical rhetoric scared him. He cautioned that socialism is valuable only to a point, as a spur to reform movements. He implored Walter Rauschenbusch and other Christian socialists to stop saying that universal education, free schools, and gas-and-water municipal socialism were socialist ideas, even though they were. These claims confused the crucial issue, despite rightly suggesting that socialism extends such things to the economy as a whole.

The crucial issue was personal freedom. Ely said the Socialist animus against private production had to be challenged as a matter of fundamental principle, not as something to be negotiated down the road. In 1889 he warned, "The danger to freedom seems a very real one." Socialism wagered everything, perilously, on a single industrial principle. It was better to expand the cooperative sector, nationalize natural monopolies, support unions, abolish child labor and other industrial abuses, and build a strong government that safeguarded individual freedom. Ely said he could have stuck with a Christian socialism that held fast to this approach. As it was, radicals like Herron, Bliss, and Rauschenbusch rushed into the movement and changed its image. Ely bailed out, calling himself a Progressive conservative. In 1892 he joined the faculty at the University of Wisconsin, helped by his former student Frederick Jackson Turner. Two years later Ely had to fight for his job before the board of regents because conservatives accused him of supporting strikes, boycotts, socialism, anarchism, and other attacks on life and property. He was exonerated, winning a landmark vindication of his academic freedom. But Ely saved his job by denying he was a socialist, an ardent prounionist, or even a social activist. He was an academic who prized his perch in the academy, wanting very much to keep it.[22]

Gladden walked a similar tightrope as a pastor and ecumenical leader, taking positions on most things that closely resembled Ely's viewpoint. But Gladden's training as a preacher and journalist made him an edgier writer than Ely, he pressed for verdicts, and he had the opposite trajectory from Ely, drifting to the left as capitalism grew increasingly predatory and the social gospel acquired an outright socialist flank. Gladden began to condemn the wage system in 1886, ten years before Debs did so. Gladden said the wage system is antisocial, immoral, and anti-Christian, so it doesn't deserve polite academic treatment. There are three fundamental choices in political economy: relations of labor and capital can be based on slavery or wages or cooperation. The wage system is better than slavery, Gladden allowed, but preserving it was not a tolerable option. The first stage of industrial progress featured the subjugation of labor by capital. The second stage was essentially a war between labor and capital. The third stage is the moral and social ideal, the cooperative commonwealth in which labor and capital have a common interest and spirit.[23]

For a while he tried to combine a structural critique of the problem with an optimistic ethical solution. In the 1880s Gladden urged business groups, workers, and reformers that the ideal was imminently attainable. The clash between labor and capital was "not a difficult problem. The solution of it is quite within the power of the Christian employer. All he has to do is admit his laborers to an *industrial partnership* with himself *by giving them a fixed share in the profits of production,* to be divided among them, in proportion to their earnings, at the end of the year." Profit sharing was the key to making the economy serve the cause of a good society. It rewarded productivity and cooperative action, channeled the virtues of self-regard and self-sacrifice, socialized the profit motive, abolished the wage system, and promoted mutuality, equality, and community. Gladden said the strongest argument for cooperative economics is its simple justice: "Experience has shown him that the wage-receiving class are getting no fair share of the enormous increase of wealth; reason teaches that they never will receive an equitable proportion of it under a wage-system that is based on sheer competition; equity demands, therefore, that some modification of the wage-system be made in the interest of the laborer. If it is made, the employer must make it."[24]

The crucial hearts and minds belonged to the business class, to which Gladden preached every Sunday. The solution was to persuade employers to set up profit-sharing enterprises, not to abolish capitalism from above or below. Gladden stressed that most employers were no less moral than the laborers they employed. It was not too late to create a cooperative alternative to the wage system. Socialism was a poor alternative because it required an overreaching bureaucracy that placed important freedoms in jeopardy. Socialists wanted to pull down the existing order. Gladden said they were right to condemn the greed and predatory competitiveness of capitalism but foolish to suppose that humanity would flourish "under a system which discards or cripples these self-regarding forces." A better system would mobilize goodwill and channel self-interest to good ends, Christianizing the social order.[25]

Gladden appealed to the rationality and moral feelings of a capitalist class confronted by embittered workers, at first resisting the implication of his assurance that business executives were at least as moral as their employees. If that was true, the remedy had to encompass more than the morality of individuals. In 1893 he still fixed on the moral feelings of the business class, arguing in *Tools and the Man* that the ideal was to create "industrial partnerships" based on profit-sharing: "I would seek to commend this scheme to the captains of industry by appealing to their humanity and their justice; by asking them to consider the welfare of their workmen as well as their own. I believe that these leaders of business are not devoid of chivalry; that they are ready to respond to the summons of good-will."[26]

By then, however, Gladden was struggling to believe it. Cooperative ownership made little headway in America, and profit sharing would not happen without strong unions. The latter realization pulled him to the left, even as he deplored union violence and featherbedding and prized his capacity to mediate between labor and capital. Gladden was insistently optimistic on other subjects, and he thrilled at the ascension of the social gospel in American churches. But he realized that the lopsided power of the capitalist class stymied any serious hope of achieving a nonsocialist, decentralized economic democracy, and he said so from the pulpit.

His critique of state socialism was sensible, prescient, and closely aligned with Ely. Gladden warned that centralized state socialism denigrates the spirit of individual creativity and invention: "It ignores or depreciates the function of mind in production—the organizing mind and the inventive mind." He spurned the Marxist doctrine that labor creates all value, not caring whether or not Marx got it from David Ricardo: "It is not true that labor is the sole cause of value or wealth. Many substances and possessions have great value on which no labor has ever been expended." He rejected the socialist promise to provide meaningful work for everyone: "Socialism takes away the burdens that are necessary for the development of strength. It undertakes too much. It removes from the individual the responsibilities and cares by which his mind is awakened and his will invigorated."[27]

Above all, state socialism is too grandiose and bureaucratic to work. It requires enormous governmental power and virtually infinite bureaucratic wisdom. Gladden explained: "The theory that it proposes is too vast for human power. It requires the state to take possession of all the lands, the mines, the houses, the stores, the railroads, the furnaces, the factories, the ships—all the capital of the country of every description." Under a socialist order, American government bureaucrats would be vested with the power to set wages, prices, and production quotas for a sprawling continent of consumers and producers: "What an enormous undertaking it must be to discover all the multiform, the infinite variety of wants of sixty millions of people, and to supply all these wants, by governmental machinery! What a tremendous machine a government must be which undertakes, in a country like ours, to perform such a service as this!" Americans were not accustomed to viewing government as an agent of redemption. Gladden linked arms with socialists to make gains toward economic democracy, while spurning socialist promises to make centralized government "the medium and minister of all social good."[28]

Gladden and Ely built a movement that radiated their ethical enthusiasm for cooperatives, democracy, Progressivism, and being peaceable. Ely was more attuned than Gladden to Christian socialist trends in England and Germany and more inclined to herald them, although Gladden also cheered that he had English and German allies. Gladden and Ely were moralistic without apology, allergic to Marxist rhetoric about smashing capitalism, and committed to Christianizing society. Society would be Christianized through further progress, reforms, and evangelization. Francis Greenwood Peabody, Graham Taylor,

Shailer Mathews, Charles Mason North, William Adams Brown, Albion Small, Jane Addams, Richard R. Wright Jr., and Adam Clayton Powell Sr. shared this concept of the social gospel. In 1906 Ely helped Catholic social ethicist John Ryan acquire a publisher for his book advocating a living wage, hoping to spark an American Catholic social gospel movement. The seeds of a movement already existed in the Catholics who belonged to unions. Why not dream of a Catholic social gospel that built political organizations and was taught at Catholic universities?[29]

But the Catholic social gospel remained confined to the unions, and Gladden kept moving leftward, always with regret, protesting that corporate capitalism demolished better possibilities. Capitalism had to be fought off with organized power and conviction, which only the Socialists and unions mustered. Thus he counted socialists as indispensable allies in the struggle against the wage system and called himself "enough of a Socialist" to embrace socialist antiwar internationalism. Since working people were losing the class struggle, and the rights to life and freedom outranked the right to property, he defended the union movement and qualified his opposition to nationalization. In the early 1890s Gladden made exceptions for the entire class of economic monopolies, including the railroads, telegraph, gas, and electric companies, sometimes citing Ely. Later he added mines, watercourses, water suppliers, and telephone services. The railroad companies in particular, he said, were "gigantic instruments of oppression." In any industry where no effective competition exists, the only just recourse is state control. The railroad and electric companies did not operate under the law of supply and demand or offer their commodities or services in an open market. In effect, they closed the market: "This is not, in any proper sense, trade; this is essentially taxation. And, therefore, I think that all virtual monopolies must eventually belong to the state."[30]

Gladden's deepening realism about the class struggle lessened his qualms about hardball union tactics. He emoted about social justice more readily than Ely and welcomed outright socialists to the social gospel. He entreated union organizers to work for human solidarity, not mere proletarian solidarity, but in 1897 he conceded that unions had legitimate reasons to intimidate scab-laborers. In his memoir, *Recollections* (1909), Gladden judged that America was probably heading "into a Socialistic experiment." Expanding the cooperative sector would be better, he said, but Americans were probably too selfish and benighted for either approach.[31]

Two years later, in *The Labor Question*, he did not share Rauschenbusch's faith that the last unregenerate sector of American society—the economy—was being Christianized. Real progress on that front would have bridged the chasm between labor and capital. As it was, Gladden lamented, corporations were more ruthless than ever, and labor organizing yielded harsh outfits like the National Association of Manufacturers and the revolutionary anarchist Industrial Workers of the World. Gladden gave up his fantasy of a paternalistic share-economy featuring profit sharing and cooperatives, taking his stand with a flawed labor movement. Unorganized labor, he said, was "steadily forced down toward starvation and misery." Elsewhere he lamented that corporate capitalism was utterly vengeful toward unions, "maintaining toward them an attitude of almost vindictive opposition." In this context, unionism was the only serious force of resistance against the corporate degradation of labor. If economic democracy was to be achieved, it had to come through industrial unionism.[32]

The socialists who streamed into the social gospel in the 1890s agreed with Gladden about industrial unionism and the importance of freedom. They had no fantasy of shareholding generosity to dispel, and they believed that socialism would unleash a gusher of unprecedented freedoms. They built organizations as energetically as Gladden and Ely. In 1889 William Dwight Porter Bliss founded the nation's first Christian Socialist organization, the first of many such organizations he would found or join. He found a comrade in English professor Vida Scudder, who joined Bliss's Episcopal parish and wrote for his socialist and reform organizations. Scudder became a distinctive figure in these circles for her gender, lesbian sexuality, genteel background, social settlement legacy, and socialist militancy. Both began in the wing of American Protestantism boasting the strongest progressive tradition, Congregationalism, but converted to Anglicanism.

SOCIAL REDEMPTION: BLISS, SCUDDER, AND DEBS

Bliss was born in 1856 to Congregational missionary parents in Constantinople. He studied at Robert College in Constantinople before completing the troika of New England Congregationalism: boarding school at Phillips Academy in Andover, Massachusetts; college at Amherst College in Amherst, Massachusetts; and seminary at Hartford Theological Seminary in Hartford, Connecticut. He began his ministerial career in Denver in 1882 but washed out from poor health. The following year he took a parish in South Natick, Massachusetts, where he did better, but two things worked on his feelings: the plight of poor workers in his village and the Catholic concept of a sacramental church. In 1885 Bliss read Henry George's articles in the *Christian Union* and studied English Anglican Socialism. The following year he joined the Knights of Labor and the Episcopal Church. Christ founded one Church, Bliss reasoned, not a bunch of rival denominations. Protestantism fragmented

Christianity into competing sects, a disaster for the Church's spiritual and social witness. Bliss was ordained a deacon in the Episcopal Church in 1886 and a priest the following year. He served a congregation in Lee, Massachusetts, and became a master workman in the local Knights Assembly, serving as a delegate to the Union Labor Convention of 1887 in Cincinnati. That year he ran for lieutenant governor of Massachusetts as the Labor candidate. In 1888 he accepted a call as rector to Grace Church in South Boston, where he organized an inner-city mission church called the Church of the Carpenter and cofounded an Episcopalian Social Gospel organization, the Church Association for the Advancement of the Interests of Labor, which enlisted thirty-eight bishops.[33]

Bliss dutifully studied Marx and Marxists but favored writers with a moral bent, especially Maurice, U.S. American Socialist Laurence Gronlund, and Italian nationalist Giuseppe Mazzini. Gronlund's book *The Cooperative Commonwealth* (1884) contained the signature phrase of the social gospel in its title and was the chief inspiration for Bellamy's *Looking Backward.* In his 1890 edition Gronlund declared, "Everything is ripe, especially in the United States, for the great change, except leaders. I am convinced they will come out from among the deeply religious minds among us." Bliss befriended Gronlund, Baptist Social Gospel pastor O. P. Gifford, and Edward Bellamy's cousin, Francis Bellamy, who shared Bliss's yearning for a union of the reform movements. In January 1889 Bliss cofounded a Bellamy Nationalist chapter in Boston and called Christian socialists to a meeting at the Tremont Temple. The latter group became, in April, the Society of Christian Socialists.[34]

For two years Bliss failed to persuade Bellamy Nationalists to work with unions, socialists, and others not fitting their bookish ethos and agenda, so he quit the Nationalists. For the rest of his life he stuck with Christian socialism and the dream of a united reformism, founding a succession of groups. Every group had a journal, a lending library, a lecture bureau, and a lecture tour, all run by Bliss. The Society of Christian Socialists was his least successful venture, topping out at twenty-five members. Bliss pledged to "show that the aim of Socialism is embraced in the aim of Christianity." The society sought to fulfill "the social principles of Christianity" out of "simple obedience to Christ." Gifford, Scudder, and upcoming Baptist minister Leighton Williams were charter members, Rauschenbusch soon joined, and Bliss launched a monthly journal, *The Dawn*, publishing articles on poverty, plutocracy, industrial policy, and the land issue and not on theology or ecclesiology, since Bliss aimed for ecumenical inclusion. His mainstay contributors were Herron, Scudder, Bellamy, Gladden, Gifford, Gronlund, Small, P. W. Sprague, and Frances Willard.[35]

Scudder was born in 1861 in India, where her Congregational missionary father drowned when she was an infant. Her given name was Julia, but there were already two Aunt Julias at home when her widowed mother returned to Auburndale, Massachusetts, and renamed her with the feminine form of her father's name. Scudder's mother, Harriet Louisa Dutton Scudder, was wealthy, mannered, and highly literate. She treasured the glory and beauty of Europe's Catholic past and raised her daughter in it, taking her to Rome for four years of elementary school. Vida Scudder was deeply attached to her mother for the rest of her mother's life. In Europe they attended Anglican churches whenever possible. In 1875 they joined Trinity Church in Boston, giving in to their love of Anglican liturgy and the sermons of Phillips Brooks. Both said that Broad Church Anglicanism provided the spiritual air they craved at Congregational services. Scudder sailed through Boston's Latin School and Smith College, finding both to be pedestrian compared to her learned family of book readers. She graduated from Smith in 1884 and enrolled at Oxford, accompanied by her mother. Scudder treasured Maurice for his culturally refined theology and puzzled at his socialism. She and her mother were devotees of Victorian higher things; politics was beneath them. Then John Ruskin made Scudder ashamed of her haughty elitism.[36]

Scudder had savored Ruskin's art criticism for years. She adored his descriptions of sunsets and Venetian palaces, owing to Ruskin her love of painting, architecture, and what she called the "portals of the temple of beauty." But Ruskin no longer wrote about such things, sadly to Scudder. His recent books blathered about wage rates, modes of production, and similar dismal fare, and he had apparently become a socialist. Scudder lamented that Ruskin wasted his spirit on issues that should have been beneath him. He had become an embarrassment. In fact, Ruskin had begun to lose his mind, which Scudder delicately did not mention when she told this story. She caught him at an early stage of decline, when his mental breakdown came off as riveting moral intensity. Ruskin's rage at social injustice and his passionate concern for the poor got to Scudder. He made her question her love of art, something monopolized by the privileged, and her privileges. Ruskin railed at students who asked to hear about impressionism. He said that a morally healthy nation cares about its poor, and caring about the poor is the essential prerequisite of moral health. Reading Ruskin's slashing attack on capitalism, *Unto This Last*, Scudder repented of her class snobbery.[37]

She vowed to spend the rest of her life serving the needs of the poor, which drove her to Maurice's socialism. Scudder had come to Oxford in a self-congratulatory frame of mind as the first American woman to study there, along with her friend and romantic partner Clara French. She returned to Boston as a Ruskin idealist. For two years Scudder wrote articles about Ruskin, Tolstoy, and Percy Bysshe Shelley, and floundered. Her beloved partner French died in 1888, Scudder grieved and kept writing, her articles were rejected as immature, and her mother despaired at her radical turn. Scudder worried that she was lapsing into dreamland. To keep her social passion alive and real she had to belong to something besides her mother's family and church. Wellesley College became part of the solution in 1887, hiring Scudder to teach English literature. In 1888 she joined a community of Episcopalian women dedicated to social activism, the Society of the Companions of the Holy Cross. Then she joined the Society of Christian Socialists in 1889, having read Marx and the Fabian socialists in the meantime.

Scudder joined Bliss's Church of the Carpenter, as did the soon-to-be famous muckraking journalist Henry Demarest Lloyd, and got her first taste of political activism. She wrote in *The Dawn* that meeting the needs of the body is part of the work of saving souls, for bodies and souls are complementary. By 1890 she had a signature theme: Socialism must stand for more than a better economic order. The hope of socialism is that a better economic order might allow people to act out of their better nature. "We are all talking about socialism today," she wrote. Activists spoke constantly about the methods, principles, and machinery of socialism, "but there is just one thing we do not talk much about, and that is, supposing we arrive, what sort of men and women shall we be when we get there?" Scudder said the main issue between socialism and capitalism was vital, not technical. History is made by those who see truly because they see simply; they glow with moral passion, perceiving a great principle in the confused disorder of life. History remembers Luther as the hero of the Reformation, not Erasmus. Utopian writers, she said, miss the essential thing: moral passion. Utopias are dreary, dull, colorless, and philistine. *Looking Backward* epitomized the problem: "I confess that the life which *Looking Backward* describes for us does not attract me in the least."[38]

Her socialist ideal was middle-class and Christian, like Bellamy's, but also liberating. Scudder said the rich and poor classes are never creative or free; the rich are stifled by overabundance, and the poor are starved by material want and oppression. The great reformers always come from the middle class. She wanted nothing to do with socialist utopias that create an "infesting horde of deadbeats." The goal of socialism is "the uplift of the struggle of humanity to a higher plane, the removal of certain external clogs and shackles that bind down to the earth the free spirit of man." The goal is not to eliminate private property, an unreal vision that only utopians find attractive. Socialism is about lifting humanity through collective ownership of the means of production and the redistribution of wealth on the basis of need. The promise of socialism is to make it possible to obey the commands of Christ: "It would enable men to 'take no thought for the morrow,' for it would remove from them the necessity of constant thought for what they shall eat, what they shall drink, and wherewithal they shall be clothed."[39]

Scudder was a popular teacher at Wellesley, where she settled into a five-track orbit of teaching, settlement work, literary writing, political activism, and spiritual practice. In 1890 she cofounded Denison House in Boston, serving from 1893 to 1913 as its primary administrator. Like Jane Addams at Hull House, Scudder conceived settlement work as a ministry, struggled with her class and race privilege, and found a supportive community for her quietly lesbian sexuality. She said white activists needed to acknowledge their privileges and be grateful for the privilege to serve others. She loved the settlement movement for providing helping opportunities for women, many of whom were lesbian or bisexual. And she led the minority wing of the movement that held out against professionalizing settlement work. Scudder did not want settlement workers to become social workers or to conceive settlements as laboratories for the advancement of social science. She wanted the settlements to be centers of Christian activism and spiritual practice. She wrote prolifically about settlements, spirituality, church affairs, and, especially, literary criticism, using her courses as source material. *The Life of the Spirit in the Modern English Poets* (1895) portrayed Shelley, Wordsworth, Tennyson, and Browning as champions of cultural progress who paved the way to Fabian socialism. *Social Ideals in English Letters* (1898) similarly portrayed Ruskin, Carlyle, and Arnold as advocates of social progress who cared about the poor, albeit with caveats about democracy. Scudder argued that the best dreams of Victorian England remained to be fulfilled in a new synthesis, ending with a question: "Will that synthesis be the social democracy of the future? Will it be the socialist state?"[40]

She treasured Bliss's evening services at Church of the Carpenter, where they feasted on the "hope of an imminent revolution." *The Dawn*, she said, "was sunlight to some of us." Grace Church did not warm to socialism, so Bliss resigned to concentrate on activism and his mission church. He emulated all of England's Christian socialist organizations simultaneously. The Society of Christian Socialists was ecumenical like Britain's Christian Socialist Society; the Church of the Carpenter was Anglo-Catholic like the Church Socialist League; the Christian Social Union was broadly Anglican like its British namesake; his labor activism in the Knights and SLP resembled how the British Labour Party was founded; and he reached out to secular middle-class intellectuals in Fabian fashion. In 1891 he founded a settlement house for Christian socialist and labor union gatherings, the Wendell Phillips Union, and urged the newfound Christian Social Union not to settle for half measures like producer cooperatives and the Single Tax. Bliss told an SLP gathering that profit sharing was "a capitalist dodge to reduce wages." Cooperatives and the Single Tax, he said, undercut the right of communities to commonly own industries. Bliss had a signature cause, contending that Christian socialism should unite the reform movements.[41]

To him, Christian socialism was freedom loving, capacious, nondogmatic, and averse to ideal systems. It was not a Christianized version of Bellamy Nationalism, Fourier communalism, or Marxian revolution, because it was not a theoretical system. Neither was it a utopian vision because utopian visions of socialism were "vague, negative, denunciatory" and destructive, much like socialist systems: "Life demands freedom, variety, change. Christian Socialists believe in life; they believe in true individual freedom." Bliss taught that Maurice was right to oppose all systems. Christian socialism was society conforming to God's free and beneficent order. It believed in progress through constructive reforms and opposed Communism, allowing people to own their own houses, belongings, and money. Christian socialists shuddered at antifamily versions of socialism and did not attack the rich for being rich or the poor for being poor. They attacked the capitalist system that rewarded selfishness and predatory behavior and struggled to unite the reform movements.[42]

Bliss reveled in the history of Christian socialism, especially the band of Maurice disciples who founded British Christian socialism in 1848 and the Anglo-Catholics who revived it in the 1880s. He grieved that French socialism was anti-Christian and nearly always medieval, "striving to revive the medieval guild." He was double minded about Ely and Gladden. Sometimes Bliss said that proponents of producer cooperatives and of public ownership of natural monopolies should call themselves socialists, and sometimes he said it was better if they didn't because the real thing is bigger. Christian socialism applies the Christian law of sacrifice to the social sphere. It is a name for Christ's moral principle that whoever would be great must be the servant of all: "He spoke to the social in man. He came to found a kingdom. He preached a Social Gospel. Jesus Christ was the seed-sower. It is for us to reap."[43]

Under socialism, associated or cooperating workers who jointly owned the means of production would conduct industry. Bliss said socialism had to be something this definite; otherwise, anyone could hijack the name. Cooperatives, profit sharing, and the Single Tax were commendable if they did not thwart the real thing—public ownership and control. Bliss taught that socialism transforms private and competing capital into united and collective capital. It can have a state or not have one, but if it has a state, the state must be democratic: "The expansion of the State is Socialistic only when the State is the people, a true democracy, the organic unity of the whole people." The so-called state socialism of Germany under Bismarck, for example, was an imperialist tyranny having nothing to do with socialism, a point pressed brilliantly by "the true Socialist of Germany," Karl Marx.[44]

Since Socialism was a principle of social action to Bliss, not a plan, it was always being worked on and never definitively established. Thus he could commend Marxism and Fabian socialism in successive paragraphs. Socialism is the democracy principle applied to the economy. Bliss said that history does not evolve backward, so capital would never regress to the private capitalist model after learning the value of combination. Trusts had come to stay. The crucial question was whether the triumphant principle of economic combination would have a democratic future or a plutocratic future. Socialism, Bliss urged, was a democratic alternative to the rule of Jay Gould plutocrats. It was advancing rapidly, exactly as Fabian ringleader Sidney Webb said; every collectivizing act was a step toward it. Even Spencer believed that Socialism was winning, though he dourly called it "The Coming Slavery."

Bliss countered that being liberated from economic pressure would free people to be more creative, interesting, and hospitable. Business competition produced stunted human beings at both ends. Under socialism, "a nobler individuality" would arise: "We shall have a renaissance in art, a revival of learning, a reformation in religion." Lecture audience critics told Bliss the poor were poor through their own fault. He replied that the poor were poor because the average worker made $350 per year, not enough to raise a family. Socialism was "the community caring for its weaker members, educating them, placing them in a proper environment." Nationalizing enterprises, he argued, was not the best way to do it. He believed that taxing them sufficiently worked better, and socialists should not disparage the term "gradual."[45]

Churches had a special role to play in the struggle for socialism, and clergy had a special role in the churches. Bliss did not say that congregations would flourish if ministers preached the gospel as they should. He said ministers had to be willing to empty the pews and sacrifice their jobs. He did not say it with Herron's air of martyrdom because Bliss cherished the Church and had no self-dramatizing martyr complex. But he said as forcefully as Herron that ministers needed to reclaim the gospel of Jesus, devote themselves to the cause of the poor, and stop toadying to the rich: "We must appeal to love by love; to brotherhood by brotherly kindness; to sacrifice by sacrifice. 'If any man would be chief among you let him be servant of all.' This is Christian Socialism."[46]

What he should say was clearer to Bliss than what he should join; thus he kept founding organizations. The Socialist Party did not exist until 1901, and Bliss put off joining it until 1912. He worked hard for the SLP, but in 1891 he endorsed the People's Party, judging that its Populist platform had a better chance of attracting radicals. In 1895 he founded the National Educational and Economic League, a Fabian-like educational outreach vehicle to trade unionists. The following year he went along with the Populist endorsement of Democrat William Jennings Bryan for president, which outraged many of his Socialist friends. Bliss did not believe that coining free silver would strike a blow against capitalism, but he was always ready to support a reform movement that caught fire, so he supported Bryan. That riled De Leon just as De Leon tried to take over the Knights and the AFL. Bliss stuck with the SLP through the 1890s while lamenting its "needlessly censorious and vindictive" leadership.[47]

For a while he tried to support the Christian Commonwealth Colony at Commonwealth, Georgia, a community of four hundred Christian Socialists that published a spunky journal, *The Social Gospel.* Founded in 1896 by two followers of Herron, Ralph Albertson and George Gibson, the Commonwealth colony sought to build a school modeled on Booker T. Washington's trinity of work, education, and Christianity at Tuskegee Institute. Early issues of the journal featured sermons and lectures by Herron, who served as a coeditor; many expounded on the journal's motto, "The Kingdom of Heaven is at hand." Except for Herron, Bliss was the supporter the colonists most wanted. Briefly he indulged them as an associate editor, but Bliss did not like communalism, which smacked of small-bore, self-indulgent, escapist religion to him. There was too much of Tolstoy in *The Social Gospel.* He said so in a long letter to the journal, admonishing that Christ's social gospel aimed at changing the world, not providing a refuge for individuals. The editors dutifully published it under the title "Self-Serving Colonies Condemned." Bliss urged the colonists back to the city and its teeming hordes of tenement dwellers: "I have always thought that the Christian's place of honor was not in heaven, but in hell, trying to turn that into heaven."[48]

He kept founding new organizations, always to mobilize the scattered reform groups. In 1897 he founded the Union Reform League (URL), which morphed two years later into a nonpartisan Fabian federation, the Social Reform Union (SRU). Bliss served as president or secretary or both in every organization he launched, serving as editor of *The Dawn* (1889–96), *The American Fabian* (1895–96), *The Social Forum* (1899–1901), *The Social Economist* (1898–1901), and *The Social Unity* (1901). He and Henry Demarest Lloyd tried to build a Fabian movement on the British model, permeating society and every political party with a vision of gradual Fabian socialism. But Fabian socialism smacked of British peculiarities, and Debs sabotaged Lloyd's attempt to make him the presidential nominee of the People's Party in 1896. Then the party cut its throat by endorsing Bryan. Bliss, characteristically, backed Bryan with determined optimism, while Lloyd was devastated, giving up on the People's Party. In 1895 Bliss wrote a landmark textbook, *A Handbook of Socialism.* Two years later he published a mammoth textbook, *The Encyclopedia of Social Reform,* which had a long run in its revised two-volume edition as the bible of social reform scholarship.[49]

Bliss founded the URL in the same year he filled San Francisco's largest auditorium every night for two weeks and called for a revolution against the city's "real governing power," the Southern Pacific Railway. He and Herron dominated the URL, which debated whether it should back a political party. In 1899 the group changed its name at a convention in Buffalo and adopted Bliss's platform—direct legislation, public ownership of monopolies, taxation of land values and income, and anti-imperialism. Herron was against platforms; this was decidedly Bliss's group. Many delegates blanched when Bliss unveiled a red banner with a white cross; Bliss explained that red symbolized fraternity, not something to be feared, and the cross was a "symbol of peace, of life, of sacrifice. It would mean brotherhood realized through sacrifice, humanity made one in love." Every Bliss sermon and lecture contained a variation on this theme. He lost count of the countless churches he addressed for the CSU and the URL/SRU, but the election of 1900 sundered the unity of the SRU and it fell apart.[50]

The SLP had a bitter faction fight in 1899 that led, two years later, to the Socialist Party. In between, the election of 1900 pitted Bryan and Republican William McKinley against Debs, the candidate of a fledgling party of railroad unionists and Populists, Social Democracy of America. Herron supported Debs, while Bliss, holding out for reformer unity, stuck with Bryan. The dream of reformer unity defined his last magazine, *The Social Unity.* Bliss implored reformers to become socialists and socialists not to give up on reformers. To him, being a socialist within reform movements was like being a Christian within socialism. The two things went together, and socialism was "the only way out." Sometimes Bliss described socialism as the principle that the community—national, state, and local—should gradually own the land and capital collectively, organizing both on a cooperative basis for the equitable good of all. Sometimes he said that socialism was greater than any principle, even cooperation: "Socialism is a collection of principles including a thousand detailed acts. It is the ism that there is no ism. It is the appeal from sectarian reforms to the essential unity of society. Even as a philosophy too, it does not claim to be universal. It recognizes truth in Individualism, in Anarchism, in

Paternalism, even in Capitalism; it simply holds that Socialism is the one social principle that industry most needs today."[51]

Debs came slower than Bliss and Scudder to socialism because he believed in the individualistic values of Anglo-Saxon Protestantism, and his BLF comrades were truer believers than he was. Yet when Debs belatedly converted to socialism in 1897, he embraced it as a cure-all, rejecting outright the Bliss strategy of uniting the reform movements. Debs was routinely florid about American liberty and individual virtue. The conservative BLF majority barely crawled into unionism; then it adopted the Gompers fixation on wages, working conditions, and skilled workers. Gompers trusted that Debs would stifle his romantic solidarity streak enough to remain a constructive unionist. He counted on Debs to nudge the Firemen closer to the AFL. He did not know that Debs crossed a line in 1890, at least inwardly. Debs concluded belatedly that labor would never thwart the power of capital if it did not unify. In 1891 he announced that he would resign as a BLF official in 1893, without explaining why. He hinted that he might found a magazine covering the entire labor movement. He did not say, until 1893, that the railroad Brotherhoods were obstacles to what mattered, uniting all railroad workers. Thus his exit was tortured, messy, and half-aborted.

No candidate had ever been nominated against Debs at a BLF convention, and no vote had ever been cast against him. In 1893 he was more popular than ever, although he skipped the previous year's convention out of apprehension that hard things might be said about his resignation. Debs seemed to be the ideal BLF leader, giving lip service to labor solidarity while defending craft unionism, small-town superiority, and Anglo-Saxon values, replete with casual backroom slurs against blacks, Italians, Irish, and Chinese. Surely he was one of them, wanting what they wanted. The delegates begged him not to resign. Debs stunned them speechless by declaring that craft unionism was useful only to a point long past; the craft model fostered class prejudices and selfishness that blocked any hope of progress. The Firemen gasped at realizing they had lost Debs but persuaded him to stay on as editor of the magazine. He resigned from the BLF without managing to get away. In June 1893 he and Conductors leader George Howard convened with fifty Conductors, Carmen, and Firemen to found the ARU. Fatefully, Debs put off fighting over racism, accepting the group's declaration that the ARU was open to all white railroad workers except managerial employees. Later he deeply regretted this blot on its record, and his. The ARU founders were done with Brotherhood provincialism, except regarding the humanity of all on the nonwhite side of the color line.[52]

Many workers rushed into the ARU, especially from the Union Pacific and Southern Pacific lines. The ARU conducted revival-like meetings along the lines, inviting Brotherhood members to join. The union grew fast, struggling to keep up with its mail and organizational challenges. In 1894 Debs won a dramatic strike against the Great Northern Railroad in St. Paul, Minnesota. No railroad brotherhood had ever won a strike, and no railroad union had ever won a strike as big as this one. Workers lined the tracks to honor Debs as he departed from St. Paul. He told crowds for years afterward that the sight of these workers, bent and withered from years of grinding toil, lifting their hats to him, was the greatest thrill of his life. In Terre Haute he got a hero's welcome that moved him to gush with tender gratitude, lifted to prominence by a union that had not yet held a national convention. By the end of the year the ARU had 150,000 members, surpassing the combined 90,000 of the Brotherhoods. Gompers reeled at the upsurge of industrial unionism, which thwarted him from recruiting Brotherhoods into the AFL and heightened the pressure he felt from Socialists in the AFL. Meanwhile Debs tamped down messianic fantasies, pleading that the ARU could not rescue all railroad workers at once; first it had to build an organization.[53]

Pullman Car workers struck against their autocratic Chicago owner, George Pullman, and begged the ARU to support them. Pullman had cut worker pay to near-starvation wages while continuing to pay dividends to shareholders. Debs said he would help as much as possible but could not go all-in; the fledgling ARU was already overstretched. The union held its first convention in June 1894 in Chicago, in a buoyant mood despite a punishing economic depression. Debs proposed to abolish the color line, implored the ARU to do the right thing, and lost the vote by 112 to 100. The winners exulted that Debs was their leader, but the ARU was a democratic organization. Pullman strikers begged the delegates to help them, and the delegates defied Debs again by voting to boycott all Pullman sleeping cars and to shut down any train that refused to detach Pullman cars. Debs accepted the challenge, acknowledging that all peaceful means of obtaining a just settlement had been exhausted. He asked the AFL and the Brotherhoods for help, to little avail. Gompers said nothing in public, only the Mineworkers pledged to help, most of the Brotherhoods were vehemently opposed, and some Brotherhoods were quietly opposed. It did not matter to the Brotherhoods that the Pullman workers had a just cause; industrial unionism was anathema to craft unionism, so the boycott was indefensible. Yet the boycott surged in its first week. Railroad workers along the Union Pacific, Southern Pacific, and Santa Fe lines refused to work whenever managements refused to detach the Pullman cars. By the fourth day 125,000 workers had joined the boycott, traffic ceased on all lines west of Chicago, and sympathy strikes erupted in many cities west of Chicago. Debs pleaded constantly against violence and ordered that no mail trains were to be stopped, but workers did stop many mail trains.[54]

The Knights of Labor and the Chicago Federation of Labor rallied in support, even floating the idea of a general strike, which Debs ruled out. He surprised reporters with his immaculate tweed suits and hard white collars. Debs stuck out incongruously among rough and exhausted ARU officials working frantic twenty-hour days, and he was never frantic. Even hostile newspapers remarked on his steely calm and dignity. Nothing remotely like the Pullman strike had ever occurred on the railroad lines, but the railroad corporations welcomed it as an opportunity to destroy militant unionism in the entire industry. A powerful corporate consortium, the General Managers Association (GMA), combined the twenty-four railroad corporations with terminals at Chicago. They were determined to break the strike and prevent its spread to New York, Pennsylvania, and the Southeast, where the ARU had few members. Debs was fully prepared to fight the railroad corporations straight up. What he naively did not expect was that the federal government would aggressively intervene on behalf of the corporations.

He was still a political innocent in 1894, believing the federal government was a neutral arbiter in the struggle between labor and capital. Grover Cleveland, now in his second term as president, had won Debs's energetic campaign support three times. Debs believed that Cleveland was more or less sympathetic to labor, though Cleveland's new attorney general, Richard Olney, was a longtime Boston corporation lawyer specializing in railroad interests and trust estates. Olney regarded Debs's pleas for peaceful protest and delivering the mail as posturing lies. He set a fateful precedent by securing injunctions from federal courts against the strikers, contending that national strikes are illegal, railroads are public highways, interstate railroads are federal highways, any obstruction of a federal highway is illegal, and thus the strikers violated the Sherman Anti-Trust Act of 1890. The causes of the strike, on this telling, were irrelevant to the legality of the boycott. The ARU defied an injunction to end the boycott, and Olney persuaded Cleveland to send the U.S. Army to Chicago, claiming that Illinois governor John Peter Altgeld—a progressive Democrat—could not be trusted to enforce the law. On July 4 Debs watched federal troops stack armaments just outside his hotel window in Chicago. At first he was delighted, trusting that the army was intervening to maintain order and allow the strike to proceed without violence. Then he realized with horror that the troops were there to incite violence against the strikers. Debs held the strikers to nonviolence, but six thousand state and federal troops fired into outraged crowds, and many protesters erupted. Thirteen people were killed in Chicago, and riots broke out in other cities.

The spectacle of federal troops slaughtering U.S. American citizens doomed Cleveland's political career. Many troops came straight from the last battles of the so-called Indian Wars. Meanwhile Debs was hauled to jail, where Kate Debs came to visit, wowing reporters with her diamond earrings, two diamond rings, a gold watch fastened to her belt, a double gold necklace, and her stately, dignified bearing. She got favorable treatment in the same papers that pilloried the strikers as nihilistic wreckers. Kate Debs resented that her husband threw away his respectable career path and indulged his brother Theodore, his constant companion and helper. But to reporters she put it positively, stressing that Debs was generous to a fault, had no hobbies, and was completely devoted to the workers.

Debs offered to call off the strike, asking only that the railroad companies take back the striking workers. Surely, he appealed, the railroad barons had enough patriotism to do what was best for the country. At the same time he called for a general strike to force Pullman and the GMA to rehire the strikers. Debs realized that if the government destroyed the ARU, and the strikers were prohibited from working in the railroad industry, industrial unionism would be devastated. The general strike fizzled, and Debs played his last card, appealing to Gompers, who replied that Debs got what he deserved, and the ARU was not worth saving. If railroad workers who did not strike wanted to join a union, Gompers was eager to welcome them into the AFL. Debs seethed with offended rage at this response. He said Gompers was a traitor to the labor movement whose callous opportunism left Debs with no option to accepting defeat. Taking on the government was a nonstarter, though, of course, Gompers made the same calculation about a strike that was already lost anyway. Debs bitterly observed: "The crime of the American Railway Union was the practical exhibition of sympathy for the Pullman employees. Humanity and Christianity, undebauched and unperverted, are forever pleading for sympathy for the poor and oppressed."[55]

Next came the vengeance of the GMA and the federal government. The government failed to convict Debs of conspiracy but won a contempt charge that jailed him for six months in Woodstock, Illinois. The railroad corporations blacklisted strikers from ever working in the railroad industry again. The same Firemen who cheered Debs after the St. Paul victory now condemned him furiously. The ARU unraveled, Debs grieved for strikers who could not find work, and he burned with anger at the Firemen who condemned him. The failure of the Pullman strike crushed the ARU and the cause of radical industrial unionism, drove the Brotherhoods into compliant relationships with the corporations, and confirmed Gompers's judgment that pacifying the employers was the only constructive option. Economic protest didn't work because it evoked the repression of the state, while electoral politics divided the unions. Perhaps Gompers was right to spurn his socialist past?

Gompers had fought off the demand of the SLP to be admitted to the AFL as a bona fide labor organization. He beat the SLP at a showdown vote in 1890, which enraged De Leon and his majority wing of the SLP, setting off three years of contention over this verdict. Gompers declared that if the SLP were admitted there would be no stopping the Single Taxers, anarchists, and Greenback populists from joining too. He put it aptly in what became his epitaph: "Unions, pure and simple, are the natural organization of wageworkers to secure their present material and practical improvement and to achieve their final emancipation." He was not antisocialist, he said, but socialism is a dreamy vision, and workers had immediate needs: "The way out of the wage system is through higher wages." A growing number of unions within the AFL disagreed, voting with the Socialists who demanded socialist policy planks at AFL conventions. At the 1894 convention they pushed hard for a proposal advocating collective ownership of all means of production and distribution and narrowly lost the vote. They gave themselves a consolation prize by deposing Gompers as president, replacing him with miner John McBride.[56]

Gompers burned with resentment at being sidelined by the Socialists, although he climbed back into office the following year. He went on to thwart the call for a labor party that the industrial unions in the AFL—the United Mine Workers, Ladies' Garment Workers, and Brewery Workers—persistently led. To Gompers, De Leon was a mendacious snake, while Debs was a bewildering disappointment. Gompers said he was shocked when Debs took the ARU presidency, since Debs had always been sensible and agreeable. Then he became someone Gompers did not recognize. Gompers took for granted that monopoly is a natural outcome of economic development. Since monopolies are inevitable, he did not inveigh against them. He conceived the labor movement as a living organism that passes through natural stages of growth. It changed by growing gradually into something different, not by rallying to an ethical imperative, something that idealistic reformers didn't fathom. Debs, Gompers said, cast aside what he knew "in favor of his emotions," disastrously.[57]

Debs grew famous in jail, greeting a stream of visitors. One was Scottish labor leader Keir Hardie, who had just founded Britain's first labor party, the Independent Labour Party (ILP), in 1893. Debs recognized a kindred spirit in Hardie a dozen years before the ILP played the leading role in founding the British Labour Party. Debs told many visitors he had learned a crucial lesson— the corporations and their allies in the federal government would never allow a union to disrupt business as usual on the rail lines. The alliance between the government and the corporations was too strong for any union movement to challenge the rule of capital. Any union that struck a blow for labor would be crushed, just like the ARU. Now he believed exactly what Gompers had always assumed about the government, but Debs could not put it that way or tack back to Gompers. *Marbury v. Madison* (1803) unilaterally endowed the Supreme Court with quasi-legislative authority, the 14th Amendment expanded the reach of the court, and the capitalist class took full advantage of government by judiciary. Debs concluded that nothing could be done to keep the state from protecting the vested interests of the ruling class, lacking a Populist government. He had always believed more deeply in the republican power of the vote than in unionism. In jail Debs fell back on his deeper belief by changing political parties.

He was done with the Democratic Party because a Democratic president smashed the ARU. Debs, his lawyer Clarence Darrow, and Lloyd plotted to take over the left wing of the People's Party. Darrow overcame rural Ohio poverty and poor training to become a legendary superlawyer. Lloyd was a millionaire social gospel journalist, longtime editorialist for the *Chicago Tribune*, and author of a best-selling attack on Standard Oil, *Wealth Against Commonwealth* (1894). Debs and his six ARU jail mates tried to beef up their knowledge base by reading Lloyd, Gronlund, Bellamy, Herron, George, the British Fabians, and Irish American Catholic populist Ignatius Donnelly. Debs said Bellamy's utopia struck him more favorably when he read it in jail. Milwaukee socialist Victor Berger, a scholarly immigrant from Austria-Hungary, came to see him, lectured Debs about Marxism, and gave him a copy of Marx's *Capital*. Debs found it dreadfully dull, settling gratefully for accessible pamphlets by Karl Kautsky. Debs did not study very much in jail, contrary to subsequent lore he fed. The local post office struggled with the crush of mail that came to him—over a hundred letters and packages per day. Debs spent most of his time writing letters and granting newspaper interviews. He conducted interviews in the sheriff's dining room and opined on politics, news, life, and the future, contending that the Pullman strike would surely deliver a tremendous windfall to the People's Party in 1896. Debs said he bore no grudge against Olney, whose job was to enforce bad laws; when the Populists won, the laws would be much better.[58]

He spent his fortieth birthday in Woodstock jail, pondering his trajectory. On his release on November 22, 1895, Debs regaled a gigantic crowd at Battery D in Chicago with an oration on radical democratic liberty, declaring that he believed more than ever in the principles of government expounded in the Declaration of Independence. Debs said the principles of life, liberty, and the pursuit of happiness stood against "the absolute sway of the money power," but the government conspired with the money power to thwart America's constitutional order and imprison ARU officials. His cause was to recover the sacred principles on which America was founded, especially liberty. Liberty and slavery are primal realities, he explained, "like good and evil, right and wrong: they are opposites and coexistent." To steal the liberty of any individual in defiance of the Constitution is to endanger the liberty of all others: "In saying this, I conjecture I have struck the keynote of alarm that has convoked this vast audience." Debs invoked Jefferson, who warned that the money power "menaced the integrity of the Republic" by controlling the judiciary. He set Jefferson against Cleveland and Olney, successors to the capitalist vultures and slavemasters of Jefferson's time who ravaged the government and tyrannized chattel slaves. No one cried out that Jefferson owned slaves and did nothing to abolish slavery; Debs got his usual pass on Jefferson veneration. Jefferson saw clearly that the money power had to be blocked from dominating the political system and government. It didn't happen, so by 1895 not much was left of American liberty, to judge from the fate of the ARU. Debs called on Shakespeare and Patrick Henry for inspirational fare, driving toward a James Russell Lowell sermonic close: "I am standing here without a self-accusation of crime or criminal intent festering in my conscience, in the sunlight once more, among my fellowmen, contributing as best I can to make this 'Liberation Day' from Woodstock prison a memorial day, realizing that, as Lowell sang:

'He's true to God who's true to man; wherever wrong is done,
To the humblest and the weakest, 'neath the all-beholding sun.
That wrong is also done to us, and they are slaves most base,
Whose love of right is for themselves and not for all the race.' "[59]

For the rest of his life Debs said his life turned a corner in jail. A group of Chicago socialists asked him to lead a socialist union they were founding, but Debs was not yet a socialist and another dose of unionism did not tempt him. He gave speeches to rebuild the ARU, pay its debts, and raise money for blacklisted workers but said he would never have another official connection to a strike. That part of his life was over. Now he tried to fuse Gronlund, Bellamy, Herron, and Kautsky without displacing the primacy he gave to Jefferson and Lincoln. For the first time, he said the wage system had to be abolished, which propelled him through a maze of ideologies on his way to founding the Socialist Party. Between 1894 and 1901 Debs lurched from industrial unionism and the Democratic Party to radical Populism in the People's Party to a populist colony version of American Social Democracy to an uneasy partnership with Berger in

Social Democracy of America to the American brand of democratic socialism he championed as a comrade of Berger, Herron, and Hillquit in the Socialist Party.

Three decades of mounting political dissension climaxed in 1896. Debs barnstormed across the country, drawing huge crowds wherever he went, especially in the prairie states between Illinois and the Rocky Mountains. He stressed that unions could not break the dominating power of the capitalist class, while denying that the ARU was dying. He also denied that he wanted the Populist presidential nomination. In city after city Debs sent his lecture fees to ARU creditors and plugged for Populist anticapitalist democracy. The People's Party had a small Socialist faction, a fusionist faction that wanted a close alliance or merger with the Democratic Party, and a third faction that opposed any alliance with the Democrats. For Debs to be nominated, the third group had to back him. He encouraged Lloyd's politicking on his behalf while quietly cheering that agrarians and silverites won control of the Democratic Party, repudiating Cleveland. Altgeld led the anti-Cleveland rebellion, but he could not run for president because he was born in Germany.

The Democrats nominated Bryan two weeks before the Populists convened in St. Louis. For three days at the Populist convention Debs ran far ahead in the informal balloting, Lloyd whipped votes for him, and Debs remained in Terre Haute. Debs could not bear convention banter and wrangling, then or later. On the fourth day, just before the convention probably would have chosen Debs, he wired Lloyd not to place his name in nomination. Lloyd and the left-Populists were crestfallen to the point of folding, conceding the convention to the pro-Bryan fusionists. Black Populists from the South were especially distraught, as supporting the Democrats was a nonstarter for them. Had Debs been sure that he wanted to lead the People's Party, he might have showed up at the convention and battled for the nomination. But that was not how he operated anyway. He had to be admired, he was willing to lead only if he didn't have to compete for the job, he hated conventions, and he liked Bryan. So Debs cast aside his recent attacks on the Democratic Party and campaigned strenuously for Bryan, even claiming in Bryan-mode that the gold standard was the cause of America's social crisis. On New Year's Day 1897, two months after William McKinley won the presidency, Debs announced that he was a socialist: "I am for Socialism because I am for humanity. We have been cursed with the reign of gold long enough. Money constitutes no proper basis of civilization. The time has come to regenerate society."[60]

He was instantly America's leading socialist, albeit lacking an organization. Grieving over the blacklisted ARU workers lacking work, Debs resolved to create a party from the remnants of the ARU, the socialist wing of the prostrate People's Party, and exiles from the SLP. He was determined to provide a refuge for the ARU workers; thus he opted for a colony socialist party. The idea was to build a socialist community in a western state and call the unemployed masses to join it. Lloyd had founded a group the previous summer called the Brotherhood of the Cooperative Commonwealth that floated this proposal, which Debs supported without joining the group. Now Debs endorsed the colony strategy as the basis of a new party, which Lloyd declined to organize because Debs did not want to merge with Lloyd's group. In June 1897 Debs gathered the national officers of the ARU and dissolved it, founding the Social Democracy of America. De Leon and Berger showed up, for different reasons, to say that colony strategies are utopian, insular, and pointless. De Leon was always in the market for recruits he could dominate, and Berger was finished with De Leon, having served as a delegate to the People's Party convention in 1896. Berger pleaded that America needed a good Socialist party with a political agenda. Why should anyone in New York or Wisconsin join a party operating solely in a western outpost? Debs persuaded the convention to adopt a two-track program of colony building plus advocacy of public ownership of monopolies and utilities, a shortened workday, and public works for the unemployed. The executive board consisted entirely of Debs's former ARU inmates at Woodstock. Lloyd shook his head that they couldn't help themselves, despite knowing that insularity is deadly.[61]

Social Democracy in America fought from the beginning over colony communalism versus class struggle socialism since almost no one wanted both things. James Hogan, Roy Goodwin, William Burns, and other former ARU officers were against class struggle rhetoric and platform political demands, while Berger, Isaac Hurwich, G. A. Hoehn, and other former SLP members were adamantly opposed to the colony plan. Debs had no stomach for the bitter wrangling that followed. The two sides warred against each other, while the colony group had contentious internal fights between employers and workers. Each of the two main factions believed it won over Debs at some point. Anarchist Emma Goldman, lobbying Debs for the colony group, tried to persuade him that he was an anarchist without realizing it. One year into the party's vindictive fighting over its mission, Debs was torn between his head and heart. In his head he believed that Berger and the class struggle socialists were right, but he didn't love them; in fact he recoiled at Berger's know-it-all lectures about socialist ideology. Debs loved his ARU brothers, who won a showdown vote at the group's second convention in 1898. The losing socialists bolted the convention, convened at a neighboring hall, and founded the Social Democratic

Party. Debs skipped the vote, characteristically, staying in bed. Then he announced he was joining the Social Democratic Party because socialists had to confront the class struggle. America needed a party of full-fledged Socialists that took the fight to all forty-five states.

The fledgling Social Democratic Party endorsed strikes, boycotts, and an eight-hour workday and blasted the SLP for needlessly antagonizing the AFL. Berger wanted a close relationship with Gompers, and Debs went along. The Debs wing wanted a plank about leasing public land to farmers, but the Berger socialists said that farmer planks are reactionary—that is, populist. So the new party said nothing about the farm issue and nothing about African Americans, again at the insistence of the Berger faction. The party was willing to make select immediate demands but not on issues that consumed farmers, the labor movement, and neo-abolitionists since that distracted from believing in social-ism. The colony socialists wailed that Debs capitulated to an un-American ide-ology, though Debs still called for a union of all citizens to oppose industrial capitalism, telling audiences that strikes are a calamity. He stressed the abject condition of the unions to the point of being deflating, adding that the true aim of the labor movement is a good society, not a powerful unionism.

Debs sprinkled bits of Marx, Kautsky, and Lassalle into his talks, but mostly for show. Berger tried to instruct him, which stiffened Debs's resolve to make socialism speak American. What mattered was to win the right of individuals to share in the value of their work. Debs disseminated this message in Berger's *Social Democratic Herald* and Cahan's *Forward*, but his favorite venue by far was Julius Wayland's *Appeal to Reason*. Wayland grew up poor and bereft in Versailles, Indiana, where his father and four siblings died in a cholera epi-demic. He apprenticed at the age of fifteen to a printer, learned the publishing business, proved very enterprising, and bought the *Versailles Index* in 1874, helped by local Republicans. In 1877 he moved to Harrison, Missouri, where he won a postmaster appointment and launched a Republican paper. In 1882 he hauled his family to Pueblo, Colorado, just in time to capitalize on its explosive growth.

Wayland made a fortune in real estate. He thought that being a lefty Republican was as radical as an enterprising type like himself should be, but in 1890 he read *The Cooperative Commonwealth* and converted to socialism. Wayland said Gronlund "landed me good and hard. I saw a new light." In 1893 he returned to Indiana and launched a socialist paper, *The Coming Nation*. It was very successful, soaring to sixty thousand subscribers, but Wayland wanted to do more for socialism. News and propaganda were not as important as build-ing a socialist community. In that mood Wayland founded a socialist colony named Ruskin Colony in Dickson County, Tennessee. He brought the paper with him but soon wearied of endless meetings, maintenance, and querulous personalities. Wayland bailed out in 1895, moved to Kansas City, Missouri, founded *Appeal to Reason*, and kept *The Coming Nation* going. His new paper was not an immediate success, finding only eleven thousand subscribers, which drained his bank account.[62]

Wayland made two desperation moves—running cheesy contests and moving in 1897 to Girard, Kansas. Gronlund opined that Kansas was ripe for socialism, so Wayland took a chance on an intensely conservative community of retired merchants who turned out to loathe socialism and him. The citizens of Girard castigated Wayland and his family in the streets, telling them to go home. He won them over when the paper succeeded spectacularly. Wayland got Debs, legendary union organizer Mary "Mother" Jones, and upcoming novelists Jack London and Upton Sinclair to write for *Appeal to Reason*. He hitched the paper in 1900 to Debs and the Social Democratic Party, risking a huge press run of 927,000 for its election-day issue. By the end of 1900 the paper had a paid readership of 141,000; by the end of the decade it exceeded 500,000; some of its single-issue press runs topped 4 million copies. Wayland made it punchy, colloquial, nervy, comical, and fearless, like him, stressing that socialism was not un-American, anti-individualistic, or anti-Christian. He put Fred Warren in charge of *The Coming Nation*, merged the two papers in 1904, and kicked back, letting Warren run the merged paper. Debs told Wayland he saw the friendly face of *Appeal to Reason* wherever he journeyed, taking heart that light was spreading.

Bliss founded the Union Reform Party in 1899, and Debs refused to join, being for socialism-only, not reforms. Berger claimed to know that Gompers was still a socialist, which set off Debs whenever he said it. Berger was smart, grumpy, arrogant, intellectual, steeped in German Social Democracy, and already on his way to building a political base on his local German audience. Debs was his emotional opposite, attracting huge crowds wherever he spoke. Debs said his theme was liberty, and republican values defined his context. But America betrayed both by shamefully exploiting its people and waging an imperial war against Spain. The only war he supported liberated all nations from capitalism. In 1900 the party had to beg him to accept its presidential nomination, exactly as Debs required. He was not a distant leader who battled for position. He was a self-sacrificing hero who needed close contact and affirmation.

Hillquit's band of SLP exiles, calling themselves the Kangaroos, showed up at the convention of March 1900. The ringleaders besides Hillquit were Cleveland printer Max Hayes, California lawyer Job Harriman, and journalist

Algie M. Simons. The Social Democrats despised the SLP, so they distrusted the exiles. If the Kangaroos stuck this long with De Leon, how could they be trustworthy? To Debs and the Berger group, the Kangaroos were obviously a threat to overtake them, being steeped in sectarian warfare and deceit. Many came from the New York Jewish textile unions, a foreign culture to Debs and even to Berger. Debs routinely described De Leon as a scoundrel and did not pretend to welcome the Kangaroos, although he grudgingly accepted the personable Harriman as a running mate. Accusations of bad faith rocketed back and forth through the campaign, scorching everyone except Debs. The Social Democrats said the Kangaroos were "impossibilists" for sneering at immediate demands, and the Kangaroos said the Social Democrats were opportunists for making immediate demands. It was never so bad that union seemed impossible; American Socialists did not assign such disputes to right–center–left categories until the IWW arose in 1905. Meanwhile both sides debated what the name of a merged party should be. The Kangaroos refused to be absorbed; if a merger occurred, there had to be a new name.

Debs campaigned tirelessly, exhorting that the "working class must get rid of the whole brood of masters and exploiters." To choose between the party of large trusts and the party of small capitalists was pointless. Socialism, he said, socializes the capital goods of the nation—the factories, railroads, and banks—not anybody's house or clothing. Generously he praised the early SLP, declaring that he felt "profound obligation, akin to reverence" for the early Socialist immigrants, grateful that they withstood immense abuse. He blasted America's imperial war in the Philippines and ridiculed the Democratic Party for claiming to stand against imperialism and monopoly. Only socialism, Debs contended, would rid capitalist America of its growing appetite for empire; all campaign rhetoric against imperialism and the gold standard was meaningless to the wageworker apart from socialism. He lauded the radical Western Federation of Miners, founded in 1893, praising Ed Boyce and Bill Haywood for building a fierce, scrappy, militant union that showed up the AFL. Debs didn't care that Berger loathed his romanticism on this subject. On many subjects Debs took instruction from Berger. On the Miners he was unabashedly a booster and friend, telling audiences the Miners were the real thing because they waged ferocious battles far outstripping anything in the eastern United States. Wherever he went Debs enthralled huge audiences with passionate, perspiring, two-hour performances. Afterward he could not resist the long evenings of socializing with admirers and old friends that exhausted him. He won ninety-seven thousand votes in the election, nearly three times as many as the SLP—a good beginning, except for the contrast to the enormous crowds he attracted.

He grappled with the difference for the next twenty years, outdrawing candidates who crushed him at the polls.[63]

In January 1901 the party of Debs and Berger merged with the party of Hillquit and Harriman, calling itself the Socialist Party of America. Herron chaired the unity convention and drafted its manifesto. Debs skipped the convention, attending only one over the next twenty years. He never developed a tolerance of party infighting. To the general public the party had a simple message, as conveyed by Debs: Crises are endemic under capitalism because workers are exploited, and the capitalist cannot find adequate markets. Centralized industries eliminate the small entrepreneur and middle class, requiring socialist salvation. Internally, however, the party had bruising fights over good versus bad unionism and whether anarcho-syndicalists belonged in the party. Four ideological tendencies gradually emerged in the party, plus a cultural divide that preceded the ideological factions. The Berger right wing prized its perch in the AFL and its electoral success. The Hillquit center-right regarded itself as the party's ideological mainstream. Debs spoke for the party's populist left that disliked the AFL and scholastic Marxism. Haywood led the ultraleft wing that reveled in direct action and inclined toward anarcho-syndicalism. Berger, Hillquit, and Haywood had national reputations, but Debs was the only national leader the party produced until the coming of Norman Thomas.

The deepest chasm in the early Socialist Party was cultural, setting eastern leaders schooled in European Marxism against radical, old-American farmers, lumberjacks, miners, railroad workers, and clerics who lived in the western states and were usually averse to socialist theory. The eastern leaders and Berger, having fled the dictatorial De Leon, devised a party structure meant to thwart centralization and bureaucracy. Basically the Socialist Party was designed like the U.S. government, making each state a bulwark against federal oppression. The party constitution was an echo of the Continental Congress, granting to each state sole control of all things pertaining to party affairs within the given state. In this sense, the Socialist Party never even tried to become an organized political party that overcame its factional disagreements. The Socialists bequeathed immense organizational problems upon themselves by imposing a federalist structure on a cultural divide that counted some influential racists on both sides.

Berger was the party's most influential bigot, steeped in the proudly racist white supremacy of his family and his native Austrian-Hungarian culture. He was born in 1860 in Nieder-Rehbach, Austria-Hungary, where his parents were conservative innkeepers who lost their business when he was young. Berger was educated at the Gymnasium at Leutschau and the universities of Budapest and

Vienna. In 1878 he immigrated to Bridgeport, Connecticut, to avoid military conscription and in 1881 moved to Milwaukee. He bonded with right-wing German American Social Democrats, taught German in the public school system, and joined the SLP. German-style Social Democracy was already a culture in Milwaukee when Berger got there; he made it more so by running popular newspapers. One was the German language *Wisconsin Vorwaerts* (Forward), which he carried successively from the SLP to the People's Party, the Social Democracy of America, and the Socialist Party. Another was a mainstay of the Socialist Party, the *Social Democratic Herald*, which Berger edited from 1901 to 1913. Another was the official paper of the local and state labor federations, the *Milwaukee Leader*, which Berger edited from 1911 to 1929.

Many who disliked Berger for his bullying arrogance stressed that he was highly able and accomplished. Hillquit said Berger was "sublimely egotistic" without being conceited or offensive. Many quietly demurred on conceited and offensive; Debs was one of them, knowing what the party owed to Berger. In 1904 Berger started running for Congress. His name recognition, labor movement support, strong opinions, abundant self-confidence, and prodigious energy made him a major political player in Milwaukee. In 1910 he won Wisconsin's Fifth Congressional District seat, becoming the first Socialist to serve in the U.S. Congress. Berger prized his high standing in the AFL and pointed to himself as the model of how American Socialists should operate. He said that major industries should be socialized, the U.S. Senate should be abolished as an affront to democracy, and socialism was sure to be achieved first in the most advanced nations. He wore the name sewer socialist proudly, assuring audiences that powerful union movements allied with socialism would achieve socialism, beginning with municipal sewers. Berger and his wife, Meta Schlichting Berger, spoke only German in their home and were deeply attached to German culture and socialism. He and Hillquit were allies most of the time in the Socialist Party—to many party members, Old Guard referred to Berger, Hillquit, their followers, and a handful of party officials—but Hillquit was suave and diplomatic, better at dealing with the party's swirl of nationalities, cultures, and ideologies. Hillquit lost U.S. congressional races in 1906 and 1908, never winning the congressional prize that Berger won five times. Hillquit was not viscerally bigoted like Berger, but both of them stooped to AFL racism to curry favor with the AFL.[64]

Berger, Hillquit, and Debs realized that workers alone could not achieve socialism. It was pointless to run for office if Socialists did not try to win friends and allies outside the labor movement. Debs blistered Berger for kowtowing to Gompers and begged Hillquit to stop placating Gompers. But Debs and

Hillquit were allies on most issues, especially after 1912, when they formed a genuine friendship. Both were advocates of industrial unionism and opponents of violence and industrial sabotage. Both were resolutely committed to political activism and running candidates for election. Both opposed the dual unionist tactic of creating a union or political organization within or parallel to an existing union; meanwhile the party debated what counted as dual unionism. To Gompers, socialism was dual. The crucial difference between Debs and the Old Guard Socialists was that Debs loved the western radicals and shared their feelings. He came to socialism after the government smashed his industrial union and threw him in jail. He spoke a radical Protestant rhetoric of freedom that did not sound like Marxism. He sympathized with the western radicals who told him they distrusted Hillquit and couldn't stand doctrinal debates.

The unions in the West chafed at being ignored by the AFL. In 1898 they banded together to form the Western Labor Union, federating the unions west of the Mississippi River. The Western Federation of Miners was the leading player in this drama. In 1902 Debs gave a fiery address at the Western Labor Union convention that rolled together the grievances and occasional exaggerations of western unionists against the AFL. He blasted Gompers for hobnobbing with industrialists in the National Civic Federation who pretended to care about workers. He tried to recall a single instance in which the AFL ever supported the western miners and couldn't think of one, notwithstanding that the western miners supported AFL unions. Debs entreated the delegates to change their name to the American Labor Union, come out for socialism, and campaign for industrial unionism. They adopted these proposals with roaring approval, and the Socialist Party leaders cringed with embarrassment. The Old Guard was building a solid base of power in the AFL. Berger and Fred Heath controlled the Central Labor Union of Milwaukee; Hillquit worked for Jewish textile unions and other craft unions as an attorney and advisor; Hayes and Barnes played prominent roles in the printing and cigar-making unions. Why antagonize their allies in the nation's only powerful union federation? Why provoke Gompers on what he hated most, dual unionism? Debs replied that he was not against the AFL; he was only against the way it operated. In this case, the AFL had no right to wail about dual unionism because it did nothing for western workers. Debs exaggerated the negligence of the AFL and, especially, Gompers's antipathy for the western miners, but to him there were worse things than exaggeration and dual unionism.[65]

The Socialist Party grew impressively in Iowa, Ohio, Kansas, the Dakotas, and Minnesota, buoyed by Debs's charisma and a surge of Populist converts. By 1904 the party had twenty-five thousand members, all pledged to the view that the class struggle is the basic fact of capitalist society. The party convened on May Day in Chicago. Debs took his usual pass at declining the nomination for president, and printer Ben Hanford was selected as his running mate. Hanford created the mythical figure Jimmie Higgins, a rank and filer who swept the meeting halls, passed out leaflets, sold subscriptions and tickets, was blacklisted for his job, and got beaten on picket lines. The platform featured Debs's claim that only the Socialist Party defended the founding American commitment to liberty and self-government, espousing the only program "by which the liberty of the individual may become a fact." Herron gave a nominating speech for Debs that repeated what he said when he nominated Debs in 1900: He and Debs embraced the party's class-based platform without aiming only at workers. The goal of the movement was to liberate all human beings on earth. Debs told the convention the Republican Party was too dominant not to be totally corrupt, the Democratic Party was dying and bankrupt, and if Lincoln and Jefferson were alive "they would be delegates to this convention." He said it constantly on the campaign trail, quadrupling his vote tally with four hundred thousand votes, including more than ten thousand each in thirteen states.[66]

Wayland told readers that people become socialists to realize an ideal, not because they have a certain kind of job. Debs said that was exactly right. He loved the reunions that occurred every week on the road, constantly delighting former railroad workers when it turned out that he remembered their names. He had a similar reunion with Anthony in Rochester, New York, and grieved at her distress. Anthony despaired that suffrage was not in sight after fifty years of struggling for it. Debs told campaign crowds that the working class "must be emancipated by the working class," society "must be reconstructed by the working class," women must be uplifted "by the working class," the working class "must be employed by the working class," the fruits of labor "must be enjoyed by the working class," and war "must be ended by the working class." Sometimes Kate Debs told Debs that one of his rhetorical flights soared into stupidity; usually he reconsidered and agreed. On the campaign trail he wrote a sentimental letter to her from the Pittsburgh hotel at which they spent their wedding night. Debs said she was more beautiful and precious to him than ever, and he was grateful not to have lost her as a friend and comrade. When the campaign ended he collapsed into bed for a week. Debs always risked ruining his health permanently, but his exhaustion in 1904 was distinctive for emotional reasons; the party's war over the AFL tormented him.[67]

He wrote the two longest pieces he ever wrote for *Appeal to Reason*, which became pamphlets titled *The American Movement* and *Unionism and Socialism*. Debs said the centuries past were a parade of tyranny and exploitation, the nineteenth century caught a glimpse of liberation from the rule of despots and parasites, and the twentieth century was destined to be "the century of humanity." He told an optimistic story that began with Robert Owen and Charles Fourier and carried into the United States through the Transcendentalists, Albert Brisbane, and Horace Greeley. He sprinkled his account with a nod to Marx and quotes from Ely and Hillquit, working up to the Knights of Labor, the SLP, the first May Day, and the Haymarket tragedy. Debs painted the Knights in heroic colors and skipped over the AFL, not crediting its role in the first May Day. He lingered over the smashing of the ARU and the lessons it taught him, which led to the Socialist Party. In barely a few years, he boasted, the Socialist Party became a player in almost every state and territory of the nation. It struggled for the freedom of all humanity, not just the labor movement, and it was surging: "Its members are filled with enthusiasm and working with an energy born of the throb and thrill of revolution. The party has a press supporting it that extends from sea to sea, and is as vigilant and tireless in its labors as it is steadfast and true to the party principles."[68]

That was the buoyant, hopeful, political story. Meanwhile the labor movement story was more troubling. Debs began with early capitalism, which wrested from workers the ownership of their tools. Technological advances swelled the size of factories and the power of corporations. Workers were helpless as individuals, so they founded local craft unions for protection. Local unions were pitifully overmatched, so they merged to form national craft unions. Employers tried to crush the craft unions, which led to the founding of trade unions, which caused employers to bargain with the craft unions. Debs leaned on Ely to trace the recent history, recycling Ely's points that unions are civilizing forces that cultivate personal virtues and strengthen communities. Sharper than Ely, he said that late capitalism bought off the skilled workers to prevent the craft unions from organizing the unskilled trades. Then it enlisted the government to smash all attempts to form industrial unions. Debs observed ruefully that trade union leaders were slow to grasp their actual role in this story but "fresh object lessons are prepared for them every day." He refused to believe that AFL leaders would continue to betray the poor and vulnerable, insisting that betrayal was precisely the issue. Debs cited a very long quote from Herron for support. On the one hand, Herron allowed, trade unionists benefited one class of workers by organizing "on the firing line of the class struggle." On the other hand, trade unionism "is by no means the solution of the workers' problem, nor is it the goal of the labor struggle. It is merely a capitalist line of defense within the capitalist system. Its existence and its struggles are necessitated only by the existence and predatory nature of capitalism."[69]

Debs said the same thing, pressing hard on corruption and shame. It was shameful to abandon most of the working class and indefensible that working-class children had to drop out of school to take lousy jobs to support their families: "What a picture! Yet so common that the multitude do not see it." He asked unionists to think about the women in their lives, who could not vote, had no voice, and were forced to bear silent witness to their "legally ordained inferiority." Socialism would sweep all of that away, without losing tender Victorian feelings about femininity: "In Socialism, woman would stand forth the equal of man—all the avenues would be open to her and she would naturally find her fitting place and rise from the low plane of menial servility to the dignity of ideal womanhood." The entire working class had to unite to abolish wage slavery, creating a revolutionary union that bonded with the Socialist Party: "Cooperative industry in which all shall work together in harmony as the basis of a new social order, a higher civilization, a real republic!"[70]

Hayes announced at the AFL convention of 1904 that AFL Socialists would no longer try to win control of the unions. He said it two years after Socialist resolutions were narrowly defeated at the AFL convention and a year after Gompers taunted the Socialists at the November 1903 convention: "Economically you are unsound, socially you are wrong, industrially you are an impossibility." Hayes declared in 1904 that the Socialist Party existed to run for political offices, not to capture the AFL. That did not mean that he folded on the AFL Socialist issue. Hayes kept running against Gompers, offering a Socialist alternative that tried to expand the Socialist wing of the AFL. But to Debs, Hayes's peacemaking retreat confirmed that striving for power within the AFL was pointless and self-defeating for Socialists. In December 1904 Thomas Hagerty, a former Catholic priest with whom Debs toured the West in 1902, and William Trautmann, who edited the Brewery Workers journal, pitched an idea to Debs that he loved: Create a radical rival to the AFL that competed with it across the nation. If AFL Socialists sought to make nice with Gompers, the time had come to smash the taboo on dual unionism. Haywood, Hagerty, Trautmann, and Mother Jones convened a group in January 1905 to launch the IWW.[71]

The founding convention took place on June 27, 1905, in Chicago. It was studded with radical stars and short on actual unions. Debs, Haywood, De Leon, Jones, *International Socialist Review* editor Simons, and Lucy Parsons furnished star power; the only major union represented was the twenty-seven-thousand-member Western Federation of Miners; and the press howled that this was the most ridiculous confection of radicalisms ever assembled. How could the socialist Debs, syndicalist Haywood, sectarian De Leon, trade union socialist Jones, and anarchist Parsons agree about anything? Debs pleaded for unity in his speech to the convention, conceding the problem. De Leon wrote the organizational platform, exactly as Berger feared, calling workers to organize as a class and seize the means of production. Major organs of the Socialist Party howled at the outrageous spectacle of Debs and Simons joining forces with De Leon and Parsons; the IWW was a very bad thing, not merely an absurd thing. Hayes's Cleveland *Citizen,* the New York *Forward,* and the *Social Democratic Herald* said it vehemently. Debs worked up to boiling anger as the condemnations piled up; then Berger admonished Debs to return to the labor movement and the Socialist Party, and Debs broke his silence.

It galled him that Berger and Hillquit treated dual unionism as the worst of all sins, scorning the dream of One Big Union. Debs chastised Berger for making his paper "the official organ and special champion" of the AFL, as though belonging to it was "a condition of membership in the Socialist Party." He said the Berger socialists knew very well that the AFL was utterly rotten. Yet it was "good enough for them, in fact just what they want, for a rotten labor movement is their salvation." The Berger types liked their perches in the AFL and their cheap superiority in it. They posed as Socialists without doing anything for socialism, making a nice living off it. Debs claimed that Berger and Heath had no trade and never worked for a wage for a day of their lives, forgetting that Berger and Heath had longer records of wage earning than he did. Berger had offended him by charging that Debs deserted the labor movement and the Socialist Party; Debs struck back: "I have simply joined a labor union that suits me. That's all." He assured *Social Democratic Herald* readers that the IWW would not split the labor movement; Berger alarmism on this topic was "nothing short of idiotic."[72]

Heath replied that every union, including the ARU, had some bad characters. The polemics about rottenness were off-kilter, especially from a Socialist leader who embraced a snake and an anarchist—De Leon and Parsons. Heath charged that Debs betrayed the upright unionists he served for decades. Back-and-forth ensued about corruption, personal foibles, and who was tolerable. Debs said most of the Socialist Party animus against the SLP had no basis besides personal animus against De Leon. He didn't have to like De Leon to work with him in the IWW. For a while Berger and Hillquit treated Debs and Haywood as outcasts, but the party needed Debs more than he needed the party. Debs wasn't like Berger and Hillquit in caring about where he stood in the party; in 1906 he put it quotably at Turner Hall in Detroit: "I am no labor leader. I don't want you to follow me, or anyone else. If you are looking for a Moses to lead you out of this capitalist wilderness, you will stay right where you are. I would not lead you into the promised land if I could, because if I could lead you in someone else could lead you out. You must use your heads as well as your hands and get yourselves out of your present condition."[73]

The prairie Socialists trusted him all the more for saying it. They had fiery leaders in North Dakota (Arthur Le Sueur) and Oklahoma (Tad Cumbie) who loved Debs and cheered his strident attacks on the AFL. Cumbie flaunted his radicalism, always wearing a flaming red shirt at party conventions. His Oklahoma comrades were angry, dirt poor, and dispossessed—virtual serfs toiling on tenant farms. Some were blacklisted former ARU workers. Oklahoma gave proletarians to the party despite lacking a working class in the Marxian sense. Berger likened them to the ancient Hebrews who traveled with bundles of hay to avoid sleeping on spots contaminated by Gentiles. Cumbie pinned a thicket of hay to his red shirt in reply. Oscar Ameringer, a Bavarian immigrant steeped in the SPD who joined the Socialist Party in 1905 and drifted to Oklahoma to run its state organization, vividly described what drew him to the center of the old Populist heartland: "These people were not wops and bohunks. They were not Jewish needle slaves, escaped from the ghettos and pogroms of Czarist Russia and Poland. Their forefathers had been starved, driven, shipped and sold over here long before and shortly after the Revolution. They were more American than the population of any present-day New England town. They were Washington's ragged, starving, shivering army at Valley Forge, pushed ever westward by beneficiaries of the Revolution. They had followed on the heels of the Cherokees, Choctaws, Chickasaws, Creeks, and Seminoles, like the stragglers of ragged armies. Always hoping that somewhere in their America there would be a piece of dirt for them."[74]

CHRISTIAN SOCIALISM IN THE SOCIALIST PARTY

Christian socialists immortalized the Moses statement and urged the party to welcome religious people. They reached middle-class audiences that were otherwise out of reach to the party and won mayoral elections. They came from every region and background and were thus harder to categorize than the Berger, Hillquit, Debs, and Haywood camps. Herron was famous when the party was founded, Bliss recruited many to join without himself joining, and J. Stitt Wilson led a band of "Social Crusade" evangelists featuring Herron, William H. Wise, William T. Brown, and James H. Hollingsworth. Congregational cleric Carl Thompson was a party bigwig recruited by Berger in Milwaukee, and Christian socialist Walter Thomas Mills ran the socialist school in Girard, Kansas, that trained a generation of socialist leaders. Other prominent Christian socialists included Edward Ellis Carr, Lewis Duncan,

George Lunn, Kate Richards O'Hare, George W. Slater, and George W. Woodbey. All were committed to establishing Christian socialism inside and outside the party, overcoming a spectacular controversy over Herron's divorce and remarriage in 1901.

Christian socialists rode Herron's meteoric career and fame until he flamed out. Then they founded a paper and organization, vowing not to be derailed by Herron's scandalous divorce. Carr ministered at a People's Church in Danville, Illinois, and founded *The Christian Socialist* in 1903. He recruited Wilson and Thompson to help run the magazine, which set Wilson on his way to winning the mayoralty of Berkeley, California—one of fifty Socialists to win mayoral posts during the party's pre–World War I boom. *The Christian Socialist* offered eight pages of commentary, news, and propaganda biweekly. It reached two thousand clerical subscribers by 1909 and peaked at twenty thousand during World War I. Carr boosted circulation by publishing special issues on specific denominations, sending complimentary copies to all clergy of the featured denomination. The Baptist issue had articles by Rauschenbusch and Leighton Williams, Carr broke ecumenical ground by publishing a Roman Catholic issue, and there was a temperance issue featuring Frances Willard.

The paper's success yielded a call for a Christian socialist organization allied with the Socialist Party. Carr and Wilson organized the founding convention of the Christian Socialist Fellowship (CSF) in 1906 in Louisville, which vowed "to show that Socialism is the necessary economic expression of the Christian life, to end the class struggle by establishing industrial democracy and to hasten the reign of justice and brotherhood upon earth." Carr, Thompson, Wilson, and lay intellectual Rufus W. Weeks were its ringleaders, behind Bliss, who argued that Christian socialism was not a Christian version of socialism because there is no such thing. Socialism is a political force for a transformation of the economy. It does not change when Christians support it, although Christians hold special reasons for supporting it, especially the desire to follow the way of Jesus.[75]

The CSF sought to win Christians to socialism without claiming that the church should be socialist. Bliss said it pointedly at the founding convention: "I do not ask that the Church declare for a Socialist program or for a Socialist party. That is a small affair. It is not the function of the Church to adopt programs or endorse parties. I simply ask that the Church dare to preach and to live her own Gospel, and be true to her own Christ." He dreamed that socialists would someday outnumber Republicans and Democrats at diocesan conventions, but Bliss did not want any diocese to endorse any party.[76]

Bliss reasoned that he would bring more Christians into socialism if he declined to join the party. The CSF started strong, creating local chapters across the nation and holding a national convention in 1907 in Chicago at which Jane Addams headed the speaker lineup. The following year the convention in New York exceeded three thousand participants. Debs, Hillquit, Spargo, and Reform Rabbi Stephen Wise congratulated the CSF for existing and thriving. Socialist Episcopal bishop Franklin S. Spalding sent a congratulatory telegram from Utah. Debs, surveying the crowd, observed that Christian socialism had come remarkably far, remarkably fast: "I am glad I can call you ministers of the Man of Galilee my comrades, for it isn't long ago that I felt a great prejudice against you as a class."[77]

Bliss spoke constantly for the CSF and served on its executive committee. He tried to keep religious humanists out of the CSF, pleading that a nominally Christian organization would be too lukewarm to change anything, but lost the vote at the founding convention. For three years Bliss and the CSF haggled over the member pledge, especially its reference to the "Social Message of Jesus," which religious humanists opposed. Finally the group opted for two kinds of membership, pro-Jesus and no-Jesus. By 1909 Bliss began to teeter on whether he should join the party. He bridled when socialists told him that Christian socialists were milk-and-water types, because Bliss regarded himself as a fire-and-iron type. He regretted that the party refused to ally with reform groups but refused to believe this issue had been settled, touting the British Labour Party as his model. In November 1911 Bliss announced that he was joining the party, boasting to Debs that he introduced more nonsocialists to socialism than Debs.[78]

Bliss and Scudder got their red cards together, capping a difficult period for Scudder. In 1896 she instigated a faculty protest against Wellesley's acceptance of tainted money from Standard Oil and nearly got fired. Lloyd saved Scudder's job by persuading her to back down, counseling that self-righteous career martyrdom does not build movements. Five years later Scudder had a devastating breakdown that disabled her for four years, largely the result of nervous exhaustion. She pulled back from activism, with guilty regret. She cultivated new interests in the saints, especially Francis of Assisi and Catherine of Siena. She chafed at having to work for a salary, being criticized for propagandizing in class and lacking a focus.

Later she recalled, "I hated my salary." Scudder hated that she needed the money and that needing it kept her from speaking out. She studied for a year in Italy and France to earn a doctorate, never wrote the dissertation, came back to it several years later to qualify for a promotion but quit in frustration: "I was indifferent to rummaging about in literary byways in pursuit of unimportant information." She told herself to count her blessings and lighten up but frustration mounted. She wrote to Rauschenbusch: "Do you speak out to your students? I can't to mine." Wellesley had canceled her best course even though she strained not to propagandize. On the other hand, Scudder admonished Rauschenbusch that if she could join the Socialist Party despite all her problems, he had no excuse for declining. She said he should get over his qualms about anti-Christian socialists: "I never regret having joined the Socialist Party. I am sure that it is immensely important for people of our type to be *within* the political movement, both in order to preserve it so far as possible from that hard dogmatism of which you speak (& it *can* be preserved if sufficient numbers of persons with religious tradition get into it) *and* to vindicate the honor of Christianity."[79]

People of their type had to join the party if it was to overcome its desolate dogmatism and materialism. Scudder said her membership counted for little but Rauschenbusch joining would be a game-changer: "Nothing but party-membership convinces these men that one is in earnest. I covet you for the party! It would draw many, and we could get a political socialism of a better type. After all, the thing has got to get out into the political arena, you know. It can't stay a tendency or a theory." Waiting for socialists to get more decent was not defensible; Christian socialists had to take the initiative.[80]

She added that Rauschenbusch also needed very much to stop bashing Catholicism. It really was bigotry, even if he thought he was scoring points for democracy and progressivism: "You make me cross, in *Christianity and the Social Crisis*, when you inveigh against priestcraft and the ecclesiastical animus." Catholicism was wiser and more biblical than he imagined: "All heresies mean partial emphases, and I hate to have you a heretic. Christianity in all its synthetic glory of the mystical and the social, blended in the sacramental, is none too big for us."[81]

Scudder believed that even the Vatican would someday realize that Catholic socialism is the hope of the world. Christianity had to be reinterpreted along Marxian lines much as Thomas Aquinas reinterpreted Catholic teaching via Aristotle. She reasoned that the Catholic and Anglican churches were better suited for it than the Protestant churches. Every Protestant church was individualistic, but the high sacramental churches were holistic and solidaristic. Moreover, the game of teasing out the true essence of Christianity was a liberal Protestant enterprise, always yielding a shrunken theology. Scudder despaired of kernel-and-husk strategies: "Must we not rather find that distinctive strength in the help that religion affords our whole thinking and feeling being to relate itself to the eternal?"[82]

In 1912 she had two experiences of liberating solidarity. One was the "bread and roses" strike in Lawrence, Massachusetts, where she gave a strong prounion speech, now prepared to accept the inevitable condemnations of Wellesley trustees and alums. The second was the publication of her book *Socialism and Character*. Scudder bade farewell to "timid platitudes concerning brotherhood and democracy," calling all Christians, socialists, and Christian socialists to the hard work of "moral preparation for a New Order." Human nature had to change; thus she was not cowed by objections about human nature. She was a "class-conscious, revolutionary socialist" who believed that socialism would create better human beings. Ruskin asked whether it was possible for manufacturers to care about the manufacture of good souls and whether socialism was the system for making it happen. *Socialism and Character* said these were the right questions, and the answer to both was yes.[83]

Moral idealism was indispensable and not enough. Scudder said Dickens and Hugo were long on moral idealism but believed in it too much. Carlyle and Ruskin had a similar idealism, but the democratic revolution left them looking quaint. Tolstoy was greater than Ruskin but both preached a reductionist salvation of simplifying wants, returning to manual labor, and being good. Maurice grasped why socialism mattered but had only a trickle of a legacy, unlike Marx, the greatest theorist of socialism. Scudder was a Marxian on the class struggle, the labor theory of value, and socializing the means of production. She argued that Marx was right about bourgeois morality but wrong to deride moral reason as a whole. In addition, Marx had good reasons to deride Christian socialism, which did not mean that Christianity could not be revolutionary. She cited Rauschenbusch to make the point, claiming he opposed the doctrine of the class struggle "in horror," apparently forgetting the last chapter of *Christianity and the Social Crisis*. Scudder said the class struggle idea is "dangerous and misleading" in its cruder forms *and* utterly indispensable in its Marxian sense. Socialism is essentially a movement of the downtrodden working class to remake the world.[84]

The time had come for all people of good will to join the socialist movement, the first movement in history "to look beyond its own corporate aim," being truly universal in its spirit and aims. Scudder explained that socialism struggles even for the good of its enemies, caring about everyone. *New Republic* founder Herbert Croly worried that socialism was hostile to the national principle; Scudder replied that socialists were perfectly capable of being faithful to their nation while holding to a higher loyalty. To exalt the good of humanity over patriotic loyalty is exactly right. At the same time, "patriotism has deep roots, and socialists are men." American nationalists had nothing to fear from the rise of socialism.[85]

She touted the affinity between the kingdom of God and socialism. Christianity teaches that the kingdom of God cannot be fully realized in history, and Christians are called to struggle for a redeemed social order that always lies beyond their horizon. Socialism, Scudder noted, has a similar here-yet-not-here eschatology. A socialist order cannot be built without extensive govern-ment action, yet socialist theory abounds in images of stateless utopias. The deepest political impulse of the socialist imagination is the anarchist dream of a transformed state that votes itself out of existence. When the revolution comes, instinctive harmony will control all human relations, and governments will not be needed. She believed it and not: "We can hardly evoke the picture without a shrug and a sigh. But the philosophical anarchist can. It is conceivable that he reads to a greater depth than we the ultimate hope in the Mind of Jesus."[86]

"I suppose it was a queer book," she later recalled. "I am sure it was premature." *Socialism and Character* won nowhere near the acclaim of Rauschenbusch's book of the same year, *Christianizing the Social Order* (1912). Then both books suddenly became very dated. Scudder and Bliss felt the hey-day ending when Europe plunged into war. They took the usual social gospel view of the war, plugging against intervention until the United States inter-vened, although Scudder confessed to feeling "something like relief when the great explosion came." At least the conceits of the ruling class were finally dis-credited. Scudder faulted her pacifist friends for preaching that war was the ultimate evil. Until 1917 she stressed that capitalist greed and imperialism caused the war; then she accepted Wilson's reasons for intervening. Scudder believed in chivalry as deeply as she believed in anything. The world is a battle-field, and the weak must be defended against their oppressors. On occasion she said the Bhagavad Gita trumped Tolstoy and the Sermon on the Mount on the spirituality of armed resistance.[87]

Christian socialism contributed greatly to the geographic diffusion of the Socialist Party and was the party's only conduit to middle-class audiences aside from the intellectuals who wrote for middle-class magazines. The party's great-est voting strength lay west of the Mississippi River among miners, tenant farm-ers, and lumberjacks. Hillquit felt the anomaly of living in the one place—New York City—where Socialist intellectuals existed; he remarked with slight exag-geration that the rest of the party was "overwhelmingly proletarian." Even in New York State the party's greatest strength was upstate. Schenectady, New York, was a Socialist stronghold, boasting a Christian socialist mayor and a socialist state assembly representative. Before 1918 the states with the highest percentages of socialist voters were Oklahoma, Nevada, Montana, Washington, California, Idaho, Florida, Arizona, Wisconsin, and Texas. The Texas party had roots in the most radical wing of the Populist movement and published a flam-ing, millenarian, Christian socialist paper, *The Rebel*. These states turned out strong for Debs in 1908 and 1912. Oklahoma—not even a state until 1907—had the strongest party organization, boasting 12,000 members, 960 locals, and 38,000 *Appeal to Reason* subscribers. Berger loathed *Appeal to Reason* as an unworthy lowball rival, but to its many readers the radical, fearless, religion-friendly, very American *Appeal to Reason* was the socialist Bible and tame by comparison to the *Rebel*.[88]

THE HERRON PHENOMENON

Bliss believed the crucial difference between Herron and him was that he loved and served the Church, a difference that Christian socialists needed to build on if they hoped to persuade the churches. He believed it long before Herron wrecked his career in the Congregational Church and the United States. Herron was the wild man of the social gospel, a preacher of socialist salvation who did not bother with policies or ideology. His hero, besides Jesus, was a Romantic spinner of inspiring words, spoken and written: Giuseppe Mazzini. Every Herron lecture was a revival sermon, a familiar genre to the Midwest audiences that he dazzled in the years that Populism raged through the West and the call for free silver reverberated in presidential elections. Thus he was a model for Debs before he bonded with Debs.

Herron was born into a poor and devout Scottish American Congregational family in Montezuma, Indiana, in 1862. He had little formal education, working in his youth as a compositor apprenticed to a printer. His father taught him to revere the Bible, hate unrighteousness, and think constantly of God. Herron later recalled that he had no childhood because the Kingdom of God and its righteousness pervaded his every waking moment. John Wesley and Boston abolitionist senator Charles Sumner were his imaginary playmates "in the company of God, with a daily deepening sense of a divine call which sooner or later I must obey."[89]

His only formal education lasted three years, in the preparatory department at Ripon College in Wisconsin. Herron devoured books on economics, religion, and philosophy, especially by Hegel, Maurice, Rudolf Lotze, and, above all, Mazzini, whose intense moral religion transfixed him. Mazzini was a Christ figure to Herron, the socialist prophet from Genoa who unified Italy, clashed with Marx in the First International, opposed Marx on idealistic and radical republican grounds, and spearheaded the Italian revolution. These influences carried Herron into the Congregational ministry, the only vocation he considered, in 1883, the same year he married Mary Everhard. In the mid-1880s he read Ely, Gladden, and Gronlund, befriended social gospel leader Josiah

Strong, and preached intense sermons on personal and social religion. To Herron, the cross of Jesus was the center of Christianity and not a vehicle of substitutionary atonement. It was the way of sacrificial suffering through which the world is saved.

He made a splash in 1890 with a speech in Minneapolis titled "The Message of Jesus to Men of Wealth." Herron said the message of Jesus to all people, but especially to the rich, is that self-sacrifice is the law of life. Jesus preached and showed that giving one's life for others, and nothing less, is saving. If the rich men of America were to become true followers of Jesus, devoting themselves to the hungry and providing work for the jobless, the kingdom of God would come to America. Lyman Abbott published the sermon in the *Christian Union*, a pamphlet version got wide circulation, and Herron received many ministerial offers from congregations. He chose First Congregational Church of Burlington, Iowa, where he was installed in December 1891. There he became a national phenomenon in eighteen months, publishing books that recycled his sensational sermons and road lectures: *The Larger Christ* (1891), *The Call of the Cross* (1892), and *A Plea for the Gospel* (1892).[90]

Herron burned with charismatic evangelical rage at the corruption of the age. Every Herron sermon condemned the atheism and social anarchy of capitalism in colorful phrases. Many Herron sermons proclaimed that a revolution was coming; the question was whether it would be saving or destructive. He anticipated what came to be called political theology, including its fundamental insight that all forms of political thinking rest on theological claims. Herron told his audiences that every social system is based on theological concepts. The wellsprings of every human virtue flow from God into human beings through their conceptions of the divine character. The character of human society approximates how human beings conceive the character of God: "A selfish God on the throne of human thought, existing, creating, redeeming for his own glory, means an earthly civilization of 'organized selfishness.'" Nothing, he said, causes more evil than bad theology. The classical idea of God as a self-glorifying monarch is Satanic, "for it is the ground of the most arrogant falsehoods, and subtlest and cruelest forms of wickedness, that dominate society." To fathom anything about the God of Jesus Christ, one must look to Jesus humbling himself, resisting worldly temptations, suffering, preaching the kingdom of God, and dying on a cross: "The cross is the expression of self-giving as the glory of God's being. All God is and has he gives. He creates and redeems to glorify others than himself."[91]

Herron did not say he learned his theology of divine suffering from Maurice, because he hardly ever cited theologians, and he held the Church in minimum low regard. But his stump speaking overflowed with theopassionism, a recent novelty in theology, and the claim that all institutions must be Christianized: "To be fully saved is to be a Christ-man instead of a self-sufficient man; a man in whom the Incarnation is continued, through whom Christ can still be the Savior of the world, who beseeches men in Christ's stead to be reconciled to God." God draws all human beings to God's self through the cross, the principle of universal salvation and harmony, and God's design for the world is social, not merely for individuals. Society is a subject of redemption. Human beings, he said, hold no rights in their selves or for their things that Christ lacked in his body. Anything that would have been wrong for Jesus is wrong in the stock exchange, a bank, a corporation, a church, or a textbook on political economics. We must not accept or admire things that we would be repelled to find in Jesus. The cross of Jesus "is the sign that Christendom has only begun to interpret; the sign which is to heal the world's sin-smitten civilizations." Everything that human beings prize "must be forever nailed on that cross, sacrificed to the same end that Christ was there sacrificed."[92]

Herron meant *everything*, including the state. He excoriated people who professed religion in their private lives while acting as atheists in their public lives. Political atheism, he warned, leads straight to political anarchy. The state is more divine than the church and is no less compelled to seek and serve the righteousness of God. Majorities are no substitute for God, for majorities can be as vicious and tyrannical as kings. Herron said it categorically: "Except the state believe on Christ it cannot be saved any more than a man." The state must be converted to righteousness to be an instrument for good. He did not worry how that sounded to non-Christians, and he demurred only slightly about latter-day Puritan theocracy, explaining that the state did not need to brandish a theology. What matters is to act like Jesus. It would be disgusting to read in the gospels that Jesus protected the rich, harmed the poor, or ran a saloon. Herron said one judges the state differently if one takes the religion of Jesus seriously. It seemed jarring to say so only because Gilded Age America was so corrupt.[93]

The early Herron blasted bad theology without saying much about politics. Every sermon text became the occasion to decry how Christianity distorts the prophetic religion of Jesus into something grotesque and anti-Christian. Paul had no concept of the cross as something reserved for Jesus; it was the church that tortured this idea out of Paul's letters. Objective atonement theory is even worse: "For God to punish Christ for our sins would be infinite wickedness, and would not make us a whit the better." Orthodoxy turns God into the problem, making God a monster to be appeased, which does nothing to eliminate sin. Jesus did not come to defend us from God. It is *God* who loves radically and saves, "a love that needs no bribing, nor buying." Jesus suffered for the same reason he expounded ethical teaching: To bring all human beings and the world to God, realizing in all humanity the goodness of God, making humanity and the world the bearers of God's righteousness. But organized Christianity, Herron said, was a conspiracy against this objective.[94]

His preaching centered forcefully on Jesus, the cross, and personal righteousness. Herron lit up the social gospel circuit like no one else, growing the movement wherever he went. Josiah Strong, already slightly skittish about where this was heading, said Herron spoke with the "intense earnestness" of a Hebrew prophet, although no one was obliged "to indorse every position" he expounded. Herron rapidly outgrew his congregation, doused with speaking invitations. One of his Burlington parishioners, Elizabeth Rand, solved his job problem in 1893 by endowing a chair for him in Applied Christianity at Iowa College in Grinnell, Iowa—a Congregational school renamed Grinnell College in 1909. Rand moved to Grinnell in the company of her daughter Carrie Rand, who was appointed principal of women. Herron's ministry went wildly national as soon as he got to Grinnell. George Gates, another Christian socialist neo-abolitionist inspired by Mazzini, was president of the college and a strong supporter of Herron. Herron taught his personal canon—Hegel, Maurice, Ruskin, Mazzini, Gronlund, Gladden, Ely, and Herron—to overflow classes and streams of visitors. He and Gates published a weekly paper, *The Kingdom,* which ran for five years until the American Book Company won a lawsuit against Gates for criticizing its monopoly of school textbooks.[95]

On the platform Herron had a hypnotic intensity that riveted audiences. His message was a social gospel version of the sermon that sparked the two Great Awakenings: Americans have fallen into corruption. In 1894 his sensational spring tour drew enormous crowds at the University of Michigan, Indiana University, Princeton University, and Union Theological Seminary. Heron told them, "I am haunted continually with the vision of the living Jesus weeping over our majestic temples of worship, our halls of theology, our conventions of religion, as though he were again in the sacred sorrow of that weeping over Jerusalem, his heart again broken because only the remnant may receive the mission which the institution rejects." Sometimes he said it would be a great privilege for him to offend people and suffer for it like Jesus. Herron wept for the church while setting off controversies about his theology, politics, and celebrity. Sometimes the controversy broke out before he left the platform. He gave a commencement speech at the University of Nebraska that the state governor promptly excoriated as an anarchist outrage. Herron never learned to shuck off the anarchist accusation. He was sensitive, tenderhearted, and vain; it offended him when critics failed to perceive his righteousness. He could be scathing in reply, especially after he got more political.[96]

He grew more socialist and political through the 1890s. In *The New Redemption* (1893), which coincided with his move to Grinnell, Herron reprised his stock themes about righteousness and sacrifice, now with a stronger revolutionary flair, describing revolutions as "the impulses of God moving in tides of fire through the life of man." It is spiritually wrong to resist a revolution, he said, for God's wild dissatisfaction with every regnant order is the life force of every revolution. The truly dangerous people are those who claim that selfishness and injustice cannot be set right.[97]

Every Herron book insisted that selfishness is always spiritually and socially destructive. Competition is anarchy, not law—the toxic evil of a deformed civilization. He allowed that the old passion for liberty in religion and politics accomplished "a great work," but industrial capitalism changed what mattered, exactly as Mazzini said. In the crisis of modern society, moral duty trumped everything else, including political rights: "The selfishness that poisons every noble passion, when it rules rather than serves, has transformed the liberty of our fathers into the most intolerable despotism the world has ever suffered." To focus merely on the rights of labor versus the rights of capital is superficial. The state must become Christian. The state is *the* organism of society, so every revolution aims at the state and is a crisis for it. Herron declared: "The state must be redeemed from the worship of property and from commercial theories of government. It can prove its right to be only by procuring a greater measure of social justice and giving a larger recognition to the sacredness of man."[98]

Domesticated American preachers said that Jesus was not a political economist, and his teaching does not apply to matters of state. Herron countered that the Sermon on the Mount is nothing less than a prescription of how we should live and how society should be organized. To dismiss the teaching of Jesus in this area is the worst kind of apostasy. To call oneself a Christian and then deny "the practicability of the Sermon of the Mount as industrial law" is the worst kind of hypocrisy. Nothing is more anti-Christian than to justify the existing order.[99]

Herron said capitalism "shuts God out of human affairs and denies the brotherhood of man. It is social anarchism. It is the declaration on the part of capital that it will not submit to law." For centuries people believed that only the divine right of kings secures political order and justice. That day was gone, and democracy was gaining everywhere, except in industry. Capitalist ownership abolished actual private ownership for most people, turning laborers who create capitalist wealth into slaves of the owners. Herron described democracy in industry and politics as the triumph of true theocracy: "It is the government of the people and their activities by the immediate inspiration of God. Democracy is religion: it is the communion of the people with God as the Spirit of their life and institutions." He pioneered the social gospel trope that democracy gaining is redemption occurring, but Herron put it in martyr-language that soon felt off key: "To look the present evil age squarely in the face, and decide to follow Christ through the midst of it, and teach his love as the curse of its evil and as the law its activities must obey, is to make up one's mind to accept some form of a crucifixion at the hands of those who want not the reign of Christ or the dominion of his love."[100]

He talked that way even as huge crowds showered him with praise and standing ovations. For a while Herron played the largest role in raising the social gospel to Great Awakening status. He wrote regularly for *The Kingdom* and *The Social Gospel*, helped Ely and Strong run the American Institute of Christian Sociology at Chautauqua, and set up a summer Chautauqua at Grinnell. Both he and Rauschenbusch ran summer institutes, admired Mazzini, and published papers titled *The Kingdom*, although neither invited the other to his summer gathering. Herron supported the SLP until it split in 1899, without writing about socialism per se. To many readers he was not as radical as Bliss because Herron focused strenuously on Jesus. In 1895 Herron developed his theocratic political theology in *The Christian State*, arguing that the state is the only organ through which all citizens of a nation act as one person in the pursuit of righteousness. Only through the state do people act together to pursue social justice. If history has a moral purpose, the state must be the organ for accomplishing it. The mission of the state begins with the achievement of individual liberty, but if liberty does not lead to the achievement of the divine good it becomes an instrument of evil.[101]

Whatever is right for the state must be right for the individual and vice versa. So-called political realism rationalized social evil by compartmentalizing the political sphere, rendering the state as something unavoidably odious. Herron said it took an "evil imagination" to imagine there are different kinds of right. The will of God cannot be different in the political sphere than in economics or personal life. If there is a divine will or right it must be universal in operation and universally particular in application. He reached for the strongest negative way of saying it: To say that Christ's teaching is saving in the individual realm, but destructive if practiced collectively in the social realm, is to commit the most wicked form of infidelity. Jesus is the world's greatest spiritual teacher: "The mind of Jesus is the right mind to have." If the state is to fulfill its mission as the organ of social unity, it must become Christian, and if Christianity is to be true to Christ, it must become political. The worst evil is the status quo, which unites "unspiritual religion and immoral politics."[102]

Herron did not appeal to his Puritan forerunners except to say they founded an American tradition of liberty that capitalism destroyed. His political theology was a vision of Christian democracy, a moral government of the people by the people. Nothing like it existed, Herron said, or had ever existed because true democracy was in its infancy. U.S. Americans did not make their laws or select their politicians or govern themselves. Instead Americans had corrupt political parties that served the capitalist class. These parties were "parasites upon the body politic, giving us the most corrupting and humiliating despotisms in polit-ical history, and tending to destroy all political faith in righteousness." He implored readers not to write off the political sphere as a zone of immorality and tyranny: "A true social democracy is the only ultimate political realization of Christianity, and industrial freedom through economic association is the only Christian realization of democracy."[103]

Herron assured his audiences that Christian collectivism would replenish by a hundredfold any individual liberty it abolished. The real property rights of the people would be established, and the needs of families would be fulfilled under "the guardianship of the state as the social organ of a Christian democracy." In 1898 he told a commencement gathering that common ownership of the earth and of industrial production is "the only ground upon which personal property and liberty can be built, the only soil in which individuality may take root." In 1900 he told a mass meeting of the Social Democratic Party that he had voted for the SLP for the past eight years and long considered himself a Socialist. "But before I am a socialist, I am a free man; I am a socialist because I am free. I have paid too great a price for my freedom, and have left too many blood stains upon the capitalistic order, to make any compromise with what I have won and intend to keep."[104]

The references to blood and paying a price were newly earned. Herron set off a backlash that far exceeded anything that Bliss, Scudder, or Rauschenbusch endured. Gates stuck by him, but the board of trustees at Iowa College tired of hearing that they foisted an anti-American anarchist on the American public and Iowa College. In 1897 they told Herron to stifle his radicalism. He replied with seven pages of gracious concessions followed by thirty pages of righteous self-defense. He would not betray Jesus or the college. A public anti-Herron campaign demanding his resignation started up, Herron got more scathing in reply, and locals noticed that he spent more time in the home of his adoring benefactress, Elizabeth Rand, and her daughter. By 1899 Herron was exhausted from the public battering. He took a sabbatical in Egypt, Syria, and Italy to recharge. In April he returned dramatically with a blistering attack on the

Spanish-American War that refueled a trustee attempt in June to fire him, although Gates and Elizabeth Rand saved him from being fired.[105]

Herron told two thousand Christian progressives at Central Music Hall in Chicago that the war betrayed George Washington, America's anticolonial heritage, and Christian decency. He put it with typical histrionic drama: "Never in history was a nation falser to its opportunity; never has a nation more shamefully and ignobly failed, and chosen such darkness in the midst of the full shining of so great a light." The United States had a golden chance, Herron said, to show what anti-imperial greatness looks like. Instead, it took the usual imperial path of killing, abusing, and stealing, plus lying about all of it. He argued that if the United States had supported Cuba's rebellion against Spain and opened U.S. American ports to Cubans, the Cubans would have achieved their freedom "without the imperialism of American speculators." The United States went to war against Spain for commercial reasons, and it blustered and dissembled every step of the way. The rampaging carried on to the Philippine Islands, where "a worthy people, simple, truthful, and easily governed," got a savage display of U.S. American destruction and lying—killing more Filipinos in three months than the Spanish killed in three centuries. The killing was not the worst part: "The American Government is remorselessly enlisted in destroying the sacredest thing that can ever be touched upon this earth—the liberty of a people seeking to express themselves in freedom and self-government."[106]

He read two long quotes from William James and Cincinnati Congregationalist pastor Herbert Bigelow protesting that the United States barreled down the violent, plundering, lying, colonizing road of empires past. Then Herron said it sharper, tying U.S. American imperialism to the demands of capitalism to plunder faraway lands and dominate their markets: "American Imperialism is merely the carrying out of the program of greed by which the holders of stocks and bonds propose to industrially subject the world—the bond-holders and stockholders who are today the emperors of the emperors and their empires." It didn't have to be this way, he said. The United States was not immutably stuck with this system, and he was not anti-American for saying so. The real traitors were those who destroyed the nation for private profit. The real anarchists were the corporate anarchists, who abolished the nation's true liberties. The worst traitors were those who branded as traitors those who protested against the nation's wrongs. He built up to a thundering conclusion: "I love my country, my fellow-citizens, too much to be silent while step by step, stealth by stealth, fraudulent effort by fraudulent effort, the liberties of the people are being stolen away, while the life and hope and self-government of the people are being ground in the industrial mill; while the peoples of the islands of the seas are betrayed and massacred in order that you may be still further betrayed and economically massacred. I love my country and my fellow-citizens too much to be silent and complacent about the monstrous wrongs that are destroying human life the world over. . . . It is time that we have done—and we will have done!—with this flagrant and arrogant hypocrisy that cries, 'patriotism,' whenever its tyranny and debauchery are attacked." Herron implored U.S. Americans to say to the Filipino people, "Forgive our shame and treason; and suffer us to wipe out our shame in service for liberty's sake."[107]

He had anti-imperialist company in the social gospel and not only among Christian socialists. Edward Everett Hale, Henry van Dyke, and Graham Taylor were leading social gospel anti-imperialists, and Bigelow was not yet a socialist in 1899. But condemning U.S. imperialism carried special dangers that most progressives averted. Strong, Abbott, Rauschenbusch, and Reverdy Ransom cheered for the Spanish-American War and did not accept aspersions on their nation's supposedly noble intentions. Gladden said the United States intervened only to liberate and civilize, never to conquer, and those who said otherwise on both sides defamed their nation. Herron heard a great deal of that while his crowds shriveled. He bristled at having to defend his chair at a school he put on the map, and in October he resigned, submitting an eloquent letter that enhanced his martyr status. Herron thanked the board for compelling him, albeit inadvertently, to practice what he preached. He plunged into Socialist activism, befriending Debs and joining him in the Social Democratic Party. Herron said the moment had come to create a strong Socialist party, even if it felt premature. His place was with his comrades, "sharing with them in the troubles that are always involved in the first creative steps of an organized movement."[108]

It seemed to him that three great lines of socialist conviction were converging. The SLP stalwarts were the first line—hard men from Europe schooled in misery, exploitation, and Marx. These old-style Socialists often seemed "sectarian and harsh," Herron allowed, plus bitter, fierce, dogmatic, and obsessed with class to the point of class hatred. Still, he admired them: "They were socialists when it took a fanatic and a hero to be a socialist; socialists, when to be known as a socialist meant hunger or starvation for themselves and their families." The SLP founders suffered for founding America's first Socialist party, a beacon of egalitarian generosity. They adapted Marxism to America and did not worship Marx, contrary to their reputation. The second line consisted of the freedom-loving individualistic children of Rousseau, Jefferson, and the French Revolution. Herron was fond of telling audiences that only the coming of Jesus outranked the French Revolution as the greatest thing to happen in history. Socialism, to the socialist children of Rousseau, fulfilled the ideals of liberty, equality, and fraternity. Liberty, a social achievement, had to be achieved by people working together, not in competition with each other. Individuality would flourish under democratic socialism, and only there. Herron treasured the socialist children of Rousseau and Jefferson, especially Debs, but this was not quite his group.[109]

The third line consisted of religious socialists. Many did not belong to an organized religion, and many were regular church ministers. Herron said more of both existed than Social Democrats presumed. He explained how religious socialists viewed the world, and argued that the movement needed them. The goal of history is for each soul to become a law unto itself. All human beings deserve to be able to individualize nature and truth for themselves. History is a story about the human struggle for freedom. Herron explained that religious socialists roared for spiritual freedom because they knew they were spiritual beings. Since they were in touch with their spiritual selves, they struggled for the good and did not apologize for trafficking in human souls. Like many religious people he knew, Herron worried that he admired Tolstoy too much. He yearned to withdraw in Tolstoy-fashion and would have done so had he been able to justify it: "It would be an unspeakable relief to me to pay my world-debt so cheaply." But no spiritually sensitive person withdraws from the suffering of others: "My place is in the thick of social pain and travail, in the depth of the resolving chaos, even if I have to bear this ethical strain and shame to the end. The least that I can do to pay my debt to my brothers, the least that I can do to be decent, is to contribute the whole of my life to the emancipation of labor from that capitalistic order which makes the product of the millions the profit and luxury of the few."[110]

On that basis, religious people were pouring into the socialist movement and the old-style radicals needed to welcome them. Herron saw two kinds of socialism coming. One would be democratic, freedom loving, religiously musical, and ethical. The other socialism would be imperialist in the manner of Bismarck or the Tory flank of the Fabian movement. Herron believed, and wanted to say, that no true socialist accepts imperialism. But he cautioned the Social Democrats that they did not control what others said and how they defined themselves. Capitalism was unsustainable because it depended evermore on finding new lands and peoples to exploit. For this reason, Herron said, some form of collective production and distribution was surely coming to replace capitalism. The future would be socialist and not far off. In that case, a bad kind of socialism was sure to emerge because there was always a party of greed to battle against. To Herron, that was the trump reason for democratic socialists to pull together. Capitalism had no future, and the great fight that was coming would pit true socialists against imperial imposters who claimed the socialist name.

Meanwhile there was a presidential election to address. Herron credited the Republicans for honestly defending the interests of the rich, being the party of the capitalist class. The Democrats were more vexing, as some were sincere reformers; some even believed their childish talk about antitrust legislation. Herron said antitrust bills had the same relationship to serious economic reform that Theodore Roosevelt had to modesty. Bryan had nothing in mind that would curb the rule of the capitalists. America needed a party that explained why predatory capitalism led to imperial smashing and killing: "The capitalistic order of America has debauched the conscience of the nation, and used its government to betray and conquer weaker peoples, in order to find markets for the produce of the struggling and blighted lives of the laborers, who cannot buy what they produce." Capitalism, upon absorbing the purchasing power of the actual producers, destroyed the freedoms of vulnerable peoples in order to furnish a market. Socialism begins with the principle of the unity and equality of the human race. It proposes that social will—not Darwinian natural selection—should be the supreme factor in evolution. As long as some people own what all people need, all are degraded and enslaved. Even the owners are less human and free than they should be. Herron yearned for "the commonwealth, the common wholeness, the common freedom, the common abundance and gladness of all men and women."[111]

Are human beings good enough to make socialism work? To answer no, Herron said, is no different from refusing to fight disease or moral evil. Nobody says that people should not be cured of their diseases until they get well, or that evil should not be opposed until people are ready to be good. It is never too soon to learn how to cooperate with others. People learn how to cooperate only by doing it, just as they learn to be free only in liberty. Some objected that socialists spoke harshly about hating the rich and the middle class. Herron said they were right to object; class hatred had to be stripped out of the socialist movement as something alien to the ethical spirit of socialism. He also acknowledged there were risks in struggling for socialism, but they were nothing compared to the risks of sticking with capitalism. Conservatism is the cause of every violent revolution. Socialism is an alternative to watching capitalism plunge the entire planet into some-against-many wars. As for socialist materialism, Herron said it was like the class hatred issue: the real thing is much better because it is ethical, universal, and even religious: "In its essence, socialism is a religion; it stands for the harmonious relating of the whole life of man; it stands for a vast and collective fulfilling of the law of love. As the socialist movement grows, its religious forces will come forth from the furnace of experience."[112]

Herron enthused that the right leader of America's first real Socialist movement came just in time. Debs proved his mettle as a labor leader and was now prepared to do the same thing for socialism. Herron worked hard for Debs in 1900, joined Wilson's Social Crusade the following year, and denied that he had ditched Christianity for socialism. He played a leading role in creating the Socialist Party and speaking for it, playing the Debs role to Christian audiences.[113]

But Herron lost his embattled Christian standing after his personal life blew up. His marriage waned in the 1890s; he depended on Elizabeth and Carrie Rand for emotional support; he rationalized that they understood him and his wife did not; and in March 1901 Mary Everhard Herron sued for a divorce and support of their four children. Herron resisted her compensation demands but lost in court. Carrie Rand gave her entire personal fortune of sixty thousand dollars to Herron's ex-wife, and in May she and Herron were married in a nontraditional ceremony that disavowed coercive institutions. Herron stoked a media firestorm by repudiating the sanctity of marriage vows and declaring that he embraced his status as an outcast. Two weeks later the Grinnell Association of Congregational Churches deposed him from the ministry for immoral conduct. Herron replied with a gracious letter, accepting his fate, but it won martyr points for him only on the left, and even there only sporadically.[114]

He was vilified. Editorialists religious and secular condemned him ferociously as a worthless, cruel, monstrous, contemptible, hypocritical wretch. Editors urged readers to picture the sobs of Herron's deserted children. Strong called Herron's conduct "despicable and a crime against society." *The Outlook* said Herron expelled himself from decent society, and no honorable paper should mention his name heretofore. Many periodicals took that counsel except for recycled condemnations. The pounding was unrelenting for the newlyweds; everywhere they went they were scolded and spurned. Progressive journalist William Allen White later recalled that Herron, his wife, and his mother-in-law were hounded constantly in public, sometimes in the streets. For a while Herron tried to tough it out. He gave the keynote address at the Socialist Party's unity convention in Indianapolis in July 1901, declaring, "Socialist unity has passed from desire and struggle into accomplished fact; and it is important that all forces related to the socialist movement should now be centered upon the one work of building up a great revolutionary party, that shall conquer all the seats of power in the nation." But in September he gave up on living in the United States. Herron moved with his wife and mother-in-law to a sixteenth-century villa near Florence, Italy, transferred his devotion to the land of Mazzini, and worked for the Second International.[115]

He had not meant to hurt Christian socialism or socialism in his quest for martyrdom. Herron recognized that he harmed his causes by showing up for them, which left him no reason not to flee. He ended up more like Tolstoy than he sought, although he said he disapproved of self-dramatizing withdrawal. Herron and Hillquit were close friends, despite clashing over racial justice and immigration. They bonded over their mutual passion to build a socialist movement, and Hillquit grieved at losing Herron to Italy; yet he did not blame Herron for fleeing. To polite society, Hillquit reasoned, it was bad enough to be an apostate minister or a radical revolutionist. Herron became distinctly offensive by being both. Thus no insult was too insulting for him; no words quite registered how reprehensible Herron had become. He gave the nominating speech for Debs at the 1904 Socialist convention and stayed in touch with American comrades but made his life in Italy. Herron's best historians, Robert Handy and Peter Frederick, both stressed that Herron relied on female devotion to an unusual degree. He could endure whatever abuse he incurred as long as he had an adoring female partner. Carrie Rand Herron died in 1914; a few months later Herron married a wealthy German woman; and he married again shortly after his German wife died, near the end of World War I.[116]

The war destroyed the Second International, but Herron compensated by joining the American Socialist "social patriots" who embraced Wilsonian idealism. For a while he was Woodrow Wilson's favorite expatriate, cheering the Fourteen Points and the League of Nations. Herron poured out books on the idealistic meaning of the war, which set him up for another crushing disappointment. The Treaty of Versailles savaged Wilsonian idealism and Herron's expectations for it. He told Hillquit he could barely stand to consider how badly the world was turning out. He went back to believing that Italy was the hope of the world, even after Benito Mussolini's fascist government took over in 1922. White aptly described Herron as "one of God's pedestal dwellers, always moving about in bronze or marble." Impressionable, intemperate, and oracular, Herron abided with Mazzini, which made him fit only for Italy. To the end of his days in 1925 Herron declaimed in Romantic mode that the kingdom was at hand.[117]

BUILDING TO THE SOCIALIST/CHRISTIAN SOCIALIST APEX

The IWW split the labor movement and the Socialist Party into warring camps. Nobody bridged the enmity between the IWW and AFL, and nobody in the Socialist Party was a candidate for this role. One storied episode briefly united the antagonists in both contexts. On December 30, 1905, former Idaho governor Frank Steunenberg was killed by a bomb at the gate of his home in Caldwell, Idaho. A Western Federation of Miners (WFM) worker arrested on suspicion of the crime claimed that IWW leaders Haywood and Charles Moyer had hired him to kill Steunenberg as payback for calling out the militia against the miners in 1899 during a strike. Newspaper barons whipped up a hang-the-anarchists frenzy, which evoked awkward silence in the labor movement until Debs pushed back hard in *Appeal to Reason*. Debs rallied the labor movement and both wings of the Socialist Party to defend the IWW leaders and George Pettibone, a Denver businessman accused mostly for appearances. In January 1907 Debs joined the *Appeal* staff, campaigned full-time on behalf of the accused, and clashed with President Theodore Roosevelt over who was a liar and who cared about social decency. The trial acquitted the accused men, and the labor movement celebrated.[118]

But this ordeal drove Haywood and Moyer into outright anarcho-syndicalism. Their opponents in the WFM captured the union during the fifteen months Haywood and Moyer were imprisoned, pulling it out of the IWW. Losing the miners erased Haywood's willingness to perform organizing drudgework. He drifted for years as an itinerant evangelist of direct action; meanwhile the IWW was reduced to organizers and strike leaders. It was great at street theater but lacked a single business agent. Now it opposed not only capitalist politics but also socialist politics, speaking a colorful language of breaking the state and seizing power. De Leon insisted that American capitalism had to be overthrown in civilized fashion, in the political realm, so the IWW expelled him, denying his credentials at the 1908 convention. This convention dropped the last remaining reference to political action from the IWW constitution. Elections were bogus because government itself is pernicious; unions themselves should run the nation. To Debs, the twin pillars of left politics were industrial unionism and Socialist political activism—organize workers and run for office. Now the IWW had renounced both pillars. Debs quietly let his membership in the IWW expire, grieving at losing what should have been. Previously, when he left a group he issued a public statement of his reasons—a ritual of ideological seriousness on the left. This time he said nothing. He loved his friends in the IWW, Haywood remained a Socialist Party leader, and Debs believed the fierce, romantic, militant spirit of the IWW had a role to play in breaking capitalism.

Debs knew very well why workers joined the AFL and employers preferred to bargain with the AFL. AFL unionists had financial stakes in the insurance funds of their unions, and their very sense of labor solidarity drew them to the nation's largest federation. Stable locals, signed contracts, rising wages, control of working conditions, and the protection of a national federation were important to them. Thus Debs always claimed he was not out to destroy the AFL; he simply wanted to belong to a union that was not an auxiliary of the capitalist class and its posturing front of alleged civic leaders, the Civic Federation, to which Gompers belonged. Debs was against the AFL for the same reason he opposed working with civic and political reform groups. He was against everything that detracted from capitalism versus socialism. Had the IWW not zoomed into political nowhere, Debs might have sabotaged even his place in the Socialist Party. As it was, he spoke for the party as no one else could.

The Socialist Party doubled its membership between 1904 and 1908, entering the 1908 campaign with forty-one thousand members and over three thousand locals. Its top officers were lawyers (Hillquit, Seymour Stedman, and Job Harriman), editor-writers (Berger, Hayes, Simons, Spargo, Heath, and John Work), and executive secretary Barnes. All wanted to base the party on craft unionism and the reform vote. All recoiled at the left-wing emphasis of Debs and Haywood on the poor, the unorganized, the unskilled, the vulnerable, and industrial unionism. The party convened in Chicago in May 1908 to select a presidential ticket. It strongly reaffirmed its commitment to political action, in contrast to the IWW. It divided five ways over small farms, large farms, and farmland in general. The Old Guard leaders could not nominate Hillquit or Berger for president because both were foreign born and both were unacceptable anyway to the midwestern and western socialists who regarded Hillquit and Berger as oily backroom operators. Thus the Old Guard tried to unseat Debs with homegrown personal favorites. Hillquit pushed for James Carey, Steadman for Simons, and Berger for Carl Thompson. The last move roiled the convention, as Thompson had a large following on his own, and Berger made a patronizing speech against Debs. In the end Debs routed Thompson and Simons, while Hillquit completely lost control of his New York delegation, delivering nobody to Carey.[119]

The party rallied behind Debs and an inspired gambit arranged by Barnes—the Red Special, a three-car railroad train carrying Debs to three hundred events in thirty-three states. It featured a brass band, a festive atmosphere, and a growing Debs cult. The CSF and the Intercollegiate Socialist Society produced streams of testimony to Debs's noble soul. Charles Kerr, succeeding Simon as editor of the *International Socialist Review* (ISR), turned it into a glossy magazine that celebrated Debs and the IWW and played down theoretical debates. Debs fed his growing legend with Jesus-like rhetoric that smacked of Herron's most florid. On May 23, 1908, he told a gathering in Girard, Kansas: "I have said so often, and I wish to repeat it on this occasion, that mankind have always crowned their oppressors, and they have as uniformly crucified their saviors, and this has been true all along the highway of the centuries. It is true today. It will not always be so. I am opposed to capitalism because I love my fellow men, and if I am opposing you I am opposing you for what I believe to be your good, and though you spat upon me with contempt I should still oppose you to the extent of my power."[120]

Prominent journalist Lincoln Steffens interviewed Debs in Milwaukee, at Berger's home. Debs said he ran for president to grow the Socialist movement, not because he wanted to be president. When the movement got within reach of winning, it would be time to run somebody else. Steffens asked why it was necessary to fight capitalism; won't it just break down inevitably? Debs shuddered visibly, replying, "Because we have minds." Human beings are not helpless against the economic forces that toss them about; human intelligence is a force of nature that enables people to abolish the misery of boom-and-bust economics. Socialism is the producers getting what they produce, ending the system where some live off the exploitation of many. Steffens asked how Socialists would socialize the trusts when they took power. Debs replied, "Take them." Berger leaped to his feet and stood over Debs angrily, retorting that Debs did not speak for him or the party; when the day came, the trusts would be paid for whatever was confiscated. Steffens told readers this exchange symbolized the revolutionary versus evolutionary divide in the Socialist Party. Debs told Steffens he accepted the traditional definition of socialism as the cooperative control and democratic management of the means of production. But he believed it was something bigger: Socialism is the next stage of human society in which human beings find a common purpose by building a cooperative commonwealth.[121]

Debs and the Red Special got a rush of good press that alarmed Roosevelt, Gompers, the antisocialist press, and Republican candidate William Howard Taft. Roosevelt said the growing Debs legend scared him. Gompers broke his twenty-two-year record of political neutrality to back Bryan, charging that the Republican Party secretly financed the Red Special. Many newspapers warned that Socialists were anti-American, and some claimed the party consisted almost entirely of foreigners. Barnes countered that the Socialists raised their own money, more than 70 percent were born in the United States, and 20 percent were immigrants from western Europe. Debs alternated between shucking off the anti-American accusation and trusting that his Americanism was obvious. He was buoyant and hopeful, enjoying the 1908 campaign like no other, until constant speaking exhausted him. It felt as if the party was growing. He told audiences the ides of November had a surprise in store "for both Republicans and Democrats." He said there was "no middle ground possible" between the capitalist parties and achieving socialism; the "sporadic reform movements" were ludicrous for contending otherwise. But the Republican platform made a pitch to Progressive reformers, Bryan won the votes of Progressive reformers by attacking monopoly, and Debs increased his 1904 total by only eighteen thousand votes.[122]

It was one thing to ask left-liberals to throw away their vote when there was nobody to vote for. In 1904 the Democrats ran a conservative lawyer, Alton B. Parker, so Debs captured the protest vote. Four years later he split the protest vote with Bryan. The Gompers factor also hurt Debs, as the Old Guard stressed. Keir Hardie, visiting the United States in June 1908, accused the American Socialists of operating too narrowly. His Independent Labour Party had a better idea, building a Socialist movement within the Labour Party. The Old Guard leaders agreed and began to scheme. They had no answer to their Debs problem aside from reasserting their control of the party machinery. They controlled the National Executive Committee (NEC) because they were writers, lawyers, and party founders. NEC membership was determined by a direct vote of all members, the rank and file of every state voted for local favorites, and the same notables got elected every year with 5 to 10 percent of the vote. In August 1909 a local in Denver bolted the party as a protest against this arrangement. Other locals soon followed suit, alarming Debs. He believed he held the party together, not belonging to the Old Guard or the anarcho-syndicalists, while feeling select affinities with both sides. In December 1909 he made an exception to butting out, writing to William English Walling that the party had to do something to stop the exodus of western locals: "The Socialist Party has already CATERED FAR TOO MUCH to the American Federation of Labor and there is no doubt that A HALT WILL HAVE TO BE CALLED. The REVOLUTIONARY character of our party and the movement MUST be preserved in all its integrity AT ALL COST, for if that be compromised, it had better cease to exist."[123]

Walling was born into wealth in Louisville, Kentucky. His father was a Louisville physician and real estate baron descended from the planter class of the South, and his mother came from a prominent Democratic family in Indiana. Walling was educated at a private school in Louisville, turned Progressive while studying in the 1890s at the University of Chicago and Harvard Law School, and moved to New York and further leftward in 1900. He founded the National Women's Trade Union League in 1903, married a Jewish immigrant writer who kept her name, Anna Strunsky, made two trips to Russia, and wrote a book in 1908 lauding the socialist movement in Russia. The following year he joined the Socialist Party and played a major role in founding the

NAACP. Debs respected Walling immensely and thanked him for opposing the Old Guard. He told Walling he was ready for a showdown with the Old Guard: "If the trimmers had their way, we should degenerate into bourgeois reform. But THEY WILL NOT HAVE THEIR WAY." That proved to be misleading for Walling because Debs did nothing until the party convened at Chicago in May 1910. There the party's committee on immigration proposed to call for the exclusion of all Asian immigrants to the United States. The Old Guard sought the approval of the AFL so desperately that it proposed to exceed the AFL's racism. Debs was apoplectic. He called the proposal "unsocialistic, reactionary and in truth outrageous." For a "bourgeois convention of self-seekers," a racist immigration policy made sense. For socialists, it was unbelievable. Debs said it was too obscene for words, a "heartless exclusion."[124]

But Debs did not attend the convention, his letter arrived too late to be read, and the Socialist Party passed a so-called compromise authored by Hillquit. It mimicked how the AFL masked its racism, calling for immigration exclusions solely to limit the number of wage earners competing for jobs, not on the basis of race or nationality. The Old Guard seized its majority advantage, proceeding to a vote on the perennial question of industrial unionism. It wanted the party to say it took no position on unionism, exactly as Gompers wanted. It was not the business of the Socialist Party to hold positions concerning the policies or structures of unions. The resolution passed, and the party's left wing bitterly assailed the vote as a betrayal of socialism. Debs was more moderate, sticking to his middling position in the party. He said he supported industrial unionism but opposed dual unionism, recognized that AFL unions held the field, and respected the right of workers to prefer and join craft unions. On that basis he tried to hold the party together while curtailing the power of the Old Guard.

The surge for socialism that Debs thought he felt in 1908 turned out to be real. Party membership doubled between 1909 and 1911, helped by Bryan voters who felt stranded and defeated, and increased another 40 percent in 1912, peaking at 118,000. In 1910 Socialists won mayoral races in Milwaukee and Schenectady, many state legislature races, and Berger's seat in Congress. The following year seventy-four cities and towns elected a Socialist mayor or at least one major city official; the three most prominent Socialist mayors were Christian clerics J. Stitt Wilson in Berkeley, California, George Lunn in Schenectady, New York, and Lewis Duncan in Butte, Montana. Debs exulted in the upward climb of *Appeal to Reason* and sneered at the party's electoral victories. By 1910 the paper reached 475,000 paid subscribers, buoyed by his articles as a staff writer. Meanwhile the election winners nearly always won by touting reform issues. If a Socialist ran on Progressive issues and took Progressive positions, what good was that? Debs irked the Old Guard leaders whenever he said it. They came from miserable urban poverty, where small gains marked the difference between surviving and not. They worked harder than ever to gain control of the party's machinery and political direction, hoping to reduce Debs to a figurehead at most.

If they pushed Debs to the sideline, perhaps they could swing the party to the labor party option. Simons began to scheme it out, persuading Hillquit, Spargo, and other Old Guard leaders to work on the AFL angle. He wrote to Walling that he didn't really like the British model, but it was better than what they had; perhaps Americans could do it better? Walling went ballistic, warning *ISR* readers that leaders of the Socialist Party were plotting to create a new party. He and his fellow millionaire socialist Robert Hunter slugged it out in *ISR*, with Walling demanding the expulsion of Simons, Hillquit, Berger, Thompson, and Graham Stokes from the NEC. Debs wailed his customary riposte that the party "CATERED FAR TOO MUCH" to the AFL. Rose Pastor Stokes and her millionaire husband, J. G. Phelps Stokes, agreed with Debs, charging that the Old Guard just wanted to get into office. Hillquit replied that no conspiracy existed; he had always said the mission of the Socialist Party was to organize the working class politically. This was an open discussion about how to do it. Berger urged Hillquit and Spargo to concentrate on winning control of the Socialist Party, which might work better than launching a new party. Debs took back every nice thing he ever said about Berger, telling Hunter that Berger's performance was "disgraceful and contemptible beyond words." He told Thompson he put up with Berger's bullying for too long. In 1911 Debs wrote that he welcomed the support of trade unionists, "but only of those who believe in Socialism and are ready to vote and work with us for the overthrow of capitalism." The AFL was "deadly hostile to the Socialist Party and to any and every revolutionary movement of the working class." How could there be Socialist leaders who preferred the AFL to socialism and its party? Debs admonished: "Voting for Socialism is not Socialism any more than a menu is a meal. Socialism must be organized, drilled, equipped and the place to begin is in the industries where the workers are employed."[125]

For a brief, thrilling, misleading moment there was a prospect of socialist unity because of the Lawrence strike. The textile mills in Lawrence, Massachusetts, employed thirty-five thousand workers; the English-speaking United Textile Workers craft union, consisting mostly of Germans, Irish, and English, had twenty-five hundred members; and scrappy IWW Local 20 had three hundred members, consisting mostly of Italians, Poles, Franco-Belgians, and Syrians. There were numerous French-Canadians and Jews in the craft union and the IWW. On January 11 a group of Polish female loom operators went on strike after receiving an unannounced wage cut. The strike spread immediately to ten thousand textile workers from forty nationalities. IWW organizers, spurning their usual exaltation of direct action, counseled the strikers against violence and helped them to make specific demands through negotiations. The local Socialist Party was deeply involved in the strike, mostly through French Canadian Wobbly organizer Louis Picavet and the party's new Italian federation. Haywood got a hero's welcome upon entering Lawrence on January 24, marking his dramatic return to the IWW after four years of drifting. In mid-March the strikers won their four major demands. It was an electrifying, stand-out, mythical moment. Even Berger celebrated the victory, obtaining a congressional investigation of the strike, while touting his cooperation with Haywood. Historian Melvyn Dubofsky said Lawrence mattered so much because the Wobblies "discovered that their tactics worked." They had talked about striking at the point of production for years without doing it. Now they fanned out to Ohio, Louisiana, Texas, Oregon, and Vancouver, Canada, taking the fight directly to industrial enterprises, waging twenty-eight strikes in 1912.[126]

But the Wobblies did not embrace the nonviolent tactics that worked at Lawrence. Haywood ridiculed Hillquit and other law-abiding Socialists, declaring that no real socialist boasts of being law-abiding. He and Wobbly comrade Frank Bohn said it aggressively in various contexts, contending that real socialists held no respect whatsoever for the property rights of capitalists and did not hesitate to use every available weapon to win the war against the capitalists. Debs shook with revulsion, objecting that Haywood erased a crucial distinction. Yes, capitalist property laws were fraudulent and corrupt but committing the Socialist movement to a strategy of violence, "butting my head against the stone wall of existing property laws," was idiotic, immoral, and counterproductive. Debs said American workers were law abiding "and no amount of sneering or derision will alter that fact." He loved the IWW for espousing industrial unionism but loathed its anarchist tactics: "Sabotage repels the American worker. He is ready for the industrial union, but he is opposed to the 'propaganda of the deed,' and as long as the IWW adheres to its present tactics and ignores political action, or treats it with contempt by advising the workers to 'strike at the ballot box with an ax,' they will regard it as an anarchist organization, and it will never be more than a small fraction of the labor movement." Direct action and sabotage are reactionary, he said, not revolutionary. Socialists must unite with tactics that foster solidarity and don't offend the moral values of workers. Looking ahead to the Socialist convention in May, Debs said he hoped the party would "place itself squarely on record at the upcoming national convention against sabotage and every other form of violence and destructiveness suggested by what is known as 'direct action.' "[127]

Briefly he believed there might be a chance to unify the Socialist Party. Perhaps the Lawrence breakthrough could be a reset moment for the entire movement. Debs had broken his rule about factional contention, but he still refused to attend the 1912 convention in Indianapolis. He figured the two main factions were equal, so at worst they would neutralize each other. The Old Guard, however, had no interest in reconciling with the radical wing, especially now that the radicals were ascendant and more anarchist sounding than ever. Haywood attended the convention as a newly elected member of the NEC, rankling the Old Guard by his presence and enhanced national stature. The resolutions committee asked the party to endorse the AFL, a counter group asked the party to endorse industrial unionism, and the party wrangled a vague compromise that left both camps feeling victorious. Hayward, for one day, thought the party had made a historic breakthrough.[128]

Then the Old Guard proposed a constitutional amendment calling for the expulsion of any member who opposed political action or advocated any form of crime, sabotage, or violence. A state senator and cleric from Wisconsin, W. R. Gaylord, conferred moral unction on the amendment. Many cited Haywood on law-abiding dopes and Debs on the necessity of moral decency. Berger seized the moment, charging that the party had a group of anarchists who only pretended to believe in political action. They used the party, he said, as a cloak for direct action, sabotage, and syndicalism, which needed to be called by its right name, anarchism, and recognized for what it was: a party-killing cancer that had to be cut out of the party. The amendment passed by a vote of 191 to 90, which set off an exodus of syndicalists from the party. Berger and Hillquit tried to push aside Debs, hustling presidential votes, respectively, for Milwaukee mayor Emil Seidel and magazine writer Charles Edward Russell. The two candidates split 40 percent of the delegate vote, failing to stop Debs from running again, this time with Seidel as his running mate. Debs won the nomination in the fashion he expected, but the 1912 convention was a fateful turning point.[129]

He realized immediately that Berger and the Old Guard went too far, but Debs was conflicted about how far. Basically he wanted the party to champion his brand of revolutionary democracy without castigating comrades as enemies, driving them out, or devising an expulsion apparatus—at least, until the election was over. In *ISR* Debs said the convention united the party "on a solid basis," and surely there would be no split. The party stood, or needed to stand, on moral ground, oppose anarchist tactics, and "reduce to the minimum the offenses punishable by expulsion from the party." He believed that expelling people would not be necessary as long as the party stood clearly for revolutionary democracy. Debs admonished Berger privately for going too far but added that the party should clean house as soon as the election was over, expelling everyone who preferred violence to the ballot. In short, it was true that Socialists had to get rid of the anarchists, but the crisis was not as bad as Berger said, so the housecleaning could wait. In that state of mind Debs hit the campaign trail.[130]

This was the year that four candidates vied for the votes of progressives, though of course Debs refused to put it that way. Theodore Roosevelt split the Republican Party and took a band of liberals into a party of their own, the Progressive Party. Incumbent Republican president Taft denied that Republicans had become merely the party of the economic establishment; otherwise they could not have dominated American politics for so long. Woodrow Wilson campaigned to break Republican dominance and nationalize the Democratic Party. Debs urged audiences not to be distracted by the noisy Progressives and Democrats. Workers were slaves under capitalism, and only the Socialists sought to abolish working-class slavery. If Roosevelt deserved to be called a Progressive, why did he cater to the trusts when he occupied the White House? The new Progressive Party was "lavishly financed and shrewdly advertised" but offered nothing new besides legalized trusts. Debs was simultaneously apocalyptic and hopeful, contending that "capitalism is rushing blindly to its impending doom" and Socialist deliverance was coming. It could not be that a system featuring so much poverty, unemployment, suicide, and crime "in a land bursting with abundance" would be able to sustain itself. The party of progress and the future, he said, was the Socialist Party. Many large gatherings roared in agreement.[131]

The Socialists lost many Socialist and Progressive votes to Roosevelt, including Gladden and Addams, and many to Wilson, notably Du Bois, yet they doubled their vote total in 1912. Wilson crushed the field in the electoral college, but the popular vote confirmed that the left was surging. Wilson won 41 percent of the vote, Roosevelt won 27 percent, Taft won 23 percent, and Debs won 6 percent with nine hundred thousand votes. Socialists had almost every reason to believe, as they did, that they were ascending. They would not have to run against Roosevelt again, and Wilson was sure to disappoint every Socialist who voted for him. Another twenty Socialists won seats in state legislatures, and eight more cities elected Socialist officials. Meanwhile Socialists made a strong showing in the AFL, not that Debs cared. Hayes ran against Gompers in 1912 and won 36 percent of the vote, buoyed by support from the Machinists, Brewery Workers, Bakers, Mine Workers, Painters, Quarry Workers, and Tailors. Socialist William Johnson won the presidency of the Machinists, and Socialist James Maurer won the presidency of the State Federation of Pennsylvania.

But even this heyday moment contained cautionary signs. The voting surge in the presidential election occurred mostly in southern and western states, especially Oklahoma, Washington, and California, while the Socialist vote sagged in the Old Guard strongholds of Wisconsin and New York. The party had an inside faction fight over Barnes's moral fitness for leadership positions and a public schism over Haywood and the IWW. Debs, while pleading for unity, played a role in purging the Socialists of anarchists. In 1913 the New York state Socialist Party sponsored a national referendum calling for Haywood's expulsion from the NEC. It passed overwhelmingly, as Haywood won less than one-third of the votes and only ten state organizations. Debs cheered the outcome, contending that the IWW had become an anarchist organization in all but name. He said it more and more angrily in reaction to bitter setbacks in Lawrence and West Virginia.

In Lawrence employers infiltrated the IWW with spies, and the IWW got a relentlessly bad press. Haywood and Elizabeth Gurley Flynn, an IWW leader from a working-class New Hampshire background, left town never to return, and local IWW leaders never built a stable organization. Local 20 collapsed, and workers lost the gains they had won. In 1912 the United Mine Workers of America (UMWA) struck in Kanawha County, West Virginia. The operators raised a private army to suppress the miners, martial law dispatched state troops to the mines, and the IWW rushed to Kanawha County. Debs accepted the usual verdict about Lawrence—the Wobblies thrived on confrontation and quickly grew bored with collective bargaining and organization building. But he wanted the Socialists to support the Wobblies in West Virginia—until he went there in April 1913 and hated what he saw.

The Wobblies flagrantly scorned the UMWA and incited the striking miners to wage an armed battle. Both things deeply offended Debs. He recoiled at hearing from Wobblies and West Virginians that socialism was about arming workers to clash with the state. The UMWA was a comparatively progressive industrial union—enough for Debs to take the side of national UMWA officials against the local miners organized by Haywood. An angry controversy ensued in the Socialist Party, two months after Haywood was expelled from the NEC. The Haywood flank—twenty-three thousand members—bolted the party, driving Debs to a bitter verdict: There was no third way. Socialists were compelled to stand wholly with the IWW or against it.[132]

On the stump Debs continued to say that Socialists needed to unite on the basis of a revolutionary democratic politics allied with industrial unionism. Routinely he said that uniting the UMWA and the Western Federation of Miners would be a good start. But his dream of uniting the Socialist Party on the basis of industrial unionism collapsed in 1913. The cause of national industrial unionism died for a generation. The Old Guard, resented as it was, kept the party going. It was never just one thing, being a patchwork of notables and party officials, and it braved the firestorm to come with courage and conviction. It held out against World War I, and after the Communist explosion shattered the party the Old Guard was the only group left standing.

3

SOCIALISM IS NOT ENOUGH: RACE, FEMINISM, RELIGION, WAR, AND EUGENE DEBS

The expansive and inclusive idea of socialism was not enough to overcome racial privilege, male privilege, and one-factor reductionism in the Socialist Party. Debs leashed his antiracism to the dogma that only socialism would abolish racism, and socialists had no special message for anyone except workers as workers. Hillquit wanted only white immigrants in the United States while denying that he and the AFL were racist for saying so. Berger was racist without apology, and Haywood took the Debs view. The Socialist Party thus muffled its voice on racism despite protests from its religious and secular neo-abolitionist flanks. The party gave essentially the same socialism-only answer to women, with a wrinkle of difference that made a difference. There were just enough women who protested that women had it worse under capitalism than men; if the party wanted female members it needed to provide a special place for them. This argument yielded a Woman's National Committee in the Socialist Party, but women never exceeded 15 percent of the party membership, and the party's first female star, Lena Morrow Lewis, wanted no special provisions for women. Being a person of color or a woman was usually enough to ward off one-factor socialism. Being religious had a similar upshot because religious socialists did not say that capitalism was the cause of all social harm.

The early socialist movement waged two kinds of racial justice politics. One was the true believing socialism-only espoused by Debs, and the other played a leading role in the founding of the NAACP. The true believers spurned racial reform politics as a palliative distraction, and the second group rejected socialism-only as pitifully inadequate. One could be a true believer and black, as were SLP stalwart Peter Clark and Baptist clerics George W. Woodbey and George W. Slater. Some black socialists moved from the first group to the second, notably

Hubert Henry Harrison and A. Philip Randolph. The NAACP cofounders refused to wait for the socialist deliverance that abolished racism. W. E. B. Du Bois and black socialist clerics Reverdy Ransom, George Frazier Miller, and Robert Bagnall were leading figures in it, as were white NAACP socialists William English Walling, Mary White Ovington, and Charles Edward Russell.

Du Bois was the ringleader of the racial justice movement that made history, but the NAACP was a middle-class outfit that succeeded only because Du Bois was willing to cut a deal with white liberals. Most in the black socialist following that ultimately made an impact were Baptist and poor. They had no publishing houses but packed lectures and street rallies. They had a marginal role in the Socialist Party and the IWW, mostly in California and New York. They lived in segregated social space without having much choice in the matter. And their champion was Woodbey.

GEORGE W. WOODBEY AND THE DILEMMA OF BLACK CHRISTIAN SOCIALISM

Woodbey preached Christian socialism with Herron-like brilliance and incomparable bravery. He was a pioneer of the black social gospel and a product of the socialist and Christian socialist movements of his time who insisted that he had no original ideas. He got his ideas from the Bible, Marx, Bellamy, Debs, and the Christian socialist currents inspired by Herron and Bliss, but Woodbey did not talk about these sources, except for an occasional reference to Marx, and except for the Bible. Claiming originality would have undermined his purpose, for Woodbey said Christian socialism was not new. It was merely a new name for the golden rule and the biblical teaching that God identifies with the oppressed.

He was born a slave in Johnson County, Tennessee, in 1854. Nothing is known of Woodbey's early life except that he studied for two terms in a common school and was otherwise self-educated. At the age of nineteen he married Annie R. Goodin of Kansas, with whom he had five children. The following year Woodbey was ordained to the Baptist ministry in Emporia, Kansas. In the 1880s he worked in mines and factories in Kansas and Missouri, was active in Republican politics in both states, and ministered to several Baptist congregations. Later he moved to Nebraska and joined the Prohibition Party, where his speaking skills and activist temperament lifted him to a prominent party role. In 1896 Woodbey ran for lieutenant governor of Nebraska and for Congress on the Prohibition ticket. That year marked a turning point in his ideological development. Bellamy's *Looking Backward* enthralled Woodbey with its vision of a socialist America in which all means of production were nationally owned, social goods were distributed equally to all citizens, everyone ate at public kitchens, and all people retired at the age of forty-five with full benefits. That led Woodbey to Wayland's *Appeal to Reason*, which he devoured, though he hedged politically, joining the Populist Party.[1]

The presidential election of 1900 completed Woodbey's ideological turn. He supported Bryan, giving speeches for Bryan on behalf of the Nebraska Democratic Party. Debs, however, came to Omaha, campaigning on the Social Democracy of America ticket. Upon hearing Debs speak, Woodbey had the conviction of hearing the real thing, although he still had qualms about throwing away his vote. For a while he gave campaign speeches for Bryan that made Bryan sound like Debs, but the Democrats stopped asking for his help, and Woodbey decided they were right: He had become a socialist. Resigning his pulpit, Woodbey announced that he would devote the rest of his life to the socialist movement. He got a movement going in Omaha, speaking every night in the streets and parks. A Nebraska comrade later told socialist organizer A. W. Ricker, "Omaha had never had the crowds that attended Woodbey's meetings."[2]

In the spring of 1902 Woodbey visited his mother in San Diego and spoke every night in the streets and lecture halls. The Socialist Party sponsored some of his speeches. Often Woodbey held forth on a soapbox. San Diego was not a likely place for him to land, as it had a small and mostly contented working class and no large industries. The area's ideal climate attracted tourists and professionals, causing IWW martyr-bard Joe Hill to remark that San Diego was "not worth a whoop in Hell from a rebel's point of view." Downtown San Diego, however, had a tradition of street oratory smacking of Hyde Park, London, which hooked Woodbey. He told crowds he came to see his mother, but, being "anxious to be free," he felt impelled to work for the cause constantly. The *Los Angeles Socialist* reported: "Comrade Woodbey is great and is a favorite with all classes. He has had very respectable audiences both on the streets and in the halls. He likes to speak on the street and it is the general verdict that he has done more good for the cause than any of our most eloquent speakers who have preceded him. He is full of resources and never repeats his speeches, but gives them something new every night." Woodbey passed a hat for contributions and branched out to Los Angeles, where the Northern Restaurant and Southern Hotel refused to deal with him when he turned out to be black. He told audiences of his welcome to the city, which set off successful boycotts of both establishments.[3]

Mt. Zion Baptist Church of San Diego called Woodbey to be its pastor and he drew large crowds to it. He won election to the state executive board of the

Socialist Party and lectured across the state, winning accolades as the Great Negro Socialist Orator. Posters heralded his appearances: "The well-known Socialist Lecturer. Quaint, Direct, Forceful. Has spoken to great audiences in all parts of the United States." That was slightly exaggerated geographically, but Woodbey worked hard at expanding his audience. In 1903 he packed a lecture hall in Los Angeles to assess Booker T. Washington's "Capitalist Argument for the Negro." Woodbey lauded Washington's gentlemanly dignity and educational accomplishments, but panned, "He has all the ability necessary to make a good servant of capitalism by educating other servants for capitalism." Washington's uplift strategy, Woodbey said, pitted black workers against white workers, which lowered wages for all laborers and their families. Washington tried to make capitalism the basis of unity between white capitalists and black workers, failing to comprehend that capitalism is inherently predatory and divisive: "There is no race division industrially, but an ever-growing antagonism between the exploiting capitalists black or white, and the exploited workers, black or white." The "only solution to the race problem," Woodbey urged, was for people of all races to share the benefits of production.[4]

Woodbey's soapbox speaking made him a frequent target of police. He was thrown in jail several times and occasionally hospitalized after the police beat him. The police in San Diego, Los Angeles, and San Francisco were especially thuggish. After he became an author and sold his socialist booklets on the streets, the beatings got worse. Woodbey was persistent and unbowed. In 1905 he led a group of protesters to a police station in San Diego after an officer clubbed him on a street corner. Woodbey's group tried to lodge a complaint, but the offending officer intervened, screaming racial epithets at Woodbey and throwing him bodily out of the station house. Woodbey pressed the charge in court, where every witness testified that Woodbey had done nothing wrong, and an all-white, middle-class jury ruled for the police. Back on his soapbox, Woodbey urged victims of police brutality to fight for their rights in court, even if they were certain to lose. He published the names of the jurors in his case, urging decent citizens to shun them.[5]

Woodbey's audiences were racially mixed, mostly working class with a sprinkling of middle-class activists and professionals, and appreciative. Every week listeners told him they had never understood socialist ideas until they heard his lucid speeches. Often they asked for a written version, which yielded his first book, *What to Do and How to Do It; or, Socialism versus Capitalism* (1903). A. W. Ricker, visiting Julius Wayland in Girard, Kansas, read the forty-page book aloud to Wayland, who published it as the August 1903 issue of *Wayland's Monthly*. Ricker declared in *Appeal to Reason* that all locals should encourage people to read it, "Negroes especially." Woodbey began with a two-sentence dedication. The first sentence paraphrased the title; the second was poignant and self-referential: "By one who was once a chattel slave freed by the proclamation and wishes to be free from the slavery of capitalism."[6]

What to Do was framed as a dialogue between Woodbey and his mother. She pitched half-incredulous questions, and he gave straightforward answers. Had he given up the Bible and the ministry to go into politics? No, socialism brought him to a deeper Christian faith, making the Bible come alive to him. More than ever he grasped what the Bible says about God giving the earth to human beings as a home, God overthrowing the Egyptian slave masters and delivering the Hebrews from oppression, God prescribing a government of the people administered by judges, which they replaced with a monarchy, God repeatedly forbidding usury, and God prescribing a jubilee law preventing the making of public debts. Woodbey's mother replied that a lot of his Socialist friends didn't believe in God or the Bible. He replied that when he worked for the Republican Party he knew a lot of atheist Republicans. He did not repudiate Socialist friends with whom he disagreed about God and eternity: "Whoever is willing to make things better here, which the Bible teaches is essential to the hereafter, I will join hands with as far as we can go."[7]

Woodbey told his mother that socialists want four things. They want all people to share the land equally "because the earth is our home and no one can live without it." They want all workers to own the tools with which they worked, "from a spade to a large factory." They want all people to own the common forms of transport, especially railroads and ships. And they want working people to make the laws governing industry by direct vote. His mother wondered what would happen to private property under this system. Woodley replied that anything produced would be justly distributed as private property to those that produced it. The crucial thing was to socialize the process by which wealth is produced, making every American an equal shareholder in the wealth of the United States.[8]

Getting control of the government, Woodbey believed, would be harder than making socialism work, but he thought both were sure to occur. Sooner or later the overwhelming majority of workers would give themselves equality by voting for it. Socialists would be elected to city and county offices, then to state offices, and finally to federal offices. Gradually they would gain control of the government. Socialism is no more radical than the golden rule or social justice, Woodbey argued; in fact, it is merely another name for these things. Public education, a socialist idea, was long considered anti-American and impossibly radical. Public industry would be similar, moving swiftly from being dangerous to being sensible and decent. As soon as socialists gained control of the government, they would take possession of the means of production and distribution by acts of legislation, replacing capitalist enterprises with public ownership, which most people would like much better.

Woodbey's mother worried that if socialists took over the government and the economy, wealthy people would launch a civil war. He replied that capitalism was too much like the old slave system to find enough mercenaries to fight its battles. The slaveholders did not dare to arm the slaves when their system was attacked, and they could only go so far to accommodate the people they needed to fight their battles without undoing the system. Capitalism had a bad case of the latter problem, Woodbey believed. Admittedly, capitalists had the law on their side because they made the laws. But as soon as socialists got elected and changed the laws, it would be game over for the capitalists.

Not many people of Woodbey's age had a mother who survived slavery and was still alive in 1903. He waxed longer than usual when she asked how women would fare under socialism. Women had it worse than men under capitalism, Woodbey acknowledged; socialism offered a better life for men and a much better life for women. In a socialist order every woman would have her own income, just like the men. Women who did society's most important work—raising children—would not have to labor anywhere else. Woodbey stressed that capitalism emptied the working-class home of its nurturing mothers, but under socialism women and their families would be lifted to the valued status they deserved. Unmarried women would be able to work in industry or have a profession. The only women who might not like socialism were the "idle parasites" under capitalism who lived off the spoils of unearned wealth. They would have to learn how to contribute something useful to society. Socialism, Woodbey observed, advocated "absolute equality of the sexes before the law," as stated in the Socialist Party platform. Capitalism exploited women and allowed society to discriminate against them, but under socialism women would be equal to men at the ballot box and everywhere else.[9]

Socialism was starting to sound pretty good to Woodbey's mother, but wouldn't it require a great deal of government and a great many laws? Woodbey's answer revealed that he was a Marxist utopian all the way down when it came to socialist government. Like most orthodox Marxists, he called his position scientific Socialism. Once the people collectively owned the land, the factories, and the means of transportation, he argued, government wouldn't be necessary and only a few laws would be needed. Capitalism had to be regulated by representative government to make it minimally tolerable, and it relied on bosses to hold workers in line. Capitalism operated on the basis of compete-or-die, but under socialism this logic would be abolished, so regulation and representative government would not be necessary. The people would make their own laws by voting directly for or against them, and they wouldn't need to be bossed by anyone since people work effectively when the firm belongs to them. Plus everyone hates to be bossed. Crime would disappear too because crime is a response to hunger and being humiliated. Woodbey figured that most people under socialism would choose to live in towns because towns are more conducive than rural areas or cities to neighborliness and community. In any case, the governance of towns and cities would be left to the direct vote of the people, just like the larger industries.[10]

According to Woodbey, he convinced his mother that socialism was the best option for African Americans and all others. He rushed past her questions about religion, however, explaining that getting into that would require another book. A year later he published a sequel, *The Bible and Socialism* (1904), this time responding to the queries of his mother's pastor. The pastor contended that Christianity is a religion, socialism is a type of politics, and religion must be separated from politics. Moreover, Woodbey's hero, Marx, was no Christian, far from it. Woodbey replied that the Bible lacks any distinction between religion and politics and that Marx, "that wonderful man," caught the justice spirit of the Bible better than any modern thinker or minister. God delivering the Hebrews from slavery was religion and politics mixed together. After the Hebrews were liberated from Egyptian rule they formed a state, replete with laws and politics, which the Bible depicts God as having remarkably detailed prescriptions about: "God is there represented as giving the Jews a regular system of government, touching every phase of human life, too numerous to mention. Indeed, I know of no relation of one man to another that is not touched upon in the Law of Moses."[11]

The Bible, Woodbey observed, is loaded with normative ethical statements bearing on politics. More precisely, the Bible is loaded with socialism. Woodbey marshaled biblical texts opposing rent, interest, profits, love of money, and the exploitation of the poor. Rent is a violation of the fundamental biblical principle that God gave the earth to all humankind as a home. To violate the law of common ownership is to commit sin. Socialism is a modern expression of the biblical right to cooperative ownership and control of the land. In the Bible the land belonged to God, and the Israelites were tenants upon it. Under capitalism a handful of cunning types stole possession of the earth to live off the labor of others. Woodbey contended that only Socialism comes close to the biblical law suspending agricultural work in the seventh year and canceling all debts in the Jubilee fiftieth year (though he conflated the Jubilee with the seventh year

Sabbath). In biblical times the aim of the Jubilee was to prevent huge debts from accumulating "for parasites to live upon from age to age, as they do today."[12]

Woodbey read Leviticus 25 as a manifesto for the "principle of universal brotherhood," the fundamental principle of socialism. Verse 35 commanded that if any of the Israelites' kin fell into difficulty, the Israelites were obligated to support them, treating the dependents as resident aliens. Woodbey universalized "kin" as "brother," preaching that God cares about all people, not just Hebrews. Verse 36 prohibited taking interest in advance or in any way making a profit off one's charity to the poor. To fear God is to take care of the poor and vulnerable without reward, another verse that Woodbey universalized. Verse 37 said the same thing more specifically, prohibiting Israelites from lending money at interest taken in advance or exacting a profit from providing food to the needy. Woodbey explained that the Bible taught a socialist ethic in a presocialist age; thus it focuses on the ethics of charity from the standpoint of social justice: "As the ultimate end, which is Socialism, was yet in the distant future, temporary relief for the brother or stranger fallen into decay is taught. But the Bible, no more than the Socialists, holds out charity as a solution of economic difficulties."[13]

Isaiah 24 was another staple of Woodbey's street preaching. Verse 5 pictured the earth lying polluted from the ravages of its inhabitants, who broke God's laws, violated the statutes, and broke the everlasting covenant. To Woodbey, this text was mostly about economic injustice—the defilement of creation by economic greed: "Socialism, or opposition to usury, has always been the relation that should be between man and man; but government has always been left to the rich, who profited through usury at the expense of the poor producer of wealth." The solution was to get the power of government into the hands of the producers, who would change the laws to gain for themselves the value of all they produced. Socialism, Woodbey said, is a bountiful vision of everyone becoming a producer. It is not about socializing poverty; it is about all people flourishing and thereby producing wealth: "Of course, the producer has the power to take over the industries now, but has yet to be convinced of it."[14]

Woodbey's ministerial interlocutor asked how he understood the teaching of Jesus, especially about patriotism and nonresistance. Woodbey replied that Christ's example is the best interpretive key to what he meant. He condemned the rich with unsparing scorn and drove the business vendors out of the temple with a whip, so "love your enemies" and "turn the other cheek" do not call his followers to be passive, cowardly, or oblivious. Woodbey claimed that Jesus, living under the Roman Empire, took the same position "that every good Socialist takes." He abided by the laws of the land until the laws could be changed.

Woodbey's exegesis of the Caesar's coin story in Matthew 22 and its Synoptic parallels took this plodding line, failing to notice the difference between Roman and Jewish coins in the story, the role of the spies, and Jesus's cagey nonanswer in front of a crowd that believed it owed nothing to Caesar. In the story some shady interrogators posing as pious Jews tried to trap Jesus with a question about paying taxes. He asked for a *denarius*, a coin minted by Rome with Caesar's image, and they whipped one out—something no righteous Jew would have done. Jesus discredited the interrogators before moving to his shape-shifting answer, laced with irony, "Render to Caesar the things that are Caesar's and render to God the things that are God's." According to Woodbey, however, "render unto Caesar" was as straightforward as it sounded: Jesus told his followers to pay their taxes to the Roman government. To Woodbey, every problem text folded into a coming socialist solution: "Like us Socialists, he meant, pay your tax and wait for better things, to be brought about by teaching the people."[15]

The war question was the last to arise before Woodbey pressed the pastor for a verdict. The key to "love your enemies" is the biblical doctrine of universal brotherhood, Woodbey argued. Socialism carries out the moral command by fashioning a politics of the biblical doctrine. What could be more loving than to treat one's enemy as a brother and an equal? The pastor countered that God commanded the Israelites to kill their enemies. Woodbey replied that as long as "robber empires" exist, war will curse the earth, and the only way oppressed people can overthrow an empire is to take up arms. War is an outgrowth of unjust economic conditions. The way to abolish it is to unite the workers of the world against economic tyranny.

That set up Woodbey's altar call. He cited Psalm 72:4, which commends those who defend the cause of the poor, bring deliverance to the needy, and crush the oppressor. Woodbey urged the pastor, "Go preach the first part of that text to the needy children of the poor in the factories, and apply the latter part to their oppressors or get out of the pulpit and make way for someone who will do it." Did the pastor hear the cry of the poor for deliverance from their oppression? Did he believe that God called him to defend the poor and afflicted and bring justice to the land? Too many ministers, Woodbey admonished, preached only about getting to heaven after one died. They ignored that the Bible resounds with admonition to pour oneself out for the poor and oppressed. Woodbey challenged the minister to preach the biblical call to social justice and to wear proudly the accusation that comes from doing so—that he was a Socialist Christian. *The Bible and Socialism* ended with the minister vowing to do so.[16]

Woodbey knew from his lecture crowds there was an audience for his message. Getting that audience to join the Socialist Party, however, was a heavy lift.

From the beginning the party had three factions on the race issue: the Berger flank that didn't want black members, the Debs majority that advocated color-blind equality and inclusion, and the Herron flank that wanted the party to make an issue of racial justice. These positions were aired at the party's founding convention in Indianapolis. For twenty years the Socialist movements gathered at Indianapolis had advocated equality "without distinction of color, race, sex or creed." This was the baseline for the new organization, a formulation already bordering on socialist cliché that rejected all distinctions except class and, arguably, nation. Most U.S. American Socialists assumed a cultural version of white supremacy, but they affirmed the traditional European socialist position that color-blind equality is a fundamental principle of justice. The issue at the party's founding convention was whether the party should issue a resolution about the special suffering of African Americans that included references to lynching, wage discrimination, and disenfranchisement.[17]

Hillquit led the opposition to a special resolution, contending that the Socialist Party could not single out blacks, Jews, Germans, or any other racial or ethnic group without contradicting the party's commitment to color-blind equality. Two of the three African American delegates at the convention—John H. Adams of Brazil, Indiana, and Edward D. McKay of Richmond, Indiana—initially supported this position, but the other black delegate, William Costley of San Francisco, contended that the Socialist movement had a legacy of evasion to overcome on this issue. Costley urged that if Socialists did not name and condemn the distinct forms of suffering imposed on black Americans, it was pointless to expect blacks to join the party. Several party leaders agreed—Herron, labor leaders Max Hayes (Printers' Union), John Collins (Machinists' Union), and William Hamilton (United Mine Workers), and the party's future secretary, William Mailley. Herron declared that he would rather lose every vote in the South than see the Socialist Party evade the race issue. Hamilton wanted the party to play a vanguard role in the trade union movement, making unionism a force for racial justice. Adams, a coal miner, changed his position on the resolution, urging delegates to seize the moment. Opponents implored that the new party would get nowhere in the South if it forthrightly advocated black equality. The wrangling over that warning produced a strong resolution with two missing planks. The Socialist Party officially condemned "color prejudice and race hatred," affirmed the equality of white and black workers, invited blacks to join the Socialist movement, and did not mention lynching or segregation.[18]

The party's racial justice wing hoped it had made a breakthrough. *Appeal to Reason* and other Socialist papers hailed the resolution as the strongest problack statement ever issued by an American political party, and the Socialist

Party distributed the resolution as a leaflet. There was some reaction in the black press, all related to the steel strike of 1901, which reignited an old debate about whether African Americans should be strikebreakers. *The Colored American* upheld the Booker Washington tradition, urging its readers to "side with the capitalists" in the steel strike. Eloquently, *The Colored American* pleaded that the black strikebreaker did not relish his role and did not wish to undermine the just demands of white workers: "It is not that he is the servant of those who would grind the poor to powder. He is not the tool of soulless opera-tors. It's because the white labor organizations refuse to make common cause with him and decline to give him the opportunity that is rightfully his to provide for his family. It is because his sympathy is alienated by treatment that drives him to the capitalist in self-defense. The corporation offers bread. The labor unions turn him away with a stone. Who can blame the Negro for thanking the Almighty for the situation that grants him what the unions deny, and establishes his power as a labor factor among those who think more of quality of servance than of the color of the servant?"[19]

Charles L. Wood of Washington, Iowa, a white socialist, replied that the Socialist Party had recently made an important statement on this matter. Wood confessed that the record of American trade unions on racial justice was "shame-ful in the extreme, and without cause." He did not blame African Americans for loathing trade unions. Still, he asked them not to give up on unionism and not to kid themselves that they had friends in the capitalist class. The capitalists sought to completely subjugate the poor and working classes, Wood contended. At the moment they used black workers as tools toward this end, but once they succeeded they would subject blacks to merciless and defenseless tyranny. Wood urged that Socialists were the only party that treated the black American as "a fellow being and a brother." He added that the union movement was changing, though he gave no specifics. The United Mine Workers opposed rac-ism, and some union leaders, notably Collins, were trying to eliminate the rac-ist policies of their organizations. Meanwhile the IWW was formally committed to organizing all workers regardless of nationality, craft, race, or gender.[20]

The Socialist Party never attracted many African Americans, as it never over-came its structural and historic impediments to doing so, and much of its inter-nal debate over the issue would have repelled African Americans who read it. *ISR* published numerous articles on this issue. *Appeal to Reason, Chicago Socialist, The Worker, Seattle Socialist,* and *Social Democratic Herald* battled over the issue, often recycling debates from *ISR.* The nakedly white suprema-cist faction (Berger, William Noyes, H. Gaylord Wilshire) contended that blacks were inferior and not worth harming the movement over. The racial justice faction (Herron, Collins, Hamilton, Costley, Quaker Caroline H. Pemberton) implored the movement not to sell its soul for a few southern chapters. The color-blind equality faction (Debs, Hillquit, the later Hayes) pleaded to stop litigating this hopelessly divisive issue that undermined the movement's influence with unions.

Debs could be blunt and emotional on this subject. In 1903 he wrote in *ISR*, "The history of the Negro in the United States is a history of crime without a parallel." White America, Debs observed, "stole him from his native land and for two centuries and a half robbed him of the fruit of his labor, kept him in beastly ignorance and subjected him to the brutal domination of the lash." But two paragraphs later Debs denied that this history of oppression made any difference to what mattered, describing social equality as a "pure fraud" that masked the real issue: "There never was any social inferiority that was not the shriveled fruit of economic inequality. The Negro, given economic freedom, will not ask the white man any social favors; and the burning question of 'social equality' will disappear like mist before the sunrise." To Debs, the class struggle was everything, and it had no color: "My heart goes to the Negro and I make no apology to any white man for it." Whenever he looked upon a brutalized black American, "I feel a burning sense of guilt for his intellectual poverty and moral debasement that makes me blush for the unspeakable crimes committed by my own race." Putting it that way helped to rationalize how little he proposed to do. Debs wanted to believe that blacks would catch up with whites, achieving equality, though he doubted it was possible since he viewed blacks chiefly as low-performing victims. In any case, the other hand prevailed: "We have nothing special to offer the Negro, and we cannot make separate appeals to all the races." No matter how badly he felt about the savageries inflicted on the basis of race, not class, Debs stuck to socialist salvation: "The capitalists, white, black and other shades, are on one side, and the workers, white, black and all other colors, on the other side."[21]

The party's openly racist wing pushed back. A self-identified "staunch member of the Socialist Party" wrote to correct Debs, informing him that Thomas Dixon was the nation's leading authority on the race issue; Debs needed to read Dixon's best seller *The Leopard's Spots*, which glorified the Ku Klux Klan. In the meantime Debs needed to stop spewing nonsense about political equality for black Americans because political equality would lead to social equality and a hellish race war. Debs rubbed his eyes that this guy claimed to be a comrade. Had he read the Socialist Party's resolution on the race issue? Debs reprinted the entire text, six paragraphs long, highlighting the part assuring "our Negro fellow worker of our sympathy with him in his subjection to lawlessness and oppression." Socialists repudiated everything that divided workers along lines of race, nationality, creed, or sex, he said. You cannot be a socialist and a bigot: "I say that the Socialist Party would be false to its historic mission, violate the fundamental principles of Socialism, deny its philosophy and repudiate its own teachings if, on account of race considerations, it sought to exclude any human being from political equality and economic freedom." He added that the party would "forfeit its very life" if it sold out the rights of blacks, "for it would soon be scorned and deserted as a thing unclean, leaving but a stench in the nostrils of honest men." Debs wanted the party to be like him: committed to color-blind justice and disinclined to talk about it since race was divisive and secondary, an epiphenomenon of economic oppression charged with toxic feelings.[22]

This was the mainstream position in the Socialist Party when it convened in 1904 in Chicago, where Woodbey was the only African American among 175 delegates representing 33 states and territories. The largest delegations were from California, Illinois, Massachusetts, Missouri, New York, and Wisconsin. Eight states—Alabama, Idaho, Indian Territory (Oklahoma), Louisiana, Mississippi, New Hampshire, Oregon, and Tennessee—had a single delegate. Woodbey spoke twice, defending a delegate who worked for the state government of Indiana (noting that German socialists boasted of serving in the German army) and defending the national secretary's salary. The color-blind faction got its way throughout the convention, as nobody said anything about race or even the fact that Woodbey was the only black delegate.[23]

Four years later he was still the only black delegate, at another convention in Chicago, but this time Woodbey put race on the agenda. He spoke four times at the 1908 convention, taking bold positions on socialization and immigration. The party was burgeoning in 1908, and socialists cheered the Social Democratic gains in Europe. Woodbey declared that soon American socialists would have a victory to deal with in some large city. What would they do upon taking power? Would they make nice with the capitalist class? Would they compensate private corporations they took over? Woodbey was for swift socialization. Every socialist mayor should take possession as soon as possible and refuse to pay compensation: "I take the ground that you have already paid for these franchises—already paid more than they are worth, and we are simply proposing to take possession of what we have already paid for." He was for socializing "everything in sight." He also wanted to build new cooperative enterprises, following the example of the Socialist municipal governments in Germany, France, England, Holland, Denmark, Norway, and Sweden. It was not enough to socialize existing enterprises, Woodbey urged: "We can't afford to wait for the alleviation of the suffering of the people. We must do it as fast as we can get in charge."[24]

Immigration was the other hot issue. In 1907 the Socialist International debated immigration at its Congress in Stuttgart, Germany. The U.S. American delegation was bitterly divided on this issue, as Hillquit led the effort to commit the International to a restrictive policy. Hillquit wanted to ban immigrants who were unlikely to join the class struggle—an oily way of saying he wanted his party to be able to take a racist position without being accused of racism by the International. This proposal was hotly debated and overwhelmingly defeated. Of the twenty-three Socialist parties at the Congress, Hillquit's position won votes only from delegates representing South Africa, Australia, and the United States. The International declared its categorical opposition to immigration restrictions based on national, racial, or ethnic grounds.[25]

That did not settle the matter for Berger, Hillquit, Ernest Untermann, and the California delegation. They brought the issue to the American convention of 1908, pushing to exclude Asian immigrants while insisting they lacked any racist motivation. Berger and Untermann said Asian immigrants were economically and psychologically backward and too many had already entered California, driving down wages. Berger warned that if the party supported admission for Chinese, Japanese, and Korean immigrants, America's (white) workers would rightly conclude that the party took no interest in helping them.[26]

Woodbey led the fight for socialist universality. Besides opposing restrictions on Asians, he opposed all immigration restrictions period: "I am in favor of throwing the entire world open to the inhabitants of the world." Many delegates erupted in agreement, and Woodbey continued: "There are no foreigners, and cannot be, unless some person came down from Mars, or Jupiter, or some place. I stand on the declaration of Thomas Paine when he said, 'The world is my country.'" Woodbey found it strange that recent immigrants from Europe denied the same right to Asians. With cutting understatement he added, "So far as making this a mere matter of race, I disagree decidedly." A committee on the issue called for a new committee to study the issue. Woodbey replied that socialists should not need committees for things like this. Concerning Berger and Untermann, he took the high road, declining to say that racism was obviously at play. Socialism was against nationalism and racism, he argued, so how could immigration be an issue at a Socialist convention? What was there to discuss? Woodbey allowed that driving down wages was a serious matter, but Socialists needed to be realistic. This problem was unavoidable as long as capitalism existed anywhere. Under capitalism either the laborer moved to the job or the job moved to the laborer. If U.S. American workers did not produce things as cheaply as workers in Asia, the capitalist class would move the means of production to Asia. Instead of betraying socialism by discriminating against Asians,

Woodbey said, it was better to fight for socialism—the "Brotherhood of Man"—everywhere.[27]

The Socialist Party kept studying the issue, debating it at its conventions of 1910 and 1912. By then Berger was the first Socialist in the U.S. House of Representatives, having been elected in 1910 to the first of his five terms in Congress representing Milwaukee. Formally the party kept faith with the Socialist International and "solidarity forever," opposing immigration restrictions, although many members disagreed, citing Berger as a symbol of Socialist success. The party's determination not to talk about race impaired its ability to discuss why the immigration issue was so unsettling. Woodbey's leadership on the immigration issue threatened but did not break the party's decorum. Only once at the 1908 convention did anyone mention the race of the party's only black delegate. Ellis Jones of Ohio, nominating Woodbey as a candidate for vice president, urged the delegates to make a statement about their commitment to racial justice. Instead, the Socialists chose Ben Hanford again. After the 1908 convention the party sent Woodbey on a lecture tour of northern cities, where he stumped for Debs and distributed a pamphlet titled "Why the Negro Should Vote the Socialist Ticket."[28]

This was the first time Woodbey ever wrote specifically for a black audience. Whatever belongs to the public, he said, belongs by right to all citizens collectively. Americans accept that public streets, schools, and libraries belong to them collectively. Socialism is about extending the same principle to land, mines, factories, shops, and railroads. Under a socialist order, "when we build a railroad, it will belong not to some Vanderbilt or Gould, but to the people. And when we ride on that railroad, or use it, we will not have to pay a profit to the capitalist." The goal is to turn all workplaces into public property. Once the public owns and democratically controls the factories and railroads everybody will have a job and nobody will suffer in poverty. Woodbey said all working people must put aside their prejudices to work for the common good: "We poor whites and blacks have fought each other long enough, and while we have fought, the capitalists have been taking everything from both of us."[29]

Under capitalism citizens see many things they cannot have. Woodbey said these things would still exist under socialism, with the difference that ordinary people could have them: "You will have a chance to get them and not have to worry about how you will live any more than you need to worry now whether you can walk on the street from this meeting." Woodbey said the Socialist Party stood for the abolition of poverty in the same way that the Republican Party once stood for the abolition of slavery. He recognized that socialism seemed too radical to most Americans, advising that the basic idea is not difficult or far out. Essentially it is to run railroads and mines like the post office. Everybody will have a job, and if they produce too much, work hours will be cut back, yielding more leisure time. Putting it this way, Woodbey realized, made socialism seem prosaic, even boring. But making socialism not-scary was crucial, and abolishing poverty would not be a prosaic achievement.[30]

Woodbey could feel that socialism was growing in 1908 even though Bryan's candidacy held back the vote for Debs. Woodbey worked hard for the party during the next electoral cycle, speaking constantly. By then he was free to speak across the nation, as his congregation in San Diego tired of socialist sermons. A parishioner later recalled that Woodbey "loosened up his flock with the Bible" but always "finished his sermon with an oration on Socialism." Woodbey stayed on good terms with Mt. Zion Church after giving up his salary, remaining on its staff while he devoted himself full time to socialist agitation. Many populists who voted for Bryan in 1908 flocked to the Socialist Party afterward. In 1909 Woodbey said agitation was the first step toward converting America to socialism. Millions of people had to imagine the cooperative commonwealth before it could be built. Socialism was "a fire in the bones of its converts and must flash out." Woodbey got some of his roughest treatment from police during this period, which he took as another sign that socialism was gaining. For one thing, it got easier to attract a crowd. He believed the socialist gains in Europe were a factor, causing even Americans to be curious about socialism.[31]

Woodbey spoke the same language about "new abolition" and "new emancipation" that NAACP liberals used, but he was a true believing Socialist who spurned reform movements. Emancipation was about liberating the vast masses of the poor from poverty. America was supposed to be a democracy, but Congress and the courts defended the right of capitalists to own what the public needed to use. To Woodbey there was little difference between the capitalist and slaveholder uses of government. Both relied on government to protect their ostensible rights to dominate people lacking effective rights. When Woodbey told the story of slavery and abolitionist rebellion, he stressed that blacks were enslaved because a profit could be made from their labor, not because they were black. The new abolition boosted the poor of all colors and benefited nearly all people: "The workers of all colors now find themselves in need of another emancipation, from a condition of wage slavery which as completely robs them of the hundreds of millions of wealth produced by their labor as did chattel slavery." Woodbey said it as emphatically as Debs: Socialism is the only solution to the race problem. When workers attain control of the economy "the race problem will be settled forever."[32]

Woodbey and Debs were the same kind of socialist, believing the IWW was too precious a dream not to try. They wanted the IWW to redeem the cause of radical industrial unionism, building one big union, while the Socialist Party ran for office, taking over the government. Debs resigned when the IWW opted for anarcho-syndicalism, but Woodbey was a creature of the streets who bonded with IWW activists, admired how they fought for free speech, and bolstered the IWW faction of the Socialist Party. In 1908 Woodbey played a leading role in the Socialist Party's defiance of a San Francisco ordinance forbidding street meetings for nonreligious groups. Speakers were arrested and dragged off to jail, outstripping the city's capacity to jail and prosecute them. Woodbey told a reporter, "The police can't stop us. They can and do arrest us when we speak, but they can't stem the tide that has been started no more than they can the ocean. The more they ill treat us, the more Socialists there are." Liberals and labor groups flocked to the socialists' defense, and the city council repealed the ordinance. Back on his soapbox, Woodbey told audiences he knew how Wendell Phillips and Frederick Douglass must have felt: "The agitation is now going for the new emancipation, and the agitators are equally hated and despised."[33]

Meanwhile the Wobblies became proficient at street theater, winning victories in municipal battles by filling jails, crowding court dockets, and draining city budgets. They clashed with governments at the city, state, and federal levels, garnering sensational publicity, which reinforced their proclivity for protest politics. Wobbly leaders Haywood, Elizabeth Gurley Flynn, and Frank Little personified the IWW's signature blend of violent rhetoric, proud rebelliousness, physical courage, and disruption. Woodbey loved them for it, imploring that Socialists and the IWW belonged together, even as he regretted the Wobbly descent into political nowhere. Until 1913 the Socialist Party vigorously supported IWW campaigns by giving them money, publicity, and activists, especially Woodbey, Flynn, and Haywood. The issue of race, however, was always there in Socialist debates about how to scale up, and the IWW had no answer either. Haywood and the IWW held the Debs view about creating a socialist world in which race did not matter, which made the IWW foreign to black Americans. Socialists paid at both ends for taking an antiracist position they tried not to talk about. Their vision of a color-blind world made no existential sense to people oppressed by racism. Moreover, Socialists were stuck with the contradiction that their positions on race, gender, and ethnicity were decades ahead of the population from which they sought votes. The IWW, seeing the contradiction, opted out of electoral politics, which did nothing to enhance its stature with black Americans.

The Socialist Party was very good at converting fraternal orders and ethnic cultural organizations to socialist politics, but these networks did not exist in African American life. To say the same thing from the other end, there was no black organization to join when an African American joined the party; it had no organizational voice that spoke to black Americans. Formally the party welcomed black members, but it made no special efforts to recruit them, hired precious few black organizers, did not assign organizers to black communities, published almost no literature specifically referring to racial justice, and in some places a welcoming attitude did not exist, to put it mildly. All the party had were Woodbey's speaking tours and the similar exertions of Woodbey protégés such as George Slater Jr. and Hubert Harrison. Woodbey and Slater came from the only black institution holding the potential to spark a movement demanding a new economic system—the church. But even Woodbey lost his congregation for talking too much about socialism, and Slater was not as accomplished as Woodbey.[34]

Woodbey was the party's best example that socialists and anarchists could forge solidarity in protest, if not in ideology. In 1912 the IWW staged a fateful free speech fight in San Diego after the Wobblies organized workers neglected by the AFL, and streetcar franchise owner John Spreckels urged the city to abolish all speaking on soapbox row. The fight began immediately after the city banned all street speaking, even revival preaching, in January 1912. The Wobblies and the California Free Speech League spearheaded a resistance campaign joined by Socialists, Single Taxers, AFL unionists, and church groups. They filled the jails with speakers, the police were ferociously brutal, and local vigilantes were allowed to seize prisoners from the jails. The seized prisoners were escorted across the county line and warned not to return; those that returned got savage beatings. Woodbey was beaten several times at speaking events and in jail. The Free Speech League patrolled his home with armed guards to protect him from being killed. After four months of this battle Emma Goldman came to San Diego to give a speech and lend support, accompanied by her partner, Ben Reitman. Reitman was captured, tortured with a lighted cigar, sexually assaulted, and tarred, while Goldman fled to Los Angeles. That was an omen of how this fight would end. The vigilante tactics defeated the Wobblies, convincing some to give up on nonviolent resistance. By the fall of 1912 soapbox row had been abandoned, and the Wobblies waited two years to return.[35]

Woodbey persisted to the end of his days, speaking for the Socialist Party, running in 1914 as its candidate for state treasurer, and still listed as a pastor at Mt. Zion Church. In 1915 he published an article fittingly titled "Why the Socialists Must Reach the Churches with Their Message." American socialists, he declared, would never get anywhere if they didn't reach the millions of working people who belonged to churches. Too many comrades tried to do it by attacking Christianity. Woodbey lamented that he spent much of his life trying to repair the damage. It was self-destructive, plus factually wrong, for socialists to claim that socialism and Christianity are incompatible. Woodbey countered, "The Bible, in every line of it, is with the poor as against their oppressors." Everywhere he went Woodbey had to contend with a stupid debate between atheist socialists and antisocialist Christians in which both sides failed or refused to see the social justice perspective of biblical faith.[36]

Woodbey had no solution to the problem except to bravely give witness, speaking as simply and clearly as he could, hoping to be heard. All he could do was preach the next sermon and head to the next town. He did not talk about things that distracted from the simple aim of converting his audiences to Christian socialism. He did not cite Du Bois or any Christian socialist to seal his points. In his later work he did not cite any authors, even Marx. The only authority to which he appealed was the Bible. To the extent that he had a model, it was Debs, but Woodbey was an accomplished speaker and political activist before Debs converted him to socialism. Woodbey did not reflect on himself or the structural obstacles to success, at least in public. He did not believe he had failed. He knew that socialism was new and growing, and he could not have worked harder to spread it.

Hubert Henry Harrison, born in Concordia, Danish West Indies (later St. Croix, U.S. Virgin Islands), had an early career as a soapbox speaker for the Socialist Party in Harlem before he struck out on his own, frustrated by the party's racial blinders and Marxist dogmatism. In his early career Harrison carried on Woodbey's work, striking with the Wobblies and silk workers in Paterson, New Jersey, in 1912–13. He organized for the Socialist Party in Harlem until he got fed up with being paid less and treated worse than other organizers. In 1917 Harrison founded a race-first socialist organization, the Liberty League of Afro-Americans, forging alliances with radical black journalists A. Philip Randolph and Chandler Owen. Upon launching the Liberty League, Harrison provided an audience for Marcus Garvey, whom he soon turned against, and edited the *Negro World,* espousing a blend of black nationalism and socialist universalism that anticipated Du Bois's trajectory. In his later career Harrison specialized in Woodbey-like soapbox performances at Wall Street and Madison Square, holding forth on a wider range of subjects than Woodbey would have considered appropriate. Throughout his career Harrison wrote for radical publications such as *ISR, New York Call, Modern Quarterly,* and *The Masses.*[37]

Harrison was more reflective than Woodbey about the work they shared. In 1911 he mused in the *Call* that interracial interactions were often awkwardly self-conscious. How should one act upon encountering "strange people"? Barbarians of every color treated the other as inferior, Harrison noted. Garden-variety racists acted on their prejudices, with or without acknowledgment. The "truly civilized" treated others frankly as human beings with no special self-consciousness about doing so. Harrison offered a gentle word of counsel to white socialists. Often they told him, "I have always been friendly with colored people." Sometimes they claimed, "I have never felt any prejudice against Negroes." Harrison did not doubt that these assurances often carried good intentions and some were even true. But they were "wholly unnecessary," he advised, plus embarrassing: "If your heart be in the right place, and this is assumed at the start, it will appear in your actions. No special kindness and no condescension is either needed or expected. Treat them simply as human beings, as if you had never looked at the color of their faces. It is wonderful but true that what people will be to you depends very largely upon what you are to them."[38]

He tried in that spirit to help white socialists grasp the reality and significance of the color line. Often they told him, "Socialism is the same for all people — women, Finns, Negroes and all." Harrison agreed, with a caveat: "But the minds of all these are not the same and are not to be approached in the same way." Black Americans lived behind the color line, he explained, "where none of these social movements have come to him." The few efforts to reach African Americans where they lived "broke down as soon as they had to cross the color line." This history made black Americans more difficult to reach with the social-ist message than was the case with women or Finns. It was "really a special work" to make socialism make sense to blacks. Harrison told a story about distributing Slater's pamphlet *The Colored Man's Case as Socialism Sees It* in New York. It was hard to get street crowds to read anything, but the title of Slater's pamphlet broke through: "We would take one of these pamphlets and hold it so that the title showed plainly and walk up to a colored man with it. As soon as his eyes fell on the words, 'Colored Man's Case,' his attention was arrested." Harrison found that even Republican and Democratic party-hacks were eager to read Slater's pamphlet, based on the title alone. After all, they had to figure out how to appeal to the "strange people" on the other side of the color line.[39]

White and black socialists had to acquire "special equipment" for this work, Harrison urged: "One must know the people, their history, their manner of life, and modes of thinking and feeling. You have to know the psychology of the Negro, for if you don't you will fail to attract or impress him. You will fail to make him think — and feel. For many of your arguments must be addressed to his heart as well as to his head. This is more true of him than of most other American groups." The Socialists had to try harder, giving higher priority to enlisting black members, which began with hiring black organizers. Debs told reporters the party had three or four paid black national organizers. Harrison could think of only one, Woodbey, who had been very effective but could cover only so much territory. The party needed a bunch of Woodbeys. Harrison had a parting question: "Does the Socialist Party feel that it needs the Negroes as much as the Negro needs Socialism?" If Socialist leaders believed they could overthrow capitalism "with one part of the proletariat against us," they needed to say so. Harrison could not believe they believed that, even though their actions said so. The socialist project could not succeed if it left the black prole- tariat behind. Surely they agreed on that: "Let us act, then, in the light of this knowledge and add to the strength of the organized, all inclusive class con- scious working class movement."[40]

As it was, the white socialists remained clueless about black communities and only half interested in organizing within them. Slater won a following through his columns in the *Chicago Daily Socialist*, popularizing the concept that Socialists were "the New Abolitionists." He told readers he had lurched from one political project to another, briefly holding out for Teddy Roosevelt trust-busting, until he heard Woodbey speak in 1908. He lauded Woodbey for converting him to the "purity, simplicity, and justice" of Christian socialism, which held "the solution of the more serious phases of the so-called race problem." Debs, in turn, praised Slater as "a fine example of the educated, wide-awake teacher, of his race, whose whole heart is in the work and who ought to be encouraged in every possible way to spread the light among the masses." But Slater did not acquire Woodbey's command of his subject or enthrall lecture audiences in Woodbey's fashion, and he fixed on proving that Lincoln was a socialist. He did not criticize the Socialist Party for its failings in black communities, which won him plaudits from white Socialist leaders but no progress on what mattered.[41]

Slater spent the years 1912–19 serving as pastor of Bethel African Church in Clinton, Iowa, writing and speaking in forums sponsored by the CSF and the *Christian Socialist*. In 1913 he summarized his career as Woodbey's protégé, speaking as one who, like Woodbey, had worked "not a little among my peo- ple." Slater had three conclusions: (1) Black Americans were "very much preju- diced against the word Socialism." (2) Blacks were "quite susceptible to the doctrines of the Cooperative Commonwealth." (3) Blacks readily took an inter- est in the cooperative commonwealth as soon as someone explained it clearly. Like Woodbey, Slater had a preacher's relationship to his audience and a preacher's concept of activism: keep the faith and deliver the next sermon. He kept telling himself that African Americans simply needed more exposure to the vision of a cooperative commonwealth.[42]

But that did not happen after Woodbey and Slater were gone, for reasons that Harrison grasped. The Socialists were already perceived as being dangerously pro-Negro politically, even as they tried to downplay the subject. Organizing

African Americans sank to a lower priority after the Communist explosion of 1919 left the Socialist Party a shattered wreck. The preachers of black Baptist socialism eschewed the ecclesiastical separatism of their denomination, the National Baptist Convention, and stifled a sneer at NAACP liberalism, which did important work but never got to the root problem. Woodbey did not say that black Americans needed to build up their own organizations before they could make an impact on the political left. He could not say that when he preached the Debsian gospel that socialism is the solution to every social problem. It must have occurred to him, however, that going for the ultimate global solution without a home of one's own had taken him to a lonely place.

SOCIALIST FEMINISM, LENA MORROW LEWIS, AND KATE RICHARDS O'HARE

The Socialist Party treated women slightly better than it did African Americans because there were just enough women in it to demand better treatment. Women played active roles from the beginning, serving on subcommittees, waging floor fights, and lobbying for resolutions. In the Democratic and Republican Parties, female delegates to conventions ranged from almost none to less than 1 percent. In the Socialist Party they numbered 8 percent in 1904, 10 percent in 1908, and 10 percent in 1912.

Nearly all these women were middle-class, white, native-born, college-educated, and Protestant, hailing from the rural Midwest or Far West. Nearly all came from middle-class Christian churches, the Christian temperance movement, Christian settlements, the suffrage movement, or, most often, all of them. Most had a role model in Frances Willard, and many came to social activism through the Woman's Christian Temperance Union (WCTU). Only four of the forty-one leading female socialists came from working-class backgrounds— Elizabeth Gurley Flynn, Kate Richards O'Hare, Rose Pastor Stokes, and Theresa Malkiel. The Socialist Party women endured constantly patronizing treatment, lacking a single representative on the executive committee until 1909, notwithstanding that the party had two female stars—O'Hare and Lena Morrow Lewis— and many women toiling at the precinct level. In 1909, when Lewis was elected to the NEC, Hillquit and Berger commiserated with each other and others that the party was carrying feminism further than necessary. In 1913, when O'Hare was elected to the International Socialist Bureau, Hillquit and Berger were mortified that the party would be a laughingstock to European socialists. Neither of these breakthroughs would have occurred had the party not reluctantly created the Woman's National Committee (WNC) in 1908.[43]

May Wood Simons told the Socialist convention of 1908 that women needed a special organization because they were more oppressed than men under capitalism. She had long believed that women were more oppressed than men but had not dared to say it at a Socialist gathering until now. She had only recently decided that women should have a special organization, and she was still against any organization that focused on women's issues. But if the party wanted larger numbers of female members it had to create a women's organization. More important, the party needed to grasp that the woman question was part of the labor question. As the first head of the WNC Simons was the gatekeeper of the difference between maintaining a women's organization and allowing it to become a female-identified caucus. Stokes was another guardian of the difference. The WNC supported the party line that socialism has nothing special to say about racism or sexism. Yet the WNC sponsored a plethora of women's groups at the state and local levels in which women bonded together, supported each other, and boosted the party's leading female voices.[44]

Socialist women wrote about each other, and far more generously than men. Lewis and O'Hare counted on the admiring publicity they received from socialist sisters when they spoke to a party local, notwithstanding that Lewis vehemently opposed any autonomous collective standing for women in the party. Both came from Midwest American social gospel evangelicalism and retained its trademarks. Both got their start in the Christian temperance movement just as it acquired socialist and suffrage-feminist flanks. Both were products of the farming heartland that birthed suffrage movements. The cult of Victorian true womanhood never reached the farm, where labor was shared across gender distinctions and women seized the idea that they should be able to vote. Lewis and O'Hare joined the Socialist Party in 1902 and threw themselves headlong into it. Lewis gave compact sermons on scientific socialism, O'Hare gave inimitable performances on whatever came to mind once she had given her three-part stump speech, and both brought Christian social purity politics into socialism, making it possible for thousands of women far removed from New York Marxist salons to imagine themselves as socialists.

Martha Lena Morrow Lewis was born in 1868 in Gerlaw, Illinois, a small town in the farming district of Warren County, near Monmouth. Her father, Thomas Morrow, was the pastor of the local United Presbyterian Church, her mother, Mary Story Morrow, was active in the Woman's Missionary Association, and both were prototypes of the social gospel. Before the Civil War, congregations and missionary societies concentrated on domestic and foreign missions; after the war they poured into welfare work, founded dozens of colleges and universities for black Americans, and created the social gospel movement.

Morrow taught Sunday school in her youth and graduated in 1892 from the nearby Presbyterian college, Monmouth College. She caught the WCTU just as it peaked under Willard. Willard cofounded the WCTU in 1874 and built it up as a speaker and corresponding secretary. In 1879 she took over as president, steadily molding the organization to her left-turning politics. She broadened its Prohibition base to include women's rights, labor rights, and education reforms. Temperance and suffrage folded together as "Home Protection," she argued, because drunken men got away with their crimes against women as long as women couldn't vote. Willard and the WCTU told women they were not the weaker sex, ordained by God to be subordinate to men, or naturally dependent on men. Society would become much better in every way when women entered the political process and voted on the basis of their values. In the late 1880s Willard became a Fabian socialist, and by 1892 the WCTU was a political powerhouse of two hundred thousand members. Morrow joined its speaking staff straight out of college, preaching Willard's renowned "do everything" social gospel of temperance, women's rights, labor organizing, education, and gradual socialism.[45]

Nothing like the WCTU had ever existed. Willard justly boasted of building an army of disciplined, purposeful, virtuous feminist women. Illinois had the strongest WCTU organizations, and Morrow served as superintendent of the sixth district centered in Freeport. She admired Willard enormously, accepting personal responsibility for the success of the Freeport district, as required of all WCTU superintendents. Morrow toured the small towns and villages of northwestern Illinois, organized WCTU branches, spoke constantly to churches and women's clubs, and became a compelling platform performer. She loved temperance activism and never ceased to believe it was essential revolutionary work. In her last year as a WCTU speaker she delivered 120 addresses, all on regenerating U.S. American society by abolishing alcohol and winning the vote. Willard died in 1898, and Morrow opted for full-bore suffrage activism, becoming secretary the following year of the Illinois Equal Suffrage Society, which threw her into alliance work with Chicago unions, campaigning for women's suffrage at the state level. In 1900 the National American Woman Suffrage Association transferred her to Portland, Oregon, to work with trade unions and develop a local organization. There she met California Christian socialists who recruited her to the newly founded Socialist Party.[46]

Approximately 20 percent of the California socialists were women, and most had taken Morrow's Christian path to suffrage and socialist activism. Her life turned a corner when she joined the party. She threw herself into Socialist organizing, telling audiences she came west to fight for women's right to vote, only to learn that socialism is about something more essential. Being unable to feed your family is much worse than being unable to vote. Sexual discrimination was terrible but not as bad as class oppression; thus women suffered more from class injustice than from sex injustice. Had Morrow not believed it she could not have endured the sexism of the Socialist Party. As it was, she gave herself to grinding, rough, low-paid, tedious Socialist organizing—a far cry from the churchy powerhouse WCTU machine in which she began. Morrow judged that socialism was weak in central and northern California but long on potential. The Karl Marx Club of Oakland took up a collection to send her north. She conducted a massive canvass by herself, giving outdoor lectures in isolated villages. She spoke for six nights in a row in Eureka, California, standing on a cracker box, handing out party tracts. Merely showing up caused a stir in places that were very short on women. Morrow rode work trains into lumber camps, stunning lumberjacks; she told stories for years to come about their reactions. Her pace slowed briefly in 1903 when Morrow met a fellow Socialist speaker, Arthur Lewis, and married him. For two years she confined most of her speaking to the Bay Area. During the city election campaign of 1903 she defied the Bay Area's police crackdown against street speaking, on one occasion calling her husband to bail her out of jail. The marriage did not last because he took a full-time lecturing appointment at the old Garrick Theater in Chicago and she had wanderlust. Lewis went back to constant road speaking, keeping her married name.[47]

In Montana a runaway horse set off a panicky crowd, upending Lewis's lecture stand, bruising her badly, and ripping apart her only platform dress. This story entered her stock speech to illustrate that nothing could thwart her or socialism. She crisscrossed the nation from Texas camps to West Virginia mining fields to small towns to the party's metropolitan strongholds in California, Missouri, Wisconsin, Michigan, upstate New York, and New York City. Always she said that gender should not matter. Many of the socialist women Lewis met were older than she and determined to create their own sector of the Socialist Party. Most had worked for the WCTU at some point and internalized Willard's lesson about the importance of having their own organization. Some organized socialist women's clubs, especially in California and Kansas. By 1907 they had a national monthly paper, *Socialist Woman*, and welcomed the call of the Socialist International to create programs and organizations advocating woman's suffrage. An opposing faction of socialist women—mostly Germans and Jews from metropolitan areas—opposed any special programs or organizations for women. The founding of the WNC struck a compromise between these positions. It created a national women's organization that propagandized for suffrage and denied that socialist women needed any special treatment to achieve equality. All they needed was to be freed from sexist exclusions and protection. This compromise suited Lewis perfectly. She detested women's clubs and their service mentality, contending that achieving real equality would be far better. She reasoned that under the current system most women identified with their own sex, but suffrage would turn women into full citizens, diminishing their gender identification, and socialism would make it superfluous. Mary Jo Buhle observes that Lewis "purposefully flaunted her own achievements not to brag but to set an example for others to emulate." Socialism would have plenty of female leaders, Lewis believed, as soon as it had more women like her.[48]

Suffrage was about the emancipation of individuals and so was socialism, on a bigger scale. From the beginning of her socialist career she said the point of feminism was "to develop the idea that woman is a human being." To Lewis, socialism dispensed with the cloying cult of womanhood that too much of the WCTU still purveyed. Only in the Socialist Party did she get to struggle for a revolution with no particular mention of her gender. Lewis wrote in 1905, "The woman who will be a real and permanent service to the Party is the one who maintains her place in the movement and her right to work solely and only on the grounds of her merit and fitness to do things." She did not tell women that becoming a socialist would be good for them, for the Socialist Party was not some kind of church. She said women should join the party for the same reason men joined it, to overthrow capitalism. Lewis put it bluntly, telling her audiences that abolishing capitalism "is no prayer-meeting job, and the woman who is afraid of a few men who are trying to secure the same thing she is working for, or who can be driven away by the men who persist in smoking, even at the inconvenience of others, had better go back to her sheltered nook and give place to the women of courage."[49]

Putting it so vehemently did not diminish her commitment to women's rights. Lewis was like Woodbey in fiercely upholding her personal dignity and defending her rights on socialist terms. She staunchly defended the right of women to be leaders at every level of the party's life and was the strongest proponent of woman suffrage and her brand of feminism in the Socialist Party. Lewis took for granted that women were more moral and social than men. Protestant morality, neo-Lamarckian social science, WCTU politics, suffrage feminism, and socialism folded together for her on these two points. She told her audiences that an infusion of morally superior women into socialism would be very good for the character of the Socialist Party. Though she kept up with the social-historical turn in social science, to her it merely modified the explanation for female superiority that she took from college, the WCTU, and the suffrage movement. Lester Ward said the female principle is the basis of the human race, and the male is an evolution in the course of nature for the purpose of differentiation. Succinctly, the female *is* the human race and the male is a development, *sex*. Lewis extrapolated from Ward that the woman question in modern society should be uncoupled from the sex question in nature. Doing so was exceedingly difficult because private property "completely changed the status of women in society." Lewis reprised Engels on private property and the turning of males into anxious patriarchs and transmitters of property. Women, she said, fell from being the head of the human race to being defined by their maternal functions: "MARRIAGE BECAME THE ALL-IMPORTANT OBJECT IN WOMAN'S LIFE." She appreciated that in some states women could work as clerks in department stores. However, American women had no hope of becoming full human beings until America abolished private property and created a socialist society: "The Cooperative Commonwealth will give us a new and higher standard of morality."[50]

By 1911 she had spoken in every state of the nation. *The Masses,* a fiery New York radical paper edited by Max Eastman and founded in 1911, profiled her that year. Lewis reflected, "The price I personally have paid has been to relinquish any and all ideas of a home. Not that it matters. I am used to it now." She said she never slept in the same place for fourteen consecutive nights at any time during her seventeen years of lecturing: "To be truthful, I have quite forgotten the sensation of having personal belongings about me, other than my clothing." She did not believe her unusual vantage point marred her perception of what women were up against; the class struggle trumped women's emancipation, and the party needed more rugged, crusading female organizers like her. Meanwhile she criticized the very women who lifted her up, seeming not to notice the irony. Socialism made all things new to Lewis, as it did to Debs and Woodbey. On the stump she proclaimed that knowledge is power, so capitalism was doomed. Capitalism educated working-class people to prop up the system and make more money, ensuring its downfall by doing so: "That which has served the capitalist class will someday serve the working class. The trained minds that create profits for the masters of today will create wealth for the producers to enjoy tomorrow."[51]

She endured hard-to-bear comments, sometimes in lecture introductions, from socialist men who couldn't resist remarking on her surprising femininity or tiny hands. It galled Lewis that Socialist men were no better than churchmen in how they treated women. She knew that many of them never accepted that she was as fearless an organizer as any of them. In 1911 her friendship with National Secretary J. Mahlon Barnes singed her reputation when Barnes's reputation as an adulterer set off a proxy fight for control of the party. Christian socialists and the party's left flank demanded a new secretary; Hillquit and Berger defended Barnes as an Old Guard stalwart; Debs resented both sides for pressuring him and making the party look bad; and Lewis got burned merely for hanging out with Barnes and not being ladylike. This drama took two years to play out, ending Lewis's desire to serve on the NEC. She shunned the spotlight, went back to lecturing in small towns, and opted for party organizing in Alaska. By the time she left Alaska for Seattle in 1917, her beloved party was unrecognizable and teetering on catastrophe.[52]

Buhle aptly judges that Lewis had an ambiguous legacy in the party matching the ambiguity of her position. By rising to the top of the party hierarchy and achieving a national reputation Lewis showed that the party held a serious commitment to women's equality, but her scorn for women's clubs and anything smacking of gender politics thwarted what she devoted her life to achieving — recruiting women into socialism. *ISR* editor Mary Marcy lauded Lewis for taking the high road, asking no favors, and blazing a path for others. Lewis, Marcy said, did not need "to be pampered with easy tasks that nobody else thinks are worth doing." *Call* editor Anita Block replied that indeed, Lewis didn't need anybody. Neither did Susan B. Anthony or Mary Marcy. But meanwhile, Block said, most women needed somebody because most women were "so atrophied by sex-slavery that they actually barricade themselves within their own prison, the Home." Block suggested that the socialist movement needed feminist leaders who did not scorn the helping hands of women's clubs, service auxiliaries, and making an issue of gender differences.[53]

The cultural federations and women's organizations of the Socialist Party strengthened the party through its boom years and helped to generate audiences for Lewis and O'Hare. Many of the women's groups forged links with the semiautonomous immigrant organizations. The new immigrants related to the party and acted in it through their own organizations. By 1912 there were Finnish, Bohemian, Hungarian, Italian, Jewish, Polish, Scandinavian, South Slav, German, Slovak, and Polish federations in the Socialist Party, all carrying forward the languages and cultural traditions of European socialism.[54]

Meanwhile the party's other female star came from prairie country. Kathleen Richards was born in 1877 in Ottawa County, Kansas. Her father's family moved from Wales to Virginia in the colonial period and to Kentucky in the early national period. Andrew Richards homesteaded to Kansas just before the Civil War and fought for the Union Army. He married Lucy Sullivan after the war, raised five children surrounded by extensive kinship networks from both sides of the family, and built a prosperous ranch. He was a Universalist, teaching his

children that God loves and saves everyone, though much of his family belonged
to the Disciples of Christ (Campbellites). The Disciples were minimalist on
church dogma and fervently evangelical, having originated among noncreedal
Scottish immigrants in the Ohio Valley. Kate Richards absorbed both religious
traditions while growing up happy in a world of herds roaming over hills, cow-
punchers brandishing spurs and big hats, and extended family picnics. She
bathed in "freedom and security and plenty," loving her intimacy with nature
and four-legged creatures. She said that growing up in this environment established her character and laid the foundation of her life. Then came the drought
and financial panic of 1887, and her idyllic childhood ended.[55]

There were weeks of tension as the recession wiped out jobs and mortgages.
Farms were abandoned, and Ottawa County lost 20 percent of its population.
O'Hare later remembered that her mother smiled bravely when her children
were nearby but cried when she thought they were out of sight: "A horrible
something that we could not fathom had settled down over our lives, but the day
when the realness of it all was forced home came all too soon." The home was
dismantled, and her father departed alone for Kansas City to find work. It cut
him to beg for a job after building a ranch from nothing. She traced her compassion for wounded people to the grief she felt for her father. The family moved to
the poor side of Kansas City, joining "the poverty, the misery, the want, the wan-
faced women and hunger-pinched children, men tramping the streets by day
and begging for a place in the police stations." Richards never lost the searing
memory of the "sordid, grinding, pinching poverty of the workless workers and
the frightful, stinging, piercing cold of that winter in Kansas City." Her father
found getting-by jobs and she took refuge in church worship, prayers, and
church service. She had religious-meaning questions to ask, but beyond that the
church was literally a refuge from the shock of urban misery and squalor.[56]

The Disciples and WCTU stumped hard for Prohibition in Kansas, keeping
many counties dry. Richards came of age on Prohibition preaching, while her
father started up a machine shop. Clerics said the key to abolishing urban squalor was to get rid of alcohol, which rang true to her since outbreaks of violence
always seemed to begin with somebody getting drunk. Richards looked up to
the clerics, aspiring to be a Disciples missionary or a minister, not realizing at
first that only the mission field was a possibility for women. Evangelical traditions became more restrictive in the late nineteenth century, disavowing their
own histories of allowing women to preach. As a teenager Richards roamed the
central business district of Kansas City with the Florence Crittenton Mission
and Home, inviting sex workers, alcoholics, and the homeless into the mission's
services and programs. For a while rescue mission work was uplifting to her,

until it began to feel futile and smug. Praying was a waste of time, and the flow of sex workers and alcoholics was unending. She floundered, not knowing what to do with her life. She read *Progress and Poverty*, *Wealth Against Commonwealth*, and a third best seller on social ills, *Caesar's Column*, by Ignatius Donnelly. Richards took an office job in her father's machine shop, where she botched every task and pleaded to be trained as a machinist until her father relented. She worked for four years as a machine shop apprentice, forging and lathing alongside skilled mechanics—union workers she admired enormously.[57]

One night in 1901 Richards attended a ball sponsored by the Cigar Makers Union, where she heard a speech by Mother Jones. Jones told the crowd that a scab at a ballot box was more contemptible than a scab at a factory. Workers needed to build their own party—the Socialist Party—instead of scabbing for capitalist parties. Richards asked Jones what a Socialist was, and Jones escorted her to a gaggle of men talking about it. The next day Richards went to the local Socialist Party office, was handed a pile of books, and took them home. All were completely incomprehensible. The last one was *The Communist Manifesto*, which for some reason never mentioned socialism. She returned to the party office to report that she couldn't understand anything in these books, which evoked much expounding from the socialists until Julius Wayland intervened, asking what she had tried to read. Wayland gave her copies of Herron's *Between Jesus and Caesar*, Bellamy's *Looking Backward*, and Robert Blatchford's British classic *Merrie England*, saying these should work much better. Richards became a socialist upon reading them: "For a time I lived in a dazed dream while my mental structure was being ruthlessly torn asunder and rebuilt on a new foundation." She found it painful to adopt a new worldview or even to try: "At last I awoke in a new world, with new viewpoints, and a new outlook. Recreated, I lived again with new aims, new hopes, new aspirations, and the dazzling view of the new and wonderful work to do."[58]

Walter Thomas Mills launched a school for socialist organizers in Girard, Kansas. He was a social gospel cleric, prohibitionist, and former Bryan supporter with a colorful personality and a lecture circuit following who had previously run a socialist night school in Chicago. His International School of Socialist Economy, partly funded by Wayland, was located over a furniture store. Mills taught the canon of socialist theory and organizing, including his own book *The Struggle for Existence*. Richards enrolled in Mills's first three-month class in Girard, enthralled by the teaching and the socialist community gathered around Wayland. One of her twenty-four full-time classmates was a second-generation Irish American from St. Louis, Francis Patrick O'Hare. He had grown up poor and virtually orphaned, with one year of high school, when

Appeal to Reason hooked him. He was already writing for the labor press when he took the course. O'Hare and Richards fell in love, deciding within four days to marry; years afterward she still described the experience rhapsodically. The course ended on December 30, 1901, and they were married at Wayland's home on New Year's Day. Their honeymoon was a socialist road show that started in Kansas City, caught media attention, and became the template of their careers in the Socialist Party.[59]

The O'Hares evangelized for socialism in Kansas, Oklahoma Territory, Texas, Arkansas, Missouri, Iowa, and Tennessee. They took their first extended trip in 1902 to the Pennsylvania mines, moved on to New York City, and boarded with party comrades wherever they went, lacking any money. They met the party bigwigs and wrote for socialist papers, already noting that Kate had a better knack than Frank for stirring attention, although Frank gave the featured lectures on their speaking tours. It took her several years to develop her speaking prowess. The couple returned to Kansas City to start a family, moved to Oklahoma Territory in 1904 after their first child was born, and tried to eke out a living in Oklahoma City. Their son Richard was born in 1903, daughter Kathleen came in 1905, and twin sons Eugene and Victor—named after Debs—were born in 1908. Frank and Kate conducted speaking tours alternately, relying on the Richards grandparents and other relatives for financial help and child care.

Meanwhile Kate O'Hare became a sensational speaker. Frank never learned how to talk to rural audiences, but Kate dazzled them with local color, knowing zingers, and a photographic eye for detail. She grew famous for her speaking and writing, conducting lengthy speaking tours arranged by the lecture bureau of *Appeal to Reason*. Wayland got the state socialist parties to bid for her services, telling them she could only accommodate two or three events per state, in suitable venues. O'Hare did not perform on soapboxes; she lectured in rented halls and to the vast, weeklong summer camps that infused the Oklahoma Socialist Party and other state organizations. Only Debs and, in some places, Jones outdrew her as a speaker. O'Hare had a triangular stump speech on politics, economics, and social issues that she gave every day for weeks at a time with local adaptations. She relied especially on Frank's sister Gertrude to care for the children during her speaking tours, an arrangement Gertrude came to resent. O'Hare's letters emoted too much, for Gertrude and Frank, about beautiful scenery and what a great time she was having. He had a nervous breakdown that diminished his road speaking and wiped out his ebullience. She felt bad about her family situation but reasoned that it couldn't be helped as long as socialism didn't exist. Sally Miller observes that O'Hare was truthfully described as "not only the foremost woman orator but also the busiest woman in America."[60]

She raged against tenant farm slavery, the convict lease system, young girls slaving in factories for two dollars a week, and the sheer badness of a society that offered no other options to hopeless millions. O'Hare blasted the state of Arkansas and "many other Southern states" for selling convicts to the highest bidder, charging that the "convict lumber camps, cotton farms and turpentine camps and [railroad] tie camps are all owned by a gang of the most greedy, soulless capitalists on earth." She condemned the system that condemned fourteen-year-old girls to perpetuate the system in brutal factories: "They all worked because they were compelled to work. No feminine unrest there; no struggle for a 'wider life,' no suffragette tendencies, no revolt against home, husbands, and babies. The whole question resolved itself into the problem of bread. If the girls expected to eat they must go out and earn their bread; not only earn their own bread but earn bread for the mother who must stay at home and act as a breeding machine to provide children like themselves for the factory. The girl must sometimes earn bread for the father, who had been worn out or broken at his job and tossed on the human scrap pile, a human wreck, whose only value now is to act as a fertilizing machine for a human breeding machine, who are breeding more children for the factory boss."[61]

O'Hare lacked any such feeling about the oppression of black Americans. One reason that certain audiences adored her was that she was as racist as they were. They loved her casual banter featuring the n-word and her bigoted asides about the supposed inferiority of black people. She told southern audiences she didn't blame them for loathing Negro Rule or the idea of social equality. "Reconstruction," to O'Hare, evoked only "the stinging disgrace of having ignorant blacks placed in positions of power and authority." She employed the vile phrase "nigger equality" as a substitute for social equality, claiming that social equality perverted the principle of equality before the law. Socialists, in her telling, wanted to "put the Negro where he can't compete with the white man." O'Hare explained that capitalism bound whites and blacks together in economic servitude. Under the equal opportunity achieved by socialism, white Americans would be liberated from having to deal with black people and vice versa: "We Socialists don't love the 'nigger' any better than he loves us." Black people repulsed her, and she took for granted that they felt the same way about whites. She tried to put it neutrally: "I neither love nor hate a negro. I am no more anxious to associate with him as he is to associate with me. I don't want to associate on terms of social equality with him and I know he is just as willing to dispense with my society as I am with his, but capitalism forces us into a social, economic, and physical relation which is just as revolting to the negro as it is to me, and as both the negro and I want to escape, the only way we can do so is by Socialism giving us both an equal opportunity to have access to the means of life and the product of our labor; then we can dump the capitalist off our back and work out our own problems, freed from the curse of race antagonism."[62]

The closing phrase was the closest she came to acknowledging that black Americans might turn out to be human beings worth knowing. Her concern was to refute the number one objection to socialism: Socialism was about equality, which led to n-word equality. O'Hare told her audiences that segregation was the only solution to the race problem. Black Americans should be given their own section of the country and left alone. If they developed a decent civilization, "well and good; if not, and he prefers to hunt and fish and live idly, no one will be injured but him and that will be his business." Two hundred forty-six years of slavery did not matter in this telling, nor a half century and counting of segregation, which had too much integration for her. Meanwhile southern whites needed to stop voting for Democrats who brayed about n-word equality, which changed nothing and kept them in power. O'Hare believed her racism wasn't the hateful kind, unlike that of Texas socialist publicist J. L. Hicks, who did not express her "I neither love nor hate" disclaimer. Her racism was just normal white self-respect that took for granted that whites and blacks could never mix in a good way. She did not apologize for her "normal" bigotry when she traveled north, and there is little evidence that audiences called her on it. In theory, the Socialist Party's support of civil rights for all Americans compelled the party in Oklahoma to welcome any blacks who wanted to join. In fact, precious few black Oklahomans pressed the issue. The prospect of dealing with O'Hare was ample reason not to bother.[63]

Her racism was layered and selective, as O'Hare was sympathetic toward Native Americans and censured anti-Jewish bigotry when she encountered it. Native Americans were individual human beings to her in ways that African Americans were not, even though O'Hare judged that nearby Cherokee, Choctaw, Creek, Seminole, and Chickasaw tribes had no hope of surviving Darwinian weeding out. She talked about intrusive white settlers and violated treaties with a moral feeling she never conveyed about Jim Crow. The difference could not have been proximity alone because Native Americans were 4.5 percent of Oklahoma's population in 1910, as compared to the black American proportion of 8.3 percent. Being a socialist also helped O'Hare acquire a more favorable view of Jews than she learned growing up, though on the stump she occasionally made a rueful aside based on a stereotype about Jews.

O'Hare never forgot how she began, as a prohibitionist. She had become a socialist in the first place because religious activism did not abolish alcoholism and poverty. She believed the best temperance activism was socialist and focused on abolishing alcoholism, not alcohol. But two contrasting sides dominated the argument about temperance, creating an impasse. One side whipped up fear against alcohol; the other side made a freedom argument that ridiculed prohibitionists. O'Hare wanted the socialist movement to oppose drunkenness with the same moral passion it conveyed about poverty, child labor, sex work, and overwork. Socialism, she said, held up to the working class the "ideal of a clear-brained, clean-bodied, conquering proletariat. We believe we have the right answer to the problem. We have found intemperance to be a disease, the fruit of capitalism." She reasoned that drunkenness was like other diseases in being largely vocational and correlated with specific trades. Miners suffered from rheumatism, railroad workers got kidney disease, printers came down with consumption, and hair workers contracted anthrax. Each trade developed a disease peculiar to its surroundings and correlated with factors of idleness, work, temperature, speed, nervous tension, and muscular strain. Coal mining and metal mining, she observed, were notorious for producing alcoholics: "Their work is excessively hard, carried on underground, in constant danger, and always in darkness, slime, and damp air. They live and labor knowing that every moment of their life hangs by the slenderest thread." O'Hare described telegraph operating and glass manufacturing with similarly vivid imagery, having listened intently to workers. She understood why they drank to the point of self-oblivion, urging readers that society needed a solution. Religion was suited to help, but churches wasted their time and money on fancy buildings. Socialism was the answer because it took over the mines, communication systems, and factories and took the profit out of alcohol. Under socialism, nobody would get rich by turning vulnerable and hurting workers into alcoholics.[64]

On the stump she railed against the hypocrisy and conservatism of churches, always contending that churches shirked their true mission. O'Hare was a Jesus-versus-Christianity Christian, deeply identified with Jesus as she interpreted him. Socialist leaders who were not social gospel clerics usually said as little as possible about religion. Even Debs was wary of controversy in this area. O'Hare did not shy away from blasting churches, partly because she demanded so much more from them. It galled her that clerics casually blamed God for everything from war to syphilis while crying "blasphemy!" when socialists laid the blame on capitalism. Somehow it was blasphemous to oppose war, poverty, and the economic slavery of women but not blasphemous to blame God for World War I, starvation, and prostitution? O'Hare was incredulous: "Sure! Blame it on poor God; He can't help Himself, and it's so much easier to sit down and twiddle our thumbs and mumble, 'God's will be done,' than it is to stand up like men and women, give God a square deal and rebuild society in a decent, sane, humane manner."[65]

O'Hare was steeped in the Marxian canon of Darwin, Morgan, Marx, Engels, and Bebel that she learned from Mills. She cited all of them when she wrote about the subjection of women, reprising Mills's Christian socialist theme that it took a thousand centuries before men realized they could hoard the earth's resources for themselves, cheating women. The rule of private property and the subjugation of women, she said, were very tightly linked. Usually her socialist critique drove the argument. In February 1917, while America geared for war and she felt the horror of the moment, she featured the feminist argument—a cry of the heart against the rule of males. Women have written no history, O'Hare lamented: "No book has ever yet been written that lays bare the woman heart and soul, and no voice has ever spoken the secrets of her mind. No man can know what women feel and no woman dare tell it. If, for but a single day, every woman spoke the exact truth and expressed her thoughts without disguise, chaos would reign and society would be turned up-side-down." Women do not speak anywhere by right, she wrote; they speak only by permission. Perhaps a few generations hence, when women owned publishing houses and were economically free, "our great-great-grand-daughters may write exactly what they feel to be true, but it is not for the women of my generation."[66]

Then men called the nation to war, and O'Hare joined Debs in lonely socialist criminal protest.

DU BOIS, OVINGTON, WALLING, AND THE NAACP

The path to a better U.S. American socialist politics of racial justice ran through left-liberalism. It did not come from the one-factor socialism of Debs and Woodbey, which was too true-believing to be creative about racial justice, and it had to fight off the sectors of the party that were outright racist. Mary White Ovington and William English Walling were socialists who flushed with shame at their party's feckless record on racial justice and did not believe in one-factor salvation. They took the Bliss view about making alliances with left-liberals, which tagged them as revisionists in their crowd. Ovington helped Du Bois find his socialist anchor, and in 1909 the three socialists plus Charles Edward Russell played major roles in founding the NAACP. Their racial justice activism was always implicitly a reproach of the Socialist Party to which they belonged and an augur of a better socialism.

The NAACP was a successor to twenty years of failing to build a protest organization for racial justice. The National Afro-American League, a black-only organization founded by Thomas Fortune in 1890, had come and gone, followed by the National Afro-American Council founded in 1898 by Fortune and

Alexander Walters, the National Negro Suffrage League founded by William Monroe Trotter in 1905, the Niagara Movement founded by Du Bois and Trotter in 1905, and the Negro American Political League founded by Trotter in 1908. White neo-abolitionists Albion Tourgée and John Milholland founded multiracial organizations that protested for racial justice, also of short duration. The Niagara Movement was in its dying phase when Du Bois cut a deal with white socialists and liberals to form the NAACP. His friendship with Ovington was crucial to the founding, survival, and flourishing of the NAACP.[67]

Ovington grew up in a cultured, Brooklyn, abolitionist, feminist, Unitarian family and was deeply involved in reform movements. In 1904 she had recently cofounded a settlement in San Juan Hill, an African American neighborhood just north of Hell's Kitchen in New York City, when Du Bois invited her to his annual spring conference at Atlanta University. Du Bois was embroiled at the time in the fight against Booker T. Washington, who became famous by contending that black Americans made progress by learning trades and eschewing politics. Du Bois roared against the self-abasement of Bookerism, founding the Niagara Movement to oppose it. Ovington had friends across the spectrum of left-wing movements; her friendship with Du Bois soon became foundational for both of them. In 1905 she joined the Socialist Party and urged Du Bois that combating capitalism was essential to the struggle against racism. She got him to read socialist writers, especially her friend John Spargo. She also worked on Ray Stannard Baker, whose journalism helped to create the activist community that founded the NAACP. By 1907 Du Bois was sprinkling prosocialist statements into his writings, calling himself a "Socialist of the path" and declaring that in socialism lay "the one great hope of the Negro American."[68]

On August 14, 1908, Springfield, Illinois, erupted in a devastating race riot. Racial tension had built up in Springfield over competition for jobs in mining and rail transportation between black and white newcomers from the South. A white woman charged that a young black man raped her; another woman egged on a mob that gathered at the jail; and hundreds of marauding white rioters killed seven black Americans by gunfire and two by lynching. Thousands of white citizens calmly looked on for two days while the mob chased down every black person it could find.

The Springfield riot shocked northern white progressives into action. Walling called the NAACP into existence with a searing article in *The Independent* titled "The Race War in the North." He was nearly as outraged by the public reaction to the riot as by the marauders. Walling and Anna Strunsky traveled to Springfield as the riot occurred, expecting to meet horrified onlookers. Civic and political leaders responded appropriately, but the "masses of the people" in the shops and streets were another story: "We at once discovered, to our amazement, that Springfield had no shame. She stood for the action of the mob. She hoped the rest of the negroes might flee. She threatened that the movement to drive them out would continue." Then the press coverage mused about "mitigating circumstances" that made such a thing possible in the home of Lincoln. Walling replied that Springfield exploded because of race hatred, not mitigating circumstances. The whole country was becoming like the worst parts of the South, and America was overdue to become alarmed about it: "Either the spirit of the abolitionists, of Lincoln and of Lovejoy, must be revived and we must come to treat the negro on a plane of absolute political and social equality, or Vardaman and Tillman will soon have transferred the race war to the North." On the basis of that either/or, Walling ended with a question: "Who realizes the seriousness of the situation, and what large and powerful body of citizens is ready to come to their aid?"[69]

Ovington, reading Walling's article, vowed to build a large and powerful national organization to fight racism. She prodded Walling to get something started. The two of them plus social worker Henry Moskowitz drafted a call for a meeting on Lincoln's one-hundredth birthday, February 12, 1909, which they sent to Ovington's contacts in reform circles. Muckraking journalist Charles Edward Russell became the fourth member of the original group, which knowingly added a fifth member, Oswald Garrison Villard, before the meetings began in earnest. Villard inherited the *New York Evening Post* from his father; his mother was the daughter of abolitionist William Lloyd Garrison; and he had been calling for a "Committee for the Advancement of the Negro Race" since 1906. Reading *The Souls of Black Folk*, by Du Bois, was a crucial influence on Villard. He investigated the peonage system and was appalled, protesting that it reinstated slavery in the South. He said America needed a civil rights organization with a research and publicity bureau, a legal division to fight court cases against racial discrimination, a special committee to investigate lynching and peonage, a lobbying operation at the federal and state levels, a committee to organize mass protest meetings, and a monthly magazine. This was a blueprint for what became the NAACP. The socialists approached Villard knowing he was already committed to the idea, plus he was rich, smart, aggressive, connected, and far more influential than any of them.[70]

From the beginning Ovington was the key to the group's unusual bridging of racial, gender, and class lines. The early meetings convened at Walling's apartment on West Thirty-Ninth Street in Manhattan, adding Baker, social worker Lillian Wald, Rabbi Stephen Wise, Unitarian minister John Haynes Holmes, and two African American members—AME Zion bishop Alexander Walters and Ovington's friend William Henry Brooks, pastor of St. Mark's Methodist

Episcopal Church in New York. Villard wrote a call signed by sixty endorsers for a new organization. Eight were black Americans: Du Bois, Walters, Brooks, school principal William Bulkley, antilynching crusader Ida Wells-Barnett, Baptist cleric J. Milton Waldron, Presbyterian cleric Francis Grimké, and civic activist Mary Church Terrell. Many of the sixty signers did not know each other, but they all knew Ovington.[71]

The founding conference took place at New York's Charity Organization Hall in 1909. Three hundred delegates attended and approximately eleven hundred spectators. Nearly one-third of the delegates were women, an echo of the abolitionist past before abolitionism and woman suffrage split over the Fifteenth Amendment. Jane Addams, Mary McDowell, Lillian Wald, and Florence Kelley headed a formidable group of social workers. Other white female delegates included labor lawyer Inez Milholland, suffrage activist Fanny Garrison Villard (Oswald's mother), and Unitarian minister Celia Parker Woolley, a founder of Chicago's Frederick Douglass Center. Politically, the white progressives divided into three groups—Socialists in the orbit of Ovington, Walling, and Russell, old-style Republican Protestants like Villard, William Hayes Ward, and John Milholland, and liberal reformers less defined by ideology or religion.

Ward gave the opening keynote, a ringing call to build a movement for equal rights. White academics spoke for the rest of the morning on an assigned subject: scientific evidence of human equality. The afternoon speakers were Woolley, Du Bois, Bulkley, and Walling. Woolley argued that a racial justice organization should treat racial, gender, and economic injustice as interlocking variables. Du Bois argued that blacks needed political power to abolish the new slavery of disenfranchisement, Jim Crow, and poverty. Bulkley argued that southern racism stupidly did not recognize the value of developing an intelligent laboring class and drove skilled workers into the ranks of unskilled labor. Walling argued that a movement opposing racial injustice should target the antilabor alliances of northern and southern economic elites.[72]

By emphasizing economic justice the early speakers displayed their yearning for a labor movement not overwhelmingly segregated and hostile to black workers. Meanwhile the organization being birthed needed to find some wealthy white backers who were unlikely to prize trade unions. The success of this enterprise depended on Villard, who was still friendly with Washington. That provoked much anxiety that Washington would take over the later-named NAACP much as he took over the Afro-American Council. But the NAACP had Socialists at the helm who forged the organization into what it needed to be. Du Bois quit his position at Atlanta University to launch the flagship magazine of the NAACP, *Crisis*. Ovington devoted her life to Du Bois and the

NAACP. Walling chaired the NAACP and was a counterweight to Villard whenever Du Bois needed counterweight help.

Ovington, Walling, and Du Bois christened the magazine *The Crisis* after James Russell Lowell's abolitionist poem of 1844 "The Present Crisis." They identified with Lowell's sentiment: "Once to every man and nation comes the moment to decide, / In the strife of Truth with Falsehood, for the good or evil side." From the beginning the magazine featured a section on politics and society titled "Along the Color Line," a canvass of press coverage and correspondence titled "Opinion," an editorial section, a section on recent atrocities against Afro-Americans titled "The Burden," and a section describing not-to-miss recent articles and books. Soon it added a section on "women's issues." From the beginning it was a sensational success. In its first year it climbed to 9,000 net paid copies per month. Afterward it climbed by over 1,000 per month for years to come, soaring to 75,000 in 1918 and peaking at 104,000 the following year.[73]

The Crisis outstripped all sources of information about Afro-Americans, and it said so stridently. It was strong and unbridled about the black church, black women, white women, the politics of gender, and electoral politics. Du Bois, putting it aptly years later, recalled that when he wrote an editorial, he "talked turkey." Repeatedly he editorialized about women and feminism, refusing to be locked into a sorry either/or that pitted abolitionism against woman suffrage. Du Bois believed that the best measure of any society's civilization was the status of women within it. The ultimate measure of a society's enlightenment was its willingness to emancipate women—especially black women. His novel *The Quest of the Silver Fleece* (1912) pressed on this theme, suggesting that even the race question ultimately reduced to the ownership of women. White men wanted to own and control all women, having their way with them sexually whenever they felt like it. They resented any infringement on this desire, such as the existence of black men. Du Bois believed that this explained the explosion of white male rage in the South during and after Reconstruction. White men had to do something with the rage and lust that consumed them after they lost their ready access to black women's bodies. They had already sentimentalized white women as delicate types lacking sexual desire, so they had a problem with their own sexuality after they could not control or rape black women with impunity. *The Quest of the Silver Fleece* conjured a black heroine antithesis of rapist white culture—the luminous Zora, a dark-skinned, self-cultured embodiment of intuition and humanity who read Plato, Tennyson, and even Herbert Spencer, symbolizing the hope of human redemption.[74]

Zora was nothing like the symbol of obsequious, sexless, uneducated, matronly black humanity that the white South proposed to immortalize. In 1911 the

Athens, Georgia, *Banner* kicked off an outbreak of nostalgia for the old black mammies of the South that turned into a movement. This movement was still building steam in 1923 when the United Daughters of the Confederacy pushed for a statue in the nation's capital to commemorate how the bucolic plantation families of old loved their mammies. Du Bois took an early shot, in 1912, at burgeoning mammy nostalgia, noting that the black mammy of the proposed statues was always "of the foster mammy, not of the mother in her home, attending to her own babies." After slavery, when the black mammy retreated to her home, white mothers condemned her for selfishly, lazily caring for her own children. Then they condemned her when she trained to be a teacher instead of nursing white children. Du Bois celebrated black motherhood as a rebellion against racism: "Let the present-day mammies suckle their own children. Let them walk in the sunshine with their own toddling boys and girls and put their own sleepy little brothers and sisters to bed. As their girls grow to womanhood, let them see to it that, if possible, they do not enter domestic service in those homes where they are unprotected, and where their womanhood is not treated with respect. In the midst of immense difficulties, surrounded by caste, and hemmed in by restricted economic opportunity, let the colored mother of today build her own statue, and let it be the four walls of her own unsullied home."[75]

Du Bois on women is a minefield. He pushed aside Wells-Barnett and Terrell when they gained spotlight attention and humiliated his wife, Nina, by carrying on with numerous mistresses. Yet his writing expressed vividly that nothing cut him deeper than everything he knew about the vile mistreatment of black women. Du Bois expected, on judgment day, to forgive the white South for many things. He expected to forgive slavery, "for slavery is a world-old habit." He expected to forgive the South for defending the Confederacy, remembering its rebellion "with tender tears," and wailing and strutting about its Lost Cause and its pride of race: "But one thing I shall never forgive, neither in this world nor the world to come: its wanton and continued and persistent insulting of the black womanhood which it sought and seeks to prostitute to its lust." Du Bois thought about it whenever somebody invoked President Taft's statement about allowing the gentlemen of the South to take control of America's race problem: "I cannot forget that it is such Southern gentlemen into whose hands smug Northern hypocrites of today are seeking to place our women's eternal destiny — men who insist upon withholding from my mother and wife and daughter those signs and appellations of courtesy and respect which elsewhere he withholds only from bawds and courtesans."[76]

The 1912 presidential race tested and broke his commitment to the Socialist Party. Du Bois would have supported Debs had the Socialists held any chance of winning or had Debs dropped his evasiveness about race. Du Bois voted for Debs in 1904 and was a member of the Socialist Party when the 1912 campaign season began. He admired Debs for his passion for justice, inspiring oratory, French Protestant background, and personal antiracism. But Debs offended him every time he spoke about racism. Du Bois bristled at the sophistry of the Debs maxim that he offered nothing to blacks except Socialism, which would abolish racism. Sometimes Du Bois said Debs was not worth supporting as long as he dodged the race issue, pretending there was no race problem apart from the labor problem. Sometimes he acknowledged that Debs took a "manly stand for human rights irrespective of color," which was brave in America. In either case, Du Bois argued, Debs was not going to win, so blacks needed to choose among the other three parties. Some Socialists replied that Du Bois was not much of a Socialist if he could not muster a vote for Debs. Du Bois, respecting this sentiment, resigned from the party, later observing that the average American Socialist could scarcely grasp the hatred blacks experienced in the South. Socialists did not see the socialist imperative of becoming "a party of the Negro." Du Bois said they should face up to reality instead of betraying social-ism: "The Negro Problem is the great test of the American Socialist."[77]

That left a choice between Taft, who perfected the political art of racial den-igration; Roosevelt, who insulted and enraged black Americans during his pres-idency; and Wilson, who had no political record. Du Bois would have backed Roosevelt had TR supported a civil rights plank in his platform, but TR had not changed. Thus Du Bois chose Wilson, while counting the risks. Wilson was studiously vague about the rights of African Americans. He had kept Princeton University black-free during his presidency there, and his southern-based party was solidly caste-ridden. There had not been a southern president since Zachary Taylor or a Democratic president since Grover Cleveland. Du Bois told *Crisis* readers it was worth finding out if the Democratic Party could be democratic at the national level, not just in the north. Wilson was the best bet: "He will not advance the cause of oligarchy in the South, he will not seek further means of 'Jim Crow' insult, he will not dismiss black men wholesale from office, and he will remember that the Negro in the United States has a right to be heard and considered."[78]

President Wilson promptly falsified every one of these predictions, purging a dozen African Americans from the federal government, segregating clerks in the Treasury and Postal Departments, and bragging about it to southern Democrats. In places where herding was impossible, the government installed cages around black employees to separate them from longtime white cowork-ers. Du Bois observed that many Democrats apparently believed there was no limit to the abuse that white America should be able to inflict on black Americans. Democrats had not controlled the presidency *and* Congress since before the Civil War; southern Democrats seized the moment, proposing bills to ban interracial marriage, extend residential and transportation segregation, ban African Americans from the army and navy, and bar people of African descent from immigrating to the United States. Du Bois appealed to Wilson as a human being, a statesman, a person who touted his sense of fairness, and a cosmopolitan sophisticate: Please stop abusing us. Moreover, if politics negated all that, there was one thing more: Please remember that "we black men of the North have a growing nest egg of 500,000 ballots." If Wilson wanted any black votes next time, he had to change course. Du Bois ended on a personal note. He had not yet apologized to readers of *The Crisis* for supporting Wilson. "But at the present rate it looks as though some apology or explanation is going to be in order very soon."[79]

Crisis was a major player in black politics. The magazine soared because it radiated Du Bois's fearless spirit and brilliantly covered the issues. He shredded the journalistic convention that nobody wanted to look at pictures of African Americans. The only blacks that white newspapers pictured were accused or convicted criminals. Even black newspapers spurned pictures of ordinary black Americans. Du Bois observed, "In general, the Negro race was just a little afraid to see itself in plain ink." *Crisis* conveyed and displayed Du Bois's contrary conviction that black embodiment is beautiful.[80]

Du Bois celebrated the early courtroom victories of the NAACP that built a legal powerhouse, but winning legal battles was never the ultimate objective to him. He conceived the NAACP as the driving wedge of a global movement to empower black people. Every board meeting had an argument about that. Some liberals pleaded with Du Bois to stop talking about social equality since that reduced to interracial sex, a losing issue for the NAACP. Some insiders were more liberal but wanted Du Bois to cool the race-talk. Race should not matter, they argued; the job of the NAACP was to delegitimize race-talk and racial favoritism. Jane Addams and John Haynes Holmes were in that wing of the NAACP. Many said the purpose of the NAACP was to restore the Fourteenth and Fifteenth Amendments and abolish lynching, not to promote a worldwide liberation movement stressing black consciousness. This was not just an argument between Du Bois and white liberals. Black NAACP insiders Archibald Grimké, Butler Wilson, William A. Sinclair, and William Pickens vehemently objected to Du Bois's approach. They said Du Bois was too radical about social equality and global racialism, treated them rudely, spent too much money, and bypassed opportunities to promote the NAACP.[81]

Ovington mediated this conflict constantly in the organization. She defended Du Bois against all critics even as she struggled to hold the organization together. Ovington tried repeatedly to help Villard see the world as Du Bois did, from the perspective of an oppressed people that struggled not to be shackled, denigrated, and otherwise ignored. Joel Spingarn, a former Columbia professor, succeeded Villard as board chair and basically sided with Du Bois. Du Bois eventually got through the NAACP's organizational crisis by bonding with Spingarn, exactly as Ovington sought. Walling implored board directors that Du Bois was their star. If they didn't learn how to work with Du Bois, it would look as if they could not abide being led by a black intellectual with star power. Du Bois made the same argument, pointing to the success of the magazine, which had thirty-three thousand subscribers by early 1914.

In April 1914 Ovington asked Du Bois to imagine that the editor of *Crisis* was a white abolitionist with all the right views. This imaginary editor would sometimes offend black American readers without being conscious of it. He would patronize more than he realized, dictate too much, and rub readers the wrong way, all as he felt that he did nothing but speak the truth. If he said anything other than what he did say, he would feel that he had compromised his conscience and principles: "He would be absolutely honorable and yet he would offend."[82]

Ovington said this was happening to Du Bois, inevitably. No black man could espouse the NAACP's principles without setting off white readers in various ways without realizing it. The trick was to become more sensitive to how and why it happened. The NAACP, she argued, had to care about the problem because it was a biracial organization that spoke to black and white audiences. Villard offended black allies by giving them orders, and Du Bois offended white allies by calling them hogs and bigots. Ovington asked Du Bois to think about the difference between a biracial civil rights organization and a socialist organization. Du Bois wanted to preach race consciousness in the same way socialists preached class-consciousness, but NAACP liberals had not signed up for that. She urged him to stop saying that he stood for NAACP principles while his critics stood for selling out. Together they were building a national movement to abolish lynching and segregation. All the previous organizations had failed. What they were doing was surely worth saving.[83]

The NAACP, for all its tensions, stepped up under Spingarn's leadership. It threw itself against a flood of Jim Crow legislation in Congress and played a key role in defeating most of it. It fought court battles against segregation and disenfranchisement, especially southern grandfather clauses. By mid-1917 the NAACP had nine thousand members. Two years later it had ninety thousand members and more than three hundred local branches—a windfall from the group's court victories, its appointment of James Weldon Johnson as field secretary, and a decision by Spingarn and Johnson to capitalize on the court publicity by recruiting black members in the South. Pushing into the South carried immense risks for the NAACP that it bravely withstood for decades while morphing into a black-led and predominantly black organization.[84]

The NAACP had plenty of liberals, black and white, for whom capitalism was a name for the freedom principle. Du Bois offended both groups every time he editorialized about the ravages of capitalism. Until World War I he recycled conventional socialist critiques of capitalist inequality and commercialism. But after Europe plunged into war in 1914 Du Bois leaned on John Hobson and the British ethical socialists for a deeper critique of capitalist imperialism.

Hobson was a nineteenth-century English polymath and radical liberal who originated the critique of economic imperialism and later became a Labour Party socialist. British anti-imperialists described empire as a problem of power lust and military overreach to be cured by ethically decent politics. Tories were the bad party because they were shameless imperialists. Hobson said a new kind of imperialism emerged in the 1880s, one driven by fierce economic competition for new markets and the discovery of natural riches in Africa. He pointed to the English depression of the 1880s, the rise of economic competitors, and the plunder of Central Africa that began with Belgium's investment in Henry Stanley's exploration of the Congo River. The European powers devoured Africa with despicable regimes of brutality and thievery. In 1875 they controlled one-tenth of the African continent. By 1900 they controlled virtually the entire continent.[85]

Hobson wrote about this historical turn as it happened, publishing ten books before his famous book *Imperialism* in 1902, contending that modern capitalism is unsustainable without exploiting colonized markets. In 1915 Du Bois powerfully amplified Hobson's argument that the plunder of Africa relied on the equation of color with inferiority. This was the crucial point, Du Bois said. The European powers took an important lesson from the British and American slave trades. The pillage and rape of Africa could be called something else if black people were less than human. France sought to build a northern African empire stretching from the Atlantic Ocean to the Red Sea. Germany, shut out from Central and South America by the Monroe Doctrine, sought colonies in Africa and Asia. Portugal renewed and expanded its historic claims to African territory.[86]

Du Bois said Western movements for democracy and progress played crucial roles in accelerating the flow of finance capital to far-off lands, thus ratcheting up the clash of empires. Democracy was supposed to be the answer to the terrible problems of inequality, exploitation, and oppression. The ship of state was supposedly launched on the great tide of democratic expansion. Yet as democracy spread, so did the rule of might, regardless of which party won office. Democracy and imperialism grew together, unless—what? In England, the Labour Party became the vehicle of the ethical socialist and Christian socialist answer. In the United States, Du Bois went back to voting for Socialists after the 1912 Wilson debacle, sharing the democratic faith of radical liberals and socialists. Du Bois was a progressive who believed in radical democracy. But he cautioned that the seemingly paradoxical wedding of democracy and imperialism was not really puzzling. White workers were asked to share the spoils of exploiting people of color. The chief exploiter role that passed historically from the merchant prince to the aristocratic monopoly to the capitalist class now belonged to the democratic nation. The only solution to this miserable picture, he said, was for democratic socialism to reach all the way to the poor and excluded, not stopping with white workers.

The movements for socialism, union organizing, and democracy had made a beginning. The capitalist class would yield to the unions as long as it found new markets to exploit. Under modern capitalism, the national bond was not based on something flimsy like patriotism, loyalty, or ancestor-worship. It was based on the wealth that creates a middle class and flows to the working class. But most of this new wealth rested on the exploitation of Asians, Africans, South Americans, and West Indians. Du Bois believed the old capitalist exploitation was fading, and it was not the reason Germans and Britons were slaughtering each other in World War I. Socialism was advancing in Germany and Britain, while both governments took for granted their right to rule and exploit nonwhite peoples. World War I was about which group of white nations would do so.

Du Bois acknowledged that Japan did not play along because Japan demanded white treatment without allying with white nations. China, too, was increasingly independent, complicating the Western domination of China. But everything depended on how far the logic of democracy extended. In this sense, Du Bois was a Fabian Socialist minus the usual Fabian racism. If progressive movements accelerated the imperial logic of modern capitalism, the only solution was to universalize democracy. If the movements for liberalism, unionism, anti-imperialism, and socialism were to create a decent world, they had to struggle for democracy everywhere, not just at home: "We must go further. We must extend the democratic ideal to the yellow, brown, and black peoples." Du Bois implored that democracy is distinctly powerful and transformative; it is "a method of doing the impossible." First the movements for democratic socialism had to win power wherever they existed. Then they had to fulfill the universalism of their creed; otherwise socialism was the worst form of hypocrisy. Du Bois believed that for the rest of his life.[87]

CHRISTIAN SOCIALIST THEOLOGY:
WALTER RAUSCHENBUSCH

Christian socialism, for all its impact and varieties within the Socialist Party, had a greater impact outside the party. Franklin Spalding, an Episcopal bishop with a national following, championed Christian socialism without joining the party. So did Methodist cleric Harry Ward, the leading and most left-wing exponent of the social gospel after World War I, who was too much an independent radical to join anything. Socialist clerics belonged to congregations, denominations, ecumenical organizations, and sectors of the academy that were otherwise unavailable to the party, which made them valuable even when they didn't join it. The leading Christian socialists became prominent in the same way their secular counterparts won elections to the executive committee of the Socialist Party: by writing prolifically for socialist, popular, and academic audiences. One Christian socialist towered above all others during the heyday of the social gospel: Walter Rauschenbusch.[88]

Oedipal issues weigh heavily in Protestant theology because many theologians have been the sons or daughters of formidable clerics. Walter Rauschenbusch is a chief example. His father, August Rauschenbusch, overwhelmed him, and his mother, Caroline Rauschenbusch, paid dearly for a bad marriage decision. August's German family claimed five successive generations of Lutheran pastors, which he extended to six before converting to the Baptist faith while serving as a missionary in the United States. On the rebound from a broken romance he married a former confirmation student and soon regretted it. In the United States he became a prominent Baptist professor in the German Department at Rochester Theological Seminary. August Rauschenbusch was headstrong, irritable, accomplished, a gifted teacher, and, to his family, prone to self-pitying meanness. His nervous bullying made him a bad husband and, at best, a difficult father; Walter spent his childhood sympathizing with his mother and trying to please his father. He spent four years of his childhood in Germany in the company of his mother and sisters and later returned for four years of Gymnasium training. August Rauschenbusch wanted his son to be better educated than Americans and not to be Americanized; he also sought lengthy separations from his wife, whose death he sometimes asked God to arrange.[89]

Rauschenbusch sailed through the University of Rochester and Rochester Seminary simultaneously, finding American schools as easy as his father complained. Theologically he turned slightly liberal during seminary, trying hard to withhold this information from his parents. His first call out of seminary was to Second German Baptist in New York City, located on West Forty-Fifth Street near Tenth Avenue on Manhattan's West Side. It bordered the northern edge of gang-ruled Hell's Kitchen and was a few blocks west of the Tenderloin district, where gambling and prostitution flourished. The church was poor, hurting, small, and crumbling, numbering 125 recent immigrants. Rauschenbusch lacked any concept of social ministry; on the other hand, he vowed to live according to the way and spirit of Jesus, conceiving the Christian life as a king-dom-building journey from sin to salvation. He preached that the church existed to hasten and participate in the coming of God's kingdom: Christians were called to insinuate God's love and justice into the world.[90]

His congregants lived in squalid five-story tenements pressing more than twenty families into each building. The malnutrition and diseases of the chil-dren tore at him. Performing funerals for children drove him into the social gospel. Politics became unavoidable; if people suffered because of politics and economics, the church had to deal with politics and economics. He joined Henry George's mayoral campaign, devoured *Progress and Poverty*, befriended two Baptist clerics on a similar journey—Leighton Williams and Nathaniel Schmidt—and read Ely's books. He and Williams launched a Christian social-ist paper in 1889, *For the Right*, shortly after Bliss founded the Society of Christian Socialists. *For the Right* was cheeky, aggressive, reformist, sometimes maudlin, and short-lived, much like *The Dawn*. Rauschenbusch later recalled that he had six books in his head; five were scholarly, one was dangerous. Three times he tried to write the dangerous one but never finished it.[91]

In 1891 he proposed to resign because he was going deaf. Rochester Seminary offered his father's former position, but Rauschenbusch doubted that teaching would work any better than ministry for a deaf person. His loving congregation insisted instead that he take a paid sabbatical. He went to England and Germany, studied the movements for socialism, and went back to his dangerous book on social Christianity. In England he liked what Christian socialists were doing but was repulsed by Anglo-Catholicism; thus he stopped writing nice things about British Christian socialism. In Germany he labored on a book titled *Revolutionary Christianity*, which argued that Christianity should be rev-olutionary, like Jesus. Rauschenbusch later romanticized this part of his story, claiming that he fixed on the kingdom of God only after he had an epiphany in Germany. In truth he emphasized the kingdom before he took his sabbatical, and his radical concept of it was U.S. American, not Ritschlian.

The German theological schools of Kant, Hegel, and Schleiermacher claimed to reconcile theology with historical criticism, but German theologian Albrecht Ritschl claimed in the 1870s that none of them actually did. The prestige theo-logical schools and the mediating versions of them were strategies to circumvent the destructive consequences of historical criticism. Ritschl said this defensive posture was a loser for theology. Theologians needed to make theology explicitly historicist by recovering the historical Jesus and the faith of the early church. The school that formed around Ritschl taught that Christianity is essentially a Jesus movement focused on the kingdom of God, not a structure of (Hellenistic) doctrine. The Ritschlian School dominated late nineteenth-century theology by solving the problem of historicism, accepting the Kantian divide between science and religion, focusing on the person and kingdom language of Jesus, and providing a theological basis for Culture Protestantism, the civil religion of the German state. Rauschenbusch absorbed from Ritschl and Adolf von Harnack that theology should be historicist and social ethical. But the Ritschlians were bourgeois nationalists who feared Social Democracy, teetered on militarism, supported the German welfare state, and rendered the kingdom of God accordingly.[92]

Rauschenbusch took Ritschlian theology where no German Ritschlian wanted to go, construing the kingdom of God as revolutionary. *Revolutionary Christianity* argued that Jesus proclaimed a postmillennial idea of the coming reign of God, and the church is supposed to transform the world by the power of Christ's Spirit. Rauschenbusch later recalled: "Here was a religious conception that embraced it all. Here was something so big that absolutely nothing that interested me was excluded from it. . . . It carries God into everything that you do." The kingdom of God includes the heavenly realm, the presence of God in the soul, the church as the body of Christ, the cooperative commonwealth, and the promise of an eschatological end of history. Rauschenbusch stressed that this idea is beautiful, comprehensive, filled with justice-making ethical content, *and* evangelical: "You have the authority of the Lord Jesus in it."[93]

But the book never quite came together, Rauschenbusch returned to his congregation in New York, and he married a schoolteacher, Pauline Rother, who helped him cope with his worsening deafness. They made pastoral calls together, expressions of love and affection passed easily between them, and their marriage was a sustained love affair that pulled him out of his depressive spiral. The next time Rochester Seminary called, in 1897, Rauschenbusch felt he was ready for an academic career, carrying on his father's work, which he did for five years, teaching English and American literature, physiology, physics, civil government, political economy, astronomy, zoology, and New Testament, all in German, in addition to raising money for the German Department.

The cliché about Rauschenbusch is that he was hopelessly idealistic. Yet he cowered on racism and militarism for most of his career; he could not conceive his beloved American nation as an empire; he gave special permission to German nationalism; and his feminism was tepid, late Victorian, and highly selective. On anti-imperialism, Rauschenbusch knew what the real thing looked like because he knew the British Christian socialists. Charles Marson, Stewart Headlam, Thomas Hancock, Scott Holland, Charles Gore, Maurice Reckett, John Clifford, and S. G. Hobson roared against British imperialism, racism, and militarism. Rauschenbusch opposed racism and immigration restrictions in his early career, and he believed that anti-imperialism in England was a very good thing. But he made allowances for the two nations he loved. American imperialism was not imperialist, Germany should not be blamed for catching up to England, and America needed more Germans.

In 1895, two years before he returned to Rochester, he wrote a racist fundraising letter for the German Department: "Are the whites of this continent so sure of their possession against the blacks of the South and the seething yellow flocks beyond the Pacific that they need no reinforcement of men of their own blood while yet it is time?" Two years later he wrote a similar letter, now as a faculty colleague, and in 1902 Rauschenbusch stood before a commencement assembly and said it aggressively: Germans were first cousins of the British Anglo-Saxons, they helped to build modern democracy, and they deserved to be included in Manifest Destiny. It was shortsighted to give British Anglo-Saxons exclusive credit for civilization. Modern democracy was created by a single Teutonic racial stock, an achievement imperiled by what he called alien strains arriving from places like France, Spain, the Slavic lands, Bohemia, Poland, and the Russian Jewish territories.[94]

That was a frightening spectacle to his German American audience. Rauschenbusch cheered his nation's victory in the Spanish-American War and its imperial frenzy in Puerto Rico and the Philippines, later to his shame. In 1902 the seminary's position in church history opened up, which is why the classic works of the social gospel have a strong historical bent. Rauschenbusch made his living as a professor of church history. He felt acutely the historical implausibility of the basic social gospel argument. If he and Gladden were right about the kingdom basis of Christianity, why was social Christianity so novel? Rauschenbusch approached his teaching and scholarship with this question in mind, making the unlikely field of church history an ally of the social gospel.

He went back to his manuscript to see what he could salvage from it, putting the kingdom of God at the center of a new book, *Christianity and the Social Crisis*. The old book had patches of labored writing and clumsy connections, but all was smooth and sparkling in the new book. It enthralled a huge audience with its flowing style and charming metaphors. The first part said the purpose of prophetic biblical religion is to transform society into the kingdom of God. The second part made an argument about why the Christian church never carried out this mission. The third part said it was not too late for the church to follow Jesus. The key to the book was part two, but Rauschenbusch feared that part three would get him fired. It was a blazing argument for radical Christian socialism.[95]

Most religions, he argued, are priestly and power worshipping—reconciling human beings with the powers of nature or force or wealth. Prophetic religion rejects the worship of power, condemns the evils of injustice and oppression, and insists that good religion is ethical. Rauschenbusch did not spurn the recent claim of the German history of religions school that Jesus and early Christianity were apocalyptical. First-century Judaism was apocalyptical, he allowed; Jesus was probably influenced by it, and the early church was apocalyptical, eager for the world to end. But Rauschenbusch countered that the social ethical sayings of Jesus far outnumbered the apocalyptical and more broadly eschatological sayings. Johannes Weiss treated Mark 13 as a master-text of apocalyptic smashing; Rauschenbusch replied that Mark 13 sounded more like the early church than like Jesus. Early Christianity was too pervaded by apocalyptic dreams to conceive the kingdom as a worldly social hope; moreover, it was too repressed by a dominating external power to think otherwise. The kingdom, Rauschenbusch said, took a further beating after Christianity became thoroughly Hellenistic. Hellenistic Christianity was ascetic, setting body and spirit against each other, conceiving salvation as the eternal life of an individual soul, and establishing a priestly hierarchical church—all disastrously for Christianity.[96]

Christianity and the Social Crisis was unabashedly socialist, describing the crisis of capitalist civilization as an opportunity to recover the lost kingdom ideal of Jesus. Production could be organized on a cooperative basis. Distribution could be organized by principles of justice. Workers could be treated as children of God. Parasitic wealth and predatory commerce could be abolished. These things are possible, Rauschenbusch urged. He took moral idealism as far as possible without believing it was enough to create a just society. Rauschenbusch taught that idealism alone is pitifully inadequate: "We must not blink the fact that the idealists alone have never carried through any great social change. In vain they dash their fair ideas against the solid granite of human selfishness." The possessing classes rule by force, cunning, and entrenched monopoly power: "They control nearly all property. The law is on their side, for they have made it. They control the machinery of government and can use force under the form of law." For these reasons, he argued, the capitalist and aristocratic classes were nearly impervious to moral truth. Being morally right, against them, is never enough: "For a definite historical victory a given truth must depend on the class which makes that truth its own and fights for it."[97]

Rauschenbusch stressed that no movement for a just commonwealth will ever fully succeed. Movements must be willing to struggle for ideals that cannot be fully attained. Yet we cannot know how much is attainable without struggling for the whole thing. To spurn the struggle for the ideal is to preempt otherwise attainable gains toward it: "At best there is always an approximation to a perfect social order. The kingdom of God is always but coming. But every approximation to it is worth while."[98]

Christianity and the Social Crisis was a supercharger for the social gospel. It ran through thirteen printings in five years and wiped out the Herron embarrassment. Rauschenbusch returned from a German sabbatical to find himself cast as a movement leader and religious celebrity, just in time to help launch the Federal Council of Churches—a federation of thirty-three denominations—and its Social Creed. The creed called for "equal rights and complete justice for all men in all stations of life," abolition of child labor, safe working conditions, special provisions for female workers, a living wage in every industry, poverty abatement, old age insurance, and equitable distribution of wealth. Harry Ward wrote the Methodist and Federal Council versions, and Rauschenbusch had a hand in the Federal Council version.[99]

Rauschenbusch expected to write no more books on the social question. He put everything he knew into *Christianity and the Social Crisis,* so why write more? Lecture audiences told him that was ridiculous; now he had obligations as a movement leader. He recalled that before 1900 his little group of ministers shouted in the wilderness: "It was always a happy surprise when we found a new man who had seen the light. We used to form a kind of flying wedge to support a man who was preparing to attack a ministers' conference with the social Gospel." Now he had to write *Christianizing the Social Order* (1912) just to meet the demand for more. Rauschenbusch said social Christianity was a new Reformation. The first Reformation worked back to Paul, reviving Pauline theology. The new Reformation "is a revival of the spirit and aims of Jesus himself." To be sure, Jesus retained the thought-forms of his background. What matters is the spirit and trajectory of his religion, not the dogmas he inherited.[100]

This time he lingered longer over the Reformation. Luther and Calvin had little feeling for the kingdom and precious little democratic spirit. Theologically they were authoritarians, lacking the imagination to appreciate the book of Revelation. They did not rescue the kingdom idea, even as they broke the Catholic prison: "The eclipse of the Kingdom idea was an eclipse of Jesus. We had listened too much to voices talking about him, and not enough to his own voice. Now his own thoughts in their lifelike simplicity and open-air fragrance have become a fresh religious possession, and when we listen to Jesus, we cannot help thinking about the Kingdom of God."[101]

The book's title was a provocation even at the high tide of the social gospel. Rauschenbusch realized that "Christianizing" rhetoric was risky, and Herron's theocratic fantasies tainted Christian socialism. The social gospel, to Rauschenbusch, was about social transformation, not state religion. He used the words "Christianize," "moralize," "humanize," and "democratize" interchangeably, identifying all with the ethical values of freedom, sacrificial love, compassion, justice, humility, fraternity, and equality: "Christianizing means humanizing in the highest sense." Most of America's social order, he claimed, was already Christianized/humanized/democratized. Bad social systems make good people do bad things; a humanized order makes bad people do good things. By his account American society in 1912 was semi-Christian. American churches, families, political institutions, and schools were more Christian than not, but all were threatened by a corrupting and predatory economic system.[102]

The despotic authority of the premodern church and the oppression of women were closely linked. As an institution, Rauschenbusch argued, the premodern church was reactionary, coercive, and politically cunning, and as a moral power it conspired with society in condemning females to subservience. But the democratizing spirit of the modern age broke the arrogance of the church and raised the legal status of women nearly to the point of equality with men. Rauschenbusch looked forward to the next stage of women's progress: "The suffrage will abolish one of the last remnants of patriarchal autocracy by giving woman a direct relation to the political organism of society, instead of allowing man to exercise her political rights for her." Meanwhile churches learned that coercion has the same relation to true religion that rape has to love. Rauschenbusch stressed that churches did not welcome their salvation; they had to be converted against their will, losing their temporal authority, and many churches were still reactionary on "the public activities and the emancipation of women."[103]

Rauschenbusch was a good enough Victorian to be conflicted about feminism. He supported the right of women to equal rights in society while believing fervently that wives and mothers should stay home to take care of their families; it grieved him that college-educated women usually did not marry. He implored his audiences not to erode the late Victorian middle-class ideal of family life in the name of individual progress for women. What made the middle-class family ideal was precisely that it allowed women not to work outside the home. Rauschenbusch could be florid on true womanhood, shuddering to imagine homes without children and mothers. He blamed capitalism for emptying the home of its nurturing wives and mothers.[104]

Christian socialism was the wholesome alternative. It lifted women to the equality they deserved while supporting the mother-nurtured family as the key to a healthy society. Christianized forms of socialism, he said, were distinctly suited to get the balance right. Just as Christianity needed the socialist passion for justice to fulfill the social ideals of the gospel, socialism needed the spiritual and moral conscience of Christianity to be saved from vulgar materialism. In 1912 he believed it was happening. Education was no longer the privilege of the few, and democracy did the same thing to politics: "Democracy stands for the cooperative idea applied to politics." Rauschenbusch allowed that democracy is not quite the same thing as Christianity, but in the political sphere "democracy is the expression and method of the Christian spirit." By this criterion America was nearly Christianized.[105]

The holdout was the economic system, "the unregenerate section of our social order." Sadly, Christian moralists looked away from the sins of capitalism, failing even to ask if the system makes it harder or easier to do the good thing. Rauschenbusch argued that capitalism is essentially corrupting. It degrades every profession it touches, turns citizens into small-minded consumers, and extends its reach to every sector of society. Thus it undermines the gains of all other spheres of society. Even the learned professions were being corrupted, and the law was the worst: " 'Commercializing a profession' always means degrading it." Wherever capitalism goes, it causes "a surrender of the human point of view, a relaxing of the sense of duty, and a willingness to betray the public."[106]

The problem was the autocratic power "unrestrained by democratic checks" that capitalism gives to owners and managers, allowing them to make unearned profits off the exploited labors of the weak; Rauschenbusch called it "a tribute collected by power." The solution was to democratize the ownership of industry and the process of investment: "Political democracy without economic democracy is an uncashed promissory note, a pot without the roast, a form without substance. But in so far as democracy has become effective, it has quickened everything it has touched." America needed economic democracy for the same reason it needed political democracy—to achieve freedom and equality, legitimate the necessary exercise of authority, and thwart the will to power of the privileged classes.[107]

Rauschenbusch conceived economic democracy as the expansion of property rights under new forms, not the elimination of property rights. Under capitalism the capitalist class wrote its own interests into the law; under a fully realized democracy the nation's property laws would serve the interests of the public. He combined the historic Christian socialist emphasis on producer cooperatives, the liberal socialism of John Stuart Mill, the Fabian progress motif, a few Marxian tropes, and a general endorsement of Social Democracy without delineating what any of these things meant in distinction from each other. Rauschenbusch took capitalist markets for granted *and* assumed that prices under socialism would be based entirely on service rendered. Economic democracy, he promised, runs straight from the farm to the kitchen: "It means the power to cut all monopoly prices out of business and to base prices solely on service rendered." Thus he recycled utopian socialist tropes while assuming that markets cannot be abolished in a free society.[108]

Rauschenbusch exaggerated the capacity of economic democracy to replace economic competition and failed to absorb Eduard Bernstein's critique of Marx's theory of surplus value. He was like Bliss in believing it was best not to sign up for one theory or model of socialism. The exception was the central place he gave to Mill's vision of worker-owned firms operating in capitalist markets to create a liberal socialist society. Mill envisioned workers "collectively owning the capital with which they carry on their operations, and working under managers elected and removable by themselves." *Christianizing the Social Order* commended this idea of economic democracy, claiming that only socialism had any prospect of competing with nationalistic militarism as a unifying social force in American life.[109]

Rauschenbusch tried to be optimistic that Americans were up to it. He said liberalism was too weak to compete with the spirit of capitalism or militarism; perhaps Christianity bonded with socialism could overcome American selfishness: "Capitalism has overdeveloped the selfish instincts in us all and left the capacity of devotion to larger ends shrunken and atrophied." But democracy was gaining, he believed, and real democracy leads to democratic socialism, which is not a monolithic idea: "There is unity of movement, and yet endless diversity of life." He held the same hope for socialism and for Christianity: Each should become more truly itself. He conceded to Francis Greenwood Peabody that most Socialists were antireligious, but if Christians could aim to Christianize China, surely they could Christianize socialism, which came from Christianity: "The Socialists are hopeless about the social regeneration of the Church. Yet it has come faster than I dared to hope. At any rate I am not going to tell the Socialists that I expect them to remain atheists. I shall tell them that they are now religious in spite of themselves and that an increased approach to religion is inevitable as they emerge from the age of polemics and dogmatism."[110]

Christianizing the Social Order was so hopeful about the progress of Christian socialism that Rauschenbusch dropped his warning about the class struggle. The social gospel was soaring and churches were scrambling to get on the right side of the social question. He dared to hope that idealism might prevail without bloodshed. Rauschenbusch urged liberals and progressives to acknowledge the socialism in their creed: "Every reformer is charged with socialism, because no constructive reform is possible without taking a leaf from the book of social-ism." It was better to wear the label as a badge of honor than to cower from it. He insisted that *Christianizing the Social Order* did not fall off the "high reli-gious ground." All 476 pages were religious because every page was about the kingdom of God: "We do not want less religion; we want more; but it must be a religion that gets its orientation from the Kingdom of God. To concentrate our efforts on personal salvation, as orthodoxy has done, or on soul culture, as liber-alism has done, comes close to refined selfishness. All of us who have been trained in egotistic religion need a conversion to Christian Christianity, even if we are bishops or theological professors. Seek ye first the Kingdom of God and God's righteousness, and the salvation of your souls will be added to you."[111]

Rauschenbusch was more anxious than the book let on. In 1910 he returned from Germany alarmed that militarism and fear mongering were out of control. He warned lecture audiences that Europe was not too civilized to be safe from plunging into a catastrophic war. In January 1914 he said in New York that his-toric opportunities for social progress rarely last more than a few years. Rauschenbusch felt the threat of World War I very personally. His widowed sister Frida and her daughters lived in Germany, as did numerous Westphalian relatives, many of whom fought in the war. Some wrote letters to him defending Germany's invasion of Belgium and France.[112]

His revulsion for war deepened as Europe teetered on catastrophe and swal-lowed him as soon as the war began. Rauschenbusch's sparkling optimism and humor vanished; battling a deep sadness, he told *The Congregationalist* he felt overcome by "profound grief and depression of spirit." He wore a piece of black crepe—a symbol of mourning—on his lapel, asked American Baptists to aid afflicted Baptists on both sides of the war, and pleaded for American neutrality.[113]

It pained him that Americans overwhelmingly favored England and were fine with aiding the British war effort. Rauschenbusch loved Germany only a little less than he loved the United States. In 1902 he told a commencement crowd he was deeply bonded to both nations: "My cradle stood on American soil, but my mother's cradle-song was German as her heart. Will you blame me if I love both countries and defend each in turn?" By 1914 that was not a toler-able perspective in American life. Rauschenbusch claimed that Germany was no more militaristic than its neighbors and no more imperialist than England. The following year he protested against America's policy of selling armaments to the Allied powers, calling for a government prohibition of all arms ship-ments. This plea provoked a firestorm of outrage. Editorialists railed against Rauschenbusch and many friends dropped away. Rauschenbusch grieved at his downfall, regretting especially the loss of longtime friends.[114]

He protested that his antimilitarism was a Christian conviction and not a recent turn: "I have been a Christian supporter of the peace idea for some years. During the Spanish-American War I took the average attitude and voiced it effectively. But shortly afterward the peace movement got a strong grip on me." He denied that he favored Germany over the United States: "I have always expressed strongly my preference for America." Gradually Rauschenbusch withdrew from the public debate, feeling its futility for him. He agonized that militarism soared in his nation and church: "It was hard enough to combine Christianity and capitalistic business. Now we are asked to combine Christianity and war." He said he could not relate to Luther and Oliver Cromwell, who despised the lower classes and "cheerfully" supported mass killing. He could not combine Christianity and war without losing his faith: "Don't ask me to combine religion and the war spirit. I don't want to lose my religion; it's all I've got."[115]

He told Gladden the greatest illusion of all was the Allied conceit of an idealistic victory: "Their entire scheme of morality is based on the premise of a successful democratic termination. But under the table they will be making very different deals." He confessed to Episcopal cleric Algernon Crapsey, "I am glad I shall not live forever. I am afraid of those who want to drag our country in to satisfy their partisan hate, or because they think universal peace will result from the victory of the allies." In 1916 Rauschenbusch joined the newly founded Fellowship of Reconciliation (FOR), emoting that he was delighted to find people more radical than he.[116]

His last two books fought off his sorrow and depression. In 1916 Rauschenbusch wrote a book for the Sunday School Council of Evangelical Denominations, *The Social Principles of Jesus*. It summarized the teachings of Jesus on poverty, property, compassion, violence, justice, and the kingdom of God, declaring that the kingdom "is a real thing, now in operation." It is within and among human beings: "It overlaps and interpenetrates all existing organizations, raising them to a higher level when they are good, resisting them when they are evil, quietly revolutionizing the old social order and changing it into the new." Sometimes the kingdom suffers terrible reversals—"we are in the midst of one now." But God wrings victory from defeat: "The Kingdom of God is always coming; you can never lay your hand on it and say, 'It is here.' But such fragmentary realizations of it as we have, alone make life worth living."[117]

That was the tone of his last book, *A Theology of the Social Gospel* (1917). Rauschenbusch acknowledged that many people said the social gospel was doing very well; churches had rallied in wartime solidarity, surging with a sense of moral purpose. He said that actually the war destroyed the social gospel, which survived only on the hope that the real thing might revive after the war:

"The Great War has dwarfed and submerged all other issues, including our social problems. But in fact the war is the most acute and tremendous social problem of all."[118]

He wearied of conservatives who said the social gospel did not believe in sin. Some liberals deserved criticism on this count, he allowed, and it was true that the social gospel emphasis on social environment tended to overlook personal responsibility for sin. But orthodoxy did the same thing with the doctrines of original sin and the divine decrees. The old theology prattled about sin while unloading responsibility for it on Adam, the devil, and predestination. More important, Rauschenbusch said, orthodoxy obsessed over personal vices while ignoring the oppression of millions "sucked dry by the parasitic classes of society." When did the great theologians ever condemn "these magnificent manifestations of the wickedness of the human heart?"[119]

Sin is fundamentally selfishness but not as construed by the old orthodoxy, which rested on an unreal doctrine of uniform corruption; thus it overlooked that sin is transmitted through social tradition and institutions. Rauschenbusch argued that society is at least as important as innate human selfishness, plus more amenable to moral correction. Human beings are bonded to each other in their bondage to sin, which is not uniform essential depravity. Some people are more sinful than others, and some traditions bear greater moral guilt than others. The orthodox emphasis on uniform depravity obscures the transmission of evil through social tradition. Drug addiction, social cruelty, ethnic feuds, and racism are transmitted from one generation to the next through socialization, not heredity.[120]

Rauschenbusch said precious little until 1917 about the evils of racism. He had no moral authority on this subject, having disgraced himself by playing to the prejudices of German Department donors. He knew only a few African Americans personally, and everything he knew about American racism contradicted his claim that Americans were building the kingdom of God. He wrote optimistic books about achieving democracy while black Americans were terrorized by a mania of lynching and subjected to a racial caste system of abuse. In *Christianizing the Social Order* he finally managed to say that the spirit of Jesus "smites race pride and prejudice in the face in the name of humanity." In 1914 he explained why it took him so long to write even a sentence: "For years, the problem of the two races in the South has seemed to me so tragic, so insoluble, that I have never yet ventured to discuss it in public."[121]

If he was to be an agent of hope in racist America, he could not mention racism, a hopelessly depressing topic. So he rationalized for most of his career. In his last book Rauschenbusch refuted the impression of his previous books that racism was just one evil among others and not as terrible as some. He described America's racial pathology as the crowning example of social evil — the ultimate example of sin making white America sick and depraved: "When negroes are hunted from a Northern city like beasts, or when a Southern city degrades the whole nation by turning the savage inhumanity of a mob into a public festivity, we are continuing to sin because our fathers created the conditions of sin by the African slave trade and by the unearned wealth they gathered from slave labour for generations."[122]

He called the sum of these social evils the kingdom of evil. Rauschenbusch retrieved this ancient concept without its superstitious baggage, explaining that he didn't believe in demons or a kingdom of evil spirits. His idea of the kingdom of evil was social and historical, conceiving evil as real, powerful, organic, and solidaristic in modern life, not mere ignorance or disjointed events. All people are bound together in the condition of bearing the yoke of evil and suffering. But only the social gospel theologized this condition of bondage and responded to it by democratizing politics, the church, economics, evil, *and the divine*. Rauschenbusch said the social gospel had to go all the way to democratizing God. If the kingdom of God is democratizing in its ethical and spiritual character, so must be the God of the kingdom. God is creative, loving, and ethical, not a feudal monarch: "A God who strives within our striving, who kindles his flame in our intellect, sends the impact of his energy to make our will restless for righteousness, floods our sub-conscious mind with dreams and longings, and always urges the race on toward a higher combination of freedom and solidarity — that would be a God with whom democratic and religious men could hold converse as their chief fellow-worker, the source of their energies, the ground of their hopes."[123]

He began to feel desperately tired just after A *Theology for the Social Gospel* was published. Rauschenbusch surmised that he was exhausted and deeply depressed. He canceled outside lectures, kept teaching until March 1918, sensed that he was dying, and wrote several final statements. One accepted his early death as God's will: "Since 1914 the world is full of hate, and I cannot expect to be happy again in my lifetime." He tried to help Rochester Seminary, declaring that a German victory would be a calamity for the world. That was less than the seminary wanted, but the most he could offer. He died of brain cancer on July 25, 1918, at the age of fifty-six.[124]

Rauschenbusch was the greatest of the social gospel theologians because he epitomized its socialist idealism. Some were better scholars or organizers, some had longer activist careers, and many were better on racial justice and feminism, but Rauschenbusch was the icon of Christian socialism who exemplified why the social gospel at its best was socialist. Many whose thought he shaped—especially Norman Thomas, Sherwood Eddy, Kirby Page, Mordecai Johnson, Justin Wroe Nixon, Walter Muelder, and, indirectly, Reinhold Niebuhr—found their way to the Socialist Party after the party lost nearly all its intellectuals in the American rush to war. Rauschenbusch was their symbol of this possibility, even though he was too sensitive to join the party. To the black social gospel leaders who subsequently mentored Martin Luther King Jr. and served as his role models—Johnson, Benjamin E. Mays, J. Pius Barbour, and Howard Thurman—the Rauschenbusch socialist factor was crucially important. They didn't need Rauschenbusch to be brave about racial injustice to love him. They loved him for championing Christian socialism, passing to King that America needed Rauschenbusch-style economic democracy almost as much as it needed to abolish its despicable regime of racial caste.

DEBS, HILLQUIT, AND THE CRISIS OF SOCIALISM

Debs was like Woodbey, Lewis, and O'Hare in living for the next speech and battle and being averse to bosses and bureaucrats. His favorite people were emotional, turbulent, dissident types who rushed to help workers in need and pushed themselves to exhaustion. Debs was fifty-seven years old when the 1912 campaign ended and more deeply exhausted than ever. The four presidential candidates said almost nothing about foreign policy or the threat of war; soon this insularity seemed incredible. Debs had just suffered his usual post-campaign collapse when Wayland committed suicide. Wayland's wife had been killed the previous year in a car accident; he had never crawled out from the trauma and depression, and in his last months he endured a right-wing smear campaign against him. Wayland left a note saying that living in a competitive society wasn't worth the struggle. Debs took it very hard, while brushing off Kate Debs's contention that he should retire from politics, spend time with her, and stop supporting his freeloading brother Theodore. Freeloading was not an issue for Debs since his brother's companionship meant that Debs was never alone, or lonely.

In September 1913 he tried to gear up for a western speaking tour but suffered a physical-emotional collapse and retreated to a sanitarium in Estes Park, Colorado. Debs was there for a month before he realized he was seriously ill. He vowed to retire, telling Theodore he got to Colorado barely in time to save his life. Debs had just finished paying off the twenty-two-thousand-dollar debt of the ARU, which ended an eighteen-year psychic torment he never considered writing off. He still wrote for *Appeal to Reason*, but every article reminded

him of Wayland, and Debs had a frosty relationship with editor Fred Warren, so
he resigned his position. He tried to imagine retiring in Terre Haute, living off
his writing, and letting admirers come to him. But the mountain air and forced
vacation revived him, and Debs realized he would go crazy in retirement. He
told Hillquit he couldn't stand to live if he couldn't be useful to socialism. His
friends Kate and Frank O'Hare realized it too. They had turned the *National
Rip-Saw* into a major socialist vehicle with Frank as editor and Kate as star
writer. They asked Debs to lecture tour for the paper, and by February 1914 he
was gladly on the road again. Audiences noticed he had changed in two ways.
The years of speaking, traveling, drinking, and raucous reunions took a toll on
his appearance, and he rarely criticized party leaders.[125]

He was tired of fighting with the Old Guard and the AFL. More important,
he believed the destiny of the working class depended entirely on its solidarity.
Debs said it through Texas, Oklahoma, Kansas, Nebraska, Colorado, Wyoming,
and Idaho. He still urged the UMWA and WFM to unite and leave the AFL,
but in the next breath he said that solidarity is the Holy Grail and proponents of
industrial unionism had already won the argument. Hardly anyone claimed
anymore that craft unionism is better: "I know of no essential distinction
between skilled and unskilled salary and wage-workers. They are all in the same
economic class and in their aggregate constitute the proletariat or working
class, and the hair-splitting attempts that are made to differentiate them in the
class struggle give rise to endless lines of cleavage and are inimical if not fatal to
solidarity." Workers had to unite, Debs exhorted; this mattered more than anything. After one hundred years of organizing, only one worker in fifteen
belonged to a union. That was pitiful; nothing would change if this ratio did not
dramatically change. But he also believed it is darkest just before the dawn.[126]

In his telling, the IWW made a splash because it recognized that the dormant unskilled masses were ripe for revolt. Debs took pride that the Socialist
Party backed the IWW in every possible way during its glory run. But that
already felt long ago. In March 1914 Debs said the IWW could have taken a
different path, but anarchists won the factional argument, yielding what anarchism always yields. He did not say it vengefully: "They are entitled to their
opinion the same as the rest of us." However, socialists and anarchists had never
worked together in the entire history of socialism "and probably never will."
Three months later the IWW local in Butte, Montana, blew up the WFM local
during a copper mine strike, and Debs furiously said he would no longer work
with Wobblies or even talk about them. He turned his attention to the development that mattered: Most industrial unionists advocated independent political
action, and most Socialists favored industrial unionism. Many of both belonged

to the AFL, where WFM president Charles Moyer blistered Gompers for selling out miners. Debs reconciled his double-minded message about unionism
by contending that a merged UMWA–WFM could be the catalyst to unite and
radicalize the labor movement. In politics he had a similar vision. The two
Socialist parties needed to bury their mutual grudges and join forces. If unionists united and Socialists united, America would "soon have the foremost proletarian revolutionary movement in the world."[127]

In April 1914 Colorado National Guard troops slaughtered eleven adults and
eleven children encamped in a tent colony in Ludlow, Colorado. Approximately
eleven thousand UMWA miners had struck against the Rockefeller-owned
Colorado Fuel and Iron Company, protesting against low pay, terrible working
conditions, and demeaning treatment in company towns. Most were Greeks,
Italians, or Serbs. The evicted strikers built tent colonies while National Guard
troops escorted strikebreakers to the mines. The largest colony, numbering
twelve hundred strikers, was in Ludlow. On April 20 National Guard troops
encircled the Ludlow camp from an overlooking bluff and opened fire; many in
the camp were killed by a machine gun. The Guardsmen lured a strike leader,
Lou Tikas, into the hills to discuss a truce and executed him. A pitched battle
ensued in which strikers took over mines and attacked strikebreakers, and fifty
people, including three National Guard soldiers, were killed before President
Wilson dispatched federal troops to end the fighting. Debs, aiming for historical
perspective, paired Ludlow with the Homestead Steel strike massacre of 1892.
Famous industrialists—John D. Rockefeller Jr. and Andrew Carnegie—were
the perpetrators. Both were renowned for being philanthropic and civic-minded,
and both deserved to go down in history as "cold-blooded murderers."[128]

On the few occasions Debs felt compelled to say something about foreign
policy, he said the American government was an armed guard for capitalist
interests. When America invaded somebody, it was always to serve the capitalist
clique that ruled the United States, not to serve humanitarian ends or any such
thing. Socialism was the only solution to class war, imperialism, and imperial
wars, and socialists were internationalists. Believing it without much further
reflection left Debs and many American Socialists flabbergasted on August 4,
1914. The same SPD that railed against war as late as August 1 rolled over when
German rulers called the nation to vanquish France, Russia, and England,
starting with Belgium. The German Social Democrats were terrified of being
crushed in a prowar stampede and spending World War I in prison cells. Debs
was appalled that the world's greatest Socialist party capitulated overnight, followed swiftly by most European socialists. He blistered the socialists who rolled
over for the war, telling audiences the war would have been thwarted had social-

ists stuck by their principles. Every belligerent nation got a pass from its socialists; Debs stressed that the Russian Bolsheviks—the left wing of Russia's socialist movement—were the only exception. He called American socialists to resist everything smacking of preparation for war.

In November 1914 he put it scathingly: "We socialists are not wanting in genuine patriotism but we are deadly hostile to the fraudulent species which is 'the last refuge of the scoundrel' and which prompts every crook and grafter and every blood-sucking vampire to wrap his reeking carcass in the folds of the national flag that he may carry on his piracy and plunder in the name of 'patriotism.' " The only true patriotism is universal, embracing all human beings. He said it on speaking tours down the West Coast, across Texas, into the prairie states, and through the Midwest. People rode in wagons for a hundred miles to hear him plead for peace. He kept going until he collapsed again in the spring of 1915, landing in a sanitarium for six weeks, this time bedridden with muscle spasms and congestion. In the fall he was back on the lecture trail, railing against America's first war loan to England and Wilson's placement of the National Guard on a war footing. Debs warned that every act of preparing for war was an incitement to war. In December 1915 he declared that he had no country to defend: "My country is the earth; I am a citizen of the world. . . . I am not a capitalist soldier; I am a proletarian revolutionist. . . . I am opposed to every war but one; I am for that war with heart and soul, and that is the worldwide war of the social revolution. In that way, I am prepared to fight in any way the ruling class may make necessary, even to the barricades."[129]

Debs called for a Third International to replace the collection of national socialisms that perished in August 1914. He offended Hillquit and Berger every time he said it, already consigning the Second International to disgraced oblivion, but his proposal was impossible in every way. Europe was in flames; France's antiwar Socialist leader Jean Jaurès had been assassinated; and even America's two Socialist parties failed to merge. It sickened Debs to watch the economy of the United States become intertwined with the war making of the Allies. Wheat and cotton prices boomed on the world market, and munitions workers made stunning salaries. By the end of the year Debs retreated to his Terre Haute porch, welcoming streams of visitors. Kate Debs hated the traffic, especially the bar and brothel owners who carried on uproariously and loved Debs. She tried not to draw the obvious conclusion about why brothel owners loved him so. Walling, Russell, Herron, Simons, Upton Sinclair, and other socialists tacked away from antiwar activism, contending that defeating Germany was paramount, which repelled Debs. He found himself cheering for mere liberals who campaigned against war and preparedness—Gladden, Bryan,

Addams, and Wisconsin U.S. Senator Robert La Follette. He implored socialists to keep their eye on the goal, resist the siren of war, stop recycling the
nationalist anxieties of bourgeois newspapers, and stay out of "this unholy massacre" in Europe. Their goal was the real peace based on social justice, which
"will never prevail until national industrial despotism has been supplanted by
international industrial democracy."[130]

Party membership slid to eighty thousand in 1914 but rebounded in 1915,
mostly via the new foreign-language federations. The Old Guard took heart that
Debs was fading, believing the party needed a standard-bearer who didn't insult
the AFL and the patriotic feelings of American voters. Debs realized that
another national campaign would kill him. Running for president again was
out of the question. He said so in April 1916, insisting he was too ill to run for
anything, which did not stop Terre Haute socialists from nominating him for
Indiana's Fifth Congressional District seat. Debs felt trapped and defeated,
unable to disappoint socialists camped on his porch. Since the locals forced the
issue, he could not say no; meanwhile the national party skipped the bother of
a convention, choosing its candidate by a mail-in referendum.[131]

Debs rallied in his customary fashion, racing to campaign appearances in all
six counties of the Fifth District's assortment of coal miners and German,
Italian, Quaker, and assorted rural communities. He gave fifty-five speeches in
the first two weeks of September alone, traversing rutted roads in a Model T
touring car. Wherever he went Debs said the exploiting and exploited classes
had nothing in common. "Preparedness" was the buzzword of the day but what
mattered was to get ready for universal democracy. The coming socialist society
"knows no race or nationality; no creed, no color, no sex. It stands loyally,
unflinchingly, for equal rights, equal freedom, and equal opportunity for all."
He was tough on capitalist politicians and militaristic preachers, calling them
"the real betrayers of the people, the hypocrites that Christ denounced and for
which He was crucified; the slimy, oily-tongued deceivers of the ignorant, trusting followers, who traffic in the slavery and misery of their fellow-beings that
they may tread the paths of ease and bask in the favors of their masters." Behind
both groups stood "the whole burglarizing gang" of capitalist barons who shook
down the government, brayed about preparedness, got rich off war, and assumed
that exploited people should die for them.[132]

Debs told Indiana farmers they should read *International Socialist Review*—
otherwise they wouldn't know what was happening in their country, such as that
ironworkers on the Mesaba Range in Minnesota were fighting to unionize.
Renowned Italian IWW anarchist Carlo Tresca wrote his first English-language
letter from a jail cell on the Mesaba Range, urging Debs onward: "Help, Gene!

You are the heart, the brain of the worker in America and your voice is the voice of labor. Not make difference what will be, in this fight, the consequence for me and my fellowworkers in cell, arise, comrade Debs, arise the workers and let them realize the necessity of the stand, one for all and all for one." "Arise" was ironic in context since Debs dragged his emaciated body to three speeches per day. Tresca wanted Debs to run for president, not caring that anarchists spurned such things. The trickle of prowar socialist defectors kept increasing, adding Mother Jones and radical journalists Eastman and John Reed. Terre Haute Democrats enlisted Jones to campaign against Debs, who said nothing about the spectacle of his longtime comrade campaigning against him. In Terre Haute he tripled the party's vote of 1914 but finished second to a Republican.[133]

He took some romantic compensation by starting up with Mabel Dunlap Curry, a firebrand speaker on suffrage, birth control, marriage, and other feminist issues. Curry had a national reputation on the Chautauqua lecture circuit and was more or less happily married to an English professor at Indiana State Normal in Terre Haute, with whom she raised three children. She was gregarious, funny, warm, strong-willed, plump, razor-sharp, and a skillful platform performer. She and Debs had a mutual attraction based on being much alike, and they lived a few blocks from each other. Mabel Curry was the partner Debs had always wanted. He loved her for the rest of his life, in circumspect fashion.

Theodore Debs and his wife, Gertrude, were happy for Debs and Curry, regretting only that they had to be secretive. In 1917 Debs collapsed on the lecture circuit and was hospitalized in Boulder, Colorado. Curry was frustrated at being the other woman, unable to visit him. She had to communicate with Debs through Theodore and was guilt-ridden about damaging her marriage, while Debs said he was pretty much guilt-free in this area. He idealized Curry, saying she was more sensitive than he, so she suffered a guilty conscience. For a while Curry pressed for marriage, but Debs said it was better to remain secret lovers and not hurt their spouses. Debs confided his situation to close friends, notably Rose Pastor Stokes; lesser friends got breezy assurances that the two marriages were just fine. Curry explained to Stokes, "His wife and my husband cannot be hurt and humiliated for the sake of our happiness."[134]

Debs and Hillquit forged a genuine friendship during the war years. It helped that each had a capacity for transcending grudges and sometimes relinquishing them. Hillquit took pride in being diplomatic, drawing on what he called "my mellowest tones and suavest manner." Being a Marxist, Russian, Jewish, Old Guard, New York City intellectual defined him in the party, especially New York City intellectual. There was no place like New York, and it housed virtually all the party's intellectuals. Hillquit wrote prolifically on socialism, recycling his

campaign speeches and talks to civic groups. His closest party comrades—
Walling, Simons, Spargo, Robert Hunter, and W. J. Ghent—wrote similar fare,
spreading the message. In *Socialism in Theory and Practice* (1909), Hillquit
defined socialism as the transfer of ownership of the social tools of production
from individual capitalists to the people. Socialism is no more confiscatory than
abolishing slavery, he argued; in fact it *is* abolitionism—capitalists hold no more
right to "modern social tools" than slaveholders held to enslaved human beings.
Just as liberalism abolished the privileges of birth and abolitionism abolished
chattel slavery, socialism was the next stage of society civilizing itself on the way
to creating a "perfect democracy."[135]

It didn't matter to Hillquit that idealistic talk about perfecting democratic
civilization is not Marxist; orthodox Marxism was an adaptable tradition to him.
He said the three defining theorists of socialism were Marx, Engels, and
Lassalle, in that order, and the greatest contemporary Marxist was Kautsky, a
master at adjusting Marxism to current circumstances. Hillquit conceived
Marxian orthodoxy as resting on the economic interpretation of history, the
doctrine of the class struggle, and the theory of surplus value. Structural economic relationships determine the character of societies. The class struggle is
an antagonism of economic interests created by the inexorable conditions of
capitalist production, not by the will of individuals. Surplus value is the difference between the actual price of labor paid in wages and the value of the product produced by labor. Ricardo taught that human labor is the source of
economic value, but Marx added that the capitalist pays to workers less than the
value that their labor adds to the goods. Capitalism is based on the capitalist's
confiscation of the value added to labor value by the labor power of workers.
Hillquit said the doctrine of surplus value is not merely that the capitalist ownership of modern social tools allows capitalists to exploit workers—a point too
obvious to need Marx's confirmation. Marxism is an argument about why the
capitalist mode of production *is* exploitation at its core, and through and
through.[136]

Hillquit disliked the Kautsky versus Bernstein controversy that rocked the
SPD near the turn of the twentieth century. Bernstein argued that orthodox
Marxism undermined liberal rights and democracy, was grievously steeped in a
catastrophe mentality of revolutionary terrorism and deliverance, recycled
repugnant slogans about the dictatorship of the proletariat, exaggerated the all-
determinative role of economic structures, wrongly denigrated the importance
of individual subjectivity and moral willing, and exaggerated its capacity to
quantify impossibly complex surplus values. He added that the SPD was better
in practice than in theory since in practice it respected liberal rights and democ-

racy and eschewed violence. Kautsky made small concessions and adjustments on these issues but reproved Bernstein for discarding fundamental Marxian principles that define what socialism is about, whatever miscalculations Marx made in elaborating them. Bernstein denied that socialists had a definite final end; Kautsky was incredulous, countering that only the final end of achieving a classless society justified the tactical compromises the SPD had to make. Hillquit endorsed the bilevel scheme Kautsky devised for the SPD in the 1890 Erfurt Program, joining the revolutionary worldview of *The Communist Manifesto* to the everyday politics of the SPD. Kautsky, he said, was the "acutest thinker and observer of modern socialism" because he vindicated Marxian orthodoxy by updating, adjusting, and defending it.[137]

Hillquit likened his role in the Socialist Party to Kautsky's role in the SPD. Like Kautsky, he believed that correct Marxian doctrine held Social Democracy together. At the worldview level, Marxian Socialism was internationalist and proletarian; at the level of current politics, it respected the national principle, as Kautsky said, and did not have to shout. Hillquit was the same everywhere, prizing his reasonableness. In May 1914 Gompers challenged him to a debate, and Hillquit gladly accepted, bantering with Gompers in a friendly manner and opining that Gompers was a socialist at heart. Hillquit was diplomatic even when he battled for factional victories, as on Kautsky versus Bernstein. He observed that few American socialists knew anything about this debate and that Kautsky stopped feuding with Bernstein after Bernstein won the battle to establish revisionist socialism as a legitimate option in the SPD. Hillquit said he had a similar relationship to Berger on friendlier terms. In 1913, debating a Catholic opponent who drew on Bernstein's arguments, Hillquit did not describe Bernstein as a traitor or a bad socialist. He said Bernstein was "an active and militant Socialist" who belonged to the other wing of the Socialist movement.[138]

John A. Ryan, in 1913, taught moral theology at St. Paul Seminary in St. Paul, Minnesota, and was the only Catholic intellectual in American social Christianity before World War I. He based his position on Thomist natural law theory and Leo XIII's papal encyclical *Rerum Novarum* (1891), writing his first book in 1906 on the right to a living wage. Ryan reasoned that the rights to live and marry inhere in all persons regardless of condition and the right to a living wage, pertaining only to wage earners, is derivative and secondary, deduced from the right to subsist on the earth's bounty. His first book put off the complex problem of the just wage, aspiring only to say what is minimally decent. Ryan was deeply conservative on Catholic doctrine, vehemently conservative on marriage and family issues, and progressive on economic issues. He supported minimum wage laws, an eight-hour workday, labor arbitration boards, municipal housing, state government unemployment and health insurance, national and state government ownership of railroads and telephone companies, municipal ownership of essential utilities and streetcars, national ownership of forestlands, and progressive taxes on income and inheritance.

Since Ryan owed his career to *Rerum Novarum,* he claimed not to worry in 1899 when Leo XIII condemned Americanism by name in the encyclical *Testem benevolentiae.* Eight years later Pope Pius X exhaustively condemned all forms of modernism, including evolutionary theory and biblical criticism, and biblical scholar Francis E. Gigot despairingly warned Ryan not to be smug; he could be next. Ryan fretted about it until 1911, when an Irish Franciscan with Vatican connections, Peter Fleming, told him he would be okay as long as he stuck to I-oppose-socialism. Ryan reached out to Hillquit, asking for a debate in which he attacked socialism and Hillquit responded. That sounded fine to Hillquit.[139]

Hillquit vowed to defend only the actual Socialist movement of the Second International, explaining that he took no interest in "bastard offshoots" of the real thing such as state socialism and Christian socialism. These were heterogeneous and heterodox distractions serving only to confuse people. Ryan happily agreed, delighted to have socialism defined as a foe of Christianity. Hillquit argued that anarchy reigned supreme under capitalism, energy and resources were wasted on a monumental scale, pauperism was rampant, the working class got poorer, and the American nation stood helpless before mighty economic trusts. Ryan said Hillquit trafficked in exaggeration and half truths. How could Hillquit know that reforming the trusts is pointless? The great trusts were barely twenty years old, and American politics was just beginning to respond to them. Far from getting poorer, American workers had more discretionary income, leisure, recreation, and access to culture than their parents or grandparents; this was why socialism did not tempt them. Ryan acknowledged that capitalism is wasteful and anarchic, but these were small evils compared to Hillquit's remedy of abolishing individual liberty and making everyone a servant of the state. It was much better to reform capitalism. Economic conditions for the masses were better in 1913 than for any previous generation, and the key to making America more just was to employ state power toward the end of attaining equality of opportunity.[140]

Ryan cautioned that many of America's social problems sprang directly from ignorance, greed, and other defects in human nature that would exist under any system. Other evils are more distinctive to capitalism: oppression of labor, dramatic inequalities of income, and unjust distribution of productive property and capital ownership. The solution was a reform politics that respected the right of individuals to use the bounty of nature toward the end of their self-development, not to build a vast, despotic socialist bureaucracy. Ryan said he hated the predatory aspects of capitalism as much as any socialist and "quite as strongly as Mr. Hillquit." He did not care for "the Capitalist Type," and he expected future generations to judge that the greed, materialism, labor oppression, and hideous inequalities of the present amounted to essential barbarism. But socialism had no substitute for the two "powerful springs of effort and efficiency" it eliminated: the hope of reward and the fear of loss. It wrongly made social expediency the test of morality instead of the other way around. Ryan said he began with the indestructible rights of the individual—the opposite of the socialist view that the individual has no rights against the state. The socialist State was the reason no one should be a socialist.[141]

Hillquit replied that he did not recognize this socialist State that wiped out individual rights. He had no idea where Ryan got the "notion of a sudden break," unless it was from reading critics who didn't understand Marx and Engels. Ryan condemned an imaginary socialist state: "The Socialists have no such romantic conceptions. To them the 'Socialist state' is nothing but a more advanced phase of modern civilization." Hillquit seized on Ryan's declaration that he wanted to radically amend the existing system, not abolish it. Socialism, Hillquit said, is precisely about radically amending the existing system: "Amended by the elimination of industrial warfare and economic exploitation and by a relative equalization in the enjoyment of wealth and opportunities, but still a system of human beings as we know them today, with all their frailty and weakness, passions and ambitions—except with less incentive and fewer opportunities for evil doing."[142]

The Ryan–Hillquit debate went on for four months and was published in *Everybody's Magazine* as a seven-part series. Both contestants were praised for their lucidity, intelligence, and civility, and both got what they wanted, each savoring his first exposure to a mass circulation audience. Ryan won a coveted chair at Catholic University in Washington, DC, which put him on the path to becoming a New Deal insider. Back in St. Paul he had felt vulnerable to complaints that he made Catholic social teaching sound too much like socialism. Afterward he heard it more than ever but from a position of strength and renown. Hillquit realized that Ryan scored against him concerning the growing middle class and the value of reform movements. For the rest of his life Hillquit lauded Ryan as the "most gratifying opponent" he ever debated—"well informed, painstaking, broad-minded, and scrupulously fair." Hillquit's allies said similar things about him right up until they repudiated him.[143]

Hillquit turned out to be better than his idol Kautsky on the war issue, guarding his party's antiwar unity during World War I, such as it was. From August 1914 to February 1917 the Socialist Party had a trickle of outright pro-German boosters led by Cahan and *The Forward*, a rival faction led by Walling, Herron, and Simons that agitated for America to side with England, and a dominant mainstream that held fast to Socialism-opposes-war. Cahan got a pass for pro-German utterances that no German American was allowed to say because he was a Russian American Jew who longed for someone—even Germany—to overthrow Russia. Cahan said it with typical candor, observing in August 1914 that if the war were only between Germany and Russia surely every Socialist in the world would favor Germany. As it was, he reasoned that a German victory would be terrible for England, Belgium, and France but deposing Russian autocracy would be worth it: "I am convinced that in the interests of progress generally and Jews specifically, a Russian defeat would be fortunate: I am convinced that it would be fortunate for all of Europe and for the entire Jewish population if Germany would take all Poland and Lithuania too, from Russia." Cahan lauded German socialism as though the war were not occurring. He published articles by prowar SPD leader Philipp Scheidemann and took a press junket to Germany in 1915 to hobnob with his SPD friends. He stuck to this position until the Russian Revolution of February 1917, whereupon *The Forward* whipsawed 180°, exulting that Jews were free in Russia so there was no need to cheer for Germany. To Cahan and the *Forward*, World War I had already yielded a wondrous outcome just as America geared up to enter it.[144]

Meanwhile the pro-England interventionist faction blistered Hillquit and Berger for supposedly harboring pro-German feelings under a cloak of neutrality. For two years the strongest prowar agitation in the Socialist Party came from the left-wing. Walling, Herron, and Simons implored that what mattered was to oppose German militarism; there was no neutral option. In November 1914 Hillquit grieved for Kautsky and his SPD comrades more than Herron and Walling could stand, telling an audience at Cooper Union that national feeling is existential, embracing "everything we hold dear—home, language, family, and friends." Every worker has a country "even before he has a class." Herron and Walling raged against Hillquit and Berger on this subject. Herron warned that pious sympathy for the German socialists would lead American socialists to the same disaster that occurred in Germany. Walling was so offended he called for Hillquit's expulsion from the party. Alarm spread through the ranks of Socialist intellectuals. Hillquit tried to smooth things over as usual, but Berger upped the ante by calling for compulsory national service emphasizing military and industrial training of America's youth, which set off a protest that nearly expelled him from the party.[145]

Hillquit needed his touted urbanity to get through 1915, while speaking for the party as chair of the NEC. In May 1915 he drafted a Socialist program for "democratic peace" that anticipated by three years Wilson's Fourteen Points. It called for no indemnities, no transfer of territories without democratic consent, political independence for all nations wanting it, an international parliament with legislative and administrative powers over international affairs, universal disarmament, and political and industrial democracy. It asked Wilson to convoke a congress of neutral nations that mediated between the belligerents and remained in session until the war ended. Meyer London, New York's newly elected Socialist in the U.S. House of Representatives, offered the resolution in the House and set up a meeting with Wilson slated for January 25, 1916. The NEC designated Debs, Hillquit, and James Maurer to join the group. Maurer had come up through the Knights of Labor and the People's Party, joined the Plumbers and Steamfitters Union in 1901, joined the Socialist Party at its founding that year, won a seat in the Pennsylvania House of Representatives in 1910, and was elected in 1912 as president of the Pennsylvania Federation of Labor, his power base until he retired in 1930. Debs said meeting with Wilson was pointless, Maurer was skeptical but willing, and the Socialist threesome met with Wilson in the White House.

Wilson was tired and preoccupied at first, but he perked up as the conversation wore on, confiding that he was considering a similar plan. He said the problem was that only the United States was both neutral and a real power; all other putatively neutral powers were beholden to one of the belligerents. Wilson suggested that a direct offer of mediation from the United States might work better, but that would require further study. Hillquit and London glowed at how well this was going; Maurer said he liked what he heard but knew that Wilson was beholden to "capitalist and militarist interests who want the war to continue." Wilson replied that he was accused more often of being owned by liberals. A month later Maurer put himself on Wilson's calendar for a follow-up session. Wilson said he would like to hear on a later occasion how Maurer might react to a preparedness plan. Maurer said there was no need to wait: "The idea of preparing for peace by creating a huge military establishment could fool no one capable of distinguishing fact from fiction." In March the Socialist Party conducted a mail-in referendum to determine its presidential slate. Maurer and O'Hare would have been the strongest ticket, but both came in second, as Maurer lost to a popular antiwar writer, Alan Benson, and O'Hare lost to a Rand School economist, George Kirkpatrick.[46]

Wilson won reelection in November 1916 by boasting that he kept America out of the war. Two months later Germany tried to starve Britain into surrender by resuming unrestricted submarine warfare, attacking neutral ships without the warnings that Wilson had extracted in 1915. To Germany, trying to end the war

was worth the risk of bringing the United States into it. Wilson broke off diplomatic relations with Germany on February 3, and Germany sank the American
steamship *Housatonic* on the same day. Three weeks later Americans learned
via the British Secret Service that Germany offered to help Mexico regain territories lost in the Mexican-American War. Debs froze in horror as a rising
clamor for war shouted, "Stand by the president!" In March he spoke to anxious
crowds on the East Coast, declaring that he would stand by Wilson only if he
refused to enter the war. To a huge gathering at Cooper Union he said Americans
should respond to any declaration of war by waging a general strike. On March
18 Germany sank three American ships without warning, and Wilson geared for
war. Germany ended America's capacity to make money off both sides of the war
and in a way that put maximum pressure on Wilson. On April 2 he asked
Congress to declare war on Germany to make the world safe for democracy.
Four days later Congress did so, overwhelmingly, with only five dissenting votes.

The Socialist Party NEC cried against this stampede, beseeching Americans
not to join the orgy of slaughter and destruction. A stunning parade of Socialist
intellectuals bolted the party. Eastman, Ghent, Herron, Hunter, Jack London,
Pastor Stokes, Phelps Stokes, Russell, Sinclair, Walling, J. Stitt Wilson, *New
York Call* editor Chester Wright, and writers Frank Bohn, Robert W. Bruere,
Arthur Bullard, Charlotte Perkins Gilman, Walter E. Kreusi, Leroy Scott,
Henry Slobodkin, and William L. Stoddard fled the party to stand with Wilson.
Even Benson embraced Wilson after years of warning against executive authority and stampedes to war. Nearly all the party's union leaders joined the exodus,
especially from unions indispensable to military production—coal miners,
machinists, needle trades, and building trades; Maurer was a rare exception,
enlisting his state federation against the war. On March 24 eleven Socialists
headed by Phelps Stokes and Russell issued a prowar manifesto: "To refuse to
resist international crime is to be unworthy of the name of Socialist. It is our
present duty to the cause of Internationalism to support our government in any
sacrifice it requires in defense of those principles of international law and order
which are essential alike to Socialism and to civilization." They implied that
Hillquit surely agreed with them, which prompted Hillquit to refuse the "unexpected honor" of enlistment in their cause: "The task to which our pro-war
American Socialists are volunteering their support is one of building up a new
system of militarism." He was incredulous and unequivocal. Had they forgotten
how they felt on August 4, 1914? "Can our American 'internationalists' of the
new brand learn nothing from the lessons of history?"[147]

The Socialist Party lost almost its entire intelligentsia in the rush to war. Nearly
all the party's American-born leaders abandoned the party, embracing their tag,

the "social patriots." The new internationalism, as they called it, was very much about American patriotism and Wilson's claim to stand for a new international order. A similar gusher of non–Socialist Party intellectuals poured into Wilson's camp, notably Clarence Darrow, John Dewey, Du Bois, Gladden, Shailer Mathews, Spingarn, and *New Republic* ringleaders Herbert Croly, Walter Lippmann, and Walter Weyl. Some war boosters were Anglophiles who said Wilson had waited too long to intervene and most came along in step with Wilson. Republicans had long been the war party in American politics while Democrats were skeptical of Republican wars. Had Wilson lost the election to Republican Charles Hughes, some progressive and Democratic intellectuals might have resisted following a Republican into war. As it was, the Wilson factor wiped out normal politics for most non-Socialist intellectuals. Gladden epitomized the non-Socialist anti-interventionists who made a very swift reversal.

Gladden campaigned through 1915–16 against preparedness and war. He said he was ready to give his life for America but not to kill for it. He told audiences across the Midwest that war is madness and this particular war lacked any moral purpose. Imperial greed fueled the war on both sides, and no warring party showed any interest in brokering terms of peace. In December 1915 Wilson announced that the United States had to prepare for war; three days later he implored a Federal Council of Churches convention to help him keep America out of the war. Wilson sprinkled his speech with social gospel bromides, knowing how to talk to liberal clergy, and Gladden was not assuaged. Gladden and Addams barnstormed through New England, pleading that war is abominable, America should not fight Germany, and America lacked a vision of postwar Europe. Gladden published a book version, *The Forks of the Road*, insisting it was not too late to stay out of the war. He wanted the United States to organize a League of Peace that outlawed war and enforced the moral law with international police power. He voted for Wilson in 1916 on the hope that Wilson would not intervene. After the election Wilson asked the warring powers to state their war aims, and Gladden was briefly hopeful. He met with Wilson, who said he planned to broker terms of peace. Wilson addressed the U.S. Senate on January 22, 1917, calling for a League of Peace and urging the warring parties to negotiate a "peace without victory." The peace had to guard against vengeance and the peace federation would keep the peace: "The equality of nations upon which peace must be founded if it is to last must be an equality of rights. Only a peace between equals can last. Only a peace the very principle of which is equality and a common participation in a common benefit."[148]

It was a stirring moment for Gladden-type progressives. Wilson's dramatic address resembled the diplomatic section of *The Forks of the Road*. He seemed to be sincere about living up to Gladden's ideals, exactly as he told Gladden. But the warring powers on both sides were determined to gain victory, and the rush of crushing disappointments ensued. Gladden sadly accepted that Wilson had no choice because no president could withstand losing three ships in one day. Gladden struggled longer with his own choice. He wrote a book, "Killing Wrong-Doers as a Cure for Wrong-Doing," while Americans decided for war. The title brought a smile to Rauschenbusch's face just before America intervened, but the book was never published. Gladden mused from the pulpit that perhaps this war — "the darkest cloud that has ever obscured the sky" — contained a glimmer of light. European leaders were sick of the war, he said; many were wailing that war must cease, "that this is the last war." Going to war to end war was the kind of rationale Gladden needed.[149]

Wilson expressed it in political terms, telling a joint session of Congress on April 2, 1917, that entering the war served the world's greater good: "The world must be made safe for democracy. Its peace must be planted upon the tested foundations of political liberty." Gladden promptly reversed course, citing Wilson's idealistic claims and contending that America fought for democracy and world peace, though with regret: "War, even when a nation accepts it with chagrin and without any expectation of exclusive gain, is a devilish business. He who sups with the devil must fish with a long spoon." He reasoned that Wilson did not actually declare war; Wilson merely acknowledged that Germany was warring against the United States. America entered the war because war-making "has been thrust upon us."[150]

Now Gladden's sermons featured Wilson's jeweled words about fighting for justice, not revenge, seeking no selfish ends, and championing the rights of humankind. "I believe that these words are true," Gladden said. "And I thank God that I have lived to hear them spoken. They can never be recalled. They can never be forgotten. They will live as long as freedom lives. They will be emblazoned on the banners of the Universal Brotherhood. And when their full meaning is grasped by the great nations of the earth war will be no more." He said Americans had a "right to believe" in the sincerity and truth of Wilson's pledge to make the world safe for democracy, "the greatest word I think that this generation has heard. It defines our destiny."[151]

Certainly it impressed nearly the entire class of progressive and Socialist intellectuals. Even Du Bois declared that black Americans needed to put aside their special concerns about racial justice to get behind Wilson. German militarism, Du Bois warned, posed a life-or-death threat to the aspirations of the darker races for equality, freedom, and democracy: "Let us, while this war lasts, forget our special grievances and close our ranks shoulder to shoulder with our own fellow white citizens and the allied nations that are fighting for democracy." Many black editorialists inveighed against this stunning counsel. Du Bois conceded nothing: "Our country is at war. The war is critical, dangerous, and world-wide. If this is our country, then this is our war. We must fight it with every ounce of blood and treasure." To most American-born intellectuals, opposing their nation at war was not an option; they could barely imagine it. Many of Gladden's admirers in the CSF bailed out of the Socialist Party, disavowing three years of sermons against the murderous, anti-Christian, antisocialist evils of war.[152]

On April 7, 1917, the Socialists held an emergency convention in St. Louis amid this torrent of repudiation and patriotic gore. It turned out to be the day after war was declared. They met in St. Louis because it had a strong local party headed by Frank and Kate O'Hare, who moved there in 1912 to run the *National Rip-Saw*. The Socialists had not conducted a national convention since 1912. Hillquit spoke as chair of the convention, ruing the "fatal blunder" of not having met, because now they were strangers to each other. When last they met, "our organization was flushed and conscious of youthful vigor. Our movement was buoyant with enthusiasm, and the men and women in it were joyous with struggle, conscious of conquest." Then the destructive forces of capitalism wreaked catastrophe in Europe. Hillquit said American socialists should not pass judgment on their European comrades; history would judge why working-class solidarity suddenly disintegrated. Meanwhile the International was torn asunder, devoured by the "Moloch of militarism and war," and American socialism deteriorated. Every measure of the party's trajectory was negative: "Our membership has been reduced to about 80,000 from 125,000. [Precisely, membership fell from 118,045 in 1912 to 83,284 in 1916.] We have lost votes in the last election. And worst of all, we have lost some of our spirit, some of our buoyant, enthusiastic, militant spirit which is so essential, so very vital for the success of any movement like ours."[153]

Now the nation was rushing to war, and the only organized force standing against it was the Socialist Party: "It falls to us to continue our opposition to this criminal war." Hillquit lamented that millions of Americans could not resist a cheap slogan, "Stand By Our President." American socialists, he vowed, "will never subscribe to so meaningless, so undemocratic a phrase by which the people of the United States surrender their sold birthright." The Socialists applauded thunderously. Hillquit shook his head at Wilson's self-righteousness. Who was Wilson to sneer about European autocracies dragging Europe into war? "If ever a great people has allowed itself to be stampeded into death and destruction, it is this great democratic people of the United States." War, Hillquit warned, means "horribly mangled bodies" and early death for millions of soldiers mostly drawn from the working class. It also means reaction at home: "War creates conditions under which all the powers of reaction, all the predatory powers of the country, can satisfy their desires, and accomplish their attacks upon popular liberty, upon popular rights with absolute impunity." No group was willing to defy the forces of reaction under the conditions of war, "unless it be the voice of the Socialist Party of the United States."[154]

For eight days 193 delegates strenuously debated the moment, although the essential outcome was never in doubt. Kate O'Hare chaired a fifteen-member Committee on War and Militarism that drafted a majority resolution and two dissenting minority resolutions. Hillquit holed up with Charles E. Ruthenberg and Algernon Lee, strategically. Ruthenberg grew up in Cleveland, worked in his early career as a sales manager of a publishing company, joined the Socialist Party in 1909, and became the leader of the party's left wing after the anarcho-syndicalists bolted. He was very tightly wound and serious, with a romantic streak, which made him a fierce factional leader, especially in his later career. Lee was a stalwart of the New York Old Guard, decidedly to Hillquit's right. Hillquit, Ruthenberg, and Lee drafted the majority resolution while Spargo and Louis Boudin authored dissenting resolutions. Spargo contended that the social patriots were not wrong, because internationalism presupposes nationalism. Pure internationalism does not exist. Nations exist, and internationalism is the interrelation of nations. The integrity and independence of nations are essential conditions of internationalism, as the Socialist International assumed in defending Ireland's struggle for national independence and Finland's fight against Russian despotism. Spargo said Germany's wanton invasion of Belgium was a crime against internationalism deserving the reaction it received. Boudin wrote a muddled resolution draped in *ISR* phraseology that he deemed to be suitably left wing and intellectual. Hillquit said Spargo made good points but drew the wrong conclusion, and Boudin was a cranky type who always had to draw attention to himself.[155]

The Hillquit resolution channeled the passionate feeling of the majority: "The Socialist Party of the United States in the present grave crisis solemnly reaffirms its allegiance to the principle of internationalism and working-class solidarity the world over, and proclaims its unalterable opposition to the war just declared by the government of the United States." Killing for capitalism was a nonstarter. This "mad orgy of death and destruction" was caused by "the conflict of capitalist interests in the European countries" because the capitalist class needed foreign markets to dispose of its accumulated surplus wealth: "The huge profits made by the capitalists could not be profitably reinvested in their own countries, hence, they were driven to look for foreign fields of investment.

The geographical boundaries of each modern capitalist country thus became too narrow for the industrial and commercial operations of its capitalist class." Imperialism, the party explained, thus became "the dominant note in the politics of Europe." Europe plunged into self-annihilation because every European power was driven to exploit world markets: "The ghastly war in Europe was not caused by an accidental event, nor by the policy or institutions of any single nation. It was the logical outcome of the competitive capitalist system."[156]

The American Socialists said the United States was no exception to this logic. When Germany invaded Belgium, the American government said nothing about the dictates of humanity, protecting small nations, and the fate of democracy. Neutrality suited the government and capitalist class just fine as long as American capitalists made huge profits off the war. Then Germany disrupted "our enormous war traffic," and suddenly the government blathered about defending democracy and civilization. The Socialists declared, "We brand the declaration of war by our government as a crime against the people of the United States and against the nations of the world. In all modern history there has been no war more unjustifiable than the war in which we are about to engage." They called for antiwar demonstrations and petitions, opposition to conscription, vigorous resistance to censorship and all other reactionary measures, consistent propaganda against prowar propaganda in public schools, and educational campaigns to organize workers "into strong, class-conscious and closely unified political and industrial organizations."[157]

Eighty percent of the delegates endorsed the Hillquit resolution, Boudin's dissent won thirty-one votes, and Spargo's got only five, as the social patriots had already resigned and didn't bother trekking to St. Louis. Hillquit co-opted his left-wing opponents by enlisting Ruthenberg, which didn't stop the left wing from steaming at Hillquit. This left was different from the one that confronted Hillquit in 1912. Immigrants poured into the party during the war years, joined the federations, and swelled its revolutionary flank. The new left was predominantly east European, committed to revolutionary working-class internationalism, sprinkled with Christian pacifists, and vocal. Some were Jewish exiles from the 1905 Russian Revolution. Most had firsthand experience of industrial capitalism in Russia, Finland, or Poland. They were unskilled workers in basic industries not belonging to a union and too recently arrived to possess the vote. They equated socialism with revolutionary industrial unionism, sharing Leon Trotsky's contempt for Hillquit and Social Democrats. Lev Davidovich Bronstein arrived in New York on January 13, 1917, already known to American Socialists by the name he stole from the warden of a Siberian prison, Leon Trotsky. He was utterly contemptuous of American Socialist leaders, deriding

Hillquit as the ideal leader of a party of dentists. To the new left-wing immigrants, as for Trotsky, the Old Guard had nothing to do with socialism. Having Hillquit speak for them was very hard to take. Ruthenberg begged Debs to come to Cincinnati to rally the left wing against Hillquit and Berger. He loaded two cars with delegates, drove 150 miles to Terre Haute, and pleaded with Debs in vain. Not even World War I could drag Debs to a convention, and he still hated faction fighting.[158]

Meanwhile Benson and Simons charged that Hillquit harmonized the contradictory and treasonous ravings of an unhinged party remnant. According to Benson, four kinds of people showed up in St. Louis: excitable "young hotheads" who wailed about having no country; German Americans who had previously been "the most conservative and stable" faction of the party until fighting against Germany became the issue; Hillquit-types who were desperate to unify the party; and newcomers too easily wowed by antiwar radicals and r-r-revolutionaries. Benson said Hillquit, Ruthenberg, and Lee lacked "the slightest intention" of rioting against any military draft that came to pass, but that didn't matter. The courts would take their words seriously; riots would occur; protesters would be gunned down in the streets; and Socialists would be convicted of treason for words they didn't really mean. Simons said the same thing more bitterly. Hillquit and Berger could not possibly believe that America's entry into the war was criminal or that World War I was the most unjustifiable war in modern history. These "grotesque falsehoods," Simon charged, were far beneath Hillquit and Berger, betraying socialism and their country just to unify a gang of "nationalistic pro-Germans, violent syndicalists, and foreign-speaking organizations ignorant of American institutions."[159]

Simons claimed that Hillquit would never publicly defend the statements he propounded in St. Louis. Hillquit refuted him immediately, declaring that he stood by every word of the declaration, which contained no expression of treason. What puzzled him was the vengeance of Simons and Benson. Hillquit noted archly that the U.S. government was amply stocked with secret service officials and public prosecutors: "If there is anything in the utterances of any Socialist or body of Socialists that may be twisted into a violation of the law, these agencies may be relied on to deal with the offenders promptly and drastically, particularly in these war-crazed times." Why were his longtime comrades so eager to get him into trouble? But that question answered itself since Benson and Simons went out of their way to say that Hillquit was not their comrade. Branding Hillquit was an act of dissociation. Meanwhile for much of the party's left flank Hillquit's insistence that he said nothing remotely anti-American confirmed that he was a cunning operator not to be trusted.[160]

The fallout was devastating. Wilson gave a preview in April 1917, telling the Democratic *New York World*, "Once lead this people into war, and they'll forget there ever was such a thing as tolerance. To fight you must be ruthless and brutal, and the spirit of ruthless brutality will enter into the very fiber of our national life, infecting Congress, the courts, the policeman on the beat, the man in the street." The Espionage Act of June 15, 1917, prohibited any interference with military operations or recruitment, promotion of insubordination in the military, or giving aid to America's wartime enemies. The law was construed broadly and applied vengefully, notably in Boston, Detroit, Grand Rapids, Kansas City, Minneapolis, St. Paul, and Seattle. Ohio Socialist leaders Ruthenberg, Charles Baker, and Alfred Wagenknecht were jailed for obstructing the conscription law. In Butte, Montana, antiwar IWW organizer Frank Little was dragged from his bed, tortured, and lynched by vigilantes. In Bisbee, Arizona, vigilantes worked hand in hand with state officials, seizing over twelve hundred IWW copper miners, loading them into cattle cars, and deporting them to the New Mexico desert. In July 1917 O'Hare was indicted for interfering with enlistment. In August twelve radical publications were banned. In September federal agents raided state Socialist Party headquarters across the nation. *American Socialist* editors J. Louis Engdahl and Irwin St. John Tucker were raided several times and waited for the inevitable indictment, which came in March 1918. Theodore Roosevelt opined that suspect German Americans should be shot. A socialist coal miner in Terre Haute was lynched for refusing to buy a Liberty Bond. The Terre Haute *Tribune*, always friendly to Debs in the past, called for his execution by firing squad. Meanwhile Debs was too ill to leave his house.[161]

Debs blasted the assaults on civil liberties, writing in *Social Revolution*, the new name of the *National Rip-Saw*, while trying to stay within the law. Previously he had carefully refrained from condemning the Liberty Loan drives and America's subsidies to England and France; now he refrained from attacking the Espionage Act itself and from telling Americans not to enlist. Neither did he rail against the intellectuals and unionists streaming out of the party. Keeping his friends, especially Pastor Stokes, was very important to him. Debs bantered affectionately with her, sympathizing that the war caused tension in her marriage, and downplayed attacks from former comrades. Russell said the Socialists were dirty traitors who should be driven out of the country. Debs replied that Russell would recover his senses when the war ended. He stayed in this cautious mode until November 1917, when the Bolshevik Revolution and a new wave of government repression lit a fire. The Bolshevik victory enthralled nearly the entire Socialist Party. Now the Socialists had to decide whether they cared more about defending the Bolsheviks or opposing the war. There were tricky trade-offs to consider because the war belligerents on both sides sought to destroy the Bolshevik Revolution. Wilson unveiled his Fourteen Points in January 1918, and the social patriots exulted that all were socialist policies, especially open covenants of peace, freedom of navigation, equality of trade conditions, disarmament, and decolonization. Debs said he hoped for a German revolution that ended the war, which set off a frenzy of speculation: Was he preparing to support the Allied cause? Instead, in January 1918 Debs repeated his general condemnation of militarism and geared up to fight for revolutionary socialism.[162]

Hillquit and O'Hare tried to stay within the law, with dissimilar results owing to their locations and standing. Hillquit ran for mayor of New York in 1917, bravely and with immense dignity. His opponents were incumbent independent Democrat John Purroy Mitchel, Republican William F. Bennett, and Tammany Democrat John Hylan. Mitchel campaigned full bore for Wilson's war, Bennett did not bother to campaign, and Hylan supported the war halfheartedly like his political boss, newspaper titan William Randolph Hearst. Hillquit tapped into a larger antiwar sentiment than he realized was there. He spoke to the biggest crowds he ever attracted and got through a flap over his admission that he did not buy Liberty Bonds. New York papers that previously treated him respectfully now exhausted the lexicon of "traitor" and "enemy," but Hillquit stayed in character and avoided legal tripwires.

Theodore Roosevelt inveighed hysterically against Hillquit, calling him a slew of bad names headed by "Hun inside our gates." Anyone who did not buy Liberty Bonds was at best a "half and half American" not to be tolerated; TR worked up to a screaming climax: "Yellow calls to yellow!" The social patriots excoriated Hillquit as a terrible danger to America and the world. He later recalled, "Only war can inspire such a spirit of passion and hate." Being pilloried by his friends wounded him. Inevitably he was accused of having German friends and wanting "the German vote." Hillquit modeled, in reply, what decency looked like, asking people not to make judgments on the basis of prejudices. He pushed for woman suffrage, compelling the other candidates to take a position on something they did not want to discuss. All four candidates came out for it, which put New York on the path to becoming the twelfth woman suffrage state. Hylan crushed the incumbent mayor by 46 to 23 percent; Hillquit won 21 percent, and Bennett won the irreducible Republican 8 percent. Meanwhile Hillquit took heart that Socialist candidates performed equally well in Chicago, Cleveland, and Buffalo. For years afterward his press antagonists described him as "the unindicted Mr. Hillquit," ruing that Hillquit was too respected in New York to be prosecuted.[163]

O'Hare had the comparative disadvantage of speaking in a different town every night, which guaranteed that somebody would haul her to court. The war became her chief subject as soon as it began in 1914. It repelled her when Hillquit apologized for the German socialists in 1914, and it disgusted her when the social patriots Americanized the same argument in 1917. She protested in April 1917 that Europe was on fire because Europeans put nationalism first and everything else second: "Because nationalism was exalted above all else, Europe is one vast charnelhouse, soaked with blood, reeking with the stench of putrid human bodies, scarred by trenches and devastated by shot and shell, while famine and pestilence rage throughout the continent, kindling the fires of misery and hunger-maddened revolt." Putting country first was exactly what the world did not need. If God transcends nationalism and socialism is international and the labor movement knows no boundaries, how could any Christian, Socialist, or unionist put nationalism first? O'Hare countered: "I am a Socialist, a labor unionist and a follower of the Prince of Peace, FIRST; and an American, second." She wrote a carefully crafted speech, sprinkled it with I-am-not-saying disclaimers, took it on the road, and gave it, by her count, 75 times before she delivered it fatefully in Bowman, North Dakota, on July 17, 1917—though her calendar indicates that O'Hare probably gave it 150 times.[164]

She began ironically, observing that the war gave her a belated opportunity to talk about socialism instead of batting away the usual prejudices against it. For seventeen years it was her dismal fate to explain that socialists did not plan to confiscate everything, had no desire to start a war, and were not bad people who hated God and families. Socialists did not believe that children are the property of the state, and many socialists were Christians, like her. O'Hare said at least she was done with having to talk about all that. Now people asked why socialists failed to prevent the capitalists from starting World War I. They voted for Wilson only to learn "that your sons do not belong to you" or themselves. Their sons were literally the property of the U.S. government. O'Hare said she made no argument about whether conscription was morally right or wrong, unconstitutional, or any such thing: "I am not making any argument whatever; I am just telling you what happened to you, that is all." What happened was that suddenly Americans were not supposed to think for themselves; the government would do the thinking, and Americans were supposed to obey.[165]

That was enough to yield trouble sooner or later; O'Hare also had socialist feminist things to say about the war. She skewered the claim that America did not intervene to benefit the capitalist class. First, the war itself was a struggle to determine which group of capitalists would dominate world markets; second, the United States entered the war because Germany sank American ships laden with food and war munitions. O'Hare said number two was a deathblow to the heart of the capitalist system. Capitalism is based on the right to trade wherever and whenever profits can be made: "If that right of free and unrestricted trade can be denied, the whole fabric of capitalism crumbles like a house of sand." If one believed that capitalism is good, the war was probably worth fighting. O'Hare did not believe it, especially because she was a woman with a long memory and the heart of a mother. When men thought of humanity they pictured barter and trade, ocean lines, and war munitions and forgot the past. When women thought of humanity "we think of living, breathing, suffering human beings," remembering the invasion of Belgium, the desolation of France and Poland, and the crushing of Ireland.[166]

At the end she circled back to conscription peril. Editorialists and politicians, O'Hare observed, brayed that Socialists were unpatriotic, seditious, and treasonable: "I will simply leave you to judge from what I have said whether you think this true or not." But she closed with three flat denials. First, Socialists did not hinder Wilson from waging the war. As it was, socialism was coming faster than ever because of the war; even England now had a thriving socialist movement. Second, she denied that socialists opposed enlistment: "Please understand me now and do not misquote what I say. If any young man feels that it is his duty to enlist, then with all my heart I say—'Go and God bless you. Your blood may enrich the battlefields of France, but that may be for the best.'" Third, she tweaked them about confiscation—for so long the first thing she had to deny as a socialist. Look who the confiscators turned out to be! Socialists used to call for the railroads to be socialized, and editorialists said it would be too expensive. O'Hare chided that buying the railroads would have been a drop in the bucket compared to what this war was costing.[167]

The following day a navy enlistee on furlough, M. S. Byrne, sent a telegram to his superior officer in Minneapolis reporting that he heard a "highly unpatriotic" lecture in Bowman "tending to discourage enlistments and resisting draft." According to Byrne, O'Hare declared that anyone who enlisted was "no good for anything but fertilizer anyhow." That ensnared O'Hare in the machinery of repression. Every day on the speaking trail she had catered to government agents, transcribing her remarks for them, developing personal relationships with them, and making sure they quoted her correctly. None of that helped her at the trial in Bismarck, North Dakota. O'Hare explained that she stayed within the law and never used the word "fertilizer," to no avail. A jury of businessmen briskly convicted her of impeding the war effort. They knew what she was and didn't care how carefully she played the game. At her sentencing before Judge Martin Wade, O'Hare said she was guilty only of stirring up the people, something she shared with Moses, Spartacus, Cromwell, George Washington, William Lloyd Garrison, Wendell Phillips, and Jesus. She did not believe that

Wade and the court were tools of the war profiteers, but her following exceeded one hundred thousand readers. If she went to prison, they would believe it. In fact, "I say that the great mass of the people of the United States are going to have that thing burned into their souls if I go to prison." Knowing she was headed to prison, O'Hare said she hoped the Spirit of Jesus was in her. If Jesus could relinquish everything and suffer for others, she was willing "to become a convict among criminals in order that I may serve my country there." Reporters expected a six-month sentence; Wade chastised O'Hare for criticizing America and slammed her with a five-year sentence.[168]

She was forty-two years old when her appeals ran out in 1919, and she entered Missouri State Penitentiary in Jefferson City, joining ninety women in the female wing. The inmates respected O'Hare for being famous and a political prisoner, and they revered Emma Goldman, who served for several months with them. O'Hare's twin sons, Eugene and Victor, were eleven years old when she entered prison. Her son Dick visited on his own and with Frank; on one occasion Dick serenaded his mother across the street when the warden wouldn't allow him to enter with a cornet. O'Hare suffered in prison, was scarred by it, and grieved that her daughter Kathleen rarely wrote to her. She hated the miserable conditions, convict labor, striped uniforms, and, above all, constant danger of infectious disease. She wrote infuriated letters about sharing baths with syphilitic inmates. Yet she also said she was grateful to suffer in prison and was not "gloomy and lonely and unloved here." On her first Easter in prison, O'Hare said it was her best Easter ever: "I think that I have come just a little nearer the soul of the universe; that I can touch hands across the ages with all who have walked through Gethsemane and who have found peace for their own souls in service for others." She sprinkled religious images through her letters and occasionally a prayer: "Oh God, deliver us from hate, that we may love and live."[169]

Nearly all the letters O'Hare wrote were to her family, with a public angle, since Frank O'Hare published them. She was an assiduous reader of the Socialist papers the government didn't shut down—*New York Call*, *Milwaukee Leader*, *St. Louis Labor*. O'Hare loved the *Call*, repeatedly praising its brave and powerful journalism, and took delight that the *Leader* was almost as good, reflecting Berger's recent militancy. She wrote letters about the rush of supportive letters she received, mostly from people she didn't know. It surprised her that Catholic priests and nuns wrote deeply thoughtful letters to her. O'Hare had never heard of just war theory, wishing she had known of it before she was imprisoned. Among her Socialist comrades she noted that Jews were singularly faithful, though not the leaders. O'Hare winced that very few of her big-name socialist friends wrote to her aside from Debs and Episcopal cleric Irwin St. John Tucker.

On her second Easter in prison she wrote that she felt closer to Jesus than ever, imbued by the Spirit of Jesus, though her cellmates merely liked her, nothing like the love and adoration they had felt for the nurturing Goldman. In May 1920 Wilson and U.S. Attorney General A. Mitchell Palmer set O'Hare free, not because she was unjustly convicted, as she protested, but because she was a mother of young children, an argument she never used. The nation and party to which she returned felt far diminished to her.[170]

It galled O'Hare that so few Christians remembered Jesus after Wilson called them to war. Prowar Christian apologetics on this theme were unbearable to her, as were the rationalizations of CSF stalwarts who bailed out of the party. Opposing their country's war, whether for Christian reasons or socialist reasons, was not an option for them. Bliss was an exception, never changing. Tucker campaigned in tireless, early-Bliss antiwar fashion, writing and speaking for the Church Socialist League and the *American Socialist*, though he turned conservative in the mid-1930s. Scudder stayed in the party but capitulated to the war; *Christian Socialist*, struggling to stay relevant, also caved to the war. In 1918 *Christian Socialist* changed its name to *Real Democracy*, explaining that the war changed almost everything. The following year the paper declared that the antiwar holdovers in the party were "a bigoted, bitter, unscientific, foolish, anti-religious sect"—not a very generous description of the comrades they abandoned.[171]

When O'Hare was indicted Debs tried to believe she would not be convicted. He told her he couldn't stand to be at large if she went to prison. This feeling grew after O'Hare was convicted. Pastor Stokes turned against the war, was arrested in March 1918 for a speech in Willow Springs, Missouri, and further goaded Debs. Berger stridently defended the party's antiwar position and made himself a highly visible target of prosecution. He said Wilson's idealistic perorations were pure "hypocrisy and humbug"; America got into the war because American capitalists were closely aligned with British capitalists. The raids on the party yielded indictments in April 1918 against Berger, Tucker, and Engdahl while Berger campaigned in a special election for the U.S. Senate. The following November Berger was elected to the U.S. House of Representatives, but Congress refused to seat him. Debs realized that he looked strangely passive compared to O'Hare, Pastor Stokes, and Berger. He could not make an impact from his sickbed because the government shut down or hampered *American Socialist*, *The Masses*, *ISR*, and *Social Revolution*; moreover, *Appeal to Reason* went over to Wilson in December 1917. To rejoin the fight Debs had to get back on the road *and* persuade the party to hold a national convention.[172]

He had two main arguments for convening: The St. Louis Manifesto was open to various interpretations, and the Bolshevik Revolution changed the world picture. Some socialists wanted to take credit for the Fourteen Points or get on the comfortable side of the Liberty Loan issue. Hillquit, London, and Berger touted that Wilson got the core of his peace plan from them. Mother Jones urged workers to buy government bonds; Algernon Lee and five other New York City Council socialists voted to support the third Liberty Loan; and three socialists on the Chicago City Council voted for a loyalty resolution. The second argument was a harder call for Debs, raising the question whether he cared more about opposing the war or helping the Bolsheviks. He greatly feared that Germany would destroy the Bolshevik Revolution, and he lacerated the progovernment German socialists who supported the slaughter of Russians. But whenever Debs warmed to this theme he stirred expectations that he would come out for the war. He got his way on the convention shortly before he stopped warning that Germany had to be stopped in Russia.[173]

Debs spoke a dozen times in Indiana and Illinois in early June of 1918. He blasted capitalist militarism, ridiculed Wilson's military idealism, called for a global socialist revolution, and baited district attorneys, without getting arrested. Debs was incredulous. No one was willing to give him a spotlight trial. He made his way to Canton, Ohio, where Ruthenberg, Baker, and Wagenknecht were imprisoned at Stark County Workhouse for opposing the draft act. The party shrewdly held its convention across the street from the prison, in Nimisilla Park. Ohio was the epicenter of the party's left wing—the only state that voted in 1912 against the anti-IWW amendment. Debs stoked his fury by visiting the imprisoned trio before the speech. In the park he said he could not say exactly what he believed, but he would not say anything he did not think. He would rather "a thousand times" be a free soul in jail than a coward in the streets. His famous antiwar speech said almost nothing about the war or the Espionage Act. Debs said the essential thing was to be faithful to the principles of the international socialist movement. If socialists did that, there was nothing to fear. He refused to be discouraged, because socialism was winning—look at Russia! He made a glancing reference to the war, observing that socialists had been fighting Prussian militarism "since the day the Socialist movement was born." Socialists needed no pious lectures about the evils of Prussian militarism. Briefly he turned scathing: "They tell us that we live in a great free republic; that our institutions are democratic; that we are a free and self-governing people. This is too much, even for a joke."[174]

The capitalist class owned the industries and politicians, made the laws, and appointed all 121 of the federal judges. Meanwhile Debs felt privileged to have served the movement to abolish capitalism: "I have regretted a thousand times that I can do so little for the movement that has done so much for me." He exulted that the movement won a spectacular victory in Russia, proclaiming as its first act "a state of peace with all mankind, coupled with a fervent moral appeal, not to kings, not to emperors, rulers, or diplomats but to *the people* of all nations." Debs said socialists had no fight with any individuals as such, even those who hated socialists: "We do not hate them. We know better." Socialists were moving toward the sunrise with faces aglow with the light of the coming day, "toward democracy and the dawn." He called for converts: "You will lose nothing; you will gain everything. Not only will you lose nothing but you will find something of infinite value, and that something will be yourself. And that is your supreme need—to find yourself—to really know yourself and your purpose in life."[175]

They needed to rise above the animal plane of existence, learn literature and science and art, and stick together, for they would be exploited, degraded, have to beg for a job, and be scorned by the very parasites that lived off their unpaid labor. They were in the crucible, about to be tried by fire. The weak and faint-hearted would be lost, just like the intellectuals who thought they were movement leaders until socialism threatened to cost them something. Debs said the movement lost nothing when the intellectuals fled. It was a rare thing for an intellectual to become a true socialist; most intellectuals who joined just wanted to be bosses. It took little to scare them away. He put in a nice word for the IWW, saying he respected Wobbly organizers far more than he respected their detractors and persecutors. An evil time had descended on the United States, when calling someone a Wobbly was enough to get the person lynched. Debs closed with his creed: Political action and industrial action go together, supplement each other, and sustain each other: "You will never vote the Socialist republic into existence. You will have to lay its foundations in industrial organization." It started with industrial unions, which create industrial democracy, allowing workers to control their jobs by owning their tools. The purpose of the Socialist Party was to unite democratized industries. Someday, Debs said, the entire economy will be organized on a cooperative basis. The title deeds of the railroads, mines, mills, and essential industries will be transferred to the people in their collective capacity. But industrial democracy—a goal for nations and the world—begins with the organization of industrial unions.[176]

Debs refused to believe that Americans would always find themselves through private endeavors that exclude others. He knew what he owed to the socialist movement and overflowed with gratitude to it. If Paine, Jefferson, Lincoln, Phillips, and craft unionism led him to socialism, it could not be that socialism was un-American. He got a thundering, waving, chanting ovation at Nimisilla Park for believing it and giving voice to it. E. S. Wertz, U.S. attorney for northern Ohio, was in the audience, with two stenographers. Wertz was most offended by the sympathetic word for the IWW; second place went to Debs's scorn for corporate and government leaders. Justice Department officials in Washington took three days to decide that Debs did not cross the line, so Wertz had to obtain his own grand jury indictment in Cleveland. Debs was arrested on June 30 and tried in September in Cleveland. He was accused of inciting insubordination in the military and obstructing the enlistment process. Debs declined on principle to make any defense. Darrow wanted to defend him, but Debs refused because Darrow supported the war. Hillquit would have defended him but was hospitalized with tuberculosis. Four competent socialist lawyers aided Debs and were allowed to do nothing, on his insistence. No witnesses were called, and Debs spoke to the jury after the prosecution finished.

He said there was nothing in his speech that warranted the charges, and he would not dispute the charges, except the insinuation that he advocated violence: "I have never advocated violence in any form." This point aside, he stood by the speech in question. Debs ran through his usual American story: Paine, Washington, and Jefferson were rebels who had to endure shunning and persecution to create a free nation, and Garrison, Phillips, and Anthony redeemed the dream of the founders by rebelling against chattel slavery. He stressed that American history books celebrated them: "You are now teaching your children to revere their memories, while all of their detractors are in oblivion." In the First Amendment the founders declared that Congress shall make no law abridging the freedom of speech or the press, so why was he on trial? Debs believed in the right of free speech and saw nothing in the Constitution about war abridging the right to it. It seemed to him that the Espionage Act violated the Constitution: "If the Espionage Law finally stands, then the Constitution of the United States is dead." There was a motion for a new trial, which the judge overruled before asking Debs if he had anything to say before sentence was passed. Debs began another run of oratory with his most famous utterance: "While there is a lower class, I am in it, while there is a criminal element I am of it, and while there is a soul in prison, I am not free." He said he could have been elected to Congress long ago but preferred to go to prison, already seeing the dawn "of the better day for humanity." At the age of sixty-three he was sentenced to ten years of prison.[177]

The Canton and trial speeches electrified demoralized American socialists. Both were widely reprinted, snatches were immortalized by citation, and, very briefly, Socialists united in praise of Debs. He was gratified and embarrassed by the outpouring, protesting that his feeble efforts were nothing compared to what Lenin, Trotsky, Karl Liebknecht, and Rosa Luxemburg did for socialism. Even to say it, however, implicitly put him in the same class as the Bolshevik leaders and the two stars of radical socialism imprisoned in Germany. Whether

Debs belonged to such company was a question of two kinds. The first kind spoke to his point—no, he had no achievements that compared to them. The second was whether he believed in their brand of socialism—just before Lenin decreed that genuine revolutionary socialists were Communists, and the Social Democratic tradition was socialist only in a mutilated sense of what Marx intended. Debs never shared Lenin's ruthless fixation on seizing and wielding power. This mentality was so foreign to him that he literally didn't understand it. Emotionally, however, Debs was a 100 percent Bolshevik on his way to prison, to the point of confusing himself and many others.

The Bolshevik Revolution of October–November 1917 thrilled American Socialists and evoked their passionate loyalty. This was not a point of contention in the Socialist Party; the entire party was strongly pro-Bolshevik. Hillquit and Berger defended the Bolsheviks so resolutely that the party's Leninist left wing was deprived of a wedge issue to split the party. Debs was enthralled by the Bolshevik victory story. In February 1919 the leader of the Socialist Party's Leninist faction, Louis Fraina, called for a left-wing organization within the party that espoused Bolshevik ideology, charged dues, and repudiated reformers. Fraina reached out to Debs, who gave his blessing, agreeing to serve on the editorial board of Fraina's periodical *Class Struggle*. Debs said he was a Bolshevik "from the crown of my head to the soles of my feet." He idealized Lenin and Trotsky as "fearless, incorruptible, and uncompromising" heroes who galvanized the greatest revolution ever seen: "It stirs the blood and warms the heart of every revolutionist, and it challenges the admiration of all the world." Debs confirmed to New York City local secretary Julius Gerber that he supported the radical wing of the party, yet he insisted he was adamantly opposed to splitting the party. If *he* was a Leninist, surely Leninism was not divisive. Debs thus endorsed an ideological agenda he did not understand that ravaged his party in remarkably short order.[178]

On his way to prison Debs sabotaged Wilson's consideration of clemency for him by lionizing the Bolshevik Revolution, emoting that the "magnificent spectacle" in Russia showed the way for all oppressed people. This message perplexed and wounded many of the humble union workers who lined his rail path from Terre Haute to Cleveland to Youngstown to the penitentiary at Moundsville, West Virginia. Debs noted that most of them wore the button of their craft in their hats. Mabel Curry had to bear her grief in private, avoiding the train station spectacle at which her lover bade farewell to his wife and Terre Haute. In prison Debs calmed down, belatedly realizing that he could not be a radical democrat and a Leninist simultaneously. But the Socialist Party in which he stayed was devastated by the Communist eruption.[179]

4

COMMUNIST TRAUMA AND
NORMAN THOMAS SOCIALISM

A potent postwar Socialist Party is imaginable. The party was viciously persecuted and dismembered for opposing the war, pulverized almost beyond recognition, and yet new members poured into it. In April 1919 the party reached a
peak of 104,822 members. Being attacked by the government unified Socialist
leaders as never before; former antagonists lauded each other for opposing the
war. Nearly everything they had claimed about the war had turned out to be
true, as they noted. Briefly the party was simultaneously devastated, reeling,
defiantly buoyant, still persecuted, and flush with new members. But the eighteen-year period in which one party held together all left-wing ideologies ended
dramatically. The siren call of Communist revolution crushed what might have
been. Factional tendencies that had previously coexisted within the Socialist
Party ripped it apart. It didn't matter that Hillquit and Berger had opposed the
war and supported the Bolshevik Revolution. Communism blew apart the entire
Socialist world. In the fevered atmosphere of 1919 that created the Communist
International (Comintern), Socialists who didn't espouse Leninism in their own
contexts were repudiated. By 1920 the Socialist Party was a shattered wreck kept
alive by AFL social democrats, who fought to keep Communists from doing to
unions what they did to the party. Afterward the Socialists found a compelling
leader straight out of the social gospel, Norman Thomas, who revived the party
with his passionate idealism—but not enough and not for long.

Lenin convinced the Bolsheviks that if they spurned alliances and ruthlessly
seized power their victory would spark a wildfire of proletarian revolutions
through Europe. He said it first upon returning to Russia from Switzerland on
April 16, 1917, in the tsar's former restroom at the Finland Station in Petrograd,

where Mensheviks came to greet him. That night he said it for two hours in a speech at Kshesinskaya Palace, the new Bolshevik headquarters after the February Revolution. Lenin mocked the agrarian reforms of the provisional government and condemned its continuation of the war. He blistered the Bolsheviks for jockeying with six socialist groups, not caring if Joseph Stalin and other party bigwigs were offended. Russia didn't need bourgeois democracy and a parliamentary republic. It needed a new order led by Bolsheviks. After the provisional government reorganized in July, appointing Aleksandr Kerensky as prime minister, Lenin thwarted all backsliding tendencies in his group. Kerensky had scaled the ranks of the peasant-based Socialist Revolutionary Party. He instituted freedoms of speech, press, assembly, religion, suffrage, and women's suffrage, laying plans for a Constituent Assembly election to be held in January 1918. But Kerensky kept the war going and never gained control of Russian politics, which enabled Lenin, Trotsky, and the Bolshevik Red Guard to overthrow him on November 7, 1917, before Kerensky could claim a democratic mandate. After the Bolsheviks seized power, Lenin was boastfully reassuring in one breath and anxiously vulnerable in the next. The Bolshevik Revolution was invincible, he claimed, yet it could not survive lacking a chain reaction of European revolutions. This fear turned out to be untrue and fateful.[1]

The Socialist Party united in supporting the Bolsheviks. Berger exemplified its consensus, boasting that the party had no equivalent of SPD leader Philipp Scheidemann. He rebuked Gompers and the AFL in stunning fashion by describing Gompers as the American equivalent. In 1918 Congress debated whether Berger deserved to be seated in the House of Representatives. He did not beg for his seat by criticizing the Bolsheviks, blasting the IWW, or qualifying his opposition to the war. Berger defiantly contended that all true Socialists defended the Soviet government, the IWW was a better class organization than the AFL, albeit with faulty tactics, and the war was imperialist and criminal. Very briefly the pulverized and persecuted Socialist Party appeared to be large and united despite its intense misery. The party's union leaders guardedly sympathized with the Bolshevik eruption, reflecting the anxieties of the rank and file. Then Lenin's call for a Third International in January 1919 set off a schism stampede. Lenin still believed the Soviet government could not survive on its own. He reclaimed the term "Communist" to dramatize that the Third International repudiated the Social Democratic tradition it surpassed. The founding of the Comintern compelled Socialists to decide whether they were Social Democrats or Communists.[2]

In August 1918 Lenin reached out to Americans, declaring that American workers "will not follow the bourgeoisie. They will be with us, for civil war against the bourgeoisie." Merely three years earlier Lenin had been little known to U.S. Americans. Now he imperiously brushed aside his critics, "people whose minds are incurably stuffed with bourgeois-democratic or parliamentary prejudices." He was commanding and triumphal: "Our Republic of Soviets is invincible." He said the Bolshevik Revolution was invincible because it was the first wave of an invincible global revolution. Every blow against the imperialists inspired more blows, engendering "new heroism on a mass scale," though Lenin allowed that the American movement lagged behind Europe. Trotsky, a latecomer from the Mensheviks to the Bolsheviks, scorned American Socialists as immigrants who forgot what socialism was about after they got to America. Lenin said some revolutions take longer, and he understood it would be a long time before Americans could help their Russian comrades. The latter point registered a note of vulnerability and precariousness, the most quoted line of his letter: "We are now, as it were, in a besieged fortress, waiting for the other detachments of the world socialist revolution to come to our relief." The Bolshevik Revolution, to be frank for a moment, desperately needed rescuing by the armies of revolutionary European governments. Lenin assured Americans it would happen because the one revolution grew stronger every day: "We are firmly convinced that we are invincible, because the spirit of mankind will not be broken by the imperialist slaughter. Mankind will vanquish it."[3]

The entire American socialist movement took this summons seriously, and aspiring American communists applied it literally to their context. Two new organs of left-wing socialism, the *Class Struggle* and *Revolutionary Age*, both coedited by Louis Fraina, spoke for the American-born radicals and recent immigrants who swelled the left wing. In 1917 the foreign-language federations constituted 35 percent of the Socialist Party; by 1919 they were 53 percent, numbering 57,000 members. The Russian factor alone was crucial. In January 1918 the party had 792 Russian-speaking members. A year later there were 3,985—immediately the most vociferous force in the party, pressing for revolution-now. They toiled in the worst sweatshops, revered Lenin and Trotsky, were excluded from most trade unions, and couldn't vote, not that they cared about voting. They scorned the party's social democratic ethos, especially its emphasis on voting. Most of them knew very little about Marxism or Bolshevism but played their welcome to the hilt, leveraging their Russian heritage. They clustered in New York and Boston, where left-wing socialists launched the New York bimonthly *Class Struggle* and the Boston semiweekly *Revolutionary Age*. *Class Struggle* covered the American situation and international socialism, while *Revolutionary Age* focused almost entirely on revolutions abroad.[4]

Both organs pushed for influence in the Socialist Party just as the party lost its base in the west and south. Entire state organizations were wiped out by the war and government repression. When the war began, the Oklahoma Socialist Party had 12,000 members, 900 locals, and 6 state legislators, and the state's radical union of tenant farmers, the Working Class Union (WCU), claimed over 30,000 members. The WCU had the spirit of the IWW in a field the IWW declined to organize, plus loose affiliations with a self-defense gang called the Jones Family. In August 1917 WCU leaders spearheaded the Green Corn Rebellion, a revolt of white and black farmers, Seminoles, and Muscogee Creeks against conscription. They destroyed pipelines, cut telephone lines, burned railroad bridges, and raided county offices in Seminole County, trying to thwart Oklahoma's participation in the war. They dreamed of marching to Washington, DC, to overthrow Wilson, subsisting on green corn. Instead, the insurrection phase lasted two days, collapsing after the government arrested 450 rebels and others fled to Arkansas, Texas, and Colorado. Approximately 150 rebels were convicted. No Socialist official was connected to the rebellion, but hundreds of Socialists were arrested, a few were convicted, and the Socialist Party and IWW were excoriated for fomenting radicalism across the state. The party held an emergency convention and disbanded, seeking to prevent the government from linking the rebellion to Berger in his espionage trial in Chicago. Socialism never rebounded in Oklahoma or any neighboring state. It was eviscerated by patriotic militarism and repression.[5]

The star of the new socialist left wing was Louis Fraina. Born Luigi Carlo Fraina in Italy in 1892, he followed his radical Republican father to New York in 1897, struggled with his mother to survive poverty and the death of his father, and taught himself literature, philosophy, and political economics while missing out on high school. He joined the Socialist Party in 1909 at the age of fifteen and switched six months later to the SLP, enticed by De Leon's dogmatic intellectualism. Fraina became the boy wonder of the SLP, wowing party stalwarts and newcomers with his didactic brilliance. He mastered soapbox oratory, wrote prolifically for the SLP paper the *Daily People*, and usually outflanked everyone to the left. In 1914 he resigned from the SLP and took over a new intellectual magazine founded by New York Socialists, the *New Review*, which had a heady run through 1915 but couldn't pay the bills. The following year Fraina edited a dance magazine, Isadora Duncan's *Modern Dance*, making ends meet. He stayed in touch with Bolshevik leaders and American left-wing socialists, cofounding *Class Struggle* in May 1917, just after rejoining the Socialist Party. His coeditors, Ludwig Lore and Louis Boudin, were left-wing party stalwarts, but Fraina derided the party, lionizing Lenin and Trotsky as world-historical heroes.[6]

Lettish revolutionaries were key players in the Socialist left wing. During the war the Russian Federation dominated the Communist Propaganda League in Chicago, and the Lettish Federation dominated the Socialist Propaganda League in Boston. Both identified with the Bolsheviks, and the Lettish Federation subsequently provided leaders for the first Soviet Latvian government. Fricis Roziš, a refugee from political exile in eastern Siberia, published a pro-Bolshevik paper, *Rabochii,* in Boston and returned to Latvia during the Bolshevik insurrection. He headed the first Soviet Latvian government as chair of Iskolat—the Executive Committee of the Soviet of Workers, Soldiers, and Landless Deputies of Latvia. In Boston the Letts controlled the left wing of the Socialist Party until 1918. Then they took over the Boston local, conceiving socialism as the rule of revolutionary councils—soviets. Aside from the Boston local, however, the left-wing faction led by Ruthenberg was peripheral in the party until just before the breakup of 1919. One measure of its marginality was that Fraina became its dominant figure in barely a few weeks. Fraina would have split the party right away had the left wing been less marginal or had Trotsky believed he should try; as it was, he settled for propaganda work and building up the left wing. To Fraina, Russia and Germany were the focal points of the one true revolution.[7]

The German socialists who mattered to American socialists were the Independent Social Democrats (USPD), who left the SPD during the war. The USPD had three factions. Karl Liebknecht and Rosa Luxemburg led the radical left, calling it the Spartacus League; Karl Kautsky and Hugo Haase led the mainstream; and Eduard Bernstein led the right flank. After the German Revolution ended the war on November 9, 1918, the USPD and SPD briefly split the governing duties of a six-member ruling council that tried to wrest a good outcome from the revolution. The provisional cabinet instituted historic reforms, including an eight-hour workday, worker councils, collective bargaining rights, national health insurance, the abolition of press censorship, and universal suffrage in local and national elections. It also contained the November Revolution within bourgeois boundaries, cutting deals with the capitalist class and royalist-reactionary military officers, which sundered the SPD/USPD coalition.[8]

The two German Social Democratic parties held contrasting concepts of socialism and the aims of the revolution. Bernstein tried to unite the SPD and USPD, but that was impossible. SPD leaders Friedrich Ebert and Philipp Scheidemann bought off every power bloc except those demanding a socialist republic, which drove out the USPD. Bernstein, alone among USPD officials, did not walk out. He rejoined the SPD, kept his membership in the USPD, and pleaded for Social Democratic unity. On the last day of 1918 Liebknecht and

Luxemburg founded the Communist Party of Germany (KPD), announcing they were done with every version of Social Democracy.[9]

Luxemburg hailed the Bolshevik Revolution as the greatest event in history and a refutation of Social Democracy. She wrote a manifesto on this twofold theme just before the German Revolution freed her from prison. The Bolsheviks, she argued, knew better than Kautsky, the Mensheviks, the opportunistic unions, and everyone else who said that only a bourgeois revolution was feasible in Russia. The Bolsheviks rightly based their actions on the global proletarian revolution proclaimed in the *The Communist Manifesto*. They cast aside the "parliamentary cretinism" of the "parliamentary nursery" about first winning a majority of the people. The true dialectic of revolutions is: First the revolution, then democracy: "That is the way the road runs. Only a party which knows how to lead, that is, to advance things, wins support in stormy times." Luxemburg embraced the Bolshevik principle that bourgeois democracy is the enemy of socialist democracy, not the road to it. She lauded the Bolsheviks for saving the Russian Revolution and the honor of international socialism by audaciously imposing "a dictatorship of the proletariat for the purpose of realizing social-ism." Now the challenge was to create a revolutionary democracy after the sei-zure of power.[10]

Here there were serious problems because Lenin and Trotsky still thought like Kautsky about the dictatorship of the proletariat. Luxemburg said socialism did not work without a flourishing, educated, liberated mass of the people. Bourgeois class rule worked without it, which Lenin overlooked, but not social-ism, which Lenin denied. Luxemburg lamented that Lenin and Trotsky con-ceived the dictatorship of the proletariat as a ready-made formula owned by the revolutionary party that officials carried out. Like Kautsky, they conceived dic-tatorship as the opposite of democracy, except that Kautsky accepted bourgeois democracy. Luxemburg feared that Lenin and Trotsky used the dictatorship of the proletariat as a club to silence and smash the democratic aspirations of the masses. Trotsky famously sneered that Marxists did not worship formal democ-racy; Luxemburg replied that true Marxists did not worship socialism or Marxism either.

She believed in the dictatorship of the proletariat, "but this dictatorship con-sists in the *manner of applying democracy*, not in its *elimination*, in energetic, resolute attacks upon the well-entrenched rights and economic relationships of bourgeois society, without which a socialist transformation cannot be accom-plished." Marxian dictatorship had to be the work of the entire proletarian class. It was not something owned by a revolutionary elite. It had to flow out of the active participation and direct influence of the masses; otherwise it was another form of tyranny. Luxemburg granted that Lenin and Trotsky had to use brutal tactics to gain power and defend the revolution. She feared they made a virtue of necessity, building a suffocating system out of tactics forced upon them and calling it Marxism. Still, she said, only the Bolsheviks had earned the right to say, "'I have dared!'"[11]

Luxemburg had not finished this article when she was released from prison in November 1918. It was not published until 1922, when her lawyer, Paul Levi, published it as a marker of his expulsion from the KPD. She plunged into the revolutionary ferment of the moment, producing a daily paper for the Spartacus League, conferring with the Berlin USPD and Revolutionary Shop Stewards, and giving speeches. She came out of prison declaring that the monarchy had never been the real enemy but merely the façade of the ruling imperialist capitalist class—"This is the criminal who must be held accountable for the genocide." The real German Revolution put all power in the hands of the working masses through the new workers' and soldiers' councils and a not-yet-organized national council of workers and soldiers. It had begun, she said, and it would not stand still because the vital law of a revolution is to outgrow itself. It would sweep away the Junker landowning aristocracy that still owned everything in eastern Germany and the private capitalists that owned everything else. Luxemburg implored readers they could not build socialism "with lazy, frivolous, egoistic, thoughtless and indifferent human beings." Socialism was about the many coming alive, overthrowing barbarism.[12]

She riffed on John 1:4, declaring that only the organized and active working class "can make the word flesh." To achieve control over production and acquire real power, workers had to struggle with capital on a shop-by-shop basis, hand-to-hand, with strikes and direct mass pressure. They had to disarm the police, confiscate all weapons, create a peoples' militia, expel all officers from the soldiers' councils, prosecute the war criminals, replace all parliaments and municipal councils with workers' and soldiers' councils, abolish all differences of rank and sexual discrimination, confiscate all dynastic wealth and income, repudiate war debts, and support socialist revolutionaries across the world. Luxemburg invoked the gospel passion narrative, with the socialist movement in the role of Jesus. Capitalists, the petty bourgeois, military officers, the anti-Semites, the press lackeys, and the SPD social imperialists called out for crucifixion. Socialists took over the Jesus role of struggling "for the highest aims of humanity."[13]

Upon cofounding the KPD with Liebknecht, Luxemburg repudiated the entire Social Democratic tradition that created and ruined the Second International. Finally she was free to say why it was flawed from the beginning. Marx and Engels got it right in the *Manifesto*—all that is necessary is to spark a political revolution, seize the power of the state, and fulfill the socialist idea. But Marx and Engels abandoned this belief after the Paris Commune, for what seemed like good reasons at the time. Social Democracy replaced the original Marxian scheme with a compound of reform and revolution that Marx endorsed, more or less. A decade after Marx died, Engels wrote a dispiriting preface to Marx's *Class Struggles in France* acknowledging how wrong he and Marx had been about the near future of capitalism. Engels went on to say that parliamentary socialism worked better than street fighting. Luxemburg believed that Engels would have scorned the SPD that fixed on election victories and capitulated in 1914, but she said he paved the way to it: "The Preface was the proclamation of the parliamentarism only tactic."[14]

Engels gave way to the Kautsky era of sterility and degradation. To Luxemburg and other left radicals these were years of bitterness at every party congress, where everything that was not parliament-only was stigmatized as "anarchism, anarcho-socialism, or at least anti-Marxism." Then came the debasement of 1914, to the last day of 1918, when Luxemburg declared that true Marxism was reborn in Germany. False Marxism led to "the henchmen of Ebert." True Marxism repudiated the debilitating dualism of the SPD Erfurt Program, which separated the minimal demands of politics from the maximal demands of the struggle for a classless society. Founding the KPD was a repudiation of Erfurt: "For us there is no minimal and no maximal program; socialism is one and the same thing; this is the minimum we have to realize today." The movement began on November 9, it was not about the monarchy, and the external form of the revolutionary struggle was the strike. Luxemburg half expected that a National Assembly would be created, and she did not say the KPD would have nothing to do with it. Neither point really mattered because both looked in the wrong place. What mattered was to build the soviets—a revolutionary order at the base. The masses would learn how to use power by using power. In the beginning is the act.[15]

Luxemburg could only hope that the worker and soldier councils would support the KPD. Berlin radicals counted on sympathetic treatment from the chief of police, USPD member Emil Eichhorn, but on January 4, 1919, the provincial government fired Eichhorn. The following day over one hundred thousand workers responded to a call from the Berlin USPD, the Revolutionary Shop Stewards, and the KPD, protesting the firing. Liebknecht and other leaders of the three groups, impressed by the turnout, formed an emergency committee that voted the same night to overthrow the Ebert government. On January 6 over half a million workers, fatefully lacking soldiers, marched in Berlin demanding a new government. The following day three hundred Spartacists tried to overthrow the government and were crushed by government forces. Luxemburg probably believed the insurrection was premature, but she did not oppose it, after which she and Liebknecht were forced into hiding. Ebert enlisted the Freikorps—paramilitary thugs armed by the government—to hunt down Luxemburg and Liebknecht.[16]

The Freikorps captured Luxemburg and Liebknecht on January 15, interrogated and tortured them, and murdered them. His body was dumped at the city morgue. Her disfigured body was discovered months afterward in the Landwehr canal. The tacit consent of Ebert and Gustav Noske conferred a special odium on the SPD in the orbits of the USPD and KPD. Socialists had not merely slaughtered socialists to preserve the bourgeois order. They commissioned the forerunners of the Nazi Brown Shirts to do their dirty work. The SPD officials who ran the provincial government were terrified of Bolshevism, contemptuous of left-wing socialists, unprepared to govern, obsessed with law and order, and timid before the old bureaucracy. In February and March 1919, after the German Republic was founded at Weimar, Ebert went on to suppress Communist uprisings in Berlin and Munich, with over one thousand casualties. In April the Communists briefly set up a republic in Bavaria, the heart of Catholic Germany, which was liquidated the following month, yielding a Red scare in Munich that persisted for decades and gave Adolf Hitler his start. To Lenin, Trotsky, Nikolai Bukharin, and Comintern leader Grigory Zinoviev, everything depended on the Communist revolution in Germany; Lenin began to say it as early as January 1918.

The SPD won the National Assembly elections of January 19, 1919, achieving the goal it held since 1875—control of the government through electoral victory. It won almost 38 percent of the vote in the nation's first free and fair election and the first one with women's suffrage. The three parties that supported the new republic—the SPD, Centre Party, and German Democratic Party (DDP)—formed a majority governing coalition, with Ebert as president of the German Reich. Scheidemann became minister president, an office later renamed chancellor after the Weimar Constitution came into force in August 1919, without Scheidemann. The SPD retained its wartime practice of calling itself the Majority Social Democratic Party, a reminder that most Social Democrats supported the war and the USPD was a fringe group. "One man, one vote," now improved to "one man or woman, one vote," was deeply ingrained in the SPD. Dictatorship of the proletariat, whatever its force as a rhetorical totem, had nothing to do with depriving the bourgeoisie of the vote. SPD officials did not regard the worker and soldier councils of the November Revolution as viable state organs, unlike the USPD, which pushed for a council system *(Räterepublik)*. To the radical majority of the USPD, council Marxism was better than parliamentary democracy. To the newly empowered SPD, the worker councils were not foundations of an alternative government or society. Syndicalism was imaginable only on the basis of an actual dictatorship of the proletariat, a nonstarter.[17]

Thus the SPD fought off the radical socialists and Communists, while right-wing nationalists vilified the SPD as a traitorous enemy. The SPD became a scapegoat for losing the war and accepting the punishing terms of the Versailles Treaty. Article 231 decreed that Germany was solely responsible for the war and its carnage. Most SPD officials in the Reichstag voted to swallow it on June 23, 1919, although Scheidemann resigned as minister president in protest, warning that Versailles put Germans in chains. Scheidemann went on to defend all the Weimar governments, making himself a symbol of Weimar treachery to the right wing. Meanwhile the USPD debated and split over joining the Comintern; the slight-majority half joined it, and the minority half eventually reunited with the SPD.

Revolutionary Age and *Class Struggle* tracked this drama intently, identifying with the KPD and the USPD leftists who ended up in it. Both organs read the American situation through a Bolshevik lens, shucking off the contrasts between Russia and the United States. It was considered bad form in these circles to observe that the Bolsheviks took power by exploiting the weaknesses of a war-ravaged, starving, unstable, basically agrarian nation steeped in autocracy. That was how Social Democrats talked, and they were the worst enemies of revolutionary socialism.

Internally, schism talk went back to the meeting on January 14, 1917, in New York that created *Class Struggle* and rebooted the paper of the Socialist Propaganda League (SPL), *The Internationalist*. Ludwig Lore convened a gathering at his home on the Brooklyn waterfront, inviting Fraina, Boudin, SPL representative John D. Williams, and four soon-to-be members of Russia's first Bolshevik Central Committee: Trotsky, Bukharin, Alexandra Kollontai, and V. Volodarsky. Bukharin, a Lenin protégé, said the revolutionaries should split the American party. Trotsky said they should stay in the party but create their own organ. A European faction fight unknown to America was thus transplanted to Lore's living room, giving birth to the paper proposed by Trotsky, *Class Struggle*, and an overhauled version of the SPL paper, now called the *New International*. Fraina was the only American in the room who identified wholeheartedly with the Bolsheviks, and even his support was qualified by his syndicalism and the fact that he favored Trotsky. Lore and Boudin were old-style left-wing Marxists; Fraina idolized Trotsky for his heroic flair and his banter about permanent revolution. The Russians hustled home after a general strike in Petrograd forced Nicholas II to abdicate the throne, leaving the Americans to plot on their own.

In public there was no glimmer of schism talk until November 1918, when the Boston local called for an emergency convention to address how the Socialist Party should counteract demands to overthrow the Bolsheviks. An inward-looking debate ensued over the party's performance, usually focused on the ostensible failings of the *New York Call*, the symbol of Hillquit socialism. Then Lenin called for a Third International. Nicholas Hourwich, a Russian Federation leader, made the first public call for splitting the Socialist Party, on February 1, 1919. It was pure Leninist projection, completely disregarding that the United States came out of World War I as a thriving world power, the apotheosis of liberal state capitalism. Hourwich heralded the Bolshevik and German Revolutions, stressed that both were responses to war-patriotism, and declared that the unity of the Socialist Party was "the chief weakness of the Socialist movement and is a continual burden to the revolutionary wing of the party." American socialists were too proud of their unity, which constrained them by making room for nonrevolutionaries. The way forward cast aside Social Democratic pretenders in Lenin's fashion. Russia and Germany had just shown how this process unfolds. Lenin was the model revolutionary because he was willing to be divisive and ruthless, insisting that building the soviets was far more important than electing a parliament.[18]

Lenin had contended for twelve years that the demand for a democratically elected assembly was a pillar of Bolshevism. For five months he pressed Kerensky to call an election, but only to weaken Kerensky while Lenin plotted to seize power. His plan was to take over the government, build up the soviets, and arm the working class; *then* democracy would strengthen the revolution by electing an assembly. After the Bolsheviks seized power, Lenin wanted to postpone the election, but Trotsky and Bukharin prevailed against him, pleading that they couldn't begin by abrogating democracy. The election proceeded and the Socialist Revolutionaries won a clear majority, winning nearly 16 million votes and 370 assembly seats. The Bolsheviks won nearly 10 million votes — nearly one-quarter of the total — and 175 seats; the Mensheviks won over 1 million votes and 16 seats; other parties split the remaining votes. The Bolsheviks were strong in the cities and industrial towns in the center of the country, and the Socialist Revolutionaries controlled the black-earth zone, the valley of the Volga, and Siberia. Thus the Socialist Revolutionaries dominated the Constituent Assembly, which met for one day — January 5, 1918. Lenin issued a Bolshevik Declaration of Rights: All power to the Soviets, nationalization of land, and workers' control over production. The assembly rejected it outright, and the following day the Bolshevik rulers dissolved the assembly.[19]

The willingness of the Socialist Party to swallow Lenin's dissolution of the assembly deprived the left wing of a schism issue until Lenin founded the

Comintern. Trotsky urged proletarians everywhere to overthrow capitalism through mass action, seize power immediately, repudiate nonrevolutionary Socialists, and establish a dictatorship of the working class. Lenin told the founding Comintern Congress in March 1919 that the "bourgeois are terror-stricken at the growing workers' revolutionary movement." The revolution was powerful and growing, needing only "to find the practical form to enable the proletariat to establish its rule. Such a form is the Soviet system with the dictatorship of the proletariat." He boasted that "dictatorship of the proletariat" sounded like Latin to the masses until the Bolsheviks showed what it meant. Now everyone knew it was the revolutionary form by which the proletariat exercised its rule.[20]

Fraina had waited for this moment. The Leninist chain reaction seemed to be happening. Finland had a Socialist government, revolution brewed in Hungary, the German emperor abdicated, the Austrian emperor fled, and the Romanovs were brutally executed, though Lenin dissembled for years about what happened to the imperial family. In February 1919 Fraina called for a formal left-wing organization within the Socialist Party that operated on its own, charged dues, imposed Leninist discipline, purged reformers, and captured the party. The Socialist Party, he said, had "no clear call to accept the new purposes and tactics of the revolutionary Third International." On his telling, the party was "part of the governing system of things, indirectly its ally and protector." It didn't matter that the Socialist Party opposed capitalism and was persecuted by the government. It didn't matter either that America had a tradition of liberal democracy and intellectual freedom—Boudin's objection, causing him to resign from *Class Struggle* in September 1918. Fraina and his comrades were infatuated with the Bolsheviks, conspiring to capture their own party.[21]

The Old Guard was slow to fathom its situation. Hillquit took pride in heading a department of the Russian Soviet Government Information Bureau, a propaganda vehicle established in January 1919. Berger was convicted of espionage in February 1919 and sentenced to twenty years in federal prison. His appeal, which he won in the Supreme Court in 1921, kept him out of prison. Hillquit and Berger believed the party would withstand any takeover attempt, until April 1919, when the left wing won twelve of fifteen seats on the NEC plus four of the five international delegates, counting O'Hare as a leftist. The international delegate winners were Fraina, Ruthenberg, O'Hare, John Reed, and, in fifth place, Hillquit. The left-wing socialists called for a June convention in New York, and the Old Guard leaders who controlled the executive committee lurched from overconfidence to panic, conjuring a dire either/or. Either they would save the party from itself or it would be destroyed. If they let the election stand the left wing would take over the party, turn it into a Bolshevik clone, and expel the Hillquit and Berger types. If the Old Guard nullified the election, the left wing would form its own party, rank-and-file members would resign in disgust, and the remaining party would be a shattered wreck.[22]

The Old Guard took option two. It expelled all seven of the so-called Russian Federations, lumping together the Russian, Ukrainian, Polish, South Slavic, Latvian, Lithuanian, and Hungarian federations. The Finnish, Jewish (Yiddish), German, and Bohemian (Czech) federations were exempt, never mind that Finnish and Yiddish speakers came from the former Romanov Empire, while the South Slavic and Hungarian federations did not. This was about getting rid of the federations infected by Leninism, and Jews in this category usually belonged to the Russian Federation; Hourwich and Chicago-based Alexander Stoklitsky were the ringleaders. For good measure the Old Guard expelled the Michigan chapter for wayward behavior and nullified the election, reasoning that the election results were tainted.

The reaction of the rank and file was outraged and incredulous. Hundreds of socialists sent angry resignation letters to the national secretary, Adolph Germer. The Old Guard's long history of bulldozing tactics was cited repeatedly. Many said the party leaders had never been democrats or socialists; they were boss rulers just like the hacks who ran Democratic machines. Alfred Wagenknecht, a left-wing member of the executive committee, issued a public letter protesting that no committee had the right to expel forty thousand members. O'Hare said many of the letters she received in prison were hot with rage, though she doubted the Old Guard had a better option. A general strike in Seattle and the founding of worker councils in Seattle and Portland enthralled the left-wing socialists who gathered in June. Perhaps the Leninist flood had begun? In that mood they debated whether they should split immediately or capture the Socialist Party. Hourwich and expelled Michigan leader Dennis Batt demanded a new organization immediately, but nearly all the English-speakers agreed with Fraina, Reed, Ruthenberg, Benjamin Gitlow, Bertram Wolfe, and Jay Lovestone that capturing the Socialist Party would be better.[23]

This disagreement eventually produced a three-way schism. At the convention it produced a grandiose document written by Fraina called the "Manifesto of the Left Wing Section Socialist Party Local Greater New York." Written in the oracular style of *The Communist Manifesto*, the left-wing manifesto pilloried Social Democrats for feeding workers reform legislation. It called on Americans to organize worker councils as the vehicle for seizing power and facilitating the dictatorship of the proletariat, prescribing a revolutionary party with centralized discipline and centralized party propaganda, leaving no room for individual opinions. Bolshevik discipline sounded liberating to most of the would-be Leninists who broke up the Socialist Party. Fraina enthused in his keynote address: "In spite of a reactionary bureaucracy, revolutionary Socialism is conquering the Socialist Party, proclaiming that in spite of the dead policies of the past, it will lay the basis for a revolutionary Socialist movement." He featured this quote in his report in *Revolutionary Age*, stressing what it did not mean: The aim of the new, self-standing, left wing of the Socialist Party was not to launch an immediate revolution or even to leave the party. It was to capture the party and prepare for the revolutionary struggle "in accord with the militant traditions of revolutionary Socialism."[24]

Hourwich, Batt, and Harry Paton led the first Communist splinter group out of the party, in July, which stole the thunder and outflanked to the left the Fraina group that wanted to take over the Socialist Party. That was intolerable to Fraina, Ruthenberg, Wolfe, and most of the left-wing caucus, which surrendered its position in early August, joining the Hourwich group. The Hourwich/Fraina communists held their founding convention on September 1, 1919, in Chicago, near the Socialist convention. Reed and Gitlow led a diehard faction at the Socialist convention, where the party split again after the Old Guard barred various left-wing delegates from entering. Reed, Gitlow, and Lovestone proceeded to the basement and founded the Communist Labor Party, shortly before Reed published his best seller on the Bolshevik Revolution, *Ten Days That Shook the World*. Now there was a Socialist Party, a Communist Party, and a Communist Labor Party. Nearly all the foreign-speaking Communists went into the Communist Party, and nearly all the English-speaking Communists went into the Communist Labor Party. The Socialist Party, boasting nearly 105,000 members in April, had 27,000 by September.

This breathtaking fall could be read as a colossal tragedy, or a sign of creative ferment, or both, although no one who stayed in the party said it was equally both. O'Hare and Debs had an awestruck sense of the Bolshevik moment as a meteor that crashed into the Socialist world, blew it apart, and couldn't be helped. Even Fraina remembered it that way seven years later, when he reinvented himself as a left-liberal named Lewis Corey. The Socialists and Communists were so consumed by their internal dramas that they played almost no role in the two great strikes of 1919– in September, 365,000 steelmakers walking out in defiance of Gompers, followed by 500,000 coal miners in November. O'Hare and Debs cheered the strikes from their prison cells and tried to be optimistic about their party.[25]

Both interpreted their lives in religious terms, admonished sad-sack socialists, and occasionally dropped the mask. O'Hare believed that socialism lost its way by giving too much power to manic dogmatists, but she said it only in occasional asides, trying not to scold. She noted that "theoretical hair-splitters and hobby-riders" did not get hauled to court and prison; maybe they would be less dogmatic if it happened? She loathed that Socialists sabotaged the party, calling it criminal, yet she insisted that the splitting and crashing did not upset her. A better socialist movement would come from the turmoil. She said it in contradictory ways, having it both ways. O'Hare said the dross would burn out "and only the pure metal remain," which was an argument for staying in a purified party, but she also said she did not weep over outworn things; moreover, the postwar tumult thrilled her. She wrote a long message to the Socialist convention, pondered her irresolution, and didn't send it because she couldn't decide whether her imprisonment obscured her vision or made her better able to see what was wrong. In either case, she argued that 1919 was a spectacular year for the world, and losing most of the Socialist Party along the way was a price worth paying.[26]

That was her response to the many grieving letters she received. Buck up! Our work has not been in vain! Socialism is transforming the world! O'Hare pointed to the achievements of the Non-Partisan League (NPL) in the Dakotas and the founding of a Labor Party in upper Minnesota. The NPL, founded in 1915 by North Dakota Socialist farmer Arthur Charles Townley, demanded and won tax reforms, state-owned storage elevators and mills, package plants, state hail insurance, and rural credits. The Labor Party, which later morphed into the Farmer-Labor Party, renewed the dream of a radical-progressive coalition uniting reformers, farmers, reform socialists, unionists, and NPL members. O'Hare stuck to the Bliss argument that this was how socialism grew and changed the world. Socialism was ordinary people gaining popular control over the economic forces governing their lives. It was reform movements finding their dynamism and unity in socialism. She had never bought the Marxist denigration of reform movements and believed more than ever in 1919 in populist socialism. The following year, receiving her pardon from Wilson, she and Frank O'Hare revived the *National Rip-Saw*.[27]

Debs had a similar trajectory with more complications. For two months he repeated his celebrity experience at Woodstock while imprisoned in Moundsville, West Virginia, basking in friendly treatment. The warden liked him, the prisoners fawned over him, and Debs stayed in touch with Mabel Curry and the world. Then Mitchell Palmer transferred Debs in June 1919 to the maximum-security penitentiary in Atlanta, where he earned the Christ-figure imagery that pervaded much of the literature about him. The oppressive summer heat alone nearly killed him. Confined to a small cell with five other prisoners, Debs wilted from blinding headaches, lumbago, kidney failure, and crushing depression, though he wrote cheery letters home. The only outsider who knew he was deathly ill was Curry. Debs affixed a single picture to his cell wall—a crucified Jesus contorted in pain and crowned with thorns. The inmates called him little Jesus and looked out for him. Debs told his brother he knew what Lincoln meant when he said he pitied anyone in purgatory who suffered more than he did: "It seems to me that my heart is the very heart and center of all the sadness and sorrow, all the pain and misery, and all the suffering and agony in the world. I don't know why it is so, I only know that deep melancholy is so completely a part of me, and I have been so often under its chastening influence, that it has become sacred to me, and costly as it is, I should not wish it taken out of my life."[28]

Debs tried to believe that uniting the Socialist parties was possible. He shared this faith with Hillquit, who told him that only Debs could bring the parties together. Debs said he would accept the Socialist nomination for president for this reason, not realizing how bad it was out there. Reconciling with the Communist Party was utterly hopeless. The Communist Labor Party was willing to support Debs but with no promise of uniting. Many Old Guard stalwarts did not want Debs as their candidate and opposed any reconciling gestures to either of the Communist parties; Algernon Lee and Julius Gerber were the ringleaders of no-Debs and no-reconciliation. Debs said most members of the three parties were comrades, and the party leaders made mistakes that could be corrected—a statement that offended the Old Guard. The party nominated federal prisoner 9653 anyway in May 1920, and Debs chastised the eight Socialists who came to see him. Seymour Stedman, James Oneal, Julius Gerber, Madge Stephens, and four others proffered the nomination, posing for an iconic picture. Debs respected Oneal as a Socialist founder with resolute integrity, but he blasted the group for adopting a weak platform and hesitating to join the Third International. He suggested that he was closer to Pastor Stokes, Reed, Ruthenberg, Wagenknecht, Ella Reeve Blor, and other Communists than with any of them. He didn't blame Lenin for resorting to armed insurrection or depriving the capitalist class of its civil liberties.[29]

Hillquit refused to believe that this version of Debs was the real one. The party had conducted a strenuous debate over the Third International and voted at its 1919 convention to apply for membership, but its application letter to Zinoviev affirmed its commitment to Social Democratic principles. If the Socialist Party was to join the Third International, the Comintern had to be open to Social Democrats. Hillquit put it eloquently at the party's May 1920 convention. The Bolsheviks, he said, dictated completely what the Third International stood for; nobody else had any say in the matter. He sympathized "absolutely" with the Soviet government and hoped always to do so: "But that does not mean, Comrades, that we abdicate our own reason, forget the circumstances surrounding us, and blindly accept every formula, every dogma coming from Soviet Russia as holy, as a Papal decree. By no means. It also does not mean that because we support the struggles of the working class in Russia, we accept for this country the special institutions and forms into which these struggles have been molded by the historical conditions of Russia." In September 1919 the Executive Committee of the Comintern lauded the IWW as the real thing and declared that so-called socialists such as Hillquit were traitors because they did not fight for the soviet power of the proletariat. Hillquit replied: "Now, comrades, with all my cordial sympathy for the Russian Soviet Government, I say, if I considered this document authentic, final, and authoritative, I could, speaking for myself, see no possible way to honestly remain in a party which accepts this as a universal program." But he did not believe this matter was settled, so he supported the party's decision to apply for membership and press for a real discussion.[30]

Hillquit wrote an earnest letter to Debs outlining the position he urged upon the party. He distinguished between the Bolshevik government and the Third International, telling Debs the Bolsheviks had achieved magnificent things, and he believed they would build a model socialist society. However, to elevate Lenin's approach to the level of a socialist model or ideological norm was unacceptable. Lenin branded all non-Bolshevik Russian socialists as foes and now imposed the same mentality on the Third International. The Socialist Party could not join the Comintern as a vassal of the Bolsheviks or an advocate of its hostility to Social Democracy. Hillquit refused to bow to "every dictum that comes from Moscow." He could not believe that Debs did not agree with him, despite how Debs treated the Socialist delegation in Atlanta.[31]

Debs was deeply affected by Hillquit's letter. He realized that Hillquit had thought carefully about this issue and fought for a commendable position in the party while Debs just reacted emotionally. Hillquit was not like the anti-Communists who condemned "the dictatorship of the proletariat" on shock value. He said it was a problematic way of describing the rule of the majority—a limited, insufficient form of democracy but superior to bourgeois democracy. Marx coined the phrase in *Critique of the Gotha Program*, describing the transition phase to communism, and Engels described the Paris Commune as an example of it. The Paris Commune was elected on the principle of universal suffrage, excluded no class from voting, and allowed every type of socialist to vote, plus nonsocialists. Marx and Engels, Hillquit reasoned, conceived the dictatorship of the proletariat as the political, "even parliamentary" majority rule of the proletariat. He stressed that the Soviets instituted no such thing, despite invoking the phrase constantly. They justified everything they did by invoking a phrase that meant, to them, that the bourgeoisie must be disarmed, disenfranchised, and outlawed. Hillquit said Social Democrats had to be clearly and resolutely against any such doctrine. Otherwise they virtually invited the bourgeoisie to disarm, disenfranchise, and outlaw socialists.[32]

Debs had long relied on Hillquit to help him keep his balance, never more importantly than now. He thanked Hillquit for helping him to frame the issue with better information. He said he agreed with Hillquit's position and would try to live up to it. He repeated this vow to O'Hare, who visited Debs shortly after her release from prison. On July 30 the Second Congress of the Comintern discussed what to do about the USPD, the French Socialist Party, and other parties with large Social Democratic factions, formally adopting Zinoviev's twenty-one rules of membership. Number 1 was that all propaganda must bear "a really communist character" and carry out the program and decisions of the Comintern. Number 2 was that every member party "must regularly and methodically remove reformists and centrists" from the labor movement. Number 3 commanded all parties to create parallel illegal organizations. Number 4 compelled "forceful and systematic propaganda in the army." Number 7 said the Comintern would not tolerate any notorious opportunists in its ranks like Kautsky, USPD economist Rudolf Hilferding, Italian Socialist Filippo Turati, or Hillquit. Number 12 said every party must be based on the principle of democratic centralism, organized in "as centralized a manner as possible" and sustaining "iron discipline." Number 21 decreed that anyone who disputed any of the twenty-one rules was to be expelled. In October Debs summarized the upshot, telling socialist interviewer William Feigenbaum, "If you were to commit the party in America to the International program laid down by Lenin, you would kill the party." The Bolshevik Revolution was one thing, and magnificent; he was "heart and soul with our Russian comrades and the Soviet Republic." It was something else to compel a program of splitting the parties and imposing Bolshevik discipline: "The Moscow Program would commit us to a policy of armed insurrection. It is outrageous, autocratic, ridiculous."[33]

Hillquit had never believed that Debs was a different kind of socialist than he was, aside from the AFL issue and the temperamental contrast. Thus he was in a position to remind Debs that his life was not a journey to Leninism. For twenty years Hillquit had relied on the humanity and ethical idealism of Debs, who rejected the violent tactics of the IWW in 1913, when it mattered. Hillquit also knew that Debs rebuffed entreaties from the Communist Party to denounce Berger and him. Debs was isolated, poorly informed, suffering, and stuck in a previous moment when the nomination group visited him. He had to be brought back to his senses and values by someone who had the moral authority and Socialist standing to tell him.

Debs enjoyed the campaign visits from reporters and began to feel better. Federal authorities allowed him to issue one bulletin per week to the United Press. Debs barely mentioned his rivals Warren G. Harding and James Cox, while calling Wilson an arrogant tool of Wall Street. The Socialists hoped their long advocacy of woman suffrage and Debs's heroic moral stature would be rewarded, but he barely topped his 1912 total, winning 919,000 votes. The Socialists were crestfallen by this result; the protest vote should have been bigger since there was no one to vote for. Meanwhile Debs relapsed into depression and physical illness. Palmer advised Wilson to release Debs from prison, and Wilson replied that Debs was a traitor to his country; he didn't care how many people cried for Debs's pardon. Debs responded that Wilson was the one who needed to be pardoned for the suffering he caused.

It got worse in February 1921, when Palmer cut off all visiting and mailing privileges for Debs, probably at Wilson's behest. Debs claimed that God gave him an inner light to guide him through dark places, "and it has never led me astray," but his darkest days occurred during Wilson's last weeks in office. Debs forbade the party to ask the new Republican president, Harding, for his individual release. If he came out, he said, it had to be with other political prisoners. On December 23, 1921, Harding commuted the sentences of Debs and twenty-three other political prisoners. A long, passionate roar of farewell welled up in the prison cells as Debs departed. Harding brought him to the White House just for the privilege of meeting him, and Debs got a tumultuous welcome in Terre Haute. Journalist David Karsner, describing the outpouring, said Debs was "the biggest public figure in the United States."[34]

He begged for the right not to make pronouncements about the strife between Socialists and Communists, pleading that he was old, sick, exhausted, and had friends on both sides. Debs said both sides made serious mistakes, and all of it happened after he went to prison, so none of it was his fault. He retreated to a sanitarium in Chicago and begged friends to send him no books because he was too ill to read them. It stunned him to see how vicious the polemics had become. In May 1921 Zinoviev chided the American Socialists for bothering to apply, sneering that the Third International was an army in wartime, not a hotel. Sneering and vituperation were the norm when Debs got out. Lenin's prosecution of the Socialist Revolutionaries in June 1922, the precursor of the Moscow Trials, provoked a plea from Debs not to kill anti-Bolsheviks: "I protest with all the civilized people in the name of humanity against the execution of any of the

Social Revolutionaries or the unjust denial of their liberty." That brought a wind-fall of applause and condemnation, plus a stream of Communists to the sanitar-ium, trying to sway Debs. In October he announced that he was staying in the Socialist Party and everyone should stop badgering him about it. The party was not what it should be, he said, but there was no better place to fight for socialism.[35]

That did not ring true to the socialists who joined the Farmer-Labor move-ments. In North Dakota the NPL ran its candidates in 1916 on the Republican line, won the governorship (Lynn Frazier) and control of the state legislature, and in 1919 enacted much of its platform, albeit briefly. In Minnesota, where the first Farmer-Labor Party arose in 1918, farmers played the catalyzing role in making common cause with unionists. In Seattle, left-wing socialists played the catalyzing role, though more often it was right-wing socialists who founded the Farmer-Labor parties. Chicago Federation of Labor president John Fitzpatrick and former social-ist stalwart Duncan McDonald forged a strong Labor Party in Illinois and built a national party on it. In Pennsylvania former socialist R. J. Wheeler was the chief founder of a Labor Party, and in Ohio Max Hayes got a Labor Party going. Fitzpatrick founded the national party in December 1919, teaming with the left wing of a civic organization called the Committee of 48 to campaign in 1920. It got on the ballot in nineteen states and called for disarmament, civil rights legislation, an eight-hour day and forty-hour week, and government ownership of all essential industries. The Farmer-Labor Party polled 290,000 votes and collapsed everywhere but Illinois after the election, but the state parties gave disaffected socialists some-where to go, prefiguring the next dream of the liberal-left: What if the progressives, agrarians, socialists, and left-unionists pulled together to offer an alternative to the Republican and Democratic parties?[36]

That was the consuming question for the entire American left in the early 1920s. Unions were seething and striking, farmers were allying with unionists to attain political leverage, leftists and liberals were enraged by the Red Scare and the bankruptcy of the Republican and Democratic parties, and yet Socialists and Communists were mired in tiny, irrelevant, anachronistic parties. Palmer arrested 6,000 suspected radicals in 30 cities and deported 550 Communists. He claimed there were 300,000 dangerous Communists still to be tracked down, which backfired, turning public sentiment against him. The two Communist parties reeled from defections and merged in 1921 as the United Communist Party of America. By then they were down to 10,000 members. The simplistic strategy of calling workers to rise and seize power caused barely a ripple in American politics. Lenin realized the chain reaction was not occurring and the Third International needed a different strategy.

Meanwhile Socialists were equally bereft. O'Hare prodded her party to learn how to work with others. Debs went back to lecture touring but was too depleted for it and had no message that spoke to the moment; he did not draw a large second crowd anywhere. Hillquit revived the British Labour Party idea, stressing that Labour adopted a Fabian Socialist constitution in 1918 and was surging. The relevant model was the Independent Labour Party, the socialist group within the Labour Party that provided yeast for its doughy blend of unions, cooperatives, socialist organizations, and caucuses. Hillquit noted that American Socialists organized their party on the German model, where socialism was older than the unions and socialist organizations charged individual dues to members, but American socialism was like its British counterpart in arising later. The Labour Party had grown into a socialist identity and verged on attaining power, wielding a mishmash of Fabian-union-Christian socialisms; Hillquit said American socialists were overdue to learn from their British counterparts. Oneal and German Federation leader Adolph Dreifuss agreed that the umbrella strategy for working-class political unity was the way to go, notwithstanding that American socialists had little experience of it.[37]

Lenin announced in April 1921 that he had a coalition strategy too, although he did not present it as a change of mind. In *Left-Wing Communism: An Infantile Disorder* he censured Communists to his left. In Russia they called for worker control of industry; in Germany they refused to work with the SPD; across Europe they made a fetish of world revolution and opposed parliamentary activism. Lenin said infantile leftism was an outgrowth of the long Bolshevik illegal struggle for power. Working underground made the Bolsheviks tougher and more disciplined than the soft Social Democrats who rolled over for World War I, but Bolshevik heroism yielded the left-wing disorder under which Communists refused to work with anyone to the right of them. Lenin rued that this reflexive extremism was commonly described as Leninism. He protested that ultraleft extremism cut off Communists from the very workers they claimed to represent. Communism did constructive work in every sphere of society; it was so much more than the insurrection and violence that obsessed the bourgeoisie. But too many Communists played into the stereotype, obsessing over old forms and "failing to see that the new content is forcing its way through all and sundry forms." Lenin told Communists they were duty bound "to master all forms, to learn how, with the maximum rapidity, to supplement one form with another, to substitute one for another, and to adapt our tactics to any such change that does not come from our class or from our efforts."[38]

American Communists puzzled over what that meant. Most persisted in the infantile mode, splitting into new splinter groups; by the end of 1921 there were twelve Communist organizations. One was led by J. Louis Engdahl and came from the Socialist Party, bolting in September 1921. It took no interest in joining the Communist Party but was very keen to join the Third International. Three months later this group played a key role in cofounding the Workers Party, which tried to unite the aboveground Communist sects and the underground Communist Party. The Workers Party was a legal united-front extension of an illegal party totaling twelve thousand members and claiming twenty thousand. At first the Communist Party stayed intact, requiring its members to also join the aboveground Workers Party. A farcical sectarian fight ensued over who controlled the party apparatus and how the underground and aboveground parties should relate to each other. The "Liquidator" faction led by Ruthenberg, Jay Lovestone, William Z. Foster, Earl Browder, and James P. Cannon won the battle. Most American Communists didn't want the Workers Party, but the Comintern told them to get in line; infantile leftism had to be eradicated. By 1923 there was no Communist Party of America; there was only the Workers Party, which sought united fronts with liberals and unionists. To put it differently, two years after American Communists ravaged the Socialist Party for operating like Social Democrats, they obeyed Lenin's order to operate like coalition-minded liberals—during the same period that Lenin instituted a one-step-backward "New Economic Policy" permitting peasant farmers and others at the low end of the economy to make capitalist transactions.[39]

The new program of the Workers Party said nothing about the dictatorship of the proletariat, worker soviets, violent revolution, or seizing power immediately. Instead, it featured the usual demands of the Socialist Party: protection of labor unions and the right to strike; unemployment relief administered through unions; respect for civil liberties; protection of civil rights for African Americans; no preparation for new wars; withdrawal of U.S. military forces from Haiti, Santo Domingo, Puerto Rico, and the Philippines (here the Socialists had a patchy history); and recognition of the Soviet Union. This was a weak version of the Socialist platform, minimizing socialism itself. So why was it necessary to destroy the Socialist Party? Caleb Harrison, national secretary of the Workers Party, explained that it differed because the Socialists were opportunists who didn't believe what they proclaimed in the St. Louis Manifesto. That was it: the Socialists had good positions but were insincere since they were opportunists. The SLP, on the other hand, was doctrinaire. The Workers Party showed the way between socialist opportunism and socialist sectarianism.[40]

The united front pioneered by the Workers Party was a tacit admission of failure, seeking to win real relationships with workers. On this count it differed from the united fronts of the 1930s that coalesced around specific issues. It was a vexing time to infiltrate American politics or know what Moscow wanted, and American Communists got burned on both fronts. Two groups vied for power in the Workers Party. Ruthenberg, Lovestone, Benjamin Gitlow, Jack Stachel, and Hungarian economist John Pepper headed the entrenched camp, riding Ruthenberg's role in founding the party and Pepper's personal connection to Zinoviev. Foster led the upstart camp along with his lieutenants Browder, Cannon, Lore, William Dunne, and the chair of the party's Jewish federation, Alexander Bittelman; they touted Foster's union-organizing expertise.

Foster grew up Irish and poor in Massachusetts and Philadelphia, entered the workforce at the age of ten, joined the Socialist Party, worked in logging camps, and drifted to the IWW. He decided it made no sense for the IWW to lure workers from existing unions, which isolated them and the IWW. The answer was to plant IWW cells in the AFL and take it over. Foster pitched this proposal to the Wobbly convention of 1911, lost the argument, and founded his own organization, the Syndicalist League of North America. He was a brilliant organizer, with bad judgment. Foster enlisted Browder and Cannon, built an educational arm he called the International Trade Union Educational League, and trained cadres for union activism. He became a player in the Chicago labor movement, befriended Fitzpatrick, and sold war bonds in 1918, which smacked of selling out, but that year he successfully organized packinghouse workers as general organizer for the Railway Carmen. Then he ran the great steel strike of 1919, which made him a major player. Foster never formally joined the Communist underground, but his educational league was suddenly flush with money he didn't get from the AFL; it came from Profintern, the Communist trade union international. He secretly joined the Communist Party in 1921 and was exposed in 1923, all the while contending that American Communism should be entirely aboveground and legal. Going underground was a loser in every way. If the party operated legally and focused on union work, it could overtake the AFL in short order. His camp championed this agenda.[41]

Clearly, or so it seemed, Foster's argument was in line with Lenin's new directive. He moved up quickly on this account, compelling Ruthenberg to curry Lenin's favor, until Lenin died of a stroke in January 1924. Immediately Moscow fell into Trotsky versus Stalin versus Bukharin. Ideological lines shifted and sometimes switched. The American analogue, Foster versus Ruthenberg–Lovestone, was always about who got in with whom at the right time. Both camps authorized Pepper to infiltrate the Farmer-Labor movements, and in 1923 Fitzpatrick invited the Communists to help him reboot the Farmer-Labor Party. The Workers Party eagerly accepted and the Socialists declined, believing Fitzpatrick would do no better than in 1920. Fitzpatrick allotted ten votes to the Workers Party, whereupon Ruthenberg and Foster stacked the convention with two hundred delegates ostensibly representing tiny groups. They couldn't stop themselves from conspiring against Fitzpatrick and alienating him, even though the whole point was to work with him.

Fitzpatrick was so enraged by Ruthenberg and Foster that he let them have his party, stormily walking out of his own convention. They were incredulous at this reaction. By their inflated count, the Farmer-Labor Party represented six hundred thousand workers. Ruthenberg and Foster claimed they tried only to win a vital role in the party, not take it over. Foster gushed that the convention was "a landmark in the history of the working class. . . . Marked by a tremendous outburst of militancy and enthusiasm, it was a vibrant, thrilling, overwhelming demand by the rank and file of agricultural and industrial labor for the formation of a powerful political party of the toilers. Nobody who attended its sessions will ever forget them." Actually, he and Ruthenberg killed the renamed Federated Farmer-Labor Party by hijacking it. It began to lose members immediately, and the Comintern noticed that the first attempt by American Communists to infiltrate Farmer-Labor politics did not go well.[42]

The Conference for Progressive Political Action (CPPA) and the Minnesota Farmer-Labor Party made stronger runs at uniting the political left that overlapped without quite uniting. Sixteen major railway unions founded the CPPA in 1922 to unite progressive organizations around a common program for independent activism. Led by Machinist union president William H. Johnston, a highly respected Socialist, it was a nonpartisan lobby group disclaiming any desire for a third party. "Nonpartisan," in this idiom, meant that it pressured both political parties to enact prolabor policies and supported the friendliest available Democrat or Republican. The railroad unions were still the most conservative sector of the labor movement, boasting 1.5 million members. Venturing this far into political activism was a breakthrough for them. Hillquit, Berger, Oneal, and Milwaukee mayor Daniel Hoan headed a Socialist delegation at the founding convention of the CPPA, which adopted the name Hillquit suggested. Ruthenberg, Lore, Harrison, and Dunne showed up at the group's second conference in December 1922, whereupon the CPPA ruled that Communists were not welcome. By 1923 the CPPA had 30 state organizations.[43]

The Minnesota Farmer-Labor Party was the first and strongest of the Farmer-Labor parties. In 1922 and 1923 it put Henrik Shipstead and Magnus Johnson in the U.S. Senate, and its ringleaders were Nonpartisan League officials Henry G. Teigan and William Mahoney. Teigan and Mahoney were unaffiliated Socialists, highly accomplished, and fond of Fitzpatrick, while believing he went national prematurely. Mahoney entered a delicate dance with the CPPA, trying to shame it or co-opt it or swing it to his purpose. He taunted its Socialist leaders for backsliding into nonpartisan nowhere and for hiding behind a nonpartisan pose. Most of the CPPA union leaders wanted to win the 1924 Democratic presidential nomination for William Gibbs McAdoo, a former director general of railroads under Wilson and Wilson's son-in-law. Mahoney chided that only a radical third party with a farmer-labor base could unite progressives and achieve something. The party already existed, in Minnesota. It needed the nationwide network and muscle of the CPPA.

Mahoney called every left-liberal group in his network to convene in St. Paul, Minnesota, in November 1923. Most accepted except for the Socialists. Hillquit said he half wanted to come but feared splitting the unions. O'Hare despaired at this decision, imploring that Socialists had to change with the times or die; the only hope politically was the Farmer-Labor movement. Mahoney welcomed the Workers Party and the Federated Farmer-Labor Party into his coalition, swallowing his previous criticism of Fitzpatrick for opening the door to Communists. The Workers Party ran candidates in Minnesota primaries under the Farmer-Labor banner, and Ruthenberg directed them to announce they were Communists. Ruthenberg wanted to be known as the American Lenin. He was steely and stern but with a romantic streak that could be reckless. The Farmer-Labor episode brought out his bravado. He declared, "Let us say frankly that each time we show our Communist face and our Communist policy in a United Front, we endanger the United Front." This risk had to be taken, he argued. Otherwise what was the point of joining a united front?[44]

Mahoney and Teigan were wary of the Communists but did not try to dissuade Ruthenberg. Nobody else had to hide who they were. Mahoney wrangled to get what he wanted from his stew of unions and activist organizations—left unity, a new party, and a presidential candidate, hopefully Wisconsin Republican U.S. Senator Robert La Follette. Only the unity part appealed to everyone, but the prospect of running La Follette for president got many skeptics on board.

La Follette was a unique figure in American politics. He was wildly popular in Wisconsin for clashing with party bosses and appealing directly to the people. He founded the Progressive wing of the Republican Party in 1900, first won a Senate seat in 1905, fought Roosevelt in 1912 for control of the Progressive Party and lost, and was the only Republican senator to vote for the federal income tax in 1913. He opposed the war, the Selective Service Act, the Espionage Act, the Allied intervention in Russia's civil war, and the Palmer Raids, enduring ferocious criticism. The only group in Mahoney's coalition that didn't want La Follette was the Workers Party. In 1923 La Follette visited the Soviet Union and dropped his pro-Bolshevik stance, telling audiences it was descending to a police state. That made him suddenly odious to Communists. He made it worse in May 1924 by declaring that Mahoney committed a terrible mistake by letting

Communists into the Farmer-Labor coalition. This was less than three weeks before the Farmer-Labor coalition planned to nominate him for president. Meanwhile McAdoo and Palmer slugged it out for the Democratic nomination, both failed, and the CPPA had only one alternative it could stand—La Follette. The solution was to run La Follette without creating a third party or helping the Farmer-Labor Party.[45]

The coalition complexities grew intense and exotic. Mahoney and Teigan cheered when the CPPA turned to La Follette; surely this was a victory for their cause. But the CPPA liked its dealmaking independence, wanting no part of a third party, let alone a class party. Moreover, it was determined to destroy the Farmer-Labor movement. The Communist issue burned the Farmer-Labor Party and helped the CPPA. La Follette charged that Communists took orders from the Comintern and helped to organize the St. Paul convention. Neither charge was hard to prove; all he had to do was cite what Ruthenberg and Foster said in the Communist *Daily Worker*. The fallout devastated Maloney's convention, reducing by 80 percent the expected turnout, which shredded his plan to create a national party. La Follette did it to prevent Maloney from founding a third party, not because a few Communists at a convention would have scared him. This controversy provided ironic cover for American Communists because Foster had just returned from a Comintern executive meeting in May at which he was excoriated for working with the Farmer-Labor movement. He and Ruthenberg thought they were doing what Moscow wanted, but Moscow had changed. Now they had to reverse everything the party claimed for five months about its political work. La Follette's attack on them made it easier for the party to say, "Never mind." Foster retracted his gushy articles about the magnificent Farmer-Labor enterprise, claiming the whole Farmer-Labor blunder was Pepper's idea. Meanwhile Foster stuck closely to Stalin, pegging him as the likely Moscow victor.[46]

The CPPA ran La Follette for president; the Socialist Party endorsed him after he was nominated in July 1924; the Farmer-Labor parties gave him gestural support; and the Workers Party ran its first presidential candidate, Foster. Debs and Du Bois offered welcome endorsements of La Follette, as did future New Deal heavyweight Harold L. Ickes. The CPPA fielded no candidates for other races, and La Follette variously appeared on ballots under the labels Progressive, Socialist, Non-Partisan, and Independent. Republican incumbent Calvin Coolidge, riding an economic boom and national gratitude for cleaning up the corruption mess of Harding's cabinet, did not bother to campaign against his hapless conservative Democratic rival, John W. Davis. Both advocated lower taxes, less regulation, and as little government as possible. Coolidge aimed his fire at La Follette, his competition for votes in the North and West. La Follette called for government ownership of railroads and electric utilities, cheap credit for farmers, prolabor legislation, civil rights for racial minorities, terminating U.S. imperialism in Latin America, banning child labor, and a national referendum before any president could lead the nation to war. He won his home state and finished second in eleven states, winning 16.6 percent of the vote.[47]

Officially, the Socialists made a decent showing, credited with 858,264 of La Follette's votes. But that was misleading since all his California votes were marked as Socialist. The Socialists realized that 1924 marked a new low for them and everything they cared about. They had never learned how to work with Farmer-Labor movements, and the version they backed, the CPPA, was unwilling to found a political party. Farmer-Labor politicking in general seemed retrogressive to socialists—piecemeal, provincial, and compromised. In addition, the socialists who rushed into it were readily tagged as backsliders. Socialist veterans struggled to comprehend why they should defer to people who opposed Debs in 1920 by running a little-known Utah lawyer (Parley P. Christensen) and a too-familiar backslider (Max Hayes). O'Hare saw the issue differently because she lived in the regional arc that produced Farmer-Labor movements and her socialism was fundamentally populist.

La Follette's turn from a pro-Bolshevik position to a critical view had plenty of company in the Socialist Party. In 1923 Cahan gave a vehemently anti-Soviet speech at the Socialist Party convention, personally attacking Trotsky, Lenin, Zinoviev, and Bukharin, condemning the prison camps in Siberia, and disavowing his previous support of the Soviet regime. Cahan said Trotsky was a windbag who completely collapsed morally, and Lenin was a lunatic. There was scattered applause, a lot of blank staring, and nervous quiet. Officially, the party still supported the Soviet government, but Socialists got increasingly insistent that democratic socialism was very different from what existed in Russia.[48]

The Socialists got behind the CPPA because it was a plausible vehicle for an American version of the British Labour Party. Hillquit entreated the CPPA leaders to reconsider their aversion to a new party. If La Follette lost and the CPPA resorted to business as usual, all their work would be wasted. This was the moment to create a Labor Party, or a Farmer-Labor-Progressive Party, or whatever it would be called. Hillquit had a moment when it might have happened, at the CPPA convention in July 1924. He got the most passionate ovation he ever received, from the delegates who wanted to form a party. It occurred to him that if he went rogue and called for a new party, the delegates would vote yes overwhelmingly. But Hillquit was not the type to go rogue. The leaders were against it and so were most of their constituents; only the types that attended conventions were for it. That was not enough, and Hillquit was not the person to swing the convention. Only La Follette had the standing to do that, and he declined. The CPPA National Committee appeased the delegates by promising to hold a special convention the following year to consider the third-party question. By the time it occurred in February 1925 the union officials had returned to business as usual, and Hillquit grieved that the British option was still remote.[49]

That was the closest the Socialists came to pulling off the Farmer-Labor option. Even La Follette could not break 20 percent in the middle of a low, crass, venal decade defined by the smugness of the business class, and he died the following year. To Gompers, the lesson of 1924 was that independent political action was a self-defeating waste of time. To Debs, the lesson was that labor leaders could not save America. He dragged himself to the 1925 CPPA convention, reminiscing with the railroad leaders who showed up, and pleaded for a radical working-class party. Only the rank and file could save America, he said, but they swam in political waters "foul and stagnant." Debs's last audiences judged that he lingered too long over his prison experiences, a judgment that vanquished his compulsion to give speeches. Near the end—he died in 1926—he said that during his imprisonment, in the nighttime quiet, he often beheld as in a vision the march of events that transformed the world: "I saw the working class in which I was born and reared, and to whom I owe my all, engaged in the last great conflict to break the fetters that have bound them for ages, and to stand forth at last, emancipated from every form of servitude, the sovereign rulers of the world. It was this vision that sustained me in every hour of my imprisonment, for I felt deep within me, in a way that made it prophecy fulfilled, that the long night was far spent and that the dawn of the glad new day was near at hand."[50]

The La Follette campaign was an equally fateful marker for American Communists, in the year of Lenin's death. Ruthenberg tried to work with the CPPA and was noncommittal about La Follette after the CPPA barred Communists from participating. Foster urged the party to endorse La Follette until refutation came from Moscow. Lore railed against the entire Farmer-Labor enterprise as it transpired, which should have been good for his career after Stalin agreed with him, except Lore thought Trotsky made good points about world revolution and permanent revolution, so Lore was expelled. This verdict came down in 1925 from Moscow. It said Ruthenberg was closer than Foster to the Comintern, Ruthenberg was to remain secretary of the party and Lovestone a member of the Central Executive Committee, and Ruthenberg was to continue coediting *Daily Worker*. Foster, to see a better day, had to capitulate completely, which he did, while flattering Stalin. Ruthenberg died in 1927 and was succeeded by Lovestone, the same year Stalin expelled Trotsky and Zinoviev. The expulsion order rattled on about Trotsky deviating to the left, never being a real Leninist, masking petty-bourgeois opportunism with ultra-revolutionary phrases, remaining a Menshevik at heart, lacking faith in the Soviet revolution, and substituting his lack of faith with a pet doctrine of permanent revolution. Trotsky chafed at the Soviet bureaucracy in which Stalin reveled. He criticized Lenin's New Economic Policy and rejected Stalin's doctrine of "socialism in one country," which gave Stalin ample ammunition to banish him. Stalin got Bukharin to inveigh against Trotsky and Zinoviev; then he purged Bukharin the following year for deviating to the right.[51]

By 1928 Stalin had eliminated the revolutionary heroes who threatened his supremacy, and the following year he dealt with his American problem. He bridled at the Foster group for boasting that they were better Stalinists than the Lovestone group. This was a disgraceful situation, he said, for Stalinism was not a thing; on the other hand, the Lovestone group was even more disgraceful. The Comintern demanded Pepper's return to Moscow, and Lovestone refused to send him. The Foster group blasted the Lovestone group for refusing to dispatch Pepper, so the Lovestone group said it was prepared to expel Pepper. Stalin admonished that the Comintern was not a stock market: "The Comintern is the holy of holies of the working class." He announced that he was done with this stock market mentality.[52]

Foster, in fact, had only a slight following in the Workers Party, but he secretly won a pledge of support from Stalin, who appointed a commission to settle the matter. Lovestone and Gitlow were fired from their leadership positions. The Foster group was promoted, except Stalin lifted Browder above his boss, chastising Foster for playing factional hardball too zealously. With Foster's lieutenant on top, it no longer mattered who held the top position; American party leaders were simply tools of Stalin. Pepper was dispatched to Moscow and disappeared in a purge. Lovestone and Gitlow got their revenge against Stalin by becoming professional anti-Stalinists; Lovestone ran the anti-Communist bureau of the AFL, and Gitlow advised exposure groups. Lore became a spy for the Soviet government to prove his loyalty to it. Reed died in Russia in 1920 of a chronic kidney ailment. Fraina had a stormy Communist career fraught with spy allegations on both sides, undertook Comintern work in Mexico, and resurfaced in 1926 as left-liberal economist Lewis Corey. Cannon was expelled as a Trotskyist and went on to head the (Trotskyist) Socialist Workers Party. Stalin conducted a deportation and terror campaign between 1930 and 1933 that stuffed millions of independent farmers into cattle cars, shipped them to arctic wastelands, and killed approximately fourteen million of them. He also built the Soviet Union into a command economy powerhouse that escaped the ravages of the Depression. Browder served as general secretary through the 1930s, held on until 1945, and was dumped by Stalin for being too friendly to the United States. Foster climbed back on top in 1945, as chair of the Communist Party, a figure-head position he held until 1957. The real leader of the later Communist Party was former Ruthenberg and Lovestone aide Stachel, who attached himself to the Comintern and kept his name out of the papers.[53]

NORMAN THOMAS SOCIALISM

There was nothing that Socialists could have done in the 1920s to reverse their dismal condition. Hillquit, describing in 1932 the past decade of Socialist Party history, did so in one sentence, claiming there was nothing to say: "For ten years the Socialist movement of America was virtually dormant." Two figures put American socialism on a better path, Norman Thomas and A. Philip Randolph. Thomas, an idealistic intellectual and Princeton graduate straight out of social gospel ministry in the Presbyterian Church, changed the image of the Socialist Party. Randolph was a transplanted black Floridian who followed Hubert Harrison into the Socialist Party and became a legendary trade union leader. Both cut their teeth on Socialist politics by campaigning for Hillquit in 1917, appreciating that Hillquit had the courage to oppose his nation at war.[54]

Thomas was America's foremost democratic socialist for forty years; Randolph exceeded Thomas as a historic figure; and both married well enough to be delivered from day job anxiety. The two Socialists worked together on countless social justice campaigns, and Thomas ran for the presidency six times. In his later career, when interviewers tried to console Thomas by noting that Franklin Roosevelt carried out much of the Socialist platform, Thomas invariably replied that he carried it out on a stretcher. That was his epitaph for U.S. American democratic socialism, which in his generation was called Norman Thomas Socialism.

Born in 1884 in Marion, Ohio, Thomas was the son and grandson of conserva-tive Welsh Presbyterian ministers and the son of a strong-minded Welsh mother who was the real keeper of the family's Calvinist orthodoxy. He grew up happy and content, delivering newspapers for Warren Harding's *Marion Daily Star*. According to Thomas, Harding lounged and chatted through the day while his wife ran the business. Thomas insisted he never felt the slightest need to rebel from his upbring-ing; the social gospel provided the only adjustment he needed. He studied briefly at Bucknell University after his father took a church in Lewisburg, Pennsylvania, and transferred in 1902 to Princeton, where Woodrow Wilson got his attention.

Wilson taught political science while doubling as university president. Thomas took his courses, admiring Wilson's intellectual command and his determination to boost Princeton's academic reputation. Princeton was a country club for privileged males of modest achievement until Wilson demanded that it reach higher. On the other hand, Thomas said, Wilson was already fully himself at Princeton—autocratic and self-righteous, abstracting politics from economics, and regarding any challenge to his opinion as "a sin against the Holy Ghost." Thomas was only slightly more liberal when he graduated in 1905 than when he entered. Not sure if he had a religious vocation, he tested it at a Presbyterian Church and settlement house in Greenwich Village and got shocked into the social gospel.[55]

Gently raised, Thomas was wholly unprepared for the chaotic violence and poverty of Lower East Side Manhattan. Decades later he still registered the shock, recalling that much of his Spring Street neighborhood "was lost in a kind of sodden apathy to which drunken quarrels brought release." He surprised himself by enduring two years of street ministry and warming to New York City. Not quite ready for seminary but getting closer, he moved to a tenement church bordering Hell's Kitchen, Christ Church, guided by his clerical Presbyterian friend Henry Sloane Coffin. Frances Violet Stewart, a Christ Church volunteer worker, taught home nursing care to tenement families. She was wealthy through her paternal grandfather, who served in Abraham Lincoln's cabinet. Thomas married Violet shortly before he enrolled at Union Theological Seminary, where patrician liberal theologian William Adams Brown taught a mild version of the social gospel. Thomas had a convicting sense of encountering the real thing when he read *Christianity and the Social Crisis*, later telling audiences that insofar as any one person converted him to socialism, it was Rauschenbusch. The New York presbytery divided over Thomas's theology, causing his father to write that rumors of his heterodoxy pained him. To Thomas, the old orthodoxy was a nonstarter; even liberal theology held little interest as theology. Only the social gospel made liberal theology relevant. He turned down upscale Brick Church on Fifth Avenue to minister at a poor, mixed ethnic immigrant church, East Harlem Presbyterian Church, where Thomas stayed for seven years and got more radical.[56]

He had never worried about how his career was doing, and now he was financially secure anyway. Thomas tried to help local workers organize unions and failed. Though not a pacifist in August 1914, he gave antiwar sermons that gradually converted him. Later he recalled that none of his conversions had a story or a moment. In November 1915 his father died, and Thomas discovered that his father's last sermon would have come out against the war. Thomas delivered it the following Sunday, moved that his conservative father ended up so close to his position.

Thomas came to pacifism through the church and let go of the church because of it. He preached that Jesus was a pacifist, urged church leaders to take a stand against war, and buttressed his case with socialist arguments. In 1916 he joined the newly founded pacifist FOR, taking over its pacifist-socialist magazine, *World Tomorrow*. Thomas conceded that war might be a tragic necessity in some circumstances, but World War I was an imperial struggle to control markets in China, India, Africa, and the Middle East, lacking any moral basis. In January 1917 he beseeched the New York presbytery to oppose America's looming intervention: "It is this which tempts me to despair for the future of the church. Even in war the church ought to stand for a form of society transcending nationalism and national boundaries." That became his staple theme— even if America could not resist Wilson's march to war, the church should have the moral courage to do so. He told a fellow Presbyterian pastor in January that Christianity and war are incompatible: "You cannot conquer war by war; cast out Satan by Satan; or do the enormous evil of war that good may come. It seems to me that the validity of Christ's method of dealing with life's problems almost stands or falls with this test."[57]

He despaired when Wilson got a stampede going: "How can we accept Christ as Lord and Master and deny his spirit by sharing responsibility for the unutterable horrors of war? Shall we cast out Satan by Satan?" It galled Thomas that the Federal Council of Churches made itself useful to society by mobilizing support for the war. He cofounded the American Civil Liberties Union with his friend Roger Baldwin and joined the American Union Against Militarism, campaigning against conscription. He balked at joining the Socialist Party because Marxism repelled him, especially its rhetoric of class war and proletarian dictatorship. Thomas abhorred authoritarianism, prizing civil liberty above all other causes. But he admired the moral defiance of the St. Louis Manifesto and the fact that Hillquit used his mayoral campaign to speak against the war; meanwhile Thomas dreaded presbytery meetings. He reached out to Hillquit, writing that war is the evilest fruit of capitalist exploitation: "To vote for you is to voice that demand and to express a hope in the sort of internationalism in which alone is our confidence for the future." Hillquit promptly enlisted Thomas in his campaign and got him to introduce Hillquit at a Madison Square Garden rally.[58]

Joining the Socialist campaign rocked his church world and family. Thomas had voted for Taft in 1908, Roosevelt in 1912, and Wilson in 1916, hoping Wilson would stay out of the war. His mother was appalled that he fell in with godless antiwar Socialists and imperiled his church ministry. Thomas replied that he hoped the presbytery would tolerate his position, but if it didn't, "it will injure herself far more than it will injure me, and I say this without conceit." Church leaders, he said, would eventually regret being on the wrong side of the war issue. Thomas wrote in December 1917 that war knows no crime but disobedience and commits the crime of forcing young men to kill. He attended church meetings that alienated him further from the church. William Adams Brown, chair of the presbytery's Home Missions Committee, asked his former student to back down before the presbytery defunded his congregation. That got to Thomas, not wanting to hurt his mission church. In April 1918 he resigned his pastorate; six months later he joined the Socialist Party, just before it blew up. Thomas told the party he was joining because this was a moment for radicals to stand up and be counted. He was for the cooperative commonwealth and against left authoritarianism, holding "a profound fear of the undue exaltation of the state." The new society "must depend upon freedom and fellowship rather than upon any sort of coercion." On these terms he and Violet Thomas threw in with the Socialists.[59]

Privately he wavered on whether he had found a political home; in public Thomas said the future belonged to freedom-loving democratic socialism. He used the term "democratic socialism" insistently, stressing his opposition to Communist rule and conspiratorial tactics. Thomas told socialists not to grieve at the party's breakup; it was good to clarify that their party stood for liberal rights and democracy. His civil liberties activism had a personal motivation— his youngest brother, Evan Thomas, was one of the almost four thousand draftees to claim conscientious objector status. Evan Thomas refused all military commands and was sentenced to life imprisonment at hard labor. Eventually his sentence was reduced to twenty-five years at Fort Leavenworth. Thomas tried to enlist churches in anticonscription activism, vaguely expecting to return to ministry after the war ended, but the churches spurned conscientious objectors, and Thomas turned away in disgust. He resented that churches risked nothing for people who refused to kill. In the early 1920s church leaders began to repent of this record, and Thomas welcomed a gusher of Christian pacifism that carried through the 1930s. But it came too late to repair his feeling about church religion. When it mattered, the Socialist Party responded bravely while mainline Protestantism catered to its interests. Thomas was grateful to learn where he belonged, at the same time and from the other side of the color line as his Harlem neighbor Randolph.[60]

Asa Philip Randolph was born in 1889 in Crescent City, Florida. Highly cordial and reticent but extroverted in public activism, he cultivated his courtly style of speech and manner by absorbing his father's sermons, reading his father's idol, AME bishop Henry McNeal Turner, and studying Shakespeare.

His father, James William Randolph, preached a black nationalist version of the social gospel, telling his AME congregants and two sons that only their Christian moral character could overcome what white oppressors did to them. His mother, Elizabeth Randolph, a seamstress, was deeply religious and filtered out her husband's sermonic excurses on racial politics. In 1891 the Randolph family moved to Jacksonville, where James Randolph ministered to a tiny congregation in a rented room. He never got a big church, lacking the educated polish of preachers who commanded large congregations. Jacksonville was not yet the racist cauldron it soon became for blacks. The city had black police officers, black members of the city council, and a black judge, plus Florida's only academic high school for African Americans, Cookman Institute. Randolph and his older brother James, while growing up, watched Jacksonville become a total-cracker bastion of Jim Crow vengeance. The Randolphs steeled their children against it, telling them to defend themselves and never surrender their dignity. On one occasion Randolph's father was called away to encircle Duval County jail to prevent a lynching; Elizabeth Randolph sat up all night with a shotgun across her lap, protecting her home and terrified sons. The following morning they learned that the lynching had been prevented.[61]

Randolph was an assiduous reader of his father's library, studying Shakespeare, Sir Walter Scott and Charles Dickens, Turner's *Voice of the Negro*, and two AME organs, *Christian Recorder* and *AME Church Review*. His father told him that nearly all the great men in the world were black, especially antislavery rebels Turner, Nat Turner, Denmark Vesey, and Frederick Douglass, and AME founder Richard Allen. James William Randolph ranked Booker T. Washington just below Allen and Turner, catching his nationalist undercurrent, which made him ambivalent about Washington versus Du Bois. Du Bois was right about black pride, but Du Bois was an elitist who cared mostly about the Talented Tenth. Washington was too accommodating but stayed in touch with ordinary people and had a strategy that helped them get ahead. Randolph's father clung to this seesaw for the rest of his life. Schoolbooks bored Randolph until a white Methodist missionary teacher at Cookman, Mary Neff, got hold of him, drawing out his talent in literature and drama. He graduated in 1907 and floundered for four years, disqualified by race from landing a job he wanted. He read Du Bois and was enthralled, realizing what it meant for him: Randolph could not thrive in Florida or his father's separatist church world; he needed to move to New York. In 1911 he joined the flow of southern blacks to Harlem.

Black Harlem, just before Randolph got there, had North–South boundaries (145th to 128th Streets) and East–West boundaries (Fifth and Seventh Avenues), but both were being erased by white flight. Randolph joined a Shakespearian theater club, hoping for an acting career until his parents demanded that he not humiliate them by taking to the stage. He learned that City College charged no tuition, so Randolph took night courses in public speaking, history, and political science. His life turned a corner when historian J. Salwyn Shapiro introduced him to European socialism. Randolph seized on Marxism, excited by the idea of a super-explanation of how societies develop. He later recalled that he read Marx as avidly as a child reads *Alice in Wonderland.* If Marxism was true, he didn't need a college degree; he already knew the big picture. Randolph thought about black freedom all the time and took interest only in people who shared his preoccupation—with one exception. Lucille Campbell Green, a young widow who owned a hair salon on 135th Street, was a protégée of hair-straightener millionaire Madame C. J. Walker. Her salon was very successful, and Randolph married her in 1914, though he refused to attend her high-society parties. One night in 1915, at a party at Walker's penthouse, Lucille Randolph met a livewire Columbia sociology student, Chandler Owen. She indulged his cascade of opinions before remarking that her husband sounded just like Owen; they should get together.[62]

Actually, Randolph and Owen were more dissimilar than alike. Owen was sarcastic and cynical, especially about women, wholly unlike Randolph. Owen knew nothing about socialism, and Randolph was obsessed with it. But they bonded to the point that Harlemites dubbed them Lenin and Trotsky, with Randolph as Lenin. Randolph dragged Owen to speeches by Debs and Hillquit, watched Harrison perform on the corner of Lenox Avenue and 135th Street, and modeled his soapbox oratory after Harrison. To Randolph, nobody ranked with Debs and no white person came close. He told friends he admired Debs above all others because Debs was a radical socialist with a deep spiritual and humanist character. Randolph and Owen joined the Socialist Party in 1916, just before Harrison resigned out of frustration. Night after night they took up Harrison's former post on Lenox and 135th. Randolph shucked off hecklers who chided him for living off his wife, replying that his loving wife was happy to support him. He and Owen launched an activist vehicle, the Independent Political Council, and took a job editing a headwaiters' trade magazine, *Hotel Messenger.* The magazine folded in eight months because Randolph and Owen exposed their boss for pocketing kickbacks. They were undaunted, enlisting Lucille Randolph to finance a new magazine called *The Messenger,* helped by a subsidy from the Socialist Party.

The party appointed Randolph and Owen to coordinate Hillquit's campaign in Harlem, and the inaugural issue of *The Messenger* came out just before the election of November 1917. It vowed to enter "the broad world of human action," opening with an editorial on rioting black soldiers in Houston, followed by editorials on La Follette, schools, woman suffrage, local organizing, peace, Germany, paying for war, friends of Irish freedom, organizing black actors, making the world safe for democracy, and recent speeches by Randolph and Owen. There were sections on economics and politics, education and litera-ture, poetry, music, and theater, and special "messages from the *Messenger*," including twenty-five reasons black Americans should support Hillquit and the Socialists. Randolph and Owen were biting, cheeky, and confrontational: "Our aim is to appeal to reason, to lift our pens above the cringing demagogy of the times, and above the cheap peanut politics of the old reactionary Negro leaders. Patriotism has no appeal to us, justice has. Party has no weight with us, principle has. Loyalty is meaningless, it depends on what one is loyal to." The second issue hailed the Bolshevik Revolution, lauding Lenin and Trotsky as brilliant world-historical heroes who knew what they were doing. In between these issues Hillquit won 25 percent of the black vote, which felt like a breakthrough for the Socialist Party.[63]

The Messenger had a dramatic run of rhetorical fireworks, ideological battles, edgy editorializing, and boastful name changes. Originally it called itself *The Only Radical Negro Magazine in America*. In 1920 the header changed to *Only Radical Magazine Published by Negroes*; four years and three name changes later, it became *World's Greatest Negro Monthly*. Randolph and Owen railed against lynching, Jim Crow, and the war. They named names and skewered foes, accenting the absurdity of black Americans fighting in France for rights they lacked in America. They admonished that black Americans had far more to fear from white terrorists in Alabama, Georgia, Mississippi, and Louisiana than from any presumed enemies in Germany. When did Germans ever oppress or lynch black Americans? A judge in Cleveland, presented with Randolph, Owen, and the July 1918 issue, could not believe they wrote such red-hot stuff, ordering them to stop fronting for evil white Socialists. The same month Du Bois came out with his "close ranks" pronouncement; the *Messenger* editors were incredulous. How had their former hero become such an idiot? Owen said if Du Bois was so gung-ho to kill Germans he should get himself to France. Meanwhile the *Messenger* urged young black Americans not to get killed for nothing.[64]

The magazine attracted strong writers, notably Jamaican nationalist and socialist W. A. Domingo, Episcopalian Socialist clerics George Frazier Miller and Robert Bagnall, Morgan State College political scientist William Pickens, and quirky, cynical, anti-Christian cultural critic George Schuyler, who gyrated politically from left to right during his run at the *Messenger*. Randolph lost his second-class mailing privileges and Owen got drafted, but there were no further scrapes with the government, despite a hefty Justice Department file on the *Messenger*. Randolph and Owen prized their location in Harlem and their contribution to a burgeoning "New Negro" movement, later called the Harlem Renaissance. They believed their independent radicalism gave them a crucial advantage over Du Bois, since *Crisis* belonged to the NAACP. They faulted Harrison for replacing socialism with black nationalism, an old song that had already failed more than once. But Randolph, Owen, and Du Bois struggled to cope with the spectacular revival of black nationalism that erupted in 1917 in response to one person, Marcus Garvey.

Marcus Garvey set off the first popular black explosion from below—a mass movement of downtrodden black Americans and West Indian immigrants. Born in St. Ann's Bay, Jamaica, in 1887, he worked in a printing firm in Kingston and joined a union, which got him blacklisted in the private sector. He traveled through Central America in 1910, studied at Birkbeck College in London in 1912, and returned to Kingston in 1914 to found the Universal Negro Improvement Association (UNIA). He said the UNIA got nowhere because the island's biracial population identified with the white colonizers. Assimilation worked for Jamaica's mixed-race population but not for its pure black majority. Garvey moved to New York in 1916 and spoke nightly on Harlem street corners, calling black people to rise up.[65]

His breakthrough came on June 12, 1917, when Harrison invited him to address his new group, the Liberty League for Colored Americans. Garvey electrified the audience and was launched, overtaking Harrison as a race leader in Harlem. Liberty League rallies turned into UNIA rallies, drawing enormous crowds. Thirty thousand West Indians, pouring into Harlem between 1915 and 1924, had to deal with being black in the racist United States and not being welcome in African American neighborhoods. Garvey took little interest in African American history and culture, a point that Du Bois eventually pressed against him.

But Garvey was gifted at expressing racial grievance, connecting with audiences that Du Bois and Randolph did not reach. Garvey said NAACP liberals like Du Bois were elitists who just wanted a place at the white man's table. The Garvey movement lifted up black people who were nobody in U.S. American society. They marched in colorful uniforms at night under black, red, and green banners calling for a black empire in Africa. They packed the largest venues they could find, overflowing the old Madison Square Garden. In August 1920 twenty-five thousand marched through Harlem, replete with Knight Commanders of the Distinguished Order of Ethiopia, Knight Commanders of the Sublime Order of the Nile, Black Cross Nurses, African Legions, and high school bands. Garvey rode in a convertible, resplendent in a regal plumed helmet. He claimed the UNIA had four million members, issuing a "Declaration of the Rights of the Negro People of the World." There were fifty-four, including the right of all black people to live freely as citizens of Africa and the principle of "the supreme authority of our race in all things racial."[66]

Garvey bought ocean vessels, purged the UNIA of leftists, celebrated black capitalism, and ramped up his rhetoric about pure black people returning to Africa to build an empire. Randolph and Du Bois wrote about him gingerly, trying not to offend. In December 1920 Du Bois was still trying to balance pro and con on Garvey, and Randolph said his early praise of Garvey occurred before he went full-bore on race baiting and back-to-Africa. The following month Du Bois implored Garvey to stop attacking biracial people; black Americans recognized no color line "in or out of the race, and they will in the end punish the man who attempts to establish it." It was absurd to talk about uniting all blacks while smearing light-colored blacks.[67]

In 1922 Garvey was indicted for fraud. His fantastical bookkeeping was exposed, the gingerly treatment ended, and Garvey claimed that light-colored blacks caused all his problems. Politically he lurched to the far right, pandering to the Ku Klux Klan, linking arms with Mississippi senator Theodore Bilbo and other white nationalists, and stooping to anti-Semitism. Randolph went full-bore against Garvey, mounting a "Garvey Must Go" campaign in the *Messenger*. Two *Messenger* writers associated with the NAACP, Bagnall and Pickens, organized anti-Garvey rallies in Harlem. Garvey gave it right back, declaring that Randolph and Owen were incompetent hacks who never succeeded at anything. Randolph got the immortalized last word by publishing a scathing takedown by Bagnall. It began viciously—somehow counting Garvey's physique as fair game for ridicule—before moving on to personal character: "Boastful, egotistic, tyrannical, intolerant, cunning, shifty, smooth and suave, avaricious, as adroit as a fencer in changing front, as adept as a cuttle-fish in beclouding an issue he cannot meet, prolix to the 'nth degree in devising new schemes to gain the money of poor ignorant Negroes; gifted at self-advertisement, without shame in self-adulation, promising ever, but never fulfilling, without regard for veracity; a lover of pomp and tawdry finery and garish display, a bully with his own folk but servile in the presence of the Klan, a sheer opportunist and a demagogic charlatan." The Garvey movement, Bagnall declared, was insane, "whether Garvey is or not."[68]

That was in March 1923, very near the end of the *Messenger*'s run as a political force. Owen left in 1921, Schuyler took his place, and the magazine held on until

1928, mostly as a cultural organ featuring Schuyler's commentary. In 1920 the *Messenger* stopped calling itself the "only radical magazine published by Negroes," since there were four others: *Crusader*, published by Communist former *Messenger* writer Cyril Briggs; *Emancipator*, another *Messenger* spin-off, published by W. A. Domingo; *Challenge*, published by William Bridges; and *Voice*, published by Harrison. *Messenger* staffers clashed over Garvey, Communism, Socialism, and immigration during their glory run, yielding rival magazines. Randolph's harsh treatment of Garvey alienated many of the neighbors he wanted to mobilize. Many Harlem radicals followed Briggs, Otto Huiswood, Lovett Fort-Whiteman, and Richard B. Moore into the Communist Party. The Socialist Party was too effete for them, smacking of downtown intellectuals. Moreover, Randolph supported the AFL position on immigration, contending that African Americans should not have to compete with Asians, east Europeans, and West Indians for low-wage jobs. One of his best-known sayings was that Garvey should have stayed in Jamaica instead of imposing himself on black Harlem.[69]

Between 1917 and 1923 Randolph and Owen launched six political and trade union organizations. All of them failed, while Randolph kept the *Messenger* going. His best early union venture was with dockworkers—the National Brotherhood of Workers of America, which he founded in 1919. For a while it was the nation's largest African American union, but Randolph dissolved it in 1921 under pressure from the AFL. By June 1925 he had given up, sick of failing, when Harlem porter Ashley Totten asked him to speak to the Pullman Porters Athletic Association about how to organize a trade union. Two months later Randolph founded the Brotherhood of Sleeping Car Porters, running it for three years out of the *Messenger* office in Harlem; then it inherited the *Messenger* office. Pullman porters were African American, and all were called George in homage to the founder, George Pullman—a throwback to slavery and Pullman family self-congratulation. In a desperate time for Socialists, a black Socialist unionized part of the very company that drove Debs to socialism.

The bedrock of the Socialist Party was the Socialist flank of the AFL—Maurer and the Pennsylvania federation, the New York textile unions, the *Call*, the *Forward*, and the Berger wing. In 1921 Maurer and Christian pacifist socialist A. J. Muste founded another bellwether institution, Brookwood Labor College, the nation's first labor college. Social gospel cleric William Mann Fincke established the Brookwood School in 1914 in Katonah, New York, as a center for social justice education and service. Maurer and Muste converted it to a labor college by enlisting financial support from Maurer's Pennsylvania Federation of Labor, Muste's Amalgamated Textile Workers of America (ATWU), the International Ladies' Garment Workers' Union (ILGWU), the American Federation of

Teachers, and the Women's Trade Union League. Board chair Maurer and ATWU president Rose Schneiderman were the early ringleaders on the board, which consisted mostly of Socialist AFL officials ranging from center-left to hard left. Muste was the key to Brookwood's existence and development, serving as its director from 1921 to 1933.[70]

Thomas and Muste were intertwined from seminary onward. Muste migrated as a youth from the Netherlands to Grand Rapids, Michigan, sailed through Hope College at the top of his class, and graduated in 1909 from the Dutch Reformed seminary in New Brunswick, New Jersey. He took his first pastorate at the Fort Washington Collegiate Church in Manhattan and obtained a second seminary education on the side at Union Theological Seminary, where he converted to the social gospel and met Thomas. Muste settled on his core convictions sooner than Thomas. He voted for Debs in 1912, drifted to the Congregational ministry in 1915 and the Quaker ministry in 1918, and found his religious home in 1916 when FOR was founded. He and Thomas worked together in FOR and, after the war ended, emphasized their socialism. In 1919 Muste threw himself into the Lawrence, Massachusetts, textile strike, becoming the spokesperson for thirty thousand striking workers from more than twenty nations. He adhered to nonviolence, was beaten by police and jailed for a week, and cofounded ATWU, serving as its national secretary for two years before taking over at Brookwood. Muste personally intersected the labor radicalisms of the time. He appointed Thomas and labor scholars David Saposs and J. B. S. Hardman to the faculty and founded a political arm called the Conference for Progressive Labor Action (CPLA) to renew the dream of a Farmer-Labor party. He worked with John Dewey in the Independent League for Political Action but resigned in 1930 because Dewey ran it undemocratically. In 1933 Muste turned the CPLA into an actual party, the American Workers Party, which got him fired from Brookwood. The following year he merged it disastrously with the Trotskyite Communist League of America, learning a brutal lesson about vulture leftism that Thomas failed to learn from him. Getting burned by Trotskyites propelled Muste back to Christian pacifism and his home at FOR, where he mentored a generation of civil rights and antiwar activists.

Thomas was grateful for the teaching perch Muste gave him at Brookwood, which relieved him from the church-leader ethos of FOR. The League for Industrial Democracy (LID) afforded a similar respite from church activism. LID was a new version of the Intercollegiate Socialist Society (ISS). Jack London, Upton Sinclair, and Clarence Darrow founded ISS in 1905 to promote socialism on college campuses. It morphed into LID in 1921 when the organization expanded its mission from colleges to the general public. Thomas and

Harry Laidler, a cofounder of ISS and longtime official in it, were codirectors of LID, producing literature on the philosophy and mission of democratic socialism. In socialist terms LID was a secular equivalent of *World Tomorrow*. It was not made up of Old Guard lawyers fixed on European Social Democracy and their own working-class orientation. LID's constituency was middle class and college educated, overlapping significantly with the *World Tomorrow* orbit, though it pitched its brand of socialism to unions.

In 1923 the same unions that supported Brookwood founded a daily paper, *The New Leader*, installing Thomas as editor. It folded after a brief run and he blamed himself, calling it the most humiliating experience of his life. AFL leaders tried to thwart Communists from infiltrating the unions and working their way upward. Muste, Maurer, and Amalgamated Clothing Workers of America (ACWA) leader Sidney Hillman were exceptions in this area, but many union leaders demanded that Thomas condemn Communism as vehemently as they did. He disappointed them, so they pulled the plug financially, later reinventing the *New Leader* as a weekly. The Old Guard controlled the financial basis of the party and its institutions—the *New Leader*, *Forward*, the textile unions, the Rand School, and a flock of summer camps. It was the organizational backbone of the La Follette coalition, being the only group in it that was equipped to run a national campaign. The Socialists ran Thomas for governor of New York in 1924, and he worked hard for La Follette, shucking off that La Follette did nothing for Thomas and the Socialists.[71]

In 1925 the Socialists ran Thomas for mayor of New York and Debs came to campaign for him. It was a passing of the torch. Debs roared at Carnegie Hall, "Not only the political parties but the press and the churches have become frank agents of capitalism. Just let Wall Street get us into a new war tomorrow and see how every preacher in the country will yell for blood!" Thomas flushed with embarrassment. He shared the feeling but would never have said it so aggressively, believing that the party needed to rebuild its stock of social gospel clerics. Future New York City mayor Fiorello La Guardia, at the time a member of Congress, supported Thomas over Tammany Democrat Jimmy Walker; Benjamin Gitlow, at the time a high-ranking Communist, spent his entire campaign attacking Thomas, as ordered by Moscow.[72]

Meanwhile another kind of turn occurred in 1925. Cahan had spurned the Zionist dream throughout his career, telling *Forward* readers that fantasizing about a Jewish state in Palestine distracted Jews from solving their problems. He stuck to this line in November 1917 after British foreign secretary Arthur James Balfour declared that Britain supported the establishment of a national home for Jews in Palestine. Cahan panned that attaining a state would change "none of our problems," citing his own 1915 editorial: "Economic interests will ensure that millions and millions of Jews will, when Jews will have their own state, still follow the old Jewish saying, 'One should lie among Jews in the grave but make a living among *goyim.*' " But Cahan had street savvy, many American Jews surprised him by welcoming the Balfour Declaration, and he noticed that Meyer London hurt himself with Jewish voters by scoffing at a Jewish state. Zionist leaders went to work on Cahan to sway him.[73]

Max Pine was the chair of United Hebrew Trades and fundraising chair of Histadrut, a Zionist labor organization in Palestine founded in 1920. In 1925 he invited Cahan to behold the miracle he said Jewish workers were accomplishing in Eretz Yisrael. The *Forward* told its 200,000 subscribers that Cahan would arrive in September. It mounted a massive publicity campaign announcing his forthcoming dispatches, running ads in national magazines and plastering New York and Boston with 25,000 half-Yiddish and half-English posters. An immigration wave called the Fourth Aliyah, which brought 80,000 Jews to Palestine from eastern Europe, was then in its second year; by 1925 there were approximately 122,000 Jews in Palestine, 16 percent of the total population of 757,000. Just before he arrived Cahan told an interviewer he didn't believe in Zionism, but he didn't hate it either; he would evaluate it as a nonpartisan.

For four days he visited kibbutzim and a few collective communities with private farm plots and lost his onlooker neutrality. He wrote glowing stories lauding Histadrut secretary David Ben-Gurion and the idealism of the kibbutzim, describing Ben-Gurion as the best kind of labor leader. On the other hand, Cahan couldn't stand the kind of Zionism that spurned socialist principles: "Zionist chauvinism is so strong that it has become something like a superstition. Free thinking has no meaning here, and revolutionary aims are denied everywhere. The fire of Zionist nationalism has melted all the class and ideological conflicts." The only kind of Zionism Cahan could imagine supporting was Labor Zionism. He loathed the Revisionist Zionism of Russian Jewish journalist Vladimir Jabotinsky, who said that Zionists had to impose their will on Palestine Arabs because Arabs would never consent to a Jewish state. Jabotinsky later called for an "iron wall" separating two nations in Palestine. To Cahan, Jabotinsky-Zionism was toxic, reactionary, and a nonstarter—mere nationalism based on pure chauvinism.[74]

Back-and-forth ensued for months over Cahan's articles. Some charged that he betrayed socialism by gushing over Zionists and capitulating to nationalism; some criticized his refusal to acknowledge that he had become a Zionist; many tussled over Palestine alone versus Palestine also. Baruch Charney Vladeck, the *Forward*'s longtime general manager, said he thanked God that Jews had no state of their own. Why should they want the problems of the Bulgarians, Estonians, Latvians, Lithuanians, and Poles? It was just as wrong to say that Jews had to believe in Zionism as to say they had to speak Yiddish or observe Orthodox religion. Cahan protégé Harry Rogoff countered that Ben-Gurion's Labor Zionist party and the socialists who supported it already outnumbered the Jewish anti-Zionists in the international Socialist movement. American Jewish socialists, to keep up, needed to rethink their anti-Zionism, especially now that the U.S. Congress closed America to east European Jewish immigrants.

Jacob Panken replied that Arabs outnumbered Jews by six to one in Palestine; how could Rogoff not see the peril? Cahan protégé Alexander Kahn enthused that Zionism was a flame of world-changing idealism wholly to be praised. Hillquit said he was not a Zionist or an anti-Zionist: "Clearly, a sharp line has to be drawn between legitimate demands for national equality and the absurd attitude that claims racial or national superiority." In May 1926 Cahan declared that he still was not a Zionist, but he felt far more positively about the socialist wing of the Zionist movement than he felt before he went to Palestine. He had only warm feelings for the communes and the Histadrut, whatever might be said about the rest of the Zionist project; it offended him when anyone besmirched the Labor Zionists. Pine could not have hoped for more; Zionism subsequently got much more favorable treatment in America's leading Jewish publication.[75]

In January 1928 the American Socialists debated an excruciating question: Did the Soviet Union deserve to be described as socialist? Thomas and Maurer said yes, Hillquit and Lee said no, and all four criticized Soviet repression and brutality. Thomas commended the Russians for trying to build a society not based on the love of money; it was too soon to conclude that they would not achieve a decent outcome. Lee said Thomas was kidding himself, and Hillquit put it dramatically: "The Soviet government has been the greatest disaster and calamity that has occurred in the Socialist movement. Norman Thomas has expressed fears as to what might happen if the experiment fails. I say the experiment has already failed." Hillquit denied there was any difference between the Soviet government and the Communist movement. These two things were the same thing. If the Soviet government fell, American Communism would vanish: "Let us dissociate ourselves from the Soviet government and thereby make clear that the Social Democrats have no connection with it, bear no relation to it." Maurer had just returned from Russia at the breakpoint of Stalin versus Trotsky. He said if he lived in Russia he would probably be a Communist since he cared only about being with the workers in their struggle. American Communism, by contrast, was a bad joke. Maurer said Stalin laughed when he told him that American Communist leaders were low-performing idiots.[76]

This fissure in the party threatened to crack it wide open, but Thomas and Hillquit supported each other and tried to be agreeable, so the party got through its 1928 convention with minimal acrimony. Thomas wanted the Socialists to run Maurer, a heavyweight and accomplished, for president; Maurer countered that Thomas should be the nominee, and he would be the running mate. Old Guard labor lawyer Louis Waldman, nominating Thomas at the 1928 convention, summarized his significance: "He was one of the few intellectuals who instead of running away from us, came to us." Nominating Thomas meant that Socialists were hoping to entice progressive intellectuals back to the party, though Waldman and Hillquit had no intention of allowing them to control the party. The delegates debated whether they should support the repeal of Prohibition and endorse the League of Nations. They took no position on Prohibition because Thomas said that would help him recruit social gospel clergy, and they agreed to endorse the League of Nations without actively supporting it, since many Socialists regarded the league as a plot by Britain, France, Japan, and the United States to rule the world. Thus the Socialists agreed to say as little as possible about the two burning issues of 1928, which offended voters in their strongest city, beer-making Milwaukee.[77]

Nominating Thomas attracted a slew of intellectuals. Du Bois, *Christian Century* editor Harold Fey, University of Chicago economist Paul Douglas, and *Nation* editors Oswald Garrison Villard and Freda Kirchwey supported Thomas, as did his former editorial colleagues at *World Tomorrow*, Devere Allen and Reinhold Niebuhr. They could relate to a party that nominated one of their own. They liked that Thomas was painfully honest about the condition of the party and his concept of its purpose. The Socialists were down to eight thousand members, so winning a Debs-like vote total was not in play. Thomas deflated the delegates by declaring that he viewed the party as a catalyst for a political movement, not an electoral player in itself. Screaming about "socialism now" would be ridiculous, plus self-defeating. They were not on the cusp of gaining power. They had to plan for the long haul, unify the left, and educate the public about democratic socialism, conceived as economic democracy and antimilitarism.[78]

Thomas campaigned for peace, freedom, and plenty. Peace meant removing the Marines from Nicaragua, canceling war debts, reducing the military budget, entering the League of Nations and democratizing it. Freedom meant liberating African Americans from Jim Crow tyranny, eliminating child labor, obtaining justice for the poor, and repudiating the bigoted smears against the nation's first Catholic presidential candidate, Democrat Al Smith. Thomas blasted anti-Catholic prejudice whenever he heard it. "Plenty," in his lexicon, was about creating good jobs for all workers and establishing federal old-age pensions. Thomas mentioned only in passing his party's platform commitment to socializing major enterprises. He said the capitalist expansion of the 1920s did not solve America's terrible problems of poverty and inequality, and the two major parties didn't even try. He turned out to be a happy warrior, enduring countless train sleepers and speeches cheerfully, projecting winsome sincerity. People told him they liked him better than Smith or Herbert Hoover but declined to throw away their vote. Thomas had a favorite reply: "Thanks for the flowers, but I wish you hadn't waited for the funeral." The 1928 campaign dramatized that the Socialist Party was ascending on college campuses and receding in the unions, very uncomfortably for the Old Guard. Thomas-for-President clubs sprouted at colleges across New England and the Atlantic states; meanwhile the candidate won less than 1 percent of the national vote.[79]

Thomas said the party had to move forward, not regain what used to work. Shortly after the election the party eliminated its warhorse requirement that every member had to believe in the class struggle. Thomas protégé Clarence Senior, a twenty-seven-year-old recent graduate of the University of Kansas, announced the change in his new role as the party's national secretary. The Old Guard Social Democrats fumed that Thomas didn't understand what he was rejecting and neither did this kid in the national office. Senior revived the party's youth section, the Young People's Socialist League (YPSL), which was battered during the Communist implosion of 1919, then reenergized during the La Follette campaign of 1924, and declined again until Senior poured time and resources into it; by 1930 YPSL had sixty-five branches. Meanwhile a debate ensued about how to build a coalition party of the left. Should Socialists base it upon an imagined farmer-labor fusion or upon middle-class liberals and progressives? In both scenarios Socialists were supposed to supply inspiration, ideas, infrastructure, and glue, but to build something significant they had to make a choice.

Thomas advocated the Socialist-liberal-Progressive strategy. His concept of socialism was middle class and his crowds were mostly middle class. His home base, besides the party, was LID, where he enlisted intellectuals to speak and write about democratic socialism. Thomas knew from the LID conferences he organized that a significant more or less socialist intelligentsia existed. To break through in American society, he believed, the Socialist Party had to persuade middle-class Americans that socialism would be good for them. The party could not rest on a trade union or Marxist appeal to working-class self-interest. Formally, LID was committed to the Farmer-Labor strategy, but running LID convinced Thomas that Socialists needed to bond with their natural middle-class allies—the very types that bolted the party in 1917. Many of them were repentant by 1928, and the next generation of progressive intellectuals cut its teeth on the shame of the intellectuals under Wilson.

Everything the Old Guard feared about the direction Thomas took the party was confirmed in 1929 when the League for Independent Political Action made him its candidate for mayor of New York. Now he was running on a liberal ticket! Worse yet, he made a very strong showing, exceeding Hillquit's tally in the 1917 race. Thomas gained the upper hand and used it—building on a middle-class base, forging alliances with youthful leftists, and proposing united fronts with non-Stalinists. He said the Communists who wrecked the party in 1919 were not his enemies, at least not if he could help it. To Thomas, Communists were socialists who went astray. They employed reprehensible tactics, but at least some of them might be won back. His great fear was the ascendancy of fascism in Europe and the United States, a specter so terrible it dwarfed everything else. When Wall Street crashed in October 1929 Thomas already had the message he took into the Depression. He was an advocate, as he wrote in May 1930, of public works, unemployment insurance, a shortened workweek, a coordinated public employment system, worker retraining, a minimum wage, the abolition of child labor, and a conditional united front against fascism.[80]

Thomas did not view the Depression as a great opportunity for socialism. He viewed it as catastrophic suffering that Socialists had to try to relieve. Often he said that shrieking did little good and the left shrieked too much. In *America's Way Out: A Program for Democracy* (1931) Thomas made a case for nationalizing the banks and essential industries. In *As I See It* (1932) he explained why he made little resort to Marx or Marxism, contending that Marxism was just one of the approaches to socialism and not the best one: "I think that in some degree the comparative failure of the Socialist Party in America has been due to its iteration of dogmas in terms that were not self explanatory and which antagonized farmers, intellectuals, and the majority of wage workers who would have been with us if they had understood." He aimed to win the La Follette voters who wanted things the Democratic and Republican Parties had no intention of delivering.[81]

As I See It had a chapter about Christian socialism and his religious pilgrimage. Thomas said he had long struggled with the contradiction between the pacifism of Jesus and the racist imperialism of the Christian Church. Christianity had a record of racism lacking any parallel in Islam and a leading role in "the most despicable slave trade in history." He admired Rauschenbusch and his successor, Harry Ward, for digging a genuinely Christian radicalism out of Christianity but no longer shared their faith: "Outstanding men in pew and pulpit are doing this very thing. That is good, but the promise of their power does not seem great. I doubt if they can win their own organizations." Thomas scoffed at the surge of pacifism in mainline Protestant denominations. He believed it was strictly a between-wars reaction, aside from the historic peace churches. The next time the government called the nation to war, the churches would fall in line. As for the "humanistic version of Protestant Christianity" taught at the University of Chicago Divinity School and similar bastions of liberal theology, Thomas doubted it was "a valid development from Christianity" and believed it was ineffective in the struggle for justice. Many social gospel liberals were religious humanists who didn't really believe in God. Thomas was describing himself, so he demitted from the ministry in 1931. High-flying religious philosophy of the Hegelian or Whiteheadian type was incomprehensible to him, and low-flying Chicago School theology was mere humanism. If Thomas no longer believed in a sky-father God, it seemed pointless to him to make a home in the watered-down remains of liberal Christianity.[82]

Socialism was the last best hope of the world, "a society from which poverty and war are forever banished." It had nothing to do with proletarian explosions or Leninist vanguard tactics: "Wretched, half-starved children are not the builders of a beautiful cooperative commonwealth. Never was mere revolt, however justified, less likely to succeed in building the new order than today." Thomas feared that the Depression pushed Americans toward some kind of dictatorial salvation. Between the two options—Communism and Fascism—he had no doubt which one Americans would embrace. In the United States any political stampede was sure to rush to the right. Thomas knew from his speaking tours that much of his ravaged nation was ripe for fascism, though he agreed with Louisiana protofascist Huey Long that American fascism would have to be called something else. The Democrats galled Thomas with opportunistic campaigns lacking any ideas besides electoral posturing and servicing the business class. Their campaign slogan was "Hee, haw, we're coming back," which perfectly suited a party lacking vision, courage, principle, and intelligence. Thomas warned, "We drift, and we drift toward disaster." To him, Herbert Hoover had already failed, and Franklin Roosevelt was a rich and shallow opportunist with a mediocre record as governor of New York.[83]

Thomas versus Hillquit had been simmering for four years when it erupted very publicly at the Socialist convention of 1932. Hillquit believed that Thomas bankrupted the Labour Party option. In England the ILP was resolutely socialist, pulling the Labour Party mishmash of progressives, liberals, unionists, and socialists to the left. But Thomas socialism was the triumph of the Labour Party mishmash itself. Moreover, to use a phrase not yet ubiquitous in American politics, Thomas was soft on Communism. In 1932 the Socialist Party had three camps on the Communist issue. The Old Guard was staunchly anti-Communist, loathing Communism for harming the Socialist movement.

Nobody in the Old Guard claimed that Soviet Communism might have turned out all right had Stalin lost. Oneal became an Old Guard intellectual leader on the strength of this issue, joining Hillquit and Lee. They contended forcefully that Communism was the enemy of democratic socialism, not a hurried version of it. The left wing of the party was friendly to Leninism and called itself the Militants. Most were young, having joined the party in the 1920s. Some were pro-Leninists and others were soft on Leninism in the fellow traveler fashion; together they claimed that the Soviets had to impose a dictatorship to industrialize Russia. Humanist author Paul Blanshard and young University of Chicago economist Maynard Krueger were leading Militants, along with numerous organizers destined for careers in the Congress of Industrial Organizations (CIO), notably Franz Daniel. The third camp consisted of the middle-class progressives led by Thomas. They had little in common with the Militants besides an openness to united fronts and, more important, a determination to break the power of the Old Guard. Thomas formed an alliance with them on that basis.

He liked having youthful allies, and the Militants indulged Thomas when he emoted about forging a unified left; they warmed to the latter spiel when Moscow tacked back to it in 1935, calling for a Popular Front. Berger had died in 1929, Hillquit was fading, and the Socialists had no future if they perpetuated Berger–Hillquit socialism. So it seemed to Thomas. Two issues roiled the 1932 Socialist convention in Milwaukee: What should the party say about the Soviet Union? And should Hillquit be replaced as national chair? The convention debated heatedly whether to disavow its previous sympathy for the Soviet government. Condemning Soviet brutality was a given; condemning the Soviet Union itself would have torn the party asunder. Finally the Socialists endorsed a policy of friendly neutrality while demanding the release of all Soviet political prisoners and the restoration of civil rights for all Soviet citizens. The convention moved to the Hillquit question and fumbled awkwardly until a Milwaukee delegate said the national chair should not be a New Yorker. Hillquit supporters pounced on this howler, charging that "New Yorker" was code for foreign and Jewish. The dump-Hillquit side vehemently denied the accusation, vainly defending its moral pride. Thomas lieutenants Blanshard and Heywood Broun led this self-defense and welcomed Vladeck's validation of their sincerity, which did not swing the vote. Hillquit dramatically said he could not help that he was born abroad, was a Jew, and lived in New York. That ended the debate, and he remained chair by a vote of 105 to 80, just before Thomas was nominated by acclamation.[84]

The Socialist platform of 1932 turned out to be historically significant. It demanded constitutional guarantees of economic, political, and legal equality for all African Americans and the nationalization of basic industries—planks that Roosevelt and the New Deal carefully left aside. It also called for federal programs that Roosevelt said nothing about during the campaign and that shortly thereafter became pillars of the New Deal. The Socialists called for immediate federal relief for the poor and unemployed to supplement state appropriations. A year later this plank became law as the Federal Emergency Relief Act. The Socialists called for federal funds for public works, road construction, reforestation, slum clearance, and homes for workers. These programs were enacted through the Public Works Administration established by the National Industrial Recovery Act (NIRA) of 1933; the Civilian Conservation Corps (Reforestation) Act of 1933; and the Home Owners Loan Corporation established by the Home Owners Refinancing Act of 1933. The Socialists demanded the right of unions to organize and bargain and called for worker compensation and accident insurance. The National Labor Relations Act of 1935—the Wagner Act—achieved these demands. The Socialists called for old-age pensions for men and women that were achieved by the Social Security Act of 1936 and for national health coverage that the Social Security Act partly achieved. The Socialists called for a six-hour day and a five-day workweek, which failed in Congress. They called for protection against mortgage foreclosures for farmers and small homeowners, which became law under the Agricultural Adjustment Act (AAA) of 1933, the Farm Credit Administration of 1933, and the Federal National Mortgage Association of 1938. They called for minimum wage laws that were established in 1933 through the National Recovery Administration (NRA), though the Supreme Court struck it down in 1935.[85]

The Thomas campaign confirmed the trend of 1928: the party had a diminished union base, and it thrived among progressive intellectuals. Douglas organized a pro-Thomas group that glittered with intellectual stars: Allen, poet Stephen Vincent Benét, Blanshard, newscaster Elmer Davis, Dewey, Du Bois, YMCA leader Sherwood Eddy, composer George Gershwin, Holmes, Krueger, poet Edna St. Vincent Millay, Niebuhr, Randolph, and cultural critic Alexander Woollcott. A similar array of literary stars endorsed Foster for president: Sherwood Anderson, Erskine Caldwell, Malcolm Cowley, Waldo Frank, Granville Hicks, Sidney Hook, Langston Hughes, John Dos Passos, James Rorty, and Edmund Wilson. Taken together the two campaigns displayed a stunning migration of intellectuals to the socialist left. Krueger served as research director of the Socialist Party and became a leader of its left wing. Nearly three hundred Thomas for President clubs formed on college campuses, forty-six members of the Harvard faculty announced their support for Thomas, and he made the cover of *Time* magazine. All of it yielded merely 2.2 percent of the national vote, the best Thomas ever attained. He knew it was coming from the admirers who said they had to vote for Roosevelt because the nation couldn't bear four more years of Hoover. Thomas became the symbol of progressive intellectual dissent. He revived the party, in a fashion; even Hillquit said in 1933, just before he died, that the party was "getting a new lease of life." But nothing devastated American socialism like its success in the New Deal.[86]

The worst days of the Depression occurred between the November election and Roosevelt's inauguration in March. FDR campaigned so blandly in 1932 that Thomas worried he was too superficial and privileged to grasp how bad things were. Roosevelt soon proved him wrong, choosing a labor secretary he knew would push him, Frances Perkins. She had grown up middle-class and Republican in Worcester, Massachusetts, graduated from Mount Holyoke College in 1902, became a social reformer through the settlement movement in Philadelphia, and joined the Socialist Party in 1908. Perkins switched to the Democrats in time to vote for Wilson in 1912, committing herself to labor reform activism. In 1918 Al Smith appointed her to the New York State Industrial Commission; in 1926 she took over as chair of the commission; in 1929 the new governor, Roosevelt, reappointed her. After the 1932 election Perkins told FDR that she would join his cabinet only if he pushed for unemployment relief and public works, an old age pension, child labor legislation, and fair labor standards. He said he was for all those things, and she signed on. Two weeks into his presidency, FDR invited Thomas and Hillquit to the White House. They urged him to nationalize the banks and obtain a $12 billion relief and public works bond issue. Roosevelt said he supported most of what they wanted, except nationalizing the banks. A few months later, after Roosevelt had secured the Emergency Banking Act, the Federal Emergency Relief Act, the AAA, the Tennessee Valley Authority Act, and the NIRA, a stunned Thomas was reduced to reminding audiences that these programs came from the Socialist platform. Hoover later told interviewers the resemblance between the New Deal and the Socialist platform was uncanny. A stream of figures in the Socialist orbit, recalculating the politics, became New Dealers. Blanshard joined the La Guardia administration in New York. ILGWU president David Dubinsky and ACWU president Sidney Hillman became New Dealers as beneficiaries of the NIRA. Both were controversial for being Socialists in the Roosevelt coalition, but both exerted a powerful influence in the Socialist and Democratic parties. Historian Arthur M. Schlesinger Jr., exaggerating only slightly, remarked that by the end of 1933 "most of those who voted for Thomas were shouting for Roosevelt."[87]

Young Irving Howe joined the Socialists during this period and idolized Thomas. Born and raised in the East Bronx, a working-class, Yiddish-speaking world much like the Lower East Side except lacking its cultural vibrancy, Howe grew up reading the *Forward* and didn't know anyone who admitted to reading the *New York Times*. His parents were garment workers, his father was ashamed of failing at business, and his strong, humorless mother held the family together. Howe assumed that Jews everywhere must be like those he knew—poor, anxious, and, especially, fearful, "the intuitive Jewish response to authority." East Bronx Jews were voluble about public matters and fearfully shy about everything private. In 1933 the ILGWU called out the entire dress trade and won the strike. It pulled Howe's grimly weary parents out of poverty, a story he told for the rest of his life. The following year he joined YPSL at the age of fourteen. Howe studied the speaking styles of YPSL debaters, awed by those with a command of the Marxian lexicon. He learned that socialists were doing badly everywhere in the world, but capitalism was in its death agony. He imbibed the Militants' contempt for the Old Guard—grizzled old unionists who cheered for Roosevelt and played pinochle at the party headquarters. If only they could drop the stodgy Social Democrats who treated socialism as a hangout! Thomas was nothing like the sour, worn-out, obsessed-with-Communism Old Guard: "Norman Thomas had it. Pure in spirit, brave, selfless to a fault, and wonderfully free of the public man's self-importance, Thomas was in some ways too large for the movement in behalf of which he spoke. With his crackling voice and rapid wit, he would often rise to an eloquence that could sway even skeptics and opponents. This was no demagogue or soapbox ranter. He spoke with logic, he marshaled arguments and facts, he came out with comely sentences and paragraphs." Thomas made Howe believe the New Deal was socialism on a stretcher, and the real thing was coming soon.[88]

Thomas and Niebuhr were leading proponents of the stretcher argument and its either/or corollary. The New Deal was gently carting the system to its death. Mere reforms would not save the system now that it had collapsed. There was no third way; sooner or later every capitalist nation would swerve to the Fascist right or the Socialist left. In Britain Harold Laski and John Strachey moved straight to the either/or, lacking a New Deal to oppose. In the United States Niebuhr and Thomas warned that New Deal reforms would never heal a sick and dying system. Thomas said FDR could have gone further on his terms by nationalizing the banks without directing credit toward production for use. A New Deal worthy of the name would have created nationalized institutions that produced for profit. Instead, Roosevelt closed the banks, patched up the system, "and gave it back to the bankers to see if they could ruin it again." The New Deal used public money and federal government power to shore up private enterprises for the sake of private profit. Thomas argued that this approach, blandly called state capitalism, had another name—fascism. FDR was not a fascist, Thomas assured his crowds; FDR was an aristocrat "in the best sense of the word." As long as Roosevelt was president, the outright fascist strain in American society would be thwarted. But Thomas warned that the New Deal was a stopgap, not a solution. The differences between Socialism and New Deal reformism were crucial, cutting to a fundamental socialist principle: Public money should be spent directly on the public interest.[89]

The Old Guard Socialists indulged union racketeering, purged Communists from the unions, and resented Thomas for rattling on about union corruption and a united front. Waldman became the leader of the Old Guard, along with Lee and Cahan, after Hillquit died. Thomas said no actual unity was possible as long as Communists clung "to their notion of a rigid dictatorship of a party controlled from Russia and by Russia." At the same time, he campaigned for a tactical united front on specific antifascist causes, "especially if and when that united front includes elements which as yet are neither Socialist nor Communist." He said it was up to democratic socialists in England, France, and the United States to stand for democratic principles against the tide of left-wing and right-wing totalitarianisms. Meanwhile he sowed confusion on the stump by mocking Roosevelt's programs. The TVA, Thomas chided, was state capitalism; the NIRA was state paternalism; and the Civilian Conservation Corps looked like forced labor to him. On these points he recycled arguments by Oneal and Waldman, who kept alive in the Old Guard the venerable social-ist antipathy for state paternalism and excessive centralization. The Old Guard, even in the 1930s, was never just one ideological group. Oneal became an Old Guard stalwart on the basis of longevity and anti-Communism, while still believing in worker self-determination. Thomas could see on the speaking trail that he was losing the argument about the New Deal; these socialist programs could not be bad just because FDR implemented them.[90]

In 1934 the Socialist Party had a histrionic blowout at a convention in Detroit. The Old Guard proposed a Declaration of Principles expounding its Social Democratic viewpoint, the Militants demanded something closer to *The Communist Manifesto*, and Allen was asked to write a consensus statement. Devere Allen was a kindly Quaker graduate of Oberlin who had run *World Tomorrow* for ten years. He got the manifesto job for being a Thomas lieutenant, a wordsmith, and a genial type. His draft declared that capitalism was doomed, and Socialists hoped it would be superseded by a majority vote. But if the whole thing collapsed into chaos, Socialists would not shrink from the responsibility "of organizing and maintaining a government under the workers' rule." This ludicrous specter—a twenty-three-thousand-member party pledging to assume command of the American colossus—set off a wild three-hour debate.

Waldman, a big personality, charged that Allen's draft was anarchist, Communist, and illegal. Militants countered that workers were on the march and the party had to catch up. Thomas tried to tone down the rhetoric, but the Old Guard and the Militants demanded a vote on the draft, and Thomas supported it. The declaration passed by ninety-nine to forty-seven. Only one Old Guardsman, Oneal, was elected to the NEC—even Waldman lost. Leo Krzycki, a left-wing ACWU vice president, was elected national chair, and the *New York Times* announced on page 1 that Thomas and the left wing had seized the party. *Times* reporter Joseph Shaplen registered how it looked to him, an Old Guard rank-and-filer. Thomas winced at being typed as a left-wing wrecker. He believed the Old Guard was corrupted by its access to Hillman–Dubinsky union power and the Militants were all he had in trying to steer the party to a better future. The Militants got their way with Thomas by appealing to his idealism.[91]

The debate over united leftism roiled the Socialist Party during the volatile mid-1930s period when unions clashed over what they should do about Communist organizers. In 1935 UMWA president John L. Lewis and the heads of seven other AFL unions formed a Committee for Industrial Organization to organize the mass-production steel, rubber, automobile, and packing industries. Both incarnations of this group were known by their acronym, CIO. Hillman and Dubinsky were ringleaders in the new group, which AFL leaders treated from the beginning as an enemy within. This was the dream of industrial unionism coming true. The CIO needed hundreds of experienced organizers, who came from the Socialist and Communist movements. It sought originally to concentrate on the steel industry and build from there, but the CIO grew explosively in the auto industry and won a breakthrough victory at the General Electric plant in Schenectady, New York. It captured the coalfields in a few months and sprawled across Pittsburgh, Buffalo, Cleveland, Toledo, Detroit, Gary, and Chicago. Many of its greatest organizers were Communists, notably Harry Bridges, Joe Curran, Wyndham Mortimer, Mike Quill, Reid Robinson, and James Matles. Lewis prevented Communists from gaining a foothold in his union but did not stop them from securing offices in other CIO unions they organized.

Communists had their largest followings in the United Auto Workers (UAW) and the new United Electrical Workers (UE). By 1938, when the entire CIO was expelled from the AFL and reorganized as the Congress of Industrial Organizations (CIO), Communists controlled a dozen CIO unions. Hillman took ILGWU back into the AFL after the CIO was expelled, having clashed with Lewis over Hillman's determination to back Roosevelt. To the Old Guard, fending off Communism was not corrupting, and united fronts were perilous at best. The schism they set off in the Socialist Party was triply ironic. They defected to a capitalist president who went on to form an alliance with Stalin. Thomas had excluded Stalinists from his united front schemes. And in 1937, returning from Russia, Thomas changed his mind anyway about Russia and collaborating with Communists.

REINHOLD NIEBUHR AND THE NEW DEAL

One figure perfectly symbolized the Socialist fights of the thirties and forties over the New Deal, Communism, united fronts, pragmatism, the Old Guard, pacifism, and the meaning of socialism—Reinhold Niebuhr. In the early and mid-1920s he was a social gospel pacifist and idealist who succeeded Thomas as a leader of FOR. In 1928 he joined the Socialist Party and moved swiftly to its left wing, devising a neo-Marxian critique of capitalism and liberal idealism that Thomas appropriated selectively. Niebuhr blasted the New Deal mercilessly through the 1930s, convinced it was as stupid and naive as the secular and Christian liberalisms he ridiculed. Then he changed again, more than once, always in the name of realism. Niebuhr's willingness to change saved him from the fate of his social ethicist colleague at Union Theological Seminary, Harry Ward, who fixed on one thing—united front leftism—and destroyed his legacy. But Niebuhr could have ended better had he made fewer course corrections.

He attacked the social gospel so powerfully that he changed the trajectory of American theology and social ethics. Niebuhr drew from Martin Luther, Thomas Hobbes, Karl Marx, and, eventually, Augustine an imperative about separating politics from morality and a personal aversion to moralizing politics. Like the other theological giants of his generation—Karl Barth, Emil Brunner, Rudolf Bultmann, and Paul Tillich—Niebuhr was trained in liberal theology, turned against it vehemently, and was tagged as neo-orthodox. In Europe, where the antiliberal revolt following World War I was called crisis theology, the leading figure was Barth. In the United States, where the crisis occurred a decade later, Niebuhr had the Barth role.[92]

But Niebuhr took for granted the fundamental principles of the social gospel and liberal theology. He epitomized the social activism of the social gospel and was never theologically neo-orthodox. The field he taught, social ethics, had no history or basis whatsoever apart from the social gospel. Niebuhr exuded the social gospel assumption that Christians are called to the ethical and political struggle for social justice. He embraced the bedrock commitment of liberal theology to intellectual freedom and the defining principles that came from it: Religious beliefs must not be established or compelled on the basis of authority, theology must allow science to explain the physical world, theology must look beyond the Bible and church tradition for answers, and biblical criticism rightly treats biblical myths as myths. To Niebuhr and Tillich, liberal theology and the social gospel did not go wrong by being liberal and pursuing social justice causes. They went wrong by being too idealistic, moralistic, rationalistic, and prone to pacifism—the very things that Thomas retained from the social gospel.

Niebuhr was born in Wright City, Missouri, in 1892, to Gustav Niebuhr, an Evangelical Synod pastor who immigrated to the United States in 1881, and Lydia Hosto Niebuhr, the daughter of an Evangelical Synod missionary based in northern California. Gustav Niebuhr grew up on a German family farm dating to the thirteenth century and fled to America at the age of eighteen. He said he dreaded his father's autocratic bearing, not mentioning that he also fled from Germany's required military service. Gustav and Lydia Niebuhr were married in 1887, two years after he graduated from Eden Seminary, and their first three children—Hulda, Walter, and Herbert—were born in San Francisco. In 1892 they moved to Wright City, where Karl Paul Reinhold was born the same year, and Helmut Richard followed in 1894.

Niebuhr excelled at two humble Evangelical Synod schools—Elmhurst College and Eden Seminary—and felt acutely his country bumpkin background when he enrolled at Yale Divinity School in 1913. He dreaded that his rough manners, mishmash of German and English, and Midwest accent marked him as a rube, telling a former teacher that his dominant feeling was humiliation: "I feel all the time like a mongrel among thoroughbreds and that's what I am." That was a clue to his overachieving hyperactivity, then and later. At Yale Niebuhr embraced the pragmatism of William James and did not read Rauschenbusch, as Niebuhr's two years at Yale were absorbed with the problems of belief. Aspiring to a doctorate in theology, he took four courses in the college's philosophy department but earned mediocre grades and lost his enthusiasm, plus any hope of being admitted to a doctoral program. Two years of Americanizing education at Yale was all he got before heading into the Evangelical and Reformed ministry.[93]

Niebuhr asked for a progressive, Americanized, reasonably well-paying church, only to get a Detroit German-speaking mission church long on pro-German nationalists. His first cause was to make German American Protestantism unabashedly American. Niebuhr poured out articles on this topic while enlisting his mother to run the congregation's daily business. His first article for a national magazine, "The Failure of German-Americanism," was published in July 1916, during the run-up to America's intervention in World War I. Niebuhr said German culture at its best was liberal, cosmopolitan, and forward-looking, but German American Protestantism smacked of German culture at its worst—conservative, provincial, and stodgy. German Americans, he admonished, needed very much to become better Americans; moreover, Americans were not wrong in disliking German militarism.[94]

Niebuhr's fixation with America and being American never ended. His entire theological career was a love affair with the United States that diagnosed its neuroses and pretensions, defended its interests, and envisaged America as the key to a just world order. After the United States intervened in World War I Niebuhr wanted desperately to enlist as a military chaplain but had to settle for running the synod's War Welfare Commission, touring military training camps. He preached Wilsonian sermons about creating a new world order based on reconciliation, democracy, free trade, and the League of Nations, until the Paris Peace Conference made a mockery of Wilson's Fourteen Points. In June 1919, while the conference was still convening, Niebuhr said it was a vengeful disaster exposing the literal weakness of liberal idealism. Wilson was a "typical son of the manse," believing too much in words and ideals: "We need something less circumspect than liberalism to save the world."[95]

This sentiment eventually made Niebuhr famous. Bethel Church grew tremendously in the early 1920s, feeding off the skyrocketing growth of the automobile industry, despite Niebuhr's frequent absence. Americanization was the wave of the future in the Evangelical Synod, and Niebuhr was its apostle, winning a following on the social gospel lecture circuit. In 1922 he caught the attention of Charles Clayton Morrison, editor of the liberal Protestant flagship, *Christian Century*. Morrison focused on two issues—defending Prohibition and opposing war—and encouraged Niebuhr to write about whatever interested him. Sherwood Eddy organized travel tours of European trade unions and occupied zones. Niebuhr joined Eddy's tour of 1923 and crossed a fateful line, repelled by France's abuse of Germans in the occupied Ruhr valley. Like many clerics of the time, Niebuhr vowed to never preach another prowar sermon: "This is as good a time as any to make up my mind that I am done with the war business. . . . I am done with this business. I hope I can make that resolution stick."[96]

For nearly ten years he struggled to keep this resolution, all the while objecting that his colleagues in FOR were naive and idealistic. Niebuhr chafed at social gospel idealism while calling for more of it, not knowing what else to say. In 1928 he moved to New York and joined the Socialist Party. Eddy proposed to pay Niebuhr's entire salary to edit *World Tomorrow* and teach half time at Union Theological Seminary. This proposal squeaked through the Union faculty by one vote, as the faculty considered him unqualified to teach at Union. Niebuhr won them over by teaching overflow classes and plugging Union students into his activist network. He taught that the capitalist lust for profit and new markets was the chief cause of World War I; then it caused the collapse of an unsustainable system. The Depression drove Niebuhr to Marx's conclusion that capitalism is inherently self-destructive. In 1930 Niebuhr cofounded, with Eddy, Kirby Page, and John C. Bennett, the Fellowship of Socialist Christians.[97]

Though Niebuhr was slow to say that his socialism trumped his antiwar convictions, he believed it propelled him beyond his social gospel milieu. The social gospel of Bliss, Herron, and Rauschenbusch belonged to a past era. In Niebuhr's experience the social gospel was overwhelmingly a pacifist phenomenon. It preached about responding to evil with love, following Jesus to the cross, loving enemies, and following the example of Mohandas Gandhi. This was the gospel to FOR, the social gospel fellowships in the denominations, and many of Niebuhr's students at Union. In 1932 he ran for Congress on the Socialist Party ticket and told New Yorkers that only socialism could save Western civilization, warning in *Harper's* magazine, "It will be practically impossible to secure social change in America without the use of very considerable violence." The terrible wreckage of the Depression overcame Niebuhr's misgivings about Marxian violence. He was done with imploring that socialism and pacifism had to go together. Most of his readers did not realize he had changed until December 1932, when Niebuhr published the most important American theological work of the twentieth century, *Moral Man and Immoral Society*.[98]

The book had an icy, aggressive, sarcastic tone, with an eerie sense of omniscience reflecting Niebuhr's recently acquired Marxism. What did it mean to be a social ethicist if one did not believe in redeemed institutions, the progressive character of history, or an idealistic theology of social salvation? Niebuhr's answer launched a new era in U.S. American theology and ethics. Politics is about struggling for power. Human groups never willingly subordinate their interests to the interests of others. Liberal denials of this truism are stupid. Morality belongs to the sphere of individual action. On occasion, individuals rise above self-interest, motivated by compassion or love, but groups never overcome the power of self-interest and collective egotism that sustains their existence. Any attempt to moralize society is not only futile but also desperately lacking intelligence. Niebuhr said that social scientists betrayed their middle-class prejudices "in almost everything they write." They believed in rational suasion and morality; thus they wrote nonsense about social change: "Conflict is inevitable, and in this conflict power must be challenged by power."[99]

With this book, "stupid" became Niebuhr's favorite epithet, followed closely by "naive." Liberal idealists failed to realize there is no such thing as a moral group. Secular liberals like John Dewey appealed to instrumental reason; social gospel liberals like Shailer Mathews and Justin Wroe Nixon appealed to reason

and love. Niebuhr said all were maddeningly stupid, failing to grasp that relations between groups are predominantly political, not ethical: "Failure to recognize the stubborn resistance of group egoism to all moral and inclusive social
objectives involves them in unrealistic and confused political thought." *Moral
Man and Immoral Society* seethed with Niebuhr's anger at the ravages of the
Depression and his frustration at America's aversion to socialism. The Marxist
idea of collective emancipation, he said, was "a very valuable illusion for the
moment" because only a "sublime madness in the soul" would take the fight to
"malignant power and 'spiritual wickedness in high places.' "[100]

Marxism, besides offering the best analysis of the Depression, held the key to
America's future. Niebuhr said it boldly: "Marxian socialism is a true enough
interpretation of what the industrial worker feels about society and history, to
have become the accepted social and political philosophy of all self-conscious
and politically intelligent industrial workers." Admittedly, American workers
did not belong to the ranks of the self-conscious and intelligent, but that would
change: "The full maturity of American capitalism will inevitably be followed
by the emergence of the American Marxian proletarian." Niebuhr said Marx
was brilliantly perceptive in his "complete moral cynicism," conceiving the
relation of social classes in society "wholly in terms of the conflict of power with
power." Equally important, Marx's realism had a utopian expectation, like
Christianity at its best. Marx espoused a tragic view of history tempered by a
vision of revolutionary transformation. So did Christianity, except that modern
Christianity dropped its realistic sense of the tragedy of life, substituting a myth
of enlightened Progress. Niebuhr said the historical sweep of human life reflects
the predatory world of nature, not the Progress myth. Only political struggle
achieves the good that is attainable for groups—justice. When revolutionaries
bend the forces of nature to achieve socialist equality, it is possible to achieve
approximate justice—as good as it gets in the social sphere.[101]

Liberal Protestant leaders howled that Niebuhr ignored Jesus, paraded his
cynicism, and said very mean things about liberalism and them. Some protested that he had no theology of the church or the kingdom and no belief in
God's regenerative grace. Some said he had no discernible theology at all.
Theologians Henry P. Van Dusen and Francis Miller could not find the gospel
anywhere in the book. Thomas, Holmes, and the *Christian Century* lamented
that Niebuhr had become a purveyor of cynicism and ethical defeat; what was
happening to their friend? University of Chicago chaplain Charles Gilkey told
his family their dear friend Reinie had apparently lost his mind. Niebuhr replied
that they were too comfortable in their idealism and humanism to understand
him; he had moved to the right theologically and the left politically: "If such a

position seems unduly cynical and pessimistic to the American mind my own feeling is that this judgment is due to the fact that the American mind is still pretty deeply immersed in the sentimentalities of a dying culture."[102]

H[elmut] Richard Niebuhr saw an opportunity. In 1930 he had begun teaching at Yale and started going by his "American" middle name. He was habituated to competing with his brother, assisting him, arguing with him, and looking up to him. Outside the public eye the brothers regularly scrutinized each other's work. In public they debated only once, in 1932, in the *Christian Century*, responding to the Japanese invasion of Manchuria. Richard spoke for nonintervention, invoking what he called "the grace of doing nothing." God has God's own plans for history, and Christians are not called to make history come out right. Reinhold countered that Christians are called to serve the cause of justice, and there is no grace in doing nothing. Richard said they had been having this argument for thirty years, and it was pointless to comment any further; there would be no more debates with his brother in public.[103]

Privately, the controversy over *Moral Man and Immoral Society* provoked Richard Niebuhr to say, "I have no defense of idealism to offer. I hate it with all my heart as an expression of our original sin." He commended Reinhold for offending so many liberals but admonished that Reinhold was still one of them in his assumptions about human nature, religion, and activism. On the virtue of "moral man," for example, Richard asked him to consider brotherly love; for example, Richard's own. He took pride in Reinhold's achievements, basked in his reflected glory, struggled to stand on his own feet, resented being compared to him, and felt jealous of him, all at the same time. If he could love his brother despite resenting him so much it wasn't because any ideal or will to love prevailed over his selfishness or resentment. It was because something else that was not his will was at work long before he had a will or an ideal. Richard argued that human beings possess a moral gift of judging right and wrong, not a gift of goodness. All morally reflective people know they are bad. Therefore he rejected Reinhold's claim that individuals are morally superior to their groups. Individuals only appear to have a higher capacity for moral self-giving because coercion works better in face-to-face relationships, and in the private realm it's easier to see that morality and enlightened self-interest go together.[104]

More important, Niebuhr was still a liberal in the way he thought about religion, conceiving it as a power for good or ill that he wanted to use for good. Richard countered that true religion is directed toward God, not society: "I think that liberal religion is thoroughly bad. It is a first-aid to hypocrisy. It is the exaltation of goodwill, moral idealism. . . . It is sentimental and romantic. Has it ever struck you that you read religion through the mystics and ascetics? You scarcely think of Paul, Augustine, Luther, Calvin. You're speaking of humanistic religion so far as I can see. You come close to breaking with it at times but you don't quite do it." Luther and Calvin did not moralize Christianity or make it a vehicle for social activism. Reinhold's frenetic chasing after social causes was spiritually corrupting. Richard put it sharply: "I do think that an activism which stresses immediate results is the cancer of our modern life. . . . We want to be saviors of civilization and simply bring down new destruction. . . . You are about ready to break with that activism. I think I discern that."[105]

Richard Niebuhr was wrong about the last part. Reinhold Niebuhr took for granted the social gospel concept of religion as energy for the social struggle. He would never say that social activism is the cancer of modern life. He assumed religion should be a power for social good, and it depends on human capacities for transcendence, good, and evil. But Richard Niebuhr exposed his brother's theology problem more deeply than the complaints of liberals about the same thing. Reinhold Niebuhr had replaced the Reformation language of grace alone, faith alone, and scripture alone with a pastiche of liberal theology and politics; then he turned Socialist; then he renounced the idealistic parts of liberal theology as a neo-Marxist. His brother got to him by protesting that he wrote as though Paul and Calvin never existed. Niebuhr's next book, *Reflections on the End of an Era* (1934), added a concluding excursus on providence and grace to its Marxian analysis. Thereafter Niebuhr drew more deeply on Augustine, Luther, and Calvin, remarking in 1939, "Even while imagining myself to be preaching the Gospel, I had really experimented with many modern alternatives to Christian faith, until one by one they proved unavailing."[106]

In the 1930s he contended that the right combination was Marxist radicalism and the biblical doctrine of sin. If politics is about struggling for power and radical politics is about struggling for a just redistribution of power, religion serves the cause of justice only if it takes a realistic attitude toward power, interest, and evil. Marx's theory of the falling rate of profit was the ground of Niebuhr's certainty that the New Deal was pitiful and futile. The problem was the system itself, Niebuhr argued, not a correctable flaw in it or even the greed of capitalists: "The sickness from which modern civilization suffers is organic and constitutional. It is not due to an incidental defect in the mechanism of production or distribution but to the very character of the social system. . . . Private ownership means social power; and the unequal distribution of social power leads automatically to inequality and injustice."[107]

Capitalist productivity inevitably outraced the system's ability to sustain a growing middle class of consumers. Sooner or later the system stopped being able to squeeze growing profits from national economies. Thus it was disintegrating, exactly as Marx predicted, although later than he expected. Liberalism and capitalism were finished. Niebuhr insisted that no amount of reformist tinkering would stop the world-historical drift toward fascism. The ravages of capitalism would never be removed by moral effort, political reformism, or even the recognition that capitalism was destroying modern civilization. The only way to avert a fascist takeover of the entire Western world was for the West to embrace radical state socialism.[108]

This part of Niebuhr's argument was a hard-edged version of a resurgent Christian socialism. In 1932 the Federal Council of Churches issued a new Social Creed calling for social planning and control of the credit and monetary systems, economic democracy, redistribution of wealth, a living wage, collective profit sharing, social security, the right to organize unions and bargain collectively, abolition of child labor, prison reform, equal rights for all, the repudiation of war, and the building of a cooperative world order. Basically it reaffirmed Harry Ward's original 1908 version with a socialist twist. Two years later Kirby Page enlisted ten Protestant denominations in a questionnaire sent to 99,890 ministers and 609 rabbis, receiving 20,870 replies. Approximately 51 percent of the respondents said they favored a "drastically reformed capitalism," and 28 percent were for Socialism, defined as the democratic socialism of the Socialist Party or something like it. Methodism had the highest number of Socialist clergy, at 34 percent, followed by Evangelical (33 percent), Congregational (33 percent), Reformed (32 percent), Disciples (30 percent), Episcopal (24 percent), Baptist (22 percent), Presbyterian (19 percent), and Lutheran (12 percent). Eighty-seven percent of the respondents gave their permission to be quoted on their economic position. Certainly, American Protestant clergy as a whole were not as left wing as these results. Only 14 percent of Lutheran pastors responded, and 9 percent of the Baptists, compared to the average of 21 percent. Still, in 1934 nearly 6,000 Protestant ministers declared themselves to be socialists.[109]

Niebuhr urged them to drop their pacifist idealism in his fashion. In 1934 he resigned from FOR, dramatically declaring that liberal Christian pacifism was too consumed with its pretense of virtue to make gains toward justice: "Recognizing, as liberal Christianity does not, that the world of politics is full of demonic forces, we have chosen on the whole to support the devil of vengeance against the devil of hypocrisy." He chose to support Marxist vengeance, knowing there was a devil in it, rather than allow the devil of hypocrisy to avoid conflict and preserve the status quo. To avoid any traffic with devils is simply to make oneself an accomplice to injustice and perhaps genocide; moral purity is an illusion.[110]

These were political arguments, however, with very hard edges. Liberal Protestants did not talk about supporting the devil of vengeance or trafficking with devils. They said that gospel idealism applied everywhere, including international politics. In their revulsion against the vengeful outcome of World War I they had turned against war. Pacifism was ascending in the mainline denominations; it spoke mostly in religious terms; and its leaders included popular religious writers such as Harry Emerson Fosdick, Georgia Harkness, Kirby Page, John Haynes Holmes, Walter Russell Bowie, Edmund Chaffee, Richard Roberts, and John Nevin Sayre. They appealed to the nonviolent way of Jesus as the normative way of Christian discipleship. In the mid-1930s nearly every mainline Protestant denomination vowed never to support another war. The Disciples of Christ, the Northern Baptist Convention, the Episcopal Church, the General Council of Congregational and Christian Churches, the two major Presbyterian churches, and the two major Methodist churches said it categorically. Niebuhr had played a role in bringing about this outcome; now he sought to undo it. But to challenge the pacifist ethos of American liberal Protestantism, he had to deal with Jesus, not rest with politics.

This was the burden of his signature work, *The Interpretation of Christian Ethics* (1935). Niebuhr said that Jesus taught an ethic of love perfectionism, which is not socially relevant: "The ethic of Jesus does not deal at all with the immediate moral problem of every human life—the problem of attempting some kind of armistice between various contending factions and forces. It has nothing to say about the relativities of politics and economics or of the necessary balances of power which exist and must exist in even the most intimate social relationships."[111]

The teachings of Jesus were counsels of perfection, not prescriptions for social order or justice. Jesus had nothing to say about how a good society should be organized. According to Niebuhr, Jesus lacked any horizontal point of reference and any hint of prudential calculation. His points of reference were always vertical, defining the moral ideal for individuals in their relationship to God. Jesus called his followers to forgive because God forgives; he called them to love their enemies because God's love is impartial. He did not teach that enmity could be transmuted into friendship by returning evil with love. He did not teach his followers to redeem the world through their care or moral effort. These Gandhian sentiments were commonplace in liberal sermons, but Jesus-style love perfectionism is not a social ethic.

Niebuhr said the teaching of Jesus has social relevance in only one sense: It affirmed that a moral ideal exists, which judges all forms of social order or rule. It's a good thing to have an ideal, but the ethic of Jesus, being impossible, offers no guidance on how to hold the world in check. The central problem of politics—justice—is about gaining and defending a relative balance of power. Jesus is no help with that. Niebuhr explained: "The very essence of politics is the achievement of justice through equilibria of power. A balance of power is not conflict; but a tension between opposing forces underlies it. Where there is tension there is potential conflict, and where there is conflict there is potential violence." Since the highest good in the political sphere is to establish justice, justice-making politics cannot disavow resorting to violence. Liberal Christian leaders refused to accept this elementary truism; Niebuhr blasted them repeatedly, especially Mathews, who taught that Christianity is committed to a moral process of regeneration and cooperation. Niebuhr acidly replied, "Christianity, in other words, is interpreted as the preaching of a moral ideal, which men do not follow, but which they ought to."[112]

There is such a thing as legitimate Christian pacifism, Niebuhr allowed, but it was not what liberal pastors in mainline denominations preached, and the Quakers fell short of it too. The real thing was the pacifism of the Franciscans, Mennonites, Amish, and Brethren, which accepted the love perfectionism of Jesus's ethic in a literal way and thus withdrew from active involvement in politics. These communities grasped the vertical orientation of Jesus's teaching and tried to organize their entire lives in accord with its literal meaning. Niebuhr allowed that under sectarian circumstances some practical teaching might be derived from the teaching of Jesus, though he was skeptical. Resistance to violence would be forbidden. Rewards for work or service would be eschewed. Resentment against wrongdoers would be forbidden. Love of enemies would be commanded. This was a tall order even in sectarian communities. Everywhere else, the love perfectionism of Jesus was a relevant impossibility only for individuals in their lives before God. No part of Jesus's ethic is applicable to the problems of social relationships in a fallen world outside the confines of countercultural sects.[113]

The peace of the world in a fallen world cannot be gained by following the way of Christ. Neither is it attainable by turning the perfectionism of Jesus into a social ethic. Peace movements do not bring peace. Niebuhr stressed that middle-class professionals always lead the peace movements—people whose social and economic privileges are made possible by the unacknowledged struggles and violence of others. To inject a perfectionist ethic into politics is to imperil the interests of justice. Realism rests on the Augustinian maxim that the peace of the world is gained by strife.

Niebuhr implored that liberal idealism was no match for the cynical evils of fascism or the enormous savageries of Stalinism and capitalism. Terrible things were happening in the world, yet liberals called for more reason and goodwill. In 1936 Niebuhr scathingly summarized what liberals purported to believe: Injustice is caused by ignorance and cured by education; civilization is gradually becoming more ethically decent; moral individuals are the basis of a decent society; appeals to love and goodwill are always in order; goodness creates happiness; and wars are stupid, prevented by intelligence.[114]

He poured out a torrent of contrary words, charging that liberalism was blind to "the inevitable tragedy of human existence, the irreducible irrationality of human behavior and the tortuous character of human history." Niebuhr blasted Dewey for purveying liberal nonsense, notwithstanding that he and Dewey had nearly the same politics. Both believed that democracy had to be extended into the economic system and that only democratic socialism could achieve social justice, which Niebuhr defined as "a tolerable equilibrium of economic power." Both voted for Thomas on that basis and employed the rhetoric of progress in claiming that socialism was the next step for history to take. In 1936 Niebuhr explained: "Socialism is the logical next step in a technical society, just as certainly as capitalism was a logical first step. First private enterprise developed vast social progress. Then history proved that the private possession of these social processes is incompatible with the necessities of a technical age." To Niebuhr, as for Dewey, modern civilization had to choose between retrogression and progress.[115]

By this reckoning fascism was not a genuine historical alternative but "a frantic effort to escape the logic of history by returning to the primitive." Whatever victories it won, it would produce only "pathological perversities" with no staying power. The real choice, Niebuhr claimed, was between retrogression and radical socialism: "Socialism means the next step forward. That next step is the elimination of the specific causes of anarchy in our present society. The basic specific cause of anarchy and injustice is the disproportion of social power which arises from the private possession of social process." Niebuhr urged that social ownership of the means of production was "a minimal requirement of social health in a technical age."[116]

New Deal reforms, by comparison, were Band-Aids for a dying patient. Niebuhr said capitalism was obviously destroying itself; more important, it had to *be* destroyed before it reduced the Western democracies to barbarism. He stuck to that line through the 1930s. Nothing short of centralized government ownership and control of the economy would save Western civilization. Niebuhr seemed not to notice that his own penetrating analysis of ruling group egotism applied to his solution. Instead of questioning the immense power that state socialism placed in a self-interested, technocratic planning elite, he invoked a dogma: History would move forward to radical state socialism or backward to a barbaric capitalism.

Meanwhile Niebuhr took balanced budget orthodoxy for granted, imploring that budget deficits ruin any chance of an economic recovery, an assumption he shared with leading Socialist officials of the time. In the early 1930s economist John Maynard Keynes urged the British Labour Party coalition government of Ramsay MacDonald to break the downward spiral of the Depression with massive government spending. MacDonald's cabinet argued about it constantly, divided, could not get to yes, and perished. A similar scenario played out in Germany in 1930, with catastrophic consequences. In both cases the finance ministers were prominent Socialists—Philip Snowden and Rudolf Hilferding. Niebuhr agreed with them that Keynesian gas was the worst possible solution; as long as capitalism existed, the responsible policy was to maintain a balanced budget. Niebuhr said Keynes's call for stimulus spending was absurd, and the United States was no place to try it. Thus he ridiculed and condemned the timid, semi-Keynesian policies of Franklin Roosevelt. In FDR's first term the New Deal reduced national unemployment from 25 to 14 percent, and only once, in 1936, did his budget deficit exceed $4 billion. To Niebuhr, however, the serious choice was between nationalizing essential enterprises and balancing the federal budget. Tragically, Roosevelt didn't manage either one; he refused to nationalize the economy and mortgaged the future with budget deficits. Niebuhr urged Roosevelt to raise taxes during the recession of 1937–38, which would have worsened the recession and unemployment.[117]

Three developments in 1935 drove the politics that split the Socialist Party the following year. (1) Moscow called for a Popular Front against fascism. (2) Thomas dragged the party into solidarity work with the Southern Tenant Farmers' Union (STFU), which he helped to found in 1934 in Poinsett County, Tennessee. The AAA, written by Agriculture Secretary Henry Wallace, tried to raise the price of food by paying farmers not to grow crops. Deep South planters were expected to share the funds with tenant farmers, but many evicted the tenants instead, leaving them homeless. Thomas helped two Socialists in Poinsett County, H. L. Mitchell and H. Clay East, found the STFU. The original group consisted of seven black men and eleven white men, which enraged segregationists. The STFU grew rapidly, singing and praying at meetings in the cadences of black church religion. Union members were beaten and murdered by armed thugs, the union was accused of being Communist, and it adopted a black church hymn, "We Shall Not Be Moved." Thomas risked his life in March 1935 by speaking to a large crowd of terrorized sharecroppers in Arkansas. He and Mitchell tried to expel the Communists who joined the STFU, but the union joined its CIO agricultural affiliate, which ensnared the STFU in the usual battle over Communism, exactly as the Old Guard objected. (3) Meanwhile the left wing of the party achieved a dream by founding its own paper, the weekly *Socialist Call.* Its ringleaders were New York Militants Jack Altman, Amicus Most, and Max Delson. Thomas tried to talk them out of it but went along as usual, partly to avoid alienating YPSL.

Youthful converts to radicalism wandered in and out of all the left-wing parties. Those who applied to the Socialists nearly always gravitated to the Militant wing. Some were drawn to the party's sharecropper solidarity work, joining a struggle rife with danger and intense debates over United Front pro-Communism and the threat of being taken over by Communists. The STFU bolted the CIO in 1939 over the latter issue, defending its identity as an alliance of white and black rank-and-file laborers, very few of whom were Communists. The Old Guard did not wait for this story or the larger drama over Communism to play out. It tried to exclude young leftists from joining the party, while the Thomas progressives voted for admission.

The Socialists were too consumed in 1935 with their battles against each other to do much else. Thomas chafed at being censored by *New Leader* editors. The Militants organized a debate between Thomas and Communist Party general secretary Earl Browder at Madison Square Garden, and Julius Gerber threatened Thomas with expulsion if he appeared alongside Browder. Browder flattered Thomas assiduously at the debate, pleading for a united front. Thomas gave his usual mixed message about Moscow. If Soviet Communism was so great, why did Russians have no freedom? He rebuffed Browder on a formal alliance, declaring that Communists behaved too badly for it to be possible. That did not appease the Old Guard, which seethed that Thomas bantered with Browder and sang the International with him. The Old Guard struck back by dissolving twelve New York City branches dominated by Militants; it swung the vote in the NEC by persuading just enough Progressives to take a stand against the Militants. Thomas and the Militants formed a rump party of upstate locals, calling itself the Socialist Party in New York State, and Waldman declared that if the party did not disavow the Detroit Declaration the Old Guard would walk out.[118]

Meanwhile the leading American left-wing youth organizations surged into the Popular Front, though confusedly, uniting ostensibly on the basis of antiwar commitments. YPSL, the Young Communist League, the Student League for Industrial Democracy, and the National Students League merged in 1936, forming the American Student Union (ASU). The group's national secretary was Socialist pacifist Joseph Lash, who was veering at the time from pacifism to

an idea that fit the Popular Front better, collective security. ASU held its founding convention in Columbus, Ohio, inviting Niebuhr to give the keynote
address. Niebuhr stunned the convention with a blistering attack on socialist
pacifism, calling ASU to unite on the basis of collective security against fascism,
not pacifism. The Young Communist League, from the beginning, had the
inside track on taking over ASU and determining how it conceived unity leftism. Niebuhr played an inadvertent role in helping it succeed.[119]

Niebuhr began voting for FDR in 1936, in accord with his later pragmatism
but not in accord with what he said at the time. The later Niebuhrian explanation was that socialism barely existed politically, FDR carried out most of the
Socialist platform, and FDR advocated collective security, so Niebuhr held his
nose and voted Democrat. The later Niebuhr exemplified the pragmatism that
brought Hillman, Dubinsky, and other Socialists into the Democratic Party.
Why stick with a Socialist sect if Roosevelt enacted most of the socialist agenda?

But in 1936 Niebuhr said the New Deal was disastrously wrong and America
needed to move sharply left. Thus he urged Thomas to embrace the Militants
and drive out the Old Guard, claiming it would energize the real socialists and
renew the party. The fatal problem of the Socialist Party, on this reading, was
the existence of its grumpy conservative wing that clung to the AFL unions,
scrupulously obeyed the law, and railed against Communism, both real and
imagined. Niebuhr said the Old Guard "has not learned a single lesson from
events." Only a spiritually corrupted socialism would have an Old Guard: "The
touching devotion of right-wing socialism to legality and the constitution is
proof either of inability or unwillingness to profit from the clear lessons of
recent history or it is merely a convenient ideological tool for suppressing new
life in the party."[120]

The rival factions slugged it out at the 1936 convention in Cleveland. Allen,
Krueger, Krzycki, Niebuhr, and physicist Alfred Sprague Coolidge exhorted
Thomas to break the Old Guard. Thomas told them that losing the Old Guard
strongholds in New York and Massachusetts would not hurt very much, even if
they also lost Connecticut and Pennsylvania. Niebuhr said that was exactly
right. The convention split the party, the Old Guard walked out, and the toll of
losses included the *Forward*, the *New Leader*, radio station WEVD, the Rand
School, several summer camps, the garment unions, and the party's municipal
political machines in Bridgeport, Connecticut, and Reading, Pennsylvania.
Niebuhr wrote in *Radical Religion*, "Many friendly critics of the party think
that this split will destroy whatever prospects of future usefulness the party may
have had. They are in error." The vital forces of the party, he explained, did not
belong to the Old Guard: "In New York there is already a remarkable burst of

new energy in the party since the hand of the Old Guard has been removed from the wheel of power."[121]

That was pure projection fueled by ideology, personal animus, and left-wing New York noise. The Militants made a lot of noise, but Niebuhr was guilty of the very naïveté and self-delusion he attributed to social gospel progressives. He and the Militants harmed the party by stereotyping the Old Guard as a grumpy machine club that clung to its union perches, excessively criticized Communism, and stifled the youth. The Old Guard was not monolithic in its ideology or even its grumpiness. It had a lot of stodgy types fitting the stereotype, but it also had able leaders who were chastened by their collective history. The foremost Old Guard leaders after Hillquit died, Waldman and Oneal, were principled democrats who defended the socialist conviction that socialists are supposed to believe in decentralized worker self-determination, not the salvation of a centralized state. To the extent that the Old Guard leaders approximated a monolith, it was on anti-Communism, where they were more right than wrong, and sometimes very wrong. They remembered vividly what it felt like to be destroyed in 1919. They rightly refused to join the Comintern and rightly thwarted Communists from controlling the unions. Many were too eager to believe that Communists ruined everything they touched, which allowed the Old Guard Socialists to excuse their weak record in racial justice organizing. The Old Guard Socialists overreacted against a surge of youthful Leninism because they had seen an earlier version destroy their party in a few months. Then they watched the party take a beating from a band of Trotskyites.

During the clamor for unity leftism in 1935 Thomas invited various non-Stalinist Communist sects to join the Socialist Party. Gitlow, midway on his journey from Lenin to the Republican right, and Lovestone, not yet ensconced in the ILGWU, had tiny groups that came aboard. Fatefully, three hundred Trotskyites also entered the party. The Trotskyites were a breed apart. They were Leninist revolutionaries who hated Stalin for hijacking Soviet Communism. They annoyed liberals and fellow travelers by harping on Stalin's crimes, which curtailed their prospects for united fronts. They had no party until 1937, but they had brilliant propagandists and a distinct bravado, in the fashion of Trotsky himself. Former *Masses* editor Eastman was the original American Trotskyite. James Cannon, falling from the Communist hierarchy after Trotsky fell, led the American Trotskyites into the Socialist Party. Max Shachtman, an autodidactic intellectual, built the American Trotskyite movement with Cannon after the Communist Party expelled them. James Burnham, a New York University philosopher, helped Muste found the American Workers Party just before he helped Trotsky take it over. Sidney Hook, another New York University philosophy professor, facilitated the entry of the Trotskyites into the Socialist Party, though Hook never quite joined the Trotskyites. The Trotskyite tradition lacked deep roots in American unionism, but it was a magnet for intellectuals thriving on Marxology and factional intrigue. Thomas forced the Trotskyites to join as individuals subject to local branch approval, which did not stop them from carrying out a classic sabotage campaign of rule or ruin, orchestrated by Trotsky in Norway. The Trotskyites had honed their vulture skills by devouring Muste's party. Now they sought a bigger prize.

Some of them sincerely sought to create a united left party on the basis of Trotsky's anti-Stalinism. Trinidadian historian C. L. R. James was a Trotskyite in the mid-1930s, writing an acclaimed history of the Communist International in 1937 and a history of the Haitian revolution in 1938. The Trotskyites wanted James to be the herald of black Trotskyism, but Trotsky's model for that was the Bolshevik domination of ethnic minorities in Russia. Trotsky and Cannon were contemptuous of the entire Socialist Party. Trotsky said Thomas counted himself a Socialist because of a misunderstanding. Cannon said the Militants were "ignorant, untalented, petty-minded, weak, cowardly, treacherous, and vain. They had other faults too." They saw themselves in a distorting mirror while imagining themselves to be Socialists. It repelled Cannon to consort with them, but "a Trotskyist will do anything for the party, even if he has to crawl on his belly in the mud." Thomas and the Socialists tried to create a broad antifascist unity. Cannon found their innocence pathetically laughable, chortling that the Socialists soon wished they had never heard of Trotskyism. By the time Thomas campaigned for votes in the 1936 election he realized that the Trotskyite experiment was another disaster, without knowing what to do about it.[122]

Losing the Old Guard reframed the bitter factionalism in the party. Herbert Zam, Gus Tyler, and Max Delson rebooted the Militants as the Clarity caucus, adopting the name of their doctrinaire periodical, *Socialist Clarity*. The Progressives instantly became the right wing of the party, to their discomfort. Meanwhile the Old Guard reorganized as the Social Democratic Federation (SDF), enlisting Hillman and Dubinsky to help finance a new organization. Hillman and Dubinsky cofounded the American Labor Party (ALP), which operated almost exclusively in New York State, allowing them to support FDR without being tainted by Tammany. The SDF reestablished its political base by aligning with the ALP, revamping so readily that Thomas had to reply. He panned that the SDF was not socialist or democratic or even a federation; it was a halfway port to Tammany Hall. That was quotably snarky but didn't stop party chair Krzycki from defecting to Hillman and FDR, embarrassing Thomas. The Socialists boasted high-ranking CIO officials Franz Daniel and Powers Hapgood, but they kept a low profile, striving not to offend their pro-FDR bosses. Historian David Shannon said the 1936 schism reduced the party from a political force to a political sect. That was not quite right because a sect has a prescribed creed or ideology. The Socialists became something between a party and a sect, retaining party-like flexibility in a tiny group. The bitter irony was that it happened amid the worst economic crisis in American history.[123]

Thomas felt the fallout from the schism on the campaign trail. He stressed that FDR did nothing for racial justice or southern sharecroppers and that twelve million men and women were jobless. He said FDR wisely ransacked the Socialist platform instead of his own campaign speeches, but the New Deal was a shaky house that would not stand. Thomas got anemic responses and knew what was coming—humiliation. On the last day of the campaign he confessed to Krueger that he was depressed and near despairing. He won 0.4 percent of the vote; meanwhile in New York State the ALP racked up three times as many votes as the Socialists.

Roosevelt co-opted and outsmarted the entire left, humiliating the Socialists who held out against him. Within the Socialist Party the Militants had only a rebellious attitude and no real anchor, and Trotskyite sabotage had to be confronted. First, Thomas went to Europe to clear his head and answer two questions: Why did England and France not help the Spanish Republic repel fascism? And what was the state of the Russian situation? Britons told Thomas the French didn't want to intervene, and French officials said they deferred to Britain. Thomas was appalled that Britain and France wrote off Spain so cavalierly. In Russia he saw things he liked—a certain national vigor, better racial relations than in the United States, and, most important, a determination to help the Republican Loyalists repel fascism in Spain. But mostly, Russia distressed him. Thomas was repulsed by the enormous throngs of political prisoners enslaved under armed guards, an entitled political class and Red Army that lived far better than the impoverished masses, wretched housing conditions, nothing close to intellectual or press freedom, and a palpable pall of fear. He and Violet Thomas were happy to leave Russia, stopping in three nations they liked, Finland, Sweden, and Denmark. They toured Poland, Germany, Czechoslovakia, and Austria on their way to Spain, where Thomas met with Republican prime minister Juan Negrín and visited the front, near Teruel, of the Spanish Civil War. Negrín said the republic needed war equipment and mechanics, which they got only from Russia.[124]

Thomas called on FDR at the White House, who wanted no part of an arms or supplies embargo on Spanish fascists. Nearly three thousand American volunteers called the Abraham Lincoln Brigade took up arms to defend the

Spanish Republic against fascist general Francisco Franco, who was aided by Hitler and Mussolini. Upward of 60 percent of the Lincoln volunteers came from the Young Communist League, and the Socialists sponsored a unit called the Debs Column. FDR jauntily called it the Debutantes Column. Thomas implored Roosevelt to enforce the Neutrality Law against the Germans and Italians fighting an undeclared war against the legal Spanish government. He warned that Spain could be the tripwire for World War II. Franco had to be stopped; otherwise fascists would surround France on three sides. Roosevelt listened intently but laughed off the warning about World War II and assured Thomas that few American arms were getting to Franco. Then he changed the subject to the Catholic vote in the United States. Thomas got the message — Roosevelt believed in collective security, more or less, but he cared mostly about domestic politics. His respect for Roosevelt plummeted.[125]

Meanwhile Thomas faced up to his sabotage problem, expelling the Trotskyites in August 1937. They took 1,000 members with them, including most of the youth section, YPSL. Howe, Hal Draper, and YPSL national chair Ernest Erber followed Cannon and Shachtman into a new party in 1938, the Socialist Workers Party (SWP). Cannon appealed to old-school radicals who were not from New York or college educated. He grew up in Kansas as the son of Irish immigrants and came to Communism through hobo organizing in the IWW. He was steely, resolute, plodding, a bombastic speaker, and not much for theory, wearing proudly his status as a founder of American Communism. Shachtman was a Jewish New Yorker to the core, excitable, passionate, funny, and prone to ironic asides, with an occasional suggestion of independence. Many of the YPSL radicals who bolted to the SWP were Shachtmanites, enthralled by his high-flying Leninist oratory and bawdy humor. The Trotskyite episode humiliated Thomas and further impaired his ability to lead the party. He told friends the Socialist Party was bound to be small with or without Communists of any kind, and he wished he had seen it earlier. Everything seemed to go against him; even American Communists outperformed the Socialists and him. In 1932 Foster won only 103,000 votes, and Thomas won almost 900,000, yet by 1936 the Communist Party was surging, accomplished, and the strongest force on the left.

American Stalinists had several factors working in their favor. The prestige of the Soviet Union grew through the mid-1930s as Russia evaded the ravages of the Depression. The Soviets touted the success of their planned economy and heightened their moral stature by leading the fight for collective security against fascism, especially in Spain. Moreover, by 1935 Communists applauded the New Deal and surpassed Socialists in the organizing fields. In 1936 they ran a token campaign for Browder while working to reelect Roosevelt. They built CIO unions and fought for racial justice, winning deserved credit in both causes. They rose to power in unions they organized, plowing money and organizers into civil rights organizations.

Socialists did not lack important successes in the CIO unions, especially in the dominant CIO union, the UAW. Roy Reuther and Victor Reuther were Socialists, Roy was a member of the NEC, he brought the party into the UAW, and he pulled his volatile pro-Communist brother Walter Reuther into the Socialist orbit. The Reuthers built the UAW into a progressive powerhouse that changed the auto industry, supported the civil rights movement, and forged alliances with other unions sprinkled with Socialists. But Thomas grieved that American Communists raced past his party on his watch, despite the cascade of repellent spectacles in Russia. He wished he had understood better what was occurring in Russia. The Moscow Trials of 1936–38 sickened and turned him. Stalin tried and executed former comrades in the Trotsky–Zinoviev left, the Pyatakov–Radek Trotskyite center, and the Bukharin–Rykov right. Thomas said it should not have taken the purges and slave labor camps to awaken him. The party suffered accordingly, but it was pointless to mope about the party now that the threat of another world war overshadowed everything. Thomas fixed fervently on preventing the next war.

He was no longer a pacifist. Being vehemently antifascist in the mid-1930s dispelled Thomas's aspiration to be like Gandhi. He said so when people queried how he could support the Lincoln Brigade. But Thomas was still passionately antiwar, and by 1939 he was crestfallen at realizing that Communists controlled the Lincoln Brigade. Moreover, even Niebuhr was still passionately antiwar in 1938. Both implored FDR to prevent another march to war. Contrary to countless renderings of Niebuhr, he did not spend the 1930s urging his nation to arm for a war against fascism. As late as March 1939 Niebuhr was opposed to preparing for war. FDR gave his famous Quarantine Speech on October 5, 1937, to rally peaceful nations to isolate the aggressive nations. Japan had invaded China; Italy had invaded Abyssinia and was helping Germany topple the Second Spanish Republic; and Hitler had remilitarized the Rhineland, violating the Treaty of Versailles. FDR said that just as a community quarantines a few members who are afflicted by a disease, the peace-loving nations had to quarantine aggressive powers that endangered world peace. He did not recommend specific policies or even cite Japan, Italy, and Germany by name, which sparked contrary interpretations of his intention and a raging debate about specific forms of intervention, isolation, and collective security. FDR built up the navy and vastly expanded the military, preparing for options that pacifists and anti-interventionists did not want.[126]

Niebuhr stridently condemned Roosevelt's naval buildup in 1937, describing it as a sinister evil to be resisted at all costs. The next year Niebuhr blasted Roosevelt's billion-dollar defense budget as "the worst piece of militarism in modern history," a stunning exaggeration considering what the Empire of Japan and Nazi Germany were doing. Right up to the Munich crisis of September 1938, Niebuhr insisted that the best way to avoid war is not to prepare for one; collective security is the realistic alternative to war. He wanted the United States to enact neutrality legislation and voluntarily support League of Nations sanctions. He and Thomas were allies on this subject, though Thomas recoiled at Niebuhr's attacks on ethical idealism. Thomas concluded in 1937 that a world war was inevitable and imminent. He responded to his dismal meeting with FDR by founding the Keep America out of War Congress, warning that another war was coming and America needed desperately to stay out of it.[127]

By the end of the 1930s Niebuhr was willing to say that the New Deal got America through the worst of the Depression, and Socialists needed to defend it against its reactionary critics. But he persisted that Roosevelt's deficit spending was a form of insulin "which wards off dissolution without giving the patient health." The New Dealers were quacks who pretended not to realize that their cure worked only for a short while: "This quackery must be recognized and exposed." Sometimes he called it "whirligig reform." In 1938 Niebuhr exclaimed, "If that man could only make up his mind to cross the Rubicon! A better metaphor is that he is like Lot's wife. Let him beware lest he turn into a pillar of salt." Meanwhile he opposed Roosevelt's preparation for war until 1939, when he flipped to urging FDR and the United States to support embattled Britain. Upon calling his nation to rally behind Britain, Niebuhr announced almost casually that he had resigned from the Socialist Party. Socialists needed to get this issue right, and by his lights the party had already failed.[128]

A GLIMMER OF HOPE: THE BROTHERHOOD OF PORTERS

For many years Du Bois and Mary White Ovington had held a running debate about Communists. Du Bois found them crude and dishonest, chiding Ovington for having Communist friends. She said he was too snooty in his intellectualism and that "workers of the world unite" was the essence of radicalism. Du Bois shucked off much of his scorn when he visited Russia in 1926 at the height of the New Economic Policy, catching the Soviet experiment in a hopeful moment. Five years later, in "The Negro and Communism," he said Communism was powered by the mighty truth that capitalism is inherently predatory and unsustainable, resting on "the slavery and semi-slavery of the colored world." White capital kept white labor in chains by oppressing people of color. To Du Bois, the Marxist dream of a united proletariat was the answer, but white labor had to take the "first step toward the emancipation of colored labor."[129]

In 1933 he rued that it was not happening, despite all the crashing. Du Bois had not studied Marx seriously until he wrote "Marxism and the Negro Problem." He ran through the labor theory of value; capital as machines, materials, and wages paid for labor; surplus value; the exploitation of laborers; and the inevitability of revolution. Whatever might be wrong about these ideas, Du Bois said, it was hard to deny that labor is the foundation of value and capitalism is stupendously exploitative and destructive. The Depression was a textbook Marxian crisis of exploitation and overproduction. Du Bois deeply admired Marx, "a colossal genius of infinite sacrifice and monumental industry." He especially prized Marx's analysis of boom-and-bust cycles. Marx explained nineteenth-century capitalism better than anybody, and his theory offered the best explanation of why capitalist civilization collapsed in 1929.[130]

Except Marxist theory and strategy did not apply straightaway to the problem of the color line. Du Bois put it sharply: "Colored labor has no common ground with white labor." No white proletariat anywhere, he observed, sought to make people of color equal to it economically, politically, and socially. The Socialist Party was clear and brave about socialism but vague and tongue-tied about the rights of blacks. Du Bois said black Americans were exploited "to a degree that means poverty, crime, delinquency, and indigence." This exploitation came from white capitalists and the white proletariat, not from an almost nonexistent black capitalist class. The white proletariat and the white capitalist class were equally hostile to blacks. Elsewhere Du Bois clarified that actually the white proletariat was worse because some white capitalists cared about black Americans, unlike the AFL. To white unionists, African Americans were subservient to their interests, just as white unionists were subservient to the interests of capital. Black Americans were left with no choice. They built survival organizations protecting them from both white enemies, and they cut deals with the handful of white capitalists and professional class liberals who had a conscience about racism.[131]

Du Bois still hoped the Depression might open the door to global revolution. America's fantastic industrial machine teetered on ruination. The trade unions representing skilled labor were "double-tongued and helpless." Unskilled white labor was too frightened by competition from blacks to unite with them, "it only begs a dole." Du Bois cried out, "There is not at present the slightest indication that a Marxian revolution based on a united class-conscious proletariat is anywhere on the American far horizon." All he could do was hope that black workers alone, the only true believers in political and economic democracy, might "in time make the workers of the world effective dictators of civilization."[132]

To him, this was an argument against the draining and perhaps futile politics of racial integration, the only kind the NAACP practiced. Du Bois was plotting his exit from the NAACP. If there was a way forward, it had to be through black-controlled institutions, schools, and businesses—a black cooperative economy modeled on nineteenth-century utopian socialism, linked with friendly Socialist or Communist parties. It surprised Du Bois to end up with a solution that barely existed in American society. He reached near-despair just before the colossal crashing and suffering of the Depression enabled one socialist dream to come true—the rise of CIO industrial unions lacking a color bar.

Yet the great breakthrough for black American unionism was built on the old craft model within the bastion of craft unionism, the AFL. Randolph had retired from union organizing in 1925 when Ashley Totten got him to speak to the Pullman Porters Athletic Association in New York. He was sick of failing and finished with unions, lacking any clue that this was the exception knocking at his door. Randolph inspired his usual handful of enthusiasts at the athletic association and insisted he was not the answer. They persisted, and he yielded, launching the Brotherhood of Sleeping Car Porters (BSCP) at the Elks lodge in Harlem on August 25, 1925.

Five hundred porters attended the founding meeting; two hundred joined; and Randolph shielded them from providing incriminating information to the Pullman spies. The founding was a resounding success, propelling Randolph to organize outside New York, where everything was harder. Chicago was the biggest prize for porter unionizing, followed by St. Louis and Oakland. Randolph recruited outstanding organizers in Chicago (Milton Webster), St. Louis (E. J. Bradley), and Oakland (Morris "Dad" Moore). His courtly elegance was off-putting to the rough-hewn organizers he recruited; Randolph had to win them over. The union grew because he recruited tenacious, self-sacrificing organizers who refused to be intimidated. By the end of 1926 the brotherhood had locals in sixteen cities, which proved to be the easy part.

The BSCP had to operate like a secret society because Pullman infiltrated every local and ruthlessly fired entire locals. Webster became nearly as indispensable to the brotherhood as Randolph, running the machinery and enforcing discipline while Randolph riveted lecture audiences across the country. Montgomery, Alabama, porter E. D. Nixon heard him in 1926. Years after Nixon played a key role in propelling Martin Luther King Jr. to fame he recalled that Randolph was the most eloquent speaker he ever heard: "I never knew the Negro had a right to enjoy freedom like everyone else. When Randolph stood there and talked that day it made a different man out of me. From that day on, I was determined that I was gonna fight for freedom until I was able to get some of it myself."[133]

The Railway Labor Act of 1926 seemed like a breakthrough, ordering railroad carriers to resolve their disputes with employees, but Pullman used its power to fend off complying, and the union floundered badly, losing members. Randolph found a few clerical allies in New York black social gospel churches—Lloyd Imes at St. James Presbyterian Church, Frederick Cullen at Salem Methodist Church, and Adam Clayton Powell Sr. at Abyssinian Baptist Church. But most black churches were hostile. The Harlem *Amsterdam News*, Chandler Owen at the *Chicago Bee*, and young Roy Wilkins at the *Kansas City Call* were supportive. But most of the black press was hostile, chastising Randolph for endangering the porters and sowing socialist discord. The *Pittsburgh Courier* charged that Randolph's radicalism fatally tainted the BSCP. The American Negro Labor Congress—a Communist front led by Randolph's former allies Otto Huiswood, Lovett Fort-Whiteman, and Richard B. Moore—said the opposite, charging that Randolph was a stooge of the AFL. Randolph welcomed moral support from white progressives and John L. Lewis but refused to take money from Lewis, explaining that black Americans had to win this fight on their own. In 1929 he won a half victory by wrangling a halfway entry into the AFL under the direct jurisdiction of AFL president William Green. Randolph had to eat his *Messenger* rants about the evil machine better called the American Separation of Labor. Eking into the AFL kept his tiny, fledgling, battered union barely alive. As late as 1933 the BSCP had only 650 members, nearly half from Chicago.[134]

The New Deal swiftly plugged the holes in the Railway Labor Act of 1926, affirming the right of employees to organize and bargain collectively through representatives of their choosing and prohibiting companies from requiring employees to join company unions. These provisions became law under the NIRA and the Emergency Railroad Transportation Act. Pullman concocted an independent union, but the BSCP overwhelmingly won the right to represent Pullman porters and maids in July 1935—a stupendous victory for Randolph, Webster, Bradley, and Dad Moore's successor, Socialist firebrand C. L. Dellums. It took another two years for the Pullman company to begin actual bargaining with the union—the defeat was so unbelievable and bitterly unacceptable to Pullman executives.

Black women played an important role in the survival and success of the BSCP, many served as auxiliary leaders, and some became union organizers. Lucille Randolph enlisted her fellow Walker salon operators to donate prizes for BSCP beauty contests and thus acquainted Harlem women with the union.

Her salon on 135th Street was a distribution center for the *Messenger*. Maida Springer, a Harlem labor organizer, supported the BSCP through its entire run, as did Neva Ryan and Irene Goins in Chicago. Ryan founded the Domestic Workers' Union, and Goins organized African American meatpackers. They heard Randolph insist that black women were exploited and oppressed like black men and sought freedom very much like black men. Randolph told the New York division of BSCP on its second anniversary in 1926 that women had to be organized no less than men. Thus he launched an auxiliary of the BSCP called the Colored Women's Economic Council, declaring, "Its program and mission are primarily and fundamentally economic. It is the first of its kind among Negroes in the world. Its plan is to contribute the knowledge of, and develop the interest in, the labor and competitive movements of America in particular and in the world in general, to the Negro women of the country."[135]

Melinda Chateauvert, the first scholar to give the women of the BSCP their due, stresses that "auxiliary" meant "secondary to the union," and it basically served as the wife of the brotherhood. The Colored Women's Economic Council did not advocate for Pullman maids or the right of women to join the BSCP. Halena Wilson became president of the Chicago auxiliary in 1931 and moved upward to the presidency of the international auxiliary in 1938. She was an advocate of the union wife as distinguished from the union woman, scaling the ranks of the auxiliary and the AFL by insisting on the difference. Still, she changed the conversation by being there, where she clashed with an equally formidable auxiliary leader, Rosina Corrothers Tucker, who advocated for Pullman maids and insisted that women should be able to join the brotherhood. Tucker was married to a Harlem Renaissance poet and minister, James David Corrothers, before she married a Washington, DC, Pullman porter, Berthea Tucker. She joined Fifteenth Street Presbyterian Church, dragged its class-conscious minister Francis Grimké into supporting the BSCP, and pushed the auxiliary to act like a union.[136]

Other black women became union organizers through the ILGWU and the American Federation of Teachers (AFT). Flora Pinkney, a graduate of Brookwood Labor College, became the first African American female organizer for ILGWU. Gertrude Elise MacDougald Ayers became an important AFT organizer while serving as vice principal of Public School 89 in Harlem. Both were movement pioneers during the impossible years. They watched Randolph skyrocket from scorned marginality to national fame. Writing off the unions as impossibly racist did not feel like an option to them, and there was something strangely exceptional about how unions got judged. Somehow unions were judged by a standard of moral righteousness that nobody applied to Harvard or

Princeton. If people clamored to get into Harvard and Princeton despite their miserably racist histories, how could Randolph be wrong to break into the AFL?

He accepted the presidency of a new organization, the National Negro Congress, which held its founding convention at Howard University in February 1936. Randolph had never regarded the brotherhood as merely a labor organization; to him it was the vanguard of a radical black political movement. He told the founding National Negro Congress that the New Deal was nowhere near what America needed. The New Deal did not change the profit system or lift human rights above property rights. It used the power of the state to support business interests and did nothing to thwart American fascism or the next war. Randolph commended the many Communists and pro-Communists in attendance for forging united fronts with liberals against fascism. He said he was grateful to the white and black Communists who supported the congress, while stating pointedly that black Americans could not solve their problems by relying on the favor of white Communists, white Socialists, or white liberals. Black Americans had to rely on their own ingenuity and skill.[137]

That showed his wary eye on the Communist problem and offered his response to it. Communists operated more adeptly in the National Negro Congress than they often managed elsewhere. They stayed in the background while volunteering for grunge work. They provided funding, organizers, and day-after-day volunteers without intruding on the authority of Randolph, national secretary John P. Davis, Urban League leaders Lester Granger and Elmer Carter, Howard University philosopher Alain Locke, and Rosenwald Fund official M. O. Bousfield. The congress developed active local chapters in more than seventy cities. In many cities it surpassed the NAACP as the leading black community organization, playing a crucial role in recruiting black workers into CIO unions. Randolph mixed his pride in its constructive work with a certain wariness of what he suspected but did not know for sure about the extent of its reliance on the Communist Party. In 1937 he claimed at the Second Congress in Philadelphia that the congress was solely a black American movement fighting for the rights of black Americans. He would not have said it had he not believed it.[138]

Three years later, in a very different situation, Randolph took it all back. By then he knew the congress was an outright Communist front and that much of its CIO support came from Communist-controlled unions. The Stalinist line changed again after the Nazi–Soviet pact of August 1939 left Hitler free to invade Poland. For true-believing united front leftists the Nazi–Soviet pact was shattering. Even for rationalizing fellow travelers it was very hard to swallow. Many of them packed into the Third Congress in 1940 in Washington, DC.

Randolph told them the Soviet Union operated much like the imperialist nations, pursuing its own interests; it was ludicrous to believe that Soviet leaders cared about the rights of black Americans.

He lost most of the audience as he spoke, watching entire rows of black and white Communists exit together. Randolph tried to soften the blow by saying he didn't want to be in a congress controlled by Communists *or* the CIO. He quit the National Negro Congress because it turned out not to be a Negro congress. He could not abide being in a pro-Soviet organization because Stalin annihilated the dream of democracy and liberty in Russia, blood purging anybody who didn't obey him. Then Stalin cut a deal with Hitler. Randolph worried briefly that he had sabotaged his standing, coming off as a red-baiting traitor and bully. Instead, he found that he had changed course just in time, lifting him higher than ever.[139]

5

WORLD WAR EMERGENCY, COLD WAR VOID, AND BLACK FREEDOM ERUPTION

World War II was a global emergency that split American Socialists down the middle before Pearl Harbor ended the debate. In the 1930s Norman Thomas urged Socialists to stand against militarism, imperialism, fascism, and capitalism, and by 1937 his loathing of Stalin and Communism had made him unwilling to ally with Communists in fighting any of these foes. Thus he inveighed against Franklin Roosevelt's path to war every step of the way, until December 1941. Thomas denied that defeating fascism trumped the socialist opposition to militarism and imperialism. In October 1939 he submitted a resignation letter that would have taken effect had the Socialist Party disavowed its antiwar position. Thomas and the party applied the St. Louis Manifesto to World War II, but Reinhold Niebuhr rightly countered that Nazi fascism presented a supreme emergency surpassing what was at stake in 1917. Niebuhr led a group of socialist internationalists who went on to realign left-liberal politics. He went on to mythologize the conceits and fears of the Cold War and temporize on the eruption of the 1950s against American racism, while recognizing that the Cold War had turned his beloved nation into a lethal global empire still insisting on its innocence.

Thomas agonized from the beginning of World War II that his position would alienate him from treasured friends and align him with isolationists he could barely stand. He told the *New York Herald Tribune* on September 12, 1939, that the disciples of Machiavelli changed sides so often it was pointless to judge a course of action by the company it acquired; the best policy was to stick with socialist ethical principles. The majority of New York City Socialists were Jews with persecuted relatives in Germany. Thomas urged Roosevelt to rescue European Jews, but he denied that America should go to war to do so; nobody in his group said otherwise. In October 1939 Thomas told a New York City Jewish comrade: "It is our whole philosophy of life, our whole program for Socialism which is at stake." If Debs could withstand the prowar onslaught, "we can." Thomas founded the Keep America out of War Congress (KAOWC) to unite the peace organizations—FOR, the War Resisters League (WRL), the National Council for Prevention of War, the Commission for World Peace of the Methodist General Conference, World Peaceways, the Women's International League for Peace and Freedom, the Peace Committee of the General Conference of American Rabbis, the left-wing American Peace Mobilization, and the mostly right-wing America First Committee. KAOWC implored Roosevelt to remove U.S. ships and nationals from belligerent zones and abandon his plans for conscription and industrial mobilization. Meanwhile the Socialist Party underwent what socialists sorrowfully called the silent split. Half the *Socialist Call* editorial board supported the Allied nations, opposing what Thomas was doing in the Socialist Party and KAOWC.[1]

Thomas deeply feared that going to war would shred American liberal democracy. One measure of this fear was that he spent the fall of 1939 ousting Harry Ward from chairing the American Civil Liberties Union (ACLU). Ward was a prominent united front radical, social gospel Methodist, and Union Theological Seminary professor who defended civil liberties, didn't believe in joining parties, never cast an electoral vote, and was not a Communist. But to him, good united leftism defended the Soviet Union. Ward poured out writings heralding the great socialist breakthrough in Russia and rationalizing Stalin's prison camps and purges. He chaired the American League for Peace and Democracy, a pro-Communist front that got in trouble with the House Special Committee to Investigate Un-American Activities (HUAC). Thomas fretted that HUAC would target the ACLU because of Ward and Communist board member Elizabeth Gurley Flynn. He said Ward was a dupe for a unity-leftism that would turn America red fascist or, more likely, black fascist. Defending the civil liberties of Communists or Fascists was valid only if one protected liberal institutions from being sabotaged by Communists and Fascists. Moreover, preserving the ACLU was imperative. Thomas planted a flag on this issue and fought for it aggressively, ousting his friends Ward and Flynn; John Haynes Holmes succeeded Ward as ACLU chair.[2]

KAOWC enlisted the religious pacifists in Thomas's orbit—Holmes, Muste, Riverside Church pastor Harry Emerson Fosdick, former Abyssinian Church pastor Adam Clayton Powell Sr., Rabbi Isidor Hoffman, and *Catholic Worker* founder Dorothy Day—and his Socialist allies A. Philip Randolph, Bertram D. Wolfe, Jay Lovestone, Louis Nelson, and Harry Laidler. Randolph brought

Ashley Totten into KAOWC, and Muste and Randolph brought young black FOR activist James Farmer into it. Lovestone bonded with Thomas on his way to a more rewarding refuge in the AFL. The America First Committee got the most press attention because it was nationalistic, lavishly funded, mostly right wing, and had a famous speaker, aviation celebrity Charles Lindbergh. Thomas went back and forth on whether the fascist-leaning Lindbergh was worth the trouble, and it gnawed at him that his most reliable allies were absolute pacifists since he wasn't a pacifist. He was upholding the old socialist faith that capitalist wars are imperialist struggles between capitalist powers.

Much of the silent split had already occurred when the Socialists convened in April 1940 at the National Press Club Auditorium in Washington, DC. The party was down to 5,000 members, and only a small rump group led by Jack Altman and Gus Tyler showed up to contend against neutralism. Altman careened from being close to Thomas to berating him; Tyler went on to a long career as a high-ranking ILGWU official and columnist for the English-version *Forward*, founded in 1983. The Socialists voted 159 to 28 for an antiwar platform declaring that the vengeance and imperial arrogance of the capitalist victors of World War I paved the way to fascism. Battlefield victories would not destroy Hitlerism. The roots of fascism and war had to be abolished, which would never happen if the world's leading democracy ceased being a democracy: "If America enters the war, we shall be subjected to military dictatorship, the regimentation of labor and the ultimate economic collapse that must follow war. In an effort to 'save democracy,' we shall have destroyed its only remaining citadel."[3]

The convention made two changes that marked the party in its twilight. It scrapped the timeworn socialist dichotomy between immediate demands and governing principles, now weaving its policy proposals into its declaration of principles, and it moved the national office to New York, relinquishing the party's thirty-five-year attempt to nest American socialism in Chicago. "Moved" was not quite literal in this case because the new office made no attempt to save the papers held in Chicago. They survived only because a wastepaper dealer hired to clear out the office sold them to a book dealer who sold them to Duke University. Not caring to preserve their history was a sign of demoralization. The Socialist remnant despaired at the quiet exodus of Socialists from the right and left flanks of the party. Niebuhr, meanwhile, steamed with anger that a squishy, provincial, sort-of idealistic form of isolationist pacifism had the upper hand in American politics and was sanctified by liberal Protestant leaders.

Niebuhr agreed to give the Gifford Lectures of 1939 in Edinburgh and ago-nized at his inability to write them. This was his chance to prove he was a theo-logian, not merely a social critic. He swore off political speaking while trying to torture the lectures out of his head and research. He made a speaking exception in November 1938 for Ward's American League for Peace and Democracy, blasting neutralists and isolationists while conveying his skittishness about Ward's throng of religious radicals and Communists. Niebuhr called for America to help the European democracies without saying that America should intervene if war commenced. Admittedly, the democratic empires sowed the seeds of fascism but allowing European democracy to be destroyed was unthinkable. In that frame of mind he gave his first round of Gifford Lectures at Rainy Hall in April 1939, delivering ten lectures on human nature, all in Niebuhr's inimitable whirling, pacing, gesticulating, rapid-fire, extemporaneous style. Many said they couldn't follow his train of thought or even begin to track it, yet they kept returning to hear him. On his way home Niebuhr spoke to a Christian youth conference in Amsterdam, where the government almost shut him down out of fear that he would provoke the Nazis across the border. At the last minute the Dutch government secured an assurance from William Adams Brown that Niebuhr was not a Communist before it allowed the speech to proceed.[4]

Hitler and Stalin signed their nonaggression pact on August 23, and Hitler invaded Poland on September 1; Niebuhr said the Nazi–Soviet pact shocked him and the war did not. For years he had cautioned left-wing comrades that Soviet ideology camouflaged the lion of Russian nationalism; Stalin, he judged, was a consummate realist and nationalist. Niebuhr did not swing up and down about Stalin like his Socialist friends. He respected Stalin without revering him and was not crushed, like Thomas, by the prison camps and purges. Niebuhr annoyed Trotskyites by opining that Russia was better off under Stalin than it would have been under Trotsky; Stalin was a Great Power statesman, and Trotsky was a fanatic. Yet for all of Niebuhr's Realpolitik respect for Stalin and refusal to judge him by an ethical yardstick, the Nazi–Soviet pact stunned him. In one stroke Stalin obliterated years of united leftism and freed Hitler to invade Poland. Niebuhr struggled to convey his revulsion, admitting he never dreamed that Stalin's cynical cunning would extend this far. British super-lawyer Stafford Cripps, a Christian socialist, told Niebuhr he was abandoning his law practice to help the Labour Party salvage something from the destruction the war would bring. Niebuhr was deeply moved. He commended Cripps to *Christian Century* readers, almost saying what he meant: He aspired to be like Cripps.[5]

If Cripps could shut down his law practice as a trivial irrelevance, why should Niebuhr rattle on about human destiny? This question haunted him during his second round of Gifford Lectures in October. German planes bombed a naval base a few miles from Niebuhr's lectures. The Scots squirmed at the sound of antiaircraft guns but kept coming back for the lectures, three afternoons per week for three weeks. Niebuhr developed the biblical realism he found in Augustine and outlined in the spring lectures, which he set against the classical thought of Plato, Aristotle, and the Stoics. The ancient Greeks and Romans conceived humans as spiritual beings, gifted with self-reflective reason and unique within nature. The Bible, by contrast, conceives the self as a created finite unity of body and spirit. Niebuhr said Augustine caught the significance of the biblical idea by describing the self as a mysterious integral identity transcending its mind and yet able to use mind and will for its purposes. God is beyond society and history *and* is intimately related to the world. The human spirit finds a home and catches a glimpse of its freedom in God's transcendence, but the self also finds in divine transcendence the limit of the self's freedom, a divine judgment against human pride, and divine mercy for sin. God's redeeming grace enables sinful egotists to surrender their prideful attempts to master their existence. Niebuhr warned that modern alternatives to Christianity would not save Europe from descending into fascist barbarism. Only Christianity had the moral and intellectual resources to fend off modern cynicism, nihilism, militarism, and will to power.[6]

The *Christian Century* published his diaries under a title that riffed on a former Niebuhr book title, "Leaves from the Notebook of a War-Bound American." Niebuhr's entry of September 18 contained a sentence that crystallized his coming battle with American pacifist socialists: "Whatever may be wrong with the British empire or with American imperialism or French nationalism, it is still obvious that these nations preserve certain values of civilization, and that the terror which is sweeping over Europe is not civilization. A moralism which dulls the conscience over this kind of evil is perverse." On October 17 he surmised that the battle against German U-boats was likely to be decisive. U-boat attacks were sporadic that fall but escalated dramatically the following May after Denmark, Norway, the Low Countries, and France fell to Germany, and Britain stood alone.[7]

Niebuhr girded personally for the battle for Britain, hustling back to Union in November 1939, tossing off articles for the *Nation* and the *Christian Century*, turning his Gifford outlines into a book, and stewing over the problem of the *Century*. Richard W. Fox, Niebuhr's best biographer, misconstrues him twice during this period. Fox claims that Niebuhr abandoned his secular political activism in the mid-1930s and believed that democratic socialism was a lost cause throughout Europe. On the contrary, Niebuhr was an important player in the crack-up of the Socialist Party in 1936, was a left-wing critic of the Old Guard, and he published a magazine—*Radical Religion*—that was drenched in secular politics. Moreover, Niebuhr treasured Labour Party socialism and did not believe it was exhausted or shattered or any such thing. He identified with the Labour Party of Cripps, R. H. Tawney, and Clement Attlee. Had Niebuhr been an English citizen like his wife, Ursula Keppel-Compton Niebuhr—who studied under him as a visiting English Fellow at Union in 1931—he would have supported Labour. As it was, he had very deep feelings about the urgent necessity of aiding England.[8]

Freda Kirchwey succeeded Oswald Garrison Villard as editor of the *Nation* in 1933 and swung it away from Villard's pacifism, turning the magazine into a bastion of liberal and socialist interventionism. In the spring of 1940 Niebuhr roared in the *Nation* for "all aid to the Allies short of war," as the slogan went. After the Socialist Party reaffirmed that it stood for neutrality in the war between rival European imperialisms, party executive secretary Irving Barshop admonished Niebuhr for supporting William Allen White's interventionist organization, Defend America by Aiding the Allies. Barshop observed that the party had a position about this matter, and there was such a thing as party discipline. Niebuhr promptly resigned, brusquely telling Barshop he had no intention of conforming to the party on this issue.[9]

He did not bother with sentimental asides about comradely feelings, precious memories, shared values, or the like. His note was curt and quick— good-bye. Niebuhr highlighted the curtness in the *Nation*, telling readers he got four letters that morning asking him to do something. The Socialist Party asked him to account for his nonconformity. A world federalist asked him to support a "world radio" for global peace education. A Communist union leader asked him to speak at a union rally for peace. A pacifist cleric asked him to join a Gandhi-like moral crusade against Nazi fascism. Niebuhr said he resigned summarily from the Socialist Party, the Nazis would not be thwarted by radio programs, no Communist union wanted to hear what he believed, and moral force was not terribly effective "against tanks, flame-throwers, and bombing planes." May 1940 was a world-historical emergency, and he had no patience for the moralistic idiocies that paralyzed Socialists, World Federalist liberals, and Gandhian fantasists. Pro-Communists, meanwhile, really needed to stop gazing at Russia for salvation.[10]

Niebuhr lingered over the problem of the Socialists. "The party position is that this war is a clash of rival imperialisms in which nothing significant is at stake." That was typical Niebuhr caricature, as Socialists never claimed that nothing significant was at stake. As for rival imperialisms, Niebuhr said of course the Socialists were right, just as a clash between himself and a gangster was "a conflict of rival egotisms." He and a gangster had much in common yet were crucially different: "That is a truth which the Socialists in America have not learned." To be sure, the Britons and French had bloody imperial hands, but Britain and France were the heart of European civilization. Niebuhr said American Socialists were deeply confused because their moral utopianism made them stupid, measuring all significant historical distinctions "against purely ideal perspectives," which blinded them to life-and-death differences "in a specific instance." Actually Niebuhr was cheating again because Thomas and the Socialists did not appeal to a pure ideal or claim there was no moral difference between the Allies and Fascists. They argued that going to war would obliterate, in the United States, the very things that made the United States a liberal democracy worth preserving. Niebuhr demolished a caricature instead of making a case that Socialists were wrong about what would happen in the United States.[11]

He balked at making the latter case because his own scathing judgments about U.S. American culture undermined whatever case he might have assembled. Niebuhr stressed that Britain still had a Christian ethos. No nation came close to England in combining "moral purpose with political realism," which gave it a crucial advantage in the current clash of nations. French pessimism rotted France's Christian cultural heritage; German pessimism yielded the fantastic evil of the Nazis; and U.S. American culture was predominantly secular too, though its version was innocent and utopian, not pessimistic or cynical. Niebuhr did not tell Americans he believed they were too moral to stand aside while the civilized Britons were slaughtered. He said it was very much in question whether Americans had any moral courage. Moreover, the liberal Protestant establishment was a big part of the problem. Niebuhr allowed that U.S. American culture was not *wholly* bereft of moral realism. James Madison understood what human beings are like and why multiple centers of power must be balanced against each other to prevent tyranny. On Niebuhr's telling, Madison got his defining principles from the Calvinist tradition that undergirded America's best institutions. But America in 1940 was overwhelmingly liberal, secular, commercial, and self-flattering, and to the extent that religion played a role that mattered, religion was liberal, secularizing, self-flattering, and perversely moralistic. Niebuhr tried to shame his country into changing course, without assuring readers that Socialists were wrong about what might go wrong.[12]

Politically, he said, isolationism worked better than liberal church morality, so church leaders fused these appeals. The *Christian Century* epitomized this strategy. *Century* editor Charles Clayton Morrison supported FDR in 1936, but four years later he charged that FDR was driving the United States to fascist rule and militarism. In May 1940 Morrison wanted FDR to organize a conference of neutral nations to formulate terms of an armistice. Niebuhr said this proposal was fatuous, inept, and "completely perverse." In June, two weeks before France surrendered to Germany, Morrison opined that it was too late for America to join the war. Hitler would either be stopped by the forces presently arrayed against him "or he will not be stopped."[13]

Thomas made similar claims during the 1940 campaign, watching his crowds dwindle after Germany conquered France. He said he found it amazing that newspapers routinely equated England with civilization and democracy as though British imperialism were a side issue or no issue at all. Thomas prized Dewey, Hook, Muste, Randolph, Will Herberg, and Bertram Wolfe for hanging with him through his toughest campaign, but 1940 was a new low, and even Randolph briefly resigned from the party to register that he did not agree with its antiwar absolutism. Thomas received a pathetic 117,000 votes despite being the only antiwar candidate in the race. He and Roosevelt wrote to each other frequently; FDR always wanted to know how it was going out there, and Thomas rued that FDR played his audiences masterfully. Roosevelt said he was against intervening and being unprepared; in 1940 that message had perfect pitch. A few days after the election FDR told Thomas he was "worried about the trend of undemocratic forces in this country." The Socialist fear that American democracy would not survive a war looked exaggerated in hindsight, but that was not what FDR said to Thomas at the time.[14]

Scribner's collected Niebuhr's recent salvos in 1940 in a book titled *Christianity and Power Politics*. Niebuhr's close friend Waldo Frank reached a big readership with an interventionist book titled *A Chart for Rough Water*. Niebuhr hoped his book would make a similar splash, but it was ignored outside his usual venues, which were mostly negative. The *Christian Century* denounced it as "a theological green light for the William Allen White Committee." Even the *Nation* panned the book, notwithstanding that most of it first appeared there. British poetic luminary W. H. Auden, though welcoming Niebuhr's pro-British solidarity, disliked his spiritual gloating—constantly looking down on his opponents and ridiculing them. Auden said Niebuhr conveyed no sense of shame, a serious failing in a theologian. Niebuhr, in fact, had a deep religious sincerity and humility, and he respected that British theologians did not ridicule each other at conferences, unlike German theologians. He and Ursula Niebuhr, moved by the review, reached out to Auden, kindling a lasting friendship.[15]

In December 1940 the *Christian Century* asked Niebuhr and others to address the fact that Roosevelt dragged a peaceable nation to the brink of war. Niebuhr said that was the wrong starting point. He hoped there was a morally decent way for America to stay out of the war, but he would not hesitate if

Roosevelt called the nation to it. Only Britain stood between Germany and a completely Fascist Europe. If America waited for that outcome, it faced a future *consumed* by the necessity of fighting off a Nazi conqueror. Niebuhr said the "constant appeals of the *Christian Century*" to stay perfectly neutral were so wrong he found them unfathomable:

> We have allowed ourselves to forget as much as possible that this resurgent Germany not only shares imperial ambitions with all strong nations, but that its fury is fed by a pagan religion of tribal self-glorification; that it intends to root out the Christian religion; that it defies all the universal standards of justice that ages of a Christian and humanistic culture have woven into the fabric of our civilization; that it threatens the Jewish race with annihilation and visits a maniacal fury upon these unhappy people that goes far beyond the ordinary race prejudice that is the common sin of all nations and races; that it explicitly declares its intention of subjecting the other races of Europe into slavery to the "master" race; that it intends to keep them in subjection by establishing a monopoly of military violence and of technical skill so that they will be subordinate in peace and in war; that it is already engaged in Poland and Czechoslovakia in destroying the very fabric of national existence by wholesale expulsion of nationals from their homeland and the forced colonization of Germans in their place; that, in short, it is engaged in the terrible effort to establish an empire upon the very negation of justice rather than upon that minimal justice which even ancient empires achieved.[16]

Making peace with such a tyranny is reprehensible, he warned. Without mentioning Ursula Niebuhr by name, Niebuhr denied that any ties of family or friendship motivated him. It surprised him that people said otherwise since "I am an American of pure German stock." It galled him that *Christian Century* writers prattled about fulfilling the Christian law of love by renouncing war. The nations that rolled over for the Nazis were not more virtuous than the Britons. It was more like the opposite. Niebuhr countered that no one becomes virtuous by avoiding conflict, and no form of justice has ever been achieved without a struggle between rival forces and interests. To be sure, there is a place in Christianity for following Jesus to the cross. Niebuhr respected individual pacifists who loved their enemies unconditionally and accepted whatever punishment came with doing so. But he denounced liberal pacifism, which combined gospel perfectionism with bourgeois utopianism: "This kind of pacifism is not content with martyrdom and political irresponsibility. It is always fashioning political alternatives to the tragic business of resisting tyranny and establishing justice by coercion." Liberal pacifists specialized in unctuous reasoning that delivered others to tyranny: "Now capitulation to tyranny in the name of nonre-sistant perfection may be very noble for the individual. But it becomes rather ignoble when the idealist suggests that others besides himself shall be sold into slavery and shall groan under the tyrant's heel."[17]

Niebuhr refrained from telling *Century* readers he expected nothing better from them, since this was a moment to shame them into changing course. In other contexts he doubted that U.S. American democracy deserved to survive: "The fact is that moralistic illusions of our liberal culture have been so great and its will-to-power has been so seriously enervated by a confused pacifism, in which Christian perfectionism and bourgeois love of ease have been curiously compounded, that our democratic world does not really deserve to survive. It may not survive."[18]

He plotted a rival to the *Christian Century*. In 1940 Niebuhr overhauled *Radical Religion*, renaming it *Christianity and Society*, but it was a quarterly house organ of the Fellowship of Socialist Christians (FSC). Liberal Protestantism needed a better flagship than the *Century*. Niebuhr pitched this idea to Union Theological Seminary president Henry Sloane Coffin, Union faculty colleague Henry Van Dusen, and World Student Christian Federation president Francis Miller, who helped him secure funding. He relied on his FSC friends Sherwood Eddy, Episcopal bishop Will Scarlett, and Pacific School of Religion theologian John C. Bennett. Bennett left Auburn Seminary in New York in 1938 to teach at Pacific; five years later he joined the Union faculty and became Niebuhr's partner in all things political, social ethical, and editorial. The inaugural issue of *Christianity and Crisis* appeared in February 1941. Its roster of ecumenical heavyweight supporters included William Adams Brown, Francis J. McConnell, John R. Mott, and Robert E. Speer. It looked almost exactly like the *Century* but spoke Niebuhr's language of power politics, conflict, and tragic necessity. It stumped for the Lend-Lease bill proposed by FDR in January, which vested Roosevelt with authority to lend or lease military supplies to any nation whose defense he judged to be vital to American security. Thomas and Morrison protested that Lend-Lease was a sure path to outright military intervention. Niebuhr said the importance and urgency of passing it were impossible to exaggerate.[19]

Christianity and Crisis addressed the emergency in liberal Protestantism, where Niebuhr relied on Coffin, Van Dusen, and Brown—churchy liberals who could never rub elbows with Niebuhr's secular left friends. Niebuhr trea-sured Bennett, Eddy, and Canadian Christian socialist King Gordon for strad-dling both worlds that mattered to him, grasping that he cared most about the world of secular political activism. The Union for Democratic Action (UDA) was Niebuhr's pride and joy. Its founders were Socialist Party exiles who agreed with Niebuhr about the war: George Counts (AFT), Murray Gross and Lewis Corey (ILGWU), John Childs (Columbia University Teachers College), and Freda Kirchwey and Robert Bendiner (*Nation*). They built a labor/socialist alternative to the William Allen White group that excluded conservatives by definition and barred Communists. Niebuhr and Counts were adamant about no-Communists; they were finished with fronts that imploded every time Moscow changed its line. At the same time, they rebuffed professional red-baiters like Texas congressman Martin Dies Jr., who started up HUAC in 1938. Nobody in UDA, beginning with Corey, was safe if Dies got to define what counted as un-Americanism.

Niebuhr was thrilled to launch something like a farmer-labor party, the closest he ever came to it. He had spurned the Dubinsky–Hillman ALP because it lacked intellectuals and fixed solely on New York; basically it was a vehicle for labor-socialists who wanted to support Roosevelt outside the Democratic Party. UDA, with Niebuhr as chair and Bendiner as vice chair, was much better. Bendiner had begun as Niebuhr's copy editor at *World Tomorrow*; now he was managing editor of the *Nation*. They enlisted Randolph, Franz Daniel, AFT officials James Loeb and Benjamin Davidson, *New Republic* columnist Kenneth Crawford, and Niebuhr stalwarts Frank and Gordon. UDA helped Randolph put the fellow-traveling National Negro Congress episode behind him and showed that he did not always agree with Thomas, though he otherwise remained in the Socialist Party and close to Thomas. Randolph joined UDA in calling for naval convoys to protect Lend-Lease shipments against German submarines; UDA was eager to claim him on whatever terms he established.[20]

Loeb ran the UDA office on West Fortieth Street and managed Niebuhr's frenetic speaking schedule. Nazi forces overran the Balkans in the spring of 1941 and Niebuhr rang the alarm to every civic, religious, and political group that would hear him. On June 21 the Germans invaded Russia. The *Daily Worker* fumbled briefly before reversing its line about Lend-Lease; Niebuhr admonished Americans not to say that Russian Communists could not be allies: "Not only in military but in every conceivable kind of moral and political strategy we make use of allies who do not share our dominant purpose but who, for purposes of their own, serve our ends. We shall scorn such help only if we mistake mathematical-moral abstractions for the real world." American Communists pressed the logical upshot: Can we join UDA? Niebuhr and Loeb heartily praised the Russians for fighting off Hitler, warning that it would be a catastrophe if he seized control of Ukraine grain and Caucasus oil. But Niebuhr refused the Communists; UDA was too precious to him to let them ruin it.[21]

Most of the left swung in favor of interventionism, spurning Thomas, after Germany invaded Russia. He held out against Stalin and Hitler and all forms of imperialism. Now Stalin was an ally, and only the Socialist left wing seemed to care about British imperialism. In February 1941 prominent *Herald Tribune* columnist Dorothy Thompson blasted Thomas for harping about the British Empire: "The reality is that this is not an imperialist war, except on the side of the Axis." The Allied fight, she said, was a "defense against a tidal wave of red-brown counter-revolution" aiming to obliterate all civilized institutions and values. Thomas replied that Thompson and *Time* mogul Henry Luce specialized in glorifying Anglo-American conceits. Rudyard Kipling, he said, "that British Nazi poet," was the laureate of this tradition, telling Anglo-Saxons it was their duty to police the "lesser breeds within the law." Thomas was incredulous that pundits rattled on about liberal civilization as though England had not used this very argument to justify its brutality in India, South Africa, and East Asia. He remembered bitterly that Winston Churchill didn't give a damn about saving liberal democracy in the Spanish Republic.[22]

In August 1941 Thomas protested that Roosevelt dragged America into England's imperial business in East Asia, committing America to fighting for Singapore and the Dutch East Indies on the hope of becoming a "senior partner in empire." He warned direly, "If we go to war over empire in southeastern Asia, neither our descendants nor history will grant forgiveness to those responsible." The following month Lindbergh embarrassed Thomas and KAOWC by declaring that three groups were driving America to war: Britons, Jews, and the Roosevelt administration. Lindbergh doubled down on anti-Semitic tripe, advising American Jews that their (supposed) control of Hollywood made them vulnerable to criticism unless they also opposed intervening in the war. Thomas made his usual disclaimer—he and Lindbergh were not allies except concerning nonintervention. The *New York Times* covered the flap, and Thomas thought it was over until he received a telegram from Niebuhr blasting him for associating with Lindbergh. Worse, UDA leaked it to the press, embarrassing Thomas. Thomas protested that Niebuhr knew very well how coalitions like this worked. He did not support what Lindbergh said, he criticized Lindbergh frequently, he didn't need to be chastised about his Lindbergh problem, and he resented that UDA piled on after the whole thing should have ended.[23]

Shortly before Japan attacked Pearl Harbor, Thomas and Violet Thomas received a letter from their son Evan, a senior at Princeton, reporting that he was leaving college to join the English service. He was a pacifist, so he chose to serve as an ambulance driver. Thomas replied lovingly that Evan had evidently made the best possible decision, for him, in a cruel world. On December 7 he drove with Violet to Princeton to retrieve some of Evan's belongings. There they heard that Japan had attacked Pearl Harbor. To Thomas, the news was devastating. He told Maynard Krueger, "I feel as if my world has pretty much come to an end, that what I have stood for has been defeated, and my own usefulness made small." To the party he said it was pointless to hold out against the war; that battle was lost. Now their job was to contend "for civil liberties, democratic Socialism, and an anti-imperialist peace." To Chicago comrade Ken Cuthbertson, he dropped the mask: "What is left us is a poor sort of lifeboat but I doubt if we can stop rowing now or make our main concern an attack upon the captain. . . . We are in a literal hell but the deepest pit of all would be an Axis victory."[24]

The *Christian Century* took a similar line: "We, too, must accept the war. We see no other way at the moment but the bloody way of slaughter and immeasurable sacrifice. Our government has taken a stand. It is our government." Morrison faulted Roosevelt for steering the nation to this outcome but accepted that America chose "the way of unimaginable cost and of doubtful morality." All Americans, he said, were implicated in the acts of their government. Those who took the path of war and those who opposed it were one people — "We stand with our country. We cannot do otherwise."[25]

The NEC accepted Thomas's position of "critical support," and the following May a surreal party convention debated whether it should espouse unqualified support, critical support, political nonsupport, or revolutionary socialism. Irving Barshop called for unqualified support; upcoming pacifist David Dellinger said the party should stand on its political opposition to Democratic and Republican policies; a tiny clique held fast to *The Communist Manifesto*; and incoming executive secretary Harry Fleischman said there was not enough difference between critical support and political nonsupport to fight over. The Socialists combined the Thomas position with a hollow insistence that they were still an antiwar party, which created an opening for somebody to champion old-fashioned antiwar socialism.

That group turned out to be, with screaming irony, the sect of former Trotskyites that followed Max Shachtman out of the SWP in 1940. Shachtman came to New York from Warsaw as an infant; his father was a tailor in the Lower East Side and Upper Manhattan; and he took two stabs at City College before dropping out in 1921. Poor health and the lure of radical politics ended his schooldays. His felicitous English made him suspect to Communist officials until Young Workers League national secretary Martin Abern gave him a job editing its paper, *Young Worker*. Shachtman thrived in the work. He and Abern attached themselves to Cannon and moved up, until 1928, when Trotsky fell and Cannon, Shachtman, and Abern went down with him. Cannon and Shachtman built the Trotskyite movement by dividing responsibilities and constituencies. Cannon was the public leader, while Shachtman served as Trotsky's secretary and edited the Trotskyite paper and journal *The Militant* and the *New International*. Shachtman thus had greater influence on Trotskyite recruits, especially in New York. In fact, he already had a cult following in New York when World War II posed tricky problems for the Trotskyite worldview.

The Trotskyites were the only pro-Communist group not traumatized by the Nazi–Soviet pact. Trotsky's hatred of Stalin and his shrewd reading of Stalin's foreign policy prepared his followers for a Soviet agreement with Hitler. James Burnham, still teaching at New York University, felt quite superior for a week after the pact was announced, having seen it coming. The shocker came when Trotsky suddenly reversed course and declared his support for the Soviet troops invading Poland. This was too much even for the Machiavellian–Leninist Burnham and the true-believing Trotskyite–Leninist Shachtman. Eastman had warned both of them that Trotsky was above all a Russian nationalist and a man of state. Now they realized it was true, just before Stalin declared war on Finland, and Trotsky announced that Stalin's expropriation of Polish and Ukrainian estates and his push into the eastern front were progressive. Russia was still a workers' state, Trotsky explained, albeit a degenerated version of one. Public ownership was the defining feature of Soviet society. Thus the Soviet Union at war was a deformed but objectively progressive nation that all Marxist–Leninists had to defend.[26]

Trotskyism was based on the premise that the Soviet regime would either move forward to revolutionary socialism or backward to capitalism. Burnham, Shachtman, and Joseph Carter began to challenge this premise in 1937 just after the Trotskyites were expelled from the Socialist Party. Burnham and Carter told the founding convention of the SWP that Trotsky's either/or was simplistic and misleading. The degenerated workers' state in Russia, they argued, was beginning to take on a viable structure of its own. It wasn't moving toward socialism or degenerating into capitalism. It was turning into a bureaucratic deformation of a workers' state. Trotsky replied that he expected foolish arguments of this sort from anarchists and radical dandies but not from revolutionary Marxists. There was no third option. Russia was not yet a workers' state in the Marxist sense of the term because creating a new society takes a while. Marx taught that bourgeois norms of distribution still exist in the first phase of a workers' state. Trotsky admonished, "One has to weigh well and think this thought out to the end. The workers' state itself, as a state, is necessary exactly because the bourgeois norms of distribution still remain in force."[27]

Trotsky insisted that he did not fetishize Marxian doctrine. When the facts demanded a revision of the theory, he was willing to change the theory. The American Trotskyites had no new facts, he said; Lenin admitted in 1923 that the Soviet regime was riddled with bureaucratic deformations. But with all its deformations, the Soviet state had not reverted to capitalism; thus it was worth defending. Italian Trotskyite fellow traveler Bruno Rizzi, reading the back-and-forth between Burnham/Carter and Trotsky, wrote a book in 1939 titled *La Bureaucratisation du Monde*. The idea that the Soviet regime was a state capitalist order run by a new class of professional bureaucrats was not new; Christian Rakovsky pioneered it in 1929 from internal Russian exile, drawing on anarchist criticism. Rizzi developed it into a full-fledged theory of bureaucratic collectivism, contending that the Bolshevik Revolution created a new ruling class that converted the means of production into a new form of property. The Soviet state was becoming bureaucratized, not socialized. Instead of dissolving into a society with no classes the state was growing fantastically. Rizzi charged that Trotsky fetishized Marx's mistaken predictions and refuted his critics with proof texts. Marx did not foresee the rise of a bureaucratic class that owned the state in a nationalized class form. But that was what happened.[28]

Trotsky doubled down on his position, using Rizzi to refute Burnham and Carter. He could accept losing Burnham but wanted desperately not to lose Shachtman. Trotsky said the crucial issue was whether the Soviet bureaucracy should be categorized as a caste, based on functions of control, or a class, based on ownership. Stalin's bureaucracy was a caste; in fact, no bureaucracy is correctly called a class because a class is defined by its independent role in the structure of an economy. Each class works out its own special forms of property, which is not true of bureaucracies. To call the Soviet regime a class was to obliterate the either/or. Trotsky did not dispute that the political prostration of the working class yielded something accurately described as bureaucratic collectivism: "The phenomenon itself is incontestable. But what are its limits, and what is its historical weight?" He answered that bureaucratic collectivism was a passing aberration and the socialist mission of the proletariat had not changed. The degenerated workers' state in Russia had to be defended before it could be regenerated by revolutionaries who believed in the real thing.[29]

Burnham and Shachtman, however, believed that bureaucratic collectivism had immense historical weight and applied very broadly to modern capitalism. The traditional definition of a class did not describe the new form of social organization invented in the Soviet Union. Shachtman explained: "What we have called the consummated usurpation of power by the Stalinist bureaucracy was, in reality, nothing but the self-realization of the bureaucracy as a class and its seizure of state power from the proletariat, the establishment of its own state power and its own rule." He recalled the old warning of Lenin and Trotsky that the Bolshevik Revolution would not succeed without help from the international proletariat. Shachtman said Trotsky needed to accept that he had been right. The Bolsheviks were left on their own, and the workers' state was overthrown—by a new, counterrevolutionary class, not a bourgeois restoration: "The old crap was revived in a new, unprecedented, hitherto unknown form, the rule of a new bureaucratic class."[30]

When the state owns the means of production, the crucial question becomes, who owns the state? This question eventually led Shachtman and his band of former Trotskyites to democratic state socialism. In 1940 it led them out of the SWP, still as Leninists. The Shachtman argument liberated his group from having to defend the Soviet Union in some way. They were done with the trauma that scarred a whole generation of Communists. True Bolshevism had been irreparably betrayed, and there was no further need to apologize for what happened in Russia. Trotskyites with a taste for the absurd flocked to Shachtman, especially if they were Jewish New Yorkers. He enthralled his cult with witty, dramatic, powerful, comical platform performances, gyrating through Marxist theory and current history. He sparkled at banter and repartee, oscillating between cheeky humor and heroic exhortation, specializing in dramatic litanies of the socialist comrades murdered by Stalin. He could also be mean, ridiculing his disciples behind their backs, which made them fearful of becoming the next target. Julius Jacobson, a product of Bronx socialism like Howe, said Shachtman was a bawdy kibitzer, so he attracted live-wire youth, especially college students. Howe recalled: "His mixture of irony and passion, so familiar to Jewish intellectual life, was not always appreciated by the Midwestern proletarian comrades who took earnestness as a proof of devotion."[31]

Burnham and Shachtman bolted the SWP at the same time, very briefly together before rocketing in opposite directions. Burnham made a splash with a book titled *The Managerial Revolution* that described bureaucratic collectivism as generally rational and commendable. Then he raced to the political right, where he championed the rule of elites, white supremacy, and rolling back the Soviet bloc, eventually as the *National Review* guru on foreign policy. Shachtman founded yet another group called the Workers Party; this one opposed capitalist wars, condemned Stalin's imperialism in eastern Europe, supported black revolutionary movements, and defended wartime striking CIO unions. It called itself a Third Camp revolutionary Socialist party, opposing capitalism and bureaucratic collectivism. Shachtman attracted colorful, intellectual, cunning Marxists who found Thomas boring. Erber, Howe, Jacobson, Hal Draper, Gordon Haskell,

C. L. R. James, Irving Kristol, Dwight Macdonald, Earl Raab, and Philip Selznick were early Shachtmanites, following Shachtman into the Workers Party, though Selznick and Kristol stayed for less than a year. The Shachtmanites outshone the Thomas Socialists from the left, took jobs in CIO unions, and were skilled at Marxology. They took pride in being hard and defending true Bolshevism. Thomas grieved at realizing that Shachtman won stronger upcomers. Thomas could admit certain things about what went wrong, but not the big thing.[32]

He said he had not wanted to run for New York governor in 1924 and he probably should not have accepted the role of party leader. There were better uses for his skills. But these were small matters compared to what Thomas and the Socialists got disastrously wrong: Roosevelt and the New Deal. Thomas could not bring himself to say it, even after he tried to ally with people who said it routinely. Getting the New Deal wrong lost the Old Guard, which decimated the party, after which Thomas and the party got Roosevelt and World War II wrong. Thomas admitted readily that he botched the Old Guard crisis and was wrong about Russia. For twenty years he equivocated in contrary ways about being wrong in 1940 and 1941; he had too much moral pride not to defend himself. But Thomas could not admit that opposing the New Deal was his greatest mistake. Had Thomas and the Socialists critically supported FDR and pulled him to the left, the party might have thrived as left ballast for the New Deal instead of defying the common sense and experience of left-liberal voters. Even American Stalinists and pro-Communists saw it clearly. Then Thomas and the Socialists pretended not to see the chasm difference between 1917 and 1940. The party deserved to be repudiated for telling Americans to look away from the difference.

Thomas was true, however, to his pledge that if the United States entered the war he would devote himself to refuting his prophecy that the United States would become what it hated. Antimilitarism, civil liberties, and humanitarian rescue were interlocking passions for him. In the 1930s he implored FDR to rescue Jews and other minorities fleeing Germany, the Sudetenland, and eastern Europe, finding precious few allies. Thomas entreated congressional committees to expand immigration laws and save threatened minorities. He appealed directly to Roosevelt, who brushed him off. In a few cases Thomas made a life-saving difference, rescuing former Communists Victor Serge, Marceau Pivert, and Julian Gorkin from execution by Stalin by appealing to Assistant Secretary of State Adolf Berle Jr. But mostly he failed, for reasons he loathed. The refugee cause had no constituency and was presumed to be unpopular; thus Roosevelt and American politicians did nothing.

After the war Thomas rechristened KAOWC as the Post War World Council (PWWC) and lifted it above his work for the Socialist Party, LID, and other organizations. He lobbied the Selective Service for a wider definition of conscientious objection and defended the rights of Communists and Fascists. In January 1942 he learned that "alien Japanese" had been forcibly removed from their jobs and homes in San Luis Obispo and Guadalupe, California. Thomas started with the ACLU, trying to leverage his authority as a founder and board member. Thirty-five ACLU directors voted by two to one not to fight the internment, infuriating Thomas. He appealed to Attorney General Francis Biddle and Assistant Secretary of War John McCloy, pleading that it was plainly racist to persecute Japanese Americans as a class. There was far more evidence of espionage among German Americans and Italian Americans, yet, mercifully, the government did not herd entire communities of them into concentration camps. Thomas pressed the point directly with FDR, protesting that the internment was immoral, illegal, totalitarian, destructive, and inflammatory. FDR brushed him off again, and Thomas tried to arouse public opposition, telling Americans their country had stripped 116,000 Japanese descendants of their rights. Was this the kind of country they wanted to be?[33]

PWWC became his favorite vehicle. Here there were no faction fights or political wrangles; everything he did for PWWC was flat-out advocacy for things he cared about. Thomas kept pressing FDR to save European Jews. One of his arguments was that England and the United States confirmed Hitler's conviction that no one cared about Jews anyway. This was a lonely cause before and during the war; Niebuhr was one of the very few who joined Thomas in it. Thomas understood from his speaking tours why Roosevelt had Japanese Americans in detention camps and refused to rescue Jews. This was very much like refusing to fight for black Americans or help the Spanish Loyalists. Roosevelt saved his political capital for higher priorities and was careful not to race ahead of his political base. He chided Thomas that he was much better at politics than Thomas. Thomas protested again when the Allies firebombed German cities, warning that erasing the distinction between combatants and civilians was morally indefensible and fateful. Meanwhile he spoke against America's embrace of Stalin and warned constantly that Stalin had a terrible plan for Europe.

Thomas was appalled by the American infatuation with Stalin that arose after Hitler invaded Russia. Politicians suddenly developed tender feelings for Stalin; *Collier's* and *Life* ran special issues idealizing Russian life and its supposed democratic trends; and the media hung an endearing nickname on Stalin, Uncle Joe. Airline executive Eddie Rickenbacker returned from Russia praising its wonderful lack of labor problems. American Communists seized on this turnabout, touting their support of Roosevelt and gaining thousands of members. They heckled Thomas mercilessly, disrupting his speeches. Who was he to criticize America's great president and hamper the war effort? How dare he criticize the internment camps? To Thomas and Thomas Socialists, the Uncle Joe phenomenon was an unbearable absurdity about a mass-murdering totalitarian. They filled the Mecca Temple in New York to protest Stalin's execution of the Polish Jewish Socialists Viktor Alter and Henryk Ehrlich.[34]

In 1940 Soviet troops massacred fourteen thousand Polish prisoners of war in the Katyń forest. American journalists and the State Department treated the story as Nazi propaganda, but Thomas urged Americans to take it seriously, warning that it was an augur of Stalin's designs for Europe. Thomas blasted Roosevelt's assurance that he knew how to handle Uncle Joe; Stalin was not a political hack looking to cut a deal. Moreover, Roosevelt played into Stalin's hands by wrongly insisting on an unconditional surrender by Germany. Thomas warned that Stalin was out to conquer eastern Europe, and the United States was needlessly abandoning east Europeans. He based his 1944 presidential campaign on this protest, calling for the Polish border of 1939 to be redrawn as part of a comprehensive settlement designed by an international federation. He argued that Stalin would settle for less if forced to do so; Stalin would not inflict another war on his war-ravaged nation just to get Poland. The Allies could save east Europeans from Soviet tyranny by standing up for them. But if Roosevelt did not stop Stalin from taking over eastern Europe, "the President may be committing us and our sons after us not only to the prolongation of this war but to the certainty of the next."[35]

The Katyń massacre and the massacre on the banks of the Vistula were augurs of something terrible, as Thomas pleaded. The Red Army waited near the Vistula while German troops exterminated Warsaw insurgents. Thomas wanted U.S. forces to meet the Russians as far to the east as possible. Then he charged, very angrily, that Yalta was the bitter consequence of refusing to impede Stalin's advance. By February 1945, when Roosevelt, Churchill, and Stalin met at Yalta in the Crimea, the Soviets controlled Hungary, Romania, and Bulgaria, and Stalin rejected Churchill's demand for free elections in Poland. Formally, the Yalta accords committed the Allies to recognize freely elected governments in the liberated areas, but the Allies cut a secret deal dividing occupied Europe into spheres of influence reflecting the current military situation. Upon returning from Yalta, Churchill assured the House of Commons: "Marshal Stalin and the other Soviet leaders wish to live in honorable friendship and equality with the Western democracies. I feel also that their word is their bond. I know of no government which stands to its obligations, even in its own despite, more solidly than the Russian Soviet Government."[36]

Thomas raged that that was an incredible betrayal: "A war begun ostensibly to guarantee the integrity of Poland and entered presumably by the United

States on the basis of the principles of the Atlantic Charter (which condemns 'territorial changes that do not accord with the freely expressed wishes of the peoples concerned') ends with Stalin in possession of the territory that he took forcibly from Poland in alliance with the Nazi aggressor and with a government in charge which is his creation." To Stalin, Poland was a highway for invaders, Russia needed a buffer state on the western border, and the West's call for elections in Poland was an existential threat. To Thomas, Poland was the acid test of a decent peace. He put it bitterly after Churchill, Stalin, and Harry Truman sealed the fate of Eastern Europe at Potsdam; Thomas called the Potsdam accords "a triumph of vengeance and stupidity [that] turned eastern and central Europe over to the communists."[37]

RANDOLPH AND THE MARCH ON
WASHINGTON MOVEMENT

The bond between Thomas and Randolph was deep, abiding, and mutually admiring. Randolph founded the BSCP with a grant from the Garland Fund that Thomas secured. In September 1940 the union inadvertently set into motion the March on Washington Movement at its fifteenth-anniversary banquet at the Harlem YMCA. In the presence of Eleanor Roosevelt, the BSCP called for the immediate abolition of racial discrimination in the army, navy, and air corps. She got Randolph on the president's calendar, accompanied by NAACP leader Walter White and National Urban League official T. Arnold Hill. Two weeks later the White House announced that no change had been made in the War Department's policy of racial segregation. Black Americans angrily asked if Randolph and White had consented to Franklin Roosevelt's capitulation to the War Department. Randolph and White said no, FDR subsequently offered small concessions, White was satisfied, and Randolph was not. Randolph recalled his first White House meeting in 1925, when militant Monroe Trotter blistered Calvin Coolidge about racism. Coolidge waited for him to finish and calmly bade Trotter good-day. Randolph reflected that stand-alone White House meetings were pointless; black Americans needed some mass action. In January 1941 he announced that he wanted ten thousand black Americans to march down Pennsylvania Avenue.

The idea caught fire, and Randolph was bombarded with queries and demands. In March he issued an official call for a July 1 march of ten thousand; in May he recalculated what was happening, calling for ten times that number of marchers. The New Dealers blanched at the prospect of one hundred thousand black Americans marching on the nation's capital. Perkins, as labor secretary, and

Hillman, as director of the Office of Production Management, balked at speaking invitations, as did Eleanor Roosevelt. She implored Randolph that he was making a grave mistake—why set back all the (supposedly great) progress they were making? More concessions were made, as Hillman urged defense contractors to hire black workers. Randolph took heavy fire from Communists for insisting that black Americans had to organize this march by themselves. Communists called him a chauvinist for minimizing their influence without saying no-Communists. On January 18 another meeting convened in the White House, where Randolph said blacks would either work in the defense plants and armed forces or march on Washington; there was no third option. FDR pleaded that protestors might get killed; Randolph said that would not happen if FDR addressed the rally. FDR tried to peel back to defense contractors only; Randolph said the government was the worst offender. New York mayor Fiorello La Guardia called for a settlement, young Office for Emergency Management lawyer Joseph Rauh was asked to write it, and FDR signed Executive Order 8802 on June 25, outlawing racial discrimination in the defense industries and government. White surmised that Franklin Roosevelt did what he had to do and Eleanor Roosevelt was a friend, albeit a queasy one.[38]

Randolph soared to iconic status, hearing himself described as the American Gandhi, while offending militants and Communists by suspending the march. But Randolph was not the American Gandhi, for reasons that James Farmer soon pressed upon him. Randolph had not trained anybody in nonviolent protest methods and had no idea how to go about it. His flippant response to FDR about protesters getting killed reflected the problem. Communist organizers Richard Parrish and Bayard Rustin accused Randolph of selling out to Roosevelt, which heightened the pressure on Randolph to sustain the movement. Black American politics had centered on legislation about lynching, poll taxes, separate but equal schools, and white primaries. Now the focus shifted to the interventionist role of the federal government. Randolph replaced the big march with local mass rallies, agreeing with *Amsterdam News* that holding the big march would play into Hitler's hands. One of the rallies became a historic occasion by launching Adam Clayton Powell Jr. as a national figure.

In the 1920s black Harlem began to talk about getting its own U.S. congressional seat. The 1940 census showed that redistricting was overdue in New York State, and Harlem political leader Herbert Bruce lobbied New York Democratic governor Herbert Lehman for a district. Lehman pressed for one, plans were proposed and scuttled, and Congress threatened to intervene if the state failed to act, which scared New York Republicans into dealing with Lehman. Central Harlem got a seat to be filled in the 1944 elections. *Amsterdam News* urged

Randolph to run for it, but he was devoted to the BSCP. Bruce wanted to run, but he had a rocky relationship with Tammany. Meanwhile black activist groups organized a freedom rally at Madison Square Garden. They bridged their differences by agreeing to honor Randolph, packing twenty thousand people into the Garden on June 16, 1942. Powell Jr. was a City Council member in addition to serving as pastor of Abyssinian Church. He wrangled a speaking slot, waited his turn through several long speeches, and finally stepped forward, talking about protest, pickets, himself, and the lack of protest politics in New York before he got there. The crowd could feel this speech was heading somewhere. Powell built up the drama and rocked the crowd, announcing that he would run for Harlem's seat. Black Americans needed a national voice in the nation's capital. The Garden exploded with jubilation. The cheering went on and on, rapturously loud. Randolph never got to speak, Rustin fumed that Powell hijacked the event, and Randolph took it graciously, savoring the messiah-like greeting he received upon walking down the aisle.[39]

That was the high-water mark of Randolph's influence. In December 1942 he announced that the March on Washington would conduct Gandhi-style civil disobedience campaigns aimed at forcing the hand of the federal government. All blacks not serving in the armed forces would be called upon to disobey all laws outside their own workplace that violated their civil rights. Muste and Rustin rejoiced at this announcement. George Schuyler and the *Pittsburgh Courier* denounced Randolph vehemently, accusing him of endangering blacks with incendiary demagoguery. Farmer surprised Randolph and many others by urging him to back down.[40]

Farmer was a Gandhian socialist steeped in the black social gospel. His father, James Farmer Sr., was a theologian trained at Boston University who taught at Wiley College in Marshall, Texas, before joining the Howard University faculty, and his mother was a teacher trained at Bethune-Cookman Institute. Farmer studied at Wiley, starred on its legendary debate team, graduated in 1938, and followed his father to Howard School of Religion. He studied Rauschenbusch and Gandhi under the tutelage of Howard Thurman, converting to socialism and Gandhian pacifism. He loved Thurman's mystical spirit but doubted Thurman's God. He joined FOR at Howard and joined the FOR staff in 1941 upon graduating from Howard, working as an organizer and recruiter. On the stump Farmer stressed that FOR was committed to racial justice; privately, he chafed at its Quaker-like culture. He told his father that segregation would crack and disintegrate if a Gandhian mass movement of black and white activists filled up the jails to abolish it. Farmer Senior replied that there was no comparison between the Indian and American situations. The

Britons were a tiny minority and the Indians a huge majority. Nonviolence was deeply rooted in Hindu culture, whereas in America "only women and sissies back away from a fight." Above all, he said, "don't forget, the British are the epitome of civilization, while our bigots are murderous savages."[41]

This devastating reply did not dissuade Farmer. He countered that white Americans had a pronounced need to believe they were morally decent, and most of them seriously believed their country stood for democracy, freedom, and equality. America needed a protest movement that shamed white Americans into confronting their false beliefs about themselves and their nation. Farmer acknowledged that Gandhi never faced savagery at the Klan level, so an American Gandhian movement would have to be stronger and braver than Gandhi's group. Farmer Senior asked if his son really believed he compared to Gandhi. The British imperialists threw Gandhi in jail; in Mississippi, a Gandhi-type would be swiftly murdered and dumped. Farmer said he was not Gandhi, but he might be the American Nehru—a worldlier figure.

He realized that venturing into the Deep South would provoke a bloodbath, so in the early going he would stick to northern states: "For the time being, we'll sharpen our nonviolent swords in northern settings. When we go south, we'll be ready to face their bullets. If they have the guns, we'll have the inner shields. If they have the jails, we have the bodies. No doubt, some of us will die. If we have to, we'll be ready." In that state of mind he applied for conscientious objector status to his draft board in Washington, DC, where a gruff black official refused to accept Farmer's application because he was a minister, qualifying for a defer-ral. Farmer said he was not a minister and had no intention of becoming one. This objection cut no ice with the draft board official, a lawyer, since Farmer was a recent seminary graduate and thus a plausible candidate for deferral. The draft board did not exist to provide a platform for pacifist propagandists. Farmer felt a twinge of guilt and a surge of joy at evading the whole business.[42]

He went to New York to work on his boss, Muste, whom Farmer viewed as "an old Marxist–Leninist warhorse" and ally—a revolutionary who returned to Christian pacifism after Leninism didn't work out. But the stalwart pacifists on the FOR National Council were not revolutionaries. To them, nonviolence was religious, not merely tactical. They were Christian pacifists committed to civil rights, in that order. Some were pure pacifists who opposed Gandhi's coercive tactics. Farmer, recalibrating, asked FOR to help him launch a parallel organi-zation. He needed the toughest FOR and WRL organizers, and he rightly fig-ured that FOR purists would not thwart his right to start something. Farmer told Muste that FOR would never ignite the movement that was needed because black Americans would not join it: "Being Negroes for them is tough enough without being pacifist, too." For that matter, only a select group of whites would ever join a pacifist organization. Thus did FOR give birth in 1942 to what became, after a couple of name changes, the Congress of Racial Equality (CORE).[43]

CORE was tiny, scrappy, interracial, and dispersed. Officially it was head-quartered at Woodlawn AME Church in Chicago, courtesy of AME minister Archibald J. Carey, who doubled as a Chicago alderman. But early on Farmer worked full-time for FOR in New York, FOR organizer George Houser ran a CORE chapter in Cleveland, and CORE developed a decentralized organization featuring chapter autonomy and an all-volunteer staff. CORE pioneered the strategy of using sit-ins and picket lines to break the color line. It picketed restaurants, barbershops, swimming pools, apartment complexes, banks, and department stores, winning concessions on consumer rights and jobs, though rarely with any media notice. Except for *Amsterdam News*, the New York media ignored everything Farmer did. He tried to catch some of the spotlight that shone on Randolph, but that never happened either.

Randolph was keen to take a Gandhian plunge until Farmer admonished him that civil disobedience requires trained cadre and a disciplined organization; the March on Washington had neither. Some of the march leaders were old cronies of Randolph's lacking any credibility at the grassroots level. They had no idea how to organize a civil disobedience campaign, and if they launched a sloppy one anywhere in the Deep South they would set off exactly the bloody massacres that conservatives predicted, damaging the cause of racial justice for decades. Farmer, in his role as editor of a monthly FOR news bulletin, invited a bevy of movement luminaries to assess Randolph's proposal. Thurman, Thomas, Niebuhr, Villard, Baldwin, novelist Lillian E. Smith, and Gandhian strategist Richard B. Gregg warned Randolph not to try Gandhi's strategy without trained cadre and a disciplined organization.[44]

Randolph backed down, thanking Farmer for saving him from embarrassment. He promised Farmer he would urge his followers to cooperate with CORE chapters wherever they existed. Farmer was conflicted about his victory, realizing it kept the civil rights movement small and ignorable. Randolph's help was welcome but sporadic. Randolph lived for the big rally, having little patience for the rigorous training regime in which CORE specialized. In 1948 Randolph achieved another historic victory with similar poker tactics by getting President Harry Truman to ban racial discrimination in the U.S. armed forces—Executive Order 9981. Again, Randolph was hailed as a hero; again, he offended left-wing allies, notably Muste and Rustin, by calling off a big demonstration, this time set for Harlem; again, Farmer contended that Randolph made the right call, alienating Muste and Rustin. Farmer resigned from FOR in 1945 and took a job with LID, working for Thomas, which helped him finance his work for CORE. He came to revere Thomas much as Randolph admired Debs and Thomas. But Farmer did not claim his extensive protest activism struck a blow for racial justice. He later recalled, "We knew what we were doing, but no one else did." CORE, to him, seemed like a flea gnawing on the ear of an elephant. Not only did CORE's numerous sit-ins and pickets fail to bring the beast to its knees. It was hard to pretend the beast even noticed.[45]

In 1944 the Socialists convened in Reading, Pennsylvania, just after the Commonwealth Federation of Canada won its first provincial government election in Saskatchewan. The Canadians were socialists in the Thomas mold, except successful. The American Socialists cheered heartily for their Canadian comrades, buoyed that success was possible, at least in Canada. They nominated Randolph for vice president, who cabled that he would love to run with Thomas but was swamped with BSCP business and had to decline: "Nothing would give me greater pleasure and joy than to share in the national campaign as a part of the Socialist ticket, not to achieve immediate office, but to build the intellectual and spiritual foundation for the development of a broad political movement in America in the pattern of and comparable to the Canadian Commonwealth Federation." Randolph said he believed that workers, farmers, the lower middle class, and the American people as a whole needed a socialist party that fought for production for use, not for profit: "As I see it, such a political movement can alone save the people of America from economic chaos and confusion and provide peace and plenty, democracy, and freedom."[46]

Being linked to Randolph was as important to Thomas and Niebuhr as they were to him. Niebuhr rued that it took a spectacular assault by the Empire of Japan to mobilize the American public: "We could not agree upon the peril in which we stood as a national community until the peril was upon us; that is the stupidity of collective man. And we could not agree upon our responsibilities to the victims of aggression until we had been joined to them, not by moral act but by historical fate." But as soon as the United States entered the war Niebuhr complained that Americans ridiculously idealized their march to it. To Niebuhr, World War II was strictly a lesser-evil affair; Wilsonian idealism repulsed him, and he did not believe in just wars or just war theory: "Many of the sermons which now justify the war will be hard to bear as the previous ones which proved it was our 'Christian' duty to stay out." Niebuhr said the purpose of the war was to stop fascism, not to create a new international order of liberal democracies. He surprised himself by concluding that wartime was the time to spell out what he believed about Christian political realism.[47]

CHILDREN OF LIGHT, CHILDREN OF
DARKNESS, COLD WAR VOID

The ninth chapter of Niebuhr's second volume of *The Nature and Destiny of Man* (1943) developed a vintage Niebuhr dialectic on what he called "The Kingdom of God and the Struggle for Justice." He argued that the struggle for justice is even more revealing of the possibilities and limits of human powers than the quest for truth. The relationship of the kingdom of God to history is inescapably paradoxical. History moves toward the realization of the kingdom, yet every occasion of its realization falls under divine judgment. This argument was the seed of Niebuhr's Christian political realism, which he began to develop in November 1943 while FDR, Churchill, and Stalin met in Tehran to plan the Allied invasion of Europe. In January 1944 Niebuhr presented the nub of his political philosophy in the Raymond F. West Lectures at Stanford. The following summer, as Allied forces launched D-Day, he expanded his West lectures into a book, *The Children of Light and the Children of Darkness*.[48]

Wartime had proved to be as nauseating as he expected, replete with Wilsonian appeals now applied to the 1940s. Niebuhr set himself against this cascade of idealism, deriding modern American liberals as spiritual cousins of Hegel, Locke, Rousseau, Thomas Paine, and Adam Smith. All were children of light who believed that the conflict between self-interest and the general interest could be resolved, and all were unbearably stupid on this account. Locke's social contract, Smith's harmonizing invisible hand, and Rousseau's general will needed only minimal restraints on human egotism because Locke, Smith, and Rousseau had immense confidence in reason or nature or both. Hegel believed his philosophy synthesized the national and universal interests. Niebuhr swept Marxists and Catholics into the same indictment, lumped with "other stupid children of light." Marxists, contrary to the Catholic charge of cynicism, were so sentimental they believed no state would be necessary after the proletarian revolution. Catholics, meanwhile, described feudalism as a Christian civilization: "The blindness of Catholicism to its own ideological taint is typical of the blindness of the children of light." In six torrential pages Niebuhr used the word "stupid" six times to characterize the children of light. Every strain of modern democratic theory, he said, shared this failing. Niebuhr enjoyed the irony of charging that the icons of modern culture, besides being naive, weren't very smart either.[49]

All manner of modern liberals, democrats, Marxists, and Catholics defended democracy badly against children of darkness, who were wise and strong in their cynicism. Niebuhr said the children of darkness understood self-interest terribly well and were not constrained by a moral law. Hobbes and Machiavelli theorized this option, exemplifying the toxic corruption of realism lacking a moral dimension. Luther was a child of darkness for railing against reason and morality, providing Lutheran cover for state absolutists and antidemocrats. Niebuhr did not say that Stalinism perverted Marxian lightness to the point of being dark. He judged that Stalin held essentially the same relation to Marxism that Napoleon had to the liberalism of eighteenth-century republicans. Each was a bully version of a utopian dream. The "demonic fury" of Nazi barbarism, on the other hand, was the epitome of toxic darkness. It plunged Europe into total war, imposed its collective will of "boundless ambitions and imperial desires" on everything in its way, and shredded the classic liberal picture of a benign, individualistic society. Niebuhr derided the liberal idea that democracy is an ideal that people deserve on account of their moral worth. The children of darkness better understood that will to power drives politics and history. This dialectic yielded Niebuhr's most famous epigram: "Man's capacity for justice makes democracy possible, but man's inclination to injustice makes democracy necessary." Liberal democracy is worth defending because it is the best way to restrain human egotism and will to power, not because it fulfills an ideal.[50]

Niebuhr still believed that political democracy needed to grow into economic democracy to attain social justice and protect democracy itself. Political democracy lacking socialized major enterprises led to the capitalist class owning the political system. Economic democracy was needed to break the overweening greed and will to power of the capitalist class. He said it plainly but with a subtle caveat: "Since economic power, as every other form of social power, is a defensive force when possessed in moderation and a temptation to injustice when it is great enough to give the agent power over others, it would seem that its widest and most equitable distribution would make for the highest degree of justice."[51]

"It would seem" was the caveat, a new one for Niebuhr. He still believed in economic democracy as an ideal; he even believed it was essential to social justice. But by 1944 he no longer believed that economic democracy was possible in his country, unlike what his British Labour Party friends were about to do. Sticking with socialism on ethical grounds made no sense to Niebuhr because Marx was right about ethical socialism—it was useless idealism at best. In the 1930s Niebuhr was consumed with one principle of justice, equality. In the 1940s he decided that freedom and order are equally important. In the past he took for granted that believing in a common humanity compelled him to work for a just world order. Now he was chastened by Augustine's caution that language and ethnicity, which bind communities on one level, are powerfully divisive at higher levels. Augustine's realism was excessive, Niebuhr allowed. Augustine lacked any basis for distinguishing between government and slavery or between a commonwealth and a band of robbers. All were forms of rule over human beings by human beings. Modern Christian realism had to do better, defending liberal democracy without enshrining any ideology as an object of faith.[52]

On these grounds he headed toward the Democratic Party and led many others to it, settling for a trinity of countervailing powers—big business, big labor, and big government. Gradual experimentation and renewal would get the right balance among the three economic powers. The property issue is never really solved; it must be negotiated continually within democracy, which is a method of finding proximate solutions for problems that cannot be solved. Niebuhr took a semester leave from Union after he finished *Children of Light* in August 1944. He conducted fundraising tours for UDA, worked in the state campaign of the American Labor Party, and threw in with the newly founded Liberal Party of New York—an outgrowth of the city versus state divide that split the Labor Party in March 1944. Counts, Randolph, John Childs, Alex Rose, and other state Labor Party bigwigs accused the city branch controlled by Hillman of kowtowing to Communists; thus they founded the Liberal Party. Niebuhr balked initially at breaking with Hillman, but near the end of the summer he joined the Liberals and was promptly elected vice chair of the party. The goal did not change—building a progressive prolabor party that excluded Communists, kept free of Tammany, and expanded on the New Deal. But that agenda pulled him step by step into the center-left of the Democratic Party.

Thomas entreated Niebuhr and the entire UDA to come home to the Socialist Party. In August 1944 he wrote an open letter to the *Socialist Call*, urging UDA to switch from Roosevelt to him. Thomas said FDR was dangerously enthralled with his personal rule and had become a servant of corrupt bosses of corrupt unions. FDR should have been embarrassed to seek a fourth term but was not. He had not pushed any progressive legislative cause since 1937, he dropped the foreign policy idealism of his Four Freedoms speech (1941), and he had no plan for preventing World War III. Thomas did not grasp that Niebuhr liked the later Roosevelt's foreign policy realism. Thomas was earnest and clueless: "You left us because of honest differences over an interventionist policy before Pearl Harbor." Now that the European war was almost over, "how about winning the peace? How about insisting that the demand for unconditional surrender be replaced by terms which may hasten a constructive people's revolution in Germany?"[53]

Niebuhr's reply was scathing. He sneered at Thomas's unctuous concern to win the peace, retorting that Hitler would be making the peace if America had listened to Thomas: "There is an exasperating quality of irresponsibility about the whole Socialist position, and it is difficult to take seriously your criticisms. This irresponsibility, which led to the folly of your pre–Pearl Harbor isolationism, stems from your inability to conceive of politics as the act of choosing among possible alternatives." Niebuhr said he could imagine some "basic political realignments" in the years to come but nothing that compelled a choice between socialism and reaction. Even if Thomas somehow racked up a sizable vote tally in November, it would "prove nothing and influence no one." The realistic choice, Niebuhr instructed, was between reverting to "the laissez-faire formula which failed before and ended in depression or of moving militantly forward in the determination to make the last four years of the Roosevelt era a period of social reconstruction and reform."[54]

On that ground he found his way to the Democratic Party, New York machine politics aside. If realistic politics reduced to laissez-faire versus the New Deal, there was no reason not to join Roosevelt's party. Niebuhr told himself he was building a farmer-labor alternative, but in fact he was building a former-Socialist brain trust lacking any farmers and perfectly suited for the next phase of the New Deal party. Roosevelt died five months after the 1944 election, his low-regarded vice president, Truman, replaced him, and in 1947 Niebuhr folded UDA into a new organization, Americans for Democratic Action (ADA)—a center-left caretaker of the New Deal legacy. Eleanor Roosevelt, Minneapolis mayor Hubert H. Humphrey, and Harvard historian Arthur Schlesinger Jr. were the ADA bigwigs. They had no organization of their own; they simply took over Niebuhr's organization after he and Loeb approached them. ADA swallowed the UDA, welcoming what the UDA Socialists contributed to postwar liberalism—union connections, anti-Communist street cred, and Niebuhr's convention performances. The UDA leftists were veterans of the battles to expel Communists from the unions and Socialist Party. They made the best anti-Communists because they were intimately acquainted with how Communists subverted democratic organizations. They boasted that they were the experts on thwarting Communism.

Niebuhr careened from advocating economic democracy to dropping altogether the language of economic justice. Socialists could be deeply democratic, he said, but they were never sufficiently empirical. A certain stubborn dogmatism rooted in Marxism or ethical idealism always prevented Socialists from engaging the world as it is. On his telling, every European Social Democratic party exemplified this problem. Meanwhile in the United States the New Deal and Truman's Fair Deal "equilibrated" economic power; thus good domestic politics in the economic area was just a matter of preserving and extending the

New Deal. In 1947 the Fellowship of Socialist Christians changed its name to Frontier Fellowship, befitting its decision to have no philosophy. Niebuhr said there was "a bare possibility that the kind of pragmatic political program which has been elaborated under the 'New Deal' and the 'Fair Deal' may prove to be a better answer to the problems of justice in a technical age than its critics of either right or left had assumed." This pallid prediction became his guiding truism in domestic politics. Frontier Fellowship, changing its name in 1951 to Christian Action, reduced its economic plank to a newspaper banality: "To maintain a high and stable level of economic activity, avoiding inflation and depression." The following year Niebuhr said he no longer thought in terms of positions about capitalism and economic democracy. The right and left still conceived politics ideologically, but "Vital Center" ADA Democrats had a better idea, fixing on what works.[55]

Thomas puzzled that Niebuhr, and Daniel Bell following Niebuhr, settled for vanilla Democratic politics. If you believe that economic democracy is essential to achieving justice, how can you let go of struggling for it? Thomas had the same feeling about imperialism. He raged against imperialism with an ethical passion that Niebuhr wrote off as softheaded idealism. To Thomas, imperialism was very much like slavery and racism in arising from arrogant self-worship and the evil compulsion to dominate. He could not be dispassionate about imperial abuse or fathom how it rested so lightly on the consciences of Western liberals. He opposed Roosevelt's insistence on an unconditional Japanese surrender and Roosevelt's attempt at Yalta to get the Soviets into the war against Japan. Both were terrible ideas for the same reason: the last thing the world needed was for the Soviet empire to expand into Asia. When Truman became president in April 1945 Thomas urged him to reverse Roosevelt's policies on eastern Europe, carpet-bombing, an unconditional Japanese surrender, and luring the Soviets into Asia. Japan was already prostrate; instead of inviting the Soviets into Asia, Thomas wanted Truman to negotiate a Japanese surrender.

Thomas was horrified when Truman ended the war by incinerating Hiroshima and Nagasaki. He was one of the very few public figures to say so, protesting that a decent society does not choose the most horrible option. Japan was ready to negotiate a conditional surrender; even failing one, Thomas said, Truman could have dropped a demonstration bomb before dictating the terms of surrender. Instead, the United States obliterated two crowded cities. Thomas's protests were unwelcome even in his customary lecture venues; he got a lot of blank stares and angry looking away. He criticized the United Nations and its role in founding the state of Israel, describing the UN as "a glorified and uneasy alliance which in its fundamental principles defeats its declared aims of the establishment of peace." Thomas told Congress he would have heartily supported a democratic UN; as it was, arrogant victors of a war once again presumed to rule the world; thus he endorsed the UN only reluctantly. He tried to be diplomatic about Israel, respecting that his party had many Labor Zionists, but Thomas warned that imposing a Jewish state on the Palestinians was another colonial project in a world that needed to abolish colonialism, and it would go badly, inflaming multiple kinds of nationalism and fanaticism. Meanwhile he cheered the Labour Party victory in Britain. Labour socialized essential industries, built an extensive welfare state, and got colonial England out of India, Pakistan, Burma (Myanmar), Ceylon (Sri Lanka), and Palestine. To Thomas, the meaning of the Labour victory applied directly to the United States: Labour Socialists survived the wilderness years of the 1930s by refusing to give up, and they succeeded by making stockpot unity leftism work.[56]

Thomas's antipathy toward Stalin and Soviet Communism seemed to make him a candidate for what became a significant social type, the Cold War socialist turned neoconservative. Neoconservatism germinated within his circle of militantly anticommunist socialists; the first neocons came from the Shachtman sect that entered the Socialist Party in 1958 and loathed the social movements of the 1960s. But Thomas was never a candidate to become a neocon. He lacked the obsession with American power and dominance that drove the neocons, and he warned during World War II that delusions about America's wartime Soviet ally could lead to a backlash and another avoidable war. Thus he pleaded for a realistic view of Soviet Communism. Briefly he cheered that World War II did not assault civil liberties and yield a Red Scare like World War I. Then a new Red Scare sprouted in 1946, and Thomas opposed it. His speaking tours gave him a vivid sense of America's overreaction. Thomas lectured in California at the end of 1945 and spoke in many of the same venues in the spring of 1947. The wild swing in his audiences appalled him: "Then the tendency was too much complacency about Russia and too much appeasement. Now there is a high degree of rather hysterical anticommunism, which is being exploited by reactionaries."[57]

Thomas spent his remaining twenty-one years fighting both positions and lamenting the failure of the labor party dream. One new entry was the Liberal Party that Dubinsky founded in New York after Communists took over the American Labor Party. Another was the Michigan Commonwealth Federation founded by Victor Reuther, Emil Mazey, and other Socialist leaders of the UAW. Another was the National Educational Committee for a New Party founded by Randolph and Dewey in 1946, which united disparate farmer-labor organizations and offshoots of the united fronts. These ventures were no less serious than the groups that built Canadian Social Democracy into a major political force. In Canada the Cooperative Commonwealth Federation and the Canadian Labour Congress grew through the 1950s and merged in 1961 into a major national party, the New Democratic Party (NDP). In the United States the farmer-labor-progressive parties usually folded within one election cycle and always struggled with the Communist problem.

American Communists appeared to ride high after World War II. They convened huge assemblies and spent much of 1946 fusing a flock of front groups, uniting in December as the Progressive Citizens of America (PCA). It advocated desegregation, national health insurance, the nationalization of the energy industry, and friendship with the Soviet Union. That year Truman sent naval forces to the eastern Mediterranean to push Soviet tanks out of northern Iran. Commerce Secretary Henry Wallace accused Truman of needlessly antagonizing Russia, and in September 1946 Truman fired him. The following March Truman intervened in the Greek civil war, asking Congress to take over the British role of helping royalist forces repel Communists. His appeal to Congress, dubbed the Truman Doctrine, commenced the Cold War. Though Wallace never joined the PCA, he was its voice, describing it as a Gideon's Army dedicated to peace and the general welfare. In 1948 the PCA formed the Progressive Party and ran Wallace for president, charging that Truman railroaded the United States into Cold War belligerency.[58]

Wallace called for the nationalization of banks and railroads, blasted segregation and the Cold War, and stayed in black-owned hotels. His supporters included Harlem congressman Vito Marcantonio, singer Paul Robeson, and future Democratic presidential candidate George McGovern. Niebuhr and Thomas despised Wallace for fronting for Communists, which spurred Niebuhr to found the ADA. From 1933 to 1940 Wallace had curtailed agricultural surpluses and alleviated rural poverty as secretary of agriculture. Thomas had asked Wallace to support the STFU when Thomas and H. L. Mitchell founded it, but Wallace refused to meet with him, believing the union undermined the AAA. During World War II the STFU advised its members to find work outside the plantation fields and set up an underground railroad to transport more than ten thousand workers to northern and northeastern states. After the war it changed its name to the National Farm Labor Union and joined the AFL. Thomas took pride in the STFU and fumed against Wallace for the rest of his life, bitterly recalling that Wallace did nothing for racial justice back when he had the power to do something important. Thomas chafed in 1940 when Wallace became vice president and did not feel sorry for him four years later when conservative Democrats knocked him off the ticket at the Democratic convention. Wallace got left-wing martyr points for losing the vice presidency, while positioning himself as the next champion of the New Deal. Two years later, in 1946, he became a hero to the anti-anti-Communist left by opposing the Cold War. Niebuhr and Thomas were repulsed by the prospect of a pro-Communist campaign fronted by Wallace. The ADA came about because the UDA was too small and underfinanced to combat the sizable wing of American liberalism that either sympathized with Communism or at least wanted friendly relationships with Communists. Like Du Bois in 1909, Niebuhr decided that to scale up he had to cut a deal with prominent liberals. The ADA was the product of Niebuhr's willingness to fold his treasured UDA into something new that did not revolve around him.[59]

He and Loeb reached out to anti-Communist liberals who would not have joined UDA. They started with Joseph Rauh, housing bureau official Wilson Wyatt, and journalist James Wechsler, who helped them recruit Humphrey, Schlesinger, Eleanor Roosevelt, former Office of Price Administration chair Leon Henderson, economist John Kenneth Galbraith, and former ambassador to Russia Averell Harriman. In November 1946 Niebuhr gave a hyperkinetic address to the CIO convention that brought Walter Reuther and David Dubinsky into the fold. Two months later 130 liberals convened at the Willard Hotel in Washington, DC, to form the ADA, which amplified the no-Communists rule of UDA; ADA excluded Communist sympathizers too. Roosevelt gave the keynote address, pointedly denying that Wallace was the guardian of the New Deal legacy. ADA was a vehicle for high-rolling Washington insiders absorbed in Democratic national politics. It swelled rapidly to 18,000 members, doubling the UDA base, and stressed that it supported Truman's forceful approach to the Soviet Union. Wyatt and Henderson ran it as cochairs, and Loeb became executive secretary. Niebuhr gave stem-winders at ADA conventions featuring cheeky salutations such as, "Ladies, Gentlemen, honored bigwigs, and high brass." He identified with ADA while becoming marginal to it. UDA, he explained to Loeb, had an educational mission and trafficked in ideas; ADA was consumed with the Beltway political horse race.[60]

Electoral pragmatism sharply distinguished Thomas from Niebuhr and the ADA; anti-Communism did not. Bell asked Thomas in 1947 how he responded to Niebuhr's claim that Thomas was too idealistic to be good at politics. Thomas humbly replied that he recognized that political action always requires compromise. What plagued him constantly was that he never knew in advance at what point a compromise became betrayal: "The dilemma which you state exists and I have never been able to find a perfect verbal or logical solution of it." Bell was moving inwardly from Thomas's orbit to Niebuhr's for exactly the reason he posed to Thomas. He stuck with Thomas for one more election but was leaning toward the verdict that Thomas Socialism was hopelessly idealistic, and Cold War liberalism got the right balance. Later he said the triumph of Cold War liberalism put an end to ideology itself.[61]

On anti-Communism, Niebuhr was not as vehement in 1948 as Thomas, who based his last presidential campaign on this issue. Thomas wanted Randolph to run for president but he declined, and Thomas reluctantly geared up, now as a grieving, depressed widower; Violet Thomas died in 1947. Thomas attracted his most distinguished band of intellectual supporters since 1932, headed by Bell, Holmes, Hook, Macdonald, Villard, Wolfe, sociologist C. Wright Mills, and social philosopher Erich Fromm. Dorothy Thompson joined this group, explaining that Thomas stood out by bravely condemning the Potsdam agreement and the incineration of Hiroshima. Thomas joined a picket led by Randolph outside the Democratic convention demanding desegregation of the military. He noted that Wallace was a latecomer to racial justice activism and blasted Wallace as an "apologist for the slave state of Russia, and preacher of peace by appeasement." Thomas said it was ridiculous to believe that peace could be achieved "by submission to the mightiest tyranny which has ever appeared on this earth." Communism was not socialism in a hurry, a militant version of liberal democracy, or any such thing. It was the annihilation of liberal democratic decency. Thomas targeted Wallace because his candidacy threatened to create a bad form of the unity leftist dream. Wallace pleaded for a debate with Truman and Republican candidate Thomas Dewey but refused to debate Thomas. Though Thomas won only ninety-five thousand votes, he exulted that Wallace won only 2.3 percent of the vote.[62]

It turned out that Communists were not riding as high as it seemed. Wallace got rough treatment on the road and received a surprisingly weak tally for a prominent former vice president. Even Adam Clayton Powell Jr. decided at the last minute not to back him, discerning wind direction. Moscow had dumped Browder as party chair and expelled him as soon as World War II ended, no longer prizing his cozy relationships with American officials and no longer pretending to support Democrats. Foster, rewarded for decades of obedient service, replaced Browder. Leftist historians scrounging for a usable past later described the Progressive Party with rose-colored piety, but Moscow swiftly left it behind as an embarrassment.[63]

Russia paid a horrific price for thwarting the Nazi war machine, losing more war dead—approximately twenty million—than the other warring nations combined. It emerged from World War II as a deeply battered world power. The Red Army touted itself as an antifascist liberating force, conquering territories of Eastern and Central Europe that had long loathed Russia and Communism.

Very briefly, European Social Democrats hoped the historic enmity between Social Democracy and Communism might be left behind. They admired the heroic struggle of the Russian people and tried to believe the future belonged to democratic socialism. Social Democrats made significant political gains throughout Western Europe but did not get the future they wanted. In divided Germany the enmity between Communists and Socialists worsened dramatically. In most of what became the East Bloc, twice-conquered resentment prevailed with few exceptions. Whatever chance Russia may have had to work out decent relationships with the governments on its western borders was erased by the Western demand to elect Western-style democratic governments in Eastern and Central Europe. The Cold War overshadowed everything in postwar Europe, fueled by Russia's colossal suffering, sense of vulnerability, and overcompensating belief in its messianic mission and America's determination to keep Russia as weak and constrained as possible.[64]

The American counterparts of European Social Democrats in the Socialist Party and Social Democratic Federation mostly shared Thomas's view that democratic socialists needed to be principled anticommunists of the not-fanatical sort. Many became high officials in the U.S. State Department, notably Robert Alexander, Irving Brown, Paul Porter, Clarence Senior, Frank Trager, and Morris Weisz. Lovestone, now heading the International Affairs department of the AFL, matched Socialists to State Department posts. In 1945 Thomas began to write a book on democratic socialism, labored over it, and pushed it aside two years later when Violet died. He was too depressed to finish it and then campaigned for president. Afterward he went back to the manuscript only to realize he needed to rewrite it.

His first draft stressed the threat of Soviet totalitarianism and blistered fellow travelers, but by the end of the campaign both themes felt like overkill to him. Wallace-style leftism was not the threat that Thomas had thought; meanwhile establishment Democrats had regained control, winning both houses of Congress in 1948. Dewey blew the election with front-runner platitudes: "Our future lies before us. . . . Our rivers are full of fish." Truman won a comeback victory with a feisty campaign defending the New Deal and his advocacy of civil rights and anti-Communism. To Socialists angling for a labor-progressive party, the election was a death knell. Truman in the White House and Democrats controlling Congress meant there was no opening. Schlesinger justly boasted that his band of ADA liberals represented the Vital Center of American politics; liberal anti-Communism was exactly the combination America needed.[65]

A Socialist's Faith, finally published by Thomas in 1951, opened with a believe-it-or-not chapter titled "We Believed in Progress." Thomas said the happy part of his life was when he believed along with everyone else that cultural progress was real and could be counted upon. He grew steadily more miserable as an adult upon realizing that no part of his belief in progress was true. He was more miserable in 1930 than in 1920, more in 1940 than in 1930, and more in 1950 than ever. Culturally, he said, the United States had always been a Philistine wasteland and not because it exuded an unsophisticated virtue. America had always been Philistine *and* corrupted by capitalism. Yet the America of his youth was a buoyant nation of life and hope. The Statue of Liberty symbolized something very real; immigrants flocked to the United States from everywhere, yearning for freedom, opportunity, and the desire not to live in fear of a police state. The other American story—white Americans enslaving and oppressing black Americans and poor Americans left to starve— contradicted the Statue of Liberty story, but even the racism story folded into the myth of American progress. The nation nearly destroyed itself in abolishing slavery and passed laws outlawing racial discrimination. Liberal democracy deepened and expanded, and the abolition of slavery underwrote the serious expectation that war could be abolished too. Thomas said he believed the whole thing when he entered the ministry. He had a sense of vocation and usefulness that were now almost impossible to describe, now that he spoke to audiences caught in the "vast web of impersonal forces."[66]

No one in his Princeton class could have imagined that Americans at midcentury would fear what science had wrought and feel no sense of security; Thomas believed that Hiroshima haunted Americans more than they admitted. To be sure, he said, early twentieth-century Americans lionized their amoral economic system, but they took for granted that ethical standards applied to society, and American literature exuded a healthy-minded optimism that now registered as quaint. Thomas put it categorically: "With the single and important exception of the growth of a better conscience on race relations, the years through which I have lived have been years of moral retrogression." The New Deal was not an exception, being driven by new technological capabilities, not moral commitments. In his youth vast communities could be moved to moral sympathy by the injustice done to someone outside their group; Thomas pointed to the framing of French artillery officer Alfred Dreyfus in 1895 and the execution of Italian American anarchists Nicola Sacco and Bartolomeo Vanzetti in 1927. That no longer existed, he said. Modern Americans respected power, not moral sympathy. Cruelty did not move them; only the enemy's cruelty moved them. They respected even the cruelty of their enemy "if by cruelty he gets things done."[67]

Thomas said it could not get worse than what he experienced on his lecture tours from 1945 to 1948. Appeals to Americans about the suffering, enslavement, and plight of displaced and oppressed people evoked blank stares. People told him it was best not to get worked up about social problems, aside from the Communist menace. Nobody wanted to hear about Hiroshima, Palestinians, or the poor. Americans didn't want to hear about Russians in slave labor camps *or* about the civil rights of Communists. The Marshall Plan, Thomas said, might be counted as an exception, but it wasn't. Though Americans were farsighted in rebuilding Europe, the plan was sold to them as a strategy to make money and fight Communism. If a policy didn't reward the selfishness of one's group or nation, it was laughed out of court. Capitalism alone, he argued, was not enough to yield this outcome, except in the sense that capitalism drove Europe to two apocalyptic wars. The world changed in 1914, almost entirely for the worse. Thomas corrected the convention that his generation believed that peace was assured by the march of progress. There would not have been so many peace societies had his generation believed that peace was assured. Still, it was true that "we could not imagine total war." Wilson got a stampede going by exploiting the real religion of America—nationalism. Afterward it was straight downhill for those who dreamed of a federation of cooperative commonwealths. Thomas reeled at recounting his entire Socialist career: down, down, down, down.[68]

Now he reeled at America's wild swing from Uncle Joe to rabid anti-Communism. Both reactions were wrong, he argued. Sooner or later "Russian imperial communism will perish by the violence which it has invoked." The question was whether it would first spread to the entire planet, obliterating cultures of individual liberty and tolerance that took centuries to create. Thomas said progressives needed to lead the fight against Communism; otherwise reactionaries would own it and it would go badly. On one hand, "the evidence of the essential evil of communism is strong." On the other hand, Western democracies handed cheap propaganda victories to the Soviet Union every time they bullied weaker nations or embraced dictators in the so-called Third World. Communism was growing in the Third World because Britain and the United States appeased Stalin from Casablanca to Potsdam *and* because Communism shrewdly exploited the hopes of formerly colonized peoples: "Despite its own worse crimes—which are still widely disbelieved—it has the towering advantage of being in a position to say to millions of resentful colonials and to the disinherited masses generally: 'Our enemies are your enemies. Let us make common cause!' " Thomas contended that if Western democracies did not extinguish their racist and imperialist attitudes they were sure to lose the battle for hearts and minds in the Third World.[69]

A Socialist's Faith showed that Thomas kept up with the trend in Social Democracy away from defining socialism as collective ownership. Socialism, to him, was a movement seeking to build a cooperative society that served the common good. There were many ways to democratize economic power, and nationalizing enterprises was just one of them. Social ownership itself is merely a means, not an end. Thomas advocated a commanding heights strategy in which public corporations controlled essential industries, consumer cooperatives controlled most retail outlets, and nonessential industries remained under private control. In 1934 he wanted all banks, railroads, coal mines, and power and oil companies to be socialized immediately, as well as all other monopolized or semimonopolized firms such as the dairy trust. By 1940 he favored consumer cooperatives over public corporations but treated this issue as a matter of contextual judgment. All natural monopolies should be socialized as public corporations, and all other essential industries should be socialized in some form. He stuck to that view for the rest of his life while stressing what it did not mean—socialists did not want to nationalize everything.[70]

A *Socialist's Faith* lingered longer over details and philosophy than Thomas had offered previously, advocating the socialization of natural resources, money, banking, credit, and monopolies. Private firms, he said, should be allowed to profit from the mineral wealth they discover or extract but not to own what they do not make. Mineral wealth should be public property and available to everyone. Thomas puzzled that citizens of modern democracies put up with private banks, paying interest "for no other service than what ought to be the social function of the creation of money in the form of credit." An essential function of a democratic state is to create money parallel to the creation of goods on noninflationary terms. Socialized credit is a fundamental necessity, promoting investment for the public good. Moreover, socializing natural monopolies such as water and electrical power systems and the steel, coal, and oil industries is essential—serving the common good by privileging the principle of production for use. Thomas believed that workers should be represented directly on company boards, not through unions, and that consumer associations should elect public representatives, though he did not elevate his nonunion preference to a principle or norm. He was fond of tweaking union audiences by insisting that, faced with a choice between political democracy and self-interested unions, he would take political democracy every time.[71]

He laid the blame for the Cold War squarely on Stalin. America's pushback in Iran and Greece and insistence on elections in Eastern Europe were benign compared to Stalin conquering Eastern Europe, launching the Berlin blockade, refusing to cooperate with the Marshall Plan, and rejecting American proposals for nuclear disarmament. At the same time, Thomas said that overreacting to Soviet aggression would be catastrophic, paving the way to another world war. As it was, Stalin could not have pushed so far into Europe lacking weak opposition. It haunted Thomas that large sections of formerly Social Democratic parties in Czechoslovakia, Romania, and Poland rolled over for Communism. He admonished American socialists not to say that coercion and bribery alone explained it; the Marxist denigration of democracy was a major contributing factor. Social Democrats capitulated to Communism instead of fighting for democracy, rationalizing that Marxism bonded them to Communists against their capitalist enemies. Thomas said he began his Socialist career as a non-Marxist, gravitated to semi-Marxism in the 1930s, and subsequently drifted from it. He respected Marx but disliked the very idea of orthodox Marxism and was grateful that American Socialists never said he had to be a Marxist. It seemed to him that Marxism was too much like theology, trafficking in abstract arguments, required doctrines, and a parade of authorities. Even the theologian closest to him, Niebuhr, had an abstruse theology that Thomas could not connect to "his admirable economic and political suggestions." Whatever relationship existed between Christianity and realism in Niebuhr's thought, Thomas could not fathom it, being averse to it.[72]

Thomas said he wished he could defend his positions of 1939, 1940, and 1941 but could do so only selectively, leaving to historians to say what his worst mistakes had been. "[However,] of nothing in my life am I surer than that I was right in 1944 on the policies that might have made for a decent peace." Had Roosevelt stuck to ethical principles on the road to Yalta instead of cutting cynical deals, the postwar world would have been far better. America intervened in Korea just as Thomas completed *A Socialist's Faith*. He supported the war on anticommunist grounds and as a show of support for the United Nations. In Korea, he reasoned, the United States had an important chance to teach Stalin and Mao Zedong that containment was real and further Communist aggression would be resisted: "Imperial communism seeks world power." On that consuming issue there was no daylight in the early 1950s between Thomas and Niebuhr, as Thomas echoed Niebuhr on the nature and perils of Communist evil.[73]

State Department guru George Kennan famously originated the strategy of Communist containment that Niebuhr amplified and the foreign policy establishment adopted. Kennan's "X" article of 1947 in *Foreign Affairs* portrayed the Soviet Union as a crude imperial power with a grossly inefficient economy and a war-ravaged population. Soviet leaders, he observed, blathered about the coming global triumph of Communism, but they couldn't build a decent highway system. They brandished an aggressive Marxist ideology, but its bankruptcy was increasingly evident to the masses. Kennan doubted that Soviet officials were keen to pursue dangerous operations abroad, and he believed they would retreat in the face of superior force. Containment was about keeping American power in their faces. The best policy was to maintain a "long-term, patient but firm and vigilant containment of Russian expansive tendencies," adroitly applying counterforce "at a series of constantly shifting geographical and political points." Containing the Russian bear was better than preparing for a hot war, and it might accelerate the self-destruction of the Soviet state. Sooner or later, Kennan argued, Soviet Communism would implode because Communism doesn't work. If America kept the pressure on for ten to fifteen years the Soviet state would unravel completely: "Soviet Russia might be changed overnight from one of the strongest to one of the weakest and most pitiable of national societies."[74]

Niebuhr befriended Kennan, supported his containment strategy, and prized his realistic wisdom. But Niebuhr was a theologian not to be deprived of theological glosses about perverted religion and forms of evil. Communism is evil, he insisted. It was terribly important to start with this recognition instead of timidly skirting around it or asking the wrong question. Timid souls questioned whether Communism was really as evil as Cold Warriors believed, and classic realists refused to import moral language into this subject. What if Communism was not as evil as Cold War anxiety made it out to be? What if Cold War fearfulness was a new example of the overreaction against the kaiser's Germany that sowed something far worse? Niebuhr said these were plausible but misleading questions. Soviet Communism was not merely a new form of Russian imperialism, projecting the normal lust for power of a Great Power. Communism had a "noxious demonry" owing to its deeply religious character as a utopian, global, secular totalitarian faith. Niebuhr described Communism as a monopoly of power wielded by a revolutionary elite in the name of Marxian deliverance. The logic of monopoly began with the Marxist doctrine that economic power inheres solely in the ownership of property. It combined dogmatism with tyranny, justifying the monopoly of the party claiming to be the vanguard of the entire revolutionary class. It drove to the dictatorship of a single tyrant, as Trotsky discovered. Niebuhr said Communism is impossible without ruthless totalitarian rule, so it was stupid to hope that liberalized forms of it would emerge: "Nothing modifies its evil display of tyranny."[75]

Communism was a perverted form of pseudouniversal religion transcending national boundaries; thus it had to be fought differently than the Allies fought Fascism. Fascism could be smashed by direct force, but Communism had the moral power of a utopian creed that appealed to deluded leftists and to millions in the Third World. Niebuhr said Communism was tactically flexible and inherently fanatical, resting on a simple distinction between oppressors and oppressed, simplistic concepts of class and exploitation, and a simplistic vision of world revolution. Waging a crusading hot war against it would not work. America's battle against Communism needed to walk a fine, patient, vigilant line between treating the Soviet state as a geopolitical Great Power rival and an implacable Nazi-like enemy: "We are embattled with a foe who embodies all the evils of a demonic religion. We will probably be at sword's point with this foe for generations to come."[76]

Niebuhr warned that a perverted political moralism is always more dangerous than explicit evil. For this reason Communism was capable of creating greater and longer-lasting evils than Fascism. The best analogy for the Communist threat to the West was the rise of militant Islam in the high Middle Ages, not the Third Reich: "Moslem power was consolidated in the Middle Ages and threatened the whole of Christendom much as Communist power threatens Western civilization today." Just as Islam brandished a quasi-universal ideology that transcended nationalism while being rooted in the Arab world, the Communist movement wielded a pseudouniversal creed that served Russian imperial ambitions. Niebuhr believed that equating Soviet tyranny with Islam validated his conception of Soviet Communism as an evil religion. He took for granted that his audience would not object to his slur that Islam was similarly demonic, and he was not called on it. Usually he added that the Islamic concept of a holy war against infidels was "analogous to the Communist conception of the inevitable conflict between capitalism and Communism."[77]

Niebuhr hung a vast ideological scaffolding on this argument, teaching that Communism was devoted to the establishment of a new universal order, not merely the supremacy of a race or nation; thus it had to be contained through diplomatic pressure and military force. In the early 1950s he condemned Communism as a devouring, demonic, totalitarian monolith, though he disliked it when Cold Warriors went completely Manichean. To Niebuhr, the essence of realism was recognizing that nothing is purely good or evil. He did not want to be confused with people who rattled on about America the pure and exceptional. In 1952 he said so in *The Irony of American History*, contending that America's innocent self-image inoculated Americans from recognizing their imperialism. This innocence helped America play its imperial role, except when it didn't. *Irony* made a case for a bit of modesty, countering the zealously self-righteous mood of the time. To be sure, Niebuhr said, Americans rightly admired their nation's unrivaled greatness and success: "Of all the 'knights' of bourgeois culture, our castle is the most imposing and our horse the sleekest and most impressive." Moreover, the "lady" of American dreams was more opulent and desirable than anyone else's. But Americans wrongly believed the lessons of history did not apply to them: "If only we could fully understand that the evils against which we contend are frequently the fruit of illusions which are similar to our own, we might be better prepared to save a vast uncommitted world, particularly in Asia, which lies between ourselves and communism, from being engulfed by this noxious creed."[78]

Niebuhr tried to help America do a better job of running its empire. His thought was geared to the problems of his friends in the State Department— fellow graduates of the Socialist Party and the UDA. He cautioned them that virtues turn into vices whenever virtues are complacently relied upon. America, for all its goodness and success, did not transcend the limits of all human striving, the precariousness of all configurations and uses of power, "and the mixture of good and evil in all human virtue." Meanwhile he accentuated the evil of Communism, famously describing it in 1953 as "an organized evil which spreads terror and cruelty throughout the world and confronts us everywhere with faceless men who are immune to every form of moral and political suasion." He stayed in this mode until 1954, when Joseph McCarthy self-destructed. It was an ugly, demeaning, mendacious, and frightening period. Niebuhr detested McCarthy's wild charges that vast numbers of government officials were Communists, while believing it was imperative to prevent McCarthy from monopolizing the anti-Communist issue.[79]

Niebuhr implicitly condoned parts of McCarthy's campaign to smoke out Communists from government, education, and religion. In 1953 he wrongly claimed that McCarthy's assistant J. B. Matthews accurately identified more than a dozen pro-Communist church leaders, and he strongly supported the government's execution of Julius and Ethel Rosenberg for stealing atomic secrets. In the mid-1950s Niebuhr began to pull back, asserting that containment had to be less ideological and fear mongering. He kept rethinking what that meant, deciding in 1958 that he and Kennan had been wrong about Communism being unsustainable and incapable of internal reforms. Otherwise, how was one to explain that Soviet premier Nikita Khrushchev condemned Stalin's crimes and had a reform agenda? The later Niebuhr struggled to formulate a moderate, empirical, realistic approach to containment, influencing how Thomas similarly tried to keep his balance—though Thomas grasped sooner than Niebuhr that bad containment yielded a spectacular catastrophe in Vietnam.[80]

The Socialist Party should have terminated its presidential campaigns after 1948; Thomas and the NEC pleaded for no more. But the party had newcomers to its ritual humiliation at the national level, plus members who wanted to run in municipal elections and needed the boost of a presidential candidate. First, it lost its entire anarchist-leaning youth caucus, the Chicago left wing, also called the Libertarian Caucus. Virgil Vogel chaired YPSL during the war and subsequently took over the Chicago left wing. He despaired at seeing Thomas and the NEC drift into the Old Guard–ADA wing of the Democratic Party, protesting that Thomas and the party used to be brave and principled—in 1939. Vogel admired the Thomas who refused to follow the liberals and Old Guard Social Democrats into the collective security camp. What happened to that guy? The new Thomas mumbled about founding a socialist institute and maybe voting for Democrats. Vogel felt betrayed. In 1949 he led his group into a new party, the Libertarian Socialist League, a throwback to the IWW. The following year the Socialist Party met in Detroit to decide whether it was politically dead. Thomas said it was time to stop running candidates. His 1944 running mate, Darlington Hoopes, countered that there had to be a socialist alternative; Democrats were a fraudulent gang that lied to get elected and did nothing in office. Hoopes was a Quaker lawyer from Reading, Pennsylvania, nostalgic for the robust labor socialism of his youth. He rallied the convention majority to run in 1952 and again in 1956, emoting idealistically to the end: "We must and we shall build a political movement in this country in which we can march side by side with millions of our devoted comrades throughout the world to our glorious goal of the cooperative commonwealth. We have kept the torch burning through a most difficult and trying period."[81]

But the socialists who changed America in the 1950s were African American fighters for racial justice: Randolph, Farmer, Rustin, Mordecai Johnson, and Martin Luther King Jr. All were devoted to Thomas but threw off the Socialist habit of leading with their socialism. They believed that socialists should be the best antiracist warriors, notwithstanding that black NAACP liberals and white Communists dominated this field. CORE was stocked with socialists, as were the left wing of FOR and the NAACP. Randolph, Farmer, Rustin, Johnson, and black socialist feminist Pauli Murray were stunned when America's Gandhi turned out to be a tweedy black Baptist Socialist with a freshly minted PhD and no activist record.

MARTIN LUTHER KING JR. AND AMERICAN APARTHEID

Martin Luther King Jr. did not come from nowhere. Long before he burst onto the national scene in Montgomery, Alabama, in December 1955 there was a tradition of black social gospel leaders that stretched back to the 1870s and struggled to break America's racial caste system. They took up the defining black social gospel project of asking what a new abolitionism would be in their post-Reconstruction context of repression and racial terrorism. They refuted the racist culture that demeaned their human dignity, showing that progressive theology could be combined with social justice politics in black church contexts. They refused to give up on the black churches, even as a chorus of black and white intellectuals contended that black churches were hopelessly self-centered, provincial, insular, anti-intellectual, and conservative. King's role models were church leaders who inherited the black social gospel tradition and came of age in the 1920s: Johnson, Benjamin E. Mays, J. Pius Barbour, Howard Thurman, and, with caveats, his Baptist preacher father, Daddy King.

Daddy King was pugnacious and domineering, always keeping the deacons in line, but also winsome, vibrant, and careful. He rebuked Jim Crow effrontery on the rare occasions that he failed to avoid white people, refusing to be addressed as "Boy." Being addressed by one's first name was also problematic in Jim Crow America, so black Americans often chose not to have one, opting for initials. Daddy King told his children to avoid whites; otherwise he did not talk about them or racism. To him, segregation was evil, white racism was a mystery best left to God, and there was nothing else to talk about concerning race. In the pulpit and at home he oscillated between cajoling and yelling, tirelessly admonishing about how to behave. His famous son, not coincidentally, never barked at anyone until very near the end of his life.

King absorbed the evangelical piety and social concerns of his family and church and got a more intellectual version of both things at Morehouse College, where Mays influenced him as president. He moved on to Crozer Seminary in Chester, Pennsylvania, where he read Rauschenbusch, William Newton Clarke, William Adams Brown, and other prominent liberal theologians, embracing Rauschenbusch's vision of economic democracy. King said the social gospel rightly conceived economic justice as an essential aspect of Christianity: "I am a profound advocator of the social gospel."[82]

His storied encounter with Johnson occurred during King's second year at Crozer, at Fellowship House in Philadelphia. Johnson was the first black president of Howard University and a legendary speaker who espoused liberal theology, democratic socialism, anticolonial internationalism, civil rights progressivism, anti-anti-Communism, and Gandhian nonviolence. He was a graduate of Morehouse College and Rochester Seminary who got his socialism straight from Rauschenbusch and later combined Christian socialism with Gandhi's strategy of civil disobedience. At Fellowship House he gave one of his customary bravura talks commending the anti-imperial nonviolence of the Gandhi movement. King was riveted and, to some degree, persuaded. Hearing a similar talk from Muste had brought out King's incredulity. Hearing it from a black social gospel leader enthralled King: "His message was so profound and electrifying that I left the meeting and bought a half-dozen books on Gandhi's life and works."[83]

Actually his path to Gandhian nonviolence was more complex than the story he told. King's knowledge of Gandhi was patchy and thin when the Montgomery boycott began. Rustin and FOR stalwart Glenn Smiley, rushing to Montgomery, asked King how much he knew about Gandhian nonviolence. King did not say what he later claimed, that he had studied Gandhi intently for years. He said he knew very little. At Crozer and Boston University King knew just enough about Gandhian strategy to feel attracted to it. At the level of this feeling he struggled with the implications of Niebuhrian realism. Christian socialism, he believed, had to combine the best parts of Rauschenbusch, Niebuhr, and Gandhi. But King concentrated on a different question in graduate school: How should he think about God and human beings?[84]

J. Pius Barbour, King's pastor during his Crozer years, combined the same intellectual planks that later marked King, playing a crucial role in passing them to King. Barbour was rooted in southern black Baptist religion, modernized by liberal theology and historical criticism and influenced by Rauschenbusch's socialism, Niebuhr's realism, the personal idealism of Boston University philosopher Edgar S. Brightman, and the naturalistic behaviorism of University of Chicago theologian Henry Nelson Wieman. Like Johnson, Barbour conceived social gospel socialism as a critique of capitalist exploitation and a vision of economic democracy. He organized his sermons in thesis-antithesis-synthesis fashion, sometimes announcing in advance what the synthesis would be. He mentored Crozer students in raconteur fashion and helped King decide to earn his doctorate in theology at Boston University.[85]

King loved the same thing in Hegel that Du Bois caught in graduate school—the notion that Spirit uses the passions of partly unsuspecting individuals to fulfill its aims of self-consciousness and freedom. King embraced Hegel's idea that truth is the whole, habitually thinking afterward in Hegelian triads yielding a synthesis. His socialist pacifist dean at Boston University, Walter Muelder, argued that Niebuhr's realism was fatally flawed by its lack of any concept of personal or social regeneration. How do human beings develop spiritually? How does personality actualize Christian values? What is the significance of self-sacrificing love in human nature and history? King embraced Muelder's critique of Niebuhr, observing: "All these problems are left unsolved by Niebuhr. He fails to see that the availability of the divine *Agape* is an essential affirmation of the Christian religion."[86]

Love divine is a redemptive energy that transcends and transforms individual and collective egotism. To King, dropping the language of spiritual regeneration was not an option. He conceived God in personalist fashion as the personal ground of the infinite value of human personality. This two-sided credo had a negative corollary confirming King's deepest feeling: If the worth of personality is the ultimate value in life, America's racial caste system was distinctly evil. Evil is precisely that which degrades and negates personality. The purpose of American racial caste was to humiliate, exclude, and degrade the personhood of African Americans. If Christianity meant anything in the American context, it had to speak and shout a contrary word. No philosophy countered American racism more powerfully than the one King absorbed and espoused as a graduate student. On that ground more than any other he clung to post-Kantian, Christian, personal idealism for the rest of his life.[87]

The movement made King, not the other way around, but the movement that swept him to prominence in December 1955 would not have caught fire without him. King's distinct brilliance lit up the Montgomery, Alabama, bus boycott on its first night and sustained it against enraged opposition. Montgomery happened because it had English professor Jo-Ann Robinson, the Montgomery Women's Political Council, Rosa Parks, and former NAACP leader E. D. Nixon. They were ready to challenge bus segregation when Parks provided the perfect test case by getting arrested. Somebody had to speak for the boycott, Nixon excoriated the ministers when nobody volunteered, King walked in late, and he took offense at being excoriated. History turned in a moment because the newcomer was willing to risk his life. King had twenty minutes to plan what he would say that night. He had one guiding thought as he headed to Holt Street Church: Somehow I have to be militant and moderate at the same time.

He appealed to the democratic traditions of America, the deep integrity of oppressed black Americans, and the teaching of Jesus. He made a justice run, declaring that there comes a time when people get tired of being trampled by the iron feet of oppression. The crowd erupted with passionate agreement. King made a second run. If this movement was wrong, so were the Supreme Court, the Constitution, Jesus, and God Almighty. If they were wrong, justice is a lie and love has no meaning. They were reaching for the daybreak of freedom and justice. The crowd erupted again at the stunning image of daybreak. King implored that Christian love is one side of the Christian faith, and the other side is justice. Christians live in the spirit of love divine *and* employ the tools of divine justice. They must use the tools of spiritual persuasion *and* the tools of political coercion. King ran out of metaphors for his third run, but the Holt Street Address perfectly distilled what became his message. Soon it was his trademark, helping him to personally link the fledgling, theatrical, church-based movement for racial justice in the South to the established, institutional, mostly secular movement based in New York City.[88]

Rustin and Smiley made their way to Montgomery, befriended King, and provided grist for the conspiracy theory that white locals already believed: It could not be that Montgomery blacks had mounted the boycott movement. New York radicals had to be running it. In fact, the Montgomery protest was wholly homegrown until Rustin and Smiley arrived. Rustin represented a new, eclectic, union-based activist group, In Friendship, founded in early 1956 to raise money for the Montgomery boycott and other racial justice protests in the South. Its ringleaders were Rustin, Farmer, Randolph, Thomas, Ella Baker, Stanley Levison, Harry Emerson Fosdick, and labor chief Jerry Wurf, and it was financed mostly by the Workers Defense League, American Jewish Council, and State, County, and Municipal Workers Union. The group used a donation from a WRL supporter to send Rustin to Montgomery.

Any outsider would have provoked grumbling and accusation among local whites and blacks. As it was, Rustin was impossibly controversial and exotic in Montgomery. He was eloquent, selfless, intellectual, and sometimes haughty— a Greenwich Village bohemian and minstrel activist with a criminal record for being gay and antiwar, and an incongruous British accent. Born in Chester, Pennsylvania, in 1910, Rustin was raised by a Quaker grandmother and learned as a teenager that the woman he thought was his sister was his mother. He dropped out of Wilberforce in 1934 and eked out a living as a singer in New York, performing with Josh White and Leadbelly. In the 1930s he was active in the Young Communist League, but after Hitler invaded Russia in 1941 and the Communist Party dropped its pseudopacifist line, Rustin returned to Quakerism and worked for the March on Washington movement as its youth organizer. He learned movement building through Randolph, joining the Socialist Party and FOR. As an FOR staffer he helped Farmer found CORE in 1942, and like most FOR staffers Rustin was imprisoned during World War II as a conscientious objector, serving three years in Lewisburg Penitentiary. After the war he learned Gandhian resistance strategy firsthand in India, returning to the United States in 1947. The following year he worked with Randolph to end segregation in the armed services, and in 1949 Rustin rode the CORE/FOR Journey of Reconciliation bus protesting bus segregation in North Carolina, which landed him on a chain gang. At the time of the Montgomery boycott Rustin was working for WRL, though he later remembered it as an FOR job, perhaps repressing that Muste dropped him from the FOR staff in 1953 after he was arrested on a morals charge.[89]

On Rustin's first day in Montgomery a hotel employee warned him that "Communist agitators and New Yorkers" were said to be running the boycott. On his second day he persuaded Montgomery Improvement Association (MIA) leaders to stage an almost-celebration of their arrests, in their Sunday church suits; he also recalculated what he should do in Montgomery. Instead of conducting formal training sessions on Gandhian strategy, as he had planned, Rustin worked organically with boycott leaders, reacting to situations as they unfolded. On his fifth day Rustin acquired a handbill distributed at a White Citizens Council meeting: "We hold these truths to be self-evident: that all whites are created equal with certain rights; among these are life, liberty, and the pursuit of dead niggers. In every stage of the bus boycott we have been oppressed and degraded because of black, slimy, juicy, unbearably stinking niggers." White Montgomery, the handbill urged, had to exterminate "these black devils" with guns and knives; otherwise "we will soon wake up and find Reverend King in the White House."[90]

Rustin shuddered at wondering how much of white Montgomery that represented. He lasted only a week in Montgomery, being too controversial to stay. Rustin did not need to be told by anyone that he was radioactive in Montgomery. His sexuality evoked anxiety reactions even among activist allies, and he had a grand manner, which put off many as arrogance, though he was never self-aggrandizing. He would not stay if he could not help, and he was willing to help from afar. King quickly perceived that Rustin's reputation as a brilliant organizer was fully merited. Meanwhile Smiley arrived just before Rustin departed.[91]

Rustin's FOR friends feared from the beginning that he would attract harmful police and press attention. FOR executive secretary John Swomley and national chair Charles Lawrence warned Randolph that Rustin would become a spectacle, hurt King and the MIA, and destroy any possibility of MIA cooperation with northern organizations. Randolph heard the same thing from Nixon, so he gathered Thomas, Farmer, Swomley, Lawrence, and others into his office and reconsidered: Maybe they should clear out of Montgomery and let the MIA handle things on its own? Smiley opposed Swomley on Rustin and opposed Randolph's reversal on Montgomery. Smiley admired Rustin enormously and wanted him to stay in Montgomery. He also believed that northern activist organizations had a crucial role to play in Montgomery, where the protest movement had almost petered out before King's home was bombed and the MIA leaders were indicted. Smiley brushed off Swomley's demand to stay away from Rustin, later recalling, "I don't forbid well." Rustin introduced Smiley to King, who promptly introduced Smiley to an MIA mass meeting on March First.[92]

As a white, southern, hardcore Christian socialist pacifist, dispatched from New York FOR, who idolized Rustin—"Bayard was my guru all this time"—Smiley was as foreign as Rustin at MIA meetings but less dangerous as a subject of controversy. He stuck out at MIA meetings, along with white Montgomery

Lutheran pastor Robert Graetz. Smiley told Swomley of King, "He had Gandhi in mind when this thing started, he says." King wanted to do the right thing, Smiley wrote, but he was very young "and some of his close help is violent. . . . The place is an arsenal. King sees the inconsistency, but not enough. He believes and yet he doesn't believe. . . . If he can *really* be won to a faith in non-violence there is no end to what he can do." The next day, fresh from a warm reception at an MIA meeting, Smiley wrote again to FOR leaders: "We can learn from their courage and plain earthy devices for building morale, etc., but they can learn more from us, for being so new at this, King runs out of ideas quickly and does the old things again and again. He wants help, and we can give it to him without attempting to run the movement or pretend we know it all."[93]

King smuggled Rustin to Birmingham, where he raised money for the MIA and linked King to Rustin's network in the North. Rustin ghosted King's first published article, "Our Struggle," which announced that "a new Negro" had been born in Montgomery, signaling a "revolutionary change in the Negro's evaluation of himself." The Montgomery movement, King/Rustin said, wielded a "new and powerful weapon—non-violent resistance" and demonstrated that "our church is becoming militant." Rustin sealed King's trust by writing for him in a voice that stressed moral arguments and sounded like him. Rustin perceived that King represented a major turning point in the civil rights struggle and told him so. There had not been a major southern mass leader since Booker Washington. Now the action had swung back to the South.[94]

Rustin combined Quaker, Gandhian, and Marxist perspectives, and King prized his ethical-Quaker sensibility, even as nearly everyone close to King distrusted Rustin. Smiley and white northern Unitarian minister Homer Jack were the only insiders to commend King's reliance on Rustin. Besides his vast northern network and high-powered expertise Rustin was valuable to King in demanding little of him. The same factor soon drew King close to Stanley Levison. King did not have to worry about Rustin's ego, as Rustin was unfailingly willing to forgo personal recognition. King counted on this virtue to the point of never mentioning Rustin in *Stride Toward Freedom*.

American Gandhianism was already a highly mediated tradition. Smiley, Rustin, Muste, Swomley, Farmer, and other FOR stalwarts had stripped Gandhianism to nonviolence, dropping Gandhi's doctrines about vegetarianism, celibacy, and the like. Like Thurman, they still used the Gandhian jargon of satyagraha and ahimsa but did not impose it on King, who embraced their ambition for him—to become the American Gandhi. King trusted his intuition about how to communicate the message of nonviolence to audiences that found Gandhian philosophy strange at best. The religion of Jesus, undeniably, had something to do with loving one's enemies. But King had to negotiate the seeming absurdity of a philosophy based on converting white oppressors through Christian love and self-sacrifice. His ongoing experience of assimilating Gandhian thought helped him couch the message in ways it could be heard. "Passive resistance" captured both sides of the message, he thought. Rustin and Smiley pressed him to expound the "cycle of violence" argument decrying retaliation against evil: Evil multiplies through the law of retaliation. Everything depends on holding fast to nonviolent deliverance from the cycle of violence.

On December 21, 1956, King and Smiley ceremoniously boarded Montgomery's first integrated bus. King told audiences across the nation that Montgomery was an early wave: "The oppressed people of the world are rising up. They are revolting against colonialism, imperialism, and other systems of oppression." He took a break at Barbour's home and struggled to fathom his sudden fame. Barbour reported, "He wanders around in a daze asking himself, 'Why has God seen fit to catapult me into such a situation?' " They agreed that only God knew the answer. The Holt Street Address would not have caused a sensation had King not been sensational, but he could not say that. He said the story was that Montgomery blacks turned out that night. But blacks had turned out thousands of times across the South without sparking anything. Why did lightning strike in Montgomery? King said every rational explanation broke down at some point: "There is something about the protest that is suprarational; it cannot be explained without a divine dimension." One might, King observed, call it a principle of concretion, like Alfred North Whitehead, or a process of integration, like Henry Nelson Wieman, or something else: "Whatever the name, some extra-human force labors to create a harmony out of the discords of the universe."[95]

The band of preachers King gathered around him nearly always said his preaching brilliance made him stand out. This was not easy for them to say because most of them were powerhouse preachers whose egos rested on their preaching prowess. King never tired of preaching about the sacredness of personality. His theme was the universality of divine grace in human souls. It was the bedrock of his social activism and the basis of every "you are somebody" sermon he heard growing up. It fused his black church faith and academic training, infused his willingness to preach theology at political rallies, and fused his band of Southern Christian Leadership Conference (SCLC) preachers to each other. After the Montgomery boycott ended, Smiley and the FOR tried to kindle a new organization in the South that would be an FOR affiliate or an independent offshoot like CORE. Smiley and Jack organized efforts toward this end in cooperation with King and other black leaders from Baton Rouge, Tallahassee, Birmingham, and Montgomery. King would have taken this path had Rustin, Baker, and Levison not developed an alternative with greater potential.[96]

Ella Baker had grown up in North Carolina and absorbed her mother's missionary Baptist idealism, which emphasized quiet, selfless devotion. She graduated from Shaw University in 1927, moved to New York the same year, joined the Young Negroes Cooperative League in 1930, and joined the NAACP staff in 1940, first as a field secretary and later as director of branches. Racial justice organizing was her passion. She organized dozens of NAACP youth chapters in the South, cofounded In Friendship to fight Jim Crow laws in the South, and made many friends in and near the Communist Party, notably Levison, a New York lawyer and Roosevelt Democrat who became wealthy through Ford dealerships and real estate investments. Levison devoted his spare time to the American Jewish Congress and NAACP, meeting Baker in the NAACP, where she chaired the New York branch. To Levison and Baker, the limitations of the NAACP were frustrating and obvious. Levison was a Communist in the 1940s and early 1950s, raising money for the party. Afterward he shrugged off his past, explaining that one could not be a New York intellectual of his generation without having Communist friends.[97]

Rustin, Baker, and Levison were determined to capitalize on the breakthrough in Montgomery. They envisioned a new organization that would kindle many Montgomerys. To succeed, they believed, the organization had to be led and constituted by southern blacks. CORE demonstrated the limitations of interracial Gandhian organizing. It struggled bravely and doggedly but failed to spark a mass movement. It was top-heavy with white, middle-class intellectuals that gave an impression of patronizing sincerity and earnestness. Rustin, Baker, and Levison took for granted that they needed Randolph's backing, which would not be easy to get. Randolph had tired of lending his name to groups lacking money, he had joined In Friendship reluctantly, and he recoiled at northern activist presumption. He thought southern protesters might do better by spurning all help from northern organizations. But King pleaded that the movement needed northern financial support and expertise. Randolph told Baker he would get behind a new initiative if it arose spontaneously from the South with a call from King or the Montgomery church leadership.[98]

In December 1956 King told a celebrative gathering at Holt Street Church that the goal of the movement was to "awaken a sense of shame within the oppressor and challenge his false sense of superiority," not to defeat white oppressors: "The end is reconciliation; the end is redemption; the end is the creation of a beloved community." That month Rustin introduced King and Coretta King to three of his closest white allies—Levison, Harris Wofford, and

Clare Wofford. The group bantered in friendly fashion until someone said white opponents might give the movement another boost by stupidly arresting King. Coretta King cut off the laughter, saying her nightmare was that King would be killed in jail. There was an awkward silence, which King broke by confessing that he would have run away had he seen the whirlwind coming. Now he had no choice, for "the choice leaves your own hands."[99]

The following August the SCLC held its founding convention, adopting a motto: To Redeem the Soul of America. This was emphatically a black organization stocked with powerhouse preachers, notably Baptists Fred Shuttlesworth and Ralph Abernathy and Methodist Joseph Lowery. Eight of the founding nine officers were Baptist ministers; thirteen of the additional sixteen members of the executive board were ministers; and many were current or former NAACP presidents. They were committed to building something new, keenly grasping their advantage over the NAACP. White racists did not fear black preachers the way they loathed the NAACP. SCLC was designed to seize on this advantage and avoid competition with the NAACP. It called for mass action protests using nonviolent methods, stressing that nonviolence brings out the nobility in humble people and coheres with Christian principles. The founders sought to avoid the charges of "Communist" and "radical" that plagued the NAACP; thus they stressed that the new organization was Christian.[100]

Rustin and Levison influenced King's thinking, briefed him for meetings, arranged speaking engagements, ghosted his articles and books, handled the press, and linked him to their networks. They fondly remembered how the CIO used strikes, boycotts, and marches to make gains for economic justice. They were also chastened by this history because the CIO strategy of fusing antiracism with trade unions and socialism did not succeed. SCLC was a second chance centered on the black church, never mind that Rustin was a gay Quaker former Communist, Levison was a Jewish former Communist, and Baker's experience of the black church made her averse to charismatic preachers. SCLC leaders bridled at King's reliance on Rustin, Levison, and Baker, but King was emphatic about needing them, taking in stride their left-wing backgrounds. It was one of God's mysteries why so many Communists and so few white liberals had cared about black Americans. History being what it was, his lieutenants inevitably came with Communist baggage.

Moreover, King agreed with Rustin and Levison that black Americans would never be free as long as there were large numbers of poor and underprivileged whites. Capitalism played different roles in the struggles for racial justice in the North and South. In the North, Rustin and Levison argued, blacks suffered primarily from the predatory nature of capitalism. In the South blacks suffered primarily from the tyranny of racial caste. Capitalism was increasingly an ally in the southern struggle against racial tyranny because the capitalist class experienced the demands of racial caste as a needless waste. Thus the two struggles, South and North, had to be kept separate. These arguments cut little ice with southern ministers, who could not take responsibility for the suffering of poor whites and who needed to say that SCLC was their movement regardless of what might be true about capitalism.[101]

The third anniversary of the *Brown* decision approached in 1957, and Randolph asked President Eisenhower for a meeting with black leaders to discuss school integration. The White House brushed him off, and the fledgling SCLC vowed to organize a "mighty Prayer Pilgrimage to Washington" if Eisenhower did not respond. Rustin and Levison carried the idea forward, along with King and Randolph, conceiving it as an opportunity to dramatize that the movement now had two superstars—King and NAACP leader Roy Wilkins. To pull it off, however, Rustin and Levison had to get Wilkins to support the event and secure the necessary permissions. Only the NAACP had the inside game to get the Lincoln Memorial. Wilkins reluctantly went along. He did not like marches, but at least In Friendship respected him enough to ask. Wilkins figured, rightly, that he might incur favor with Eisenhower by vowing to keep things mild, peaceable, and focused on Congress, not Eisenhower.

Rustin and Levison urged Johnson not to run overlong, and he ran less overlong than usual. They let Powell go next to last, risking that he might upstage King. Levison wrote the first draft of King's speech, and King practiced it on the road, honing the text with Rustin and Levison. Editorial smoothening went fine except for the key line. Rustin insisted that "Give us the ballot" was weak. He wanted King to say, "When we have achieved the ballot" or perhaps "We demand the ballot" because black Americans didn't want anything to be *given* to them. To Rustin, King's phrase fell "like a pile of dirt." King gave Rustin a vintage King gentle stare: "Well, Bayard, I don't mind your criticizing my ideas. But I don't like your criticizing my words, because I'm better at words than you are." Whether it sang was more important to King than a quibble about the message. That settled the issue, and King electrified the crowd with "Give us the ballot."[102]

King said the *Brown* decision came as a "joyous daybreak" to end the long night of forced segregation. It should have abolished *Plessy v. Ferguson* tyranny, but "all types of conniving methods" were still used against blacks, so democracy was still an aspiration in the United States, not a reality. One could not be a democratic citizen if one could not vote. King ran off six iterations of his title. "Give us the ballot and we will no longer have to worry the federal government about our basic rights. . . . Give us the ballot and we will fill our legislative halls with men of good will. . . . Give us the ballot and we will place judges on the benches of the South who will 'do justly and love mercy.' " The crowd picked up the refrain and chanted it back. King stressed that the South's defiance of *Brown* set off a "tragic breakdown of law and order." America desperately needed a president who restored the rule of law and defended the Constitution, and it desperately needed Congress to pass strong civil rights legislation. Instead the executive branch was "all too silent and apathetic," Democrats capitulated to Dixiecrats and Republicans capitulated to "right-wing, reactionary Northerners." Both political parties "betrayed the cause of justice."[103]

King implored liberals to defend true liberalism and implored white southern moderates to find their courage. "There is a dire need today for a liberalism which is truly liberal," he declared. True liberalism was devoted to justice, standing up for the rights of oppressed minorities. It was not the callow individualism of so many so-called liberals, who respected every viewpoint without holding one: "We call for a liberalism from the North which will be thoroughly committed to the ideal of racial justice and will not be deterred by the propaganda and subtle words of those who say, 'Slow up for a while; you are pushing too fast.' " The North needed to enlarge its meager supply of fighting liberals, and the South needed to demand moderate leaders. King said there were more moderate whites in the South than hatefully racist whites. It seemed otherwise only because the party of bigotry was more aggressive and politically active: "There are in the white South more open-minded moderates than appear on the surface. These persons are silent today because of fear of social, political, and economic reprisals." King called for an upsurge of white moderate courage in the South that dared to lead "in this tense period of transition."[104]

He had words of counsel and hope. The civil rights movement had to stand for integration and democracy, and it had to be led by people of goodwill and deep conviction. "We must be sure that our hands are clean in the struggle," King urged. "We must never struggle with falsehood, hate or malice. Let us never become bitter." In other contexts he turned theological at this point; to this gathering he cautioned against black supremacist versions of black nationalism. "We proudly proclaim that three-fourths of the peoples of the world are colored," King declared. The black struggle for freedom in the United States was deeply linked to similar struggles in Asia and Africa. But solidarity had to be claimed and practiced "in the right spirit." Otherwise it turned into reverse bigotry: "We must not become victimized with a philosophy of 'black supremacy.' Our aim must never be to defeat or to humiliate the white man, but to win his friendship and understanding, and thereby create a society in which all men will be able to live together as brothers."[105]

King lauded the NAACP for marching through the courts, not mentioning that Wilkins denigrated him constantly off the record. Still, court victories were not enough; thus they were gathered at the Lincoln Memorial: "We must act in such a way as to make possible a coming-together of white people and colored people on the basis of a real harmony of interest and understanding. We must seek an integration based on mutual respect." King often ended by reciting the patriotic anthem "My Country 'Tis of Thee." On this occasion he opted for the third verse of "Lift Every Voice and Sing," which James Weldon Johnson wrote in 1900 to honor Booker T. Washington's Lincoln Day visit to Johnson's segregated school in Jacksonville, Florida: "Shadowed beneath thy hand, may we forever stand / True to our God, true to our native land."[106]

This speech was too new and important for King not to have a manuscript, so he stuck to it closely until he didn't. Rustin realized immediately that King was right about the cannon shots of "Give us the ballot." He marveled that King galvanized the crowd like nobody else and puzzled that he could not say why. So much of King's stump material was straight out of a schoolbook. The crowd cheered even when King strayed from his text with an aside he could not resist about *eros*, *filios*, and *agape*. How many times could he get away with a seminary excursus on three forms of Greek love? Rustin realized, more than ever, that King distinctly understood the musical power of words. He was a once-in-a-lifetime phenomenon. Rustin, Levison, and Randolph did not say publicly what they said to each other: The event was a huge success because it put King onstage alongside Wilkins, where his star qualities showed through.[107]

That was the movement highlight of the late 1950s. Everything else was hard, grinding, and ambiguous by comparison. The bus issue was unique as a source of economic leverage for black southerners, so white officials desegregated city buses. Usually there was a one-day protest yielding the necessary arrests for a legal challenge that city officials welcomed. New Orleans, Baton Rouge, Memphis, Savannah, and Atlanta averted another Montgomery in this fashion, depriving the SCLC of its best shot at a Montgomery chain reaction. Shuttlesworth launched a bus boycott in Birmingham in October 1958, but it sputtered and failed. By then SCLC had moved to voter registration, putting off the dream of boycott wildfire.

Baker took over as executive secretary of SCLC in January 1958. She intended only to set up an office and launch a voter registration program, "Crusade for Citizenship," as her appointment was temporary. But there was no organization without her, so Baker stayed for two years, single-handedly holding it together. Fatefully, she found SCLC leaders to be arrogant and self-centered. In her telling, they looked down on women, wasted her time, habitually came late to

meetings, and did not respect her. Her expertise did not seem to count for anything, nor did the fact that she was old enough to be their mother. King was
habitually chauvinistic. Baker found him pompous, spoiled, condescending,
and eager to be idolized. On one occasion she asked him why he condoned
such hero worship; King replied it was what people wanted.

To Baker, that was a pathetic answer. She believed that mass movements
should be organized from the ground up, with a radically democratic ethos.
Instead SCLC was building a personality cult that impeded the movement
from growing. Baker respected King enough to work with him; years later she
denied King family accusations that she hated King. She had never despised
King, but she very much disliked the kind of organization he fostered. The
ministers expected Baker to wait on them and defer to them while they deferred
to King. Baker's response, at the time and later, was blunt: "I have no respect for
that." Septima Clark, the other woman besides Baker to serve on the SCLC's
executive staff in the 1960s, had the same experience of chauvinistic treatment.
The word of a woman had no weight "whatsoever," she said. SCLC ministers
had a dramatic idea of activism centered on their heroics and supported by others consigned to underling roles.[108]

There were others who felt pushed aside, excluded for not belonging to a
southern clerical elite or the right northern socialist elite. Brilliant, prolific,
energetic Pauli Murray was one of them. Born in Baltimore and raised by her
light-colored Episcopalian maternal grandparents in Durham, North Carolina,
Murray graduated from Hunter College in New York in 1933, joined the
Socialist Party and worked for the Workers' Defense League, studied at Howard
Law School in the early 1940s, was active in CORE, and kept voting for Thomas
long after she befriended Eleanor Roosevelt. Murray advocated for civil rights
and women's rights as a lawyer but spent the entire 1950s on the margins of
causes, jobs, and organizations, never quite sure in each case which factor marginalized her the most—being female, black, gay, queer, Episcopalian, or
socialist. King had come and gone before Murray stopped being marginalized,
ending her career as an Episcopal priest. Nixon, too, was stung at being pushed
aside: "I'm proud that I was part of it, even though so many people got famous
out of it and I was still left here. And I'm still here servin' the people and the rest
of 'em are gone." SCLC leaders told a different story of creating the very protest
organization that Rustin and Baker originally proposed. They appreciated
King's distinct ability and accepted that his word was the final authority. They
never claimed to be grassroots organizers in Baker's mold. They were committed to a charismatic leadership model, cultivated a chaotic style, and paid little
attention to their affiliates. SCLC needed to be a hit-and-run operation led by

ministerial firebrands who supported King. Whether or not they were right, it was emphatically what existed, featuring far more socialist input than any insider wanted to talk about publicly.[109]

The switch to voter registration seemed more doable for SCLC than its original dream of boycott wildfire; meanwhile Wilkins smoldered at King and the new organization. Wilkins had four top-drawer complaints. He did not like having a personal rival, let alone a neophyte rival. He fumed that King and SCLC soaked up money that should have gone to the NAACP. He protested that SCLC cut into the NAACP's following and organizations in the South. And the very existence of SCLC felt like a reproach to Wilkins. Anything that hurt the NAACP in the South hurt the civil rights movement; moreover, SCLC had it both ways with the NAACP, taunting the organization for its conservatism while benefiting from southern repression of the supposedly radical NAACP. Wilkins thus forbade NAACP officials to join or work with SCLC. His operatives planted articles ridiculing King's identification with Gandhi and nonviolence. Privately King burned at feeling unfairly attacked. Publicly he turned the other cheek, claiming to feel no rivalry with Wilkins or the NAACP.

King's ascendancy was laced with irony. He became famous while the movement stalled and faded. Insiders called it the Movement even as it floundered. King's defenders claimed he was not a radical: He belonged to the black church, was trained in mainline seminaries, and was a bourgeois moderate in all things. Historian L. D. Reddick, the only SCLC insider who was not a minister, made an often-quoted case for this view in 1958 after a woman nearly killed King by stabbing him in the chest. Reddick said King was like Gandhi in being vulnerable to crazy people or nationalists harboring murderous ambitions, and he had nothing to do with Marxism or Communism: "Neither by experience nor reading is King a political radical. There is not a Marxist bone in his body. He accepts his society save where injustice and violence defile it. In the classic phrase, Martin Luther King is a bourgeois leader of the masses."[110]

That was the official line, which King both encouraged and bridled against. He was mindful that Du Bois joined the Communist Party the same year King founded SCLC. Acknowledging he was a democratic socialist would have gone badly. Spelling out the socialist worldview he took from Rauschenbusch, Du Bois, Johnson, Randolph, Barbour, the early Niebuhr, Mays, Muelder, and Rustin would have yielded turmoil and vilification, not a chance to educate the public about Socialism versus Communism. Every insider in the Randolph/Thomas/Farmer network was intimately acquainted with this problem and wanted King to finesse it. They could be open about being socialists, but not King. The next star of American democratic socialism, Michael Harrington, belatedly learned how delicately Rustin, Randolph, Levison, and even Reddick handled this hazard.

MICHAEL HARRINGTON AND THE OLD LEFT

Edward Michael Harrington grew up far from New York socialism, in St. Louis, Missouri, where his middle-class family was Irish Catholic on both sides. His father, Edward Harrington, was a mild-mannered patent lawyer who fought in France during World War I and whom Harrington described as a gentle soul. His mother, Catherine Harrington, was a domineering personality and teacher whom Harrington described, with more reserve, as a public-spirited volunteer in Catholic and civic organizations. Harrington let on to friends that his mother was a militant Catholic whose dogmatism and forcefulness gave him much to overcome. His father taught him by word and example to do whatever Catherine Harrington wanted.

Precocious and eager to please, Harrington was twelve years old when he started high school. His neighborhood, in his telling, was a "pleasant Irish Catholic ghetto" where everyone believed in God and the United States. He studied under Jesuits at St. Louis University High School and at Holy Cross College in Worcester, Massachusetts, always the youngest in his class. Harrington's training in Thomist scholasticism showed through for the rest of his life, yielding three-point lectures, syllogisms, and a powerful attraction to Marxian scholasticism. In high school he puzzled about why Immanuel Kant could be so famous for arguments that Harrington's teachers destroyed in a few sentences. Skepticism is self-refuting! Worcester was a cultural shock to Harrington because he had grown up in assimilated, mildly nostalgic, Midwest Irish-Americanism. In Worcester he met Irish Americans whose memories of persecution centered on New England, not Ireland. They hated the Yankees who had driven them to a sullen ethnic chauvinism that looked down on Jews, blacks, Italians, Lithuanians, Poles, and all non-Irish Catholics. Not all St. Louis Irish Americans had lace curtains, but his upbringing wholly unprepared him for hardened ethnic enmity.[111]

Graduating from Holy Cross at the age of nineteen, Harrington indulged his parents by studying law for a year at Yale, which bored him, and English for a year at the University of Chicago, which he liked, but not enough to hang on for a doctorate. He said he first rebelled against Irish Catholicism by becoming a Taft Republican at Yale; he switched to democratic socialism on his last day at Yale; and he had a conversion experience while working in a summer job for the St. Louis Pupil Welfare Department. Harrington took the job to save up for a move to New York to become a Bohemian poet. One day he recoiled at finding himself in a decayed building near the Mississippi River that reeked of garbage, dead rats, broken toilets, and overcrowded habitation: "Suddenly the abstract and statistical and aesthetic outrages I had reacted to at Yale and Chicago became real and personal and insistent. A few hours later, riding the Grand Avenue streetcar, I realized that somehow I must spend my life trying to obliterate that kind of house and to work with the people who lived there." Perhaps the job got to him that quickly, but Harrington's biographer Maurice Isserman discovered that he worked for the Welfare Department for three days.[112]

The Korean War broke out in 1950 and Harrington wanted to be a conscientious objector, but that was unbearable to his parents, so he volunteered for the Army Medical Reserve on the understanding that he would soon be shipped to Korea. Instead, the Pentagon declined to call up the federal reserves. Harrington transferred in January 1951 to a unit in New York, finding his way the following month to the Catholic Worker House of Hospitality on Chrystie Street in the Bowery. He was twenty-three years old and knew only two things about the Catholic Worker: Dorothy Day was its leader, and it was as far to the left as one could get in the Catholic Church. Catholic Workers were committed to voluntary poverty, serving the poor, and seeing Christ in everyone. They repeated Day's mantra: They were there to become saints. Harrington dutifully said the words but spent little time actually ministering to the poor. He took over the *Catholic Worker* paper and gave evening lectures; the first was on Martin Buber's communitarian socialism. His boyish affability and brilliance quickly made him a favorite of the founder. Day had a colorful past as a Bohemian Greenwich Village anarchist, but she shushed Workers who asked about it. The Catholic Church had saved her life, and she committed herself to it before she had any inkling of founding the Catholic Worker or the *Catholic Worker*. She brooked no dissent from Catholic orthodoxy or her personal authority at the Worker. At the time, Day was deeply embattled because of the war. In between wars the Worker surged and the Catholic hierarchy mostly put up with Day's radicalism. Every time there was a war to oppose, the Worker lost followers and readers, and Day fended off attacks from bishops.[113]

For nearly two years Harrington tried to adopt Day's anarcho-pacifist politics and her devotion to Catholic orthodoxy, while spending his evenings at the White Horse tavern. Dylan Thomas, Delmore Schwartz, Norman Mailer, William Styron, Dan Wakefield, and other poets and writers were regulars at the White Horse. Young Democratic Party operative Daniel Patrick Moynihan was another regular. Harrington wrote poems about bohemian freedom, smoked and drank every night, held court on politics and literature, and became a fixture at the White Horse, dropping Day's anarchism, pacifism, and religion in succession. Day had long arguments with him about socialism versus anarchism and pacifism, trying to hold onto him. Finally in December 1952 he dropped Catholicism, breaking the news to her over lunch. Day asked fearfully if a woman was the reason. He said no, he just couldn't accept Catholic theology anymore. Day said that made her happy. Intellectual dissent was perfectly respectable to her; sins of the flesh were not. Soon afterward he was taking women home nearly every night.

Bogdan Denitch recruited Harrington to YPSL, spotting him in March 1952 on a picket line. To Denitch, the Catholic Worker anarchists were flaky moral perfectionists; Harrington seemed misplaced among them. Denitch plied him with Marxian books, stressing that socialism was about abolishing the system that produced so much poverty and misery. Harrington had never met anyone like Denitch, a Serb from Kosovo born in 1929 in Sofia, Bulgaria, where his father was the Yugoslav ambassador. Denitch's father was ambassador to Egypt when World War II began, forced into exile by the Nazis, and later exiled again by Marshal Josip Broz Tito's Communist regime. As Denitch told the story, he fought in a Yugoslav unit in the British Eighth Army—at the age of fifteen—and was wounded in Italy. He served with the British occupying forces in Vienna and had bruising encounters with the Red Army. After the war the British government asked him to fight insurgents in Malaya or, if he preferred, to mine coal. Denitch's military service, however, entitled him to first-class passage anywhere in the British Empire. He chose Canada and promptly slipped into the United States illegally. In 1946 he enrolled at City College in New York, majoring, in effect, in student politics. Denitch joined YPSL and CORE in 1948 and was a tireless organizer in both organizations, exuding a bluff, garrulous, cunning, gunslinger style. He was exuberantly promiscuous and dramatic, enthralling women with highly fictional tales of his resistance adventures in Yugoslavia, in a thick Serbo-Croatian accent. He worked for thirteen years as a journeyman machinist and tool and die maker, joining the International Association of Machinists, and boasted of proving that not all CORE activists were pacifists.[114]

Harrington was his prize recruit and closest friend, joining the Socialist movement in the same year—1952—that Daniel Bell famously described socialists as prisoners of an "unhappy problem" and Howe left the Shachtmanites for clinging to Leninism. Socialists, Bell said, lived in the world but were not of it. They could only act—like Thomas—as the Niebuhrian "moral man in immoral society," not as political agents. Bell had come up through YPSL in the early 1930s and stuck with Thomas until just after the 1948 election. Harrington wrestled with Bell's argument, especially its irony for him: Was he dropping one form of politically irrelevant moral perfectionism for another? He could join YPSL only if he believed the answer was no. Bell did not say that democratic socialism was too otherworldly only in the United States. He said democratic socialism in every context was in the world but not of it, lacking empirical discipline, just as Niebuhr said. Denitch countered that Bell overgeneralized his U.S. American experience, because socialism was far from transpolitical in Europe.[115]

Bell had joined YPSL when capitalism was imploding and sectarian Marxists thrilled at knowing the secret of history. He described the thrill vividly, recalling that lefty sectarians enjoyed "the illusions of settling the fate of history, the mimetic combat on the plains of destiny, and the victorious sense of power in demolishing opponents." Howe was equally quotable about his experience as a Shachtmanite: "Never before, and surely never since, have I lived at so high, so intense a pitch, or been so absorbed in ideas beyond the smallness of the self. It began to seem as if the very shape of reality could be molded by our will, as if those really attuned to the inner rhythms of History might bend it to submission." Bell and Howe had lived for the movement, caught in its vortex of meetings, actions, and tournament, embracing its discipline of heroic asceticism. The Shachtmanites still had this sectarian fervor in the 1950s, proclaiming portentously about the sweep of history and demands of the age. But now American capitalism was booming, necessitating ever more reliance on sectarian obsession.[116]

Denitch and Harrington gravitated to Shachtman for the same reasons that Hal Draper, Gordon Haskell, Howe, Julius Jacobson, Macdonald, Stanley Plastrik, and others had flocked to him as Trotskyites. But Shachtman founded the Workers Party on doubt. Breaking with Trotsky was the turning point of his life; then he struggled to decide how much Leninism he should drop. In 1944 he reflected, "Doubts are bridges you cannot stand on for long. Either you go back to the old views or move on to new ones." Shachtman moved on, but ambiguously. He allowed vigorous in-house debate but furiously condemned apostates who made a show of leaving. Thus they tended to slip away quietly at leaving time. The war enabled the Shachtmanites to make an impact far beyond their tiny group. They took jobs in the war industry and paid steep taxes to the party. They fanned out to unions across the country, vowing to "colonize" the labor movement. They defied the no-strike pledge that union bosses made after Pearl Harbor, supporting wildcat strikes. They clashed with Walter Reuther for upholding the no-strike pledge in the UAW and blasted CIO Communists for supporting the war, reclaiming Bolshevik "revolutionary defeatism." The Shachtmanites had the best paper on the left, *Labor Action*, edited by Draper. By 1943 its circulation was forty thousand, a stunning accomplishment for a scattered sect numbering five hundred dues payers.[117]

They reflected painfully on why they were so tiny despite stirring up so much attention. Erber said they were too much like the Jesuits: "We live a life apart from our surroundings. We develop our own sense of values, our own moral concepts, our own habits, and even our own jargon." Howe said Marx turned out to be wrong about the working class being the driving force of social change. Stalinism and Fascism shredded the working class, and the emergence of mass society corrupted it, making class-struggle rhetoric quaint. Howe pointed to the pathetic spectacle of Czech workers embracing Stalinism. Shachtman raged that such critiques smacked of petit bourgeois twaddle, but his postwar actions told a different story. The Labour Party breakthrough in England belatedly shook some of the Leninism out of him. For the first time Shachtman considered that perhaps socialism did not have to emerge from a catastrophe convulsion. Erber resigned in 1948, and the following year Shachtman stopped calling his group a party, selecting a modest moniker, the Independent Socialist League (ISL). ISL reconciled with Walter Reuther, dropped its membership in the Trotskyite Fourth International, supported the purge of Communists from the CIO, and aligned with the left wings of the British Labour Party and the Continental Social Democratic parties. Officially the ISL was still Leninist, but it was heading in a Social Democratic direction when Howe bailed out and Harrington and Denitch entered.[118]

Were the Shachtmanites becoming Social Democrats, or was this just another Leninist ruse? Did even Shachtman know for sure? Thomas and his Socialist lieutenants did not trust Shachtman, believing he was still a Trotskyite who made a few adjustments. But every left-wing group struggled to recruit members, and raiding each other was easier than attracting newcomers. Denitch was legendarily good at it. According to the often-told joke on this topic, "If you sent Bogdan onto campus for 12 hours he will end up with a party group. If you sent him onto campus for 24 hours he will end up with a party group and two pregnancies. If you leave him on campus for 36 hours you will have three pregnancies and three factions." On the surface Denitch and Harrington were a bad cop/good cop duo; Denitch gave hard-left talks and poached recruits for YPSL, and Harrington gave winsome talks about democratic socialism. In fact they were equally devoted to sectarian intrigue, reviving a left-wing art that had faded in YPSL. Denitch and Harrington didn't care if the party elders disapproved because their generation was getting drafted and the Socialist Party caved on the Korean War. To the Socialist elders the party's tradition of antiwar militancy was gone, and the war was a test of containment and the United Nations. YPSL members rued that these claims put their lives in danger, which made them ripe for raiding by the youth wing of the ISL, the Socialist Youth League (SYL).[119]

In 1952 the Shachtmanites founded an independent antiwar journal called the *Anvil*. It brought together the SYL and both factions of the YPSL left wing—the Third Camp revolutionaries led by Denitch and the pacifist wing led by David McReynolds, which violated the Socialist Party ban on collaborating with any totalitarian organization, defined as any organization holding an affinity with Leninism, Stalinism, or Fascism. McReynolds tried to stay on good terms with party leaders; he was a UCLA student who wanted the party to return to its antiwar position. He fought against Denitch and Harrington for control of the YPSL left wing and narrowly lost. Denitch and Harrington organized a unity conference with SYL featuring a keynote by Shachtman. They designed a conference poster adorned with a quote from e. e. cummings—"there is some shit i will not eat." The Thomas Socialists pushed back, suspending the New York chapter of YPSL. Denitch and Harrington responded in 1953 by pulling most of YPSL out of the Socialist Party, and the party responded by expelling Denitch, Harrington, and their followers; McReynolds stayed in what remained of YPSL.[120]

In 1954 Denitch and Harrington founded a new organization with SYL leader Max Dombrow, inevitably called the Young Socialist League (YSL); now they were officially Shachtmanites. Dombrow was the group's first chair, but a year later Harrington won an election to chair the group and was launched as the golden boy of the new generation. SYL veteran Deborah Meier voted for Harrington without expecting him to stay. To her, it was obvious that he would find a more rewarding perch sooner or later. Harrington was good at winning admirers who didn't like his sectarian loyalties; he had the Thomas charisma with broadly middle-class audiences. But he loved the socialist left in which he found himself. He never really considered a career as a Democratic politician, though many urged him to consider it. His FBI file mushroomed after he took over YSL. Harrington helped YSL members deal with their draft boards, safeguarding the distinction between YSL and ISL, since the federal government classified ISL as a subversive organization. Shachtman was deprived of a passport for ten years, and Harrington didn't bother to apply for one. ISL, though justly proud of *Labor Action*, fixed on a narrow range of ideas and issues, especially Third Camp socialism versus bureaucratic collectivism. Somehow Draper never tired of articles condemning Stalinism. Harrington wrote many of them under his own byline, plus "Edward Hill" and "Eli Fishman," the latter a parody of the Anglo-Saxon pseudonyms his Jewish comrades employed.

YSL forged its best alliances with Muste at FOR and David Dellinger at WRL. Left-wing pacifists knew where they stood, always looked for alliances, and were more comfortable with Harrington than he was with them. Most of them were socialists or anarchists anyway, but he strained to claim pacifist commonality with them. Sometimes he called himself a Pacifist-Socialist, rationalizing that socialism modified the kind of pacifist he was. It wasn't his fault that absolute pacifists changed what the word meant. FOR, WRL, and Catholic Worker pacifists were dedicated to civil disobedience; Harrington confined his direct-action protests to the legal picket. He picketed more than other Shachtmanites because they were indoor types fixed on their scholastic debates and raiding peer organizations. Shachtman confined himself to grand appearances, hibernating in Floral Park, Long Island, where he grew orchids and ran a mail order business hawking hi-fi components. Harrington described his comrades as "determined, but unhysterical anticommunists engaged in seemingly Talmudic exegeses of the holy writ according to Karl Marx." When Shachtman gave one of his three-hour perorations on comrades murdered by Stalin, "it was like hearing the roll call of revolutionary martyrs who were bone of our bone, flesh of our flesh."[121]

Harrington and Denitch had ascended in New York socialism by forging their own group from a split they fomented, exuding the Trotskyite mentality that other groups were rivals and thus candidates for raiding. In 1955 they took over the New York chapter of the ADA's youth division, Students for Democratic Action (SDA). They did it in classic sectarian fashion—attending every meeting to the end and voting as a bloc. Harrington exploited the same generational split between ADA and its youth that he exploited in the Socialist–YPSL episode, in this case by defending the rights of Communists. But more was at stake in ADA. McCarthyism terrorized American politics, ADA was the flagship of American liberalism, and it was Red-baited constantly despite supporting anti-Communist legislation. Hubert Humphrey steered the Communist Control Act of 1954 through the U.S. Senate, making membership in the Communist Party a federal crime. Harrington taunted the ADA/SDA liberals—you call that liberalism? He accused ADA leaders of betraying liberalism and the rights of American Communists just to win some votes, incurring their resentment, especially because he spent their money. They couldn't expel him because they were not the SDA, and he had won his position legitimately. They stewed for months over the problem before making a drastic decision in the summer of 1956, abolishing their youth section. If the youth organization was going to call them out, it was better not to have one.[122]

This was a dubious beginning to Harrington's socialist career. Years later Denitch teased Harrington admirers that he remembered the Harrington who lacked a halo. Though Harrington absorbed the Marxian fetish with being hard, YSL stalwarts never thought he was hard like them. He grew up middle class, tried to please his mother, was educated at elite schools, ministered at a Catholic pacifist sect, and still preferred the literary dilettantes at the White Horse over his socialist comrades. On certain issues he sounded like a Catholic, not like them. YSL leaders did not conceive the atomic bomb issue as primarily moral since they were hard, and nothing was primarily moral to them. Harrington did not subordinate his moral revulsion to the class struggle; in fact, his answer to Bell invoked the idea of the witness, a pacifist trope. Harrington admired that pacifists stubbornly witnessed to claims lacking any immediate practical relevance. To a point, he accepted the Bell critique that socialism is not of this world. Socialism was a struggle to transform the world according to socialist values. It was worthwhile even in losing battles: "If the choice for the modern world is between socialism and barbarism (and I think it is), the answer is not to support barbarism because it is on the ascendant, but to continue to struggle for socialism."[123]

May Wood Simons and Kate O'Hare would have recognized the cult of Marxian hardness and dread of feminine everything that prevailed in Old Left culture. Midcentury socialism was like turn-of-the-century socialism in welcoming female members without asking how they felt or what they wanted. The difference was that early socialism had prominent female leaders and the post–Nineteenth Amendment era did not. The women who joined the Socialist Party and ISL were usually students or recent college graduates, often with backgrounds in religious service. They signed up for organizing tasks, typed stencils, handed out leaflets, spoke up in meetings (or not), and did not complain about supporting male leaders. They embraced socialism as a movement for freedom without protesting that the socialist movement treated them no differently than the rest of society.

The movement as a whole had an ethos of ascetic self-sacrifice. Women could not call attention to their needs and desires without suggesting that they lacked the requisite self-sacrifice, never mind that they were the ones who cared for children and families. The old socialist objection—Why should women get special treatment?—was as forbidding as ever but now in movements that did not raise up female leaders and did not ask if they should. Midcentury socialists lacked the sense of feminist solidarity that might have asked the question, or any language for it. Howe later reflected, after the feminist eruption of the late 1960s stunned and challenged him, that he never previously thought about the feelings of female comrades. There was something pitiful about this fact and its prevalence, he acknowledged. But the pity may have surpassed the gender factor alone; Howe confessed that his band of male intellectual socialists was "programmatically untrained" to engage *anyone's* feelings, pain, vulnerability, or personal experience: "The fate of the world hung heavily on our shoulders, yet we asked few questions about the lives, feelings, inner thoughts of those who were supposed to be our partners in making a new society."[124]

Meier and Brooklyn College SDA activist Ruth Jordan attested that the early Harrington was slightly more sensitive about gender discrimination than his peers, just as he was slightly more committed to antiracist activism through his friendship with Rustin, whom he first met at an antiwar demonstration in 1951. Until 1954 Harrington held the usual socialist view that antiracist activism was important but not a top socialist priority. The few black Americans he knew personally were socialists, and he held the usual snooty Marxist view of the NAACP—a vehicle of the black bourgeoisie. Until the *Brown* decision of 1954 struck down "separate but equal" segregated education, Harrington had no concept of a mass movement or acquaintance with one. He felt vaguely that Rustin, Randolph, and Farmer hit on something important, whatever it was. Reflecting on the *Brown* decision and his own half-formed thoughts about black socialists, Harrington conjectured that the struggle against racism might be the next great "Social Force" in U.S. American politics. He winced at his calculating mindset while deciding that socialists had to become better known for caring about racial justice.[125]

He joined the Manhattan branch of the NAACP, connecting with NAACP national labor secretary Herbert Hill. Hill was a white socialist who joined the NAACP on the Marxian model, conceiving it as mass work. Then he shifted his fundamental loyalty to the NAACP, dropping his Marxian premise that privileging racial justice was provincial compared to socialism. Hill stressed to Harrington that the NAACP was a mass organization far outstripping anything in the socialist left, and in some contexts it was predominantly working class. The position of the black middle class confuted the Marxian analysis of how change occurs. Only "bourgeois" black leaders had the money, connections, and confidence to challenge Jim Crow. Thus the most militant and courageous black leaders nearly always came from the middle class. Harrington applied what Hill told him: go to branch meetings, shut your mouth, and try to learn. He later reflected that the Social Force began to show its human face to him, "if only as a well-meaning socialist tourist."[126]

He reached out to Rustin, who was feeling more isolated than ever: "We had the comradeship and closeness that political irrelevance had imposed upon us." Then lightning struck in Montgomery, and Rustin knew what it meant. The struggle had returned to the South, it was not based on unions or the Talented Tenth, and it ran through the black church. Harrington knew almost nothing about the black church freedom struggle that produced King. For the rest of his life he wrote clichéd cant about King "utterly transforming that passive faith" that King inherited. But Harrington worked on all the mobilizations of the 1950s that Rustin directed from the offices of BSCP and the Negro Labor Committee, both located on 125th Street. He introduced to Rustin his two best YSL organizers, Rachelle Horowitz and Tom Kahn, who became Rustin's chief organizers. Both were Brooklyn College undergraduates who joined YSL in 1956 after hearing Shachtman condemn the Soviet invasion of Hungary; Shachtman's musical speaking voice and intellectual power mesmerized Kahn. Rustin and Kahn became lovers; Kahn later recalled that Rustin drew him into "his endless campaigns and projects," introducing him to Bach, Brahms, and the importance of balancing a personal life with social justice work: "He believed that no class, caste or genre of people were exempt from this obligation." The Rustin trio organized the Prayer Pilgrimage for Freedom, where Harrington met King for the first time.[127]

YSL was growing because Harrington won converts on his speaking tours and American Communism disintegrated. In January 1956 the American Communist Party had twenty thousand members, still bigger than the entire organized anti-Stalinist left had ever been. The following month Khrushchev condemned Stalin as a paranoid, mass-murdering tyrant. His secret speech, published in June, split the American Communist Party into a small hard-line faction led by Foster and a small reform faction led by John Gates. More important, it drove out most of the party, leaving a shell of three thousand members jostling with FBI infiltrators. Harrington was careful not to crow about the downfall of the Communist Party. Even Shachtman tempered his rhetoric, urging his disciples to think about where all those ex-Communists might go— perhaps a new configuration was possible. Ex-Communists would never join ISL outright—there was too much enmity to overcome—and the upcoming generation of independent radicals had no interest in the sectarian wars of the 1930s that created Trotskyites, Shachtmanites, Stalinists, and the rest. McReynolds, chairing the Socialist Party's Committee for a Socialist Program, came up with a plan: The Shachtmanites and Socialists should reconcile to renew democratic socialism.[128]

McReynolds pitched this proposal to the Socialists in 1956, and they turned it down resoundingly by more than three to one. How could they work with Leninists? Why would they want to? McReynolds persisted for two years that Shachtman had changed and his group would energize the party. Meanwhile the Socialist Party carried out a separate merger in 1957 with a seemingly opposite outfit—the Old Guard dead-enders of the SDF. There was something pathetic and irresistible about trying to reach back to 1936. Thomas, Milwaukee mayor Frank Zeidler, and party cofounder Jasper McLevy worked with SDF stalwarts Louis Goldberg, Morris Polin, and party cofounder James Oneal to end a painful separation. Many sentimental things were said at the unity convention in New York, which created the Socialist Party–Social Democratic Federation (SP-SDF), though nearly everyone still called it the Socialist Party. McReynolds quelled left-wing Socialist opposition to the merger by vowing to bring in the Shachtmanites as soon as the SDF merger occurred. Concerted opposition to the merger came entirely from the SDF: specifically, New York SDF chair James Glaser, the *Forward*, and the Jewish Socialist Verband. *Forward* editor Harry Rogoff resented Thomas for criticizing Zionism and its impact on the Jewish labor movement. In 1958 Thomas still had protégés at the American Jewish Committee (Harry Fleischman) and Jewish Labor Committee (Emanuel Muravchik), but these organizations had ambiguous positions about Zionism. The clear trajectory was toward pro-Zionism, which shrank the Jewish socialist milieu in which Thomas had spent his entire socialist career, very sadly to him.[129]

As soon as the SDF merger was done, McReynolds and the Committee for a Socialist Program returned to the merger that mattered to them. McReynolds appealed to the party's new executive secretary, Irwin Saull, who consented, and to Thomas, who said he knew these Shachtmanites and they would devour the party within a year. McReynolds insisted the Shachtmanites were sincere. Thomas hedged in 1957, telling McReynolds and Saull he would accept all the Shachtmanites except Harrington and Denitch, two conniving liars who were beyond tolerating. Shachtman said he was willing to beg to be admitted. In September 1957 Thomas asked him for honest replies to two questions: Was he still a Leninist? Would his group agree not to be an organized caucus, either open or secret, within the party? Shachtman said he would "lean over back-wards" to prove he did not intend to raid or capture the party. As for Leninism, he still believed the Bolshevik Revolution had a democratic potential at its inception that Stalin obliterated, but he would not impose this view on the party. Thomas balked at Harrington and Denitch, and Shachtman made a goodwill move by asking Denitch to move away from New York; Denitch moved to Berkeley, California.[130]

Winning over Thomas swung the vote, though not without impassioned objections that Leninists could not be trusted. Zeidler resigned as national chair, explaining that he could not associate with Leninists. Former national secretary Robin Myers led the opposition, pleading that the ISL was still Leninist and it changed course only after the Soviet meltdown created a new opportunity. Myers did not want to absorb a gusher of former Communists and she took for granted that Shachtman's no-capture pledge was a lie. Maybe the party had a worthwhile future and maybe it didn't, but welcoming Leninists was wrong in either case. The merger passed by a narrow margin, but just as the votes were arriving in the mail Shachtman called McReynolds to an emergency meeting. He said the merger wasn't worth the turmoil it caused; maybe they should put it off for a while. McReynolds was incredulous, imploring Shachtman not to walk away from two years of reconciling work. Veteran Canadian Trotskyite Maurice Spector, witnessing this exchange, lingered after the meeting to explain to McReynolds what was happening. He could read the signs and knew what would happen next. As soon as Shachtman got into the party, Spector predicted, "he's going to go so far to the right that you won't believe it." McReynolds couldn't believe it, but he had never been a Trotskyite.[131]

Shachtman captured the party as swiftly as Myers feared but very differently than she expected. Spector was spot-on about Shachtman careening to the right. In 1958 Shachtman cared about only one thing—currying favor with the Socialist Party's right wing. This was a group he could dominate for the rest of his days. The merger with the SDF swung the math in his favor, making him willing to do anything to win over the party officials and Old Guard, even temporarily back out of the merger if necessary. The bitter irony was that McReynolds engineered the merger precisely to undermine the control of the Old Guard. The vaunted opening to former Communists never happened. Had the party welcomed respected ex-Communists like John Gates and Steve Nelson, Shachtman would not have been able to control it. Once he saw his opportunity he dropped any interest he might have held in the ex-Communist infusion. Shachtman entered the party committed to a strategy of political realignment that he fostered among his disciples and publicly disavowed—until he captured most of the party apparatus. He took contradictory positions and denied there was any contradiction, ostensibly on the ground that "realignment" could mean different things but really because he had to wait until he controlled the party machinery. The Shachtmanites swiftly took over the party press, LID, and YPSL, falling short of complete control until July 1968, when they finally secured a majority on the national committee. Meanwhile young activists from the civil rights and antiwar movements came into the party lacking any concept of an Old Guard socialist or a Shachtmanite. They were surprised at what they encountered when they joined; it wasn't like the Harrington speech at their college.[132]

At first Shachtman held back Harrington from the party chair, not wanting to convey that a coup had taken place. YPSL activist Eldon Clingon acted as party chair while the Shachtmanites thrashed out among themselves which version of political realignment they supported. They conducted secret meetings and spoke a coded Trotskyite language to each other, still operating like cunning Leninists. They cast all others as types—Muste types, Thomas types, *Monthly Review* types—reserving their greatest scorn for any soft type. The later Harrington admitted that he and the Shachtmanites acted like Bolshevik jerks but denied they were wrong to capture the party. The party was weak and they were strong. The Shachtmanites debated varieties of the realignment idea, buoyed by the AFL-CIO merger of 1955 and the rise of the civil rights movement, before settling on the view that socialists did not need to create a labor party because the Democrats were becoming a labor party.

The first version of realignment envisioned an exodus of black and white progressives, socialists, and unionists out of the Democratic Party. Socialists streamed into the civil rights movement through Randolph's Harlem office, where Rustin, Horowitz, and Kahn built on the successful Prayer Pilgrimage for Freedom by organizing in 1958 and 1959 the historic Youth Marches for Integrated Schools. The second one gathered twenty-five thousand marchers in Washington, DC, fusing socialists and ex-communists united only by the songs and the civil rights movement. Shachtman formed a fatherly-guru bond with Horowitz and Kahn, at first assuming that the political goal was to set off an exodus. But the Shachtmanites had begun in 1956 to debate another version of realignment, questioning whether it might be internal instead. Haskell and Herman Benson were the first proponents of a Democratic version. Why should leftists and liberals have to leave the Democratic Party? Why not the Dixiecrats? If southern blacks got to vote again and the AFL-CIO used its political muscle, a new Democratic Party would emerge. Shachtman gamed out his group's interest, denying he would ever vote for a capitalist, while plotting his path into the Socialist Party. In 1959 Harrington made a case for realignment that was still ambiguous about inside-versus-outside the Democratic Party. He could see where this argument was heading, but emotionally he couldn't bear the thought of voting for a Democrat. Weren't they still Marxists?[133]

Meanwhile in 1959 the nearly defunct youth section of LID reinvented itself, spurred by University of Michigan undergraduate Al Haber and Student League for Industrial Democracy president André Schiffrin. It was anchored on the Michigan campus, renamed itself on January 1, 1960, as Students for a Democratic Society (SDS), and had to defend its right to be a protest organization. YPSL wanted no left-wing competition just before the sit-in explosion of January set off protest wildfire.[134]

By 1960 it was pointless for the Shachtmanites to deny they were running the Socialist Party. Harrington took over the party's new biweekly paper, *New America*, which replaced *Socialist Call*. The lead story of his inaugural issue was by Randolph, who chastised the Democratic and Republican Parties for doing as little as possible on civil rights. Now the Shachtmanites knew what they believed about realignment, declaring that the civil rights movement and AFL-CIO were transforming the Democratic Party into a labor party. They put it aggressively at the party convention of May 1960, establishing a new Socialist position on electoral politics. New political forces, they observed, were changing the Democratic Party—"the new Negro, labor's immensely powerful political machine, the liberal and peace organizations." Sooner or later these forces would seize control of the party and change its fundamental character. The Socialists said they were "wholeheartedly dedicated to the fight for realignment." Seemingly overnight they had developed warm feelings for liberals and a sunny optimism about American politics. They shared the fight for realignment with the UAW, the ADA, the New York Liberal Party, and "other outstanding progressive movements." Moreover, "the SP-SDF is ideally suited to spearhead the drive for realignment in that it is an independent organization, free of any compromising ties with the old party machines." In other words, the party was undertaking "a basic shift in tactics," volunteering to be "the most courageous and intransigent force for realignment." The Democratic Party was becoming "a new liberal-labor second party" and democratic socialists had the program for it.[135]

Shachtmanite strategy was always about riding into power by latching onto somebody. The realignment strategy radiated an ambitious swagger that Socialists hadn't displayed in decades. They adopted the Shachtmanite line with few objections—Darlington Hoopes was the leading holdout, pleading that he wanted to be in a good party, not a corrupt one. To him, the Shachtmanites were conniving leaches. The Socialists debated realignment for the next two years, but the 1960 convention was a turning point. On the opening day of the Socialist convention an Alabama jury near miraculously acquitted King of tax fraud. King and Randolph immediately called for demonstrations at the upcoming Democratic and Republican Conventions, which they named the March on the Conventions Movement for Freedom Now. The organizing burden fell on Rustin, who turned to Harrington. The sit-in explosion of January 1960 unleashed a flood of student protesters who challenged King to get arrested with them. King sent Harrington to speak for him at a sit-in in Washington; a decade later, recalling the moment self-consciously in a different time, Harrington explained: "It was not then considered preposterous for a white radical to be a spokesman for a black leader."[136]

Rustin sent Harrington to organize the protest at the mid-July Democratic Convention in Los Angeles. Harrington went to Los Angeles "filled with a romantic image of myself" and was swiftly disabused of it. Why would King send a white socialist outsider to organize in Los Angeles? Harrington never came up with a better answer than the lame and clueless one that King actually believed in racial integration. He had never organized in a black community without Rustin and did not know Clarence Jones, a black conservative entertainment lawyer and friend of King's with whom he worked in Los Angeles. The desolation of black life in Los Angeles stunned Harrington. He thought constantly about James Baldwin's saying that a black American must always be on guard and never relax. Harrington saw it as never before, fretting that *he* was edgy and defensive in Los Angeles.[137]

In New York, black Americans lived in sprawling tenements that fostered a sense of community. In Los Angeles they were spread out over huge geographic distances in decaying individual houses. Harrington winced at the isolation and anomie he encountered. He tried to organize with Communists and the NAACP and failed. The Communists red-baited him since he was open about being a Socialist, and they lied about being Communists, and the NAACP was unwilling to demonstrate. Plus the Communists and NAACP officials detested each other. Harrington caught his first glimmer of a self-recognition that haunted him for years—his simple belief in racial integration rested on the false assumptions that he was good, white society was normative, and black Americans wanted to be assimilated into white society. For six weeks Harrington worked around the clock to organize a mass march. He failed abysmally, telling Rustin, who told him to get back to work; there would be a march even if no one else came. Harrington wrangled with hostile, dishonest police officials, pretending not to see through them, needing their cooperation. He and Jones broke through with a handful of ministers and union officials, or so they thought; on demonstration day the ministers came in droves, surprising Harrington and Jones.

Meanwhile Rustin's life exploded because Powell wanted the civil rights movement to run through himself and the Democratic Party, not King and Rustin. Powell had just come through a contentious period in his life by playing an insider role in the Eisenhower administration. Democrats fumed at him for years, but in 1958 he defeated a Tammany attempt to unseat him and returned to the party on his terms, refuting everyone who said he was politically dead. Like all civil rights leaders, Powell did not like John F. Kennedy, who voted against the Civil Rights Act of 1957 and courted Dixiecrat support. Kennedy had no gut-level passion for justice, he was soft on McCarthyism, and being Roman Catholic did not help him at Abyssinian Church. Kennedy reminded Powell of the feckless Adlai Stevenson, except Kennedy was worse. Powell's favorites for the Democratic nomination were Humphrey, Michigan governor G. Mennen Williams, and Missouri senator Stuart Symington—fighting liberals who cared about racial justice.

By July 1960 the only liberal with a chance was Symington, and he had little chance. Kennedy swept the primaries, Lyndon Johnson had party bosses in his corner, and some old-timers wanted Stevenson to get a third chance. Powell mounted the pulpit at Abyssinian to make a risky, breathtaking case for Johnson. Admittedly, Johnson mutilated the civil rights bill of 1957, but he whipped it through the Senate. It would not have passed without him, and he did it as a Texas southerner. Powell said Johnson had a ruthless tenacity that he respected and the movement needed. If it came down to Kennedy versus Johnson there was no contest. Abyssinians had to support Johnson, and to get there they had to work on themselves. Powell declared, "Any Negro who automatically dismisses Lyndon Johnson because of the accident of birth automatically qualifies himself as an immature captive Negro, and a captive of his own prejudices." He made it stronger: "This is a test of your own Christianity and if you rise to the heights you will be putting the reactionary segregationists of the South squarely on the spot so that all Americans, Northerners and Southerners, will know that they alone are the immature people. Let us not be captives of our own prejudices."[138]

Heading into the Democratic Convention, Powell enjoyed his resurgence. The Democratic nominee, whoever it turned out to be, would need Powell to swing the votes of black Americans away from Richard Nixon. On his way to Los Angeles Powell aggressively reclaimed his importance in Democratic politics. Students had ignited sit-in wildfire in Nashville, Greensboro, and far beyond. Older movement leaders welcomed the surge while waiting anxiously for King's trial in Montgomery for tax fraud. They were astonished when King was acquitted. It was hard to say, when King called for the convention protests, where the movement was going or if it tilted toward the Democrats. To Powell, the flip side was equally relevant. Regular Democrats needed him more than ever. If Democrats were to be the party of civil rights or even aspire to that status Powell was indispensable. King, Randolph, and Rustin formulated platform demands for both party conventions backed by picketers, and Rustin claimed the NAACP supported the pickets.

That was a blunder, evoking Wilkins's wrath. Wilkins had not agreed to any specific plan, and he was outraged that Rustin misrepresented him. Wilkins was angry anyway because he resented King's celebrity and now a youth movement evolving out of SCLC—the Student Nonviolent Coordinating Committee (SNCC)—openly derided the NAACP. Trained by Methodist pastor James Lawson and Ella Baker, SNCC was founded on April 15, 1960. Lawson said the NAACP was a stodgy vehicle of the black bourgeoisie, offending Wilkins. Who was Lawson, a mere youth organizer in Nashville, to sneer at the NAACP? Then Rustin pulled a fast one and Wilkins erupted. He fired off an angry, accusatory letter to Randolph, who waited eight days to reply. Wilkins took his complaint to Powell, who seized the moment. On June 18 King spoke to the National Sunday School Congress in Buffalo. The next day Powell told the Sunday School Congress that King and Randolph had bullied Wilkins. Moreover, Powell said, this had become a pattern. King and Randolph arrogated themselves over other civil rights leaders and relied too much on two advisors, Rustin and Levison, who were outright socialists. Powell posed as an apostle of unity, albeit by red-baiting Rustin and Levison. King and Randolph, Powell said, had good intentions, but they needed to play better with others; otherwise the movement would be hopelessly splintered.[139]

The *Pittsburgh Courier* ran the story, which Rustin and Randolph shrugged off. Powell was always angling to make himself the center of attention. Randolph chuckled at the suggestion that he was a Socialist because of Levison's influence over him. King, however, was stung by Powell's attack, and said so. Powell retreated, telling King the *Courier* misquoted him. King went to Rio de Janeiro for the Baptist World Alliance, believing the episode was over, but in Rio he received a stunning message from Powell through an emissary, Ann Arnold Hastings. Powell demanded that King cancel the pickets at the Democratic Convention. If King refused to cancel, Powell would announce at a press conference that King was sexually involved with Rustin.[140]

This totally fabricated threat horrified King. He tried to call Randolph in New York, but Rustin picked up the phone; Randolph was out of the office. Mortified and panic stricken, King conveyed the message to Rustin. The two men tried to gauge if Powell would do it. They had never trusted Powell, but this was fantastically over the top. Finally Rustin reached Randolph, who surmised that Powell was desperate to shore up his standing with party regulars who would vote on Powell's chairmanship of the Education and Labor Committee. Randolph told Rustin to tell King they had to carry out the conventions project. They could not control what Powell did, and if King canceled the picket, Randolph would have to explain that King did so at Powell's insistence.

That left King stranded with no guarantee that Powell would not smear him anyway. Rustin agreed with Randolph, but King hesitated. Rustin, hoping to force King's hand, offered to resign his position with King and SCLC. King did not reject the offer, which wounded Rustin. The SCLC board had never wanted Rustin, it chafed at King's reliance on him, and it blamed Rustin for King's legal peril in Alabama. The board was already screaming to fire Rustin when Powell shrewdly blackmailed King on Rustin's vulnerability points. Rustin later recalled: "Martin had one very major defect. He did not like contention with people who were supposed to be friends. . . . He sort of folded on in-fighting." Rustin announced his resignation, declaring that Powell had sought "to weaken, if not destroy, the march on the conventions for his own obvious political reasons."[141]

The convention demonstrations went on without Rustin, who lost his relationship with King for three years. The NAACP held rallies at both conventions and refused to demonstrate. In Los Angeles Kennedy was roundly booed upon entering an NAACP rally. He won a few grudging claps with a game performance, but the crowd saved its acclaim for Humphrey, who declared that he would rather stand up for civil rights than win any election at any level. After the candidates departed Powell gave a barnburner speech about retaking the White House and fulfilling American democracy. He rocked the house with acidic jibes at white cluelessness; Harrington winced that he went too far, scaring off white moderates. Then the pickets went up, and Powell skipped out, along with Wilkins. The following day Kennedy racked up a first-ballot victory and Powell seethed with frustration. Blacks across the convention shook their heads, crying out, "No, no, no." The scene unnerved the Kennedy team—people who thought their suave gentility entitled them to the votes of black Americans. Robert Kennedy, Theodore Sorensen, Kenneth O'Donnell, Pierre Salinger, and Lawrence O'Brien guided the Kennedy team. They had no connection to black communities and no idea how to engage black voters. Powell, on second thought, realized that that fact played to his advantage.

Harrington and Jones got five thousand people to protest and march. It was a modest turnout but a huge relief to Harrington after weeks of stone-cold failure. King impressed Harrington enormously: "I marveled that he had the emotional strength and maturity to keep his equilibrium given the fantastic pressures to which he was subjected." King was bombarded with phone messages and people pulling at him constantly. He was "like the eye of a storm, calm and self-possessed while a tempest whirled around him." Before the convention started King told Harrington he was leaning toward Kennedy because Kennedy told him personally he would push for a civil rights bill. Harrington begged King to hold back. Harrington later reflected that he had a stupid reason and a good one. The stupid reason was that he hadn't adjusted to supporting any Democrat, no matter what Shachtman said; he wrote in Norman Thomas on voting day. The serious reason was that Nixon might win the election, and King needed to sustain his reasonably good relationship with him.[142]

But King had known Nixon for several years and had a hunch that Kennedy was a better bet. They turned to political philosophy and Harrington gasped at realizing that King was a flat-out democratic socialist. King was not influenced merely by social gospel socialism or his friendship with Rustin. His worldview was socialist: "He understood the need for a thoroughgoing democratization of the economy and the political structure of society. He understood that full civil rights for an exploited and hungry mass of black Americans constituted only a first step in the transformation of the intolerable conditions under which they lived." The conversation made Harrington anxious before it yielded a bit of ideological pride. This could not get out; it would ruin King if people knew how closely he agreed with Rustin, Randolph, Harrington, and Rauschenbusch. Harrington did not even want to hear King say it. Nonetheless, "it was a revelation to me that this warm and luminous man of the South had, in the course of a much more profound political and intellectual journey than mine, come to a view of America and the world that I largely shared."[143]

6

NEW LEFT, OLD LEFT, AND
MICHAEL HARRINGTON

The New Left ascended dramatically, bristling with the idealism of privileged youth, and crashed spectacularly, while sprouting liberationist movements. It brought the first wave of the baby boom generation into radical politics by defying the complacency and parental conformism of the 1950s. It brushed aside the doctrines of the Old Left only to recycle some of the worst ones. It was humanistic, integrationist, and consumed with making the world better for others until it turned self-destructive and disintegrated. It birthed a brilliant racial justice organization, the Student Nonviolent Coordinating Committee (SNCC), and a storied campus organization, Students for a Democratic Society (SDS), both of which changed dramatically in 1965. SNCC embraced Black Power, SDS turned revolutionary, and both played roles in founding the women's liberation movement. SDS had a fractious relationship with Old Left Socialists until it broke into Maoist proto-Leninist factions; meanwhile the Socialists splintered too. Nearly all the creativity, scheming, failing, and angst of the Socialists revolved around Michael Harrington, who refused to believe, for too long, that his friends were creating a new kind of conservatism.

Harrington resigned as cochair of the Socialist Party in 1972 as a protest against comrades who supported the Vietnam War, sneered at feminism, reflexively took the AFL-CIO line, and supported Richard Nixon over George McGovern. Then he led two successive organizations—the Democratic Socialist Organizing Committee (DSOC) and Democratic Socialists of America (DSA). DSOC was a union of Old Left Social Democrats, trade union leaders, and progressive youth, and DSA was the same thing plus a strong dose of New Left veterans and former Communists. Both organizations touted multi-tendency fusions of red, green, pink, and feminist socialism; Harrington took pride in leading very different kinds of Socialist organizations from the one he joined in his youth. But DSOC and DSA were short on cadres who put socialism first or even high up. Harrington's later comrades related democratic socialism in some way to what they really cared about. It was hard for newcomers to identify what democratic socialism was per se or what kind of activism it entailed. That was a sea change from the cadre movement he joined in 1952.

Being a veteran of the civil rights struggle during its idealistic-integrationist phase marked Harrington for the rest of his life. He was nostalgic for his early organizing with Bayard Rustin; in later life he lit up when he recalled it. The early movement preached a simple ethical message of integration that didn't require Harrington to look within. In 1960, organizing a civil rights demonstration in Los Angeles, he had to look within to fathom why he was failing, defensive, and despairing. It pained him to realize that his supposed antiracism was a species of white liberal racism. Harrington learned to say he was grateful to be corrected, but he said it with a tinge of regret and bruised feelings, usually adding that Martin Luther King Jr. espoused racial integration. The struggle for racial justice, it turned out, was more complex than the blend of moral feeling and Marxism he brought to it. As for the white-dominated SDS, he was steeped in regret. If anyone could have bridged the divide between the Old and New Left it was Harrington. He failed when it mattered and spent the rest of his life trying, mostly commendably, to make up for it.

The call for a New Left originated in the late 1950s breakup of British Communism and crossed the Atlantic in the early 1960s. The first concerted use of the term was made by British intellectual exiles from the Communist Party who joined a younger generation of antinuclear activists on college campuses to create New Left Clubs. In 1959 two British left-wing journals—*New Reasoner* and *Universities and Left Review*—merged to form *New Left Review*, the flagship of the New Left Clubs. Stuart Hall, a West Indian student at Oxford, was a key figure in the early New Left, describing it as the crossroads of an expiring Stalinism and a reconstructed Social Democracy. Similar currents sprouted in France, where a band of independent intellectuals called themselves the Nouvelle Gauche, and the United States, where a group of ex-Trotskyites founded the *American Socialist* magazine shortly after leaving the SWP. All associated the New Left with generational change and rethinking. There were contentious arguments about which parts of Marxism were obsolete, but "New Left" always meant that control of production was just one issue among others and proletarian deliverance was no longer expected.[1]

Two conventions of June 1962 framed the Old Left's attempt to bond with the next generation. One was the Socialist convention in Washington, DC, at which the party formally settled its position on political realignment. The second was the SDS convention in Port Huron, Michigan, that issued the *Port Huron Statement*. The Socialist Party had three camps on electoral politics. YPSL and its old-school allies led by William Briggs of Los Angeles wanted the party to return to independent socialist campaigning or the dream of creating a labor party or both. They had not become socialists to work in the Democratic Party. The Shachtmanites made their customary case for Democratic realignment, and a third camp led by former Shachtmanites Deborah Meier and Saul Mendelson said the Shachtman position focused too exclusively on the Democratic Party, alienating young radicals. The three camps evenly split the first vote, momentarily putting realignment in jeopardy, since the first and third groups held the same objection: Why should we alienate newcomers who don't want to work in the Democratic Party? The Shachtmanites shrewdly averted defeat by swinging behind the Meier–Mendelson group. They didn't have to say the party worked only in the Democratic Party. It was enough to save the realignment doctrine in a broadly inclusive form for those who couldn't deal with Democrats. A year later political scientist James MacGregor Burns said the United States had four parties—liberal presidential Democrats, moderate presidential Republicans, conservative congressional Democrats, and traditional congressional Republicans. All the presidents since 1932 were liberals or moderates, but the nation's real political power resided in the coalition of Dixiecrats and Republicans that controlled Congress. The Shachtmanites embraced this description as ballast for their realignment goal of defeating the Dixiecrats.[2]

Meier was a public-school teacher and subsequent founder of the small schools movement who wanted the party to attract the kind of young radicals who joined SDS. Al Haber, an eccentric, ponderous, sometime graduate student at the University of Michigan and son of a former Michigan economics professor and dean, was the founder of SDS. He persuaded the LID to sponsor SDS and recruited a scruffy college student, Tom Hayden, who didn't so much join as fail to fend off Haber. Hayden grew up in a middle-class, Irish American, devout Catholic family in Royal Oak, Michigan. He enrolled at Michigan in 1957, edited the *Michigan Daily*, spurned YPSL, and savored C. Wright Mills's acid description of accountants and clerks—pathetic, numb, thoughtless little men. Hayden thought that perfectly captured his father. He met Harrington on the Michigan campus on May Day 1960 and two months later at the Democratic Convention. Hayden respected Harrington but told him that Americans instantly rejected socialism, a European word; U.S. American radicalism needed a fresh start in an American idiom. Meanwhile Hayden latched onto the newborn SNCC, especially SNCC activist Casey Cason, a University of

Texas graduate student he married in 1961. Tom and Casey Hayden helped SNCC and SDS bond with each other.[3]

Hayden's clenched-fist reserve struck Harrington immediately. Old Left leaders radiated a heroic presence; Hayden was antiheroic, with a flat affect and no personality save for his burning intensity. He and Casey Hayden believed that what mattered was to change the values of American society, not to reform governmental structures. They laughed at Harrington's ardor for realignment, as if the Democratic Party were a vehicle with faulty axles. They were slow to fathom how deeply American they and their values were. Hayden later recalled that he and early SNCC were imbued with an idealistic version of the American story, believing in racial integration "not just as a future ideal, but as an ideal to be practiced in the here and now; a belief that places like Mississippi were not part of the American dream, but nightmares that America would awaken from; a belief, finally, that the Constitution, the president, and the American people were really on our side." He rode a Freedom Bus from Atlanta to Albany, Georgia, was thrown into jail on his twenty-second birthday in December 1961, and decided that SDS needed him, not SNCC. Hayden worried that SNCC was doomed by its lack of administrative structure, running entirely on spontaneity and moral passion. Maybe SDS was the answer.[4]

For weeks he labored on a manifesto for SDS that sprawled to seventy-five pages. Hayden took his moral philosophy from French novelist Albert Camus, his political philosophy from his former Michigan teacher Arnold Kaufman, and his politics from Mills. He rejected Reinhold Niebuhr's scathing attack on children of light but also recognized that love alone does not achieve justice; Hayden followed Camus in contending that struggling for a better world is the only way to live. From Kaufman he adopted the idea of participatory democracy; from Mills he adopted the idea that interlocking elites of corporate, political, and military leaders—not an economic class—run the world. Mills said the new rulers needed no coordinated conspiracy to get their way; it was enough to have a bureaucratic convergence of interests, which the Cold War provided. Hayden's draft ran long on Mills and ethical idealism. Meanwhile he declared shortly before SDS convened in Port Huron that his generation trusted only three people older than thirty: Mills, Norman Thomas, and Harrington. Thomas made the list for his ethical idealism and because he urged students to join SDS instead of YPSL. Harrington fell off on the first night of the Port Huron conference.[5]

Fifty-nine members of SDS—representing eight hundred dues payers—convened in June 1962 at a UAW retreat center in Port Huron. The ringleaders were Hayden, Haber, former Michigan undergraduates Sharon Jeffrey and Bob

Ross, Michigan social psychology graduate student Dick Flacks, Swarthmore College student Paul Booth, and SDS field secretary Steve Max. For three days they stewed over Hayden's draft, dropped entire sections, and whittled and smoothened. Their opening sentence, much quoted, which Hayden wrote as a revision, touted their distinct experience and college student outlook: "We are people of this generation, bred in at least modest comfort, housed now in universities, looking uncomfortably to the world we inherit." The delegates said they were born into the world's mightiest nation and raised to believe that America stood for freedom, equality, and democracy—"these American values we found god." They told a story of disillusionment centered on the "permeating and victimizing fact of human degradation, symbolized by the Southern struggle against racial bigotry" and the "enclosing fact of the Cold War, symbolized by the presence of the Bomb." They spoke of fearing a nuclear apocalypse amid fellow citizens who were too numb and lacking in imagination to respond. They skewered America's self-congratulation about being a democracy and leading the "free world," bade farewell to Old Left slogans such as "Capitalism cannot reform itself," "General Strike," and "All Out on May Day," and waved off Daniel Bell, since ideology was far from dead. America abounded in technical expertise, they observed, but it was terribly short on life-affirming values and idealism.[6]

The *Port Huron Statement* began with a purportedly self-evident humanistic truism in the fashion of the Declaration of Independence: "We regard *men* as infinitely precious and possessed of unfulfilled capacities for reason, freedom, and love." The goal of every individual and society, SDS said, should be human independence, enabling all persons to achieve their maximal capacities for self-cultivation, self-direction, self-understanding, and creativity. Conventional U.S. American individualism glorified possession and privilege, producing isolated, lonely, shrunken individuals. SDS commended a generous individuality that nurtured social relations and concern: "We would replace power rooted in possession, privilege, or circumstance by power and uniqueness rooted in love, reflectiveness, reason, and creativity." It described participatory democracy as a system in which individuals share in the social decisions that affect their lives through media that facilitate their common participation. Work should be educative, creative, and self-directed, fostering independence and respect for others. No healthy democracy tolerates stultifying or degrading work. SDS enthused that students were rising up to claim their humanity. It concluded with six imperatives about what the New Left needed to be: intellectually skilled, socially diverse, young, inclusive of liberals and socialists, willing to cause controversy, and good at finding solutions. Implicit in all six points: the best site for a New Left was the university.[7]

Kaufman had not yet published his thoughts about participatory democracy when the *Port Huron Statement* embraced them. Later he published a book titled *The Radical Liberal: New Man in American Politics* (1968). Kaufman placed himself in the liberal tradition of John Stuart Mill, Leonard Hobhouse, and John Dewey, accentuating Dewey's idea that ethical individuality flourishes only within a shared political community of democratic engagement. He argued that liberalism should be based on the right of each person to develop his or her potentialities as fully as possible. "Participatory democracy" named what was missing in reductionist forms of liberalism such as entrepreneurial individualism and democratic realism. Liberalism is fundamentally about liberty and equal opportunity, which should apply to all citizens. It is truly liberal only if it enables all citizens to develop their essential human capacities, including their powers of shared deliberative action. Kaufman appropriated the romantic-participatory strain in Jean-Jacques Rousseau's social contract theory and the indictment of the U.S. American ruling class offered by Mill. American democracy was merely formal and exclusive at best, excluding the many from the promise of equal opportunity. The idea of participatory democracy gave Hayden a counter-concept to YPSL's proletarian fantasy that similarly rejected reform politics. The movement itself was the point of the movement. It fired Hayden with a soaring self-confidence he later found hard to explain: "I still don't know where this messianic sense, this belief in being right, this confidence that we could speak for a generation came from. But the time was ripe, vibrating with potential."[8]

The Student League for Industrial Democracy (SLID) had long espoused democratic socialism and barred proponents of totalitarian doctrines from joining. Harrington bristled that Hayden's draft seemed to brush aside these identity markers. Did Hayden not understand why the clause excluding Communists and Fascists mattered? Did he even know that SLID endured a wretched Communist takeover in the 1930s? How could he believe that privileging the shallow progressivism of white college students was better than democratic socialism? Harrington commiserated with Rachelle Horowitz and Tom Kahn before they arrived in Port Huron, where Horowitz and Kahn represented YPSL. Flacks picked up Harrington and Shachtman protégé Donald Slaiman at the airport, finding both in a combative mood; Slaiman was a civil rights department official in the AFL-CIO. Harrington came to defend an entire left-wing tradition and to correct SDS about anti-Communism. It didn't matter to him that participatory democracy was contrary to Communism or that SDS was groping for an identity. Hayden offended him by treating anti-Communist socialism as obsolete. As Harrington later put it, he came to fight "in solidarity with the Russian oppositionists, the Left Socialists and anarchists in the Spanish Civil War, the Hungarians invaded by the Red Army in 1956, and the Poles in their endless struggle for freedom and decency in the shadow of Soviet power."[9]

Harrington could stay only for the opening night, so he blasted Hayden right away for dismissing anti-Communism, the labor movement, and liberal Democrats. No record of his speech and postlecture banter exists, but everyone said both were blistering. Hayden later described the speech as "paranoid, hysterical, anti-communist mud-slinging." Slaiman piled on: Who was Hayden to sneer at AFL-CIO chief George Meany? Hayden replied that America used anti-Communism to excuse every bad thing it did in the world; he didn't believe the Soviet Union was inherently aggressive or that American troops belonged in Vietnam; most unions were conservative; and liberal Democrats were part of the problem. Otherwise, what was the point of creating SDS? Harrington came off as an Old Left bully, as he later grasped: "My notion of a progressive, Leftist anti-Communist made as much existential sense to them as a purple cow." To him, the Red Army smashing into Hungary was a fresh outrage compelling condemnation; nobody in SDS shared that feeling. Harrington implored that realignment was the key to changing America, and liberals were essential to it. It didn't matter that his group adopted this position only recently. The Shachtmanites had let go of their Marxian cynicism about U.S. American politics. They became optimists during the very years Hayden's generation discovered that America was surprisingly bad. The ironies sailed past each other at Port Huron. The Marxian Socialists wanted to renew the Democratic Party from within, and the recently alienated SDS youth wanted an alternative to Democratic Party liberalism.[10]

The next day the convention debated whether to grant visitor status to a seventeen-year-old from the Communist Party's new youth group, the Progressive Youth Organizing Committee. Horowitz, Kahn, and YPSL chair Richard Roman filled in for Harrington, insisting that this issue had been settled on the left decades ago; didn't SDS know anything about Communist subversion? Democratic leftists don't invite Communists to their meetings. By the time SDS voted to seat the Communist teenager, he had gone home. The rest of the convention revised Hayden's draft, deciding to accentuate the generational theme, keep the emphasis on participatory democracy, and support civil rights legislation, antipoverty programs, and increased spending on education. Ross added a sentence that admonished college students not to be snooty about union bureaucrats, and Flacks added that SDS was fundamentally opposed to Communism because it rested on the "total suppression of organized opposition." Roman pushed Flacks to say it categorically; it seemed to SDS that

Roman, Horowitz, and Kahn cared only about anti-Communism. But the SDS ringleaders left the convention believing they had created something new while dealing constructively with Old Left criticism. Had Roman, Horowitz, and Kahn taken credit for improving the *Port Huron Statement*, SDS would have let them. That is not what happened.[11]

Hayden, Haber, Max, Ross, Booth, Flacks, Mickey Flacks, Casey Hayden, and Paul Potter had believed that Harrington was better than his group; now they knew otherwise. Harrington asked Horowitz if SDS responded constructively to his criticisms, and she said no. This fateful deception launched him into bully mode, pressing the LID board to void all decisions made at Port Huron, fire Haber and Hayden, remove Max from the payroll, censure SDS materials coming from the central office, and replace Max as secretary with Roman. In July the LID board locked SDS out of its office in downtown Manhattan, which reduced Hayden to begging LID to stop slandering and abusing SDS. Kahn faced off with SDS leaders, insisting that LID had every right to their files. SDS, he warned, was vulnerable to being branded as Communist: "People are going to attack us." Hayden shot back, "Yeah, and you're going to be one of them. Our greatest enemy is not HUAC or the Right, it's you." Hayden said the treacherous Kahn would surely try to destroy SDS.[12]

This drama seeped into other venues. Harrington imagined he was curbing some unruly youngsters, much as Thomas dealt with Denitch and him in 1953, but Thomas didn't see it that way, despite having reconciled with Harrington. In September 1962 Thomas and LID stalwart Paul Taylor, a former president of Sarah Lawrence College, persuaded the LID board to reconcile with SDS. The *Port Huron Statement* was allowed to stand and SDS got its office back. Two weeks later Hayden, Booth, Potter, and Todd Gitlin met with *Dissent* magazine editors Irving Howe, Michael Walzer, Emanuel Geltman, and Joseph Buttinger. *Dissent*, founded in 1954 by Howe and Lewis A. Coser, was the flagship of the social democratic left. It was urbane, anti-Communist, antibureaucratic, and erudite, featuring radical democrats like Mills and Paul Goodman among its dominant cast of social democrats. The SDS leaders and *Dissent* editors met at the elegant Upper East Side Manhattan home of Buttinger, a former Austrian Socialist leader and veteran of its underground resistance against Hitler.

Howe later described the scene: "Two generations sat facing each other, fumbling to reach across the spaces of time. We were scarred, they untouched. We bore marks of 'corrosion and distrust,' they looked forward to clusterings of fraternity. We had grown skeptical of Marxism, they were still unchained to system. We had pulled ourselves out of an immigrant working class, an experience not likely to produce romantic views about the poor; they, children of warm liberals and cooled radicals, were hoping to find a way into the lives and wisdom of the oppressed." Could they bond over their devotion to freedom and penchant for social criticism? The *Dissent* editors were fine with participatory democracy but not with contrasting it to representative democracy, as SDS did. The two sides clashed over anti-Communism. Howe and Geltman made windy speeches assailing SDS for romanticizing Fidel Castro and not caring about oppressed East Europeans. Howe distrusted Hayden, seeing the "beginnings of a commissar" in Hayden's clenched air of distance: "Pinched in manner, holding in some obscure personal rage, he spoke as if he were already an experienced, canny 'political.'" Gitlin later countered: "In truth Hayden was a dynamo. The two of us shared a house that year; I was awed by his nonstop schedule." The clash over Cuba rolled off Gitlin; what caught him was Howe's disgust when Hayden quoted Gandhi about nonviolence and redeeming the enemy. You have to love everyone, Hayden said. Redeeming the enemy is as important as changing society. Gitlin recalled, "To me, this was Hayden at his most eloquent, the New Left at its most stirring."[13]

SDS needed an institutional base and LID needed to repair its image, so the two sides negotiated a truce. By then Harrington fathomed how bad he looked. SDS leaders couldn't look at him, his reputation plummeted on the left, and embarrassment swept over him. He was humiliated, belatedly realizing what he had squandered. Harrington apologized for being stupid, irrational, and thuggish. He should have perceived the difference between SDS youths trying out a position and Old Left faction fighters holding a line, but alas. He said it repeatedly for the rest of his life.

The early fallout was mostly a grapevine affair. This was an intra-left scandal that didn't make the *New York Times*. A few SDS leaders forgave him, especially Ross, but most did not. Many were quotably scathing for many years. Casey Hayden was much quoted: "I know now what it must have been like to be attacked by Stalinists." Tom Hayden said he learned at Port Huron "that Social Democrats aren't radicals and can't be trusted." Hayden's contempt had a touch of gratitude for finding a perfect foil: "He was the perfect guy for everybody to overthrow." SDS had a fledgling identity before Port Huron and an uncertain relationship to the old socialism. Hayden said Harrington and LID established a sharp dichotomy between the Old Left and New Left that SDS could not have achieved on its own: "The names they called us reinforced our new left identity." Journalist Jack Newfield, writing a popular history of the New Left in 1966, featured quotable anti-Harrington zingers and the fact that Harrington apologized profusely. Hayden's snarky quotes about Harrington kept coming for over twenty years, until 1988, when he buried the hatchet. Harrington's early apologies said he made some important points about Communism in a bad way. Later he said he was blind and dense in ways he found inexplicable. Still later his therapist helped him comprehend the colossal screw-up of his life. Harrington had always been the youngest at everything he did. His self-image, he reflected, was that of a young person: "Up comes this younger generation. I think that they are ignoring my honest, sincere, and absolutely profound advice. And this struck at my self-image."[14]

He never got over it. The fallout dogged him for the rest of his life, lingering wherever he went on lecture tours, yielding hostile questions that he fielded with apologies that sometimes ran too long. SDS founders nurtured their victim story beyond its reasonable shelf life, refusing for over twenty years to accept Harrington's apology, fueling a left-wing tradition of Harrington-ridicule. The solidarity organizations of the 1980s memorialized it; I heard it often through those years. Some interpreters thus exaggerate the fallout for Harrington's psyche and legacy. Political scientist Robert A. Gorman lurches too far on both: "Psychologically, he was devastated, his self-image shattered. Having spent over a decade cultivating an image and a constituency, he destroyed both in one foolish night and its aftermath. Professionally, Harrington was now a man without turf. Stereotyped as a strident anti-communist, anti-capitalist, and anti–New Leftist, he was simply ignored altogether by scholars."[15]

That does not describe the ebullient founder and leader of DSOC and DSA that I knew from 1974 to 1989 who poured out scholarly books, averaged one hundred lectures per year, and regularly editorialized on radio and television. Even as a description of Harrington in the aftermath of Port Huron, it misses that his unexpected fame caused greater inner turmoil for him, he spoke to SDS chapters through the years of his grapevine beatings, and he stuck to his baseline points about Communism. Harrington was too defensive in 1962 about YPSL to acknowledge its repellent features, and the SDS founders were perceptive about the upshot of his anti-Communism. To the end of the 1960s he spoke for the most conservative flank of the antiwar movement, exactly as SDS expected. Meanwhile SDS descended into revolutionary delusions, both Leninist and not, that destroyed the organization in 1969, having learned nothing from the history of Leninist sabotage that Harrington warned about in Port Huron.

Harrington won national renown during the very months he sabotaged his reputation on the left. To a larger audience than joined SDS, he was the author of *The Other America*, nearly always called "the book that launched the war on poverty." In December 1958 *Commentary* editor Anatole Shub asked him for an article on poverty, notwithstanding that Harrington knew little about it. His many articles for *Commonweal* and *Dissent* never mentioned this issue, and the only reference to it in his entire corpus was an article on public housing in *Commentary*. But Shub figured his speaking tours and the Catholic Worker stint must have taught him something, and Harrington was always a quick study. Liberal journals of the 1950s did not discuss poverty. Economic growth expanded the middle class, and poverty was said to be a marginal hangover from the Depression lacking any importance as a political issue. More growth would mop up whatever was left of poverty.[16]

Two Harvard doyens of ADA, Arthur Schlesinger Jr. and John Kenneth Galbraith, confirmed this complacent reading while scrounging for something for liberals to do. Schlesinger said in 1956 that liberals faced a "challenge of abundance." America had no structural economic problems to solve, so liberals needed to move on to "qualitative liberalism," helping to improve the quality of (middle-class) life. Schlesinger wasn't sure what he meant, but two years later Galbraith offered an answer in the bible of prosperity liberalism, *The Affluent Society*. The title was (ostensibly) the thesis—America is incredibly rich. Galbraith said liberals still had work to do because America needed a better balance between its private opulence and public bankruptcy. Liberals believed in government and cared about education, the environment, and cities. Galbraith allowed that poverty still existed in America but not in a general sense, being restricted to individual cases and islands of backwardness such as Appalachia. The book instantly symbolized an era, causing Galbraith to plead against its reputation; we're-so-rich was not his point. *The Affluent Society*, however, reinforced the convention that Americans should not worry overmuch about whoever it was who missed out on the wealth boom.[17]

A few critics objected. Economist Leon Keyserling said in 1958 that establishment liberals might be too complacent, noting that more than a quarter of U.S. American families reported annual incomes below four thousand dollars. Keyserling suggested there was a stronger case to be made for a New Deal–like employment policy than Schlesinger and Galbraith recognized. A few months later U.S. Senator Paul Douglas of Illinois put it more strongly in a surprising venue. *The Affluent Society* won an award from the Tamiment Institute in New York, and Douglas—an ADA stalwart and former University of Chicago economist—was asked to present it. He spoiled the party by observing that according to the Census Bureau approximately 25 percent of the nation earned incomes of less than three thousand dollars—a figure low enough to count as poor, though Galbraith pegged the poverty cutoff at one thousand dollars. If one-fourth of the nation was poor, how was this an affluent society? Galbraith responded graciously that the title of his book was a Madison Avenue misfortune that now he had to bear.[18]

Harrington drew a picture of the problem, explained it with an ill-considered version of a dubious concept, and proposed a solution. His article "Our Fifty Million Poor" derived the fifty-million figure from the Federal Reserve Board and U.S. Commerce Department. To explain why rich America had so much poverty he said that poverty creates a culture of its own that cuts across regional and national boundaries. Anthropologist Oscar Lewis originated the "culture of poverty" idea in his book *Five Families: Mexican Case Studies in the Culture of Poverty* (1959), contending that the poor of Mexico City, San Juan, and New York had more in common with each other in terms of interpersonal relations, family structure, time orientation, value systems, and spending patterns than with middle-class people of their own nations. Harrington agreed that the poor lived in a culture of poverty, though he employed this idea in a broad fashion that played down Lewis's emphasis on cultural norms, replacing it with Harrington's emphasis on economics and social policy. According to Harrington, the reality of the culture of poverty thwarted all piecemeal attempts to abolish poverty. America needed a comprehensive program dealing with housing, schools, medical care, labor rights, and communal institutions.[19]

In a subsequent article titled "Slums, Old and New" Harrington argued that the new poverty was more degrading than the poverty of nineteenth-century immigrant communities because the latter were bound together by strong families, neighborliness, ethnic and religious bonds, and aspirations of a better life. The new slums were sites of broken families and anomic despair lacking any sustaining culture. Harrington said the United States needed housing programs that interspersed the poor among working-class and middle-class communities. His articles appeared just as poverty emerged as a public issue, catalyzed by John Kennedy's primary campaign in West Virginia and a storied CBS broadcast by Edward R. Murrow on migrant farmworkers, *Harvest of Shame*. Several publishers asked Harrington to write a book, but he declined because Shachtman told him to concentrate on building the party. Harrington's friend Herman Roseman, an economist, countered that he had a moral duty to illumine a social problem that economists ignored. Macmillan offered Harrington a five-hundred-dollar advance, a huge sum for an activist always pinched for bus fare.[20]

The Other America said fifty million poor Americans lived in a world invisible to middle-class Americans, existing mostly in rural isolation and crowded urban slums. They were unskilled workers, migrant farmworkers, the elderly, and oppressed racial minorities. Most black Americans were poor, Harrington wrote, because "the American economy, the American society, and the American unconscious are all racist." He described the situation of the American poor in two interchangeable ways: "The poor are caught in a vicious circle; or, the poor live in a culture of poverty." In fact, these were not inter-changeable conceptions; Harrington misconstrued the problematic idea he took from Lewis. Lewis described the culture of poverty as a system of cultural values contrasting with middle-class values, which he said described perhaps one-fifth of the U.S. American poor. Harrington played down the idea that the poor subscribed to alternative norms, yet he heightened its stigma by describing *all* impoverished Americans as victims of the culture of poverty. To Harrington, the culture of poverty was a vicious circle, not a choice. The poor got sick more than others and stayed ill longer than others because they lived in unhealthy neighborhoods, ate bad food, and lacked decent medical care, all of which prevented them from holding a steady job: "At any given point in the circle, particularly when there is a major illness, their prospect is to move to an even lower level and to begin the cycle, round and round, toward even more suffer-ing." Only rarely do individuals break out of the vicious circle, and groups lack the social and political agency to do it: "Only the larger society, with its help and resources, can really make it possible for these people to help themselves."[21]

Lewis disliked Harrington's economic interpretation of the culture of pov-erty and took no interest in his policy proposals, believing that revolutionary socialism was the only cure for the culture of poverty and thus for poverty. Harrington applied his newfound optimistic politics to the poverty issue. Only the government was big enough to finance a comprehensive national program. Harrington wanted community organizers and other local agencies to organize the poor and coordinate antipoverty programs funded by the government, for "only the Federal Government has the power to abolish poverty." He said Americans needed to be shamed by the facts and stirred to action. Until that happened, "the other America will continue to exist, a monstrous example of needless suffering in the most advanced society in the world."[22]

The Other America was published in March 1962 and won just enough notice for Penguin to buy the paperback rights. Harrington pocketed fifteen hundred dollars, enough to live in Paris for several months. He made plans to spend 1963 in France but commenced a romantic relationship with a Greenwich Village culture writer for the *Village Voice*, Stephanie Gervis, in the summer of 1962. Gervis was a few years out of Cornell and an exception to his succession of fashion models. She held Harrington in low-medium regard until she heard him give a bravura speech outside the United Nations at a rally protesting nuclear testing. Her initial disinterest made her more interesting to him than his long run of apolitical girlfriends. Harrington left for Paris in January 1963, just before Dwight Macdonald emoted for forty pages in the *New Yorker* about *The Other America*. Gervis joined Harrington in Paris in May, and the following month they married. He wanted to love France but lamented that the French were rude and snobbish, and French Socialists were no better. He had no inkling that the Macdonald review changed his life. Harrington's political highlight of 1963 was to represent the SP-SDF at the Eighth Congress of the Socialist International in Amsterdam. West Berlin mayor Willy Brandt, the star of the surging German Social Democratic Party, gave a buoyant keynote address; British Labour Party leader Harold Wilson, a year before he became prime minister, also spoke. Harrington delighted at hanging out with European Socialists, regretted missing the March on Washington, and was still in France when President Kennedy was assassinated in Dallas.[23]

The March on Washington of August 28, 1963, was conceived and organized by socialists. Rustin, Kahn, and CORE socialist Norman Hill drafted a proposal for a two-day protest in Washington, DC. Randolph became its director after the NAACP came aboard; he asked Rustin to run what became a one-day extravaganza; Rustin appointed Kahn as chief of staff and Horowitz as head of transportation logistics; and Walter Reuther mobilized the UAW. King electrified the nation with a closing run from his "I Have a Dream" speech, feeling the need to soar with something after he wandered off his text. His dream was "deeply rooted in the American dream that one day this nation will rise up and live out the true meaning of its creed—we hold these truths to be self-evident, that all men are created equal." He dreamed that the sons of former slaves and slave owners would eat together "at the table of brotherhood" on the red hills of Georgia and that Mississippi, "sweltering with the heat of oppression," would be "transformed into an oasis of freedom and justice." His long ending rang nine rounds of chimes on "Let Freedom Ring," the closing phrase of "My Country 'Tis of Thee."[24]

The speakers trooped to the White House and King was showered with effusive gratitude along the way. His powerful unscripted ending impressed JFK, who told an aide, "He's damn good." King, growing embarrassed, asked the president if he heard Reuther's forceful speech; JFK said he had heard Reuther plenty of times. Randolph, Wilkins, and Reuther seized the moment, pressing Kennedy to fight for a strong civil rights bill. JFK said the vote looked close in the House and bad in the Senate; they needed a bipartisan consensus on civil rights, not a Democratic crusade. The March on Washington was about winning the nation's attention and mobilizing support for the civil rights bill. On these counts it was a smashing success. The demands were moderate, only prescribed picket signs were allowed, and liberals experienced it as a day of triumph and mobilization. Now came the messy, grinding, and very political work of pushing the bill through. The march started Rustin on the path from Old Left pacifist protester to regular Democrat, and it insulted every female leader in the movement, although Rosa Parks and Diane Nash Bevel were allowed to take a bow. Ella Baker said quotable things about why this kept happening, while Malcolm X, James Baldwin, and Adam Clayton Powell Jr. delivered quotable zingers about the limitations of King's coalition. Malcolm derided the performers for letting Randolph tell them what song to sing and what speech to make.[25]

The march alienated the SNCC militants whom King lauded in his speech. SNCC leaders Courtland Cox, Charles McDew, Charles McLaurin, Robert Moses, Avon Rollins, and Charles Sherrod had just spent three years being persecuted for community organizing in the Deep South. The experience had hardened them, yielding a contradictory agenda. SNCC had two defining objectives: Provoke the federal government to smash segregationist resistance in the Deep South, and build strong black organizations. These objectives conflicted with each other, while SNCC became a magnet for militants who did not care for King's theology and did not speak his language of redemptive suffering and Christian love.[26]

The socialists who organized the march conducted a conference of their own two days after the march. Rustin, Randolph, Thomas, and Farmer gave speeches basking in the moment and their achievement. Legendary journalist I. F. Stone, covering the conference, said it made sense that socialists organized the march because only socialism had an answer for "the lower third of our society, white as well as black." Stone commended Rustin, Randolph, Thomas, and other socialists for infusing socialism with "fresh meaning and revived urgency." Socialists played key roles in two new, fast-growing peace organizations, the Committee for a Sane Nuclear Policy (SANE) and the Student Peace Union. They had a rising intellectual star in Harrington, who didn't realize *The Other America* was hot. The book became required reading for social scientists, government officials, student activists, and intellectuals. Economic advisor Walter Heller gave a copy to Kennedy, who may have read it before ordering a federal war on poverty three days before his death. Harrington returned to New York just before Christmas 1963, not yet fathoming that his life had changed. He struggled to cope with a barrage of media calls, stunned at becoming somebody that ABC News would call. Lyndon Johnson, in his first State of the Union Address, declared war on poverty, telling Heller that abolishing poverty was his kind of program.[27]

Harrington chafed whenever someone said he was moving up in the world. People told him he should drop socialism and get into politics; sometimes they said he had already started, since *The Other America* never mentioned socialism. Harrington pondered three explanations for this omission. Pragmatism: He didn't want to detract attention from the poverty issue; Marxism: He was corrupted by the seduction of bourgeois status, urging the masses to accept a few crumbs instead of claiming the whole loaf that was rightly theirs; Weber: He exchanged his ethic of ultimate ends for a sensible ethic of responsibility. Harrington recognized a bit of himself in all three explanations, reasoning that all were baked into his realignment politics. In the 1950s he had bought the Trotskyite dogma that any compromise with the bourgeoisie impeded the coming surge of proletarian consciousness. Trotsky said Stalinist treachery and Social Democratic ineptitude were the twin roadblocks to socialist revolution. This argument got the Trotskyites and Shachtmanites through the 1940s, until Shachtman cast away his anchor, joining the Socialist Party. Harrington said democratic socialism was better, but he remembered what it felt like to really believe in the revolution. This wasn't like that.[28]

For a moment—basically, 1964—his standing held up in the New Left and soared on the liberal left. Harrington attracted large lecture audiences and helped to organize the Freedom Summer infusion of northern college students into the struggle for voting rights in Mississippi. *The Other America* played a key role in Freedom Summer, assigned to all project volunteers, though Harrington's speaking tour kept him out of Mississippi until September. SNCC leader Moses and former Stanford dean Allard Lowenstein founded the Mississippi Freedom Democratic Party (MFDP) to create opportunities for black political agency in Mississippi, registering seventeen thousand brave black Mississippians to vote. Two weeks after Johnson signed the Civil Rights Act of 1964 Republicans raged against it at their presidential convention, nominating far-right icon Barry Goldwater. Black Mississippians showed up at Democratic gatherings and were excluded, so the Freedom Democrats offered their own slate of sixty-eight delegates to the Democratic Convention in Atlantic City. Johnson erupted with alarm, fearing the Freedom Democrats would ruin his convention and campaign. He wheedled and threatened in customary LBJ fashion, forcing his wannabe running mate Humphrey to champion his compromise: Two seats for the MFDP, with LBJ choosing the delegates. Johnson strong-armed MFDP attorney Joseph Rauh and his UAW boss Reuther into submission; Rustin, King, Wilkins, and SCLC lieutenant Andrew Young fell into line.

For Rustin, it was a coming-out moment. He was shedding his longtime identity as a selfless agitator to become a regular Democrat—at least, as regular as a gay black Quaker socialist could be. Rustin implored the Freedom Democrats not to wreck the convention. They needed to pull together and focus on the November elections. A new Democratic Party was emerging that would change what was politically possible. The time had come, Rustin said, for the new Democrats to move beyond moral protest, claim their political victory, build on it, and change the nation by governing effectively. The Freedom Democrats listened to Rustin politely but disagreed; he did not speak their language and they did not know him. King went next, more gingerly. He said he hoped they would accept the compromise and move on: "But if I were a Mississippi Negro, I would vote against it."[29]

That was exactly what happened, as the Freedom Democrats voted unanimously for self-respect and defying Johnson. They had risked their lives to vote at this convention, not to win a symbolic victory. A compromise that did not acknowledge their right to represent Mississippi and choose their own representatives failed the test of decency, no matter that Rustin, King, Wilkins, Andrew Young, and a chorus of white liberals implored them to swallow it. Johnson's insistence on naming the delegates cut deeper than the two token seats he offered, but both were offensive, and his so-called solution would have opened party meetings to blacks with no guarantee they would be allowed to register to vote. SNCC and the Freedom Democrats were exhausted and scarred at Atlantic City. In two months the Mississippi Summer Project had yielded sixty beatings, eight unsolved killings, seventeen church burnings, thirteen bombings, and twenty-three shootings. Casey Hayden, divorced from Tom Hayden and deeply involved in the Summer Project, wrote to him before he got to Atlantic City: "I am tense and pretty high strung lately, find myself being really grumpy, which I hate." She said she might be in love but was too stressed to know: "Just realized I have no home address. Hope this reaches you. Are you happy? I can't really analyze me anymore." SNCC called Rustin a traitor, and Harrington defended his friend, arguing that ethically, the Freedom Democrats were right, but politically they succeeded tremendously, just as Rustin said. The Freedom Democrats kept battling within the Democratic Party, campaigning for the Johnson–Humphrey ticket in a state that cast 87 percent of its votes for Goldwater. But SNCC was done with the Democratic Party.[30]

Atlantic City convinced Moses that his brave registration work was pointless. He swore off working with whites or in the system, walking out of SNCC in February 1965, telling SNCC leaders they should leave too. Sherrod took a similarly dramatic turn but within SNCC, joining the swing toward racial militancy that redefined SNCC. He argued that the crucial question for black Americans was whether they wanted to share power in reconciliation with whites or seize power "in rioting and blood." Winning a few positions changed nothing, he said. The Freedom Democrats were defeated because blacks had no real power at the convention. Black Americans needed to build their own base of political power, not make alliances with white liberals that forced blacks to be satisfied with token gains. Black Americans needed to become powerful as a people and for their own people, instead of linking arms with white liberals. SNCC stalwart Cleveland Sellers put it summarily: "Never again were we lulled into believing that our task was exposing injustices so that the 'good' people of America could eliminate them. We left Atlantic City with the knowledge that the movement had turned into something else. After Atlantic City, our struggle was not for civil rights, but for liberation."[31]

Freedom Summer exhausted SNCC, especially its leader John Lewis, who said in Atlantic City that the Freedom Democrats shed too much blood to be treated as honorary guests. Lewis epitomized early SNCC, fired by social gospel conviction. He grieved that King sided with the liberals at Atlantic City but was grateful that King found the least offensive way of selling out. Then Lewis offended SNCC comrades by refusing to join them in bashing King. Lewis never wavered in admiring and emulating King, which made him quaint within SNCC by the end of Freedom Summer. SNCC needed an organizational overhaul with structures of accountability or, failing that, a galvanizing leader who held things together. It needed money to pay its mushroomed staff, and a sage or therapist to help with burnout. None of these things happened. Lewis was marginalized, the insurgent faction disdained organizational restructuring and accountability, Christian moral language became passé, Moses refused to be the unifying leader, SNCC got terrible publicity coming out of Atlantic City, burnout spread like a contagion, and SNCC clashed internally over its objectives.[32]

SNCC gathered in November 1964 at a retreat in Waveland, Mississippi, to rethink its agenda. Position papers were placed on a pile. Casey Hayden and her SNCC roommate Mary King slipped a paper titled "Women in the Movement" into the pile anonymously, fearing a hostile reaction. Hayden had organized Freedom Rides and King assisted SNCC press secretary Julian Bond. White female southerners from northern colleges constituted the largest group of Freedom Summer volunteers. "Women in the Movement" held them in mind without putting it that way. Hayden and King said SNCC took male dominance for granted and routinely mistreated its female workers, citing eleven examples of male chauvinism. The constitutional revision committee consisted only of males, as did the leadership of the Mississippi Summer Project; women were assigned to secretarial roles regardless of their experience; and even the women who held leadership positions were expected to defer to men. Hayden and King said the average SNCC worker assumed male superiority in the same way the average white person assumed white superiority. In both cases the assumption was so deep that people didn't realize they held it and weren't willing to discuss it. Hayden and King pleaded that male supremacism is as destructive as racism:

"Assumptions of male superiority are as widespread and deep rooted and every much as crippling to the woman as the assumptions of white supremacy are to the Negro."[33]

This brave intervention was the first of its kind in the New Left. In 1963 Betty Friedan sparked a middle-class feminist movement with her best-selling book *The Feminine Mystique,* famously describing a problem lacking a name: Suburban women were miserable, despite living comfortably. The mystique, Friedan said, identified womanhood with marriage and motherhood, to their detriment. Women needed professional careers no less than men. "Women in the Movement" came from a site of death-risking struggle, far from the culture of suburbia and careerism described by Friedan. Hayden and King noted poignantly why it had to be anonymous: "Think about the kinds of things the author, if made known, would have to suffer because of raising this kind of discussion." The reaction was as bad as they feared. Ridicule abounded, and Stokely Carmichael countered that the position of women in SNCC was prone. Hayden and King generously said for years afterward that they caught the humor in Carmichael's jest and were not offended by it, although he also said it numerous times afterward in contexts where it meant exactly what he said.[34]

More troubling to Hayden and King was that black women in SNCC did not endorse their critique. Ella Baker had called SNCC into existence at Shaw University in 1960 and nurtured its growth. Diane Nash was the first paid field staff worker in SNCC and played a high-level leadership in it. Ruby Doris Smith (Robinson) was a legendary SNCC veteran of Freedom Ride jails and organizing campaigns. Cynthia Washington, Donna Richards, Muriel Tillinghast, and other black women directed their own local SNCC projects. None felt represented by the sweeping claims of Hayden and King to speak for them. Hayden and King criticized, with prophetic force, their experience of being denigrated and having their talents wasted in SNCC. They described something terribly real—only it was not the experience of their rooted and accomplished black female counterparts. Black women in SNCC were becoming more powerful. They reproved the comments of Carmichael and others like it but knew immediately what was awry with the Hayden–King critique. Hayden and King subsumed black women under a gender category that erased their racial particularity. They wrongly generalized their own experience as white women bearing white middle-class privilege, which masked their anxiety about the swing away from racial integration after Atlantic City. Hayden and King were losing status in SNCC not because they were women but because they were white. They called for feminist justice without acknowledging the difference that race made to their conception of it.[35]

The eruption of feminist criticism in SNCC spread directly to SDS through the SDS spinoff that Tom Hayden and outgoing SDS president Todd Gitlin founded in 1963, the Economic Research and Action Project (ERAP). ERAP sent student organizers into northern cities to lead the poor into battles against city governments. Hayden launched an ERAP project in Newark, New Jersey, contending that the liberal establishment was the enemy. Rennie Davis and Richie Rothstein launched an ERAP project in Chicago, as did Sharon Jeffry and Carol McEldowney in Cleveland, among many others. Women poured into ERAP straight out of college, making the transition more readily than SDS men. SDS was more male dominated than SNCC because SDS was a campus organization and SNCC was an organization of organizers. SNCC organizers listened patiently to ordinary people, empathized with them, and validated their concerns. Their work relied on cooperative virtues and habits that SDS women already had when they joined ERAP; thus they often made better organizers than the men and were more attracted to the work. ERAP leaders Jeffry, McEldowney, Harriet Stulman, and Connie Brown read the Hayden–King memo and initiated a similar discussion in SDS. They planned a workshop for the SDS convention of December 1965, but 1965 was the year that everything changed. SDS was a different organization by the time it convened in December.[36]

Atlantic City went down in New Left lore as the epitome of liberal betrayal and the proof that civil rights liberalism was bankrupt. SNCC and SDS debated from the beginning whether white activists should organize in black communities. Atlantic City swung this debate to a negative verdict, ending the innocence phase for white liberals who were not willfully oblivious. Singing "We Shall Overcome" now evoked awkward feelings of self-consciousness in white liberals and white Socialists. Harrington felt the change but repressed it, clinging to the hope of political salvation he shared with Rustin and King. Congress passed the Economic Opportunity Act in August 1964, appropriating $800 million to fund the new Office of Economic Opportunity headed by Peace Corps director Sargent Shriver, who appointed Harrington to the program's organizing group. Shriver briefed Harrington on the program's mandate and budget, and Harrington objected that America could not abolish poverty by spending "nickels and dimes." Shriver archly replied, "Oh, really, Mr. Harrington. I don't know about you, but this is the first time I've spent a billion dollars."[37]

As Harrington told the story, this exchange symbolized why the United States lost its vaunted war on poverty. LBJ didn't think big enough when it mattered and he lost interest after Democrats got blown away in the backlash elections of 1966. In the early going Harrington and Assistant Secretary of Labor Daniel Patrick Moynihan drafted a proposal to create full employment through large-scale public works projects. They argued that America needed to spend $100 billion over ten years to abolish poverty, investing heavily in preschool education, public works programs, Social Security increases, and universal healthcare. This estimate was in line with a study by the University of Michigan's Survey Research Center and with Shriver's plea to Johnson in 1965. But funding that war was not to be after the United States massively escalated in Vietnam.[38]

In October 1964 Harrington addressed a rally at the University of California-Berkeley sponsored by SDS. He got a resounding welcome; the crowd roared approvingly when rally organizer Lewis Feuer said he would rather vote for Harrington than LBJ. That carried Harrington through the November election. Later that month he was installed with fanfare as the new chair of LID. Jack Newfield charted Harrington's ascension, noting that barely three years previously he ruled one faction of YPSL and the back room of the White Horse. Now Harrington was knighted by Schlesinger as America's "only responsible radical" and feted at the Fifth Avenue Hotel by Thomas, Rustin, Bell, and James Wechsler. In his acceptance speech Harrington said he planned to organize a conference of American and European Socialists to envision the future of left-liberal politics and would continue to fund the rapidly growing SDS. Wechsler editorialized in the *New York Post* that the commitment and conscience of a single person sometimes yielded small miracles. Harrington, he said, was a rare voice breaking through the gridlock of consensus politics.[39]

It was a strange moment. Harrington's conflict with SDS was known only to movement lefties, SDS still depended on LID, and Democratic realignment was happening. Johnson and the Democrats won a landslide victory in 1964 that seated fifty-one new Democrats in the House. Great Society legislation made 1965 the highlight year of every liberal Democratic politician's career. Five Deep South states lacking any Republican tradition switched to Goldwater, Meany proclaimed that the moment had come to fulfill the promises of the New Deal, and Shachtmanites took high positions in the AFL-CIO. Slaiman enlisted Kahn as a speechwriter for Meany; Hill moved up the ranks of the Industrial Union Department; Sam Fishman was elected president of the Michigan AFL-CIO; Shachtman's wife, Yetta Shachtman, and Sandra Feldman ran the office of Al Shanker, head of the AFT of New York; and Meany established the A. Philip Randolph Institute, a major patronage sinecure employing Rustin as executive director and Horowitz as secretary.

Realignment had a brief heyday that changed the nation permanently. As long as civil rights, poverty, and social insurance were the defining issues on the left, Harrington's prominence was secure. He was still the bridge between the Old Left and New Left despite Port Huron and Atlantic City. Agenda items left over from the dismal end of the Truman administration barreled through Congress. A huge bill supporting elementary and secondary education passed in April 1965 after Powell pushed it through the House. Johnson signed it in the one-room schoolhouse in Stonewall, Texas, where his schooling began, thanking Powell and Oregon senator Wayne Morse effusively. Major legislation established Medicare and Medicaid, national endowments for the arts and humanities, new environmental standards, immigration reform, and a federally guaranteed right to vote. Harrington called for a "Third New Deal" to abolish poverty that created a "new human care sector of the economy." In the fall of 1965 he attended a Texas-style buffet dinner in the White House to plan a conference on civil rights. Johnson welcomed the participants and Mississippi civil rights leader Aaron Henry marveled to Harrington, "Mike, we're eating barbecue in the White House."[40]

THE OTHER SIXTIES: THE WAR AND THE END OF THE KING ERA

To Harrington, that was the last gasp of the good-feeling era. Johnson promised in 1964 not to escalate the war in Vietnam; then in February 1965 he massively escalated, bombing North Vietnam and instituting a military draft. Protests erupted immediately on campuses. SDS organized marathon all-night teach-ins to educate students about Vietnam and American foreign policy. In December 1964 SDS called for a national demonstration in April 1965 opposing the war. At the time it would have been pleased to gather two thousand protesters. By April 17, 1965, when the first big SDS antiwar demonstration occurred, SDS was the epicenter of a burgeoning antiwar movement. The call to the April demonstration didn't exclude Communists or the Leninist sects from participating, which alarmed Rustin, who issued a protest cosigned by Muste and Thomas. Twenty-five thousand protesters showed up in Washington for a demonstration that was mild and nice compared to its successors. SDS president Paul Potter said the movement needed to name the evil that sent Americans to kill Vietnamese, though he did not do so, adding that a Communist victory in South Vietnam would be better than a prolonged American war. No Vietcong flags were unfurled on April 17, no American flags were burned, no declarations of solidarity with Hanoi were issued, and civil rights anthems were not yet reprised in homage to Vietnamese Communist leader Ho Chi Minh. But all of that came swiftly afterward as the antiwar movement grew radical very fast.[41]

Defenders of Kennedy's intervention in Vietnam said losing South Vietnam to Communism would be an unacceptable blow to American prestige and its

Cold War leadership. Reinhold Niebuhr and the foreign policy establishment took for granted the domino theory that Communists would conquer Southeast Asia if the United States pulled out of South Vietnam, though Niebuhr regarded Vietnam as a hard case because it was both a civil war and a Soviet proxy war, in this case backing a repressive dictatorship in South Vietnam. Had the government of Ngo Dinh Diem been less thuggish, Niebuhr would have felt better about Kennedy's lesser-evil choice. As it was, he anguished over the lesser evil, not sure that Kennedy found it. Then Diem was killed in a CIA-backed military coup, Kennedy was assassinated, and Johnson dramatically escalated the bombing and troop deployments. Niebuhr said Vietnam was an impossible problem, so Johnson should not be faulted for lacking an answer: "Our hegemonous position and military strategy force us to create a 'democracy' in a peasant culture."[42]

By July 1965 the United States had tried every conceivable military strategy in Vietnam except using atomic weapons and waging the search and destroy missions it tried for the next three years. Counterinsurgency failed, and bombing North Vietnam merely strengthened the determination of the insurgents. Vietnamese insurgents and villagers were attacked and bombed by jets, AC-47 rapid-fire miniguns, Huey Cobras, flamethrowers, and artillery. They were poisoned and incinerated with chemical defoliants, napalm, and white phosphorus that turned entire villages into lakes of fire. Insurgents were forced to live for years in tunnels, coming out only at night, subsisting on rationed balls of rice — all to avoid losing a colonial war. Niebuhr believed that winning the war was impossible and losing South Vietnam to Communism was intolerable. He urged Johnson to take a bizarre third option, building a fortress asylum in Thailand. America needed to stand tall, Niebuhr contended, reminding the world of its superior might and will. If Johnson kept escalating there would be no alternative to making South Vietnam an American colony. Taking a stand in Thailand would be much better, and if that failed the Philippines would be second best. Niebuhr stuck to this fantasy for five months.[43]

Meanwhile Thomas embarked on a nationwide campus tour to plead for an antiwar movement that did not burn U.S. flags or romanticize Vietnamese Communists. He implored students to cleanse the American flag, not burn it. He said it at a massive teach-in at Berkeley in May 1965 and at both of the enormous rallies sponsored by SANE later that year in New York and Washington. At Berkeley Thomas commended the New Left for opposing American intervention in Vietnam and criticized its leading organizations for denigrating Social Democratic values: "The new left is very amorphous in program, inclined to be nihilistic, anarchistic rather than Socialist. Freedom from dogmatism is a good thing but lack of program is not. I deeply regret the tendency of some rather conspicuous members of the new left to appear more interested in a Communist victory than in a constructive peace."[44]

That put it with customary Thomas sincerity. Harrington put it more aggressively, protesting that the commendable end-the-war message of the first SDS demonstration gave way to rallies at which speakers offered "explicit or covert political support to the Viet Cong." End-the-war was not the point for them, Harrington objected; rally speakers competed with each other to incite the crowds against their government. Harrington warned that pro-Communist rhetoric was not innocent, and apocalyptic final-conflict rhetoric would not remain mere performance. He said that Ho Chi Minh's mass-murdering collectivization of North Vietnam was an ugly preview of what a communist victory would look like in South Vietnam. The Communists and procommunists who waved Vietcong flags made it harder to end the war. His position fixed on negotiations and was willing to accept a tragic result: "I believe that the domestic and international consequences of the war there are so disastrous that we must negotiate even if, tragically, the negotiations would open up the way to a Vietcong victory—and I would regard that victory as a defeat for human freedom."[45]

Howe put it scathingly in a rambling article on "new styles in leftism." The New Left was mostly about sneering and posturing, he argued, especially about seven things. (1) It was extremely hostile toward liberalism, which it wholly identified with a current institutional version bearing no relation to Dewey or John Stuart Mill; thus it trafficked in shallow caricatures. (2) It refused to learn anything from older generations of radicals, especially about Communism. (3) Lately it acquired a "vicarious indulgence in violence," sneering at King for holding fast to nonviolence. (4) It constantly condemned something called the Establishment, which it never defined except as an "all-purpose put-down." (5) It carried on about the decline of the West without mentioning the long, anti-democratic, antirational, reactionary history of this trope. (6) Its crude anti-Americanism welcomed anti-Americanisms of every sort, "even if one contradicts another." (7) It celebrated fusions of nationalism and Communism wherever they existed in the Third World, while scorning East European reformers. Here the scriptural text was *The Wretched of the Earth* by Martinique psychiatrist Frantz Fanon. Howe acknowledged that Fanon powerfully expressed the rage of nationalist-revolutionaries who despised their bourgeois governments and didn't want to be ruled by dictators like Ghanaian strongman Kwame Nkrumah. Fanon skillfully refashioned Trotsky's theory of permanent revolution, now with Third World peasants and the urban poor in the vanguard role. Howe sympathized with Fanon's desire to mobilize the masses to remake their nations: "But what if the masses do not wish to participate?" Liberal democracy, Howe argued, was at least a democratic answer; Fanon had no answer.[46]

New Left leaders were willing to hear such criticism from people they respected and felt respected by. They gave a platform to Thomas and Stone, both of whom blasted the same conceits criticized by Harrington and Howe. Moreover, the Communist issue was not the firewall in the United States that Harrington and Howe made it out to be. Communists played a conservative role in the antiwar movement. They did not burn American flags, wave Vietcong flags, or commit any form of violence, and the Communist Party called for negotiations to end the war—the most conservative form of antiwar protest. Harrington said the peace movement had to be open to Communists while repudiating their views. Every time he said it he contradicted the experience of protesters who met their first Communists at an antiwar rally. Most antiwar protesters did not romanticize the Vietcong or believe it was their business to decide how Vietnam should govern itself. McReynolds championed this principled pacifist position in the Socialist Party, trying to pull the party into the antiwar movement and Harrington away from the Shachtmanites. Maurice Isserman aptly notes that Harrington versus McReynolds was fateful for the party. Harrington viewed McReynolds as a muddled pacifist dilettante, McReynolds distrusted Harrington, and McReynolds resented that Thomas favored Harrington over him.[47]

The tiny generation differently represented by McReynolds and Harrington was the one that didn't exist on the left. Basically the left was a thirties generation facing off against a sixties generation. It didn't help that Harrington imbibed the badgering style of the Shachtmanites and looked down on McReynolds. Howe was a brawler who could turn caustic and accusatory at the slightest provocation; he was elderly and an esteemed literary critic before he acquired social democratic manners. Harrington's affable charm sometimes did not extend to people who set off one of his ideological tripwires. Harrington and Howe waited for many years for a left resurgence—only to alienate the one that emerged.

Harrington bottled up his intense inner conflicts to the point that Howe and Meier didn't know he had a nervous breakdown. They had to read about it in his memoir, somehow not noticing that for four years he drastically curtailed his speaking engagements. Harrington attended the antiwar rallies of 1965 at which Thomas spoke but held back from speaking, no longer trusting his emotional health. On March 14, 1965, Harrington ended a California lecture tour by speaking at a Unitarian Universalist church in San Diego about poverty. He got his customary introduction, strode to the lectern, and nearly fell to the floor. He couldn't stand, feeling he was on the verge of fainting. He got through the talk by sitting in a chair and pressing his legs into it, distracting himself with induced pain. It was the first flash of his breakdown, which he blamed on over-work. He proceeded to the Selma demonstration march to Montgomery, accompanied by Randolph and Rustin, fixing on the stares of disbelief and the tears of Montgomery blacks. Harrington told himself that nothing about him had changed; he was a civil rights militant, and his health was sure to improve.[48]

Instead, his anxiety took hold of him, exploding at trivial intrusions, setting off profuse sweating and tremors in his chest, and turning streets into angled distortions, like the mirrors of a fun house. Reluctantly Harrington accepted that he was not exhausted and had no physical ailment. This crisis came straight from his psyche, requiring four years of psychoanalysis to determine that he did not know how to be the minor celebrity who took calls from ABC, delivered thousand-dollar lectures, and should have been a father figure to the New Left. His disdain for middle-class life had taken him to the Catholic Worker and to Shachtmanite Marxism, a utopian vision of catastrophe yielding revolutionary change. Now he was some kind of middle-class Marxist, surely an absurdity—which set him on the path of proving otherwise. Harrington denied, when he got married, that marriage would change him, only to learn that the nuclear family is "profoundly bourgeois" for a reason. In 1964 he earned twenty thou-sand dollars, a mortifying sum for him, never mind that for eight more years he relied on Stephanie Harrington's health insurance policy at the *Village Voice*. Even his place in the civil rights movement became uncertain after Atlantic City. As he put it: "The itinerant radical agitator, the writer of articles with long titles for magazines of small circulation, the practitioner of a comfortable pov-erty on the margin of the affluent society, could not recognize the middle-aging participant in the discussions with men of power, who was married and received middle-class fees for giving anti-capitalist speeches."[49]

Harrington's therapist, Elizabeth Thorne, helped him realize that his fre-netic speaking schedule was a symptom of his breakdown, not its cause. He converted repressed emotions into physical symptoms, obtaining no relief from the two free lectures he gave for every one that paid him. He told himself he was still a servant of social justice causes, not a star who floated above them, but denial intensified the war within. Harrington experienced his Freudian uncon-scious as a terribly real and alien thing that took over his life, dictated imperi-ously to his rational self, and dragged him to therapy: "It was the force that was dominating my life and the experience was about as subtle as being hit over the head with a brick." He was less certain that Freud's id–ego–superego model was right, and he outright doubted that the unconscious functions within a matrix primarily determined by one's relationship to one's mother and father. But that made Freud like Marx: an original, profoundly dialectical, indisputably important theorist of primal realities, however much he got wrong. As it was, four years of therapy persuaded Harrington to be mindful of what he repressed and helped him clarify what he retained from Marx. He never grew comfortable with making a nice living off criticizing capitalism, and he keenly regretted that his Old Left complex twisted and contorted him on Vietnam.[50]

The long-anticipated SDS convention of December 1965 took place in Kewadin, Michigan. Newcomers had poured into SDS from across the country, overwhelming its Berkeley–Ann Arbor–Boston–New York axis. They didn't accept the leadership of the leaders and they took for granted that the draft issue trumped everything else. Female leaders felt more invisible than ever, swept aside by an angry, anarchic, draft-resisting tide. All the veteran male leaders and most of the veteran female leaders of SDS later described the convention as a chaotic disaster. The primacy of the draft issue reinforced the dominance of the males, both old and new. The long-awaited workshop on women occurred in this context. It broke into a mixed group and an all-female group because the men chafed at being criticized and some women concluded it was pointless to discuss feminism in the presence of defensive males. Neither discussion got very far, but the National Council endorsed a statement from the all-female group led by Heather Tobis and Sarah Murphy. SDS, it said, prized uniformity of language and values far too much: "Men must learn and understand the problem of free independent women and encourage full participation by each woman as she defines herself, as should be the case with any individual." That was tame and liberal, but it launched what became a fiery movement for women's liberation.[51]

SDS lurched to chaotic radicalism just as Cold War liberals began to turn against the war. In February 1966 *Christianity and Crisis* celebrated its twenty-fifth anniversary. Humphrey was the keynote speaker for a banquet centered on Niebuhr. Niebuhr's declining health prevented him from attending, so Humphrey paid him a visit before heading to the banquet. He told Niebuhr that America was winning in Vietnam; Niebuhr cringed at realizing that Humphrey was too honest to hold a public opinion that contradicted his personal opinion, unlike war architects Robert McNamara and George Ball. To shill for the war, Humphrey had to convince himself. Niebuhr turned against the war, telling his friend Will Scarlett, "I am scared by my own lack of patriotism. . . . For the first time I fear I am ashamed of our beloved nation."[52]

That summer Black Power swept like fire through U.S. American cities. On May 9, 1966, Carmichael replaced Lewis as head of SNCC at a raucous meeting that redefined the organization. Shortly afterward James Meredith, conducting a solo March Against Fear from Memphis, Tennessee, to Jackson, Mississippi, was shot and wounded, and civil rights leaders converged on Memphis to complete Meredith's march. SNCC staffer Willie Ricks riled up small gatherings by referring to "black power," which intrigued Carmichael. In Greenwood, Mississippi, Carmichael tried out the phrase and electrified the crowd: "We been sayin' 'Freedom Now' for six years and we ain't got nothin'. What we gonna start sayin' now is *Black Power!*" Black Power repudiated King's theology of redemptive suffering and racial integration. It disavowed liberal democracy, nonviolence, working with whites, and America. It expelled all whites from SNCC—exceeding what Carmichael wanted—and scared the hell out of white America.[53]

Carmichael skyrocketed to national fame, declaring that black Americans were colonized subjects and integration was a middle-class goal championed by a professional elite of middle-class blacks. More important, integration was "a subterfuge for the maintenance of white supremacy," a despicable scheme that sprinkled a few blacks into the white middle class on token terms to hold down all others. Carmichael was done with that and redemptive suffering. He said the Deep South blacks he tried to organize were "steaming mad" at being oppressed: "We had nothing to offer that they could see, except to go out and be beaten again. We helped to build their frustration. We had only the old language of love and suffering. And in most places—that is, from the liberals and middle-class—we got back the old language of patience and progress." Carmichael implored black Americans to ally with revolutionary struggles in the Third World, overthrowing racism itself. If that sounded like "black racism" to fearful whites, he could not help them: "The final truth is that the white society is not entitled to reassurances, even if it were possible to offer them."[54]

King coped with the Black Power challenge for the rest of his life, delineating what was true in it and what he rejected. He admitted to friends that the Meredith March pulled him to a new low and he doubted he could work with SNCC anymore. He was asked about Black Power wherever he went. Repeatedly he said he was dedicated to transforming black powerlessness into constructive and creative power. Power is not an end in itself; it is the means to achieving a good society. Black Americans needed power desperately—the ability to achieve a constructive purpose. The Black Power movement would not achieve it by being threatening and separatist. Rustin pressed King to say it aggressively, as Rustin did.

Rustin was scathing about the Black Power eruption. He hated the masculine bravado of Black Power and its repudiation of coalition politics. "Anybody who talks about a black agenda is a reactionary," Rustin said. "As soon as you move into the economic struggle you're in a totally new universal ball game with universal objectives." In that vein he wrote a declaration titled "Crisis and Commitment" that Randolph and Wilkins promptly endorsed. It reaffirmed the movement's commitment to integration, nonviolence, and democracy, without referring explicitly to Black Power. King balked at signing the statement, and Rustin implored that it expounded King's core beliefs. King, Andrew Young, and Stanley Levison worried that the subtext was obvious and damaging: Rustin was blaming an ascending white backlash on Black Power. King did not want to be associated with this accusation, so he turned down Rustin. He was still the apostle of bringing people together, as he emphasized to reporters. But after the statement was published King told reporters that of course he agreed with its substance; he refused to sign only because he stood for unity. That was a serious mistake. King realized it after his endorsement became the story and Levison told him he had to take it back; he was in danger of sabotaging his unifying capacity. King, deeply embarrassed, agreed to eat some crow. He told Levison he made mistakes of this kind only when he dealt with Rustin.[55]

The election of 1966 approached and King oscillated between saying what he really believed and trying not to hurt liberals running for office. He had not said previously that white Americans never intended to integrate their schools or neighborhoods or to support economic equality. Then he got pelted with rocks in Chicago, and King began to say it. He said it bitterly to the Alabama Christian Movement at its tenth anniversary dinner in Birmingham. He turned it around in *Ebony*, mocking black Americans who told him they would not march because they didn't believe in nonretaliation. Every facet of their lives reeked of oppression, King said, yet they were willing to fight only if someone spat on them at a demonstration! The election came, and the backlash was fierce. Democrats lost 47 House seats, 3 Senate seats, 8 governorships, and 677 seats in state legislatures. Ronald Reagan won a landslide victory for California governor and was crowned as the new leader of the American right.[56]

King denied that a backlash was occurring because that story always blamed him for something and obscured what mattered: The civil rights movement merely surfaced the animosity that had always existed. Calling it a backlash suggested that racism was increasing and he should do something differently. Backlash talk was a species of denial. After the election King convened a retreat for the financially bleeding SCLC, now down to seventy-five staffers, at Frogmore, near Savannah. He was bleak and grim, admitting he didn't know what to do next. King gave a long, personal, vulnerable summary of the movement's shortcomings and a lowball assessment of its accomplishments from 1954 to 1965. He appreciated that some legislative and judicial victories had been won, but they "did very little to improve the lot of millions of Negroes in the teeming ghettos of the North." The movement did not touch "the lower depths of Negro deprivation." It was hard to say this but "we must admit it: the changes that came about during this period were at best surface changes, they were not really substantive changes." American racism, King noted, was distinctly vicious: "The white man literally sought to annihilate the Indian. If you look through the history of the world this very seldom happened." That was what black Americans were up against—a genocidal impulse fueled by the pervasive white American belief in white superiority. "The ultimate logic of racism is genocide."[57]

King sympathized with Black Power because it instilled racial pride and sought real power. But the Black Power ideology currently in vogue, he said, had three fatal problems: It was nihilistic and separatist, and these things combined to justify violence. SCLC had to stand for power as "the right use of strength." They could not wave off the problem of how things were heard. King believed that Swedish Social Democracy was better than American capitalism, but he couldn't say that without hurting the movement, so he said that SCLC needed to reinvent itself as an antipoverty organization demanding a minimum guaranteed income. It took Gandhi forty years to liberate India, King observed, so SCLC needed to think in a longer time frame than previously: "I believe that with this kind of moral power, with this kind of determination, with this willingness to suffer, we'll get across the goal-line."[58]

Back in Chicago Young and the SCLC fought losing battles with Mayor Richard Daley on voter registration, job training, slumlords, and open occupancy. Daley kept voting rolls low and wanted all Chicago patronage to come through him. He fought off downstate Republican voters by tightening his urban machine—a shortsighted strategy as the suburbs grew larger. King and Young implored Daley to work with them to change Chicago, but that was never a serious option for Daley, who used his leverage with the federal government to get his way. SCLC got very little for its grinding, battered, much-criticized work in Chicago. Rustin and others admonished that they had warned King that Daley would play him. King responded by doubling down on his recent drift to the outside. Everything that mattered to the later King pushed him to the outside, where he embraced a bold, wonky, magic-bullet approach to antipoverty politics—a guaranteed annual individual income of four thousand dollars—and became an antiwar leader.

Levison pushed the idea of a new book featuring the income idea. By January 1967 spending for the Equal Opportunity Program had flattened at $1.5 billion while the low-balled estimate for Vietnam zoomed to $10 billion. Thomas and

Yale chaplain William Sloane Coffin Jr. urged King to campaign against Vietnam. King greatly admired Thomas, calling him "the bravest man I ever met" and an unsurpassed champion of peace and "a society free of injustice and exploitation." He wanted to give Thomas-like antiwar speeches but told Levison he was not ready to burn his bridge to LBJ. In January he holed up in Ocho Rios, Jamaica, to write the antipoverty book. King had barely arrived to the only extended getaway he ever made when he had a turning point. Leafing through the January *Ramparts*, he came across a twenty-four-page photo essay depicting the burned and mutilated bodies of Vietnamese war victims. The pictures filled him with revulsion. He vowed face up to being an antiwar leader.[59]

Clergy and Laity Concerned About Vietnam (CALCAV, the group's next-to-last name) had pined for that decision for months. Coffin, Union Theological Seminary president John C. Bennett, Union theologian Robert McAfee Brown, and Jewish Theological Seminary theologian Abraham Joshua Heschel were its ringleaders. All were close to King and implored him to speak out. Levison was wary of doing so, and Rustin was outright opposed, both fretting that King would diminish his standing by speaking for two movements that did not work together. Becoming an antiwar leader would mean losing LBJ, probably the Ford Foundation, and much of the Democratic Party and civil rights establishment. If King lost influence in civil rights to become one peace leader among others, what good was that? King wrestled with this question, criticized the war, agreed with Levison, agonized, and felt he should do more. He crossed a line in Jamaica, opting for risky out-there righteousness.

King granted James Bevel a brief leave from SCLC to join Muste's staff at FOR, where Bevel organized a huge antiwar demonstration scheduled for April 15 at the United Nations Plaza. Shortly after Bevel moved to New York and before King left Jamaica, Muste died of a heart attack. Muste had trained the people who trained King in Gandhian nonviolence. His last antiwar coalition was dominated by SDS and other left groups holding little interest in Gandhian nonviolence. Rustin, Bevel, and Thomas spoke at Muste's memorial service, emphasizing his religious wellspring; meanwhile King's advisors and the SCLC board entreated King to reject Bevel's invitation to speak at the UN protest. They dreaded that King seemed bent on squandering his civil rights leadership for a role in a shrill antiwar movement. Young attended a meeting of the April 15 organizers and was appalled. Wild talk about smashing the fascist American government prevailed. Young told King the only sane organizer was the Communist representative. King took seriously Young's warning about SDS and the pleas of his advisors that Bevel was emotionally unstable. Young worried that King would not have time, at a rally speech, to develop a thoughtful argument and that media coverage would not distinguish King from ranting SDS speakers.[60]

King turned the issue over and over in his mind. At least he was refreshed, zinging Young and others with his mimicry and bawdy humor. Insiders measured King's exhaustion by how much they saw his comic side; it came back briefly after Jamaica. April 15 approached, King accepted a speaking role, and Young scrambled to cushion the impact. King had to speak first and leave, to avoid being associated with Carmichael and other extremists. In addition, King needed to make a thoughtful speech to his wing of the movement—religious progressives—before the April 15 rally defined him. Young made arrangements with Bennett and Heschel for King to speak at Union. But the buffer event grew too large for Union's chapel, necessitating a move across the street to Riverside Church and its seating capacity of thirty-nine hundred.

The Riverside speech required special preparation. None of King's advisors wanted to write it, so Young farmed it out to two professors—Vincent Harding of Spelman College and John Maguire of Wesleyan University. Meanwhile King gave an antiwar speech in Beverly Hills, California, and reprised it at Chicago's Coliseum. He wanted Rustin to write the Beverly Hills speech, still underestimating Rustin's loyalty to Johnson–Humphrey Democrats and the AFL-CIO. LBJ demanded to know why King canceled two meetings with him; the speeches provided the answer. The Riverside buffer event, by the time it occurred on April 4, 1967, was a very big deal. Levison could not bring himself to attend, as King's ex-communist was cautious about politics.

King declared that he came to Riverside "because my conscience leaves me no other choice." He saluted CALCAV and a recent statement by its executive committee, written by Brown: "A time comes when silence is betrayal." King felt morally obligated "to break the betrayal of my own silences and to speak from the burnings of my own heart." For a while he had been hopeful about the fight against poverty but "then came the build-up in Vietnam, and I watched the program broken and eviscerated as if it were some idle political plaything of a society gone mad on war, and I knew that America would never invest the necessary funds or energies in rehabilitation of its poor so long as Vietnam continued to draw men and skills and money like some demonic, destructive suction tube."[61]

The Two Viet-Nams, by French-American critic Bernard Fall, was an essential text for war resisters. King read it in Jamaica to bolster his contention that Vietnam was a recycled colonial war. At Riverside he recounted that France and Japan colonized Vietnam, which declared its independence in 1945, yielding nine years of French colonial aggression backed by the United States, followed by America's takeover of the colonizer role. King ridiculed America's liberator self-image: "We have destroyed their two most cherished institutions: the family and the village. We have destroyed their land and their crops. We have cooperated in the crushing of the nation's only non-Communist revolutionary political force—the unified Buddhist church. We have supported the enemies of the peasants of Saigon. We have corrupted their women and children and killed their men. What liberators!"[62]

Sadly he declared that the United States was on the wrong side of anticolonial movements throughout the world. King still believed in the dream of America realizing the revolutionary promise of its Declaration of Independence, but he said America was rich, privileged, short on compassion, and morbidly afraid of Communism. Thus the first modern country became the world's foremost counterrevolutionary power: "I am convinced that if we are to get on the right side of the world revolution, we as a nation must undergo a radical revolution of values." King charged that Americans prized profit, property, and machines above human beings. This profoundly warped value system defeated all attempts to overcome "the giant triplets of racism, materialism, and militarism." The revolution that was needed—"a true revolution of values"—would not tolerate extreme inequality in the United States or the pillage of Third World countries by American capitalism. Neither would it stand for imperial U.S. American wars: "This business of burning human beings with napalm, of filling our nation's homes with orphans and widows, of injecting poisonous drugs of hate into veins of peoples normally humane, of sending men home from dark and bloody battlefields physically handicapped and psychologically deranged, cannot be reconciled with wisdom, justice and love. A nation that continues year after year to spend more money on military defense than on programs of social uplift is approaching spiritual death."[63]

America needed a spiritual reawakening to its own revolutionary democratic ideals: "Our only hope today lies in our ability to recapture the revolutionary spirit and go out into a sometimes hostile world declaring eternal hostility to poverty, racism and militarism." Personally, King could not go on speaking for nonviolence or against the violence of the oppressed in America's cities "without having first spoken clearly to the greatest purveyor of violence in the world today—my own government." The war poisoned America's soul, he pleaded: "It can never be saved so long as it destroys the deepest hopes of men the world over." At the end he reached for his biggest what-is-needed statement, a creed about love divine that he called "this Hindu-Moslem-Christian-Jewish-Buddhist belief about ultimate reality," citing 1 John 4: "Let us love one another; for love is God and everyone that loves is born of God and knows God. He that loves not knows not God; for God is love. If we love one another God dwells in us, and his love is perfected in us."[64]

At Riverside there were two standing ovations, a burst of applause when King endorsed draft resistance, and no real surprises. The crowd hushed when King described America as the world's leading purveyor of violence, and Bennett declared that King spoke to America's conscience more powerfully than anyone. Daddy King astonished himself by changing his mind about the war and his son's opposition to it. The Riverside crowd knew that King had said most of this before and much of it numerous times. Many knew his favorite riffs and set pieces by heart, joining in when King closed with eight lines of James Russell Lowell's "Once to Every Man and Nation." Elsewhere shock and condemnation prevailed. King assumed that this episode would be like the Birmingham demonstration: White editorialists would disapprove, middle-class black journalists would say that King was egotistical and harmful to blacks, the usual defenders would push back, and the story would turn in his favor. That *is* what happened eventually, but each part went worse than he expected.

The chief organs of liberal Protestantism, *Christian Century* and *Christianity and Crisis*, and the left-liberal *Nation* were exceptions to an onslaught of condemnation. The *Century* praised the speech as "a magnificent blend of eloquence and raw fact, of searing denunciation and tender wooing, of political sagacity and Christian insight, of tough realism and infinite compassion." *Life* countered that King exceeded his "personal right to dissent" by connecting civil rights to his espousal of "abject surrender in Vietnam." Former U.S. Information Agency chief Carl Rowan skewered King in *Reader's Digest*. The real civil rights leaders, Rowan claimed, grieved over King's egotism. They also chafed at his habit of fleeing jail to accept honors, his rude treatment of White House allies, and his reliance on Communist advisors. Wilkins, the *New York Times*, and the *Washington Post* denounced the speech as politically disastrous. The *Post* put it frostily, charging that King's "sheer inventions of unsupported fantasy" inflicted "grave injury" on his allies and worse injury on himself: "Many who have listened to him with respect will never again accord him the same confidence. He has diminished his usefulness to his cause, to his country and to his people. And that is a great tragedy." The *Pittsburgh Courier* said the same thing, ripping King for "tragically misleading" black Americans about issues that were "too complex for simple debate." Levison defended King publicly but told him privately the speech was politically inept and rambled overlong about distant matters. Rustin and Randolph refused to comment publicly. King reeled at the outpouring of condemnation, the worst he ever received.[65]

The battering went on, stunning King and shaming him. Friends saw him shed tears more than once. For a while it seemed that Levison and Rustin were right, but the controversy helped to lift the April 15 mobilization into a spectacle—the takeoff of a skyrocketing antiwar movement. King felt it happening as huge crowds surged into Central Park. He marched with Young from Central Park down Fifth Avenue to Forty-Second Street and the UN Plaza. Vietcong flags were unfurled, and the first mass burning of draft cards occurred. King compared the mobilization to the March on Washington. Security concerns kept him off the platform, which was fine with him; his camp did not want him on stage with Carmichael. King repeated much of the Riverside speech, to tumultuous acclaim, adding, "I am disappointed with our failure to deal positively and forthrightly with the triple evils of racism, extreme materialism, and militarism. We are presently moving down a dead-end road that can only lead to national disaster."[66]

Harrington later regretted that he and Rustin fell short of King's political bravery, though he said it in contortionist fashion, describing Rustin as "the bravest man I have ever known, and certainly one of the most dedicated and committed militants." Harrington reasoned that King made the right decision, despite damaging his political efficacy, while Rustin did the "wrong thing for the right reason." He refused to censure his friend's wrong decision, insisting that it took rare bravery in 1967, especially since Rustin had to forsake his long-time pacifism to do what seemed politically right to him. Harrington twisted himself into a similar contortion through the 1960s. Shachtmanite realignment was nothing without the AFL-CIO; everything that made it powerful had the AFL-CIO at its center. In 1966 Rustin hosted a gathering of *Dissent* writers to ponder the war and the antiwar movement. Shachtman made a rare appearance, dragging himself from Floral Park to Rustin's apartment. Harrington reprised his argument that a Communist victory was inevitable in Vietnam, and it would be a lesser evil to an unending or expanded war. Shachtman raged in refutation. Communism was the greater evil, the war was not lost, and he was appalled that *Dissent* had become a bunch of hand-wringing pacifists. America had to keep fighting until the Communists were defeated. Shachtman was fine with "we want negotiations" as long as the conditions were such that Ho Chi Minh would never agree.[67]

On that dubious ground the Shachtmanites founded a group in the spring of 1967 called Negotiations Now. It posed as the moderate alternative to SDS radicalism, giving Galbraith, Schlesinger, and other ADA leaders a foothold in the antiwar movement. Negotiations Now existed primarily to provide a platform for the Socialist Party, which touted its mostly imaginary contributions to ending the war in responsible fashion. *New America* covered the great demonstrations with disapproving superiority, objecting that rally speakers spewed anti-Americanism and made no demands on the Communists. Editor Paul

Feldman had a special animus for folk singer Pete Seeger, an old Popular Frontist who gave offense by showing up and singing. Harrington was a mainstay of Negotiations Now and open about his conflicted feelings. He envied McReynolds for his simple revolutionary pacifism, but it was simplistic; he wanted to cheer the antiwar speakers, but many were shrilly anti-American; emotionally he disliked his own position: "This war is so ugly and horrible that I want to do something more personal, more involved than simply being rational and political. But I can't participate in demonstrations that will alienate people from the antiwar cause; I can't condone 'leftist' attacks on the First Amendment freedoms; I can't endorse middle-class elitism or regard middle-class psychodrama as a substitute for serious politics."[68]

By 1966 he no longer had to beg off from antiwar speaking invitations, because rally organizers didn't want him. In 1967 Harrington began to say that the hope of realignment and social transformation rested on America's emerging "conscience constituency," not the working class. His book *Toward a Democratic Left* (1968) described Americans as utopian pragmatists who believed that social problems are solved in the middle of the road. Harrington allowed that Americans had reason to believe their nation was an exception to the European curse of ideology. Geographic location and expanse, the American constitutional order, capitalist prosperity, and new technologies dashed the dreams of American socialists, past and current. A new crop of social scientists recycled Bell on the end of ideology, happy to leave social problems to specialized experts such as themselves. Harrington said the regnant pragmatic utopianism underestimated the importance of realigning elections in American history. The Republican victory of 1860 was not a mere adjustment. Neither was the triumph of the East and Midwest over the Populist South and West in 1896 or the election of 1932 that yielded the New Deal. Journalist Theodore White reported that Johnson's speechwriters realized the 1964 election held a similar potential. They implored campaign strategists to decide whether their mission was to broaden the base or shape the mandate. White claimed that Johnson achieved both. Harrington countered that LBJ merely hustled for new votes, expounding no new ideas, which brought on the backlash elections of 1966 that diminished his historic 1964 victory.[69]

Harrington told the Shriver billions story to substantiate his thesis: Johnson tried to retain the "fantastic coalition" that elected him instead of leading it to a new progressive project. Admittedly, LBJ spent some political capital fulfilling the promises of the 1930s, but he settled for half versions of old policy goals and offered no vision of future transformation. Truman's call for universal health insurance was turned into a Medicare program covering the elderly "and some of the poor." Nothing that Johnson said or did suggested that liberalism was a "prophetic force" with a bold vision of a better America. Johnson-style liberalism, Harrington argued, was merely what its New Left critics said, the establishment.[70]

Harrington wanted Democrats to transform society in the direction of equality and racial justice, not settle for reform tinkering. He committed wholly to the conscience constituency thesis, even calling it the New Class. Sociologist David Bazelon, retrieving the New Class argument from its anarchist and post-Trotskyite history, said there was a great new mass of people who benefited from the economic prosperity of the 1950s, went to college, moved to the suburbs, and swung every recent election. The political identity of this new political force, he observed, was not yet established. Perhaps it would use its newly minted degrees and professional-class jobs to enrich itself, or perhaps it would ally with the poor to realign U.S. American politics in a progressive direction. Harrington bet on the latter possibility. Blue-collar workers were a minority of the labor force, white-collar work was expanding dramatically, and the meaning of the middle-class category was changing. Harrington argued that technological change was creating "politically and socially unprecedented types of human beings" never imagined in Marxist theory.[71]

The entire Marxian tradition from Marx to Mills skewered the middle class as a stratum of vacillating rear-guarders, but Marx fixed on small-property owners and entrepreneurs, and Mills blasted the managers described by Burnham and Shachtman. Harrington took a page from the New Left exaltation of the university as the site of the next left-wing upsurge. The growing core of the New Class was university educated and worked in the public sphere—scientists, technicians, teachers, policy experts, consultants, and other professionals. It gained social leverage through position and the use of its special expertise, not by making money. By education and work experience, Harrington argued, the New Class "is predisposed to planning." He allowed that the rush to graduate education reinforced some of the worst competitive instincts in American life; middle-class parents obsessed about getting their kids into Harvard. But Harrington countered that education is distinctly broadening and subversive: "A school is a dangerous place, for it exposes people to ideas." Like it or not, the New Class was growing and increasingly powerful. What kind of values would the newly educated take into their careers as scientists, professionals, and social planners? Harrington said everything was at stake in this question. The New Class might become an ally of the poor and the unions or "their sophisticated enemy."[72]

Toward a Democratic Left was geared to the 1968 campaign, but it applied to a later moment, not its own. It was an argument for precisely the conscience constituency that won the Democratic nomination for George McGovern in 1972. Harrington refashioned his role on the left by heralding the vision of a new progressive politics. His version of it had room for people like himself who held a muddled position on Vietnam and respected the moral sensibilities of regular Democrats. But America exploded in 1968, shattering what might have been in the election.

Newark and Detroit erupted in riots in July 1967, convulsing King. Fire and gunfire ravaged a 140-block area of Detroit, pitched battles raged between snipers and police, the National Guard moved in with armored personnel carriers, and forty-three people were killed before army paratroopers restored order. King told a conference call of advisors he had hit bottom; Detroit marked a new low in modern American history. He proceeded to a New Left conference in Chicago, the National Conference for New Politics, which gathered three hundred groups. King was greeted with jeers of "Kill whitey, kill whitey" before he said anything. More-radical-than-you was much in fashion, with much chanting about burning down fascist Amerika. Black nationalists heckled King, and he struggled to be heard. It was awful, he told Levison: "The black nationalists gave me trouble. They kept interrupting me, kept yelling things at me." White wannabe radicals came out against liberalism and all things American. One day of this was enough for King, who made an early exit with four days of conferencing still to go. The atmosphere of chaotic hostility repulsed him. If the antiwar coalition he wanted had veered into crazed ultra-leftism, he could not speak for it.[73]

SCLC boiled over with problems deferred and worsening. There were bruising arguments over its highest priority. Antipoverty? The war? Open housing? Voter registration? Marian Wright, a lawyer working for the NAACP Legal Defense Fund in Mississippi, had an idea that King liked—marching poor people from Mississippi to Washington to stage sit-ins. Levison added the idea of a tent city, recalling the Bonus March of 1932. King had come to regret that he cut short the campaign in Chicago. Had he marched into Cicero, a Klan stronghold, it would have been bloody, but he would have earned street credibility before Newark and Detroit erupted. King's lieutenants objected that poverty was an abstraction and squatting in the nation's capital would go badly. King took their brusque rebuttals personally; his fractious lieutenants no longer seemed creative to him. Against Rustin and nearly the entire SCLC staff, King decided for a Poor People's Campaign for Jobs or Income. Bevel and Jesse Jackson told him vehemently he was wrong.

In November and December 1967 King gave the Massey Lectures, broadcast by the Canadian Broadcasting Corporation. He moved straight to a two-sided argument about the decade from 1955 to 1965: "Everyone underestimated the amount of violence and rage Negroes were suppressing and the amount of bigotry the white majority was disguising." Both illusions were dispelled, he said, because for three summers in a row Americans watched their cities burn. King argued that the crimes committed by black looters were small offshoots of the colossal crimes of white society. In a crucial sense the civil rights movement had ended. The SCLC demonstrations in the South felt like earthquakes; in the North they caused barely a ripple. More important to King, something had happened to young people. During the heyday of SCLC young people flocked to the protests and felt represented by them. But that fell apart "under the impact of failures, discouragement, and consequent extremism and polarization."[74]

They had to march on the nation's capital to spark a new generation of protest against denigration and oppression. King put it dramatically in his last Massey Lecture, a Christmas sermon. It was his usual message in a context of worse-than-ever despair: "Somehow we must be able to stand up before our most bitter opponents and say, 'We shall match your capacity to inflict suffering by our capacity to endure suffering. We will meet your physical force with soul force. Do us what you will and we will still love you.' " Now, however, he said it by counterposing the dream and the nightmare, invoking four nightmares. He had a dream but saw it turn into a nightmare when four young girls were murdered. He saw the nightmare again in the vicious poverty gripping urban black American communities. He saw it again as black Americans set fire to their neighborhoods. He saw a fourth nightmare rage out of control as America ravaged Vietnam. King lived on the edge of despair but dared not give up hope: "Yes, I am personally the victim of deferred dreams, of blasted hopes, but in spite of that I close today by saying I still have a dream, because, you know, you can't give up in life."[75]

Erecting a city of the poor in Washington would show dramatically that he had not given up. There was much grumbling that King committed SCLC to a bad campaign and stiffed his top aides by asking Bernard Lafayette to run it. Bevel and Jackson angered King by continuing to deride the campaign after King committed to it. Rustin said that herding poor people to Washington would not accomplish anything. King said they had to find a way to dramatize what poor people were up against. He wished he could do it without protesting and going to jail because he was tired of both. He wanted to talk about democratic socialism but that was out of play. All he could do was stand with the poor and dramatize their situation. This was the way to expand the civil rights movement into a human rights movement that showcased the struggles of oppressed peoples across racial lines. King asked Harrington to help, who agreed with Rustin that King needed a political victory, not a sprawling shantytown spectacle in the nation's capital. Harrington was stunned by King's battered condition. The King he knew was ebullient, warm, funny, and self-confident. Now King seemed grimly sad and barely recognizable—a tortured figure who looked seriously ill. But Harrington could not say no to King, so he set aside his personal opinion to work on the Washington campaign, which was slated to begin on April 22, 1968.[76]

King had two months left, and nothing came easily anymore. At the end he was tense, drained, overweight, and constantly teetering on collapse. He could not sleep, and he startled friends by snapping at them. Longtimers who had never seen him yell at anyone were stunned to see him yell at Young and Jackson. In February King headlined a tribute to Du Bois at Carnegie Hall in New York. Thinking about Du Bois lifted him to special eloquence, brushing off how it might play in the *New York Times*. King said Du Bois was an intellectual giant and teacher who surpassed all others in demolishing the pernicious idea of racial inferiority, shredding "the army of white propagandists—the myth-makers of Negro history." Du Bois was "first and always a black man," in later life he became a Communist, and he was persecuted by the U.S. government. King was defiantly admiring: "He confronted the establishment as a model of militant manhood and integrity. He defied them and though they heaped venom and scorn on him his powerful voice was never stilled." More than ever King appreciated what it must have been like for Du Bois—"a radical all his life"—to battle on. It was time to stop "muting the fact" that Du Bois was a genius *and* a Communist, for "irrational, obsessive anti-Communism has led us into too many quagmires." The crowd erupted in passionate applause; King concluded that Du Bois's greatest virtue "was his committed empathy with all the oppressed and his divine dissatisfaction with all forms of injustice."[77]

The Poor People's Campaign called for a $30 billion federal antipoverty program, a full-employment bill, a guaranteed annual income, and at least $500,000 for low-cost housing per year. King and Young designed a plan for SCLC's most ambitious protest ever. It would begin with a lobbying campaign, caravans of the poor would descend on Washington, and on March 5 the marching around Capital Hill would commence. King said they had to march on Washington because the government "declared an armistice in the war on poverty while squandering billions to expand a senseless, cruel, unjust war in Vietnam." He acknowledged there would be traffic jams and disruption, plus a spectacle encampment. Rustin pleaded with King to call off the whole thing. Electing Democrats and stumping for a new civil rights bill for open housing were crucial. Making a mess in Washington was crazy.[78]

But King had grown accustomed to being more radical than everyone around him. In his last weeks he doubled down on the path of public sacrifice, dragging others along. He had never taken care of himself, and he was not about to change merely because he was ill and exhausted. As a child he sang that he wanted to be more like Jesus. In his last years he came very close to it. The Poor People's Campaign topped King's previous forays into risky, controversial, chaotic protest. He would not be shamed into reverting to middle-class politics. Now he outflanked even Bevel, his usual barometer of too-far extremism. King had to stand with the poorest of the poor and afflicted. He told the SCLC staff, "When I took up the Cross, I recognized its meaning. The Cross is something that you bear, and ultimately that you die on."[79]

At the end, in Memphis, King was struggling to help garbage workers attain decent treatment. On April 3, 1968, he closed his last sermon with the set piece he always used when he hit bottom, "I've Been to the Mountaintop." The next day he was assassinated.

King's battered lieutenants carried out the Poor People's Campaign, which Robert Kennedy supported before and while he ran for president. Harrington had implored Kennedy to run, switched to antiwar challenger Eugene McCarthy when Kennedy declined, and switched back to Kennedy after McCarthy's strong showing in the New Hampshire primary lured Kennedy into the race and pushed Johnson to bail out, just before King was killed. Harrington, Lewis, and Young tried to salvage something from King's death, campaigning for Kennedy in Indiana, Oregon, and California. In California Harrington and Lewis teamed with farmworker leader Cesar Chavez—a trio that symbolized to Harrington the hope of a Kennedy presidency. On June 5 Kennedy won the California primary and was assassinated. Young said the King era ended that day. The Kennedy campaign had impelled Young to go on after King's death. Now there was nothing to salvage from losing Martin, and Young fell into a deep depression. It was no longer possible to repress what happened in April. Kennedy's assassination ended the denials: "We were all trying to pretend that Martin's death had not devastated us, but it had. And with the compounding shock and grief of Robert Kennedy's murder, I couldn't even pretend anymore."[80]

Harrington went back to McCarthy, campaigning in New York, but could not drag himself to the Democratic Convention in Chicago, where Hayden led antiwar protesters in bloody clashes with Daley's police. The Democrats nominated Humphrey—the winner of zero primaries—amid riotous dissension and fury, all benefiting Richard Nixon. To Democratic Party bosses, the party belonged to them; democracy had nothing to do with it. To Young and Lewis, Humphrey was a longtime friend of the movement and a hapless casualty of Johnson's blunder in Vietnam. To Harrington, Humphrey was a bad choice but the lesser evil to Nixon; in October 1968 Harrington founded an alliance of

Kennedy and McCarthy supporters, the New Democratic Coalition. To Rustin, Humphrey was a model liberal meriting full-throttle support. Rustin worked hard for Humphrey, riding with him in motorcades and speaking alongside him at rallies. But many white liberals spurned Humphrey, resenting his record on Vietnam and his dependence on party bosses, and black voters supported Humphrey in lukewarm fashion, convulsed by trauma and rage. Rustin believed that white antiwar liberals were the key to the election. He beseeched them not to stay home out of anger or despair; too much was at stake. Instead Rustin's nightmare came to be. Nixon won the presidency with a racially coded appeal to a newly Republican South, and the King era ended.

NEW LEFT IMPLOSION, NEW LIBERALISM, AND STRUCTURAL CRISIS

The Shachtmanites did not like Harrington's campaigning for McCarthy; in fact they hated it. McCarthy was an effete liberal with a spotty record on labor issues who based his campaign on opposing the war. Everything about him offended the Shachtmanites, who resented that Harrington contorted realignment into a conscience constituency shibboleth centered on college-educated McCarthy types. Still, Harrington was their ostensible leader, aside from the semiretired Shachtman. Thomas faded in the summer of 1968, and Harrington was elected as party chair. In September, Thomas wrote to Shachtmanite operative Penn Kemble that in the aftermath of the Chicago catastrophe, "I look forward to even greater efforts by the Socialists to end this obscene war." That was wildly out of touch with the party's trajectory. Thomas had been mortified in 1967 when he learned that the CIA secretly funded his anti-Communist work for the Institute for International Labor Research. The Shachtmanites were not embarrassed and not shy about vitiating Thomas's legacy as soon as they won complete control of the party.[81]

Harrington had been useful to the Shachtmanites for the ten years they controlled the party machinery but not the national committee. In July 1968 they won a majority on the committee and no longer needed Harrington. His influence in the party plummeted just as he became party chair. McReynolds and Briggs organized a rival caucus at the 1968 convention, the Debs Caucus, while Seymour Steinsapir led a group of dissidents out of the party, forming the Union for Democratic Socialism. Thomas died in December 1968, and Harrington lauded him as a blend of Lincoln, Protestant conscience, and Debs, "a man for whom socialism was personal and ethical." Now the mantle of Debs and Thomas fell on Harrington. But to the Shachtmanites Harrington was just for show. Kahn, Kemble, and Irwin Saull ran the party and broadcast their contempt for Harrington's squishy-liberal turn. In 1969 Kahn bestowed LID's "man of the year" award on Humphrey. Harrington skipped the ceremony out of embarrassment and piqued the Shachtmanites in October by speaking at the first Moratorium March to End the War in Vietnam. The following month former McCarthy aides David Hawk and Sam Brown organized the second moratorium, a mammoth spectacle bringing five hundred thousand demonstrators to Washington, DC. The movement was now so huge and mainstream it didn't matter that SDS imploded.[82]

SDS disintegrated as dramatically as it ascended. It launched two forms of liberationist feminism and was taken over by three forms of revolutionary vanguard Maoism, one of which called itself Leninist along with its campus front. The war pushed aside the feminist issue until June 1967, when a women's liberation workshop at the SDS national convention declared that the world divided into three camps: capitalist, socialist, and Third World. Feminism, the workshop argued, aligned with Third World struggles for liberation because all women were in a colonial relationship with men. Feminism is about fighting for liberation from male oppression, a struggle best conceived in relation to Third World revolutionary movements. SDS men countered that women were not colonized and SDS men were not oppressors; otherwise, why should feminists stay in SDS? The logic of the colonizer claim was that women should separate from men. They said it so aggressively that many SDS women not previously disposed to join the separatist camp did so.[83]

Two schools of SDS feminism emerged from the 1967 convention. Shulamith Firestone, Judith Brown, Beverly Jones, Jo Freeman, and Roxanne Dunbar applied the logic of Black Power to feminism, contending that women's liberation is an end in itself, the ultimate revolution. Radical women needed to be independent from the New Left, not a caucus within it. "Politico" feminists Heather Tobis Booth, Naomi Weisstein, Marilyn Salzman Webb, and Alice Lynd implored against separatism, contending that feminism is not liberating if it opts out of politics, working with males, and struggling for social justice. Both types of SDS feminism tapped into gushers of repressed anger and frustration. Both founded groups that told their stories, compared notes, spawned more groups, and drafted manifestos. Both derided the National Organization for Women as bourgeois and careerist, "the NAACP of the women's movement," as the saying went, although politicos were sometimes willing to work with it. Both made claims about the liberation of women that did not distinguish between white women and women of color, claiming to speak for women as a class. And both forms of SDS feminism spoke of revolutionary upheaval, much like the drift of SDS generally. In the spring of 1968 SDS led a spectacular student rebellion at Columbia University, seized the administration building, and became a household name. SDS called itself an agent of revolution, except that it had no philosophy of revolution. What was the theory that defined SDS as a revolutionary organization? This question set up SDS to be devoured by Maoist Leninists who had an answer.[84]

The Maoist–Leninist group Progressive Labor (PL) and an aspiring terrorist group called the Revolutionary Youth Movement (RYM) devoured SDS in eighteen months. Maoist proto-Leninism combined the Maoist emphasis on peasant revolutionary struggle with Leninist vanguard ideology. PL injected it into SDS, where it spread like wildfire. The Worker–Student Alliance (WSA) was PL's front on campus, fixing on the Third World generally, not China. RYM, a magnet for the privileged students that shut down Columbia, was led by Columbia strike leader Mark Rudd and University of Chicago law school graduate Bernardine Dohrn. Dohrn reframed the split between politico feminists and radical feminists, describing the politicos as full-time movement organizers and the radicals as professional women who made a profession out of being women. The politicos, Dohrn said, raised the issue of women's liberation as part of their overall work, while the radicals were self-centered types concerned only with themselves as women. The radicals were long on lawyers, teachers, and other professional class women, but Dohrn stressed that the profession at issue was self-promoting feminism: "Most of the women's groups are bourgeois, unconscious or unconcerned about the class struggle and the exploitation of working-class women, and chauvinists concerning the oppression of black and brown women." Dohrn aptly scorned the pretensions of white "sisterhood is powerful" rhetoric while exaggerating the apolitical thrust of SDS radical feminism. As long as SDS existed, Firestone, Brown, Jones, and other SDS radical feminists were not completely apolitical; they espoused separatist cultural feminism only after SDS disintegrated.[85]

Dohrn played a major role in sundering SDS. PL, WSA, and RYM clashed with each other in 1969 at the ninth national convention in Chicago, each vying for control of the organization. WSA was fresh from its success in the Third World Student Strike at San Francisco State College. RYM declared that the Black Panther Party was the vanguard of the black liberation movement in the United States, and RYM was in solidarity with the party and its Black People's Army. Black Panthers were being jailed, killed in shootouts with police, and driven into exile. RYM said SDS had no reason to exist if it did not rally behind the Panthers in their life-and-death crisis. RYM wanted SDS to sign up for revolutionary violence, taking for granted its right to determine who it was—the Panthers—that black Americans should follow. Debates over direct action split RYM into a dominant actionist faction led by Dohrn, Rudd, and Bill Ayers (RYM 1) and a more conventionally Marxist faction led by SDS national secretary Mike Klonsky, Walter Coleman, and Bob Avakian (RYM 2). RYM 1 and RYM 2 both claimed they were more revolutionary and devoted to the Panthers than PL, which PL vehemently disputed. SDS tore itself apart in Chicago. Southern California SDS had nominated its regional leader Klonsky to the national office to get rid of him, believing the national office was irrelevant. RYM split the convention, and SDS broke into two organizations, SDS-WSA and SDS-RYM. But most of its chapters disintegrated, SDS-RYM dissolved in 1970, and only the RYM 1 faction of RYM continued—as the terrorist Weather Underground, blowing up buildings.[86]

Radical feminists were on a separatist cultural trajectory regardless of what happened in SDS. As it was, the implosion of SDS framed their descriptions of the radical feminist difference. Firestone, in *The Dialectic of Sex* (1970), quoted Black Panther women who said it was imperative to focus on the primary struggle against racial oppression and turn away from the "petit bourgeois little cliques" that changed the subject. Firestone said this was precisely what radical feminists rejected: "We have here a complete denial by blacks (and women, no less) of their own principles of Black Power as applied to another group: the right of the oppressed to organize around their oppression *as they see and define it.* It is sad that the Black Power movement, which taught women so much about their political needs through the obvious parallels, should be the last to see that parallel in reverse." Radical feminists applied the principles of radical politics to women, leaving behind those who did not. Women were oppressed as a class very much like black Americans, and the principles of liberation were the same for women as for blacks. She said the women's liberation groups that remained "within the larger leftist movement haven't a chance, for their line is dictated from above, their analysis and tactics shaped by the very class whose legitimate power they are protesting." All they could accomplish, at most, was to increase the tension "that already threatens their frayed leftist groups with extinction." Firestone argued that any surge of real feminism within any left-wing organization would destroy the organization, so radical feminists should just leave. She pointed to the SDS men who glorified Dohrn for winning first place "on the *Ten Most Wanted* list of Weathermen and assorted guerrillas." These same men previously derided women's liberation. Firestone allowed that their cheers for Dohrn registered progress of a sort, but radical feminists were done with trying to win that kind of favor.[87]

The wild implosion of SDS repulsed Harrington; thus he learned almost nothing from the struggle for women's liberation that played out within it. LID and SDS severed their relationship in 1966 before SDS turned on itself. Then the escalations of more-militant-than-thou took over. Harrington reflected that SDS lurched to the logical conclusion of its impossible premises: "Americans could not help America, only an uncorrupted and Fanonist Third World could do that; and therefore it was the duty of American radicals to become an armed, terrorist column of the international revolution." His situation in the Socialist Party was prosaic by comparison. There was never a Harrington faction in the party. He was against the war, but in the party he stood for muddled unity. He kept his distance from the Debs Caucus, which said the party lost its way when it resolved to go wherever the labor movement happened to be. In January 1970 Harrington finally declared that he was for pulling out of Vietnam; 40 percent of the public had preceded him in reaching this verdict. It helped that a Republican was president and some of Harrington's favorite union leaders—Reuther, Victor Reuther, UAW secretary-treasurer Emil Mazey, and American Federation of State, County and Municipal Employees (AFSCME) District 37 (New York City) president Victor Gotbaum—called for America to withdraw. Harrington had assumed that Cold War conservatism was a given in the AFL-CIO; now he mused that perhaps realignment applied to the labor movement too.[88]

Prime Minister Olof Palme of Sweden invited Harrington to Stockholm, and he thrilled at Palme's bold antiwar criticism; Social Democracy felt fresh and healthy in Sweden, unlike Harrington's situation. Yet Harrington still could not break with the Shachtmanites. In 1970 he and Kemble wrote a party resolution on the war that muddled its ostensible call for a ceasefire and disengagement. McReynolds resigned in disgust, despairing that he had brought into the party the group that ruined it. A trickle of others followed him out and the Shachtmanites responded by throwing off their pretense that "Negotiations Now" was some kind of antiwar position. In October 1970 Shachtman wrote a prowar missive declaring that the issue in Vietnam was democracy versus totalitarianism. Communism had to be defeated, preferably by building up the South Vietnamese army and decreasing American forces.[89]

Harrington replied that this position was abstract, ahistorical, and wrong. The United States was not defending self-determination in South Vietnam, and the Socialist Party should not support anti-Communist wars wherever Communism advanced. He said it was unconscionable to defend reactionary anticommunists as a lesser evil to Communism. The lesser evil was to get out of Vietnam and accept a Communist victory. This declaration enraged Shachtman. He never spoke to Harrington again, offended that Harrington betrayed his office, the party, and him. Now the fight was on for the soul of the Socialist Party. The Shachtmanites renamed themselves the Majority Tendency caucus, and Harrington rallied his friends. He told Chicago UAW leader Carl Shier and Boston Jewish Labor Committee director Julius Bernstein that he didn't want a faction fight; he just wanted the Shachtmanites to accept that the party was a coalition with an antiwar wing. He still believed in coalition politics; it was the Shachtmanites who reduced socialism to a union ideology. But the socialists who agreed with him had streamed out of the party. Harrington begged them, one by one, to return. He got some blistering replies from former comrades who resented that it took him so long to defy Shachtman. Meier and Denitch, however, came back, and Howe joined for the first time out of loyalty to Harrington.[90]

In March 1972 the Shachtmanites strengthened their control by merging with the Democratic Socialist Federation (DSF), a small group of elderly Jewish Social Democrats that bolted the party in 1936 and never came back out of dislike of Thomas. Now the party had three factions represented by three coequal chairs, demoting Harrington to a shared leadership status with Rustin and DSF leader Sasha Zimmerman. The factional struggle for the Socialist Party mapped onto the 1972 Democratic primary campaigns. Harrington supported Maine senator Edmund Muskie, the party's best chance to unseat Nixon, until Muskie dropped out in March, and Harrington switched to antiwar candidate George McGovern, a South Dakota senator. The Shachtmanites and their DSF allies supported the Pentagon's favorite Democrat, Senator Henry Jackson of Washington, until he dropped out, after which they supported Humphrey.[91]

The new liberalism came into full bloom in 1972. Liberals of the 1950s were quiet and restrained. They campaigned for decorous types like Adlai Stevenson and G. Mennen Williams, were cowed by the Cold War, and did not speak for mass movements. The social movements of the 1960s produced a different kind of liberal—outspokenly antiwar, feminist, and movement-oriented. The Democrats adopted new rules after the 1968 election that reduced the influence of party insiders and tripled the number of female and African American delegates to the 1972 convention. McGovern played a leading role in changing the rules; then he beat Humphrey for the nomination with a grassroots campaign that galvanized progressives.

McGovern was steeped in Midwest social gospel Methodism. He won the Distinguished Flying Cross as an army bomber in World War II, studied for two years at Garrett Evangelical Theological Seminary, voted for Henry Wallace, and earned a doctorate in history at Northwestern University, writing a dissertation on the Ludlow massacre. He taught at Dakota Wesleyan University and was elected in 1962 to the U.S. Senate. McGovern was mildly liberal in his early Senate career and got more outspoken through the 1960s. He entered the presidential nomination race in 1968 just before the convention, taking up Robert Kennedy's fallen banner, which put him on track for a reform candidacy in 1972. In 1969 McGovern called for outright withdrawal from Vietnam; in 1972 his campaign also supported amnesty for draft evaders. McGovern espoused both positions with understated moral eloquence in the face of volatile opposition. To the Shachtmanites and the CIO hierarchy he was a catastrophe—preachy, idealistic, feminized, and anti-interventionist. It didn't matter that McGovern was the most prounion nominee in the history of the Democratic Party. He called America to come home, and he owed nothing to the AFL-CIO. Thus he was anathema to Meany.[92]

The AFL-CIO voted 27 to 3 to take no position on Nixon versus McGovern. The UAW, AFSCME, Machinists, and Communications Workers endorsed McGovern on their own, but losing the AFL-CIO hurt the Democrats badly. Meany ridiculed "the gay-lib people" who ran the Democratic convention: "The people who look like Jacks, acted like Jills, and had the odor of johns about them." Some insiders assumed that Kahn supplied Meany with this gay-bashing tripe, which is unlikely; Meany had three speechwriters, and, as Horowitz observed, by the time Meany or his successor, Lane Kirkland, gave a speech it was almost impossible to sort out which hand had written which line. The Kahn story stayed in circulation mostly because the Shachtmanites did play a similar game on other subjects. *New America* derided McGovern as a squishy, pink, New Class idealist not deserving its endorsement. Shachtman said McGovern reminded him of Wallace, except McGovern was worse. Formally, the party endorsed McGovern in the same disingenuous way it previously endorsed the antiwar movement—by showering him with insults and faint praise. Socialist stalwart and AFT president David Selden protested that McGovern was the most Thomas-like candidate ever nominated by the Democrats; had the Shachtmanites lost their minds? A National Committee meeting of October 1972 was the last straw for Harrington. Some in the Majority Tendency vehemently opposed McGovern, and others gave lip service to supporting him despite disdaining him. Harrington resigned as chair, protesting that most of the Shachtmanites, one way or another, were pro-Nixon.[93]

A week before Nixon crushed McGovern, Shachtman died of a heart attack. The Shachtmanites rejoiced that McGovern liberalism got the thrashing it deserved, while Kahn lamented that Shachtman expired just when the "full fruits of his achievements" were realized in a renovated social democratic movement. In December 1972 the Shachtmanites renamed the party Social Democrats, USA, marking that it was their party and the Harrington types were defeated. Shachtman had taught Harrington that American power in Third

World contexts is an incitement to Communism, not an alternative to it. Harrington struggled to explain Shachtman's retrogression, speculating that perhaps he relinquished the Third Camp argument without acknowledging it. Shachtman shucked off what he knew to be true because losing in Vietnam was intolerable, and he no longer believed there was a third way between capitalism and Communism. Thus his legacy, Harrington said, became the sad spectacle of socialists for Nixon: "My friends had turned themselves into a fanatically anti-Communist clique of people with staff jobs in unions and related institutions." He did not believe they were corrupted by careers; the real corruption was political and ideological: "They were not scoundrels who were bought and paid for. That is why they are tragic."[94]

Perhaps they were tragic, but the Shachtmanites came from tiny sectarian nowhere to capture the Socialist Party and scale the ranks of the labor movement. They financed nearly everything they did with money from their historic enemy, the Old Guard textile unions, until they reached the apex of the AFL-CIO and funded themselves. Then they cofounded the most consequential political-intellectual movement of the late twentieth century, neoconservatism, the name that Harrington hung on them in September 1973 as an act of dissociation. The mission of the original neocons was to retake the Democratic Party from McGovern liberals. Two groups came together to try it. One consisted of the Shachtmanites — Kahn, Kemble, Horowitz, Sidney Hook, Rustin, Feldman, Shanker, Arnold Beichman, Carl Gershman, Emanuel Muravchik, Arch Puddington, and others. The second group consisted of intellectuals from the Humphrey and Jackson camps, especially *Public Interest* editors Bell and Irving Kristol, *Commentary* editor Norman Podhoretz, and sociologist Daniel Patrick Moynihan, plus Midge Decter, Nathan Glazer, Max Kampelman, Jeane Kirkpatrick, Seymour Martin Lipset, Richard Perle, John Roche, Ben Wattenberg, and Paul Wolfowitz. These two groups melded together in a classic Leninist vehicle that Kahn founded with AFL-CIO money, the Coalition for a Democratic Majority (CDM). They disputed the right of Harrington and *Dissent* to name them, but the name stuck because it perfectly captured the rush of Shachtmanites and Jackson liberals to the political right.[95]

Two magazines, *Commentary* and *The Public Interest*, played leading roles in the neocon upsurge. *Commentary*, the liberal flagship of the American Jewish Committee, took a sharp right turn in 1970, blasting the antiwar movement, feminism, Black Power, McGovern liberalism, gay rights, and liberation theology. It did not say that some feminists went too far; it said all feminists were pathetic and ridiculous. *Commentary* polemics were more knowing and effective than similar fare on the traditional right because nearly everybody who wrote for *Commentary* was a former lefty or still claimed to be one. They claimed they had not changed. It was the Democratic Party that changed, leaving them without a political home, unless they could retake the party.

The neoconservatives charged that affirmative action and Black Power destroyed the civil rights movement, the Great Society created a New Class of parasitic bureaucrats and social workers, and McGovern liberalism betrayed the fight against Communism. Podhoretz's wife, Decter, joined Kemble at CDM and perfected the neocon style of polemic against feminists and "New Politics" liberals. A few refugees from the New Left joined the neocons, notably theologians Richard John Neuhaus and Michael Novak, as did a few politically homeless conservatives, notably sociologists Peter Berger and James Q. Wilson. But most neocon criticism bore the trademarks of the Old Left, resounding with Shachtmanite contempt for the liberal intelligentsia and the "fashionable liberal elite." *Dissent* and the *Nation* were execrable but so were the *New Yorker* and the *New York Times*. The early neocons said Harrington betrayed pro-American Social Democracy in the hope of winning plaudits in the *New Yorker*. They resented his implication that they were the left wing of the right, not the right wing of the left. The difference was crucial, as the labeled party keenly understood.[96]

Neoconservatives believed in democratic rule by elites and lacked conservative nostalgia. They did not yearn for medieval Christendom, Tory England, the Old South, or Gilded Age capitalism. They were modernists, comfortable with a minimal welfare state, schooled in the social sciences, and allergic to Old Right xenophobia and anti-Semitism. Calling them conservatives of any kind was insulting. But the neocons were changing more than they acknowledged, gradually aligning objectively with the political right. Kristol described himself as a "neo-liberal" like Niebuhr and literary critic Lionel Trilling. In the 1950s he blasted liberals for abetting the Communist conspiracy, notoriously suggesting that Joseph McCarthy was more loyal to America than liberals. By the mid-1960s he believed that liberals were equally naive about eradicating poverty. Kristol and Bell, judging that government policymakers were operating with a shortage of hard information, founded *The Public Interest* in 1965 as an antidote to Great Society idealism.[97]

The Other America was Exhibit A of what they opposed. Bell said that social policy intellectuals fell for Harrington's sermonic effusions; Kristol reasoned that the best research was not getting filtered to government policymakers; together they described *The Public Interest* as "a middle-aged magazine for middle-aged readers." Kristol later recalled: "Conservatism in the United States at that time was represented by the Goldwater campaign against the New Deal, with which none of us had any sympathy, and by *National Review*, which we regarded as too right-wing. We considered ourselves to be realistic meliorists, skeptical of government programs that ignored history and experience in favor of then-fashionable ideas spawned by the academy."[98]

This wet-blanket empiricism played a secondary role in the neocon upsurge. On the day after Nixon was reelected in 1972, he told a reporter that "throwing money at problems" caused the Great Society to fail. Harrington often cited this remark because it wrongly implied that Johnson spent huge sums to eradicate poverty, and it echoed Bell's critique that Harrington had no answer—all Harrington could say was that LBJ should have spent more money to abolish poverty. Bell and Kristol admonished that no amount of government spending changed the dysfunctional attitudes and habits of the poor. To them, the corrective began with go-slow prudence. Isserman notes insightfully that Harrington had Bell in his head as "a kind of skeptical political conscience."[99]

But neoconservatism surged in American politics by fighting, not by casting a wet blanket. It was fiercely ideological in the fashion of its Trotskyite, *Partisan Review*, "New York intellectual" roots. William Phillips and Philip Rahv, in 1937, turned the Communist *Partisan Review* into a storied independent Marxist forum blending anti-Stalinist politics and modernist aestheticism. Rahv, Hook, James Burnham, Lionel Trilling, Diana Trilling, and Lionel Abel were its ringleaders. The next generation of New York intellectuals, younger by ten to fifteen years, included Howe, Kristol, William Barrett, Alfred Kazin, and Delmore Schwartz. A third generation subsequently included Hilton Kramer, Steven Marcus, and Podhoretz. The New York intellectuals were deeply politicized thinkers who believed in the social and political power of ideas. They did not allow their training in deterministic social science to quell their belief that powerful ideas can change the world—a faith that later gave them ample advantage over liberal academics in the political realm. Adept at launching magazines, especially when their politics changed, they scattered across the map politically but always with a style that reflected their background in the Old Left.[100]

The Public Interest warned that social engineering often had predictable bad consequences and worse unanticipated ones. Glazer, Edward C. Banfield, Roger Starr, and Aaron Wildavsky sharply criticized Great Society housing and welfare policies; James Q. Wilson censured liberal strategies to overcome racism; Moynihan said the war on poverty was faring badly; and John H. Bunzel inveighed against black studies. In the name of promoting equal opportunity— a liberal ideal—the journal warned that a bad mutation of liberalism was breeding dependency in the welfare class, legitimizing reverse racism through affirmative action, impeding America's economic growth, and creating a New Class of parasitic public sector functionaries.[101]

At first the neocons said they opposed social engineering only if the evidence weighed against it, not because they opposed government programs on principle. But by 1970 the difference was already blurred. *The Public Interest* took on a movement character, blasting social justice as a goal of government policy. Kristol later recalled that the rise of the antiwar counterculture drove his group to draw lines and make unexpected alliances: "Suddenly we discovered that we had been cultural conservatives all along. Now, we had to decide what we were for, and why. Cool criticism of the prevailing liberal-left orthodoxy was not enough at a time when liberalism itself was crumbling before the resurgent Left." *Commentary* specialized in hot criticism, offended that privileged American youths chanted slogans against their country. Podhoretz had struggled to assimilate to American society and be accepted as a U.S. American not requiring a hyphen. It galled him when a slightly younger generation denounced America in the streets. He said he tried to return to the liberal anticommunist establishment only to find it no longer existed. The old "Vital Center" liberals lost their will and coherence. Schlesinger and Galbraith accommodated feminism, Black Power, and other radicalisms, while the fiasco in Vietnam sapped the will of liberals to fight Communism. Kemble helped Podhoretz find writers for the new *Commentary*, a bastion of aggressive criticism specializing in personal attacks on former friends.[102]

Samuel McCracken blasted the new academic leftism, Dorothy Rabinowitz took aim at activist professors and clergy, Decter and Arlene Croce said feminism destroyed families and society, and Kristol skewered the liberal "religion of democracy." A bit later Kirkpatrick denounced the politics of McGovernism, and Novak condemned the moralistic hypocrisy of the New Class. Podhoretz touted the advantage his writers held over the traditional right in attacking the left: "We knew what they really thought and felt, which did not always coincide with what they considered it expedient to say in public; and we knew how to penetrate their self-protective rhetoric."[103]

Kristol explained what that meant: "The neoconservatives are the political intellectuals, and that's what the Trotskyists were. The Trotskyist movement produced political intellectuals, which is why so many went into sociology and achieved distinction. It was much more rigorous intellectual training than you could get in college. If someone came up with some matter on which you were not well read, my God, you were humiliated. It was Jesuitical. The Republican Party, meanwhile, produced antipolitical intellectuals. Those people are not in my tradition."[104]

Neocons said it was not too late for the Democratic Party to regain its self-respect and anti-Communist militancy; otherwise the United States would lose the struggle for the world. They claimed the Soviet Union was preparing to fight and win a nuclear war against a cowardly America that feared the Soviet Union too much to resist it. Neocons opposed the Strategic Arms Limitation Treaty because they opposed détente, charging that Henry Kissinger's diplomacy in the Nixon and Gerald Ford administrations enabled the Soviet Union to stabilize its empire. In 1976 the neocons backed Henry Jackson and founded the Committee on the Present Danger, warning that Kissinger-style coexistence dangerously weakened the United States. This contention won no appointments in the Democratic administration of Jimmy Carter, which propelled the neocons to bond with Ronald Reagan.[105]

Harrington battled the neocons for the rest of his life. He was tied to some by friendship and to most by history. The turning point of his life occurred when he realized "that I had trusted them longer than I should have, that I kept giving noble socialist speeches to the public while they were plotting and conniving behind my back." Later it galled and fascinated him that the most successful socialists in American history succeeded by taking over the foreign policy and education wings of the Republican Party. In September 1972 he took his first real job, teaching political science at Queens College—part of the City University system in New York—because he was the father of two sons and needed health insurance; Stephanie Harrington switched to freelance journalism. The following February Harrington convened a weekend conference, "The Future of the Democratic Left," at New York University. A hundred friends came, melting to eighty on Sunday morning at a decayed West Side hotel, deciding to start over. They didn't belong in the Socialist Party, which wasn't even called the Socialist Party anymore. Many had cut their activist teeth in the Kennedy and McGovern campaigns; Howe, Meier, and Denitch provided older-generation gravitas; and the group resolved to launch a new organization modestly called the Democratic Socialist Organizing Committee (DSOC).

This was decidedly a friends-of-Mike outfit. McReynolds founded a tiny Debs Caucus group in Milwaukee called the Socialist Party USA; it was hardy but never grew. Harrington low-balled his expectations, claiming he sought merely to create a pluralistic socialist group that survived. But DSOC fixed from the beginning on Harrington's ambition for the conscience constituency. He knew from his board membership in ADA that many of its sixty thousand members were closet socialists, and so were many of the McGovern workers. He said America had more socialists than ever; the mission of DSOC was to lure them out of the closet.[106]

He wrote a charter statement for DSOC, "We Are Socialists of the Democratic Left," declaring, "We identify with the tradition of Eugene Victor Debs and

Norman Thomas—with a socialism which is democratic, humanist, and anti-war." Harrington said DSOC would have no doctrinal line and no cadre disciplined by a vanguard pretension. In October 1973 he presided over its founding convention in New York. Denitch, Howe, Meier, Julius Bernstein, Harry Fleishman, Victor Reuther, Carl Shier, former Packinghouse Workers president Ralph Helstein, union journalist Ruth Jordan, and veteran UAW socialists Irving Bluestone, Martin Gerber, and Emil Mazey played leading roles, as did Harrington campus protégés Steve Kelman and Ben Ross (Harvard), Alex Spinrad (Yale), and Ronnie Steinberg (New York University). Harrington told the four hundred delegates, "Today we begin the work of building the seventies Left." That was a gloss on Lenin's greeting to the Soviet delegates in revolutionary Petrograd in 1917, "We shall now proceed to construct the Socialist order." It evoked a wry smile from the knowing and sounded impressive to those unschooled in Leninism. Jack Ross, averse to Harrington, says this reference registered that he "still viewed politics through rigid and doctrinaire categories."[107]

Harrington told DSOC it needed to go where the people were, in the liberal wing of the Democratic Party. Many politically homeless veterans of SDS showed up to see what would be said and who would show up. Few of them joined right away, but Ron Radosh wrote a mostly favorable report on the conference for *Socialist Revolution*, a New Left flagship. Radosh caught the irony that veteran anti-Communists were trying to achieve the Communist dream of a united front. The convention agreed to support one paid staffer, UMass-Amherst graduate Jack Clark, a former YPSL activist who worked out of Meier's spare room on the Upper West Side. Clark was a Julius Bernstein protégé who began working for Harrington in 1972, originally to organize the caucus that lost the battle for the Socialist Party. Harrington thought the convention went amazingly well until he reached Meier's apartment after the second day and was immediately pulled into a heated, tearful, intense confrontation between feminists and stunned old-timers. Harrington and the old-timers thought they were covered on the feminist issue. They supported the Equal Rights Amendment and every policy reform related to feminism and had strong female leaders on the national committee, especially Meier, Jordan, and union official Liz McPike. Steinberg, a sociology graduate student, informed her socialist friends that they had just spent two days offending every young feminist in the hall.[108]

Steinberg had tried to tell the organizers at the planning meetings that feminism is not about policy alone—to no avail. They were Old Left socialists who equated justice with egalitarian policies. They knew very little about the rebellions against male rule that flared in SNCC and SDS and were disinclined to take lessons from them anyway. Steinberg, Nancy Shier, and Gretchen Donart spelled out what DSOC needed to learn from the New Left. The Old Left women, though wonderful, did not identify with the feminist movement as such. They had feminist goals, but feminism did not define them. To New Left feminists, feminism had to be as basic to socialism as its commitment to workers and racial justice. Feminism was deeply personal *and* political, a challenge to the most primordial form of human domination. Steinberg said DSOC Old Lefties had to change, absorbing feminist values; otherwise DSOC had no chance of attracting young feminist members. They needed to prefigure what a feminist society would be like. Sexism, she argued, is not simply a characteristic of individual males; it is a cultural and political dimension of a society that degrades women. DSOC had no hope of building the seventies left if it replicated the prefeminist Old Left.

Harrington didn't fathom the transformation of feeling and style that was being demanded; it took him several years to get a clue. But he realized that he and DSOC needed to try. Promises were made, workshops were held, the women's caucus grew, and by 1975 the women's caucus trusted the organization sufficiently not to run its own slate of candidates for the national committee. Few women were elected, and the women's caucus regretted having trusted the organization, though DSOC ran an end-around the election to place women on the national committee. Two years later Nancy Shier pushed for a provision guaranteeing that 50 percent of the national board would be female; DSOC was 70 percent male. Harrington, still not getting it, asked Shier if she wanted the size of the national committee to be determined by the pool of available women. She surprised him by saying yes, and he got his first clue at a feeling level of what feminism is about.[109]

He built up DSOC by touring on campuses, stressing that its pragmatic multiplicity embraced feminists, Fabians, democratic Marxists, religious socialists, gay rights activists, Zionists, non-Zionists, pacifists, nonpacifists, former Communists, and environmentalists. Harrington said he was definitely some of these things and not others, but DSOC was emphatically all of them. Radosh joined the national board over the angry objections of Howe and others. James Weinstein, though linked, like Radosh, to the New Left spinoff New American Movement, joined DSOC and launched his paper, *In These Times*. Veteran New Leftists streamed into the organization, changing its collective personality. Many of us who joined in the mid-1970s came from colleges where the Old Left was unknown and the New Left never happened, unless the McGovern campaign counted as New Left. It was puzzling to learn about Shachtmanites and Harrington's only recent break from them. He seemed nothing like the neocons who decried the McGovern campaign as an atrocity. Some DSOC stalwarts radiated Old Left conservatism, but not Harrington. The New Left, too, belonged to the past, a tale of idealistic initiatives that crashed during or before our college years. We heard Harrington's recruiting lecture as a left-of-McGovern call to work in the left wing of the Democratic Party.[110]

His stump speech during this period was titled "Liberalism is not enough." It commended the *New York Times* on social issues, Nixon, and the war but said the *Times* was bad on labor issues and economic justice in general. Harrington called the McGovern youth to battle for the soul of the Democratic Party in the "left wing of possibility." On occasion he made a Marxian point ("Here's a note for Marxologists") but was careful to confine Marxian debates to his books and keep his sectarian past in the past. DSOC would not have succeeded had Harrington felt compelled to rehash either thing. I first heard his recruiting speech in 1974 at Harvard, where I cofounded a DSOC chapter, and first heard the introduction that always made him cringe. Harrington was introduced as the author of *The Other America*, "the book that launched the war on poverty." He gently reintroduced himself: "I've written several other books that might interest you." His other books were important to him, and he hoped they were better than *The Other America*, a puffed-up version of a journalistic article he wrote on the run during his Greyhound Bus years.

His big-book case for democratic Marxism, *Socialism*, was published the year before he founded DSOC; four years later there was a sequel, *The Twilight of Capitalism* (1976), which Harrington dedicated to "the foe of every dogma, champion of human freedom and democratic socialist," Karl Marx. Both books argued that Marx was a democratic socialist very much like Harrington. To be sure, Harrington said, Marx contributed to the utopian problem in socialism, he was dramatically wrong about the trajectory of capitalism, and certain things that he wrote fell short of championing human freedom. On utopianism, "it is important to root out every bit of messianism from the socialist vision, to reject the notion of a secular redemption that, like the incarnation of Christ, claims to make all things new." On capitalism, Marx mistook its takeoff for its decline and wrongly predicted that workers would get poorer. As for the bad parts of Marx that Lenin seized upon, Harrington said they were temporary lapses, which Engels compounded by grafting onto Marx his pet theory of dialectical materialism.[111]

Much of Harrington's argument rehashed signature tropes of Eduard Bernstein and the Social Democratic tradition. He said *The Communist Manifesto* featured a schizophrenic exaggeration of capitalist achievements and communist promise. Its opening line about the "specter of communism" haunting Europe was absurd since Europe in 1848 was at war over bourgeois freedoms, not communism. Marx and Engels knew they were blowing smoke, for motivational purposes. In section 2 they announced the funeral of the bourgeoisie, but in the final section they advocated an alliance with it. Marx furiously denounced the bourgeoisie while trying to bring it to power. Harrington explained that Marx had a weakness for dramatic rhetoric, parading specter and funeral language while advocating tactical alliances with Chartists in England, agrarian reformers in the United States, petty-bourgeois radicals in France, and the bourgeoisie itself in Germany.[112]

Orthodox Marxism teetered on the contradiction between Marx's apocalyptic vision of imminent revolutionary deliverance and the tactical reform politics he espoused for the interim. Harrington stressed that this contradiction already pervaded the *Manifesto*; it was not just an early Marx versus later Marx issue, though there were special problems with the early Marx. Nearly everything that Kautsky-Marxists and Bernstein-revisionists contested for decades traced back to whether they kept a two-story structure in place (Kautsky) or judged that Marx's utopianism and denigration of liberal democracy compelled the democratic socialist corrective (Bernstein). Harrington was in the Bernstein tradition, but he believed it was short on militant conviction and seriously understated Marx's commitment to democracy. The latter deficiency was already defining for the democratic socialist tradition before Leninism existed. Then democratic socialists insisted on it to dissociate themselves from Lenin and Soviet Communism.

Near the end of the *Manifesto*, Marx and Engels contended that the bourgeoisie was fundamentally hostile to proletarian interests, and in Germany the bourgeois revolution would be the "immediate prelude" to a proletarian revolution. That smacked of an immediate transition from a bourgeois to a communist revolution, skipping an intervening period of bourgeois government. Was Leninism Marxist? Harrington argued that instead of taking Marx's "immediate prelude" statement literally it was better to understand Marx by what he did in 1848, advocating long-term alliances with bourgeois democrats. Admittedly, this was not much of a difference at first because later in 1848 Marx urged workers to form secret armed organizations that prepared for immediate class war. In 1850 he went full bore ultra-leftist, urging workers to set up revolutionary proletarian regimes alongside the victorious bourgeois governments.[113]

Harrington employed a stage theory to dispose of these problems, explaining that the bad Marx prevailed through 1850. For two years Marx was an ultra-leftist who envisioned the proletarian revolution as a popular explosion or insurrection from below. But even during Marx's bad phase, Harrington argued, he was a Jacobin democrat, never a proto-Leninist. Marx advocated independent revolutionary regimes that stoked popular explosions, not vanguard dictatorships that deceitfully manipulated proletarians or conspired coups. Admittedly, on several occasions during this phase Marx used the fateful phrase "dictatorship of the proletariat."[114]

Harrington invoked the early Sidney Hook on Marx's peculiar understanding of dictatorship. Marx conceived dictatorship as the class basis of precommunist societies, not as revolutionary repression. Every state was a dictatorship, including the bourgeois democracies, because the state exists to uphold the economic and political power of the ruling class. Marx believed the state was necessary only in class societies. Once the proletarian revolution overthrew capitalism and the capitalist state, the state would be unnecessary. A communist state was a contradiction in terms. Marx described the Paris Commune as a dictatorship because its property forms organized a proletarian form of class rule. He defended it forcefully, lauding the Paris Commune for paying all officials the same wages that workers received and making all administrative, judicial, and educational officers recallable by universal suffrage. In Marx's lexicon, a proletarian dictatorship brought about the fulfillment of democracy.[115]

But in Marxist-Leninism, dictatorship of the proletariat was about depriving the bourgeoisie of the right to vote, an indefensible objective to which Marx contributed mightily. Though Harrington was persistently anti-utopian, he passed lightly over Marx's immense contribution to socialist utopianism and the harm it caused. His emotional commitment to proving that Marx was a deep-down democrat always trumped what he wrote on this subject. Marx resorted to violent tactics and vicious rhetoric that flunked minimal tests of democratic principle. He flirted with the vanguard conspiracy theories of Louis Auguste Blanqui, called for insurrections from below, advocated secret societies, and skewered opponents, factional rivals, and hapless followers with violent invective, calling them toads and vermin. Harrington's "Marxism" did not include the quintessential Marxian belief that a proletarian revolution abolishes classes and the state, and it denied that Marx was an economic determinist except on occasions when he was "unjust to his ideas." Marx's preface to the *Critique of Political Economy* (1859) contended that all intellectual, political, and religious phenomena are superstructural rationalizations of economic interests. Harrington said this formulation fell under the rule "Even Homer nods." The real Marx was not the economic determinist of the preface but the antimechanistic neo-Hegelian of the *Grundrisse* who taught that the economic, political, and cultural dimensions of society interact and mutually determine each other.[116]

Harrington was surely right that Marx, a thinker of enormous power, was not a vulgar Marxist and the *Critique of Political Economy* oversimplified his argument by trying to summarize it concisely. But here the rule of watching what Marx did is instructive. Marx published the preface, stood by it, repeated it in other contexts, and republished it; meanwhile he did not publish the *Grundrisse*. Had Marx shared Harrington's concern to absolve Marxism of economic determinism, he would not have disseminated and recycled his formulation about it so determinedly, which supported his concept of class. Harrington did not believe the mode of production determined the organization of slave and feudal societies, but Marx emphatically believed it, defining a class precisely by its function in the mode of production.

Harrington allowed that Marx overbelieved in the emancipating and transforming power of democratic action. Thus Marx did not grasp that the problem of bureaucracy would bedevil every form of liberal capitalism, Social Democracy, Marxism, and Communism. But Harrington read the *Wall Street Journal* every day and seethed when it sneered at Marx or misrepresented him. It galled Harrington that he had to spend so much time explaining to reporters that Marx was not a Stalinist or Leninist. The biggest problem with Marxism, he would say, was that Marx trusted too much in democracy. Marx made errors large and small, but he saw in the struggling, hurting, ragged proletariat of the mid-nineteenth century the human builders of a good society. Reformist trade unions, of all things, were the cells of social revolution: "If the more extravagant of his hopes have been disappointed, the basic social forces to which he looked have done much to change the world." Harrington believed they held the power to change it even more.[117]

German sociologist Werner Sombart opined in 1906 that the United States was hostile to socialism because American prosperity prevented revolutionary consciousness from arising, the American economy had access to enormous natural resources, and American workers were obsessed with getting ahead; socialism might hold them back. Harrington countered that America had enough suffering and exploitation to give rise to socialism. Sombart's famous brief for American exceptionalism made sense only in its immigrant context. Many immigrants found a better life in the United States after they fled from degrading conditions in the homelands. Moreover, America's ethnic pluralism turned workers against each other, and the introduction of labor-saving machinery set native-born skilled workers in the craft unions against unskilled immigrant laborers. Harrington lamented that the AFL and the Socialist Party therefore had anti-immigrant legacies. Capitalism was the problem, not immigrants, but the AFL and the Socialists treated immigrants as a problem. American capitalism split the working class, the mainly immigrant industrial workers stood outside the organized labor movement, and American socialism never quite became what it should have been.[118]

Socialism, to Harrington, was the idea of a new society in which certain fundamental limitations of human existence are transcended. It was a vision of ample social goods being shared and enjoyed. His premise was a throwback to nineteenth-century Marxism and Fabianism: The human battle with nature has been won, making it possible to create a different kind of society. The struggle for scarce resources programmed invidious competition into life, but now there is more than enough for everyone—the prerequisite for cooperation, community, and equality to become natural. Harrington said the specter of eco-catastrophe painted by economists Kenneth Boulding and Robert Heilbroner underestimated human ingenuity. He believed that people do not respond generously to doomsday threats. Tidal, solar, and geothermal power, he said, remain to be tapped; the benefits of space exploration are unknowable; modern assumptions about consumption are not immutable. Harrington was stubbornly optimistic in order to safeguard his premise that the means exist to create cooperative societies: "For if abundance is not possible, then neither is socialism." Good socialism cannot be created under conditions of scarcity. Even dictatorial socialism cannot cope with scarcity because it engenders competition for limited resources. For socialism to be achievable, the battle for survival and the predatory culture of winning at the expense of others must be overcome.[119]

DSOC projected a harder edge than the Thomas-era Socialist Party, though some DSOC Marxists objected that Harrington was no more Marxist than Bernstein and his central trope—bureaucratic collectivism—did not come from Marx. Harrington described bureaucratic collectivism as the defining feature and problem of "late capitalism," contending that the old pro-and-con debate about economic planning has been obsolete ever since late capitalism commenced in the 1940s. What matters is the form in which economic planning takes place. Corporate capitalism is a top-down form of bureaucratic collectivism in which huge oligopolies administer prices, control the politics of investment, buy off the political system, and define cultural tastes and values while obtaining protection and support from the state. It shakes down the state for subsidies and favors and socializes its losses with government bailouts, all the while claiming to believe in private enterprise. Late capitalism vests managerial elites bent on increasing their own wealth and power with the power to determine the social order.[120]

Harrington's books of the 1970s copiously detailed how corporations determine governmental priorities, socialize their losses, and buy off compliant politicians, which he called the "antisocial socialization of the economy." His favorite sources on this theme were California State University political economist James O'Connor and two German socialists associated with the Frankfurt School, Claus Offe and Jürgen Habermas. All contended that the state is constantly in crisis because it cannot meet the demands of modern society to simultaneously solve social problems, advance democracy, clean up the antisocial ravages of capitalism, and support cultural identity. Habermas said this situation ended the era in which philosophy could be the sole basis of normative reflection. Philosophy needed to work in tandem with social science, in his case to reconstruct the universal conditions of understanding through a philosophy of language, speech-act theory. Harrington, Habermas, and Offe shared a similar concept of democratic socialism as the democratization of the collectivist logic of modernity, and Harrington took much of his detailed argument about the structural fiscal crisis of government from O'Connor. To Harrington, democratic socialism was an every-week lecture circuit mission. He was a message speaker about the unavoidability of bureaucratic collectivism and the imperative of creating bottom-up forms of pluralistic economic democracy. Nationalization, he would say, is only one of the forms of socialization and usually the last resort — exactly as the Socialist International said in the Frankfurt Declaration (1951).[121]

DSOC compensated for its tiny membership by attracting high achievers in the unions, the academy, social activism, and the Democratic Party. In December 1974 DSOC faced off against the CDM at the midterm conference of the Democratic Party in Kansas City. Harrington and fellow DSOC Democratic delegate Marjorie Phyfe Gellerman defended the reforms that democratized the presidential nominating process, opposing the neocon effort to roll back the reforms. For DSOC it was a modest intervention that led to a breakthrough in 1976. DSOC played a major role in writing the 1976 Democratic Party platform, comparable to the role of the American Conservative Union (ACU) in the Republican Party. The ACU, however, had three hundred thousand members in 1976; DSOC had two thousand. Two things enabled DSOC to play an outsized role in Democratic politics: Harrington and DSOC were better than liberals at defending the welfare state, and DSOC had powerful union allies, especially AFSCME national president Jerry Wurf, AFSCME New York president Victor Gotbaum, UAW president Doug Fraser, and Machinists president William Winpisinger. These unions generously financed Democratic Agenda, showing that progressive unionism was a real thing and growing.[122]

Wurf was a gruff fighter who never forgot that he began as a Brooklyn socialist agitator. He took it personally, as the leader of a thriving public sector union, when Republicans denigrated government spending. Wurf bridled at the conservatism of the AFL-CIO hierarchy, detested the Shachtmanites, and liked Harrington. Gotbaum provided invaluable organizing assistance to Democratic Agenda. Fraser came into Harrington's orbit without having previously belonged to any left-wing group. Winpisinger began as an auto mechanic, scaled the ranks of the Machinists, befriended Harrington, and joined DSOC. It delighted

Harrington that DSOC became a home for union leaders who were radicalized on the job, lacking any connection to the Old Left. By 1976 four members of Congress openly identified with DSOC: John Conyers (Michigan), Bella Abzug (New York), Ron Dellums (California), and Robert Kastenmeier (Wisconsin). Feminist icon Gloria Steinem, the founding editor of *Ms.* magazine, was active in Democratic Agenda and DSOC, as was AFSCME secretary-treasurer and Coalition of Black Trade Unionists official Bill Lucy.

The centerpiece of Democratic Agenda was the Humphrey-Hawkins bill for full employment. Hubert Humphrey was its Senate sponsor; Congressional Black Caucus leader Gus Hawkins was its House sponsor; and DSOC sociologist Bertram Gross was its principal author, modeling it on the original full employment bill of 1944. Humphrey-Hawkins committed the federal government to achieve an adult unemployment level of 3 percent or less. Morris Udall, an Arizona liberal and Humphrey-Hawkins advocate, won Harrington's backing for president; Jimmy Carter, a Humphrey-Hawkins skeptic who did not support McGovern in 1972, won the nomination; and left-liberals consoled themselves that Carter was electable and perhaps could be pulled to the left. Briefly they were encouraged. Carter delivered a liberal speech at the Democratic Convention, named Minnesota liberal Walter Mondale as his running mate, and told his platform operator, Joe Duffy, to accommodate the Democratic Agenda caucus. Carter ran on Humphrey-Hawkins and a pledge to limit defense spending, defeating President Gerald Ford in November 1976.[123]

Carter was unlucky and politically inept. He became president just after the post-1946 economic boom ran out and the bill came due for years of farming and factory overproduction. Factories retooled for computerized production while coping with unsold inventories. The Organization of Petroleum Exporting Countries (OPEC) pulled off an oil embargo, the workforce changed from blue to white collar, and standard Keynesian tools no longer flattened economic cycles to keep the economy on a steady growth course. Harrington claimed that Carter owed his victory to the coalition of unionists, blacks, Hispanics, feminists, and liberals represented by Democratic Agenda, but Carter drew a different conclusion, having won ten of the eleven former Confederate states. He believed that being an outsider was the key to his election and presidency. Thus he took pride in his bad relationship with a Democratic Congress, counting it as evidence of his virtue. Carter was a moralistic-technocratic throwback to the pre–New Deal Democratic Party, albeit with updated views about racial justice, feminism, and human rights. DSOC and the labor movement seethed that Carter did almost nothing to stem a tidal wave of layoffs, plant closings, and union busting. The economy slid into a miserable recession, and a chorus of liberals joined Harrington in imploring Carter to enact the strong Keynesian policies he had run on.[124]

Carter tuned out the liberals *and* the neocons. Inflation was terrible because of concentrated industrial production and the OPEC embargo; he dared not make it worse with Keynesian gas. Meanwhile he stiffed the neocons on cabinet appointments and, for most of his term, militarism. In 1978 Harrington and Fraser organized an anti-Carter challenge at the Democratic Party midterm convention in Memphis. They blasted Carter's entire record while young Hillary Clinton whipped a floor vote to prevent the party from censuring its incumbent president. This convention was an augur of Senator Edward Kennedy's primary challenge against Carter. In December 1979 the Soviets invaded Afghanistan, and Carter dramatically increased defense spending, which did not dissuade neocons from joining Reagan's camp. Harrington had a standing offer to take over the leadership of ADA, but he dreamed of riding into power in Kennedy's administration. Kennedy challenged Carter for the nomination, DSOC went full bore for Kennedy, and he ran a strange, timid, vacuous campaign, deflating DSOC. Harrington and DSOC had everything at stake in the Kennedy campaign. He and Kennedy were friends who idealized each other, each seeing himself in the other. Kennedy's dismal campaign devastated Harrington and DSOC. Carter won the nomination, leveraging the hostage crisis in Iran to his advantage and putting the squeeze on big-city black mayors. DSOC refused to slink back to him. Harrington could not muster his usual appeal about the lesser evil and holding your nose. He was too disgusted with the odd, isolated, tone-deaf Carter to try and too deflated by how close he came to achieving his fantasy.[125]

As much as Harrington despaired over Carter's bad luck and failure, he realized that both reflected the structural crisis of the welfare state. Rational-choice Marxism had its heyday during this period, proposing to explain the combination of stagnation and inflation that blighted the Carter years. G. A. Cohen, John Roemer, Jon Elster, and Eric Olin Wright argued that welfare state capitalism features a structural conflict among capitalists, state managers, and workers in which each group rationally maximizes its material interests. State managers provide public services and impose regulations up to the point that capitalists allow, but capitalists have the upper hand because the legitimacy of the managers depends on the health of the economy. State power is exercised within class configurations that condition how it is exercised. Harrington resisted the vogue of rational-choice Marxism because its vaunted rationality tied the interests and behavior of classes and state managers to capitalist structures. If a state manager's self-interests define what rationality means, and the state is free, how is this still a Marxian theory of the state? How is it even radical? Rational-choice Marxism was great for making Marxism make sense, as Elster put it, to neoclassical economists and rational-choice social theorists, but it stripped Marxism of its distinct power—Marxian dialectic. Wright's version was closer to Harrington than to Elster, but Harrington judged that the entire rational-choice school was too individualistic. Real Marxism takes the class struggle more seriously than rational-choice Marxism.[126]

James O'Connor was more helpful to him, developing the analysis under-girding Harrington's theory of the social costs of capitalist expansion. In his book *The Fiscal Crisis of the State* (1973) O'Connor argued that the growth of the state sector is a cause of the expansion of monopoly capital and an effect of its expansion. The state sector causes monopoly industries to expand *and* the state expands as an effect of monopoly growth. As technology advances and production becomes specialized, big firms swallow small ones, creating an economy that is much more difficult to regulate, facilitate, support, clean up, and bail out than the economy of smaller enterprises it replaced. O'Connor argued that the state under welfare state capitalism performs two basic and often contradictory functions—sustaining or creating the conditions for profit-able capital accumulation and sustaining or creating the conditions for social harmony. He called the first function accumulation and the second function legitimization, which corresponded with two kinds of expenditures, social capi-tal and social expenses, which corresponded with the Marxian categories of social constant capital and social variable capital.[127]

Social capital includes investments in roads, airports, railroads, education, administration, job training, child care, urban renewal, retirement, unemploy-ment, health, medical care, and the like. Social expenses are unproductive in the Marxian sense, securing contented workers and favorable environments for investment and trade. O'Connor counted social welfare, military spending, and foreign aid as social expenses. He regretted that state governments do not cate-gorize their budgets in Marxian class terms; as it was, O'Connor stressed that nearly every state agency performs accumulation and legitimization functions, and nearly every state expense has a corresponding twofold character. Some education spending is social capital (teachers and equipment) and some is a social expense (campus police). Social insurance reproduces the workforce, while income subsidies to the poor pacify the surplus population, in the Marxian phrase. Against modern conservatives, O'Connor showed that the growth of the state is indispensable to the expansion of capitalism, especially the monopoly industries. Against liberal theory, he denied that the expansion of monopoly industries inhibits the growth of the state.[128]

As monopoly capital grows, so do social expenses. The more that social capital grows, the more the monopoly sector grows. The more the monopoly sector grows, the more the state expends on social expenses of production. O'Connor argued that this accumulation of social capital and social expenses is a contradictory process yielding the fiscal crisis of the modern state. The state that increasingly socializes capital costs does not appropriate the social surplus. Welfare state capitalism is about capitalists socializing their losses and keeping the profits. The fiscal crisis of the state is the upshot of the structural gap between state expenditures and state revenues. Expenditures increase more rapidly than the means of financing them. O'Connor developed his basic argument in two detailed chapters before turning to the familiar problem of corporations, industries, and other groups making special interest claims on the budget. Some special interests are litigated in public view, including all that unions and the poor request, and others are carefully screened from public view. In both cases, he argued, the market is almost never the coordinating agency for a special interest. Special interests are processed by the political system and either succeed or fail there, yielding the staggering waste and duplication of welfare capitalism.[129]

This analysis and a similar Germany-based account by Offe undergirded Harrington's argument about the social costs of late capitalism. The government is charged with arranging the preconditions for profitable production, and its rule depends on its success in doing so. Offe tartly explained that because the capitalist state is not itself capitalist, it depends on capitalists. Every public servant works for the benefit of monopoly interests. Harrington, building on O'Connor and Offe, described three kinds of compensatory mechanisms by which late capitalism sustains its rule and bonds the state to its interests. (1) Monopolies, oligopolies, cartels, and transnational corporations organize markets to permit managerial planning and the elimination of price competition. (2) Technological innovation is institutionalized to create new needs and markets. (3) The state intervenes in the economy with countercyclical policies that serve the interests of the major capitalist players. Like O'Connor, Harrington lingered over the labyrinthine process that produces a federal budget, cautioning that its procorporate outcome is only partly explained by the political power of corporations and the rich. Government acts as the representative of the capitalist class as a whole, something no enterprise can do. Marx famously described the democratic state under capitalism as the executive committee of the bourgeoisie. Offe and Harrington said this is a true insight into the function of the state under late capitalism. The capitalist class is anarchic and competitive, and it must be more discreet in democratic societies than was true in Marx's time. Under late capitalism the state plays the indispensable role of articulating a unifying national interest and ideology that transcends all business rivalries. In the United States the state sustains the functional illusion that all Americans have equal opportunity, freely choose their work, and freely choose their rulers.[130]

Harrington departed from O'Connor on one point, believing that he exaggerated the cooptation of the organized working class by capitalist ideology. O'Connor said unions are completely coopted—cooperating smoothly with monopoly capital to export capitalist conflicts to the small business and state sectors. Union wage increases in the monopoly sector are passed on to the society, while big business and big labor share the benefits of social investments, social consumption, and defense outlays. To be sure, O'Connor said, unions are not hostile to direct government production of any goods or services, but otherwise big business and big labor were partners. That consigned the Marxian class struggle to a bygone phase of capitalism, resembling too closely what Harrington disliked about rational-choice Marxism. O'Connor relied on the conscience constituency fallback even more than Harrington, contending that any plausible resistance to capitalism must come from alliances of teachers and administrators, transport workers and transit users, welfare workers and welfare recipients, and the like. Autoworkers, steelworkers, and other big unions had no place in the next left, having bonded with monopoly capital.[131]

Harrington refused to believe it, just as he denied that the New Left had been right to spurn union bureaucrats. The welfare state, he allowed, is an arena of struggle that is systematically biased in favor of monopoly capital. In the 1970s America suffered mightily for the fact that the government paid the corporations to make the nation evermore dependent on oil from the Middle East. Since the same corporations controlled the natural gas, coal, and nuclear industries, they even got the government to subsidize them for not developing alternative technologies. Harrington admitted that the case for fatalistic resignation is awfully strong. The game is rigged and the welfare state is deeply implicated in it. But he insisted that the welfare state is more dialectical and complex than O'Connor said. It mattered that there was such a thing as a progressive union. It mattered that the union struggles of the 1930s helped to produce the New Deal and successful industrial unions. The welfare state, Harrington argued, will never produce anything more than very limited concessions to the needs of the vast majority. Almost nothing that left-liberals want in the economic arena can be achieved without mobilizing progressive unions. Price controls on oligopolies, universal health insurance, quality education, full employment, redistribution of wealth and income, and a minimum guaranteed income are out of reach if big labor rests content with sharing the spoils of monopoly capitalism. The spoils, however, were diminishing in 1980, which ruined Carter's presidency and yielded the presidency of Ronald Reagan, a fire alarm crisis for the left.[132]

THE CRISIS OF THE EIGHTIES AND THE REAGAN RIGHT

DSOC was slow to mobilize for the Reagan onslaught because the national office was demoralized, and in December 1980 the Institute for Democratic Socialism staged a showcase event—a conference titled "Eurosocialism and America" in Washington, DC. DSOC had achieved full-member status in the Socialist International (SI) in 1978, the same year SPD leader Willy Brandt became SI president. The Eurosocialism conference was a reward to Harrington for devoting himself to the SI. The four heavyweights of European Socialism gave keynote speeches: Brandt, Palme, British Labour Party left-wing leader Tony Benn, and French Socialist leader François Mitterrand. Brandt called for a massive redistribution of wealth and resources from the rich northern nations to the nations of the global South. Palme advocated an economic democracy program featuring full employment, democratic economic planning, and democratization of the process of capital formation and investment. Benn, a former cabinet member in the Wilson and Callaghan Labour governments, gave a preview of the argument he made throughout the 1980s for nationalizing essential industries and abolishing the House of Lords. Mitterrand argued that socialists must organize society to abolish the power of fear, the power of lies, and the power of money. Dutch Labor Party leader Joop Den Uyl, the fifth European keynoter of the conference, recounted his run as prime minister from 1973 to 1977 and the socialist response to the New Left, and Spanish Socialist leader Felipe González joined the discussion from the audience.[133]

Harrington's address to the conference told an appreciative story of European Social Democratic success. In the late 1940s, he said, Social Democrats stressed nationalization and central planning and built the European welfare states. But capitalism rebounded in the 1950s and socialists responded by socializing consumption through income redistribution, stepping back from socializing production. The revisionist movement in British, German, and Swedish Social Democracy adjusted to late capitalism by redefining socialism. Harrington said the revisionists drifted too far from socialist militancy yet mounted a valuable and radical critique of outmoded socialist doctrines. British socialist Anthony Crosland was the paradigmatic revisionist. Though overimpressed by 1950s affluence, Crosland was singularly effective in persuading European socialists to stop fixing on how many enterprises they nationalized. Crosland's magisterial *Future of Socialism* (1957) contended that social ownership is an empirical question to be decided on a case-by-case basis, not a matter of socialist principle. Harrington said that is exactly right.[134]

He commended the French Socialists for constructively engaging the New Left and seeking to atone for socialist complicity in French colonialism. It helped that they started over in a new party. The Socialist Party (PS) grew out of the old French Section of the Workers' International (Section française de l'Internationale ouvrière, SFIO), but the PS appealed to young people, professionals, Catholics, and anti-imperialists, unlike the SFIO. Socialist leader Guy Mollet led the SFIO to ignominious oblivion by opposing the Algerian struggle for independence. Harrington commended Brandt and Palme for steering the SI to a constructive engagement with democratic revolutionary movements in the Third World. The SI supported Michael Manley's socialist government in Jamaica, Guillermo Ungo's Democratic Revolutionary Front in El Salvador, and the Sandinista government in Nicaragua. Harington said socialists needed to take up this work without betraying Social Democratic values.[135]

Nothing like the Eurosocialism conference had ever occurred in the United States. Tom Kahn tried to sabotage it by enlisting AFL-CIO chief Lane Kirkland against it—falsely claiming that Harrington brushed aside the AFL-CIO—and entreated the German Marshall Plan to pull its funding. Kahn succeeded with Kirkland, failed with the Germans, and may have played a role in the American media's unbelievable decision to ignore the conference. No television network showed up, and the only major U.S. newspaper to report on it was the *Washington Post*. Harrington burned at this rebuff for the rest of his life. It was small consolation to him that European outlets gave the event extensive coverage. Harrington understood that Americans do not look beyond the United States for guidance about how to improve their society, yet he overinvested emotionally in the conference. Meanwhile the American media blew off an easy chance to catch the next prime ministers of Spain and Sweden and the next president of France.

I cofounded a DSOC chapter in Albany, New York, during the month of the Eurosocialism conference, and two months later I cofounded a highly active chapter of the Committee in Solidarity with the People of El Salvador (CISPES). I served as president of Albany DSOC while our chief founder, historian Larry Wittner, served as secretary and newsletter editor. Within a year we had a bustling local of 165 members consisting mostly of professors, students, social workers, and state government workers. The ethos of Albany DSOC was middle-class, bookish, deeply civil, and policy oriented, fostering strong personal and political connections to AFSCME, the Amalgamated Clothing and Textile Workers Union (ACTWU), and the Public Employees Federation. CISPES was completely different, consisting of young radicals fresh out of college, way-left-of-DSOC academics, and church peace and justice activists.

I failed to persuade almost anyone in either organization to join the other one. A cultural chasm divided DSOC from the Central American solidarity organizations of the 1980s, notwithstanding that DSOC actively opposed Reagan's policies in Central America and Harrington was the U.S. American member of the SI's Committee to Defend the Nicaraguan Revolution. Albany CISPES began as a response to the mass-murdering rampages of Salvadoran death squads, including the assassination of Archbishop Oscar Romero in March 1980 and the rape and murder of four Catholic female missionaries in December 1980. I spoke every week for CISPES, raising medical aid money and contending against Reagan's right-wing policies toward El Salvador and Nicaragua. Albany CISPES had an emergency mentality; Salvadorans were being killed and we felt compelled to stop it. Albany DSOC met once a month and averaged three major events per year. We endorsed the activities of other groups and supported striking unions but made no attempt to match the intensity of CISPES. My friends in CISPES—the Nicaraguan Solidarity Network, the Sanctuary movement, the Anti-Apartheid Coalition, the SWP, and even a local middle-class antinuclear organization—did not regard DSOC as a radical organization. I was reduced almost to begging when we founded a social justice center in downtown Albany, and my friends balked at allowing DSOC to join. In DSOC we believed that being socialists made us radical and that the U.S. government should keep its imperial hands off Central America. The solidarity organizations judged that we were no more radical than the Nuclear Freeze movement and the National Organization for Women—middle-class, upwardly mobile, credentialed, and mindful of our careers.

DSOC came from a decade that never quite began. In historical-political terms there were no 1970s. The 1930s belonged to Franklin Roosevelt and the New Deal, which extended through Harry Truman's surprise victory of 1948, holding off the Republican attempt to end the Roosevelt era. Dwight Eisenhower clearly marked the 1950s as a political era, and the 1960s were dramatically marked by King, Kennedy, the New Left, the Vietnam War, and the Great Society, though Harrington, enlarging on this theme, always said there were two 1960s, divided by 1965. Nixon blew his chance to stamp the 1970s, and Carter was too ineffectual even to try. Nixon owed his presidency to the backlash against the 1960s, and Carter owed his to being a moralistic contrast to Nixon. The backlash reached full throttle in 1980, electing Reagan. The 1980s turned the 1960s upside down, though Harrington could never bring himself to admit that Reagan ranked with Roosevelt, Eisenhower, or LBJ. Harrington insisted until his death in 1989 that the eighties were simply another lost decade that would soon be left behind in memory and feeling. Reagan, he said, was lucky, charming, cruel, an earnest ideologue, and a conceptual incompetent "who tried to take revenge on the past rather than creating the future he so often proclaimed."[136]

Harrington and Carter held a similar incredulity about Reagan. Carter spent the last days of the 1980 campaign trying to awaken a sense of revulsion about Reagan, reminding Americans of his ugly opposition to the civil rights movement. That was futile; the overwhelming majority that elected Reagan was finished with feeling bad about African Americans, Vietnam, the poor, and America. Reagan heaped vile ridicule on women of his imagination, "welfare queens." He told Americans their country was in economic decline because labor elites strangled productivity, liberals created government jobs for themselves, and welfare mothers were addicted to welfare. Liberals coddled America's criminal class (coded black) and welfare class (also coded black). The poor became the underclass, a coded term meant to repel. The word "liberal," on Reagan's watch, became an epithet in American politics. Nearly every Democratic presidential candidate in 1960 proudly claimed the term — Kennedy, Humphrey, Stevenson, and Stuart Symington; LBJ was the ironic exception. The 1980s obliterated this self-description for politicians. In September 1981 Harrington blasted Democrats for capitulating to all of it. Except for the Congressional Black Caucus, he wrote, "the Democratic party either stood idly by while reactionaries mounted their savage attack on social programs, particularly those aimed at helping the working poor, or worse joined in the destruction of gains they themselves had pioneered." Harrington's disgust, however, still registered his belief that the reactionary turn in American politics would not last. Neocons read the political trends more shrewdly.[137]

Jeane Kirkpatrick became Reagan's ambassador to the United Nations; Elliott Abrams ran Reagan's Central American policy as assistant secretary of state for inter-American affairs; Richard Perle became assistant secretary of defense; Paul Wolfowitz directed policy planning at the State Department; Eugene Rostow and Kenneth Adelman successively ran the Arms Control and Disarmament Agency; Max Kampelman headed arms control negotiations; Richard Pipes directed the Soviet and East European division of the National Security Council; and William Bennett ran the education department. All these neocons appointed other neocons, notably Carl Gershman by Kirkpatrick and William Kristol by Bennett. The rush of neocons was strong at the beginning and grew through Reagan's presidency. The *New Republic* warned half seriously that "Trotsky's orphans" took over the government. Irving Kristol said the neocons flourished because the Republican Party needed intellectuals who knew how to fight and rationalize: "We had to tell businessmen that they needed us. . . . It is very hard for business to understand how to think politically." Neocons won Reagan's favor and captured Old Right foundation money by approaching politics as factional tournament, turning every issue into a referendum on pro-Americanism. They specialized at first in anti-Communism, education, and culture war, not being trustworthy on economics; then they became Reagan-conservatives on economics too.[138]

Three celebrated books epitomized what was called Reaganomics: George Gilder's *Wealth and Poverty* (1980), Charles Murray's *Losing Ground: American Social Policy 1950–1980* (1984), and David Stockman's *The Triumph of Politics* (1986). Gilder said the other Americans who mattered were the nation's long-suffering capitalists, who produced the nation's wealth and were never thanked for it. He thanked them profusely for "the enriching mysteries of inequality" and "the multiplying miracles of market economics." Stockman ecstatically lauded Gilder's book just before Stockman slashed Aid to Families with Dependent Children (AFDC) and other welfare programs as Reagan's budget director. Reagan cut AFDC by 11.7 percent, food stamps by 18.8 percent, and other food programs by 13.3 percent. Republican Senator Robert Dole told Reagan and Stockman that somebody "besides welfare recipients" needed to take a hit, if only for appearances. But that never happened.[139]

Murray made a classic case for hitting the poor again, agreeing with Harrington that the system should be faulted for American poverty. But the system he meant was the "entire federal welfare and income-support structure for working-age persons." Murray argued that welfare perversely persuaded nonachievers to get on the dole instead of working. The culture of poverty, though terribly real and insidious, did not prevent Americans from rising into the middle class—until the welfare state created a structural system of dependency. Murray said the solution was to abolish the entire federal welfare state. Poor Americans would be better off if they had no alternative to getting a job and leaning on their families or local charity. The Manhattan Institute funded Murray's research for the express purpose of providing a right-wing counter to *The Other America* and its legacy. Stockman, later recounting that he was able to gouge only the poor, said the poor were always first in line because they made "weak claims." Everybody else had lobbying power, which he called, in now-I-get-it mode, "the triumph of politics."[140]

Gilder popularized the ideological basis of Reaganomics—supply-side economics. It was a pure fantasy that captivated the Republican right in the late

1970s, championed by economist Arthur Laffer, *Wall Street Journal* editorial writer Jude Wanniski, and Buffalo House Republican Jack Kemp. The Laffer Curve supposedly showed that massive tax cuts would generate far more revenue than they lost in cuts. For a half century Republicans had scolded that Democrats were bad because they handed out a free lunch at taxpayer expense. Republicans were the party of fiscal responsibility, and Democrats were the party of irresponsibility. Reagan turned this tradition on its head by embracing the magical world of supply-side deliverance. Now Republicans offered a free lunch bonanza to all taxpayers, especially the rich. Everybody except the poor would get something, and the tax cuts would generate a historic windfall of economic growth. The Reagan White House had to forecast how the economy would develop as a basis for calculating its proposals. Supply-side advisors wanted a very high figure for real growth in gross domestic product (GDP) in order to prove that their proposals worked. Monetarists wanted a low "in money" GDP (real GDP plus the rate of inflation) to prove that their policies held down prices. The two camps figured out what would have to happen to make their contradictory policies come true; then they claimed it would happen. Stockman subsequently provided a mind-boggling account of the unhinged mentality that tripled the nation's debt in eight years. Every prediction of the Reagan White House failed, except the political one that tax cuts are wildly popular.[141]

Reagan led the Republican Party and a host of enabling Reagan Democrats into temptation by persuading both that deficits don't matter because tax cuts more than pay for themselves, especially at the upper end. When he took office in 1981 the national debt was $907 billion, approximately 26 percent of GDP. Eight years later the tripled debt represented 40 percent of GDP. Reagan did it by cutting the marginal tax rate from 70 percent to 28 percent, cutting the top rate on capital gains from 49 percent to 20 percent, and dramatically hiking military spending—an additional 4 percent increase on top of the 5 percent increase for 1981 authorized by Carter. This staggering splurge of social engineering fueled a huge inequality surge, which Reagan officials described as a return to the economic state of nature. The promised trickle-down effect of Reaganomics never materialized because only corporations and the wealthy gained new disposable income. Nationwide, savings actually declined under Reagan. On his watch the United States went from being the world's leading creditor nation to being its leading debtor nation. The nation's historic reliance on corporate taxes as a chief source of revenue was rescinded, as was its half century of assuming that decent treatment of the poor and vulnerable is an American value.[142]

Harrington described Reaganomics as "Keynesianism for the rich" and inveighed against its cruelty to the poor. But he could not take Reagan seriously as a political thinker or leader. Reagan, he said, was a symptom of a massive structural change and a political backlash. Harrington argued that the first wave of deindustrialization affected black males before it ravaged entire industries and regions. Deindustrialization created different kinds of structural poverty, driven by impersonal economic forces, eliminating the kinds of jobs that previously lifted the poor out of poverty. In *The New American Poverty* (1984) Harrington highlighted the differences from 1962. He said he would rather write in the style of *The Other America:* "I wish I could once more evoke poverty, suggest its look, its smell, its often twisted spirit, with just a few rudimentary references to the underlying trends." But wretched sweatshops had returned to American cities because of the macroeconomic structures. He cautioned that the transition to a global economy could not be avoided, which was very different from the policy of punishing the most vulnerable Americans: "We have done that to ourselves." *The New American Poverty* grimly reflected that crises do not make people compassionate: "They are frightening, and most people concentrate on saving themselves. Thoughts of 'brothers' or 'sisters,' who are moral kin but not one's blood relatives, are a luxury many cannot afford."[143]

It repelled Harrington that the political right became powerful by blaming the victims for their poverty. He drew upon sociologist Leonard Goodwin's study of the attitudes of poor Americans toward work. Goodwin found that poor people overwhelmingly expressed a strong desire to work that crossed racial, gender, and regional lines. What distinguished their attitude toward work was their estimate of their chance to succeed, not their desire to work. They held a work ethic but had little confidence that they would be able to act on it. Goodwin said poor whites had more confidence in their life chances than black Americans who were not poor; otherwise the crucial factor in the so-called culture of poverty was that the poor experienced failure and humiliation in the labor market. Thus they settled for welfare dependency and were branded as deviants in blame-the-victim books and political speeches.[144]

Harrington grew more chastened with each year of Reagan's first term. Leftist historians, following Italian Communist Antonio Gramsci, tellingly named the entire capitalist era from 1920 to 1973 after car baron Henry Ford. Harrington followed convention, describing Ford as the first to understand that the new technology of the early twentieth century required a transformation of the society, not just the factory or the economy. Ford made cars with clever ingenuity, borrowing ideas from bicycle producers, sewing machine producers, cigarette makers, and meat packers. He mechanized the flow of auto production and its individual components, creating the greatest factory ever seen, the Model T assembly line. But his genius move was to take seriously the old

Socialist slogan that workers should be paid enough to buy what they produce. Ford paid his workers high wages, treated them decently, created his own distribution system of franchised auto dealers, and provided cheap credit for car buyers. Gramsci, pondering Ford's business model from a prison cell in 1929, said Ford inaugurated a new epoch in capitalism—Fordism, a form of rationalized production that created a new type of consumer and citizen. It helped that Ford was an American who lacked feudal encumbrances to throw off. Harrington noted that Fordism had an ironic relationship to the New Deal. Ford knew what he was doing at the business level, but he bitterly opposed the New Deal, like the entire capitalist class. FDR only half believed in Keynesian medicine, but he saved American capitalism by nationalizing Fordism, forging a new social contract that worked until the 1970s.[145]

Harrington grappled anxiously with the stagflation, uneven growth, and threats to the welfare state that were the legacy of the 1970s. He said he felt closer on this subject to free enterprise conservative Friedrich Hayek than to liberals because Hayek understood that the prosperity of the fifties and sixties was not coming back, and liberals refused to believe the world had changed. Hayek claimed that the New Deal violated eternal laws of economics and human nature, eventually reaping what it sowed. The crisis of the seventies and eighties was the natural free market punishing Keynesian hubris. Harrington acknowledged that liberalism collided head-on with the structural limitations of the system it improved. Working- and middle-class Americans no longer expected to live better than their parents. America's decline as a world economic power cost Carter his second term. Then America turned to Reagan, an amiable ideologue lacking a vision for the really existing world.[146]

In May 1981 Mitterrand was elected as the first Socialist president of the Fifth Republic. The following month the PS won an absolute majority in parliament and Mitterrand named Socialist Pierre Mauroy as prime minister, appointing four Communists to the cabinet. Mitterrand campaigned on a detailed economic program called 110 Propositions for France that the PS crafted in alliance with the Communist Party and the Left Radical Party. The PS said it was socialist, not social democratic; it sought to transform society, not make capitalism more humane. Mitterrand enacted his entire campaign program, nationalizing banks and key industries, increasing social benefits, instituting a 10 percent increase in the minimum wage, and enacting a solidarity tax on wealth. He sought to boost economic demand and achieve full employment with a stimulus specifically designed to help the poorest the most. His stimulus did help the poorest French citizens, but the economy stagnated, unemployment worsened, the Bank of France maintained a stringent monetary policy, and the franc was devalued three times.

Mitterrand began to retreat in 1982, while police battled right-wing students in the streets. In March 1983 he capitulated, switching to an austerity plan that gave highest priority to wringing inflation out of the economy. Mitterrand figured, rightly, that his best chance of staying in power was to make France competitive in the European Monetary System. Reagan could run up colossal trade and government deficits and get away with it as long as the American majority felt better by November 1984, but smaller deficits mortally threatened France's standing in the world market. Mitterrand carried out France's greatest political decentralization since Napoleon, workers won the right to speak on workplace economic issues, and Mitterrand won plaudits from the *Wall Street Journal* for refusing to bail out France's largest industrial equipment maker, Creusot-Loire. In political terms Mitterrand's adjustment worked, more or less. He had a respectable run as a social democratic manager, winning reelection in 1988 and remaining in office until 1995. Harrington, however, took little consolation that French Socialists held on to power. Nationalizing the banks had not helped and neither did Mitterrand's Keynesian stimulus. Harrington said the only nation where Mitterrand's aggressive approach might have worked was the United States, but the United States instituted Keynesianism for the rich. It was easy to say that Mitterrand should have stuck to his convictions the way Reagan stuck to his. Many said so, but not Harrington. The world was going through a wrenching transition that couldn't be helped. What mattered was to limit the harm to workers and the poor.[147]

For two years Reagan presided over worse misery than anything Mitterrand could stand or survive. When Reagan took office, unemployment was slightly under 7 percent; by November 1982 it was just under 11 percent, the worst since the Depression, while safety net assistance was slashed. Many of the four million Americans who lost their jobs lost well-paying industrial jobs that never came back. Liberals crowed that Reagan was sure to be a one-term failure like Carter. The Democratic establishment played it safe by limiting the 1982 Philadelphia midterm convention to party appointees and officials—quashing Democratic Agenda. Harrington warned in November 1982 that Democrats were overconfident and shortsighted. Lower wages, reduced inflation, lower interest rates, fear of unemployment, and shuttered plants might combine to revive the economy just in time to reelect Reagan. All of it would be on the backs of the poor and downsized, but Republicans had that figured. Harrington's prediction bore out after the defense buildup and consumer spending on credit kicked in. Unemployment was down to 3.5 percent when Reagan crushed Democratic candidate Walter Mondale in 1984. Mondale was scorned as a tax-and-spend liberal *and* for warning about Reagan's deficits and militarism.

Harrington rued that Mondale united all the forces in the Democratic coalition and still got blown away by a brief recovery. This wasn't like Carter losing because Mondale was a good candidate.[148]

Harrington said too many liberals reminded him of Herbert Hoover in 1932, believing that a bit of growth and lower exchange rates for the dollar would bring back prosperity. Mondale called for industrial policies that resisted runaway deindustrialization, but Americans rewarded Reagan's version of happy talk, and Harrington urged the left to rethink its basic orientation. The welfare state did not come into existence in any nation through a thought-out plan. It was the piece of socialism that Social Democrats found they could achieve after World War II; even Sweden is only a half exception to the rule that the welfare state is a hodgepodge of political compromises founded on the postwar economic boom. Harrington argued that socialists should not treat the welfare state as their definitive achievement. Democratic socialists differed from liberals in regarding the structural limits of the system as historical and changeable. To socialists, winning democratic control was primary and shoring up the welfare state was secondary.[149]

"We never said the welfare state is a substitute for socialism." This staple of Harrington's lecture touring had a flip side, his retort to old-school socialists: "Any idiot can nationalize a bank." He said both things frequently after Mitterrand retreated to inflation-fighting stability. Reviewer Christopher Lehmann-Haupt noted that Harrington wrote a lot of meandering sentences and vague exhortations after his perplexities set in. Harrington's book *The Next Left* (1986) skillfully weaved patterns out of the past that never quite built up to its title. But he stuck to his core message, sometimes putting it succinctly: "The issue of the twenty-first century and of the late twentieth century is, can that collective tendency be made democratic and responsible? Can it be made compatible with freedom?" He believed that freedom will survive the ascendance of globalized markets and corporations only if it takes the form of decentralized economic democracy. Into the early 1980s Harrington said the market should operate within an economic plan without determining its basic priorities. He spoke for the rest of his life about the market operating within a plan, but in the mid-1980s his actual position shifted to the opposite. He conceived planning within a market framework on the model of Swedish and German Social Democracy—solidarity wages, full employment, codetermination, and collective worker funds. The later Harrington was an advocate of plans operating within the market. To many critics that smacked of selling out socialism; he replied: "To think that 'socialization' is a panacea is to ignore the socialist history of the twentieth century, including the experience of France under

Mitterrand. I am for worker- and community-controlled ownership and for an immediate and practical program for full employment which approximates as much of that ideal as possible. No more. No less."[150]

DSOC never scaled up to what it wanted to be. Always there were anxieties about its image, its position, and Harrington's limitations. Was DSOC too close to Kennedy and the liberal Democrats? Should the conventions cut back on union speakers? How could the union leaders be slighted when they paid for everything? One telling problem was that DSOC had very few people from the generation slightly older than me. In 1980 most of our members were either older than forty or younger than twenty-five. At two national board meetings we discussed this problem uncomfortably. Some of us had friends who wanted to join a democratic socialist organization, but not DSOC. They were not going to hang out with Old Left Social Democrats and Harrington's union buddies. Harrington took this problem personally; there seemed to be no end to paying for his past. Thus he was willing to merge with the New American Movement (NAM).

NAM was a New Left socialist organization that morphed into a U.S. American version of Euro-Communism. Former SDS leader Michael Lerner called it into existence in 1971 to create something from the ruins of SDS. He had grown up in a nonreligious Zionist family in Newark, New Jersey, met Heschel at a Hebrew-speaking Conservative religious camp, and at the age of twelve become a religious non-Zionist. Later he studied under Heschel at Jewish Theological Seminary during his college days at Columbia University. In the 1960s Lerner earned a PhD in philosophy at Berkeley, turned radical, and chaired its SDS chapter from 1966 to 1968. He lurched to the action faction of SDS, which spurned theory in the name of "super-democracy." Lerner organized sit-ins against CIA and ROTC recruiters on campus and felt no allegiance to the national SDS organization, believing it was irrelevant.

Then SDS exploded in June 1969, and Lerner was devastated, "a heartbreaking experience for me and many others." In September he began teaching philosophy at the University of Washington at Seattle, where he founded the Seattle Liberation Front (SLF) and puzzled over what went wrong in SDS. Lerner pointed to three things—the cult of Third World revolution, the cult of violence in the Black Power movement, and the contempt of SDS for working-class whites. He vowed to create a liberationist organization that didn't make these mistakes, modeling what sane radical socialism looked like. Lerner organized a statewide ballot initiative to lower the tax burden on working people, clashing with SLF comrades who opposed bourgeois tax reforms and aligning with working-class whites. He also organized a major antiwar demonstration and was indicted for it—"I was indicted for my role as the supposedly evil professor who was turning my students into revolutionaries." In 1971 he co-organized the biggest of the Washington, DC, antiwar demonstrations and was still under indictment when he founded NAM and wrote its declaration of principles.[151]

Lerner was determined to recover the humanistic, revolutionary SDS that was lost. The Weathermen had taken over the SDS national office, dissolved SDS, and destroyed its records, ostensibly to thwart the FBI. That eliminated the information needed to reconstruct SDS, an organization of nearly one hundred thousand members. The Weathermen construed their terrorism and hooliganism as antiracist solidarity, accusing Lerner of betraying the revolution with a frivolous tax reform. He later recalled, "I was increasingly thinking that we needed to understand the psychological dynamics that led people to self-destroy their own movement, that manifested both in the way that SDS self-destroyed at its national convention in Chicago and in the way that the Seattle Liberation Front was being torn apart by people who claimed they wanted a revolution but simultaneously were characterizing working people as irredeemably reactionary because of their white skin privilege."[152]

Lerner, SLF leader Chip Marshall, and Lerner's partner Theirrie Evelyn Cook founded NAM in Davenport, Iowa, in November 1971, eschewing the usual university towns. Lerner's call letter said the new organization should reach out to working people and reject all forms of Communist dictatorship: "I wanted this organization to overcome the anti-intellectualism that had come into fashion in SDS around 1968 and cease romanticizing the anti-imperialist and anti-racist struggles that led to a fawning acceptance of anything that came from nonwhite sources no matter how immoral or self-destructive." He thought the call would draw perhaps a hundred like-minded people. Instead, four hundred came to Davenport, sorting into four groups. One was a mixture of anarchists and self-styled Maoists averse to all leaders. Another consisted of refugees from the Communist Party who chafed at criticism of "real existing socialism" in Russia, China, and Eastern Europe. A group of radical feminists wanted NAM to emphasize woman-identified feminism and contest the leadership of Lerner and Cook. The fourth group was more or less what Lerner wanted, eager to base a new organization on a campaign for tax justice. Lerner despaired at his invention: "I was shocked and profoundly disappointed." He also felt hijacked: "We imagined that their disagreements with us would lead them to ignore and denounce our efforts rather than cause them to show up and take over what we started." Some founders wanted to form a cadre organization, some wanted to reinvent SDS anarchy, and some just didn't like Lerner. He won a few arguments. The convention resolved that NAM would be a democratic socialist mass organization that worked in multiple ways and incorporated the liberation of women and nonwhites into every NAM program. But Lerner knew he couldn't play a leadership role in this group and doubted he could be in it: "In front of our eyes, the antileadership and superdemocracy tendencies reemerged in precisely the ways that would guarantee endless debate and no serious unified strategy."[153]

NAM churned through nonleading leaders in its early years until SDS veterans Richard Healey and Roberta Lynch filled the vacuum. Healey was a gifted Chicago organizer and mathematician with a legendary mother, longtime California Communist leader Dorothy Healey, and Lynch was a Chicago organizer with a strong leadership style. Healey's geniality enabled the organization to finesse its faction that wanted no leaders. Then he judged that NAM had a bigger problem with perfectionist leftism. NAM had the intensity and ethos of a cadre organization but could not agree on a political program. Every reform proposal elicited the objection that reformism strengthens the system by acknowledging bourgeois legality. Lerner and his original ten organizers, including Lynd and Weinstein, drifted away, and NAM lost its three biggest chapters when the Maoists walked out. By 1975 NAM was down to 350 members. In 1974 Healey slowed the downward spiral by persuading his mother to join. Dorothy Healey had joined the Communist Party in 1928, led its Los Angeles district for over twenty years, spread its message as a radio commentator, denounced the Soviet invasion of Czechoslovakia, tried to bend the party to her anti-authoritarian beliefs, and resigned in 1973. She brought her friends into NAM, which bolstered its Euro-Communist wing.[154]

In Europe Euro-Communism was a major movement of parties and organizations founded by Communist Party leaders. It adopted reformist and parliamentary methods for adjusted pro-Communist ends. NAM became the closest thing to an American equivalent. The name New American Movement was literal for the New Leftists and symbolically loaded for the former Communists, allowing both to affirm their Americanism. Richard Healey had joined in the first place when he read Lerner's call for a New American Movement; the name seemed exactly right to him. By 1975 he was deeply chastened, realizing that coming of age in the 1960s had not prepared him or his friends for the crushing neoliberal turn in capitalism. They were children of the greatest mass mobilization since the 1930s, but the mass movements were dying and trade unions were under assault. NAM renewed itself by running socialist schools in church basements, emphasizing its socialist feminism, conducting grassroots direct action and anticorporate organizing, and adopting Gramsci-style cultural Marxism. It built strong chapters in Los Angeles, San Francisco, Chicago, Pittsburgh, and Dayton, and 50 percent of its leaders were female.

Socialist feminism was fundamental to NAM, where feminism did not escalate into more-radical-than-thou attacks on other women. NAM leaders Lynch, Barbara Ehrenreich, Judith Kegan Gardiner, Holly Graff, Torie Osborn, and Chris Riddiough combined gender criticism with an emphasis on the necessity of political struggle. Ehrenreich got her start as a writer by writing about it. She grew up in Butte, Montana, graduated in 1963 from Reed College, and earned a PhD in cellular immunology in 1968 from Rockefeller University but never pursued a career in science. In 1970 she gave birth to a daughter at a public clinic in New York and instantly became a feminist in reaction to a physician who induced labor so the staff could go home. Ehrenreich taught and wrote in the 1970s about women's health, teaming with feminist journalist Deirdre English. She joined New York NAM and wrote its signature statement on socialist feminism, calling for "a socialist feminist kind of feminism and a socialist feminist kind of socialism." Radical feminism that failed to struggle for political justice was not very radical, she argued; at the same time, mechanical Marxism wholly misconstrued what feminism is about by consigning the so-called woman question to a compartmentalized superstructure. Ehrenreich said Marxism and feminism hold a crucial thing in common—both are critical ways of interpreting the world that shred social conventions, construing the world in terms of antagonisms. You can't be a Marxist or a feminist, she said, and remain a spectator; to grasp the reality exposed by Marxism and feminism is "to move into action to change it."[155]

Marxism is a theory of economic exploitation, showing that inequality arises from social processes that are intrinsic to capitalism as an economic system; the system of class rule rests directly on forcible exploitation. Feminism is a theory about the universality of sexual oppression, showing that male rule rests on the fact of male violence; the threat of male assault coerces rebellious women to conform and drives compliant women into complicity with male rule. Ehrenreich said it was fine to combine Marxism and feminism as a hybrid but better to aim for a synthesis. The hybrid pairing always raises the question of which form of oppression cuts deeper, and it gets in the way of understanding sexism within the historical context of capitalism. Integrated socialist feminism construes monopoly capitalism as a political-economic-cultural totality. It has room for feminist issues having nothing to do with modes of production, and the room is not a superstructure. Ehrenreich said the promise of socialist feminism, yet to be realized, was to be the common ground between Marxism and feminism, synthesizing class and sex, and capitalism and male domination.

NAM contributed mightily to the Gramsci boom of the 1970s and 1980s. Stanley Aronowitz taught in the early 1970s at Meier's public high school in East

Harlem, published a noted book in 1973 on the American working class, and joined NAM in 1976 upon moving to the University of California-Irvine. He and Carl Boggs, a NAM stalwart and prolific social theorist, also taught at the Los Angeles Socialist School, housed in a Unitarian Universalist church. NAM did its most influential work in the schools, where Aronowitz, Healey, and Boggs grafted Gramsci into the organization and built relationships with activists. Aronowitz and Healey taught a weeklong school on Gramsci each year before the national meeting, fixing on Gramsci's distinction between wars of maneuver and position. Wars of maneuver are revolutionary struggles for power, as occurred between 1917 and 1920. Wars of position are party-building struggles featuring united fronts, reform programs, and battles on the cultural level against bourgeois conventions. NAM identified with Gramsci's signature prescription, "Pessimism of the mind, optimism of the will," and embraced his distinct emphasis on the importance of culture war. Gramsci taught that radical intellectuals have a crucial role to play in wars of position—building counter-hegemonic institutions such as schools, newspapers, journals, and other media.[156]

Yet NAM lacked the intellectual firepower and social impact of DSOC. NAM said it was the real thing because it was democratic socialist, whereas DSOC was social democratic. But by Gramsci's standard, NAM didn't compare to DSOC. In the mid-1970s NAM and DSOC gingerly drew closer to each other. Some individuals followed Radosh and Weinstein in joining both groups, and NAM and DSOC cooperated on a few projects. In 1977 Lynch attended the DSOC convention as an invited guest, still with her guard up. She said DSOC was misguided because aligning with Democrats and labor bosses doesn't build socialism. Healey decided, however, that NAM needed to imagine a merger; NAM organizer Harry Boyte agreed; DSOC insider Jim Chapin encouraged Harrington to consider it; and Lynch began to waver. Healey envied the success of Democratic Agenda. He pressed the case for a merger, never mind that his mother led the opposition to it. Lynch rued that NAM played no role—unlike DSOC—in the Progressive Chicago Action Network that bridged the racial divide in Chicago politics and later helped elect Harold Washington as mayor. DSOC had impressive youth leaders that NAM could not dismiss as Old Left knockoffs: Joe Schwartz, Mark Levinson, Penny Schantz, and Jeremy Karpatkin. Many NAM activists relinquished their romanticism about Third World revolutions after Pol Pot conducted a horrible genocide in Cambodia and the Communist takeover in Vietnam was as brutal as the social democrats had warned. A certain grudging respect for social democratic circumspection took hold. In 1980 NAM voted by two to one to negotiate with DSOC. New Left academics, searching for a usable past, were seizing on

Popular Front Communism, which strengthened Healey's hand as he negotiated with DSOC. Harrington was no help with the usable past problem; he was trying to overcome his past. But he had built the united front of the 1970s.[157]

Ben Ross and Alex Spinrad led the fight against merging with NAM, welcoming the support of Howe and Michael Walzer. The Committee Against the NAM Merger charged that NAM was bad on Israel and incompatible with DSOC. Why should DSOC bond with SDS exiles and pro-Communists who trashed Socialists for years, indulged Communists, turned Communist, and destroyed their own movement? Exaggerated things were said at the 1981 DSOC convention in Philadelphia about the supposed anti-Israel stance of NAM. A tone of anger I never heard previously in DSOC raged in factional caucuses that were also new to DSOC. NAM called for recognition of the Palestine Liberation Organization (PLO) but so did most of the SI parties. NAM had only a handful of pro-Palestinian activists, a group outnumbered by its Jewish Zionist former Communist flank in the orbit of *Jewish Currents*, edited by Zionist NAM stalwart Morris Schappes. In the end the two organizations agreed to support negotiations with the PLO *and* U.S. military aid to Israel. This was the only issue on which DSOC demanded a specific commitment. NAM accepted the DSOC position that Communist parties are not socialist, and DSOC agreed that the merged organization would establish regional offices in Chicago and San Francisco.[158]

The unity convention of March 20–21, 1982, founded DSA. Harrington chaired the new organization; NAM members Lynch, Ehrenreich, Richard Healey, and black historian Manning Marable were named to the national board, as were DSOC members Meier, Howe, Winpisinger, and gay rights activist Harry Britt. The word "synergy" was invoked several times, registering the conviction that the merger would attract new members. DSOC had four thousand members, NAM had thirteen hundred, and the following year DSA counted seven thousand members; Cornel West was one of the newcomers. DSA boasted that it was the nation's largest democratic socialist organization since 1935, but it melted as fast as it grew, shrinking to five thousand by 1987. The offices in Chicago and San Francisco were lost, leaving chagrined former NAM members in a New York–based organization. Healey and Boyte fell away from the organization, pursuing independent grassroots organizing projects; Harrington and Ehrenreich disliked each other, co-convening awkward meetings; and it became hard not to notice that synergy had not happened.

DSA was a better organization than DSOC had been, but DSA accentuated the old DSOC problem of uniting activists primarily devoted to feminism, antiracism, gay and lesbian rights, antimilitarism, labor, Third World solidarity, religious socialism, environmentalism, and other causes. It featured even less of a distinct socialist perspective than DSOC had managed, with a higher quotient of identity politics. DSA became a significant player in Central American solidarity activism, which helped to propel Radosh and Robert Lieber into the neocon right. It launched Lynch and Jo Ann Mort into prominent union careers; Lynch scaled the ranks of AFSCME to become executive director of AFSCME Council 31, and Mort moved from directing Democratic Agenda to serving as director of communications for Unite and ACTWU, the predecessor unions to Workers United, an affiliate of Service Employees International Union. DSA boosted the writing careers of Ehrenreich, Marable, Kate Ellis, John Judis, Harold Meyerson, and Adolph Reed Jr. It stressed the interconnectedness of all social justice, peace, postcolonial, and ecological issues. West explained that he joined DSA and stayed in it because he needed to belong to some organization that cared about everything he cared about. That was the best argument for DSA, but there were never enough people who felt that way.

Ehrenreich and Harrington became cochairs in 1983, with mixed results at best. Many of us puzzled over and regretted the aversion between them, delicately steering around it. Ehrenreich wrote funny, sharp, wonderfully snarky op-eds on Nancy Reagan, housework, religious cults, television sitcoms, obnoxious males, political hacks, corporate greed, and other tribulations; two of her collections were titled *The Worst Years of Our Lives* (1990) and *The Snarling Citizen* (1995). On occasion she admonished women to stop peddling guilt about abortion, declaring that she felt none about her two abortions. In 2001 she wrote an instant classic of muckraking journalism, *Nickel and Dimed,* a chronicle of her three months of labor as a waitress, hotel maid, house cleaner, nursing-home aide, and Walmart clerk. Ehrenreich helped DSA survive the wilderness years, writing restless, scathing, passionate, plucky, luminous op-eds and books. Many DSA members were volunteer workers in Jesse Jackson's Democratic primary campaigns of 1984 and 1988; I was one of them. Harrington was skittish about Jackson in 1984 because electing Mondale seemed imperative. Afterward Jackson won him over and Harrington wrote speeches for him in 1988. Jackson tried to build a Rainbow Coalition of social movements that outlasted the election cycle, extending the legacy of the civil rights movement. Many of us Jackson volunteers worked harder for Mondale in the general election than we managed four years later for Michael Dukakis, and others dropped out completely by Dukakis time. We did not talk about realignment except to say that we no longer believed in it. Even Harrington said there were no political parties anymore. Hollowed out "dealignment" was the reality, organized anarchism. Political adventurers roamed the countryside to build their personal following, armed with state-of-the-art technology, battling each other like rival warlords. When they won they tried to govern by patching together ad hoc coalitions. Harrington believed this trajectory would eventually throw the entire system into a crisis. He didn't claim to know what would happen next. He said he just wanted democratic socialists to be ready to be relevant.[159]

In 1985 he learned he had metastatic carcinoma, a secondary growth indicating that he had a serious primary cancer lurking somewhere, which was found at the base of his tongue. Harrington underwent treatment and had a successful operation. For two years he returned to road lecturing, bringing more newcomers into DSA than it lost from death or drifting away. The Youth Section was active in the Central American and South African solidarity struggles, and in 1987 a DSA-led coalition called Justice for All held rallies, teach-ins, and press conferences in more than one hundred cities protesting against cuts in Medicaid, food stamps, welfare, and federal aid to housing. Harrington had reason to believe, as he did, that DSA was doing reasonably well despite everything. Sometimes he read too much into drawing a big crowd.

In November 1987 he struggled to swallow, went back for a checkup, and learned he had a new and inoperable tumor in his esophagus. The verdict was that he had six months to two years left. Harrington vowed immediately to write a capstone book. Meanwhile he wrote a public letter declaring that ever since Nixon was elected in 1968 and especially since Reagan was elected and reelected, "I have been waiting for the wind to shift, for the turn to the left to begin. But now it is utterly clear that that long awaited moment is coming in the foreseeable future." Surely America was about to turn away from "the meanness and greed and militarism that have dominated us for so long." Harrington lamented that his cancer "could not have come at a worse time. . . . Here I am trying to deal with chemotherapy when I want to be out there pushing the movement forward when the change comes." He said the sixties might have gone better had the socialists of the fifties not been weak and divided and unimaginative. Now the next great left opportunity was approaching and it was imperative to build a strong, united, imaginative movement: "I hope I have a future and I fight each day to see that I will have one. But I *know* that *we* have a future—I long ago wagered my life on that—and I ask you to do as much as you can to make it happen."[160]

In June 1988 his friends organized a sixtieth birthday celebration at the Roseland Dance Hall in New York. Kennedy, Winpisinger, Steinem, Chavez, and Canadian Socialist leader Ed Broadbent spoke. Kennedy said, "In our lifetime it is Michael Harrington who has come the closest to fulfilling the vision of America that my brother Robert Kennedy had, when he said, 'Some men see things as they are and say, Why? But I dream things that never were and say,

Why not?' Some call it Socialism; I call it the Sermon on the Mount."
Harrington responded with his favorite set piece, the water parable. In desert
societies, he said, water is so precious it is money. People fight and die for it;
marriages are arranged to secure it; and governments rise and fall in pursuit of
it. Entire societies stretched over several millennia have taken for granted that
fighting over water is ingrained in human nature. Many such deserts still exist,
deeply conditioning the human beings that live within them. Yet in modern
societies we expect not to die of thirst: "Water is the one thing that has been
socialized. Hoarding it, fighting over it, marrying for it are *not* part of human
nature after all—*because we have confidence that it will be shared.* So why can't
we go a little further and imagine societies in which each person also has food
and shelter? In which everybody has an education and a chance to know their
value? Why not?"[161]

Harrington took seriously the necessity of believing in ordinary people.
Often he told campus audiences, "If you consider your country capable of democratic socialism, you must do two things. First you must deeply love and trust
your country. You must sense the dignity and humanity of the people who survive and grow within your country despite the injustices of its system. And second, you must recognize that the social vision to which you are committing
yourself will never be fulfilled in your lifetime." Sometimes he put it with a
Christianized gloss: "I am running toward the kingdom of humanity and I am
aware that I will never see it. Perhaps no one will." After the lecture was over
and Heineken time had commenced at a hotel bar, he could be bleak about
where history was going. He hated the kind of leftism that paraded self-righteous superiority and tagged every opponent as a fascist, but in private he would
allow that the emerging system of global corporate giants wedded to pliant governments was "a kind of fascism."

Every Harrington lecture had three points that he announced at the outset.
His last book, *Socialism: Past and Future* (1989), expounded his signature tril-
ogy of points: (1) Socialism is the hope of human freedom and justice under the
conditions of bureaucratic collectivism. (2) The fate of freedom and justice
depends upon social and economic structures. (3) Capitalism will subvert the
possibilities of freedom and justice that capitalism fostered unless it is subjected
to democratic control from below. Harrington fastened on the contradictory
meanings of "socialization" and the ambiguous legacy of Marx related to them.
Marx caught the crucial contradiction of capitalism by describing it as private
collectivism. Capitalism is an antisocial form of socialization that began by
expropriating the labor power of the individual. Peasants were driven from their
land, artisans were deskilled, and a regime of collective property replaced indi-

vidualistic private property in the name of securing it. Harrington allowed that Marx overbelieved in contradiction dialectics, believing that capitalism would abolish itself after it abolished feudalism—the negation of the negation. This mistake about capitalist self-abolition, however, obscures that Marx was right about capitalism destroying its own best achievement. Harrington's last book updated his argument that late capitalism subverts freedom and justice by enlisting the state to subsidize its interests, socialize its losses, and protect the rule of elites.[162]

Socialization can refer to the centralization and interdependence of capitalist society under the control of an elite or to bottom-up democratic control. Harrington wanted to say that socialization is really only the latter, while the former should be called collectivism. But that would have been misleading. Socialization can mean different things, capitalism is often subtle, and there is such a thing as state collectivist socialism. On capitalist subtlety, he pointed to Reagan, who employed the power of the state to carry out a class-based reduction of taxes to subsidize a rich minority. Reagan used social power on behalf of an elite, but it would be strange to describe Reaganomics as collectivization. On the other hand, conservatives constantly describe socialism as collectivist, not without warrant in many cases, but state ownership and control is not the objective of good socialism. Harrington said nationalization suited the socialist movement in only one brief phase of its history, and in modern times it "has become the nostalgia of a flawed memory at best, and reactionary at worst."[163]

Good socialism is about "empowering people at the base, which can animate a whole range of measures, some of which we do not even yet imagine." Harrington's favorite current example was in trouble in 1989, as he knew. The star of the Eurosocialism conference in 1980, from a policy standpoint, was Rudolf Meidner, a German economist for the Confederation of Swedish Trade Unions (LO). He was a Jewish socialist from Breslau who fled Nazi Germany in 1933 at the age of nineteen and became a Swedish citizen ten years later. Meidner and LO economist Gösta Rehn devised the economic policy undergirding Sweden's advanced welfare state, the Rehn–Meidner Model. It was instituted in 1951, three years before Meidner earned his doctorate under Gunnar Myrdal at the Stockholm School of Economics. Rehn–Meidner featured a centralized system of wage bargaining combining a solidarity wage policy and a state-run pension system built on collective savings, both in tandem with Sweden's high-tech, export-oriented focus on international trade.[164]

Wages were set to ensure approximately equal pay for equal work, assigning high rates to inefficient firms and low rates to productive, competitive firms. The model deliberately forced inefficient firms to improve or die, simultaneously promoting efficiency and equality. It committed the state to retrain and relocate displaced workers and promoted decommodification by eroding the connection between the marginal productivity of individual firms and wage rates. Rehn–Meidner helped to create the most egalitarian society in Europe, while Sweden's focus on high-tech exports avoided the inefficiency problems that plagued insular welfare states. Swedish Social Democracy was so successful in the 1950s and 1960s that even Meidner felt no need to supplement the nation's wage policy with a profit-sharing scheme. In 1975 he changed his mind, partly by studying Germany's debate over profit sharing.[165]

The German Trade Union Confederation (DGB) was the first, in the late 1960s, to push for social funds, proposing to create worker-controlled company funds by taxing major company profits. The DGB failed to enact it, but Meidner picked it up in 1975, when the proposal acquired a name: the Meidner Plan. It called for an annual 20 percent tax on major company profits to be paid in the form of stock to eight regional mutual funds. Worker, consumer, and government representatives controlled the funds. As their proportion of stock ownership grew, these groups were collectively entitled to representation on company boards. Locals and branch funds jointly held voting rights of the employee shares. In 1976 the LO embraced the Meidner Plan, and the Social Democrats had an anguished debate over it. Palme pleaded that Sweden didn't need to socialize the economy; ordinary Social Democracy worked just fine. In 1976 the Social Democrats beat the second-place Centre Party by 18 percent but lost the election, thwarted by campaign attacks on Meidner socialism. Forty-four years of Social Democratic governance in Sweden came to an end. In 1982 the Social Democrats regained power and enacted a weak version of the Meidner Plan but downplayed it as much as possible, trying not to scare the investor class.[166]

A 40 percent ceiling was placed on the amount of stock the eight funds in total could own of any single firm, and the funds were managed conventionally. Still, even with a 40 percent ceiling the Meidner Plan would have eventually rendered effective control over Swedish companies to the worker and public organizations. Since the funds represented part of workers' compensation, the plan contained a built-in system of wage restraints and facilitated a new form of capital formation. It required no program of nationalization, and investors still sought the highest rate of return. Like most public bank models, the Meidner Plan separated risk in production from entrepreneurial risk, assigning production risks to worker-managed enterprises and entrepreneurial risks to the holding companies.[167]

The labor movement and Social Democrats stressed that benefits from the capital fund accrued to all wage earners, and the plan traded wage restraint for greater control over investment capital. Big-business groups howled against it incessantly, determined to kill it. They protested that small businesses didn't have to pay the tax and charged that unions were consumed with power lust. The capitalist class inveighed against its loss of control. Stock markets are the home turf of financiers, a privilege that Swedish capitalists defended aggressively. Managers of the worker funds, trying to legitimize themselves to the financial class, managed like ordinary fund managers, but that made the whole enterprise abstract to the general population.

Palme did the minimum for the worker funds, and in 1986 he was assassinated—a shock to Swedes that reverberated beyond everything political. To stir popular support for the Meidner Plan, Social Democrats needed to back it with industrial policies targeting specific needs—things that citizens could see at work in their communities during the period that Sweden's shipbuilding industry and other pillars of the manufacturing base were restructured. Harrington tracked this drama in his last days with disappointment and frustration. The charter for the Meidner Plan expired in 1990, and the Social Democrats lost the 1991 election; Harrington could see both outcomes coming. He lamented that Swedish workers took little interest in their nation's historic experiment in decentralized economic democracy, a greater venture than the Mondragon cooperatives in Spain or German codetermination. Only a small minority of Swedish workers wanted to take on the responsibility. Most were indifferent, and some were hostile. Harrington said this is what capitalism has done to working-class and middle-class people: "The capitalist attack on artisanal skill, the whole historic process that created a semi- and unskilled work force, has left a deep impression on society. Labor was widely degraded to the status of a painful means to the pleasurable end of consumption."[168]

Capitalism has created societies in which hardly anyone in the working class believes their work has a positive value. Harrington sympathized with the verdict of French social theorist André Gorz, as expressed in the title of his book *Farewell to the Working Class* (1982). Gorz said the left was overdue to sweep away the entire category and problematic of human experience as work. Postindustrial capitalism changed what socialism needs to be. Social salvation must be pursued in the domain of leisure time, the only place that workers and consumers experience social and political agency. Instead of pressing for the right to work or the rights of workers in workplaces, the left should press for an income regardless of work. Gorz argued that the green movement and the women's movement are the keys to the next socialism. Both refuse to accept the work ethic that was fundamental to early capitalism and every form of socialism. Gorz did not mean that the ecology movement or even an ecofeminist version of it is an end in itself. He said the green movement is a stage in the larger struggle for a society in which the only things of worth to each person are those that are good for all. In *Ecology as Politics* (1980) he argued that the left must not settle for a capitalism that adapts to some ecological restraints. The left must be a green-driven "social, economic, and cultural revolution that abolishes the constraints of capitalism and, in so doing, establishes a new relationship between the individual and society and between people and nature."[169]

Harrington embraced much of Gorz's argument about postindustrial realities, the importance of the green and feminist movements, and the political upshot of consumption-based identity. Workers want to spend less time thinking about their jobs or workplaces, period, even in Sweden. But Harrington countered that work is far too important in human experience to be consigned to the history and politics of a past era. Farewell ecologists like Gorz were stuck in a transition phase that was already passing. The new technologies were creating new kinds of work that demand reskilled workers and new kinds of workplaces. New forms of work were coming that engage and stimulate the intelligence of workers. Harrington began to write his last book on the day he was told his cancer was inoperable and he had little time left. *Socialism: Past and Future* was a letter to the next left. He implored it not to take a passive attitude toward the rush of forthcoming technology: "We should make the engineering of technology a political question, insisting that industry of every kind try to create machines that make jobs creative and interesting."[170]

The last new book he absorbed was *In the Age of the Smart Machine* (1988) by Harvard Business School social psychologist Shoshana Zuboff. It was an instantly classic study of information technology in the workplace. Zuboff described the duality of information technology in its informing and automating capacities, the range of intellectual skills demanded by information technology, the challenges of information technology to managerial authority and control, the tendency of information technology to turn the division of labor into a division of learning, and the collaborative nature of information work. Harrington seized on Zuboff's two-sided argument about the new technology and the old hierarchies. The same managerial class that introduced information technology did everything in its power to maintain the old hierarchies that information technology undermined. Zuboff explained that the managers of old justified their hierarchical status on the basis of their expertise. The justifying liberal right of private property did not work for them since they were paid functionaries of capital. They were bosses because they had a self-created monopoly of knowledge on how enterprises produce things and make money. But information technology introduced machines that are smarter than the corporate bureaucrats, and its logic is the opposite of the old capitalist de-skilling logic. Information technology is all about using minds and re-skilling. Drawing on Zuboff's account, Harrington asked, "If the managerial elite is no longer the monopolist of productive knowledge, why should it be accorded the obedience and prerequisites claimed in the past? Isn't there a disturbing egalitarianism implicit in the new means of production?"[171]

Zuboff told stories about psychologically conflicted managers summarizing the data on the transition to automated corporate systems. Repeatedly they gave lip service to using the new program to expand the initiative of workers *and* chose the program that invested in the intelligence of the machines, not human beings. The managers recognized the liberating potential of information technology but repressed it because it delegitimized their authority. The moral of the story, Harrington said: "The habits of the obsolete past dominate the possibility of a radically humane future." He did not mean the new technology would shower humane blessings on society if only the managers got out of the way. Harrington believed more than ever in bureaucratic collectivism and the rock-bottom necessity of radical democratic politics. The new technology, he warned, might very well create a reactionary social structure of accumulation: "There could be a future in which an elite patronizes a sophisticated work force, the middle of the class structure exists somewhat precariously outside the charmed circle of high technology, and a new poverty flourishes in a growing underclass at the bottom of the most productive society in history."[172]

That was spot-on in 1989. Harrington said it was "outrageous but inevitable" that the struggle over the ends of information technology would begin and be focused on "the societies of the privileged fifth of the race." Four centuries of colonial exploitation and oppression ensured this outcome. Even if "giant strides" toward global economic integration occurred, there was no chance of overcoming the four-century deficit "within the next fifty years." This was a major reason, he argued, why socialism needed to have a future. Only Socialists have a record of caring about everybody in entire societies and the world. Socialists do not let go of demanding freedom, equality, and community for everyone. Socialism is an invaluable tradition of anticapitalist criticism and is inherently international "for pragmatic reasons as well as for moral solidarity."[173]

Democratic socialism, on this telling, was gradualist but visionary—a stubborn and persistently reformist pressure for gains toward democratic self-determination. Harrington knew how that sounded to many of the readers he wanted. "Many people, still under the spell of the recent past, will find my futurism quixotic because it is so much at odds with the age of Reagan and Thatcher and Kohl." But Reagan, British Tory Margaret Thatcher, and German Conservative Helmut Kohl

depended on eighteenth-century rationales to justify their authoritarianism—
"myths of the invisible hand that justify the elitist maneuvers of the visible hand,
idylls of the organic community that facilitate the growth of mass society and create both a new poverty and a vacuous hedonism." Harrington urged socialists to
learn from their past failures how to create a better future. If they were willing,
"there is hope for freedom, solidarity, and justice" and perhaps even hope for a
visionary gradualism that meets the challenge of its time.[174]

Religion gnawed at him. Marx persuaded Harrington that religion was passing into oblivion, but Harrington worried about something that Marx lost no
sleep over: How shall Western societies inspire people to care about their own
moral character or that of their society? If religious ideas about the existence of
moral truth go down with the religions, what will happen to the virtues and to
common values? Harrington wrote a book on this problem in 1983, *The Politics
at God's Funeral*. He assigned a staggering ambition to democratic socialism—
to provide the legitimizing and integrating principle for Western societies that
Christianity once provided. Harrington called for a united front of religious and
secular socialists to redeem the values of religious socialism and fill the void left
by terminal Western religions. The new socialist united front, he said, would
recover the values of progressive Judaism and Christianity, but not in religious
form. It would require the religious wing to subordinate its religious concerns
to the needs of the movement in order to promote the ethical values it held in
common with other socialists. Harrington believed that progressive religious
values could survive without religion, and he assumed the religions were dying
anyway. Socialism was a vehicle to keep progressive religious values alive.[175]

"But Mike," I would say, "what if religion isn't dying? What if religion has a
better chance of surviving than socialism, because Schleiermacher was right
about the human impulse for mystery and sacred relationship? And what if the
socialist movement you want needs living, vital religious communities to sustain itself?" I never got very far with him on this subject. Marx and Freud set
Harrington straight about religion, and he didn't care to rethink that business,
much as it gnawed at him. The Christian flanks of DSOC and DSA were really
strong. We puzzled at the lack of a similar self-identifying Jewish-religious con-
tingent, grateful for the exceptions of Arthur Waskow and Arnold Jacob Wolf,
but the Christians in the Religion and Socialism committee provided ample
leadership for DSOC and DSA: James Luther Adams, John C. Cort, Harvey
Cox, Judith Deutsch, Marcia Dyson, Michael Eric Dyson, Mary Emil, John
Endler, Norm Faramelli, George G. Higgins, Joe Holland, Peter Laarman, Alex
Mikulich, David O'Brien, Maxine Phillips, Richard Poethig, Michael Rivas,
Rosemary Radford Ruether, Rod Ryon, David Seymour, Jack Spooner, Peter

Steinfels, Juanita Webster, Charles C. West, Cornel West, Loretta Williams, and others. Harrington liked that DSOC and DSA had so many theological types. He was religiously musical, calling himself a Catholic atheist. But his upbringing drilled into him that religion is about *believing certain things.* He could never quite fathom that many theologians and most religious studies scholars don't believe it.

Upward of one-third of the DSOC–DSA religious socialists were Catholics, notably Cort, Emil, Higgins, Holland, Mikulich, O'Brien, Ruether, and Steinfels, and hardly any were theologically conservative. The leading exception, Cort, edited the DSOC–DSA magazine *Religious Socialism* for many years and was sufficiently stubborn to make a ruckus at DSOC and DSA conventions about votes over abortion that he lost overwhelmingly. Cort ran the magazine with an ecumenical spirit. More important, he exemplified the history of American Catholic socialism. For decades, Catholics were there but not in the lead. They were there from the early worker parties and the Knights of Labor onward, but the Vatican railed against socialism until the 1960s, so Catholic unionists and progressives did not call themselves socialists, even when they were. Cort symbolized how that changed.

JOHN C. CORT, THE ACTU, AND CATHOLIC SOCIALISM

Cort grew up middle class and Episcopalian in Woodmere, Long Island, where his father was a schoolteacher. The family emphasis on school achievement enabled Cort to win a scholarship to a prep school in Watertown, Connecticut, which put him on track to get into Harvard in 1931. He remained blissfully unaware of the Depression until 1936. The poor sections of New York City that he glimpsed from a train window looked no worse to him in 1933 than in 1923, and none of his Harvard teachers talked about the catastrophe ravaging the poor, the entire working class, and much of the former middle class. The poor were always there, remote and unknown. At Harvard he studied the classic humanism of Irving Babbitt, enjoying Babbitt's shooting-gallery approach to intellectual history but questioning whether humanism provides enough meaning to live by. Cort asked local Episcopal priests what they really believed; they replied that theological language is symbolic and historically relative. This answer repelled him but explained a lot about the Episcopal Church. Cort vowed not to stay in a church that didn't believe in Christian teaching. He joined the Catholic Church, graduated from Harvard in 1935, took a job writing for a Boston weekly, and moved to the New York Catholic Worker in 1936 upon hearing a speech by Dorothy Day.[176]

Cort was drawn to Day's saintly intensity and her familiar Episcopal-to-agnostic-to-Catholic conversion story. He liked that she was a literature buff who wrote for socialist papers before she converted to Catholicism. Day pushed Cort into his first calling, labor journalism. The *Catholic Worker* needed a labor journalist and Cort was willing. He wrote about union organizing, strikes, and strikebreaking and taught a course at the CW on the 1931 papal encyclical of Pius XI, *Quadragesimo Anno*, which updated the 1891 encyclical of Leo XIII, *Rerum Novarum*. Both encyclicals harshly criticized capitalism and socialism, calling for a new social order based on the principles of solidarity, subsidiarity, and the rights to private property and collective bargaining. Cort taught himself the encyclical tradition as he taught the course, barely keeping ahead of the class. His articles cheered for John Lewis and the CIO, vividly conveying that Lewis was the leader of the just side in a just war. Cort caught some flack from CW pacifists for siding too clearly with the CIO but not from Day.[177]

He crafted a speech for Catholic audiences that quoted *Quadragesimo Anno* about capitalist monopoly power, asked the crowd to identify the source, and corrected them when they guessed it must be Karl Marx or the Communist *Daily Worker*. Cort touted the balanced wisdom of the papal tradition. On the one hand, the church condemned the fundamental capitalist principle that production is primarily for profit and not for the satisfaction of human needs; on the other hand, the church did not claim that the wage system is essentially unjust or inevitably exploitative. Cort gathered a Catholic Worker group in 1937 to launch the Association of Catholic Trade Unionists (ACTU), an educational association for Catholic members of unions. What good was Catholic social teaching if Catholics didn't know what it was? This question drove Cort to cofound ACTU, which subsequently branched into labor activism.

He gave five years of full-time service to ACTU and for twenty years wrote for its national weekly newspaper, *The Labor Leader*. Cort expounded the teaching of *Quadragesimo Anno* that workers have a right to share in the control and decision making of plants and industries through worker groups called industry councils or vocational groups or guilds. He defended the CIO sit-down strikes of the late 1930s, denying that sit-downs violated the property rights of owners, though the Supreme Court ruled otherwise in 1939. Cort steered ACTU and the paper entirely toward the nexus of labor news and Catholic social teaching, which gradually took him outside the orbit of the *Catholic Worker*. *The Labor Leader* did not expound on agrarianism, pacifism, anarchism, and spirituality. Cort became wholly absorbed in Catholic union activism while Day drifted from it except for Cesar Chavez and the United Farm Workers.

ACTU supported a dozen different strikes, mostly by new CIO unions. Cort played down the Communist role in founding CIO unions, claiming that only a small minority of CIO founding organizers were Communists. This was his genuine belief in the late 1930s, though Cort felt pressured to say it because Detroit radio priest Charles Coughlin thundered every week to his national audience that FDR was a Communist and the CIO was almost entirely Communist. ACTU supported the UAW and campaigned against Coughlin's profascist demagoguery. Cort argued that good Catholic unionism steered between the Communist problem in the CIO and the racketeering problem in the AFL. The latter problem, he contended, was worse by far. Gangsters controlled waterfront docks on the East Coast, the Gulf of Mexico, and the Great Lakes through the International Longshoremen's Association (ILA). They got their way by dispatching goon squads to club and shoot whoever defied them. *The Labor Leader* published exposés of the dockworker rackets and cheered for David Dubinsky in 1940 when he called for the firing of corrupt union leaders.[178]

But ACTU was a moral gadfly, and the Dubinsky resolution was overwhelmingly voted down. AFL president William Green was willfully oblivious to the racketeering problem in his federation. It didn't help that the AFL's best organizers defected to the CIO. Lewis directed spectacular coal strikes in 1945 and 1946, unions struck against other industries across the nation, and ACTU called for unions cleansed of racketeer AFL leaders and Communist CIO leaders. Public anger against the unions swelled to a fateful peak, yielding a Republican-dominated Congress in 1946. The following year the Taft-Hartley Act outlawed most forms of striking and required union officers to sign affidavits vowing that they weren't Communists. Cort and ACTU opposed Taft-Hartley, commended Truman for vetoing it, and grieved when Congress overrode Truman's veto.

Cort took pride in belonging to the Catholic wing of the anti-Stalinist left, and in later life he read critiques of ACTU anti-Communism that made his head spin. He tried to be gracious with young scholars who romanticized the Popular Fronts or the postwar period when Communists nearly captured the UAW. "Perhaps if you had been there, you would get it," he would say. ACTU was quiet during World War II. Unions pledged not to strike, many ACTU leaders served in the armed forces, and Cort was hospitalized with tuberculosis. After the war ACTU came back strong, scaling up to 6,000 members, though it was still dwarfed by 60,000 Communist Party Stalinists. Stalinists controlled or dominated fifteen CIO unions representing 1.4 million members within the thirty-nine unions and 5.4 million members of the CIO. The battle for the CIO centered in the million-member UAW. Pro-Communists lamented what might have been had Communists defeated Reuther for control of the UAW.

Cort never bought that he should apologize for opposing Stalinism in the unions. American workers, he said, rightly rejected Communism on political, religious, and economic grounds. The political objection was usually paramount, though for Day the religious factor was paramount—she always quoted Lenin's statement that atheism is an essential component of Marxism, a door-slammer for her. Cort noted that ACTU leaders never had to defend their anti-Communism within the organization. Soviet totalitarianism repelled American Catholics, who noticed that American Communists had to change their position every time the line changed in Moscow. Cort, Detroit ACTU, New York ACTU, and *The Labor Leader* pushed hard for Reuther. In March 1946 Reuther won the UAW presidency; in December 1947 he won control of the union and pressed CIO leader Philip Murray to nullify the charters of Stalinist unions; in 1949 Murray engineered the expulsion of the (Stalinist) United Electrical Workers. Cort cheered that America had no legal or moral obligation to allow Stalinist labor leaders to carry out orders from Moscow, exactly as Reuther and Murray said.

Meanwhile Cort grimly tracked the racketeering problem in the AFL. Green died in 1952, and George Meany succeeded him, sparking a burst of hope among reformers. Meany's many flaws did not include tolerating the ILA. He got the AFL to expel the ILA in 1953, which did not cripple it. Dockworkers voted in 1954 to stick with the ILA instead of joining the new union chartered by the AFL. Two years later it happened again, dockworkers now spurning the AFL-CIO, which merged in 1955. In 1959 the ILA was admitted to the AFL-CIO on the fallacious ground that it had reformed. The dockworker defeats of 1954 and 1956 nearly destroyed Cort's faith in democracy. Even a celebrated Marlon Brando movie, *On the Waterfront*, didn't turn the tide against the ILA. Industrial democracy failed; had Cort wasted his career advocating for it? He teetered on yes and tacked in a political direction, joining ADA. Perhaps political democracy was the answer. Cort met lots of Democratic bigwigs through the ADA and befriended some who opened career doors he did not expect.

His meager diet at Hospitality House inflicted him in 1938 with tuberculosis, which Cort struggled for twelve years to overcome. He and his wife, Helen Haye Cort, raised ten children through years of tenuous health and austerity. Cort often said he was "totally Catholic" when it came to marriage and family, believing in "seek ye first the kingdom of God and all shall be added to you." The expulsion of the Stalinist unions from the AFL-CIO ironically devitalized ACTU, depriving it of a galvanizing opponent. *The Labor Leader* ran its last issue in November 1959, though New York ACTU kept going into the 1970s. Cort served on the editorial staff of *Commonweal* from 1943 to 1959, forging friendships across its liberal Catholic readership. He worked successively as a business agent of the Boston Newspaper Guild, regional director of the Peace Corps in the Philippines, director of the Massachusetts Commonwealth Service Corps, and director of the Model Cities Program in Lynn, Massachusetts. In 1965 he moved his family to Roxbury, a predominantly African American section of Boston, believing that white liberals like him needed to prove their commitment to racial integration, especially if they ran an antipoverty agency, which he did.[179]

In his last paycheck job he funded sixteen projects, including a Meals on Wheels program, a senior citizens' center, and a housing rehab program. It was good work tied to political vicissitudes that ran out in 1973, when an unfriendly mayor pushed him out. Cort was sixty years old when he stopped earning paychecks and vowed to figure out the meaning of his life. In January 1974 he attended a conference at Massachusetts Institute of Technology sponsored by a new organization called People for Self-Management (PSM). There he met a scholar of worker ownership, Cornell political economist Jaroslav Vanek, and was deeply impressed by keynote speaker Irving Bluestone, a UAW economist and vice president. Bluestone said workplaces needed to become more interesting, complex, democratic, and humane. Cort joined PSM and attended a meeting of Boston DSOC.

Boston DSOC was religion-friendly, sometimes meeting at the Paulist Center, where Cort heard speeches by *Commonweal* editor Peter Steinfels and Holy Cross College historian David O'Brien. Cort asked them the same question he had asked Norman Thomas at a Harvard venue forty years previously. If they believed in freedom as much as they claimed, how could they believe in state ownership of the means of production? It seemed to Cort they had no better answer than Thomas, but he had a worker ownership answer in his head, and he pored over Harrington's books. Two Harrington factors won him over: Harrington was unquestionably devoted to freedom and democracy, and he denied that socialism should be equated with nationalizing the economy.

Cort began to think that perhaps he had been a socialist ever since he founded ACTU. He greatly admired Julius Bernstein, the ringleader of Boston DSOC. In September 1975 Cort told Bernstein he was ready to join. He wrote an article announcing his decision, leading with a typically puckish Cort anecdote plucked from Dostoevsky's *The Brothers Karamazov*. A French police official professed that he didn't fear the socialists, anarchists, infidels, and revolutionaries. He understood them and kept watch over them. The people he feared were the Christian socialists: "They are dreadful people! The socialist who is a Christian is more to be dreaded than the socialist who is an atheist." Cort enjoyed the suggestion that he became dangerous after many years of respectable work as a professional service director. But he also played up that DSOC operated in the Democratic Party and was loaded with renowned intellectuals.[180]

Cort observed that DSOC proposed to nationalize the big banks and place employee and public representatives on the boards of all major industrial and financial corporations. If that was democratic socialism, he had been a democratic socialist for a long time: "Since conversion to Catholicism in 1933 I have always been rather conservative in theology and inclined to take seriously the opinions of the Popes as expressed in their encyclicals." From the popes he absorbed that socialism is about nationalizing the economy and abolishing private property. But what if socialism is more complex and various than that— and always has been? Cort stressed that producer and consumer cooperatives are forms of social ownership, and West Germany had codetermined enterprises. He noted that John XXIII, in *Mater et Magistra* (1961), improved on *Quadragesimo Anno*: It was not merely a good idea to grant to workers some share in their enterprises; Pope John said it was a demand of justice.[181]

Briefly he touted the Frankfurt Declaration statement that Marxism is only one of the three major roads to socialism; the other two are ethical humanism and religious socialism. Subsequently Cort treated the Frankfurt Declaration as the authoritative description of democratic socialism. In 1977 a group of religious socialists gathered at the DSOC convention in Chicago to organize a Religion and Socialism group and its publication, *Religious Socialism*. Cort ran the magazine for eleven years, handed it to Jack Spooner for ten years, and picked it up again in 1998 for two more years. To read the magazine in its early years was to get very familiar with the Frankfurt Declaration, since Cort quoted it constantly. Later he treated the Stockholm Declaration of the Socialist International (1989) with similar reverence. The analogy was obvious: To Cort, the Frankfurt and Stockholm Declarations were the encyclicals of democratic socialism.

The Socialist International called at Frankfurt for "a system of social justice, better living, freedom, and world peace," affirming the universal right to freedom of thought, expression, education, organization, and religion and the right "of every human being to a private life, protected from arbitrary invasion by the state." The Frankfurt Declaration said that various forms of social ownership are adaptable means of serving the welfare of the community and that unions are indispensable to a democratic society, but not as tools of a central bureaucracy or a corporative system. It supported the universal rights to work, healthcare, child care, leisure, education, economic security, and housing, condemned all forms of imperialism, and commended liberation struggles throughout the world for self-determination, freedom, and justice.[182]

Cort stressed four aspects of the Frankfurt Declaration. He loved to quote its assertion that Communism falsely claimed a role in the socialist tradition. He cited repeatedly its affirmation of mixed-economy pluralism, urging socialism-bashers to get their clocks fixed. He celebrated that Frankfurt formally welcomed ethical humanist and religious comrades; Social Democrats no longer said that Marxism is the real thing, and other kinds of socialists should be tolerated. And he prized above all the Frankfurt assertion that the guiding principle of capitalism is private profit and the guiding principle of socialism is the satisfaction of human needs. That was an echo of *Quadragesimo Anno*.

In 1989 the International replaced Frankfurt with the Stockholm Declaration, and Cort jubilantly embraced it. Harrington was one of its coauthors, just before he died. Cort exulted that the Stockholm Declaration *didn't even mention* Marxism, featuring signature Harrington arguments—state ownership does not guarantee economic efficiency or social justice, equality is the condition of the development of individual personality, and equality and personal freedom are indivisible. In Cort's last issue of *Religious Socialism* he bowed out with what he called "a public service," reprinting the entire text of the Stockholm Declaration under the title "This Is Socialism," which he juxtaposed to a passage from *The Communist Manifesto* under the title "This Is Not Socialism—This Is Communism." The latter passage was the Marx–Engels exhortation about over-throwing the capitalist class, centralizing all instruments of production in the hands of the state, and abolishing private property. Cort grieved that the latter type of thinking continued to infiltrate DSA, perhaps "by a kind of secret seduction."[183]

Cort deeply admired Harrington, grateful that he built good-spirited socialist organizations. He bristled when Harrington took heat at DSA conventions for opposing nationalization and embracing the Socialist International. Then Harrington died, and Cort rued that two kinds of radicalism ascended in his wake. One was the old religion, revolutionary Marxism. The other was a powerful cultural leftism that spoke the language of deconstructionist disruption. There were fervent contentions between the two groups, but Cort felt alienated from both sides. He had a longtime editor's sense of wind direction. He fretted that the sheer frustration of being a democratic socialist in the 1990s was pushing DSA away from social democracy. If he made it to his one hundredth birthday would he still feel welcome in DSA? Cort fell seven years short of finding out, dying in 2006, eleven years before DSA voted to leave the Socialist International.

7

CULTURAL LEFTISM, CORNEL WEST, MARKET SOCIALISM, AND NANCY FRASER

Antonio Gramsci, imprisoned in 1926 for leading the Italian Communist Party, famously asked himself why the right was better at politics than the left. He answered that the right speaks to people where they live, exercising hegemony over their ideas at the cultural level. Orthodox Marxists dismissed the cultural realm as epiphenomenal, the superstructure, never mind that capitalism lives in schools, communications media, religious communities, political parties, and civic organizations. Gramsci said these institutions permeate the society with bourgeois values, augmenting the power of capitalism. Hegemony is the process by which a ruling class makes its domination appear natural by grafting its worldview onto society. Gramsci lauded Lenin for eliminating Kautsky's division of labor between intellectuals who led and workers who followed; the revolutionary party was a single, cohesive unit, not a society with a division of labor. But that still brought socialist consciousness to the working class from outside — the vanguard party as the agent of revolutionary struggle.

Gramsci warned that if socialists continued to fixate on seizing political power, they would keep failing. The capitalist state is an integral constellation of political, economic, and civic forces. Its power includes all the cultural institutions through which power relations are mediated. Lenin grasped better than Kautsky the totality of the capitalist state, but neither took seriously the cultural problems of the working class as a whole. Gramsci went back to the role of intellectuals, distinguishing between traditional and organic intellectuals. Traditional intellectuals legitimize the structures, myths, and norms of the dominant order even as they affect a certain interclass aura in the interstices of society. Organic intellectuals are radical thinkers who identify with the working class, know what working people feel and think, and criticize the bourgeois conventions of capitalist culture.

They work at various professions while shaping the ideas of the class to which they organically belong.[1]

This argument swept much of the socialist Left in the 1980s, lifting Gramsci into the top rank of Marxian thinkers. He died in prison in 1937; his notebooks were published after World War II; his thought seeped into Marxist theory; and English editions of his work appeared in the 1970s. Gramsci died a true-believing Communist who argued that Communism and Fascism operate by the same method—totalitarianism. Communism and Fascism, he said, differ only in their objective impact on history. Soviet Russia had a right to use the same methods as the Fascists because Russia used them to create a liberating socialist society. Hardly anyone believed that by the time Gramsci became the icon of cultural Leftism. The Gramscian turn addressed key shortcomings of Marxian theory, boosted the rise of cultural studies and postcolonial theory, and responded to the culture wars of the right. Harrington beheld it with conflicted feelings. He was a truer organic intellectual than most of the professors who wrote books on Gramsci. He regretted that he fixed too long on realigning the Democratic Party. And the Gramsci boom gave ballast to Harrington's signature contention: the crucial thing is to permeate society with socialist values. Yet Gramsci was a Leninist who inadvertently authorized socialists to take a light pass at political economics. Harrington wished that Leninism had never happened and he puzzled at socialists who played down economics.[2]

He died just before the Communist governments of Eastern Europe perished and the Berlin Wall came down. The collapse of Communism in 1989 briefly buoyed the hope of democratic socialists that the way had cleared for a straight-up debate about democratic socialism. I wrote three books and many articles making this argument. In 1990 I wrote that the democratic socialist commitment to universal rights of freedom and well-being contrasted with "Communist terror, totalitarian rule, and economic bankruptcy." Two years later I protested against the widespread claim that the implosion of Soviet Communism made democratic socialism irrelevant: "The need for greater social and economic equality has not vanished with the passing of the Soviet bloc. The ravages of imperialism, oppression, structural dependency, environmental destruction, and world poverty have not diminished with the triumph of liberal capitalism." I plugged for liberation theology, ecofeminism, and economic democracy, conceiving economic democracy as common ground for liberation movements and as a bottom-up alternative to social democratic interventions from above.[3]

But we democratic socialists did not get the debate we wanted. The political right took credit for winning the Cold War, neoliberal globalization turned the entire planet into a single economic market, and Bill Clinton won the White House in 1992 after George H. W. Bush raised taxes and lost the Reagan right. Factories rushed to new plantations in the global South, devastating American industrial communities. Clinton was a master of opportunistic triangulation, refashioning Republican causes as technocratic neoliberal wisdom. He punished welfare recipients far beyond anything Bush had dared, gutting Aid to Families with Dependent Children (AFDC). Clinton pushed a crime bill through Congress that worsened the trend of draconian prison sentences, securing three-strike laws and harsher penalties for crack cocaine that condemned urban black males to life sentences. He won a huge victory for deindustrialization by championing the North American Free Trade Agreement (NAFTA), a monument to the determination of corporate executives to relocate in cheap-labor, no-tax havens. He tore down the New Deal wall between investment and commercial banks, paving the way to the bank empires and fantastic financial speculation of the George W. Bush years.[4]

Clinton occasionally did something DSA liked, such as achieving a hard-won gas tax of 4.3 cents per gallon, but, mostly, DSA opposed him. It fought against the federal three-strikes law and, in 1997, founded the Prison Moratorium Project, one of the first campaigns opposing what was later called the New Jim Crow. DSA was a player in the Medicare for All movement, advocating a Canadian-style single-payer healthcare system, and joined a growing movement for global justice, forging ties with global solidarity groups. It worked with the Congressional Progressive Caucus to oppose the (failed) Multilateral Agreement on Investment, which would have stripped national governments of the right to regulate foreign investment. The willingness of DSA to fight a Democratic president and party establishment on welfare, incarceration, healthcare, global solidarity, and the banks attracted new members. DSA climbed in the mid-1990s from seven thousand to ten thousand members. In 1995 it revised the organization's original founding document of 1982, "Where We Stand: Building the Next Left." The revised version put economic globalization at the center of its analysis and strategy. DSA knew where it stood before and after it lost Harrington, and its dedicated national office kept the organization relevant in Left-coalition campaigns for social justice. But in many locales DSA became a study group that showed up for occasional forums and rallies. Mostly it was a home for scattered, stubborn types holding out against the 1990s.[5]

DSA acknowledged that Clinton governed much like his governing Social Democratic peers, British Labour Party leader Tony Blair and German Social Democratic Party leader Gerhard Schröder. The 1995 version of "Where We Stand" declared that global economic integration rendered obsolete the Social

Democratic model of independent welfare states, compelling Socialists to revise their vision and tactics. Socialism was still the belief that people should freely and democratically control their community and society, and the struggle for it was still led by the excluded, workers, minorities, and women. DSA described itself negatively and positively: "We are socialists because we reject an international economic order sustained by private profit, alienated labor, race and gender discrimination, environmental destruction, and brutality and violence in defense of the status quo. We are socialists because we share a vision of a humane international social order based both on democratic planning and market mechanisms to achieve equitable distribution of resources, meaningful work, a healthy environment, sustainable growth, gender and racial equality, and non-oppressive relationships."[6]

"Where We Stand" contended that individuals reach their full potential only in a society that embodies the values of liberty, equality, and solidarity. Socialism is about creating material and cultural bonds of solidarity across racial, gender, age, national, and class lines. DSA said it was deeply feminist and antiracist and committed to one voice, one vote political democracy. It stressed that non-unionized enterprises fire workers at will and that corporations govern through hierarchical power relations resembling monopolies, not free markets. It protested that the defense establishment was pursuing a military policy of imperial overreach, treating the preservation of America's global military dominance as a top objective. It contrasted economic democracy to the tax-free maquiladora zones on the U.S.–Mexico border, where abuse of workers and the environment were standard fare. Economic democracy does not abolish all forms of domination, DSA allowed, but it is crucial to all social justice struggles and the building of a green economy. Economic democracy works differently from democratic state socialism, to the same historic end: "If socialism cannot be achieved primarily from above, through a democratic government that owns, controls, and regulates the major corporations, then it must emerge from below, through a democratic transformation of the institutions of civil society, particularly those in the economic sphere—in other words, a program for economic democracy."[7]

The Clinton administration drove DSA to say outright that sometimes it worked in the Democratic Party and sometimes it didn't. In 1995 DSA formally declared that it took no either/or position on building a new party or trying to change the Democratic Party. When I spoke to DSA locals it usually took only a few minutes to gauge whether it was basically a Harrington crowd or a gathering of independent progressives, people flirting with the Green Party, and anarchists. These were wilderness years of intense demoralization on the left. DSA asked me in 1999 and 2000 if I could write an encouraging word about any-thing. I could not, noting that Clinton mustered deep-down conviction and sought to change public opinion on only one issue in his entire presidency, NAFTA: "Clinton's 'third way' keeps tacking further and further to the right, because you can't triangulate with a Left that doesn't exist." I didn't mean there was no left. I meant there was no left that pulled Clinton to the left or that com-pelled him to take it seriously. Harrington built DSOC on the conviction that radical ideas advance during periods of liberal ascendancy in solidarity with mass movements. But liberalism was dead, replaced by a neoliberal counterfeit, and you had to be middle-aged even to remember what a mass movement looked like.[8]

Remnants of the left that founded DSOC and NAM still existed in the unions, grassroots advocacy organizations, Democratic Party, and progressive foundations, but the left was strong in only one place: the academy. DSA over-flowed with academics. Some paid their dues every year, many operated in the DSA orbit with occasional dues paying, and some were just outside the DSA orbit. Political theorists, historians, and social critics included Stanley Aronowitz, Ronald Aronson, Benjamin Barber, Joanne Barkan, Kenneth Baynes, Robert Bellah, David Bensman, Sheri Berman, Fred Block, Harry Boyte, David Bromwich, Mary Jo Buhle, Paul Buhle, Craig Calhoun, Don Cooney, Harvey Cox, Robert Dahl, Alan Dawley, Bogdan Denitch, Jacob Dorn, Ken Estey, Herbert Gintis, Todd Gitlin, Amy Gutmann, Michael Hirsch, Gerald Horne, Irving Howe, Maurice Isserman, John Judis, Harvey Kaye, Michael Kazin, Ron Kramer, Mark Levinson, Harold Meyerson, Bruce Miroff, Frances Fox Piven, Joerg Rieger, Richard Rorty, Joseph Schwartz, Philip Selznick, John D. Stephens, William Sullivan, Todd Swanstrom, Michael Walzer, and Lawrence Wittner. Political economists included Gar Alperovitz, Bill Barclay, David Belkin, Samuel Bowles, Severyn T. Bruyn, Martin Carnoy, David Ellerman, Jeff Faux, David M. Gordon, Robert Heilbroner, John Roemer, Frank Roosevelt, Leland Stauber, Thomas E. Weisskopf, Richard Wolff, and Erik Olin Wright. DSA contributed to the broad field of cultural Leftism and the Gramsci boom, attracting intellectuals who focused primarily on the cultural reproduction of domination. African American critics in this field included Michael Eric Dyson, Bill Fletcher Jr., Obery M. Hendricks Jr., bell hooks, Manning Marable, Adolph Reed Jr., Corey D. B. Walker, Juanita Webster, and Cornel West. Feminist critics within and outside the academy and DSA included Linda Alcoff, Sheila D. Collins, Barbara Ehrenreich, Zillah Eisenstein, Kate Ellis, Nancy Fraser, Chris Riddiough, Ruth Rosen, Rosemary Radford Ruether, Ronnie Steinberg, Gloria Steinem, and Iris Marion Young.

Harrington was right that the children of the 1960s would change the academy *and* socialism. Some of them changed socialism more than he anticipated, lifting the struggle for cultural recognition above the devotion to class and distributive justice. Judith Butler, Michael Eric Dyson, bell hooks, Cornel West, and Iris Marion Young made seminal cultural left contributions to this debate. David Bromwich, Bogdan Denitch, Todd Gitlin, Irving Howe, and Richard Rorty upheld the old social democracy defensively, contending that the politics of cultural difference fragmented the left and thwarted its struggle for economic justice. Joseph Schwartz and Michael Walzer sought to temper the social democratic critique of cultural leftism, while West, hooks, Young, and Fraser made notable attempts to fuse socialist and cultural left criticism, sometimes very differently from each other. The feeling of siege expressed by many social democrats heightened as the right carried out its loud attack on the welfare state. Neoliberals responded to the surging right and economic globalization by rolling back welfare entitlements and liberating market forces from public control. Difference feminists and multicultural leftists responded to the social democrats, democratic socialists, conservatives, and neoliberals by attacking difference-blind liberalism, conceiving justice as the recognition of group specificity. Butler and Young, in importantly different ways, were leading advocates of difference feminism, compelling the left to confront the ways it demeaned marginalized identities. Communitarians made a highly influential contribution to these debates by adopting the cultural-difference model to their own social ethical ends.[9]

Communitarians criticized the liberal devotion to individual rights and the egocentrism of American culture, upholding the importance of community- and character-forming institutions. They retrieved Aristotle's concept of justice as a community bound by a shared understanding of the good and Hegel's concepts of social subjectivity and recognition, spanning a broad political spectrum ranging from democratic socialists (Benjamin Barber, Robert Bellah, Rosemary Radford Ruether, Philip Selznick, William Sullivan, Michael Walzer) to moderate progressives (Amitai Etzioni, William Galston, Jane J. Mansbridge, Michael Sandel, Charles Taylor) to conservatives (William Bennett, Alasdair MacIntyre, Robert Nisbet, Christina Hoff Sommers). Ruether conceived communitarian socialism as the integration of liberal, socialist, and radical feminisms; Walzer developed a pluralistic theory of equality; Sandel made a highly influential critique of John Rawls's liberal neo-Kantian theory of justice. The communitarian surge revived the entire field of political theory, yet the communitarians were brushed aside when the left debated cultural recognition versus redistribution. The leading theorist of this defining debate was—and is—Nancy Fraser. Communitarians disqualified themselves from her purview by blurring the categories that mattered and sprawling across nearly the entire political spectrum. What mattered to Fraser was to unite the two central competing traditions of the left. She said it was wrong for the Marxist/social democratic left and the cultural feminist/multicultural left to fight over the hierarchy of oppression, a mistaken debate with harmful consequences. In the realm of theory Fraser stands out among U.S. American socialist thinkers of the past generation for creatively addressing most of the field. In the realm of public discussion the leading American socialist intellectual is Cornel West.[10]

West has long championed and represented the ideal of uniting socialist struggles for social justice by privileging the issues of people of color, in his case as honorary vice chair of DSA. For many years he wrote books and conducted lecture tours with bell hooks and Michael Lerner, exploring with hooks the cultural politics of black feminism and socialist feminism and with Lerner the relationships between blacks and Jews within and outside the left. hooks began her career with a blistering black feminist critique of white feminism, *Ain't I a Woman* (1981), that changed the landscape of women's studies and feminist theory. She fixed on the academy in her early career before shifting to the broader reading public she attracted. Lerner cut loose from the academy and built *Tikkun* magazine into an important vehicle of the interreligious left, while remaining on the outskirts of DSA, having felt mistreated by Harrington at the turning point of Lerner's career. Had Lerner joined DSA its religious caucus would not have been so lopsidedly Christian. As it was, most of the prosocialist readership that Lerner and Peter Gabel forged at *Tikkun* was lost to the leading democratic socialist organization. Meanwhile the political economists and political theorists plugged away at market socialism and economic democracy during the heyday of TINA—There Is No Alternative. One political dissenter from TINA, Bernie Sanders, kept alive for many years the stubborn insistence that there must be an alternative. Then he tapped into a groundswell of revulsion demanding one.

CORNEL WEST AND THE CULTURAL POLITICS OF SOCIALISM

West came to academic philosophy and socialist activism from the black church, the civil rights movement, and the Black Panther Party. He was born in 1953 in Tulsa, Oklahoma, where his grandfather was a Baptist minister. He spent two weeks in Tulsa, moved with his parents to Topeka, Kansas, where his father was a civilian air force administrator, and moved in 1958 with his family to Sacramento, California. There he grew up in a totally segregated world, very happily, absorbing the music, ethos, and rhetoric of black culture. West knew whites only from television, much to his benefit: "Whiteness was really not a point of reference for me because the world was all black. . . . That was a very positive thing, because it gave me a chance to really revel in black humanity." Had he been forced to deal with whites, it would have been harder to perceive their humanity: "I didn't have to either deify them or demonize them. . . . I could just view them as human beings, and I think that was quite a contribution of my own context."[11]

As a youth he reveled in the preaching of Shiloh Baptist Church pastor Willie P. Cooke, admired Malcolm X and Martin Luther King Jr., was hooked by Søren Kierkegaard's struggle with melancholia and mortality, and came of age politically by attending Black Panther meetings. Kierkegaard taught him that philosophy should be about the human experiences of living, suffering, and finding hope. The Panthers taught him that politics should combine the best available theory with concrete strategies. West absorbed Panther teaching about Malcolm and socialism but viewed both through a Christian lens, steeped in the black church and King. At seventeen he enrolled at Harvard, already knowing who he was and what he aimed to do: "Owing to my family, church, and the black social movements of the 1960s, I arrived at Harvard unashamed of my African, Christian, and militant decolonized outlooks." He was determined to shape his own image, not have it shaped for him: "I've always wanted to be myself, and, of course, that is a perennial process." At Harvard he studied philosophy under Robert Nozick, John Rawls, Hilary Putnam, and Stanley Cavell in addition to his major, Near Eastern languages and literature, which he undertook so he could read ancient religious texts and graduate in three years.[12]

That made him twenty years old when he began his doctoral program in philosophy at Princeton University. West worried that Princeton philosophers would undermine his Christian faith and denigrate his attraction to Frankfurt School neo-Marxism. Instead, his teachers took no interest in religion; his advisor, Richard Rorty, had a pragmatic historicist turn that influenced West; and Sheldon Wolin urged him to study the Hegelian Marxist background to the Frankfurt School. West started with a dissertation on British neo-Hegelian T. H. Green, switched to the Aristotelian aspects of Marx's thought, and settled on Marx's ethical commitments. He argued that Marx's historicism and anticapitalism were informed by ethical values of individuality and democracy, notwithstanding his attacks on moral reason. By the mid-1970s West was already acquiring a reputation as an intellectual spellbinder. The first time I saw him, in 1975, he had attracted a sidewalk crowd of a dozen people at Harvard Divinity

School and was expounding exuberantly on varieties of black nationalism. The crowd got larger and I surmised, "That must be Cornel West." Two years later he began his teaching career at Union Theological Seminary.[13]

"You know, my aim was always to teach at Union Seminary," he later reflected. "Union Seminary, for me, was the real institutional site that brought together all of my interests. It was a Christian seminary, it was deeply shaped by progressive politics, Marxism, feminism, antihomophobic thought and black liberation theology." Union had a storied history starring Reinhold Niebuhr and Paul Tillich, but the crucial factor for West was that Union was the epicenter of black liberation theology.[14]

Union theologian James Cone, the founder of black theology, conceived it as the religious self-expression of oppressed black Americans. Cone earned his doctorate in theology in 1965 at Garrett Evangelical Theological Seminary in Chicago and stewed over the irrelevance of his field. He taught at Adrian College in Michigan, wrote articles that meant nothing to him, and hated his situation until Detroit exploded in 1967. The Black Power Movement expressed his rage and perspective. Cone later recalled that he found his voice upon hearing pastors and theologians exhort black Americans to follow Jesus instead of resorting to violence: "I was so furious that I could hardly contain my rage. The very sight of white people made me want to vomit." His revulsion was motivating and clarifying: "My rage was intensified because most whites seemed not to recognize the contradictions that were so obvious to black people."[15]

This rush of emotion and conviction produced his electrifying first book, *Black Theology and Black Power* (1969), the founding text of black liberation theology. By the summer of 1968, Cone said, "I had so much anger pent up in me I had to let it out or be destroyed by it." King's murder was merely the last straw. Cone vowed that he would not compromise with the evils of white racists: "Racism is a deadly disease that must be resisted by any means necessary. Never again would I ever expect white racists to do right in relation to the black community." He wrote *Black Theology and Black Power* in four weeks, describing it as a conversion experience: "It was like experiencing the death of white theology and being born again into the theology of the black experience."[16]

Malcolm's phrase "by any means necessary" was fundamental to Cone's definition of his object, Black Power: "Complete emancipation of black people from white oppression by whatever means black people deem necessary." Black Power, he said, used boycotts when necessary, demonstrations when necessary, and violence when necessary. Cone's first book contained the liberationist principle of responding to a world that defined the oppressed as nonpersons; however, neither personhood nor the word "liberation" was a key concept to him as yet. He focused on why Black Power rejected white liberalism and black reform-ism. Black Power was an announcement that all whites are responsible for white oppression. Cone respected King but preferred Malcolm, who was "not far wrong when he called the white man 'the devil.' "[17]

Black Power was against integration, especially its humiliating assumption that white institutions were superior. Cone said the last thing black people needed was to be assimilated into white culture. White people persecuted blacks viciously for centuries but puzzled over the black anger that sparked urban riots. White liberals, in particular, wanted to be morally innocent of racism while enjoying the privileges of whiteness. Cone said the black struggle for liberation would get nowhere if blacks got tied up with the anxieties of white liberals. In America the liberating Christ of the gospels had to be black, "working through the activity of Black Power."[18]

Cone developed his theological argument in A *Black Theology of Liberation* (1970), conceptualizing blackness as a racial marker and a symbol of liberation from various forms of oppression. At the time he was unaware of similar stirrings in Latin America and South Africa, but Cone defined "blackness" as a symbol of oppression extending beyond the North American context. The object of black theology was "liberation from whiteness." It was "theology of and for the black community, seeking to interpret the religious dimensions of the forces of liberation in that community." Cone stressed that whites were "in no position whatever" to make judgments about the truth claims of black theology. The very point of black theology was to "analyze the satanic nature of whiteness" and offer an alternative to it.[19]

God is black because liberation is the essence of the divine nature: "White religionists are not capable of perceiving the blackness of God, because their satanic whiteness is a denial of the very essence of divinity." Cone said evil, to blacks, is anything that arrests or negates liberation; salvation is liberation. To whites, evil is normal life, benefiting from the privileges of whiteness; salvation would be the abolition of whiteness—becoming black with God. Cone repudi-ated the entire intellectual agenda and ethos of liberal theology, declaring that Aristotle, Kant, Hegel, and Schleiermacher meant nothing to him. The test of black theology is whether it reflects the religious experience of blacks and con-tributes to their liberation.[20]

Cone was extremely important to West and significantly different from him. "Cone provided a space for radical Black Christians to be affirmed," West explained. "Here was somebody who was trying to hold onto some spiritual issues while making the link to radical political struggles." But West cared about Aristotle and Kant, and he didn't share Cone's opposition to working in interracial social justice organizations. When Cone burst into prominence, West was already steeped in Black Panther debates between what he called "porkchop nationalists and serious socialist internationalists." The first time West read Cone's book on Black Power he pegged it as "petit-bourgeois nationalism." Cone later clarified that he supported liberationist movements in the Third World and regarded himself as a socialist, which narrowed the differences between Cone and West—but only to a point. Cone was the apostle of the liberationist departure in American theology, applying Du Bois, Malcolm, King, Fanon, and James Baldwin to theology and claiming that only liberation theology was biblically orthodox. West was equally devoted to Du Bois, Malcolm, King, Fanon, and Baldwin, but the claim of orthodoxy was alien to him.[21]

Liberation theology was at the heart of West's pragmatic, postmodern, anti-imperial, historicist, black Christian liberationist work, but he stressed that he was not a theologian. He told his classes they could not understand Du Bois if they didn't understand Marx, Hegel, Emerson, and Weber, so there is no alternative to absorbing Marx, Hegel, Emerson and Weber. West's bond with Aronowitz and his journal *Social Text* were formative influences. Like Aronowitz, he espoused the Council Marxism of Rosa Luxemburg and Karl Korsch while leaving room for the proto-Councilist Syndicalism of Hubert Harrison and the Wobblies. West was slow to find a Socialist organization he could join. DSOC smacked too much of social democratic anti-Communism, and NAM barely existed in New York before the DSA merger. The founding of DSA gave West a place to land during the same year he published his first, favorite, landmark book *Prophesy Deliverance! An Afro-American Revolutionary Christianity* (1982).[22]

West said democratic socialism is like liberal theology—a valuable project in its time that outlived its usefulness. Both were stepping-stones to something better. Democratic socialism is a noble vision, he allowed, but every form of it is compromised by middle-class electoral reformism. Liberal theology is similarly a creative project—of the bourgeois imagination. Both carried on long past their heyday and were superseded by liberation movements. West described six types of Marxism—Stalinism, Leninism, Trotskyism, Gramscianism, Social Democracy, and revolutionary Councilism—assigning a theological analogue to each type.

Stalinism, a total perversion of its founding symbols, is the Ku Klux Klan of Marxism. The Leninist and Trotskyist traditions are fundamentalist, marshaling proof texts for truncated versions of Marxist norms. West lauded Gramsci for his emphasis on cultural hegemony but cautioned that Gramsci was only slightly democratic, being too Leninist to defend freedom on the grounds of principle, not merely strategy. Gramscian Marxism is analogous to theological neo-orthodoxy, "an innovative revision of dogmas for dogmatic purposes." West judged that Social Democracy has the same strengths and defaults as the social gospel tradition. Both produced impressive critiques of capitalism but not a revolutionary praxis. Social Democracy, even when it retains the class struggle and the dialectic of history, sells out revolutionary consciousness, concentrating on electoral reformism and anti-Communism. Like the social gospel, it accommodates bourgeois modernity too deeply not to be compromised by it.[23]

The best Marxism is the revolutionary Councilism of Luxemburg, Korsch, and Anton Pannekoek, which West viewed as analogous to liberation theology. Council Marxism repudiates the class collaborationism of Social Democracy, conceiving revolutionary worker councils as prefigural incarnations of the new society. Instead of viewing workers as wage earners, voters, and consumers, it views workers as collective, self-determining producers who prefigure the coming socialist order. Council Marxism is about workers seizing power through revolutionary organizations that already prefigure a socialist society—"all power to the soviets." The early Gramsci, in 1918 and 1919, was a Council Marxist who wanted Italy's councils in Turin to take control of organizing production. He said that the worker councils were communist, not merely one organ of the revolutionary struggle against the bourgeoisie, and that Lenin agreed with him. But the worker councils did not develop into a national movement, Gramsci was accused of reducing Marxism to syndicalism, and he fell in line with actual Leninism. West believed that Gramsci should have stuck with prefigural democratic radicalism, the best of the Marxist traditions: "Councilism is to Marxism what liberation theology is to Christianity: a promotion and practice of the moral core of the perspective against overwhelming odds for success."[24]

This scheme was an effective way to teach seminary students about the varieties of Marxism, but it misrepresented the Marxian tradition, and its upshot was problematic. Orthodox Marxism, a tradition far more important historically than the Trotsky and Gramsci traditions, had no place in West's scheme. Its unwieldy two-house structure of proletarian revolution and parliamentary socialism led to the impasse in which the movement divided between Leninism and Social Democracy, but orthodox Marxism was the dominant socialist tradition for two generations, and it did not wither away after Socialist parties were compelled to choose between Leninism and Social Democracy. Moreover, the ostensible affinity between Council Marxism and liberation theology did not bode well for liberation theology since Council Marxism was a utopian construct that never worked anywhere. The "overwhelming odds" were a serious problem if the point was to change society, not merely adopt a utopian position. The democratic socialist tradition that West dismissed at least had actual parties and unions that changed society. Council Marxism, though an important variant of socialist thought, existed only in the heads of Marxian intellectuals.

West and Aronowitz pressed the argument in DSA for the superiority of Council Marxism, contending that "democratic socialism" is a euphemism for the betrayal of revolutionary consciousness, settling too readily for social democracy. I pushed back that West's radical democratic vision was unattainable on Councilist terms, he was wrong to identify liberation theology with a single form of Marxism, and democratic socialism does not reduce to the politics of defending the welfare state. It also includes a guild socialist tradition bearing complex relationships to Council Marxism, syndicalism, and anarcho-syndicalism. Council Marxism needed democratic socialism in the same way that liberation theology needed to be informed and limited by earlier forms of religious socialism, especially those in the guild socialist tradition.[25]

To a considerable degree West moved in the latter direction without relinquishing his preference for the Council Marxists. He tracked the growing literature of the 1980s on market socialism and adjusted his position to it, conceiving democratic socialism as economic democracy that allows the market to get prices right. West leaned on Croatian economist Branko Horvat, Polish economist Włodzimierz Brus, and Russian-Scottish economic historian Alec Nove, accepting that any feasible model of socialism must accept market mechanisms and mixed forms of ownership. West said his "wholesome Christian rejection" of all oppressive hierarchies drove how he thought about socialism—without quite acknowledging that Social Democrats had been right to make exactly the adjustment he made. He endorsed a mixed-model socialism featuring "a socio-economic arrangement with markets, price mechanisms, and induced (not directed) labor force, a free press, formal political rights, and a constitutionally based legal order with special protections of the marginalized." His vision of democratic socialism featured five major economic sectors: (1) state-owned industries of basic producer goods (electricity networks, oil and petrochemical companies, financial institutions); (2) independent, self-managed, socialized public enterprises; (3) cooperative enterprises controlling their own property; (4) small, private businesses; and (5) self-employed individuals.[26]

To his surprise West found himself echoing Harrington's theme that some kind of collectivism is inevitable; the question is whether it will be democratic and bottom-up or authoritarian and top-down. West and Harrington conducted a DSA road show in the 1980s and influenced each other, though Harrington never quite absorbed what West tried to teach him about white privilege. On the road, West endorsed Harrington's signature claim that the socialist struggle is to democratize collective structures. In 1986 West put it programmatically:

"The crucial question is how are various forms of centralization, hierarchy, and markets regulated—that is, to what extent can democratic mechanisms yield public accountability of limited centralization, meritorious hierarchy, and a mixture of planned, socialized, and private enterprises in the market along with indispensable democratic political institutions."[27]

Sometimes he put the Harrington argument plainly: "The basic choice in the future will be between a democratic, or 'bottom-up' socialization, and corporate, or 'top-down,' socialization." West commended Harrington for framing the issue in a way that transcended the distractions of everyday politics and noise. The point was to broaden the participation of citizens in the economic, political, and cultural dimensions of the social order "and thus control the conditions of their existence." Harrington persuaded West that socialists need to focus on democratizing the process of investment. By the end of the 1980s West could write that Harrington's democratic socialism was inspiring, "indeed visionary." But West still favored Council Marxism, and he found Harrington ironically lacking at the cultural level. West shook his head that the author of *The Other America* devoted his subsequent books to economic analysis, social theory, and political strategy. Harrington lived too far above the everyday, grasping, vacuous, nihilistic, television-watching, sometimes violent culture of ordinary consumers to write about it. He was eloquent about the structural injustices of capitalism but passed over its equally devastating operations on the cultural level.[28]

That was never true of West, who wrote about popular music, television, sexuality, identity politics, black culture, white supremacy, the culture of nihilism, and the cultural limitations of progressive organizations dominated by whites. West's pamphlet for DSA, "Toward a Socialist Theory of Racism," was a signature statement for him and the organization. He delineated four types of American socialist thinking about racism, regretting that all four were blinkered by Marxian bias. Historic socialist reductionism was the first view; double exploitation was a major corrective view; black nationalism was the third option; and Du Bois pioneered the best of the four theories, which was still inadequate.[29]

West described Eugene Debs as the American icon of the first view, socialism-is-the-answer reductionism. Debs subsumed racial injustice under the general rubric of working-class exploitation, conceiving racism as a divide-and-conquer ruse of the ruling class. West said Debs was an honorable exemplar of color-blind socialism, but socialist reductionism is too simplistic to be a serious answer. The second approach, usually taken by the socialist wing of the union movement, stuck to the class exploitation thesis while acknowledging that blacks are subjected to a second dose of exploitation through workplace discrimination and exclusion. This acknowledgment of racism as "super-exploitation" improved on

Debs but still limited the struggle against racial injustice to the workplace. The "Black Nation" thesis operated differently, conceiving black Americans as an oppressed nation within the United States. The Garvey movement, the American Communist Party, various Leninist organizations, and various black nationalist organizations and individuals espoused it, often citing Stalin's definition of a nation: "A historically constituted, stable community of people formed on the basis of a common language, territory, economic life and psychological make-up manifested in a common culture." West commended the Garvey movement and the Communist traditions for taking seriously the cultural dimension of the freedom struggle. In this respect, most black nationalists were "proto-Gramscians." But as theory, he said, the Black Nation thesis was shot through with ahistorical special pleading, and as practice the back-to-Africa campaign of Garvey was backward looking, if not reactionary.[30]

Du Bois and neo-Marxian theorist Oliver Cox formulated the fourth approach as an alternative to the Black Nation thesis: Racism is a product of class exploitation and of xenophobic attitudes not reducible to class exploitation. West commended Du Bois and Cox for contending that racism has a life of its own depending on psychological factors and cultural practices that are not necessarily or directly caused by structural economic injustices. Du Bois and Cox, West argued, had the right project, pointing to the capitalist role in modern racism while stressing psychological and cultural aspects of the problem. The struggle that is needed against racism moves further in this direction, stressing that the roots of racism lay in conflicts between the civilizations of Europe, Africa, Asia, and Latin America before capitalism arose, while retaining the Marxist emphasis on class exploitation. Moreover, all four of the dominant socialist approaches operate largely or exclusively on the macrostructural level, concentrating on the dynamics of racism within and between social institutions. West called for a full-orbed theory of racism that deals with the genealogy of racism, the ideological dimensions of racism, and micro-institutional factors.[31]

This all-encompassing socialist theory of racism would be Gramscian, emphasizing culture and ideology while extending beyond Gramsci's formulations. It would assume that cultural practices of racism have a reality of their own that does not reduce to class exploitation, that cultural practices are the medium through which selves are produced, and that cultural practices are shaped and bounded by civilizations, including the modes of production of civilizations. It would offer a genealogical account of the ideology of racism, examining the modes of European domination of non-European peoples. It would analyze the micro-institutional mechanisms that sustain white supremacy, highlighting the various forms of Eurocentric dominance. It would provide a macrostructural analysis of the exploitation and oppression of non-European peoples, tracking the variety and relationships between the various types of oppression.

This was a project for theorists of a scholarly bent, a title West declined. He explained that he was an intellectual freedom fighter, not a writer of scholarly tomes geared to disciplinary conversations. For forty years he averaged over one hundred lectures per year and showed up for television interviews, speaking to academic and nonacademic audiences on his broad range of topics. To social activists he often expounded on the cultural limitations of progressive organizations dominated by whites. DSA was the primary case in point. DSA touted its gallery of black intellectual stars, but that did not change its ethos or image sufficiently to attract more than a modicum of black members. The organization looked white and sounded white to the black Americans it tried to recruit. West observed that this cycle of trying and failing ensnared progressive organizations like DSA in a vicious circle. Even when white progressives made serious attempts to diversify they were too remote from the everyday lives of people of color to succeed. The remoteness was geographical and cultural, and the failure it caused discouraged white organizations from struggling against white supremacy, which further widened the cultural gap between people of color and white activists.

West said the only way to break this vicious circle is for progressive organizations to privilege the issues of people of color, taking the liberationist option of siding with the excluded and oppressed. Strategies based on white guilt are paralyzing, both psychologically and politically, while strategies based on making white organizations more attractive to racial minorities don't work. The answer is for organizations to make a commitment of will to the specific struggles of people of color. West said it is pointless for such organizations to pursue diversity campaigns if they do not make the struggle against white supremacy their highest priority. There must be a transformation of consciousness that is practical, convinced that antiracism trumps other causes, and not overburdened with useless guilt: "What is needed is more widespread participation by predominantly white democratic socialist organizations in antiracist struggles—whether those struggles be for the political, economic, and cultural empowerment of Latinos, blacks, Asians, and North Americans or anti-imperialist struggles against U.S. support for oppressive regimes in South Africa, Chile, the Philippines, and the occupied West Bank."[32]

He invoked the term used in liberation theology, "conscientization"—a transformation of consciousness that occurs through an act of commitment, creating a new awareness of marginalization, exclusion, and oppression. Only by taking the liberationist option would white activists comprehend why they should privilege the struggle against racism. Bonds of trust across racial lines must be forged within contexts of struggle. West cautioned, "This interracial interaction guarantees neither love nor friendship. Yet it can yield more understanding and the realization of two overlapping goals—democratic socialism and antiracism. While engaging in antiracist struggles, democratic socialists can also enter into a dialogue on the power relationships and misconceptions that often emerge in multiracial movements for social justice in a racist society. Honest and trusting coalition work can help socialists unlearn Eurocentrism in a self-critical manner and can also demystify the motivations of white progressives in the movement for social justice."[33]

White liberals blanched that West limited his effectiveness by identifying with DSA, conservatives Red-baited him for it, and black nationalists heaped scorn on him for it. He replied, "I've got to be organized with some group." Socialism alone will never eradicate racism, and antiracist struggle is fundamental to any progressive politics worth pursuing: "Yet a democratic socialist society is the best hope for alleviating and minimizing racism, particularly institutional forms of racism." He chose DSA because it was multiracial, multitendency, and comprehensive, standing for racial justice, economic democracy, feminism, environmentalism, and anti-imperialism: "We need the groups highlighting connection and linkage in a time of balkanization and polarization and fragmentation. There's got to be some group that does this."[34]

In his early career West did not regard King as a prophetic model or believe that he compared to Malcolm as an inspiring figure: "King was for us the Great Man who died for us—but not yet the voice we had to listen to, question, learn from and build on." That began to change in the 1980s as scholars paid attention to King's socialism, anti-imperialism, antimilitarism, and nuanced response to Black Power. West took back his mildly patronizing view of King, explaining that it took a while to recognize that King embodied "the best of American Christianity." Now West described King as an organic intellectual, nonviolent resister, American prophet, and egalitarian internationalist: "As an organic intellectual, he exemplifies the best of the life of the mind involved in public affairs; as a proponent of nonviolent resistance he holds out the only slim hope for social sanity in a violence-ridden world; as an American prophet he commands the respect even of those who opposed him; and as an egalitarian internationalist he inspires all oppressed peoples around the world who struggle for democracy, freedom, and equality."[35]

In 1984 West moved to Yale Divinity School and joined campus protests for a clerical union and South African divestment that got him arrested and jailed. The university punished him by cancelling his leave for spring 1987, which forced him to spend the semester commuting between Yale and the University of Paris. The following year he returned to Union, but in 1988 he moved to Princeton University as professor of religion and director of Afro-American studies. Princeton asked what it would take to get him; West said it would take a serious commitment to build a premier black studies program. He gave six years to building one centered on novelist Toni Morrison, then moved to Harvard in 1994 to join its black studies program, with a joint appointment at the Divinity School. Literary critic Henry Louis Gates Jr., the architect of Harvard's program, famously called it the Dream Team of black studies.

West's renown ascended with each of these moves. To the extent that he hung his reputation on conventional academic categories he was a philosopher of religion and a left-pragmatist. In *The American Evasion of Philosophy* (1989) he argued that the pragmatic, Marxist, and Christian intellectual traditions are the best sources for countering the hegemonic canons and conventions of the regnant order. West described Charles S. Peirce as the founder and methodologist of American pragmatism, William James as an Emersonian moralist fixed on the powers and anxieties of individuals, and John Dewey as a theorist of historical consciousness and creative democracy. Like Rorty, West espoused a historicist neopragmatism that rejected all claims to objective knowledge, but, unlike Rorty, West was religious. He said Christian insights into "the crises and traumas of life" were indispensable to his sanity, holding at bay "the sheer absurdity so evident in life, without erasing or eliding the tragedy of life." West's pragmatism fixed on transient matters, ruling out truth claims about extrahistorical realities, yet as a Christian pragmatist his hope transcended the transient matters. In the realm of faith, he argued, the ultimate issue is life or death, not rational consistency.[36]

If one seeks to be in solidarity with the oppressed it helps to be religious, which avails wider access to the lifeworlds of the oppressed, and it helps to be a pragmatist, though West did not believe that one must be religious or a pragmatist. He treasured the pragmatism of Du Bois, Gramsci, Dewey, James, Niebuhr, C. Wright Mills, literary critic Lionel Trilling, and political philosopher Roberto M. Unger, but he also treasured nonpragmatists King, Rauschenbusch, Sojourner Truth, Elizabeth Cady Stanton, and Dorothy Day. What matters, he said, is to struggle against oppression everywhere.[37]

For all his success, and to some degree because of it, despair was a real option for West. He wrote constantly about keeping faith and sustaining hope partly as an admonition to himself. In 1993 he published two books that differently registered his deepening gloom about U.S. American society and the condition of black America. *Keeping Faith* collected his articles on pragmatism, Marxism, racial justice, and progressive politics. *Race Matters* launched him into the realm of American public celebrity just as he began to talk about taking leave of the United States.

Keeping Faith vividly expressed West's deepening alienation. To be a black American intellectual, he said, is to be caught "between an insolent American society and an insouciant black community." White Americans are unwilling to learn from black people, while black Americans take little interest in the life of the mind. Thus "the African American who takes seriously the life of the mind inhabits an isolated and insulated world." West said this problem is objective, not something that anyone can overcome. There is no African American intellectual tradition to support black intellectuals, so the few that emerge are condemned to "dangling status." Black Americans, he argued, have only two organic intellectual traditions: musical performance and church preaching. Both are oral, improvisational, histrionic, and rooted in black life, containing canons for assessing performance and models of past achievement. West said nothing comparable exists in the intellectual field. Du Bois, Baldwin, Zora Neale Hurston, E. Franklin Frazier, and Ralph Ellison are exceptions to a degree but do not compare to the best black preachers and musicians. The only great black American intellectual was Morrison. Aside from the handful of exceptions, black American intellectuals either capitulated to the white academy or catered to the "cathartic provincialism" of a black community lacking any use for intellectuals. West said this grim picture was getting worse, and he struggled not to despair.[38]

Race Matters said the same thing for the trade market, contending that the "decline and decay in American life" applied especially to black America. West took a hard line on what he called "nihilism in black America" and the shortcomings of contemporary black leaders. America as a whole, he said, shared the problem of nihilism, but it harmed black Americans with a special vengeance. Two sentences prepared readers for the jeremiad to come: "We have created rootless, dangling people with little link to the supportive networks—family, friends, school—that sustain some sense of purpose in life. . . . Post-modern culture is more and more a market culture dominated by gangster mentalities and self-destructive wantonness."[39]

West argued that capitalist culture bombards its youthful consumers with titillating images designed to stimulate self-preoccupation, materialism, and antisocial attitudes, corrupts them, and leaves most of them untethered: "Most of our children—neglected by overburdened parents and bombarded by the market values of profit-hungry corporations—are ill-equipped to live lives of spiritual and cultural quality." Capitalist postmodernity, he charged, is deeply nihilistic. At the street level nihilism is the experience of "horrifying meaning-lessness, hopelessness, and (most important) lovelessness." West said the culture of nihilism is more destructive than oppression or exploitation in poor black neighborhoods—the "major enemy of black survival in America." As recently as the early 1970s black Americans had the lowest suicide rate in the United States. A generation later young black Americans had the highest rate. What changed? What caused "this shattering of black civil society"?[40]

West recognized that bitter experiences of integration took a toll, and black optimism collapsed after the King years passed. But he judged that two other factors were more important—"the saturation of market forces and market moralities in black life and the present crisis in black leadership." He pointed to the flood of violence and sexual titillation pouring through the media and culture industries. This cascade of depravity degrades all Americans, he argued, but it damages poor young black Americans most of all: "The predominance of this way of life among those living in poverty-ridden conditions, with a limited capacity to ward off self-contempt and self-hatred, results in the possible triumph of the nihilistic threat in black America."[41]

More than ever, West contended, black Americans needed compelling leaders; instead, it got mediocrities with little moral character: "The present-day black middle class is not simply different than its predecessors—it is more deficient and, to put it strongly, more decadent. For the most part, the dominant outlooks and life-styles of today's black middle class discourage the development of high quality political and intellectual leaders." In fact, the worst aspects of America's general cultural decadence were "accentuated among black middle-class Americans."[42]

West recalled that the great black leaders of the past carried themselves with moral dignity. They wore suits and white shirts, conveyed a serious moral purpose, treated ordinary people with humble respect, and projected a bold, gut-level anger at American racism. "In stark contrast, most present-day black political leaders appear too hungry for status to be angry, too eager for acceptance to be bold, too self-invested in advancement to be defiant." On the rare occasions that they struck a prophetic note, it was for show, "more performance than personal, more play-acting than heartfelt." Middle-class black leaders were just like other entrants to middle-class consumption, obsessed with status and addicted to self-gratification. Instead of raging against "the gross deterioration of personal, familial, and communal relations among African-Americans," they looked away from it.[43]

West delineated three types of contemporary black leaders: race-effacing managers, race-identifying protest leaders, and race-transcending prophets. Los

Angeles mayor Thomas Bradley exemplified the first type, relying on political savvy and diplomacy to claim a place at the establishment table. Black nationalist leaders and most leaders of the civil rights organizations belonged to the second category. The third type was West's ideal—standing boldly for racial justice while transcending race as a category of personal identity and collective loyalty. He pegged Adam Clayton Powell Jr. and Harold Washington as race-transcending prophets. Jesse Jackson tried to be one in his 1988 presidential race but never quite overcame his opportunistic past; West judged that his own generation had yet to produce one.

He sorted black intellectuals into similar types: race-distancing elitists, race-embracing rebels, and race-transcending prophets. The first type, impressed by their own cultivation and accomplishments, held themselves above other blacks; West named Adolph Reed Jr. as an example. The second type rebelled against the snobbish insularity of the white academy by creating a black-space version of it; West put most Afrocentrists in this category. The ideal, the race-transcending prophets, fused the life of the mind with the struggle for justice without paying heed to social standing, career advancement, or intellectual fashions. West's exemplar was Baldwin; Oliver Cox also qualified; currently only Morrison deserved to be called a race-transcending prophetic intellectual. West lamented: "This vacuum continues to aggravate the crisis of black leadership—and the plight of the wretched of the earth deteriorates."[44]

He knew he would be accused of being too harsh or ungenerous, though the backlash roared for years, more than he expected, which played a role in making him famous. West tried to limit the damage by detailing what he did not mean. He was not calling for a Messiah to replace Malcolm or King because that was not the point and messiah figures are problematic anyway. Malcolm said nothing about "the vicious role of priestly versions of Islam in the modern world," and King was sexist and antigay. West said what mattered was to develop "new models of leadership and forge the kind of persons to actualize these models." America needed race-transcending prophets who raged for justice.[45]

BELL HOOKS AND BLACK FEMINIST LIBERATIONISM

Race Matters brought West a crush of publicity and changed his life. From there he climbed higher, attaining fixture status in the media while conducting long-running dialogues with bell hooks and Michael Lerner. West met hooks at the Socialist Scholars Conference of 1985 and befriended her later that year when they became faculty colleagues at Yale, and he befriended Lerner in 1989 when Harrington brought them together for a conference shortly before Harrington died. Each dialogue went on for many years and produced a coauthored book. The book version of his dialogue with hooks was titled *Breaking Bread: Insurgent Black Intellectual Life* (1991). His book dialogue with Lerner was titled *Jews and Blacks: Let the Healing Begin* (1995). West's dialogue with hooks carried on throughout their careers while both became fixtures of the cultural studies canon.

hooks was born Gloria Jean Watkins in 1952 in Hopkinsville, Kentucky. Her father worked as a post office janitor, her mother worked as a maid, and both struggled to comprehend and control their brilliant, volatile, unhappy daughter. She bridled at her father's patriarchal rule and mood swings, both fearing him and defying him. She had a closer relationship with her mother but described her family background as dysfunctional. Her teachers in segregated schools, mostly single black women, gave her role models of accomplishment but admonished against her penchant for talking back. At the age of ten hooks began to write searing poems, adopting her maternal great-grandmother's name as a pseudonym. She later recalled that writing was how she carried out her desperate need to kill herself without having to die: "It was clearly the Gloria Jean of my tormented and anguished childhood that I wanted to be rid of, the girl who was always wrong, always punished, always subjected to some humiliation or other, always crying, the girl who was to end up in a mental institution because she could not be anything but crazy, or so they told her." On one occasion she pressed a hot iron to her arm, imploring her parents and five siblings to leave her alone; she wore her scar as a brand "marking her madness."[46]

Her brilliance marked her for college if she survived, but to her parents any local college would do. They opposed her vehemently, especially her father, when hooks won a scholarship to Stanford and accepted it. Stanford was even more foreign and bewildering than she expected. She barely survived, feeling impossibly isolated, unable to justify to herself why she was there. Various kinds of radical politics were prevalent on campus, yet hooks had white male professors who were unabashedly racist, sexist, and classist and others who would have been offended at being called racist or sexist but were both all the same. She took a women's studies class with a leading white feminist scholar, Tillie Olsen, whose work focused on the silencing of women in Western literature. hooks anguished at the complete absence of any mention of black women. She confronted Olsen, who was remorseful, and the class, which resented hooks for "spoiling their celebration, their 'sisterhood,' their 'togetherness.' " She survived by working on a book about what was missing.[47]

Olsen's remorse was completely unhelpful because hooks was not looking for sympathy. She needed help with what was missing. Somehow, even in women's studies, black women did not matter; they had no history that qualified for inclusion. She later recalled, "Attending such classes, I reached a very real point of desperation and urgency; I needed to know about black woman's reality. I needed even to understand this feeling of difference and separation from white women peers." Her manuscript was a response to the indignity of being rendered invisible. She rued that her social reality as a black woman made her different from her white male, white female, and black male peers at Stanford, where hooks met highly assimilated black males who mystified her. She pored over the indexes of history and sociology textbooks looking for anything about black women, finding almost nothing. She was nineteen years old when the first draft of *Ain't I a Woman* reached five hundred sprawling pages of self-taught history and analysis: "The book emerged out of my longing for self-recovery, for education for critical consciousness—for a way of understanding black female experience that would liberate us from the colonizing mentality fostered in a racist, sexist context."[48]

That put it in language she acquired in graduate school from Brazilian Christian socialist educator Paolo Freire, who fixed on Fanon questions—What would liberationist anticolonial pedagogy be? How should education be conceived if it is not an instrument of colonization? These became burning questions to hooks after she entered graduate school and anticipated her teaching career. As an undergraduate she consumed the essays of Morrison and ransacked history books for clues about black women. hooks was not political when she began to write *Ain't I a Woman*. She was a lonely, autodidactic black female poet just trying not to drown. It took her seven years and many rewrites to finish the book. She worked for the telephone company after graduating from Stanford, tried to wrestle her unwieldy manuscript into shape, and got no encouragement from anyone. She tried to bond with exploited black female coworkers, which deepened her discouragement: "I often felt an intense despair that was so overwhelming I really questioned how we could bear being alive in this society, how we could stay alive."[49]

It galled her that so much of the literature on black women celebrated strong superwomen, looking away from the suffering and oppression of black women. Her pain at the phone company drove her to graduate school, very unhappily. hooks drifted from the University of Wisconsin to the University of Southern California to UC-Santa Cruz, studying English literature in departments where she never had a black female teacher. She had one black male professor at Stanford and one at USC, both of whom discouraged black female students. She later recalled that she spent her entire graduate school career waiting for a discussion of critical pedagogy that never occurred; somehow graduate professors were not reflective about what they did every week in the classroom. She tried to take no courses from outright racists, but that proved to be impossible: "It was often in the very areas of British and American literature where racism abounds in the texts studied that I would encounter racist individuals." She found a godsend guide on the pedagogy question in the writings of Freire, who said exactly what she already believed: Education is never a neutral process. Education either integrates students into the dominant system, facilitating conformity to it, or it is a practice of freedom that seeks to transform the system.[50]

Professors and classmates told hooks repeatedly that she lacked "the proper demeanor of a graduate student." Finally she stopped rewriting *Ain't I a Woman*, sent it to a succession of publishers, and was rejected. She pushed it aside, concentrating on earning her doctorate at UC–Santa Cruz, "despite the prevalence of racism and sexism." Her manuscript would have stayed in the drawer if not for three developments in 1980: white feminists began to talk about racism, hooks gave a bookstore talk in San Francisco that got a stormy reaction, and she learned at the bookstore that South End Press—a new left-wing publishing collective in Boston—was looking for manuscripts on race and feminism. At South End the editors wanted the book but worried it was too angry. hooks said she wasn't really angry; this was an issue of cultural difference distinguishing her intense black culture expressiveness from the opaque indirectness of white culture. *Ain't I a Woman* paid homage to the famous speech of Sojourner Truth in its title, underscoring Truth's rhetorical question by dropping the question mark. It ranged over the impact of sexism on black women during slavery, the denigration of black women after slavery, black male sexism, white feminist racism, and the politics of black feminism. It skewered the toxic blend of Jim Crow racist and sexist stereotypes that demonized black women for surviving. It protested that black women were routinely marginalized in black freedom movements and that white feminists reinforced the historic cultural stigmas put upon black women.[51]

hooks named names and talked turkey, angering many who did not appreciate being criticized. She ripped renowned white lesbian feminist poet Adrienne Rich for lauding a "strong anti-racist female tradition" that did not exist. She rehearsed the story of nineteenth-century white feminist racism and ran through the canon of modern white feminism from Betty Friedan's *The Feminine Mystique* to Barbara Berg's *The Remembered Gate* to Zillah Eisenstein's edited *Capitalist Patriarchy and the Case for Socialist Feminism*. All perpetuated racist ideology, she charged, generalizing about American women entirely from the perspective of white women. hooks said an unspoken force allowed white feminists to ignore black women without mentioning their own racial identity: "That force is racism. In a racially imperialist nation such as ours, it is the dominant race that reserves for itself the luxury of dismissing racial identity while the oppressed race is made daily aware of their racial identity." She sympathized with black feminists who joined separatist groups but said they were wrong too; in fact they allowed white racism to turn them into mirror-image reactionaries: "By creating segregated feminist groups, they both endorsed and perpetuated the very 'racism' they were supposedly attacking." hooks lingered over the manifesto of the Combahee River Collective, charging that this black lesbian separatist classic gave white feminists permission to care only about themselves and led black women's groups into political nowhere: "Many black women who had never participated in the women's movement saw the formation of separate black groups as confirmation of their belief that no alliance could ever take place between black and white women."[52]

That was a disaster for feminism, she argued, pointing to black lesbian feminist Lorraine Bethel's contention that white women were soft, privileged parasites living off white men and black domestic workers. hooks disliked the trend among lesbian black feminists to say that a real feminist cannot be heterosexual. Her draft delved into this issue, but the editors asked her not to go there, and she eliminated the entire section except for one sentence stating that nothing good would come from attacking heterosexuality per se. She got furious replies from Cheryl Clarke, Barbara Smith, and other black lesbian feminists claiming that she insulted them without even granting them the dignity of using the word "lesbian." hooks regretted that she deferred to her editors; at least her draft would have shown that she engaged this issue seriously. *Ain't I a Woman* drove to a plea for an interracial feminist movement that united against racism, sexism, and capitalism. The rebellious rhetoric of white feminism, hooks said, created an illusion of radicalism and militancy. Feminism needed to *become* radical by uniting against everything feminists should oppose: "Women's liberationists, white and black, will always be at odds with one another as long as our idea of liberation is based on having the power white men have. For that power denies unity, denies common connection, and is inherently divisive." All feminists, she argued, must accept responsibility for abolishing the forces that divide women.[53]

Ain't I a Woman was a sensational debut that opened career doors for hooks. It got many harsh reviews, some of which wounded her deeply. She said the hostile reviews nearly crushed her. The book version of her doctoral dissertation, *Feminist Theory: From Margin to Center* (1984), addressed the hostile reviews immediately, confessing that the attacks from black feminists hurt most: "Some of the most outspoken black women active in feminist movement responded by trashing both it and me. While I expected serious, rigorous evaluation of my work I was totally unprepared for the hostility and contempt shown me by women whom I did not and do not see as enemies." hooks said she would not have been able to carry on had there been no positive response; later she recalled that it came mostly from readers outside the academy. *Feminist Theory* doubled down on her argument that all feminists needed to band together to make feminism antiracist, antisexist, and anticapitalist. hooks decried that most of the white feminist movement fit into capitalism with no problem, equating feminism with professional careers for white, middle-class women. It started with Friedan focusing on white suburban housewives "bored with leisure, with the home, with buying products." hooks said the feminist mainstream still sounded like Friedan: "Racism abounds in the writings of white feminists, reinforcing white supremacy and negating the possibility that women will bond politically across racial and ethnic boundaries."[54]

hooks denied that she said it to disparage "sisterhood is powerful" rhetoric; shaming white feminists out of aspiring to solidarity was the last thing she intended. Sisterhood is powerful was exactly the right idea except for the racist and procapitalist ways white feminists construed it. *Feminist Theory* revisited the issue of lesbian sexuality and her disagreements with black feminist separatists. hooks said she was strongly prolesbian and that Clarke and others had misread her. Her previous book tried to make one point on this subject: "Feminism will never appeal to a mass-based group of women in our society who are heterosexual if they think that they will be looked down upon or seen as doing something wrong." She had not meant to single out lesbian feminists for criticism because other feminist groups also derided heterosexual relationships with men. hooks said the feminist movement must not condone any form of antilesbian prejudice *or* condemnation of heterosexual practice: "As feminists, we must confront those women who do in fact believe that women with heterosexual preferences are either traitors or likely to be anti-lesbian. Condemnation of heterosexual practice has led women who desire sexual relationships with men to feel they cannot participate in feminist movement. They have gotten the message that to be 'truly' feminist is not to be heterosexual."[55]

hooks grieved that when feminism went radical it opted for some kind of separatism; meanwhile white liberal feminists dominated what the media called feminism. It was not too late to build a radical feminist movement that approximated the sisterhood ideal. Feminism would fail if it did not forge an interracial united front to abolish racism, sexism, and capitalism: "Women must take the initiative and demonstrate the power of solidarity. Unless we can show that barriers separating women can be eliminated, that solidarity can exist, we cannot hope to change and transform society as a whole." She built up to Freire's theme that a liberationist movement must be infused with love and fired by it. Freire taught in *Pedagogy of the Oppressed* that domination reflects the pathology of love; the dominators become sadists and the dominated become masochists: "Because love is an act of courage, not of fear, love is commitment to others. No matter where the oppressed are found, the act of love is commitment to their cause—the cause of liberation."[56]

hooks was sensitive to criticism that her subsequent books quoted Freire too much and she wrote them too hurriedly. She completed her PhD in English literature at Santa Cruz in 1983, taught there in her early career, joined the Yale faculty in 1985, and moved to Oberlin College in 1988. Her three years at Yale were dramatic and scarring. Teaching in the English Department and African American Studies, she attracted large classes, took pride in confronting her students, and deflated Yale's self-congratulatory pieties about itself. Yale president Benno Schmidt declared in his inaugural address of 1986 that Yale's mission was to "preserve, disseminate, and advance knowledge through teaching and research." That perfectly summarized what hooks rejected: "Again and again, academic freedom is evoked to deflect attention away from the ways knowledge is used to reinforce and perpetuate domination, away from the ways in which education is not a neutral process. Whenever this happens, the very idea of academic freedom loses its meaning and integrity."[57]

Yale was obviously a bastion of privilege and elitism, she said. What galled her was that Yale employed a superficial rhetoric of diversity and academic freedom to guard its privileges. It wasn't just Yale; the academy as a whole was self-serving and conformist. hooks lamented students who cared only about their prospective careers and at black students who questioned whether blackness exists. Many believed that assimilation to the existing academy was the only way to succeed. She objected: "We must ask ourselves how it can be that many of us lack critical consciousness, have little or no understanding of the politics of race, deny that white supremacy threatens our existence and well-being, and act in complicity by internalizing racism and denigrating and devaluing blackness." The logic of assimilation, she implored, rests on the white supremacist idea that eradicating blackness will allow blacks to become white: "Of course, since we who are black can never be white, this very effort promotes and fosters serious psychological stress and even severe mental illness." hooks grieved at the pain and confusion of her black students at Yale. She told them that winning a perch in elite society was not worth killing themselves. She charged that women's studies was becoming as careerist and elitist as the rest of the academy: "Feminist theory is rapidly becoming another sphere of academic elitism, wherein work that is linguistically convoluted, which draws on other such works, is deemed more intellectually sophisticated, in fact is deemed more theoretical." hooks chided that writing snooty, unintelligible articles in peer-reviewed journals is not radical; it's another version of becoming complicit in structures of domination.[58]

She was keenly mindful of the difference between attracting an audience and being liked. hooks was embattled in her overflow classes and lecture venues. She wanted to be liked but not enough to betray her idea of what a liberationist teacher should do in her context. She sympathized with students who stirred with excitement at the feminist slogan that the personal is the political. She remembered what this slogan once meant to her but pressed a critical question: What comes of beginning with yourself when your self is a product of white supremacist, sexist, capitalist America? hooks cautioned that too many feminists reduced the political to themselves and their career aspirations. The feminists of SDS had strong political convictions, but student feminists of the 1980s and 1990s mostly did not. The dominant culture and their own narcissism taught them to stick with the personal: "Then the self does not become that which one moves into to move beyond, or to connect with. It stays in place, the starting point from which one need never move." Feminism cannot be transformative, she insisted, if it never becomes politicized.[59]

At Yale and later at Oberlin hooks had to deal with select antagonistic colleagues who never grasped that she was not an exponent of identity politics. She plainly decried the separatist, individualistic, and narcissistic perils of identity politics, while affirming simultaneously that identity politics was right to roar for personal dignity and personality. Feminism, she argued, lost its way when it capitulated to capitalism. hooks said it had already happened when she came of age at Stanford: "Obsessive, narcissistic concern with 'finding an identity' was already a popular cultural preoccupation, one that deflected attention away from radical politics." She exhorted her students not to settle for capitalist success: "To challenge identity politics we must offer strategies of politicization that enlarge our conception of who we are, that intensify our sense of intersubjectivity, our relation to a collective reality. We do this by reemphasizing how history, political science, psychoanalysis, and diverse ways of knowing can be used to inform our ideas of self and identity."[60]

That made her very much like West, urging audiences to aim higher and love radically. hooks denied that West overdid the nihilism theme. "Nihilism is everywhere," she said. It struck deep into assimilated middle-class blacks who felt a sense of loss and meaninglessness, cut off from themselves and their history: "These feelings of alienation and estrangement create suffering." hooks told West she had recently shared a conference forum with a privileged black woman who mocked her emphasis on struggle while the audience cheered. hooks lamented that this speaker and the audience had no personal acquaintance with any justice movement; thus they did not know the joy of struggling for justice: "We must teach young Black folks to understand that struggle is process, that one moves from circumstances of difficulty and pain to awareness, joy, fulfillment." She gave a personal example: "When I was here at Yale I felt that my labor was not appreciated. It was not clear that my work was having a meaningful impact. Yet I feel that impact today."[61]

West lauded hooks for willingly paying the price of defying the self-perpetuating rules of the academy. He said she braved the scorn of ensconced academics to reach a much larger public than the academy, calling out the "surreptitious self-loathing" that paralyzes much of the academy. He appreciated especially that she was an African American writer "without being an Afro-centric thinker," grounding her work in black life while refusing to conceive black life in competitive relation to European or Euro-American life. Black American culture, West observed, has a hybrid character. Since hooks was rooted in black American life, "she feels no need to spend her energy fighting off White influences, extricating White elements, or teasing out only African sources for her thought." hooks reflected in reply that she came of age at a hot time in the academy, when women's studies was fresh and promising, and black women demanded a place in it. It made her sad to see what came of academic feminism. She shifted away from it in reaction, rooting herself even more in black life than she intended when she began: "Feminist theory does not emerge as a discourse rooted in any kind of discussion of Blackness, so to some extent, Black women, like myself, who entered that discourse did not enter it through the door of gender, race, and class. We came to it in terms of gender alone and have been struggling ever since for recognition of race and class."[62]

MICHAEL LERNER AND THE POLITICS OF MEANING

West's ongoing dialogue with hooks was a model for his dialogue with Lerner, who told his story—recounted in the previous chapter—of growing up in Newark and rebelling against his secular Zionist parents. They sent him to a progressive Christian school in Short Hills instead of the local public school, where 80 percent of the students were Jewish. Hebrew School in the late afternoons was torture to his classmates but not to Lerner, who yearned for Jewish companions and Judaism. Lerner disdained the overassimilated path of his parents. Both became prominent players in New Jersey Democratic politics, ascended into the upper middle class, moved to the suburbs when blacks moved into their neighborhood, and reduced their Jewish identity to Zionism. Lerner put it bluntly: "By the time I was eleven or twelve I was seeing that it was actually their ability to sell themselves to one WASP after another who would offer them some reward in return for help in getting elected" that advanced their careers. "My parents' own power was completely derivative and dependent on their fawning over these various WASP politicians, who in turn served a ruling elite of wealthy WASPS." His father became a judge, his mother ran the campaigns of three New Jersey governors, and she took it hard when Lerner took a religious turn. Lerner's father accepted that he had religious feelings, but his mother read it as retrogression—choosing to be downwardly mobile.[63]

Heschel drew Lerner into his deep Jewish learning and piety, though neither of them was involved in protest politics before 1965. Lerner grew up fearing the tougher black kids at school and was skeptical during his college years at Columbia about political activism. At college he did not admire Jewish literary stars such as Lionel Trilling and Saul Bellow because they reminded him of his parents. Lerner studied philosophy under Herbert Marcuse at Berkeley, was swept into the Free Speech Movement, and careened to the SDS left wing. He founded NAM to resurrect the democratic socialist wing of SDS, but that didn't work out. In *The New Socialist Revolution* (1973) he expounded his original vision for NAM, contending that the left shared with ordinary people the corrupting condition of powerlessness. A tiny capitalist class held most of the economic power and bought commensurate political power, yielding a depressed majority population and a dysfunctional left. Lerner argued that the next revolution depended on the growing radical consciousness of students, youth, blacks, women, the working class, and radicalized professional men. These social forces needed to form revolutionary peoples' councils in neighborhoods and schools and create a mass democratic socialist party to support the councils. Then the many would be empowered to take back their country.[64]

The memory of France in May 1968 haunted Lerner's argument. France teetered on a revolution that the French Communist Party thwarted out of solicitude for the security interests of Moscow. American anarchists proclaimed that the French disaster showed why no socialist party should be trusted. Lerner argued that no socialist government existed anywhere on earth and the French Communist Party was a status-quo outfit dominated by Moscow. The imperative of the next revolution was to build something lacking any precedent: a democratic socialist society based on peoples' councils and facilitated by a mass socialist party. Nothing got better as long as the many had almost no power. Harrington panned Lerner's book as warmed-over SDS utopianism. He said he wanted to commend the book but couldn't because Lerner recycled the SDS disdain for liberals and exaggerated the capitalist hegemony over the academy. The academy was changing, Harrington observed; it mattered that radical children of the 1960s were obtaining tenure in it. His review wounded Lerner; forty years later Lerner cited it when he told me he forbade articles about Harrington in *Tikkun*.[65]

The New Socialist Revolution won little notice, and Lerner stewed over his situation. NAM had gone awry, and his book was ignored. Lerner rethought what his life was about, knowing that his two selves did not fit together. One was a political performer still radiating the more-radical-than-you spirit of SDS and aspiring to be the next great left-wing leader. The other Lerner had religious feelings that he repressed in lefty circles and empathy for working-class people that his lefty friends disparaged. He was tired of stifling his religious feelings to fit in with the left, regretting especially that Jewish socialism was overwhelmingly antireligious: "Whenever I brought up religion, all sides agreed that I should shut up about it. They argued that religion was fundamentally a reactionary force, and that my own personal commitments as a religious Jew were not welcome." Lerner subsequently regretted that he tried so hard to conform to antireligious leftism. He shuddered to remember how deeply self-divided he had been, which yielded "indefensible distortions in my thinking and behavior."[66]

Meanwhile he pondered the writings of Austrian American psychiatrist Wilhelm Reich, which focused on overall character structure, not individual neurotic symptoms. What would a mass psychology of empowerment be? This question drew Lerner back to school. In 1977 he earned a PhD in clinical psychology and cofounded the Institute for Labor and Mental Health, joining a group of psychiatrists, psychologists, social workers, family therapists, union officials, and community activists. They shared Lerner's conviction that psychology wrongly fixes on individual neuroses, explaining powerlessness as the product of an individual's personal failure. There had to be an approach to therapy that did not replicate American individualism, did not repel working-class people, and promoted social change.

The New Socialist Revolution had a glimmer of where Lerner was headed. At the end of a long chapter describing the social forces of the next revolution, he said that powerlessness was not the only power problem that radical movements faced. The New Left was too utopian and alienated to acknowledge the gains it made. It forced Lyndon Johnson to resign his presidency but fell into crazed despair when the war didn't end. The New Left failed to build on its achievements because it never took satisfaction in anything it achieved. The only criterion of success it respected was utopian. Thus it undermined its sense of self-worth at the very moment that it swayed much of the nation to criticize the war and American society: "Failing to sense its own importance, the Left indulged in inwardness and sectarianism and finally fell apart." Later he hung a psychosocial name on this affliction: "surplus powerlessness."[67]

Most radicals are afraid of winning, Lerner argued. This fear is rooted in their belief that they don't have a right to win. Being isolated and marginal comes naturally to radicals, who strive to stay that way despite claiming otherwise. Lerner observed that most radicals give the impression to outsiders of being strangely arrogant and elitist. They demean ordinary people as greedy, stupid, bigoted, opportunistic, and six kinds of backward, conveying superiority. Lerner said radicals would not be so judgmental if they didn't assume that people like them had no chance of succeeding. The pronounced tendency of left-wing people to sneer at others reflects a pathological commitment to being alienated losers. Radicals believe they deserve to be isolated, being the kinds of people that conventional society will never respect. Lerner's work with the Institute for Labor and Mental Health yielded, in 1986, a "new kind of self-help book," *Surplus Powerlessness,* and led him to found *Tikkun* magazine the same year, both in partnership with legal scholar Peter Gabel. Both were dedicated to creating a healthier left than the one Lerner joined as a Berkeley philosophy student. He credited Reich, Marcuse, and Gabel as major influences on his thinking, but the foremost influence was Heschel, who taught him that prophetic justice is central to Judaism and compassion is the guiding value of Jewish tradition. Like Heschel, Lerner conceived his writing as Midrash on Torah written in contemporary language.[68]

He wrote as an advocate of the Jewish Renewal Movement based in Philadelphia around the organization Aleph and founded by Rabbi Zalman Schachter-Shalomi, though Lerner opposed its tendency to lift spiritual concerns above the political struggle for justice. He wrote as an ally of Peace Now, New Israel Fund, New Jewish Agenda, Israel Peace Lobby, Mazon, Jewish Fund for Justice, various Jewish feminist collectives, and all synagogues affirming gay, lesbian, and queer members. Lerner told readers that feminism liberated him "from the sterile world of academic philosophy to a much deeper understanding of human reality." Editing *Tikkun* and serving as rabbi of Beyt Tikkun synagogue in San Francisco suited him better than the academy. He stressed that Hebrew religion is rooted in the experience of deliverance from slavery in Egypt and the teaching of the Hebrew prophets. Judaism is supposed to be radical, prophetic, devoted to justice, and compassionate. Lerner argued that Judaism was drained of its prophetic character by the persecution of Jews in Christian Europe and the attempts of Jews to assimilate. Assimilation didn't work very well anyway because Europeans reserved a special loathing for Jews.

In the United States, assimilation worked much better because white America had Native Americans and African Americans to hate. Lerner sympathized with the many Jews who swallowed American materialism and selfishness on their way to feeling like real Americans. His parents were prototypes, at least with decent liberal politics. But his parents were spiritually desiccated, a dead end. They lacked any feeling for what made Judaism a great religion. Then came a type of Jewish consciousness that lacked even halfway decent politics.[69]

The role of Jews in the neocon movement distressed Lerner and motivated him. Neoconservatism was a much broader phenomenon than its Jewish component, but the substantial Jewish presence in it struck him as the old assimilation story on steroids—Jews absorbing and championing the most selfish, predatory, and boorish aspects of the dominant culture. Lerner decried that neocons lacked any feeling for the downtrodden and that many neocon leaders were Jews: "The celebration of selfishness that forms the core of the neoconservative-style Jewish identity leads to a dead end." He said it various ways, usually pairing selfishness and cynicism as twin neocon traits. He also turned it over, charging that anti-Semitism was escalating on the left in response to Israeli brutality against the Palestinians, accusatory back-and-forth between American blacks and Jews, and the neocon phenomenon. In *The Socialism of Fools* (1992) Lerner said anti-Semitism was mostly a right-wing pathology, but the left had plenty of it too, not least among self-hating Jews. He implored non-Jewish left-wing readers: Don't wait for Jews to raise this issue. Raise it yourself, refute anti-Semitic comments immediately, and don't reward self-hating Jews with leadership positions.[70]

Lerner grieved in the early 1990s that blacks and Jews were growing estranged from each other. Jews wanted to be appreciated by blacks for supporting the civil rights movement and often felt scorned instead, which made them angry. Lerner allowed that Jews sometimes acted like white racists in demeaning blacks, but "their Jewishness has nothing to do with this behavior." They didn't behave badly because they were Jews; black nationalist accusations to this effect were racist: "The willingness to generalize from the behavior of some to the larger group to which they belong is illegitimate and a classic characteristic of racism." Lerner said the opposition of the American Jewish Committee and other Jewish organizations to affirmative action belonged to a different category because here Jews acted as Jews. He supported affirmative action for African Americans just as he supported the Zionist position that all Jews hold an automatic right to Israeli citizenship based on the Law of Return. In both cases a controversial policy sought to rectify a past wrong. But Lerner asked black readers to understand why Jewish organizations opposed any policy favoring any group. Jews had only bad experiences with quota systems and were thus strongly predisposed to oppose them.[71]

Lerner asked Jesse Jackson to join him in a campaign to condemn racism in black and Jewish American communities, but Jackson turned him down. He made a similar pitch to West, who said he would prefer a dialogue project. They began taping in 1990, and both ascended dramatically in 1993 as West published *Race Matters* and Hillary Clinton gave a famous speech expounding Lerner's idea of the "politics of meaning," which called for a new ethos of caring and community. Lerner said that mean-spirited cynicism ruled in American public life but not inevitably. He and Clinton got roasted in a blaze of media ridicule after Clinton voiced his argument. Lerner's splash of fame and brief association with Clinton helped to extract an advance of one hundred thousand dollars from Penguin, which set up Lerner and West for years of envious takedown.

Lerner told West that Jewish Americans have a history of caring about black Americans, there is no reciprocal history, and neither black Americans nor African nationalists respected why Jews felt compelled to establish the State of Israel. West replied that Du Bois and Paul Robeson supported Zionism and that black Americans generally perceive Israel as part of British and American imperialism; moreover, Israel supported South Africa during the apartheid era. They agreed that Du Bois and Robeson were exceptions and that *Tikkun* stoutly condemned Israel's support of South Africa. They disagreed about the upshot of the Jewish chosen people doctrine. West said it was an impediment to judging all nations by one ethical standard. Lerner said it commendably created a higher standard: "I wish that every other people in the world would similarly see themselves as chosen. There's nothing in Jewish texts saying that God didn't make any deals with other peoples, or that only Jews were given the duty of moral responsibility." The problem, he argued, is that Israel is constantly judged more stringently than other nations, a bad game in which assimilated American left-wing Jews play a key role—they are Jews only for the purpose of condemning Israel: "There is something deeply 'off' in this pattern of claiming one's Jewishness only when Jewishness is something to be critiqued."[72]

West doubted that invoking the higher standard in this context is always anti-Semitic: "If you project yourselves as more enlightened and moral than other nations you are going to solicit attention." Lerner took another run at his point, observing that anti-Semites have long justified their hatred of Jews by demanding a higher standard of them than Jews can fulfill: "We don't hear from Blacks in this country any agitation about the non-democratic nature of African states that is vaguely comparable to the amount that progressive American Jews agitate about the lack of democratic equality in Israel. Even though the level of democracy in Israel is higher than virtually every African state. Yet African Americans make demands on Israel. We have a genocidal slaughter of hundreds of thousands of people in Rwanda, and yet African Americans have more to say about the undemocratic nature of Israel than they do about the oppression of Blacks by Blacks in Africa. I don't see Jews going around saying that African states should be eliminated, or that they don't have a right to exist because they oppress minority groups—even though there's a long history of minority groups being oppressed in African states."[73]

Lerner cited his magazine's repeated call for real rights, real self-determination, and real land for the Palestinians in a two-state solution. He embodied the difference between pro-Zionism and Zionism, taking pride that he had never been a Zionist. But Lerner would not be shamed by anyone who singled out Israel for criticism. He said he would feel differently if blacks learned about anti-Semitism at church or criticized African oppression with the outrage they mustered for Israel: "A whole continent of Black folk are oppressing each other whilst Black folk in the U.S. don't give a damn—but they know about Jews and our shortcomings. This is wrong." West said black Americans knew a lot about Israel and very little about African nations because America is deeply involved in Israel and the American media surveys the world from the standpoint of American interests. White supremacy, he observed, is the paramount issue for black Americans, and white Jews with an anti-Arab mentality play the dominant role in Israel. Lerner countered that the media argument is spurious—how would West feel if Lerner said that Jewish antiblack racism is attributable to media coverage of black crime? Moreover, 60 percent of the Israeli population consists of people of color—Sephardim from North Africa and Spain and Mizrahi from Yemen, Iraq, and other Arab nations: "Their culture isn't white; Europe doesn't mean a thing to them. They don't have the European history of equality and democracy. The fact is it's the Jews who come from Arab lands who are the most anti-Arab." West replied that these points do not change the dominance equation. The dominant power in Israel is white, Euro-American, and allied with U.S. imperial power. Black Americans identify with Jews because of the Exodus narrative and historical oppression, but they also see clearly where the parallels disappear.[74]

Lerner and West agreed that accusatory language about racial privilege is fraught with peril while disagreeing about what must be risked. Lerner argued that talking about racial privilege implicates all whites in the benefits of black oppression and thereby shuts down any chance of changing society: "White-skin privilege is a category that undermines social change, because it emphasizes what the majority of people have in common with the white ruling class." The left, he charged, has been making this mistake since 1965, constantly insulting the majority of Americans. The left tells white Americans they are bad, they should feel bad about it, and their only hope of salvation is to renounce who they are. Lerner put it sharply: "It tells them how much privilege they have, how they are just like the ruling class. And this, because of something about the color of their skin, something they can't possibly change!" He said America's terribly real problem of racism would not improve as long as progressives impugn the humanity of all white Americans. Lerner added that anti-imperial accusation works the same way, making all Americans guilty of something they did not create. West replied that he walked a rhetorical tightrope every day, but declining to name the social evils at work was not an option: "Pointing out the facts of American imperial privilege, white privilege, male and heterosexual privilege in no way undermines the legitimacy of the struggle against white supremacy, male supremacy, class inequality, and homophobia." Anyone who plays down the evil of white supremacy, he said, is not a reliable ally in the struggle against it.[75]

Lerner held his ground, contending for the left he wanted, which did not compete for victim status. He charged that "comparative victimology" seized the left in the late 1960s and identity victimology has ruled ever since. Native Americans win the contest of who-is-most-oppressed, black Americans hold second place, and everyone else competes for victim status in a bad game: "People are constantly trumping each other over this both in individual arguments and in terms of framing what it is we should be working on together. In fact, many of the struggles around identity politics revolve around the dynamics of claims to oppression. The result has been to push away many people who feel inadequate to press their claim to being most oppressed." Lerner said there are only two good options for the left. One is to struggle for a society in which race, gender, ethnicity, sexuality, and the like do not matter. The other is to expand the category of oppression "to include the spiritually, ethically, and psychologically debilitating consequences of the competitive market. Then more and more people will see how there are various ways of being oppressed and that they are equally valid, politically and psychologically."[76]

Tikkun pushed for option two—an expansive progressivism mindful of how Jewish-affirming Jews hear the American debate over identity politics. West said he opposed the victimology game *and* playing down the facts of oppression, while recognizing that some value-laden framework drives, frames, and weighs the facts of every factual argument. Lerner said his reality was that the Jewish right has a powerful value framework, constantly invoking the Holocaust to win the victim status game. Lerner could not win the argument for progressive Judaism within the Jewish community on a victim status basis. Moreover, he argued, fixing on privilege creates a bad left: "To most people, it feels like the Left is putting them down. By focusing on their relative privilege and ignoring their own oppression by the social system, it has driven away millions of people who came into the Left at the height of the antiwar movement. If the Left is continually making people feel bad about themselves, they will clearly want no more to do with it. And that's what has actually happened in the past twenty-five years." West replied that he and Lerner had found their fundamental disagreement. He didn't carry around the sense of all-is-lost post-1960s devastation that Lerner felt. The left that nurtured West did not fix on making whites feel bad; it cast the freedom struggle in a way that recognized the facts of racial oppression and made a moral appeal. West allowed that victim-righteousness defined too much of the left but that was not the left to which he belonged. Moreover, Lerner fretted too much about white fragility: "The Left must provide meaning to those facts in such a way that the beneficiaries of privilege recognize their role but are not solely defined by it."[77]

Lerner acknowledged that no true left could play down antiblack racism. He wanted the left to include anti-Semitism as a category of oppression and to help relatively privileged people perceive how the prevailing system oppresses them too. *Tikkun* pressed the latter theme, refashioning the Friedan argument about a problem lacking a name: Millions of white Americans are chewed up by the system but do not perceive the left as an ally and do not know how to name their sense of meaninglessness and hopelessness. Lerner argued that liberal and progressive movements needed to change. America needed a new kind of progressive politics, which he called the politics of meaning. Basically it was a type of cultural politics that vests spirituality, hope, and ethical values with progressive political meaning. Lerner said there is no good reason why the right dominates American political discourse about spirituality and values. There are only bad reasons deriving from the antireligious rationalism and materialism of secular progressivism. Americans, Lerner argued, were caught in cynicism and desperate for hope: "We hunger to be recognized by others, to be cherished for our own sakes and not for what we have accomplished or possess, and to be acknowledged as people who care about something higher and more important than our own self-interest."[78]

The idea of the politics of meaning emerged from Lerner's work in the Institute for Labor and Mental Health. The institute set up a stress clinic that created occupational stress groups and family support groups, eschewing the individual therapy model. Lerner's work with these groups convinced him that most middle-class Americans are not motivated primarily by material self-interest. His group-clients were unhappy, wanted meaningful work, blamed themselves for their failures, and assumed that Americans succeed or fail based on merit. Lerner observed, "Most people have developed a complex personal story of how they screwed things up. It explains why they have been unable to find work that would more than adequately fulfill their need for meaning and purpose, and why they have failed to build lives in which they receive greater recognition and caring from others." It took weeks of talking to get people to open up; at first they assured Lerner that everything was fine. Then they told their stories of pain and regret. Lerner said the political right got the attention of ordinary people by talking about family breakdown, children, crime, moral dilemmas, and spiritual hunger. The liberal-left, meanwhile, took pride in being above such things. Lerner argued that American politics was deeply cynical and getting worse. Republican Newt Gingrich of Georgia became the star of the U.S. Congress by assuring Americans they could not afford to care for each other. Lerner said Gingrich succeeded because predatory individualism destroys the faith that others can be counted on to care for the hurting and to solve common problems.[79]

Politics as the struggle for power to run the government was of secondary importance to Lerner. The politics that mattered to him was about organizing a common public life. Lerner said the best model for the politics of meaning is the feminist movement, which is not primarily about changing laws or government programs. Feminism focuses primarily on changing the ways that women are treated and talked about. Every human interaction and aspect of culture is of concern to it. Feminists pursue power politics to achieve feminist legislative goals, but feminism itself transcends its advocacy of rights and new entitlements. The politics of meaning, he argued, works the same way: "A politics of meaning is as much about changing how we deal with one another in our daily lives as it is about social policies or narrowly defined legislative programs."[80]

He got a splash of fame that quickly turned ugly when Hillary Clinton extolled the politics of meaning. Lerner and Clinton were excoriated for blathering New Age platitudes, pretending that liberals have moral values, and presuming to admonish. Pundits accused Lerner of scolding individuals, never mind that he was against scolding and shaming. The *New Republic* said Clinton was welcome to confess her own moral failures but had no business projecting them onto others. Neocon pundit Charles Krauthammer said Clinton's speech was a species of adolescent, breathless, conceited self-congratulation. Rush Limbaugh bashed Clinton and Lerner for an entire chapter of one of his best sellers, dredging up howlers about Lerner from his SDS days. Lerner defended Clinton, but she dropped him and the politics of meaning. Lerner said the cynical meanness out there was much worse than he had realized.[81]

When the book version appeared in 1996 he was steeled for hostile reviews. Many were brutal; Lerner seemed to evoke a need to ridicule. Some reviewers skipped past the book to attack Lerner personally, describing him as overbearing, cloying, and relentlessly self-promoting. *Atlantic* reviewer Lee Siegel rolled together the usual anti-Lerner hits, depicting the politics of meaning as a "coat of crazy colors" and deriding Lerner's "loony visions of a brave new consciousness." Siegel said the book was "an unreadable compendium of gaseous bromides that Lerner has been repeating for ten years." He howled at Lerner's supposedly idiotic belief that he could be feminist and profamily simultaneously or a radical Jew but still religious. *The Politics of Meaning*, Siegel warned, was the worst part of *Tikkun*—the editorial column—spread over 326 pages. Since Siegel was synthesizing years of anti-Lerner fodder, he reached for historical perspective, assuring *Atlantic* readers that Lerner's "publicity-hungry maneuverings earned him whatever vituperation he received."[82]

BROTHER WEST: LIVING OUT LOUD

As bad as the pounding got for Lerner, it did not compare to what West got. His unparalleled career in public intellectualism set him up for critics envious, hostile, and pedantic. West appeared regularly on cable news shows, commented weekly on Tavis Smiley's National Public Radio program, served as a senior advisor to presidential candidate Bill Bradley in the 2000 Democratic primaries, campaigned for Green Party nominee Ralph Nader in the 2000 presidential election, supported Al Sharpton's brief presidential bid in 2004, cut two rap CD's, *Sketches of My Culture* (2001, Artemis) and *Street Knowledge* (2004, Roc Diamond), and played the role of Councilor West, a member of the Council of Zion, in two of the *Matrix* movies, *The Matrix Reloaded* and *The Matrix Revolutions*. He enjoyed being famous but rued its perils. West was keenly aware that the more famous he became, the more *he* became the subject instead of anything he said. Having stressed the shortcomings of others on his way up, he got a barrage of payback. Black nationalists and black radicals charged that he got famous by criticizing black Americans and playing to white audiences. Many reviewers, friendly and hostile, said his writings were vague, rhetorical, and utopian.[83]

On the right, hostility was routinized, constantly depicting West as the epitome of the corruption of the academy. In 1995 *New Republic* literary editor Leon Wieseltier wrote the mother lode of hostile criticism, declaring that West's work was "noisy, tedious, slippery . . . sectarian, humorless, pedantic and self endeared." According to Wieseltier, West did not make arguments, he merely declaimed. He was not a philosopher but merely cobbled together snatches of philosophies. His eccentricity was surpassed only by his enormous vanity. His books were monuments "to the devastation of a mind by the squalls of theory." In sum, in a quote immortalized by repeated citation: "They are almost completely worthless."[84]

Wieseltier's parade of mean-spirited exaggerations heightened West's vulnerability to non-right-wing criticism, usually without citation. It also fueled ferocious ridicule from the right, where Wieseltier was nearly always cited gleefully. Conservative activist David Horowitz, reviewing *The Cornel West Reader* in 1999, recycled Wieseltier's charges, added a few of his own about West's "intellectual superficiality" and "blasts of hot air," and condemned West's friendships with Sharpton and Black Muslim leader Louis Farrakhan. West tried to build bridges between black nationalists and Jewish critics. To Horowitz, this was the key to West's eminent stature: his oxymoronic capacity to pose simultaneously as a racial healer and a "bedfellow of racial extremists." He said West got away with it only because no one took him seriously: "He is the quintessential nonthreatening radical, an African American who can wave the bloody shirt to orchestrate the heartstrings of white guilt, while coming to dinner at the Harvard faculty club and acting as a gentleman host."[85]

West spent his social capital trying to bring enemies together, taking risks that few others dared. In his early career he censured Farrakhan's characterization of Judaism as a "gutter religion" as despicable, but later he spoke more guardedly about the "underdog resentment and envy" that fueled black anti-Semitism, and in 1995 he supported Farrakhan's Million Man March. West entreated black nationalists that overcoming white supremacism was something they could not do by themselves. He urged Farrakhan to repudiate anti-Semitism and to acknowledge the equal humanity of all persons. Lerner drew a sharp line at Farrakhan, calling him a "racist dog." Both terms repelled West, eliciting his reply: "I wouldn't call the brother a racist dog, but a xenophobic spokesperson when it comes to dealing with Jewish humanity." Farrakhan, West said, "loves Black folk deeply, and that love is what we see first."[86]

Conservatives charged repeatedly that only they and a few neoliberals dared to criticize West. This convention was stupendously false. Many scholars blasted West for blaming the victim in his critique of black nihilism. Cultural critic Nick De Genova said West sounded "like the classic example of a colonized elite, trapped in an existential condition of self-hatred and shame because he has come to view his own people as undignified, indecent, backward, and uncouth." Social critic Eric Lott said West's entire "lexicon of urban savagery" was frightening, reactionary, and factually wrong, coming perilously close to denying the humanity of poor black Americans. Political scientist Floyd W. Hayes III, black studies scholars Lewis Gordon and Peniel E. Joseph, and philosophers Charles Mills and Clevis Headley concurred that West's critique of Afro-nihilism was hard to distinguish from blame-the-victim conservatism. Hayes said West balefully recycled the old culture-of-poverty elitism. Gordon objected that West had no business putting down the black Marxist tradition, especially C. L. R. James and Walter Rodney. Joseph hotly accused West of "demonization and invocation," lifting Morrison above all others by invocation and putting down everyone else.[87]

Iris Marion Young concurred with Hayes, Gordon, Joseph, Mills, and Headley that West wrongly blamed black Americans for their nihilism, adding that West and Sylvia Hewlett stooped to a similar antifeminism in their critique of American family life. West and Hewlett argued that children do better in two-parent families, and the left needs to care about eroding family structures. Young said it appalled her to read such counsel from supposed progressives: "Privileging marriage and genetic ties of parenting in this way is heterosexist and insulting to adoptive parents, and wrongfully supports continued stigmatization of single mothers." Philosopher John Pittman said West conjured an ethical pragmatist like himself when he described Marx. Philosopher George Yancy said he relied too heavily on religion, in his case a thin crypto-fideism. How could much of a religion come from merely pragmatic religion?[88]

West endured right-wing attacks with as little replying as possible. Defending himself from ridicule was pointless, as was responding to people with whom he shared nothing. He engaged other critics wholeheartedly, often explaining that public intellectualism and original scholarship are different things. The Gramscian task of engaging the dominant culture was vocation enough for him. He denied that he blamed the victim in *Race Matters*; was there no statute of limitations on this "leftist knee-jerk" myth? He respected the black intellectual tradition but not to the point of Gordon's filio-piety; Du Bois was a Victorian elitist and Enlightenment rationalist, and most of Gordon's treasured black Marxists were Leninists. He did not dismiss black nationalism, contrary to Joseph, nor share Headley's devotion to the philosophy guild. To Young he replied that it should be possible to defend the progressive possibilities of heterosexual marriage from a feminist standpoint without being accused of bigotry against gays, lesbians, and single parents. He told Pittman that every insightful interpretation of Marx has background premises; Georg Lukács described a neo-Hegelian Marx, Alexandre Kojève described a Heideggerian Marx, Louis Althusser described a structuralist Marx, and West played up Marx's ethical rudder. To Yancy he acknowledged that the "more" beyond utility and politics was not his

subject. He avoided onto-theology, though he also avoided pragmatic reductionism. West appreciated the irreducible mystery of life and the tragicomic "funk"
of living, suffering, struggling, and dying. He prized Anton Chekhov above all
thinkers because Chekhov grappled with the tragicomic darkness and incongru-
ity of life. West espoused a "blues-ridden gospel" of resistance to evil, trusting
in the possibility of divine goodness: "Ours is in the trying—the rest is not our
business."[89]

He looked at the world through various lenses, not a grand theory. Marxism
alone was a collection of lenses, much like liberation theology and the varieties
of feminism. West did not sell out his early socialism or Marxism or liberationist
radicalism in his later career, though many claimed otherwise. He was keenly
aware that his prominence had much to do with having come along at the right
moment: "My sheer level of privilege and scope of exposure is unprecedented."
He stressed that the academy needs to address audiences and topics outside the
academy.[90]

In 2001 he acquired a president at Harvard, economist Lawrence Summers,
who did not fathom West's value to the university, holding the Wieseltier view
of his work. Summers accused West of embarrassing Harvard, admonished him
to write a scholarly work that peer-reviewed academic journals would review,
and challenged him to justify his position at Harvard. West decided to resign
quietly and return to Princeton; it seemed pointless to fight with Summers. For
two months he shunned reporters, but the story exploded into a page one spectacle anyway. The *Harvard Crimson* recycled Wieseltier's polemic and mocked
West's purported vanity and hypocrisy. Fareed Zakaria piled on in *Newsweek*,
recycling Wieseltier yet again; *Newsweek* readers were assured that "noisy, self-
endeared, completely worthless," and all the rest were exactly right. The *New
Republic* said West epitomized the mutation of the public intellectual into a
celebrity master of public relations. The media bashing exceeded West's collective past experience. To him, the entire episode was pathetic and damaging,
driving him back to Princeton, where he had colleagues and administrators
who fathomed his immense value to the university.[91]

IMPERIAL COLOSSUS AND GLOBAL CAPITALISM

DSA took no official position in the watershed presidential election of 2000.
West worked hard for Bradley in the Democratic primaries, came to loathe
Bradley's opponent Al Gore in the process, and switched to Green Party candi-
date Ralph Nader after Gore won the nomination. Barbara Ehrenreich, Black
Radical Congress official Juanita Webster, and other prominent DSA members

supported Nader. Many DSA members stuck with Gore, notably AFL-CIO president John Sweeney, but ramming through a majority endorsement would have torn the organization apart after years of Clinton demoralization. Those of us who worked for Gore usually led with our misgivings about him, which worsened as he ran a dismal campaign and performed poorly in the first two presidential debates. Former DSA national director Jack Clark said he supported Gore with the same lukewarm feeling he mustered for Carter. Clark motivated himself by fixing on the negative: If George W. Bush won the White House, public services would be privatized and public employee unions would be savaged. Theologian Harvey Cox lauded Nader for opposing Clinton's neoliberal trade deal with China but said that in the privacy of the voting booth, "I am not going to do anything that might help elect the lethal-injection butcher from Texas."[92]

Nader was polling 7 percent nationally at the time; the prospect of a spoiler vote that elected Bush weighed heavily on many of us. National Political Committee member Andrew Hammer said he could not support any of the proffered candidates but planned to send a check to Bernie Sanders. Longtime interfaith labor activist Norm Faramelli, fretting over the spoiler scenario, beseeched DSA not to exaggerate Gore's deficiencies. Gore was better than Bill Clinton, he said. Gore was a person of depth and substance who cared about racial justice, worker justice, and foreign policy decency, and his environmentalism was far ahead of the political curve. Faramelli suggested that too much bad-mouthing of Gore could yield a very bad consequence.[93]

Years of compacted disgust with Clinton prevented many DSA members from settling for Gore. Nader won 97,000 votes in Florida, where Bush edged Gore by 537 votes, and the U.S. Supreme Court decreed that democracy wasn't worth a Florida recount. Gore, as president, would not have invaded Iraq, bestowed another tax cut on the rich, or let the oil companies devise his energy and environmental policies. Bush claimed in the 2000 campaign that tax cuts pay for themselves—the Laffer Curve lived on despite the 1980s. The national debt crossed the $4 trillion mark in 1993, Clinton's first year in office. Clinton raised the marginal income tax rate to 39.6 percent, which Republicans predicted would destroy the economy. At the end of Clinton's run the national debt was $5.6 trillion and heading downward, as Clinton rang up budget surpluses of $70 billion in 1998, $124 billion in 1999, and $237 billion in 2000. According to the Congressional Budget Office, had the United States stuck with Clinton's fiscal policy the cumulative budget surplus would have reached $5.6 trillion by 2011, wiping out the national debt.[94]

Bush squandered that inheritance with tax cuts and wars. His tax cuts blew a $2 trillion hole in the deficit, while Bush became the first president in American history not to raise taxes to pay for an expensive war. The total costs of Bush's wars are still mounting and will surpass $5 trillion. He added a $1 trillion Medicare prescription drug benefit without paying for it either—a windfall for the pharmaceutical industry. In eight years Bush's administration piled up new debt and new accrued obligations of $10.35 trillion, and it doubled the national debt from $5.7 trillion to $11.3 trillion, not counting the $5.4 trillion of debt inherited from the federal takeovers of Fannie Mae and Freddie Mac, the home mortgage guarantors. Bush amassed more debt in eight years than America's previous forty-two presidents combined, breaking the record of the previous debt champion, Ronald Reagan.[95]

More important than the fiscal chaos of Bush's presidency was its colossal foreign policy wreckage. Clinton grappled throughout his presidency with the natural tendency of an unrivaled power to regard the entire world as its geopolitical neighborhood. Neocons protested through the 1990s that America didn't *do* anything with its unrivaled military power. On their telling, Clinton took a holiday from history, dangerously diminishing America's role in world affairs. This exaggeration served a fateful purpose. Even if terrorists had not struck the United States on September 11, 2001, it would have been overdue for a moral and political reckoning with the compulsive expansionism of unrivaled power. But the crisis of American imperialism increased by several orders of magnitude with Bush's election, his selection of a neoconservative foreign policy team, their urging after the fiendish attacks of 9/11 to conceive the struggle against terrorism as a world war, and his decision to do so.

Many clueless obituaries were written for the neocons after Soviet Communism perished and neocons lost their unifying enemy. Did anything justify the "neo" any more? Many observers said no, overlooking that neoconservatives held a more aggressive view of America's role in the world than other conservatives. Charles Krauthammer, William Kristol, Joshua Muravchik, Michael Novak, Richard Perle, Norman Podhoretz, Ben Wattenberg, and Paul Wolfowitz pressed the difference through the 1990s. Instead of reducing military spending, they contended, the United States needed to expand its military reach to every region of the world, using its tremendous military and economic power to consolidate America's global supremacy. Krauthammer gave this doctrine a name, "unipolarism," admonishing Americans to relinquish their innocent denial that they had an empire. It was a very good thing that a single pole of world power now dominated the world. A serious American foreign policy would strive to sustain this dominance. Krauthammer said the United States should leave prodemocracy projects and peacekeeping to third-rate democratic powers like Canada and Sweden. No self-respecting unipolar superpower does windows. The mission of the United States was to create a new world order shaped by American power.[96]

This prescription struck most neocons as a too-cynical version of the right idea. They embraced the goal of unipolar dominance while qualifying or rejecting Krauthammer's haughty disregard of missionary enterprises. Sustaining American dominance and planting more democracies, they argued, go together. Podhoretz told me he had been a unipolarist for more than twenty years, though he recognized that politically it represented a new movement within neoconservatism that had to be led by younger neocons like Krauthammer and Wolfowitz. Novak said unipolarism was the positive side of anti-Communism, and pro-American global democracy was an indispensable feature of it. Wattenberg told nervous politicians not to be shy about asserting American superiority: "We are the first universal nation. 'First' as in the first one, 'first' as in 'number one.' And 'universal' within our borders and globally." Because the United States is uniquely universal, Wattenberg claimed, it has a unique right to impose its will on other nations on behalf of a democratic world order.[97]

Krauthammer, Wattenberg, and Muravchik crafted a new ideological grammar, stressing that ideological wars begin with new creeds. The Cold War rhetoric of totalitarianism, Finlandization, Present Danger, fifth columnist, infiltration, and choke point went down the Orwellian memory hole; only "appeasement" survived the death of Soviet Communism. The new neoconservatism spoke of neo-universalism, neo–manifest destiny, benevolent global hegemony, waging democracy, democratic idealism, liberal imperialism, declinism, and unipolarism. Not all neoconservatives went along with this transition. A few defected from the neocon movement, notably military strategist Edward Luttwak and political writer Michael Lind; neocon sociologist Peter Berger shook his head at the imperial chauvinism of his friends; and some neocons distinguished between defending American superiority and assuming the burdens of a global Pax Americana. From the beginning the neocons divided between nationalistic realists (Krauthammer, Jeane Kirkpatrick and Irving Kristol) and democratic globalists (the vast majority of neocons).[98]

Unipolarism was not an exclusively neoconservative enterprise. Unipolarist conservative hawks Donald Rumsfeld, William F. Buckley Jr., and Dick Cheney did not come from the neoconservative movement, nor did unipolarist conservative realists Colin Powell, Dick Armitage, Condoleezza Rice, and Henry Kissinger. The Democratic Party sprouted milder versions of unipolarism, notably by Zbigniew Brzezinski. But the ideology of American unipolarism was largely a neoconservative phenomenon, which caused Cheney to strengthen his alliances with neocons.[99]

The hallmark of the new neoconservatism was its radical faith that the maximal use of U.S. American power is good for America and the world. Neocons despised Clinton for wasting America's hegemonic power: Clinton was solicitous of world opinion; he intervened in nations that didn't matter like Somalia and Haiti; and he indulged Iraq, Iran, North Korea, China, and the Palestinians. The neocons tightened their hold over conservative think tanks and magazines, cultivated alliances with Cheney and Rumsfeld, founded the *Weekly Standard* magazine with Rupert Murdoch money, and got a huge boost from the rise of the Fox network, also a Murdoch production. They were deeply involved in the culture wars of the 1990s, which enhanced their standing in the Republican Party. In 1997 they founded the Project for the New American Century (PNAC), which called for a foreign policy of global dominion; the following year they implored Clinton to overthrow the Baathist regime in Iraq. Most neocons supported Arizona senator John McCain in the 2000 Republican presidential primaries, but Wolfowitz and Perle judged that George W. Bush looked more electable and teachable. Two months before the election of 2000 PNAC spelled out its global empire strategy: repudiate the Anti-Ballistic Missile (ABM) treaty, build a global missile defense system, develop a strategic dominance of space, increase defense spending by $20 billion per year, establish permanent new bases in southern Europe, Southeast Asia, and the Middle East, and reinvent the U.S. military to "fight and decisively win multiple, simultaneous major theater wars." PNAC added that it might take "a new Pearl Harbor" for Americans to realize they needed to dramatically expand America's force structure.[100]

When Bush won the presidency, the neocons came with him. Wolfowitz and Perle headed the list, followed by Elliott Abrams, John Bolton, Stephen Cambone, Devon Cross, Paula Dobriansky, John Hannah, Robert Joseph, Zalmay Khalilzad, Scooter Libby, William Luti, Peter W. Rodman, William Schneider Jr., Abram Shulsky, David Wurmser, and Robert B. Zoellick. Cheney was the key to this windfall of appointments. For seven months Bush frustrated his neocon aides, rejecting their demands for a big increase in the Pentagon budget. He talked about invading Iraq but spent his political capital on a tax cut for the rich. He quashed the ABM Treaty and America's support of the Kyoto Protocol and the International Criminal Court, but these were second-rate issues to the neocons. He took little interest in scattered terrorist groups like al Qaeda, though the neocons shared that predisposition. They wanted Bush to overthrow Iraq, Iran, and Syria. By July the *Weekly Standard* was so frustrated it called on Rumsfeld and Wolfowitz to resign in protest.[101]

On September 11 the president found himself suddenly in need of a worldview. His advisors had one, and they were obsessed with overthrowing Iraq. In a real sense Bush joined his own administration. I do not mean that he became a puppet of Cheney or the neocons. Bush apparently made up his own mind to scuttle the doctrine of deterrence, pursue antiterrorism as a world war, propound a radical doctrine of preventive war, and invade Iraq. But these were long-standing neocon fantasies that became American policies at the urging of Bush's advisors. Wolfowitz and Rumsfeld urged Bush to respond to al Qaeda's attacks by invading . . . Iraq. It didn't matter that Iraq had nothing to do with 9/11; what mattered was to overthrow Saddam Hussein and impose a pro-American regime in the Middle East.

The Bush administration had a sloppy list of reasons to invade Iraq, which it never bothered to subject to serious internal criticism. To question any of them was to betray one's lack of right-thinking pro-Americanism. It got a stampede going by scaring the public about Saddam's supposed weapons of mass destruction. Bush sought to change the Middle East, creating a pro-American Iraq that gave the United States a direct power base, ensured the oil supply, set off a chain reaction of regime changes, gave relief to Israel, and got rid of a thuggish enemy. The visions of a new pro-American government in the Middle East and the transformation of the region were tightly intertwined. Bush wanted Arab leaders to get the picture. They kept their heads down when Bush intervened in Afghanistan; afterward they carried on as though the world had not changed. Bush resolved to smash into their terrorist-breeding world at its center.

DSA joined the antiwar opposition, which in March 2003 defied 83 percent of the American public. I spoke against the war every week for two years, though my connection to DSA during these years was through its Religion and Socialism group, since there was no DSA chapter where I lived in southwest Michigan. Sometimes I crossed paths with West. My speeches focused on "imperial designs" and sought to kindle an antiwar movement in the academy, religious communities, and civic organizations. His were lacerating by comparison, emphasizing the whiteness of American imperialism. West said three dogmas of modern American life folded together to degrade American democracy and erase whatever decent global image the United States possessed. Capitalist fundamentalism—the glorification of unfettered markets and market rationality—casts aside the public good while delivering the world to the corporations. Aggressive militarism—the pursuit of global military empire—imposes the will of American elites on other nations. Escalating authoritarianism—the diminishment of individual rights—betrays hard-won liberties in the name of national security. Taken together, he said, "we are experiencing the sad American imperial devouring of American democracy . . . an unprecedented gangsterization of America."[102]

Capitalist fundamentalism reduces all values to market value, pitting enterprises and national governments in a race to the bottom. West said American nihilism is a two-sided coin. On one side it is the despair of worthlessness and believing in nothing, which reaches all categories of Americans and especially devastates the poor. On the other side it is the ruthless abuse of power that nihilistic elites wage on a daily basis, which also falls heaviest on the most vulnerable. West depicted the Bush administration as a showcase of nihilistic rule serving up fear and greed, tax cuts for the rich, and imperialism. He said he felt some respect for old-style Democrats like FDR and even LBJ who at least cared about the poor at a gut level. By contrast, John Kerry and Hillary Clinton were "paternalistic nihilists" who spoke blandly for democracy with no gut-level rage at the injustices of the system. West had a version of American exceptionalism—America is exceptional in its conceit and self-delusion. "No other democratic nation revels so blatantly in such self-deceptive innocence, such self-paralyzing reluctance to confront the nightmare of its own history." Refusing to grow up, the American colossus shuns painful truths about its racism and imperialism: "Race has always been the crucial litmus test for such maturity in America. To acknowledge the deeply racist and imperial roots of our democratic project is anti-American only if one holds to a childish belief that America is pure and pristine, or if one opts for self-destructive nihilistic rationalizations."[103]

Sometimes West did not come through as a writer; the torrential riffs that made him a sensational speaker sometimes did not sing on the page. He enthralled lecture audiences with dazzling riffs on a range of topics that no one else matched. Most reviewers who chastised him lacked even a fraction of his intellectual range. West never really changed, notwithstanding the left critics who said his early writings were radical and then he sold out. Others wrongly said his early writings were Marxism dressed up as Christian thought. West was not really a Marxist who used Christianity; it was more like the other way around. He began as a liberationist social critic committed to building progressive multiracial coalitions, and he remained one. He moved easily among groups that had little in common with each other and that sometimes could not stand each other. Three kinds of ethical universalism compelled him to try: love for all black people, the universal love ethic of Christianity, and the universal solidarity ethic of socialism.

He played an intellectual leadership role in DSA without making it to many DSA meetings. This was the usual case for intellectual leaders in every generation of the socialist movement. Those who wrote theory and shaped the discourse were usually not the ones who kept the organization going; Hillquit and Harrington were outstanding exceptions. In West's generation, however, the role of academics specifically—not just intellectuals—changed markedly in the socialist movement. Harrington welcomed the flow of academics into DSA whether or not they came to meetings. His emphasis on the conscience constituency put off old-timers and proletarians but anticipated what happened. Democratic socialism got stronger in the academy while it weakened everywhere else.

RESTORING THE SOCIALISM IN SOCIAL DEMOCRACY: MARKET SOCIALISM

Socialists dominated two broad debates in social and political theory that remain ongoing in the academy and the socialist movement. The first is sui generis to socialism and longstanding in it: Is socialism compatible with capitalist markets? What would market socialism be? The second is the debate over the politics of economic redistribution, cultural difference, and political representation, including transnational representation. Both debates are global discussions, and the second is the key to the rise of a third wave within post-1960s feminism. Irving Howe, nobly publishing little-noticed articles on market socialism in *Dissent*, said in 1993 he realized that many readers skipped over them. He was fine with that, conceding that these articles "are provisional, a little abstract, and inclined to disagreements with one another. They don't necessarily paint a picture of an actual future—who can?" Howe reasoned that a democratic socialist has to have a certain amount of utopian imagination. Just because Communist utopianism turned out badly is no reason to condemn utopian thinking altogether. The utopian demand for a better world is a necessity of the moral imagination. If you're an American, Howe added, it isn't even possible to banish the utopian impulse, for democratic utopianism "runs like a bright thread through American intellectual life."[104]

The idea of market socialism dates back to the British and French cooperative socialist traditions of the nineteenth century, which argued that there must be a way to combine socialist cooperation with capitalist markets because abolishing markets is hostile to freedom. John Stuart Mill, England's greatest liberal socialist, said what matters is to eliminate exploitation, not markets. The growth of liberty and economic progress are linked. Any form of collectivist socialism that abolishes competitive markets is bound to thwart liberty and economic progress. Mill carefully weighed the advantages and disadvantages of capitalist, cooperative, and public ownership, advocating firm-wide (not statewide) cooperative ownership of the means of production. He stressed that competitive markets are motors of economic growth and change—not mere conduits of state planning. The crucial thing is to devise an alternative to the sorry choice between working for oneself alone or for a master: "The aim of improvement should be not solely to place human beings in a condition in which they will be able to do without one another, but to enable them to work for one another in relations not involving dependence."[105]

Mill foresaw the danger of collectivist regimes that brought about an "absolute dependence of each on all, and surveillance of each by all." Proudhon made a similar argument in France, countering Louis Blanc's advocacy of state-supported cooperatives. Mill and Proudhon insisted that retaining the rivalry among cooperatives is indispensable to clearing room for freedom and creative ingenuity within socialism. Mill explained: "It would be difficult to induce the general assembly of an association to submit to the trouble and inconvenience of altering their habits by adopting some new and promising invention, unless their knowledge of the existence of rival associations made them apprehend that what they would not consent to do, others would, and that they would be left far behind in the race." Competition is a problematic and necessary stimulant, "and no one can foresee the time when it will not be indispensable to progress."[106]

Marxian socialists heaped ridicule on this position, following Marx himself, who said Mill was fatuous like all other bourgeois economists, treating the bourgeois relations of production as eternal and their forms of distribution as historical, "and thereby shows that he understands neither the one nor the other." Morris Hillquit flatly concurred: "There is no room in a socialist commonwealth for production for sale or for commerce." But even revisionist social democrats and guild socialists did not challenge the Marxian condemnation of capitalist markets. Eduard Bernstein and guild socialist pioneer G. D. H. Cole did not say Marx was wrong to pit socialism against markets. Christian socialists had market socialism pretty much to themselves for decades, along with the much-derided *Kathedersozialisten* ("socialists of the chair") in Germany led by Albert Schäffle. The idea of worker-owned or community-owned cooperatives competing with each other in capitalist markets was not radical enough for socialists who made a substitute religion of socialism.[107]

The first break in this picture occurred in the 1930s in the historic debates over economic calculation. Austrian economist Ludwig von Mises claimed that economic calculation is impossible in any economy lacking private ownership and a full set of markets, including capital markets. Mises taught that markets work properly only when they are embedded in a system of property rights in which private individuals are allowed to buy and sell shares in the means of production. Socialist economists Evan Durbin and Oskar Lange countered that Mises smuggled too much of his individualism into neoclassical theory. The market doesn't care about individuals since ownership in a market economy belongs to *enterprises* registered with courts. Durbin taught at the London School of Economics and was the British Labour Party's leading economist. He persuaded key party leaders that central economic planning must be combined with market discipline, especially getting prices right. Lange taught in his early career in his native Poland, emigrated to the United States in 1937, taught at the University of Chicago until 1945, served as the Polish delegate to the United Nations Security Council in the mid-1940s, and published his major work in 1936, *On the Economic Theory of Socialism.* He rejected the Marxian labor theory of value, contending that socialists must accommodate neoclassical price theory.[108]

Lange and Durbin argued that socialists should retain the benefits of public ownership and centralized control by integrating market mechanisms and incentives into socialism. Lange made a detailed case for a large state sector coexisting with the pricing and market discipline of a private sector of small enterprises. State planners simulated and were instructed by the private sector's pricing system, and planning boards set prices by adjusting to shortages and surpluses. When shortages occurred prices were raised to encourage businesses to increase production. When surpluses occurred prices were lowered to encourage businesses to prevent losses by curtailing production.

This was emphatically an attempt to save the state socialist model by integrating into it an important role for the market. Lange and Durbin still had centralized planners trying to replicate the innumerable, enormously complex pricing decisions of markets—a task exceeding the competence, time constraints, and knowledge of any conceivable planning board. They did not call their economic models market socialism, and their political success was modest. Durbin and Labour economists Douglas Jay, Hugh Dalton, and Hugh Gaitskell gradually turned Labour Party economic policy in a Keynesian direction emphasizing taxation of wealth and income, macroeconomic intervention, and a shift away from its Fabian emphasis on public ownership. Jay contended that Labour should never have identified socialism with public ownership of the means of production. However, Fabians controlled the Labour Party during its postwar glory days of the late 1940s, when Labour socialized one-third of the British economy; Durbin played a mediating role between the party's mainstream Fabian and revisionist wings before he died in 1948. After Labour fell out of power in 1951 revisionists led by Gaitskell won control of the party. Lange, meanwhile, returned to Poland in 1945, renounced his American citizenship, and more or less conformed to Poland's Communist reality. He spent his last years teaching Polish Communists how to use modern economic tools of analysis and planning, with little mention of regulated markets.[109]

Gaitskell and C. A. R. Crosland championed a type of market socialism in all but name in Britain. Their revisionist movement changed the Labour Party, emphasizing the role of markets and the shortcomings of state socialism. They made detailed arguments for expanding the cooperative sector, developing cooperative-public partnerships, establishing solidarity wage policies, accepting the mixed economy, and emphasizing democratic socialist values. But in Britain the orthodoxy to be overturned was Fabian Collectivism, a subject of little interest to Continental Social Democrats and Communists. In the 1950s Lange's former students and colleagues in Poland revived the discussion of Lange-style market socialism. One Polish Communist economist, Włodzimierz Brus, was the leading figure.

Brus grew up in Poland, fled to the Soviet occupation zone in Lwów (now Lviv, Ukraine) when Germany invaded Poland in 1939, and returned to Poland in 1945 with the Polish First Army. He found that his parents had perished in the Holocaust, and his wife had remarried and become a Communist military official. In the 1950s Brus wrote propaganda for the Communist government of Władysław Gomułka, remarried his wife, and gave mostly unheeded advice to the government on economic reforms. Brus returned to the Lange idea of market socialism, distinguishing between capacity-producing long-term production decisions and capacity-using short-term decisions. He said long-term decisions should be left to central planners, but managers could make decisions in state-owned, short-term enterprises on the basis of profitability. He opposed the dictatorial collectivism of the Soviet Union *and* the decentralized self-management Communism of Yugoslavia, advocating central planning with regulated markets. His case for a refashioned Lange-style market socialism made it respectable in Eastern Europe, though Brus was expelled from the party in 1968 after he defended party reformers. He taught in the 1970s and 1980s at Oxford, writing scholarly works on Communist reforms in Hungary and Yugoslavia.[110]

Did a reform idea forged in Communist Eastern Europe have any relevance to Western socialism? The answer was yes, but Brus did not traffic in reassurance. He had hard-earned convictions about the tyranny and squalor of Communism and was dead serious about forging a better socialism. On these counts he was much like his fellow economic historian and market socialist Alec Nove, a Russian exile who taught at the University of London from 1958 to 1963 and at the University of Glasgow from 1963 to 1982. Nove went beyond the standard criticisms of Stalinist excess and deformations, laying much of the blame for dictatorial socialism on Marx himself, whose few writings about the economics of socialism were "either irrelevant or directly misleading." Nove puzzled that anyone ever took seriously Marx's projection that "brilliant multipurpose human beings" would abolish the division of labor. He was incredulous that this willful credulity carried on for decades, turning Marxian utopianism into a bad religion: "It is nonsense to assert that to be a socialist, or a revolutionary for that matter, one must believe in an unrealizable utopia." Nove and Brus took for granted the necessity of establishing political control of the major investment flows of the economy, but they were scathing about domineering central planners. So much killing and destruction had been carried out in the name of impossible goals. Market socialism, to them, was a chastened attempt to salvage something from the wreckage, focusing on the contempt for markets that too much of the socialist tradition assumed. They ended up with a feasible socialism that was hard to distinguish from Social Democracy, but being soaked in the Communist experience made them sensitive about their signature point.[111]

Nove and Brus drove European market socialists to an unwelcome verdict: Market socialism does not grow best out of socialism; to succeed it must be planted where markets are firmly established. Among its proponents are Saul Estrin, an emeritus economics professor at the London School of Economics, and David M. Miller, a political theorist at Oxford, who have been the leading theorists of market socialism since the 1970s. Estrin specializes in the microeconomics of comparative economic systems, and Miller is best known for his pluralistic theory of social justice. Indian philosopher Prabhat Ranjan Sarkar, the founder of Progressive Utilization Theory, and Dada Maheshvarananda, director of the Prout Research Institute of Venezuela, are longtime proponents of market socialism from the global South. In the United States, World Bank economist David Ellerman, Yale political theorist Robert Dahl, and Southern Illinois University economist Leland Stauber played pioneering roles in market socialist and economic democracy theory before their passing. Longtime theorists still active in this field include University of Maryland political economist Gar Alperovitz, University of California-Davis sociologist Fred Block, People-Centered Development Forum founder David C. Korten, University of California economist John Roemer, Loyola University political philosopher David Schweickart, and University of Michigan economist Thomas E. Weisskopf.[112]

Alperovitz and Korten avoid socialist language; Block, Roemer, Schweickart, and Weisskopf contend that reclaiming the socialist ownership principle is crucial, as did Stauber; and Dahl said he didn't care if his readers conceived economic democracy as a better form of capitalism or a better form of socialism. Those who embrace the market socialist name argue that European Social Democrats were wrong to discard the socialist focus on the structure of economic ownership. Reclaiming the socialist name is worth the trouble precisely because democratic ownership is a crucial factor in building a just society, but reclaiming the socialist ownership principle must be done in a way that achieves economic efficiency by accepting market discipline.

Ownership is a complex idea encompassing a variety of rights. There are four basic models of enterprise control within market socialist theory and four models of social claims to income. Social control can mean government-directed public management representing the community at the local, regional, or national level, or cooperative worker management based on individual ownership in which each member owns one share in the enterprise, or cooperative worker management in which workers own a firm collectively as a group, or a blend of public and cooperative models. Social rights to income can mean that the surplus of the enterprise accrues to the public through a local, regional, or national government agency, or to the individual members of a cooperative enterprise, or to a cooperative as a whole, or to a blend of both. These models yield multiple variations since "public" ranges from local to regional to national and the different sets of rights do not have to be assigned in the same way.

Many market socialists minimize the complexity problem by opting for the simplest model of public or cooperative control combined with a similar right to income—centralized public management combined with public surplus appropriation, or cooperative worker management combined with worker appropriation. Centralized government collectivism, with or without markets, is at least coherent. The U.S. Pacific Northwest has a longtime network of plywood cooperatives that exemplifies the traditional cooperative principle of one person, one vote, while the renowned Mondragon cooperatives in Spain vest the rights of ownership in the workers as a collectivity. Many market socialists in the cooperative self-management camp favor the Mondragon model because it avoids the self-interest traps of individuated cooperatives. Those who self-identify as economic democrats while spurning the socialist category tend to be more comfortable than market socialists with pluralistic complexity and it-all-depends local circumstances, but these are mere tendencies.[113]

Ellerman was a leading American advocate of Mondragon-style collective self-management. Schweickart devised a worker self-management model that adds one feature of public enterprise socialism, national government control over net capital formation. Roemer proposed a public enterprise model in which most of the enterprise surplus flows back to the national government and is distributed equitably to the general public as a social dividend. Stauber proposed a public enterprise model in which capital income goes to local government agencies as shareholder income and is either distributed to local citizens or used for local public purposes. Block devised a mixed model of ownership and control that makes room for workers, outside shareholders, consumers, creditors, suppliers, and environmentalists. Weisskopf devised a mixed model that features public control of large firms, worker control of smaller firms, public income rights, and worker income rights.[114]

All were chastened by the failures of market Communism in Eastern Europe, stressing that two of the three defining features of Communism—one-party politics and command allocation of resources and commodities—have nothing to do with democratic market socialism. Even the Soviet Union had notable market socialists, including Nikolai Bukharin and Nobel laureate Leonid Kantorovich, who could not overcome the Marxian and Russian Communist antipathy for the market mechanism. The founders of Anglo-American market socialism admired their forerunners in Yugoslavia, Hungary, and Poland for doing their best with the hand dealt to them, but the East European experience showed why market socialism had to build on existing markets instead of smuggling them in afterward.[115]

That did not cause them to swallow stock markets. Most market socialists have contended that control of enterprises should be vested only in public agencies serving the community or in cooperative worker councils or in a blend of both. The argument that Wall Street is hopelessly corrupt and should be abolished was a staple of market socialist theory in the 1980s and 1990s, and Schweickart and Korten were vehement on this theme during the financial crash of 2008. Stauber, however, made room for external equity ownership rights and fully functioning stock markets. He restricted equity ownership and trading to public financial institutions and public enterprises, vesting each local government with an investment fund, a publicly controlled financial institution that bought and sold securities in corporate enterprises. Stauber implored that bending capital markets to market socialist purposes retains an important engine of wealth and is workable.[116]

Roemer became prominent in market socialist theory on the strength of his analytical acumen and his throwback collectivism. For him, socialism is not socialist without state control of the commanding heights of the economy, public ownership of enterprises, a democratic distribution of society's economic surplus, and income equality. Roemer contends that all enterprises must be publicly owned and government must direct all investment. He distinguishes the commanding heights from lower heights without explaining how to do so in firms with myriad products. He tries to ward off centralized bureaucratic stagnation by appropriating the Japanese *keiretsu* model, which organizes firms into groups tied to banks that advise, lend to, and monitor firms in their group. According to Roemer, the *keiretsu* cluster model of chummy bankers, industrialists, and politicians is transferable to the United States and could be democratized by giving workers in each firm the right to elect and fire their bosses. Democratizing corporatism in this fashion would require a bit of worker control that Roemer otherwise dislikes, since he says that cooperatives are inefficient. His version of market socialism has a blueprint mentality *and* a willingness to tinker with the mechanics, but the point in both cases is to save old-style collectivism.[117]

I have argued since the early 1980s for an economic democracy model that aims for contextually optimal mixtures of public social ownership, cooperative social ownership, and private ownership. Public ownership works better than the cooperative model in industries with large economies of scale or extensive externalities, it pays greater heed than cooperatives to the needs of the entire society, and cooperatives have trouble scaling up. Cooperative ownership achieves direct, democratic, humane, interpersonal self-determination at the firm or guild level, it works better than public ownership in industries with small economies of scale and few externalities, and centralized bureaucracies tend to bloat and stagnate. Both kinds of social ownership carry the danger of discouraging entrepreneurship and innovation, and each is needed as a counterweight against too much of the other. Public enterprise socialism is susceptible to the soft-budget restraint problems that plague all public enterprises, with decisions being made on the basis of political connections and inefficient agencies or firms getting financed. Cooperatives, on the other hand, are typically underfinanced because capitalist banks don't like them and they prohibit nonworking shareholders. Cooperatives maximize net income per worker rather than profits, so they tend to favor capital-intensive investments over job creation.[118]

The latter problems reflect the virtues of cooperatives and can be mitigated via tax incentives and regulations that promote job expansion, reinvestment, innovation, and bank support. But even cooperatives aided by better financing and entrepreneurial incentives carry a bias toward capital-intensive investments. Capitalist firms readily scale up because they have structural incentives to grow under conditions of constant returns to scale. When costs-per-item are constant, capitalist firms are predisposed to grow to increase profits. Doubling the size of a capitalist firm will double its profit. Cooperatives maximize per-worker share income, not total profits, so they do not automatically expand production when demand increases. Unless sizable economies of scale are involved, cooperatives have little to gain by doubling the size of their enterprises. A cooperative hardware store run by thirty people will have the same per-worker share income as a cooperative run by sixty people.

These problems drove Estrin to his signature proposal—run the capital of cooperative enterprises through semiautonomous holding companies that don't allow cooperatives to stagnate. Estrin built on the mutual-fund model of cooperative socialism pioneered by English Anglican archbishop William Temple in 1941 and revised by Rudolf Meidner in the 1970s. Temple proposed that England should institute an excess profits tax to generate social funds that would gradually acquire decentralized democratic control of major enterprises, which he called a revised guild socialism. The Meidner Plan in Sweden was a scaled-back version of this idea, establishing eight regional social funds with public representation and limiting to 40 percent the amount of enterprise control that the funds could acquire. Temple and Meidner fixed on achieving economic democracy through the excess profits tax; the new entity needed to manage the funds was merely instrumental. Estrin fixed on the new entity, stressing that it could be a creative firewall between the state and an enterprise management. The key was to place a semiautonomous investment agency or holding company between the state and the enterprise, giving it the authority to make investment decisions. The holding company would vest the ownership of productive capital, loan capital to enterprises at the market rate of interest, pay attention to market signals, and shut down inefficient firms.[119]

Miller endorsed Estrin's scheme and shared Estrin's interest in applying it only to cooperatives. But Roemer, Nove, Block, and Weisskopf also endorsed it, reasoning that it applied better to public enterprises or mixed models. They concurred with Estrin that establishing separate entrepreneurial institutions might be the best way to solve the hard problem of making socialism more entrepreneurial. Every form of social ownership must ward off partisan interference, corrupting influences, and insularity. Estrin rightly cautioned that cooperatives have inherent limitations that often cause them to underperform at entrepreneurial creativity, innovation, and reinvestment. His scheme stretched the capital supply constraints of worker ownership by compelling the holding companies to maintain an arm's length relationship with cooperative firms. Basically it was a public bank scheme to help cooperatives scale up, which Roemer and Block subsequently applied to public enterprises.[120]

The key problem with Estrin's proposal is that it weakens workers' power at the firm level. To the extent that the holding companies are granted supervisory control over their client enterprises, worker control is diminished. To the extent that the holding companies are kept in a weak position, the advantages of the mutual fund model are traded off as the enterprises essentially revert to the cooperative model. Estrin and Miller said the holding companies should provide capital to cooperatives without exercising control rights that thwart self-management. Roemer and Block said the opposite—the holding companies should monitor the enterprises closely and undoubtedly would in any case. The latter outcome is more likely, by design or not, because Estrin's version depends on a demanding form of civil service. The asset managers maintain a supervisory distance from the asset users *and* a financial and entrepreneurial commitment to the users. The holding companies are asked to bear substantial capital risks while having little or nothing to say on decisions affecting the risks. The mutual fund model may in fact displace cooperative ownership or public ownership of the commanding heights with semidistant public bank finance.[121]

Market socialists thus generated a profusion of proposals to a debate that remains ongoing. They are willing to say that capitalist markets are economically efficient, get prices right, increase freedom of choice, and decrease the power of bureaucracy. On the other hand they insist that consumers are not sovereign, markets do not distribute goods and services justly, and markets do not foster healthy persons and communities. Market socialists usually claim to uphold the socialist principle that markets should operate within plans — until they get to specifics, where many just mean that social democratic interventions such as solidarity wage policy or codetermination should operate within markets. Nove admitted that he struggled to identify the precise difference between social democracy and market socialism. Weisskopf said there is one difference: Market socialists intervene before markets operate, and social democrats usually intervene afterward.[122]

On the latter telling, social democracy is more vulnerable to buckling under political challenge because its interventions are easier to reverse than changes in property rights. But markets already operate everywhere that market socialists propose to install socialist planning. Market socialism only sounds more radical than economic democracy. When the market-and-plan discussion cuts to specifics, market socialists and economic democrats push for the same thing: achieving as much economic democracy as possible under the constraints of politics and efficiency. This aim marks an important departure from what social democracy became in the 1950s, but it is very much in the tradition of social democratic practicality.

DISTRIBUTION, RECOGNITION, PARTICIPATION, THIRD-WAVE FEMINISM, AND NANCY FRASER

Nobody got famous on market socialism. *Dissent*, a small jewel of a magazine, has long been the best venue for it, while the best-known market socialists made their names for other things — Nove for Russian economic history, Dahl for pluralist political theory, and Roemer for analytical Marxism. Walzer sustained *Dissent* through the bitter Clinton and Bush years, generously using his perch at the Institute for Advanced Study in Princeton to keep social democratic ideas in circulation. In his early teaching career at Harvard Walzer wrote an influential book on just-war theory, *Just and Unjust Wars*, and team-taught a course with philosopher Robert Nozick that yielded Walzer's book on pluralistic justice, *Spheres of Justice*. The former book was taught in the military academies, explicating a "supreme emergency" doctrine of just war; the latter book contributed to the communitarian heyday, expounding a theory of complex equality keyed to the critique of domination in multiple spheres. Both displayed Walzer's irenic, historicist, analytical style, and his mildly social democratic perspective. These turned out to be his major works, as Walzer switched to editing and the essay format after moving in 1980 to the institute. The fact that Howe and Walzer opposed the DSOC merger with NAM proved hard to live down in much of DSA. *Dissent* was not as old-school as the reputation it held in the DSA left wing. Walzer helped to keep the magazine alive after Howe died in 1993, always astutely, albeit with a niche role in the political left. The academics that changed the left had friendlier relationships than Walzer and especially Howe to the rise of cultural leftism, changing what counted as a socialist argument.[123]

Difference feminism played the leading role in the rise of the cultural left. Two landmark books published in 1990 epitomized its challenge to Marxian, social democratic, and New Left politics: *Gender Trouble: Feminism and the Subversion of Identity* by Judith Butler and *Justice and the Politics of Difference* by Iris Marion Young. At the time, Butler taught humanities at Johns Hopkins University, and Young taught political philosophy at the University of Pittsburgh. Butler grew up in Cleveland, caught her love of philosophy at Hebrew school, earned her doctorate at Yale in 1984, and began to argue in the late 1980s that gender is a performance with a script and an audience. Young grew up in New York City, earned her doctorate at Penn State in 1974, and took her passionate commitment to feminism into antiwar activism and studies of democratic theory, racism, Michel Foucault, Jürgen Habermas, and Marxism.

Butler attacked the idea of the naturalness of gender, arguing that left-progressives were barely any better than conservatives in assuming the existence of true gender identities and natural sexes. She pushed feminists to apply their deconstructive criticism of the category of "woman" to the category of "female." Butler's subversive stew of philosophy, anthropology, literary theory, and psychoanalysis was hard for social democrats to perceive as a contribution to left politics; for several years *Dissent* mocked it as a model of how not to write for *Dissent*. Young was more troubling to social democrats for clearly belonging to the socialist left. She argued that the left had not yet allowed the social movements of the sixties and seventies to transform how it talked about justice. Justice, the primary subject of political philosophy, is not primarily a problem of distribution, contrary to positivist and reductionist political theories. Positivists take institutional structures for granted instead of criticizing them, and reductionists reduce political subjects to a unity, valuing sameness or commonality over difference or specificity. Young contended that a notion of justice informed by liberationist movements must begin with the concepts of domination and oppression, not distribution. A sense of justice must arise from listening, not from applying purportedly fundamental principles of justice to all or most societies. She affirmed that moving in this direction meant that social groups must become bearers of rights.[124]

Young placed herself more or less in the Frankfurt School critical theory tradition of Horkheimer, Marcuse, and Habermas. Marx described critical theory in 1843 as "the self-clarification of the struggles and wishes of the age." Young and Fraser liked the political character of this definition, and both drew upon Habermas's construal of human rationality as communicative action. But Habermas never privileged or even mentioned gender as a category of analysis, barely mentioning feminism as a social movement, and Young chafed at the sense of a homogeneous public pervading his *Theory of Communicative Action*. She developed a fivefold concept of oppression as exploitation, marginalization, powerlessness, cultural imperialism, and violence. Distributive injustices may contribute to or result from these forms of oppression, she reasoned, "but none is reducible to distribution and all involve social structures and relations beyond distribution." Oppression happens to entities that no theory of justice has ever conceptualized—social groups. Young argued that groups are socially prior to individuals without existing apart from individuals; the identity of every human being is partly constituted by group affinities. Equal treatment, the gold standard of fairness theories of justice, suppresses differences in ways that reinforce oppression. Young contended that when women's liberation, Native American rights, bilingual education, and similar group concerns are at stake, the only way to ensure the just outcome of full participation is to recognize particular rights for groups. She had no universal principles, and neither does anyone else. She started from a specific location and denied that anyone can justly make a comprehensive claim: "I claim to speak neither for everyone, to everyone, nor about everything."[125]

Now the left no longer knew what counted as an injustice. Three *Dissent* regulars—Bromwich, Gitlin, and Rorty—wrote books decrying the rise of the cultural left that made a splash. Bromwich charged in *Politics by Other Means* (1992) that left-wing culture warriors inside the academy and right-wing culture warriors outside the academy were ruining higher education. They combined to distort the noble word "culture" itself, construing it only as social identity, not as tacit knowledge acquired "by choice and affinity." The constant warfare between the two camps, he protested, discredited the idea of liberal education, yielding classrooms in which students were indoctrinated in liberationist agendas. Group thinking, if allowed to proceed on its present course, would destroy higher education.[126]

Gitlin concurred that the right captured political power while the cultural left marched on the English Department. He said it scathingly in *Dissent* before the book version said it for the ages under a much-quoted title, *The Twilight of Common Dreams: Why America Is Wracked by Culture Wars* (1995). Gitlin commended the universalist humanism of the New Left, a generous worldview that was ridiculed by the "late New Left politics of separatist rage." The later New Left self-destructed politically, he argued, but took over the academy. From its unchallenged perch in the academy it proceeded to take over left politics and morphed into new forms: "By 1975, the universalist Left was thoroughly defeated—pulverized, in fact. Defeat was pervasive, taken for granted." Gitlin scorned the cultural leftist jargon of disruption, subversion, and rupture and its emphasis on rape and sexual harassment, all of which conveyed that cultural leftists didn't want to relate to ordinary people; it was enough to seize the academy and reduce feminism to identity politics. Rorty's book-contribution to this nostalgic genre was titled *Achieving Our Country* (1998). He said he had nothing against black pride or gay pride—both were compelling and just responses to the "sadistic humiliation" that the dominant culture meted out to African Americans, gays, and lesbians: "But insofar as this pride prevents someone from also taking pride in being an American citizen, from thinking of his or her country as capable of reform, or from being able to join with straights or whites in reformist initiatives, it is a political disaster."[127]

Fraser was a rising academic star in 1995, when she intervened in the debate over cultural leftism. She graduated from Bryn Mawr in 1969 and earned her doctorate in philosophy in 1980 at CUNY Graduate Center. In her early career she taught at Northwestern University, and in 1997 she moved to the New School for Social Research. Her 1989 essay collection on Foucault, Rorty, Habermas, and feminism, *Unruly Practices*, established that she was a socialist feminist committed to political efficacy *and* to drawing on the deconstructive insights of postmodernists, especially Foucault and Rorty. Rorty, at the time, was better known for his skeptical pragmatic antifoundationalism and playful ironic spinning than for his social democratic politics. Fraser confessed straightaway that she struggled to hold together her patchwork of commitments: "Radicals in academia *do* find themselves subject to competing pressures and counterpressures. We *do* internalize several distinct and mutually incompatible sets of expectations. And we *do* experience identity conflicts as we try simultaneously to wear several different hats. However, we should not rush to join in the chorus of left-wing professor bashing. The real contradictions of our lives notwithstanding, the radical academic is not an oxymoron."[128]

Fraser's work had a double aim from the beginning. She wrote abstract essays about social and political theory in a way that reflected her social justice activism: "On the one hand, I write as a social theorist trained as a philosopher and influenced by recent developments in literary theory, feminist theory, and cultural studies. On the other hand, I write as a democratic socialist and feminist." Always she straddled the ground between the scholarly demands of her profession and the relevance of academic theory for her activist commitments. Foucault helped her understand her own divided consciousness, especially concerning the politics of knowledge and the role of power in creating its own knowledge. But getting anything constructive out of Foucault is impossible; Foucault wasn't helpful even with strategic questions about coordinating liberationist struggles. Rorty's deconstruction of analytic philosophy and his case for American pragmatism were formative for Fraser. Rorty single-handedly revived the academic reputation of American pragmatism, especially Dewey. But Fraser disliked the Rorty who dismissed the entire Marxist tradition with smug one-liners and celebrated the glories of North Atlantic bourgeois democracies. Fraser was a bridge builder who respected the academy, shared the social justice ambitions of the socialist tradition, and responded to the pain of marginalized individuals and communities.[129]

In 1995 she intervened in the roaring debate over cultural leftism and its elevation of recognition over distribution. Fraser said the uncoupling of these two concepts of justice was baleful for the left. The best response to this sorry situation was to reconstruct the concept of justice in a way that incorporates the best insights of both camps. The major axes of injustice, she argued, are two-dimensional. Every form of injustice is rooted simultaneously in the political economy and the status order. No struggle for justice can succeed lacking a politics of redistribution *and* a politics of recognition. The hard part comes next because real tensions exist between these two orientations. Redistribution strategies silence the most pressing causes of harm for denigrated groups, while recognition strategies try to mitigate unjust outcomes without changing the underlying structures that generate unjust outcomes. Fraser said welfare state distributive justice is inadequate and so is mainstream multiculturalism. The left needs to "add insult to injury," wedding socialist distribution to full-orbed difference feminism and the recognition of special group harms.[130]

This argument was both diagnostic and constructive, employing analytical distinctions in both cases. In the real world, Fraser acknowledged, "culture and political economy are always imbricated with one another." Every struggle

against injustice makes demands that at least implicitly call for both redistribution and recognition. But the only way to devise a conceptual scheme that
illumines the intertwined complexity of the real world is to abstract from it. The
redistribution versus recognition dilemma is terribly real. Late capitalism
decentered the importance of class, after which social movements mobilized
around crosscutting axes of difference. These movements overlap and sometimes conflict. They never proceed wholly without demands for economic
change, but identity-based claims predominate in the postmodern left. Thus
the left has lost its programmatic coherence. Fraser smuggled one assumption
into her diagnosis and constructive argument: Any version of recognition politics that fails to uphold the principle of universal human dignity is out of play,
even if it otherwise promotes social equality. She bracketed the problem of the
relation between recognition of cultural difference and liberalism; her subject
was the relation between cultural difference and social equality. But any form
of identity politics that fails to respect human rights "of the sort usually championed by left-wing liberals" is unacceptable and ruled out.[131]

Fraser accepted that the distributive theories of Rawls, economist Amartya
Sen, and political philosopher Ronald Dworkin deserve their place in the
canon. Rawls conceived justice as fairness in the distribution of primary goods.
Sen reasoned that justice ensures that people have equal capabilities to function. Dworkin taught that justice requires an approximate equality of resources.
Fraser disclaimed any need to choose among them, since all three theories offer
a rigorous way to think about distributive justice and a way to deal with cultural
injustice. Rawls argued that social bases of self-respect are primary goods to be
fairly distributed; Sen argued that one needs a sense of self to be able to function; Dworkin grounded his argument for the redistribution of resources on the
equal moral worth of persons.[132]

Cultural accounts of injustice are symbolic, rooting injustice in social patterns
of representation and interpretation. Here the defining injustices are disrespect,
being rendered invisible, and being judged by cultural norms that are alien to
one's culture. Two Hegelian philosophers with social democratic politics, Charles
Taylor and Axel Honneth, developed the two leading theories of recognition justice. Taylor described disrespect as wounding violence and recognition as a vital
human need. Honneth stressed the Hegelian point that all persons owe their
sense of personal integrity to the recognition they receive from other persons; he
argued that recognition is the fundamental principle of justice, encompassing
economic justice concerns. Fraser observed that Hegelians came naturally to the
primacy and language of recognition via Hegel, but Young and legal scholar
Patricia Williams similarly emphasized the theme of recognized personhood.

Recognition theorists do not ignore material economic causes of injustice. The question is how to relate claims for recognition aimed at remedying cultural insult with claims for redistribution aimed at remedying economic injury.[133]

Advocates of both approaches have reason to safeguard the priority of their claims against the other side. Recognition theorists advocate for specific groups, promoting group differentiation, while redistribution theorists seek to abolish group differentiation. This was the core of the redistribution-recognition dilemma as Fraser construed it. She devised a conceptual spectrum of social collectivities bordered at one end by the redistribution model and at the other end by the recognition model. In between she placed the hard cases that fit both models simultaneously. The classic redistribution example is the Marxian rendering of the exploited working class. The mission of the Marxian proletariat is to abolish itself as a class, not to get a better deal: "The last thing it needs is recognition of its difference." Justice in this case is about putting the proletariat out of business, even if one fills out Marx's account with cultural variables he screened out. Fraser placed denigrated gays and lesbians at the other extreme end—victims of a sexual mode of differentiation not rooted in political economy. Gays and lesbians occupy no distinct position in the division of labor and do not constitute an exploited economic class. "Despised sexuality" is their mode of collectivity, being oppressed by the privileging of heterosexual norms. The economic consequences that gays and lesbians suffer derive from heterosexism, not from being rooted directly in the economic structure. Therefore the remedy for the injustice inflicted upon them is recognition, not redistribution.[134]

Fraser placed gender and race in the middle of the spectrum—hybrid modes of collectivity combining features of the exploited class and the despised sexuality. Both of these collectivities suffer from maldistribution *and* misrecognition in ways in which neither injustice is an indirect effect of the other. Both forms of injustice are primary and co-original, needing both kinds of remedy. Gender is a structuring principle of political economy generating specific modes of marginalization and pink-color exploitation *and* a cultural value differentiation that devalues nearly everything marked as female. Here it matters very much that the logics of redistribution and recognition pull in opposite directions. The logic of redistribution eliminates gender as a factor; the logic of recognition valorizes gender specificity; the movement for women's rights/liberation thus oscillates recurrently between redistribution and recognition. Fraser argued that race is similarly a bivalent mode of collectivity. It structures the division of labor, the status hierarchy of work, and access to specific labor markets, reflecting the historic legacy of colonialism and slavery, *and* it justifies forms of bigotry against all persons marked as black, brown, and yellow. Like gender, the problem of race is implicated in both kinds of injustice and needs both kinds of remedy, yielding similarly oscillating forms of antiracist politics.

Fraser fixed on the problem of opposing pulls, mapping alternative conceptions of redistribution and recognition. Two injustice remedies, she argued, cut across the redistribution-recognition divide: affirmation and transformation. Affirmative remedies correct inequitable outcomes without changing the underlying framework that causes the inequities, obtaining an end-state outcome. Transformative remedies restructure the underlying framework, targeting the processes that produce outcomes. Fraser described mainstream multiculturalism as an affirmative remedy that redresses disrespect by revaluing group identities and deconstruction as a transformative remedy that attacks the underlying value structure. Gay identity politics is an affirmation remedy, enhancing existing sexual group differentiation; "gay" marks an identity group. Queer theory is a transformation remedy, deconstructing traditional constructions of sexuality and destabilizing existing sexual group differentiation; "queer" is anti-identitarian. Fraser reasoned that this point holds for recognition strategies generally. Affirmative strategies promote existing group differentiation, and transformative strategies destabilize them. She described analogous distinctions for economic justice. The welfare state offers affirmative remedies that leave the underlying structures intact, while socialists promote transformative remedies that change the relations of production.[135]

These distinctions yielded a four-celled matrix. Fraser pictured a horizontal axis comprised of affirmation and transformation remedies and a vertical axis comprised of redistribution and recognition. Redistribution and affirmation intersect in the first cell, where the welfare state reallocates resources and supports group differentiation. Redistribution and transformation intersect in the second cell, where socialists restructure relations of production and blur group differentiations. Recognition and affirmation intersect in the third cell, where mainstream multiculturalism reallocates surface respect and supports group differentiation. Recognition and transformation intersect in the fourth cell, where deconstructionists restructure the relations of production and destabilize group differentiations. Fraser thus cast mainstream multiculturalism as the cultural analogue of the welfare state and deconstruction as the cultural analogue of socialism. Certain remedies, she argued, work at cross-purposes with one another if pursued simultaneously, and others do not. Welfare state affirmative redistribution strategies do not mesh with transformative recognition strategies that destabilize group differentiation. Similarly, socialism and mainstream multiculturalism do not go together because socialism undermines group differentiation and multiculturalism promotes it.[136]

Two pairs of remedies came out better than the others. Welfare state affirmative redistribution strategies mesh with mainstream multicultural affirmative recognition strategies because both promote group differentiation. The fact that both remedies amply exist in institutional structures is a major consideration in their favor. Socialist transformative redistribution and transformative deconstruction also work together, undermining existing group differentiations. Fraser stumped for socialist economics and cultural deconstruction, admitting the problem with her remedy—it would work only in a society that doesn't (yet) exist. The socialist-deconstruction combination, she acknowledged, is feasible only in a society in which all citizens have been "weaned from their attachment to current cultural constructions of their interests and identities." Socialism is obviously a project of the utopian imagination, but so is deconstruction in its own way. Fraser argued that only the socialist-deconstruction combination is capable of doing justice to all struggles against injustice. It promotes coalition building and does not assume a zero-sum game.[137]

The redistribution-recognition dilemma does not arise only within a single bivalent collectivity. It also arises across collectivities, such as gay and working class or black and female. Fraser observed that such crosscutting forms of the redistribution-recognition dilemma tend to be especially resistant to affirmative remedies because affirmative strategies work additively and conflict with each other. Transformative solutions are especially needed when class, race, gender, and sexuality intersect. In sum, she favored transformative approaches, which promote synergy, over affirmative approaches, which are zero-sum. She drove to a doleful conclusion. The problem is terrible and daunting, and the only solution is a utopian strategy for a society that doesn't exist: "We are currently stuck in the vicious circles of mutually reinforcing cultural and economic subordination. Our best efforts to redress these injustices via the combination of the liberal welfare state plus mainstream multiculturalism are generating perverse effects. Only by looking to alternative conceptions of redistribution and recognition can we meet the requirements of justice for all."[138]

This argument put Fraser at the center of a many-sided, long-running debate in which she generously responded to critics and tweaked her position. One of her dialogues, with Honneth, turned into a coauthored book in which she defended her two-dimensional concept of justice, pitting her perspectival dualism against his Hegelian normative monism of recognition. Fraser and Honneth agreed that an adequate concept of justice must address redistribution and recognition concerns, and recognition must not be reduced to an epiphenomenon of distribution. They agreed that left-wing utopian energies were exhausted and left-Hegelians could no longer conceive society as a culturally homogeneous, bounded whole; political claims under the conditions of postmodern plurality can no longer be adjudicated ethically by appealing to a single shared-value system. They disagreed over Honneth's claim that a differentiated concept of recognition encompassing the recognition of rights, cultural appreciation, and love encompasses everything at stake in the problematic of redistribution. The Fraser–Honneth dialogue spurred both thinkers to develop implied aspects of their moral philosophy, partly because their ideological commitments were very similar. Fraser and Honneth were trying to get to a similar place via different philosophical frameworks, yielding a certain high-minded politeness in their dialogue. Other responses were not so polite.[139]

Butler was not having any of it. To her, there was no problem to solve, and Fraser was only marginally better than Gitlin and Rorty, treating the cultural left as a problem. Butler said the only left that exists anymore is the cultural left. Instead of wailing against it, social democrats should be grateful it exists. Instead they howled about the ruination of liberal education, the abandonment of Marxian materiality, the death of common dreams, and the "merely cultural" preoccupations of a reigning cultural left. Smoother versions championed "the imaginary finesse of Habermasian rationality" and middle-class socialist nostalgia for something called the common good. Butler refrained from naming names, but Habermas and Honneth were the implied champions of Habermasian rationality, and Robert Bellah's coauthored *Habits of the Heart* (1985) made a celebrated case for communities of moral memory and a progressive politics of the common good. Butler was incredulous that the very movements "that continue to keep the Left alive are credited with its paralysis." Was there no getting through to the whiners? Did they really believe that all cultural left movements are reducible to their identitarian formations? Or was this a ruse to restore white, heterosexual male socialists to their star status on the left?[140]

Describing the orthodoxy of the left as "neoconservative Marxism," Butler fixed on one issue, the orthodox disparagement of queer politics, and one theorist, Fraser. She recognized that Fraser was better than the orthodox leftists but only by degree. Fraser, after all, not only distinguished between economic and cultural injustices; she also kept old-style Social Democracy in play by granting it a privileged claim to economic justice. In the name of defending the cultural left from an onslaught of left criticism, Fraser recycled the very distinction between political economy and the cultural sphere that left orthodoxy wielded to marginalize queer politics. Butler said this distinction has no place in a serious interpretation of Marxian materialism. It was smuggled into Marxism by Kautsky-style orthodoxy, separating the material from the cultural, after which postmodern Marxists construed sexuality as the epitome of the cultural, moving sexuality as far as possible from the material relations that create society. Butler said cultural leftists were not fooled by this strategy to diminish their standing and concerns: "The neoconservatism within the Left that seeks to discount the cultural can only always be another cultural intervention, whatever else it is." Whatever else it does, it tries to reinstate the discredited idea of secondary oppression. Butler said every such strategy "will only reprovoke the resistance to the imposition of unity, strengthening the suspicion that unity is only purchased through violent excision."[141]

Rorty opposed Fraser from the opposite standpoint. He told his students at Princeton that cultural studies is a diversion from serious political activism, not a form of it, and he could not fathom why Fraser and Butler believed that cultural recognition is a useful idea. The leftism of the 1930s and 1940s that shaped him did not talk about respecting foreign cultures. Its central idea was that all human beings have a common humanity, and prejudice is a violation of this commonality. To prejudge a fellow human person as a member of a despised group is wrong. American leftists assumed that creating a decent society is about redistributing wealth and opportunity and abolishing prejudice. The left did not speak of manual workers, the poor, blacks, women, gays, or lesbians as having a culture of their own. Rorty said the feminist movement changed this picture because the language of prejudice did not quite fit what feminism is about. Male domination of females was not really a consequence of male prejudice against females. Women did not bear a stigma for being women and were not scapegoated as blacks and Jews were. "Recognition," however, worked equally well to describe what blacks need from whites, gays from straights, and women from men.[142]

That much made sense to Rorty. What puzzled him was that recognition came to be construed as recognition of cultural difference instead of a common humanity. Was it because stigmatized people were often said by prejudiced people to fail at acquiring cultural refinement? Or because prejudiced men said that women acquire only lightweight forms of culture? But Rorty said that abolishing prejudice is a more direct and effective remedy in both cases. As far as he could tell, the main driver of recognition politics was the politics of what it took to establish academic programs in women's studies, black studies, and gay studies. These programs could have been geared to eliminate prejudice, but administrators needed a more academic goal, so the programs proposed to study the cultures of stigmatized groups.

Cultural studies ascended in the academy and the left, enshrining cultural recognition as a defining leftist goal. It set off a generational fight between wave-two feminists demanding their rights and wave-three feminists speaking the language of deconstruction and recognition, but that was not Rorty's business. He said the rise of cultural studies was a kind of cultural revolution that stunned old lefty academics like himself: "Culture pushed economics aside, in part because the maturing sixties leftists had a lot of ideas about cultural change, but few ideas about how to counter Reagan's soak-the-poor policies, what to do for the unemployed in the Rust Belt, or how to make sure that a global economy did not pauperize American wage earners. Because culture pushed economics aside, the straight white male working class in America may find it tempting to think that the leftist academy is uninterested in its problems." Rorty stressed that eliminating prejudice is direct, readily understood, and achievable, whereas cultural recognition is none of these things. The only reason that cultural recognition won is that cultural leftists in the academy wanted to teach it.[143]

His young academic colleagues reminded him of the Marxists he knew in the 1930s who believed that autoworkers should learn about dialectical materialism, lest they succumb to bourgeois unionism. Rorty agreed with Taylor about the wounding power of disrespect and with Honneth about becoming a person through other persons. But the recognition that heals and enables, he countered, applies to individuals, not to cultural groups. The cultural left agenda threw the left into confusion because it contradicts the democratic individualism of the entire U.S. American progressive tradition. The diversity prized by America's exemplary philosopher, Dewey, was of self-creating individuals, not a diversity of cultures. Rorty believed that being gay should be "no big deal" in American society and the left has more important work than learning about the native cultures of immigrants. It surprised him to feel so alienated from what became the left. Rorty admired Fraser but struggled with her thicket of abstract jargon: "Do we really need to replace 'hierarchical racial dichotomies' with 'networks of multiple intersecting differences that are demassified and shifting' rather than just, for example, trying to bring up white kids to think less about differences in skin color and more about shared pains and pleasures?" He cheered for Fraser against Butler and Young but could not concur that deconstruction improves socialism. Being clever at deconstruction is great for moving up in the academy, but it doesn't equip anyone "to help our society eliminate prejudice and increase fairness." Rorty wanted the American left to pay much less attention to French deconstruction and think far more about American wages descending toward the level of the global wage market.[144]

Young blasted Fraser's bifocal ordering as disastrous for liberationist concerns and aggressively defended left-wing multicultural feminism. She shared Butler's feeling that Fraser was too friendly to social democrats, but Young spoke from a standpoint of involvement in multiple liberationist-socialist causes, unlike Butler. Young cared as much as Rorty about economic justice, but she knew at a feeling level why the left had changed, unlike Rorty. Young allowed that Fraser set herself against a genuine peril on the left—a cultural leftism based in the academy that brushed aside economic justice. Taylor was guilty of it in his book on multiculturalism and recognition, and Young had seen school multiculturalism textbooks that focused solely on recognition. But Young charged that Fraser exaggerated how often this occurred on the left; more important, her solution "is worse than the disease." Young contended that feminist, antiracist, and gay liberation movements do not demand recognition as an end in itself. Fraser contrived a worse problem than actually exists and solved it badly by dichotomizing between economic justice and cultural recognition. She portrayed working-class politics and queer politics as more one-dimensional than they are, retrogressing from the New Left theorizing that marked her own early work.[145]

Young rehearsed her rendering of the five faces of oppression, puzzling that Fraser regressed to a "brazenly dichotomous" theory. The two structures that Fraser chose left no room for the political aspect of social reality—practices of law, citizenship, institutions, administration, and political participation. This major weakness was the subject of an entire second wave of subsequent contention over Fraser's theory. Fraser expressly followed Habermas in adopting a bifocal perspective; Young noted that she did so despite previously criticizing Habermas for dichotomizing between the state-economic system and the lifeworld in which people exist as cared-for individuals. The early Fraser subverted Habermas's twofold scheme by invoking the category of political action and struggle. What happened to that person? Fraser said she opted for a bifocal approach in order to identify contradictions in reality. Young countered that the contradictions she found were mostly contrived by her brazen dichotomy. If Fraser was right, the goals of feminist and antiracist movements are internally contradictory. Transformative redistribution is supposedly incompatible with affirmative recognition because redistribution changes the underlying structure and recognition leaves it in place. Young refused to believe it, implying that she said so from closer acquaintance with liberationist movements. She added that bringing these remedies into the same basic structure was a bad move yielding a bad result: "Why not choose plural categories to distinguish and reflect those issues of justice that concern the patterns of the distribution of goods from those that concern the divisions of labor or the organization of decision-making power?"[146]

The dichotomy approach produces categories that are too stark. Young proposed a fourfold scheme for evaluating the justice of social institutions: distribution of goods and resources, division of labor, organization of decision-making power, and the creation of a culture of respect and free self-expression. She argued that no conceivable dual category scheme shows how struggles can aim at different kinds of goals. Young lauded the cultural studies movement, especially French social theorist Pierre Bourdieu, for demonstrating that political economy is always thoroughly cultural without ceasing to be political. Acquiring positions in privileged economic strata depends on cultural factors of education, family connection, taste, and social connection. Culture is one of several sites of struggle interacting with others. Young observed, "A materialist cultural approach understands that needs are contextualized in political struggle over who gets to define whose needs for what purpose." She chided that the early Fraser made exactly this argument in one of her *Unruly Practices* essays. The early Fraser said that every struggle against oppression is a struggle against cultural and economic domination because the cultural styles of the oppressed are denigrated and the denigrated are denied equal access to material goods. Young wrote, "I recommend the position of the earlier Fraser over the later."[147]

Worst of all, Fraser misrepresented cultural leftism by describing the politics of recognition as an end in itself. Young allowed that some separatist groups do treat recognition in this fashion, but otherwise it is rare that a recognition movement cuts loose from economic justice issues. When it happens, the remedy is to reconnect recognition with economic justice, affirming that recognition is an element within economic and political equality. But Fraser, Young protested, "does just the reverse," treating all group-based claims of recognition as ends in themselves. Young brushed close to Butler's accusation, observing that Fraser's position seems similar to conservatives who construe antiracist recognition as reverse racism against whites. Young allowed that the equality versus difference debate does pose a wrenching dilemma for feminists. It was a hard call whether feminists should demand gender blindness in the policies of employers or demand special provisions for the primary caretakers of children. Either choice has consequences that feminists don't like. But this dilemma, Young cautioned, has nothing to do with Fraser's redistribution-recognition contrivance. The real dilemma pits two redistribution strategies against each other. Young said feminists need places where they speak for themselves and discuss with each other how they should solve their real dilemmas. It has always been hard to do this in the glare of the general public. Then a great hue and cry went up over cultural leftism. Then Nancy Fraser, of all people, told the bashers of political correctness they made some good points.[148]

Fraser greeted Butler warmly before correcting her in detail; she greeted Rorty warmly before explaining that traditional identity politics was the only part of this subject he understood; and she gave Young short shrift. She welcomed that Butler retrieved "the genuinely valuable aspects of Marxism and the social-ist-feminism of the 1970s," linking both to the best parts of cultural studies and poststructuralism. But Fraser disagreed with Butler about what should be taken from Marxism and socialist feminism. They also disagreed about the merits of poststructuralist criticism and the nature of contemporary capitalism, and Fraser strenuously objected that Butler lumped her with "neoconservative Marxists." The latter refutation had to come first because Fraser could picture what would happen otherwise. Butler's many followers would perceive Fraser as a slick ver-sion of the enemy who construed sexual oppression as less fundamental, mate-rial, and real than class oppression. They would move to the verdict that Fraser subordinated struggles against heterosexism to struggles against the exploitation of workers. Fraser observed: "Finding me thus lumped together with 'sexually conservative orthodox' Marxists, readers could even conclude that I view gay and lesbian movements as unjustified particularisms that have split the Left and on whom I wish forcibly to impose left unity." She protested that she believed "nothing of the sort" and did not appreciate Butler's lumping move.[149]

Fraser did not derogate the injustices of recognition as merely cultural; her central objective was to conceptualize recognition and redistribution as equally primary and real kinds of harm. Butler pointed to Fraser's construal of heterosexism as a pure injustice of recognition, which Butler said underwrote Fraser's subordination of heterosexism to more fundamental forms of oppres-sion. The purity point was misleading because Fraser framed the redistribution-recognition spectrum as a thought experiment, and she later clarified her position about pure exploitation and pure heterosexism, denying that either exists in the real world. In her dialogue with Honneth, Fraser argued that all real-world forms of oppression are bivalent, ranging in more-or-less forms across the spectrum. This verdict, however, was already implicit in her 1995 essay remarks about thought experiments, Marxian exploitation, and heterosexism. Fraser never said that misrecognition is merely the experience of being looked down upon, a psychological phenomenon. She said it is about being denied the status of equal partnership in social interactions and social life, an institutional-ized social relation. Misrecognition is a fundamental injustice whether or not it is accompanied by economic injustice. Later she clarified that bivalent duality is always in play, neither misrecognition nor maldistribution is merely an indi-rect effect of the other, and each has some independent weight. Fraser came close to Weber, not Marx, on the duality of status and class. Her distinction between redistribution and recognition was not a tactic to establish a new ortho-doxy: "Contrary to Butler, I mean to defend the distinction while disclaiming the tactic."[150]

She rejected three central Butler contentions: (1) The oppression of gays and lesbians should not be categorized as misrecognition because it entails material economic harms. (2) The family is central to capitalist functionality. (3) The distinction between the material and the cultural is unstable. Butler wrongly attributed to Fraser the view that injustices of misrecognition must be immaterial and noneconomic, so she gave examples of material harms suffered by gays and lesbians, which did not refute Fraser's distinction between redistribution and recognition. Fraser conceived misrecognition as the *material* construction through which devalued persons are harmed by the imposition of privileged institutionalized cultural norms. On capitalism, Butler made two versions of a weak argument. One was definitional: Regulating sexuality is part of the economic structure by definition. This was a near-tautology explaining nothing about historical varieties of capitalism, the social division of labor, or the capitalist mode of production. Butler also invoked the functionalist argument that capitalism runs on compulsory heterosexuality. Fraser blushed to see it recycled in the age of gay-friendly corporations. Corporate capitalism is very skilled at accommodating gay rights and making money off it: "Butler has resurrected what is in my view one of the worst aspects of 1970s Marxism and socialist-feminism: the overtotalized view of capitalist society as a monolithic 'system' of interlocking structures of oppression that seamlessly reinforce one another." Fraser implored that if the left aspires to describe the real world it must pay attention to the gaps between structures. The functionalist system theories of the seventies are "better left forgotten."[151]

As for the instability of the material/cultural distinction, Butler got two things wrong. She assumed that Fraser's normative distinction between redistribution and recognition rests on an ontological distinction between the material and the cultural, and she believed that undermining the latter distinction sunders the former distinction. But Fraser held that injustices of misrecognition are as material as injustices of maldistribution; she made no ontological distinction. Her distinction between redistribution and recognition correlated under capitalism with the distinction between the economic and the cultural. That is, it correlated with a social-theoretical distinction, not an ontological distinction. Fraser said the real difference between them is over the economic/cultural distinction. Butler cited anthropologist Claude Lévi-Strauss on the processes of exchange in precapitalist societies, where kinship organized the structures of marriage, sexual relations, labor, distribution, relations of authority and obligation, and the hierarchies of status and prestige. Distinctly economic and cultural relations did not exist; Butler said the distinction between the economic and the cultural therefore has no stable ground. Fraser replied that Lévi-Strauss historicized a distinction that is central to modern capitalist societies. Societies featuring a single order of social relations led to capitalist societies in which the social structural differentiation between the economic and the cultural is crucial and amply grounded. Fraser held no brief against deconstruction; she said its approach to the politics of recognition is often better than "standard identity politics." Nonetheless, deconstructionist criticism is prone to be proud and heedless, presuming that to historicize something is to render it null and void for social theory. Fraser said good historicism assumes the opposite. Instead of claiming to destroy or destabilize useful distinctions, historicism makes it possible to wield distinctions with precision.[152]

Almost everything Rorty said against recognition politics criticized traditional identity politics, but Fraser opposed identity politics too, aiming to deinstitutionalize oppressive value hierarchies. Identity politics treats misrecognition as a freestanding cultural norm, abstracting the harm from its institutional and economic matrices, and it essentializes identity, pressing individuals to conform to a defined identity. Fraser argued that Rorty missed the better option—to reinterpret recognition in terms of status. Recognition is about the status of individual group members as partners in social interaction, not the recognition of a group-specific identity. It takes misrecognition seriously as a species of unjust subordination, an injustice institutionalized throughout the world in laws, regulations, policies, and practices that exclude same-sex partnerships, stigmatize single mothers, racially profile criminal suspects, and the like. The status model does not reify group identities or reduce all recognition injustices to an all-purpose solution such as universal opposition to prejudice. Justice, Fraser explained, sometimes requires recognition of differences; it does not contradict or supersede respect for the equal humanity that everyone shares. It deepens this respect, making it possible to fulfill the universal principle. Fraser said the left understands social justice more deeply after forty years of social movement gains; she was not for turning back the clock.[153]

The tone and mood changed markedly when Fraser responded to Young. There were no appreciative words about welcoming her perspective: "Iris Young and I seem to inhabit different worlds. In her world, there are no divisions between the social Left and the cultural Left." In Young's world, Fraser said, social democrats and cultural leftists worked together for redistribution and recognition. Almost nobody who stumped for identity politics was an essentialist, "let alone an authoritarian or chauvinist." Recognition demands were almost never put forward as ends in themselves, and all such demands were framed as transitional socialist objectives. In sum, "the divisions that inspired my article are artifacts of my 'dichotomous framework,' figments of my imagination."[154]

Fraser countered that she did not fantasize the spate of social democratic books against cultural leftism, the march of a million black men on the nation's capital in which no socioeconomic demands were voiced, or the "widespread gloating" among social democrats when Old Left Marxist Alan Sokal published a hoax send-up of deconstruction in *Social Text*. The fissures were terribly real, and her aim was to show that they rested on false antitheses, which Young should have appreciated. Fraser objected that Young "systematically distorts my argument" with arguments "more tendentious than analytical." Fraser began four sentences with the phrase "contra Young." Contrary to Young, she did not invent the distribution-recognition paradigm, contrive its breakup, describe distribution and recognition as substantial domains, change her mind, or attribute the splits between distribution and recognition proponents to false consciousness. Fraser described the interrelation of the cultural and economic spheres by tracing the unintended effects of cultural and economic claims: Cultural claims have distributive implications, and economic claims have cultural implications. She said this was a form of perspectival dualism, not dichotomy, exactly as she expounded in her early work that Young also distorted. Fraser had no idea why Young insisted so vehemently that five factors are better than two. Young's fivefold list of group oppressions was ad hoc and undertheorized, and she offered no good reasons to reject Fraser's contrast between affirmative and transformative remedies. The crucial difference between Fraser and Young was Young's passionate commitment to a movement-affirmative politics. Fraser described Young as a willful left-wing Pollyanna who refused to see any real problems with the postmodern left. Whatever problems there were "will somehow be automatically resolved in some all-encompassing 'coalition' whose basis and content need not be specified." But strong forms of affirmative recognition politics do not fight for economic justice.[155]

The Fraser debate about redistribution-recognition carried on for over a decade. The second round was grim, chastened, and sometimes despairing. It operated within Fraser's dual framework and took for granted that the split between the redistribution left and the recognition left was terribly real. Fraser, Elizabeth Anderson, Joseph Heath, Ingrid Robeyns, and others wrote about integrating redistribution and recognition in theory and practice. Fraser sharpened her critique of chauvinist elements within recognition movements. Anderson argued that affirmative action is one important recognition strategy that does not conflict with redistribution. Heath contended that Dworkin's equality of resources model is the best redistribution theory of justice, partly because it underwrites a democratic politics of recognition. Robeyns made a similar case for the capability model of Sen. A third round of debate commenced in 2002 when Leonard Feldman argued that political injustices are distinct from economic and cultural injustices. Feldman expanded on the point made by Young that Fraser's economy-culture model left no room for the vital political sphere of law, citizenship, and institutions. Kevin Olson argued that the political dimension of justice supersedes redistribution and recognition because it is normatively and conceptually prior to other forms of social participation.[156]

Fraser refashioned her theory to include a distinct political dimension of justice, adding "representation" to distribution and recognition. In effect, she updated Weber's triad of class, status, and party to include the problems of political representation as justice concerns. The critiques of Feldman and Olson persuaded her that the redistribution-recognition frame wrongly takes for granted the specific and constitutive work of politics. Politics deals with representation — who is included and what are the rules? Distribution and recognition are political in contesting for power and policy objectives, usually as adjudicated by the state, but politics determines how the state organizes itself and structures struggles for justice. Fraser took for granted the ordering role of politics until economic globalization challenged it. Globalization brought home to her that political injustice is a central category unto itself and a problem of multiplying global complexity. The image of justice as a scale held by a blindfolded judge evokes an enduring test of justice, impartiality. The image of justice as a map evokes the problems of the bounds of justice, the framing issue. Fraser argued that recognition politics throws into question what an impartial scale would be and globalization throws into question the concept of national sovereignty underlying the Westphalian map of justice. What is the scale of justice on which contested heterogeneous claims might be impartially weighed? In a world that pits environmentalists, human rights activists, nongovernmental organizations, the global poor, transnational corporations, national governments, and international institutions against each other in various shifting patterns generating multiple kinds of representation claims, how should the bounds of justice be framed?[157]

These questions shape Fraser's recent work, which runs longer on description and raising questions than on providing answers. She stresses that the image of the scale has been stretched to the breaking point because parties no longer fight over something that can be weighed on a single scale. Movements demanding economic redistribution clash with defenders of the economic status quo *and* with movements defending specific groups *and* with representational claims on behalf of the global poor, refugees, the global environment, and world peace. Redistribution, Fraser reflects, is a comparatively simple question of pro versus con or how much versus how little. When groups clash over the claims of redistribution, recognition, and representation, the threat of partiality is exceeded and changed by the specter of incommensurability. Decisions made by national governments, corporations, international organizations, currency speculators, and large institutional investors have immense impacts on national communities and parts of the world lacking any input in the decisions. First-order questions about justice are questions of substance about redistribution or recognition: How much economic inequality does justice permit? How much redistribution is required? What constitutes equal respect? Which kinds of difference merit public recognition? The metalevel questions supersede these first-order questions: What is the best frame for considering first-order questions? Who are the relevant subjects entitled to just distribution or reciprocal recognition?[158]

Politics furnishes the stage on which movements for distribution and recognition take place. Since representation is the defining issue of the political, misrepresentation is the characteristic political injustice. Fraser observes that misrepresentation occurs when political boundaries or decision rules wrongly prevent some people from participating equally with others in social interaction. It is usually intertwined with maldistribution or misrecognition but does not have to be. A second level of misrepresentation occurs when the boundaries of a community are drawn to wrongly exclude some people from participating in contests over justice. Fraser calls it misframing, the denial of a right to have any rights. Globalization generates and exposes the injustice of misframing. It grows the sector of international institutions holding little or any relationship to a national government, and it exposes that the modern state is a powerful instrument of injustice, gerrymandering political space at the expense of the poor and vulnerable. If you have no standing, you cannot struggle for redistribution or recognition.[159]

Fraser doesn't claim to know what the post-Westphalian frame should be, but she reasons that it surely begins with the principle that all affected by a given structure or institution hold moral standing as subjects of justice in relation to it. The territorial state fails the test of the all-affected principle: "Globalization is driving a widening wedge between state-territoriality and social effectivity. As these two principles increasingly diverge, the effect is to reveal the former as an inadequate surrogate for the latter." Affirmative framers seek to redraw boundaries or create new ones without challenging the authority of the territorial state to decide who deserves justice. Transformative framers contend that many injustices are not territorial in character and should not be adjudicated by territorial states. Transformative framing, on this account, is the attempt to apply the all-affected principle directly to the framing of justice, bypassing national governments. It is solidarity and peace activists pressing for transnational agreements about financial markets, biotechnology, and weap-

ons. It is environmentalists and indigenous peoples claiming standing as subjects of justice in relation to state-transcending powers that impinge on their
lives. It is the assertion of the right to make a claim of injustice against any
structure that causes harm.[160]

Fraser's work drove to this point by identifying from the beginning with
socialist feminism and applying it to a changing world. She said the conventional textbook rendering of second-wave feminism is too internal to feminism,
telling a progress story about an exclusionary movement dominated by white,
middle-class, heterosexual women that became increasingly inclusive as it
embraced the concerns of LGBTQ+ persons, women of color, and the working
class. Fraser was all for progress and inclusion, but the textbook story fails to
situate how feminism changed in relation to broader historical and global
developments. Her version divides into three phases. The first phase grew out of
the social movements of the 1960s and was closely identified with them. The
second phase commenced at the turn of the 1970s, when the utopian energies
of the New Left faded. Feminism in its second phase was drawn into the orbit
and language of identity politics, recasting itself as a politics of recognition. But
cultural feminism arose just as Fordism collapsed and the welfare state buckled
under the pressure of global neoliberalism. Fraser said identity politics feminism could not thrive in a globalizing world; it could only shrink to sectarian
status. U.S. American feminists endured the eighties and nineties in a confused
state, feeling their declining relevance; then the onslaught aftermath of 9/11
overwhelmed them. They were not prepared for the fresh burst of toxic masculinity and nationalistic militarism that engulfed them, worse than the *Rambo*
movies of the 1980s. The third phase of feminism commenced in Europe and
subaltern contexts before it spread to the United States. It is a form of transnational politics emerging in transnational spaces.[161]

Wave stories of this kind nearly always favor the perspective of the person
telling the story. Many are variations on a story about liberal feminism clashing
with cultural feminism leading to social(ist) feminism. Fraser's version is more
attuned to the radical feminism of the 1960s that was never liberal and the
socialist feminism of the 1970s that came and went. Her version registers the
surprise she felt in the early 1990s when free-market ideologies "previously
given up for dead" not only thrived but triumphed, shredding the inclusive
ethos of the welfare state and its "prosperity-securing steering capacities."
Meanwhile identity politics ruled in feminism, as feminists resorted to the
grammar of recognition: "Unable to make headway against injustices of political economy, they preferred to target harms resulting from androcentric patterns of cultural value or status hierarchies. The result was a major shift in the

feminist imaginary: whereas the previous generation pursued an expanded ideal of social equality, this one invested the bulk of its energies in cultural change." Fraser allowed that every phase of feminism talked about cultural transformation. What distinguished the identity politics phase of feminism was its retreat to an autonomous cultural project—"its decoupling from the project of political-economic transformation and distributive justice."[162]

Phase two had a mixed legacy, she judged. It found new ways to critique male dominance but lost "the socialist imaginary," subordinating social justice struggles to cultural struggles. The timing of this retreat to a truncated cultural-ism "could not have been worse." Fraser recalled that precisely at the moment that neoliberalism staged "its spectacular comeback," feminists moved up in the academy by attacking essentialism, equating feminism with jargon borrowed from French deconstructionists. The same thing happened in other sectors of progressive politics. To be sure, she allowed, identity politics carried further in the United States than anywhere else. But she saw a good deal of it while lecturing and teaching in Europe. Neoliberals combined familiar labor market flexibility with familiar cultural recognition politics, especially multiculturalism. Analogous shifts occurred in the former Communist nations and the so-called Third World. The end of the Cold War curtailed the flow of aid to the periphery and commenced neoliberal structural adjustment policies that squeezed postcolonial developmental states. Economic redistribution projects disappeared in the global South, fueling "an enormous surge of identity politics in the postcolony, much of it communalist and authoritarian." Postcolonial feminists were caught between downsized state capacities and an upsurge of communal chauvinism. Fraser sympathized with feminists wherever they felt compelled to settle for identity politics; on the other hand, she painted a doleful picture of shrinking and retreat.[163]

In the United States it was especially dreadful, she said, after 9/11. Feminists looked up from their debates over essentialism to find that an "unholy alliance of free-marketeers and fundamentalist Christians had taken over the country." Fraser shuddered at the manipulation of gender in the so-called war on terror, which cascaded through the 2004 election. Democratic candidate John Kerry, a decorated Vietnam War veteran, was cast as an effeminate girlie man who "could not be trusted to protect American women and children from the crazed violence of bearded fanatics." Fraser judged that this issue won the election for George W. Bush, overcoming that Bush was a bad president. One facet of the Bush coalition fascinated Fraser: why were so many evangelical women in it? Most did not live patriarchal lives; they were active in the labor market and empowered in their families, yet they subscribed to an ideology of traditional domesticity. Fraser reasoned that conservative evangelical religion speaks to the insecurity of the neoliberal condition. It attains no real security for anyone but offers a discourse and practices expressly addressing insecurity, telling people they are sinners, they will fail, and God will help them. To borrow a later-Foucault expression, evangelicalism is a "care of the self" regime adept at managing insecurity.[164]

The third wave of feminism began in transnational spaces, rejects the state-territorial frame, and still operates predominantly in contested transnational contexts. Fraser says the third wave is too ambitious and devoted to effective action to rest with identity politics; plus it is alarmed about the role of transnational forces in worsening gender injustice. In third-wave feminism, feminists link their claims for redistribution and recognition to struggles to change the political frame. European third-wave feminists target the economic policies and structures of the European Union. Feminists involved in protests against the World Trade Organization challenge the governance structures of the global economy.

Berkeley political theorist Wendy Brown, a third-wave feminist theorist, observes that to speak of a post-Westphalian order is not to imply that nation-state sovereignty is finished or irrelevant. "Post" signifies a specific condition "of afterness in which what is past is not left behind, but, on the contrary, relentlessly conditions, even dominates a present that nevertheless also breaks in some way with this past." Fraser argues that the third wave has already changed how recognition feminism operates, looking beyond the territorial state. Under the slogan "Women's rights are human rights" the third wave has become a global movement that links struggles against local antifeminist practices to campaigns for changes in international law. First-order injustices are specifically targeted: "In this phase, a major concern is to challenge interlinked injustices of maldistribution and misrecognition." But third-wave feminists also operate at the meta-injustice level, refiguring gender justice as a three-dimensional problem that integrates redistribution, recognition, and problems of representation transcending the demand of voting rights for women in constituted political communities.[165]

In Europe, Fraser argues, third-wave feminism is a threefold struggle. It works with other progressive forces to establish feminist social welfare protections at the transnational level, works with progressives to integrate redistributive policies with feminist recognition policies that respect European cultural heterogeneity, and struggles to accomplish both objectives without hardening external borders. She cautioned in 2009 that the threat of transnational Europe retreating to fortress Europe is terribly real; then it became more than a threat.

European feminists led the way into the third wave, followed by feminists from the global South and Asia involved in agencies of the United Nations and the World Social Forum. Here as well, Fraser observes, feminists join environmentalists, development activists, indigenous peoples, and other progressive transnational groups to challenge the linked injustices of maldistribution, misrecognition, and misrepresentation: "There, too, the task is to develop a three-dimensional politics that appropriately balances and integrates those concerns."[166]

It galls her that most feminists do not oppose neoliberalism and that the dominant culture measures feminist progress by the number of female corporation executives. In 2019 Fraser described "lean-in" corporate feminism as "equal opportunity domination," a handmaiden of capitalism that shares the managerial tasks of exploitation and oppression. Liberal feminism, she protested, asks ordinary people in the name of feminism "to be grateful that it is a woman, not a man, who busts their union, orders a drone to kill their parent, or locks their child in a cage at the border." In 2009, asking why feminism is so easily seduced, Fraser pointed to a subterranean elective affinity between feminism and neoliberalism, the critique of authority. Both movements roar for freedom, claiming to stand for the freedom principle. On the other hand, she said, feminism and neoliberalism diverge over posttraditional forms of gender subordination. The break does not occur over forms of personal domination and subjection. Feminism and neoliberalism diverge over structural processes in which the actions of many persons are impersonally mediated. For example, the traditional responsibility of women for child-rearing shapes labor markets that disadvantage women. This disadvantage makes women less powerful than men in the marketplace, which exacerbates the unequal power of women in families. Fraser said neoliberal capitalism runs on exactly such market-mediated processes of subordination; there is no capitalism without them. Feminists need to fight off their cooptation, focusing on the subordinating structural processes of neoliberalism in the fashion of socialist feminism and the third wave.[167]

That was just after the banks crashed and the Bush years ended. DSA fell off during the Bush years. In 2004 it backed Kerry after he won the Democratic nomination, reasoning that a Kerry defeat would be taken "not as a defeat of the U.S. political center, which Kerry represents, but of the mainstream Left." The nation was in an emergency situation one year after it invaded Iraq; supporting the surviving Democratic candidate seemed imperative, even when it turned out to be Kerry. Meanwhile DSA mounted an Economic Justice Agenda (EJA) campaign against the so-called Grand Compromise pushed by Bush and Wall Street Democrats: tax cuts for corporations and the wealthy in exchange for cuts in Social Security and Medicare. In the last year of Bush's presidency the EJA prefigured what became the Bernie Sanders campaign of 2016. This upward tick in activist energy continued during the Obama years, soon in frustration with Obama's lukewarm centrism.[168]

Comparisons between Franklin Roosevelt in 1933 and Barack Obama in 2009 were prevalent in 2009, until hope ran out that Obama would be a comparable figure. Like FDR, Obama accelerated Keynesian gas, battled Republicans, and refused to nationalize the banks, though the banks were small in Roosevelt's case. In Obama's case the banks were colossal and got more so after getting their bailouts, which made them sufficiently powerful to prevent real reform, at least with Obama as president. The crucial political difference between 1933 and 2009, however, was that America was deeply into a depression when FDR took office, whereas Obama's job was to prevent a depression from occurring. Obama helped to pull the economy out of its death spiral but not in a way that inspired much gratitude. Meanwhile a gusher of protest against neo-liberal priorities and consequences erupted on his watch, reviving the American version of a European tradition, democratic socialism.

8

Breaking the Oligarchy: Bernie Sanders, Alexandria Ocasio-Cortez, and the Next Left

Economic globalization integrated two radically different models of growth—debt-financed consumption and production-oriented export and saving—creating a wildly unstable world economy of asset bubbles and huge trade imbalances. Under Republican and Democratic administrations alike the United States hollowed out its industrial base that paid decent wages, gave incentives to runaway firms, condemned young black felons to draconian prison sentences, and rang up enormous trade deficits that left the nation dependent on China and Japan to finance its debt. Supposedly there was no alternative to neoliberal capitalism and the rule of the megabanks. This went on through the administrations of Bill Clinton, George W. Bush, and Barack Obama, even after bankers crashed the financial system. But the crash of 2007–8 and its aftershocks changed what people, especially young people, were willing to accept. Mass movements across the categories of identity became possible again. Many young Americans flatly demanded the same universal healthcare, free higher education, and solidarity wages that are commonplace in Europe. Democratic socialism made a comeback after the idea of a left movement lost its sense of bygone irrelevance.

The Clinton and Bush administrations sowed the seeds of the comeback by allowing Wall Street to do pretty much whatever it wanted. Wall Street fell in love with derivatives, Clinton tore down the Glass-Steagall wall separating commercial and investment banking, and the big commercial banks merged with investment banks and insurance companies, creating interconnected megabank empires. Bush cheered the megabank mergers and a frenzy of Wall Street speculation based on hashed-together subprime mortgages. In 2007 the economy cratered after the debt resort reached its outer limit in the housing market, and the mortgage bubble burst.

For twenty years securitizations and derivatives were great at concocting extra yield and allowing the banks to hide their debt. It seemed a blessing to get a low-rate mortgage. It was a mystery how the banks did it, but you trusted that they knew what they were doing. Your bank resold the mortgage to an aggregator, who bunched it up with thousands of other subprime mortgages, chopped the package into pieces, and sold them as corporate bonds to parties looking for extra yield. Your mortgage payments paid for the interest on the bonds. This scheme was ingenious for creating market value and charging fees at every link in a chain of selling, packaging, securitizing, and reselling. It worked as long as housing values always went up and there was no reckoning for the trashy assets held with borrowed money on which the whole casino was built.

Broadly speaking, a derivative is any contract that derives its value from another underlying asset, such as buying home insurance. More narrowly it's an instrument that allows investors to speculate on the future price of something without having to buy it. Derivatives were developed to allow investors to hedge their risks in financial markets—in essence, to buy insurance against market movements. In each case they quickly became major investment options in their own right, allowing executives to claim "earnings" for contracts in which money exchanged hands only at a designated future date that could be far off. Option trading—paying for the right to exercise an option in the event that prices move in a set direction—soared in the 1970s, aided by the growth of computers, which helped to gauge the volatility of assets. The more prices move, the more buyers exercise their options. Currency swaps and then interest-rate swaps emerged in the 1980s. Currency swaps exchange bonds issued in one currency for another currency, enabling both parties to seek lower interest rates. Interest rate swaps pair variable rate borrowers with borrowers on a fixed rate, as both parties try to manage their risk exposure.[1]

From there it was a short step to the credit default swaps pioneered in the late 1990s in which parties bet on, or insured against, defaults. Credit default swaps are private contracts that allow investors to bet on whether a borrower will default. This market was completely unregulated until the Dodd-Frank financial reform bill of 2010. In theory, credit default swaps are a form of insurance because sellers guarantee to pay investors if their investments go bad. In reality, the credit default mania of the Bush years was pure gambling exempted from insurance reserve requirements and state gaming laws. Credit default sellers were not required to set aside reserves to pay for claims, and in 2000 the Commodity Futures Modernization Act exempted credit default swaps from state gaming laws and other forms of regulation.

For ten years credit default swaps were fantastically lucrative. In 1998 the total value of credit default contracts was $144 billion; by 2008 it was $62 trillion and at the heart of the financial crash. The derivatives market as a whole was equally spectacular and concentrated. In 2003 seven banks owned 96 percent of the derivatives in the U.S. banking system, which had a total value of $56 trillion; by 2008 this market was estimated to be $520 trillion. Alan Greenspan, the Federal Reserve chair from 1987 to 2006 and a major proponent of derivatives, contended that the big banks and financial firms needed a market vehicle to transfer their highly leveraged risks. But these instruments offered dangerous incentives for false accounting and made it extremely difficult to ascertain a firm's true exposure. They generated huge amounts of leverage in which investors controlled assets far exceeding the original investment. They were developed with no consideration of the broad economic consequences. Securitization practically ensured unaccountability by creating new types of information asymmetries. Mortgage bundlers knew more than the buyers about what was in the bundles, but nobody knew very much, which left nobody responsible for what happened to them. Essentially, securitization allows banks to set up off-balance-sheet vehicles to hide their debt. If financial institutions could parcel out their risk, supposedly there was nothing to worry about since housing values always went up. At every link in the chain, every time a loan was sold, packaged, securitized, or resold, transaction fees were charged and somebody's "wealth" increased. Bonuses were paid for short-term paper gains on money held up for as long as ten years. The mania for extra yield fed on itself, blowing away business ethics and common sense.[2]

Finally the reckoning came. Fannie Mae and Freddie Mac owned or controlled half the nation's $12 trillion mortgage market. These congressionally chartered companies teetered on collapse in September 2008, and Treasury Secretary Hank Paulson took them over. Fannie Mae's common share price had dropped in one year from $66 to $7.32, and net losses for the two companies stood at $5.5 billion. Paulson and Federal Reserve Board chair Ben Bernanke persuaded Bush that seizing both companies simultaneously was the only alternative to a global meltdown, since nearly every American home mortgage lender and Wall Street bank relied on them to facilitate the mortgage market, and foreign investors led by Japan, China, and Russia held more than $1 trillion of the debt issued or guaranteed by the two companies. Paulson later recalled, "We had, I thought, just saved the country—and the world—from financial catastrophe."[3]

Actually the week of reckoning had just begun. Lehman Brothers screamed for rescue; Merrill Lynch and Washington Mutual were drowning too; and

General Electric CEO Jeffrey Immelt told Paulson he couldn't sell any commercial paper, a frightening sign that a systemwide liquidity crisis had begun. Lehman had $600 billion of assets and was very interconnected. But Lehman had bad timing and a fateful combination of capital and liquidity problems. Lehman's assets were believed to be worth $20 billion less than the value at which they were carried, creating a huge capital hole that caused anxious counterparties to flee, creating a huge liquidity problem. Paulson scrounged $30 billion from the big banks to broker a deal for Lehman, but nobody wanted to buy it. Meanwhile Paulson learned that the teetering American International Group (AIG) dwarfed his Lehman problem, just before he let Lehman crash.

AIG was the poster child of the derivatives fiasco. The financial products unit of AIG, a corporation of U.S.-based insurance companies claiming assets of $1 trillion, bankrupted the conglomerate by trafficking in derivatives tied to subprime mortgages. Its derivatives unit was a huge casino selling phantom insurance for credit default swaps with no backing aside from the value of dubious mortgages. The company financed long-term mortgages with short-term paper, which required more promissory notes every time the mortgages lost value, and it took huge losses in its securities lending program by lending out high-grade bonds for cash, which torpedoed its tens of billions of dollars of contracts guaranteeing 401(k)s and other retirement holdings.

AIG was the epitome of systemic risk, connected to hundreds of companies and financial institutions. If AIG went down, the process of unwinding its contracts would take many years, destroying countless lives and businesses. Bush was stunned at bailing out AIG, asking how an insurance company could be so systemically important. Paulson said AIG was an unregulated holding company of regulated insurance companies. Bernanke described it as a hedge fund sitting atop an insurance company. The Lehman crash roiled the credit and stock markets, the AIG bailout did nothing to calm the financial markets, and short sellers brought Morgan Stanley to its knees. Bernanke said they had to bail out Wall Street as a whole, not just a few firms. If Congress did not pass a whopping bailout called the Troubled Asset Relief Program (TARP), "we may not have an economy on Monday." The economy they had was teetering on the brink of an abyss.[4]

The Democratic presidential candidate, Obama, helped the Bush administration obtain its bailouts of September/October 2008. Had Obama not been a key political player in the bailout, he might have been less obsequious to Wall Street after he became president. Had the financial system crashed in December instead of September, Obama might have demanded tougher treatment of firms that caused the crash, which might have led to stronger policies of his own—assuming his election. As it was, Obama was co-opted before he began, and he stayed on that path. He inherited a global deflationary spiral that extracted portfolio contractions of 30 to 40 percent. He put his economic policy in the hands of Timothy Geithner, the Federal Reserve Bank of New York president who cut the bailout deals, and Lawrence Summers, who helped Clinton tear down the Glass-Steagall wall. Geithner became treasury secretary, and Summers chaired the National Economic Council. That was a sickening omen to many left-liberal activists who worked to elect Obama. Something precious was already slipping away before Obama was inaugurated in January 2009—the hope that he might change the system.

The left had worked hard for Obama. DSA formally supported his election, West delivered sixty-five campaign speeches on Obama's behalf, and Barbara Ehrenreich and Bill Fletcher Jr. teamed with Tom Hayden and actor Danny Glover to form a campaign vehicle, Progressives for Obama. They gasped with revulsion when Obama stocked his cabinet and staff with Wall Street insiders, Republican defense officials, and retreads from the Democratic establishment, appointing only one progressive, Labor Secretary Hilda Solis. On March 27, 2009, Obama met with the CEOs of the nation's thirteen biggest banks, famously telling them, "My administration is the only thing standing between you and the pitchforks." He said they needed to pull together, work together, and show some respect for the public's rage about excessive executive compensation. The bankers nodded in fake agreement, winning a reprieve they didn't deserve. Had Obama cut the banks down to an upper limit of 3 percent of GDP for a single bank and 2 percent for an investment holding company, he would have won a political windfall. The cheering would have resounded through the country. But Obama wanted to work with big bankers who took no interest in working with him. They created a joint lobbying powerhouse, the CDS Dealers Consortium, to oppose every financial reform that he and the Democrats proposed. Citigroup alone hired forty-six lobbyists to fight off the government that had just bailed out Citigroup.[5]

Obama inherited banks holding $2 trillion of toxic debt, but the big bankers felt better after getting their bailouts, and they didn't want to be regulated. The big private equity firms and hedge funds refused to pay more than thirty cents on the dollar for the mortgage bundles, and the banks couldn't stay in business if they booked such huge losses on their holdings. So the banks kicked the can down the road, holding out for sixty cents, lobbied furiously against financial reforms, and returned to the swaps market. Cash for trash, Paulson's original plan, was a straightforward giveaway with no public accountability and no annoying demands to do anything in particular with the taxpayers' money. Obama officials debated ramping up the insurance approach, "ring-fencing" bad assets by providing federal guarantees against losses. But that was a more-of-the-same option that coddled the banks and didn't solve the valuation problem that nobody trusted anyone's balance sheet. Obama officials debated whether to set up transitional "bad banks" to soak up toxic debt. Here the risk of getting prices wrong was even greater. If the government overpaid for toxic securities, taxpayers were cheated; if it didn't overpay and the banks took mark-to-market prices, many were sure to fail. Geithner settled on an Aggregator Bank blending the original Paulson plan with some elements of the bad bank topped off with an auction scheme. The government subsidized up to 95 percent of deals partnered with hedge funds and private equity firms to buy up toxic debt—the most cumbersome, pro-megabank, obsequious, and nontransparent option.[6]

Obama escalated the war in Afghanistan and expanded America's military empire. He watered down the financial reform bill as it moved through Congress, accepting carve-outs for corporate users of derivatives and opposing proposals to force banks to spin off their trading operations in derivatives. He killed a crucial amendment to the financial reform bill that would have imposed sensible limits on the size of megabanks. He took a passive approach to health-care reform legislation, letting a Democratic Congress write the bill, and refused to press for a public option. He put off immigration reform for a later time that did not come and broke a campaign promise by extending Bush's tax cut for the rich. Conciliation was not merely Obama's default mode, as progressives had worried in 2008; it was his chief operating mode.

Meanwhile Obama triggered a ferocious, titanic, vindictive backlash merely by living in the White House and doing his job. Every day that he served he made the nation look better than it was, which Donald Trump keenly grasped while putting it differently. Fox television and an unhinged right-blogosphere stoked the backlash, expanding the market for a best-selling conspiracy literature. A skyrocketing Tea Party movement claimed that Obama's stimulus bill was a socialist takeover of America; somehow it was outrageous to prevent the nation from reliving 1932. Impassioned rallies demanding, "I want my country back" began shortly after Obama was inaugurated. More than one-fourth of the U.S. American population claimed to believe that Obama was not born in the United States, was not a legitimate president, was a Muslim, and a Socialist, and either definitely or probably sympathized with the goals of Islamic fundamentalists wanting to impose Sharia law throughout the world. In some polling up to a third of Americans tagged Obama as sympathetic with Islamic radicalism, and over half tagged him as a Socialist. The books and right-blogosphere had random lists of bad things Obama supposedly believed, plus competing narratives about how he and his white lefty allies defrauded the nation. The shifting base of the Republican Party was told that Obama was born in Kenya, his teenaged mother forged an American birth certificate so he could run for president, he imbibed radical socialism from a father he never knew, or his real father was an American Communist poet, he wrote *Dreams from My Father* to hoodwink prospective voters, or he got a 1960s revolutionary to write the book for him, he exploited his friendships with devious white liberals and Communists to get him into Harvard Law School and the U.S. Senate, and his presidency was a conspiracy to destroy America.[7]

The birther movement rang this alarm for two years before Trump joined it in 2011. It had no basis whatsoever besides racism and backlash hysteria, being too blatant to be called a dog whistle. Trump became a major political player by lauding the birther movement and stumping for it. He flirted with the idea of running for president, shooting to the top of the prospective Republican field, but wasn't ready to mount a campaign. He was impressed at how quickly he ascended and how easy it was. All he had to do was play to the rage and not get outflanked in doing so.

The progressives and socialists who worked to elect Obama were caught between their disappointment in his tepid politics and their revulsion at what he was up against. Some fell out dramatically. West worried privately in 2008 that Obama was "the Johnny Mathis of American politics," gliding to success in the smoothly tame manner of the crooner's early career. When Obama appointed Geithner and Summers, West felt betrayed. He had similar feelings when Obama retained Bush's defense secretary, Robert Gates, and appointed a McCain Republican, retired marine general James L. Jones, as national security advisor, and recycled veteran Middle East advisor Dennis Ross. West recalled: "I said, 'Oh my God, I have really been misled at a very deep level. I have been thoroughly misled, all this populist language is just a façade.' " He had figured that Columbia University economist Joseph Stiglitz and Princeton University economist Paul Krugman, or at least progressive Keynesians of lesser stature, would run Obama's economic policy. Two years into Obama's presidency West described him bitterly as "a black mascot of Wall Street oligarchs and a black puppet of corporate plutocrats. And now he has become head of the American killing machine and is proud of it."[8]

Michael Lerner went through a similar metamorphosis more gradually. Lerner hoped that Obama would work for something like *Tikkun*'s idea of a "caring society," emphasizing environmental sustainability, nuclear disarmament, human rights, and the abolition of global poverty. For two years Lerner protested that Obama lacked a consistent worldview or vision. It was hard to say what Obama thought he was doing, besides shoring up the establishment; *Tikkun* kept editorializing that it was not too late for Obama to espouse a progressive story about cooperating with others to achieve a global common good. After Obama delivered his 2012 State of the Union Address, however, Lerner stopped complaining that Obama had no vision because he had clearly come up with one. Lerner said it was a variation on the Republican worldview: "Economic nationalism backed by a competitive ethos domestically and a strong military internationally." To Lerner, Obama's aggressive talk about competing to "win the future" was a sad echo of the Clinton administration, recycling the very slogans and corporate agenda by which Clinton demoralized the Democratic Party. Betrayal, therefore, was exactly the point. Lerner had met with Obama in 2006 and advocated on his behalf; then he regretted having believed in Obama: "We accomplish little by dwelling for the next few years on how dishonestly Obama manipulated us."[9]

The betrayal trope was exaggerated, registering surprise or double-dealing. Obama advocated the very policies and governed in the very manner of liberal-leaning moderation that he espoused in the 2008 campaign. He did not have a single risky position in his campaign agenda. His opposition to the Iraq war played to his favor in the Democratic weeding-out process, and he had committed himself to it long before he became a national figure. On everything else he was no more progressive than his chief Democratic rivals, Hillary Clinton and John Edwards, and on some things he was less so. Obama's only radical belief was that he could be elected president.

Obama did not promise to get out of Afghanistan; he promised to escalate there. He did not promise to scale back the military empire; he promised to expand the army, emphasize emergency warfare and counterterrorism, and shift the military away from preparing for World War III. He never promised to break the banking oligarchy or create a public bank. For a while he debated whether to advocate a gas tax but decided that was too risky. His campaign quietly supported a public option in healthcare, but healthcare reform was a secondary issue for most of Obama's campaign. He caved on Bush's tax cut for the rich, but that was a hostage trade after Republicans threatened not to extend unemployment benefits and the middle-class tax cut. Frustration with Obama and the Democrats sparked, in 2011, the strongest burst of DSA chapter activity in more than a decade. Then came a spectacular eruption, Occupy Wall Street.

Occupy Wall Street began in July 2011 with a poster by a Canadian environmentalist group, Adbusters, which playfully perched a ballerina atop Wall Street's iconic Charging Bull while riot police looked on in the background. U.S. Day of Rage, a mostly Internet organization, and Anonymous, a multiformation social media network, helped to turn out the original protest on

September 17. The Adbusters ad envisioned 20,000 protesters but barely 2,000 showed up. Conventional progressive organizations were leery of the call to occupy Zuccotti Park, just north of the New York Stock Exchange, which the protesters renamed Liberty Plaza. The decision-making body of Occupy, the NYC General Assembly, consisted of anarchists making no demands and refusing to be identified as leaders. They identified with the leaderless revolutionaries of the ongoing Arab Spring protests that spread across North Africa and the Middle East. The first few days of the occupation were chaotic and disappointing. The occupying group was small, never exceeding more than 150 at night. But new people joined every day, some arriving from other cities. A breakthrough occurred on Saturday, September 24, when the protesters marched to Union Square. Eighty-seven were arrested, garnering major media coverage.[10]

Occupy spread rapidly to more than fifty cities, with major protests occurring in Boston, Dallas, Oakland, Phoenix, Seattle, and Washington, D.C. To the extent that Occupy claimed an ideology, it was anarchist, which yielded an egalitarian, autonomous, leaderless protest committed to a modified model of consensus. But each protest site had its own ethos and process. The share of America's income held by the top 1 percent of the population had more than doubled since 1982. The top 1 percent held 39 percent of the nation's wealth and took in 25 percent of its annual income. Occupy Wall Street raged with colorful street theater against this situation, dramatizing that the top 1 percent plays by a different set of rules and reaps fantastic gains at the expense of everyone else. It protested that no bankers went to jail for crashing the financial system while taxpayers were compelled to clean up the mess and young people could not find a starter job.

To the core Occupiers who lit a fire, it was more important to sustain a spirit of rebellion than to agree on what the government should do about derivatives or tax justice. Their mission was to raise hell against the 1 percent, not to formulate policies. Attempts by some Occupiers to formulate demands were turned aside as premature and a violation of Occupy process. But Occupy had no trouble specifying what it was against. It raged against corporate-dominated politics, bailing out megabanks, and perpetuating inequality and discrimination based on age, race, gender identity, and sexual orientation. It was against monopoly farming and the poisoning of the food supply, the abuse of animals, unsafe working conditions, outsourcing labor, the financing of education through student debt, the legal status of corporations as persons, lack of health coverage, the erosion of privacy, and the abuse of military and police power. Occupy called for peaceable occupying protests across the nation and in all spheres of society.

There was never a profile of the crowds that showed up every day in Liberty Plaza. The movement morphed beyond its original core of alienated youth fed up with the system and willing to sleep in the cold and rain. People from every racial and ethnic community showed up, and all ages. There were tensions between hardcore types who slept there for weeks and smartly dressed professionals and students showing up after work or class. Deodorized drop-ins tried not to wince at the odor and messiness of the occupation, while the live-in protesters were quick to detect wincing and discomfort. There were hard words between left-politico activists, many from DSA, and anarchists who insisted that trying to change the system through electoral politics is pointless and corrupting. Makeshift seminars on economic alternatives abounded. Green Party activist and retired economics professor Richard Wolff stood out among the seminar conveners. Wolff taught until 2008 at the University of Massachusetts, Amherst, where he and Stephen Resnick developed a Marxian analysis of five concrete forms of surplus production and the uncountably many forms of surplus appropriation. Wolff taught Occupiers that Marxism is best interpreted as a tradition of anti-capitalist criticism. After Occupy was shut down he kept the seminars going every month at Judson Memorial Church.[11]

The Occupy slogan, "We are the 99 percent," radiated globally before the occupiers of Zuccotti Park were expelled on November 15, 2011. This message fed on a flock of media stories about Wall Street corruption and the lobbying of Wall Street against every attempt to reform the system. Simon Johnson, chief economist of the International Monetary Fund in 2007–8, observed in 2009 that the finance industry has effectively captured the American government. It goes far beyond mere access or even collusion, Johnson said. In the United States the two career tracks of government and high finance are melded together. Johnson noted that when the IMF enters the scene of a crash, the economic part is usually straightforward. Nations in crisis are told to live within their means by increasing exports, cutting imports, and breaking up bankrupt enterprises and banks. Every nation in crisis that is not the United States gets this prescription. The U.S. case was significantly different inasmuch as the United States controls the IMF, it has a powerful, well-connected oligarchy, and it pays its foreign debts in its own currency. So the U.S. recovery began by paying off Wall Street.[12]

Otherwise, all crashes of the neoliberal era are basically alike. The same thing happened in Japan in 1991, South Korea and Indonesia in 1997, Russia, Malaysia, and Argentina in 1998, and the derivatives meltdown of 2008. A financial oligarchy rigged the game in its favor, built an empire on debt, overreached in good times, and brought the house down on everybody. When the house collapsed the elites took care of their own. To get a different result a nation has to break the grip of the oligarchy. Two kinds of populism soared in the aftermath of the Wall Street payoff and Occupy Wall Street. They had almost nothing in common except revulsion at the rule of differently perceived elites. Each of these popular gushers acquired a presidential candidate in the Republican and Democratic primaries who read the signs and attracted enormous crowds. The right-wing surge elected a hatemongering Republican president who lifted white resentment, racism, xenophobia, and nationalism above the usual Republican appeal to small government. The left-wing surge, needing a language for what went wrong since 1973, reached for a democratic socialist explanation and solution.

BERNIE SANDERS AND THE AMERICAN SOCIALIST REVIVAL

Bernie Sanders inveighed against corporate greed and the gouging of the middle class for decades before he became famous for it. He was born in Brooklyn in 1941 into a family of east European Jewish immigrants. His father, Elias Ben Yehuda Sanders, was born in Galicia, Austria-Hungary (later Poland), and immigrated to the United States in 1921; his mother, Dorothy Glassberg Sanders, was born in New York City to immigrant parents from Russia and Poland. Sanders said he learned the importance of politics at an early age because all his relatives who stayed behind in Poland perished in the Holocaust. Elias Sanders got by in the Flatbush section of Brooklyn by selling paint, reminding Sanders of Willy Loman in *Death of a Salesman*, a grim figure. Sanders played stickball and punchball in the streets, cheered for the Brooklyn Dodgers as family, tagged behind his older brother Larry Sanders, and ran on the high school track team. He studied for a year at Brooklyn College, brushing off his father's objection that college was a waste of time. Dorothy Sanders died young, never achieving her dream of living in a house, and Sanders transferred in 1960 to the University of Chicago, getting away from Brooklyn and his father.

The Sanders family voted Democrat but was not political; Sanders's political awakening occurred in Chicago. He read magazines voraciously while paying little attention to schoolwork, joining YPSL, CORE, and the Student Peace Union. By the end of his sophomore year he was a hardcore lefty. In 1962 Sanders demonstrated against university-owned segregated housing by joining a CORE sit-in at the administration building, one of the first student sit-ins in the North. A bit later he joined a citywide protest organized by the Coordinating Council of Community Organizations against public school segregation, getting arrested in Englewood. Sanders also protested against police brutality and the Vietnam War. His father died in 1963, and Sanders spent his inheritance on eighty-five acres of woodland in Middlesex, Vermont. He graduated in 1964, lived on a kibbutz in Israel for six months, and worked as a Head Start teacher and carpenter in New York City. In 1968 he moved to Vermont with his partner, Susan Mott, converting a maple sugar house to a more or less livable cabin lacking indoor plumbing and electricity.[13]

Sanders wrote journalistic articles for newspapers and bought a house in Stannard, a tiny rural community in Vermont's poor, rugged, picturesque Northeast Kingdom. In 1971 he attended a meeting of the Liberty Union Party, a Vermont democratic socialist offshoot of the People's Party, at Goddard College in central Vermont. He left the meeting as the party's candidate for the U.S. Senate, developing his trademark style in his first campaign—blunt, clear, opinionated, and very far from slick. Sanders garnered 2 percent of the vote in the special election of January 1972 and ran six months later as the Liberty Union candidate for governor, campaigning with People's Party presidential candidate Benjamin Spock. Two years later he ran for the Senate again and in 1976 for the governorship again, peaking with a 6 percent vote tally. He played down the word "socialism," explaining that he didn't want to spend his time explaining what it didn't mean to him. In 1977 he resigned from the party, tired of campaigning with no money. Sanders took a writing job with the American People's Historical Society, making filmstrips for schools; his favorite was a thirty-minute documentary on Eugene Debs.

In 1981 his friend Richard Sugarman, a religion professor at the University of Vermont, told Sanders he should run for mayor of Burlington, a university town of thirty-eight thousand nestled in the gorgeous Adirondack Mountains. Contrary to later mythology, Burlington was not a counterculture enclave. The town's mostly working-class population routinely elected moderate Democrats and Republicans, and Sanders avoided the s-label without denying he was some kind of socialist. Burlington had a five-term incumbent Democrat lacking any Republican opposition. He did very little campaigning, believing that Sanders was too far-out to be a threat. Sugarman turned out to be right—the city leadership had drifted too far from working families and neighborhoods, catering overmuch to moneyed interests and the downtown business community. Running as an Independent, Sanders won by fourteen votes, shocking the Board of Aldermen. A recount confirmed that he won by ten votes, pulled to victory by the police union, opponents of a property tax hike, and environmentalists opposed to a high-rise condominium project on the waterfront of Lake Champlain.[14]

Sanders bought some halfway respectable clothes and fought off the Board of Aldermen, which rejected every one of his appointees. He surprised many by governing effectively, creating sports, concert, and tree-planting programs that improved the quality of life. The new programs and his battles with the aldermen exposed them as obstructionist hacks. Sanders cofounded a political organization aimed at putting progressives on the board from all six wards. The Progressive Coalition won three new seats, enough to protect his veto power, and went on to launch the Vermont Progressive Party, a major player in Vermont politics. Burlington flourished in the eighties, reelecting Sanders three times. He created a Community and Economic Development Office that promoted small business growth, affordable housing, and community planning. The city cleaned up Lake Champlain, won plaudits for livability, became a magnet for music festivals, and developed the nation's first community trust housing program, enabling working-class people to buy their homes. Sanders cultivated a lefty image for the city by touting his socialist beliefs and blasting Reagan's policies in Central America. He described socialism as believing in economic rights—no more and no less. He brought a succession of lefty speakers to Burlington and tossed off cheeky zingers on his radio show but did not neglect managerial tasks. In 1988 he married a social worker, Mary Jane O'Meara, and ran for Vermont's lone seat in the U.S. House of Representatives, losing to Republican lieutenant governor Peter Smith by only 3 percent. Two years later he unseated Smith, becoming the first House member in forty years who was not a Republican or a Democrat.[15]

Conservative Democrats initially blocked him from joining the House Democratic Caucus; it took several weeks of painful back-and-forth before Sanders won entry. He opposed the Gulf War of 1991 on the ground that war should be the last resort. If the United States and its allies expelled Iraq from Kuwait, war would become the norm in the post–Cold War era. Later that year he cofounded the House Progressive Caucus, through which he goaded both parties through the nineties. Sanders fought against corporate welfare and the deregulation of Wall Street, opposing Clinton's rollback of Glass-Steagall. He fought against NAFTA and the Permanent Normal Trade Relations pact with China, denying that corporate interests mesh with the needs of American workers and communities. Repeatedly he assailed the greed of the pharmaceutical industry and its success at buying politicians. He also protected his political backside in rural, gun-owning Vermont, voting five times against the Brady Bill mandating background checks and a waiting period for buying guns. In 1994 Sanders voted for Clinton's crime bill, rationalizing that the Violence Against Women Act outweighed the odious parts. He opposed the Patriot Act of October 2001 and the Iraq War of March 2003, and in 2006 he announced he would run for the U.S. Senate seat opened by retiring Republican senator Jim Jeffords.

Senate Democratic Leader Harry Reid promptly announced that he supported Sanders, as did New York senator Chuck Schumer. These endorsements smoothed the way to a straight-up contest with a Republican opponent, businessman Richie Tarrant, who ran a very negative, personal, fearmongering campaign that backfired. Sanders crushed him by 65 to 32 percent, joining the congressional body that Victor Berger had campaigned to abolish as unsuited to a democracy, too much resembling the House of Lords.[16]

The 2006 election ended with forty-nine Republicans, forty-nine Democrats, and two Independents in the Senate. Sanders and Connecticut former Democrat Joe Lieberman swung control of the Senate to the Democrats by caucusing with them. The new majority leader, Reid, showered Sanders with friendly treatment, granting his request to serve on the Health, Education, Labor, and Pensions Committee under Edward Kennedy. For Sanders it was a novel experience to be a player on legislation that got somewhere, especially after Obama was elected. Sanders grew adept at attaching small provisions to the larger bills of others. He got $11 billion for community health centers into the Affordable Care Act (ACA) of 2010 and took pride that 25 percent of Vermonters received their primary healthcare through community health centers. He blasted TARP as an outrageous gift to the banks and voted against it, subsequently voting against Geithner's appointment as treasury secretary.

On December 10, 2010, one month after the midterm elections swept away Democratic control of the House and Senate, Sanders addressed a lame-duck session of the Senate just before it voted on extending Bush's tax cut for the rich. He carried on for eight and a half hours. Sanders had no prepared text; he had only scraps of various speeches and a determination to see how long he could last. He did not deny that Obama traded the tax cut for important things— extending unemployment benefits, the earned income tax credit, and the middle-class tax cut. But Republicans had previously extended unemployment insurance when the unemployment rate exceeded 7.2 percent, and they supposedly believed in the middle-class tax cut. Would they dare to carry out their threat just to satisfy the donor class?[17]

Sanders implored the Democrats to yield no ground. This was a moment to stand and fight for a nonnegotiable imperative. Why accept a bad deal if it obtained only a month or two of relief before Republicans demanded more? Sanders said the underlying reality was that the Republican Party does not believe in Social Security, Medicare, Medicaid, the Department of Education, and the Environmental Protection Agency. This was not an argument about the Tea Party movement per se; Sanders never mentioned the Tea Party. He said the Republican Party as a collective entity is bent on abolishing the New

Deal and the Great Society. This was what mattered; the Bush tax cut was a proxy-skirmish over it. In this context, Sanders argued, Obama's deal made sense only as Beltway politics. Most Americans are opposed to giving tax breaks to the very rich: "Our job is to rally those people. I would like very much to see the American people saying to our Republican and some Democratic colleagues: 'Excuse me. Don't force my kids to have a lower standard of living in order to give tax breaks to the richest people.' " He said the war within the United States exceeded the wars in Iraq and Afghanistan: "I am talking about a war being waged by some of the wealthiest and most powerful people against working families, against the disappearing and shrinking middle class of our county. The billionaires of America are on the warpath. They want more and more and more."[18]

He got personal, naming the big-bank CEOs, reviewing their bailout figures, and citing what they would get from the pending tax bill. JP Morgan Chase CEO Jamie Dimon stood to receive a personal $1.1 million tax break. Morgan Stanley CEO John Mack came in for a $926,000 tax break after running his bank into the ground. Bank of America CEO Ken Lewis was due for a $713,000 tax break shortly after getting a $45 billion bailout from the Treasury Department. Sanders bitterly contrasted these figures to the $250 cost of living adjustment for seniors and disabled veterans that failed to get through the Senate. He said the TARP bailout was a model of transparency compared to the bailouts that Bernanke and Geithner orchestrated in secret. Sanders told the story of asking Bernanke in 2009 to publish the names of the banks receiving backdoor bailouts. Bernanke refused, and Sanders introduced legislation to make the information public. The bill passed and the information was published the week before Sanders commanded the Senate floor. He recited rows of bailout gore: Goldman Sachs, $780 billion; Morgan Stanley, $2 trillion; Citigroup, $2.4 trillion; Bear Stearns, $1 trillion. He added incredulously that the Fed bailed out Toyota, Mitsubishi, and the state-owned Bank of South Korea while the American auto industry teetered on collapse.[19]

The bailed-out banks could have been compelled to lend to small and medium-sized businesses, but that didn't happen because the government bows to the megabanks. The United States could invest in its people instead of accepting that one-fourth of Americans are poor, fifty million have no health insurance, and the United States imprisons more people than any nation on earth. Sanders said 25 percent of the nation's bridges were either structurally deficient or functionally obsolete; in Vermont 50 percent were deficient and 35 percent were obsolete. China, spending 9 percent of GDP on infrastructure, was about to open forty-two new high-speed rail lines facilitating trains zooming two hundred miles per hour; Europe, spending 5 percent, abounds with high-speed rail travel; the United States, spending 2.4 percent, pales pathetically by comparison. Sanders said the United States needs massive investments to convert to a green economy, but the oil and gas industries routinely get their way, not even paying taxes, while the chasm between the 1 percent and the bottom 90 percent grows every year. Sanders recounted the basic storyline several times. In the 1970s the 1 percent earned 8 percent of all income. In the 1980s it rose to 12 percent. By the end of the 1990s it topped out at 18 percent. In 2007 the 1 percent was up to 23.5 percent, having doubled its income between 1995 and 2007 while nearly halving its income tax rates: "How much more do they want? When is enough enough? Do they want it all?"[20]

Greed, he reflected, is a sickness much like addiction. The 1 percent is addicted to greed, much like heroin and nicotine addicts are addicted to heroin and cigarettes. Sanders said he kept hoping the 1 percent would have an epiphany of "enough," but alas—its addiction crowds out any recognition that sharing is virtuous and rewarding: "I think this is an issue we have to stay on and stay on and stay on. This greed, this reckless, uncontrollable greed is almost like a disease which is hurting this country terribly. How can anybody be proud to say they are a multimillionaire and are getting a huge tax break when one-quarter of the kids in this country are on food stamps? How can anyone be proud of that? I don't know."[21]

Sanders had the virtue of relentlessly staying on. The speech crashed the Senate website, won a huge audience on C-SPAN 2, and flooded Sanders's office with phone calls. Obama tried to divert attention from the filibuster by holding an impromptu press conference with Bill Clinton. Left-wing activists rued the obvious symbolism of the Obama–Clinton diversion. Sanders stayed on message through the gridlock of Obama's early second term, when almost nothing was achievable between a Democratic president and a Republican House of Representatives. Sanders liked and admired Obama but blasted Obama's proposed Trans-Pacific Partnership (TPP) as the latest corporate neoliberal assault on American workers, "a disaster for American workers." He defended the ACA from weekly Republican attacks in Congress but insisted that a single-payer system enrolling everyone in Medicare would be better than the Obama solution of forcing the health insurance companies to take more customers. In October 2013 Sanders began to test the waters outside Vermont; through 2014 he mulled a presidential run, encouraged by speech crowds that implored him to run.[22]

He agreed with his crowds that watching Hillary Clinton sail to the Democratic nomination was unacceptable. The centrist Democrats had gotten their way too long on neoliberalism, welfare reform, and mass incarceration, and they capitulated on marriage equality when it mattered, as Bill Clinton signed the Defense of Marriage Act in 1996, Obama coyly declined to "grow" on marriage equality until 2012, and Hillary Clinton didn't support it until 2013. Sanders ruminated on his political and policy differences with Hillary Clinton, stressing that they flat-out disagreed about the kind of party that Democrats should be. Bill and Hillary Clinton earned their name of Clinton Incorporated, epitomizing the Wall Street Democrat. Somebody from the progressive wing had to make Clinton defend her politics and policies.

Had Senator Elizabeth Warren of Massachusetts been ready to run in 2014 or early 2015 Sanders would not have run. Warren was an ally, a friend, an actual Democrat, and more popular with progressives in 2014 than Sanders. A fledgling national campaign for Warren started up in 2014, which she disappointed by declining to run. Sanders was willing to file as a Democrat to run in Democratic primaries, but he realized that he wasn't sure if working-class Democrats would rally to his emphasis on the struggles of the working class. They did in Vermont, but Vermonters do not cater to right-wing culture wars or care that Sanders is not a Democrat. Sanders tested whether he could break through in other parts of the country. He started in October 2013 with a speaking tour in Mississippi, Alabama, Georgia, and South Carolina, attracting respectable crowds for being a U.S. senator from the North. He asked plaintive questions about working-class whites voting against their economic interests and got a chorus of race, race, race in reply. Meeting progressive organizers, it humbled him to realize how hard it is to be a progressive in the Deep South. In 2014 he held encouraging events in New Hampshire, North Carolina, and South Carolina and made obligatory trips to Iowa. It was pointless to think about running without making friends in Iowa. In South Carolina many poor blacks and whites got nothing from Obamacare because their state rejected the Medicaid expansion provided by the ACA. Sanders dwelt on the outrage of their situation. Some would die from lack of health insurance despite being eligible for Medicaid paid for by the federal government.

In October 2014 Sanders spoke at a Democratic barbecue in Iowa City and realized that retiring senator Tom Harkin's successor in the midterm election, Bruce Braley, was in trouble. Braley gave a tepid speech and the crowd turned him off. The following month Braley lost Harkin's longtime seat to a right-wing Republican, Joni Ernst, swept away by a Republican tide that retook the U.S. Senate for the first time since 2006. Republicans in 2014 won their largest congressional majority since 1928. This pathetic Democratic performance was clarifying and motivating to Sanders. It smacked more of Democratic failure than of Republican success. Republicans won by running ugly television ads and keeping turnout low; Democrats won by turning out big vote tallies. Sixty-three percent of the electorate didn't bother to vote in 2014, and the figures were worse for low-income and young people.

Sanders figured that progressives had a historic opportunity to excite working-class and middle-class voters, and he rightly surmised that Iowa progressives would be fuming in 2016. Surely he could light a fire in the opening caucus state, if he built a decent campaign team. He began to assemble a team. Progressive Democrats of America, an outgrowth of the Dennis Kucinich presidential campaign of 2004, was already urging Sanders to run. DSA came aboard in December 2014, vowing to work hard for Sanders. The only national political consultant whom Sanders knew, Tad Devine, told him in April 2015 that he would need a fundraising operation, professional and volunteer staffs, a national and state media operation, a paid media program, and to deal with scheduling requirements and security issues. Beltway friends told Sanders it was pointless to contend against Hillary Clinton. She had the Clinton machine and the entire Democratic establishment behind her, including four hundred superdelegate convention votes already committed nine months before the first caucus in Iowa.[23]

In May he launched his campaign at the Lake Champlain waterfront park. Sanders delivered the campaign version of his stump speech, headed by "enough is enough." He vowed that he would not attack Clinton personally or play along with the media premise that politics is a game show or soap opera. He started with income and wealth inequality—why should they be impressed by America's wealth when nearly all of it goes to the rich? He ran through forty years of flat wages in the middle class and the catastrophic Supreme Court decision on *Citizens United*, allowing billionaires to buy candidates and elections. He lingered over the climate change eco-crisis and capped it with a pitch for green jobs and infrastructure jobs. He opposed neoliberal trade deals and called for a fifteen-dollar minimum wage, breaking up the megabanks, overturning *Citizens United*, moving away from fossil fuel energy, adopting Medicare for All, protecting Medicare and Social Security, making public college free, and espousing liberal internationalism. For a moment he got uncharacteristically personal, noting that he came from Brooklyn and his mother never got to live in her own house. Sanders remembered what it felt like to lack any discretionary money. For months afterward people asked him if he believed he could win the presidency. He was dead serious in saying yes, though he realized it was a long shot.[24]

For the next fourteen months Sanders ran the greatest political campaign ever waged by an American democratic socialist. He brought the s-word back into play in American politics, contending that democratic socialism is the fitting name for his belief that a living wage, universal healthcare, a complete

education, affordable housing, a clean environment, and a secure retirement
are economic rights. The polling data were extremely forbidding when he
began. In June 2015 Clinton polled among registered Democrats at 61 percent
nationally, followed by Sanders at 15 percent and former Maryland governor
Martin O'Malley at 1 percent. In Iowa Clinton led Sanders by 52 percent to 33
percent. Sanders called for Democratic debates and the Democratic National
Committee put him off. He spoke gamely to small crowds in Iowa, New
Hampshire, Nevada, and South Carolina, willing himself forward until ten
thousand progressives greeted him boisterously on July 1 in Madison, Wisconsin.
That was a breakthrough, although the three major television networks ignored
him until December.

Sanders rued that he lacked a single Democratic governor on his side or a
single big-city mayor. In the entire Congress he had only six supporters—
Senator Jeff Merkley (Oregon) and Representatives Keith Ellison (Minnesota),
Tulsi Gabbard (Hawaii), Raul Grijalva (Arizona), Marcy Kaptur (Ohio), and
Peter Welch (Vermont). Running against the entire Democratic establishment
hurt Sanders with African Americans and seniors. He had never learned how to
speak to black voters, which showed as soon as he belatedly tried, lacking anywhere near the credibility of Hillary Clinton. Moreover, Sanders couldn't get a
hearing from elderly voters. His puzzled team found there were three reasons:
Senior voters liked Bill and Hillary Clinton, the socialist word scared them off,
and they couldn't imagine how someone their age—Sanders turned seventy-
four in 2015—could be healthy enough to be president. Older people were out
of play for the Sanders campaign.

There were many trips to Iowa, yielding 101 rallies and town meetings, plus
campaigning in New Hampshire, Nevada, and South Carolina. The differences
between the Sanders and Clinton crowds grew pronounced. Sanders drew large,
impassioned, mostly youthful crowds while Clinton drew small, tepid, mostly
older crowds. He blasted TPP as a sellout of U.S. American workers and managed not to crow in October 2015 when Clinton reversed her position on it. He
had celebrity backers who put themselves out for him, notably West, Harry
Belafonte, Rosario Dawson, Danny DeVito, Danny Glover, Spike Lee, Mark
Ruffalo, Susan Sarandon, Sarah Silverman, and Shailene Woodley.

To ward off scare-usage of the s-word, in November 2015 Sanders gave a
speech on democratic socialism at Georgetown University. He led with FDR,
commending him for championing a bundle of New Deal policies, every one
of which was condemned as socialist. He lauded FDR's State of the Union
Address of 1944 affirming the concept of economic rights. He said he lined up
with FDR and Martin Luther King Jr. in believing that real freedom includes

economic security. Sanders drove to a credo, reeling off thirty-two paragraphs about what democratic socialism meant to him. There were eight sentences beginning with the phrase "Democratic socialism means," plus other variations on this theme: "Democratic socialism means that we must create an economy that works for all, not just the very wealthy. Democratic socialism means that we must reform a political system in America today which is not only grossly unfair, but, in many respects, corrupt."[25]

He cited King on bad socialism versus good socialism, embracing King's objection that America has socialism for the rich and rugged individualism for everyone else. Sanders said good socialism is based on the idea of economic rights for all people, exactly as King believed. Democratic socialism is about the economy working for everyone, creating a vibrant economic and political democracy, and every person having a right to healthcare, as in Denmark, Sweden, Finland, Canada, France, Germany, and Taiwan. He turned it over, detailing what he didn't believe. Sanders didn't believe the government should own the means of production, "but I do believe that the middle class and the working families who produce the wealth of America deserve a fair deal." He didn't believe in special treatment for the 1 percent, "but I do believe in equal treatment for African-Americans who are right to proclaim the moral principle that Black Lives Matter." He despised all appeals to nativism and prejudice, "and I do believe in immigration reform that gives Hispanics and others a pathway to citizenship and a better life." He didn't believe in any foreign -ism, "but I believe deeply in American idealism." He wasn't running for president because he felt it was his turn "but because it's the turn of all of us to live in a nation of hope and opportunity not for some, not for the few, but for all."[26]

By November 2015 he was riding high, welcoming a surge of idealism and youthful volunteers. The polls were encouraging, indicating that Sanders could beat Donald Trump or Republican contender Marco Rubio and in many states by larger margins than Clinton. This development was crucial to the Sanders campaign because it took away the argument that Clinton was the only Democrat who could win the White House. Sanders accentuated his theme that he was not running to fulfill a personal or family legacy; he was running to bring the Democratic Party back to the many it had abandoned.

The chaotic Iowa caucus ended strangely with a 50–50 vote split between Clinton and Sanders and coin tosses to select delegates. The media rightly played the outcome as a remarkable victory for Sanders, though his team fixed privately on two sets of figures. Sanders won 84 percent of voters aged twenty-nine or younger and 26 percent of voters aged sixty-five or older. That boded ominously for elderly-dominated southern Democratic primaries. He enjoyed a week of glory in New Hampshire, where he defeated Clinton by 60 percent to 38 percent. The Sanders campaign was geared to town halls and rallies. It reaped a windfall of publicity and campaign volunteers for its performance in the first two states, which ended the town hall phase of the primary process. Now the campaign ran out of runway. Sanders had to hope that his rush of volunteers might turn out the vote in states where he lacked much of a campaign structure. He lost a reasonably close race in Nevada — 52 to 47 percent — and was blown away in South Carolina. Clinton won 73 percent of the vote in South Carolina and 90 percent of African American votes.[27]

Then came a crush of primaries and caucuses that gyrated wildly up and down. Even the vastly superior Clinton operation held on for dear life, not knowing what would happen from state to state, with one crucial exception: Super Tuesday, March 1, featured six southern states that Clinton was sure to win big. She crushed Sanders in Alabama, Arkansas, Georgia, Tennessee, Texas, and Virginia, running up an earned delegate lead she never relinquished afterward, despite many losses afterward. The Sanders campaign performed gamely on Super Tuesday, winning strong victories in Colorado, Minnesota, Oklahoma, and Vermont and barely losing in Massachusetts. The delegate tally for Super Tuesday was 518 for Clinton and 347 for Sanders. Sanders staffers strained not to say to the media that Clinton ran up her lead in states that Democrats had no chance of winning in November.

Four days later Sanders won landslide victories in Kansas, Maine, and Nebraska, while getting crushed in Louisiana. On March 8 the Sanders campaign won a dramatic come-from-behind victory in Michigan. Morale soared at winning a big industrial state with a diverse population, but a week later Sanders lost in Florida, Illinois, Missouri, North Carolina, and Ohio. On March 22 he lost the Arizona primary despite working hard there and won Idaho and Utah in landslide fashion; four days later he won landslide victories in Alaska (82 percent), Hawaii (71 percent), and Washington (73 percent). There were calls for Sanders to bow out of the race — from a Clinton campaign that was losing primary contests by staggering margins. The Sanders victory train rolled on, winning the Wisconsin primary (57 percent) and the Wyoming caucus (56 percent). The win in Wyoming marked seven straight primary and caucus victories. Old-style, vote-suppressing New York voted on April 19. The Democratic primary was closed to registered Independents, and Sanders shook his head at New York's throwback tangle of process obstacles. His team made a valiant effort capped by an extraordinary overflow gathering in Greenwich Village's Washington Park but lost by 58 percent to 42 percent despite beating Clinton upstate.[28]

Afterward Sanders won in Rhode Island, Indiana, West Virginia, and Oregon, leaving him with 46 percent of the pledged delegates with one primary day remaining, June 7. Many times every day he was compelled to explain why he stayed in the race. Even if he swept California, New Jersey, New Mexico, South Dakota, North Dakota, and Montana on June 7 he would fall short of the nomination figure, so why bother? Sanders reasoned that if he won big in California, the superdelegates would have to think twice about supporting Clinton. On June 6 the Associated Press reported that the superdelegates were sticking with Clinton. No need to vote—Clinton had the nomination sewn up! Clinton did, in fact, have the nomination sewn up, but Sanders resented that the Associated Press drove down turnout in a race he lost by 7 percent. He fought for strong platform planks at the Democratic Convention, where the party came out for breaking up the megabanks, reinstating the Glass-Steagall wall, abolishing the death penalty, establishing a carbon tax and a fifteen-dollar minimum wage, providing free public education, expanding Social Security, closing corporate tax loopholes, rebuilding infrastructure, and overturning *Citizens United.*

This historic run pulled the Democratic Party to the left and brought newcomers into DSA, which grew from sixty-five hundred members in fall 2014 to eight-five hundred in early November 2016. Strong majorities of voters under the age of thirty-five across the nation told pollsters they favored socialism over capitalism. Every such poll yielded Google searches on "democratic socialism" in which DSA came up first. The national office of DSA dutifully explained to reporters that social democrats try to reform capitalism, democratic socialists advocate worker and public ownership, and Sanders was a social democrat. Sanders got through the entire campaign without once being asked by a reporter if he supported worker ownership or decentralized forms of public ownership. Journalists took his Denmark-model as proof positive that he equated democratic socialism with advanced welfare-state politics. That was fine with him. He had learned as mayor of Burlington that people were going to call him a socialist whether he used the word or not, and the word conveyed certain things dear to him that no other term quite conveyed. So he wore it proudly while other progressive politicians of his generation shunned it. Then came a generation that remembered not the Cold War. The young socialists who poured into the Sanders campaign confirmed to him that he made the right choice.

DSA called for Trump's defeat after Sanders failed to win the nomination, without endorsing Clinton. Resentment of the Clinton campaign and the Democratic National Committee ran high among many former Sanders workers, though Sanders did his best to rally support for Clinton in the general election. The Sanders backers mostly did support Clinton, and some worked for her, although 12 percent of the Sanders primary supporters voted for Trump. This figure, though significant, pales in comparison to the 25 percent of former Hillary Clinton supporters who voted in 2008 for Republican candidate John McCain. On the day after Trump was elected, one thousand new members joined DSA. This one-day yield exceeded entire-year totals of most of the years that DSA had existed. Over the next eight months more than thirteen thousand new members joined and over one hundred new DSA local chapters were founded. By July 2017 DSA had twenty-four thousand members. That year fifteen DSA member candidates won elections in local and state contests across thirteen states, which encouraged dozens of additional DSA members to run in the midterm elections of 2018. Many had worked in their first political campaign for Sanders. One won a spectacular victory that instantly made her the new star of the political left.[29]

THE NEXT LEFT: DSA, AOC, AND
THE SANDERS REVOLUTION

DSA caught a windfall from the Sanders campaign, another from Trump's election in 2016, and another from the midterm elections of 2018. The second and third windfalls yielded dramatic membership gains, but the Sanders campaign was the turning point. DSA issued a new mission statement in June 2016, "Resistance Rising," exulting that 2016 was "a game-changing year for leftists and progressives. We are finally reemerging as a vital and powerful force after an extended period of stagnation and demoralization, and we face a political landscape more favorable than perhaps at any time since the 1960s."[30]

The story that DSA told began with the stagflation crisis of the 1970s, when economic elites seized the moment for themselves, mobilizing politically to lower taxes for the rich and the corporations, curtail democratic rights in workplaces and politics, slash spending on education and social services, deregulate entire industries, and open flows of capital across national borders. DSA folded the race-coded attacks on welfare recipients into the neoliberal story, a game that Reagan and Clinton neoliberals played differently to a similar effect. It acknowledged that working-class Europeans got through the 1990s better than U.S. workers, but by the twenty-first century the entire planet belonged to neoliberal capitalists. As recently as 2010 there was no example anywhere of successful resistance to neoliberalism to which socialists and progressives could point. Neoliberalism prevailed everywhere as the only way.

Occupy Wall Street signaled that people were fed up with downsizing and being humiliated. New movements arose for immigration justice, a raised

minimum wage, racial justice, and equality—the Dreamer movement, Fight
for $15, Black Lives Matter, and the Sanders campaign. Meanwhile in 2014 the
left-wing Syriza Party rose to power in Greece as an outright resistance movement, and the left-wing Podemos Party in Spain emerged from anti-austerity
protests as a major political force. The following year Jeremy Corbyn became
the British Labour Party leader by opposing the party's recent neoliberal record.
DSA said the converging social movements in the United States changed what
was possible: "These movements have opened up space for a serious discussion
of capitalism, male-dominance and racism in our society that has not existed in
decades, and which provides unique opportunities for the growth of a democratic socialist movement that emphasizes the interconnectedness of all of the
struggles and the structural character of the reforms needed to make real and
lasting change."[31]

"Resistance Rising" featured DSA's customary mix of public ownership and
worker ownership, contending that housing, utilities, heavy industry, and other
large, strategically important sectors should be subject to democratic planning
outside the market and market-driven worker-owned firms should produce and
distribute consumer goods. Large-scale investments in new technology and
enterprises should be made on the basis of maximizing the public good, not to
drive up shareholder value, especially to create a green economy. Healthcare,
child care, public education from prekindergarten through college, shelter,
and transportation should be provided to all citizens free of charge, and every
citizen should receive a basic salary regardless of the person's employment status. The U.S. Senate should be abolished, replaced by a body reflecting the
political will of the electorate and based on proportional representation. Citizen
boards for government services and program councils for those who receive
government services should be established. Programs to dismantle the privileges of whiteness, maleness, and heterosexual norms must be established,
strengthening existing antidiscrimination policies. Democratic socialism, DSA
declared, connects antiracist, feminist, LGBTQ, labor, anti-ableist, and anti-
ageist movements to each other: "We consider each of these struggles to be
mutually reinforcing, and believe that the success of one ultimately depends on
the success of the others."[32]

DSA was not quite ready in June 2016 to unfurl its new strategy. Eighteen
months of intense wrangling over it lay ahead, but "Resistance Rising" accurately previewed what it would be, declaring that the organized working class
holds a tremendous potential power not to be written off. Much of DSA's youth
movement embraced the rank-and-file strategy formulated in 2000 by *Labor
Notes* staff writer Kim Moody, who argued that building a militant minority of

rank-and-file unionists is the way to renew the socialist movement. Socialists should seed unions by taking union jobs and build the movement by converting workers to socialism. Sometimes they can work with union leaders but more often the leaders must be bypassed. The rush of new members into DSA included many post-Trotskyites and semi-anarchists who clashed with each other over ideology while agreeing that DSA should disavow its social democratic legacy and reinvent itself as a working-class organization. "Resistance Rising" registered contrary pulls within the organization. DSA had long said that social movement work and public socialist education were its top priorities, whereas electoral activism was important for some and not for others, it could mean different things, and some were outright against it, so it was number three. Putting it that way felt outdated after the Sanders campaign transformed DSA. Many old-timers said the Sanders campaign vindicated the Harrington approach; many newcomers swelled the faction that opposed electoral activism on principle; and many others drew the line at Sanders: he was okay, but progressive Democrats like Warren were not because the Democratic Party is the graveyard of socialism.[33]

DSA converged on the view that electoral activism of some kind is indispensable, but the kind had to change. The organization began to speak about "building capacity" to run its own campaigns. *Democratic Left*, DSA's house organ, reflected the push for a new strategy while dealing with factions opposed to the national office or to most kinds of electoral politics or to any kind of electoral politics. *Jacobin*, a magazine founded in 2010 by DSA member Bhaskar Sunkara, pushed for a new labor party. The magazine was closely aligned with DSA's strongest caucus, a Marxian cadre organization eventually named Bread and Roses. In November 2016 Seth Ackerman wrote in *Jacobin* that the old labor parties took the wrong approach to the right idea. Building a labor party was the right idea but taking a separate ballot line was suicidal in America's two-party tyranny. The better approach is to bore from within in guerrilla insurgency fashion — building a movement organization that builds local and state chapters, binds leaders to a defined program, and treats the ballot issue on a case-by-case basis. This argument got traction in a crowded field, defining what the new DSA majority vowed to become in the medium-range future — a self-standing political force focused primarily on labor organizing. In January 2018 DSA declared, "In accordance with our long-term objective of building a mass socialist political formation in the United States, it is essential that National DSA prioritize cultivating and supporting socialist candidates who will be accountable to DSA's political agenda and who can serve as the base for increasingly assertive and widespread independent socialist electoral activity in the coming years. This work will be critical to the development of a genuine alternative to the neoliberal third-way politics of the corporate establishment within the Democratic Party."[34]

DSA vowed to up its game in environmental activism, especially the climate justice movement, giving high priority to campaigning for institutional divestment from fossil fuel capital. Serious environmentalism, it said, must be socialist: "Organizing as open socialists gives DSA members the opportunity to organize around widely supported 'green' causes under the banner of the anticapitalist 'red' movement." Positively, there is no environmental alternative to the global struggle for labor, environmental, and human rights; negatively, there is no alternative to the global ecosocialist struggle against capitalism.[35]

DSA envisioned that the transition to a new society would take place through nonreformist reforms such as nationalizing the auto industry and big banks and creating worker-controlled investment funds by taxing corporate profits. Sunkara noted elsewhere that the transition from social democracy to democratic socialism is perilous because Social Democrats in power nearly always move to the right, which buys stability from powerful interests. Moving leftward invites capital strikes and ultra-leftism. Sunkara said the transition must move quickly or be lost, and it cannot move at all without majority power in the legislatures and unions. DSA, trying in 2016 to close with visionary confidence, acknowledged that the transition issue is very speculative: "But we should never lose sight of the democratic socialist vision that serves as the guiding thread tying together the many struggles for freedom and equality in which we are constantly engaged, day in, day out."[36]

The three priorities did not change, but DSA changed how it approached them. The former electoral model conferred endorsements on progressive candidates and loaned out volunteers to them. The goal was to elect as many progressives as possible, and the connecting link between DSA and the candidate was always weak at best. Candidate accountability was pretty much nonexistent, and DSA settled for mere access, which usually diminished over time. In 2018 DSA adopted a new model focused on building up the organization as a sustainable, full-orbed political organization: "Instead of loaning out our volunteer capacity to political candidates, we have begun to build electoral capacity within DSA—capacity responsible directly to the organization and democratically controlled by its members." The organization vowed to create chapters that build their own field and canvassing operations, maintain their own data, formulate their own messaging, develop their own research capacity, and run their own campaigns, acquiring the full range of electoral skills and capacities.[37]

This ambition to become a working-class power independent of the Democratic Party is daunting for a sixty-thousand-member organization, though

not impossibly far-fetched. The Democratic and Republican Parties are drastically hollowed out, barely deserving to be called political parties. Trump conquered the Republican Party by himself despite lacking any background in
politics. The power of the political parties resides in the ability of their consultants, lawyers, and functionaries to control the means of electioneering in every
state. DSA vows to break away from the patronage networks that control
Democratic politics, aiming to become more like the Vermont Progressive
Party, Richmond Progressive Alliance (California), New Haven Rising
(Connecticut), and Malcolm X Grassroots Movement (Jackson, Mississippi)
than like Democracy in America, Progressive Democrats of America, and Move
On. The former organizations are community-based and predominantly working class, building grassroots power; the latter are predominantly middle-class
organizations founded to keep voters engaged as activists but which spend most
of their time raising funds. In 2017 Sanders launched an organization to sustain
contact with his supporters, Our Revolution. That year nearly 40 percent of
DSA's national convention delegates voted not to work with Our Revolution;
the majority had to plead that Sanders was not like Move On.

One spectacular congressional victory of 2018, another congressional victory
that year of comparable dimensions, and thirty-eight other electoral victories at
state and local levels changed the image of DSA as a political player. On June
26, 2018, DSA member Alexandria Ocasio-Cortez unseated ten-term incumbent
Democrat Joseph Crowley in New York's Fourteenth Congressional District
representing the East Bronx, part of north-central Queens, and Rikers Island.
Her stunning victory made her an instant political star ubiquitously called AOC.
Six weeks after AOC defeated Crowley for the Democratic nomination, DSA
member Rashida Harbi Tlaib won a crowded Democratic primary in Michigan's
Thirteenth Congressional District covering the western half of Detroit and sev-
eral western suburbs. Both went on to win in November.[38]

The victory by Ocasio-Cortez set off another spike in DSA's rapid growth.
More than a thousand new members joined DSA the day after she beat Crowley.
By the end of June DSA had forty-two thousand members; three months later it
was fifty thousand. Ocasio-Cortez ran on Medicare for All, abolishing U.S.
Immigration and Customs Enforcement (ICE), and representing hard-pressed
people of color who usually see no point in voting. She was born in 1989 in the
Parkchester section of the Bronx. Her father came from the South Bronx and
ran a small architecture company; her mother grew up near Arecibo, Puerto
Rico, and cleaned houses; the family moved to Yorktown Heights in Westchester
County so Ocasio-Cortez and her younger brother Gabriel could attend better
schools. They often returned to their former Bronx neighborhood to see rela-

tives; AOC said these forty-minute drives drilled into her how much it matters to live in a neighborhood with quality schooling. Her cousins were already bearing children when she enrolled at Boston University. She majored in economics and international relations, handling immigration casework as a Senate intern for Edward Kennedy, and lost her father in 2008 to lung cancer, which plunged the family into a financial crisis. Ocasio-Cortez graduated in 2011, worked for an educational nonprofit in the Bronx, took a side gig as a bartender, and worked extra shifts to keep her family afloat.[39]

She canvassed for Sanders in 2016, surprising herself at making the transition from community organizing to electoral organizing. After Trump won the election AOC piled into a borrowed car with friends to visit two sites connected by environmental degradation. They drove to Flint, Michigan, to meet people poisoned by lead leached from water pipes into the drinking water, continued to the Standing Rock Indian Reservation in North Dakota, and joined the Lakota Sioux's resistance to the Dakota Access Pipeline. Ocasio-Cortez said the trip changed her into someone willing to take risks. Meanwhile a group of former Sanders staffers led by Saikat Chakrabarti and Corbin Trent founded a group called Brand New Congress to recruit working-class leaders to run for office, soliciting nominations. Gabriel Ocasio-Cortez nominated his sister, and AOC got an out-of-the-blue call from Brand New Congress. On the campaign trail she conveyed her closeness to the struggles of hurting people. Her early campaign consisted mostly of actors living in Astoria, volunteers from Justice Democrats (an offshoot of Brand New Congress), and DSA organizers. AOC joined DSA halfway through her campaign and welcomed an onrush of DSA workers who flooded her district and turned the election.

Tlaib was equally novel in the U.S. Congress, if less sensational to the media, and a generation older. Born in 1976 to working-class Palestinian immigrants in Detroit, her mother was born near Ramallah and her father was born in East Jerusalem. Her father immigrated to Nicaragua, moved to Detroit, worked on an assembly line at Ford Motor Company, and fathered fourteen children; Tlaib is the eldest. Tlaib earned her college degree at Wayne State University in 1998 and graduated from Western Michigan University Cooley Law School in 2004. In her early career she worked for State Representative Steve Tobacman, running for his seat in 2008 when his term limit expired. Tobacman's Detroit district was 40 percent Latinx, 25 percent African American, 30 percent non-Hispanic white, and 2 percent Arab American. Tlaib bested seven Democratic contestants and won the general election to enter the Michigan House of Representatives. She was reelected twice to the Michigan House, hit her term limit in 2014, and failed that year to unseat a Republican incumbent for the

Michigan Senate. In 2018 she aimed for the congressional seat long held by Democrat John Conyers, who resigned in 2017. There was a special election to complete Conyers's twenty-seventh term and a general election the same day for the next two-year term. Tlaib lost the special election but won the Democratic primary for the general election, facing no Republican opposition in November. She became the first Palestinian American woman to be seated in Congress and one of the first two Muslim women in Congress, entering simultaneously with Ilhan Omar (D-MN).[40]

DSA had not had an outright dues-paying member in Congress since Major Owens represented Brooklyn in Congress from 1983 to 2007 and Ron Dellums retired in 1998, though Conyers and various others were virtual members in all but dues paying. Tlaib was steeped in the UAW-socialist ethos of Detroit DSA and well known in Michigan politics before she entered Congress. Her background in left-progressive organizing showed in her commanding rally speeches; at a January 2019 rally outside a ritzy auto show gala, Tlaib warned General Motors executives over a megaphone that she would demand the return of every dime of their taxpayer bailout if they shut down the plant in Poletown. AOC came from political nowhere by comparison. She stumped for candidates in Kansas, Missouri, and Michigan, contending that progressivism is the future of the Democratic Party because her generation is more left wing than older Democrats. She came to DSA meetings when she could, asking her senior legislative advisor, Randy Abreu, to host conference calls with DSA National Director Maria Svart and other DSA organizers. AOC leveraged her celebrity in February 2019 by teaming with Senator Ed Markey (D-MA) to propose the Green New Deal.[41]

The Green New Deal calls for a mobilization to reduce greenhouse gas emissions by 40–60 percent by 2030 and achieve net-zero greenhouse gas emissions by 2050, proposing that the greenhouse gases released to the atmosphere must not exceed the gases that are sequestered or removed. It is built on an infrastructure investment plan and a jobs guarantee, calling for investments to create millions of high-wage jobs in a green economy. The proposal envisions new energy-efficient power grids to outfit buildings for maximum sustainability, the eradication of fossil fuels and industrial meat, and the transformation of other industries. It stipulates that all U.S. Americans have a right to healthy food and a sustainable environment and that historically marginalized, oppressed, and neglected communities must be included in all plans for a just transition to a green economy. It contends that the United States must organize a just transition that develops new transit networks and changes the process of industrial production, all while learning to cope with the floods, heat waves, famines, and hurricanes wrought by climate change. It builds on the verdict of the October 2018 Intergovernmental Panel on Climate Change that to limit warming to 1.5 degrees Celsius above preindustrial levels and thus avoid many severe climate change impacts, the world must reach net-zero emissions of carbon dioxide by the year 2050.[42]

The House version proposed by AOC was referred to the House Subcommittee on Energy and Mineral Resources and would require separate legislation to make any of its proposals binding. It takes no explicit position on nuclear power and carbon capture, though Ocasio-Cortez opposes any new nuclear plants. The Green New Deal calls for massive investments in high-speed rail and zero-emission vehicles and favors family farming. Ocasio-Cortez and Markey deserve immense credit for making the first governmental proposal that approaches the scale of the problem, taking seriously that environmentalism must move beyond its focus on regulating destructive companies. They willingly endured the ridicule that came with doing so from Trump, House Speaker Nancy Pelosi, and many others. The Green New Deal ambitiously imagines a working-class environmental politics, lifting climate politics out of the elite confines of professional-class activism and think tanks.

Yet AOC and Markey drew it up in think tank fashion, earning a swift rebuke from the Energy Committee of the AFL-CIO, which charged that the Green New Deal would cause "immediate harm to millions of our members and their families." AOC and Markey neglected the socialist principle that the labor movement must be involved in every phase of the discussion. Unions came early to environmental activism, fighting for healthy workplace and community environments. Any plan for a just transition to a green economy must make labor rights, labor protections, and labor expertise central to the discussion. Sara Nelson, president of the Association of Flight Attendants and a leading contender to succeed Richard Trumka as president of the AFL-CIO, put it bluntly: "A few hours training is not a just transition. The transition needs to begin *before* the jobs go away." A just transition, Nelson observes, must ensure that pensions and healthcare are protected for workers in phased-out fossil fuel industries. It must draw on union expertise to prevent unintended consequences, such as losing the capacity to make the steel needed to create alternative forms of energy. A just transition must invest in technological innovation and negotiate fair-trade agreements ensuring that American workers get to manufacture wind turbines and solar panels.[43]

Nelson stressed that the labor movement has never seen a just transition. The experience of union workers is that "just transition" refers to a spate of training followed by corporate flight and community devastation. The Green New Deal cannot get anywhere without the unions, but most unionists distrust environmental activists. To build trust, Nelson argues, environmentalists must shore up the wasteland already produced by the last transition that had nothing to do with justice. It starts by working *with* battered unions instead of projecting a get-over-it attitude. The BlueGreen Alliance, a coalition of labor unions and environmental organizations operating in nine states, is a beginning. Led by the United Steelworkers and the Sierra Club, it focuses on research and advocacy for clean jobs, clean infrastructure, and fair trade. DSA aspires to play a similar synergizing role.

Two election campaigns portended contrasting possible futures for DSA. In May 2018 two DSA-endorsed candidates for the Pennsylvania state legislature, Summer Lee and Sara Innamorato, made national headlines by defeating incumbent Pittsburgh legislators in the Democratic primary. Both incumbents came from prominent Democratic families, and DSA got glowing coverage in the *New Yorker* for its "democratic socialist landslide." The following month Pittsburgh DSA elected new leaders that spurned electoral work. The chapter turned inward and fractious, driving away Lee, Innamorato, and many DSA campaign workers. Meanwhile in April 2019 six DSA members won seats on Chicago's City Council—one-eighth of the entire council. Here there were no recriminations about electoral politics since all the winners ran as democratic socialists and Democratic Party activism is deeply rooted in Chicago DSA. In Chicago there were only earnest meetings about how to keep the six new city council members accountable to democratic socialist values and politics.[44]

The new DSA envisions a new workers' party that unites grassroots working-class organizations and redefines what DSA is about. In 2017 DSA left the Socialist International, repudiating Social Democratic reformism, and birthed a flock of new ideological caucuses, contesting the redefinition issue. The Left Caucus, a Marxian cadre organization rooted in the post-Trotskyist group Solidarity, was the leading player. Solidarity struggled since the early 1970s to build a socialist movement in the unions, with marginal success; Moody's formulation of the rank-and-file strategy was written for it. Left Caucus morphed into Momentum, won the largest bloc of votes on the DSA National Political Committee, endured a bitter split over its class-first priorities, and rebooted in 2019 as Bread and Roses. Its hallmarks are echoes of the mid-twentieth-century Shachtmanites, advocating a centralized organization, a third-party insurgency, tithing dues, and rank-and-file radicalism. Another leading caucus arose to oppose everything that distinguished Bread and Roses within DSA. It began as Praxis, morphed to Build, and espouses anarchist "horizontalism," opposing all structures of leadership accountability and all forms of central organization, including the national office of DSA. Two caucuses arose to advocate red and semi-anarchist ideologies more inclusively. Socialist Majority resembles the political line of Bread and Roses without its reputation for harsh aggression, and Libertarian Socialists resembles Build without denigrating electoral work. Another new caucus, North Star, emerged to defend the social democratic heritage of DSA, reluctantly giving up the DSA tradition of no caucuses, since DSA now had many.

DSA had already agreed to formally endorse Sanders and to push hard for Medicare for All and the Green New Deal when it convened in August 2019 in Atlanta. At the convention it voted not to endorse any other candidate if Sanders failed to win the Democratic nomination for president. The convention affirmed that DSA needed to have a strong national organization and to make a sooner-or-later "dirty break" from the Democratic Party. It called for the uninhibited transnational free movement of people (open borders), and advocated the full decriminalization of sex work. The closest vote was a ten-vote victory for the rank-and-file labor strategy, reflecting that nearly half the delegates were opposed to slighting union leaders and social democratic progressives. Other proposals smacking of sectarian rigidity were defeated, notably a proposal forcing DSA chapters to endorse only avowed socialist candidates in local and state elections, though DSA reaffirmed that it would endorse only outright socialists at the national level. Many delegates were relieved that the organization did not break apart at the convention, but survival is a low bar.

Veteran DSA journalist Harold Meyerson was tellingly double-minded about DSA's 2020 presidential election strategy. He regretted that the organization would endorse only Sanders against Trump; on the other hand, no DSA endorsement at the national level carried any weight anyway except to hurt whoever the candidate turned out to be. DSA, while trying to reinvent itself as an organization that builds strong independent chapters generating grassroots power, simultaneously debated whether this strategy vests too much importance in electoral politics and whether the rank-and-file strategy unnecessarily antagonizes labor leaders and progressives.[45]

Meanwhile Sanders represents democratic socialism to millions who know nothing else about it and to many who identify with it because of him. In June 2019 he gave another speech on democratic socialism that recycled the best parts of his 2015 speech—FDR in 1944, King on socialism, and the long American history of attacking Social Security and Medicare as anti-American socialism. Sanders got very near the end before he found a way to say it differently. What does it actually mean, he asked, to be free? Are you free if you cannot afford to see a doctor or stay in a hospital? Are you free if you cannot afford the prescription drug you need to stay alive? Are you free if you spend half your limited income on housing, or have to borrow money from a payday lender, or have to keep working at the age of seventy, or cannot afford to attend college? Sanders said every American should have a right to a job paying a living wage, quality healthcare, a complete education, affordable housing, a clean environment, and a secure retirement.[46]

These six economic rights define what he calls democratic socialism. Sanders still conflated social democracy with democratic socialism, but his 2020 campaign endorsed a version of worker codetermination that traversed the line between them, calling for worker control of up to 45 percent of board seats and 20 percent of shares. Sanders is both radical and not, depending on the issue and the contextual lens. He acquired a reputation for radicalism by advocating policies that European Social Democrats achieved in the 1950s. But Sanders is radical not only in his U.S. American context. He earned his radical reputation by recovering the language of class struggle that European Social Democrats relinquished in the 1950s. Social Democrats stopped railing about the hardships of the poor after they built the welfare states, settling for the claim that they are the best defenders of their historic achievement, the welfare state. They dropped social ownership and the class struggle at the same time and for the same reasons. Sanders is like Corbyn in radiating the anger of the antineoliberal rebellion, reintroducing class struggle rhetoric to electorates that hadn't heard it in decades.

The British election of December 2019 pitted Corbyn's socialism against Tory incumbent Boris Johnson's pledge to "Get Brexit Done." Corbyn called for nationalized railways, a four-day workweek, a state-owned pharmaceutical company, new taxes on the financial industry, and worker–public representation on company boards. He urged British voters to stop corporate runaways by establishing codetermination on company boards. If Germany can place worker and public representatives on corporate boards, why should British workers and the public lack any say in the corporate race to the bottom? Corbyn got his customary treatment from the media—vindictively hostile. His actual proposals got very little play since he was easy to ridicule personally plus vulnerable to red-baiting, plus vulnerable to charges that he tolerated and stoked anti-Semitic prejudice in the party. Corbyn denied that his criticism of Israel crossed the line into anti-Semitism, but many who knew him said he definitely crossed it. He refused to address this devastating accusation with the seriousness it deserved, and he doubled the disaster by refusing to defend the party's opposition to Brexit. Labour was crushed in the election, absorbing its worst defeat in a century, losing districts it had dominated for decades. Yet Corbyn had a distinguished socialist tradition at his back marked by venerable names—Keir Hardie, John Ruskin, William Morris, George Bernard Shaw, Stewart Headlam, Sidney

Webb, Beatrice Webb, G. D. H. Cole, R. H. Tawney, William Temple, Clement Attlee, C. A. R. Crosland, Richard Crossman, and Tony Benn. Sanders had nothing like that behind him when he injected the language of democratic socialism into American politics.[47]

This injection made almost no appeal to America's democratic progressive traditions, except for token references to FDR and King. Sanders could have diminished the exotic impression of his democratic socialism by identifying with the progressive Democrats who established Social Security, Medicare, Head Start, the Civil Rights Act, and the Voting Rights Act. He could have touted the roles that socialists like Thomas, Randolph, Harrington, Rustin, and Farmer played in winning the nation's greatest legislative social justice achievements. Instead he conveyed that his brand of U.S. American social democracy was distinctive to him in American politics, not something he broadly shared with American progressivism. Sanders was too enamored of his independent image to make friends and allies in the party whose nomination he sought. His second campaign for the presidency, like his first, was very short of elected Democrats and regular Democrats. Harrington had supported and befriended liberal Democrats while building social democratic organizations that Sanders did not join. Sanders dramatically vindicated the Harrington strategy of working through the Democratic Party, but he set himself up for anachronistic red-baiting by making democratic socialism sound more novel, exotic, and distinctive to him than it was.

His achievement in his first run for president was already historic when he ran the second time. Sanders tied for first place in the 2020 Iowa caucus, won the New Hampshire primary, and crushed the field in the Nevada caucus. Suddenly he was the frontrunner with a clear path to the nomination. The Democratic establishment and the corporate media shrieked with sky-is-falling alarm, pleading that regular Democrats and Wall Street neoliberal Democrats had to consolidate before Sanders ran away with the nomination. Five candidates clogged the moderate lane—former vice president Joe Biden, Minnesota senator Amy Klobuchar, former South Bend, Indiana, mayor Pete Buttigieg, billionaire former New York City mayor Mike Bloomberg, and billionaire civic activist Tom Steyer. Biden finished fourth in Iowa, fifth in New Hampshire, and second in Nevada. He had always been a mediocre candidate, having run twice previously for the Democratic nomination and won zero primaries. He was personable and sincere, with a common touch, albeit with a long history of verbal howlers, and accused by some women of unwelcome hugs. For months Biden bumbled through debates and town halls, sometimes lapsing into babbling.

But Biden had a firewall in the state preceding Super Tuesday, South Carolina. Older black voters in South Carolina prized Biden's connection to

Obama and never warmed to anyone else in the Democratic field, even in earlier months, when black U.S. Senators Cory Booker and Kamala Harris were candidates. South Carolina black voters resurrected Biden's candidacy, powering a victory in which Biden won every county and beat Sanders by 48.7 percent to 19.8 percent. The waters parted for Biden as soon as he won in South Carolina. Steyer dropped out, Buttigieg and Klobuchar endorsed Biden just before the Super Tuesday primaries of March 3, and Super Tuesday voters streamed into Biden's camp. Biden won 10 states on Super Tuesday—Alabama, Arkansas, Maine, Massachusetts, Minnesota, North Carolina, Oklahoma, Tennessee, Texas, and Virginia. The following day Bloomberg cleared out the moderate lane by endorsing Biden, and the day after that Elizabeth Warren cleared out the progressive lane by ending her candidacy, declining to endorse anyone. Fear of Sanders and fear of a Trump reelection had driven the field to consolidate with breathtaking speed. Sanders won the Super Tuesday primaries in California, Colorado, Vermont, and Utah, but March 3 turned out very differently from what nearly happened.[48]

Perhaps Sanders could have defeated Trump, as he insisted, but a great many Democrats and independents did not believe it, or judged that Biden had a better chance of defeating Trump. In addition to fear of Trump and Sanders, a third fear helped to lift Biden above higher-ability candidates, reducing the field to Biden versus Sanders. A new form of coronavirus named SARS-Cov-2 broke out in Wuhan, China, in December 2019, causing a new disease named coronavirus disease 2019 (Covid-19). The Chinese government initially repressed the story and refused help from the World Health Organization (WHO) before it swung massively to contain the virus. Covid-19 spread beyond China, and on January 31, 2020, the WHO announced that a global public health emergency existed. Trump had dissolved the White House office dealing with global health threats. The U.S. Centers for Disease Control and Prevention (CDC) declined to use the WHO test developed by German scientists, fatefully choosing to develop a U.S. test that was delayed by manufacturing mishaps, and the Food and Drug Administration refused to speed approval for commercial labs to disseminate tests. The badly deficient U.S. healthcare system was rapidly exposed. Trump squandered the entire month of February, still claiming on February 28 that Covid-19 was a hoax. His administration provided disastrously poor guidance to governors and mayors when it was most needed. When the March 10 primaries occurred, only four thousand Americans had been tested for the virus; the following day the WHO officially described Covid-19 as a pandemic.

Now it was too late for the United States to hold off the contagion with comprehensive testing; the United States passed straight to mitigation. Italy was devastated by the disease, which spread to New York City, saturating the city in February. In March and April the disease ravaged New York worse than Italy, overwhelming the hospital system and spreading across the nation. Italy's case fatality rate topped 10 percent when American Democrats lined up to vote for Biden or Sanders. Sanders's emphasis on radical economic change felt out of sync to regular Democrats who hoped merely to survive the contagion and replace Trump. Biden raced ahead of Sanders on March 10 by winning the primaries in Michigan, Missouri, Mississippi, and Idaho. Victory celebrations were shut down as Americans were told to stop congregating in groups of every kind. "Social isolation" became a way of life, and the presidential campaign became a third-tier story with a clear heading—Biden was on course to win the Democratic nomination.

Sanders won the support of younger voters by lopsided margins and lost by similar margins among older voters, who turned out in larger numbers. The Sanders campaign was predicated upon turning out a tidal wave of new young voters, which did not materialize; instead the party mainstream of regular Democrats and neoliberals outvoted the left Democrats and independents who supported Sanders. Biden cruised to the nomination riding a widespread clamor for safety. If Biden could beat Trump in November, it was worth settling for him, despite his shortcomings. His prosaic familiarity worked for him in a primary campaign that suddenly no longer mattered very much as long as he was the frontrunner and the pandemic spread across the nation. Sanders hung on gamely until April 8, pressing Biden to move leftward on policy issues. He criticized Biden for opposing Medicare for All, supporting the fracking industry, and prizing his chummy relationships with Big Pharma and Wall Street, stressing that most Americans in their twenties, thirties, and forties agreed with him, not Biden. Sanders rued that his thriving campaign was throttled practically overnight. But the causes he cared about were more prominent than ever in American politics.

Biden coasted to the Democratic nomination while state governments quarantined Americans in their homes. New York suffered the worst, especially black and brown people in the Bronx, Harlem, Queens, and Brooklyn. Then the same thing happened wherever the disease spread, ripping through densely populated neighborhoods of the urban poor, especially the black and brown poor. Healthcare workers bore the brunt of it directly, heroically risking their lives. "We're all in this together," a public piety, acquired ritual status, belying that some were far more vulnerable than others. The rich fled to their vacation homes, many taking the virus with them to sunbelt and ski resort states. Middle-class professionals were marooned at home with their children. People with mobility, flexible professional jobs, and money in the bank experienced the contagion very differently from people lacking all three.

The burden of maintaining a civilization fell on healthcare workers, truck drivers, grocery and pharmacy workers, police officers, and warehouse and delivery workers. They did essential work and thus had to bear special risks of dying from the virus. Middle-class and wealthy Americans were suddenly compelled to contemplate the lives of people who lacked homes and the means to isolate themselves. Americans as a whole got a taste of what it feels like to be fearful and vulnerable all the time. State governors scrambled to buy ventilators on the open market, bidding against each other. Ten years of government-subsidized attempts to develop a stockpile of ventilators had yielded almost nothing because corporate mergers in the medical manufacturing industry yielded conglomerates demanding big profits. Corporate oligopolies that could have spent the recent boom years investing in their employees and building up their reserves instead bought back their own stock, reaping huge, quick profits; then they wailed for government bailouts. The nation needed the federal government to mobilize a comprehensive program of testing and contact tracing, which did not happen. Trump stuck to the sociopathic narcissism that conquered the Republican Party and put him in the White House, plotting the next round of political divide and conquer.[49]

The next round came swiftly. On May 25—Memorial Day—forty-six-year-old George Floyd was arrested in Minneapolis for allegedly using a counterfeit twenty-dollar bill at a market. An African American man described by friends as a gentle giant, Floyd had lost his job as a bouncer at a Minneapolis bar during the Covid-19 shutdown. He was handcuffed and fell to the ground, three Minneapolis police officers pinned him to the ground, one of them pressed his knee on Floyd's neck, and a fourth officer looked on. White officer Derek Chauvin drove his knee into Floyd's neck for almost nine minutes. For five minutes Floyd cried out repeatedly, "Please," "Mama," "I can't breathe," "Don't kill me." Near the end he pleaded, "I can't breathe, please, the knee in my neck, I can't breathe, Mama." He passed out, but Chauvin kept pressing for almost three minutes more, staring icily at onlookers who beseeched him to stop. Floyd lay motionless on the street, the officers made no attempt to secure medical treatment, and Floyd died of mechanical asphyxia. American cities erupted in enraged, grieving, traumatized protests. Chauvin was charged with second-degree murder, and the other three officers were charged with aiding and abetting a murder. Huge demonstrations against racism and racist policing occurred for two weeks in cities throughout the world. Trump acknowledged that Chauvin's actions were indefensible, but he quickly swung back to divide and conquer, lashing out at governors and mayors who in his view were too squeamish. If they weren't willing to retake the cities with overwhelming military force, they didn't deserve to be governors or mayors. Trump mobilized military police and deployed the 82nd Airborne Division in Washington, DC, touting his willingness to use the military wherever he saw fit.

George Floyd became the latest victim in a searing litany of black Americans cut down in similar fashion. The recent list alone included Ahmaud Arbery, Sandra Bland, Rayshard Brooks, Michael Brown, Dominique Clayton, Eric Garner, Botham Jean, Laquan McDonald, Tamir Rice, and Breonna Taylor. The two most recent helped to ignite the Floyd explosion. Arbery was murdered on February 23 while jogging in Glynn County, Georgia. His white executioners mistook him for a burglary suspect, chased him down in their pickup truck, and killed him, claiming their right under Georgia law to employ deadly force to protect themselves. Taylor, an emergency medical technician, was at home in bed in Louisville, Kentucky, on March 13 when three white police officers barged into her apartment on a no-knock search warrant. Her boyfriend called 911 and got off one shot at the invading officers, who killed Taylor by spraying her with eight bullets; later they filed a police report riddled with false information. Many of the protest speeches for Floyd began with him, moved to Taylor and Arbery, and proceeded to the long train of others cut down as though their lives did not matter, being marked black.[50]

The crises of 2020 piled on each other and compounded each other: backlash movements based on anti-racism, anti-feminism, xenophobia, and disrespect for LGBTQ+ persons; a climate crisis that has evoked only token gestures thus far in the United States; and a pandemic that will take years to play out. The United States wasted the crisis of 9/11, barging into imperial wars that did not end. It wasted the financial crisis of 2008, allowing the bailed-out megabanks to become bigger than ever. The Covid crisis stripped bare the injustices of the system and what comes from indulging the corporate race to the bottom. Just-in-time supply chains and just-in-time labor policies leave societies perilously vulnerable in a crisis. Essential goods cannot be obtained when supply chains based in Asia are disrupted. Neoliberal labor policies leave masses of workers without health insurance or paid leave or a pension. The Biden administration, elected on its promise to "Build Back Better," will be forced by structural conditions and the fallout from the crises of 2020 to dwell on "Better," pushed beyond its comfort zone. Achieving universal healthcare and addressing the climate crisis are colossal imperatives that cannot be deferred. Economies with greater resiliency and far greater ecological sustainability must be imagined. New regional trading blocks must be forged that make supply chains less dependent on exploited labor in faraway, anti-union, no-tax havens. We have seen what neoliberalism looks like under neoliberal Democratic administrations, traditional Republican administrations, and a reactionary-nationalist Republican administration. To improve on Clinton and Obama, Biden must reorder the nation's priorities.

MAKING DEMOCRATIC SOCIALISM AMERICAN

This story began with the world's first workers' party, the Workingmen's Party of New York, and the first hope of American radical industrial unionism, the Knights of Labor. It ends with twenty-something veterans of the Sanders campaign and their allies mobilizing for a Green New Deal and vowing to build new social justice networks that scale up to a new labor-socialist party. From the beginning American socialists confronted so many structural, institutional, and ideological obstacles that it is remarkable there has been so much story to track and interpret.

White Americans vested immense pride in being an exceptional New World beacon of individualistic liberty, discounting that the new Republic depended on chattel slavery and exterminated the native population. The nation came together, more or less, by codifying the antidemocratic beliefs of eighteenth-century liberals. I have stressed that the twofold catastrophe of 1917–19 obliterated whatever chance the Socialist movement had of becoming important on its terms. The vicious government persecution of the Socialist Party during and after World War I and the devastation of the Communist siren call to revolution destroyed the Socialist movement, relegating to secondary status everything else.

Yet everything else included very considerable factors. *Federalist Paper*, no. 10, decreed that democracies are "spectacles of turbulence and contention" incompatible with the rights of security and property owners. The Constitution established a simple-majority system in which a party receives no representation if it does not win more votes than all other parties within a constituency. Simple-majority representation in single-member districts puts immense lesser-evil pressure on voters not to waste their vote, deterring minor parties. Politically, the plurality model of representation turned the nation into a two-party fiefdom thwarting minor party challenges, especially from Socialists. There are almost no exceptions in the world to the rule that a simple majority, single-ballot system creates two-party fiefdoms.[51]

The United States enfranchised white males with the vote before it industrialized, which deprived Socialists of the issue that fired every Socialist movement in Continental Europe. America's federal structure deprived Socialists of a national governing focus of oppression, unlike the autocracies that European

Social Democrats opposed. The United States elects its presidents by aggregating national votes in a single round of voting for a given individual through an electoral college, putting the presidency out of reach for third parties. The American simple-majority, two-party system incentivizes interest groups to form coalitions *within* parties *before* elections take place instead of across parties after elections, as in polities with proportional representation. The Republican and Democratic Parties co-opted challenges to their rule and controlled electoral machinery at the state level, ramping up the barriers to ballot access after women won the vote. Then Franklin Roosevelt shrewdly saved the capitalist system and co-opted its left opposition when the U.S. American story might have turned out differently.[52]

Werner Sombart rightly said that socialism was no match for America's open borders, capitalist prosperity, and upward mobility. The Sombart explanation is justly famous, catching that American workers feared that socialism would prevent them from getting ahead. But America had more than enough suffering and exploitation to create a surging socialist movement, and the Sombart explanation does not explain what was distinctly odd and doomed about American socialism. Early American socialism failed, above all, because divide-and-conquer hegemony worked under the nation's extraordinary ethnic pluralism. Workers were turned against each other, the AFL pitted native-born workers in the craft unions against unskilled immigrant workers, the AFL bought into capitalism, and it excluded the mostly immigrant industrial workers. That yielded a labor movement unlike any in Europe, a crushing difference for American socialists. No factor outranked this one.

Plurality representation and single-member districts, though hostile to socialist interests, are not insurmountable obstacles. Democratic socialist parties have overcome this combination in numerous countries, notwithstanding that proportional systems eventually became the norm in Western Europe. Sweden and Denmark had plurality, single-member systems until 1907 and 1915, respectively, and Britain, Canada, and most former British colonies still do. Germany had single-member districts until 1914. The wasted-vote syndrome applies only if one of the ruling parties is perceived as being much worse than the other. Democratic socialist parties have succeeded in plurality systems where this perception did not take hold, as in Britain and Canada. Americans like voting for their presidents in national contests instead of having the leader emerge from parliamentary jockeying, and the Socialists had compelling candidates in Debs and Thomas. The "gift of the suffrage" stressed by Lenin and sociologist Selig Perlman didn't stop Australian workers from becoming class conscious. Political scientist Theodore Lowi pressed the argument about federalism, overlooking that federal constitutions in Australia, Canada, Germany, and Switzerland did not thwart socialist movements. On ballot access, the Democratic and Republican Parties have always gamed the system in ways not tolerated in other advanced democracies. Every minor party in American politics has suffered from it, but that does not explain why the Socialist Party approached only once the vote tallies of James Weaver in 1892, Theodore Roosevelt in 1912, Robert La Follette in 1924, George Wallace in 1968, and Ross Perot in 1992 and 1996.[53]

America's culture of capitalist individualism thwarted socialists from the beginning, but the foremost reason the Socialist Party failed before World War I was its distinct labor movement problem. Sociologist Seymour Martin Lipset put it sharply, stressing that the very term "labor movement" never meant in the United States what it conveys in Continental Europe and all other English-speaking societies. In the United States it refers merely to unions, not to a movement encompassing working-class economic and political organizations. American unions were founded separately from left-wing political parties. They protected their independence from all political parties, became part of the system of political control represented by the two-party system, and defeated the socialist union leaders who stumped for a labor party. Marx and Engels perceived that this exceptional characteristic would be very difficult to overcome. Then Debs condemned the socialist comrades who tried to win the AFL to socialism. Debs played a role in sealing the greatest failure of the Socialist movement by charging, justly and vehemently, that Gompers-style business unionism made the AFL beholden to the interests, worldview, and agenda of the ruling class. His pure, simplistic idea of socialist deliverance helped to keep the labor underpinning of American socialism remarkably small.[54]

The Socialist Party was too small and disorganized to spearhead the movement it wanted, U.S. American unions were too different from Continental and British unions to support the Socialist movement, and Debs was good only at running for office, an activity he disparaged. The founding Socialists, overreacting to their suffering under Daniel De Leon, created a ramshackle organization anchored by state parties. They never overcame their original decision to subordinate the national party to every state organization. Daniel Bell pressed rightly on this point; the Debs-era Socialists were too disorganized and ideological to become a real political party. Yet they made a very promising beginning. During the Debs years the American Socialists outperformed all their European counterparts in the electoral sphere. No European Socialist party before 1918 won 6 percent of the national vote, as Debs did in 1912. American socialists elected a flock of mayors and state representatives, matched the cultural diversity of the entire Second International combined, and boasted a profusion of periodicals lacking any parallel. As late as 1916 the American socialist movement seemed more promising than any other, except for two things—a small, ramshackle organization and a very slight union base.

Reaching a peak of 118,000 members in 1912 sounded impressive only in the United States; the British Labour Party boasted 1.9 million members the same year, and even New South Wales had 250,000. That year the Socialist Party of America boasted 1.2 members per 1,000 of the population. In Britain the figure was 41.7; in Germany it was 14.7. The tiny, disorganized, isolated American party was also unstable, losing members as fast as Debs and Kate O'Hare recruited them. Nathan Fine, poring over membership records, quotably noted, "The rank and file of the Socialist Party in truth made, and then, unfortunately, unmade it. But it was not altogether the same rank and file."[55]

There were never enough unionists in the Socialist Party or industrial unionists in the AFL to sustain socialism. In Britain five of the ten largest unions in 1910 were industrial unions lacking a skill bar; in the United States there were two in the top ten, the UMWA and the ILGWU. Craft unionism so dominated the AFL that craft racism and sexism were impregnable and political independence was orthodoxy. The Socialists got most of their union members from the five leading industrial unions in the AFL—the UMWA, ACWA, ILGWU, Brewery Workmen, and Western Federation of Miners. They tried to convert the AFL to socialism and nearly passed a socialist ownership plank in 1893—the high-water mark, eight years before the Socialist Party existed. Max Hayes led the fight for socialism in the AFL and caught the ferocious contempt of Debs, many prairie radicals, and the syndicalists for trying too decorously.[56]

Debs would not have become a socialist had he been able to tolerate remaining in a craft union. His fling at industrial unionism was stormy and brief, after which he converted to magical socialism, the cure for all social problems not to be sullied by reform movements or mediocre trade unions. Debs was the apostle of a true way that found strength in its evangelical purity. His socialism was a Protestant redemption strategy soaked in the idioms and assumptions of American revivalism. Being a romantic American individualist reinforced his magical socialism and his evangelical concept of his mission, making him an incomparable platform performer. He loved the workers and they loved him back, but he made it hard for them to join his party, castigating a union federation that encompassed 750,000 workers in 1900 and 2.5 million workers by 1913.

Hayes kept pushing the AFL to create a British-style labor party. In 1906 fifty-one AFL unions founded a Labor Representation Committee for this purpose, taking the name of the Labour Party forerunner organization. Six years later Hayes challenged Gompers for the AFL presidency and won 36 percent—respectable, but not gaining. Always the industrial unions played the leading role in pushing for a labor party, especially the UMW, ILGWU, and Brewery Workers. In 1920 they struck out on their own, founding the Farmer-Labor Party. The ascending Labour Party inspired them, and the Communist breakup of the Socialist Party repelled them. The Farmer-Labor pioneers waited too long and got on few ballots, making a dismal beginning. Four years later the forces that needed to come together briefly did so, for one election, running La Follette as the candidate of a Farmer-Labor-Socialist-Progressive coalition. It helped that the AFL came aboard to punish the Democrats and Republicans, but the AFL had not changed; backing La Follette was a one-off affair. To Hillquit and the Old Guard survivors of the Communist explosion, losing the La Follette coalition was desperately hard to take, ranking with the sad dictatorial turn of Soviet Communism. It was hard to imagine in 1925 how Soviet Communism would ever find its way to democracy; meanwhile the dream of a labor party stayed out of reach, condemning the Socialist Party to years of utter irrelevance kept afloat by garment union money.

Failing to win over the labor movement made American socialism wholly unlike Continental Social Democracy and British socialism. The Farmer-Labor-Socialist-Progressive coalition was never hard to imagine; it haunted the left because every election produced political victors who did not represent vast sectors of the population. But Americans had only unions, not a real labor movement.

For a while the Great Depression rewrote the script on what might be possible. Union activism rebounded dramatically, Congress passed the Wagner Act of 1935, and Communists and Socialists organized the CIO. The Wagner Act threw the weight of government behind union organizers, forcing employers to allow their plants to be unionized. FDR endorsed it shortly before it passed, determined to co-opt a tide of left-wing and right-wing populist forces—Norman Thomas Socialists, Farmer-Labor organizers, Huey Long–Charles Coughlin fascists, Republican progressives, and Communists. He did it with wily brilliance, putting left leaders on his payroll and favoring select left candidates over Democrats. Minnesota governor Floyd Olsen (Farmer-Labor Party), New York City mayor Fiorello La Guardia (American Labor Party), Nebraska senator George Norris (Independent), and Wisconsin governor Philip La Follette (Progressive Party) bonded with FDR, who told them he was on their side, determined to transform the Democrats into a progressive party. To a considerable degree the New Deal was in fact a form of socialist deliverance. The only Socialist play after failing to unite the left was to pull FDR to the left by working with him and demanding more from him. But the party opposed him for reasons that made Thomas sound strange and the Socialists look irrelevant.

The last hope of a Labor Party breakthrough was lost in the whiplash reactions of 1946, '47, and '48. The CIO struck hard for postwar wage gains, and Congress passed the Taft-Hartley Act over Truman's veto. Taft-Hartley abolished or curtailed almost every tool that built the unions, outlawing jurisdictional strikes, wildcat strikes, solidarity strikes, secondary boycotts, secondary and mass picketing, closed shops, and union monetary contributions to federal political campaigns. It gave state legislatures a green light to enact Orwellian right-to-work laws having nothing to do with the right to work. The unions had grown from three million AFL members in 1935 to fourteen million AFL and CIO members in 1945. Taft-Hartley was about making them weak and insecure again. The last hope of a Labor Party died with Truman's feisty comeback victory of 1948. Now the defanged labor movement belonged wholly to the Democratic Party.

My emphasis on the role of religious socialists highlighted that they were there in every era of American socialist history. They refused to blame capitalism for all of society's ills, connected socialism to reform movements, and made socialism more diverse in race, gender, class, and geography. Nearly always the religious socialists refused to fit their moral convictions to a socialist ideology; for them it had to work the other way around. Christian and Jewish socialists who otherwise regarded themselves as neo-Marxists, Fabians, syndicalists, or social democrats asserted the ethical difference when it arose. It arose whenever an overriding moral conviction was at stake and nearly whenever it was said that socialists must not bother with reform movements—in both cases a guardrail against magical socialism. The best religious socialists were principled anti-imperialists and neo-abolitionists, contending that religion alone or socialism alone should be enough to produce principled anti-imperialists and neo-abolitionists. As it was, they lamented that it often took both things joined together.

Always the religious socialists were tagged as squishy moralists for emphasizing their moral convictions. They just had to take it, realizing why so much of the socialist movement was antireligious. The same thing happened in the Second International, only worse, because religious socialism had no status in Continental Social Democracy. Hillquit called it a bastard offshoot of the only real socialism, Marxian social democracy. A generation later Marxists protested that Thomas substituted his religiously inspired idealism for the real thing and ruined what remained of the Socialist Party.

Thomas chose the Socialists over the church after the church rolled over for World War I, making an emblematic judgment about the future of Christian socialism—it worked better as a secularized form of ethical idealism. Certainly it did in his case. His buoyant ethical humanity was a light to many in the 1930s and 1940s, giving them a place to stand; they were Norman Thomas Socialists. But Norman Thomas Socialism was the old Christian socialism stripped of Christianity and an ideological rudder. It was the name of the moral passion that threw Thomas into struggles for social justice and an ideal that floated above them. As an ideal it became a kind of substitute faith for Thomas, explaining why the Socialist Party should keep running for office, and he should humiliate himself in its service.

Thomas was a failure as a party leader and a light to many for the same reason. He stuck to an ideal instead of getting behind Roosevelt, disastrously. He doubled down by pushing out the Old Guard, which literally bankrupted the party. He betrayed his longtime antifascism in 1940 in the name of a higher idealism, disastrously. He tried to cheer in 1944 when the Cooperative Commonwealth Federation (CCF) took power in Saskatchewan, achieving the first social democratic government in North America. The CCF dated only from 1932 and had to compete in Canada's plurality electoral system, yet it zoomed past its U.S. American counterpart, planting North America's first universal Medicare system in Saskatchewan. Thomas-style socialism, it turned out, had a robust role to play in Canada but not where Thomas lived.[57]

To my generation of democratic socialists Thomas came off as the last idealist—the last figure of consequence who became a socialist because he believed the world was progressing steadily toward unity and freedom. The early Thomas fervently believed that democratic socialism synthesized the cultural progress of modern society and was destined to become the basis of a world government. The later Thomas said his life was a succession of worse-worse-worse disillusionments that made him evermore miserable. But even putting it that way smacked of believing that idealistic socialism should be true. Thomas could not track the twists and turns of Reinhold Niebuhr's dialecticism, puzzling that anyone as hard-edged and cynical as Niebuhr could be a Christian social ethicist. Why Niebuhr spent so much time blasting liberal humanism was a mystery to Thomas.

The last comrade-disciples of Thomas loved him for persisting anyway. Julius Bernstein, James Farmer, Harry Fleischman, Michael Harrington, Irving Howe, and A. Philip Randolph did not describe Thomas as overly idealistic, willful, naive, or any such thing. They described him as fiercely truthful and wondrously courageous. They loved him for keeping the Socialist Party going and for imploring the New Left to wash the flag, not burn it. Martin Luther King Jr. said Thomas was the bravest person he ever met and the foremost advocate "of a society free of injustice and exploitation." Randolph, pressed by interviewers to identify some personal fault of Thomas, insisted that he never found one.

Howe said he treasured Thomas precisely for exemplifying how to be idealistic and realistic simultaneously: "Even after he died Thomas remained, so to say, in my head, setting a standard of right action, pointing to the elusive path where the 'ethic of ultimate ends' and the 'ethic of responsibility' join. When I did something unworthy in politics, it was to his memory I had to answer; when I acquitted myself well, it was his approval I would most have wanted."[58]

Harrington played a similar role for the social democrats and New Leftists he brought into DSOC and DSA. He was better suited to it intellectually than Thomas, though he had to grow more than Thomas personally to play the role. Harrington's self-sacrificing persona mildly amused old friends who had known him in the 1950s. He built healthy organizations bridging the Old Left–New Left rift, giving the children of the 1960s something constructive to join. Richard Healey recalled that SDS was born alienated and got worse before it blew up: "We were increasingly desperate around civil rights and the war, which only got worse after 1967 and our 'leaders' became increasingly self-referential. That sense of isolation and desperation was palpable every day." Healey admired Harrington for pulling off the dream of a united front, even as he regretted that he and Harrington never really bonded.[59]

Harrington kept his guard up with most people, habituated to platform performing and organizational leadership. He worked hard at winning influence for his organizations in the Democratic Party and the Socialist International, remembering what it felt like to live in left sectarian nowhere. He enjoyed too much his hobnobbing with Willy Brandt and Olof Palme, but there was a serious purpose in it. His former friends in Social Democrats USA (SDUSA) resented that Brandt and Palme pulled the International in a postcolonial direction, favoring DSOC and DSA. Harrington hoped it was not too late for democratic socialists to get on the right side of the postcolonial revolution, and he knew for sure that the Shachtmanites had no chance of winning the next generation of Democratic Party youth. It was strange how his battle with the neocons turned out. DSOC outperformed SDUSA in the Democratic Party, yet the neocons went on to spectacular success in the Republican Party.

The neocons made enemies on the right when they rode into the Reagan administration. Many old-style conservatives protested that the neocons won their positions with sharp elbows and shook down the Old Right foundations for money. Neocons countered that their Old Right critics were anti-Semitic, which was sometimes true, and that Harrington's name for them in the first place was really a euphemism for "Jewish conservatism," which was false. Harrington named the neocons to identify the phenomenon of socialists-and-liberals-for-Nixon. Neoconservatism was the last phase of the Old Left and a cry of revulsion against the social movements of the 1960s. Harrington never lost his appalled fascination with the march of his former socialist comrades and liberal friends into Republican power. Meanwhile he implored the left to find new answers for a changing world.[60]

This part of Harrington's legacy is still relevant. James O'Connor and Claus Offe helped him fathom the miserable stagflation of the 1970s and 1980s, the dress rehearsal of neoliberalism. Harrington pressed for bottom-up economic democracy, admonishing that any idiot in power can nationalize a bank. The left needed to sustain a socialist vision of a new society while struggling for it in grassroots, piecemeal, gradual fashion, building models of worker ownership and decentralized public control. When Harrington scaled further up he could be misleading as to whether he was still talking about markets within plans, because in fact he described social democratic plans operating within markets. To be a unifying organizational leader, he had to fudge his position. To his left flank, his position was socialism only if the Meidner Plan was a means to an actually socialist transition.

That position is the new mainstream in DSA, but even the new DSA concedes that the Meidner Plan falls under the category of far-off vision land. It is so remote from anything currently existing in the United States that arguments about its role as a means or end quickly become very academic. German codetermination and the Mondragon cooperatives are similarly otherworldly in an American context, the difference being that both are long established and venerable in Germany and Spain.

Worker councils in Germany date back to four printing houses in Ellenburg, Saxony, in 1850. Germany had worker councils in scattered areas where unions were strong until 1920, when the SPD pushed through the first codetermination law, the Works Council Act *(Betriebsrätegesetz)*. It mandated that all businesses employing more than twenty workers were required to recognize a consultative worker council that represented the social and economic interests of workers to the management. The Nazis abolished the worker councils and broke up the unions, but in 1946 the Allied Control Authority restored the councils in its *Kontrollratsgesetz Nr. 22*. After the Federal Republic was established, unions pushed hard for codetermination, threatening massive strikes. The payoff came in 1951 with the historic Coal, Steel, and Mining Codetermination Law *(Montan-Mitbestimmungsgesetz)*, requiring codetermination in all businesses employing more than one thousand workers through worker representatives constituting one-half of supervisory company boards. The following year a follow-up law mandated that all workers at the shop-floor level had to be represented by a worker council. In 1955 the *Bundespersonalvertretungsgesetz* extended similar codetermination rights to all members of the civil services in the Federation and German states.[61]

German unionists and Social Democrats claimed that workers work more effectively when they are allowed to codetermine how their company operates. They turned out to be right, at least in Germany, where coal and steel producers employing more than one thousand workers had supervisory boards composed of eleven members: five from management, five representing workers, and the eleventh being neutral. Larger boards sustained the same proportion of representation. The shareholders and trade unions elected the supervisory board, and it elected the management board. The chair of the supervisory board was always a shareholder representative, and the management board had one worker representative. Workers still worked and managers still managed, but German industries developed a cooperative culture that respected the input of workers on working conditions and industrial processes at the plant level. Many firms worked up to a consensus basis of decision making, creating sufficient trust to allow worker committees to contribute to higher-management decisions about wage rates, layoffs, financial policies, and structural reforms. One degree of codetermination led to another, winning broadly popular support, a cultural achievement. The Codetermination Act of 1976 expanded codetermination law to cover firms employing more than two thousand workers, eliminated the neutral eleventh board member, and mandated that workers and managements have the same number of representatives.

Codetermination is like social democracy in humanizing capitalism with socialist reforms without abolishing capitalism. Mondragon is simultaneously more modest and ambitious, making outright worker ownership work on a smaller but significantly large scale. The Mondragon network has existed since 1956 in the Basque region of Spain. It employs over 75,000 worker-owners in an advanced network of 102 individual cooperatives united in a cooperative federation, the Mondragon Cooperative Corporation. It has 70 industrial firms that compete in global markets, plus an agricultural cooperative, five schools, a technical college, and a central bank that is half-owned by its own employees and half-owned by other cooperatives. Each Mondragon worker-owner holds one share of voting stock, and profits are distributed in the form of additions to a capital account on which 6 percent interest is paid annually. Seventy percent of annual profits are distributed to worker-owners on the basis of salary scale and seniority, 10 percent are donated to charity, and the remaining 20 percent are reinvested.[62]

Mondragon is able to make long-term investments in expansion, diversification, research and development, and reinvestment because members cannot withdraw money from their capital accounts until they retire. It has demonstrated for decades that worker empowerment and cooperation can be turned into economic advantages. Any such experiment in economic democracy has to acquire distinct skills, habits, and technical knowledge. Select unions and worker associations in the United States began to acquire all three out of necessity after neoliberal capitalism went global. In 1980 there were fewer than two hundred American worker-owned enterprises, and most were small, isolated, and restricted to a handful of economic sectors. Globalization drove many communities and a few unions to trade wage restraint for worker ownership or, more ambitiously, worker control over investment and enterprise management. In the 1990s thousands of firms converted to worker ownership, bringing the total number by 1999 to approximately twelve thousand, where it has stayed.

Most employee-ownership plans offer shares without voting rights; most assure that employees are kept in a minority-ownership position; few provide educational opportunities to help worker-owners develop management skills; and few offer programs to help worker-owners forge links with other cooperative enterprises. Worker ownership without democratic control is a nominal version of economic democracy, thwarting the real thing. With all its limitations, however, the growth of the employee ownership sector laid the groundwork for an economic democracy movement. The United Steel Workers and the ACTWU promoted worker ownership through the AFL-CIO Employee Partnership Fund, providing capital for union-led conversions to worker ownership. The Midwest Center for Labor Research, Ohio Employee Ownership Center, National Cooperative Business Association, Employee State Ownership Plan Association, U.S. Federation of Worker Cooperatives and Democratic Workplaces, and Industrial Cooperative Association facilitated worker buyouts and developed sector-specific expertise that were unavailable to previous generations of American cooperatives.

Economic democracy at the grassroots level begins by expanding the cooperative sector. Producer cooperatives take labor out of the market by removing corporate shares from the stock market and maintaining local worker ownership. Community land trusts take land out of the market and place it under local democratic controls to serve the needs of communities. Community finance corporations take democratic control over capital to finance cooperative firms, make investments in areas of social need, and fight the redlining policies of conventional banks. Expanding the cooperative sector reclaims the socialist principle that democratic ownership is a central factor in building a just society. But expanding the cooperative sector is not enough. Cooperatives have trouble scaling up, they usually cannot compete with large, integrated corporations in industries with large economies of scale or many externalities, and they are not geared to address the needs of the entire society. In particular, cooperatives do not do enough to combat inequality.

Most cooperatives require members to sell out to the company rather than allow members to sell out to the highest bidder and take their capital gains, and most operate on the traditional principle that those who own a company's capital have the right to control the company. The former policy guards against reverting to traditional investor ownership; the latter policy assumes that property rights determine the right of effective control. But successful cooperatives impose high borrowing fees on new members, weeding out anyone who can't afford high share prices, and property rights measure human value in terms of exchange value, which leaves out people who cannot earn wages. Economic democracy cannot be merely a movement to expand the number of high-priced cooperatives. Full-orbed economic democracy creates democratic institutions that treat all citizens as stakeholders in the economic system.

We need new forms of social ownership that are entrepreneurial and innovative, facilitate capital formation, scale up, make room for everyone, and don't replicate the bloated bureaucracies of centralized state socialism. The social fund scheme underlying the Meidner Plan was, and is, a bellwether example. An excess profits tax creates social funds that entitle workers and the public to shareholding representation on company boards. In Sweden it worked very well, except politically. Swedish conservatives and finance capitalists railed against it constantly for ten years, while the Social Democrats supported it timorously. The very idea of economic democracy offended the conservatives and finance capitalists, while Swedish workers were indifferent to it. Had the Meidner Plan been allowed to run past 1992, it would have crossed the line from social democracy into democratic socialism. But even in Sweden the guardians of neoliberal capitalism do not tolerate transitions to a different kind of system, and the capitalist attack on artisanal skill has produced workers who do not respect their work.

Economic democracy has to push on both fronts simultaneously, developing forms of social ownership that are market-savvy and that build a cooperative culture. The public bank model contains a built-in system of wage restraints, requires no program of nationalization, and investors still seek the highest rate of return. Always there are trade-offs to negotiate concerning how much supervisory control to grant the holding companies. The investment agencies envisioned in public bank theory diminish democratic worker control, compelling fund managers to play a competitive game on behalf of the common good. But these trade-offs are inherent in the attempt to make democratic socialist values work within capitalist markets and capitalist societies.

"Yardstick" public corporations are another alternative to nationalizing entire industries. A publicly owned bank, pharmaceutical manufacturer, health insurance company, or auto company can measure what the market actually requires in industries that tend to become oligopolies. The case for establishing a public bank that funds green jobs was powerful in 2009, but the Obama Administration preferred to placate the megabank oligarchy. Meanwhile a plank establishing a public option in healthcare was included in the original ACA, passed the House of Representatives, and was supported by a majority in the Senate. The public option would have competed with private plans in national or regional purchasing pools. It would have eliminated high deductibles, allowed members to choose their own doctors, and allowed members to negotiate reimbursement rates and drug prices.

The public option was, and is, a glide path to Medicare for All. Health care is a fundamental human right that should be available to all people regardless of their economic resources. A decent society does not relegate the poor and underemployed to second-class status. When middle-class and upper-middle-class people have to rely on the same healthcare system as the poor, they use their political power to make sure it's a good system. The public option was the acid test of whether Obamacare was going to structurally reform the system or just make the insurance companies take more customers. Had citizens been allowed to choose a government plan, they would have done so—which could have led to a universal Medicare, with everybody in and nobody out. As it was, Obama bailed out from the fight to defeat a Senate filibuster, and the cause of structural reform was lost. Sanders, the only Senator to call for Medicare for All in 2009, swung the left wing of the Democratic Party in his direction afterward, believing that the moment for the glide path had passed. But establishing a public option, a public bank, or a public pharmaceutical company would be a major breakthrough for economic democracy.

Economic democracy needs no blueprint; the crucial thing is to find out which models work best in particular communities. Economic democracy and ecological survival are linked by the necessity of creating alternatives to the capitalist fantasy of unlimited growth. Climate change is melting the polar caps and vast areas of permafrost at a catastrophic pace, destroying wetlands and forests around the world, harming first the world's poorest and most vulnerable. Corporate giants like ExxonMobil succeed as businesses and investments while treating the destructive aspects of their behavior as someone else's problem.

Neoclassical theory is about acquiring as many goods as possible for as little labor as possible, picturing the economy as an isolated system through which exchange value circulates between firms and households. But the global capitalist market cannot be the model for a sustainable society. The environment is everything bundled together from the inside-out, with feedback loops and interconnected wholes. Lacking a fundamental course correction, the earth is condemned to overheat, choke on its waste, exhaust its resources, and turn on its human destroyers. Today the link between economic democracy and the struggle for sustainable ecological communities is a matter of life and death for the entire planet.

The irony of economic democracy is that it fulfills the central conceit of neoclassical economics by actually giving choices to workers. The neoclassical conceit is that capitalism doesn't exploit anyone because labor employs capital as much as capital employs labor. But in the real world the owners of capital nearly always organize the factors of production. To expand the cooperative, public, and social fund sectors would give choices to workers that neoclassical theory does not deliver. It would show that there are alternatives to a system that stokes and celebrates greed and consumption to the point of self-destruction. Nobody is willing anymore to build a fossil fuel plant without the promise of endless government subsidies. Instead of subsidizing more of that, the U.S. could invest in the green economy of a shared future, guided by the values of democratic socialism, with or without the name.

Democratic socialists do not have to agree about the ideal state in order to struggle for an ecosocialist society in which no group dominates any other and the dignity of every person is recognized. The strategic focal point of the next democratic socialism is grassroots organizing. The legacy of the Sanders movement—a campaign for the Democratic Party presidential nomination by an independent socialist—is thousands of local organizing initiatives and down-ballot campaigns. The next generation of democratic socialists is geared to grassroots organizing and boasts many of the best organizers in the country. In the Harrington era, democratic socialism was a catchall for other commitments that democratic socialists cared about more. Today it is the top priority of a new generation of democratic socialists. The next generation is big enough to show up anywhere and is too outraged to melt away.

NOTES

1. RADICAL DEMOCRACY, JEWISH UNIVERSALISM, AND SOCIAL DEMOCRACY

1. Gary Dorrien, *Social Democracy in the Making: Political and Religious Roots of European Socialism* (New Haven: Yale University Press, 2019).
2. Ira Kipnis, *The American Socialist Movement, 1897–1912* (New York: Columbia University Press, 1952).
3. Daniel Bell, *Marxian Socialism in the United States* (Princeton: Princeton University Press, 1952; repr., 1967); Bell, *The End of Ideology: On the Exhaustion of Political Ideas in the 1950s* (New York: Free Press, 1960).
4. Howard Quint, *The Forging of American Socialism: Origins of the Modern Movement* (Columbia: University of South Carolina Press, 1953); David Shannon, *The Socialist Party of America: A History* (New York: Macmillan, 1955).
5. Theodore Draper, *The Roots of American Communism* (New York: Viking, 1957); Draper, *American Communism and Soviet Russia: The Formative Period* (New York: Viking, 1961); David A. Shannon, *The Decline of American Communism: A History of the Communist Party of the United States since 1945* (New York: Harcourt, Brace, 1959); Irving Howe and Lewis Coser, *The American Communist Party: A Critical History* (New York: Frederick A. Praeger, 1957); Harry Overstreet and Bonaro Overstreet, *What We Must Know about Communism: Its Beginnings, Its Growth, Its Present Status* (New York: W. W. Norton, 1958).
6. Maurice Isserman, *Which Side Were You On? The American Communist Party during the Second World War* (Middletown, CT: Wesleyan University Press, 1982); Ronald Schatz, *The Electrical Workers: A History of Labor at General Electric and Westinghouse* (Urbana: University of Illinois Press, 1983); Mark Naison, *Communists in Harlem During the Depression* (Urbana: University of Illinois Press, 1983); Bruce Nelson, *Workers on the Waterfront: Seamen, Longshoremen, and Unionism in the 1930s* (Urbana: University of Illinois Press, 1988); Robin D. G. Kelley, *Hammer and Hoe: Alabama Communists during the Great Depression* (Chapel Hill: University of North

Carolina Press, 1990), "patiently," xiv; Michael Goldfield, "Race and the CIO: The Possibilities for Racial Egalitarianism during the 1930s and 1940s," *International Labor and Working-Class History* 44 (Fall 1993), 1–32.

7. James Weinstein, *The Decline of Socialism in the United States, 1912–1925* (New York: Monthly Review Press, 1967; repr., New Brunswick: Rutgers University Press, 1984).

8. Mary Jo Buhle, *Women and American Socialism, 1870–1920* (Urbana: University of Illinois Press, 1981); Sally M. Miller, "For White Men Only: The Socialist Party of America and Issues of Gender, Ethnicity and Race," *Journal of the Gilded Age and Progressive Era* 2 (July 2003), 284–96; Jack Ross, *The Socialist Party of America: A Complete History* (Lincoln: University of Nebraska Press, 2015); Heath W. Carter, *Union Made: Working People and the Rise of Social Christianity in Chicago* (Oxford: Oxford University Press, 2015); Philip S. Foner, *Black Socialism and Black Americans: From the Age of Jackson to World War II* (Westport, CT: Greenwood Press, 1977).

9. Kipnis, *The American Socialist Movement*, 44, 269, quote 269.

10. Bell, *Marxian Socialism in the United States*, 52, 58, quote 61; James Dombrowski, *The Early Days of Christian Socialism in America* (New York: Columbia University Press, 1936).

11. A. E. Bestor Jr., "The Evolution of the Socialist Vocabulary," *Journal of the History of Ideas* 9 (June 1948), "a social," 263; Frank T. Carlton, "The Workingmen's Party of New York City, 1829–1831," *Political Science Quarterly* 22 (September 1907), 402–13.

12. Adam Tuchinsky, *Horace Greeley's "New York Tribune": Civil War–Era Socialism and the Crisis of Free Labor* (Ithaca: Cornell University Press, 2009); Robert C. Williams, *Horace Greeley: Champion of American Freedom* (New York: New York University Press, 2006); Henry Mayer, *All on Fire: William Lloyd Garrison and the Abolition of Slavery* (New York: St. Martin's Press, 1998); James M. McPherson, *The Struggle for Equality: Abolitionists and the Negro in the Civil War and Reconstruction* (Princeton: Princeton University Press, 1964).

13. Karl Marx, *Dispatches for the New York Tribune: Selected Journalism of Karl Marx*, ed. James Ledbetter (New York: Penguin Books, 2007).

14. Karl Marx, *On the First International: The Karl Marx Library*, vol. 3, ed. and trans. Saul K. Padover (New York: McGraw Hill, 1973), 157–270; Marx, "Critique of the Gotha Program: Marginal Notes to the Program of the German Workers' Party" (1875), in *On Revolution: The Karl Marx Library*, vol. 1, ed. and trans. Saul K. Padover (New York: McGraw-Hill, 1971), 488–506; other editions in *Karl Marx: Selected Writings*, ed. David McLellan (New York: Oxford University Press, 1977), 564–70; and *The Marx-Engels Reader*, 2nd ed., ed. Robert C. Tucker (New York: W. W. Norton, 1978), 525–41; Marx and Engels, "The Communist Manifesto," in *Karl Marx: Selected Writings*, 219–47, and *The Marx-Engels Reader*, 469–500.

15. Wolfgang Stüken, "Biographien wichtiger Personen der deutschen Demokratie-geschichte und Demokratiebewegung: Gustav Körner (1809–1896)" (Mainz: Institut für Geschichtliche Landeskunde; May 7, 2009); "Gustave Koerner House Restoration," https://gustavekoerner.org; Gustave Koerner, *Memoirs of Gustave Koerner, 1809–1896*, ed. Thomas J. McCormack (Cedar Rapids, IA: Torch Press, 1909).

16. Elliot Shore, Ken Fones-Wolf, and James Philip Danky, *The German-American Radical Press: The Shaping of a Left Political Culture, 1850–1940* (Urbana: University of Illinois Press, 1992); Karl Obermann, *Joseph Weydemeyer* (New York: International Publishers, 1947); Hans L. Trefousse, *Carl Schurz: A Biography* (New York: Fordham University Press, 1998); John Nichols, *The "S" Word: A Short History of an American Tradition . . . Socialism* (London: Verso, 2011), 61–99.

17. Theodore Parker, "Hildreth's United States," in *The Works of Theodore Parker*, 15 vols., Centenary Edition (Boston: American Unitarian Association, 1907–11), 8: 270–71; Parker, "The American Idea: Speech at the New England Anti-Slavery Convention, Boston" (May 29, 1850), https://www.bartleby.com/100/459.html; Garry Wills, *Lincoln at Gettysburg: The Words That Remade America* (New York: Simon and Schuster, 1992), 107.

18. Abraham Lincoln, Address to the Wisconsin State Agricultural Society, September 30, 1859, Milwaukee, Wisconsin; http://www.abrahamlincolnonline.org/lincoln/speeches/fair.htm.

19. George W. Slater Jr., "Abraham Lincoln a Socialist," *Chicago Daily Socialist* (October 6, 1908).

20. Dorrien, *Social Democracy in the Making*, 27–113.

21. Karl Marx, "Inaugural Address to the First International" (1864), in *Karl Marx: Selected Writings*, 531–37; Marx, "Policies and Programs," *On the First International*, 79–152; William H. Dawson, *German Socialism and Ferdinand Lassalle* (London: Swan Sonnenschein, 1891), 114–32; Ferdinand Lassalle, *Gesammelte Reden und Schriften*, 12 vols., ed. Eduard Bernstein (Berlin: P. Cassirer, 1919–20); Roger Morgan, *The German Social Democrats and the First International, 1864–1872* (Cambridge: Cambridge University Press, 1965); Julius Braunthal, *History of the International*, 3 vols. (New York: Praeger, 1967–80), 1: 75–87.

22. Samuel Gompers, *Seventy Years of Life and Labor*, 2 vols. (New York: E. P. Dutton, 1925), quote 1: 55; Barbara Goldsmith, *Other Powers: The Age of Suffrage, Spiritualism, and the Scandalous Victoria Woodhull* (New York: HarperPerennial, 1999), 18–37, 142–208, 246–86; Myra McPherson, *The Scarlet Sisters: Sex, Suffrage, and Scandal in the Gilded Age* (New York: Twelve, 2014), 344–47.

23. Morris Hillquit, *History of Socialism in the United States* (New York: Funk and Wagnalls, 1910), 186–89; Frederick Heath, *Social Democracy Red Book* (Terre Haute, IN: Standard Publishing, 1900), 32–35; Frank Girard and Ben Perry, *The Socialist Labor Party, 1876–1991* (Philadelphia: Livra Books, 1991), 3–5. Engels published the first attempt to codify essential Marxism in 1880, *Socialism: Utopian and Scientific*. An English edition was published in 1892: Friedrich Engels, *Socialism: Utopian and Scientific*, trans. Edward Aveling (New York: International Publishers, 2015).

24. Carol Conell and Kim Voss, "Formal Organization and the Fate of Social Movements: Craft Association and Class Alliance in the Knights of Labor," *American Sociological Review* 55 (April 1990), 255–69; Leon Fink, "The New Labor History and the Powers of Historical Pessimism: Consensus, Hegemony, and the Case of the Knights of Labor," *Journal of American History* 75 (June 1988), 115–36; Fink, *Workingmen's Democracy: The Knights of Labor and American Politics* (Urbana: University of Illinois

Press, 1983); Gerald N. Grob, "The Knights of Labor and the Trade Unions, 1878–1886," *Journal of Economic History* 18 (June 1958), 176–92; Sidney H. Kessler, "The Organization of Negroes in the Knights of Labor," *Journal of Negro History* 37 (July 1952), 248–76; Susan Levine, "Labor's True Woman: Domesticity and Equal Rights in the Knights of Labor," *Journal of American History* 70 (September 1983), 323–39; Robert E. Weir, *Beyond Labor's Veil: The Culture of the Knights of Labor* (State College: Pennsylvania State University Press, 1996).

25. Henry George, *Progress and Poverty*, 2nd ed. (1879; New York: Robert Shalkenbach, 1919).

26. Ibid., quote 469.

27. Karl Marx to Friedrich Sorge, June 30, 1881, in *Marx-Engels Correspondence*, 394–96.

28. Philip S. Foner, *History of the Labor Movement in the United States*, 4 vols. (New York: International Publishers, 1955), 2: 132–55; Gompers, *Seventy Years of Life and Labor*, 1: 235–77.

29. Jeremy Brecher, *Strike!* (Boston: South End Press, 1997), 44–64; Gompers, *Seventy Years of Life and Labor*, 1: 292–315; *Almanac of American History*, ed. Arthur M. Schlesinger Jr. (New York: Barnes and Noble, 1993), 359–61.

30. L. Glen Seretan, *Daniel De Leon: The Odyssey of an American Marxist* (Cambridge: Harvard University Press, 1979), 4–18; Seretan, "Daniel De Leon as an American," *Wisconsin Magazine of History* 61 (Spring 1978), 210–23; Carl Reeve, *The Life and Times of Daniel De Leon* (New York: Humanities Press, 1972), 17–30; Charles A. Madison, "Daniel De Leon: Apostle of Socialism," *Antioch Review* 5 (Autumn 1945), 402–14; Marx-Engels Correspondence, 467, 87; Melvyn Dubofsky, *We Shall Be All: A History of the Industrial Workers of the World* (New York: Quadrangle, 1969), quotes 133.

31. Daniel De Leon, *Socialist Reconstruction of Society* (New York: New York Labor News, 1905), "the weapon," 59.

32. Bell, *Marxian Socialism in the United States*, 33–35, "union wrecking" and "a professor," 41; Madison, "Daniel De Leon: Apostle of Socialism," 405–12.

33. Morris Hillquit, *Loose Leaves from a Busy Life* (New York: Macmillan, 1934), "a religious," 10; see Irving Howe, *World of Our Fathers* (New York: Simon and Schuster, 1976).

34. Abraham Cahan, *The Education of Abraham Cahan*, 2 vols., trans. Leon Stein, Abraham P. Conan, and Lynn Davidson (Philadelphia: Jewish Publication Society of America, 1969), "we regarded," 1: 158; Sanford E. Marovitz, *Abraham Cahan* (New York: Twayne Publishers, 1996), 2–32; Jeffrey S. Gurock, *American Jewish History: East European Jews in America, 1880–1920* (New York: Routledge, 1998), 59–77; Seth Lipsky, *The Rise of Abraham Cahan* (New York: Schocken Books, 2013), 17–32.

35. Hillquit, *Loose Leaves from a Busy Life*, 19–48, "he excelled," 47; Norma Fain Pratt, *Morris Hillquit: A Political History of the American Jewish Socialist* (Westport, CT: Greenwood Press, 1979), 3–19.

36. David Karsner, *Debs: His Authorized Life and Letters* (New York: 1919), 175–79; McAlister Coleman, *Pioneers of Freedom* (New York: Vanguard Press, 1929), 150–51; Nathan Fine, *Farmer and Labor Parties in the United States, 1828–1928* (New York: Rand School of Social Science, 1928), 187–89; Ray Ginger, *The Bending Cross: A Biography of Eugene Victor Debs* (New Brunswick, NJ: Rutgers University Press,

1949); Nick Salvatore, *Eugene V. Debs: Citizen and Socialist* (Urbana: University of Illinois Press, 1982).

37. Lewis Henry Morgan, *Ancient Society* (Cambridge: Harvard University Press, 1964); "Lewis Henry Morgan, LL.D.," *Proceedings of the American Academy of Arts and Sciences* 17 (June 1881–June 1882), 429–36; Steven Conn, *History's Shadow: Native Americans and Historical Consciousness in the Nineteenth Century* (Chicago: University of Chicago Press, 2004), 136–39, 210–27.

38. Friedrich Engels, *The Origin of the Family, Private Property, and the State* (1884), in *The Marx-Engels Reader*, 734–59, quotes 745, 741.

39. Ibid., quotes 745, 746.

40. May Wood Simons, *Woman and the Social Problem* (Chicago: Charles Kerr, 1899), 5–29, quotes 21, 23.

41. Socialist Party of America, *Proceedings of the 1908 National Convention* (Chicago: Socialist Party, 1908), 303–4.

2. SOCIAL GOSPEL SOCIALISM, THE LABOR MOVEMENT, AND THE SOCIALIST PARTY

1. Washington Gladden, *Being a Christian: What It Means and How to Begin* (Boston: Congregational Publishing Society, 1876); Gladden, *The Christian Way: Whither It Leads and How to Go On* (New York: Dodd, Mead, 1877).

2. Richard T. Ely, *Ground under Our Feet: An Autobiography* (New York: Macmillan, 1938), 3–22, "offered," 16; Benjamin G. Rader, "Richard T. Ely: Lay Spokesman for the Social Gospel," *Journal of American History* 53 (June 1966), 61–74; John R. Everett, *Religion in Economics: A Study of John Bates Clark, Richard T. Ely, and Simon N. Patten* (Philadelphia: Porcupine Press, 1981), 75–79.

3. Richard T. Ely, *French and German Socialism in Modern Times* (New York: Harper and Brothers, 1883), "professorial," 245; Ely, *The Past and the Present of Political Economy* (Baltimore: Johns Hopkins University Press, 1884); Ely, *Recent American Socialism* (Baltimore: Johns Hopkins University Press, 1885).

4. Richard T. Ely, *The Labor Movement in America* (New York: Thomas Y. Crowell, 1886), "today," 121; Ely, *Ground under Our Feet*, "this spectacular" and "an unprecedented," 72.

5. Josiah Strong, *Our Country, Its Possible Future and Its Present Crisis* (New York: American Home Missionary Society, 1886; rev. ed., New York: Baker and Taylor, 1891); Charles H. Hopkins, *The Rise of the Social Gospel in American Protestantism, 1865–1915* (New Haven: Yale University Press, 1940); James Dombrowski, *The Early Days of Christian Socialism in America* (New York: Columbia University Press, 1936); Paul A. Carter, *The Decline and Revival of the Social Gospel* (Ithaca: Cornell University Press, 1954); Henry F. May, *Protestant Churches and Industrial America* (New York: Harper and Brothers, 1949), 250–55; Robert T. Handy, ed., *The Social Gospel in America, 1870–1920* (New York: Oxford University Press, 1966), 179–80; Ely, *Ground under Our Feet*, 79, 140–43. My discussion of Gladden and Social Darwinism in this chapter adapts material from Gary Dorrien, *The Making of American Liberal*

Theology: Imagining Progressive Religion (Louisville: Westminster John Knox Press, 2001), 304–24.

6. Herbert Spencer, *First Principles* (New York: D. Appleton, 1864); Spencer, *The Principles of Sociology*, 3 vols. (New York: D. Appleton, 1876–97); Richard Hofstadter, *Social Darwinism in American Thought* (Boston: Beacon Press, 1955), 31–50; George W. Stocking Jr., *Race, Culture, and Evolution: Essays in the History of Anthropology* (Chicago: University of Chicago Press, 1968), 234–69; Stephen Jay Gould, *Ontogeny and Phylogeny* (Cambridge: Harvard University Press, 1977); Charles Darwin, *The Descent of Man* (New York: John Murray, 1874), 166–68.

7. Ernst Haeckel, *The History of Creation*, 2 vols. (1876; 6th ed., New York: D. Appleton, 1914), quote 2: 249; Robert J. Richards, *The Tragic Sense of Life: Ernst Haeckel and the Struggle over Evolutionary Thought* (Chicago: University of Chicago Press, 2008), 255–61.

8. W. E. B. Du Bois, "The Conservation of Races" (1897), in *W. E. B. Du Bois: A Reader*, ed. David Levering Lewis (New York: Henry Holt, 1995), 20–27; Du Bois, *The Philadelphia Negro: A Social Study* (1899; repr., Philadelphia: University of Pennsylvania Press, 1996), 385–97; Thomas F. Gossett, *Race: The History of an Idea in America* (New York: Schocken Books, 1965), 54–83; George M. Frederickson, *Race: A Short History* (Princeton: Princeton University Press), 51–75; M. K. Richardson and G. Keuck, "Haeckel's ABC of Evolution and Development," *Biological Reviews* 77 (2002), 495–528.

9. Robert G. McCloskey, *American Conservatism in the Age of Enterprise: A Study of William Graham Sumner, Stephen J. Field, and Andrew Carnegie* (Cambridge: Harvard University Press, 1951); Bruce Curtis, *William Graham Sumner* (Boston: Twayne, 1981); William Thomas O'Connor, *Naturalism and the Pioneers of American Sociology* (Washington, DC, Catholic University of America Press, 1942).

10. William Graham Sumner, *Social Darwinism: Selected Essays*, ed. Albert Galloway Keller (Englewood Cliffs, NJ: Prentice-Hall, 1963), quotes 94, 95; see Sumner, *The Challenge of Facts and Other Essays* (New Haven: Yale University Press, 1914).

11. Gary Dorrien, *Social Ethics in the Making: Interpreting an American Tradition* (Oxford: Wiley-Blackwell, 2009), 15–51.

12. John Fiske, *Through Nature to God* (Boston: Houghton Mifflin, 1899); Fiske, *The Destiny of Man Viewed in the Light of His Origin* (Boston: Houghton Mifflin, 1884); Fiske, *A Century of Science and Other Essays* (Boston: Houghton Mifflin, 1899); Albion W. Small, *An Introduction to the Study of Society* (New York: American Book Company, 1894). Small founded the *American Journal of Sociology* in 1895.

13. "Principles of the American Economic Association," in Richard T. Ely, "The Founding and Early History of the American Economic Association" 26 (March 1936), 141–50; Dombrowski, *The Early Days of Christian Socialism in America*, "we who," 51; Hopkins, *The Rise of the Social Gospel*, 116–17.

14. Eugene V. Debs to Daniel and Marguerite Debs, September 12, 1904, Eugene V. Debs Collection, Cunningham Library, Indiana State University, Terre Haute; David F. Karsner, *Talks with Debs in Terre Haute* (New York: New York Call, 1922), 80–81; Debs, "How I Became a Socialist," *New York Comrade* (April 1902), in

Writings and Speeches of Eugene V. Debs, ed. Joseph M. Bernstein (New York: Hermitage Press, 1948), 43–44; Nick Salvatore, *Eugene V. Debs: Citizen and Socialist* (Urbana: University of Illinois Press, 1982), 4–22; Ray Ginger, *The Bending Cross: A Biography of Eugene Debs* (New Brunswick, NJ: Rutgers University Press, 1949), 3–19.

15. Samuel Gompers, *Seventy Years of Life and Labor*, 2 vols. (New York: E. P. Dutton, 1925), "is the basis," 1: 286.

16. Fifty-Third Congress, Third Session, "Testimony of Samuel Gompers," Senate Executive Document 7, *Report on the Chicago Strike of June–July, 1894, by the United States Strike Commission* (Washington, DC: United States Strike Commission, 1895), 200–205, "the ethics," 205; Gompers, *Seventy Years of Life and Labor*, 1: 235–87; Salvatore, *Eugene V. Debs*, 56–87.

17. Ginger, *The Bending Cross*, 61–80; Salvatore, *Eugene V. Debs*, 91–97.

18. Richard T. Ely, *Taxation in American States and Cities* (New York: Thomas Y. Crowell, 1888); Ely, *Problems of Today* (New York: Thomas Y. Crowell, 1888); Ely, *An Introduction to Political Economy* (New York: Chautauqua Press, 1889), quotes 17; Ely, *Social Aspects of Christianity and Other Essays* (New York: Thomas Y. Crowell, 1889), 9; Ely, "The Founding and Early History of the American Economic Association," 146; Sidney Fine, "Richard T. Ely: Forerunner of Progressivism, 1880–1901," *Mississippi Valley Historical Review* 37 (March 1951), 599–624.

19. Ely, *The Labor Movement in America*, 325–27, 332–33; Richard T. Ely, "Fundamental Beliefs in My Social Philosophy," *The Forum* 18 (September 1894–February 1895), 210–13.

20. Ely, *Social Aspects of Christianity*, quotes 11, 22, 24, 25; Ely, "Fundamental Beliefs in My Social Philosophy," 173–83; Theron F. Schlabach, "An Aristocrat on Trial: The Case of Richard T. Ely," *Wisconsin Magazine of History* 47 (Winter 1963–64), 140–59; Rader, "Richard T. Ely: Lay Spokesman for the Social Gospel," 61–74; Handy, *The Social Gospel in America*, 181; Arthur M. Lewis, *Ten Blind Leaders of the Blind* (Chicago: Charles H. Kerr, 1910), 65–82.

21. Ely, *French and German Socialism in Modern Times*, 28–29; Ely, "Competition, Its Nature, Its Permanency, and Its Beneficence," December 27, 1900, Speech in Detroit, Michigan; Ely, "Needs of the Day," *The Dawn* (May 1890), in Dombrowski, *The Early Days of Christian Socialism in America*, quote 55; Edward Bellamy, *Looking Backward, 2000–1887* (Boston: Houghton Mifflin, 1888).

22. Ely, *An Introduction to Political Economy*, 240–47, quote 245; Merle Curti and Vernon Cartensen, *The University of Wisconsin: A History, 1848–1925*, 2 vols. (Madison: University of Wisconsin Press, 1949), 1: 508–27.

23. Washington Gladden, *Applied Christianity: Moral Aspects of Social Questions* (Boston: Houghton Mifflin, 1886), 25–33; Gladden, *Working People and Their Employers* (New York: Funk and Wagnalls, 1894), 44–45.

24. Gladden, *Applied Christianity*, quotes 34–35; Richard T. Ely, ed., *A History of Cooperation in America* (Baltimore: Johns Hopkins University Press, 1888); Nicholas Paine Gilman, *Profit Sharing between Employer and Employee: A Study in the Evolution of the Wages System* (London: Macmillan, 1890); Gladden's thinking on

profit sharing was strongly influenced by Sedley Taylor, _Profit-Sharing Between Labor and Capital, Six Essays_ (New York: Humboldt, 1886).

25. Gladden, _Applied Christianity_, 53–101, quotes 98, 100.

26. Washington Gladden, _Tools and the Man: Property and Industry under the Christian Law_ (Boston: Houghton Mifflin, 1893), quotes 214, 124; discussion of cooperative ownership, 190–203.

27. Ibid., 130, 271.

28. Ibid., 264–65; closing quote in Washington Gladden, _Christianity and Socialism_ (New York: Eaton and Mains, 1905), 141.

29. John A. Ryan, _A Living Wage_ (New York: Macmillan, 1906; rev. ed., 1920), with an introduction by Richard T. Ely.

30. Gladden, _Christianity and Socialism_, 102–38, right to property statement, 92; Washington Gladden, _Social Facts and Forces_ (New York: G. P. Putnam's Sons, 1897), 80–86; Gladden, _Recollections_, 308–9; Gladden, _Tools and the Man_, 294–302, quotes 299, 300.

31. Gladden, _Social Facts and Forces_, 81–82; Gladden, _Recollections_, 305–8; see John L. Shover, "Washington Gladden and the Labor Question," _Ohio Historical Quarterly_ 68 (October 1959), 344–45.

32. Washington Gladden, _The Labor Question_ (Boston: Pilgrim Press, 1911), 3–55, 98–110, "steadily," 55; Gladden, _Recollections_, 305–8, "maintaining," 305.

33. W. D. P. Bliss, _Socialism in the Church of England_ (Boston: n.p., 1888); _The New Encyclopedia of Social Reform_, ed. Bliss, Rudolf M. Binder, and Edward P. Gaston (New York: Funk and Wagnall, 1908); Richard B. Dressner, "William Dwight Porter Bliss's Christian Socialism," _Church History_ 47 (March 1978), 66–68; Christopher L. Webber, "William Dwight Porter Bliss (1856–1926): Priest and Socialist," _Historical Magazine of the Protestant Episcopal Church_ 38 (March 1959), 9–39.

34. Laurence Gronlund, _The Co-operative Commonwealth in Its Outlines: An Exposition of Modern Socialism_, 2d ed. (1884; Boston: Lee and Shepard, 1890), viii.

35. "Declaration of Principles of the Society of Christian Socialists," _The Dawn_ 1 (May 15, 1889), quotes 1.

36. Vida Dutton Scudder, _On Journey_ (New York: E. P. Dutton, 1937), 15–30; Theresa Corcoran, _Vida Dutton Scudder_ (Boston: Twayne Publishers, 1982), 9–19; Arthur Mann, _Yankee Reformers in an Urban Age_ (Cambridge: Harvard University Press, 1954), 217–28; Peter J. Frederick, "Vida Dutton Scudder: The Professor as Social Activist," _New England Quarterly_ 43 (September 1970), 407–33; Elizabeth Hinson-Hasty, _Beyond the Social Maze: Exploring Vida Dutton Scudder's Theological Ethics_ (New York: T. and T. Clark, 2006), 7–15.

37. Vida D. Scudder, "Recollections of Ruskin," _Atlantic Monthly_ 85 (April 1900), 568–71, "portals," 568; Scudder, _On Journey_, 33–74; Derrick Lane, _Ruskin the Great Victorian_ (London: Routledge and Kegan Paul, 1969), 500–509, 540–44; John Ruskin, _Fors Clavigera_, 4 vols. (New York: J. Wiley and Sons, 1871); Ruskin, _Praeterita_ (New York: J. Wiley and Sons, 1886); Jon Abse, _John Ruskin: The Passionate Moralist_ (New York: Alfred Knopf, 1982).

38. Vida D. Scudder, "The Socialism of Christ," *The Dawn* 3 (December 18, 1890), 3–4; Scudder, "Socialism and Spiritual Progress—A Speculation," Address to the Society of Christian Socialists, March 1891, *Andover Review* 16 (July–December, 1891), 49–67, "we are" and "but there," 49; "I confess," 53.

39. Scudder, "Socialism and Spiritual Progress," "infesting," 58, "the uplift," 61, "it would," 62.

40. Vida D. Scudder, "The College Settlements Movement," *Smith College Monthly* (May 1900), 447–54; Scudder, "College Settlements and College Women," *Outlook* 70 (April 19, 1902), 973–76; Scudder, "The Place of College Settlements," *Andover Review* 18 (October 1892), 339–50; Scudder, "A Shadow of Gold," *Overland Monthly* (October 1887), 380–89; Scudder, "The Poetry of Matthew Arnold," *Andover Review* 10 (September 1888), 232–49; Scudder, "Arnold as an Abiding Force," *The Dial* 27 (December 16, 1899), 481–82; Scudder, "Democracy and Education," *Atlantic Monthly* 89 (June 1902), 816–22; Scudder, *The Life of the Spirit in the Modern English Poets* (Boston: Houghton Mifflin, 1895); Scudder, *Social Ideals in English Letters* (Boston: Houghton Mifflin, 1898), "will that," 275.

41. Scudder, *On Journey*, "the hope" and "was sunlight," 165; W. D. P. Bliss, "Profit-sharing a Capitalistic Dodge to Reduce Wages," quoted in "Comrade Bliss," *Workmen's Advocate* 6 (May 3, 1890), 1; Bliss, "The Single Tax," in *The New Encyclopedia of Social Reform*, 1250–55.

42. W. D. P. Bliss, "What Is Christian Socialism?" *The Dawn* (January and February 1890), reprinted as a Society of Christian Socialists pamphlet, *What Is Christian Socialism?* (1890), quotes 4.

43. *What Is Christian Socialism?*, "the deep" and "striving," 9; "he spoke," 15.

44. Ibid., "scientific," 18; "the expansion" and "the true," 21.

45. Ibid., "the coming," 32; "a nobler" and "we shall," 33; "the community," 38.

46. Ibid., "we must," 48.

47. W. D. P. Bliss, "The Church of the Carpenter and Thirty Years After," *Social Preparation for the Kingdom of God* 9 (January 1922), 12–13; Bliss, "Why Socialists Should Vote for Mr. Bryan," *American Fabian* 2 (October 1896), 1–11; Dressner, "William Dwight Porter Bliss's Christian Socialism," "needlessly," 74.

48. W. D. P. Bliss, "Self-Serving Colonies Condemned," *The Social Gospel* 2 (April 1899), "I have," 17.

49. W. D. P. Bliss, *A Handbook of Socialism* (London: Swan Sonnenschein; New York: Charles Scribner's, 1895); textbook, *The Encyclopedia of Social Reform* (New York: Funk and Wagnalls, 1897).

50. Dombrowski, *The Early Days of Christian Socialism in America*, "real governing" and "a symbol," 106; Bliss, "The Church of the Carpenter and Thirty Years After," 14–15; "General Treasurer Bliss's Lecture Trip," *The Christian Socialist* 8 (June 13, 1911), 3; Peter J. Frederick, *Knights of the Golden Rule: The Intellectual as Christian Social Reformer in the 1890s* (Lexington: University of Kentucky Press, 1976), 95; Hopkins, *The Rise of the Social Gospel*, 179.

51. Bliss, *A Handbook of Socialism*, "the only" and "Socialism is," 182.

52. Gompers, *Seventy Years of Life and Labor*, 1: 282–84; Salvatore, *Eugene V. Debs*, 114–32; Ginger, *The Bending Cross*, 108–20.

53. Eugene V. Debs, "Proclamation to the American Railway Union," June 1, 1895, in *Writings and Speeches of Eugene V. Debs*, 1–4; Leonard Painter, *Through Fifty Years with the Brotherhood of Railway Carmen of America* (Kansas City, MO: Brotherhood Railway Carmen of America, 1941), 50–59; F. Ruth Painter, *That Man Debs and His Work* (Bloomington: Indiana University Graduate Council, 1929), 16–17.

54. Almont Lindsey, *The Pullman Strike: The Story of a Unique Experiment and of a Great Labor Upheaval* (Chicago: University of Chicago Press, 1967), 115–54; William H. Carwardine, *The Pullman Strike* (Chicago: C. H. Kerr, for the Illinois Labor History Society, 1971), 41–83; Ginger, *The Bending Cross*, 114–20; Salvatore, *Eugene V. Debs*, 126–28; *Senate Executive Document 7*, 6–33. O. D. Boyle, *History of Railroad Strikes: A History of the Railroad Revolt of 1877, the American Railroad Union Strike on the Great Northern in 1894 and Its Participation in the Pullman Car Strikes of the Same Year, the Eight-Hour Strike of 1917 and the Runaway Switchmen's Strike of 1920* (Washington, DC: Brotherhood Publishing, 1935), 55–59.

55. Eugene V. Debs, "Labor Strikes and Their Lessons," in *Striking for Life*, ed. John Swinton (New York, 1894), "the crime," 324–25; Debs, "Proclamation to the American Railway Union," 2; Gompers, *Seventy Years of Life and Labor*, 1: 411–14; "Testimony of Samuel Gompers," *Senate Executive Document 7*, 192–93; Ginger, *The Bending Cross*, 128–51; Lindsey, *The Pullman Strike*, 225–27; Karsner, *Talks with Debs*, 60–61.

56. Gompers, *Seventy Years of Life and Labor*, "unions, pure" and "the way out," 1: 385.

57. Ibid., 411–13, "in favor" 412.

58. Henry Demarest Lloyd, *Wealth against Commonwealth* (New York: Harper and Brothers, 1894); Irving Stone, *Clarence Darrow for the Defense: A Biography* (Garden City: Doubleday, Doran, 1941).

59. Eugene V. Debs, "Liberty," Speech at Battery D., Chicago, November 22, 1895, in *Writings and Speeches of Eugene V. Debs*, 6–20, quotes 7, 8, 15, 20.

60. Eugene V. Debs, Letter to the American Railway Union, *Railway Times* (January 1, 1897), quote 1; Lawrence Goodwyn, *Democratic Promise: The Populist Movement in America* (New York: Oxford University Press, 1976), 520–25; Ginger, *The Bending Cross*, 187–91; Salvatore, *Eugene V. Debs*, 158–61.

61. Eugene V. Debs to Henry Demarest Lloyd, July 10, 1897, and January 7, 1899, Henry Demarest Lloyd Collection, Wisconsin State Historical Society, Madison; Chester M. Destler, *Henry Demarest Lloyd and the Empire of Reform* (Philadelphia: University of Pennsylvania Press, 1963), 381–82; Salvatore, *Eugene V. Debs*, 162–66; Ginger, *The Bending Cross*, 197–99.

62. J. A. Wayland, *Leaves of My Life: A Story of Twenty Years of Socialist Agitation* (Girard, KS: Appeal to Reason, 1912), 9–38, quote 27; Elliott Shore, *Talkin' Socialism: J. A. Wayland and the Role of the Press in American Radicalism, 1890–1912* (Lawrence: University Press of Kansas, 1988), 8–28; Howard H. Quint, "Julius A. Wayland, Pioneer Socialist Propagandist," *Mississippi Valley Historical Review* 35 (March 1949), 585–606; Quint, *The Forging of American Socialism: Origins of the American Movement* (Columbia: University of South Carolina Press, 1953), 192–99; George Allen England,

The Story of the Appeal (Girard, KS: Appeal to Reason, 1913); *Social Democracy Red Book*, 132–33.

63. Eugene V. Debs, "On Unity," *Social Democratic Herald* (January 20, 1900); Debs, "The Issue of Unity," *Social Democratic Herald* (April 21, 1900); Debs, "No Organic Unity Has Been Effected," *Social Democratic Herald* (July 21, 1900); Debs, "The Progress of the Social Revolution," *Social Democratic Herald* (December 1, 1900); Debs, "Outlook for Socialism in the United States," *International Socialist Review* 1 (September 1, 1900), quotes 130, 131; Morris Hillquit, *History of Socialism in the United States* (New York: Russell and Russell, 1910), 294–310; Quint, *The Forging of American Socialism*, 332–43.

64. Victor Berger, "How Will Socialism Come?" in Berger, *Broadsides* (Milwaukee: Social-Democratic, 1912), 25–30; Berger, "Socialism or Communism?" ibid., 35–39; Berger, "Down with the Senate," ibid., 43–54; Berger, "For Whom Is There Freedom?" ibid., 83–87; Berger, "A Socialist's View of the Single Tax," ibid., 126–31; Berger, "Labor Learns in the School of Experience," ibid., 159–65; Berger, "Abolish Parties? What For?" ibid., 187–92; Berger, "Do We Want Progress by Catastrophe and Bloodshed or by Common Sense?" ibid., 228–35; "How to Make the Change," ibid., 240–44; Morris Hillquit, *Loose Leaves from a Busy Life* (New York: Macmillan, 1934), "sublimely," 53; Sally M. Miller, *Victor L. Berger and the Promise of Constructive Socialism* (Westport, CT: Greenwood Press, 1973), 16–33; Miller, "Victor Louis Berger," *Historical Dictionary of the Progressive Era, 1890–1920* (Westport, CT: Greenwood Press, 1973), 28.

65. Eugene V. Debs, "The Western Labor Movement," *International Socialist Review* (November 1902), in Debs, *Writings and Speeches of Eugene V. Debs*, 54–63; McAlister Coleman, *Eugene V. Debs: A Man Unafraid* (New York: Greenberg, 1930), 219; Bell, *Marxian Socialism in the United States*, 64.

66. Eugene V. Debs, "Speech of Acceptance," *International Socialist Review* (May 1904), in Debs, *Writings and Speeches of Eugene V. Debs*, 73–76, "they would," 74; "Socialist Party of America Platform, 1904," https://medium.com/@reidkane/socialist-party-of-america-platform-1904-d6da4cad879e, "by which"; Debs, "How I Became a Socialist," *New York Comrade* (April 1902), in Debs, *Writings and Speeches of Eugene V. Debs*, 43–47; Quint, *The Forging of American Socialism*, 135–36.

67. Eugene V. Debs, "The Socialist Party and the Working Class," Speech in Indianapolis on September 1, 1904, in Debs, *Writings and Speeches of Eugene V. Debs*, 125–39, quotes 139.

68. Eugene V. Debs, "The American Movement," *Appeal to Reason* (1904), in Debs, *Writings and Speeches of Eugene V. Debs*, 76–95, quotes 76, 95, 94.

69. Eugene V. Debs, "Unionism and Socialism," *Appeal to Reason* (1904), in Debs, *Writings and Speeches of Eugene V. Debs*, 95–125, "fresh object," 106, Herron quote 112.

70. Debs, "Unionism and Socialism," quotes 122, 123, 125.

71. Gompers, *Seventy Years of Life and Labor*, quote 1: 397.

72. "Preamble to the IWW Constitution," http://www.iww.org/en/culture/official; Eugene V. Debs, letter to the *Social Democratic Herald*, in Ginger, *The Bending Cross*, quotes

240; Debs, "The Coming Labor Union," *Miners' Magazine* 7 (October 26, 1905), 13; Melvyn Dubofsky, *We Shall Be All: A History of the Industrial Workers of the World* (New York: Quadrangle, 1969), 91–109; Ginger, *The Bending Cross*, 238–44; A. M. Simons, "IWW," *International Socialist Review* 6 (August 1905), 76–77.

73. Ginger, *The Bending Cross*, quote 244.

74. Oscar Ameringer, *If You Don't Weaken: The Autobiography of Oscar Ameringer* (New York: Henry Holt, 1940), quote 233–34.

75. "Constitution of the Christian Socialist Fellowship," *The Christian Socialist* 3 (July 1, 1906), "to permeate," 41; Robert T. Handy, "Christianity and Socialism in America, 1900–1920," *Church History* 21 (March 1952), 39–54; John Spargo, "Christian Socialism in America," *American Journal of Sociology* 15 (July 1909), 16–20; Eliot White, "The Christian Socialist Fellowship," *The Arena* 41 (January 1909), 47–52.

76. W. D. P. Bliss, "The Gospel for Today," Speech to the Founding Conference of the Christian Socialist Fellowship, *The Christian Socialist* 3 (July 1, 1906), 5–8, "I do not," 8.

77. Debs quoted in *New York Herald* (June 1, 1908), cited in Handy, "Christianity and Socialism in America," "I am glad," 50; Hopkins, *The Rise of the Social Gospel*, 237–38.

78. W. D. P. Bliss, "The Social Faith of the Holy Catholic Church," *The Christian Socialist* 8 (November 19, 1911), 9–12; Dressner, "William Dwight Porter Bliss's Christian Socialism," 79–80.

79. Scudder, *On Journey*, 175–82, "I hated," 178, "I was," 179; Vida Scudder, *A Listener in Babel: Being a Series of Imaginary Conversations* (Boston: Houghton Mifflin, 1903); Vida Scudder to Walter Rauschenbusch, October 9, 1912, Rauschenbusch Family Collection, "do you" and "I never"; "Miss Scudder's Criticized Speech: Just What She Said at a Citizens' Meeting in Lawrence, to Which Exception Has Been So Excitedly Taken by the Brahmins," *Boston Common* (March 9, 1912), 7. This section adapts material from Gary Dorrien, *The Making of American Liberal Theology: Idealism, Realism, and Modernity* (Louisville: Westminster John Knox, 2003), 135–37.

80. Vida Scudder to Walter Rauschenbusch, September 21, 1912, Rauschenbusch Family Collection.

81. Vida Scudder to Walter Rauschenbusch, August 8, 1911, "you make me" and "I know many"; Scudder to Rauschenbusch, September 21, 1912, "There is also."

82. Vida D. Scudder, "Christianity in the Socialist State," *The Hibbert Journal* 8 (April 1910), 562–81, "must we not," 567; Scudder, "Religion and Socialism," *Harvard Theological Review* 3 (April 1910), 230–47; Scudder, "Why Doesn't the Church Turn Socialist?" *The Coming Nation* (March 29, 1913), 9–10; Scudder, "Socialism as the Basis of Religious Unity," *The Unity of Life*, ed. Henry W. Wilbur (Philadelphia: National Association of Religious Liberals, 1911).

83. Vida D. Scudder, *Socialism and Character* (Boston: Houghton Mifflin, 1912), "timid," vi, "moral," 4, "class-conscious" and "the spiritual," 5–6.

84. Ibid., "in horror," 279, "dangerous," 145.

85. Ibid., "to look," 167, "patriotism," 171; Herbert Croly, *The Promise of American Life* (1909; repr., Boston: Northeastern University Press, 1989), 210–11.

86. Scudder, *Socialism and Character*, "we can hardly" and "but the," 400.
87. Scudder, *On Journey*, "I suppose," 191, "something like," 279; Vida D. Scudder, "Some Signs of Hope," *The Intercollegiate Socialist* 3 (April–May 1915), 6–8; Scudder, *The Church and the Hour: Reflections of a Socialist Churchwoman* (New York: E. P. Dutton, 1917), 40–73, 95–102.
88. Hillquit, *Loose Leaves from a Busy Life*, "overwhelmingly," 70; Weinstein, *The Decline of Socialism in America*, 24.
89. George D. Herron, "At the Shrine of Mazzini," *Kingdom* 10 (February 24, 1898), 379; Charles Beardsley, "Professor Herron: A Character Sketch," *Arena* 15 (April 1896), 784–96, "in the company," 786; W. H. Denison, "Professor George D. Herron, D.D.—A Sketch of His Life and Character," *The Social Gospel* 1 (July 1898), 18; Hopkins, *The Rise of the Social Gospel*, 185; Robert T. Handy, "The Influence of Mazzini on the American Social Gospel," *Journal of Religion* 29 (April 1949), 118; Handy, "George D. Herron and the Social Gospel in American Protestantism, 1890–1901," PhD diss., University of Chicago, 1849, 7–15.
90. George D. Herron, "The Message of Jesus to Men of Wealth," *Christian Union* 42 (1890), 804–5, reprinted, Herron, *The Message of Jesus to Men of Wealth* (New York: Fleming H. Revell, 1891); Herron, *The Larger Christ* (Chicago: Revell, 1891); Herron, *The Call of the Cross: Four College Sermons* (Chicago: Revell, 1892); Herron, *A Plea for the Gospel* (Boston: Thomas Y. Crowell, 1892).
91. Herron, *The Larger Christ*, "a selfish," 25; "for it is," 26; "the cross is," 25–26.
92. Ibid., "to be fully," 30; "is the sign" and "must be," 33.
93. Ibid., "except the state," 37.
94. Ibid., "for God," 51; "a love," 70.
95. Josiah Strong, Introduction to *The Larger Christ*, quotes 9, 10; Handy, "George D. Herron and the Social Gospel in American Protestantism," 57–64.
96. George D. Herron, *The Christian Society* (Chicago: Fleming H. Revell, 1894), "I am haunted," 9; Herron, "The Opportunity of the Church," *Arena* 15 (December 1895), 42–45; Herron, *A Plea for the Gospel*, 33–41.
97. George D. Herron, *The New Redemption: A Call to the Church to Reconstruct Society According to the Gospel of Christ* (Boston: Thomas Y. Crowell, 1893), "the impulses," 15.
98. Ibid., "a great" and "the selfishness," 20; "the state," 29–30.
99. Ibid., "the practicability," 56; "there is no," 143.
100. Ibid., "shuts God out," 32; "it is," 62–63; "to look," 97–98.
101. George D. Herron, *The Christian State: A Political Vision of Christ* (New York: Thomas Y. Crowell, 1895), 36–55.
102. Ibid., "the evil," 56; "the mind," 59; "morally" and "unspiritual," 65.
103. Ibid., "parasites," 77; "a true," 88; George D. Herron, "The Quality of Revolution," *The Social Gospel* 1 (June 1898), 8.
104. Herron, *The Christian State*, "the guardianship," 106; George D. Herron, "The Social System and the Christian Conscience," *The Kingdom* 10 (June 1898), "the only ground," 827; Herron, *Why I Am a Socialist*, Address to the Social Democratic Party,

Central Music Hall, Chicago, September 29, 1900, Pocket Library of Socialism pamphlet Number 20 (Chicago: Charles H. Kerr, 1900), "But before," 1.

105. Handy, "George D. Herron and the Social Gospel," 91–99, 133–43; George D. Herron, *Between Caesar and Jesus* (Boston: Thomas Y. Crowell, 1899), 22–28; Herron, *A Confession of Social Faith: An Address Before the Chicago Single Tax Club*, pamphlet (Chicago: Chicago Single Tax Club, 1899).

106. George D. Herron, "American Imperialism: An Address," Address to the National Christian Citizenship League, April 12, 1899, *The Social Forum* (June 1, 1899), "never in history," 3; "without the imperialism," 4; "a worthy," 8; "the American," 10.

107. Ibid., "American," 15; "corporate anarchists," 16; "I love," 17; "forgive," 18.

108. Herron, *Why I Am a Socialist*, "sharing," 1; Josiah Strong, *Expansion, under New World-Conditions* (New York: Baker and Taylor, 1900), 280–81; editorial, *The Outlook* 70 (July 29, 1899), 699; Lyman Abbott, *The Rights of Man: A Study in Twentieth-Century Problems* (Boston: Houghton Mifflin, 1901), 274; Graham Taylor, "Social Under-Tow of the War," *The Commons* 3 (June 1898), 5–6; Taylor, "Social 'Overflow' of the War," *The Commons* 3 (August 1898), 2–3; Washington Gladden, "The Issues of the War," *The Outlook* 59 (July 16, 1898), 673–75; Winthrop S. Hudson, "Protestant Clergy Debate the Nation's Vocation, 1898–1899," *Church History* 42 (1973), 110–18; Robert T. Handy, *A Christian America: Protestant Hopes and Historical Realities*, 2d ed. (New York: Oxford University Press, 1984), 243.

109. Herron, *Why I Am a Socialist*, "sectarian" and "they were," 2.

110. Ibid., "wide," 2; "It would be" and "My place," 3.

111. Ibid., "childish," 4; "the capitalistic," 5; "the commonwealth," 7.

112. Ibid., "in its essence," 9.

113. George D. Herron, "The New Religious Movement," *The Kingdom* 11 (April 20, 1899), 485; Herron and C. B. Patterson, "The New Social Apostolate," *Arena* 25 (May 1901), 490–91.

114. George D. Herron, "Letter to Grinnell Church Committee," *The Social Crusader* 3 (June 1901), 18–24. Dombrowski confused many readers by construing the entire divorce episode as having happened in 1891, and Hopkins, still too embarrassed in 1940 to recount what happened, gave it a terse, one-paragraph summary with a spot-on final sentence: "Such was the tragic end of the most brilliant episode in social-gospel history." Dombrowski, *The Early Days of Christian Socialism in America*, 172–73; Hopkins, *The Rise of the Social Gospel*, "such," 200.

115. Handy, "George D. Herron and the Social Gospel," 21–23, "despicable," 21; William Allen White, *The Autobiography of William Allen White* (New York: Macmillan, 1946), 561; George D. Herron, Address to the Socialist Party Unity Convention, *The Social Crusader* 3 (August 1901), "Socialist unity," 2; Frederick, *Knights of the Golden Rule*, 174–75.

116. Quint, *The Forging of American Socialism*, 140–41; Handy, "George D. Herron and the Social Gospel," 170; Frederick, *Knights of the Golden Rule*, 177.

117. George D. Herron, *The Menace of Peace* (New York: M. Kennerley, 1917); Herron, *Woodrow Wilson and the World's Peace* (New York: M. Kennerley, 1917); Herron, *Germanism and the American Crusade* (New York: M. Kennerley, 1918); Herron, *The*

Greater War (New York: M. Kennerley, 1919); Herron, *The Defeat in the Victory* (London: C. Palmer, 1921); Herron, *The Revival of Italy* (London: Allen and Unwin, 1922); Frederick, *Knights of the Golden Rule,* "one of," 182.

118. Dubofsky, *We Shall Be All,* 96–109; Ginger, *The Bending Cross,* 244–56.

119. Max Hayes, "The World of Labor," *International Socialist Review* 8 (June 1908), 788–91; Salvatore, *Eugene V. Debs,* 221–23; Ginger, *The Bending Cross,* 266–67.

120. Eugene V. Debs, "The Issue," Speech on May 23, 1908, in Girard, Kansas, *Writings and Speeches of Eugene V. Debs,* 293–310, quote 298.

121. Lincoln Steffens, "Eugene V. Debs on What the Matter Is in America and What to Do About It," *Everybody's Magazine* (October 1908), http://www.weneverforget.org/hellraisers-journal-lincoln-steffens-interviews-eugene-debs-labor-agitator-the-keeper-of-the-socialist-heaven/.

122. Eugene V. Debs, "Railroad Employees and Socialism," *International Socialist Review* (October 1908), *Writings and Speeches of Eugene V. Debs,* 311–17, "for both," 317; Debs, "The Socialist Party's Appeal," *Independent* (July–December, 1908), Debs, *Writings and Speeches of Eugene V. Debs,* 317–23, "no middle," "sporadic," and "ludicrous," 322.

123. Eugene V. Debs to William English Walling, December 7, 1909, *Writings and Speeches of Eugene V. Debs,* 326; Seymour Martin Lipset and Gary Marks, *It Didn't Happen Here: Why Socialism Failed in the United States* (New York: W. W. Norton, 2000), 174.

124. William English Walling, *Russia's Message: The True World Import of the Revolution* (New York: Doubleday, Page, 1908); Richard Schneirov, "The Odyssey of William English Walling: Revisionism, Social Democracy, and Evolutionary Pragmatism," *The Journal of the Gilded Age and Progressive Era* 2 (October 2003), 403–30; James Boylan, *Revolutionary Lives: Anna Strunsky and William English Walling* (Amherst: University of Massachusetts Press, 1998); Debs to Walling, "if the trimmers," 296; Eugene Debs to the Socialist Party of America, May 1910, *International Socialist Review* (July 1910), *Writings and Speeches of Eugene V. Debs,* 326–28, "utterly unsocialistic," 326, "bourgeois," "such," "swept," and "barring," 327.

125. William English Walling, "Laborism versus Socialism," *International Socialist Review* 9 (March 1909), 683–89; Robert Hunter, "The British Labour Party: A Reply," ibid. (April 1909), 753–64; Salvatore, *Eugene V. Debs,* "disgraceful," 245; Eugene V. Debs, "A Letter from Debs," *International Socialist Review* 10 (January 1910), "has already," 609; Debs, "Danger Ahead," *International Socialist Review* (January 1911), Debs, *Writings and Speeches of Eugene V. Debs,* 333–36, "but only," 334–35; "deadly hostile" and "is not," 335; David Shannon, *The Socialist Party of America: A History* (New York: Macmillan, 1955), 63–66; Robert D. Reynolds, "The Millionaire Socialists: J. G. Phelps Stokes and His Circle of Friends," PhD diss., University of South Carolina, 1953, 210.

126. Dubofsky, *We Shall Be All,* 227–62, "Wobblies had," 260.

127. Eugene V. Debs, "Sound Socialist Tactics," *International Socialist Review* 12 (February 1912), 481–86, in Debs, *Writings and Speeches of Eugene V. Debs,* 350–57, "butting," 351; "no amount," "sabotage repels," and "place itself," 353.

128. "The National Socialist Convention of 1912," *International Socialist Review* (June 1912), 808; *Proceedings of the National Congress of the Socialist Party, 1912*, 195.

129. Kipnis, *The American Socialist Movement*, 400–404; Shannon, *The Socialist Party of America*, 84–86; Bell, *Marxian Socialism in the United States*, 74–75; Ross, *The Socialist Party of America*, 130–31.

130. Eugene V. Debs, "This Is Our Year," *International Socialist Review* 13 (July 1912), quotes 17; Salvatore, *Eugene V. Debs*, 254–55.

131. Eugene V. Debs, "Speech of Acceptance," *International Socialist Review* 13 (October 1912), in Debs, *Writings and Speeches of Eugene V. Debs*, 361–66, "lavishly," 363; "capitalism is rushing" and "in a land," 365.

132. Eugene V. Debs, "The Party Builder," (August 9, 1913); "Debs Denounces Critics," *International Socialist Review* 14 (August 1913), 105; Debs, "A Plea for Solidarity," *International Socialist Review* 14 (March 1914), 538; Paul Buhle, "Debsian Socialism and the 'New Immigrant' Workers," in *Insights and Parallels: Problems and Issues of American Social History*, ed. William L. O'Neill (Minneapolis: University of Minnesota Press, 1973), 263–64; Salvatore, *Eugene V. Debs*, 256–57; Weinstein, *The Decline of Socialism in America*, 341

3. SOCIALISM IS NOT ENOUGH

1. "George Washington Woodbey," *Who's Who of the Colored Race*, ed. Frank Lincoln Mather (Chicago: Memento Edition, Half-Century Anniversary of Negro Freedom in U.S., 1915), 290–91; Edward Bellamy, *Looking Backward: 2000–1887* (Boston: Houghton Mifflin, 1888); Philip S. Foner, *American Socialism and Black Americans: From the Age of Jackson to World War II* (Westport, CT: Greenwood Press, 1977), 45–60, 151–52; Foner, "Reverend George Washington Woodbey: Early Twentieth Century California Black Socialist," *Journal of Negro History* 61 (April 1976), 136–57. This section on Woodbey adapts material from Gary Dorrien, *The New Abolition: W. E. B. Du Bois and the Black Social Gospel* (New Haven: Yale University Press, 2015), 458–82.

2. A. W. Ricker, *Appeal to Reason* (October 31, 1903), in Foner, *American Socialism and Black Americans*, 152.

3. *Los Angeles Socialist* (July 12, 1902), in Foner, *American Socialism and Black Americans*, 153; Joe Hill to E. W. Vanderleith, n.d., in Melvyn Dubofsky, *We Shall Be All: A History of the Industrial Workers of the World* (New York: Quadrangle, 1969), 190.

4. *Common Sense* (October 27, 1906), "well-known," and *Los Angeles Socialist* (May 2, 1903), "he has," "there is," in Foner, *American Socialism and Black Americans*, 153–54.

5. "Battery Charge," *San Diegan-Sun* (July 11, 1905), in Foner, *American Socialism and Black Americans*, 154.

6. A. W. Ricker, *Appeal to Reason* (October 31, 1903); George Washington Woodbey, *What to Do and How to Do It, or, Socialism vs. Capitalism* (1903), reprinted in George W. Woodbey, *Black Socialist Preacher*, ed. Philip S. Foner (San Francisco: Synthesis Publications, 1983), quote 40.

7. Woodbey, *What to Do and How to Do It, or, Socialism vs. Capitalism*, quote 43.

8. Ibid., quotes 48.

9. Ibid., 79–80.

10. Ibid., 82–83.

11. George Washington Woodbey, *The Bible and Socialism* (1904), in Woodbey, *Black Socialist Preacher*, quotes 91, 92.

12. Ibid., 102.

13. Ibid., 105.

14. Ibid., 117.

15. Ibid., 133.

16. Ibid., 145.

17. Morris Hillquit, *History of Socialism in the United States* (New York: Funk and Wagnalls, 1910), 309–10; "Comrade Debs Is Pleased," *The Worker* (August 11, 1901); Eugene V. Debs, "The Socialist Movement in America," *Social Democratic Herald* (April 26, 1902); Ira Kipnis, *The American Socialist Movement, 1897–1912* (New York: Columbia University Press, 1952), 105–6.

18. Charles H. Vail, "The Negro Problem," *International Socialist Review* 1 (February 1901), 464–70; "The Negro Resolution," *International Socialist Review* 5 (January 1905), 192–93; Foner, *American Socialism and Black Americans*, 94–98; Sally M. Miller, "The Socialist Party and the Negro, 1901–1920," *Journal of Negro History* 56 (July 1971), 220–29; Howard H. Quint, *The Forging of American Socialism: Origins of the Modern Movement* (Columbia: University of South Carolina Press, 1953), 42–43; James Dombrowski, *The Early Days of Christian Socialism in America* (New York: Columbia University Press, 1936), 187–90; Laurence R. Moore, "Flawed Fraternity: American Socialist Response to the Negro, 1901–1912," *Historian* 32 (November 1969), 1–18.

19. Editorial, *The Colored American* (August 18, 1901), quotes; Foner, *American Socialism and Black Americans*, 100; *Appeal to Reason* (August 17, 1901).

20. Charles L. Wood to *The Colored American*, September 14, 1901, September 28, 1901, and October 26, 1901, in Foner, *American Socialism and Black Americans*, 101–2.

21. Eugene V. Debs, "The Negro in the Class Struggle," *International Socialist Review* (November 1903), reprinted in Debs, *Writings and Speeches of Eugene V. Debs*, ed. Joseph M. Bernstein (New York: Hermitage Press, 1948), quotes 64, 65, 66.

22. Eugene V. Debs, "The Negro and His Nemesis," *International Socialist Review* (January 1904), in *Writings and Speeches of Eugene V. Debs*, quotes 68, 69.

23. "1904 Socialist Party Convention," *International Socialist Review* 4 (May 1904), 686–87.

24. *Proceedings, National Convention of the Socialist Party, Held at Chicago, Illinois, May 10–17, 1908*, Chicago, 1908, quotes 208–9, in George W. Woodbey, "Remarks of Rev. Woodbey at the 1908 Socialist Party Convention," Woodbey, *Black Socialist Preacher*, 243.

25. Morris Hillquit, "Immigration in the United States," *International Socialist Review* 8 (August 1907), 65–75; Sally M. Miller, "For White Men Only: The Socialist Party of America and Issues of Gender, Ethnicity and Race," *Journal of the Gilded Age and*

Progressive Era 2 (July 2003), 295; Victor Berger, "The Misfortunes of the Negroes," *Social Democratic Herald* (May 31, 1902).

26. Socialist Party, *Proceedings, National Convention of the Socialist Party, Held at Chicago, Illinois, May 10–17, 1908,* Chicago, 1908, 106–21; Cameron H. King Jr., "Asiatic Exclusion," *International Socialist Review* 8 (May 1908), 61–69; Bruce Rogers, "Our Asiatic Fellows," *International Socialist Review* 15 (April 1915), 626; Miller, "For White Men Only: The Socialist Party of America and Issues of Gender, Ethnicity and Race," 295–96; Kipnis, *The American Socialist Movement,* 279–88.

27. *Proceedings, National Convention of the Socialist Party, Held at Chicago, Illinois, May 10–17, 1908,* Chicago, 1908, quotes 106; Woodbey, "Remarks of Rev. Woodbey at the 1908 Socialist Party Convention," Woodbey, *Black Socialist Preacher,* 244.

28. Sally M. Miller, *Victor L. Berger and the Promise of Constructive Socialism, 1910–1920* (Westport, CT: Greenwood Press, 1973); Marvin Wachman, *History of the Social Democratic Party of Milwaukee, 1897–1910* (Urbana: University of Illinois Press, 1945); Victor L. Berger, *Voice and Pen of Victor L. Berger: Congressional Speeches and Editorials* (Milwaukee: Milwaukee Leader, 1929).

29. George W. Woodbey, "Why the Negro Should Vote the Socialist Ticket," Socialist Party Leaflet, 1908, in Woodbey, *Black Socialist Preacher,* 252–53.

30. Ibid., 254.

31. George W. Woodbey, "Socialist Agitation," *Chicago Daily Socialist* (January 3, 1909), in Woodbey, *Black Socialist Preacher,* "a fire," 245; Foner, *American Socialism and Black Americans,* "loosened," 170.

32. George W. Woodbey, "The New Emancipation," *Chicago Daily Socialist* (January 18, 1909), in Woodbey, *Black Socialist Preacher,* 245–46.

33. *Chicago Daily Socialist* (May 11, 1908), "the police," in Foner, *American Socialism and Black Americans,* 169–70; Woodbey, "The New Emancipation," "the agitation," 249; Dubofsky, *We Shall Be All: A History of the Industrial Workers of the World,* 91–109, 120–70; Ray Ginger, *The Bending Cross: A Biography of Eugene Victor Debs* (New Brunswick, NJ: Rutgers University Press, 1949), 238–58; A. M. Simons, "IWW," *International Socialist Review* 6 (August 1905), 76–77.

34. Mark Naison, *Communists in Harlem During the Depression* (Urbana: University of Illinois Press, 1983), 4; Miller, "For White Men Only: The Socialist Party of America and Issues of Gender, Ethnicity and Race," 297–98; George W. Slater Jr., "Negroes Becoming Socialists," *Chicago Daily Socialist* (September 15, 1908); Slater, "Booker T. Washington's Error," *Chicago Daily Socialist* (September 22, 1908), reprinted in *Black Socialist Preacher,* 299–301, 302–4.

35. Grace L. Miller, "The IWW Free Speech Fight: San Diego, 1912," *Southern California Quarterly* 54 (1972), 211–38; Dubofsky, *We Shall Be All: A History of the Industrial Workers of the World,* 189–97; Foner, *American Socialism and Black Americans,* 171–72; Rosalie Shanks, "The IWW Free Speech Movement: San Diego, 1912," *Journal of San Diego History* 19 (Winter 1973), 25–33.

36. George W. Woodbey, "Why the Socialists Must Reach the Churches with Their Message," *The Christian Socialist* (February 1915), in *Black Socialist Preacher,* quote 261. For brief accounts of Woodbey's career, see Robert H. Craig, *Religion and Radical*

Politics: An Alternative Christian Tradition in the United States (Philadelphia: Temple University Press, 1992), 116–20; Allen Dwight Callahan, "Remembering Nehemiah: A Note on Biblical Theology," in *Black Zion: African American Religious Encounters with Zionism*, ed. Yvonne Chireau and Nathaniel Deutsch (New York: Oxford University Press, 2000), 161–62; Juan M. Floyd-Thomas, *The Origins of Black Humanism in America: Reverend Ethelred Brown and the Unitarian Church* (New York: Palgrave Macmillan, 2008), 105–6; Winston A. James, "Being Black and Red in Jim Crow America: Notes on the Ideology and Travails of Afro-America's Socialist Pioneers, 1877–1930," *Souls* 1 (Fall 1999), 47–48.

37. Jeffrey B. Perry, *Hubert Henry Harrison: The Voice of Harlem Radicalism, 1882–1918* (New York: Columbia University Press, 2008); Richard B. Moore, "Harrison, Hubert Henry," *Dictionary of American Negro Biography*, 292–93.

38. Hubert Henry Harrison, "How to Do It—And How Not," *New York Call* (December 16, 1911), reprinted in Harrison, *A Hubert Harrison Reader*, ed. Jeffrey B. Perry (Middletown, CT: Wesleyan University Press, 2001), 60.

39. Ibid., 61.

40. Ibid., 61–62.

41. George W. Slater Jr., "The New Abolitionists," *Chicago Daily Socialist* (January 4, 1909); Slater, "How and Why I Became a Socialist," *Chicago Daily Socialist* (September 8, 1908), "purity" and "the solution," 298; Slater, "Abraham Lincoln a Socialist," *Chicago Daily Socialist* (October 6, 1908); Eugene Debs to *Chicago Daily Socialist* (January 4, 1909), "a fine," 336; in *Black Socialist Preacher*, 334–35, 296–98, 309–11, 336.

42. George W. Slater Jr., "The Negro and Socialism," *The Christian Socialist* (July 1, 1913), in *Black Socialist Preacher*, 346.

43. Sally M. Miller, "Women in the Party Bureaucracy: Subservient Functionaries," in *Flawed Liberation: Socialism and Feminism*, ed. Sally M. Miller (Westport, CT: Greenwood Press, 1981), 13–35; Neil K. Basen, "The 'Jennie Higginses' of the 'New South in the West': A Regional Survey of Socialist Activists, Agitators, and Organizers, 1901–1917," in *Flawed Liberation*, 87–112.

44. Socialist Party, *Proceedings of the 1908 National Convention* (Chicago: Socialist Party, 1908), 302; May Wood Simons, "Aims and Purposes of Women Committee," *Progressive Woman* 3 (October 1909), 2; Gretchen and Kent Kreuter, "May Wood Simons: Party Theorist," in *Flawed Liberation*, 37–60.

45. Lena Morrow Lewis, "Experiences of a Socialist Propagandist," *Common Sense* (April 1, 1905); Mary Jo Buhle, *Women and American Socialism, 1870–1920* (Urbana: University of Illinois Press, 1981), 162–63; John W. Leonard, "Lena Morrow Lewis," in *Woman's Who's Who of America: A Biographical Dictionary of Contemporary Women of the United States and Canada* (New York: American Commonwealth Company, 1914), 489; Frances Willard, *Glimpses of Fifty Years* (Chicago: Woman's Temperance Publishing Association, 1889), 470–77; *Let Something Good Be Said: Speeches and Writings of Frances E. Willard*, ed. Carolyn De Swarte Gifford and Amy R. Slagell (Urbana: University of Illinois Press, 2007); Ruth B. Bordin, *Frances Willard: A Biography* (Chapel Hill: University of North Carolina Press, 1986).

46. Lena Morrow, "Alumni et Alumnae," *The Annex* 3 (November 11, 1892), 11–12; Mary Jo Buhle, "Lena Morrow Lewis: Her Rise and Fall," *Flawed Liberation*, 64–65.

47. Lewis, "Experiences of a Socialist Propagandist"; Buhle, *Women and American Socialism*, 163–64; Buhle, "Lena Morrow Lewis," 67; Ethel Lloyd Patterson, "Lena Morrow Lewis: Agitator," *Masses* 1 (July 1911), 13.

48. Lewis, "Experiences of a Socialist Propagandist"; Buhle, *Women and American Socialism*, 163–64; Buhle, "Lena Morrow Lewis," 67; Patterson, "Lena Morrow Lewis: Agitator," 13. Lena Morrow Lewis, "Woman Suffragists and Woman Suffragists," *Socialist Woman* 1 (February 1908), 3; Lewis, "The Woman Suffrage Movement," *Progressive Woman* 4 (March 1911), 4; Buhle, *Women and Socialism*, quote 162.

49. Lewis, "Experiences of a Socialist Propagandist," quotes; Lena Morrow Lewis, "Woman's Day," *New York Call* (February 27, 1910).

50. Lena Morrow Lewis, "The Sex and Woman Questions," *Masses* 1 (December 1911), quotes 7.

51. Patterson, "Lena Morrow Lewis: Agitator," "the price" and "to be," 13; Lena Morrow Lewis, "The Materialist Basis of Education," *Masses* (March 1912), "that which."

52. "Barnes Forced to Resign," *Christian Socialist* (August 17, 1911); "National Executive Committee's Great Contortion Act," *Christian Socialist* (August 31, 1911); Buhle, "Lena Morrow Lewis," 80.

53. Buhle, *Women and American Socialism*, 166; Buhle, "Lena Morrow Lewis," 77; Mary E. Marcy, "Efficiency the Test," *New York Call* (May 8, 1910); Anita Block, "A Reply to Mary E. Marcy," *New York Call* (May 15, 1910).

54. Sally M. Miller, "Other Socialists: Native-born and Immigrant Women in the Socialist Party of America, 1901–1917," *Labor History* 24 (Winter 1983), 84–102; Miller, "For White Men Only: The Socialist Party of America and Issues of Gender, Ethnicity and Race," 288–91; Charles Leinenweber, "The American Socialist Party and 'New' Immigrants," *Science and Society* 32 (Winter 1968), 2–25; Kipnis, *The American Socialist Movement, 1897–1912*, 272–88; "A Letter from Japanese Socialists to Their Comrades in the United States," *Socialist Party Weekly Bulletin* (January 19, 1907).

55. Kate Richards O'Hare, "How I Became a Socialist Agitator," *Socialist Woman* (October 1908), 4; O'Hare, *Kate O'Hare's Prison Letters* (Girard, KS: Appeal to Reason, 1919), 21–23; Sally M. Miller, *From Prairie to Prison: The Life of Social Activist Kate Richards O'Hare* (Columbia: University of Missouri Press, 1993), 4–14.

56. O'Hare, "How I Became a Socialist Agitator," 4.

57. Ibid., 4–5; Ignatius Donnelly, *Caesar's Column*; Miller, *From Prairie to Prison*, 15–19.

58. O'Hare, "How I Became a Socialist Agitator," 5.

59. Kate Richards O'Hare, "The Girl Who Would," *Wilshire's Magazine* (January 1903), 27–29; Miller, *From Prairie to Prison*, 26–27.

60. Miller, *From Prairie to Prison*, quote 49.

61. Kate Richards O'Hare, "The Leaven Doing Its Work," *National Rip-Saw* (March 1913), 3–12, in O'Hare, *Kate Richards O'Hare: Selected Writings and Speeches*, ed. Philip S. Foner and Sally M. Miller (Baton Rouge: Louisiana State University Press, 1982), 56–62, "many other" and "convict," 60, 61; O'Hare, "The Wages of Women," *National Rip-Saw* (July 1913), 2, 6–9, in *Kate Richards O'Hare*, 63–70, "they all," 65.

62. Kate Richards O'Hare, *"Nigger" Equality*, pamphlet (St. Louis: *National Rip-Saw*, 1912), in *Kate Richards O'Hare*, 44–49, "the stinging," 44; "put the," 45; "we Socialists," 46; "I neither," 48."

63. Ibid., "well and," 48.

64. Kate Richards O'Hare, "Drink, Its Cause and Cure," *National Rip-Saw* (September 1913), 3, 6, in *Kate Richards O'Hare*, 78–85, quotes 79.

65. Kate Richards O'Hare, "Blame It On God," *National Rip-Saw* (February 1916), 18–19.

66. Kate Richards O'Hare, "The Tale of a Rib," *National Rip-Saw* (February 1917), 5, in *Kate Richards O'Hare*, 114–18, quotes 118.

67. This section on Du Bois adapts material from Dorrien, *The New Abolition*, 233–48.

68. W. E. B. Du Bois, "Socialist of the Path" and "The Negro and Socialism," *Horizon* 1 (February 1907), 3–4, 6–10; in Du Bois, *Selections from the Horizon*, 5–7, quotes 6; Mary White Ovington to W. E. B. Du Bois, June 10, 1904, *The Correspondence of W. E. B. Du Bois*, 1: 76–77; Mary White Ovington, *Half a Man: The Status of the Negro in New York* (New York: Longmans, Green, 1911); Ovington, *The Walls Came Tumbling Down* (New York: Harcourt, Brace, 1947), 13–54; R. Stannard Baker, *Following the Color Line: An Account of Negro Citizenship in the American Democracy* (London: Forgotten Books, 2015).

69. William English Walling, "The Race War in the North," *Independent* 63 (September 3, 1908), 529–34, quotes 531, 534; Walling, *Socialism As It Is: A Survey of the World-wide Revolutionary Movement* (New York: Macmillan, 1912); Walling, *The Larger Aspects of Socialism* (New York: Macmillan, 1913).

70. Edgar Gardner Murphy to Oswald Garrison Villard, May 2, 1903; May 29, 1903; and June 10, 1903, Oswald Garrison Villard Papers, Houghton Library, Harvard University; Villard to Murphy, February 23, 1906, Villard Papers; Mary White Ovington to Oswald Garrison Villard, October 8, 1906, Villard Papers; Villard, Speech to the Afro-American Council, October 10, 1906, in *Colored American Magazine*, undated clipping, Villard Papers; Mary White Ovington, "Reminiscences," *Baltimore Afro-American* (November 26, 1932), 24–26, reprinted as "The NAACP Begins," in Ovington, *Black and White Sit Down Together: The Reminiscences of an NAACP Founder* (New York: The Feminist Press, 1995), 56–60; Ovington, *The Walls Came Tumbling Down* (New York: Harcourt, Brace, 1947), 103–4; James M. McPherson, *The Abolitionist Legacy: From Reconstruction to the NAACP* (Princeton: Princeton University Press, 1975), 374–88; Patricia Sullivan, *Lift Every Voice: The NAACP and the Making of the Civil Rights Movement* (New York: New Press 2009), 4–5.

71. Oswald Garrison Villard, *Fighting Years: Memoirs of a Liberal Editor* (New York: Harcourt, Brace, 1939), 192; Mary White Ovington, *How the National Association for the Advancement of Colored People Began*, pamphlet (New York: NAACP, 1914), 1; Charles Flint Kellogg, *NAACP: A History of the National Association for the Advancement of Colored People* (Baltimore: Johns Hopkins University Press, 1967), 11–13; Villard, "The Call," Appendix A, in Kellogg, *NAACP: A History of the National Association for the Advancement of Colored People*, 298; Ovington, *The Walls Came Tumbling Down*, 100–107; Carolyn Wedin, *Inheritors of the Spirit: Mary White Ovington and the Founding of the NAACP* (New York: John Wiley and Sons, 1998),

106–7; August Meier and John H. Bracey Jr., "The NAACP as a Reform Movement, 1900–1965: 'To Reach the Conscience of America,' " *Journal of Southern History* 49 (February 1993), 3–30.

72. William H. Ward, "Address of William Hayes Ward," *Proceedings of the National Negro Conference, 1909* (1909; repr., New York: Arno Press, 1969), 9–13; Celia Parker Woolley, "Race Reconciliation," ibid., 74–78; W. E. B. Du Bois, "Politics and Industry," ibid., 79–88; William L. Bulkley, "Race Prejudice as Viewed from an Economic Standpoint," ibid., 89–97; William English Walling, "The Negro and the South," ibid., 98–109.

73. *The Crisis: A Record of the Darker Races* 1 (November 1910); Mary Dunlop Maclean, "African Civilization," *The Crisis* 1 (March 1911), 23–25; Kellogg, *NAACP: A History of the National Association for the Advancement of Colored People*, 52–54; Ovington, *Black and White Sit Down Together: The Reminiscences of an NAACP Founder*, 66–67.

74. W. E. B. Du Bois, "Editing *The Crisis*," March 1951, reprinted in *The Crisis Reader: Stories, Poetry, and Essays from the NAACP's Crisis Magazine* (New York: Modern Library, 1999), "talked turkey," xxviii; Du Bois, *The Quest of the Silver Fleece: A Novel* (1911; repr., New York: Harlem Moon, 2004); Lewis, *W. E. B. Du Bois: Biography of a Race*, 449; Irene Diggs, "Du Bois and Women: A Short History of Black Women, 1910–1934," *Current Bibliography on African Affairs* 7 (Summer 1974), 260–79.

75. W. E. B. Du Bois, "The Black Mother," *The Crisis* 5 (December 1912), 21. The Mammy statue movement was widely noted in the black press, notably the Nashville, Tennessee, *National Baptist Union Review* (May 4, 1923), the Jackson, Tennessee, *Christian Index* (February 22, 1923), and the New York *Age* (January 6, 1923); see Marilyn Kern-Foxworth, *Aunt Jemima, Uncle Ben, and Rastus: Blacks in Advertising Yesterday, Today, and Tomorrow* (Westport, CT: Praeger, 1994), 88, and Emilie M. Townes, *Womanist Ethics and the Cultural Production of Evil* (New York: Palgrave Macmillan, 2006), 36.

76. W. E. B. Du Bois, "Hail Columbia!" *The Crisis* 5 (April 1913), 289–90; Du Bois, "Forward Backward," *The Crisis* 2 (October 1911), 243–44; Du Bois, "Votes for Women," *The Crisis* 4 (September 1912), 234; Du Bois, "Woman Suffrage," *The Crisis* 9 (April 1915), 284–85; Du Bois, "Woman Suffrage," *The Crisis* 11 (November 1915), 29–30; Kelly Miller, "The Risk of Woman Suffrage," *The Crisis* 11 (November 1915), 37–38; Lewis, *W. E. B. Du Bois: Biography of a Race*, 463–65; W. E. B. Du Bois, *Darkwater: Voices from Within the Veil* (New York: Harcourt, Brace, 1920), quotes 100.

77. Eugene Debs, "The Negro in the Class Struggle," *International Socialist Review* (November 1903), and Debs, "The Negro and His Nemesis," *International Socialist Review* (January 1904), in Debs, *Writings and Speeches of Eugene V. Debs* (New York: Hermitage Press, 1948), 63–66, 66–73; Nick Salvatore, *Eugene V. Debs: Citizen and Socialist* (Urbana: University of Illinois Press, 1982), 225–30; W. E. B. Du Bois, "The Last Word in Politics," *The Crisis* 5 (November 1912), "manly" and "the Negro," 29; Du Bois, "Socialism and the Negro Problem," *New Review* 1 (February 1, 1913), 138–41, "scarcely" and "a party," 139; Du Bois to Carolina M. Dexter, November 6, 1812, *The Correspondence of W. E. B. Du Bois*, 1: 180.

78. W. E. B. Du Bois, "Politics," *The Crisis* 4 (August 1912), 180–81, quote 181; Du Bois, "The Election," *The Crisis* 5 (December 1912), 75; Du Bois, *Dusk of Dawn: An Essay toward an Autobiography of a Race Concept* (New York: Harcourt, Brace and World, 1940), 234–35.

79. W. E. B. Du Bois, "Another Open Letter to Woodrow Wilson," *The Crisis* 6 (September 1913), 232–36, quotes 235–36; Du Bois, "An Open Letter to Woodrow Wilson," *The Crisis* 5 (March 1913), 236–37.

80. Du Bois, "Editing *The Crisis*," quote xxix.

81. W. E. B. Du Bois to Oswald Garrison Villard, March 18, 1913, *The Correspondence of W. E. B. Du Bois*, 1: 181; Du Bois, *Dusk of Dawn*, 240–41; Kellogg, *NAACP: A History of the National Association for the Advancement of Colored People*, 93–110; Sullivan, *Lift Every Voice: The NAACP and the Making of the Civil Rights Movement*, 35–48; Du Bois, "Intermarriage," *The Crisis* 5 (February 1913), 180–81; Lewis, *W. E. B. Du Bois: Biography of a Race*, 474–77; Ovington, *Black and White Sit Down Together*, 67; Thomas Lee Philpott, *The Slum and the Ghetto: Neighborhood Deterioration and Middle-Class Reform, Chicago, 1880–1930* (New York: Oxford University Press, 1978), 299–300.

82. Mary White Ovington to W. E. B. Du Bois, April 11, 1914, *The Correspondence of W. E. B. Du Bois*, 1: 191–93, quotes 192.

83. Ibid., 192–93.

84. W. E. B. Du Bois, "We Come of Age," *The Crisis* 11 (December 1915), 25–28; Du Bois, "The Drama among Black Folk," *The Crisis* 12 (August 1916), 169–73; Kellogg, *NAACP: A History of the National Association for the Advancement of Colored People*, 117–37, 165–87.

85. John A. Hobson, *Imperialism* (1902; repr., London: Allen and Unwin, 1948); Adam Hochschild, *King Leopold's Ghost: A Story of Greed, Terror, and Heroism in Colonial Africa* (Boston: Houghton Mifflin, 1998).

86. John A. Hobson and A. F. Mummery, *The Physiology of Industry: Being an Exposure of Certain Fallacies in Existing Theories of Economics* (London: John Murray, 1889); Hobson, *The Problem of the Unemployed: An Inquiry and an Economic Policy* (London: Methuen, 1896); Hobson, *The War in South Africa: Its Causes and Effects* (London: J. Nisbet, 1900); W. E. B. Du Bois, "The African Roots of the War," *Atlantic Monthly* 115 (May 1915), 707–14.

87. Du Bois, "The African Roots of the War," quote 712–13.

88. Gary Dorrien, *Social Ethics in the Making: Interpreting an American Tradition* (Oxford: Wiley-Blackwell, 2011), 109–45.

89. August Rauschenbusch, *Leben und Wirken von August Rauschenbusch*, ed. Walter Rauschenbusch (Cassel: J. G. Oncken, 1901), 15–97; Dores Robinson Sharpe, *Walter Rauschenbusch* (New York: Macmillan, 1942), 20–22; Walter Rauschenbusch, "Augustus Rauschenbusch, D.D.," *Baptist Home Missions Monthly* (September 1898), 323–24; Paul M. Minus, *Walter Rauschenbusch: American Reformer* (New York: Macmillan, 1988), 2–4; August Rauschenbusch to Maria Ehrhardt, 24 July 1873, Archives, North American Baptist Conference, Sioux Falls, South Dakota; Walter Rauschenbusch to August Rauschenbusch, 15 October 1882, Box 34, Rauschenbusch Family Collection, American Baptist-Samuel Colgate Historical Library, Rochester,

New York. This section on Rauschenbusch adapts material from Gary Dorrien, *The Making of American Liberal Theology: Idealism, Realism, and Modernity* (Louisville: Westminster John Knox Press, 2003), 74–117.

90. Walter Rauschenbusch to Munson Ford, 30 June 1886, Box 23, Rauschenbusch Family Collection; Rauschenbusch, "Genesis of 'Christianity and the Social Crisis,'" *Rochester Theological Seminary Bulletin: The Record* (November 1918), 51; Walter Rauschenbusch, Sermon Notebook 2, 1886, Box 150, Rauschenbusch Family Collection.

91. Leighton Williams, "The Brotherhood of the Kingdom and Its Work," Brotherhood Leaflet No. 10. in *The Kingdom* 1 (August 1907), no pagination; Williams, "The Reign of the New Humanity," *The Kingdom* 1 (December 1907); E. F. Merriam, "The Brotherhood of the Kingdom," *The Watchman* (13 August 1908); Editorial, *For the Right* 1 (November 1889).

92. See Gary Dorrien, *Kantian Reason and Hegelian Spirit: The Idealistic Logic of Modern Theology* (Oxford: Wiley-Blackwell, 2012), 314–77.

93. Walter Rauschenbusch, "The Kingdom of God," Cleveland YMCA Lecture, 1913, in Robert T. Handy, ed., *The Social Gospel in America: 1870–1920* (New York: Oxford University Press, 1966), quotes 267; Rauschenbusch, *The Righteousness of the Kingdom*, ed. Max L. Stackhouse (Lewistown, NY: Edwin Mellen Press, 1999), 79–116; Rauschenbusch, "A Conquering Idea," (1892), in *Walter Rauschenbusch: Selected Writings*, ed. Winthrop S. Hudson (New York: Paulist Press, 1984), 71–74.

94. Walter Rauschenbusch (unsigned), *What Shall We Do with the Germans?* Pamphlet, 1895, "are the whites," Box 47, Rauschenbusch Family Collection; Rauschenbusch (unsigned), *The German Seminary in Rochester*, pamphlet, 1897, Box 47; Rauschenbusch, Commencement Address, "The Contribution of Germany to the National Life of America," 1902, "alien," Box 92.

95. Walter Rauschenbusch, *Christianity and the Social Crisis* (New York: Macmillan, 1907; repr., Louisville: Westminster John Knox Press, 1991), xxxvii; citations of Harnack on 95, 112, 129, 130, 132, 156, 191, 298.

96. Rauschenbusch, *Christianity and the Social Crisis*, 62–63.

97. Ibid., quotes 400, 401.

98. Ibid., 421.

99. *The Social Creed of the Churches*, ed. Harry F. Ward (Cincinnati: Eaton and Maine, 1912); Frank Mason North to Walter Rauschenbusch, 3 August 1908, Box 25, Rauschenbusch Family Collection.

100. Walter Rauschenbusch, *Christianizing the Social Order* (New York: Macmillan, 1912), quotes 9, 58, 56.

101. Ibid., 89–90.

102. Ibid., 123–30, quote 125.

103. Ibid., 130–38, quotes 131, 135.

104. Rauschenbusch, *Christianity and the Social Crisis*, quotes 279, 276; see Walter Rauschenbusch, "Some Moral Aspects of the 'Woman Movement,'" *Biblical World* 42 (October 1913), 195–98; Walter Rauschenbusch, "What About the Woman?" Box 20, Rauschenbusch Family Papers; Peter Gabriel Filene, *Him Her Self: Sex Roles in Modern America* (New York: Harcourt Brace Jovanovich, 1974), 23–29; Janet Forsythe

Fishburn, *The Fatherhood of God and the Victorian Family: The Social Gospel in America* (Philadelphia: Fortress Press, 1981), 120–27; Fishburn, "Walter Rauschenbusch and 'The Women Movement': A Gender Analysis," paper delivered at the 1999 Social Gospel Conference, Colgate Rochester Divinity School, Rochester, New York, March 18, 1999; Susan Curtis, *A Consuming Faith: The Social Gospel and Modern American Culture* (Baltimore: Johns Hopkins University Press, 1991), 107–8, 112.

105. Rauschenbusch, *Christianizing the Social Order*, 137–55, quotes 152, 153.

106. Ibid., quotes 156, 317.

107. Ibid., quotes 314, 341–43, 352–56.

108. Ibid., quote 361.

109. John Stuart Mill, *Principles of Political Economy*, 2 vols. (New York: Appleton, 1884), 2: 357–59; Rauschenbusch, *Christianizing the Social Order*, 356–71; Walter Rauschenbusch, "Christian Socialism," *A Dictionary of Religion and Ethics*, ed. Shailer Mathews and Gerald Birney Smith (New York: Macmillan, 1923), 90–91.

110. Rauschenbusch, *Christianizing the Social Order*, "Capitalism has," 369; "there is," 329; Walter Rauschenbusch to Francis G. Peabody, 14 December 1912, Box 26, Rauschenbusch Family Collection.

111. Rauschenbusch, *Christianizing the Social Order*, 458–66, quotes 433, 464–65.

112. Walter Rauschenbusch, Address to Religious Citizenship League, 30 January 1914; Rauschenbusch, "The Contribution of Germany to the National Life of America," Box 92; Walter Rauschenbusch to Hilmar Rauschenbusch, 23 September 1914, Box 37, Rauschenbusch Family Collection.

113. Walter Rauschenbusch to *The Congregationalist*, 24 September 1914.

114. Rauschenbusch, "The Contribution of Germany to the National Life of America," "my cradle," Box 92; Walter Rauschenbusch to "a Friend," 7 March 1917, Box 32, Rauschenbusch Family Collection; Walter Rauschenbusch, "Be Fair to Germany: A Plea for Open-mindedness," *The Congregationalist*, 15 October 1914; "Methodists Do Not Want to Hear Pro-German Divine," *Regina Morning Leader* (5 November 1914).

115. Rauschenbusch to "a Friend," 7 March 1917, "I have been," "I have always," "It was hard"; Walter Rauschenbusch to John S. Phillips, 16 May 1917, "don't ask me," Box 32, Rauschenbusch Family Collection.

116. Walter Rauschenbusch to Washington Gladden, 17 January 1917, Box 32, "their entire," Rauschenbusch Family Collection; Walter Rauschenbusch to Algernon Crapsey, open letter published in *Rochester Herald*, 23 August 1915, "I am glad"; Rauschenbusch to Dores Robinson Sharpe, 21 April 1916; Minus, *Walter Rauschenbusch*, 179–82; Sharpe, *Walter Rauschenbusch*, 378–79. A decade earlier Rauschenbusch was one of Crapsey's few defenders when he was tried for heresy; his letter to Crapsey in 1915 was a reply to a quite formal letter in which Crapsey questioned the soundness of his ideology and theology.

117. Walter Rauschenbusch, *The Social Principles of Jesus* (New York: Association Press, 1916), quotes 196–97.

118. Walter Rauschenbusch, *A Theology for the Social Gospel* (New York: Macmillan, 1917; repr., Louisville: Westminster John Knox Press, 1997), 4.

119. Ibid., quotes 33–34, 53.

120. Ibid., 59–60.

121. Rauschenbusch, *Christianizing the Social Order*, "smites," 60; Walter Rauschenbusch, "The Belated Races and the Social Problem," *Methodist Review* 40 (April 1914), "for years," 258.

122. Rauschenbusch, *A Theology for the Social Gospel*, "when," 79.

123. Ibid., 81–92, 159–87, quotes 174, 179.

124. Walter Rauschenbusch to Herbert White, 18 January 1918, Box 32; Walter Rauschenbusch to Clarence A. Barbour, 25 February 1918, Box 32; Walter Rauschenbusch, "Instructions in Case of My Death," 31 March 1918, "since 1914," Box 87, Rauschenbusch Family Collection; Walter Rauschenbusch to Cornelius Woelfkin, first draft, 25 April 1918; published version, 1 May 1918; Rochester Seminary press release version subtitled "ALWAYS AN AMERICAN," 11 July 1918, Box 91, Rauschenbusch Family Collection.

125. Ginger, *The Bending Cross*, 317–22; Salvatore, *Eugene V. Debs*, 272–74.

126. Eugene V. Debs, "A Plea for Solidarity," *International Socialist Review* (March 1914), in Debs, *Writings and Speeches of Eugene V. Debs*, 366–73, quote 367.

127. Ibid., quotes 369, 370, 373; Eugene V. Debs, "Revolt of the Railroad Workers," *International Socialist Review* (June 1914), in *Writings and Speeches of Eugene V. Debs*, 373–78.

128. Eugene V. Debs, "Homestead and Ludlow," *International Socialist Review* (August 1914), in *Writings and Speeches of Eugene V. Debs*, 378–83, quote 378; Debs, "The Gunmen and the Miners," *International Socialist Review* (September 1914), ibid., 383–86; Anthony DeStefanis, "Violence and the Colorado National Guard: Masculinity, Race, Class and Identity in the 1913–1914 Southern Colorado Coal Strike," in *Mining Women: Gender in the Development of a Global Industry*, ed. Laurie Mercier and Jaclyn Gier (New York: Palgrave, 2010), 195–212; Howard Zinn, *A People's History of the United States* (New York: HarperPerennial, 2015), 354–57.

129. Ginger, *The Bending Cross*, "we socialists," 329; Eugene V. Debs, "Even to the Barricades," *Rebellion* (December 1915), "my country," 37; Salvatore, *Eugene V. Debs*, 274–75.

130. Eugene V. Debs, "The Prospect for Peace," *American Socialist* (February 19, 1916), in *Writings and Speeches of Eugene V. Debs*, quotes 391, 392; David F. Karsner, *Talks with Debs in Terre Haute* (New York: New York *Call*, 1922), 116–20, 132–44.

131. Eugene V. Debs, "Letter of Acceptance," *American Socialist* (April 2, 1916), in *Writings and Speeches of Eugene V. Debs*, 395–97.

132. Ibid., "knows no," 396; Eugene V. Debs, "Politicians and Preachers," *American Socialist* (June 24, 1916), in *Writings and Speeches of Eugene V. Debs*, "the real," 398; Debs, "Ruling Class Robbers," *American Socialist* (July 1, 1916), ibid., "the whole burglarizing," 400.

133. Eugene V. Debs, "The Class War and Its Outlook," *International Socialist Review* (September 1916), 400–403; Carlo Tresca to Eugene V. Debs, n.d. (September 18, 1916), in Salvatore, *Eugene V. Debs*, 276.

134. Salvatore, *Eugene V. Debs*, 277–80, quote 280. Ginger was among either the unknowing or the embarrassedly circumspect, saying nothing of this relationship.

135. Morris Hillquit, *Loose Leaves from a Busy Life* (New York: Macmillan, 1934), "my mellowest," 59; Hillquit, *Socialism in Theory and Practice* (New York: Macmillan, 1909), "modern" and "perfect," 11.

136. Hillquit, *Socialism in Theory and Practice*, 18–35; Morris Hillquit and John A. Ryan, *Socialism: Promise or Menace?* (New York: Macmillan, 1914), 122–33; Frederick Engels, *Socialism: Utopian and Scientific*, trans. Edward Aveling (New York: International Publishers, 2015); Karl Kautsky, *The Class Struggle (Erfurt Program)*, trans. William E. Bohn (Chicago: Charles H. Kerr, 1910); Kautsky, *The Social Revolution*, trans. A. M. Simons and May Wood Simons (Chicago: Charles H. Kerr, 1916).

137. Eduard Bernstein, *The Preconditions of Socialism*, trans. Henry Tudor (Cambridge: Cambridge University Press, 2004); Hillquit, *Socialism in Theory and Practice*, 100–111, "acutest," 133; Hillquit and Ryan, *Socialism*, 131–32; Gary Dorrien, *Social Democracy in the Making: Political and Religious Roots of European Socialism* (New Haven: Yale University Press, 2019).

138. Hillquit and Ryan, *Socialism*, "an active," 133; Hillquit, *Loose Leaves from a Busy Life*, 103–5.

139. John A. Ryan, *A Living Wage* (New York: Macmillan, 1906); Ryan, "Program of Social Reform by Legislation," Part 1, *Catholic World* (July 1909), 433–44; Ryan, "Program of Social Reform by Legislation," Part 2, *Catholic World* (August 1909), 608–14; Ryan, "The Method of Teleology in Ethics," *New York Review* 2 (January–February 1907), 402–29; Ryan, "The Fallacy of 'Bettering One's Position,' " *Catholic World* (November 1907), 145–56; Edward F. McSweeney, "The Minimum Wage and Other Economic Quackeries," *Columbiad* (April 1913), 3–4; Pope Pius X, *Lamentabili Sane*, July 3, 1907; Pius X, *Pascendi Dominici Gregis*, September 8, 1907, *The Papal Encyclicals*, ed. Anne Freemantle (New York: New American Library, 1963), 202–7, 197–201; James F. Driscoll, S.S., "Recent Views on Biblical Inspiration," *New York Review* 1 (June–July 1905), 4–11; Francis E. Gigot, "The Higher Criticism of the Bible: Its Constructive Aspect," *New York Review* 2 (November–December 1906), 302–5; Gigot, "The Higher Criticism of the Bible: Its Relation to Tradition," *New York Review* 2 (January–February 1907), 442–44; R. Scott Appleby, *"Church and Age Unite!": The Modernist Impulse in American Catholicism* (Notre Dame: University of Notre Dame Press, 1992), 117–67; Ryan, *Social Doctrine in Action* (New York: Harper and Brothers, 1941), 116–17.

140. Hillquit and Ryan, *Socialism*, 1–38.

141. Ibid., quotes 246, 247, 250.

142. Ibid., quotes 239, 240.

143. Hillquit, *Loose Leaves from a Busy Life*, quote 89.

144. Seth Lipsky, *The Rise of Abraham Cahan* (New York: Schocken, 1913), 119–24, quote 120.

145. William E. Walling, "The Remedy: Anti-Nationalism," *The New Review* (3 February 1915), 77–83, quotes 78; Salvatore, *Eugene V. Debs*, 281; David Shannon, *The Socialist Party of America: A History* (New York: Macmillan, 1955), 85; Sally M. Miller, "Socialist Party Decline and World War I, Bibliography and Interpretation," *Science and Society* 34 (Winter 1971), 398–411.

146. James Maurer, *It Can Be Done: The Autobiography of James Hudson Maurer* (New York: Rand School Press, 1938), quotes 216–17; Hillquit, *Loose Leaves from a Busy Life*, 160–62.

147. J. G. Phelps Stokes, Charles Edward Russell, Walter E. Kreusi, William English Walling, Charlotte Kimball Kreusi, Robert W. Bruere, Leroy Scott, William L. Stoddard, Charlotte Perkins Gilman, W. J. Ghent, and Upton Sinclair, "The Question of War: Letter to the Editor of the *New York Call*," *New York Call* 10 (March 24, 1917), "to refuse," 6; Morris Hillquit to the *New York Call* 10 (March 27, 1917), Hillquit quotes 6.

148. Washington Gladden, *The Great War—Six Sermons* (Columbus, Ohio: McClelland, 1915), 8–9; Gladden, *Is War a Moral Necessity? Sermon Preached before First Congregational Church of Detroit, April 18, 1915* (Detroit: Printed by Friends, 1915), 6–15; Gladden, "What War Must Bring," *War and Peace* (Columbus, Ohio: First Congregational Church, 1914), 30–31; Gladden, "Universal Righteousness," sermon, March 29, 1915, Gladden Papers, Washington Gladden, Ohio Historical Society, Columbus, Ohio; Gladden, "Nations Are Members One of Another," sermon, April 11, 1915, Gladden Papers; Gladden, "A Communication: A Pacifist's Apology," *The New Republic* 5 (November 20, 1915), 75–76; Woodrow Wilson, "An Annual Message on the State of the Union," December 7, 1915, *The Papers of Woodrow Wilson*, 69 vols., ed. Arthur S. Link (Princeton: Princeton University Press, 1980), 35: 293–310; Wilson, "An Address to the Federal Council of Churches," December 10, 1915, ibid., 35: 329–36; Washington Gladden to Woodrow Wilson, December 11, 1915, ibid., 35: 344–45; Woodrow Wilson to Washington Gladden, December 14, 1915, ibid., 35: 353; Gladden, *The Forks of the Road* (New York: Macmillan, 1916), 31–32, 98, 106–7; Woodrow Wilson, "An Appeal for a Statement of War Aims," December 18, 1916, *The Papers of Woodrow Wilson*, 40: 273–76; Wilson, "An Address to the Senate," January 22, 1917, ibid., 40: 533–39, quotes 536.

149. Thomas J. Knock, *To End All Wars: Woodrow Wilson and the Quest for a New World Order* (Princeton: Princeton University Press, 1992), 108–22; Ronald Schaffer, *America in the Great War: The Rise of the Welfare State* (New York: Oxford University Press, 1991), xiv–xvii; Henry F. May, *The End of American Innocence: A Study of the First Years of Our Own Time, 1912–1917* (New York: Alfred A. Knopf, 1959), 355–86; Washington Gladden, "High Lights of Mercy," quotes February 11, 1917, Gladden Papers.

150. Woodrow Wilson, "An Address to a Joint Session of Congress," April 2, 1917, *The Papers of Woodrow Wilson*, 41: 519–27, "the world," 525; Washington Gladden, "America at War," April 29, 1917, "war" and "an acceptance," Gladden Papers.

151. Gladden, "America at War," quotes.

152. W. E. B. Du Bois, "Close Ranks," *Crisis* 16 (July 1918), "let us not," 111; Du Bois, "A Philosophy in Time of War," *Crisis* 16 (August 1918), "our country," 164–65.

153. Morris Hillquit, "Keynote Address to the 1917 Emergency Convention of the Socialist Party, St. Louis, Mo.—April 7, 1917," *The World* 578 (April 20, 1917), quotes 6.

154. Ibid., quotes 6.

155. John Spargo, "Second Minority Report of the Committee on War and Militarism, St. Louis—April 11, 1917," *Milwaukee Leader* 6 (April 12, 1917), 9; Louis Boudin, "First Minority Report of the Committee on War and Militarism: St. Louis—April 11, 1917," *Milwaukee Leader* 6 (April 12, 1917), 9; "Hillquit Starts Debate on Party War Resolutions: Declares Report of Majority Takes Absolute Position against Conflict: Scores Minority's Views," *Milwaukee Leader* 6 (April 12, 1917), 1, 12; Oakley C. Johnson, *The Day Is Coming: Life and Work of Charles E. Ruthenberg, 1882–1927* (New York: International Publishers, 1957), 19–27; Charles E. Ruthenberg, *Are We Growing toward Socialism?* (Cleveland: Cleveland Socialist Party, 1917), pamphlet.

156. [Morris Hillquit, Algernon Lee, and Charles Ruthenberg], "The Socialist Party and the War: Adopted at the St. Louis National Emergency Convention, April 7–14, 1917 and Ratified by Referendum," *The American Labor Year Book, 1917–1918*, ed. Alexander Trachtenberg (New York: Rand School of Social Science, 1918), 50–53, quotes 50, 51.

157. Ibid., quotes 52, 53.

158. Leon Trotsky, *My Life* (New York: Charles Scribner's Sons, 1930), 213.

159. Allan L. Benson, "Why the Majority Report Should Be Defeated," *New York Call* (April 22, 1917), 3–4; A. M. Simons, "Dishonesty and Treason," *New York Call* 10 (April 25, 1917), 6.

160. Morris Hillquit, "As to Treason," *New York Call* 10 (April 26, 1917), 6.

161. Woodrow Wilson to Frank I. Cobb, editor, *New York World*, in *The Papers of Woodrow Wilson*, "once lead," 5: 399; Ginger, *The Bending Cross*, 343–44; Dubofsky, *We Shall Be All*, 376–93; Eugene Debs, "The IWW Bogey," *International Socialist Review* (February 1918), in *Writings and Speeches of Eugene V. Debs*, 405–8; *A Communist Trial: Extracts from the Testimony of C. E. Ruthenberg and Closing Remarks to the Jury by Isaac E. Ferguson* (New York: National Defense Committee, n.d.), 6–31; William Preston, *Aliens and Dissenters: Federal Suppression of Radicals, 1903–1933* (Cambridge: Harvard University Press, 1963); H. C. Peterson and Gilbert C. Fite, *Opponents of War, 1917–1918* (Madison: University of Wisconsin Press, 1957).

162. Ginger, *The Bending Cross*, "dirty" and "driven," 346.

163. "Roosevelt Calls Support of Mayor Duty to Nation," *New York Times* (October 30, 1917), "Hun" and "half," 1; Hillquit, *Loose Leaves from a Busy Life*, "yellow," 193; "only war," 192; "the unindicted," 234; James Weinstein, *The Decline of Socialism in America, 1912–1925* (New Brunswick, NJ: Rutgers University Press, 1984), 151.

164. Kate Richards O'Hare, "My Country," *National Rip-Saw*, renamed *Social Revolution* (April 1917), "because" and "I am," 5.

165. Kate Richards O'Hare, *Socialism and the War*, pamphlet (St. Louis, MO: Frank O'Hare, 1919), in *Kate Richards O'Hare*, 122–43, quotes 134.

166. Ibid., "if that," 137; "we think," 138.

167. Ibid., quotes 142.

168. Miller, *From Prairie to Prison*, 145–57, "highly," "tending," and "no good," 145; Kate Richards O'Hare, "Speech Delivered in Court by Kate Richards O'Hare Before Being Sentenced by Judge Wade," *Social Revolution* (February 1918), 6–7, in *Kate Richards O'Hare*, 170–81, "I say," 177; "to become," 178.

169. Kate Richards O'Hare to her family, April 20, 1919, *Kate Richards O'Hare,* "gloomy," 205; "I think," 208; June 8, 1919, "Oh God," 220.

170. Kate Richards O'Hare to her family, May 10, 1919, ibid., 214–217; June 8, 1919, 217–220; June 15, 1919, 220–23; July 26, 1919, 225–27; Kate Richards O'Hare, *Kate O'Hare's Prison Letters* (St. Louis: Frank O'Hare, 1920), 12, 16, 34, 53.

171. Editorial, *Real Democracy* (December 1919), "a bigoted," 1; Irwin St. John Tucker, *Out of the Hell-Box* (New York: Morehouse-Gorham, 1945); Jacob H. Dorn, " 'Not a Substitute for Religion, but a Means of Fulfilling It': The Sacramental Socialism of Irwin St. John Tucker," in *Socialism and Christianity in Early Twentieth Century America,* 137–64.

172. *Hearings Before the Special Committee Concerning the Right of Victor L. Berger to be Sworn in as a Member of the Sixty-Sixth Congress,* 2 vols. (Washington, DC: Government Printing Office, 1919), "hypocrisy," 1: 65, 92; Weinstein, *The Decline of Socialism in America,* 166–67.

173. Eugene V. Debs, "The Socialist Party and the War," *The Social Builder* (May 1918).

174. Eugene V. Debs, "The Canton, Ohio Speech," June 16, 1918, in *Writings and Speeches of Eugene V. Debs,* 417–33, "a thousand," 418; "since the day," 421; "they tell," 422.

175. Ibid., "I have" and "a state," 424; "we do," 426; "toward democracy" and "you will," 427.

176. Ibid., quote 432.

177. Eugene V. Debs, "Address to the Jury," September 12, 1918, *Writings and Speeches of Eugene V. Debs,* 433–37, "I have," 434; "you are, " 435; "if the," 436; Debs, "Statement to the Court," ibid., 437–39, "while there is," 437; "of the better," 439.

178. Eugene V. Debs, "The Day of the People," *The Class Struggle* 3 (February 1919), 1–4, in Debs, *Writings and Speeches of Eugene V. Debs,* 440–42, "from the," 442; "fearless," 440; "it stirs," 440–41; V. I. Lenin, "Letter to American Workers," August 20, 1918, in Lenin, *Selected Works* (New York: International Publishers, 1971), 462.

179. Debs, "The Day of the People," "magnificent," 440; Debs, "Our Opportunity," *The Illinois Comrade* 1 (March 1919); Salvatore, *Eugene V. Debs,* 296–302.

4. COMMUNIST TRAUMA AND NORMAN THOMAS SOCIALISM

1. V. I. Lenin, *The State and Revolution: The Marxist Theory of the State and the Tasks of the Proletariat in the Revolution* (August 1917), in Lenin, *Selected Works* (New York: International Publishers, 1971), 264–356; Edmund Wilson, *To the Finland Station: A Study in the Writing and Acting of History* (New York: Harcourt, Brace, 1940), 471–75; John Reed, *Ten Days That Shook the World* (New York: Boni and Liveright, 1919; New York: Penguin Classics, 1980).

2. *Hearings Before the Special Committee Appointed under the Authority of House Resolution No. 6 Concerning the Right of Victor L. Berger to be Sworn In as a Member of the Sixty-Sixth Congress,* 2 vols. (U.S. Circuit Court of Appeals for the Seventh Circuit, Government Printing Office, October 1918), 1: 295–99; 2: 575–76; Ludwig Lore, "The Elections," *The Class Struggle* 2 (December 1918), 621; James Weinstein, *The Decline of Socialism in America, 1912–1925* (New Brunswick, NJ: Rutgers University Press, 1984), 177–81.

3. V. I. Lenin, "A Letter to American Workingmen," August 20, 1918, *The Class Struggle* I (December 1918), 532–33; Lenin, "Letter to American Workers," August 20, 1918, Lenin, *Selected Works*, 456–67, "will not," 462; "people whose," 465; "our Republic" and "we are firmly," 466; "we are now," 467; Leon Trotsky, *My Life* (New York: Charles Scribner's Sons, 1930), 274.

4. Weinstein, *The Decline of Socialism in America*, 177–84; Theodore Draper, *Roots of American Communism* (New York: Viking Press, 1957), 132–39.

5. Garin Burbank, *When Farmers Voted Red: The Gospel of Socialism in the Oklahoma Countryside, 1910–1924* (Westport, CT: Greenwood Press, 1976), 134–46; H. C. Peterson and Gilbert C. Fite, *Opponents of War, 1917–1918* (Madison: University of Wisconsin Press, 1957), 23–30; "Socialist Gets 20 Years for Draft Opposition," *Los Angeles Herald* 43 (June 12, 1918); Nigel Anthony Sellars, "Treasonous Tenant Farmers and Seditious Sharecroppers: The 1917 Green Corn Rebellion Trials," *Oklahoma City University Law Review* 27 (Fall 2002), 1097–1141.

6. Louis C. Fraina, "Labor and Democracy," *The Class Struggle* 1 (September–October 1917), 61–62; Draper, *Roots of American Communism*, 62–68, 130–35; Paul M. Buhle, *A Dreamer's Paradise Lost: Louis C. Fraina/Lewis Corey (1892–1953) and the Decline of Radicalism in the United States* (Atlantic Highlands, NJ: Humanities Press, 1995), 2–13; Weinstein, *The Decline of Socialism in America*, 184–86.

7. *Revolutionary Radicalism: Report of the Joint Legislative Committee Investigating Seditious Activities Filed April 24, 1920, in the Senate of the State of New York*, 4 vols. (Albany: New York State Senate, 1920), 1: 261; Draper, *Roots of American Communism*, 62–67, 132; Weinstein, *The Decline of Socialism in America*, 184; "Fricis Rozins," *The Great Soviet Encyclopedia* (1979), https://encyclopedia2.thefreedictionary.com/Fricis+Rozins.

8. Eduard Bernstein, *Die deutsche Revolution* (Berlin: Gesellschaft und Erziehung, 1921), 126–57; A. Joseph Berlau, *The German Social Democratic Party, 1914–1921* (New York: Columbia University Press, 1950), 251–63; Bertram D. Wolfe, *Three Who Made a Revolution* (New York: Stein and Day, 1984), 620–37; Leopald Haimson, *The Russian Marxists and the Origins of Bolshevism* (Cambridge: Harvard University Press, 1955), 87–111; Mikhail Heller and Aleksandr M. Nekrich, *Utopia in Power: The History of the Soviet Union from 1917 to the Present*, trans. Phyllis B. Carlos (New York: Summit Books, 1986), 50–110.

9. Rosa Luxemburg, "Our Program and the Political Situation" (1918), *The Rosa Luxemburg Reader*, ed. Peter Hudis and Kevin B. Anderson (New York: Monthly Review Press, 2004), 357–78; Luxemburg to Emanuel and Mathilde Wurm, December 28, 1916, *The Rosa Luxemburg Reader*, 362–64; Luxemburg to Emanuel and Mathilde Wurm, February 16, 1917, *The Rosa Luxemburg Reader*, 373–77.

10. Rosa Luxemburg, "The Russian Revolution," (September 1918), in *The Rosa Luxemburg Reader*, 281–310, "parliamentary" and "that is," 289; "a dictatorship," 290. This section on Luxemburg adapts material from Gary Dorrien, *Social Democracy in the Making: Political and Religious Roots of European Socialism* (New Haven: Yale University Press, 2019), 202–5.

11. Luxemburg, "The Russian Revolution," "but this," 308; "I have," 310.

12. Rosa Luxemburg, "The Beginning," *Die Rote Fahne* (November 18, 1918), in *The Rosa Luxemburg Reader*, 343–45, "this is," 343; Luxemburg, "The Socialization of Society," *Die Junge Garde* (December 1918), in *The Rosa Luxemburg Reader*, 346–48, "with lazy," 348.

13. Rosa Luxemburg, "What Does the Spartacus League Want?" *Die Rote Fahne* (December 14, 1918), in *The Rosa Luxemburg Reader*, 349–57, "acquire" and "can make," 351; "for the highest," 357.

14. Rosa Luxemburg, "Our Program and the Political Situation" (December 31, 1918), *The Rosa Luxemburg Reader*, 357–73, "the Preface," 362.

15. Luxemburg, "Our Program and the Political Situation," "anarchism" and "the henchmen," 363; "for us," 365.

16. Rosa Luxemburg, "Order Reigns in Berlin," *Die Rote Fahne* (January 14, 1919), in *The Rosa Luxemburg Reader*, 373–78.

17. Bernstein, *Die deutsche Revolution*, 143–45, 158–60; Philipp Scheidemann, "Bericht über den 9. November 1918," Deutsches Historisches Museum, https://web.archive.org/web/20140712054628/http://www.dhm.de/lemo/html/dokumente/scheidemann; *Biographisches Lexikon des Sozialismus: Verstorbene Persönlichkeiten*, ed. Franz Osterroth (Hannover: J. H. W. Dietz, 1960), 1: 262–63; Detlef Lehnert, "The SPD in German Politics and Society, 1919–1929," in *Bernstein to Brandt: A Short History of German Social Democracy*, ed. Roger Fletcher (London: Edward Arnold, 1987), 115–16.

18. "The Crisis in the Socialist Party," *Revolutionary Age* (November 30, 1918); Editorial, *Revolutionary Age* (December 11, 1918); Ludwig Lore, "The Elections," *The Class Struggle* 2 (November–December 1918), 338; Nicholas I. Hourwich, "The Left Wing in the American Socialist Party," *Revolutionary Age* (February 1, 1919), quote; Weinstein, *The Decline of Socialism in America*, 186–87; Draper, *Roots of American Communism*, 78–87.

19. O. H. Radkey, *The Elections to the Russian Constituent Assembly of 1917* (Cambridge: Harvard University Press, 1950), 16–39; Lenin, "Can the Bolsheviks Retain State Power?" November 9, 1917, *Selected Works*, 362–95; Lenin, "The Immediate Tasks of the Soviet Government," *Selected Works*, 401–31.

20. Leon Trotsky, "Letter of Invitation to the Congress: First Congress of the Communist International," January 24, 1919, https://www.marxists.org/history/international/comintern/1st-congress/invitation.htm; V. I. Lenin, "Speech at the Opening Session of the Congress," March 2, 1919, https://www.marxists.org/archive/lenin/works/1919/mar/comintern.htm#s1.

21. Louis C. Fraina, "Problems of American Socialism," *The Class Struggle* 2 (January–February 1919), quotes 32–33; Fraina, "The Bolsheviki — Socialism in Action!" *Evening Call* 11 (January 5, 1918), 7.

22. *Berger et al. v. United States*, 255 U.S. 22, 41 S. Ct. 230 (1921); *Hearings Before the Special Committee Appointed under the Authority of House Resolution No. 6 Concerning the Right of Victor L. Berger to be Sworn In*; Weinstein, *The Decline of Socialism in America*, 194–96.

23. Nathan L. Welch to Adolph Germer, June 6, 1919; Alfred Wagenknecht to All Members and Locals of the Socialist Party, June 6, 1919; Kate O'Hare to Otto Branstetter, February 24, 1920, in Weinstein, *The Decline of Socialism in America*, 198–99; [Louis Fraina], "The National Left Wing Conference," *Revolutionary Age* 2 (July 5, 1919), 4–5.

24. [Louis Fraina], "Manifesto of the Left Wing Section Socialist Party Local Greater New York," in *Revolutionary Radicalism*, 1: 706–14; *Revolutionary Radicalism*, 1: 531–36; Fraina, "The National Left Wing Conference," "in spite of" and "in accord with," 4; Weinstein, *The Decline of Socialism in America*, 111–12; Draper, *Roots of American Communism*, 165–68.

25. Lewis Corey, "How Is Ownership Distributed?" *New Republic* (May 5, 1926); Corey, "Is Income More Equally Distributed?" *New Republic* (January 26, 1927); Corey, *The House of Morgan: A Social Biography of the Masters of Money* (New York: Grosset and Dunlap, 1930).

26. Kate Richards O'Hare to the O'Hare Family, June 15, 1919, *Kate Richards O'Hare*, "theoretical," 222; July 26, 1919, "and only the," 227; August 28, 1919, 236–38.

27. Herbert E. Gaston, *The Nonpartisan League* (New York: Harcourt, Brace and Howe, 1920); Samuel P. Huntington, "The Election Tactics of the Nonpartisan League," *Mississippi Valley Historical Review* 36 (March 1950), 613–32; Michael Lansing, *Insurgent Democracy: The Nonpartisan League in North American Politics* (Chicago: University of Chicago Press, 2015); Seymour Martin Lipset, *Agrarian Socialism* (Berkeley: University of California Press, 1971); Nathan Fine, *Labor and Farmer Parties in the United States, 1828–1928* (New York: Rand School of Social Science, 1928); Richard Valelly, *Radicalism in the States: The Minnesota Farmer-Labor Party and the American Political Economy* (Chicago: University of Chicago Press, 1989).

28. Nick Salvatore, *Eugene V. Debs: Citizen and Socialist* (Urbana: University of Illinois Press, 1982), quote 316; Ray Ginger, *The Bending Cross: A Biography of Eugene Victor Debs* (New Brunswick, NJ: Rutgers University Press, 1949), 390–91.

29. Ginger, *The Bending Cross*, 397–98; Salvatore, *Eugene V. Debs*, 322.

30. *Proceedings of the National Convention, 1919* (New York: Socialist Party, 1919), 715–17; Morris Hillquit, "Dictatorship and the International," *Socialist World* 1 (August 15, 1920), 1–4, "absolutely" and "but that does not," 2; "now, comrades," 3; *Revolutionary Radicalism*, 1: 624–26; Harry W. Laidler, "The Socialist Convention," *Socialist Review* (June 1920), 28–29.

31. Morris Hillquit to Eugene V. Debs, June 30, 1920, text in Weinstein, *The Decline of Socialism in America*, "every dictum," 220.

32. Hillquit, "Dictatorship and the International," "even parliamentary," 3; Morris Hillquit, *From Marx to Lenin* (New York: Hanford Press, 1921), 57–59.

33. "Minutes of the Second Congress of the Communist International: Seventh Session, July 30, 1920," https://www.marxists.org/history/international/comintern/2nd-congress/ch07.htm; "Kate O'Hare Visits Debs," *Socialist World* 1 (July 1920), 8–9; William Feigenbaum, "Debs to the Socialist Party," *Socialist World* 1 (October 1920), "If you were," "heart and soul," and "the Moscow Program," 17–18.

34. Ginger, *The Bending Cross*, 405–6; Salvatore, *Eugene V. Debs*, 325, "and it has," 323; David Karsner, *Talks with Debs in Terre Haute* (New York: New York *Call*, 1922), "the biggest," 17.

35. Eugene V. Debs to David Karsner, July 28, 1922, in *Talks with Debs in Terre Haute*, 192–195; Salvatore, *Eugene V. Debs*, "I protest," 331; Eugene V. Debs, "Review and Personal Statement," October 2, 1922, Press Release, National Office of the Socialist Party.

36. Robert Minor, "A Yankee Convention," *The Liberator* 3 (April 1920), 28–34; A. S. Carm, "The Labor Party Convention," *The Weekly People* 29 (December 6, 1919), 1; Morris Hillquit, "Radicalism in America," *Socialist World* 1 (October 15, 1920), 18–19; Stanley Shapiro, "Hand and Brain: The Farmer-Labor Party of 1920," *Labor History* 26 (Summer 1985), 405–22; Hamilton Cravens, "The Emergence of the Farmer-Labor Party in Washington Politics, 1919–1920," *Pacific Northwest Quarterly* 57 (October 1966), 148–57; David Montgomery, "The Farmer-Labor Party," in *American Workers from the Revolution to the Present*, ed. Paul Buhle and Allan Dawley (Urbana: University of Illinois Press, 1985).

37. Morris Hillquit, "Working Class Political Unity," *New York Call* 14 (September 7, 1921), 7; James Oneal, "The Detroit Resolution," *New York Call* 14 (September 19, 1921), 7; Adolph Dreifuss, "For a Mass Movement," *New York Call* 14 (September 22, 1921), 7.

38. V. I. Lenin, *Left-Wing Communism: An Infantile Disorder* (April 27, 1920), in Lenin, *Selected Works*, 516–81, quotes 581.

39. Workers Party of America, pamphlet, *For a Labor Party: Recent Revolutionary Changes in American Politics; A Statement of the Workers Party, October 15, 1922* (New York: Workers Party of America, 1922), 1–18; C. E. Ruthenberg, "The Workers Party and the Labor Party," *Bulletin of the Workers Party of America* (New York: Workers Party of America, November 27, 1922), 1–2; "The Open Communist Party—The Task of the Hour," *Workers' Council* 1 (October 15, 1921), 120–21; A. Rafael (Alexander Bittelman), "The Task of the Hour," *The Communist* (October 1921); James Oneal, *American Communism: A Critical Analysis of Its Origins, Development and Programs* (New York: Rand Book Store, 1927), 138–45; Weinstein, *The Decline of Socialism in America*, 254–57; Draper, *Roots of American Communism*, 341–95; Bell, *Marxian Socialism in the United States*, 126–28; Benjamin Gitlow, *I Confess: The Truth about American Communism* (New York: E. P. Dutton, 1940), 131–59.

40. Caleb Harrison, Preface of the *Program and Constitution of the Workers Party of America Adopted at the National Convention in New York City, December 24-25-26, 1921* (New York: Workers Party of America, 1921), 1–14; Weinstein, *Decline of Socialism in America*, 258–61; Draper, *Roots of American Communism*, ch. 21–23.

41. William Z. Foster, *The Great Steel Strike and Its Lessons* (New York: B. W. Huebsch, 1920); Foster, *The Revolutionary Crisis of 1918–1921: In Germany, England, Italy and France* (Chicago: Trade Union Educational League, 1922); Foster, *The Bankruptcy of the American Labor Movement* (Chicago: Trade Union Educational League, 1922); Foster, *Organize the Unorganized* (Chicago: Trade Union Educational League, 1926); Foster, *Misleaders of Labor* (Chicago: Trade Union Educational League, 1927); Victor

G. Devinatz, "The Labor Philosophy of William Z. Foster: From the IWW to the TUEL," *International Social Science Review* 71 (1996), 3–13; Bell, *Marxian Socialism in the United States*, 129; Edward Johanningsmeirer, *Forging American Communism: The Life of William Z. Foster* (Princeton: Princeton University Press, 1994), 34–44, 75–82.

42. William Z. Foster, "The Federated Farmer-Labor Party," *The Labor Herald* 2 (August 1923), 2–7, quote 2; John Pepper, "For a Labor Party: Addenda to the Second Edition, May 15, 1923, in *For a Labor Party: Recent Revolutionary Changes in American Politics*, pamphlet, 2nd ed. (New York: Workers Party of America, 1923), 5–7, 49–68; *Statement of Principles of the Federated Farmer-Labor Party*, pamphlet (Chicago: Federated Farmer-Labor Party, 1923), 1–3; Pepper, "William Z. Foster—Revolutionary Leader," *The Worker* (April 14, 1923); Pepper, "The First Mass Party of American Workers and Farmers," *The Worker* (July 21, 1923); John C. Kennedy, "The Outlook for a Labor Party," *American Labor Monthly* 1 (June 1923), 23; Weinstein, *The Decline of Socialism in America*, 279–85; Bell, *Marxian Socialism in the United States*, 128–29; Theodore Draper, *American Communism and Soviet Russia* (New York: Vintage, 1960), 42–46.

43. "Address to the American People: Adopted by the Conference for Progressive Political Action at its Founding Conference, Chicago, Ill. Feb. 20–21, 1922," *Socialist World* 3 (February 1922), 3–4; Otto Branstetter et al., "The Conference for Progressive Political Action," *Socialist World* 3 (February 1922), 1–3; Jay Lovestone, "Our Next Step," *The Worker* 5 (February 25, 1922), 6.

44. "Farmer-Labor Convention and the Communists," *Minnesota Union Advocate* (June 21, 1923); "The Problem of a Third Party," *Minnesota Union Advocate* (November 15, 1923); Kate Richards O'Hare, "Are We Headed Straight for Perdition?" *American Vanguard* (November 1923), 1; C. E. Ruthenberg to District Executive Committee, District 9, Minneapolis, March 27, 1924, in *Daily Worker* (March 31, 1924), and Weinstein, *The Decline of Socialism in America*, "let us," 300–301.

45. David P. Thelen, *Robert M. La Follette and the Insurgent Spirit* (New York: Little, Brown, 1976), 178–90; Nancy Unger, *Fighting Bob La Follette: The Righteous Reformer*, 2nd ed. (Madison: Wisconsin Historical Society Press, 2008), 215–38; James H. Shideler, "The La Follette Progressive Party Campaign of 1924," *Wisconsin Magazine of History* 33 (Autumn 1950), 444–57; John D. Buenker, "Robert M. La Follette's Progressive Odyssey," *Wisconsin Magazine of History* 82 (Autumn 1998), 2–31.

46. Alexander Bittelman, "Farmer-Labor Opportunism," *Daily Worker Magazine Supplement* (December 13, 1924); Weinstein, *The Decline of Socialism in America*, 307–21; Thelen, *Robert M. La Follette and the Insurgent Spirit*, 181–88.

47. Unger, *Fighting Bob La Follette*, 272–303; Herbert F. Margulies, *The Decline of the Progressive Movement in Wisconsin, 1890–1920* (Madison: State Historical Society of Wisconsin, 1968), 244–90; K. C. Mackay, *The Progressive Movement of 1924* (New York: Columbia University Press, 1947).

48. "Socialist Party National Convention Delegates Remain Silent in Face of Attack on Soviet Russia: Cahan Rages in Attack on Soviet Rule," *The Worker* (June 2, 1923); Steve Fraser, *Labor Will Rule: Sidney Hillman and the Rise of American Labor* (Ithaca: Cornell University Press, 1993), 178–81.

49. Morris Hillquit, *Loose Leaves from a Busy Life* (New York: Macmillan, 1934), 300–323.

50. Eugene V. Debs, "The American Labor Party," *Socialist World* (January 1925), "foul"; Debs, *Walls and Bars* (Chicago: Socialist Party, 1927), in Debs, *Writings and Speeches of Eugene V. Debs*, "as in" and "I saw," 483.

51. "Expulsion of Trotsky and Zinoviev: Statement of the Central Executive Committee of the Workers Party of America, November 20, 1927," *Daily Worker* 4 (November 21, 1927), 2; J. V. Stalin, "The Fight against Right and 'Ultra-Left' Deviations," *Pravda* 40 (February 18, 1926) https://www.marxists.org/reference/archive/stalin/wowks/1926.

52. J. V. Stalin, "Speech Delivered to the American Commission of the Presidium of the Executive Committee of the Communist International, May 6, 1929," https://www.marxists.org/reference/archive/stalin/works/1929, quote.

53. Bell, *Marxian Socialism in the United States*, 133–34; Paul Buhle, *Marxism in the United States* (London: Verso, 2013), 132–38; William Z. Foster, *Our Country Needs a Strong Communist Party* (New York: New Century Publishers, 1946).

54. Hillquit, *Loose Leaves from a Busy Life*, "for ten," 326.

55. Norman Thomas, "Autobiography," unpublished, 1–36, "a sin," 32, New York City Public Library, Fifth Avenue, Manhattan. Harry Fleishman told me in 1982 that he regretted deeply that the published version of his excellent biography of Thomas was only half as long as the book he wrote. See Harry Fleischman, *Norman Thomas: A Biography* (New York: W. W. Norton, 1964); W. A. Swanberg, *Norman Thomas: The Last Idealist* (New York: Scribner's, 1976); Raymond F. Gregory, *Norman Thomas: The Great Dissenter* (New York: Algora, 2008).

56. Thomas, "Autobiography," 41–49, "was lost," 46.

57. Murray B. Seidler, *Norman Thomas: Respectable Rebel* (Syracuse: Syracuse University Press, 1961), "it is this," 21; Norman Thomas to Rev. Howard A. Walter, January 31, 1917.

58. Bernard Johnpoll, *Pacifist's Progress: Norman Thomas and the Decline of American Socialism* (Chicago: Quadrangle Books, 1970), "how can," 22; Norman Thomas to Morris Hillquit, October 2, 1917.

59. Norman Thomas to Emma Mattoon Thomas, November 2, 1917; Thomas, *The Christian Patriot* (December 1917), in *Norman Thomas on War*, ed. Bernard Johnpoll (New York: Garland, 1974), 44–50; Thomas, "Autobiography," 64–70, "was lost," 46; Thomas to Alexander Trachtenberg, October 18, 1918, "profound" and "must defend"; Thomas, *We Have a Future* (Princeton: Princeton University Press, 1941), 29–30.

60. Norman Thomas, "Conscience and the Church," *Nation* (August 23, 1917), 198; Thomas, "Justice to War's Heretics," *Nation* (November 9, 1918), 547; Thomas, *The Conscientious Objector in America* (New York: B. W. Huebsch, 1923).

61. Paula F. Pfeffer, *A. Philip Randolph: Pioneer of the Civil Rights Movement* (Baton Rouge: Louisiana State University Press, 1990), 7–22; Jervis Anderson, *A. Philip Randolph: A Biographical Portrait* (New York: Harcourt Brace, 1973), 29–42.

62. Anderson, *A. Philip Randolph*, 68–73.

63. A. Philip Randolph and Chandler Owen, *The Messenger* (November 1917), quotes 2, editorials 6–10, politics 11–20; education 22–27; poetry 27–28; theatre 29–30; messages, 31.

64. A. Philip Randolph and Chandler Owen, "Pro-Germanism Among Negroes," *Messenger* (July 1918); W. E. B. Du Bois, "Close Ranks," *Crisis* 16 (July 1918), 111; Anderson, *A. Philip Randolph*, 105–7; Lowther, "A. Philip Randolph and the *Messenger*," 8.

65. Marcus Garvey, "The West Indies in the Mirror of Truth," *The Champion Magazine* (January 1917), reprinted in *Selected Writings and Speeches of Marcus Garvey*, ed. Bob Blaisdell (Mineola, NY: Dover Publications, 14–16); Garvey, "A Journey of Self-Discovery," *Current History* (September 1963), reprinted in John Henrik Clarke, ed., *Marcus Garvey and the Vision of Africa* (New York: Vintage Books, 1974), 71–81; Rupert Lewis, *Marcus Garvey: Anti-Colonial Champion* (Trenton, NJ: Africa World Press, 1988); Judith Stein, *The World of Marcus Garvey: Race and Class in Modern Society* (Baton Rouge: Louisiana State University Press, 1986); E. David Cronon, *Black Moses: The Story of Marcus Garvey and the Universal Negro Improvement Association* (Madison: University of Wisconsin Press, 1955); Tony Martin, *Race First: The Ideological and Organizational Struggle of Marcus Garvey and the Universal Negro Improvement Association* (Westport, CT: Greenwood Press, 1976).

66. Manifesto: "Declaration of the Rights of the Negro Peoples of the World," International Convention of the Negroes of the World, New York City, August 31, 1920, in *Selected Writings and Speeches of Marcus Garvey*, 16–24, quote 18.

67. W. E. B. Du Bois, "Marcus Garvey," *The Crisis* 21 (December 1920), 58–60; Du Bois, "Marcus Garvey," *The Crisis* 21 (January 1921), 112–15, "in or," 114; Du Bois, "The Black Star Line," *The Crisis* 24 (September 1922), 210; Du Bois, "A Lunatic or a Traitor," *Crisis* (May 1924), in Du Bois, *W. E. B. Du Bois: A Reader*, ed. David Levering Lewis (New York: Henry Holt, 1995), 340–42.

68. Marcus Garvey, "The Negro's Greatest Enemy," *Current History* (September 1923), in *The Marcus Garvey and Universal Negro Improvement Association Papers*, 1: 3; Garvey, "An Appeal to the Soul of White America," October 2, 1923, in *The Marcus Garvey and Universal Negro Improvement Association Papers*, 5: 464–68; Robert W. Bagnall, "The Madness of Marcus Garvey," *Messenger* (March 1923), 638–48, "boastful," 638, "whether," 648.

69. Daryl Scott, "Immigrant Indigestion: A. Philip Randolph, Radical and Restrictionist," Center for Immigration Studies (June 1, 1999), http://cis.org.; Arnold Shankman, *Ambivalent Friends: Afro-Americans View the Immigrant* (Westport, CT: Greenwood Press, 1982), 46–47.

70. Richard Altenbaugh, "The Children and the Instruments of Militant Labor Progressivism: Brookwood Labor College and the American Labor College Movement of the 1920s and 1930s," *History of Education Quarterly* 23 (Winter 1983), 395–411; Charles F. Howlett, "Workers' Education and World Peace: The Case of Brookwood Labor College," *Journal for Peace and Justice Studies* 4 (1991), 33–34; A. J. Muste, "Brookwood Labor College," *The Railway Conductor* (April 1927), 155; Nat Hentoff, *Peace Agitator: The Story of A. J. Muste* (New York: Macmillan, 1963), 25–58; Jo Ann Robinson, *Abraham Went Out: A Biography of A. J. Muste* (Philadelphia: Temple University Press, 1981), 18–55; Norman Thomas, "On the Death of A. J. Muste," *New America* 6 (February 16, 1967), 2.

71. Thomas, "Autobiography," 82–90.

72. Swanberg, *Norman Thomas*, quote 98; Gitlow, *I Confess: The Truth about American Communism*, 364.

73. Abraham Cahan, "The 'Victory' of Zionism and the Socialist Enlightenment of the Masses," *Forward* (December 1, 1917); Seth Lipsky, *The Rise of Abraham Cahan* (New York: Schocken, 2013), quote 126.

74. Lipsky, *The Rise of Abraham Cahan*, 147–58; Vladimir Jabotinsky, "The Iron Wall," *Jewish Herald* (November 26, 1937).

75. Yaacov Goldstein, *Jewish Socialists in the United States: The Cahan Debate, 1925–1926* (Portland: Sussex Academic Press, 1998), 87–88, 161–63, 182–83, 188–91, 209–10; "clearly, a sharp," 228; Jack Ross, *The Socialist Party of America* (Lincoln: University of Nebraska Press, 2015), 286–88.

76. "Socialism and Soviet Russia," *The New Leader* (February 4, 1928); Nathan Fine, *Labor and Farmer Parties in the United States: 1828–1928* (New York: Rand School of Social Science, 1928), 428–29, Hillquit quotes 428; Ross, *The Socialist Party of America*, 296; James Maurer, *It Can Be Done: The Autobiography of James Hudson Maurer* (New York: Rand School, 1938), 290–91.

77. Johnpoll, *Pacifist's Progress*, "he was," 55; Ross, *The Socialist Party of America*, 297–300; Louis Waldman, *Labor Lawyer* (New York: E. P. Dutton, 1944), 189.

78. "Socialists Likely to Name Thomas," *New York Times* (March 18, 1928); "Socialists Name Thomas at Convention," *New York Times* (April 13, 1928).

79. Thomas, "Autobiography," 106–11; Fleischmann, *Norman Thomas*, 116–20, "thanks," 116; David Shannon, *The Socialist Party of America: A History* (New York: Macmillan, 1955), 193–97.

80. Norman Thomas, "A Program for Unemployment," *World Tomorrow* (May 1930), 215–17.

81. Norman Thomas, *America's Way Out: A Program for Democracy* (New York: Macmillan, 1931); Thomas, *As I See It* (New York: Macmillan, 1932), "I think," 20; Thomas, *Human Exploitation in the United States* (New York: Frederick A. Stokes, 1934).

82. Thomas, *As I See It*, "the most," 143; "outstanding," 150; "humanistic" and "a valid," 141.

83. Ibid., "a society" and "wretched," 171; "hee haw," 167; "we drift," 166.

84. Shannon, *The Socialist Party of America*, 216–19; J. W., "Socialist Party Convention: Opportunism and Petty Bourgeois Reform Mark Outstanding Traits of Convention and Standard-Bearers," *Proletarian News* 1 (June 14, 1932), 1, 7.

85. Fleischman, *Norman Thomas*, 140; Arthur M. Schlesinger Jr., *The Age of Roosevelt: The Politics of Upheaval* (Boston: Houghton Mifflin, 1960), 176–80.

86. Paul H. Douglas, "An Idealist Masters Realities," *World Tomorrow* (May 1932), 151; Devere Allen, "Presidential Possibilities: Norman Thomas—Why Not?" *The Nation* (March 30, 1932), 365; Hillquit, *Loose Leaves from a Busy Life*, "getting," 327; Shannon, *The Socialist Party of America*, 222; Thomas, "An Autobiography," 94–95.

87. Schlesinger, *The Age of Roosevelt*, "most of," 180. Kirstin Downey, *The Woman behind the New Deal: The Life of Frances Perkins, FDR's Secretary of Labor and His Moral*

Conscience (New York: Doubleday, 2009); Naomi Pasachoff, *Frances Perkins: Champion of the New Deal* (New York: Oxford University Press, 1999).

88. Irving Howe, *A Margin of Hope: An Intellectual Autobiography* (New York: Harcourt Brace Jovanovich, 1982), "the intuitive," 6; "Norman Thomas," 19–20.

89. Norman Thomas, *The Choice Before Us: Mankind at the Crossroads* (New York: Macmillan, 1934), 83–127, 162–99, "and gave it," 89; "in the best," 164; Reinhold Niebuhr, *Reflections on the End of an Era* (New York: Scribner's, 1934), 17–30; Niebuhr, "After Capitalism—What?" *The World Tomorrow* 16 (1 March 1933), 203–4.

90. Thomas, *The Choice Before Us,* "to their notion," 79; "especially if," 81; Norman Thomas, *The New Deal: A Socialist Analysis,* pamphlet (Chicago: Socialist Party of America, December 1933), 3.

91. Socialist Party of America, "Declaration of Principles," *American Socialist Quarterly* (July 1934), quote 6; Joseph Shaplen, "Left Wing Seizes Socialist Party," *New York Times* (June 4, 1934); Waldman, *Labor Lawyer,* 267; Swanberg, *Norman Thomas,* 168; Bell, *Marxian Socialism in the United States,* 166–67.

92. This section on Niebuhr adapts material from Gary Dorrien, *The Making of American Liberal Theology: Idealism, Realism, and Modernity* (Louisville: Westminster John Knox Press, 2003), 432–48; and Dorrien, *Soul in Society: The Making and Renewal of Social Christianity* (Minneapolis: Fortress Press, 1995), 102–16.

93. Reinhold Niebuhr to Samuel D. Press, March 3, 1914, Reinhold Niebuhr Papers, Library of Congress, Washington, DC.

94. Reinhold Niebuhr, "The Failure of German-Americanism," *Atlantic* (July 1916), 16–18.

95. Reinhold Niebuhr, *Leaves from the Notebook of a Tamed Cynic* (1929; repr., New York: Meridian Books, 1966), "typical," 40; Niebuhr, Letter to the Editor, *The New Republic* (June 14, 1919), "we need," 218.

96. Niebuhr, *Leaves from the Notebook of a Tamed Cynic,* quotes 68, 69.

97. Reinhold Niebuhr, *Does Civilization Need Religion?* (New York: Macmillan, 1928), 1–28.

98. Reinhold Niebuhr, "Catastrophe or Social Control?" *Harper's* 165 (June 1932), 118.

99. Reinhold Niebuhr, *Moral Man and Immoral Society: A Study in Ethics and Politics* (New York: Scribner's 1932), quotes xiv, xv.

100. Ibid., "failure to," xx; "a very," "sublime," and "malignant," 277.

101. Ibid., "Marxian socialism" and "the full," 144; "complete moral," 145; "wholly in terms," 146.

102. Reinhold Niebuhr, "Dr. Niebuhr's Position," *Christian Century* 50 (January 18, 1933), quote 91–92; Theodore C. Hume, "Prophet of Disillusion," *Christian Century* 50 (January 4, 1933), 18–19; Norman Thomas, review of *Moral Man and Immoral Society,* by Reinhold Niebuhr, *The World Tomorrow* 15 (December 14, 1932), 565, 567; John Haynes Holmes, review of *Moral Man and Immoral Society, Herald Tribune Books* (January 8, 1933), 13; John Haynes Holmes, "Reinhold Niebuhr's Philosophy of Despair," *Herald Tribune Books* (March 18, 1934), 7; Reinhold Niebuhr, "Ten Years That Shook My World," *Christian Century* 56 (April 26, 1939), 546; Niebuhr, "After Capitalism—What?" *The World Tomorrow* (March 1, 1933), 204.

103. H. Richard Niebuhr, "The Grace of Doing Nothing," *Christian Century* 49 (March 23, 1932), 379; Reinhold Niebuhr, "Must We Do Nothing?" *Christian Century* 49 (March 30, 1932), 416–17; H. Richard Niebuhr, "The Only Way into the Kingdom of God," *Christian Century* 49 (April 6, 1932), 447; see [Reinhold Niebuhr], "The League and Japan," *World Tomorrow* 15 (March 1932), 4; *Remembering Reinhold Niebuhr: Letters of Reinhold and Ursula M. Niebuhr*, ed. Ursula M. Niebuhr (San Francisco: HarperSanFrancisco, 1991); H. Richard Niebuhr, *The Social Sources of Denominationalism* (New York: Henry Holt, 1929); H. Richard Niebuhr, *The Kingdom of God in America* (New York: Harper and Row, 1937).

104. H. Richard Niebuhr to Reinhold Niebuhr, n.d. [mid-January, 1933], Reinhold Niebuhr Papers; Library of Congress, Washington, DC; cited in Richard W. Fox, *Reinhold Niebuhr: A Biography* (New York: Pantheon Books, 1985; 2nd ed., Ithaca: Cornell University Press, 1996), 144–45.

105. Ibid.; see discussion in Fox, *Reinhold Niebuhr*, 145–46.

106. Niebuhr, "Ten Years That Shook My World," quote 546; Reinhold Niebuhr, *Reflections on the End of an Era* (New York: Charles Scribner's Sons, 1934), 279–96.

107. Niebuhr, *Reflections on the End of an Era*, quote 24.

108. Niebuhr, "After Capitalism—What?" 203–4; Niebuhr, *Reflections on the End of an Era*, 27–30; see Niebuhr, "Is Religion Counter-Revolutionary?" *Radical Religion* 1 (Autumn 1935), 14–20.

109. Federal Council of the Churches of Christ in America, *Quadrennial Report* (1932); Robert Moats Miller, *American Protestantism and Social Issues, 1919–1939* (Chapel Hill: University of North Carolina Press, 1958), 101–2.

110. Reinhold Niebuhr, "Why I Leave the F.O.R.," *Christian Century* 51 (January 3, 1934); reprinted in Reinhold Niebuhr, *Love and Justice: Selections from the Shorter Writings of Reinhold Niebuhr*, ed. D. B. Robertson (1957; repr., Louisville: Westminster John Knox, 1992), 254–59.

111. Reinhold Niebuhr, *An Interpretation of Christian Ethics* (New York: Harper and Brothers, 1935; repr., New York: Harper and Row, 1963), quote 23.

112. Ibid., 106–7, 116.

113. Ibid., 114–15; Reinhold Niebuhr, "Religion and Marxism," *Modern Monthly* 8 (February 1935), 714.

114. Reinhold Niebuhr, "The Blindness of Liberalism, *Radical Religion* 1 (Autumn 1936), 4.

115. Ibid., "the inevitable," 4; Reinhold Niebuhr, "The Idea of Progress and Socialism," *Radical Religion* 1 (Spring 1936), "tolerable" and "socialism is," 28. Niebuhr's "tolerable equilibrium" phrase appeared frequently in his writings, as in Niebuhr, "Ten Years That Shook My World," 545.

116. Niebuhr, "The Idea of Progress and Socialism," "a frantic," "pathological," and "socialism means," 28; Reinhold Niebuhr, "The Creed of Modern Christian Socialists," *Radical Religion* 3 (Spring 1938), "a minimal," 16.

117. Dorrien, *Social Democracy in the Making*, 371–74; Arthur M. Schlesinger Jr., "Reinhold Niebuhr's Role in Political Thought," in *Reinhold Niebuhr: His Religious, Social, and Political Thought*, 140; Schlesinger, *The Politics of Upheaval* (Boston:

Houghton Mifflin, 1960), 626–57; John C. Bennett, "Reinhold Niebuhr's Social Ethics," in *Reinhold Niebuhr: His Religious, Social and Political Thought*, 73.

118. Eric Leif Davin, "The Very Last Hurrah? The Defeat of the Labor Party Idea, 1934–36," in *"We Are All Leaders": The Alternative Unionism of the Early 1930s*, ed. Staughton Lynd (Urbana: University of Illinois Press, 1996), 124–25; Bell, *Marxian Socialism in the United States*, 168–69; Johnpoll, *Pacifist's Progress*, 165–67; Swanberg, *Norman Thomas*, 194–95; Shannon, *The Socialist Party of America*, 242–43; Donald H. Grubbs, *Cry from the Cotton: The Southern Tenant Farmers' Union and the New Deal* (Chapel Hill, NC: University of North Carolina Press, 1971); Lowell K. Dyson, "The Southern Tenant Farmers Union and Depression Politics," *Political Science Quarterly* 88 (1973), 230–52.

119. Ross, *The Socialist Party of America*, 368–69; Student Section of the Independent Communist Labor League, "Which Road Shall the A.S.U. Take?" (November 1937), https://archive.org/details/WhichRoadShallTheAsuTake; American Student Union, *Toward a "Closed Shop" on the Campus* (New York: American Student Union, 1936); Fox, *Reinhold Niebuhr*, 170–71; Lawrence S. Wittner, *Rebels against War: The American Peace Movement, 1933–1983* (Philadelphia: Temple University Press, 1984), 20; Robert Cohen, *When the Old Left Was Young: Student Radicals and America's First Mass Student Movement, 1929–1941* (New York: Oxford University Press, 1993).

120. Reinhold Niebuhr, "The Revolutionary Moment," *American Socialist Quarterly* (June 1935), quotes 9.

121. "Thomas Wins Nomination But Wrecks Party"; Reinhold Niebuhr, "The Conflict in the Socialist Party," *Radical Religion* 1 (Winter 1936), "many" and "in New York," 1; Shannon, *The Socialist Party of America*, 245.

122. James P. Cannon, *History of American Trotskyism* (New York: Pioneer Press, 1944), 222–27, "ignorant," 227, "a Trotskyist," 223; Bell, *Marxian Socialism in the United States*, 170–74; C. L. R. James, *World Revolution, 1917–1936: The Rise and Fall of the Communist International* (London: Secker and Warburg, 1937); James, *The Black Jacobins: Toussaint L'Ouverture and the San Domingo Revolution* (London: Secker and Warburg, 1938).

123. Socialist Party, *For a Socialist America*, party platform leaflet, 1936; Bell, *Marxian Socialism in the United States*, 171; Shannon, *The Socialist Party of America*, 250; Swanberg, *Norman Thomas*, 200–205; Matthew Josephson, *Sidney Hillman* (New York: Doubleday, 1952), 398; "National Convention Convenes March 26," *Socialist Call* 3 (March 20, 1937).

124. Thomas, "An Autobiography," 183–90; Swanberg, *Norman Thomas*, 214–15.

125. Norman Thomas, *A Socialist's Faith* (New York: W. W. Norton, 1951), 311; Fleischman, *Norman Thomas*, 179; Swanberg, *Norman Thomas*, 216.

126. Dorothy Borg, "Notes on Roosevelt's 'Quarantine' Speech," *Political Science Quarterly* 72 (1957), 405–33; John M. Haight, "Roosevelt and the Aftermath of the 'Quarantine Speech,'" *Review of Politics* 24 (1962), 233–59; Haight, "France and the Aftermath of Roosevelt's 'Quarantine Speech,'" *World Politics* 14 (January 1962), 283–306.

127. Reinhold Niebuhr, "Brief Comments," *Radical Religion* 3 (Winter 1937), quote 7; Niebuhr, "Brief Notes," *Radical Religion* 3 (Spring 1938), quote 7; Niebuhr, "European Impressions," *Radical Religion* 2 (Autumn 1937), 31–33.

128. Reinhold Niebuhr, "New Deal Medicine," *Radical Religion* 4 (Spring 1939), "reactionary," "which wards," and "this quackery," 1–2; Niebuhr, "Roosevelt's Merry-Go-Round," *Radical Religion* 3 (Spring 1938), "if that man," 4; Schlesinger, "Reinhold Niebuhr's Role in Political Thought," 142.

129. W. E. B. Du Bois, "Russia, 1926," *The Crisis* 33 (November 1926), 7–8; Du Bois, "My Recent Journey," *The Crisis* 33 (December 1926), 66; Du Bois, "Judging Russia," *The Crisis* 33 (February 1927), 189–90; Du Bois, "The Negro and Communism," *The Crisis* (September 1931), 313–15, 318, 320, quote 319.

130. W. E. B. Du Bois, "Marxism and the Negro Problem," *The Crisis* 40 (May 1933), quote 103–4; Du Bois, "Communist Strategy," *The Crisis* 38 (September 1931), 313–14; Du Bois, "Our Class Struggle," *The Crisis* 40 (July 1933), 164–65.

131. Du Bois, "Marxism and the Negro Problem," quotes 104, 118.

132. Ibid., quotes 118.

133. Anderson, *A. Philip Randolph*, "I never," 177.

134. Ibid., 187–215; Larry Tye, *Rising from the Rails: Pullman Porters and the Making of the Black Middle Class* (New York: Macmillan, 2005), 40–57; Samuel Lubell, *The Future of American Politics* (Garden City, NY: Doubleday, 1956), 232; Jack Santino, *Miles of Smiles, Years of Struggle: Stories of Black Pullman Porters* (Urbana: University of Illinois Press, 1989).

135. Melinda Chateauvert, *Marching Together: Women of the Brotherhood of Sleeping Car Porters* (Urbana: University of Illinois Press, 1998), 43–45, quote 8.

136. Ibid., 11–13.

137. *Official Proceedings of the National Negro Conference* (Chicago: National Negro Conference, February 14–16, 1936), 7–12; Thomas C. Fleming, "The National Negro Congress of 1936," *Columbus Free Press* (September 22, 1999); Wilson Record, *The Negro and the Communist Party* (Chapel Hill: University of North Carolina Press, 1951), 153–99; Ralph Bunche, "The Programs, Ideologies, Tactics, and Achievements of Negro Betterment Organizations" (Pittsburgh: Carnegie Foundation Study, June 1940), 319–41; Horace R. Cayton and George S. Mitchell, *Black Workers and the New Unions* (Chapel Hill: University of North Carolina Press, 1939), 414–24; Anderson, *A. Philip Randolph*, 231–33; Irving Howe and Lewis Coser, *The American Communist Party* (New York: Praeger, 1962), 356–58.

138. Mark Naison, "Harlem Communists and the Politics of Black Protest," *Marxist Perspectives* 1 (Fall 1978), 33–35; Lawrence S. Wittner, "The National Negro Congress: A Reassessment," *American Quarterly* 22 (Winter 1970), 885–99.

139. Bunche, "The Programs, Ideologies, Tactics, and Achievements of Negro Betterment Organizations," 357–71; Howe and Coser, *The American Communist Party*, 358; Anderson, *A. Philip Randolph*, 234–36.

5. WORLD WAR EMERGENCY, COLD WAR VOID, AND BLACK FREEDOM ERUPTION

1. Norman Thomas to the *New York Herald Tribune* (September 12, 1939); Thomas to Aaron Levenstein (October 23, 1939)," "it is" and "we can," Norman Thomas

Papers, New York Public Library; W. A. Swanberg, *Norman Thomas: The Last Idealist* (New York: Scribner's, 1976), 235–38; Collection Overview, "Keep America Out of War Congress Collected Records, 1938–1942," Swarthmore College Peace Collection, Swarthmore, PA; Thomas and Bertram D. Wolfe, *Keep America Out of War: A Program* (New York: Frederick A. Stokes, 1939); Lawrence S. Wittner, *Rebels against War: The American Peace Movement 1933–1983* (Philadelphia: Temple University Press, 1984), 21; David A. Shannon, *The Socialist Party of America: A History* (New York: Macmillan, 1955), 255; Harry Fleischman, *Norman Thomas: A Biography* (New York: W. W. Norton, 1964), 199.

2. Gary Dorrien, *Social Ethics in the Making: Interpreting an American Tradition* (Oxford: Wiley-Blackwell, 2011), 109–30; Norman Thomas to Harry F. Ward, October 10, 1939, Harry F. Ward Papers, Burke Library, Columbia University; Ward, "Statement by Dr. Harry F. Ward, National Chairman," American League for Peace and Democracy, November 1938, Ward Papers; Ward, *In Place of Profit: Social Incentives in the Soviet Union* (New York: Charles Scribner's Sons, 1933); Ward, *The Soviet Spirit* (New York: International Publishers, 1944).

3. Socialist Party of America, "We Take Our Stand! 1940 Socialist Platform"; Jack Ross, *The Socialist Party of America: A Complete History* (Lincoln: University of Nebraska Press, 2015), 401; Shannon, *The Socialist Party of America*, 271.

4. [Reinhold Niebuhr], "The International Situation," *Radical Religion* 4 (Fall 1938), 1–2; Richard W. Fox, *Reinhold Niebuhr: A Biography* (Ithaca: Cornell University Press, 1996), 185–89.

5. Reinhold Niebuhr, "Leaves from the Notebook of a War-Bound American," August 25 and September 1, 1939 entries, *Christian Century* (October 25, 1939), 1298; September 18 and 21, 1939 entries, *Christian Century* (November 15, 1939), 1406; October 17 entry, *Christian Century* (December 27, 1939), 1607; Niebuhr, "The Ambiguity of Human Decisions," *Radical Religion* 5 (Summer 1939), 3–4.

6. Reinhold Niebuhr, *The Nature and Destiny of Man*, 2 vols., vol. 1: *Human Nature*; vol. 2: *Human Destiny*. (New York: Charles Scribner's Sons, 1941, 1943).

7. Niebuhr, "Leaves from the Notebook of a War-Bound American," *Christian Century* (November 15, 1939), "whatever," 1406; Niebuhr, "Leaves from the Notebook of a War-Bound American," (December 17, 1939), 1607.

8. Fox, *Reinhold Niebuhr*, 193. Another leading biographer, Charles C. Brown, conveys a simplistic understanding of Niebuhr's Socialism during this period and does not grasp that Niebuhr remained a Socialist until 1945; Charles C. Brown, *Niebuhr and His Age: Reinhold Niebuhr's Prophetic Role and Legacy* (Harrisburg, PA: Trinity Press, 2002), 100.

9. Irving Barshop to Reinhold Niebuhr, May 22, 1940, Reinhold Niebuhr Papers, Library of Congress, Washington, DC; Niebuhr to Barshop, May 24, 1940; Niebuhr, "An End to Illusions," *Nation* (June 29, 1940), 778; Niebuhr, "Idealists as Cynics," "Peace and the Liberal Illusion," "Greek Tragedy and Modern Politics," and "Ideology and Pretense," *Nation* articles reprinted in Niebuhr, *Christianity and Power Politics* (New York: Charles Scribner's Sons, 1940), 75–82, 83–94, 95–106, 107–16; Fox, *Reinhold Niebuhr*, 193.

10. Reinhold Niebuhr, "An End to Illusions," *Nation* (June 29, 1940), in *Christianity and Power Politics*, 167–75, "world radio," 167; "against tanks," 168.

11. Ibid., "the party," 167; "a conflict," "that is," "against purely," and "in a specific," 169.

12. Reinhold Niebuhr, "Germany and the Western World," in *Christianity and Power Politics*, 49–64, "moral purpose," 60.

13. [Charles Clayton Morrison], "Defending Democracy," *Christian Century* 57 (June 5, 1940), "or he will," 841; [Morrison], "No Third Term!" *Christian Century* 57 (October 16, 1940), 1273; Morrison, *The Christian and the War* (Chicago: Willett, Clark, 1942); Reinhold Niebuhr, "An Open Letter," *Christianity and Society* 5 (Summer 1940), 30–33, "completely," 31.

14. Franklin D. Roosevelt to Norman Thomas, November 9, 1940, Thomas Papers; Fleischman, *Norman Thomas*, 193–97; Bernard Johnpoll, *Pacifist's Progress: Norman Thomas and the Decline of American Socialism* (Chicago: Quadrangle, 1970), 224–27.

15. Waldo Frank, *A Chart for Rough Water: Our Role in a New World* (New York: Doubleday, Doran, 1940); Harold Bosley, "Illusion of the Disillusioned," *Christian Century* 58 (January 1, 1941), "a theological," 14–15; W. H. Auden, "Tract for the Times," *Nation* 152 (January 4, 1941), 24–25.

16. Reinhold Niebuhr, "To Prevent the Triumph of an Intolerable Tyranny," *Christian Century* 57 (December 18, 1940), quotes 1579; Niebuhr, "Editorial Notes," *Christianity and Society* 5 (Spring 1940), 10; [Charles C. Morrison], "Why We Differ," *Christian Century* 58 (December 10, 1941), 1534–38; [Morrison], "The Neutrality Act Is Discarded," *Christian Century* 58 (November 26, 1941), 1459.

17. Niebuhr, "To Prevent the Triumph of an Intolerable Tyranny," quotes 1579–80.

18. Niebuhr, "The War and American Churches," in *Christianity and Power Politics*, quote 47.

19. Reinhold Niebuhr, "The Lend-Lease Bill," *Christianity and Crisis* 1 (February 10, 1941), 2; "Niebuhr Launches New Journal," *Christian Century* 58 (January 22, 1941), 133.

20. "Union for Democratic Action," *Christianity and Society* 6 (Summer 1941), 6; Steven M. Gillon, *Politics and Vision: The ADA and American Liberalism, 1947–1985* (New York: Oxford University Press, 1987), 8–12.

21. Reinhold Niebuhr, "New Allies, Old Issues," *Nation* 153 (July 19, 1941), quote 50–51; Niebuhr, "The Crisis Deepens," *Christianity and Crisis* 1 (May 5, 1941), 1–2.

22. Dorothy Thompson, *New York Herald Tribune* (February 24, 1941), "the reality" and "defense," and Norman Thomas, "How to Fight for Democracy," *Annals of the American Academy* (July 1941), "that British" and "lesser" in Swanberg, *Norman Thomas*, 246–47.

23. Norman Thomas to Burton Wheeler, August 25, 1941, "senior partner" and "if we," Thomas Papers; Charles A. Lindbergh, *Wartime Journals of Charles A. Lindbergh* (New York: Harcourt, 1970), 539; Norman Thomas to Bertram Wolfe and Emanuel Muravchik, September 16, 1941, Thomas Papers; Thomas to Reinhold Niebuhr, September 15, 1941; Swanberg, *Norman Thomas*, 254–55; Wayne S. Cole, *America First* (Madison: University of Wisconsin Press, 1953), 147–48.

24. Norman Thomas to Maynard Krueger, December 11, 1941, "I feel"; Thomas to the National Executive Committee, Socialist Party of America, December 9, 1941, "for civil"; Thomas to Ken Cuthbertson, January 2, 1942, "what is," Thomas Papers.

25. [Charles C. Morrison], "An Unnecessary Necessity," *Christian Century* 58 (December 17, 1941), 1565–67, quotes 1565.

26. Leon Trotsky, "The USSR in War," *New International* 5 (November 1939), 325–32; reprinted in Trotsky, *In Defense of Marxism: Against the Petty-Bourgeois Opposition* (New York: Merit Publishers, 1965), 3–21, and *The Basic Writings of Trotsky*, ed. Irving Howe (New York: Random House, 1963), 305–14; Trotsky, "The Twin-Stars: Hitler-Stalin," "The World Situation and Perspectives," and "Stalin after the Finnish Experience," in *Writings of Leon Trotsky (1939–1940)*, ed. Naomi Allen and George Breitman (New York: Pathfinder Press, 1973), 113–24, 139–57, 160–64; Peter Drucker, *Max Shachtman and His Left: A Socialist's Odyssey Through the American Century* (Highland Park, NJ: Humanities Press, 1994), 145–53; Maurice Isserman, *If I Had a Hammer: The Death of the Old Left and the Birth of the New Left* (New York: Basic Books, 1987), 38–39.

27. Leon Trotsky, "'Not a Workers' and Not a Bourgeois State?" in *Writings of Leon Trotsky (1937–1938)* (New York: Pathfinder Press, 1970), 60–71, "one has," 66–67; Trotsky, "Once Again on the 'Crisis of Marxism,'" *Writings of Leon Trotsky (1938–1939)* (New York: Pathfinder Press, 1974), 204–206; Trotsky, "Bureaucratism and the Revolution" and "Is the Bureaucracy a Ruling Class?" in *Basic Writings of Trotsky*, 170–77, 216–22; James Burnham, "Science and Style: A Reply to Comrade Trotsky," in Trotsky, *In Defense of Marxism*, 187–206.

28. Bruno Rizzi, *The Bureaucratization of the World*, trans Adam Westoby (1939; repr., New York: Free Press, 1985), 50–56.

29. Leon Trotsky, "The USSR in War," Trotsky, *In Defense of Marxism*, "the phenomenon," 10.

30. Max Shachtman, untitled essay of 1940, reprinted in Shachtman, *The Bureaucratic Revolution: The Rise of the Stalinist State* (New York: Ronald Press, 1962), and reprinted under the title "Stalinism: A New Social Order," in *Essential Works of Socialism*, ed. Irving Howe (New Haven: Yale University Press, 1976), 526–46.

31. Gary Dorrien, *The Neoconservative Mind: Politics, Culture, and the War of Ideology* (Philadelphia: Temple University Press, 1992), 28–34; Isserman, *If I Had a Hammer*, "a kibitzer," 116; Irving Howe, *A Margin of Hope: An Intellectual Autobiography* (New York: Harcourt Brace Jovanovich, 1982), "his mixture," 40.

32. Dorrien, *The Neoconservative Mind*, 34–67; Johnpoll, *Pacifist's Progress*, 233–34; Swanberg, *Norman Thomas*, 262; Ross, *The Socialist Party of America*, 417; Drucker, *Max Shachtman and His Left*, 145–53; Isserman, *If I Had a Hammer*, 40–41; James Burnham, *The Managerial Revolution: What Is Happening in the World* (New York: John Day, 1941); Burnham, *The Struggle for the World* (New York: John Day, 1947); Burnham, *Containment or Liberation? An Inquiry into the Aims of United States Foreign Policy* (New York: John Day, 1952).

33. Norman Thomas, *We Have a Future* (Princeton: Princeton University Press, 1941), 42–43, 124; Swanberg, *Norman Thomas*, 267.

34. Norman Thomas, *A Socialist's Faith* (New York: W. W. Norton, 1951), 46; Swanberg, *Norman Thomas*, 282; Fleischman, *Norman Thomas*, 206–7.

35. Johnpoll, *Pacifist's Progress*, quote 237.

36. Winston Churchill, *The Second World War: Triumph and Tragedy* (Boston: Houghton Mifflin, 1953), 400–401.

37. Fleischman, *Norman Thomas: A Biography*, "a war," 213–14; Thomas, *A Socialist's Faith*, 67.

38. Herbert Garfinkel, *When Negroes March: The March on Washington Movement in the Organizational Politics for FEPC* (New York: Atheneum, 1969), 18–31; Jervis Anderson, *A. Philip Randolph: A Biographical Portrait* (New York: Harcourt Brace, 1973), 244–61; Walter White, *A Man Called White* (New York: Viking, 1948), 186–93; David Lucander, *Winning the War for Democracy: The March on Washington Movement, 1941–1946* (Urbana: University of Illinois Press, 2014).

39. Adam Clayton Powell Jr., "Soap Box," *The People's Voice* (April 18, 1942), 5; Powell Jr., Speech at Madison Square Garden, June 16, 1942, in Powell, *The People's Voice* (June 19, 1942); Charles V. Hamilton, *Adam Clayton Powell Jr.: The Political Biography of an American Dilemma* (New York: Scribner, 1991), 140; Wil Haygood, *King of the Cats: The Life and Times of Adam Clayton Powell Jr.* (Boston: Houghton Mifflin, 1993), 93.

40. Garfinkel, *When Negroes March*, 41–59; James Farmer, *Lay Bare the Heart: An Autobiography of the Civil Rights Movement* (New York: Arbor House, 1985; repr., Fort Worth: Texas Christian University Press, 1998), 154–56; White, *A Man Called White*, 190–94.

41. Farmer, *Lay Bare the Heart*, quote 79–80.

42. Ibid., 80.

43. Ibid., "an old," 85, "being Negroes," 111; A. J. Muste, *The Essays of A. J. Muste*, ed. Nat Hentoff (New York: Simon and Schuster, 1967); Nat Hentoff, *Peace Agitator: The Story of A. J. Muste* (New York: Macmillan, 1963), 25–44; Jo Ann Robinson, *Abraham Went Out: A Biography of A. J. Muste* (Philadelphia: Temple University Press, 1982), 29–38.

44. Farmer, *Lay Bare the Heart*, 156; Editorial, "To March or Not to March," *Pittsburgh Courier* (January 2, 1943); A. Philip Randolph, "A Reply to My Critics," *Chicago Defender* (July 17, 1943).

45. Farmer, *Lay Bare the Heart*, "we knew," 153.

46. A. Philip Randolph, Message to the 24th National Convention, "Minutes of the 24th National Convention," 1944, Socialist Party of America; Ross, *The Socialist Party of America*, 424.

47. Reinhold Niebuhr, "History (God) Has Overtaken Us," *Christianity and Society* 7 (Winter 1941–42), in Niebuhr, *Love and Justice: Selections from the Shorter Writings of Reinhold Niebuhr*, ed. D. B. Robertson (Philadelphia: Westminster Press, 1957), 292–96, "we could," 293; Niebuhr, "Editorial Notes," *Christianity and Society* 7 (Winter 1941–42), "many of," 9.

48. Niebuhr, *The Nature and Destiny of Man*, 2: 244–86.

49. Reinhold Niebuhr, *The Children of Light and the Children of Darkness* (New York: Scribner's, 1944), "other stupid," 32, "the blindness," 13.

50. Niebuhr, *The Children of Light and the Children of Darkness,* "demonic" and "boundless,"" 23; "man's capacity," xi.

51. Ibid., quote 113–14.

52. Reinhold Niebuhr, *Christian Realism and Political Problems* (New York: Scribner's, 1953), quote 127.

53. Norman Thomas, "Open Letter to Reinhold Niebuhr," *Socialist Call* (August 4, 1944), in Swanberg, *Norman Thomas,* 288, and Frank Warren, *An Alternative Vision: The Socialist Party in the 1930s* (Bloomington: Indiana University Press, 1974), 180.

54. Reinhold Niebuhr, "Reply to Norman Thomas," *Socialist Call* (September 8, 1944), in Swanberg, *Norman Thomas,* 290, and Warren, *An Alternative Vision,* 181.

55. Reinhold Niebuhr, "Plutocracy and World Responsibilities," *Christianity and Society* 14 (Autumn 1949), "a bare," 7–8; Niebuhr, "Frontier Fellowship," *Christianity and Society* 13 (Autumn 1948), 4; Niebuhr, "The Organization of the Liberal Movement," *Christianity and Society* 12 (Spring 1947), 8–10; Niebuhr et al., "Christian Action Statement of Purpose," *Christianity and Crisis* 11 (October 1, 1951), "to maintain," 126; Niebuhr, "The Anomaly of European Socialism," *Yale Review* 42 (December 1952), 166–67.

56. Johnpoll, *Pacifist's Progress,* 250–54, "a glorified," 253; Norman Thomas to Maurice Specter, May 5, 1950, Thomas Papers; Swanberg, *Norman Thomas,* 291–93; Jack Ross, *Rabbi Outcast: Elmer Berger and American Jewish Anti-Zionism* (Washington, DC: Potomac Books, 2011), 105–6.

57. Daniel Yergin, *Shattered Peace: The Origins of the Cold War and the National Security State* (Boston: Houghton Mifflin, 1977), "then the," 285; Dorrien, *The Neoconservative Mind,* 72–84.

58. Keith Archer, *Political Choices and Electoral Consequences: A Study of Organized Labour and the New Democratic Party* (Montreal: McGill–Queen's University Press, 1990), 15–29; Ross, *The Socialist Party of America,* 431; Hugh T. Lovin, "New Deal Leftists, Henry Wallace and 'Gideon's Army,' and the Progressive Party in Montana, 1937–1952," *Great Plains Quarterly* (Fall 2012), 273–86; Lawrence S. Wittner, *American Intervention in Greece, 1943–1949* (New York: Columbia University Press, 1982), 180–97; Karl M. Schmidt, *Henry A. Wallace: Quixotic Crusade 1948* (Syracuse: Syracuse University Press, 1960), 91–95.

59. Gary Dorrien, *Breaking White Supremacy: Martin Luther King Jr. and the Black Social Gospel* (New Haven: Yale University Press, 2018), 204–5; Reinhold Niebuhr, "The Organization of the Liberal Movement," *Christianity and Society* 12 (Spring 1947), 8; John C. Culver and John Hyde, *American Dreamer: A Life of Henry A. Wallace* (New York: W. W. Norton, 2000), 408–66.

60. Niebuhr, "The Organization of the Liberal Movement," 8; Fox, *Reinhold Niebuhr,* "ladies," 230; Brown, *Niebuhr and His Age,* 128.

61. Norman Thomas to Daniel Bell, November 4, 1947, Thomas Papers; Daniel Bell, *The End of Ideology: On the Exhaustion of Political Ideas in the Fifties* (New York: Free Press, 1960).

62. Johnpoll, *Pacifist's Progress,* quotes 256; Norman Thomas to A. Philip Randolph, November 10, 1947, Thomas Papers; Randolph, "Why I Am for Thomas," *Socialist Call* (October 19, 1948); Fleischman, *Norman Thomas,* 235–37.

63. Dorrien, *Breaking White Supremacy,* 205.

64. Mikhail Heller and Aleksandr M. Nekrich, *Utopia in Power: The History of the Soviet Union from 1917 to the Present,* trans. Phyllis B. Carlos (New York: Summit Books, 1986), 370–511; Robert Leckie, *Delivered from Evil: The Saga of World War II* (New York: Harper and Row, 1987), 648–64; John Lewis Gaddis, *The United States and the Origins of the Cold War, 1941–1947* (New York: Columbia University Press, 1972), 230–43.

65. Robert A. Divine, "The Cold War and the Election of 1948," *Journal of American History* 59 (1972), 90–110; Thomas W. Devine, *Henry Wallace's 1948 Presidential Campaign and the Future of Postwar Liberalism* (Chapel Hill: University of North Carolina Press, 2013); Zachary Karabell, *The Last Campaign: How Harry Truman Won the 1948 Election* (New York: Knopf, 2001); Arthur Schlesinger Jr., *The Vital Center: The Politics of Freedom* (Boston: Houghton Mifflin, 1949).

66. Thomas, *A Socialist's Faith,* 9–21, "vast," 12.

67. Ibid., "with the," 13; "if by," 14.

68. Ibid., "we could," 15.

69. Ibid., "hard," 37; "Russian," viii; "the evidence" and "despite," 47.

70. Ibid., 3; Norman Thomas, *The Choice before Us: Mankind at the Crossroads* (New York: Macmillan, 1934), 219–21; Thomas, *We Have a Future,* 150–58.

71. Thomas, *A Socialist's Faith,* quote 191; Norman Thomas, *Socialism Re-examined* (New York: W. W. Norton, 1963), 137–43.

72. Thomas, *A Socialist's Faith,* 4–8, "his admirable," 121; Norman Thomas, *The Prerequisites for Peace* (New York: W. W. Norton, 1959).

73. Thomas, *A Socialist's Faith,* "of nothing," 317; "imperial," viii.

74. [George F. Kennan], "The Sources of Soviet Conduct," *Foreign Affairs* 25 (July 1947), "long-term," 576; "Soviet," 579–80.

75. Reinhold Niebuhr, "Why Is Communism So Evil?" *The New Leader* (June 8, 1953), in Niebuhr, *Christian Realism and Political Problems* (New York: Scribner's, 1953), 33–42, "noxious," 34; "nothing," 41.

76. Reinhold Niebuhr, "The Change in Russia," *The New Leader* 38 (October 3, 1955), "simple," 18–19; Niebuhr, "Why Is Communism So Evil?" 37; Niebuhr, "The Peril of Complacency in Our Nation," *Christianity and Crisis* 14 (February 8, 1954), "we are embattled," 1.

77. Niebuhr, "The Change in Russia," quotes 18–19.

78. Reinhold Niebuhr, *The Irony of American History* (New York: Scribner's, 1952), "of all," 15; "if only," 16.

79. Ibid., "and the mixture," 133; Niebuhr, "Why Is Communism So Evil?" "an organized," 34.

80. Reinhold Niebuhr, "Communism and the Protestant Clergy," *Look* (November 17, 1953), 37; Niebuhr, "Uneasy Peace or Catastrophe," *Christianity and Crisis* 18 (April 28, 1958), 53; Niebuhr, *The Structure of Nations and Empires* (New York: Charles Scribner's Sons, 1959), 282.

81. "Why We Are Leaving the Socialist Party, by the Chicago Left Wing—June 1949," in Ross, *The Socialist Party of America,* 454; J. Paul Henderson, *Darlington Hoopes: The*

Political Biography of an American Socialist (Glasgow: Humming Earth, 2005), "we must," 137.

82. Martin Luther King, Jr., to Alberta Williams King, October 1948, *The Papers of Martin Luther King, Jr.*, ed. Clayborne Carson, Ralph E. Luker, Penny A. Russell, vol. 1, *Called to Serve, January 1929–June 1951* (Berkeley: University of California Press, 1992), 161; King, "The Christian Pertinence of Eschatological Hope," 29 November 1949–15 February 1950, *The Papers of Martin Luther King, Jr.*, 1: 268–73; King, "Preaching Ministry," September 14–November 24, 1948, *The Papers of Martin Luther King, Jr.*, ed. Clayborne Carson et al., vol. 6, *Advocate of the Social Gospel* (Berkeley: University of California Press, 2007), 69–72, "I am a," 72. This section summarizes themes and arguments in *Breaking White Supremacy*.

83. Martin Luther King Jr., *Stride toward Freedom: The Montgomery Story* (1958; repr., Boston: Beacon Press, 2010), "his message," 84; Martin Luther King Jr., "Pilgrimage to Nonviolence," *Christian Century* 77 (13 April 1960), 439–41; Coretta Scott King, *My Life with Martin Luther King, Jr.* (New York: Holt, Rinehart and Winston, 1969), 71; David Garrow, *Bearing the Cross: Martin Luther King, Jr., and the Southern Christian Leadership Conference* (New York: Quill, 1986), 41.

84. Martin Luther King, Jr. Papers Project, "The Student Papers of Martin Luther King, Jr.: A Summary Statement on Research," *Journal of American History* 78 (June 1991), 23–31; Keith D. Miller, "Composing Martin Luther King, Jr.," *PMLA* 105 (January 1990), 70–82; Miller, *Voice of Deliverance: The Language of Martin Luther King, Jr., and Its Sources* (New York: Free Press, 1992; repr., Athens: University of Georgia Press, 1998), 45–92; Miller, "Martin Luther King, Jr., Borrows a Revolution: Argument, Audience and Implications of a Secondhand Universe," *College English* 48 (March 1986), 249–65; David Levering Lewis, *King: A Biography* (1970; 3rd ed., Urbana: University of Illinois Press, 2003); Lewis V. Baldwin, "Martin Luther King, Jr., the Black Church, and the Black Messianic Vision," *Journal of the Interdenominational Theological Center* 12 (Fall 1984/Spring 1985), 93–108.

85. J. Pius Barbour to Martin Luther King, Jr., 21 July 1955, *The Papers of Martin Luther King, Jr.*, 2: 564–66; Lischer, *The Preacher King*, 68–69; Lewis, *King*, 33; Garrow, *Bearing the Cross*, 41.

86. Martin Luther King, Jr., "Reinhold Niebuhr's Ethical Dualism," 9 May 1952, *The Papers of Martin Luther King, Jr.*, 2: 142–51, "all these," 150; Walter Muelder, "Reinhold Niebuhr's Conception of Man," *The Personalist* 26 (July 1945), 284–92; King Jr., *Stride toward Freedom*, 100; King Jr., "The Theology of Reinhold Niebuhr," April 1953–June 1954, *The Papers of Martin Luther King, Jr.*, 2: 269–79.

87. Dorrien, *Breaking White Supremacy*, 271–81.

88. Martin Luther King, Jr., "MIA Mass Meeting at Holt Street Baptist Church," December 5, 1955, *The Papers of Martin Luther King, Jr.*, 3: 71–74; King, Holt Street Baptist Church Address, December 5, 1955, audiotape, Martin Luther King Jr. Center, Atlanta, GA; King, *Stride toward Freedom*, 48–52.

89. Bayard Rustin, "Nonviolence vs. Jim Crow" (1942), Rustin, "The Negro and Nonviolence" (1942), and Rustin, "Twenty-Two Days on a Chain Gang," in Rustin, *Time on Two Crosses: The Collected Writings of Bayard Rustin*, ed. Devon W. Carbado

and Donald Wise (San Francisco: Cleis Press, 2003), 1–5, 6–10, 31–57; Howell Raines, *My Soul Is Rested* (New York: G. P. Putnam's, 1977), 53–56; August Meier and Elliott Rudwick, *CORE: A Study in the Civil Rights Movement, 1942–1968* (Urbana: University of Illinois Press, 1975), 9–38; John D'Emilio, *Lost Prophet: The Life and Times of Bayard Rustin* (Chicago: University of Chicago Press, 2003), 7–38; Milton Viorst, *Fire in the Streets: America in the 1960s* (New York: Simon and Schuster, 1979), 200–211.

90. Bayard Rustin, Montgomery Diary, February 21, 25, and 26, 1956, in *Time on Two Crosses*, quotes 59, 63; D'Emilio, *Lost Prophet*, 224–29.

91. Rustin, Montgomery Diary, 64–65; Bayard Rustin, "New South, Old Politics," *Liberation* (October 1956), 23–26.

92. D'Emilio, *Lost Prophet*, quote 234; Farmer, *Lay Bare the Heart*, 178, 186–87.

93. Glenn Smiley to John Swomley and Alfred Hassler, February 29, 1956, Fellowship of Reconciliation Papers, John Swomley Files, Swarthmore College, "he had"; Smiley to Swomley, n.d. [March 1, 1956], "we can"; D'Emilio, *Lost Prophet*, "Bayard was," 234; Garrow, *Bearing the Cross*, 70; L. D. Reddick, *Crusader Without Violence* (New York: Harper and Row, 1959), 123–24.

94. Martin Luther King, Jr., "Our Struggle," *Liberation* (April 1956), 3–6; Michael Harrington, *Fragments of the Century* (New York: Saturday Review, 1973), 101–2.

95. King, *Stride toward Freedom*, "there is," "whatever," 54, 55; Garrow, *Bearing the Cross*, "the oppressed" and "he wanders," 63, 76; Reddick, *Crusader without Violence*, 129–30; L. D. Reddick, "The Bus Boycott in Montgomery," *Dissent* (Spring 1956), 111.

96. Martin Luther King, Jr., "The Ethical Demands of Integration," *Religion and Labor* (May 1963), 4; Anders Nygren, *Agape and Eros*, trans. Philip S. Watson (Philadelphia: Westminster Press, 1953), 75–81; Paul Ramsey, *Basic Christian Ethics* (New York: Charles Scribner's Sons, 1950), 2–3, 13, 94–105; Kenneth L. Smith and Ira G. Zepp, Jr., *Search for the Beloved Community: The Thinking of Martin Luther King, Jr.* (Valley Forge, PA: Judson Press, 1998), 61–66.

97. Ella Baker, "Bigger than a Hamburger," *Southern Patriot* 18 (June 1960), 4; Baker, "Tent City: Freedom's Front Line," *Southern Patriot* 19 (February 1961), 1; Barbara Ransby, *Ella Baker and the Black Freedom Movement: A Radical Democratic Vision* (Chapel Hill: University of North Carolina Press, 2003); Reddick, *Crusader Without Violence*, 157; David J. Garrow, *The FBI and Martin Luther King, Jr., from "Solo" to Memphis* (New York: W. W. Norton, 1981), 42–45; Adam Fairclough, *To Redeem the Soul of America: The Southern Christian Leadership Conference and Martin Luther King, Jr.* (Athens: University of Georgia Press, 1987), 29–31.

98. A. Philip Randolph to Ella Baker, March 7, 1956, A. Philip Randolph Papers, Library of Congress; Fairclough, *To Redeem the Soul of America*, 32; Aldon D. Morris, *The Origins of the Civil Rights Movement: Black Communities Organizing for Change* (New York: Free Press, 1984), 82–83; Ella Baker, "The Black Woman in the Civil Rights Struggle," in *Ella Baker: Freedom Bound*, ed. Joanne Grant (New York: Wiley, 1998), 227–31.

99. Taylor Branch, *Parting the Waters: America in the King Years, 1954–63* (New York: Simon and Schuster, 1988), 185–86; Garrow, *Bearing the Cross*, quotes 81, 84; King,

Stride toward Freedom, 163–65; Reddick, *Crusader Without Violence*, 154; Harris Wofford, *Of Kennedys and Kings: Making Sense of the Sixties* (New York: Farrar, Straus and Giroux, 1980; repr., Pittsburgh: University of Pittsburgh Press, 1992), 115.

100. Morris, *Origins of the Civil Rights Movement*, 84–87; Fairclough, *To Redeem the Soul of America*, 32–34; Reddick, *Crusader Without Violence*, 184–86; King, *Stride toward Freedom*, 167–68; Branch, *Parting the Waters*, 199; Kenneth B. Clark, "The Civil Rights Movement: Momentum and Organizations," *Daedalus* 95 (Winter 1996), 611–12.

101. Bayard Rustin, "New South . . . Old Politics" (1956), in Rustin, *Time on Two Crosses*, 95–101; Fairclough, *To Redeem the Soul of America*, 37–55; Adam Fairclough, *Martin Luther King, Jr.* (Athens: University of Georgia Press, 1995), 34–47; Branch, *Parting the Waters*, 206–16.

102. Branch, *Parting the Waters*, quotes 217; Reddick, *Crusader Without Victory*, 194–96.

103. Martin Luther King Jr., "Give Us the Ballot—We Will Transform the South," May 17, 1957, in King, *Testament of Hope: The Essential Writings and Speeches of Martin Luther King, Jr.*, ed. James M. Washington (New York: HarperCollins, 1991), quotes 197, 198.

104. Ibid., 198, 199.

105. Ibid., 199, 200.

106. Ibid., 200.

107. Fairclough, *To Redeem the Soul of America*, 42–46; Morris, *Origins of the Civil Rights Movement*, 126–28; Farmer, *Lay Bare the Heart*, 190.

108. Ransby, *Ella Baker and the Black Freedom Movement*, 180–92; Stephen B. Oates, *Let the Trumpet Sound: The Life of Martin Luther King Jr.* (New York: Harper and Row, 1982), 514; Morris, *Origins of the Civil Rights Movement*, "I have," 113; Fairclough, *To Redeem the Soul of America*, "whatsoever," 50.

109. Raines, *My Soul Is Rested*, "I'm proud," 50; Morris, *Origins of the Civil Rights Movement*, 93; Dorrien, *Breaking White Supremacy*, 470–504.

110. Reddick, *Crusader Without Violence*, "neither by," 233.

111. Harrington, *Fragments of the Century*, 71–77, "public" and "pleasant," 1; Maurice Isserman, *The Other American: The Life of Michael Harrington* (New York: PublicAffairs, 2000), 9–14; Marion Magid, "The Man Who Discovered Poverty," *New York Herald Tribune Magazine* (27 December 1964), 9.

112. Harrington, *Fragments of the Century*, "suddenly," 66; Michael Harrington, *The Long-Distance Runner: An Autobiography* (New York: Henry Holt, 1988), 1; Isserman, *The Other American*, 54–55.

113. Dorrien, *Social Ethics in the Making*, 361–77; Dorothy Day, *The Long Loneliness* (New York: Harper and Row, 1952).

114. Ian Williams, "Remembering Bogdan Denitch," *Nation* (April 5, 2016); Harrington, *The Long-Distance Runner*, 22; Isserman, *The Other American*, 102–5.

115. Daniel Bell, "Marxian Socialism in the United States," in *Socialism and American Life*, 2 vols., ed. Donald Drew Egbert and Stow Persons (Princeton: Princeton University Press, 1952), "unhappy" and "moral man," 1: 217; Howard Brick, *Daniel Bell and the Decline of Intellectual Radicalism: Social Theory and Political*

Reconciliation in the 1940s (Madison: University of Wisconsin Press, 1986), 171; Michael Kazin, "The Agony and Romance of the American Left," *American Historical Review* 100 (December 1995), 1488–1512.

116. Bell, "Marxian Socialism in the United States," "the illusions," 222; Howe, *A Margin of Hope*, "never before," 42.

117. Max Shachtman, "An Epigone of Trotsky," *New International* 10 (August 1944), "doubts," 266; Isserman, *If I Had a Hammer*, 46.

118. Ernest Lund [Ernest Erber], "The Turn to a Mass Party," private circular to the Workers Party, 1943; Isserman, *If I Had a Hammer*, 47–51, "we live," 47; Howe, *A Margin of Hope*, 50–51.

119. This version of the Denitch joke came from David McReynolds, to Isserman on September 16, 1991; Isserman, *The Other American*, 121.

120. David McReynolds, "On Cooperation with the Socialist Youth League," *Young Socialist Review* (Winter 1952), 5; Isserman, *The Other American*, 123; Bogdan Denitch, "YPSL Breaks Ties with Socialist Party," *Labor Action* (July 13, 1953), 3.

121. Harrington, *Fragments of the Century*, quotes 76, 77; Michael Harrington, "An Appeal to Militant Pacifists by a Pacifist-Socialist: For Unity," *Labor Action* (February 8, 1954), 8; Edward Hill [Michael Harrington], "Pacifists Join the YSL" (March 1, 1954), 7.

122. Edward Hill [Michael Harrington], "What Does Liberalism Offer Youth?" *Young Socialist Challenge* (October 3, 1955), 2; Isserman, *The Other American*, 133; Arthur Mitzman, "The Campus Radical in 1960," *Dissent* (Spring 1960), 143–45; Harrington, *Fragments of the Century*, 79.

123. Michael Harrington, "A Discussion: The Third-Camp Socialist as 'Witness,'" *Labor Action* (May 17, 1954), "if the," 2-C; Harrington, "An Appeal to Militant Pacifists," 8; Harrington, "Plenty of Common Ground," *Young Socialist Challenge* (March 28, 1955), 1-C; Isserman, *The Other American*, 138.

124. Howe, *A Margin of Hope*, "programmatically" and "the fate," 45.

125. Harrington, *Fragments of the Century*, "Social," 96.

126. Ibid., "if only," 98.

127. Ibid., "we had," 101; "utterly," 102; Rachelle Horowitz, "Tom Kahn and the Fight for Democracy: A Political Portrait and Personal Recollection," *Democratiya* 11 (Winter 2007), 204–51, "he believed," 213.

128. Michael Harrington, "Communism after Hungary: In the United States," *Commonweal* 65 (February 1, 1957), 455–56; Bogdan Denitch, "Gates Case Touches Off Defense of Academic Freedom," *Young Socialist Challenge* (March 25, 1957), 1-C; Denitch, "The Campus Shows Signs of Perking Up," *Young Socialist Challenge* (April 22, 1957), 1-C; Isserman, *The Other American*, 164–65.

129. Norman Thomas to Morris Polin, January 23, 1957, Thomas Papers; Elmer Berger to Norman Thomas, March 22, 1957; Ross, *Rabbi Outcast*, 124–25; Ross, *The Socialist Party of America*, 468–70.

130. Isserman, *If I Had a Hammer*, 70–71, "lean," 71; Isserman, *The Other American*, 396.

131. Isserman, *If I Had a Hammer*, "he's going," 73; Henderson, *Darlington Hoopes*, 156; Ross, *The Socialist Party of America*, 472; Isserman, *The Other American*, 163–65.

132. Max Shachtman, "What Program for Democratic Socialists?" *Labor Action* (March 14, 1958), 3.

133. Gordon Haskell, "Labor Movement Too Is Put on the Spot by the Historic Negro Fight in the South," *Labor Action* 5 (March 1956), 2; Herman Benson, "The Communist Party at the Crossroads," *New International* 22 (Fall 1956); Shachtman, "What Program for Democratic Socialists?" 3; Michael Harrington, "The New Left," YPSL mimeograph (1959), 6–7.

134. George R. Vickers, *The Formation of the New Left: The Early Years* (Lexington, MA: D. C. Heath, 1975), 68–70; Kirkpatrick Sale, SDS: *The Rise and Development of the Students for a Democratic Society* (New York: Vintage, 1974), 24–35; Isserman, *If I Had a Hammer*, 204.

135. A. Philip Randolph, "The Cruel Deception," *New America* (September 5, 1960), 1; Socialist Party–Social Democratic Federation, "A Way Forward: Political Realignment in America," (1960), in Ross, *The Socialist Party of America*, quotes 476–77; *Proceedings: 1960 National Convention, Socialist Party–Social Democratic Federation*, May 28–30, 1960, Washington, DC, 1–28.

136. Harrington, *Fragments of the Century*, "it was," 107; "Political Action Is Focus of SP Convention Debate," *New America* (June 29, 1962), 6.

137. Harrington, *Fragments of the Century*, "filled with," 108.

138. Adam Clayton Powell Jr., "Let's Give Up Our Own Prejudices," Sermon on July 3, 1960, in Powell, *Keep the Faith, Baby!* (New York: Trident Press, 1967), quotes 79, 80; this section on Powell adapts my discussion in Dorrien, *Breaking White Supremacy*, 224–26.

139. Garrow, *Bearing the Cross*, 138; Branch, *Parting the Waters*, 314–15, quote 291; D'Emilio, *Lost Prophet:*, 296–97.

140. Branch, *Parting the Waters*, 315; D'Emilio, *Lost Prophet*, 298; Garrow, *Bearing the Cross*, 138.

141. D'Emilio, *Lost Prophet*, quotes 298–99; Branch, *Parting the Waters*, 329; Clayborne Carson, *In Struggle: SNCC and the Black Awakening of the 1960s* (Cambridge: Harvard University Press, 1995), 26–27.

142. Harrington, *Fragments of the Century*, "I marveled" and "like," 114.

143. Ibid., "he understood," 114–15, "it was," 115.

6. NEW LEFT, OLD LEFT, AND MICHAEL HARRINGTON

1. Michael Harrington, "Yvon Craipeau's New Book 'The Coming Revolution,' " *Young Socialist Challenge* (January 27, 1958), 10; Harrington, "The New Left: The Relevance of Democratic Socialism in Contemporary America" (New York: YPSL pamphlet, 1959), 1, 9–10; Norman Birnbaum, "British Opinion on Marchers," *Nation* (April 18, 1959), 339; Andrew Hacker, "The Rebelling Young Scholars," *Commentary* 30 (November 1960), 409–10; Maurice Isserman, *The Other American: The Life of Michael Harrington* (New York: PublicAffairs, 2000), 168; Stuart Hall, "Culture, the Media, and the 'Ideological Effect,' " in *Mass Communication and Society*, ed. J. Curran and J. Woollacott (London: Edward Arnold, 1977), 315–48.

2. "Political Action Is Focus of SP Convention Debate," *New America* (June 29, 1962), 6; James MacGregor Burns, *The Deadlock of Democracy: Four-Party Politics in America* (New York: Prentice Hall, 1963).

3. Casey Hayden, "Onto Open Ground" and "In the Attics of My Mind," in *Hands on the Freedom Plow: Personal Accounts by Women in SNCC*, ed. Faith S. Holsaert, Martha Prescod Norman Noonan, Judy Richardson, Betty Garman Robinson, Jean Smith Young, and Dorothy M. Zellner (Urbana: University of Illinois Press, 2012), 49–52, 381–88; Tom Hayden, *Reunion: A Memoir* (New York: Collier Books, 1988), 15–52; James Miller, *Democracy Is in the Streets: From Port Huron to the Siege of Chicago* (New York: Simon and Schuster, 1987), 154; Michael Harrington, *Fragments of the Century* (New York: Saturday Review Press/E. P. Dutton, 1973), 132–33; C. Wright Mills, *White Collar: The American Middle Classes* (New York: Oxford University Press, 1953); Isserman, *The Other American*, 228; Kirkpatrick Sale, *SDS* (New York: Random House, 1993), 57–60.

4. Hayden, *Reunion*, "not just," 54; Harrington, *Fragments of the Century*, 133; Casey Hayden, "Onto Open Ground," 52.

5. Tom Hayden, "Writing the Port Huron Statement," in *The Sixties*, ed. Linda Rosen Obst (San Francisco: Rolling Stone Press, 1977), 71; Hayden, *Reunion*, 94–95; C. Wright Mills, *The Power Elite* (New York: Oxford University Press, 1956).

6. Tom Hayden, "Draft Paper for S.D.S. Manifesto, for Consideration in Convention 11–15 June, F.D.R. Labor Center, Port Huron, Michigan," DSA Collection, Tamiment Library, New York University; Students for a Democratic Society, *The Port Huron Statement*, at http://www2.iath.virginia.edu/sixties/HTML_docs/Resources/Primary/Manifestos/SDS_Port_Huron.html.

7. SDS, *The Port Huron Statement*.

8. Arnold S. Kaufman, *The Radical Liberal: New Man in American Politics* (New York: Atherton Press, 1968); Hayden, *Reunion*, "I still," 74.

9. Michael Harrington, *The Long-Distance Runner: An Autobiography* (New York: Henry Holt, 1988), "in solidarity," 57; Harrington, *Fragments of the Century*, 143–45.

10. Ron Chernow, "An Irresistible Profile of Michael Harrington (You Must Be Kidding)," *Mother Jones* 2 (July 1977), "paranoid," 32; Miller, *Democracy Is in the Streets*, 111–16; Harrington, *Fragments of the Century*, "my notion," 145.

11. Todd Gitlin, *The Sixties: Years of Hope, Days of Rage* (New York: Bantam Books, 1987), 115; Isserman, *The Other American*, 238; Harrington, *Fragments of the Century*, 146.

12. Gitlin, *The Sixties*, "People are," "yeah," and "treacherous," 119.

13. Irving Howe, *A Margin of Hope: An Intellectual Autobiography* (New York: Harcourt Brace Jovanovich, 1982), "two generations," 291–92; "pinched," 293; Gitlin, *The Sixties*, "in truth," 172; "to me," 173.

14. Miller, *Democracy Is in the Streets*, "I know," 140, "he was," 115; Jack Newfield, *A Prophetic Minority* (New York: New American Library, 1966), "the Social," 134; Hayden, "Writing the Port Huron Statement," "the names," 71; Chernow, "An Irresistible Profile of Michael Harrington," 32; Hayden, *Reunion*, 88; Miller, *Democracy Is in the Streets*, "up comes," 115; Harrington, *Fragments of the Century*, 148.

15. Robert A. Gorman, *Michael Harrington: Speaking American* (New York: Routledge, 1995), "psychologically," xxii.

16. Michael Harrington, "The Housing Scandal," *Commentary* 60 (July 2, 1954), 311–13; Harrington, "Marxist Literary Critics," *Commonweal* 62 (December 11, 1959), 324–26.

17. Arthur Schlesinger Jr., "The Challenge of Abundance," *The Reporter* (3 May 1956), 8–11; John Kenneth Galbraith, *The Affluent Society* (Boston: Houghton Mifflin, 1958), 250–58; Galbraith, "How Affluent Is Our Society?" *New Leader* 42 (February 2, 1959), 16–19.

18. Leon Keyserling, "Eggheads and Politics," *New Republic* (October 27, 1958), 15; Galbraith, "How Affluent Is Our Society?" 19; Helen Hill Miller, "Today's 'One Third of a Nation,' " *New Republic* (November 17, 1958), 13–15.

19. Michael Harrington, "Our Fifty Million Poor," *Commentary* 28 (July 1959), 19–27; Harrington, "Slums, Old and New," *Commentary* 30 (August 1960), 118–24; Oscar Lewis, *Five Families: Mexican Case Studies in the Culture of Poverty* (New York: Basic Books, 1959).

20. Harrington, "Slums, Old and New," 118–24; Harrington, "Notes on the Left," *New Leader* 44 (May 22, 1961), 17; Harrington, "The Economics of Racism," *Commonweal* 74 (July 7, 1961), 367–70; Isserman, *The Other American*, 181.

21. Michael Harrington, *The Other America: Poverty in the United States* (New York: 1962; repr. Macmillan, 1993), "the American," 71; "the poor," "at any," and "only the larger," 15.

22. Harrington, *The Other America*, "only the," 171; "the other," 191; Oscar Lewis, "The Culture of Poverty," in *On Understanding Poverty: Perspectives from the Social Sciences*, ed. Daniel Patrick Moynihan (New York: American Academy of Arts and Sciences, 1969), 194–95.

23. Dwight Macdonald, "Our Invisible Poor," *New Yorker* (January 19, 1963). Here, as elsewhere, I am drawing on personal conversations with Harrington.

24. Martin Luther King Jr., "I Have a Dream," August 28, 1963, in King, *A Testament of Hope: The Essential Writings and Speeches of Martin Luther King Jr.*, ed. James M. Washington (San Francisco: HarperSanFrancisco, 1986), 217–20.

25. Gary Dorrien, *Breaking White Supremacy: Martin Luther King Jr. and the Black Social Gospel* (New Haven: Yale University Press, 2018), 351–54, "he's," 352.

26. Clayborne Carson, *In Struggle: SNCC and the Black Awakening of the 1960s* (Cambridge: Harvard University Press, 1995), 96–99.

27. I. F. Stone, "Civil Rights Movement Moves Back towards Socialism for Answers," *I. F. Stone's Weekly* (September 16, 1963), "the lower" and "fresh," 2; Isserman, *The Other American*, 225.

28. Harrington, *Fragments of the Century*, 176–77.

29. Adam Fairclough, *To Redeem the Soul of America: The Southern Christian Leadership Conference and Martin Luther King Jr.* (Athens: University of Georgia Press, 1987), "but if," 204; Bayard Rustin, "From Protest to Politics: The Future of the Civil Rights Movement," *Commentary* (February 1965), reprinted in Rustin, *Time on Two Crosses: The Collected Writings of Bayard Rustin*, ed. Devon W. Carbado and Donald Weise (San Francisco: Cleis Press, 2003), 116–29; John Lewis, *Walking with the Wind: A Memoir of the Movement* (New York: Harcourt Brace, 1998), 286–91.

30. Michael Harrington, "Should the Left Support Johnson?" *New Politics* 3 (Summer 1964), "succeeded," 6; Carson, *In Struggle*, 127–35; Lewis, *Walking with the Wind*, 289; Hayden, *Reunion*, "I am" and "just realized," 117.

31. Carson, *In Struggle*, "in rioting," 127; Cleveland Sellers, *River of No Return: The Autobiography of a Black Militant* (New York: William Morrow, 2018), "never again," 111.

32. Carson, *In Struggle*, 134–35; Lewis, *Walking with the Wind*, 308–11; this section adapts material from Dorrien, *Breaking White Supremacy*, 372–74.

33. Name Withheld By Request [Casey Hayden and Mary E. King], "Women in the Movement," SNCC Position Paper, November 1964, Appendix to Sara Evans, *Personal Politics: The Roots of Women's Liberation in the Civil Rights Movement and the New Left* (New York: Vintage, 1979), 233–35, quotes 234.

34. Hayden and King, "Women in the Movement," "think about," 234; Mary King, *Freedom Song: A Personal Story of the 1960s Civil Rights Movement* (New York: Morrow, 1987), 452; Evans, *Personal Politics*, 88; Betty Friedan, *The Feminine Mystique* (New York: W. W. Norton, 2013).

35. On the clash of gender and race in SNCC, see Cynthia Washington, "We Started from Different Ends of the Spectrum," *Southern Exposure* (Winter 1997), 14; Muriel Tillinghast, "Depending on Ourselves," *Hands on the Freedom Plow*, 250–56; Paula Giddings, *When and Where I Enter: The Impact of Black Women on Race and Sex in America* (New York: William Morrow, 1984), 302; Belinda Robnett, *How Long? How Long? African American Women in the Struggle for Civil Rights* (New York: Oxford University Press, 1997), 115–17.

36. Connie Brown, "Cleveland: Conference of the Poor," *Studies on the Left* 5 (Spring 1965), 71–74; Gitlin, *The Sixties*, 162–63; Evans, *Personal Politics*, 126–55; Hayden, *Reunion*, 123–50.

37. The Shriver story was one of Harrington's lecture circuit favorites.

38. James N. Morgan, Martin H. David, William J. Cohen, and Harvey H. Brazer, *Income and Welfare in the United States* (New York: McGraw-Hill, 1962), 3–7.

39. Jack Newfield, "Poverty Crusader Named Chairman of the Board," *Village Voice* (November 26, 1964), "only," 3; James Wechsler, "Man of His Times," *New York Post* (November 19, 1964); Isserman, *The Other American*, 147, 219; Harrington, *Fragments of the Century*, 166.

40. Michael Harrington, "A New Populism," *New York Herald Tribune* (March 28, 1965); Harrington, "The Politics of Poverty," *Dissent* 12 (Autumn 1965), "third" and "new human," 429; Harrington, *Fragments of the Century*, "Mike," 128.

41. Students for a Democratic Society, "March on Washington to End the War in Vietnam," Paid Advertisement, *Nation* (March 12, 1965), 32; Lucy Komisar and Paul Feldman, "Student March on Washington Calls for End to Vietnam War," *New America* (April 30, 1965), 1; Sale, *SDS*, 177–81.

42. Reinhold Niebuhr, "The Problem of Vietnam," *Christianity and Crisis* 23 (August 5, 1963), 12; Niebuhr, "Prospects of the Johnson Era," *Christianity and Crisis* 25 (February 22, 1965), "our hegemonous," 14.

43. Niebuhr, "Consensus at the Price of Flexibility," *New Leader* 48 (September 27, 1965), 20.

44. W. A. Swanberg, *Norman Thomas: The Last Idealist* (New York: Charles Scribner's Sons, 1976), "the new," 459.

45. Michael Harrington, "Disloyalty? Or Dissent?" *New York Herald Tribune* (October 17, 1965), "explicit," 4; Harrington, "Does the Peace Movement Need the Communists?" *Village Voice* (November 11, 1965), in Harrington, *Taking Sides: The Education of a Militant Mind* (New York: Holt, Rinehart and Winston, 1985), 106–15, "I believe," 112–13; Isserman, *Other American*, 259; Harrington, *Fragments of the Century*, 199.

46. Irving Howe, "New Styles in Leftism," *Dissent* (Summer 1965), in Howe, *Steady Work: Essays in the Politics of Democratic Radicalism, 1953–1966* (New York: Harcourt, Brace and World, 1966), 41–78, "vicarious," 70; "the Establishment" and "all-purpose," 72; "even if," 73; "but what," 77.

47. Harrington, "Does the Peace Movement Need the Communists?" 106–15; "Harrington Replies," in *Taking Sides*, 116–25; I. F. Stone, "Daydreams and Suicide Tactics," *New America* (June 18, 1965), 5; Howe, "New Styles in Leftism," 47; Isserman, *The Other American*, 260, 273; Gitlin, *The Sixties*, 175.

48. Harrington, *Fragments of the Century*, 166–69; Michael Harrington, "The Mystical Miltants," in *Beyond the New Left*, ed. Irving Howe (New York: McCall, 1965), 33–39; Harrington, "Radicals Old and New," *New Republic* 153 (July 3, 1965), 29.

49. Harrington, *Fragments of the Century*, "profoundly," 182; "the itinerant," 183; Michael Harrington, "The New Radicalism," *Commonweal* 82 (September 3, 1965), 623–27.

50. Harrington, *Fragments of the Century*, "it was," 186.

51. "On Roles in SDS," *New Left Notes* (January 28, 1966), in Evans, *Personal Politics*, 168.

52. "Reinhold Niebuhr Discusses the War in Vietnam," *New Republic* (January 29, 1966), 16; Niebuhr to Will Scarlott, April 1, 1966, "I am"; Niebuhr to Scarlott, April 4, 1966, "for the," Reinhold Niebuhr Papers.

53. Carson, *In Struggle*, "we been," 209–10; Lewis, *Walking with the Wind*, 388–89; Stokely Carmichael and Charles Hamilton, *Black Power: The Politics of Liberation in America* (New York: Random House, 1967; repr., Kwame Ture and Charles Hamilton, Vintage, 1992), 34–56; this section adapts material from Dorrien, *Breaking White Supremacy*, 393–403, 410–18.

54. Carmichael and Hamilton, *Black Power*, quotes 53, 54, 50, 49.

55. "Dr. King Weighing Plan to Repudiate 'Black Power' Bloc," *New York Times* (October 10, 1966); "Crisis and Commitment," *New York Times* (October 14, 1966); "King Clarifies His Stand," *New York Times* (October 18, 1966); Bayard Rustin interview with Milton Viorst, cited in John D'Emilio, *Lost Prophet: The Life and Times of Bayard Rustin* (Chicago: University of Chicago Press, 2003), "anybody," 449; Thomas Brooks, "A Strategist Without a Movement," *New York Times Magazine* (February 16, 1969), 24–27; David Garrow, *Bearing the Cross: Martin Luther King Jr. and the Southern Christian Leadership Conference* (New York: Quill, 1986), 533–34.

56. Garrow, *Bearing the Cross*, 536; Martin Luther King Jr., "Nonviolence: The Only Road to Freedom," *Ebony* 21 (October 1966), 27–30; "Reagan Emerging in 1968 Spotlight,"

New York Times (November 10, 1966); Alan J. Matusow, *The Unraveling of America* (New York: Harper and Row, 1984), 214; John L. Sullivan and Robert E. O'Connor, "Electoral Choice and Popular Control of Public Policy: The Case of the 1966 House Elections," *American Political Science Review* 66 (December 1972), 1256–68.

57. Martin Luther King Jr., "Dr. King's Speech—Frogmore—November 14, 1966," The King Center, www.thekingcenter.org/archive, quotes 6, 7.

58. Ibid., quotes 13, 30.

59. Martin Luther King Jr., Testimony to the Subcommittee on Executive Reorganization of the Committee on Government Operations, U.S. Senate, 89th Congress, 2nd Session, December 15, 1966, college.cengage.com/history; King, "The Bravest Man I Ever Met," *Pageant* (June 1965), reprinted in Cornel West, ed., *The Radical King* (Boston: Beacon Press, 2015), 229–34, quotes 225; "Dr. King Will Write Book During Leave," *New York Times* (December 14, 1966); William F. Pepper, "The Children of Vietnam," with a preface by Dr. Benjamin Spock, *Ramparts* (January 1967), 44–67; Garrow, *Bearing the Cross*, 544.

60. Michael B. Friedland, *Lift Up Your Voice Like a Trumpet: White Clergy and the Civil Rights and Antiwar Movements, 1954–73* (Chapel Hill: University of North Carolina Press, 1998), 177–78; William Sloane Coffin Jr., *Once to Every Man* (New York: Atheneum, 1977), 223–29; Andrew Young, *An Easy Burden: The Civil Rights Movement and the Transformation of America* (New York: HarperCollins, 1996), 425–28; Taylor Branch, *At Canaan's Edge: America in the King Years* (New York: Simon and Schuster, 2007), 584–88; Garrow, *Bearing the Cross*, 549–50.

61. Martin Luther King Jr., "A Time to Break Silence," Speech at Riverside Church, April 4, 1967, in King, *A Testament of Hope*, quotes 231, 232–33.

62. Ibid., quote 236; Bernard Fall, *The Two Viet-Nams: A Political and Military Analysis* (New York: Praeger, 1963).

63. King, "A Time to Break Silence," quotes 240, 241.

64. Ibid., "our only" and "this Hindu," 242; Martin Luther King Jr., "Declaration of Independence from the War in Vietnam," April 4, 1967, in *Two, Three . . . Many Vietnams: A Radical Reader on the Wars in Southeast Asia and the Conflicts at Home*, ed. Banning Garrett and Katherine Barkley (San Francisco: Harper and Row, 1971), "without having" and "it can never," 207, 208.

65. Editorial, *Christian Century* (April 19, 1967), "a magnificent," 492–93; Editorial, *Christianity and Crisis* (May 1, 1967), 89–90; Editorial, *Nation* (April 24, 1967), 515–16; "Dr. King's Disservice to His Cause," *Life* (April 21, 1967), "his personal" and "abject," 4; Carl Rowan, "Martin Luther King's Tragic Decision," *Reader's Digest* (September 1967), 37–42; Rowan, *Breaking Barriers: A Memoir* (Boston: Little, Brown, 1991), 246–48; Editorial, "Dr. King's Error," *New York Times* (April 7, 1967); Editorial, "A Tragedy," *Washington Post* (April 6, 1967), "sheer inventions" and "many who"; "NAACP Decries Stand," *New York Times*, April 11, 1967; Editorial, *Pittsburgh Courier*, April 16, 1967, "tragically"; Max Lerner, "The Color of War," *New York Post* (April 7, 1967); Garrow, *Bearing the Cross*, 553–54; Branch, *At Canaan's Edge*, 595.

66. Martin Luther King Jr., "Dr. King's Speech in Front of U.N., April 15, 1967," "I am," www.thekingcenter.org/archive/document; Harris Wofford, *Of Kennedys and Kings:*

Making Sense of the Sixties (New York: Farrar, Straus and Giroux, 1980; repr., Pittsburgh: University of Pittsburgh Press, 1992), 223.

67. Harrington, *Fragments of the Century*, "the bravest," 205; "wrong thing," 206; Michael Harrington, "America in Vietnam: From Here to Nowhere," *Village Voice* (April 14, 1966), 1; Harrington, "Answering McReynolds: A Question of Philosophy, A Question of Tactics," *Village Voice* (December 7, 1967), reprinted in Harrington, *Taking Sides*, 126–36; Isserman, *The Other American*, 271.

68. Paul Feldman, "Peace Movement at Crossroads," *New America* (December 15, 1966), 3; Harrington, "Answering McReynolds," "this war," 135–36.

69. Michael Harrington, *Toward a Democratic Left: A Radical Program for a New Majority* (New York: Macmillan, 1968), 8–14; Theodore White, *The Making of the President 1964* (New York: Atheneum House, 1965); Harrington, "Wisdom and Unwisdom," *New Republic* 159 (July 20, 1968), 24–25.

70. Harrington, *Toward a Democratic Left*, "fantastic," 13; "and some" and "prophetic," 15; Michael Harrington, "Who Are the True Redeemers?" *New Republic* 160 (April 12, 1969), 25–27.

71. David Bazelon, *Power in America: The Politics of the New Class* (New York: New American Library, 1967); Harrington, *Toward a Democratic Left*, 282–305, "politically and," 285; Michael Harrington, "Radical Strategy: Don't Form a Fourth Party, Form a New First Party," *New York Times Magazine* (October 11, 1970), 28–29.

72. Harrington, *Toward a Democratic Left*, "the Left," "is predisposed," and "their sophisticated," 290; "a school," 289; Michael Harrington, "What's Left," *New Republic* 159 (September 21, 1968), 34.

73. Branch, *At Canaan's Edge*, "awful," 637–38; John Hersey, *The Algiers Hotel Incident* (New York: Knopf, 1968), 90–91; Kerner Commission, *Report of the National Advisory Commission on Civil Disorders* (New York: Bantam, 1968), 20–32; Nancy Zaroulis and Gerald Sullivan, *Who Spoke Up? American Protest against the War in Vietnam* (New York: Doubleday, 1984), 128–29; Renata Adler, "Letter from the Palmer House," *New Yorker* (September 23, 1967), 71.

74. Martin Luther King Jr., *Conscience for Change* (Boston: Beacon Press, 1968); reprinted as *The Trumpet of Conscience* (Boston: Beacon Press, 2010), quotes 7, 48; Dorrien, *Breaking White Supremacy*, 423–26.

75. King, *Conscience for Change*, quotes 76, 78, 79.

76. D'Emilio, *Lost Prophet*, 457–71; Fairclough, *To Redeem the Soul of America*, 364; Branch, *At Canaan's Edge*, 678–79; Harrington, *Fragments of the Century*, 128–29.

77. Martin Luther King Jr., "Honoring Dr. Du Bois," in John Henrik Clarke, Esther Jackson, Ernest Kaiser, and James H. O'Dell, *Black Titan: W. E. B. Du Bois* (Boston: Beacon Press, 1970), reprinted in Cornel West, ed., *The Radical King* (Boston: Beacon Press, 2015), 113–21, quotes 114, 118, 119, 120.

78. King, "Honoring Dr. Du Bois," quote 120.

79. Martin Luther King Jr., Address to the Southern Christian Leadership Conference, Penn Community Center, Frogmore, SC, May 22, 1967, in West, *The Radical King*, 126.

80. Young, *An Easy Burden*, "after he" and "we were," 486; Lewis, *Walking with the Wind*, 415; Michael Harrington, "Poverty in the Seventies," foreword to *The Other America*,

revised edition (New York: Penguin, 1981), xix; Harrington, "The Will to Abolish Poverty," *Saturday Review* 51 (July 27, 1968), 41.

81. Norman Thomas to Penn Kemble, September 12, 1968, Norman Thomas Papers, "I look"; Bernard Johnpoll, *Pacifist's Progress: Norman Thomas and the Decline of American Socialism* (Chicago: Quadrangle Books, 1970), 280–82; Swanberg, *Norman Thomas*, 477–80; Peter Coleman, *The Liberal Conspiracy: The Congress for Cultural Freedom and the Struggle for the Mind of Postwar Europe* (New York: Free Press, 1989).

82. Michael Harrington, "Norman Thomas Was a Socialist," *Village Voice* (January 2, 1969), "a man," 13; Mary Breasted, "Old Left Gives Hubert Its Academy Award," *Village Voice* (April 24, 1969), 3; Harrington, "The Vietnam Moratorium," *New America* (October 25, 1969), 2; Rachelle Horowitz, "Tom Kahn and the Fight for Democracy: A Political Portrait and Personal Recollection," *Democratiya* 11 (Winter 2007), 228–30; Isserman, *The Other American*, 287; Jack Ross, *The Socialist Party of America: A Complete History* (Lincoln: University of Nebraska Press, 2015), 505.

83. Carl Oglesby, "Notes on a Decade Ready for the Dustbin," *Liberation* (August-September 1969), 6–9; Evans, *Personal Politics*, 193–211; David Barber, *A Hard Rain Fell: SDS and Why It Failed* (Jackson: University Press of Mississippi, 2008), 116–19; Gitlin, *The Sixties*, 381–95.

84. Shulamith Firestone, *The Dialectic of Sex: The Case for Feminist Revolution* (New York: William Morrow, 1970), 32–45; Jo Freeman, *The Politics of Women's Liberation: A Case Study of an Emerging Social Movement and Its Relation to the Policy Process* (New York: David McKay, 1975); Beverly Jones and Judith Brown, *Toward a Female Liberation Movement* (Boston: New England Free Press, 1968).

85. Bernardine Dohrn, "Toward a Revolutionary Women's Movement," *New Left Notes* (March 8, 1969); Barber, *A Hard Rain Fell*, quotes 140; Jones and Brown, *Toward a Female Liberation Movement*, 2–8.

86. Radical Education Project Collective, "Debate within SDS: RYM II vs. Weatherman," Encyclopedia of Anti-Revisionism On-Line, https://www.marxists.org/history/erol/ncm-1/debate-sds/introduction.htm; Richard Healey to author, August 10, 2019; Barber, *A Hard Rain Fell*, 152–74; Sale, *SDS*, 311–18.

87. Firestone, *The Dialectic of Sex*, quotes 42–43.

88. Harrington, *Fragments of the Century*, "Americans," 163; Michael Harrington, "Getting Out of Vietnam," *Dissent* 17 (January–February 1970), 6–7.

89. David McReynolds, "Point of Departure," *Hammer & Tongs* (May 25, 1970), 22; McReynolds, "Socialists and Liberals: The Decline of a Party," *Village Voice* (July 9, 1970), 16; Max Shachtman et al., "Statement on Vietnam," *Hammer & Tongs* (October 9, 1970), 8.

90. Michael Harrington, "Socialists and Reactionary Anti-Communism," party circular (August 1970); Harrington to Carl Shier, DSA Papers, New York University; Isserman, *The Other American*, 291–92; Ross, *The Socialist Party of America*, 509.

91. "Rustin, Harrington, and Zimmerman Head United Socialist Organization," *New America* (March 20, 1972), 1; Paul Feldman, "A New Day for American Socialism," *New America* (March 31, 1972), 1.

92. Thomas J. Knock, "Come Home, America': The Story of George McGovern," in *Vietnam and the American Political Tradition: The Politics of Dissent*, ed. Randall B.

Woods (New York: Cambridge University Press, 2003), 82–120; Knock, *The Rise of a Prairie Statesman: The Life and Times of George McGovern* (Princeton: Princeton University Press, 2016); Richard M. Marano, *Vote Your Conscience: The Last Campaign of George McGovern* (New York: Praeger Publishers, 2003); Bruce Miroff, *The Liberals' Moment: The McGovern Insurgency and the Identity Crisis of the Democratic Party* (Lawrence: University Press of Kansas, 2007).

93. "Forsaking Debs for Nixon: A Call to American Socialists: Letter of Resignation as National Co-chairman of the Socialist Party–Democratic Socialist Federation, October 23, 1972," *Nation* 215 (November 13, 1972), 454–55; "From the Steelworkers Convention at Las Vegas," *John Herling's Labor Letter* (September 12, 1972), "the gay-lib" and "the people," 1; Max Green, "McGovern Underestimates the Communists," *New America* (July 3, 1972), 6; Isserman, *The Other American*, 299; Sidney Hook, "An Open Letter to George McGovern," *New America* (September 30, 1972), 4; David Selden to Charles S. Zimmerman et al. (September 13, 1972), DSA Papers; Harrington, *Fragments of the Century*, 195; "Harrington Quits as Socialist Head," *New York Times* (October 23, 1972), 17; "Harrington Quits His Post: SP-SDF Disputes His Criticism," *New America* (October 25, 1972), 6; Horowitz, "Tom Kahn and the Fight for Democracy," 231–34.

94. Tom Kahn, "Max Shachtman—His Ideals and His Life," *New America* (November 15, 1972), "full," 4; Harrington, *Fragments of the Century*, 210, "my friends" and "they," 224; James Ring Adams, "Battle Royal among Socialists," *Wall Street Journal* (December 8, 1972).

95. Gary Dorrien, *The Neoconservative Mind: Politics, Culture, and the War of Ideology* (Philadelphia: Temple University Press, 1993); Dorrien, *Imperial Designs: Neoconservatism and the New Pax Americana* (New York: Routledge, 2004); Michael Harrington, "The Welfare State and Its Neoconservative Critics," *Dissent* 20 (Fall 1973), 398–405.

96. Social Democrats, USA, "For the Record: The Report of Social Democrats, USA on the Resignation of Michael Harrington and His Attempt to Split the American Socialist Movement," undated [1973], DSA Papers; Maurice Isserman, *If I Had a Hammer: The Death of the Old Left and the Birth of the New Left* (New York: Basic Books, 1987), 57–75; Lewis A. Coser and Irving Howe, eds., *The New Conservatives: A Critique from the Left* (New York: New American Library, 1977); Harrington, *Fragments of the Century*, 132–65, 195–225.

97. Irving Kristol, " 'Civil Liberties': 1952—A Study in Confusion," *Commentary* 13 (March 1952), 233–36; Kristol, "Liberty and the Communists," *Partisan Review* 19 (July/August 1952), 493–96; Kristol, "Facing the Facts in Vietnam," *New Leader* 46 (September 30, 1963), 7–8; Kristol, "The Poverty of Equality," *New Leader* 48 (March 1, 1965), 15–16.

98. Walter Goodman, "Irving Kristol: Patron Saint of the New Right," *New York Times Magazine* (December 6, 1981), 202; Daniel Bell and Irving Kristol, "What Is the Public Interest?" *The Public Interest* 1 (Fall 1965), "middle-aged," 4; Irving Kristol, *Neoconservatism: The Autobiography of an Idea* (New York: Free Press, 1995), "conservatism in," 31.

99. Michael Harrington, "The Big Lie about the Sixties," *New Republic* 173 (November 29, 1975), "throwing," 16; Daniel Bell to Irving Howe, April 25, 1973, DSA Papers; Isserman, *The Other American*, "a kind," 303.

100. Terry A. Cooney, *The Rise of the New York Intellectuals: "Partisan Review" and Its Circle, 1934–1945* (Madison: University of Wisconsin Press, 1986); Alan M. Wald, *The New York Intellectuals: The Rise and Decline of the Anti-Stalinist Left from the 1930s to the 1980s* (Chapel Hill: University of North Carolina Press, 1987); Richard H. Pells, *The Liberal Mind in a Conservative Age: American Intellectuals in the 1940s and 1950s* (New York: Harper and Row, 1985); William Barrett, *The Truants: Adventures among the Intellectuals* (New York: Anchor Press, 1982); William Phillips, *A Partisan View: Five Decades of the Literary Life* (New York: Stein and Day, 1983); Alexander Bloom, *Prodigal Sons: The New York Intellectuals and Their World* (New York: Oxford University Press, 1986); Neil Jumonville, *Critical Crossings: The New York Intellectuals in Postwar America* (Berkeley: University of California Press, 1991).

101. Nathan Glazer, "Housing Problems and Housing Policies," *The Public Interest* 7 (Spring 1967), 21–51; Aaron Wildavsky, "The Political Economy of Efficiency," *The Public Interest* 8 (Summer 1967), 30–48; James Q. Wilson, "The Urban Unease: Community vs. City," *The Public Interest* 12 (Summer 1968), 25–39; Daniel P. Moynihan, "A Crisis of Confidence," *The Public Interest* 7 (Spring 1967), 3–10; John H. Bunzel, "Black Studies at San Francisco State," *The Public Interest* 13 (Fall 1968), 22–38.

102. Kristol, *Neoconservatism*, 31; Harrington, "The Welfare State and Its Neoconservative Critics," 400–405; Dorrien, *The Neoconservative Mind*, 137–50; Norman Podhoretz, "Reflections on Earth Day," *Commentary* 49 (June 1970), 26; Norman Podhoretz, *Breaking Ranks: A Political Memoir* (New York: Harper and Row, 1979).

103. Samuel McCracken, "Quackery in the Classroom," *Commentary* 52 (October 1971); Dorothy Rabinowitz, "The Activist Cleric," *Commentary* 50 (September 1970); Midge Decter, "The Liberated Woman," *Commentary* 50 (October 1970); Jeane Kirkpatrick, "The Revolt of the Masses," *Commentary* 55 (February 1973); Michael Novak, "Needing Niebuhr Again," *Commentary* 54 (September 1972); Podhoretz, *Breaking Ranks*, 307.

104. Sidney Blumenthal, *The Rise of the Counter-Establishment: From Conservative Ideology to Political Power* (New York: Harper and Row, 1988), quote 154; see Norman Podhoretz, "What the Voters Sensed," *Commentary* 55, no. 1 (January 1973), 6.

105. Norman Podhoretz, "Making the World Safe for Communism," *Commentary* 61 (April 1976), 33–41; Richard Pipes, "Why the Soviet Union Thinks It Could Fight and Win a Nuclear War," *Commentary* 64 (July 1977), 24–34.

106. Harrington, *The Long-Distance Runner*, "that I," 15; Harrington, "Dee-Sock," in *Taking Sides*, 153–57; Harrington, "Say What You Mean—Socialism," *Nation* 218 (May 25, 1974), 649–50; Harrington to the National Committee of Social Democrats USA, June 21, 1973.

107. "We Are Socialists of the Democratic Left," DSOC pamphlet, 1973; Paul L. Montgomery, "Socialist Group Outlines Goals," *New York Times* (October 14, 1973), "today we begin"; Isserman, *The Other American*, 318; Harrington, *The Long-Distance Runner*, 18–24; Ross, *The Socialist Party of America*, "still," 545.

108. Ronald Radosh, "The Democratic Socialist Organizing Committee," *Socialist Revolution* (July 1973), 77; Harrington, *The Long-Distance Runner*, 26.

109. Harrington, *The Long-Distance Runner*, 25–29; I am relying on conversations with Steinberg, Harrington, and others.

110. Ronald Radosh, *Commies: A Journey through the Old Left, the New Left, and the Leftover Left* (San Francisco: Encounter Books, 2001), 138–39; Michael Harrington, "Grassroots Needs," *Nation* 218 (January 19, 1974), 68; Harrington, "Say What You Mean — Socialism," 648–51; Harrington, "Our Proposals for the Crisis," *Dissent* 22 (Spring 1975), 101–4.

111. Michael Harrington, *Socialism* (New York: Saturday Review Press, 1972), "it is important," 5; Harrington, *The Twilight of Capitalism* (New York: Simon and Schuster, 1976), "the foe," 5.

112. Harrington, *Socialism*, 36–45; Karl Marx and Frederick Engels, *The Communist Manifesto* (1848), reprinted in *Karl Marx: Selected Writings*, ed. David McLellan (Oxford: Oxford University Press, 1977), 221–47.

113. Marx and Engels, *The Communist Manifesto*, 246; Karl Marx, "Address to the Communist League" (1848), *Karl Marx: Selected Writings*, 277–85; Marx, "Speech to the Central Committee of the Communist League" (1850), *Karl Marx: Selected Writings*, 298–99; Harrington, *Socialism*, 45–49.

114. Harrington, *Socialism*, 50.

115. Ibid., 50–52; Sidney Hook, *Towards the Understanding of Karl Marx: A Revolutionary Interpretation* (New York: John Day, 1933).

116. Karl Marx to Joseph Weydemeyer, 5 March 1852, *Karl Marx: Selected Writings*, 341; Karl Marx and Frederick Engels, *The German Ideology* (1844), *Karl Marx: Selected Writings*, 159–91; Karl Marx, "On Bakunin's *State and Anarchy*," (1874), *Karl Marx: Selected Writings*, 562–63; Harrington, *The Twilight of Capitalism*, quotes 183, 42; Karl Marx, Preface to *A Critique of Political Economy*; *Karl Marx: Selected Writings*, 388–91; Marx, *Grundrisse*; *Karl Marx: Selected Writings*, 345–87.

117. Harrington, *Socialism*, "if the," 76.

118. Werner Sombart, *Why Is There No Socialism in the United States?* (London: Macmillan, 1976); Harrington, *Socialism*, 131–33.

119. Harrington, *Socialism*, "resurgence," 345; "for if," 347; Harrington, *The Twilight of Capitalism*, 174–75; Kenneth Boulding, *Beyond Economics* (Ann Arbor: University of Michigan Press, 1968); Robert Heilbroner, *An Inquiry into the Human Prospect* (New York: W. W. Norton, 1974).

120. Harrington, *The Twilight of Capitalism*, 175, 195–201; Michael Harrington, *Decade of Decision: The Crisis of the American System* (New York: Simon and Schuster, 1980); Harrington, *The Next Left: The History of a Future* (New York: Henry Holt, 1986); Harrington, *Socialism: Past and Future* (New York: Arcade Publishing, 1989).

121. Harrington, *The Twilight of Capitalism*, "antisocial," 334; Jürgen Habermas, *Legitimation Crisis*, trans. Thomas McCarthy (Boston: Beacon Press, 1975); Habermas, *Communication and the Evolution of Society*, trans. Thomas McCarthy (Boston: Beacon Press, 1979), 1–68.

122. Michael Harrington, "Can Democrats Meet the Challenge?" *Newsletter of the Democratic Left* 2 (December 1974), 1–7; Harrington, *The Long-Distance Runner*, 93–98; Isserman, *The Other American*, 329.

123. Michael Harrington, "Jobs for All," *Commonweal* (January 30, 1976), 76; Harrington, "Two Cheers for Socialism," *Harper's* (October 1976), 78–79; Harrington, *Full Employment: The Issue and the Movement* (pamphlet, New York: Institute for Democratic Socialism, 1977).

124. Michael Harrington, "Electoral Victory and Full Employment Challenge," *Newsletter of the Democratic Left* 4 (December 1976), 1; Harrington, "What Socialists Would Do in America—If They Could," *Dissent* 25 (Fall 1978), 440–52; Harrington, "A Status Quo Economy," *Harper's* 255 (September 1977), 34–35; Harrington, "Full Employment and Socialist Investment," *Dissent* 25 (Winter 1978), 125–36; Harrington, "For a Socialist Democracy," *Current* 207 (November 1978), 21–24.

125. Harrington, "Beyond November: The Democrats Remain the Real Home of the Left," *The Progressive* 44 (October 1980), 25; Harrington, "No Time for Mourning Now," *Democratic Left* (November 1980), 14; Harrington, "Social Retreat and Economic Stagnation," *Dissent* 26 (Spring 1979), 131–34; Isserman, *The Other American*, 335; Harrington, *The Long-Distance Runner*, 103–11; Dorrien, *The Neoconservative Mind*, 167–73.

126. G. A. Cohen, *Karl Marx's Theory of History* (Princeton: Princeton University Press, 1978); Cohen, "Forces and Relations in Production," in *Analytical Marxism*, ed. John Roemer (Cambridge: Cambridge University Press, 1986), 11–22; John Roemer, "New Directions in the Marxian Theory of Exploitation and Class," ibid., 81–113; Roemer, "'Rational Choice' Marxism: Some Issues of Method and Substance," ibid., 191–201; Jon Elster, "Further Thoughts on Marxism, Functionalism, and Game Theory," ibid., 202–20; Elster, *Making Sense of Marx* (Cambridge: Cambridge University Press, 1985); Eric Olin Wright, *Class, Crisis, and the State* (London: New Left Books, 1978).

127. James O'Connor, *The Fiscal Crisis of the State* (New York: St. Martin's Press, 1973), 13–39, 49–51, 82–96.

128. Ibid., "the surplus," 7.

129. Ibid., 64–96.

130. Claus Offe, *Berufsbilungsreform* (Frankfurt: Suhrkamp Verlag, 1975), 22–25; Offe, *Strukturprobleme des kapitalistischen Staates* (Frankfurt: Suhrkamp Verlag, 1973); Offe, "The Political Economy of the Labor Market," in Offe, *Disorganized Capitalism*, ed. John Keane (Cambridge: MIT Press, 1985), 10–51; Offe, "Some Contradictions of the Modern Welfare State," in Offe, *Contradictions of the Welfare State*, ed. John Keane (Cambridge: MIT Press, 1984), 147–61; Harrington, *Twilight of Capitalism*, 307–12; Harrington, *Decade of Decision: The Crisis of the American System*, 80–106.

131. O'Connor, *The Fiscal Crisis of the State*, 249–56.

132. Harrington, *Twilight of Capitalism*, 313–19; Harrington, *Decade of Decision*, 40–78, 285–316.

133. Willy Brandt, "A Program for Survival," in *Eurosocialism and America: Political Economy for the 1980s*, ed. Nancy Lieber (Philadelphia: Temple University Press, 1982), 235–44; Olof Palme, "Democratizing the Economy," ibid., 219–34; François

Mitterrand, "Democratizing the Political Process," ibid., 195–204; Joop Den Uyl, "Democratizing the Social Structure," ibid., 205–18; Tony Benn, *Arguments for Socialism* (New York: Penguin, 1980).

134. Michael Harrington, "Eurosocialism: An Overview," in *Eurosocialism and America*, 3–21; Anthony Crosland, *The Future of Socialism* (New York: Macmillan, 1957); Harrington, "Socialism Reborn in Europe," *New Republic* 178 (March 11, 1978), 19–22.

135. Harrington, "Eurosocialism: An Overview," 19; Harrington, *The Long-Distance Runner*, 153–73, 194–97; Michael Harrington, "Problems and Paradoxes of the Third World," *Dissent* 24 (Fall 1977), 379–89; Harrington, "Socialism Reborn in Europe," *New Republic* 178 (March 11, 1978), 19–22.

136. Harrington, *The Long-Distance Runner*, "who tried," 13.

137. Michael Harrington, "No to Jelly Bean Policies," *Democratic Left* 9 (September 1981), "the Democratic," 2; Herbert Gans, *The War against the Poor: The Underclass and Antipoverty Policy* (New York: Basic Books, 1995).

138. Dorrien, *The Neoconservative Mind*, 10–11; Michael Massing, "Trotsky's Orphans: From Bolshevism to Reaganism," *New Republic* 196 (June 22, 1987), 18–22; Blumenthal, *The Rise of the Counter-Establishment*, "we had to," 154.

139. George Gilder, *Wealth and Poverty* (New York: Basic Books, 1980), "the enriching" and "the multiplying," 119–20; David Stockman, *The Triumph of Politics* (New York: Harper and Row, 1986), "besides," 305; Michael Harrington, *The New American Poverty* (New York: Holt, Rinehart and Winston, 1984), 36.

140. Charles Murray, *Losing Ground: American Social Policy, 1950–1980* (New York: Basic Books, 1984), 227–34, "entire," 227; Stockman, *The Triumph of Politics*, "weak," 305; Gary Dorrien, "Blaming the Poor for Poverty," *Sojourners* (January 1986); Michael Katz, *The Undeserving Poor: From the War on Poverty to the War on Welfare* (New York: Pantheon Books, 1989), 143–56; Robert S. McElvaine, *The End of the Conservative Era: Liberalism after Reagan* (New York: Arbor House, 1987), 48–49.

141. Jude Wanniski, *The Way the World Works: How Economies Fail—And Succeed* (New York: Basic Books, 1978).

142. "Historical Debt Outstanding: Annual 1950–1999; Annual 2000–2010," *TreasuryDirect*, www.treasurydirect.gov/govt/reports.

143. Harrington, *The Next Left: The History of a Future*, 96–115; Harrington, *The New American Poverty*, 144–45, "I wish," 8; "we have," 2; "they are," 3; Harrington, "Crunched Numbers," *New Republic* (January 18, 1985), 7–10.

144. Harrington, *The New American Poverty*, 123–50; Leonard Goodwin, *Do the Poor Want to Work? A Social-Psychological Study of Work Orientations* (Washington, DC: Brookings Institution, 1972); "New Poverty: Michael Harrington Interviewed by Barbara Reynolds," *USA Today* (October 7, 1987); Harrington, "Willful Shortsightedness on Poverty," *Dissent* 33 (Winter 1986), 19.

145. Harrington, *The Next Left*, 18–46; Antonio Gramsci, "Americanism and Fordism," in Gramsci, *Selections from the Prison Notebooks*, trans. Quintin Hoare and Geoffrey Nowell Smith (New York: International Publishers, 1971), 277–318.

146. Harrington, *The Next Left*, 10–16; Friedrich A. Hayek, *Studies in Philosophy, Politics and Economics* (Chicago: University of Chicago Press, 1967); Michael Harrington, "Is Capitalism Still Viable?" *Journal of Business Ethics* 1 (Boston: D. Reidel Publishing, 1982), 283.

147. Alexandre Reichart, "French Monetary Policy (1981–1985): A Constrained Policy, between Volcker Shock, the EMS, and Macroeconomic Imbalances," *Journal of European Economic History* (2015), 11–46; Marc Lombard, "A Re-examination of the Reasons for the Failure of Keynesian Expansionary Policies in France, 1981–1983," *Cambridge Journal of Economics* (April 1995), 19; Mark Vail, *Recasting Welfare Capitalism: Economic Adjustment in Contemporary France and Germany* (Philadelphia: Temple University Press, 2009); Harrington, "Is There Socialism after France?" *Taking Sides*, 233–48; Harrington, "Mitterrand's Term: A Balance Sheet," *Dissent* 34 (Winter 1987), 82–92.

148. Michael Harrington, "Don't Bank on a Recession," *Democratic Left* 10 (November 1982), 8; Harrington, *The Long-Distance Runner*, 116.

149. Harrington, *The Next Left*, 141–94; Michael Harrington, "If There Is a Recession—and If Not," *Dissent* 32 (Spring 1985), 139–44; Harrington and Mark Levinson, "The Perils of a Dual Economy," *Dissent* 32 (Fall 1985), 417–26.

150. Harrington, "What Socialists Would Do in America—If They Could," 450; Michael Harrington, "Markets and Plans: Is the Market Necessarily Capitalist?" *Dissent* 36 (Winter 1989), 56–70; Harrington, "Harrington Replies," *The Nation* (14 June 1986), "the issue" and "to think," 3; Harrington, "Progressive Economics for 1988," *Nation* 242 (May 3, 1986), 601; Christopher Lehmann-Haupt, review of *The Next Left*, by Michael Harrington, *New York Times* (February 12, 1987).

151. Michael Lerner, "Reflections on NAM," *Works and Days* 28 (2010), 35–45, "a heart-breaking," 35; Lerner to author, May 12, 2019, "I was"; Lerner, *Jewish Renewal: A Path to Healing and Transformation* (New York: G. P. Putnam's, 1994), 16–17.

152. Lerner to author, May 12, 2019, "I was."

153. Lerner, "Reflections on NAM," "I wanted," 38; "I was," "we imagined," and "in front," 41.

154. Richard Healey interview with author, May 14, 2019; Dorothy Healey and Maurice Isserman, *Dorothy Healey Remembers: A Life in the American Communist Party* (New York: Oxford University Press, 1990), 27–79, 197–244.

155. Barbara Ehrenreich, "What Is Socialist Feminism?" *Working Papers on Socialism and Feminism* (New York: New American Movement Pamphlet, 1976), https://www.marx ists.org/subject/ . . . /ehrenreich-barbara/socialist-feminism, quotes; Roberta Lynch, "Is the Women's Movement in Trouble?" *Working Papers on Socialism and Feminism*; Judith Kegan Gardiner, "Ambitious Moderation: Socialist Feminism in the NAM Years," *Works and Days* 28 (2010), 49–63; Victor Cohen, Interview with Chris Riddiough, *Works and Days* 28 (2010), 77–86; Victor Cohen, Interview with Holly Graff, *Works and Days* 28 (2010), 107–22.

156. Stanley Aronowitz, "The New American Movement and Why It Failed," *Works and Days* 28 (2010), 21–33; Aronowitz, *False Promises: The Shape of American Working Class Consciousness* (New York: McGraw-Hill, 1973); Aronowitz, *The Crisis in Historical Materialism: Class, Politics and Culture in Marxist Theory* (New York: Praeger, 1981);

Carl Boggs, *Gramsci's Marxism* (London: Pluto Press, 1976); Boggs, *The Two Revolutions: Gramsci and the Dilemmas of Western Marxism* (Boston: South End Press, 1984).

157. Roberta Lynch, "Is DSOC on the Right Foot?" *In These Times* (March 30, 1977), 18; Healey and Isserman, *Dorothy Healey Remembers*, 246–47; Mike Davis, "The Lesser Evil? The Left and the Democratic Party," *New Left Review* 115 (1986), 5–36; Bill Barclay, "Report to New American Movement Membership" (July 1980); Richard Healey to author, August 10, 2019.

158. Isserman, *The Other American*, 348; Ross, *The Socialist Party of America*, 550.

159. Barbara Ehrenreich, *The Worst Years of Our Lives: Irreverent Notes from a Decade of Greed* (New York: Harper Perennial, 1990); Ehrenreich, *The Snarling Citizen: Essays* (New York: HarperPerennial, 1995); Ehrenreich, *Nickel and Dimed: On (Not) Getting By in America* (New York: Picador, 2001); Ehrenreich, "Owning Up to Abortion," *New York Times* (July 22, 2004); Michael Harrington, "A Case for Jackson," *Dissent* 35 (Summer 1988), 262–64; Harrington, *The Long-Distance Runner*, 67–68.

160. Michael Harrington to DSA, "From the Desk of Michael Harrington," undated 1988, author's copy.

161. Isserman, *The Other American*, "in our lifetime" 359; "water is," 359–60.

162. Harrington, *Socialism: Past and Future*, 7–15, 188–217.

163. Ibid., "has become," 197.

164. Ibid., "empowering," 197; Magnus Ryner, *Capital Restucturing, Globalization and the Third Way* (London: Routledge, 2002), 85–86; Gøsta Esping-Andersen, *Politics against Markets: The Social Democratic Road to Power* (Princeton: Princeton University Press, 1985), 240–46.

165. Gary Dorrien, *Social Democracy in the Making: Political and Religious Roots of European Socialism* (New Haven: Yale University Press, 2019), 464–66.

166. Rudolf Meidner, "A Swedish Union Proposal for Collective Capital Sharing," in *Eurosocialism and America*, 27–33; Meidner, *Employee Investment Funds: An Approach to Collective Capital Formation* (London: Allen and Unwin, 1978); Jonas Pontusson, "Radicalization and Retreat in Swedish Social Democracy," *New Left Review* 165 (September/October 1987): 5–33.

167. Meidner, "A Swedish Union Proposal for Collective Capital Sharing," 29–31; Jonas Pontusson, *The Limits of Social Democracy: Investment Politics in Sweden* (Ithaca: Cornell University Press, 1992), 237; Pontusson, *Public Pension Funds and the Politics of Capital Formation in Sweden* (Stockholm: Swedish Center for Working Life, 1984); Esping-Andersen, *Politics against Markets*.

168. Harrington, *Socialism: Past and Future*, "the capitalist," 204; Rudolf Meidner, "Why Did the Swedish Model Fail?" *Socialist Register* (1993), 211–28; Jonas Pontusson, *Swedish Social Democracy and British Labour: Essays on the Nature and Conditions of Social Democratic Hegemony* (Ithaca: Cornell University Press, 1988); Robin Blackburn, "A Visionary Pragmatist," *Counterpunch* (December 22, 2005), http://www.counterpunch.org/2005/12/22/a-visonary-pragmatist.

169. André Gorz, *Farewell to the Working Class: An Essay on Post-Industrial Socialism*, trans. Mike Sonenscher (London: Pluto Press, 1982); Gorz, *Ecology as Politics*, trans. Patsy Vigderman and Jonathan Cloud (Boston: South End Press, 1980), "social," 4.

170. Harrington, *Socialism: Past and Future*, "we should," 204–5.
171. Shoshana Zuboff, *In the Age of the Smart Machine: The Future of Work and Power* (1988); Harrington, *Socialism: Past and Future*, "if the," 192–93.
172. Harrington, *Socialism: Past and Future*, "the habits," 13; "there could," 193.
173. Ibid., quotes 194–95.
174. Ibid., quotes 278.
175. Michael Harrington, *The Politics at God's Funeral: The Spiritual Crisis of Western Civilization* (New York: Holt, Rinehart, and Winston, 1983).
176. This section condenses the first half of my foreword to John C. Cort, *Christian Socialism: An Informal History*, 2nd ed. (Maryknoll, NY: Orbis Books, 2020). It draws on numerous discussions that I held with Cort from 1977 to 2006, including the several times I heard him tell his story, and also draws on his memoir, *Dreadful Conversions: The Making of a Catholic Socialist* (New York: Fordham University Press, 2003).
177. Pope Leo XIII, *Rerum Novarum: The Condition of Labor* (1891), and Pope Pius XI, *Quadragesimo Anno: After Forty Years* (1931), in *Catholic Social Thought: The Documentary Heritage*, ed. David J. O'Brien and Thomas A. Shannon (Maryknoll, NY: Orbis Books, 2004), 12–39, 40–80.
178. Edward Swanstrom, *The Waterfront Labor Problem* (1938); Cort, *Dreadful Conversions*, 105–15.
179. Cort, *Dreadful Conversions*, 217–43.
180. John C. Cort, "Why I Became a Socialist," *Commonweal* (March 26, 1976), https://www.commonwealmagazine.org/why-i-became-socialist.
181. Ibid.; Pope John XXIII, *Mater et Magistra: Christianity and Social Progress* (1961), in *Catholic Social Thought*, 82–128.
182. First Congress of the Socialist International, "Aims and Tasks of Democratic Socialism: Declaration of the Socialist International," Frankfurt-am-Main, Federal Republic of Germany, 1951.
183. John C. Cort, "This Is Socialism . . . This Is Not Socialism—This Is Communism," *Religious Socialism* 24 (Summer 2000), 1; Cort, "The Case for Christian Socialism: Both the Capitalists and the Liberation Theologians Are Wrong," *Crisis* (September 1, 1988), https://www.crisismagazine.com/author/jcort; Cort, *Christian Socialism*, 310–27.

7. CULTURAL LEFTISM, CORNEL WEST, MARKET SOCIALISM, AND NANCY FRASER

1. Antonio Gramsci, *Selections from the Prison Notebooks*, ed. and trans. Quintin Hoare and Geoffrey Nowell Smith (New York: International Publishers, 1971), 5–23; Chantal Mouffe, *Gramsci and Marxist Theory* (London: Routledge and Kegan Paul, 1979).
2. Gramsci, *Selections from the Prison Notebooks*, 125–58; Christine Buci-Glucksmann, *Gramsci and the State* (London: Lawrence and Wishart, 1979).
3. Gary Dorrien, *Reconstructing the Common Good* (Maryknoll, NY: Orbis Books, 1990), "Communist," 155;, ibid., paperback edition 1992, "the need," vi; Dorrien, *Soul in*

Society: The Making and Renewal of American Social Christianity (Minneapolis: Fortress Press, 1995); Dorrien, "Liberal Socialism and the Legacy of the Social Gospel," *Cross Currents* (Fall 1989); Dorrien, "Economic Democracy: Common Goal for Liberation Movements?" *Christianity and Crisis* (September 10, 1990); Dorrien, "Economic Democracy and the Language of Faith," *Religious Socialism* (Winter 1990); Dorrien, "Failure of a Dream? Liberal Democracy and the Future of Economic Democracy," *Religious Socialism* (Winter 1994); Dorrien, "Beyond State and Market: Christianity and the Future of Economic Democracy," *Cross Currents* (Summer 1995).

4. Gary Dorrien, *The Obama Question: A Progressive Perspective* (Lanham, MD: Rowman and Littlefield, 2012), 6–9; Sidney Blumenthal, *The Clinton Wars* (New York: Farrar, Straus and Giroux, 2003); Bill Clinton, *My Life* (New York: Alfred A. Knopf, 2004).

5. Joseph M. Schwartz, "A History of Democratic Socialists of America, 1971–2017," https://www.dsausa.org/about-us/history.

6. Democratic Socialists of America, "Where We Stand: Building the Next Left," https://www.dsausa.org/strategy/where_we_stand, "rendered" and "workers," 2; "we are," 3.

7. Ibid., "deeply," 4; "imperial," 9; "if socialism," 11.

8. Gary Dorrien, "Triangulating to the Right: Social Democracy in Europe and the United States," *Religious Socialism* (Summer 1999), quote 9; Dorrien, "Rethinking the Theory and Politics of Christian Socialism," *Democratic Left* (January 2000), 23–26.

9. Linda Alcoff, *Visible Identities: Race, Gender, and the Self* (New York: Oxford University Press, 2006); Michael Eric Dyson, *Race Rules: Navigating the Color Line* (New York: Vintage, 1996); Frances Fox Piven and Richard A. Cloward, *The Breaking of the American Social Compact* (New York: New Press, 1998); Rosemary Radford Ruether, *Sexism and God-Talk: Toward a Feminist Theology* (Boston: Beacon Press, 1983), 216–34; Joseph Schwartz, *The Future of Democratic Equality: Rebuilding Social Solidarity in a Fragmented America* (New York: Routledge, 2009).

10. Michael Walzer, *Spheres of Justice: A Defense of Pluralism and Equality* (New York: Basic Books, 1983); Michael Sandel, *Liberalism and the Limits of Justice* (Cambridge: Cambridge University Press, 1982); William Sullivan, *Reconstructing Public Philosophy* (Berkeley: University of California Press, 1982); Alasdair MacIntyre, *After Virtue: A Study in Moral Theory* (Notre Dame: University of Notre Dame Press, 1984); Benjamin Barber, *Strong Democracy* (Berkeley: University of California Press, 1984); Amitai Etzioni, *The Spirit of Community: Rights, Responsibilities, and the Communitarian Agenda* (New York: Crown Publishers, 1993); Gary Dorrien, *Soul in Society: The Making and Renewal of Social Christianity* (Minneapolis: Fortress, 1995), 336–76.

11. Cornel West, "On My Intellectual Vocation," interview with George Yancy, in West, *The Cornel West Reader* (New York: Basic Civitas Books, 1999), 19–20.

12. Cornel West, "The Making of an American Radical Democrat of African Descent," introduction to West, *The Ethical Dimensions of Marxist Thought* (New York: Monthly Review Press, 1991), reprinted in West, *The Cornel West Reader*, 3–18, "owing to," 5; West, "On My Intellectual Vocation," "I've always," 21.

13. Ibid., 9–10.

14. West, "On My Intellectual Vocation," "you know," 22; West, "The Making of an American Radical Democrat of African Descent," 11.

15. James H. Cone, *My Soul Looks Back* (Maryknoll, NY: Orbis Books, 1986), quotes 44; Cone, *Risks of Faith: The Emergence of a Black Theology of Liberation, 1968–1998*, "devastated," xv; Cone, "*Martin & Malcolm & America:* A Response by James Cone," *Union Seminary Quarterly Review* 48 (1994), 52–57. Cone's first publication, an essay titled "Christianity and Black Power," was rejected by the *Christian Century* and *Motive* magazines before his subsequent Union colleague C. Eric Lincoln published it in his book *Is Anybody Listening to Black America?* ed. C. Eric Lincoln (New York: Seabury Press, 1968), 3–9.

16. Cone, *My Soul Looks Back*, quotes 46; James H. Cone, *Said I Wasn't Gonna Tell Nobody: The Making of a Black Theologian* (Maryknoll, NY: Orbis Books, 2018), 8–14.

17. James H. Cone, *Black Theology and Black Power* (New York: Harper and Row, 1969; 2nd ed., 1989; repr., Maryknoll, NY: Orbis Books, 2005), quotes 56.

18. Ibid., 27–28, "working," 48.

19. James H. Cone, *A Black Theology of Liberation* (Philadelphia: J. B. Lippincott, 1970; 20th anniversary edition, Maryknoll, NY: Orbis Books, 1990), "liberation," 5; "theology of," 7; "in no position," 8; "analyze," 9.

20. Ibid., "white religionists," 64; James H. Cone, "Black Theology on Revolution, Violence, and Reconciliation," *Union Seminary Quarterly Review* 31 (Fall 1975), 5–14.

21. Michael Lerner and Cornel West, *Jews and Blacks: A Dialogue on Race, Religion, and Culture in America* (New York: Penguin, 1995), "porkchop" and "petit-bourgeois," 21.

22. Cornel West, *Prophesy Deliverance! An Afro-American Revolutionary Christianity* (Philadelphia: Westminster Press, 1982); Stanley Aronowitz, *The Crisis in Historical Materialism: Class, Politics, and Culture in Marxist Theory* (New York: Praeger Publishers, 1981). This section adapts material from Gary Dorrien, *Social Ethics in the Making: Interpreting an American Tradition* (Oxford: Wiley-Blackwell, 2009), 563–83.

23. West, *Prophesy Deliverance!* 134–37; West, "Black Theology and Marxist Thought," in *Black Theology: A Documentary History, 1966–1979*, ed. Gayraud S. Wilmore and James H. Cone (Maryknoll, NY: Orbis Books, 1979), 552–67; West, "Harrington's Socialist Vision," *Christianity and Crisis* (12 December 1983), 484.

24. West, *Prophesy Deliverance!* "Councilism is," 137; Serge Bricianer, *Pannekoik and the Workers' Councils* (St. Louis: Telos Press, 1978); Rosa Luxemburg, *Selected Political Writings of Rosa Luxemburg*, ed. Dick Howard (New York: Monthly Review Press, 1971).

25. Dorrien, *Reconstructing the Common Good*, 162–64.

26. Cornel West, "Alasdair MacIntyre, Liberalism, and Socialism: A Christian Perspective," in *Christianity and Capitalism: Perspectives on Religion, Liberalism, and the Economy*, ed. Bruce Grelle and David A. Krueger (Chicago: Center for the Scientific Study of Religion, 1985), in West, *Prophetic Fragments: Illuminations of the Crisis in American Religion and Culture* (Grand Rapids: Eerdmans, 1988), "wholesome" and "socio-economic," 134–35; Alec Nove, *The Economics of Feasible Socialism* (London: Allen and Unwin, 1983); Wlodzimierz Brus, *The Economics and Politics of Socialism* (London: Routledge and

Kegan Paul, 1973); Branko Horvat, *The Political Economy of Socialism: A Marxist Social Theory* (Armonk, NY: M. E. Sharpe, 1982).

27. Cornel West, "Critical Theory and Christian Faith," *Witness* (January 1986), reprinted in West, *Prophetic Fragments*, "the crucial," 122; Michael Harrington, "Is Capitalism Still Viable?" *Journal of Business Ethics* 1 (1982), 283–84; Harrington, "Corporate Collectivism: A System of Social Injustice," in *Contemporary Readings in Social and Political Ethics*, ed. Garry Brodsky, John Troyer, David Vance (Buffalo: Prometheus Books, 1984), 245.

28. Cornel West, "Michael Harrington, Socialist," *Nation* (January 8/15, 1990), reprinted in West, *Beyond Eurocentrism and Multiculturalism: Prophetic Thought in Postmodern Times* (Monroe, ME: Common Courage Press, 1993), 181–88, quotes 183, 184.

29. Cornel West, "Toward a Socialist Theory of Racism," Institute for Democratic Socialism" (1985), in West, *Prophetic Fragments*, 97–108.

30. Ibid., 98–99, Stalin quote 98; Marcus Garvey, "Address at Newport News, October 25, 1919," *Negro World* (November 1, 1919), in *The Marcus Garvey and Universal Negro Improvement Association Papers*, ed. Robert A. Hill (Berkeley: University of California Press, 1983), 1: 112–20; Harry Haywood, *Negro Liberation* (New York: International Publishers, 1948); James Forman, *Self-Determination and the African-American People* (Seattle: Open Hand Publications, 1981).

31. West, "Toward a Socialist Theory of Racism," 99–101; Oliver C. Cox, *Caste, Class and Race* (Garden City, NY: Doubleday, 1948).

32. West, "Toward a Socialist Theory of Racism," 107–8.

33. Ibid., 108; West, "Beyond Eurocentrism and Multiculturalism," 3–30.

34. Cornel West, "We Socialists," *Crossroads* (July/August 1991), in West, *Prophetic Reflections: Notes on Race and Power in America* (Monroe, ME: Common Courage Press, 1993), 239–44, "I've got to be" and "We need," 243; West, "Toward a Socialist Theory of Racism," "yet a democratic," 108.

35. West, "The Making of an American Radical Democrat of African Descent," "King was," 7; Cornel West, "Martin Luther King Jr.: Prophetic Christian as Organic Intellectual," October 1986, in West, *Prophetic Fragments*, 3–12, "the best," 11; "as an," 11–12.

36. Cornel West, *The American Evasion of Philosophy: A Genealogy of Pragmatism* (Madison: University of Wisconsin Press, 1989), 42–111, 194–210, 226–39, quotes 233.

37. Ibid., 233–34.

38. Cornel West, *Keeping Faith: Philosophy and Race in America* (New York: Routledge, 1993), 67–85, quotes 67, 72.

39. Cornel West, *Race Matters* (Boston: Beacon Press, 1993; paperback edition, New York: Vintage Books, 1994), quotes 9, 10.

40. Ibid., quotes 12, 23.

41. Ibid., quotes 24, 27.

42. Ibid., quotes 54.

43. Ibid., quotes 56, 58.

44. Ibid., 57–66, quote 66; Adolph Reed Jr., *The Jesse Jackson Phenomenon: The Crisis of Purpose in Afro-American Politics* (New Haven: Yale University Press, 1986); Reed,

"What Are the Drums Saying, Booker? The Current Crisis of the Black Intellectual," *Village Voice* 40 (April 11, 1995), 31–36; Reed, "Dangerous Dreams: Black Boomers Wax Nostalgic for the Days of Jim Crow," *Village Voice* 41 (April 16, 1996), 24–29.

45. West, *Race Matters*, quote 69.

46. bell hooks, *Talking Back: Thinking Feminist, Thinking Black* (Boston: South End Press, 1989), "it was clearly" and "marking," 155.

47. Ibid., "spoiling," 149; Tillie Olsen, *Silences* (1965; repr., New York: Feminist Press, 2003).

48. hooks, *Talking Back*, "attending," 150; "the book," 151.

49. Ibid., "I often felt," 152; Paulo Freire, *Education, the Practice of Freedom* (1967; revised English edition published as *Education for Critical Consciousness* [New York: Seabury Press, 1973]); Freire, *Pedagogy of the Oppressed*, trans. Myra Bergman Ramos (1st ed., 1968; 1st English edition [New York: Seabury Press, 1970]).

50. hooks, *Talking Back*, quote 57.

51. Ibid., "the proper," 58; "despite," 61; bell hooks, *Ain't I a Woman: Black Women and Feminism* (Boston: South End Press, 1981; repr., New York: Routledge, 2015).

52. hooks, *Ain't I a Woman*, "strong," 125; "racist ideology," 137; "that force," 138; "by creating," 150; "many black," 152.

53. Ibid., "women's liberationists," 156; hooks, *Talking Back*, 154; Cheryl Clarke, "The Failure to Transform: Homophobia in the Black Community," in *Home Girls: A Black Feminist Anthology*, ed. Barbara Smith (New York: Kitchen Table: Women of Color Press, 1983), 197–208.

54. bell hooks, *Feminist Theory: From Margin to Center* (Boston: South End Press, 1984), "some of," i; "bored," 1; "racism," 3.

55. Ibid., "feminism will," 153; "as feminists," 152–53.

56. Ibid., "women must," 44; Freire, *Pedagogy of the Oppressed*, "because love," 77.

57. hooks, *Talking Back*, "again," 64; Schmidt quote on 64.

58. Ibid., "we must," 65; "of course," 67; "feminist theory," 36.

59. Ibid., "then the," 106.

60. Ibid., "obsessive," 106; "to challenge," 107.

61. bell hooks and Cornel West, *Breaking Bread: Insurgent Black Intellectual Life* (Boston: South End Press, 1991; repr., New York: Routledge, 2017), "nihilism" and "these feelings," 14; "we must," 16; "when I was," 17–18.

62. Ibid., "surreptitious," 60; "with being" and "she feels," 62; "hot," 70; "feminist," 106.

63. Lerner and West, *Jews and Blacks*, 26–31, "by the time," 26–27.

64. Michael P. Lerner, *The New Socialist Revolution: An Introduction to Its Theory and Strategy* (New York: Dell, 1973), 3–55, 139–230.

65. Ibid., 231–51; Michael Harrington, "Only the Convinced Can Be Persuaded," review of *The New Socialist Revolution* by Michael P. Lerner, *New York Times* (March 11, 1973).

66. Michael Lerner, "Reflections on NAM," *Works and Days* 28 (2010), "whenever I" and "indefensible," 45; Lerner, *Surplus Powerlessness: The Psychodynamics of Everyday Life . . . and the Psychology of Individual and Social Transformation* (Oakland, CA: Institute for Labor and Mental Health, 1986), vi–vii.

67. Lerner, *The New Socialist Revolution*, "failing to," 230; Lerner, *Surplus Powerlessness*, 186–202.

68. Lerner, *Surplus Powerlessness*, "new kind," xii.

69. Michael Lerner, *Jewish Renewal: A Path to Healing and Transformation* (New York: G. P. Putnam's Sons, 1994), 123–73, "from the" xiv–xv.

70. Ibid., "the celebration," xxii; Michael Lerner, *The Socialism of Fools: Anti-Semitism on the Left* (Oakland, CA: Tikkun Books, 1992), 108–16.

71. Lerner, *The Socialism of Fools*, "their Jewishness" and "the willingness," 120.

72. Lerner and West, *Jews and Blacks*, "I wish," 55; "there is," 56.

73. Ibid., "if you," 57; "we don't," 57–58.

74. Ibid., "a whole," 59; "their culture," 59–60; Michael Lerner, *Embracing Israel/ Palestine: A Strategy to Heal and Transform the Middle East* (Berkeley: North Atlantic Books, 2012).

75. Lerner and West, *Jews and Blacks*, "white-skin," 70; "it tells them," 70–71; "pointing out," 71.

76. Ibid., "comparative" and "people are," 73; "to include," 74.

77. Ibid., "to most," 75; "the Left," 76.

78. Michael Lerner, *The Politics of Meaning: Restoring Hope and Possibility in an Age of Cynicism* (New York: Addison-Wesley, 1996), "we hunger," 4.

79. Ibid., "most people," 6.

80. Ibid., "a politics," 23.

81. Michael Lerner, "Cynicism vs. the Politics of Meaning: Hillary Clinton Doesn't Deserve the Media's Sneers for Saying What Most Americans Feel," *Los Angeles Times* (June 20, 1993); Lerner, *The Politics of Meaning*, 310–15; Rush Limbaugh, *See, I Told You So* (New York: Pocket Books, 1993), 142–57.

82. Lee Siegel, "All Politics Is Cosmic: The Politics of Meaning," *Atlantic* (June 1996), https://www.theatlantic.com/magazine/archive/1996/06/all-politics-is-cosmic/37661.

83. African United Front, "Open Letter to Cornel West and the Other Uncle Toms" (1993), www.blacksandjews.com/Open_LetterAUF, accessed 3/24/07; Jack E. White, "Philosopher with a Mission," *Time* (June 7, 1993), 62.

84. Leon Wieseltier, "All and Nothing at All: The Unreal World of Cornel West," *New Republic* 212 (March 6, 1995), 31–36, quotes 31, 32; White, "Philosopher with a Mission," 62.

85. David Horowitz, "Cornel West: No Light in His Attic," salon.com (October 11, 1999), 1–6, quotes 2–3, www.frontpagemag.com/Articles, accessed March 23, 2007.

86. Cornel West, "Reconstructing the American Left: The Challenge of Jesse Jackson," *Social Text* 11 (1984), 3–19, "despicable," 14; West, *Race Matters*, "underdog," 112; West and Lerner, *Jews and Blacks*, "racist," "I wouldn't," and "loves," 191; see *Black Religion after the Million Man March*, ed. Garth Kasimu Baker-Fletcher (Maryknoll, NY: Orbis Books, 1998).

87. Nick De Genova, "Gangster Rap and Nihilism in Black America: Some Questions of Life and Death," *Social Text* 43 (1995), 89–132, quote 95; Eric Lott, *The Disappearing Intellectual* (New York: Basic Books, 2006), 114–15; Floyd W. Hayes III, "Cornel West and Afro-Nihilism: A Reconsideration," in *Cornel West: A Critical Reader*, ed.

George Yancy (Oxford: Blackwell Publishers, 2001), 245–60, quote 248; Lewis R. Gordon, "The Unacknowledged Fourth Tradition: An Essay on Nihilism, Decadence, and the Black Intellectual Tradition in the Existential Pragmatic Thought of Cornel West," ibid., 38–58; Peniel E. Joseph, " 'It's Dark and Hell Is Hot': Cornel West, the Crisis of African-American Intellectuals and the Cultural Politics of Race," ibid., 295–311, quote 299; Clevis Headley, "Cornel West on Prophesy, Pragmatism, and Philosophy: A Critical Evaluation of Prophetic Pragmatism," ibid., 59–82; Charles W. Mills, "Prophetic Pragmatism as Political Philosophy," ibid., 192–223.

88. Iris M. Young, "Cornel West on Gender and Family: Some Admiring and Critical Comments," in *Cornel West: A Critical Reader*, 179–91; Cornel West and Sylvia Ann Hewlett, *The War against Parents: What We Can Do for America's Beleaguered Moms and Dads* (Boston: Houghton Mifflin, 1998); John P. Pittman, " 'Radical Historicism,' Antiphilosophy, and Marxism," in *Cornel West: A Critical Reader*, 224–44; George Yancy, "Religion and the Mirror of God: Historicism, Truth, and Religious Pluralism," ibid., 115–35.

89. Cornel West, "Afterword: Philosophy and the Funk of Life," in *Cornel West: A Critical Reader*, 349–59, quotes 356, 358–59.

90. Ibid., quote 360.

91. Sam Tanenhaus, "The Ivy League's Angry Star," *Vanity Fair* (June 2002), 201–3, 218–23; Ross Douthat, "Let Us Now Praise Cornel West," *Harvard Crimson* (January 11, 2002), 1; Fareed Zakaria, "The Education of a President," *Newsweek* (January 14, 2002), http://fareedzakaria.com, accessed March 24, 2007; Editorial, "The Pragmatist," *The New Republic* (April 19, 2002), http://www.tnr.com/doc, accessed March 24, 2007; Cornel West, *Democracy Matters: Winning the Fight against Imperialism* (New York: Penguin Press, 2004), 193–99, "as one," 199; Lynne Duke, "Moving Target," *Washington Post* (August 11 2002), F1, F43.

92. Jack Clark, "Stop Union Busting: Vote for Gore," *Religious Socialism* 24 (Summer 2000), 4; Harvey Cox, "Threaten for Nader, Vote for Gore," ibid., "I am not," 6; Juanita Webster, "A Vote for Nader Could Help the Left," ibid., 6; Rod Ryon, "Nader's Presence Can Make a Point," ibid., 7.

93. Andrew Hammer, "Send a Check to Bernie Sanders," *Religious Socialism* 24 (Summer 2000), 5; Norm Faramelli, " 'Nobody Is Perfect'—Vote for Gore," ibid., 9–10; Gary Dorrien, "The Proximate Good Means Gore," ibid., 8.

94. "President Clinton Announces Another Record Budget Surplus," *CNN Politics* (September 27, 2000), http://articles.cnn.com; Historical Debt Outstanding: Annual 2000–2010"; Tax Policy Center, Urban Institute, and Brookings Institution, "The Tax Policy Briefing Book," 2011, www.taxpolicycenter.org.

95. Alan Greenspan, *The Age of Turbulence: Adventures in a New World* (New York: Penguin, 2008), 186; Linda J. Bilmes and Joseph E. Stiglitz, "The $10 Trillion Hangover: Paying the Price for Eight Years of Bush," *Harper's* (January 2009), 31–35; Historical Debt Outstanding: Annual 2000–2010"; "The Tax Policy Briefing Book"; Joseph E. Stiglitz and Linda J. Bilmes, *The Three Trillion Dollar War* (New York: W. W. Norton, 2008).

96. Charles Krauthammer, "Universal Dominion: Toward a Unipolar World," *National Interest* 18 (Winter 1989), 48–49; Krauthammer, "Can America Stand Alone?" *Time* (October 22, 1990), 96; Krauthammer, "The Unipolar Moment," *Foreign Affairs* 70 (1991), 25–33; Krauthammer, "How the War Can Change America," *Time* (January 28, 1991), 100; Krauthammer, "Must America Slay All the Dragons?" *Time* (March 4, 1991), 88; Krauthammer, "On Getting It Wrong," *Time* (April 15, 1991), 70; Ben J. Wattenberg, "Neo-Manifest Destinarianism," *National Interest* 21 (Fall 1990), 51–54; Joshua Muravchik, *Exporting Democracy: Fulfilling America's Destiny* (Washington, DC: American Enterprise Institute, 1991).

97. Author's interview with Norman Podhoretz, June 12, 1990; author's interviews with Michael Novak, March 20, 1990, and June 19, 1992; Ben J. Wattenberg, *The First Universal Nation: Leading Indicators and Ideas about the Surge of America in the 1990s* (New York: Free Press, 1991), "we are," 20.

98. Author's interview with Peter L. Berger, September 26, 1990; Jeane J. Kirkpatrick, "A Normal Country in a Normal Time," *National Interest* 21 (Fall 1990), 44; Irving Kristol, "Tongue-Tied in Washington," *Wall Street Journal* (April 15, 1991).

99. Department of Defense, "Defense Planning Guidance" (February 18, 1992); excerpts published in the *New York Times* (March 8, 1992) and *Washington Post* (March 11, 1992); Patrick E. Tyler, "U.S. Strategy Plan Calls for Insuring No Rivals Develop," *New York Times* (March 8, 1992), A1; Tyler, "Senior U.S. Officials Assail Lone-Superpower Policy," *New York Times* (March 11, 1992), A6; Paul Wolfowitz, "Historical Memory: Setting History Straight," *Current* 423 (June 2000), 19; Charles Krauthammer, "What's Wrong with the Pentagon Paper?" *Washington Post* (March 13, 1992), A25; James Mann, *Rise of the Vulcans: The History of Bush's War Cabinet* (New York: Viking, 2004), 212–13.

100. Project for the New American Century, *Rebuilding America's Defenses: Strategy, Forces and Resources for a New Century* (Washington, DC: Project for the New American Century, 2000), "fight," iv; "a new," 6.

101. Robert Kagan and William Kristol, "No Defense," *Weekly Standard* (July 23, 2001), 11–13; Richard A. Clarke, *Against All Enemies: Inside America's War on Terror* (New York: Free Press, 2004), 30–33.

102. Gary Dorrien, *Imperial Designs: Neoconservatism and the New Pax Americana* (New York: Routledge, 2004); West, *Democracy Matters*, "we are," 8.

103. Ibid., "paternalistic," 35; "no other" and "race has," 41.

104. Irving Howe, "The Spirit of the Times," *Dissent* (Spring 1993), 131–33, quotes 132.

105. John Stuart Mill, *Principles of Political Economy* (1st ed., 1848; 3rd ed., 1852; 6th ed., 1865; repr. 6th ed., London: Ashley, 1909), "the aim," 1st ed., 768; 6th ed., 763.

106. Mill, *Principles of Political Economy*, 6th ed., "absolute dependence," 211; "it would be" and "and no one," 793; David Belkin, "Why Market Socialism? From the Critique of Political Economy to Positive Political Economy," in *Why Market Socialism?* ed. Belkin and Frank Roosevelt (Armonk, NY: M. E. Sharpe, 1994), 10–13.

107. Karl Marx, *Grundrisse*, trans. Martin Nicolaus (London: Penguin Books, 1973), 758–59, "and thereby," 759; Morris Hillquit, *Socialism in Theory and Practice* (New York: Macmillan, 1909), "there is," 134; Walter Rauschenbusch, *Christianizing the Social*

Order (New York: Macmillan, 1912), 350–69; Albert Schäffle, *The Quintessence of Socialism* (London: Swan Sonnenschein, 1889).

108. Evan F. M. Durbin, *Purchasing Power and Trade Depression* (London: Jonathan Cape, 1933); Durbin, *Socialist Credit Policy* (London: Victor Gollancz, 1934); Durbin, *The Problem of Credit Policy* (London: Chapman and Hall, 1935); Durbin, *What Have We to Defend? A Brief Critical Examination of the British Social Tradition* (London: G. Routledge, 1942); Durbin, *Problems of Economic Planning* (London: Routledge and Kegan Paul, 1949); Ludwig von Mises, "Economic Calculation in the Socialist Commonwealth" (1920), in *Collectivist Economic Planning*, ed. F. A. Hayek (Clifton, NJ: Kelley, 1975); Ludwig von Mises, *Socialism: An Economic and Sociological Analysis* (1st ed., 1922; English ed., 1969; Indianapolis: Liberty Classics, 1981); Oskar Lange, with F. M. Taylor, *On the Economic Theory of Socialism* (1st ed., 1938; New York: McGraw Hill, 1964); Lange, "Marxian Economics and Modern Economic Theory," *Review of Economic Studies* 2 (1935), 189–201.

109. Gary Dorrien, *Social Democracy in the Making: Political and Religious Roots of European Socialism* (New Haven: Yale University Press, 2019), 385–99, 435–56; Tadeusz Kowalik, "Oscar Lange's Market Socialism: The Story of an Intellectual-Political Career," in *Why Market Socialism?* 137–54.

110. Wlodzimierz Brus, *The Market in a Socialist Economy* (London: Routledge and Kegan Paul, 1972); Brus and Kazimierz Laski, *From Marx to Market: Socialism in Search of an Economic System* (Oxford: Oxford University Press, 1989); Anne Applebaum, "The Three Lives of Helena Brus," *Washington Post* (December 6, 1998); Jan Toporowski, "Wlodzimierz Brus," *The Guardian* (November 13, 2007).

111. Alec Nove, *The Economics of Feasible Socialism* (London: Allen and Unwin, 1983), "the little" and "brilliant," 10; "it is nonsense," 14; Nove, *Socialism, Economics, and Development* (London: Allen and Unwin, 1986).

112. Saul Estrin and David Winter, "Planning in a Market Socialist Economy," in *Market Socialism*, ed. Estrin and Julian Le Grand (Oxford: Oxford University Press, 1989), 100–138; Estrin, "Workers' Cooperatives: Their Merits and the Limitations," ibid., 165–92; Estrin and Le Grand, "Market Socialism," ibid., 1–24; David Miller, "Socialism and the Market," *Political Theory* 5 (November 1977), 473–89; Miller, *Market, State and Community: Theoretical Foundations of Market Socialism* (Oxford: Oxford University Press, 1990); Frank Cunningham, *Democratic Theory and Socialism* (Cambridge: Cambridge University Press, 1987); C. B. Macpherson, *Democratic Theory: Essays in Retrieval* (Oxford: Oxford University Press, 1973); Dada Maheshvarananda, *After Capitalism: Economic Democracy in Action* (San Germán, Puerto Rico: InnerWorld Publications, 2013); Gar Alperovitz, *America beyond Capitalism: Reclaiming Our Wealth, Our Liberty, and Our Democracy* (Hoboken, NJ: John Wiley, 2005); David C. Korten, *Agenda for a New Economy: From Phantom Wealth to Real Wealth* (San Francisco: Berrett-Koehler, 2010); Robert Dahl, *A Preface to Economic Democracy* (Berkeley: University of California Press, 1985), 151–52.

113. Dahl, *A Preface to Economic Democracy*, 140–50; David P. Ellerman, "The Socialization of Entrepreneurialism: The Empresarial Division of the Caja Laboral Popular," (Somerville, MA: Industrial Cooperative Association, 1982), 13–17; H.

Thomas and C. Logan, *Mondragon: An Economic Analysis* (London: Allen and Unwin, 1982), 149–61; Miller, "Socialism and the Market," 479–85; Joyce Rothschild and J. Allen Whitt, *The Cooperative Workplace: Potentials and Dilemmas of Organizational Democracy and Participation* (Cambridge: Cambridge University Press, 1986), 73–115; Roy Morrison, *We Build the World as We Travel* (Philadelphia: New Society Publishers, 1991), 35–102; Thomas E. Weisskopf, "Challenges to Market Socialism: A Response to Critics," in *Why Market Socialism?* 298–300;

114. David P. Ellerman, "Property and Production: An Introduction to the Labor Theory of Property" (Somerville, MA: Industrial Cooperative Association, 1980); Ellerman, *The Democratic Worker-Owned Firm* (London: Unwin Hyman, 1990); John Roemer, "Market Socialism, A Blueprint: How Such an Economy Might Work," in *Why Market Socialism?* 269–95; David Schweickart, *Capitalism or Worker Control? An Ethical and Economic Appraisal* (New York: Praeger, 1980); Leland Stauber, "A Proposal for a Democratic Market Economy," *Journal of Comparative Economics* 1 (1977), 235–58; Stauber, *A New Program for Democratic Socialism: Lessons from the Market-Planning Experience in Austria* (Carbondale, IL: Four Willows Press, 1987); Fred Block, "Remaking Our Economy: New Strategies for Structural Reform," in *Why Market Socialism?* 371–82; Weisskopf, "Challenges to Market Socialism," 297–315; Samuel Bowles, David M. Gordon and Thomas E. Weisskopf, *Beyond the Waste Land: A Democratic Alternative to Economic Decline* (Garden City, NY: Doubleday, 1983), 261–390.

115. Roemer, "Market Socialism, A Blueprint," 269–70, 281; Weisskopf, "Challenges to Market Socialism," 300–301; Jaroslav Vanek, *General Theory of Labor-Managed Market Economics* (Ithaca: Cornell University Press, 1970).

116. Stauber, "A Proposal for a Democratic Market Economy," 241–55; Korten, *Agenda for a New Economy*, 65–112; David Schweickart, "What to Do When the Bailout Fails," *Tikkun* (May/June 2009), 72–73; Schweickart, *Capitalism or Worker Control?* 106–13.

117. Roemer, "Market Socialism, A Blueprint," 270–77; Joanne Barkan and David Belkin, "Comment," in *Why Market Socialism?* 282–88.

118. Dorrien, *The Democratic Socialist Vision*; Dorrien, *Reconstructing the Common Good*; Dorrien, *Soul in Society*; Gary Dorrien, *Economy, Difference, Empire: Social Ethics for Social Justice* (New York: Columbia University Press, 2010); Dorrien, *Social Democracy in the Making*.

119. Estrin and Winter, "Planning in a Market Socialist Economy," 109–29; David Miller and Saul Estrin, "A Case for Market Socialism: What Does It Mean? Why Should We Favor It?" in *Why Market Socialism?* 225–40; William Temple, *The Hope of a New World* (New York: Macmillan, 1941), 54–62; Temple, *Christianity and the Social Order* (Harmondsworth, Middlesex: Penguin Books, 1942), 77–78.

120. Saul Estrin, "Workers' Cooperatives: Their Merits and Their Limitations," in *Market Socialism*, 165–92; Estrin and Legrand, "Market Socialism," 16–20; Estrin and Winter, "Planning in a Market Socialist Economy," 125–26; Miller and Estrin, "A Case for Market Socialism," 231–32; Weisskopf, "Challenges to Market Socialism," 305–9; Ann Arbor Democratic Socialists of America, "Toward a Cooperative Commonwealth," pamphlet (Ann Arbor: Ann Arbor DSA, 1983).

121. Roemer, "Market Socialism, A Blueprint," 274–76; Block, "Remaking Our Economy, 375–80; David Belkin, "Why Market Socialism?" 29.

122. Alec Nove, " 'Market Socialism' and 'Free Economy': A Discussion of Alternatives," in *Why Market Socialism?* 369; Nove, "Feasible Socialism? Some Social-Political Assumptions," ibid., 219–23; Weisskopf, "Challenges to Market Socialism," 312–15, quote 315.

123. Michael Walzer, *Just and Unjust Wars: A Moral Argument with Historical Illustrations* (New York: Basic Books, 1977); Walzer, *Spheres of Justice*; Walzer, *Interpretation and Social Criticism* (Cambridge: Harvard University Press, 1987).

124. Judith Butler, *Gender Trouble: Feminism and the Subversion of Identity* (New York: Routledge, 1990); Iris Marion Young, *Justice and the Politics of Difference* (Princeton: Princeton University Press, 1990).

125. Karl Marx, "Letter to Arnold Ruge, September 1843," *Karl Marx: Early Writings*, ed. Lucio Coletti (New York: Penguin, 1975), "the self-clarification," 209; Young, *Justice and the Politics of Difference*, "but none," 9; "I claim," 13; Nancy Fraser, "What's Critical about Critical Theory? The Case of Habermas and Gender," in Fraser, *Unruly Practices: Power, Discourse, and Gender in Contemporary Social Theory* (Minneapolis: University of Minnesota Press, 1989), 113–43; Jürgen Habermas, *The Theory of Communicative Action*, 2 vols., trans. Thomas McCarthy (1984; repr., Boston: Beacon Press, 1989).

126. David Bromwich, *Politics by Other Means: Higher Education and Group Thinking* (New Haven: Yale University Press, 1992), "by choice," xiv.

127. Todd Gitlin, *The Twilight of Common Dreams: Why America Is Wracked by Culture Wars* (New York: Henry Holt, 1995), "late New" and "by 1975," 146; Gitlin, "The Rise of Identity Politics," *Dissent* (Spring 1993); Richard Rorty, *Achieving Our Country: Leftist Thought in Twentieth-Century America* (Cambridge: Harvard University Press, 1998), "sadistic" and "but insofar," 100.

128. Fraser, *Unruly Practices*, 17–68, 93–112, 161–90, "radicals in," 1; Richard Rorty, *Philosophy and the Mirror of Nature* (Princeton: Princeton University Press, 1979); Rorty, *Consequences of Pragmatism* (Minneapolis: University of Minnesota Press, 1982); Rorty, *Contingency, Irony, and Solidarity* (Cambridge: Cambridge University Press, 1989).

129. Fraser, *Unruly Practices*, "on the one," 3.

130. Nancy Fraser, "From Redistribution to Recognition? Dilemmas of Justice in a 'Postsocialist' Age," *New Left Review* 212 (July/August 1995), 68–93; reprinted in Fraser, *Justice Interruptus: Critical Reflections on the 'Postsocialist' Condition* (New York: Routledge, 1997), 11–39; and *Adding Insult to Injury: Nancy Fraser Debates Her Critics*, ed. Kevin Olson (London: Verso, 2008), 11–41. Citations from this article will be from the Verso edition.

131. Fraser, "From Redistribution to Recognition?" quotes 13.

132. John Rawls, *A Theory of Justice* (Cambridge: Harvard University Press, 1971); Amartya Sen, *The Idea of Justice* (Cambridge: Harvard University Press, 1979); Ronald Dworkin, *Taking Rights Seriously* (Cambridge: Harvard University Press, 1978).

133. Charles Taylor, *Multiculturalism and "The Politics of Recognition"* (Princeton: Princeton University Press, 1992); Axel Honneth, *The Struggle for Recognition*, trans. Joel Anderson (Cambridge: MIT Press, 1995); Patricia J. Williams, *The Alchemy of Race and Rights* (Cambridge: Harvard University Press, 1991).

134. Fraser, "From Redistribution to Recognition?" 18–22, quote 20.

135. Ibid., 28–33.

136. Ibid., 33–34.

137. Ibid., quote 39.

138. Ibid., quote 41.

139. Nancy Fraser and Axel Honneth, *Redistribution or Recognition? A Political-Philosophical Exchange*, trans. Joel Golb, James Ingram, Christianne Wilke (London: Verso, 2003).

140. Judith Butler, "Merely Cultural," *Social Text* 15 (1997), 265–77, reprinted in *Adding Insult to Injury*, 42–56, quotes 46; Robert Bellah, Richard Madsen, William M. Sullivan, Ann Swidler, Steven M. Tipton, *Habits of the Heart: Individualism and Commitment in American Life* (Berkeley: University of California Press, 1985).

141. Butler, "Merely Cultural," quotes 56.

142. Richard Rorty, "Is 'Cultural Recogniton' a Useful Notion for Leftist Politics?" *Critical Horizons* 1 (2000), 7–20, reprinted in *Adding Insult to Injury*, 69–81.

143. Ibid., "culture pushed," 74.

144. Ibid., "no big" and "do we," 77; "to help," 78.

145. Iris Marion Young, "Unruly Categories: A Critique of Nancy Fraser's Dual Systems Theory," *New Left Review* 222 (1997), 147–60, reprinted in *Adding Insult to Injury*, 89–106, quote 91.

146. Ibid., "brazenly," 93; "why not," 96; Fraser, "What's Critical about Critical Theory?" 114–29; Christopher F. Zurn, "Arguing over Participatory Power: On Nancy Fraser's Conception of Social Justice," *Adding Insult to Injury*, 142–63; Elizabeth Anderson, "Affirmative Action and Fraser's Redistribution–Recognition Dilemma," ibid., 164–75; Ingrid Robeyns, "Is Nancy Fraser's Critique of Theories of Distributive Justice Justified?" ibid., 176–95; Joseph Heath, "Resource Egalitarianism and the Politics of Recognition," ibid., 196–220.

147. Young, "Unruly Categories," "a materialist," 99; "I recommend," 100; Christian Hunold and Iris Marion Young, "Justice, Democracy, and Hazardous Siting," *Political Studies* 46 (1998), 82–95; Pierre Bourdieu, *Distinction: A Social Critique of the Judgment of Taste* (Cambridge: Harvard University Press, 1979); Bourdieu, "What Makes a Social Class?" *Berkeley Journal of Sociology* 32 (1988), 1–18; Nancy Fraser, "Struggle over Needs: Outline of a Socialist–Feminist Critical Theory of Late Capitalist Political Culture," *Unruly Practices*, 161–90.

148. Young, "Unruly Categories," "does just," 101; "seems similar," 103.

149. Nancy Fraser, "Heterosexism, Misrecognition, and Capitalism: A Response to Judith Butler," *Social Text* 15 (1997), 279–89, in *Adding Insult to Injury*, 57–68, "the genuinely" and "neoconservative," 57; "finding me" and "nothing," 58.

150. Ibid., "contrary to," 59–60; Fraser and Honneth, *Redistribution or Recognition?* 7–26.

151. Fraser, "Heterosexism, Misrecognition, and Capitalism," quotes 65.

152. Ibid., "standard," 66; Claude Lévi-Strauss, *The Elementary Structures of Kinship* (Boston: Beacon Press, 1969).

153. Nancy Fraser, "Why Overcoming Prejudice Is Not Enough: A Rejoinder to Richard Rorty," *Critical Horizons* 1 (2000), 21–28, in *Adding Insult to Injury*, 82–88.

154. Nancy Fraser, "Against Pollyanna-ism: A Reply to Iris Young," *New Left Review* 223 (1997), 126–29, in *Adding Insult to Injury*, 107–11, quotes 107.

155. Ibid., "widespread," 107; "systematically" and "more," 108; "will somehow," 110–11; Nancy Fraser, "Social Justice in the Age of Identity Politics," 11–26; Fraser, "Culture, Political Economy, and Difference: On Iris Young's *Justice and the Politics of Difference*," in *Justice Interruptus*, 189–206; Alan D. Sokal, "Transgressing the Boundaries: Towards a Transformative Hermeneutics of Quantum Gravity," *Social Text* 46–47 (Spring/Summer 1996), 217–52.

156. Nancy Fraser, "Rethinking Recognition: Overcoming Displacement and Reification in Cultural Politics," *New Left Review* 2 (2000), 107–20, in *Adding Insult to Injury*, 129–41; Elizabeth Anderson, "Affirmative Action and Fraser's Redistribution–Recognition Dilemma," *Adding Insult to Injury*, 164–75; Joseph Heath, "Resource Egalitarianism and the Politics of Recognition," ibid., 196–220; Robeyns, "Is Nancy Fraser's Critique of Theories of Distributive Justice Justified?" ibid., 176–95; Leonard Feldman, "Status Injustice: The Role of the State," ibid., 221–45; Kevin Olson, "Participatory Democracy and Democratic Justice," ibid., 246–72.

157. Nancy Fraser, "Reframing Justice in a Globalizing World," *Adding Insult to Injury*, 273–94; Fraser, *Scales of Justice: Reimagining Political Space in a Globalizing World* (New York: Columbia University Press, 2009), 1–11.

158. Fraser, *Scales of Justice*, 12–15.

159. Ibid., 16–22, 76–99.

160. Ibid., quote 24–25.

161. Ibid., 100–101; Nancy Fraser, *Fortunes of Feminism: From State-Managed Capitalism to Neoliberal Crisis* (London: Verso, 2013), 209–26.

162. Julia Kristeva, "Women's Time," *Signs: Journal of Women in Culture and Society* 7 (1981), 13–35; Zillah R. Eisenstein, *The Radical Future of Liberal Feminism* (New York: Longman, 1981); hooks, *Feminist Theory*; Alison Jagger, *Feminist Politics and Human Nature* (Totowa, NJ: Rowman and Allanheld, 1983), 169–350; Rosemary R. Ruether, *Sexism and God-Talk: Toward a Feminist Theology* (Boston: Beacon Press, 1983), 216–22; Catherine Keller, *Apocalypse Now and Then: A Feminist Guide to the End of the World* (Boston: Beacon Press, 1996), 128–30; Ruth Rosen, *The World Split Open: How the Modern Women's Movement Changed America* (New York: Penguin, 2001); Stacey M. Floyd-Thomas, *Mining the Motherlode: Methods in Womanist Ethics* (Cleveland: Pilgrim Press, 2006), 1–14; Fraser, *Scales of Justice*, "previously" and "prosperity," 104; "unable" and "its decoupling," 105.

163. Fraser, *Scales of Justice*, "the socialist," 105; "could not" and "its spectacular," 106; "an enormous," 108.

164. Ibid., "unholy," 108; "could not," 109; Michel Foucault, *The Care of the Self*, trans. Robert Hurley (New York: Vintage Books, 1986).

165. Wendy Brown, *Walled States, Waning Sovereignty* (New York: Zone Books, 2010), "of afterness," 21; Brown, *Edgework: Critical Essays on Knowledge and Politics* (Princeton: Princeton University Press, 2005); Virginia Vargas, "Feminism, Globalization, and the Global Justice and Solidarity Movement," *Cultural Studies* 17 (2003), 905–20; Donna Dickenson, "Counting Women In: Globalization, Democratization, and the Women's Movement," in *The Transformation of Democracy? Globalization and Territorial Democracy*, ed. Anthony McGrew (Cambridge: Polity, 1997), 97–120; Fraser, *Scales of Justice*, "in this," 113.

166. Fraser, *Scales of Justice*, quote 115.

167. Cinzia Arruzza, Tithi Bhattacharya, and Nancy Fraser, *Feminism for the 99%: A Manifesto* (London: Verso, 2019), "equal opportunity" and "to be grateful," 2; Fraser, *The Old Is Dying and the New Cannot Be Born* (London: Verso, 2019), 14; Fraser, *Fortunes of Feminism*, 224–26; Susan Moller Okin, *Justice, Gender, and the Family* (New York: Basic Books, 1989), 138–39.

168. "DSA PAC Statement on Kerry Campaign," *Democratic Left* 32 (Fall 2004), quote 8; Gary Dorrien, "Kerry to Beat Bush," *Religious Socialism* 28 (Winter 2004), 5; Michael Hirsch, "Economic Justice Agenda Adopted," *Democratic Left* 35 (Winter 2008), 4.

8. BREAKING THE OLIGARCHY

1. This opening section adapts material from Gary Dorrien, *The Obama Question: A Progressive Perspective* (Lanham: Rowman and Littlefield, 2012), 73–84.

2. Alan Greenspan, *The Age of Turbulence: Adventures in a New World* (New York: Penguin, 2008), 366–73; Peter Coy, "Are Derivatives Dangerous?" *Business Week* (March 31, 2003), www.businessweek.com, accessed December 1, 2008; see R. Batra, *Greenspan's Fraud: How Two Decades of His Policies Have Undermined the Global Economy* (New York: Palgrave Macmillan), 2005; Gary Dorsch, "Weapons of Financial Mass Destruction," Financial Sense University, October 8, 2008, wwwfinancialsense.com, accessed October 30, 2008; "A Nuclear Winter?" *The Economist* (September 18, 2008), 12.

3. Henry M. Paulson Jr., *On the Brink: Inside the Race to Stop the Collapse of the Global Financial System* (New York: Business Plus, 2010), quote 18.

4. Andrew Ross Sorkin, *Too Big to Fail: The Inside Story of How Wall Street and Washington Fought to Save the Financial System—and Themselves* (New York: Penguin Books, 2010), 299–307; Paulson Jr., *On the Brink: Inside the Race to Stop the Collapse of the Global Financial System*, 171–221; William D. Cohan, *House of Cards: A Tale of Hubris and Wretched Excess on Wall Street* (New York: Anchor Books, 2010), 56–154; Bernanke quote "The Reckoning—As Crisis Spiraled, Alarm Led to Action," *New York Times*, http://www.nytimes.com/2008/10/02/business, accessed March 19. 2011.

5. Tom Hayden, Barbara Ehrenreich, Bill Fletcher Jr., and Danny Glover, "Progressives for Obama," *Nation* (March 25, 2008); Eric Dash, "Bankers Pledge Cooperation with Obama," *New York Times* (March 27, 2009); Eamon Javers, "Inside Obama's Bank CEOs Meeting," *Politico* (April 3, 2009), http://www.politico.com/news; Rick Klein,

"Obama to Bankers: I'm Standing 'Between You and the Pitchforks,'" ABC News, The Note Blog, http://blogs.abcnews.com/thenote/2009/04.

6. "Bailed-Out Banks," *CNN Money.com*, n.d., accessed June 9, 2009; Rick Newman, "The Best and Worst Bailed-Out Banks," *U.S. News and World Report.com*, June 9, 2009, accessed June 9, 2009; Paulson Jr., *On the Brink*, 360–64; Michael Lewis and David Einhorn, "The End of the Financial World as We Know It," *New York Times* (January 4, 2009), 9–10; Eric Dash, Louise Story, and Andrew Ross Sorkin, "Bank of America to Receive $20 Billion More," *New York Times* (January 16, 2009), B1, 6; Edmund L. Andrews and Eric Dash, "Deeper Hole for Bankers: Need Keeps Growing for Funds in Bailout," *New York Times* (January 14, 2009), A1, 22; Eric Lipton and Ron Nixon, "A Bank with Its Own Woes Lends Only a Trickle of Bailout," *New York Times* (January 14, 2009), A1, 24; David M. Herszenhorn, "Senate Releases Second Portion of Bailout Fund," *New York Times* (January 16, 2009), A1, 16.

7. Dorrien, *The Obama Question*, 207–16; Jerome R. Corsi, *The Obama Nation: Leftist Politics and the Cult of Personality* (New York: Threshold Editions, 2008); Corsi, *Where's the Birth Certificate?: The Case That Barack Obama Is Not Eligible to be President* (Washington, DC: WND Books, 2011); Brad O'Leary, *The Audacity of Deceit: Barack Obama's War on American Values* (Los Angeles: WND Books, 2008); Aaron Klein, *The Manchurian President: Barack Obama's Ties to Communists, Socialists, and Other Anti-American Extremists* (Washington, DC: WND Books, 2010); Jack Cashill, *Deconstructing Obama* (New York: Threshold Editions, 2011); Cashill, "Is Khalid al-Mansour the Man behind Obama Myth?" *WorldNetDaily* (August 28, 2008), www.wnd.com; Michelle Malkin, *Culture of Corruption: Obama and His Team of Tax Cheats, Crooks, and Cronies* (Washington, DC: Regnery, 2009); Pamela Geller (with Robert Spencer), *The Post-American Presidency: The Obama Administration's War on America* (New York: Threshold Editions, 2010); Webster Griffon Tarpley, *Obama: The Postmodern Coup* (Joshua Tree, CA: Progressive Press, 2008); Dinesh D'Souza, "How Obama Thinks," *Forbes* (September 27, 2010); D'Souza, *The Roots of Obama's Rage* (Washington, DC: Regnery, 2010).

8. Chris Hedges, "The Obama Deception: Why Cornel West Went Ballistic," *truthdig* (May 16, 2011), www.truthdig.com.

9. Michael Lerner, "A Progressive Strategy for 2011–2012," *Tikkun* (Spring 2011), 6–7.

10. Gary Dorrien, "Occupy the Future: Can a Protest Movement Find a Path to Economic Democracy?" *America* (March 12, 2012); "Questions for Gary Dorrien: On the Ethical Roots and Uncertain Future of Occupy Wall Street," *America* (March 12, 2012); and "Savvy Occupiers: An Interview with Gary Dorrien," *Christian Century* (November 15, 2011).

11. "The Declaration of the Occupation of New York City," Sparrow Project (November 1, 2011), https://www.sparrowmedia.net/2011/11/the-declaration-of-the-occupation-of-new-york-city; David Graeber, "Occupy's Liberation from Liberalism: The Real Meaning of May Day," *Guardian* (May 7, 2012); Richard D. Wolff and Stephen A. Resnick, *Knowledge and Class: A Marxian Critique of Political Economy* (Chicago: University of Chicago Press, 1987); Wolff, Resnick, and J. K. Gibson-Graham, *Class and Its Others* (Minneapolis: University of Minnesota Press, 2000); Wolff, *Democracy at Work: A Cure for Capitalism* (Chicago: Haymarket, 2012).

12. Simon Johnson, "The Quiet Coup: How Bankers Took Power, and How They're Impeding Recovery," *The Atlantic* (May 2009), 46–56.

13. Linda Feldmann, "Bernie Sanders: 'I'm Proud to be Jewish,'" *Christian Science Monitor* (June 11, 2015); Tamara Keith, "Sanders Could Be the First Jewish President, but He Doesn't Like to Talk about It," National Public Radio (November 2, 2015), https://www.npr.org/2015/11/02/454051697/sanders-could-be-the-first-jewish-president-but-doesnt-like-to-talk-about-it; Jason Horowitz, "Bernie Sanders's '100% Brooklyn' Roots Are as Unshakable as His Accent," *New York Times* (July 24, 2015); Carol Felsenthal, "Bernie Sanders Found Socialism at the University of Chicago," *Chicago Magazine* (May 4, 2015), https://www.chicagomag.com/Chicago-Magazine/Felsenthal-Files/May-2015/Bernie-Sanders-University-of-Chicago; Bernie Sanders, *Our Revolution: A Future to Believe In* (New York: Thomas Dunne Books, 2017), 7–22.

14. "Sen. Bernie Sanders, I-Vt.," *Roll Call*, http://media.cq.com/members/509?rc=1; Greg Guma, *The People's Republic: Vermont and the Sanders Revolution* (South Burlington, VT: New England Press, 1989), 15–45; Sanders, *Our Revolution*, 25–30; Peter Dreier and Pierre Clavel, "What Kind of Mayor Was Bernie Sanders?" *The Nation* (June 2, 2015), https://www.thenation.com/article/bernies-burlington-city-sustainable-future.

15. Russell Banks, "Bernie Sanders, the Socialist Mayor," *Atlantic* (October 5, 2015), https://www.theatlantic.com/politics/archive/2015/10/bernie-sanders-mayor/407413; Guma, *The People's Republic*, 40–55; Michael Kruse, "14 Things Bernie Sanders Has Said about Socialism," *Politico* (July 17, 2015), https://www.politico.com/story/2015/07/14-things-berne-sanders-has-said-about-socialism-120265; Sanders, *Our Revolution*, 32–40.

16. Linda Qiu, "Did Bernie Sanders Vote against Background Checks and Waiting Periods for Gun Purchases?" *Politifact* (July 10, 2015), https://www.politifact.com/truth-o-meter/statements/2015/jul/10/generation-forward-pac/did-bernie-sanders-vote-against-background-checks; Bonnie Kristian, "Bernie Sanders Is Not Nearly as Progressive as You Think He Is," *The Week* (February 9, 2016), https://theweek.com/articles/603044/bernie-sanders-not-nearly-progressive-think.

17. Bernie Sanders, *The Speech: On Corporate Greed and the Decline of the Middle Class* (New York: Nation Books, 2015), 13–17.

18. Ibid., "our job," 19; "I am," 20.

19. Ibid., 25–32.

20. Ibid., "how much," 73.

21. Ibid., "I think," 126.

22. Sanders, *Our Revolution*, "a disaster," 46.

23. Ibid., 48–85; Jeff Weaver, *How Bernie Won: Inside the Revolution That's Taking Back Our Country—and Where We Go from Here* (New York: Thomas Dunne Books, 2018), 43–48; DSAUSA.org, "#WeNeedBernie—Democratic Socialists of America," http://www.dsausa.org/weneedbernie.

24. Sanders, *Our Revolution*, 115–29; Weaver, *How Bernie Won*, 57–65.

25. Bernie Sanders, "Speech on Democratic Socialism in the United States," Georgetown University, November 19, 2015, https://www.vox.com/2015/11/19/9762028/bernie-sanders-democratic-socialism, 1–13, quote 5.

26. Ibid., quotes 9.

27. Sanders, *Our Revolution*, 167–72; Weaver, *How Bernie Won*, 171–218; Patrick Healy and Jonathan Martin, "Donald Trump and Bernie Sanders Win in New Hampshire Primary," *New York Times* (February 9, 2016).

28. Sanders, *Our Revolution*, 170–78; Weaver, *How Bernie Won*, 219–32; "Super Tuesday State Results," *Washington Post* (March 1, 2016).

29. Democratic Socialists of America, "Dump the Racist Trump; Continue the Political Revolution Down-Ballot; Build Multiracial Coalitions and Socialist Organization for Long-term Change," August 16, 2016, http://www.dsausa.org/election2016; Joel Bleifuss, "Trump's Path to Victory," *In These Times* (June 2019), 3; Democratic Socialists of America, "15 DSA Members Elected! 2017 Election," http://www.dsausa. org/15_dsa_members_elected.

30. Democratic Socialists of America, "Resistance Rising: Socialist Strategy in the Age of Political Revolution," June 2016, 1–12, "a game-changing," 1.

31. Ibid., 2–3, "these movements," 3.

32. Ibid., "we consider," 8.

33. Ibid., 9; Kim Moody, "A Solidarity Working Paper," *Solidarity* (2000), reprinted as "The Rank and File Strategy: Building a Socialist Movement in the U.S.," *Solidarity* "Reflections on the Rank and File Strategy," *Jacobin* (August 10, 2018), https://www. jacobinmag.com/2018/08/rankandfilestrategy; Democratic Socialists of America, "Our Electoral Strategy," National Political Committee, January 27, 2018, https://electoral. dsausa.org.

34. DSA, "Resistance Rising," "medium," 10; DSA, "Our Electoral Strategy," "in accordance"; Seth Ackerman, "A Blueprint for a New Party," *Jacobin* (November 8, 2016), https://www.jacobinmag.com/2016/11/bernie-sanders-democratic-labor-party-acker man/.

35. DSA, "Resistance Rising," "organizing," 11.

36. Bhaskar Sunkara, *The Socialist Manifesto: The Case for Radical Politics in an Era of Extreme Inequality* (New York: Basic Books, 2019), 122–23, 221–22; DSA, "Resistance Rising," "but we," 12.

37. DSA, "Our Electoral Strategy," "instead of."

38. Kate Aronoff, "The Democratic Socialists Scored Some Big Wins, Here's What They're Planning Next," *In These Times* (November 10, 2017); Aronoff, "Why the Democratic Socialists of America Won't Stop Growing: The Inside Story of DSA's Dramatic Ascent," *In These Times* (August 12, 2018); Avery Anapol, "Four Socialist-backed Candidates Win Pennsylvania Legislative Primaries," *The Hill* (May 16, 2018); Li Zhou, "Alexandria Ocasio-Cortez Is Now the Youngest Woman Elected to Congress," *Vox* (November 7, 2018), https://www.vox.com/2018/11/6/18070704/election-results-alexandria-ocasio-cortez-wins; Maurice Isserman, "Socialists in the House: A 100-Year History from Victor Berger to Alexandria Ocasio-Cortez," *In These Times* (November 8, 2018); Miriam Bensman, "They Had Money, We Had People," *Dissent* (July 9, 2018), https://www.dissentmagazine.org/blog/they-had-money-we-had-people-alexandria-ocasio-cortez.

39. "Meet Alexandria: Early Life, Experience," https://ocasio2018.com/about; Alix Langone, "Meet the 28-Year-Old Former Bartender Who Will Likely Become the Youngest Congresswoman Ever," *Money* (June 27, 2018), http://money.com/money/5323399/alexandria-ocasio-cortez-career; Charlotte Alter, "The Making of AOC," *Time* (April 1, 2019), 25–26; "Democratic Socialists of America Membership Surges after Alexandria Ocasio-Cortez's Stunning Victory," *Daily Beast,* June 28, 2028, https://www.thedailybeast.com/democrratic-socialists-of-america-membership-surges-after-alexandria-ocasio-cortezs-stunning-victory.

40. Astead W. Herndon, "Rashida Tlaib, With Primary Win, Is Poised to Become First Muslim Woman in Congress," *New York Times* (August 8, 2008); Todd Spangler, "How Detroit's Rashida Tlaib Will Make History in Washington," *Detroit Free Press* (September 9, 2018); Erin Kelly, "Six Things about Rashida Tlaib, Who Will Likely Become First Muslim Woman in Congress," *USA Today* (August 8, 2018); Natasha Fernández-Silber, "Making Detroit the Engine of a Green New Deal," *Democratic Left* (Spring 2019), 10–11.

41. Alexi McCammond, "Alexandria Ocasio-Cortez Has as Much Social Media Clout as Her Fellow Freshman Democrats Combined," *Axios* (November 28, 2018); Jennie Neufeld, "Alexandria Ocasio-Cortez Is a Democratic Socialists of America Member: Here's What That Means," *Vox* (June 27, 2018); Emma Whitford, "The Socialists' Dilemma: We Elected Them to Office, Now What?" *In These Times* (June 2019), 26–30.

42. Rep. Alexandria Ocasio-Cortez (D-NY-14), H. Res. 109 — "Recognizing the Duty of the Federal Government to Create a Green New Deal," 116th Congress (2019–20), Introduced February 7, 2019, https://www.congress.gov/bill/116th-congress/house-resolution/109/text.

43. Sarah Lazare, "The Green New Deal Needs Support from Labor: Here's How to Get It," *In These Times* (June 2019), "immediate," 31; "a few," 32; BlueGreen Alliance, "About Us," https://www.bluegreenalliance.org/about/members.

44. Eliza Griswold, "A Democratic-Socialist Landslide in Pennsylvania," *New Yorker* (May 16, 2018), https://www.newyorker.com/news/dispatch/a-democratic-socialist-landslide-in-pennsylvania; Anapol, "Four Socialist-Backed Candidates Win Pennsylvania Legislative Primaries"; Whitford, "The Socialists' Dilemma," 26–29; Eric Lutz, "Chicago's Democratic Socialists Promise Change as They Take Office," *The Guardian* (June 29, 2019), PORTSIDE@lists.portside.org.

45. Maria Svart, "Ready to Save the Planet, and Ourselves," *Democratic Left* (Spring 2019), 2–3; Harold Meyerson, "What the Socialists Just Did — and Why," *American Prospect* (August 9, 2019), https://prospect.org/article/what-socialists-just-did-and-why; Andrew Sernatinger, "DSA Is Leading the Charge," *Jacobin* (August 11, 2019), https://www.jacobinmag.com/2019/08/democratic-socialists-for-america-dsa-convention-2019-atlanta; Andrew Sernatinger, "Moving Targets: DSA's 2019 Convention," *New Politics* (August 21, 2019), https://newpol.org/moving-targets-dsas-2019-convention/; Meagan Day, "Using Power Builds Power," *Democratic Left* (Fall 2019), 4–5.

46. Bernie Sanders, Speech on Democratic Socialism, June 12, 2019, George Washington University, *Vox,* httpps://www.vox.com/2019/6/12/18663217/bernie-sanders-democratic-socialism-speech-transcript.

47. Gary Dorrien, *Social Democracy in the Making: Political and Religious Roots of European Socialism* (New Haven: Yale University Press, 2019), 311–78; Benjamin Mueller, "Safe Choice amid Chaos of Brexit: A Socialist?" *New York Times* (October 7, 2019); Jamie Stern-Werner, "We Need to Learn Lessons from Labour's 'Antisemitism Crisis,'" *Jacobin* (February 21, 2020), https://jacobinmag.com/2020/02/labours-party-anti semitism-crisis-corbyn-sanders?utm_source=Jacobin&utm_campaign=ad10d82549; Alan Johnson, "Institutionally Anti-Semitic: Contemporary Left Antisemitism and the Crisis in the British Labour Party," *Fathom* (2020), https://fathomjournal.org/wp-content/uploads/2019/03/Institutionally-Antisemitic-Report-FINAL-6.pdf.

48. Gary Dorrien, "Bernie Sanders, Social Democracy, and Democratic Socialism," *History News Network* (February 23, 2020), http://hnn.us/article/174385; Jonathan Martin and Alexander Burns, "Biden and Sanders Duel for Clear Edge," *New York Times* (March 4, 2020); Joey Garrison, "Warren Ends Presidential Campaign," *USA Today* (March 6, 2020); Alexander Burns and Jonathan Martin, "Biden Wins in 3 States to Widen Delegate Advantage," *New York Times* (March 11, 2020).

49. Sheri Fink and Mike Baker, "A Lab Pushed for Early Tests, But Federal Officials Said No," *New York Times* (March 11, 2020); Beth Cameron, "I Ran the White House Pandemic Office: Trump Closed It," *Washington Post* (March 13, 2020); Alexander Burns and Jonathan Martin, "How It All Came Apart for Bernie Sanders," *New York Times* (March 21, 2020); Nicholas Kulish, Sarah Kliff, and Jessica Silver-Greenberg, "The U.S. Tried to Build a New Fleet of Ventilators: The Mission Failed," *New York Times* (March 29, 2020); James E. Baker, "It's High Time We Fought This Virus the American Way," *New York Times* (April 3, 2020); Sydney Ember, "Bernie Sanders Drops Out of 2020 Democratic Race for President," *New York Times* (April 8, 2020); Peter Baker and Maggie Haberman, "Trump Leaps to Call Shots on Reopening Nation, Setting Up Standoff with Governors," *New York Times* (April 13, 2020).

50. Joe Barrett, Ern Ailworth, and Ben Kesling, "Demonstrations Spread across U.S. as Ex-Officer Charged with Murder in George Floyd's Death," *Wall Street Journal* (May 29, 2020); Evan Hill, Ainara Tiefenthäler, Christiaan Triebert, Drew Jordan, Haley Willis, and Roin Stein, "8 Minutes and 46 Seconds: How George Floyd Was Killed in Police Custody," *New York Times* (May 31, 2020); Neil MacFarquhar, "Many Claim Extremists Are Sparking Protest Violence. But Which Extremists?" *New York Times* (May 31, 2020); Katie Rogers, Jonathan Martin, and Maggie Haberman, "As Chaos Spreads, Trump Vows to 'End It Now,'" *New York Times* (June 2, 2020); Tom Cotton, "Send in the Troops," *New York Times* (June 3, 2020); Richard Fausset, "What We Know about the Shooting Death of Ahmaud Arbery," *New York Times* (June 4, 2020); Christina Carrega, "FBI Opens an Investigation into the Death of Breonna Taylor," *ABC News*, May 22, 2020, https://abcnews.go.com/US/fbi-opens-investigation-death-breonna-taylor/story?id=70829091; Sabina Ghebremedhin and Christina Carrega, "Breonna Taylor, Kentucky EMT, Allegedly Killed by Police Executing Search Warrant," *ABC News* (May 13, 2020), https://abcnews.go.com/US/breonna-taylor-kentucky-emt-allegedly-killed-police-executing/story?id=70657850.

51. James Madison, *The Federalist* No. 10, in *The Federalist*, ed. Jacob E. Cooke (Middletown, CT: Wesleyan University Press, 1961), 56–65, "spectacles," 61; Maurice

Duverger, *Political Parties: Their Organization and Activity in the Modern State*, trans. Barbara North and Robert North (London: Methuen, 1954), 217; Douglas W. Rae, *The Political Consequences of Election Laws* (New Haven: Yale University Press, 1967); Arendt Lijphart "The Political Consequences of Electoral Laws, 1945–85," *American Political Science Review* (June 1990), 481–96; Page Smith, *The Constitution: A Documentary and Narrative History* (New York: Morrow, 1980), 265–302.

52. Selig Perlman, *A Theory of the Labor Movement* (New York: Macmillan, 1928), 169–71; Theodore J. Lowi, "Why Is There No Socialism in the United States? A Federal Analysis," in *Why Is There No Socialism in the United States?* (Paris: L'Ecole des Hautes Etudes en Sciences Sociales, 1987), 39–40; Seymour Martin Lipset, *Political Man: The Social Basis of Politics*, 2nd ed. (Baltimore: Johns Hopkins University Press, 1982), 199–215, 265–66.

53. John H. M. Laslett and Seymour Martin Lipset, "Social Scientists View the Problem," in *Failure of a Dream? Essays in the History of American Socialism*, ed. Laslett and Lipset (Garden City, NY: Anchor Books, 1974), 25–82; Werner Sombart, "American Capitalism's Economic Rewards," in *Failure of a Dream?* 593–608; Daniel Bell, "The Problem of Ideological Rigidity," in *Failure of a Dream?* 85–111; Lipset and Gary Marks, *It Didn't Happen Here: Why Socialism Failed in the United States* (New York: W. W. Norton, 2000), 43–83.

54. Laslett and Lipset, "Social Scientists View the Problem," 38–40; Lipset and Marks, *It Didn't Happen Here*, 85–86.

55. Nathan Fine, *Labor and Farmer Parties in the United States 1828–1928* (New York: Rand School of Social Science, 1928), 325–26, "the rank," 249; Richard W. Judd, *Socialist Cities: Municipal Politics and the Grass Roots of American Socialism* (Albany: State University of New York Press, 1989), 14–19; Lipset and Marks, *It Didn't Happen Here*, 110–11; Duverger, *Political Parties*, 68–69.

56. Theodore Saloutos, "Radicalism and the Agrarian Tradition," in *Failure of a Dream?*, 142–44; Lipset and Marks, *It Didn't Happen Here*, 102–3; Philip Taft, *The AF of L in the Time of Gompers* (New York: Harper and Brothers, 1957), 68–74.

57. Dean Eugene McHenry, *The Third Force in Canada: The Co-operative Commonwealth Federation, 1932–1948* (Berkeley: University of California Press, 1950); Patrick Lacroix, "From Strangers to 'Humanity First': Canadian Social Democracy and Immigration Policy, 1932–1961," *Canadian Journal of History* 51 (2016), 58–82; Seymour Martin Lipset, *Agrarian Socialism: The Cooperative Commonwealth Federation in Saskatchewan: A Study in Political Sociology* (Berkeley: University of California Press, 1971).

58. Martin Luther King Jr., "The Bravest Man I Ever Met," *Pageant* (June 1965), reprinted in Cornel West, *The Radical King* (Boston: Beacon Press, 2015), 225–34, "of a society," 225; Irving Howe, *A Margin of Hope: An Intellectual Autobiography* (New York: Harcourt Brace Jovanovich, 1982), quote 304.

59. Richard Healey to author, August 10, 2019.

60. Gary Dorrien, *The Neoconservative Mind: Politics, Culture, and the War of Ideology* (Philadelphia: Temple University Press, 1993); Dorrien, *Imperial Designs: Neoconservatism and the New Pax Americana* (New York: Routledge, 2004).

61. Sarah Bormann, *Angriff auf die Mitbestimmung. Unternehmensstrategien gegen Betriebsräte—der Fall Schlecker* (Berlin: Sigma, 2007); *Mitbestimmung und Betriebsverfassung in Deutschland, Frankreich und Großbritannien seit dem 19. Jahrhundert.' Tagungsband zum 16. wissenschaftlichen Symposium auf Schloss Quint bei Trier 1993*, ed. Hans Pohl (Stuttgart: Steiner, 1996); Petra Junghans, *Mitwirkung und Mitbestimmung der Betriebsgewerkschaftsleitung in den Betrieben der DDR. Eine empirische Untersuchung in Ost-Berliner Industriebetrieben* (Berlin: WVB, 2004).

62. Ana Gutiérrez Johnson and William Foote Whyte, "The Mondragon System of Worker Production Cooperatives," in *Workplace Democracy and Social Change*, ed. Frank Lindenfeld and Joyce Rothschild-Whitt (Boston: Porter-Sargent, 1982), 177–98; Joyce Rothschild and J. Allen Whitt, *The Cooperative Workplace: Potentials and Dilemmas of Organizational Democracy and Participation* (Cambridge: Cambridge University Press, 1986); Karl Ove Moene, "Strong Unions or Worker Control?" in *Alternatives to Capitalism*, ed. Jon Elster and Karl Ove Moene (Cambridge: Cambridge University Press, 1989), 83–97; Roy Morrison, *We Build the Road as We Travel* (Philadelphia: New Society Publishers, 1991); John Logue and Jacquelyn Yates, *The Real World of Employee Ownership* (Ithaca: Cornell University Press, 2001); Gary Dorrien, *Reconstructing the Common Good* (Maryknoll, NY: Orbis Books, 1992); Dorrien, *Economy, Difference, Empire: Social Ethics for Social Justice* (New York: Columbia University Press, 2010).

INDEX